ASIA PACIFIC
BUSINESS
TRAVEL GUIDE 1997/98

The business and independent traveller's guide to Australia, Bangladesh, Cambodia, China, Fiji, Hong Kong, India, Indonesia, Japan, Korea (N & S), Laos, Macau, Malaysia, Myanmar, Nepal, New Zealand, The Pacific Islands, Pakistan, Papua New Guinea, The Philippines, Singapore, Sri Lanka, Taiwan, Thailand and Vietnam

PRIORY PUBLICATIONS LTD

Syresham, Brackley, Northants NN13 5HH, UK
Tel: (+44) 1280 850 603. Fax: (+44) 1280 850 576

ISBN 1 871985 25 0

Editors: Jonathan Hart (Business), Travel Business Analyst Hong Kong (Tourism);
Publisher: Malcolm Orr-Ewing

© Priory Publications Ltd 1997

All rights reserved. No part of this publication may be reproduced, stored in a retrieval system or recorded by any means without the prior permission of the Publishers. Whilst every effort is made to obtain accurate information, the Publishers cannot accept liability for any errors.

The views expressed in this publication and of its constituent Country Reports are those of the contributors and publishers and do not necessarily represent those of the Pacific Asia Travel Association.

Photographs. The publishers would like to express their thanks to various National Tourism Organisations for the provision of photographs used in this publication and to the contributors as named in the Myanmar and Vietnam sections. Front cover photograph by courtesy of the Hong Kong Tourist Assiciation, London. Malaysia, Singapore & Thailand photographs by courtesy of C K Photography, Gillingham, Kent, UK.

Printed in Singapore by Eurasia Press (Offset) Pte Ltd

We're all over the Pacific Rim but... we're easy to PFind.

Conveniently located throughout the Pacific Rim, Pan Pacific Hotels and Resorts has 16 hotels ideally located to look after your accommodation needs.

From Bangkok to Singapore to the West Coast Of America, we offer quality accommodation, excellent business, entertainment and recreational facilities combined with personal and attentive services.

And soon, we can be found in these new locations; Yokohama (Aug.97), Manila (Dec.97), Kota Kinabalu (Dec.97), Malacca (Dec.97), Penang (Dec.97) KL International Airport (Dec. 97).

For reservations, contact any Pan Pacific Hotel, reservation office or your travel agent. Reservations can also be made using our PF access code.

PAN PACIFIC
Hotels and Resorts

ASIA: Singapore, Kuala Lumpur, Johor Bahru, Pangkor, Jakarta, Bangkok, Hong Kong, Dhaka, Wuxi, Narita. **PACIFIC**: Gold Coast, Palau. **NORTH AMERICA**: Vancouver, San Francisco, Isle of Hawaii.

Contents

AUSTRALIA

What to See & Tourism	8
Key Facts/Useful Addresses	11
Hotels	12
Restaurants	25
Car Hire	26

BANGLADESH

What to See/Tourism	27
Restaurants/Dacca plan	28
Key Facts/Airlines/Car Hire	29
Addresses/Hotels	30

CAMBODIA

Doing Business	31
Tourism Update	32
What to See	33
KeyFacts/Addresses/Airlines/Restaurants	34
Hotels	35

CHINA

Doing Business	39
Tourism Update	40
What to See	42
Key Facts	45
Useful Addresses	46
Hotels	50
Restaurants	60
Airline Departures & Offices	61
Major Exhibitions	63
Background/Events in 1997	I-IV

FIJI

What to See	65
Car Hire/Key Facts/Airlines	66
Airline Departures & Restaurants	67
Hotels	68

HONG KONG

Doing Business	70
Tourism Update	71
What to See	72
Key Facts	75
Hotels	76
Restaurants	84
Airlines/Car Hire	86
Airline Departures	87
Major Exhibitions	88

INDIA

Doing Business	91
Tourism Update	92
What to See	93
Key Facts/Useful Addresses	96
Hotels	99
Airline Departures & Offices	118

INDONESIA

Doing Business	123
Tourism Update	124
What to See	125
Key Facts/Useful Addresses	127
Hotels	129
Restaurants/Car Hire/Airlines	138
Exhibitions	141

JAPAN

Doing Business	143
Tourism Update	145
What to See	146
Key Facts/Useful Addresses	148
Hotels	150
Restaurants	160
Car Hire/Airline Offices	161
Airline Departures	162
Major Exhibitions	165

KOREA, North

Doing Business	166
Tourism Update/What to See	166
Key Facts	167
Hotels/Useful Addresses	168

KOREA, South

Doing Business	169
Tourism Update	171
What to See	172
Key Facts/Useful Addresses	174
Hotels	176
Restaurants/Airline Offices	180
Major Exhibitions/Car Hire	181
Airline Departures	182

LAOS

Doing Business	183
Tourism Update	183
What to See	184
Key Facts	185
Hotels/Useful Addresses	186

MACAU

Doing Business	187
Tourism Update	188
Key Facts	190
Hotels	192
Restaurants/Airlines/Addresses	193

MALAYSIA

Doing Business	197
Tourism Update	197
What to See	199
Key Facts/Useful Addresses	201
Hotels	203
Restaurants/Airline Offices/Car Hire	213
Airline Departures	214
Major Exhibitions	218

MYANMAR

Doing Business	216
Tourism Update	217
What to See	218
Key Fact File	220
Hotels	221

NEPAL

What to See	222
Restaurants	223
Key Facts/Addresses/Car Hire	224
Hotels/Airline Departures	225

NEW ZEALAND

What to See	226
Key Facts	227
Useful Adresses/Auckland plan	228
Hotels	229
Restaurants	231
Airline Offices/Car Hire	232

PACIFIC ISLANDS

Background	233
What to See	235
Car Hire	236
Hotels	237
Airline Departures	239

PAKISTAN

What to See	241
Key Facts	242
Hotels & Restaurants	243
Car Hire/Useful Addresses	244

PAPUA NEW GUINEA

Doing Business/Tourism Update	245
What to See	246
Key Facts/Useful Addresses	248
Hotels/Restaurants/Car Hire	249

PHILIPPINES

Doing Business	252
Tourism Update	253
Useful Addresses	255
Key Facts/Car Hire	256
Hotels	258
Restaurants/Map	262
Airline Departures & Offices	263
Major Exhibitions & Conventions	264

SINGAPORE

Business Scene/Tourism Update	268
What to See	269
Car Hire	271
Useful Addresses/Key Facts	272
Hotels	274
Restaurants	281
Airline Departures	282
Major Exhibitions	283

SRI LANKA

What to See	284
Restaurants/Car Hire	285
Key Facts/Useful Addresses	286
Hotels	287
Airline Departures	288

TAIWAN

Doing Business	291
Tourism Update	292
Airline Offices/Key Facts	294
Useful Addresses/Hotels	295
Restaurants	298
Airline Departures	300
Major Exhibitions & Conferences	301

THAILAND

Doing Business	305
Tourism Update	306
What to See	308
Useful Addresses/Key Facts	310
Hotels	312
Restaurants	325
Car Hire/Airline Offices	326
Airline Departures	327
Major Exhibitions	328

VIETNAM

Doing Business	333
Tourism Update	334
Key Facts/Useful Addresses	337
Hotels	339
Restaurants/Airline Departures	341

MAJOR HOTEL CHAINS IN ASIA-PACIFIC	343
ADVERTISERS' INDEX	347

Spoiling you all over Asia at Le Méridien.

With fourteen hotels and resorts in Asia Pacific, Le Méridien is ready to spoil you wherever you go. With inimitable Asian hospitality, Le Méridien takes care of your weary travelling soul and makes you feel at home, abroad. For bookings, contact your nearest Forte and Le Méridien reservation office or for further details fax Hong Kong on (852) 2732 1204.

LE MERIDIEN NIRWANA SPA & GOLF RESORT BALI, LE MERIDIEN PRESIDENT HOTEL & TOWER BANGKOK, LE MERIDIEN CHANGI SINGAPORE, LE MERIDIEN JAKARTA, LE MERIDIEN NEW DELHI, LE MERIDIEN SINGAPORE.

Le MERIDIEN
HOTELS & RESORTS

PATA in 1997/98

Development, promotion and facilitation of tourism and travel to and within the Asia-Pacific Region

Over 2000 Membership organisations worldwide

Over 17,000 Chapter Members worldwide with 2500 in Europe

European Trade Shows:
ITB Berlin
WTM London
BIT Milan
FITUR Madrid
MITT Moscow
Holiday World Prague
CIS Travel Market St Petersburg
EIBTM Geneva

Country Trade Shows:
Norway
Finland
Sweden
Denmark
France
Benelux
Estonia
Hungary
Germany
Italy
Spain
UK

Development & Training, Heritage & Conservation, Environment & Research.
New Destinations Development

16 European Chapters located in Austria, Bavaria, Benelux, Denmark, Estonia, Finland, France, Germany, Hungary, Italy, Norway, Russia, Spain, Switzerland, Sweden, & the United Kingdom

The Pacific Asia Travel Association - (PATA) - was founded in 1951 in Hawaii as a non profit-making corporation dedicated to the development, promotion and facilitation of tourism within the Asia/Pacific region. PATA members work together to effect a synergistic approach to the challenges of the world marketplace.

PATA's role as a sharing and learning organization has enabled it to act as a catalyst for tourism development within the world's fastest growing destination - the Asia/Pacific.

The PATA region is geographically defined by longitudinal lines 110° West and 75° East, reaching from Pakistan and India across Asia to the Pacific, to the Western regions of North America, Korea, Japan and the CIS in the North, and to Australia and New Zealand in the South - 38 destinations in all.

PATA membership encompasses the globe and is open to organizations involved in or related to some phase of the travel industry within the PATA regions. Membership in the Association tops 2000 with a worldwide network of over 81 Chapters and 17,000 Chapter members.

The PATA Europe Division has taken a strong interest in the incentive and meeting planning market with organised meetings from Europe to Asia.

PATA is also organizing member Trade Missions to various European Markets in conjunction with its Chapters.

PATA's major marketing activity is its worldwide PATA Travel Mart, held annually in a different PATA member destination. Over 1200 buyers and sellers meet to make arrangements for their future services. In 1997 the PATA Travel Mart was held in Beijing, China from 16-19 April. 1998's Travel Mart takes place in Singapore, which becomes its permament home from that year, April 22-25.

PATA's annual conference is the highlight of the members' year and the Annual Conference 1997 was held in Beijing, China April 20-24. 1998's conference takes place in Manila March 29-April 2nd with the Chapters World Congress taking place in Cebu, Phlippines, March 25-27th.

PATA's research activities oversee project and statistical studies and compile an annual visitor statistical report which is used worldwide as a prime source of tourism information.

PATA has established an Antarctic Fund to promote knowledge and understanding of the benefits and effects of tourism in the Antarctic, and advocate a responsible industry perspective on Antarctic tourism. PATA also urges members to promote wherever possible the benefits of environmentally sensitive tourism.

PATA believes that the present and future success of the region's travel industry depends on environmental and cultural preservation. In 1992 PATA introduced its "Code for Environmentally Responsible Tourism" to strengthen the principles of preservation that have guided the Association since its foundation.

Headquarters

Pacific Asia Travel Association
Executive, Planning and Operations & Americas Division. Montgomery Street, West Tower, Suite 1000, San Francisco, CA 94014, USA
Tel: (415) 986 4646; Tlx: 170685;
Cable: PATA; Fax: (415) 986 3458
e-mail: patahq@ix.netcom.com

Europe Divison

Pacific Asia Travel Association
Les Eucalyptus (Block I), 11 Avenue des Guelfes, Zone E Fontvieille, MC 98000 Monaco.
Tel: (377) 9205 6132;
Fax: (377) 9205 6133;
e-mail: pata@monaco.net

Asia Division

Pacific Asia Travel Association
138 Cecil Street, # 04-02 Cecil Court, Singapore 069538
Republic of Singapore.
Tel: (065) 223 7854/7855; Tlx: RS 42035 PATA; Fax: (065) 225 6842
e-mail: patadra@singnet.com.sg

Pacific Division

Pacific Asia Travel Association
80 Wiliam Street, Suite 203, Wooloomooloo, NSW 2011, Australia. e-mail: pata@world.net.
Send all correspondence to: PO Box 645, King's Cross, NSW 2011
Tel: (02) 332 3599; Tlx: 72478;
Cable; SPATA; Fax: (02) 331 6592

PATA

The 1997/98 edition of the *Asia-Pacific Business Travel Guide* covers all the countries in PATA membership in the Pacific Rim. Myanmar joined PATA in 1996 and Laos has been included as the other countries in the former French Indo-China are featured and it is thought she will join in 1997/98.

It is a guide to doing business in the Asia-Pacific region; also to tourist developments. The countries covered, from Pakistan in the West to New Zealand in the East range from some of the poorest in the world to some of the richest. The area represents the fastest growing business and tourist destinations on the globe, with over 80 million visitors - nearly 40% of the world's international flyers. It is predicted that by the end of the century over half of all aircraft movements will be to and within this region.

The guide is aimed primarily at the business traveller and the travel trade which serves him or her. Thus we have listed some 1000 business class hotels, many including colour photographs, although we have also included incentive and conference destinations and resorts, particularly in the Pacific arena.

We have given suggestions for the business traveller's leisure time and provided him or her with key facts about each country, useful addresses, specialist exhibitions and air connections between the rest of the world and the Asia-Pacific region.

For 1997/8 we have again produced Country Reports for the leading visitor generating destinations in this guide listed in the table below (except for those marked†). These are available free-of-charge from the Publisher at the address below. The guide is also now updated quarterly and available electronically on the Internet under the site name **http://travel.cm-net.com/pata**.

About the Guide

Country Sections

Information on most of the 26 Country Sections is divided into the following categories:

Doing Business
Investment climate
Political devlopments
Business awareness & etiquette

Tourism Update
General tourism trends
Arrivals profiles
Hotel developments
Aviation news

What to See and Do
Sights not to miss
Shopping
Getting Around
Communications
Entertainment
Leisure
Arrival & departure

Key Fact File
Customs & entry
Exchange rates
Dialling codes
Business hours
Health requirements
Best time to visit
National Holidays

Useful Addresses
Government Departments
Chambers of Commerce
Business bureaux
Post Offices
Hospitals/emergencies
Air Couriers

Maps
Country Maps
City Maps

Hotels
Reference Table
Extended colour entries
A-Z Hotel listing

Restaurants
Listed by cuisine

Car Hire

Airlines
Departures & offices

Major Exhibitions
& their organisers

Visitors in 1996
Visitor arrivals in the Pacific-Asia region grew by 9% in 1995 to reach 78.5 million. First figures for 1996 indicate a further 10% increase to 86.4 million.
A trend in the past six years has been the growth of inter-Asian arrivals. These have risen from 21 million in 1989 to more than 40 million in 1996. At the same time European arrivals to the region rose from 6.5. to 10 million.

[Figures at right from Travel Business Analyst, Hong Kong. * = provisional, based on first six months' arrivals.]

Country	Visitors mn	+/-%
China	51.2	10
Hong Kong	11.5	15
Macau†	8.15	5
Malaysia	7.8	4*
Singapore	7.3	2
Thailand	7.2	10
Indonesia	4.95	15*
Australia†	4.2	14*
Japan†	3.8	15*
Korea (S)†	3.7	-2
Taiwan	2.4	1
India	2.3	7*
Philippines	1.9	10*
Vietnam	1.6	25

Priory Publications Ltd, PO Box 24, Brackley, Northants NN13 5FA.UK.Tel:(+44) 1280 850603; Fax:(+44) 1280 850576; E-mail:priory@dial.pipex.com

8 AUSTRALIA - Introduction

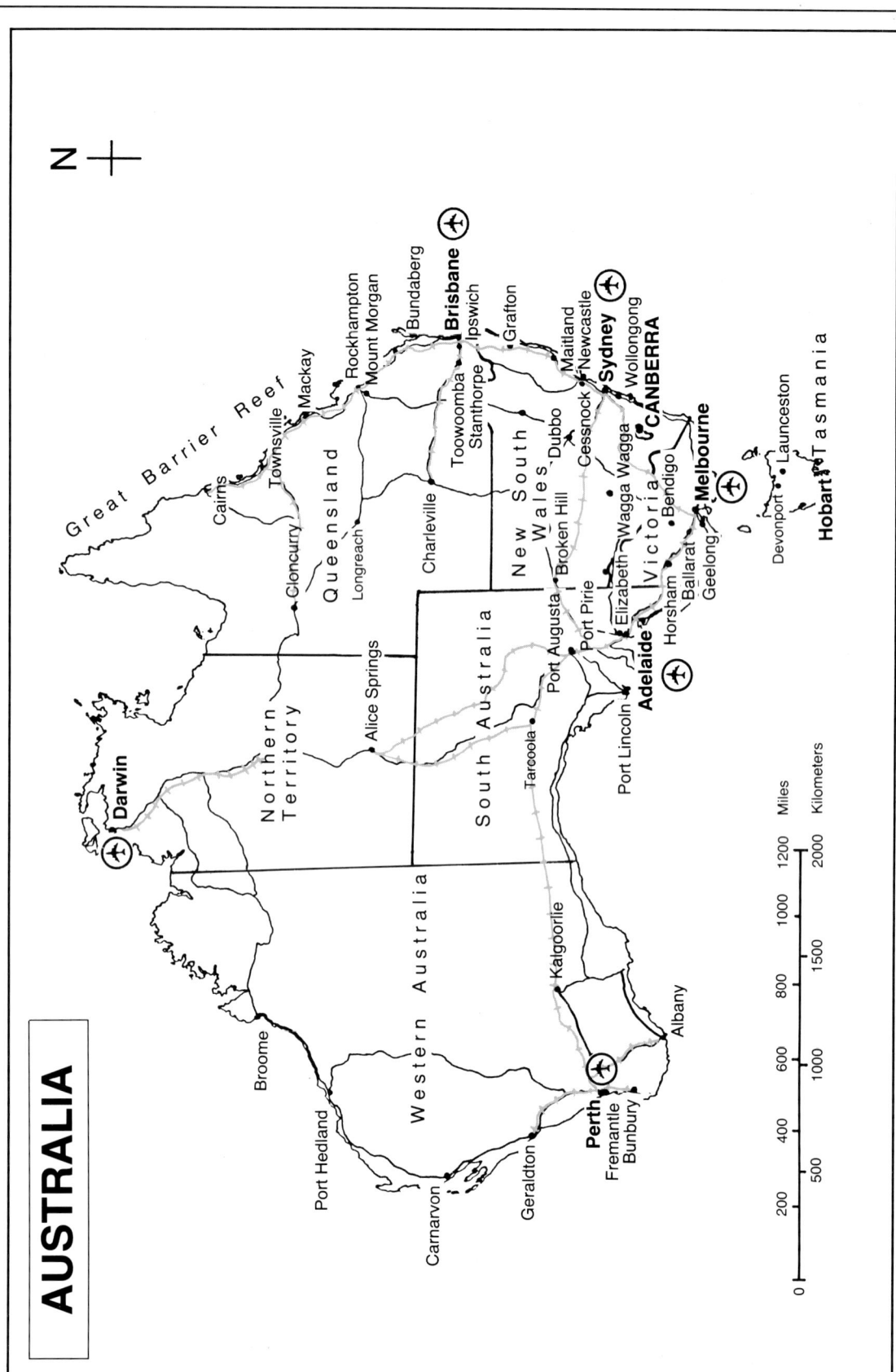

Australia

What to see

Where to start is often a more difficult question than what to see. Australia has so much to offer visitors - both in the cities and in the countryside and outback beyond.

In Sydney most visitors immediately gravitate towards the magnificent Opera House and the nearby Sydney Harbour Bridge. In the Rocks are The Observatory, including the State Archives with the records of the First Fleet which colonised Australia, the Aboriginal Arts, The Tribal Arts Centre, The Earth Exchange and the Museum of Contemporary Arts. Also worth a visit are the National Maritime Museum in Darling Harbour, the Hyde Park Barracks Museum and the Royal Botanic Gardens.

Melbourners have traditionally considered themselves more sophisticated than their Sydney counterparts. Perhaps the best way to take in the city is by using its extensive tram network. Melbourne is home to the National Gallery, which was completed in 1968. Its much newer concert hall (bigger than Sydney Opera House) can seat 2,677. The city's Performing Arts Museum is certainly worth a visit. Newly opened is the Australian Wildlife Park.

The capital Canberra, 'though, is the best place to spy fine architecture as the city carries out the plans first laid down by a US designer back in 1912. The Australian War Memorial and Museum should not be missed. Newly opened in 1992 is the Gininderra Arts & Crafts Village in Federation Square.

Adelaide, Perth and Brisbane are beautifully laid out cities and just walking around their respective central shopping districts makes for an absorbing half day. Perth's King's Park gives a fabulous view over the Swan River and the city's southern suburbs.

Beyond the cities and suburbia, the country has suddenly become famous for its adventure tours into the outback and throughout the Northern Territory - the Top End. Kakadu, the Great Barrier Reef and the far north of Queensland are also popular. The Warner Bros Movieworld opened in 1992 near Cairns. Tasmania, too, has become synonymous with wilderness adventure. But these tours appear more popular with locals than foreigners. Australia's Asian visitors such as the Japanese seem less keen to take these kind of trips.

Shopping

So long as you have the cash there is very little that can't be bought in any of Australia's big cities. Further afield, 'though, the choice becomes limited. Due to still high tariff walls, many imported goods are expensive as are locally-made items such as clothing. Bush gear like hats and long all-weather jackets are becoming increasingly fashionable.

Duty-free shops also operate in the cities and are a boon for tourists, who can find few bargains elsewhere. Anyone with an air ticket out of the country can use the stores such as Sydney's *Downtown Duty Free* and *Nicholas Duty Free*. Both are on Pitt Street.

Also in Sydney, most quality items are usually found in the large department stores around Hunter Street, Park Street, Philip Street and George Street.

The newly-opened Queen Victoria Building in Sydney, contains more than 900 shops, cafes and restaurants, including leading brand names and in Eat Street an avenue of international restaurants and takeaways. It provides one-stop shopping and eating.

Melbourne claims to be the shopping capital of Australia, with some first-class department stores such as *Myers*. The power of the central shopping district was in decline as more and more people limited their purchases to soulless suburban malls, but the downtown area has fought back with some new small specialist stores of its own.

Long underrated and little understood Aboriginal art and artefacts have grown in popularity in recent years; although some items still need an export permit. The quality of other Australian souvenirs is fast improving, with woodworkings, leatherwork, hats, rugs and boots all worth looking out for. Please note that you will be expected to pay the asking price for any item on display. As a rule Australians do not haggle in stores, but they do shop around for the best deal.

Getting Around

Australia's new deregulated domestic air network provides almost the only way of covering the huge distances involved in travelling around the country. Frequencies are excellent between the main cities and the service of a reasonable standard and getting better as competition hots up from Compass and others.

Bus and train services do link major cities, but the transit times do not in any way compare with the airlines. Nevertheless, the *Indian Pacific Highway* linking Sydney with Perth remains extremely popular despite its 65-hour journey duration.

Car rental is straightforward with all the large international groups having offices around the country. The rental market is extremely competitive so it's best to shop around for the cheapest deal. All include third-party insurance and many offer an unlimited kilometres flat charge. Expect to pay between A$100-130 for a mid-size car from the big boys, perhaps 30 per cent less with some smaller operators. One-way rentals are also possible, 'though this may incur an additional fee. Metered taxis are reasonably cheap throughout Australia and, given that most of the sights are within easy reach of city centres, it is just as easy to catch a cab as to take the bus. Also remember that tipping is not necessary, but is unfortunately becoming more commonplace. Buses, generally, are clean and well run by local transport authorities

Melbourne and Adelaide retain some eccentric looking old trams, which offer a slow if enjoyable means of getting around the two cities. Suburban rail networks vary from city to city, with Sydney probably offering the most comprehensive system.

In Sydney a fast monorail now links the City Centre, World Square, Haymarket, Darling Harbour and the Convention Centre. The below ground railway connects with other areas and the suburbs.

Entertainment

All of Australia's big five city centres provide plenty of scope for great nights out in comparative safety. What's on offer tends to vary from city to city with Sydney claiming the pot as the liveliest and brashest of all. Like any big city Sydney has a selection of pubs and clubs. The city's red light district can be found round Darlinghurst Road in the King's Cross district, although recent clean up campaigns have taken most of the drugs off the streets. It still claims plenty of strip joints and cheap porn parlours, but there are also any number of cheap eating and drinking establishments such as the highly recommended *Bourbon and Beefsteak, Real Ale Tavern (Jazz Club)* or *Round Midnight Jazz Club*. Other pubs popular with ex-pats include the *Brooklyn, Lord Nelson* and *Horizons* (ANA Hotel) in the CBD. Classical ballet, as well as opera and concerts can be seen at the Opera House and ethnic Australian dance at the Aboriginal Islander Dance Theatre at Glebe, 5 kms west of the city centre.

A slightly more discreet Melbourne does not quite match its northern rival for the pace of its nightlife, but has its own red-light area, a flourishing cultural scene and more than 40 discos. Nightlife in the other chief cities can be summed up as follows: Canberra is sleepy; Brisbane conservative, Adelaide progressive, Hobart simple, Perth 'early to bed' while the Top End's Darwin is restricted to one or two all-night discos and casinos.

The much celebrated Sydney Opera House - the home of the National Opera - is a magnet for many visitors, even if it's only to look at the place. To confirm Australia's new-found cultural credentials, the nation boasts three orchestras, some 20 or more theatres, a thriving home-ground film industry and a fair sprinkling of internationally-known artists and musicians. The sheer breadth and depth of cultural life is therefore within easy reach of the foreign visitor

Most of Australia's key cities hold large annual arts jamborees. Perhaps the best known is Adelaide's Festival of Arts, which dates back to the sixties, but both Perth and Melbourne also stage equally impressive festivals that now rival the Adelaide original.

Eating out is an entertainment in itself down under and, with the massive influx of foreign immigrants in recent years, the variety of cuisine on offer has broadened beyond the dreams of many Australians who can now dine out on a wide range of ethnic cooking.

Leisure

There is almost no limit to the recreational facilities on offer across Australia - from a host of water sports on the coast, urban activities such as squash, tennis and bowls to more adventurous and demanding pursuits in the outback. Largely spectator-based sports - cricket (summer), Rugby League (winter in NSW and Queensland), Australian Rules football (winter in Victoria, South Australia, Western Australia and Tasmania) - generate a passionate local following. Tennis and golf, too, are equally well supported - especially during their respective Australian *Opens*. For participants, tennis and golf facilities can be found in even quite small towns. Many hotels have their own courts and while clubs (often with grass courts) form the focal point for the sport, most are open to non-members. Most suburbs boast at least one squash club. While local municipalities own their own golf courses open to the public. Both sports tend to be relatively inexpensive, particularly compared with what you might expect to pay elsewhere in the Pacific-Asia region.

Queensland is the best place for water-sports - diving, sailboarding, water-skiing, sailing and big game fishing. Surfing is a way of life among the young and young at heart and good beaches can be found right around the coastline.

Horse racing is a national passion, best illustrated by the obsessive interest in the Melbourne Cup which is held on the first Tuesday of November. Race day is a public holiday in Melbourne. There are some 450 flat and harness-racing tracks around the country, so it should be possible to attend one meeting without too much trouble.

Surprisingly for a land associated with sunshine and beaches, Australia has more skiable slopes than Switzerland, although the skiing season is quite short. The season in parts of NSW, Victoria and, to a lesser extent, Tasmania, lasts from June to, perhaps, early September. Facilities in the ski resorts are generally first class. Purists, 'though, may find the quality of the snow not quite up to Alpine conditions.

Arrival & Departure

Australia's two main international gateways are Sydney's Kingsford Smith, just 8km south of the city and Melbourne's Tullamarine some 21 km from the downtown area. Perth, Brisbane, Cairns, Darwin and Hobart (only to New Zealand) also handle international flights.

Sydney badly needs a new airport so expect long waits for baggage, immigration and customs clearance. Buses and taxis operate from all of the above airports to downtown areas. From Kingsford Smith there is a Airport Express bus (No. 300) costing A$5 or the Kingsford Smith transport bus, also $5, which calls on major hotels every 30 minutes, or a cab which costs up to A$20.

Adelaide airport is 8 km from the city centre, transit bus costs A$3, taxi A$12. Brisbane airport is 13 km from the city centre, bus costs A$5.40 or taxi A$15. Darwin 18 km, bus cost A$7, taxi A$13. Melbourne 24 km, bus cost A$7, taxi A$25. Perth 10 km, bus A$6, taxi A$18.

International departure tax is now A$25.

Useful Addresses

Business: Australian Trade Commission

Austrade, departments of high commissions and embassies overseas, also has branches throughout Australia which can advise both about inward investment opportunities and joint ventures and about export markets for Australian companies.

The Austrade centre, PO Box 2386, Cnr Barry Drive/Northbourne Ave, **Canberra** City ACT 2601. Tel: (062) 765111; Tlx: 62194; Fax: (062) 765105

Stockland House, 181 Castlereagh St, **Sydney** NSW 2000. Tel (02) 9265 3555; Tlx: 121555; Fax: (02) 9264 8237

Goverment Insurance Office Centre, 5th Fl, Suite 504, 400 Hunter St, **Newcastle** NSW 2300. Tel: (049) 28331; Tlx: 28331

Level 2, 484 Queen St, **Brisbane**, Qld. Tel: (07) 832 6266; tlx: 40593; fax: 832 1529

2nd fl, Australian Central Credit Union Bldg, 70 Light Sq, **Adelaide** SA 5000. Tel: (08) 237 3444; tlx: 82521; fax: (08) 212 6791

2nd fl, Continental Bldg, 162 Macquarie St, **Hobart** TAS 7001. Tel: (002) 205111; tlx: 58907; fax: (002) 234139

5th fl, Commerce Hse, World Trade Centre, Cnr Flinders/Spencer Sts, **Melbourne** VIC 3005. Tel: (03) 611 3355; tlx: 31270; fax: 611 3527

6th fl, SGIO Atrium Bldg, 170 St Geoerges Terrace, **Perth** WA 6000. Tel: (09) 481 0677; tlx: 92424; fax: (09) 481 0531

3rd fl, Capita Bldg, 62 Cavenagh St, **Darwin** NT 0801. Tel: (089) 818686; tlx: 85210; fax: (0889) 4349

Business: other

Australian Chamber of Commerce
Mr Brent Davis, Chief Economist, PO Box E139, Queen Victoria Terr, Canberra ACT 2600. Tel: (062) 732381; tlx: AA 62507; fax: (062) 733 646

Australian Institute of Export
Mr Marina Mirolio, PO Box R215, Royal Exchange NSW 20900. Tel: (02) 9241 1745; fax: (02) 9251 3851
Confederation of Australian Industry (CAI)
Ms Sharon Green (Information Officer), PO Box E14, Qn Victoria Terr, Canberra ACT 2600. Tel: (062) 732311; tlx: AA 62733; Fax: (062) 733196
Foreign Investment Review Board
c/o The Tresury, Canberra ACT 2600. Tel: (062)633762; tlx: 62010; fax: (062) 633866
Sydney Chamber of Commerce
93 York St, Sydney NSW 2000. Tel: (02) 9299 7888; tlx: 127113
Trade Ministry/Dept of For. Affairs &Trade.
100 William St, Sydney. Tel: (02) 9358 0222

Air Couriers
Adelaide **DHL**: (08) 8371 0055;
Canberra **DHL**: (06) 280 4983
Melbourne. **DHL** (03) 372 1555; **Federal Express** (03) 338 0411; **TNT Express** (03) 329 0400; **Wards Express** (03) 329 1711.
Perth **TNT**: (9) 353 3640. *Sydney*. **DHL** (02) 9317 8300; **Federal Express** (02) 9317 6666; **TNT Express** (02) 9317 7717; **UPS** (02) 9313 1666; **DPE**: (02) 9313 1000

Australia Key Fact File

Passport Requirements:
All visitors, except those from New Zealand, must obtain a visa prior to arrival. On arrival, entry is subject to the granting of a permit for the period of stay specified in the visa.

Currency:
Australian dollar A$. 100 cents = A$1.

Exchange rate *(as at February 1997)*
US$1 = 1.30 A$; £1 = 2.11 A$

IDD Code: 61 *followed by...*
Adelaide 8; Alice Springs 89; Armidale (NSW) 67; Brisbane 7; Broken Hill 80; Cairns 70; Canberra 6; Darwin 889; Devonport (Tas) 04; Dubbo 68; Geelong 52; Gold Coast 75; Hobart 02; Kalgoorlie 90; Launceston 03; Melbourne 3; Newcastle 49; Perth 9; Sydney 2; Townsville 77; Woollongong 42.

Currency Restrictions:
None on the import of foreign currency. Exports are limited to A$5,000 in Australian currency without prior approval.

Electricity supply:
240/250 volts AC 50HZ.

Language: English

Time:
GMT: EST + 10 hrs; CST + 9 hrs; WST + 8 hrs; EDT: EST + 15 hrs; CST + 14 hrs, WST + 13 hrs. Most states observe daylight saving from October to March.

Business hours:
Commercial offices: Monday to Friday 0900-1700;
Government offices: Monday to Friday 0900-1700; Banks: Monday to Thursday: 0930-1600; Fridays 0930-1700; Shops: Monday to Friday 0830-1700; Saturday 0830-1200.

Customs & Entry:
Duty-free allowance is 200 cigarettes or equivalent in other tobacco products; one litre of alcoholic liquor and A$400 worth of dutiable goods. Strict laws prohibiting or restricting the entry of drugs, weapons, firearms and certain quarantinable articles into Australia. Furs, skins, ivory and reptile leather goods plus some other items are banned.

Health Requirements:
Vaccinations are not required unless a visitor arrives from or has recently visited a country infected by yellow fever. No health certificate is needed to enter Australia.

Climate/Best time to visit:
Australia has a generally pleasant climate without extremes in temperatures. Temperate states (the SE and extreme SW) have four seasons, while those in the tropical zone have two - wet summers, and autumns; dry winters. In the other states summers range from hot to very hot with maximum temperatures above 38°C (100°F). Beach resorts are crowded during the school holiday periods of January, Easter, last week of June/first of July, last week of September. Most popular holiday month is January, so many urban-based businesses close down completely from just before Christmas until the beginning of February.

National Holidays 1997:
1 January - New Year's Day; 26 January Australia Day; 28-31 March Easter; 25 April - Anzac Day; 10 June - Queen's Birthday (exc W. Australia); 25/6 December - Christmas/Boxing Day. Labor Day - 4 March in Western Australia & Tasmania; 11 March in Victoria; 6 May in Queensland; 7 October in other states. Some other state holidays.

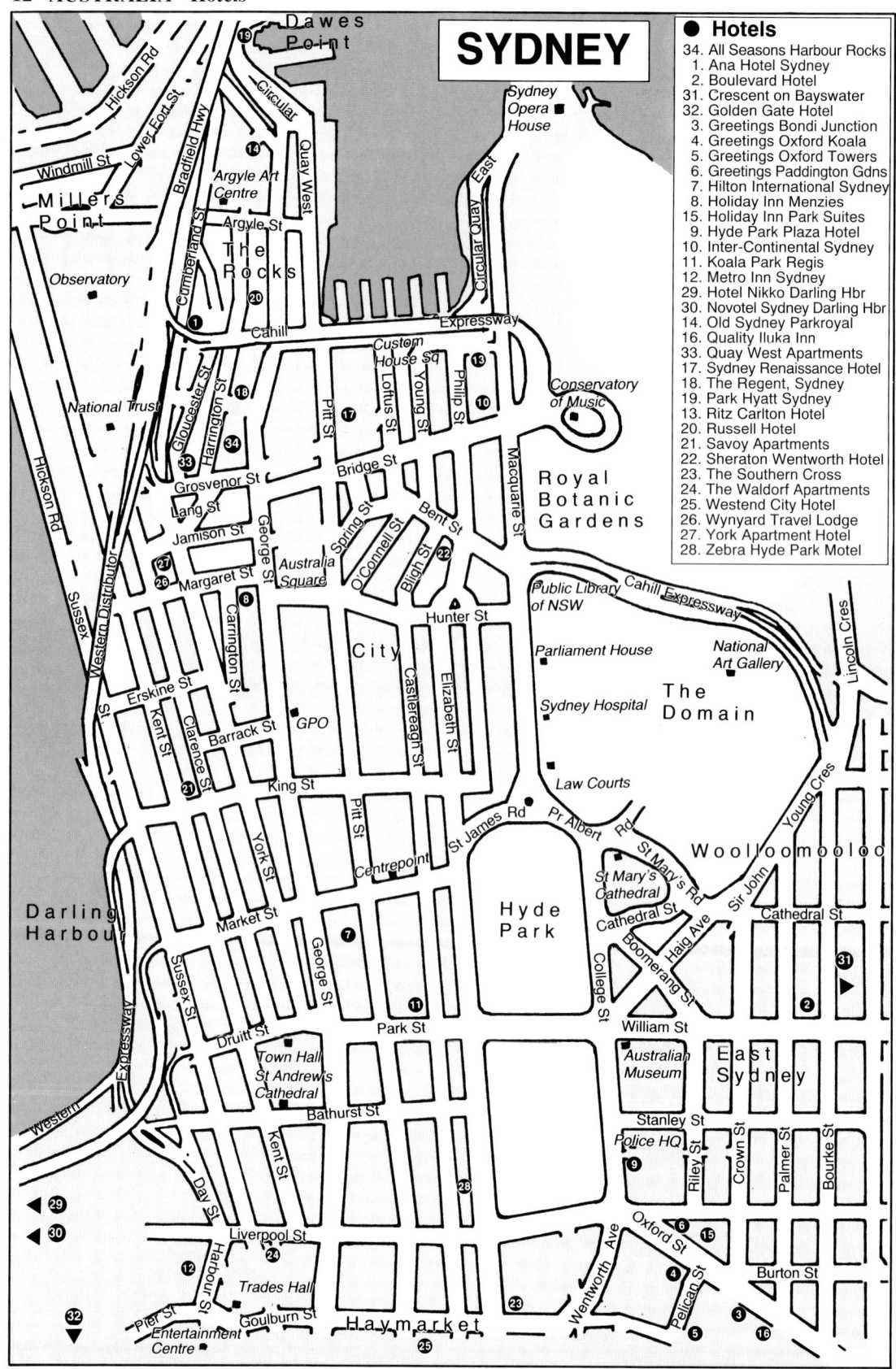

Sydney Hotel Reference Table

Hotel (listed in price order)	SINGLE ROOM RATE (AUS $)	LOCATION	NUMBER OF ROOMS	NUMBER OF SUITES	CONFERENCE FACILITIES	EXHIBITION SPACE	LARGEST BANQUET NUMBER	BUSINESS CENTRE	SWIMMING POOL (0 = indoor)	TENNIS COURT	HEALTH CLUB	VIDEO FILMS
Park Hyatt Sydney	440	Dawes Pt	159	37	●	●	500	●	●	-	●	●
The Observatory Hotel	340	Rocks	78	22	●	●	100	●	○	●	●	●
Ritz Carlton	325	CBD	93	13	●	●	500	●	●	-	●	●
The Park Sheraton	320	Kings X	550	10	●	●	500	●	●	-	-	●
Inter-Continental	310	CBD	423	42	●	●	260	●	○	-	●	●
Ana Hotel Sydney	300	Rocks	573	-	●	●	500	●	●	-	●	●
Sebel Town House	300	Eliz.Bay	139	26	-	-	200	●	●	●	●	●
Sydney Renaissance	290	CBD	534	35	●	●	170	●	●	-	●	●
Old Sydney Parkroyal	290	Rocks	142	32	●	●	30	●	●	-	●	●
The Park Lane	285	CBD	511	50	●	●	500	●	●	●	●	●
The Regent, Sydney	270	Rocks	530	66	●	●	600	●	●	-	●	●
Sheraton Wentworth	270	CBD	411	32	●	●	1000	●	●	-	●	●
Quay West	265	Rocks	116	8	●	●	60	●	○	-	●	●
Parkroyal at Darling Harb'r	255	D'ling Hrbr	273	22	●	●	200	●	●	-	●	●
Hyatt Kingsgate	250	Kings X	389	-	●	●	600	●	●	●	●	●
Sydney Hilton	250	CBD	556	29	●	●	650	●	●	-	●	●
Hotel Nikko Darling Hbr	240	Dlg Harb	589	56	●	●	300	-	○	-	●	●
Holiday Inn Menzies	230	City	221	15	●	-	400	●	○	-	●	●
Ramada Hotel North Ryde	230	Nth Ryde	-	228	●	●	180	●	●	-	●	●
Golden Gate Hotel	225	Rocks	376	4	●	●	250	●	●	-	●	●
Sydney Airport Parkroyal	210	Airport	248	-	●	-	200	●	●	●	●	●
Centra North Sydney	200	N.Sydney	430	2	-	-	-	●	●	-	●	●
Park on Oxford Apart'ts	195	Darlingh'st	-	150	●	●	50	-	○	-	●	●
Southern Cross	195	Haymkt	164	19	-	-	200	●	●	-	●	●
York Apartment Hotel	193	CBD	89	41	-	-	-	●	●	-	●	-
Sydney Airport Hilton	190	Airport	258	98	●	●	400	●	●	●	●	●
Wynyard TraveLodge	190	CBD	205	-	●	●	200	●	-	-	-	●
Manly Pacific Park Royal	185	Manly	158	11	●	●	450	●	-	-	●	●
Waldorf All-suite	185	Haymkt	91	-	-	-	-	●	●	-	-	●
Radisson Kestrel	185	Manly	83	30	-	-	80	●	-	-	-	●
Novotel Sydney	180	Drlg Hbr	506	24	●	●	110	●	●	-	●	●
Sydney Marriott	180	Hyde Park	227	14	●	-	400	●	●	-	●	●
The Cambridge	170	E.Sydney	140	40	●	-	-	-	●	-	●	●
Waratah Hotel	170	Haym'kt	143	-	-	-	-	-	-	-	-	-
Gazebo Hotel	165	Eliz.Bay	400	-	●	-	200	●	○	-	-	-
Manly Waterfront AptH	165	Manly	25	21	-	-	-	-	-	●	-	-
Swiss Grand All Suite Hotel	165	Bondi Bch	-	203	●	-	350	●	●	-	●	●
The Landmark	165	Eliz.Bay	457	13	●	●	300	●	●	-	-	●
Boulevard Hotel	160	City	274	-	●	--	200	●	--	-	●	●
Holiday Inn Park Suites	160	Hyde Park	-	135	●	-	-	-	-	-	●	●
The Westbury	160	Kings X	67	-	-	-	-	-	-	-	-	-
Metro Inn Sydney	160	Dlg Harbour	340	26	-	-	-	-	-	-	-	●
Olims Sydney Hotel	160	Potts Pt	114	4	●	●	150	●	-	-	●	-
Hyde Park Plaza	155	E.Sydney	135	45	●	-	120	●	●	-	●	●
Simpsons Potts Point	155	Potts Pt	14	-	-	-	-	-	-	-	-	-
Paramatta Parkroyal	150	Paramatta	186	1	●	●	250	-	●	-	●	●
Country Comfort Syd' Ctrl	150	City	46	4	-	-	-	-	-	-	-	●
Savoy Apartments	148	CBD	54	-	-	-	-	-	-	-	-	-
Greetings Oxford Koala	138	E.Sydney	351	-	-	-	-	-	-	-	-	●
Crescent on Bayswater	135	Kings X	57	3	●	-	-	●	-	-	●	●
Glenview Hotel/Conv. Ctre	125	N.Sydney	70	3	●	●	250	●	○	-	●	●
Parramatta Travelodge	125	Rosehill	163	2	●	●	120	-	●	●	-	●
Wooloomooloo Waters	115	W'mooloo	-	94	-	-	-	-	-	-	-	●
Top of the Town	115	Kings X	102	-	●	-	-	-	●	-	-	●
Chateau Sydney	110	Potts Pt	92	2	-	-	-	-	●	-	-	●

Melbourne Hotel Reference Table

Hotel (listed in price order)	Single Room Rate (AUS $)	Location	Number of Rooms	Number of Suites	Conference Facilities	Exhibition Space	Largest Banquet Number	Business Centre	Swimming Pool (0 = indoor)	Tennis Court	Health Club	Video Films
The Windsor Oberoi	380	CBD	160	20	●	●	600	●	-	●	●	●
Grand Hyatt Melbourne	350	CBD	540	19	●	●	900	●	●	●	●	●
Hotel Como	350	S.Yarra	-	107	●	●	80	●	●	-	●	●
Melbourne Hilton on the Park	330	E.Melbne	324	9	●	●	600	●	●	-	●	●
Le Meridien Melbourne	300	West CBD	232	9	●	●	120	●	O	-	●	●
The Sebel of Melbourne	300	CBD	100	15	-	-	100	-	●	-	●	●
Rockman's Regency	299	CBD	170	15	-	-	-	-	O	-	●	●
Melbourne Parkroyal	280	CBD	-	283	●	●	120	●	●	-	●	●
Sheraton Towers Southgate	280	South M'ne	375	13	●	●	250	●	●	-	●	●
Regent of Melbourne	280	CBD	311	52	●	●	650	●	-	-	●	-
Centra Melbourne	225	CBD	372	13	●	-	110	●	-	-	●	●
Parkroyal on St Kilda Rd	215	South	218	2	●	-	60	●	-	-	●	●
Savoy Park Plaza	198	CBD	158	4	●	-	230	●	-	-	●	●
All Seasons Swanston	198	CBD	-	197	●	-	130	●	O	-	-	-
Bryson Hotel	195	CBD	293	70	-	-	-	-	-	-	●	●
Banks Hotel	190	West CBD	204	-	-	-	-	-	-	-	-	-
St Kilda Rd TraveLodge	187	South	224	1	●	●	150	●	-	-	-	-
Novotel Melbourne on Collins	185	CBD	323	-	●	●	200	●	-	-	●	●
Melbourne Travelodge Airpt	180	Airport	205	-	●	●	160	●	-	-	●	●
Country Cmft Old Melbourne	175	North	226	-	●	●	300	●	-	-	●	-
Southern Cross Hotel	160	CBD	282	64	●	●	1000	●	-	-	●	●
All Seasons Crossley	160	CBD	88	-	-	-	-	●	-	-	-	●
Metro Inn Riverwalk	155	Richmond	72	22	●	-	100	-	-	-	-	-
Radisson President	150	Albert Pk	365	20	●	●	1000	●	-	-	-	●
Hotel Grand Chancellor	150	CBD	150	-	●	-	200	●	-	-	●	●
Eden on the Park	148	Albert Pk	202	12	●	●	240	-	-	-	●	●
Chateau Melbourne	145	CBD	159	-	●	-	150	●	-	-	●	●
Batmans Hill Hotel	120	West CBD	86	-	-	-	-	-	-	-	-	-
All Seasons Welcome	110	CBD	360	-	●	-	80	●	-	-	-	●
Hotel Ibis Melbourne	90	North CBD	250	-	●	●	160	●	-	-	●	●

Rest of Australia Hotel Reference Table

Hotel	Single Room Rate (AUS $)	Location	Number of Rooms	Number of Suites	Conference Facilities	Exhibition Space	Largest Banquet Number	Business Centre	Swimming Pool (0 = indoor)	Tennis Court	Health Club	Video Films
Green Island Resort	700	Cairns	46	-	-	-	-	-	●	●	●	-
Bedarra Bay Resort	638	Gt Barr Rf	-	16	-	-	-	-	●	●	●	-
Lizard Island Lodge	520	Gt Barr Rf	-	32	-	-	-	-	●	●	●	-
Hayman Resort	395	Gt Barr Rf	170	44	●	●	200	●	●	●	●	-
Sheraton Mirage	360	Pt Douglas	300	-	-	-	300	-	●	●	●	-
Orpheus Island Resort	350	Gt Barr Rf	-	31	-	-	-	-	●	●	●	-
Sheraton Mirage	325	Gold Coast	300	25	●	-	250	-	●	●	●	●
Holiday Inn Crowne Plaza	325	Hamilton Isd	400	-	●	●	350	●	●	●	●	-
Dunk Island Resort	324	Gt Barr Rf	135	-	-	-	-	-	●	●	●	-
Marriott Surfers Paradise	305	Surfers P	330	-	●	●	720	-	●	●	●	●
Heritage Hotel	300	Brisbane	232	20	●	●	200	●	●	-	●	●
Hyatt Hotel Canberra	290	Canberra	231	18	●	●	320	●	O	●	●	●
Hyatt Regency Coolum	290	Coolum Bch	321	9	●	●	250	●	●	●	●	●
Conrad Int'l Treasury Casino	280	Brisbane	121	16	●	-	100	●	-	-	●	●
Cooroona Ski Lodge	280	Falls Crk	-	11	-	-	-	-	-	-	-	-
Hyatt Regency Perth	270	Perth	336	28	●	●	700	●	●	●	●	●

Rest of Australia Hotel Reference Table

Hotel (listed in price order)	SINGLE ROOM RATE from (AUS $)	LOCATION	NUMBER OF ROOMS	NUMBER OF SUITES	CONFERENCE FACILITIES	EXHIBITION SPACE	LARGEST BANQUET NUMBER	BUSINESS CENTRE	SWIMMING POOL (0 = indoor)	TENNIS COURT	HEALTH CLUB	VIDEO FILMS
Hyatt Regency Adelaide	260	Adelaide	348	21	●	●	400	●	●	-	●	●
Sheraton Brisbane	260	Brisbane	404	7	●	●	500	●	●	-	●	●
Perth Parmelia Hilton	255	Perth	222	52	●	●	300	●	●	-	●	●
Sails in the Desert	245	Ayers Rk	226	4	●	-	240	-	●	●	-	-
Brampton Island Resort	241	Gt Barr Rf	108	-	-	-	-	-	●	●	●	-
Brisbane Hilton	240	Brisbane	314	6	●	●	680	●	●	●	●	●
Hyatt Regency Sanctry Cove	240	Gold Cst	247	3	●	●	350	●	●	●	●	●
Pan Pacific Gold Coast	240	Gold Cst	298	-	●	-	500	-	●	●	●	●
Radisson Plaza Hotel	240	Cairns	210	10	●	●	320	●	●	-	●	●
Adelaide Hilton	235	Adelaide	308	12	●	●	450	●	●	●	●	●
Fairmont Resort	233	Blue Mts	404	16	●	●	525	●	●	●	●	●
Cairns Hilton	230	Cairns	260	5	●	●	280	●	●	-	●	●
Plaza Hotel Darwin	225	Darwin	221	12	-	-	-	-	●	-	●	-
Royal Pines Resort/Prince Htl	225	Gold Cst	329	-	●	-	1050	-	●	●	●	●
Cairns International	225	Cairns	321	-	●	●	200	●	●	-	●	-
The Beaufort Hotel	225	Darwin	164	32	●	●	300	●	●	-	●	●
Sheraton Perth	220	Perth	396	28	●	●	750	●	●	-	●	●
Hinchinbrook Isd Resort	220	Gt Barr Rf	19	-	-	-	-	-	●	●	●	-
Capital Parkroyal	215	Canberra	266	6	●	●	80	●	●	-	●	●
Plaza Alice Springs	205	A.Springs	235	-	●	-	200	●	●	●	●	-
Hindley Park Royal	205	Adelaide	138	39	●	-	320	●	●	-	●	-
Diamond Bch Htl Casino	200	Darwin	96	-	●	●	200	●	●	●	●	-
Grand Chancellor Hobart	200	Hobart	234	12	●	-	500	-	O	-	●	●
Desert Gardens Hotel	200	Ayers Rk	100	-	-	-	-	-	●	-	-	-
Conrad Htl/Jupiters Cas.	200	Gold Cst	622	-	●	-	200	-	●	-	●	-
Brisbane Parkroyal	195	Brisbane	141	8	●	-	500	●	●	-	●	●
Pacific International	195	Cairns	170	10	-	-	-	-	●	-	-	-
Ana Hotel Gold Coast	190	Surfers P	403	-	-	-	-	-	●	-	-	-
Launceston Cntry Club/Cas.	190	Launceston	104	-	●	-	-	-	-	●	●	-
Perth Parkroyal	190	Perth	99	1	●	-	80	-	●	-	●	●
Gt Keppel Island Resort	188	Gt Barr Rf	193	-	-	-	-	●	●	●	●	-
Orchard Perth Hotel	180	Perth	260	20	●	●	200	●	●	●	●	●
Burswood Resort Hotel	180	Perth	415	-	-	-	-	-	-	-	-	-
Perth Townhouse Parkroyal	180	Perth	120	1	●	-	40	-	O	-	●	●
Esplanade Hotel	180	Fremantle	141	-	●	-	-	-	●	-	-	-
Ramada Hotel	180	Surfers P	401	2	●	-	250	-	●	●	●	-
Brisbane City TraveLodge	180	Brisbane	190	1	●	●	240	-	-	-	-	●
Noah's Lakeside Hotel	178	Canberra	205	6	●	-	-	●	●	-	●	●
Gold Coast International	175	Surfers P	296	10	-	-	-	-	●	●	●	●
Holiday Inn Cairns	175	Cairns	235	10	●	-	100	●	●	-	-	-
The Pavilion Hotel	175	Canberra	186	-	-	-	-	-	●	-	-	-
Surfers Paradise Travelodge	175	Surfers P	265	-	●	●	370	-	●	●	●	●
All Seasons Abbey Hotel	165	Brisbane	-	87	●	-	100	●	●	-	●	●
Sheraton Breakwater	165	Townsville	192	-	-	-	500	●	●	-	●	●
Ramada Grand Adelaide	165	Adelaide	188	38	●	●	620	●	●	-	●	●
Daydream Island Travelodge	160	Gt Barr Rf	302	1	●	-	200	●	●	●	●	●

Rest of Australia Hotel Reference Table

Hotel (listed in price order)	SINGLE ROOM RATE (AUS $)	LOCATION	NUMBER OF ROOMS	NUMBER OF SUITES	CONFERENCE FACILITIES	EXHIBITION SPACE	LARGEST BANQUET NUMBER	BUSINESS CENTRE	SWIMMING POOL (0 = indoor)	TENNIS COURT	HEALTH CLUB	VIDEO FILMS
Canberra International	160	Canberra	117	36	●	●	120	●	●	●	-	●
Carlton Crest Int'l	160	Brisbane	412	35	●	●	800	-	●	-	●	●
Darwin TraveLodge	160	Darwin	178	2	●	●	100	-	●	-	-	●
Ramada Gt Barr Reef Resort	160	Cairns	180	4	●	●	200	-	●	●	●	-
Novotel Launceston	160	Launceston	165	-	-	-	-	-	-	-	-	-
Terrace Intercontinental	156	Adelaide	313	21	●	-	300	●	●	●	●	●
Perth International	155	Perth	230	-	●	-	-	-	●	-	●	-
Apollo Charlestown	155	Charlestown	42	8	●	-	110	●	●	-	-	●
Pajinka Wilderness Lodge	152	Cape York	24	-	-	-	-	-	-	-	-	-
Adelaide TraveLodge	150	Adelaide	191	-	●	-	35	-	●	-	-	●
Peppers Guest House	150	Hunter Vy	47	-	-	-	-	-	-	-	-	-
Eden Coral Coast Resort	150	Cairns	330	11	-	-	-	-	●	●	●	-
Radisson Observation City	150	Perth	150	-	●	-	-	●	-	-	-	●
Townsville Travelodge	150	Townsville	306	56	●	●	450	●	●	-	●	●
Kewarra Beach Resort	145	Cairns	-	60	●	-	-	-	●	●	-	-
Four Seasons Kakadu	140	Kakadu NT	110	-	-	-	-	-	-	-	-	-
Quality Lennons Hotel	140	Brisbane	150	-	●	-	-	-	-	-	-	-
Quality Harbourside Cairns	135	Cairns	100	-	-	-	100	-	●	-	-	●
Wrest Point Htl/Casino	135	Hobart	197	-	●	-	-	-	●	●	●	-
Chancellor on the Park	130	Brisbane	108	-	●	●	140	●	●	-	●	●
Radisson Long Isd Resort	130	Gt Barr Rf	140	-	-	-	-	-	●	●	●	●
Radisson Royal Palms	130	Pt Douglas	305	10	●	●	200	-	●	●	●	●
Gazebo Hotel Brisbane	130	Brisbane	108	-	●	●	140	●	●	-	●	●
Adelaide Holiday Inn Suites	129	Adelaide	-	140	-	-	-	-	-	-	-	-
Old Adelaide Inn	129	Adelaide	64	-	●	-	-	●	●	-	●	-
Quality Pokolbin Resort	129	Hunter Vy	54	-	-	-	-	-	●	●	-	-
Lord Forrest Hotel	125	Bunbury	105	10	-	-	-	-	-	-	-	-
Canberra Rex Hotel	125	Canberra	154	-	-	-	-	-	-	-	-	-
Canberra TraveLodge	125	Canberra	156	2	●	-	280	-	O	-	●	●
Quality Langley Hotel	124	Perth	253	-	●	-	1000	-	-	-	●	●
Quality Beachcomber Hotel	123	Surfers P	300	-	-	-	80	-	●	●	●	●
Hotel Adelaide	120	Adelaide	147	-	-	-	-	-	●	-	-	-
Innkeepers Lenna	120	Hobart	50	-	●	-	-	-	-	-	-	-
All Seasons Atrium Hotel	120	Darwin	136	4	●	-	100	●	●	-	●	●
Paradise Centre Resort	115	Surfers P	80	-	-	-	-	-	●	-	-	-
Ansett Gateway Hotel	110	Adelaide	226	-	●	●	-	-	-	-	-	-
Frontier Oasis	110	A.Springs	90	-	●	-	80	-	●	-	-	-
Lasseters Hotel/Casino	110	A.Springs	75	5	●	-	160	-	●	-	-	-
Milton Pk Cntry Hse Htl	110	Bondi Jnc	46	-	-	-	-	-	-	-	-	-
Westside Motor Inn	109	Hobart	139	-	-	-	-	-	-	-	-	-
Adelaide Meridien	104	Adelaide	90	-	●	-	60	-	●	-	●	●
Yulara Resort	100	Ayers Rk	70	-	-	-	-	-	●	-	-	-
Quality Princes Hotel	98	Perth	167	-	-	-	300	●	-	-	-	●
Olim's Canberra Hotel	95	Canberra	125	33	●	●	240	-	-	-	-	-
Vista Hotel Alice Springs	93	A.Springs	140	-	-	-	-	-	-	-	●	-
All Seasons Freeway Hotel	90	Perth	77	5	●	-	120	●	●	●	-	-
Frontier Darwin	90	Darwin	83	-	●	-	-	-	●	-	-	-

Australia Hotels

Adelaide SA

Hotel Adelaide   C
62 Brougham Place, 5006
Tel: 8267 3444; Tlx:82174; Fax: 8239 0189

Adelaide Barron Town House   D
Cnr Hindley/Morphett Strs, 5000
Tel:8211 8255; Tlx:82941; Fax: 8231 1179

Adelaide Hilton
233 Victoria Square, PO Box 1871, 5000
Tel: 8217 0711; Tlx:87173; Fax: 8231 0158

The Adelaide Hilton is situated 70 metres from the GPO, central to shopping, theatre and business districts. The hotel overlooks Victoria Square, adjacent to the vibrant Central Market and surrounded by a myriad of café-bars and restaurants, 5.5 kms from the airport.

Accommodation & rates
256 double/112 twin A$ 235-345; 12 suites A$400-700

Credit cards accepted:
Amex, Diners, Visa, Mastercard, JCB

Meeting & conference facilities
15 meeting/conferencerooms, max. capacity 750 theatre-style; audio-visual equipment available; 400 sq m exhibition space; largest reception 450 seated or 600 cocktail; private dining room for 25 people

Room services
Airconditioning, colour TV, direct-dial telephone (ext in bathroom), hairdryer, laundry/valet service, minibar, music/radio, tea/coffee making facilities, 24-hr room service, non-smoker bedrooms available, video films

Business & other services
Business centre, executive floor, express checkout, airport pickup, car parking & rental, taxi service, barber shop/ beauty salon, newsstand/shops

Sports & Recreation
Billiards/snooker, fitness centre/gym,sauna jacuzzi/whirlpool, outdoor swimming pool, tennis

Restaurants & Coffee Shops
Grange Restaurant (80) - Fine dining - chef Cheong Lew, open Tues-Sat nts only;
Brasserie (80) - Popular priced menu, open daily breakfast, lunch & dinner.

Overseas Sales Representatives
Hilton International Sales Offices; Hilton Reservations worldwide.

Adelaide Holiday Inn   C
255 Hindley Road, 5000
Tel: 8231 8333; Fax: 8231 4741

All Seasons Adelaide Meridien   D
21-37 Melbourne St, North Ad' 5006
Tel: 8267 3033; Fax: 8239 0275

Adelaide Travelodge   D
208 South Terrace, 5000
Tel: 8223 2744; Tlx:89232; Fax: 8224 0519

Apartments on the Park   D
274 South Terrace, 5000
Tel: 8232 0555; Tlx:30819; Fax: 8223 3457

Country Comfort Inn   D
226 South Terrace, 5000
Tel: 8223 4355; Fax: 8232 5997

Hindley Parkroyal   B
65 Hindley Street, 5000
Tel: 8231 5552; Tlx: 186554; Fax: 8237 3800

Hyatt Regency Adelaide   B
North Terrace, 5000
Tel: 8231 1234; Tlx:88582; Fax: 8231 1120

Old Adelaide Inn   D
60 O'Connell St, 5006
Tel: 8267 5066; Tlx:89271; Fax: 8267 2946

Ramada Grand Hotel Adelaide   C
2 Jetty Road, Glenalg, 5045
Tel: 8376 1222;Tlx:186565; Fax: 8376 1111

Stamford Plaza   C
150 North Terrace, 5000
Tel: 8217 7552; Tlx:88325; Fax: 8231 7572

Hotel Classification: **A** *after name of hotel =over US$ 200 per person per night;* **B** = *between US$ 150-200;* **C** = *between US$ 100-150;* **D** = *between US$ 50-100;* **E** = *under US$ 50;* ¶ = *prices on application.* ◐ = *PATA Hotel member*

Alice Springs NT

Frontier Oasis Hotel   D
10 Gap Road, 0870
Tel: 521444; Fax: 523776

Lasseters Hotel & Casino   C
Barrett Drive, PO Box 2632, 5750
Tel: 525066; Tlx: 81126; Fax: 529816

Plaza Hotel Alice Springs   C
Barrett Drive, 0870
Tel: 528000; Tlx: 81091; Fax: 523822

The Vista Hotel Alice Springs   D
Stephens Road, PO Box 415, 0870
Tel: 526100; Fax: 521988

Ayers Rock NT

Desert Gardens Hotel   C
Yulara Resort, PO Box 121, 0872
Tel: 089 562100; Tlx: 81367; Fax: 089 562156

Sails in the Desert Hotel   B
Yulara Drive, PO Box 21, 0872
Tel: 089 562200; Tlx: 81108; Fax: 089 562018

Yulara Resort   ◐   D
PO Box 46, Yulara NT 5751
Tel: 089 562144; Tlx: 81084; Fax: 089 562222

Bowral NSW

Milton Park Country House Hotel   A
Horoerns Rd, 2576
Tel: (048) 611522; Tlx: 73958; Fax: (048) 614716

Brisbane QLD

All Seasons Abbey Hotel   C
160 Roma St, 4000
Tel: 3236 1444; Tlx: 142661; Fax: 3236 1134

The Beaufort Heritage Hotel   A
Cnr Edward/Margaret Sts, 4000
Tel: 3221 1999; Fax: 3221 6895

Brisbane City Travelodge   C
Roma St, 4003
Tel: 3238 2222; Fax: 3238 2288

Brisbane Parkroyal   C
Cnr Alice & Albert Sts, 4000
Tel: 3221 3411; Tlx:40186; Fax: 3229 9817

Carlton Crest Hotel Brisbane   C
On King George Square at City Hall, 4000
Tel: 3229 9111; Tlx: 41320; Fax: 3229 9618

Brisbane Hilton
190 Elisabeth St, PO Box 1394, Qld 4001
Tel: 3234 2000; Fax: 3231 3199

Centrally situated in the main inner city area, on Elisabeth Street and the bustling Queen Street Mall, 18 km from the airport. Spectacular atrium style hotel, with three executive floors.

Accommodation & rates
215 double/99 twin A$ 240-315 (single occ. $ 200-275); 6 suites A$ 350-1100

Credit cards accepted:
Amex, Diners, Visa, Mastercard, JCB

Meeting & conference facilities
11 meeting/conference rooms, max. capacity 800; audio-visual equipment available; largest reception 680 seated or 1100 cocktail

Room services
Airconditioning, colour TV, direct-dial telephone (ext in bathroom), hairdryer, laundry/valet service, minibar, music/radio, tea/coffee making facilities, 24-hr room service, non-smoker bedrooms available, video films

Business & other services
Business centre, executive floor, express checkout, car parking & rental, taxi service, barber shop/ beauty salon, newsstand/shops

Sports & Recreation
Fitness centre/gym, jacuzzi/whirlpool, massage, sauna, outdoor swimming pool, tennis

Restaurants & Coffee Shops
Atrium Café (250) - Casual/buffetr, open 0630-2300; *Victoria's Restaurant* (90) - Fine dining, lunch Mon-Fri; dinner Mon-Sat

Overseas Sales Representatives
Hilton International Sales Offices; Hilton Reservations worldwide.

Chancellor on the Park Hotel   C
Cnr Wickham Terrace/Leinhardt St, 4000
Tel: 3831 4055; Tlx: 144980; Fax: 3831 5031

Conrad Int'l Treasury Casino   A
William & George Sts, 4000
Tel: 3306 8888; Fax: 3306 8880

Gazebo Hotel Brisbane   D
345 Wickham Terrace, 4000
Tel: 3831 6177; Fax: 3832 5919

Holiday Inn Times Square   C
200 Creek Street, 4000
Tel: 3368 3500; Fax: 3368 3950

Quality Lennons Hotel Brisbane   C
66-76 Queens St, 4000
Tel: 3222 3222; Tlx:40252; Fax: 3221 9389

Quality River Plaza Hotel   D
21 Dock Street, South Brisbane 4101
Tel: 3844 4455; Fax: 3844 9254

Sheraton Brisbane Hotel & Towers
249 Turbot St, PO Box 1211, 4000   B
Tel: 3835 3535; Tlx: 44944; Fax: 3 835 4960

Bunbury WA

Lord Forrest Hotel   D
Symmons St, 6230
Tel: (097) 219966; Fax: (097) 211845

Cairns QLD

Cairns Hilton
Wharf St, PO Box 1114, 4870
Tel: (070) 52 1599, Fax: (070) 52 1370

The Cairns Hilton enjoys stunning views of Trinity Bay, the Pacific Ocean, and is ideally situated adjacent to the local business tourist centre

Accommodation & rates
260 double/twin A$ 230-340; 5 suites A$ 750-1200

Credit cards accepted:
Amex, Diners, Visa, Mastercard, JCB

Meeting & conference facilities
Five meeting/conference rooms, max. capacity 400; audio-visual equipment and exhibition space available; largest reception 280 seated or 340 cocktail

Room services
Airconditioning, colour TV, direct-dial telephone (ext in bathroom), hairdryer, laundry/valet service, minibar, music/radio, tea/coffee making facilities, 24-hr room service, non-smoker bedrooms available, video films

Business & other services
Business centre, executive floor, express checkout, car parking & rental, taxi service, travel centre, barber shop/ beauty salon, newsstand/shops, guided tours

Sports & Recreation
Fitness centre/gym, jacuzzi/whirlpool, massage, sauna, outdoor swimming pool, tennis

Restaurants & Coffee Shops
Breezes (180) - International, open 0600-2300; *Mondo Café* (100) - International, open 1100-midnight

Overseas Sales Representatives
Hilton International Sales Offices; Hilton Reservations worldwide.

Cairns International Hotel   C
17 Abbott St, PO Box 934, 4870
Tel: 311300; Fax: 31 1801

Eden Coral Coast Resort   C
Coral Coast Drive, 4879
Tel: 591234; Fax: 591297

Green Island Resort   A
c/o Wharf Street, 4870
Tel: 313300; Fax: 521511

Holiday Inn Cairns   D
121 the Esplanade & Florence St, 4870
Tel: 313757; Fax: 313770

Kewarra Beach Resort   C
Kewarra St, Kewarra Beach, 4878
Tel: 576666; Tlx: 48340; Fax: 577525

Pacific International Hotel   C
PO Box 2325, 4870
Tel: 517888; Tlx: 48274; Fax: 510210

Quality Harbourside Hotel   C
209-217 The Esplanade, 4870
Tel: 518999; Fax: 510317

Radisson Plaza Hotel at the Pier   B
Marlin Parade, 4870
Tel: 311411; Tlx: 148202; Fax: 313326

AUSTRALIA - Hotels

Radisson Royal Palms Resort C
Port Douglas Rd, Port Douglas 4871
Tel: 995577; Fax: 995559

Ramada Gt Barrier Reef Resort C
Velvers Rd/Williams Esplanade, 4871
Tel: 553999; Tlx: 48478; Fax: 553902

Reef Hotel Casino A
31-45 Wharf St, Cairns Qsld 4870
Tel: (70) 308888; Fax: (70) 308777

Sheraton Mirage Port Douglas Hotel A
Davidson St, PO Box 172, 4871
Tel: 995888; Tlx: 48888

Canberra ACT

Canberra City TraveLodge D
74 Northbourne Ave, 2600
Tel: 249 6911; Tlx: 62050

Canberra International C
242 Northbourne Ave, 2602
Tel: 247 6966; Tlx: 62154; Fax: 248 7823

Canberra Travelodge D
150 Northbourne Ave, PO Box 517, 2601
Tel: 248 5311; Fax: 248 8357

Capital Parkroyal C
1 Binara St, (part of National Convention Centre), 2601
Tel: 247 8999; Tlx: 61850; Fax: 257 4903

The Hyatt Hotel Canberra A
Commonwealth Ave, 2600
Tel: 270 1234; Tlx: 61362; Fax:281 5998

Lakeside Hotel C
London Circuit, City Centre, 2600
Tel: 247 6244; Tlx: 62374; Fax: 257 3071

Olims Ainslie Hotel D
Cnr Limestone/Ainslie Ave, Braddon, 2601
Tel: 248 5511; Tlx: 62988; Fax: 247 0864

The Pavilion Hotel C
Cnr Canberra Ave/National Circuit Forrest, 2603
Tel: 295 3144; Tlx: 61839; Fax: 295 3325

Charleston NSW

Apollo Charleston C
290 Pacific Highway, Charleston NSW 2290. Tel: (049) 436733; Fax: (049) 421149

Coolum Beach QLD

Hyatt Regency Coolum B
Warran Rd, PO Box 78, 4573
Tel: 71 461234; Fax: 71 462957

Darwin NT

The Beaufort Hotel ○ B
The Esplanade, 5794
Tel: 800800; Tlx: 84061; Fax: 800888

Darwin TraveLodge C
122 The Esplanade, 0800
Tel: (889) 815388; Fax: (889) 815701

Four Seasons Darwin D
Buffalo Court, PO Box 4119, 0800
Tel: 815333; Tlx: 85309; Fax: 410909

MGM Grand Darwin C
Gilruth Ave, 0801
Tel: 438888; Fax: 438999

Novotel Atrium Hotel Darwin D
Cnr Peel St/Esplanade, PO Box 1474, 5794
Tel: 410755; Fax: 819025

Plaza Darwin Hotel C
32 Mitchell St, 0800
Tel: 820000; Fax: 811765

Falls Creek VIC

Cooroona Ski Lodge A
8 Slalom St, PO Box 52
Tel: (057) 583244; Tlx: 56947

Fremantle WA

Fremantle Esplanade Hotel D
Corner Marine Terrace/Essex Street, 6160
Tel: 430 4000; Tlx: 96977 ; Fax: 430 4539

Gold Coast Area QLD

Ana Hotel Gold Coast C
22 View Avenue,(PO Box 93), Surfers' Paradise, 4217
Tel: 5579 1000; Tlx:44655; Fax: 5570 1260

Conrad Hotel & Jupiter's Casino ○ C
Gold Coast Highway, Broadbeach 4218
Tel: (07) 5592 1133; Tlx: 145127; Fax: (07) 5592 8219

Gold Coast International B
Cnr Gold Coast Highway/Staghorn Ave, Surters Paradise, 4217. Tel: (7) 5592 1200; Tlx: 42142; Fax: (7) 5592 1180

Hyatt Regency Sanctuary Cove B
Casey Rd, Hope Is, PO Box 2148, Sanctuary Cove 4215.Tel: (07) 5530 1234; Tlx: 140268; Fax: (07) 5577 8234

Marriott Surfers' Paradise Resort B
158 Ferney Avenue, Surfers' Paradise 4217.Tel: (07) 5592 9800; Fax: 5592 9888

Pan Pacific Hotel Gold Coast ○
PO Box 174, 81 Surf Parade, Broadbeach, Queensland 4218
Tel: (07) 5592 2250; Fax: (07) 5592 3747
E-Mail: panpacgc@OntheNet.com.au

Located adjacent to the beach and within 15 miles of Coolangatta domestic and 65 miles of Brisbane International Airports, the Pan Pacific offers guests an unrivalled ocean-front setting for comfort and enjoyment on Queensland's Gold Coast - Australia's prime vacation playground.

Accommodation and Rates:
298 rooms; Single/Double rate A$ 240
Special Pacific Floor.

Credit cards accepted:
Access, Visa, Diners, Amex, JCB

Meeting & banqueting facilities
Ballroom and 7 meeting rooms, capacity up to 500, with audio-visual equipment

Room services
Airconditioning, colour TV, direct-dial telephone, hairdryer, tea/coffee making facilities, minibar, 24-hr room service

Other services
Adjacent to Oasis Shopping Resort (190 shops); monorail link to Jupiters Casino

Sports & Recreation
Pool, outdoor spa, two lit tennis courts, jogging track, walkway to beach, health club and sauna

Restaurants & coffee shops
Two restaurants featuring continental cuisine and steakhouse specialities; Lobby Lounge; Pool Bar

Overseas Sales Representatives
Pan Pacific Hotels & Resorts Worldwide, SRS Steigenberger Reservation Service

Paradise Centre Resort C
Hanlan St, Surfers' Paradise 4217
Tel: (07) 5559 3399; Fax: (07) 5550 2077

Quality Beachcomber Hotel D
18 Hanlan St, Surfers Paradise 4217
Tel: (07) 5570 1000; Fax: (07) 5592 2715

Quality Inn Gold Coast D
2 Barney Street, Southport 4215
Tel: (07) 5532 7922; Fax: (07) 5532 0195

Figures in brackets after names of restaurants in long hotel entries signifies number of covers/seats available.

20 AUSTRALIA - Hotels

Ramada Hotel Surfers' Paradise   C
Cnr Gold Coast Hwy/Hanlan St, Surfers' Paradise, 4217
Tel: (07) 5579 3499; Fax: (07) 5539 8370

Royal Pines Resort and Gold Coast Prince Hotel   C
Rose Street, Ashmore, Gold Coast 4214
Tel: (7) 5597 1111; Fax: (7) 5597 2277

Sheraton Mirage Gold Coast ◯ A
Sea World Drive, PO Box 2595, Surfers' Paradise 4215
Tel: (07) 5591 1488; Fax: (07) 5591 2299

Surfers' Paradise Travelodge   C
2807 Gold Coast Highway, Surfers' Paradise, 4217.
Tel: (07) 5592 9900; Fax: (07) 5592 1519

Tropic Sands Motor Inn   E
1295 Gold Coast Highway, Gold Coast 4214
Tel: (07) 5535 1044; Fax: (07) 5535 8313

Great Barrier Reef QLD

Bedarra Bay Resort   A
GPO Box 1033, Brisbane 4001
Tel: (07) 360 2444; Fax: (07) 360 2453

Bedarra Hideaway   A
Bedarra Island 4810
Tel: (070) 688168; Fax: (070) 688552

Brampton Island Resort   A
GPO Box 1033, Brisbane 4001
Tel: (07) 360 2444; Fax: (07) 360 2453

Daydream Island Travelodge Resort   C
Whitsunday Islands, Pte Mail Bag 22, Mackay 4740.Tel: (079) 488488/ (008) 075040; Fax: (079) 488499

Dunk Island   A
GPO Box 1033, Brisbane 4001
Tel: (07) 360 2444; Fax: (07) 360 2453

Great Keppel Island Resort   C
Gt Kepple Island, PO Box 108, via Rockhampton 4700
Tel: (079) 391744; Fax: (079) 391775

Hamilton Island Resort   ◯   B
Private Mail Bag, Hamilton Island 4803
Tel: (079) 469999; Fax: (079) 468888

Hayman Resort   ◯   A
Hayman Island, Great Barrier Reef, 4801
Tel: (079) 401234; Fax:(079) 401567

Laguna Quays Resort   A
Kunpipi Springs Rd, Whitsunday 4800
Tel: (079) 466446; Fax: (079) 477770

> ◯ after name = Associated Hotel Member of the Pacific Asia Travel Association.

Latitude 19 Resort   D
Mandalay Ave, Nelly Bay, Magnetic Island, Townsville 4816
Tel: (077) 785200; Tlx: 47000

Lizard Island Lodge   A
GPO Box 1033, Brisbane 4001
Tel: (07) 360 2444; Fax: (07) 360 2453

Orpheus Island Resort   B
PMB 15, Townsville Mail Ctr, Qld 4810
Tel: (077) 777377; Fax: (077) 777533

Ramada Gt Barrier Reef Resort   C
Cnr Veivers Rd/Williams Esplanade, Palm Cove 4879
Tel: (070) 553999; Fax: (070) 553902|

Hobart TAS

Hotel Grand Chancellor   C
1Davey Street, (adj. Victoria Docks), 7000
Tel: 354535; Tlx: 58037; Fax: 238175

Innkeppers Lenna of Hobart   D
20 Runnymede St, 7004
Tel: 232911; Tlx: 58190

Westside Motor Inn   D
156 Bathurst St, 7000
Tel: 346255; Tlx: 58228

Wrest Point Hotel-Casino   C
410 Sandy Bay Rd, 7005
Tel: 250112; Tlx: 58115; Fax: 253909

Hunter Valley NSW

Peppers Guest House   C
Ekerts Rd, Pokolbin 2321
Tel: (049) 987596; Fax: (049) 987739

Quality Pokolbin Resort   D
Broke Rd, Hunter Valley, Pokolbin 2321
Tel: (049) 987600; Tlx: 73172

Injinoo QLD

Pajinka Wilderness Lodge   D
**Via Cape York, Injinoo 4876
Tel: (070) 313988; Fax: (070) 313966**

Kakadu NT

Gagudju Crocodile Hotel   C
Locked Bag No 4. Flinders St, Jabiru/ Kakadu 0886
Tel: (089) 792800; Fax: (089) 792707

Gagudju Lodge   D
Arnhem Highway, via Jim Jim, Cooinda 0886.Tel: (089) 790145; Fax: (089) 790148

Frontier Kakadu Village   D
Arnhem Highway, Kakadu National Park, 0866.Tel: (089) 790166; Fax: (089) 790147

Launceston TAS

Launceston Federal Country Club-Casino   D
Country Club Ave, 7250
Tel: 355777; Tlx: 58600; Fax: 355788

Novotel Launceston   C
29 Cameron St, 7250
Tel: 343434; Tlx: 58888; Fax: 317347

Leura, Blue Mountains NSW

Fairmont Resort & Conf. Centre   B
1 Sublime Point Road, Leura 2780
Tel: (47) 825222; Tlx: 122153; Fax: (47) 841685

Melbourne VIC

All Seasons Crossley Hotel   C
51 Little Bourke St, 3000
Tel: 9639 1639; Fax: 9639 0566

All Seasons Swanston Hotel   B
195 Swanston St, 3000
Tel: 9663 4711; Fax: 9663 8191

All Seasons Welcome Hotel   D
265-281 Little Bourke St, 3000
Tel: 9639 0555; Fax: 9639 1179

Banks Hotel   C
Cnr Spencer St & Fliners Lane, 3000
Tel: 9629 4111; Fax: 9629 4300

Batman's Hill Hotel   D
66-70 Spencer St, 3000
Tel: 9614 6344; Tlx:15808; Fax: 9614 1189

Bryson Hotel   C
186 Exhibition St, 3000
Tel: 9662 0511; Tlx:32779; Fax: 9663 6988

Carlton Court Melbourne   C
65 Queens Road, 3004
Tel: 9529 4300; Fax: 9521 3111

Centra Melbourne on the Yarra   B
Flinders & Spencer Sts, 3005
Tel: 9629 5111; Fax: 9629 5624

Chateau Melbourne Hotel   C
131 Lonsdale St, 3000
Tel: 9663 3161; Fax: 9662 3479

Hotel Como   A
630 Chapel St, South Yarra, 3141
Tel: 9824 0400; Fax: 9824 1868

Country Comfort Old Melbourne   C
5-17 Flemington Rd, 3051
Tel: 9329 9344; Tlx:32057; Fax: 9328 4870

AUSTRALIA - Hotels

Eden on the Park C
6 Queen's Rd, 3004
Tel: 9830 2222; Tlx: 135202; Fax: 9820 2553

Grand Hotel Chancellor C
131 Lonsdale street, 3000
Tel: 9663 3161; Fax: 9662 3479

Grand Hyatt Melbourne A
123 Collins Street, 3000
Tel: 9657 1234; Fax: 9650 3491

Holiday Inn Park Suites A
333 Exhibition Street, 3000
Tel: 9663 3333; Fax: 9663 8811

Hotel Ibis Melbourne D
15-21 Thiery St, 3000
Tel: 9639 2399; Tlx: 151385; Fax: 9639 1988

Melbourne Airport Travelodge C
1 Centre Road, Melbourne Airport
Tel: 9338 2332; Fax: 9330 3230

Melbourne Hilton on the Park
192 Wellington Parade. E. Melbourne, 3002
Tel: 9419 2000; Fax: 9419 2001

The Melbourne Hilton is situated just five minutes from the city's commercial and downtown shopping areas. It is a 30-minute drive from the airport and is located in a prestigious residential area overlooking the Melbourne Cricket Ground.

Accommodation & rates
212 double/112 twin A$ 230-330; 70 King A$ 330-360; 9 suites A$ 390-1500

Credit cards accepted:
Visa, Mastercard, Amex, Diners, JCB

Meeting & conference facilities
10 meeting/conference rooms with audio-visual facilities, capacity 10-1000; largest reception 600 seated or 1000 cocktail.

Room services
Airconditioning, colour TV, direct-dial telephone, hairdryer, laundry/valet service, minibar, music/radio/alarm clock, tea/coffee making facilities, 24-hr room service, non-smoker bedrooms available, video films.

Business & other services
Business centre, car parking (charged), taxi service, barber shop/hairdresser, beauty salon, guided tours, newsstand/shops, gentleman's outfitter

Sports & Recreation
Fitness centre/gym, jacuzzi/whirlpool, indoor swimming pool, sauna

Restaurants & Coffee Shops
Café Rialto (160) - International, open 0630-2300; *Chandelier Room* (90) - Continental, open Mon-Sat 1900-2300; *Franc's on Collins* (60) - bar/lounge, open Mon-Fri noon-2300; Sat 1700-0100. *Rialto Bar* (45) - open daily 1100-2300

Overseas Sales Representatives
Hilton International Co

Le Meridien at Rialto Melbourne
495 Collins St, 3000
Tel: 9620 9111; Fax: 9614 1219

Set in a unique historical environment in the heart of Melbourne, next to the Rialto Observation Deck and within walking distance to the Casino and many restaurants and shops of Melbourne, Le Meridien at Rialto promises a blend of elegant European service with natural Australian charm.

Accommodation & rates
166 doubles, 66 twin. Rack rate from A$ 300; corporate from A$ 205; 9 suites, rack rate from A$ 470; corporate rate A$ 340

Credit cards accepted:
Amex, Bankcard, Diners, JCB, Mastercard, Visa

Meeting & banqueting facilities
9 meeting/reception rooms with audio-visual facilities; 200 sq m exhibition space; largest reception 120 seated/190 cocktail

Room services
Airconditioning, colour TV, direct-dial telephone (ext. in bathroom), laundry/valet service, minibar, music/radio/alarm clock, 24-hr room service, tea/coffee making facilities, non-smoker bedrooms, video films, pay TV, toaster, scales

Business & other services
Business centre, car parking (charged), taxi service, barber shop/hairdresser, beauty salon, guided tours, newsstand/shops, gentleman's outfitter

Sports & Recreation
Fitness centre/gym, jacuzzi/whirlpool, indoor swimming pool, sauna

Restaurants & Coffee Shops
Café Rialto (160) - International, open 0630-2300; *Chandelier Room* (90) - Continental, open Mon-Sat 1900-2300; *Franc's on Collins* (60) - bar/lounge, open Mon-Fri noon-2300; Sat 1700-0100. *Rialto Bar* (45) - open daily 1100-2300

Overseas Sales Representatives
Forte & Meridien Hotels & Resorts

Metro Inn Riverwalk B
Corner Bridge Rd/River St, Richmond 3126
Tel: (03) 9246 1200; Fax: (03) 9246 1222

Novotel Melbourne on Collins C
270 Collins St, 3000
Tel: 9650 5800; Tlx: 151417; Fax: 9650 7100

Parkroyal on St Kilda Road C
562 St Kilda Rd, 3004
Tel: 9529 8888; Fax: 9525 1242

The Radisson President Hotel C
65 Queens Rd, 3004
Tel: 9529 4300; Fax: 9521 3111

The Regent of Melbourne A
25 Collins St, 3000
Tel: 9653 0000; Tlx: 37724; Fax: 9650 4261

Rockman's Regency Hotel A
Cnr Exhibition & Lonsdale Sts, 3000
Tel: 9662 3900; Tlx: 38890; Fax: 9663 4297

Savoy Park Plaza Melbourne B
630 Little Collins St, 3000
Tel: 9622 8888; Fax: 9622 8877

The Sebel of Melbourne A
321 Flinders Lane, 3000
Tel: 9629 4088; Fax: 9629 4066

The Sheraton Hotel C
13 Spring Street, 3000
Tel: 9650 5000; Fax: 9650 9622

Sheraton Towers Southgate A
1 Brown St, 3000
Tel: 9696 3100; Fax: 9690 6581

Southern Cross Hotel C
131 Exhibition St, 3000
Tel: 9653 0221; Tlx: 30193; Fax: 9650 2119

St Kilda Road TraveLodge C
Cnr St Kilda Rd/Park St, 3205
Tel: 9699 4833; Fax: 9690 1603

Photographs normally refer to the properties whose details follow them.

Stamford Plaza Melbourne A
111 Little Collins St, 3000
Tel: (03) 9659 1000; Fax: (03) 9659 0999

Victoria Hotel E
215 Little Collins St, 3000
Tel: 9653 0441; Tlx: 31264; Fax: 9650 9678

The Windsor Oberoi
103 Spring St, 3000
Tel: 9633 6000; Fax: 9633 6001

This century-old national treasure, centrally located adjacent to the Victorian Parliament House, overlooks the Treasury Gardens. The restaurants serve European cuisine complemented by a selection of Australian wines. The Windsor combines quiet elegance with every modern day convenience.

Accommodation & rates
160 rooms, single/double/twin A$ 380-600; 20 suites A$ 650-1500

Credit cards accepted:
Visa, Mastercard, Amex, Diners, JCB, Eurocard

Meeting & conference facilities
Three meeting/conference rooms, capacity 60-350; Grand Ballroom 600 seated/1000 cocktail; private meeting suites for 6-10 persons

Room services
Airconditioning, colour TV, direct-dial telephone, hairdryer, laundry/valet service, minibar, music/radio/alarm clock, 24-hr room service, video films.

Business & other services
Business centre, car parking, travel centre,

Sports & Recreation
Fitness centre/gym, golf, sauna, jacuzzi/whirlpool, massage, tennis

Restaurants
The Lounge (80) - Colonial dining room, open 0600-midnight (Mon-Fri); from 0700 Sat/Sun; *The Cricketers' Bar* (20)

Overseas Sales Representatives
Oberoi Hotels Worldwide

Newcastle NSW

Apollo Charlestown Hotel D
288-292 Pacific Hwy, PO Box 363, 2290
Tel: (049) 436733; Fax: (049) 421149

Perth WA

Airways City Hotel D
195 Adelaide Terrace, 6000
Tel: 323 7799; Tlx: 93113; Fax: 221 1956

All Seasons Freeway Hotel D
55 Mill Point Road, South Perth WA 6151
Tel: 367 7811; Fax: 367 915

Burswood Resort Hotel C
Gt Eastern Hwy, WA-6100
Tel: 362 7777; Tlx: 197224; Fax: 470 2553

Hospitality Inn E
1235 Albany Hwy, Bentley 6102
Tel: 451 6344; Tlx: 93123; Fax: 458 6679

Hyatt Regency Perth A
99 Adelaide Terrace, 6000
Tel: (9) 225 1234; Fax: (9) 325 8899

Kings Ambassador Hotel D
517 Hay Street, 6000
Tel: 325 6555; Tlx: AA 92616; Fax: 221 1539

Metro Inn Perth D
61 Cunning Highway, South Perth WA 6151
Tel: 367 6122; Fax: 367 3411

Radisson Observation City Hotel B
The Esplanade, Scarborough Beach, 6019
Tel: 245 1000; Tlx: 95782; Fax: 245 1345

Orchard Hotel C
707 Wellington St, PO Box 7244
Tel: 327 7000; Tlx: 95050; Fax: 327 7017

Perth Ambassador Hotel D
196 Adelaide Terrace, 6000
Tel: 325 1455; Tlx: 95799; Fax: 325 6317

Perth International Hotel C
10 Irwin St, 6000
Tel: 325 0481; Fax: 323 2902

Perth Parkroyal B
54 Terrace Rd, 6004
Tel: 325 3811; Fax: 221 1564

Perth Townhouse Travelodge C
778 Hay Street, 6000
Tel: 321 9141; Fax: 481 2250

Quality Langley Hotel D
221 Adelaide Terrace, 6000
Tel: 221 1200; Tlx: 197178; Fax: 221 1669

Quality Princes Hotel D
334 Murray Street, 6000
Tel: 322 2844; Fax: 321 6314

Sheraton Perth Hotel C
207 Adelaide Terrace, 6000
Tel: 325 0501; Tlx: 92938; Fax: 325 4032

For Overseas Offices of Hotel Chains, see back of this book

Perth Parmelia Hilton
Mill St, Perth, Western Australia 6000
Tel: 322 3622; Fax: 481 0857

Overlooking the Swan river in the heart of central business district and shopping area. 2.5 km to Perth Railraod Terminal, 19 km to Fremantle Port, 10 km to Perth's International Airport and 9 km to the domestic sirport

Accommodation & rates
156 single/double, 66 twin A$ 255-315 (single occ. A$ 225-285); 52 suites A$ 375-625

Credit cards accepted:
Visa, Mastercard, Amex, Diners, JCB

Meeting & conference facilities
Six meeting/conference rooms with audio-visual facilities, total capacity 1070; 343 sq m exhibition space; largest reception 300 seated or 500 cocktail; teleconferencing + ISDN line available

Room services
Airconditioning, colour TV, direct-dial telephone, hairdryer, laundry/valet service, minibar, music/radio/alarm clock, tea/coffee making facilities, 24-hr room service, in-room safe, non-smoker bedrooms available, video films

Business & other services
Express checkout, airport pickup, translation service, car parking & rental, taxi service, barber shop/beauty salon, guided tours, newsstand, gift shops

Sports & Recreation
Fitness centre/gym, sauna, outdoor swimming pool

Restaurants
Terrace Restaurant (140) - International buffet, open 0700-1430 Mon-Fri/0600-2230 Fri-Sat; *Adelphi Steakhouse* (90) - Café/steakhouse, open 1100-midnight (closed Sun lunch); *Garden Restaurant* (75) - Fine dining, open 1900-2230 Tues-Sat only

Overseas Sales Representatives
Hilton International Worldwide

Sydney NSW

All Seasons Harbour Rocks Hotel D
34-52 Harrington St, 2000
Tel: 9251 8944; Fax: 9251 8900

Ana Hotel Sydney A
176 Cumberland St, the Rocks, 2000
Tel: 9250 6000; Fax: 9223 6560

Beehive Apartments C
132-136 Sussex St, 2000
Tel: 9299 8200; Fax: 9262 3032

Best Western Oxford Koala D
Cnr Pelican & Oxford Sts, 2010
Tel: 9269 0645; Tlx:21868; Fax: 9283 2741

Boulevard Hotel A
90 William St, 2011
Tel: 9357 2277; Tlx:24350; Fax: 9356 3786

Centra North Sydney B
17 Bute Street, 2060
Tel: 9955 0499; Fax: 9922 3689

Chateau Sydney C
14 Macleay St, 2011
Tel: 9358 2500; Fax: 9358 1959

Country Comfort Hotel Sydney Central D
Cnr George & Quay Streets, 2000
Tel: 9212 2544; Fax: 9281 3794

The Crescent on Bayswater D
33 Nayswater Road, Kings Cross, 2001
Tel: 9357 7266; Fax: 9357 7418

Gazebo Hotel C
2 Elizabeth Bay Rd, PO Box 1143, 2011
Tel: 9358 1999; Fax: 9356 2951

Glenview Hotel & Reception Centre
194 Pacific Highway, PO Box 167, 2065 D
Tel: 9439 6000; Tlx:26126; Fax: 9439 6442

Golden Gate Hotel C
169-179 Thomas St, 2000
Tel: 9281 6888; Fax: 9281 6688

Greetings Bondi Junction D
79 Oxford St, Bondi Junction 2022
Tel & Fax: 9389 1761; Tlx: 122147

Greetings Paddington Gardens D
21-15 Oxford St, 2021
Tel: 360 2333; Tlx: 121868; Fax: 332 4601

The Holiday Inn Menzies B
14 Carrington St, 2000
Tel: 299 1000; Tlx: 20443; Fax: 290 3819

Holiday Inn Park Suites C
16-32 Oxford Street, 2010
Tel: 9331 7728; Fax: 9360 2583

Hyatt Regency Sydney A
Top of William Street, Kings Cross, 2011
Tel: 9356 1234; Tlx:23114; Fax: 9357 2757

Hyde Park Plaza Hotel C
38 College Street, 2010
Tel: 9331 6933; Tlx: 22450; Fax: 9331 6022

Inter-Continental Hotel Sydney A
117 Macquarie St, 2000
Tel:9230 0200; Tlx:177965; Fax:9 240 1204

Landmark Parkroyal B
81 Macleay Street, 2011
Tel: 9368 3000; Fax: 9357 6631

Manly Pacific Parkroyal B
55 North Steyne, Manly 2095
Tel: 9977 7666; Fax: 9977 7822

Manly Waterfront Apartment Hotel
1-3 Raglan Street, Manly 2095 C
Tel: 9976 1000; Fax: 9976 2226

Metro Inn Sydney C
64-67 Harbour Street, 2000
Tel: 9281 0400; Fax: 9281 1212

Metro Motor Inn Kings Cross D
40 Bayswater Road, Kings Cross, 211264
Tel: 9356 3511; Fax: 9357 1426

Hotel Nikko Darling Harbour B
161 Sussex St (Cnr Market St), 2009
Tel: 9299 1231; Tlx:20733; Fax: 9299 3340

Novotel on Darling Harbour C
100 Murray Street, Pyrmont NSW 2009
Tel: 9934 0000; Tlx:22407; Fax: 9934 0099

Observatory Hotel A
89-113 Kent Street, 2000
Tel: 9256 2222; Fax: 9256 2233

Old Sydney Parkroyal A
55 George St, 2000
Tel: 9252 0524; Tlx:72279; Fax: 9251 2093

Olims Sydney Hotel C
26/34 Macleay St, Potts Point 2011
Tel:9358 2777; Tlx:123752; Fax: 9358 3186

Oxford Towers Motor Inn E
13 Waine St, 2010
Tel: 9267 8066; Tlx:73281; Fax: 9261 8706

Paramatta Travelodge C
106 Hassall St, Rosehill, 2142
Tel: 9891 3877; Fax: 9891 3953

The Park All-Suite Hotel C
16-32 Oxford Street, Darlinghurst, 2010
Tel: 331 7728; Tlx: AA 74824; Fax: 360 2583

Sheraton on the Park A
161 Elizabeth Street, 2000
Tel: 9286 6000; Fax: 9286 6686

Park Hyatt Sydney A
7 Hickson Road, The Rocks 2000
Tel: 9241 1234; Fax: 9256 1555

Parkroyal Paramatta C
30 Philip St, PO Box 254, Paramatta 2150
Tel: 9689 3333; Tlx:26388; Fax: 9689 3959

Parkroyal at Darling Harbour A
150 Day Street, 2000
Tel: 9261 1188; Fax: 9261 8766

Quay West A
98 Gloucester Street, 2000
Tel: 9240 6000; Fax: 9240 6060

Radisson Kestrel Hotel C
8-13 South Steyne, Manly Beach, 2095
Tel: 9977 8866; Fax: 9977 8209

Ramada Hotel North Ryde B
Cnr Epping & Herring Roads, N Ryde 2113
Tel: 9888 1077; Fax: 9805 0655

Ramada Hotel Parramatta C
18-40 Anderson St, Parramatta 2150
Tel: 9259 7000; Fax: 9251 8484

The Regent, Sydney A
199 George St, PO Box N185, 2000
Tel: 9238 0000; Tlx:73023; Fax: 9251 2851

The Ritz Carlton Sydney A
Level 8, 61a Macquarie St, 2000
Tel: 9252 4600; Fax: 9252 4286

Savoy Apartments B
Cnr King & Kent Strs, 2000
Tel: 267 9211; Tlx: 121082; Fax 262 2023

Sebel of Sydney A
23 Elizabeth Bay Rd, 2011
Tel: 9358 3244; Tlx:20067; Fax: 9357 1926

Sheraton on the Park A
161 Elisabeth Street, 2000
Tel: 9286 6000; Fax: 9286 6686

The Southern Cross, Sydney C
Cnr Goulburn & Elizabeth Streets, 2000
Tel: 9282 0987; Tlx:26324; Fax: 9211 1806

Swiss Grand All Suite Hotel C
Cnr Beach Road/Campbell Pde, Bondi Beach, 2026
Tel: 9365 5666; Fax: 9365 5330

Swiss Grand Hotel Bondi Beach C
Cnr Campbell Parade/Beach Road, 2026
Tel: 9365 5666; Fax: 9365 5330

Sydney Airport Parkroyal C
Cnr Bourke Rd/O'Riordan St, Mascot, 2020
Tel: 9330 0600; Fax: 9667 4517

Sydney Marriott B
36 College Street, 2010
Tel: 9361 8400; Fax: 9361 8599

24 AUSTRALIA - Hotels

Sydney Airport Hilton
20 Levey Street, Arncliffe NSW 2205
Tel: 9518 2000; Fax: 9518 2002

The Sydney Airport Hilton is situated opposite the international terminal, just minutes from the domestic and international airports and 20 minutes from downtown Sydney

Accommodation & rates
194 double/64 twin A$ 230-330 (single occ. $ 190-290); 98 suites A$ 350-450

Credit cards accepted:
Amex, Diners, CB, JCB, Mastercard, Visa

Meeting & conference facilities
11 meeting rooms, with audio-visual facilities, capacity 600; 327 sq m exhibition space; largest reception 400 seated or 600 cocktail.

Room services
Airconditioning, colour TV, direct-dial telephone (ext. in bathroom), hairdryer, laundry/valet service, minibar, music/radio/alarm clock, 24-hr room service, tea/coffee making facilities, trouser press, non-smoker bedrooms, in-house video films

Business & other services
Business centre, express checkout, airport pickup, car parking & rental, taxi service

Sports & Recreation
Fitness centre/gym, golf, jogging track, massage, squash, outdoor swimming pool, tennis

Restaurants & Coffee Shops
Seasons (160) -A la carte/buffet, open 0600-23000

Overseas Sales Representatives
Hilton International Worldwide

Sydney Hilton
259 Pitt Street, Sydney 2000
Tel: 9266 2000; Fax: 9265 6065

The Sydney Hilton is located in the heart of the city, surrounded by the major shopping, entertainment and business districts and minutes by monorail to Darling Harbour. The team at Hilton International offers our clients years of experience for class service and hospitality. We look after our guests and we do it well!

Accommodation & rates
315 double/241 twin, A$ 250-360; executive floor A$ 350 single/A$390 double; 29 suites A$ 400-1000

Credit cards accepted:
All major

Meeting & conference facilities
10 meeting/conferencerooms, audio-visual equipment available; largest reception 650 seated or 1000 cocktail

Room services
Airconditioning, colour TV, direct-dial telephone (ext in bathroom), hairdryer, laundry/valet service, minibar, music/radio, tea/coffee making facilities, 24-hr room service, non-smoker bedrooms available, video films

Business & other services
Business centre, executive floors, Clubroom *Wa No Kutsurogi*, express checkout, car parking & rental, travel centre, taxi service, newsstand/shops

Sports & Recreation
Fitness centre/gym, jacuzzi/whirlpool, massage, sauna, outdoor swimming pool

Restaurants & Coffee Shops
The Market Place (186) popular price buffet/à la carte, open Sun-Thurs 0600-2300/Fri-Sat 0600-0100; *San Francisco Grill* (160) - International fine dining, open Mon-Fri noon-1430/Mon-Sat 1800-2300; *Café Rendezvous* (45) - Coffee, snacks, open Sun-Thur 1000-midnight/Fri-Sat 1000-0200/Sun 1000-2200

Overseas Sales Representatives
Hilton International Worldwide.

○ *after the name of the hotel signifies that the hotel is an Allied Hotel Member of the* **Pacific Asia Travel Association**

Sydney Renaissance A
30 Pitt Street, 2000
Tel: 9259 7000; Tlx: 127792; Fax: 9252 1999

Top of the Town Hotel C
227 Victoria Street, Kings Cross, 2011
Tel: 9361 0911; Fax: 9361 4972

The Waldorf Apartments B
57-67 Liverpool St, 2000
Tel: 9261 5355; Fax: 9261 3753

Waratah Central Hotel B
220 Goulburn St, PO Box 188; 2000
Tel: 9281 0333 Tlx: 20799; Fax: 9281 0222

Wentworth Hotel ○ A
61-101 Philip St, PO Box 2686, 2001
Tel: 9230 0700; Fax: 9227 9133

The Westbury Hotel C
221 Darlinghurst Rd, PO Box 464, 2010
Tel: 9360 3222; Fax: 9360 3277

Wooloomooloo Waters Apts D
48-74 Dowling St, 2011
Tel: 9358 3100; Fax: 9356 4839

Wynyard Vista C
7-9 York St, PO Box 1583, 2001
Tel: 9299 3000; Tlx:26690; Fax: 9262 2416

York Apartment Hotel B
5 York Street, 2000
Tel: 9210 5000; Fax: 9290 1487

Townsville QLD

Sheraton Breakwater Casino Hotel A
Sir Leslie Thiess Dr, 4810
Tel: (77) 222333; Fax: (77) 716505

Townsville Travelodge C
334 Flinders Mall, 4810
Tel: (77) 722477; Fax: (77) 211263

Hotel Classification: **A** *after name of hotel = over US$ 200 per person per night;* **B** *– between US$ 150-200;* **C** *= between US$ 100-150;* **D** *= between US$ 50-100;* **E** *= under US$ 50;* ¶ *= prices on application.*

Sydney Hilton

Restaurants

Below we give a selection of restaurants, with their types of cuisine, located in the State Capital Cities and which reflect the cultures and nationalities which have formed Australian society.

Adelaide

Bangkok Restaurant *(Thai/Malay)*.
1st Fl, 217 Rundle St. Tel: 8223 5406

Chief Charley's *(Fish)*
12 Grenfell St. Tel: 851 4432

The Feathers *(English/European)*
516 Glynburn Rd, Burnside.
Tel: 8332 6133

Henry Ayers Room *(International /French)*
Ayers House, 288 North Terrace.
Tel: 8224 0666

Jarmer's Restaurant *(French)*
297 Kensington Rd, Kensington Park.
Tel: 8332 2080

The Magic Flute *(International)*
109 Melbourne St, North Adelaide.
Tel: 8267 3172

Brisbane

Barrier Reef Seafood Restaurant
138 Albert St. Tel: 221 9366

David's *(Cantonese/Internat'l)*
157 Elizabeth St. Tel: 229 9033

The Drawing Room
Brisbane City TraveLodge, Roma St.
Tel: 238 2288

Michael's on the Mall *(Seafood)*
1st Fl, 164 Queen St Mall. Tel: 229 4911

Canberra

EJ's
21 Kennedy St, Kingston. Tel: 951949

Imperial Court *(Chinese)*
40 Northbourne Ave. Tel: 485547

The Lobby
King George Terrace. Tel: 731563
(Closed during Parliamentary recesses)

Rossini's *(Italian)*
Qantas House, London Circuit.
Tel: 480062

Seasons *(International)*
Canberra Theatre Centre, London Circuit.
Tel: 497700

Darwin

Beagle Restaurant
Museum of Arts & Sciences, Conacher St, Fannie Bay. Tel: 817791

Lee Dynasty *(Cantonese)*
21 Cavenagh St. Tel: 817808/812700

Seaview *(Gourmet Restaurant)*
Seaview Motor Inn, 60 East Point Rd.
Tel: 818809

Hobart

Dear Friends *(Local/Fish)*
8 Brooke St, The Waterfront. Tel: 232646

Milan's Seafood Restaurant
7 Beach Road, Sandy Bay. Tel: 252180

Mr Wooby's *(Brasserie/Pizzeria)*
Rear of 65 Salamanca Place. Tel: 343466

Mures Fish House *(Fish)*
5 Knopwood St, off Montpelier Retreat, Battery Pt. Tel: 236917

The Point Revolving Restaurant
Wrest Point Hotel-Casino, 410 Sandy Bay Rd. Tel: 250112

Sakura Japanese Restaurant
85 Salamanca Place Tel: 234773

La Suprema Pasta House *(Ital)*
255 Liverpool St. Tel: 310770

Melbourne

Cliveden Room *(International)*
Hilton Hotel, Cnr Wellington Parade & Clarendon St, East Melbourne.
Tel: 9419 3311

Empress of China *(Cantonese)*
120 Little Bourke St.
Tel: 9663 1883. **BYO.**

Florentino *(Italian)*
80 Bourke St. Tel: 9662 1811

Gourmand *(German/Internat'l)*
604 Station St, Box Hill. Tel: 9 890 8788.

Grand Dining at the Windsor
The Windsor Hotel, 115 Spring St.
Tel: 9653 0653

Mietta's *(International)*
7 Alfred Place. Tel: 9654 2366

Petty Sessions *(French)*
459 Collins St. Tel: 9614 3854

Rosati *(Italian/International)*
95 Flinders Lane. Tel: 9654 7772

Slattery's Cafe
219 King St. Tel: 9967 1360. **BYO**

Stephanie's *(French)*
405 Tooronga Rd, East Hawthorn.
Tel: 9920 8944

Two Faces *(European)*
149 Toorak Rd, South Yarra.
Tel: 9266 1547

The Willows *(French)*
462 St Kilda Rd. Tel: 9267 5252

Perth

Adelphi Steak House
Parmelia Hilton Hotel, Mill St. Tel: 322 3622

Emperor's Court *(Chinese)*
66 Lake St. Tel: 328 8860

The Establishment *(French/Australian)*
35a Hampden Rd, Nedlands.
Tel: 386 5508.

Fast Eddy's *(Burger/Steaks)*
Cnr Hay St/Milligan St.
Tel: 3212552

Hana of Perth *(Japanese)*
Mill St. Tel: 322 7908

Matilda Bay *(French/Californian)*
3 Hacket Drive, Crawley.
Tel: 386 5425

Ord Street Cafe
27 Ord St, West Perth.
Tel: 321 6021

The Plum *(French/International)*
99 Francis St. Tel: 328 5920.

River Room *(European)*
207 Adelaide Terrace. Tel: 326 0501

Sydney

Balkan II
215 Oxford St, Darlinghurst.
Tel: 9331 7670.

Bangkok *(Thai)*
234 Crown St, Darlinghurst. Tel: 9334804

Bathers Pavilion
Balmoral Beach, North Shore
Tel: 9968 1133

Bayswater Brasserie
32 Bayswater Rd, Kings Cross.
Tel: 9357 2177

Bilson's
Upper Level, Sydney Harbour Passenger Terminal
Tel: 9251 5600

Chez Oz *(Australian)*
23 Craigend St, Darlinghurst.
Tel: 9332 4866

Cicade
Potts Point. Tel: 9358 1255

Claude's *(French)*
10 Oxford St, Woollahara.
Tel: 9331 2325

Darley Street Thai
30 Bayswater Rd, Kings Cross
Tel: 9358 6530

Desaru *(Southeast Asian)*
28 Falcon St, Crow's Nest, North Sydney.
Tel: 9438 4331

Doyle's on the Beach *(Local/Fish)*
11 Marine Parade, Watson's Bay.
Tel: 9337 2007

Harpoon Harry's *(Fish)*
Macquarie Hotel, 42 Wentworth Ave.
Tel: 9264 9089

Imperial Peking Harbourside
15 Circular Quay West, The Rocks.
Tel: 9223 1128

Jordans *(Seafood)*
197 Harbourside, Darling Harbour
Tel: 9281 3711

Kables *(International)*
The Regent Hotel, 199 George St, CBD.
Tel: 9238 0000

Kim Van *(Vietnamese)*
147 Glebe Point Rd, Glebe.
Tel: 9660 5262

Marigold *(Chinese)*
299-305 Sussex St. Tel: 9264 6744

AUSTRALIA - Car Hire/Airline Offices

Marios *(Italian)*
Darlinghurst Road, Kings Cross
Tel: 9331 4945

Mayur *(Indian)*
MLC Centre, 19 Martin Place.
Tel: 9235 2361

Mixing Pot *(Italian)*
178 St John's Rd, Glebe.
Tel: 9660 7449

Prasit's *(Thai)*
Imperial Hotel, 33 Erskineville Rd,
Erskineville. Tel: 9516 4780

Suntory *(Japanese)*
529 Kent St. Tel: 9267 2900

Taylor's *(Italian)*
203-5 Albion St, Surry Hills.
Tel: 9933 5100.

(BYO = Unlicensed; bring your own wine)

Car Hire

Avis Rent-A-Car
(Head Office) 110-112 Christie St, St Leonards, NSW 2065
Tel: (02) 9437 5755; Fax: (02) 9906 1624
(+ Over 250 offices throughout Australia)

Budget Rent-A-Car
(Central Reservations HQ) Melbourne
Tel: (03) 9320 6333; tlx: 39088; fax: (03) 9206 3636. Sydney (City) Office tel: (02) 9339 8888; fax: (02) 9332 1260

Half Price Rent-A-Car
Tel: (02) 9357 1191

Hertz Rent-A-Car
Corner Riley Street/William Street, Sydney
Tel: (008) 333377 (national toll-free)
Sydney (02) 9360 6621
Melbourne (03) 9663 6244

Letz Rent a Car
116 Darlinghurst Road, PO Box 187, Kings Cross, Sydney NSW 2001.Tel: (02) 9331 3099; fax: 9331 7077; tlx: 740099 LRCCAR

Natcar
Tel (02) 9332 1233

Thrifty
Tel: (02) 9357 5399

Airline Offices

(R=reservations; F =flight information)

Air China
Level 11, 115 Pitt Street, Sydney 2000
Tel: (02) 9232 7277; Fax: (02) 9232 7465
Melbourne tel: (03) 9642 1555; fax: -0235

Air India
31 Market Street, Sydney 2000
Tel: 9261 4502

Air Lanka
c/o World Aviation Systems (Aust) Pty, 403 George St, Sydney NSW 2000
Tel: 9290 3422/9239 1722

Air New Zealand
9th fl, 115 Pitt Street, Sydney 2000
Tel: (02) 9234 4111/9223 4666
Melbourne tel: (03) 9654 3311
Perth tel: (08) 221111

Air Niugini
Tel: (02) 9232 3100

Air Pacific
Tel: (02) 9436 6151/9957 0150

Alitalia
2nd fl, Orient Overseas Building, 32 Bridge Street, Sydney 2000. Tel: (02) 9247 9133

British Airways
Level 26, AIDC Tower, 201 Kent Street, Sydney. Tel: (02) 9258 3300
Melbourne tel: (02) 9603 1133
Perth tel: (08) 425 7711

Canadian Airlines
1st fl, Clarence St, Sydney 2000
Tel: (02) 9290 6972/9299 7843
Melbourne tel: (03) 9629 6731

Cathay Pacific
Cnr Hunter/O'Connell Sts, Sydney 2000
Tel: (02) 9231 5122/9931 5555
Melbourne tel: (03) 9602 2088

Continental Airlines/Air Micronesia
321 Street, Sydney 2000
Tel: (02) 9249 0111
Melbourne tel: (03) 9602 4899

Garuda
175 Clarence St, Sydney 2000
Tel: (02) 9334 9944
Melbourne tel: (03) 9654 4311
Perth tel: (08) 9322 4000

JAL
19 Bligh Street, Sydney 2000
Tel: (02) 9233 4500

JAT
130 Philip Street, Sydney 2000
Tel: (02) 9221 2199/9221 2899

KLM
5 Elizabeth St, Sydney 2000
Tel: (02) 9231 6333
Melbourne tel: (03) 9338 4881

Lauda Air
64 York St, Sydney 2000
Tel: 9262 6500

Lufthansa
Lufthansa House, 143 Macquarie St, Sydney 2000
Tel: (02) 9240 6254/9367 3888
Melbourne tel: (03) 9602 1155

Malaysian Airlines
11th fl, American Express Tower, 388 George St, Sydney 2000
Tel: (02) 9231 5066/9232 3377
Melbourne tel: (03) 9654 6822

Olympic
1st fl, 44 Pitt St, Sydney 2000
Tel: (02) 9251 2044
Melbourne tel: (03) 9602 5400

Philippine Airlines
49 York St, Sydney 2000
Tel: (02) 9262 3333

Qantas
Qantas Int'l Centre, Internationa Square, Sydney 2000
Tel: (02) 9957 0111/9236 2636
Melbourne tel: (03) 9602 6111
Perth tel: (08) 9322 0222

Royal Brunei Airlines
3710 MLC Centre, 19 Martin Place, Sydney 2000
Tel: (02) 9223 1566

Singapore Airlines
Singapore Airline House, 17-19 Bridge St, Sydney 2000
Tel: (02) 9236 0111/9231 3522
Melbourne tel: (03) 9602 4555

Swissair
33 Pitt Street, Sydney 2000
Tel: (02) 9232 1744

Thai Airways International
75-77 Pitt St, Sydney 2000
Tel: (02) 9844 0999/9251 1722
Melbourne tel: (03) 9962 6132

United Airlines
10 Barrack Street, Sydney 2000
Tel: (02) 9237 8888

UTA
12 Castlereagh St, Sydney 2000
Tel: (02) 9233 3277
Melbourne tel: (03) 9614 2041

What's the link between business and the Asia Pacific?

BRITISH AIRWAYS
The world's favourite airline

http://www.british-airways.com

Bangladesh

What to see

Dhaka was founded in 1608 as the seat of the Imperial Mughal Viceroys of Bengal and was a thriving centre for the silm and muslim. It still also contains some fine examples of British colonial architecture - mainly north of the Old City. This area was originally set aside by the Moghuls for foreigners and later occupied by the British.

Best examples of the British presence are in the administrative infrastructure - Dhaka College, the Supreme Court (formerly the governor's residence), the Secretariat and Curzon Hall. As elsewhere in the sub-continent, many of Dhaka's modern buildings are a disappointment. The city is dotted with a series of imposing and visually striking mosques. The Khan Mohammed Mirdhai Mosque and the Hassain Dolan Mosque are particularly good examples.

Cox's Bazar boasts the world's longest beach - 120 kilometres; Nr Chittagong, the second city, Chandanpura Mosque is not to be missed - 37 kms away at Sitakund. The tea gardens of Sylhet in the Surma Valley are well worth a visit. The area enjoys a range of exotic flora and fauna. The Surma valley is also a haven for migratory birds.

Shopping

Don't expect to find many quality imported goods for sale as taxes on these items are high and local demand relatively low, so aim to look for the better quality local handicrafts. These represent remarkably good value and often involve fine craftsmanship.

Most of the large hotels boast shopping arcades, which tend to specialise in traditional handicrafts. Opposite the Dhaka Sheraton the Export Promotion Bureau has a good selection of local goods - leather, silk and cotton, garments, carpets, etc for sale in foreign currency. In the same area, the Karika Handicraft Emporium offers a similar range of items but in local currency.

Bangla jewellery is inexpensive and bargains can be had at a variety of outlets throughout Dhaka. Particularly good is Chandran in the DIT supermarket on Mymensingh Road.

Getting around

National carrier Biman operates an extensive domestic network centred on Dhaka; although frequencies are a bit patchy for business travellers in a hurry. Only flights between Dhaka and Chittagong offer better than daily frequencies. There are also services from Chittagong to Cox's Bazar, Khulna and Jessore.

Car rental is possible through Parjatan, but not especially advisable. Better to hire a car and driver for the day, which is not expensive and comes with a guarantee that you will find your destination more easily. Once again, taxis are cheap and are mainly available from ranks at the large hotels or can be hailed in the street. Otherwise motorised rickshaws may be the only means of transport around Dhaka. Buses are dirty and overcrowded and do not carry destination signs or numbers in English.

Bangladesh's well-developed river network is used by everyone and if time is not a problem then "rocket" ferries are recommended to reach a number of points from Dhaka and Chittagong.

Entertainment

There are a few exclusive discos in Dhaka where access to visitors is restricted. What's more the American Marines Club in the US Embassy has a disco every Friday night to which non-members can gain access. Other foreign-oriented clubs hold similar events at the weekend, but not all are open to visitors. In Chittagong, the Hotel Agrabad has a Friday-night disco.

But what Dhaka lacks in terms of nightlife is to some extent compensated for by some delightfully unassuming and ridiculously low-priced restaurants. Keep away from the big hotels for the best deals, but watch out for the after effects.

Nevertheless, the Sonargaon and Sheraton both have excellent buffets where the chance of catching something nasty is somewhat reduced.

Leisure

For a small fee non-guests are able to gain access to the swimming pool at the Dhaka Sheraton. Otherwise, recreational facilities are in short supply or of poor quality. Some other hotels have tennis courts, but again these are limited.

Arrival & Departure

Zia International Airport is located outside the city. A taxi is the only reliable method of travelling into Dhaka; although a bus (No.6) connects the airport with the Central Railway station at Kamalapur. Zia also handles all domestic flights.

International Airport Departure Tax, is TK200; TK20 on domestic flights. s.

Restaurants

Dacca perhaps the most reliable (and licensed) restaurants are to be found in the Dacca Sheraton and Sonargaon Hotels. Nevertheless visitors might like to try the selection in Dacca which follows as an alternative. In Chittagong there are several good Chinese restaurants, more reasonably priced than in the capital.

Ali Baba Specialised Restaurant
Mymensingh Rd (opp. Hotel Sonargaon)

Chung Wah *(Chinese)*
North-South Rd. Tel: 251044)

LaDiplomat *(Continental)*
Gulshan. Tel: 602282

Mary Anderson Floating Restaurant
Pagla (8 km from city - on Buriganga River) Tel:71288

ParjatanTouristRestaurant *(Bangladeshi)*
Mohakhali. Tel: 605398

Red Button *(Continental)*
Farm Gate. Tel: 317717

Sakura Restaurant *(Chinese/Japanese/ Continental - licensed)*.1st Fl Karika Emporium (Nr. Dacca Sheraton).Tel: 509296

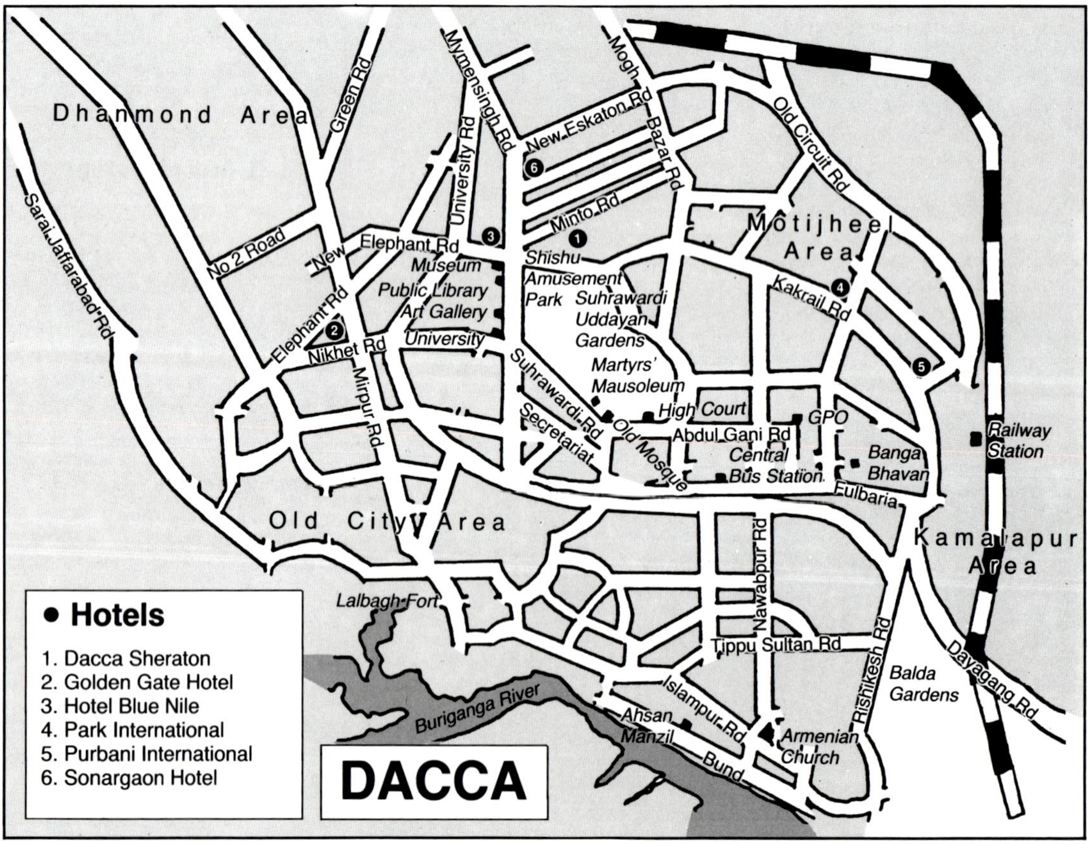

● **Hotels**
1. Dacca Sheraton
2. Golden Gate Hotel
3. Hotel Blue Nile
4. Park International
5. Purbani International
6. Sonargaon Hotel

DACCA

Bangladesh Key Fact File

Passport Requirements:
A valid passport is required by all visitors. Visas are required for travellers staying more than 15 days except those from British Commonwealth (exc the Dominions) and Bhutan, Guyana, Gabon, Ireland, W Samoa, Somalia, Tunisia & Vatican. No visa required for travellers staying up to 15 days and able to show return ticket.

Currency:
Taka (Tk). 1 poisha = 1 taka

Exchange Rate: *(February 1997)*
US$1 = 42.8 Tk; £1 = 69.3 Tk

Currency Restrictions:
Import & export of local currency limited to Tk 300. Free import of foreign currency, subject to declaration. Export of foreign currency limited to the amount declared on entry

Electricty Supply:
220/240 volts AC

Language:
Bangla and other local languages. English is spoken and widely understood and used commercially.

Time:
GMT + 6 hours; EDT + 11 hours.

IDD Code: 880 *followed by area codes*
Bogra 51; Chittagong 31; Comilla 81; Dhaka 2; Khulna 41; Kushtia 71; Mymensingh 91; Sylhet 821

Business hours:
Government offices 0730-1400 Saturday to Thursday; commercial offices 0900 to 1700 Saturday to Thursday
Shops 1000-1230 Monday to Friday; 1000-1400 Saturday. Tourist shops may stay open longer.
Banks 0900-1300 Saturday to Wednesday; 0900-1100 Thursday.

Customs & Entry:
A Customs Declaration Form is issued on arrival. This must be kept as it will be checked before a traveller is allowed to leave the country. Allowance is 200 (or two cartons) cigarettes and two litres or bottles of liquor.

Health Requirements:
Yellow fever certificate required; cholera/typhoid/malaria precautions advised tho' not mandatory and little risk in Dakha or main tourist areas. All water should be regarded as being potentially contaminated. Rabies is present.

Climate/Best Time to Visit:
Tropical, with heavy rainfall (2,450mm annually in Dhaka) and bright sunshine in the monsoon and warm for the greater part of the year. Min-max June-August 25-35˚C; The winter months - November-March - are cooler and pleasant (min-max 13-27˚C). Best time to visit is October to May.

Airport Departure Tax
Tk 200 on international flights; Tk 20 on domestic.

National Holidays 1997
6 February Shab-E-Kadar; 26 March Independence Day; 9/10 February start of Ramadan*; 21 February Shahid Dibosh; 8/10 March Eid ul-Fitr (end of Ramadan)*; 14 April Bengali New Year; 1 May Labour Day;17-19 April Eid-ul-Azha *; 18 July Eid-e-Miladunnabi (birth of the prophet Mohammed)*; 15 August National Mourning Day; 15/16 December Shab-E-Barat/Biganj Dibash (Victory Day); 25 December Christmas Day; *(* Moslem holidays; may vary by one/two days acc. to the moon).*

Airlines

Aeroflot
Sheraton Hotel, Dacca Tel: 506636

Air India.
Dacca Sheraton Hotel, Tel: 500070-71

Biman
Biman Bhaban, 100 Motijheel C/A, Dacca Tel: 240151-9/240161-9/20171-9

British Airways
8th fl, Sena Kalyan Bhaban, 195 Motijheel Commercial Area, Dacca.
Tel: 956 4869/861091-4; Fax: 003239

Gulf Air
Jahangir Tower, 10 Karwan Bazar, Dacca
Tel: 323542/323522; Fax: 863945

Indian Airlines
Sharif Manson, 56/57 Motijheel C/A, Dhaka
Tel: 256533/231687

Kuwait Airways
c/o Bengal Aviation Services, 43 Dilkusha Commercial Area, Dacca 2
Tel: 232139/232388

Lufthansa
c/o Sheraton Hotel. Tel: 502856

Myanmar (Burma) Airways
Hajhala Sein & Co, 25 Bagabandhu Ave, Dacca. Tel: 253090

PIA
Dacca Sheraton. Tel: 501112; Fax: 832985

Royal Nepal Airlines
54 Motijheel C/A, Dacca. Tel: 239353

Saudia
Sonargaon Hotel, PO Box 2772, Dacca
Tel: 311207/311969; Fax: 813145

Singapore Airlines
Yusuf Chamber, 20 Dilkusha Commercial Area, Dacca 2.Tel: 863640; Fax: 833260

Thai International
Sheraton Hotel, Minto Road, Dacca
Tel: 834711-9

What's the link between business and the Asia Pacific?

BRITISH AIRWAYS
The world's favourite airline

http://www.british-airways.com

Useful Addresses

Air Couriers

DHL: Dhaka (02) 600189
TNT: Dhaka (02) 235546
UPS: Dhaka (02) 605581

Banks, GPO

American Express
Motijheel Commercial Area,
Dacca.Tel:283173.
Off Sheikh Mujib Rahman Rd, Agrabad
Commercial Area. Tel: 501045/6

Chartered Bank
Motijheel Commercial Area, Dacca.
Tel: 251372
Suhrawardi Rd, Chittagong. Tel: 201181

GPO Dacca
Abdul Gani Rd, (off Bangbandhu Ave, near Baitul Moharram Mosque (- see town plan)

Car Hire

Bangladesh Parjatan Corporation
233 Airport Road, Tejgaon,
Dacca 1215. Tel:819193
Rajdhani Tours
Dhaka.Tel: 501263

Chambers of Commerce

Bangladesh Chamber of Industries
GPO Box 3988, BCIC Bldg (3rd Fl), 30-31
Dikusha CA, Dacca.
Tel: 252081; Tlx: 65847
Chittagong Chamber Commerce & Industry
PO Box 481, Chamber Hse, Agrabad CA, Chittagong. Tel: 50447/50448; Tlx: 66372 CHAMBER BJ
Dacca Chamber of Commerce & Industry
65-66 Motijheel CA, Dacca. Tel: 232562/232693/255106; Tlx: 642418
The Federation of Bangladesh Chambers of Commerce & Industry
60 Motijheel CA, Dacca. Tel: 282880/250566/257734
Metropolitan Chamber of Commerce & Industry
Chamber Bldg, 122-124 Motijheel CA, Dacca. Tel: 230714/257316/236168-9

Government Departments for Tourism, Trade & Investment

Bangladesh Parjaton Corporation (National Tourist Office) 233 Airport Rd, Tajgoan, Dacca. Tel: 325155-9; Tlx: 642206 TOUR BJ

Bangladesh Parjaton Corporation - Chittagong branch Motel Shaikat, Stat-ion Rd, Chittagong.Tel: 209514/204650

Board of Investment
Shilpa Bhavan, 91 Motijheel Commercial Area, Dacca. Tlx: 642212 ; Fax: 833626

Export Promotion Bureau
122-124 Motijheel Commercial Area, Dacca. Tlx: 642204. Fax: 833167

Ministry of Commerce
Bangladesh Secretariat, Dacca.
Tlx: 642201 FTD BJ

Ministry of Industries
Shilpa Bhavan, 91 Motijheel CA, Dacca.
Tlx: 642212 DGIND BJ

Trading Corporation of Bangladesh
TCB Bhaban, Kawran Bazar, Dacca. Tlx: 642217 & 642203 TCB BJ; Fax: 813582

Hotels

Dacca

Dacca Sheraton Hotel B
1 Minto Rd, PO Box 504.Tel: 863391/861191
Tlx: 642401 SHER BJ; Fax: 860468

Hotel Blue Nile E
36 New Elephant Rd. Tel: 509416

Hotel Golden Gate E
28 Mirpur Rd. Tel: 505111

Hotel Park International E
46 Kakrail Rd. Tel: 405191/2

Hotel Purbani International E
1 Dilkusha Rd, Motijheel CA.
Tel: 864926; Tlx: 642460; Fax: 833212

Pan Pacific Sonargaon Hotel
107 Kazi Nazrul Islam Ave, PO Box 3595.
Tel: 811005/812011; Fax: 813324
E-mail: ppdagst@dhaka.agni.com
With its international clientèle, Dhaka's most distinguished luxury hotel offers privacy, fine cuisine and personalized service to met the diverse needs of its guests.

Accommodation and rates:
377 rooms and suites; single/double room US$ 180; suites US$ 230-700
(subject to 35% gov't tax & service charge)
Credit cards accepted:
Access, Visa, Carte Blanche, Diners, Eurocard, Amex
Groups
8 meeting rooms with audio-visual equipment available; capacity 750; largest reception 1500

Room services
Newly renovated rooms, central air-conditioning, colour TV, radio, honesty bar, satellite TV, 24-hour room service

Business & other services
24-hour business centre, travel desk, barber shop/beauty salon, airport bus

Sports & recreation
Two pools, health club with sauna, massage, tennis & squash courts

Restaurants & coffee shops
Four restaurants offering Western, Asian, Continental and French cuisine; poolside & three other bars

Overseas Sales Representatives
Pan Pacific Hotels & Resorts worldwide.
SRS Steigenberger Resrvation Service

Hotel Zakaria International E
35 Gulshan Ave, Mohakhali, CA
Tel: 601172

Other areas

Hotel Agrabad C
Agrabad CA, PO Box 147, **Chittagong** 4100. Tel: (31) 500111; Tlx: 66237; Fax: (31) 225572

The Hilltown Hotel E
Tally Ho Rd, Slyhet, **Chittagong**.Tel: 8262

Motel Shaikat E
Station Rd. **Chittagong**.Tel: (31) 204650/209845 (Run by Parjatan Tourist Office)

Hotel Shahjahan E
Saddarghat Rd, **Chittagong**.Tel: 203446

Hotel Shaibal E
Motel Rd, **Cox's Bazar** Tel: 3275

Motel Upal E
Motel Rd, **Cox's Bazar**
Tel: 4258 (Run by Parjatan)

Hotel Nurpur E
Line Rd, Barisal, **Khulna** Tel: 3377

Hotel Rupsa International E
North Jessore Rd, **Khulna** .Tel: 60563

The Parjatan Motel E
Abdul Majid Rd, **Rajshahi**. Tel: 2099/5492

Cambodia

Doing Business

Cambodia has enjoyed relatively fruitful economic progress in recent years despite continued political in-fighting, Khmer Rouge insurgency, sporadic food shortages and rising labour costs.

A liberal foreign investment law introduced by the Phnom Penh government in 1994 produced an estimated US$2 billion worth of initial projects, thanks to incentives for investors including 9% corporation tax, free repatriation of profits, an eight-year tax holiday and exemption from import duties. Most popular investment sectors are travel and tourism, gems, food industry and wood products. The government would like also to reinvigorate investment in tobacco, paper and cement production. But the growing garment industry was hit by demonstrations in early 1997 as women factory workers pleaded for shorter working hours and higher pay - prompting the King, who is seen as a unifying influence in the country, to urge government to permit union representation and regulations.

The Asian Development Bank estimates that Cambodia will achieve real GDP growth of 7-8% in 1996/7, with inflation no more than 5% and current account deficit down to 8%. This compares with an inflation rate of 30% in 1993/4. The country is also interested in joining ASEAN and in further joint ventures to promote the Mekong Delta area. Investment pledges for 1995 came to over US$2 billion, of which some 75% were from Malaysia.

In a country ravaged by two decades of war and strife, plus hugely destructive drought and flood damage to the staple rice crop in the early 1990s and again in 1994, the IMF attributed its future optimism for the country to government programmes aimed at boosting rural development; widening privatisation (at least 70% of the economy is already in private hands) and cementing international confidence in the stability of the *riel*, the local currency, through the introduction of larger denomination bank notes.

Of the US$410 million allocated for Cambodia's 1995 budget, US$180 million was from international donors and US$230 million from Phnom Penh, with the emphasis on reducing unproductive expenditure, supporting the *riel* and bringing down inflation.

Deprived of US$100 million-a-year aid from the former Soviet Union, Cambodia's economy entered the 1990s in very poor shape. The Phnom Penh government printed excess bank notes to pay civil servants and the *riel* collapsed. By March 1993, UN economists estimated inflation was running at 340%. However, the election of a legitimate government allowed disbursement of a promised total of US$880 million in humanitarian and economic aid from Western governments and aid agencies, helping to put the country back on its economic feet.

Despite continued Khmer Rouge activity and rural food shortages caused by drought, Cambodia has since been making relatively smooth, albeit interrupted, economic progress. While rural development - including an US$85 million European Union aid programme for refugee rehabilitation, health, industry, land mine clearance, education, water supplies and wells - is officially designated as priority, international business activity centres around Phnom Penh, in three main sectors: services, timber and gemstones.

The long-standing presence of more than 20,000 UN peace-keepers was largely responsible for the services sector growth in the capital, producing a flourishing rash of new accommodation, restaurants and communications systems.

.The business environment is still largely unstructured, with its fractious politics, reputed flouting of controls, corruption and the threat of banditry, but for those willing to take the gamble, the rewards are there. Business visitors will find the need to hire a hand- or radio phone as the public phone system is still undeveloped, although some modern phoneboxes taking US$ phonecards are now sprouting up in Phnom Penh.

Etiquette & business practice

Cambodians are a peaceful nation, similar to Thais, and do not like confrontation. Political discussion should be avoided. For business meetings, men should wear a lightweight suit and tie. English and French are the business languages. Photography is permitted although it is advisable to ask the permission of Cambodian people, especially monks. Modest tips are appreciated in restaurants and hotels.

Tourism

General

If gambling is endemic to doing business in Cambodia, then it is also central to the country's efforts to promote tourism. As elsewhere in Indo-China, the building of casinos is seen by tourist authorities as a swift route to attracting big-spending visitors as well as package tourists. The difference is Cambodia is playing its casino cards close to its chest because the Khmer Rouge, with the implied threat of sabotage, has denounced casinos as "breeding grounds for corruption and vices of all kinds". Hence, details of casinos due to be built on Naga Island and in nearby Sihanoukville were shrouded in mystery in 1995.

In late 1994, the Cambodian government publicly announced it would use casino gambling as a means of promoting tourism, employment and regional economic development.

In the case of southern Naga Island, which is estimated to be within 90 minutes flying time of 450 million people, the offer to international investors was a blatant: *build an airport and you get the island*. But when the Malaysian Ariston group signed a deal with the Cambodian government in January 1995 to develop Naga and Sihanoukville, as well as neighbouring Kompong Som Beach, casinos were not mentioned: only theme parks, golf courses, marinas, hotels and an airport.

Visitor security, plus a UN recommendation for a strict limitation on tourist numbers, for preservation reasons, to the temples of Angkor Wat (Cambodia's principal tourist site initially envisaged by authorities as being able to attract up to 1 million visitors a year), are major stumbling blocks to growth. So is the lack of international standard hotel accommodation.

Although the Cambodian Tourism Ministry statistically can claim its tourist 'circuit' is as safe as those of neighbouring destinations, international perceptions of *The Killing Fields* plus the kidnapping and murdering of foreigners in 1994 remain powerful deterrents to overseas tour operators.

Official statistics are sketchy but are expected to show Cambodia failed to reach its target of 250,000 visitors in 1995. And of the total 153,535 visitors recorded during the first 11 months of 1994, compared with 104,257 in 1993, most were understood to be either business visitors, expatriate Cambodians or French, Japanese or Americans involved in the UN peacekeeping force, aid programmes or the reconstruction of Angkor Wat.

The tourism ministry estimates that some US$2 billion is currently being invested in tourist infrastructure, including the upgrading of Phnom Penh's Poechtenong Airport, additional hotels in the capital plus airport and road upgrades and resort hotels at Kompong Som Beach, Naga Island, Sihanoukville and Siem Reap (near Angkor Wat).

But it also claims the current supply of some 1,300 international standard rooms is up to 5,000 rooms short of existing needs. Essentially, Cambodia's future tourism focuses on two specific areas, each linked with Phnom Penh. To the northwest, the capital is linked with Siam Reap via Tonle Sap River and lake (casino ships, cruises, fishing) and to the south with Kompongsom Beach/Naga Island/Sihanoukville (casinos, beaches watersports combined with the offshore island of Po and Tansay plus the 1908 resort town of Kep).

The Cambodian government has signed a memorandum of understanding with a Malaysian firm to develop a vast tourism complex east of the northern provincial capital of Siam Reap - a scale model of Angkor Wat. Another Malaysian firm is installing a *son et lumière* system at Angkor Wat itself.

Hotels

Until 1995 the only hotel in Phnom Penh meeting standards of comfort and reliability for upmarket tourists and business visitors was the 280-room Sofitel Cambodiana. However now several hotel chains including Dusit and Inter-Continental (which opened a 354-room hotel in September 1996) have expressed confidence in the country. Raffles International has invested US$25 mn in Phnom Penh in refurbishing the 209-room Royal Hotel and another US$30 mn in upgrading the Grand Hotel d'Anggkor in Siem Reap. Aman Resorts is investing US$50mn in Phnom Penh, Siem Reap and Kampong Cham. Byron International is building a 250-room prperty in Siem Reap. Hotel developers currently enjoy 70-year land leases, low fees and rental values and unrestricted foreign shareholding in joint ventures, provided a local partner is involved. There is no taxation on the repatriation of funds or on profit..

Aviation

1995 was a landmark year for Cambodian aviation as the long troubled country finally re-established a flag carrier of its own. A plan to get a national airline off the ground had been around for some time but it was only in January 1995 that the talking stopped and a fledgling Royal Air Cambodge took to the skies. Malaysia Helicopter Services (MHS) has taken a 40% stake in RAC ahead of Singapore Airlines, which had previously indicated an interest in the Phnom Penh based carrier. MHS is providing management and maintenance support as well as leasing aircraft to the Cambodian airline.

RAC re-inaugurated its service with a flight from Phnom Penh to Kuala Lumpur using a B737-400 leased from Malaysian Airline Systems, in which MHS has a controlling interest. Its fleet consists of two leased 737-400s plus two ATR 72s for domestic destinations. For MHS the deal fits neatly with its other minority airline holdings such as its 49% stake in Air Maldives. It also allows its affiliate MAS to offload some surplus aircraft capacity to the Cambodian carrier. The new RAC is the first national carrier for Cambodia since 1975 when the former Royal Air Cambodge ceased operations. It also brought to an end flights by Thai-backed operators Cambodia International Airlines (CIA) and SK Air. CIA had been flying between Phnom Penh and Bangkok, Hong Kong, Vientiane, Singapore and some other cities. RAC started flying to Ho Chi Minh City, Singapore, Kuala Lumpur, Singapore, Bangkok and Hong Kong in 1996.

What to See

Phnom Penh. Most important monument is the Royal Palace (entrance US$4, open 0800-11/1400-1700) now once again occupied by the King. Its Silver Pagoda, built in 1962 in the grounds, has a silver tile floor, a 90-kg gold Buddha decorated with 10,000 diamonds, a 300-yr old small emerald Buddha and many religious relics. Also in the complex: the Chan Chay Pavilion. the Throne Hall, Napoleon III villa and the Elephant Dock Villa. The National Museum of Art exhibits pre-Angkor and Angkor sculptures. Among impressive Wats (temples) is Wat Phnom, of 1434 origin and frequently rebuilt since and Wat Ounalom, a 1443 monastery and one of the most important Buddhist sites in the country, unfortunately sacked by the Khmer Rouge but now being rebuilt, and Wat Moha Montrei with its traditional Khmer murals. Those with strong stomachs may want to see the Tuoi Sieng Prison Museum where Pol Pot imprisoned, tortured and killed some 20,000 innocent victims and Choeung Ek, the *Killing Fields*, 15 km from the city, where the Khmer Rouge exterminated some 9000 people.

Cambodia's most famous site and the world's largest temple complex spread over 228 sq kms is **Angkor Wat**, near Siem Reap, some 250 km and a US$100 flight from the capital. A day's tour costs $120. It was built by the Hindu King Suryavarman in the 12th century and comprises sandstone temples, chapels, causeways and reservoirs. When Buddhism became the main Cambodian religion in the 15th century, it was abandoned, but the French until 1970 and Indian and International archaeologists since are trying to restore its former glory. Nearby is Bayon temple (Angkor Thom) with its 200 enigmatically smiling stone faces.

Shopping

Phnom Penh is not a sophisticated shopping environment, with the best buys being *kramas* (Cambodian scarves) and jewellery made from silver, onyx and other locally mined precious stones. Khmer handicrafts can be bought at the shop in the Hotel Cambodiana, at Kheng Song Souvenirs (99 Achar Mean Boulevard) and dyed silk known as *Bang Neang Sok Kra Ob* can be bought at La Boutique (36

Sihanouk Boulevard). Best bets for jewellery purchase are stalls at The Old Market (*Psar Cha*), the Central Market, or Tuol Tum Pong Market. More expensive buys can be had at the State Jewellery Shop (junctions of 13 and 106 streets), the Silver Shop (1 Achar Mean Blvd) or the Tan Sotho Fine Antiques Shop (No 188 Street 13). Duty free produce is available at Bayon Duty Free, No 34 Street 214. The only real supermarket is the International at 35, 178 Street.

Getting Around

Safest way to travel is by air. Seats to and from Siem Reap (for Angkor Wat) are sold on an 'in principle' basis. **Do not** accept taxi rides from the capital to Siem Reap. Travelling by bus, train or boat out of Phnom Penh is illegal and travel to and from Cambodia by land is very dangerous.

No taxis cruise the streets of Phnom Penh. Service taxis can be hired at Psar Chbam Pao, a taxi station next to the Chbam Market. You can travel to Vietnam by this method for US$20. Cars can be hired from most of the first class hotels for around US$50 per day with driver. Phnom Penh Tourism charges US$40 per day with driver. Many students supplement their income by transporting tourists on motorbikes. You can get to the Killing Fields for some $5-7 per day. Travellers will also be pestered by cyclo drivers who will transport you anywhere within Phnom Penh for no more than US$1; $3 would be the price for a whole morning. Cars with driver can be hires for around US$30 per day.

Royal Air Cambodge flies daily to eight domestic destinations including Sihanoukville, Battambang and Siem Reap.

Entertainment

Phnom Penh's entertainment venues are tame in comparison with Bangkok or Manila but The *Lobby Bar* or *Cyclo Bar* at the Hotel Cambodiana and the luxury lounge at the Novotel both play live music until 11 pm nightly. *The Foreign Correspondent Club* at 363 Karl Marx (Sisowath Quay) with a good view of the river, is a good place for businessmen to meet and the *Gekho Club* on 110 Street is a favouite haunt of journalists. *The Rock Hard Café* (315 Karl Marx Blvd) opens til 11 pm; the *Heart of Darkness* Bar til 10. The *Kong Kea* Floating Restaurant has live music nightly and there is dancing at the Royal Hotel at 92 Street. There is a night club at the Cambodiana Hotel and the *Dancing Restaurant* on 128 Street lives up to its name. There are two karaoke clubs - the *China Town Karaoke* at 46-49 Street 214 and the *Pacific Nite Club KTV* at 234-238 Monivong. The best evening entertainment is to be found at the Municipal Theatre where ballet is performed. Khmer classical dance (*lamthon*) is performed at the Fine Arts Theatre. Masked theatre and shadow plays are also popular. The hotel Cambodiana features classical Khmer dancing performances on Saturday nights. There are two cinemas, the Mouscou and the Prachea Shun on Achar Mean Street, both showing Khmer language films. Westerns are shown at the Foreign Correspondents Club on Saturday nights.

Leisure

Sporting facilities in Phnom Penh are limited. Tennis is available at the *Tennis Clubs* whilst jogging, badminton and soccer are available at the *Olympic Stadium*. River trips on the Mekong or Bassac rivers can be arranged. The International Youth Club near Wat Phnom offers swimming, squash, tennis and volley ball.

Arrival & Departure

There are direct connections to Phnom Penh from Bangkok, Ho Chi Minh City, Hong Kong, Kuala Lumpur, Singapore and Vientiane. Pochentong Airport is 7 km out of the capital, along USSR Boulevard. Taxis from the major hotels charge US$15-20; a motorbike ride for those travelling light costs $2. International departure tax is US$15; domestic $4-5.

Cambodia Key Fact File

Passport Requirements:
All visitors must have a valid passport. Visa required for all visits of more than 15 days. Tourist visas valid up to 15 days issued at airport on arrival for US$20.

Currency:
New Riel (KHR). 100 Sen = 1 Riel.

Exchange Rates: *(March 1997)*
US$ 1 = KHR 2300; £1 = KHR 3728

Currency Restrictions:
Export of local currency is not permitted. Export of foreign currency is limited to the amount declared on arrival. US dollar is widely recognised and accepted; others generally not. Credit cards only accepted at large hotels and shops.

Electricity Supply:
220 volts 50 cycles AC

Language:
Khmer. English and French spoken in tourism and business circles.

Time: GMT + 7; EST + 10 hrs

IDD Code: 885 No area codes applicable

Business Hours:
Commercial offices are open from 0730-1130 and 1400-1730 Monday to Friday; Banking hours are 0800-1500 Monday to Friday; Shops 0800-2000 Monday-Sunday.

Customs & Entry:
A visitor may bring duty free: 200 cigarettes or 250 grams of cigars or 250 grams of tobacco plus one opened bottle of spirits and a reasonable amount of perfume.

Health Requirements:
Yellow fever certificate required if arriving from an infected area. Diptheria, hepatitis, malaria, polo, tetanus, typhoid immunisation recommended. Malaria exists throughout Cambodia except in Phnom Penh.

Climate/best time to visit:
Tropical humid climate with a rainy season between June and October; heaviest rainfall Sept/Oct. Dry season between November and May (temperatures 26-29%C). Humidity averages 70% in winter; 80-85% in mid-Summer

National Holidays 1997
14-16 April (Cambodian New Year); April 17 (Victory over American Imperialism Day); May 1 (Labour Day); May 2 Visaka Bocha (Buddha's birthday);6 May Royal Ploughing Ceremony; June 1 International Childrens Day; 24 September Constitution Day; 23 October Paris Peace Agreement; 30 Oct-1 Nov HM the King's Birthday; 9 November Independence Day; 24-26 November National Water Festival.

Useful Addresses

Post Office
Corner of 26 Street and Achar Mean Blvd. Tel: 23324. Open 0700-1900

Medical Emergencies
SOS International Medical Clinic
33 Issarak Blvd, tel: 912765.
Khmer Hospital (Calmette), Monivong Rd
Polyclinique Aurore
No 58-60 Street 113. Tel: 723173

Air Couriers
DHL Worldwide Express.
Tel: 18 810838/23 427726
Federal Express. Tel: 23 427633
Overseas Courier Service. c/o Sofitel Cambodiana - tel: 18 810227
TNT Express Worldwide. Tel: 23 366062
UPS. Tel: 23 366323

Government Offices
Bureau d'immigration. Pokambor Blvd. Tel: 424794
Council for the Development of Cambodia. Gov't Palace, Sisowath Quay, Wat Phnom, Phnom Penh. Fax: (23) 361616/360606
Ministry of the Interior. Jnct Tou Samouth Blvd/214 Street. Tel: 724372
Ministry of Information and Culture. Junc Achar Mean/180 Street. Tel: 426059
Press Office of Foreign Ministry. Junc 240 Street/Karl Marx Blvd.Tel: 426122

Airline Offices

Aeroflot Airlines
8 Tou Samouth Blvd. Tel: 23 362008

Air France
313 Sisowath Boulevard,Sofitel.
Tel/fax: 426426

Bangkok Airways
Hotel Dosit Pitou, 118 Achar Mean Blvd. Tel: 426298

Dragonair
No 19 ,Street 106. Tel: 23 427665

Lao Aviation
No 58 Sihanouk Blvd. Tel: 426563

Malaysian Airlines
Diamond Hotel, grd fl, 207 Monivong Blvd. Tel: 426688; fax: 810274

Royal Air Cambodge
206a Norodon Blvd. Tel: 23 360154

Silk Air
Gd fl, Palin Hotel, Monivong Blvd. Tel: (23) 722236

Thai Airways
No 19 Street 106. Tel: 722335; fax: 427211

Vietnam Airlines
36 Sihanouk Blvd. Tel: 427426

Restaurants

Khmer food is similar to Thai cuisine. Restaurants are not very developed in Phnom Penh, with the best food being found at the established hotels. Below we list a small selection.

Ban Thai *(Thai).* No 1, 306 Street.

Chao Pra Ya *(Thai)* 62 Tou Samouth.

Coca *(Thai)* Junc. Achar Mean/240 Street

Crackers Restaurant *(International)*
13 90 Street.

Gecko Club *(International)*
Junc. 114 and 61 Street

International Restaurant *(Chinese)*
Pailin Hotel. 219 Monivong Bd. Tel: 23 426697

La Paillotte *(French)*
234 Street.

Ly Ly Restaurant *(Chinese)*
117 Achar Mean Boulevard

Mekong Restaurant *(Khmer)*
Hotel Sofitel Cambodiana.
313 Karl Marx Avenue. Tel: 426288 (local)

Midori *(Japanese)*
145 Norodom Boulevard

The Royal Pavilion *(Chinese)*
Hotel Sofitel Cambodiana.
313 Karl Marx Avenue. Tel: 426288 (local)

Taj Mahal Restaurant *(Indian)*
Tou Samouth district (nr Independence Mon't)

Cambodia Hotels

Phnom Penh

Allson Star Hotel D
PO Box 533, Cnr Monivong Blvd/ Kampuchea Krom Blvd
Tel: 23 722022; Fax: 23 722021
17 standard, 40 superior rooms, 10 executive. Taxi/limo, laundry/valet, coffee shop, business centre

Ambassador Hotel C
Cnr USSR/Keo Mony Street
Tel: 726029
Restaurant, bar, swimming pool, AC

Cambodiana Inn D
313 Karl Marx Quay
Tel: 725059
AC; bar & restaurant

Diamond Hotel C
172-184 Monivong Boulevard
Tel/Fax: 23 426535
55 rooms + 13 deluxe; AC/TV+video/ IDD; business centre, bank, laundry/valet service; coffee shop.

Dusit Hotel C
No 2 St 140
Tel: 23 427483; Fax: 23 427209

Green Hotel E
145 Street, Preah Norodom Boeung Keng, Kong, Chomneas
Tel: 23 26055
23 singles, 10 doubles with AC.

Hawaii Hotel E
18 St 130 Quarter Phsar Thmey Market, Khand Daun Penh. Tel/fax: 23 726652
28 singles, 35 twin, 5 suites. AC,laundry, car rental, coffee shop

Hotel Inter-Continental Phno Penh
PO Box 2288, Regency Square, 296 Blvd Mao Ise Iung, 3 B
Tel: 23 720888; Fax: 23 720885
354 bedrooms & 29 suites, 6 apartments + shops, business centre, health & fitness club, meeting room to 600.

Holiday International Hotel D
84 Street, Monivong Blvd.
Tel: 23 427402; Fax: 23 427401
10 singles, 31 twin rooms with TV/AC/ IDD, laundry/valet service; 24 hr business centre, bank, café & lounge, 2 pools, car rental, disco/karaoke

Hotel Juliana Hotel C
16 Juliana, 152 Street, Sangkat Veal Weng, Khand 7 Makara
Tel/Fax: 23 366070
43 single, 8 twin rooms with AC/IDD/TV. Business centre, conference room, hairdresser, fitness centre, sauna, massage, money exchange, office rental,air bus service, laundry/valet service; restaurant..

Monorom Hotel E
89 Achar Mean Blvd
Tel: 26149/24951/24549

Olympic Hotel & Tower B
158-166 Preah Sihanouk Blvd
Tel: 18 811579
200 rooms, 40 service apartments; AC/TV/ IDD 'phone, business centre, swimming pool, gym, sauna.

Hotel Orchidée D
262 Achar Mean Boulevard
Tel: 22659
AC/TV.

Hotel Pacific E
200 BC Monivong Blvd
Tel: 23 23547
AC. Nightclub

Pailin Hotel E
219 BC Monivong Boulevard
Tel: 23 26697/8
(Formery White Hotel) 32 AC rooms.

La Paillotte Hotel D
234 Street Khemarak
Tel/Fax: 426513
IDD/TV + satellite, minibar; restaurant

Phnom Penh Floating Hotel B
Karl Marx Quay
Tel: 720178; Tlx: 5201; Fax: 720197
AC/TV/satellite in rooms, minibar, 2 restaurants, swimming pool.

Rama Inn §
8-10 Samdeck Louis Elm St, PO Box 936
Tel: 362161; Fax: 428381

Regent Hotel D
/ St 109, Group 41, Boeung Rang, Khand Daun Penh
Tel/fax: 23 27649
17 single, 18 twin AC rooms; postal service, laundry, car hire.Coffee shop

Le Royal Hotel C
No 26 Sotheavos Road
Tel/Fax: 427651
40 rooms, with AC/IDD/Satellite TV; limousine tour service, restaurant &nightclub.

Sofitel Cambodiana B
313 Karl Mark Avenue
Tel: 23 426288; Tlx: 583 1715426 C8DA-X; Fax: 23 426392
184 rooms, 24 suites; business centre, swimming pool, gym, boutique, travel centre, banqueting facilities; AC/IDD/TV/ video in rooms, laundry/valet service, safety deposit boxes, minibars, 3 restaurants, limo service

Wat Phnom Hotel D
Junc. 51/96 Street
Tel: 23 725320
AC/TV+video/IDD; business centre, bank, laundry/valet service; coffee shop.

Siem Reap/Angkor

Grand Hotel d'Angkor C
Vitthai Charles de Gaulle
Tel: 15 911292; Fax: 15 911291
303 AC rooms with satellite TV. Restaurant, conferece room

Hotel de la Paix/A Pavilion Resort
Savatha St, Sangkat II D
Tel: (via Bangkok) 662 247 2832; Fax: 662 247 2837
TV, Restaurant, Conference room

Nohor Kohthlok (Airport) Hotel D
Tel: 23 57505; Fax: 23 57991
84 rooms, 2 suites, restaurant, convention centre,business centre

Ta Prohm Hotel D
Tel: 15 913130
58 AC rooms with TV + satellite, minbars.

Price guide: A after name of hotel = single room rate over US$200; B = between $150-200; C = $100-150; D = $50-100; E = under $50. § = on application

CAMBODIA - Introduction

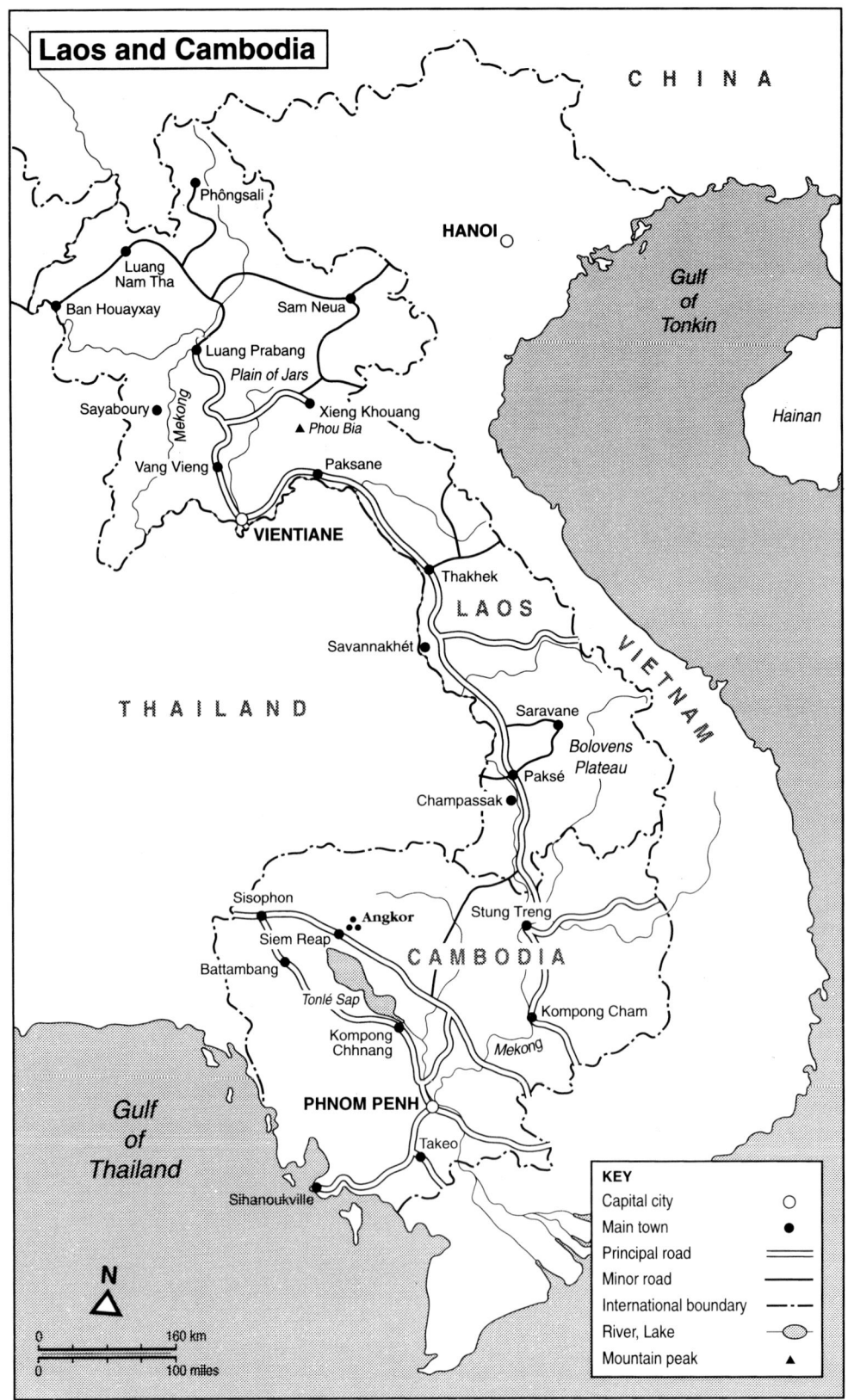

Cartography by Steve Munns, from Guide to Laos & Cambodia, *Bradt Publications, 1995*

COUNTRY REPORT
CHINA '97

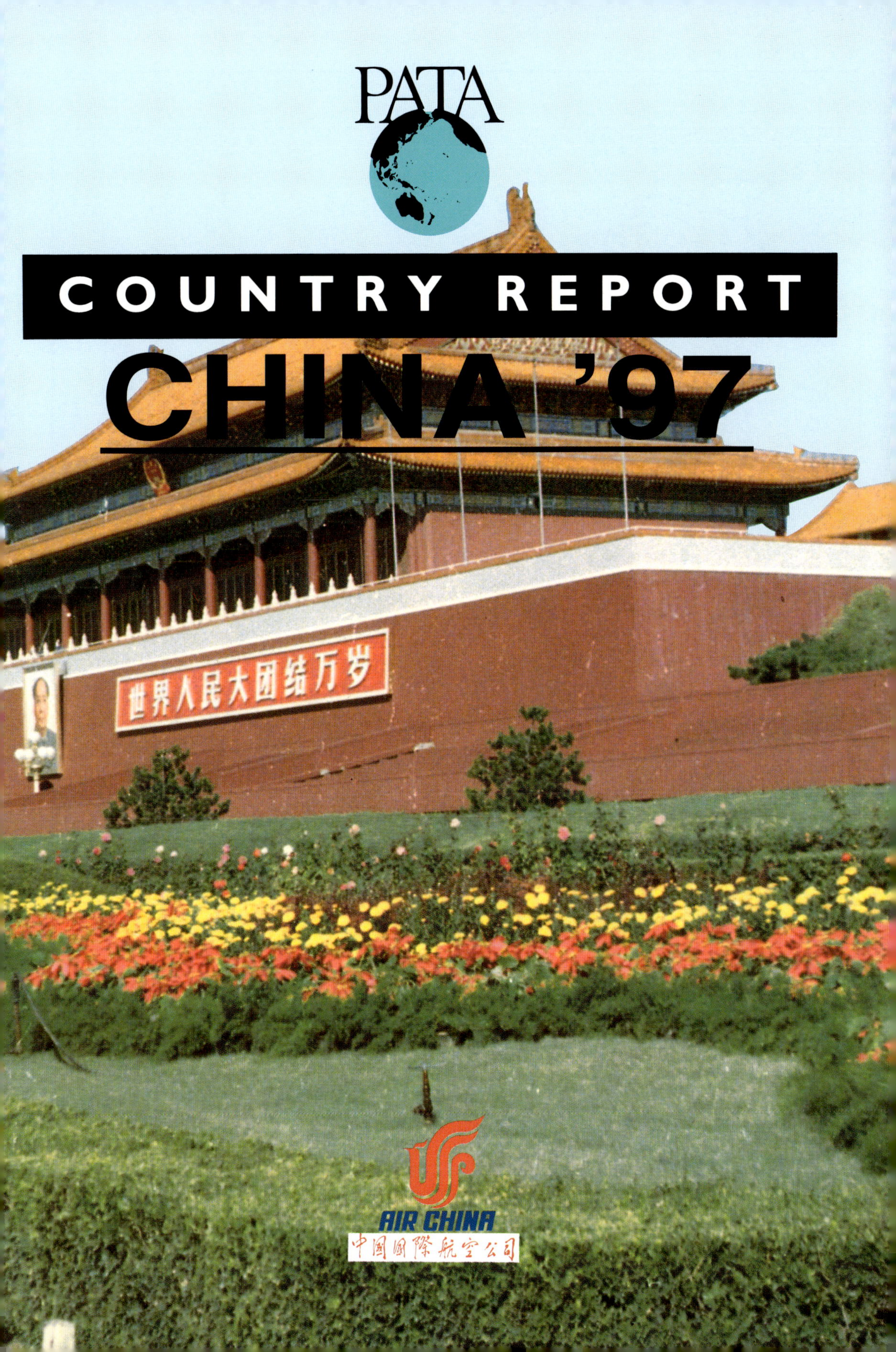

AIR CHINA
中国国际航空公司

CHINA - Introduction

China

Doing Business

Developments in 1996

Politically and economically, China began 1997 on an upbeat note. Jiang Zemin, a disciple of modern reforms, had firmly consolidated his position as successor to 92-year-old Deng Xiao Ping, the architect of China's open market policies, who died in February.

International business concerns about China's imminent takeover of Hong Kong had largely subsided. In his New Year message to the nation, Jiang promised that Hong Kong would continue to trade globally, and few multinational corporations were said to be expecting any immediate or serious interruption to the territory's established work structure. Relations with Taiwan had thawed enough for agreement to be reached on the start-up of direct freight shipping links between the two countries.

Trading was bouyant on China's two, albeit small, stock markets with a promise of foreign participation in 'A' shares. Analysts were forecasting double digit economic growth for the country in 1997, with GDP again rising above 10% after a slowdown during the previous two years. And inflation, which had been running at 20% or above in some provinces, was expected to be brought down to an average 6% during the year.

Realistically, however, China reached a half way economic house in 1997. The country's rapid transformation to a full market economy had been achieved at the expense of many of its 1.2 billion population. The gap between the new rich and poor was widening and corruption was widely accepted as being out of control. An estimated 168,000 loss-making state-run industries had been allowed to go bankrupt without a safety net, putting as many as 10 million out of work. In addition, the easing of controls on millions of farm co-operatives, allowing private enterprise and profit, left thousands of peasants roaming the streets in search of alternative work.

At the same time, rising labour costs, without equivalent improvements in efficiency or productivity, were accompanied by the official implementation of a five day, 40-hour working week, producing extra pressure on employers and their profit margins. In 1995, a 44-hour working week had been introduced, reducing the former six day working week.

Despite both government and investor sensitivity over labour problems, and the apparent lack of an immediate solution to them, the general consensus among analysts was that business and investment would continue to grow in 1997, primarily because reforms had passed the point of reversal and incentives, and potential, continued to be attractive to outsiders.

Helping optimism were a continued build-up of investment through new Special Administrative Region Hong Kong plus the prior example of China's swift economic recovery following the events in Tiananmen Square in 1989, proof that the path of business can often be separate to that of politics or world opinion.

Business Etiquette

The practicalities of doing business in China have much improved in recent years, thanks to a transportation, accommodation and commercial infrastructure lifted from the Dark Ages to challenge neighbouring countries in all but the finer elements of service and efficiency.

Even some of China's less attractive traits to foreigners are being tackled. In mid-1995, a government edict began to impose fines, or worse punishment, on all service industry workers using any of 50 bad habits - mostly instinctive gestures or phrases that can be construed as rude by customers. Given the general lack of training, and what many foreigners view as a total disregard of basic manners, first time visitors can be surprised by the formalities of doing business in China.

Punctuality at meetings is deemed an essential, whatever the delays you may have encountered en route. Dress should be formal, whatever your Chinese counterparts are wearing, and business cards, presented ceremoniously with two hands, should be fully factual, preferably with a precise Chinese translation on the reverse side.

A good local agent to guide you through an ever-changing and labyrinthine bureaucracy, plus a translator are also essentials as few Chinese, even at very senior level, speak foreign languages. Displaying status and dignity are important in a society which is welcoming but still wary of foreign ways and methods. Deference must always be shown to age and rank with both men and women, many of whom hold senior posts. Greeting is by shaking hands in the western way, but it is not unusual for Chinese to clap on your arrival. Your clapping in return shows appreciation.

Despite the formalities, the Chinese are usually straightforward to the point of being abrupt in their comments, if not their decisions - all of which require being granted a large amount of 'face'. However small the business, you are unlikely ever to deal with just one counterpart but rather a delegation sitting in a long line, each with a given separate task. Entertaining follows the same pattern, with large groups sitting around devouring endless dishes and making copious ceremonious toasts in rice liquor. Westernisation and the influx of joint-venture hotels have changed some entertainment habits, but the ground rules are the same: top quality foreign gifts such as cognac, whisky or cigarettes, plus unfailing attention and good humour are appreciated; politics are a taboo subject, and firmness with a suitable amount of flattery will get you everywhere.

Tourism Update

General

The visitor arrivals total in 1996 in China was 51.2 million, up 10%, faster than the 6% growth in 1995. The percentage increase in visitor arrivals has been smaller than those experienced in the rest of Asia Pacific. And that 10% growth in 1996 represents a high actual numerical growth - almost five million visitors - and much higher than any other destination in the region.

The 51 million total includes visitors from Hong Kong, Macau and Taiwan, but most comparative analysis takes place on the near seven million visitors with foreign passports. But even this requires caution as the breakdown is by passport - which affects some analysis, such as of expatriates living in Asia. Markets most affected (overstated) by this methodology are American and British passport holders.

The major growth market has been the Korean, which moved up six places in 1993 to become the fourth largest, then two more by 1995, to second place. Its 694,000 total in 1996 was up 31%. Growth from the largest market, Japanese travellers, was also positive, up 19% to 1,549,000. And the American market was strong, growing 12% to 576,000. The Russian total increased 14% to 556,000, and Mongolians dropped out of top five, their place being taken by Malaysians, up 19% to 299,000.

Of the non-foreign markets, the 9% growth from Hong Kong and Macau (figures are not separated), taking it to 42.5 million, represents the biggest numerical growth - almost four million. And the Taiwanese total, which more properly should be in the overseas arrivals section, grew 13% to 1.7 million in 1996. Each visitor stays in China for approximately seven days. The budget of the NTO for overseas promotion is approximately US$4 million.

The year 1997 has been designated *Visit China Year*. It is also the year the country will also host an important travel trade meeting, the annual travel mart and conference of the Pacific Asia Travel Association, in Beijing. 1997 is also the year when Hong Kong reverts to Chinese sovereignty. Travel to Hong Kong becomes part of domestic travel. However, this does not mean there will be free access for Chinese citizens into Hong Kong or for travellers to Hong Kong planning to visit China proper. As already exists with the Chinese border town of Shenzhen, travel into Hong Kong will still be controlled. And China already counts separately some visitors from Hong Kong - as 'compatriots'.

Aviation

The country's airlines are also developing rapidly. The big three - Beijing-based Air China, Shanghai-based China Eastern Airlines, and Guangzhou-based China Southern Airlines - are all members of the International Air Transport Association. And they have now been joined in IATA by Chengdu-based China Southwest Airlines. Outstanding questions on China Southern Airlines figures for 1994 make percentage growths in 1995 an estimate only. However, there was good growth for the three main airlines.

The country's major international airline, Air China, sold 1,792,000 seats, a 24.6% increase, on its international routes in 1995. Developments for 1997 include a doubling of services Heathrow-Beijing and non-stop flights London to Hong Kong, using new Boeing 747-400 aircraft. Flights to Australia (Melbourne/Sydney) are also set to be doubled.

The next largest in international terms was China Eastern, which sold 1,741,000 seats, up 16.5%. Because figures for China Southern are for 1994 there is no precise comparison with 1995, but it is believed the airline grew faster than the other two. It sold 1,350,000 seats during the year.

Airport figures are available for total traffic only, not just international. It is likely that some growth potential at Guangzhou airport was taken by the nearby Shenzhen airport, opened in late 1991 and now already China's fifth-largest. Also, a passenger total is higher than visitor totals indicate, because most travellers would be counted twice - once when arriving, and a second time when leaving.

According to *Travel Business Analyst* estimates, the number of passengers at

Beijing's main Capital airport increased 20% to 14 million in 1996. The next was believed to be Guangzhou's much stretched airport, where there were 13 million passengers, a 17% increase. And at Shanghai, there were 11 million passengers, up about 25%. The fact that some of China's airlines have joined IATA resulted in the emergence of IATA-licensed travel agencies in the country; the first, China International Travel Service, was licensed in 1995. The period of extraordinarily rapid growth of new airlines seems to be over, but there is still rapid expansion. Growth in 1995 was again at 20%.

In 1996 an important development was the first official foreign investment in a Chinese airline since the communist takeover. A US investor bought 25% of the equity in Hainan Airlines. Another development that is likely to become important is the return of the Civil Aviation Administration of China, which was China's only airline until being disbanded in the late 1980s in favour of regional, semi-independent airlines, to aviation operations. As well as being responsible for the control of civil aviation in China, a CAAC company also has investments in China Southwest Airlines, in Dragonair in Hong Kong, and Air Macau in Macau.

Hotels

Hotels in China have also developed considerably over the past five years — adding over 100,000 more rooms, representing almost 40% growth. Most of these were in the major centres. Development has been concentrated in about 10 main centres in the country.

But over the past three years, emphasis has moved to many provincial centres, and as a result substantial growth is expected there over the next few years. In 1995 the fastest growth for 10 years took place, with a 24% increase in the number of hotels to 3,720. The growth in rooms was almost as fast — 20% to 486,114 — which meant a slight fall in the average number of rooms per hotel, to 131 rooms.

In 1996 growth was not as fast. Not all the new hotels will be 400-rooms-plus typical of foreign development to date. Many are smaller, with under 200 rooms, and many are in secondary centres, not in the main cities. Hotels due to open 1996-98 include: In secondary and tertiary cities, they include Shangri La in **Beihai** with 364 rooms; in **Changchun**, Shangri La with 458 rooms, and the Swiss Belhotel with 230 rooms; Gloria Plaza in **Changsha** with 300 rooms; in **Chengdu**, the Amara with 225 rooms, Gloria Plaza with 600 rooms, Holiday Inn Crowne Plaza with 434 rooms, and the Sichuan Eaton Jinjiang with 300 rooms; Shangri La in **Dalian** with 563 rooms; Sheraton in **Dongguan** with 300 rooms; Shangri La in **Fuzhou** with 350 rooms; in **Haikou**, Club Med with 350 rooms, SMI Mandarin with 318 rooms; Novotel in **Hangzhou** with 247 rooms; in

Hefei, Holiday Inn with 320 rooms, and Novotel with 220 rooms; in **Harbin**, Inter-Continental with 228 rooms, and Shangri La with 437 rooms; Novotel in **Jilin** with 300 rooms; in **Jinan**, Century Run Hua with 151 rooms, and Novotel with 300 rooms; Club Med in **Kunming** with 200 rooms; in Nanchang, Gloria Plaza with 430 rooms, and Lake View Zenith with 320 rooms; in **Nanjing**, Holiday Inn with 350 rooms, and International with 300 rooms; Citic Byron in **Ningbo** with 288 rooms; in **Qingdao**, Amara Golf Resort with 264 rooms, Equatorial with 464 rooms, and Shangri La with 466 rooms; in **Sanya**, Banyan Tree with 200 rooms, Club Med with 350 rooms, and Gloria Resort with 410 rooms; Amara Golf Resort in **Shandong** with 264 rooms; in **Shenyang**, the Furama with about 200 rooms, Grand Stanford with 454 rooms, Regal with 400 rooms, Sheraton with 562 rooms, and Traders with 492 rooms; Centennial in **Shenzhen** with 265 rooms; Ramada in **Shunde** with 450 rooms; in **Suzhou**, Gloria Plaza with 300 rooms, Sheraton with 400 rooms, and Taihu Equatorial Resort with 252 rooms; in **Tianjin**, Holiday Inn with 215 rooms, Stanford with 250 rooms; in **Wuhan**, Marco Polo with 281 rooms, Holiday Inn Riverside with 265 rooms, Shangri La with 750 rooms; in **Wuxi**, Ramada with 325 rooms, Sheraton with 350 rooms; Marco Polo in **Xiamen** with 347 rooms; in **Xian** the Inter-Continental Xidu with 578 rooms; in **Zhuhai**, Emperor Byron with 158 rooms, Grand Bay View with 260 rooms, Pearl Island with 250 rooms.

In primary cities, they include in **Beijing**, the Beijing Ming Yang Club with 300 rooms; in **Guangzhou**, the Gloria Inn with 350 rooms, and Sheraton with 500 rooms; in **Shanghai**, all in the new business district of Pudong, the Holiday Inn with 340 rooms, Grand Hyatt with 560 rooms, Regal with 350 rooms and Shangri-La with 661.

What to see

Beijing: The Palace Museum and the Forbidden City, built between 1406 and 1420, were the imperial palaces of the Ming and Qing dynasties. Tiananmen Square with its Great Hall of the People, Mau Zedong Mausoleum and museums of Chinese History and Chinese Revolution. In the South, there is the Temple of Heaven to visit, completed in 1420. Also Beihai Park, the Summer Palace, the Fragrant Hills and

Nanjing Road, Shanghai

the Yonghegong Lamasery. Tours to the Great Wall of China can be arranged from Beijing.

Chengde. A former Imperial resort along with the eight outer temples is now a top tourist resort. The city's Puning Temple has the world's largest Buddha sculpture, with 1000 arms and eyes, weighing 110 tons.

Chengdu is the capital of Sichuan province and its best known sites are the Thatched Hut of Du Fu, Marquis Wu Memorial Temple, Wenshu Academy, Qingyang Taoist temple and the 2000 year old Dujiangyan Dam. Embroidery and cuisine style are Sichuan's best known exports.

Chongqing in southwest China is a good jumping off point to see the Three Gorges of the Changjiang River.

Dalian in the northeast is famous for its beaches and shell carvings and glassware.

Fuzhou, capital of Fujian province is called the 'hotspring' city and is also famous for lacquerware, stone and cork carving.

Guilin's exceptional deep lakes and caves have earned it the title 'best sight under heaven'; other tourist sites include Seven Star Park, Duixiu Peak and Fubo Hill.

Hangzhou, which so impressed Marco Polo, is famous for its embroidery, silk umbrellas and Longjing tea.

Guangzhou (Canton) is China's trading and economic capital where capitalism has taken something of a foothold. Worthy of interest is the Guangzhou Zoo (which has a large collection of pandas), the Pagoda, the Guangdong Provincial Museum with its offerings of priceless Ming vases and the Guangzhou Museum, which has some interesting material devoted to the Opium Wars.

Hainan Island is a province in its own right and is billed by the Chinese authorities as 'China's Hawaii'. With its many unspoiled beaches, Hainan is targeted to become a major resort centre.

Luoyang: Capital of ancient dynasties; situated near Xian. Worth seeing: the Longmen grottoes, Han Tombs, Baimasi temple and Municipal Museum.

Nanjing has been China's capital on many occasions - the last time was prior to the communist takeover in 1949. Its former pre-eminence is reflected in its many fine buildings, both ancient and modern. The Black Dragon Lake Park is a tranquil corner of the city, the Linggu Pagoda, Nanjing Museum and the tomb of the first Ming emperor should be on any sightseeing list.

Qingdao: One of China's more pleasant port cities. In the past it was strongly influenced by the Germans and there is still some surviving German-style architecture - notably the city's railway station. Qingdao has many sandy beaches and even a pier. Luxun Park is the venue for a number of summer-type concerts and exhibitions.

Quangzhou in Fujian province is famous for its stone buildings with the influence of the Tang and Song dynasties. It was one of the starting points of the silk road and as well as being host to Buddhism, has relics of Christianity, Islam and Manicheism.

Shanghai A city of 12 million and the country's biggest commercial and economic centre; also one of the best places to shop in China.

Along Shanghai's waterfront (previously known as The *Bund*) still stand the many magnificent buildings created by Shanghai's foreign-owned banks and corporations. In fact, a walk along the old *Bund* is one of the highlights of a visit to Shanghai.

The city has other attractions: the Jade Buddha Temple, the Shanghai Botanical Gardens, Shanghai Zoo, and the Longhua Pagoda and Temple. The Yu Yuan Garden is sited close to the *Bund*. A trip around the harbour is also worth arranging.

A beer or even a meal in the old (some would say decaying and seedy) Cathay Hotel - now the Heping - should be tried just for the experience. Situated in a prime position on the Bund, it was once the most fashionable in China.

Just outside Shanghai (three hours by car) is **Suzhou,** a kind of eastern Venice with a network of busy canals. It is also a major centre for the silk industry and has several pleasant gardens.

Wuxi on the northern banks of Lake Taihu is known for its Tortoise Head Peninsula, Liyuan garden, Luting Hill and Xuhui Park (with its Second Spring under

CHINA - Introduction

heaven). The Grand Canal runs through the 300-year old city.

Xian: Capital of Shaanxi province and site of the famous 6000 life-size terracotta warriors in the Emperor Qin Shi Huang Mausoleum. Also worth seeing: the Provincial Museum and the Dayen Pagoda.

Shopping

Until a few years ago, China's so-called *Friendship Stores* were about the only place where visitors could buy foreign goods as the stores were designed tom accept foreign currency payment only and to prevent Chinese from acquiring exotic imported goods. As a result, it is best to avoid them and look for items in the many large department stores, which sell largely locally made goods.

In the last two years, China has experienced a retail boom and new shopping centres have sprung up. The opulent Peking Palace Hotel has a Watsons Supermarket which, in true Hong Kong style, sells everything that anyone could conceivably want though prices are not cheap. Visitors to Beijing should also check out the Lufthansa Centre, which, apart from its hotel and office facilities, boasts the capital's largest international-style luxury shopping centre selling Chinese and foreign goods. The Swissotel's Hong Kong and Macau Center sells a wide range of furs, leather goods and suits. Other stores are the Beijing Friendship Store (drab but good value) and for carpets the Marco Polo Carpet Shop in the China World Shopping Arcade, and for women's clothing Silk Alley near the Jianguo hotel. Amongst markets, try Yabolu Market, near Riban Park, Chaowal Antiques Market or the top floor of Hong Quiao Market, east of the Temple of Heaven.

Shops specialising in arts and craft have sprung up in recent years where foreigners can buy local jewellery, silk, furs and furniture. Again prices can be high and the same kind of items are probably available in Hong Kong at cheaper prices.

Chinese "antiques" can be found in hotel lobbies or specialist shops. Few items on sale will be really old and again prices tend to be high. Customers should make sure that antiques are stamped with a government seal of authentication as only antiques dating from the Qing Dynasty (1797-1820) onwards may be legally exported. Purchasers should keep receipts carefully.

Markets have appeared everywhere in China's larger cities and some of the goods on sale are of surprisingly high quality (though many are not). Leather goods are excellent value and there are good bargains to be had. Many markets stay open until late at night as well as opening on Sundays.

Finally, access to western-style toiletries and hygienic accessories is still limited. So ensure that you have enough toothpaste, deodorant, soap, etc as you are only likely to find functional Chinese equivalents

Getting around/ Communications

For internal flights, there are two classes of ticket: first class or economy. For each class there are three fare rates: one for westerners, one for Hong Kong Chinese and one for Mainland Chinese. So don't be surprised if your Chinese interpreter or agent pays less for his seat than you do !

China's airports are undergoing an unrivalled period of expansion and modernisation. 1995 saw the completion of nine new airports and twenty morre were being expanded or modernised in 1996. However travellers are advised to arrive at least 90 minutes before their flying time.

Long-distance travel by train is a viable alternative to air travel if you have the time. Local trains are slow, often full and should be booked at least a few days in advance, but "expresses" are smooth, comfortable, fast and with steward(ess) service. Train travel is around 25% cheaper than comparable air services. Trains connecting major cities are usually equipped with sleepers.

Car hire is not developed, although Hertz opened an office in Shanghai in 1995. Until recently foreigners were forbidden to drive in China. Taxis are best ordered through your hotel and it will make life easier if you get your destination written down in Chinese before setting off. Business visitors should allow plenty of time to get to appointments as the number of cars on Beijing's roads has exploded in the past two years and traffic jams are endemic. Most taxi drivers are honest but there are some 'cowboys' about, particularly at the airport. Check to see whether cars are registered with the Beijing authorities and make sure your driver turns on his meter. Flagfalls are RMB 10.40 (ca. US$ 1.25) for the first 4 km and RMB 1.6 for each subsequent km for small cars and RMB 12 and 2 respectively for large taxis. For intermediate distances, try the square yellow *miandi* (Chinese for bread-van) who only charge RMB 10 for 10 kms. Fares should be fixed in advance.

Most of the larger, western-oriented, hotels can arrange a chauffeur-drive service. However in China's main cities taxis abound and are, by and large, good value. As well as standard cars, Peking's *mianbao chi* or *mian di* (bread wagons) are a good alternative. These are small yellow vans, so-called because they resemble a loaf of bread and they are everywhere. Comfortable and reasonably-priced, few have air-conditioning.

Buses are best avoided as they are over-crowded, noisy and hot in summer. Without some knowledge of Chinese it would be difficult to know which bus to catch or where it was going.

Entertainment

After work activities have improved radically. Until the late eighties, there were few, if any, places to drink outside the main internationally known hotels. However the 1990s has seen a deluge of new private bars opening in cities like Shanghai and Guangzhou as well as an explosion of karaoke bars catering to tourists and Chinese citizens alike. These can be entertaining and well worth a visit.

China has also experienced disco fever and many international hotels now offer dancing facilities. Recently opened independent discos include *JJs*, the *Hard Rock Café*, *Nightman* and *NASA*.

Hotels in major centres by and large have excellent bars, with a wide range of beers and spirits, but prices are high. Some smaller hotels restrict customers to locally-made beer and soft drinks. Joint venture bars in Beijing worth checking out include *Charlie's Place* in the Jianguo Hotel and the *Sports Bar* at the Jingguang Centre which claims to be Beijing's 'trendiest watering hole', featuring non-stop sports videos on TV monitors. The China World Hotel's *Red Lion Bar* is a good place for a quiet drink and there are numerous other bars within the World Trade Centre complex. For a more informal atmosphere, check out *Frank's Place* (tel: 6507 2617) or the *Mexican Wave* (tel: 6506 3961) - both run by expats. *Poachers' Inn* is a recently opened British-style pub with live music.

In Shanghai the Symphony orchestra is the best in China (tickets tel: 437 3288). There is the celebrated *Jazz Club* in the Peace Hotel (tel: 321 1244) or discos at *Nicole's* in the Hua Ting Sheraton and the *Reading Room* in the Shanghai JC Mandarin Hotel. The best after-hours pub/lounges are the *Oasis* in the Garden Hotel, the *Penthouse Bar* in the Hilton or the English-style *Traders Pub* in the JC Mandarin Hotel.

In Guangzhou the *Cultural Palace* houses opera, two theatres and a concert hall. The Sapphire Cinema in the Holiday Inn often shows Western films. Night spots include the *River Garden* Night Club in the White Swan Hotel, the *Tavern* Pub in the Garden Hotel or the *Lotus Pond* piano bar in the same hotel. There are discos at the Holiday Inn, Novotel, Garden and China hotels.

Visitors to China should remember that this is a conservative country. Most hotels carry regulations issued by the Public Security Bureau which would seem austere in other countries. One international hotel directory featured the following caveat:

'*Lecherous acts, prostitution, taking of drugs and drug trafficking, smuggling, gambling, wrestling or any other unlawful activities are strictly prohibited. In the event of violation of any of the above, the Public Security Department has the authority to take necessary action in accordance with the Security Control Regulations of the People's Republic of China and the relevant laws.*' You have been warned.

As might be expected from a country with a rich culinary heritage, China boasts excellent food to those who know where to look. Numerous new restaurants have recently opened in Beijing and foreign visitors can now eat anything from Macdonalds, Pizza Hut and Kentucky Fried Chicken to Japanese, Mongolian and Korean cuisine. (See *Selected Restaurants* after the China Hotels section of this guide). Most of the large hotels have excellent European restaurants and many offer a range of local cooking - often in separate restaurants. Some provide fast food.

First class Chinese cooking is often found in the least likely of surroundings. the *Rich and Powerful People Hot Dog City* is a stone's throw from the World Trade Centre in Beijing and features such exotica on its menu as *Korean Dog Hot Pot* and *Lovers' Hot Pot*. Some of the best meals can be had at street stalls though travellers would be advised to bring their own chopsticks or eating utensils as some of the smaller Chinese establishments are not renowned for their hygiene.

It is said that the Cantonese will eat anything that moves and some restaurants in Guangzhou sell delicacies such as dog, owl and monkey's brain. Many of the city's restaurants can at first sight be mistaken for pet shops as Chinese customers like to choose their lunch while it is still alive.

Apart from eating and drinking there is little in the way of independent entertainment and none at all outside the larger cities. This situation is changing with increased Western penetration.

Leisure

Most international-class hotels now have swimming pools and gymnasia (See Hotel Reference Tables following this section). In Beijing recreational facilities are also available at the Royal International Club (tel: 6522144) which does not charge an entrance fee and can offer tennis and badminton. The Capital Club is a social club for expat families and is a good place to make contacts both with Chinese opposite numbers. Golf is available at Beijing International Golf Club (tel: 6338731 ext 4021), situated 35 km north of the city. Kangle Palace, in the Asian Games Village is one of the largest indoor recreation centres in Asia and offers swimming, indoor tennis, sauna, squash and a gymnasium, as well as shops, a karaoke lounge and bowling alley. Jogging is popular in parks in all major cities. In Guangzhou the Luhu Park Country Club is recommended for golf, swimming and tennis but it is membership. The Shanghai Golf & Country Club (tel: 6972 8111) offers golf equipment for hire as well as providing other recreational facilities.

Arrival & Departure

The main airports for international flights are Beijing (PEK), a 40-minute, 29 km and RMB 60 taxi ride (bus RMB 10) from downtown and Shanghai (SHA) - probably the best in China. Taxis to Shanghai (Hongqiao) Airport - 15 km out, cost about RMB 16, CAAC buses RMB 2. In both cases shuttle hotel buses, costing RMB 50 are available but should be booked ahead.

The majority of foreign airlines that use these airports have attempted to improve passenger handling for their own customers. Expect to have to fight hard to regain your luggage on landing, as most airports lack a baggage reclaim carousel.

An airport tax of RMB90 is payable on all departing international flights (domestic 15-30 RMB) and must be paid at a separate desk from the check-in point.

CHINA - Introduction   45

China Key Fact File

Passport Requirements:
All visitors require a passport and a visa. Visas can be obtained at short notice and at half the price paid in Europe, in Hong Kong. For travel to Tibet, a separate approval is required from the Tourist Bureau of Tibet (Fax: 86-891-34632).

Currency:
Renminbi Yuan (RMB). 100 fen = 1 RMB

Exchange Rate:
US$1 = 8.3 RMB; £1 = 13.4 RMB
(March 1997)

IDD Code: 86 *followed by.....*
Beijing 10; Chengdu 28; Dalian 411; Fuzhou 591; Guangzhou 20; Guilin 773; Haikou 750; Hangzhou 571; Lhasa 891; Shanghai 21; Shenyang 24; Shekou/Shenzhen 755; Suzhou 512; Tianjin 22; Urumqi 991; Wuhan 27; Xiamen 592; Xian 29

Currency Restrictions:
A total ban exists on the import and export of foreign currency. RMB is not traded outside and is now available from foreign exchange dealers and Bank of China branches once arrived. Foreign Exchange Certificates (FECs) are no longer required.

Electricity Supply: 220 volts; AC/50 cyc

Language:
Basically Mandarin north of the Yangtse and Cantonese to the south. There are many regional languages and dialects.

Time: GMT + 8 hours; EDT + 13 hours

Business Hours:
Government and commercial offices are open 0800-1130, 1300-1500 Monday to Saturday.
Shops are open 0900 - 1900 every day.
Banks are open 0900-1200, 1400-1700 Monday to Saturday.

Customs & Entry:
A extensive range of items are prohibited, especially political material and anything else that might be detrimental to China's cultural, economic and moral interests. 400 cigarettes & 2 litres of wine can be imported. Baggage forms must be completed on arrival detailing all jewellery etc, a copy of which must be presented to customs upon leaving. Similarly a certificate for the export of any cultural relics, handicrafts etc, if purchased during a stay, must be presented when leaving the country.

Health Requirements/Advice:
All visitors must fill in a Health Declaration. Otherwise there are no specific regulations, except for those arriving from or having travelled through an infected area. Yellow Fever, Cholera, Typhoid/Polio & Malaria inoculation recommended. Do not drink tap water and make sure water for teeth cleaning, ice etc has been boiled or sterilised. Stick to well cooked meat, cooked vegetables and peel fruit yourself. Rables is present but dogs and cats are banned form major cities. Bilharzia is present in fresh water pools and rivers.

Climate/Best time to Visit
China's climate is highly varied from intensely cold winters in the north to the subtropical areas around Guangzhou.
Beijing in the north has four distinct seasons - one hot, one cold and two more pleasant spells between. Best time to visit is May to mid-June and late Augsut to early November; Best time to visit Guangzhou is October through March; typhoons in August & September. Shanghai is subtropical - best time to visit being Autumn.

National Holidays 1997
1 January New Year's Day; February 7-9 Chinese New Year; 8 March International Women's Day; 1 May International Labour Day; 4 May National Youth Day; 1 June International Children's Day; 1 August National Army's Day; 1/2 October National Day. Other local festivals in outlying areas.

Visitor Hotlines

A new service for problems or complaints and tour information. All centres give informarion in Chinese and English; additional languages as described below.

Region	Tel. No.	Hours	+Languages
Beijing	10-6513 0828	24 hours	Japanese
Changchun	431-809246	24 hours	Jap/Rus/Mon
Changsha	731-444 4134	0800-1730	
Chengdu	28-667 3693	0800-1200/1400-1800	
Fuzhou	591-755 4153	24 hours	Japanese
Guangzhou	20-8667 7422	0900-1830	
Guiyang	851-523516	0800-1800	
Haikou	898-677 2253	0800-1130/1430-1800	
Hangzhou	571-505 6631	0800-1800	
Harbin	451-364 1441	0830-1730	Jap/German
Hefei	551-363 1821	0800-1200/1330-1730	
Huhhot	471-665978	0800-1200/1430-1830	
Jinan	531-296 3424	0800-1800	
Kunming	871-313 5412	0630-1900	
Lanzhou	931-882 6860	0800-1800	
Lhasa	891-24584	24 hours	Tibetan (No English)
Nanchang	791-224983	0800-1800	
Nanjing	25-330 1221	0800-2000	
Nanning	771-202312	0730-1130/1430-1730	
Shanghai	21-6439 0630	0900-1700	
Shenyang	24-684 6450	0800-1200/1300-1700	
Shijiazhuang	311-601 4239	0800-1600	
Taiyuan	351-404 7544	24 hours	
Tianjin	22-331 8814	(day)	
	22-331 8812	(night)	
Urumqi	991-217119	1000-1400/1600-2000	Jap.
Wuhan	27-283 2914	0800-1700	
Xian	29-725 1480	0800-1800	
Xining	971-42931-964	0800-1200/1430-1800	(NoEng)
Yinchuan	951-622265	0800-1200/1400-1800	Jap.
Zhengzhou	371-5952484	0800-1800	

Useful Addresses

Beijing

American Chamber of Commerce
c/o General Electric Co Ltd.Tel: 6522491

China Beijing Corporation for International Economic Co-operation
Evergreen Garden, Zhong Shan Park. Tel: 6655676; Tlx: 22470 CN

China Consultancy Corporation for Industrial Co-operation & Dev'ment
3 Dongdan Bei Street, PO Box 1523

China Council for the Promotion of International Trade
4 Fuxingmenwai St. Tel: 6801 3344; Tlx: 22315 CCPITCN; Fax: 6801 1370

China Economic Development Corporation
93 Bei He Yan Dajie. Tel: 6554231; Tlx: 22044 ACFIC CN

China Economic Information Corporation
Wangfujing Dajie. Tel: 6650 7722

China International Trust & Investment Corporation (CITIC)
19 Jiangguomenwai Dajie. Tel: 6500 2255; Tlx: 22305 CITIC CN

China Investment Bank
Office Building of Media Centre B11, Fuxing Lu. Tel: 6851 5868; Tlx: 22537 CIB CN

China National Machinery Import & Export Corporation
Er Li Gou, Xi Jiao.Tel: 6831 7733; Tlx 22242 CMIEC CN; Fax: 6831 4143

China National Tourist Office
Chong Wen Men Hotel, 2 Chong Wen Men Xi Dahia. Tel: 512 2521

Couriers
DHL-Sinotrans, tel 6466 2211; Federal Express-Qian Tan Co, tel 6501 1017; TNT Express Worldwide, tel 6467 2517; UPS-Sinotrans, tel 6422 5670

Emergencies
Capital (Beijing Union) Hospital. Dongdan Bei Dajie. Tel: 6512 77331, ext. 217. (Foreigners' section ext. 274/251)
Ambulance service. Tel: 120
Police/Emergency. Tel: 110

Japan-China Association for Economy and Trade
Tel: 6521605

Japan-China Economic Relations and Trade Centre
Tel: 6507766, ext. 3008

National Tourism Administration
No 9a Jianguomennai Ave, Beijing 100740. Tel: 6513 8866 ext 1413; Fax: 6512 2096

Post Office
PTT Building, Changan Xidajie, tel: 6666215

Secretarial/Translation Services
Via Business Centres of Great Wall Sheraton, Hilton, Holiday Inn Lido, Palace, Shangri-La Hotels mentioned in Hotel Listings of this book or

Dietz Business Services Ltd
The International Club, Guoji Julebu. Tel: 652 2566

Major Foreign Trade Corporations
Known by their Cable Addresses; 'Agrimex' and so on

AGRIMEX. Agricultural Machinery & Equipment
Sanlihe. Tel: 6801 2416; Tlx: 866361; Fax: 6801 2871

ARTCHINA. Pottery & Porcelain, Jewellery, Jade etc
82 Donganmen St. Tel: 6558831; Tlx: 22155 CNART CN

AUTIMPEX. Automboliles, Motor Cycles & Accessories
8 Da Tang Fang Hutong, Xishi, Xicheng Dist, 100034. Tel: 6602 0782; Fax: 6601 5381/6401, 6568282

CATIC. China National Aero Technology Import/Export Corporation
5 Liang Guo Chang, Dong Cheng Dist, 100010. Tel: 6401 7722; Fax: 6401 5381/6401 5682

CEROILFOOD. China National Oils & Foodstuffs Import/Export Corp'n
82 Donganmen St. Tel: 6466 0854; Tlx: 22281 CEROF CN; Fax: 6466 0636

CHINAFILM. China Film Distribution & Exhibition Corp'n
25 Xinwai St. Tel: 62013493; Tlx: 22195 FILM CN; Fax: 6202 5833

CHINAMET. Mettalurgical Import/ Export Corporation
46 Dongsixi Dajie. Tel: 6513 3322 ext 4117; Tlx: 22461; Fax: 6512 3792

CHINAPACK. Packaging Import/ Export Organisation
28 Donghu Lane, Andingmenwai. Tel: 6421 17476; Tlx: 221490; Fax: 6421 2124

CHINASILK/CHINATEX. China Silk Corporation/Textiles Import-Export
82 Donganmen St. Tel: 6512 8336; Tlx: 22280 CNTEX; Fax: 6513 6838

CHINAWALL. Great Wall Industrial Corporation. Tech. Designs /Services
1 Hongqiao Dong Daije, Congwenmenwai (Box 847). Tel: 6837 2506/6837 2941; Tlx: 22484 CPMC CN; Fax: 6837 3155

CHINELECTRON. Electronics Equipment & Technology.
49 Fuxing Road. Tel: 6810910; Tlx: 22475 CEIEC CN

CHINSCICAD. Scientific Instruments Import & Export.
75 Denghsi Kou St. Tel: 6550669; Tlx: 22474 ASHICN.

CHUNGKUO. Bank of China (for foreign trade).
410 Fuchengmennei Ave, 100818; Tel: 6665325; Tlx: 22254 BCHO CN

CITIC. China International Trust & Investment Corporation.
2 Qianmen Dong Dajie, 14th fl, Box 9021.Tel: 6550905; Tlx: 22305 CITICCN

CLETC. Light Industrial Foreign Economic & Technical Corp'n
22b Fuwai Daije. Tel: 6894743/ 6895369. Tlx: 22465 LIMEX CN

CNEIC. Nuclear Energy Industry Import/Export Organisation.
1a Dong Yue Tan Bei Jie, Xi Cheng Dist.Tel: 6866415; Tlx: 22349 SSTCC

CHINA - Introduction

CNOOC. China National Offshore Oil Corporation.
29-31 Changan Dong. Tel: 6555225. Tlx: 2261 CNOOC CN

COMTRADE. China Council for the Promotion of International Trade.
Fuxingmenwai Daije. Tel: 6867229; Tlx: 22315 CCPIT CN

CONSULTEC. Trade Consultation & Technical Service Corporation.
2 Changan Street E. Tel: 6462912/ 6553031. Tlx: 22506 CTSUL CN

COSCO. Ocean Shipping Company. Vessel Charter/Cargo Booking.
6 Dong Chang An Street.
Tel: 6555431; Tlx: 22264 CPCPK CN

INDUSTRY. Light Industrial Products (Toys/paper etc) Import/Export
82 Donaganmen St. Tel: 6558831; Tlx: 22282 LIGHTCN; Fax: 6512 3763

INSTRIMPEX. Computers, Electronics, Communications Equipment Import/Export Organisation
Er Li Gou, Xijiao. Tel: 6831 7733; Tlx: 22242 CIIEC CN

JENDEV. Southwest China Joint Energy Dev't Corp's. (Coal, railways, harbour improvement etc)
16 Heping Rd N. Tel: 6446671 ext 763/776; Tlx: 22494 CNCDC CN

MACHIMPEX. National Machinery Import/Export Corp'n
Er Li Gou, Xijiao. Tel: 6891243/ 6891974. Tlx: 22242 CMIEC CN

MACHINTERCORP. Machine Building/Technical Transfers/ Engineering/Plants etc.
12 Fuxingmenwai St. Tel: 6867890/ 6865281; Tlx: 22341 CMIC CN

MINMETALS. Metals & Minerals Import/Export Corp'n
8 Chedaogou, Hai Dian Dist. Tel: 6802 1275/802 1324; Fax: 6831 5079

NEWBUILD. New Building Materials Corporation. Factories/ Advanced Equipment & Technology Importation.
Zizhuyuan Rd, Xijiao. Tel: 6891260. Cable 4454 Beijing.

NONFERMET. Non-ferrous Metals Import/Export Organisation
46 Dong Sixi Dajie. Tel: 6801 4477; Tlx: 22461 MIEC CN; Fax: 6801 5368

PETCORP. Oil Industry Development Organisation
Box 766 Liiupukang. Tel: 6444313; Tlx: 22312 PCPRC CN

PICC. People's Insurance Co of China. Marine, Hull, Aviation, Cargo & Land
Box 2149. Tel: 6335150; Tlx: 22102 PICC CN

PMIEC. Precision Machinery Import/Export Corp'n
2 Yuetan Bei Xiojie. Tel: 6895012/ 6896364; Tlx: 22484 CPMC CN

PUBLIMEX. Publications Import/ Export Corp'n. Foreign Books, newspapers etc
Chaoyangmennei, Box 88.
Tel: 6440731; Tlx: 22313 CPC CN

SINOCHART. Chartering & Space Booking for Export/Import Cargoes
Er Li Gou, Xijiao. Tel: 6890931/ 6893566. Tlx: 22265 TRANS CN

SINOCHEM. Chemicals (inc. rubber tyres) Import/Export Corp'n
Yu long Hotel, 40 Fu Cheng Rd. Tel: 6841 5588 ex 8/F; Fax: 6841 3120

SINOTRANS. Foreign Trade Transportation Corporation. Customs Clearance, delivery of import/export cargoes/joint venture couriers etc.
Er Li Gou, Xijiao. Tel: 6831773; Tlx: 22867 TRANS CN

TECHIMPORT. National Technical Import Corporation
Er Li Gou, Xijiao. Tel: 6831 7733/ 892 1160; Tlx: 22244; Fax: 6831 6696

XINSHIDAI. Imports/exports aeroproducts, electronics, ships, vehicles and machinery. Enters into joint ventures
Box 511. Tel: 6664714; Tlx: 22338 XSDCO CN

In Hong Kong:
China Resources Corporation
China Resources Building, 18th fl, 26 Harbour Rd. Tel: 2831 7111; Tlx: 73277

Guangzhou

All the following offices, opened in 1985 especially for foreign business visitors, are situated on the ground floor of the **Dong Fang Hotel,** *120 Liu Hua Road, telephone no. 8666 9900 (ask for the extension nos quoted below) opposite the Trade Fair grounds.*

Bank of China
Zhujiang Trust & Consultancy Co. Ext. 1161

China State Construction Engineering Co. Ext. 1124

External Economic Information Consultancy & Service Co. Ext. 1112

Guangzhou Administartive Bureau for Industry & Commerce. Ext 1112

Guangzhou Economic & Technical Development Office. Ext. 1123

Guangzhou Foreign Economic Law Offices. Ext. 1119

Guangzzhou Froreign Trade Corporation. Ext. 1123

Guangzhou Friendship Labour Service. Ext. 1118

Guangzhou International Trust & Investment Corporation. Ext. 1114

Guangzhou Municipal Taxation Bureau. Ext. 1115

People's Insurance Bureau. Ext. 1116

Yangcheng Certified Public Accountants. Ext. 1117

Couriers
Courier Service Company of Guangzhou, tel: 8664614; DHL-Sinotrans, tel: 8335 5041/5047. TNT: 8668 0972; UPS-Sinotrans, 35 Shamian Daije, tel: 8818 9006

Emergencies
First Municipal Hospital, 602 North Renmin Road. Tel: 833 3090
Public Security Bureau (Foreign

Affairs Section) 8331060
Foreign Guest Medical Room. Dong Fang Hotel, tel: 8669900
Police: tel 110; Ambulance: tel 8182110

Post & Telecommunications
Guangzhou Post Office, Yanjiang Rd 1, tel: 8188 6615; Telecommunications Bureau, Liu Hua Square, tel: 8777 7623/8777 5190

Tourist Office
China International Travel Service (CITS), 179 Huanshi Rd, tel: 8667 7271; Fax: 8329 1788

Shanghai

China Council for the Promotion of International Trade
27 Zhongshan East Rd. Tel: 62107221

China National Import/Export Corporations
Animal By-products. 23 Zhongshan Rd E, tel: 6321 5630
Arts & Crafts. 16 Zhongshan E Rd, tel: 6321 2100
Cereals & Oils. 11 Hangkou Rd, tel: 6321 9760
Chemicals. 27 Zhongshan E Rd, tel: 6321 1540
Foodstuffs. 26 Zhongshan E Rd, tel: 6321 6233
Light Industrial. 128 Huqin Rd, tel: 6321 6858
Machinery. 27 Zhongshan E Rd, tel: 6321 5066
Metals & Minerals. 27 Zhongshan E Rd, tel: 6321 1220
Textiles (garments). 27 Zhongshan E Rd, tel: 6321 8500
Textiles (silks). 17 Zhongshan E Rd, tel: 6321 5770
Transportation. 74 Dianchi Rd, tel: 6321 3103

Couriers
DHL-Sinotrans, tel: 6536 0705; Federal Express-Qian Tan Co, tel: 6501 4840; PO Express Mail Service Station, tel 324 5025; TNT Express Worldwide, tel: 6419 0000. UPS-Sinotrans, tel: 6321 3862

Emergencies
Shanghai No 1 Hospital, 410 Suzhou Bei Lu, tel: 6324 0100
Huashan Hospital, 12 Wulumuqi Zhong Lu, tel: 6431 1600
Police 210 Hankou Lu, tel: 6321 5380

Secretarial & Translation Services
Service Center for Overseas Traders (SCOT), Opp. Jinjiang Hotel, 58 Maoming Road. Tel: 6237 0115; Tlx: 33012 BTHJC CN. Shanghai Centre, 1376 Nanjing Xi Lu, tel: 6258 2582

Shanghai Industrial Consultants
Rm 109, 49 Sichuan Road. Tel: 6211818/6231747.Tlx: 33102SICFUCN
Also at Suite 101, Jingan Guest House, 370 Hua Shan Road. Tel: 6563050 ext. 101;Tlx: 33148 SICISCN

Shanghai International Trade Information & Exhibition Corp'n
33 Zhongshan Dong Yi Lu. Tel: 6233480; Tlx: 33290 SCPIT CN

Taxis
Friendship Taxi. Tel: 6536363
Municipal Taxi. Tel: 656444

Tourist Office/NTO
China National Tourist Office, 66 Nanjing Dong Lu, tel: 6432 4960

Main Travel Agents

Beijing

China International Travel Service Head Office (CITS)
103 Fuxingmennei Ave, 100800
Tel: 6601 1122; Tlx:22350; Fax: 6601 2013
China Travel Service Head Offlce
8 Dongjiaomingxiang, 100005
Tel: 6512 9933; Tlx:22487; Fax: 6512 9008
China Youth Travel Service Head Office (CYTS)
23b Dongjiaomingxiang, 100006
Tel: 6512 7770; Tlx:20024; Fax: 6512 0571
China International Travel Service Beijing
28 Jianguomenwai St, 100002
Tel: 6515 8562; Fax: 6515 8602
China International Sports Travel Co
4 Tiyuguan Rpad, Chongwen Dist, 100061
Tel: 6701 7364; Fax: 6701 7370
China Comfort Travel Head Office
57 Di An Men Xi Dajie, 100009
Tel: 6601 6288;Tlx:222862;Fax: 6601 6336

China Women Travel Service
103 Dongsi Nan Street, 100010
Tel: 6553307/6513 6311; Tlx: 21160; Fax: 6512 9021

Guangzhou
China Travel Service Guangdong
10 Qiaoguang Road, 510115
Tel: 8333 6888; Tlx:44217; Fax: 8333 6625
China International Travel Service Guangdong
179 Huanshi Road, 510010
Tel: 8666 6271; Tlx 44450; Fax: 8667 8048
Guangdong Railway China Youth Travel Service
69 Dadao Road, Dongshan, 510600
Tel: 8775 2401/2407; Fax: 8776 2509

Guilin
China International Travel Service Guilin
14 Ronghu Road, 541002
Tel: 223518; Fax: 222936
Guilin Overseas Tourist Corporation
8 Zhishan Road, 541002
Tel: 334026; Tlx: 48463; Fax: 335391

Kunming
The Kunming Scenery-Custom Internationa Tourist Service
2nd fl, Yunnan Hotel, Yongan Road, 650041
Tel: 313 9042/313 6594/313 5860; Fax: 313 5851

Nanning
China Guangxi Tourist Corporation
40 Xinmin Road, 530212
Tel: 202042; Tlx: 48142; Fax: 204105

Shanghai
China Internationa Travel Service Shanghai
33 Zhongshan Road E1
Tel: 6321 7200; Tlx:33277; Fax: 6329 1788
Shanghai Jinjiang Tours Ltd
27 Fl, Union Bldg, 100 Yanan Road E, 200002. Tel: 6329 0690; Tlx: 33429; Fax: 6320 0595
Shanghai CYTS Tours Corporation
2 Hengshen Road, 200031
Tel: 6433 1826; Tlx:30241; Fax: 6433 0507

Urumqi
Xinjiang Nature Travel Service
64 Dongfeng Road, 830002
Tel: 227791; Tlx: 79049; Fax: 217174

Xian
China International Travel ServiceShaanxi
32 North Changan Road, 710061
Tel: 752066; Tlx: 70115; Fax: 751453
China Travel Service Shaanxi
272 Jiefang, 710004
Tel: 712557; Tlx: 70148; Fax: 714152

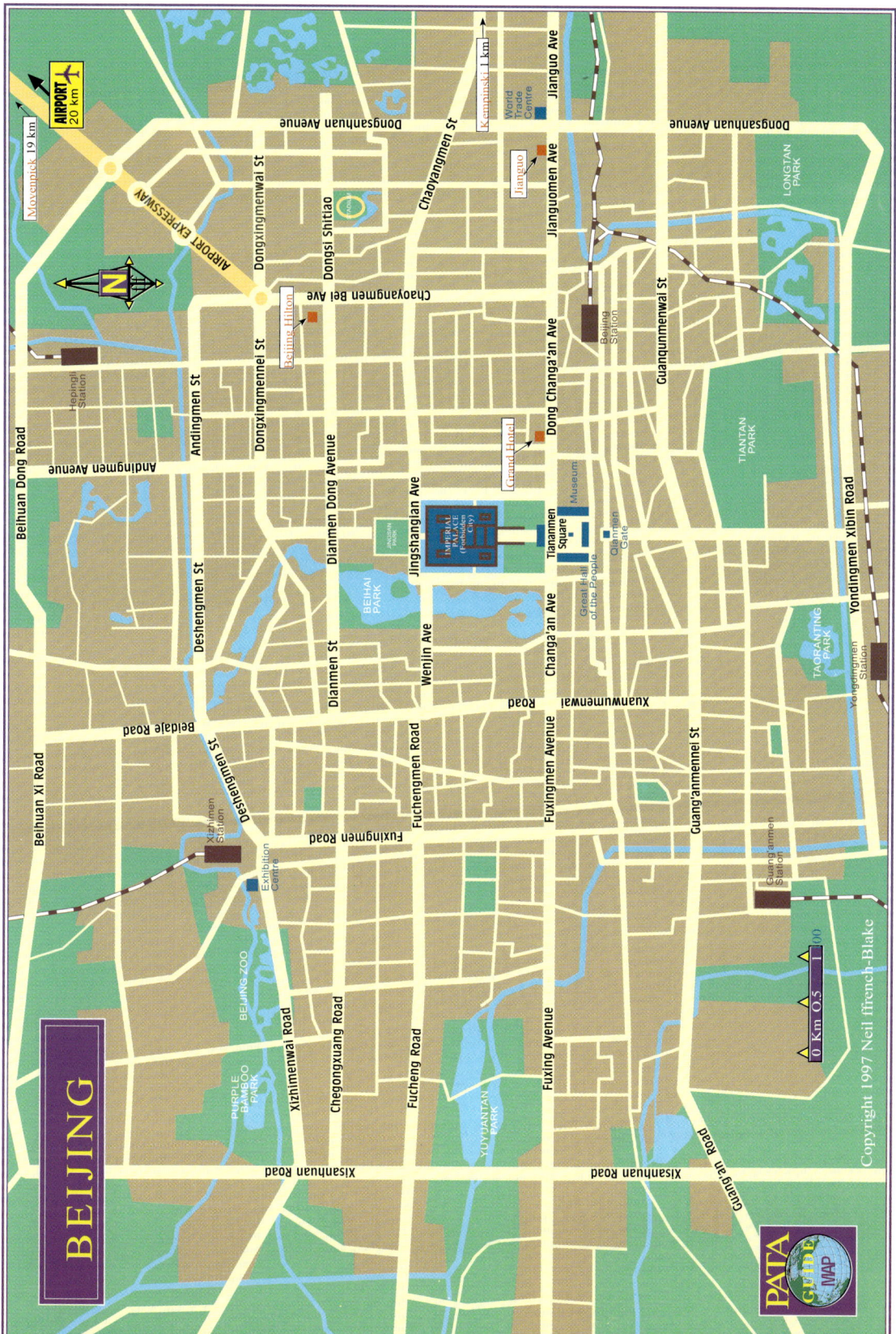

Beijing Hotel Reference Table

Hotel (listed in price order)	Single Room Rate (From) US$	Location	Number of Rooms	Number of Suites	Conference Facilities	Exhibition Space	Largest Banquet	Business Centre	Swimming Pool (O=Indoor)	Tennis Court	Health Club	Video Films
Kempinski Lufthansa Center	280	Chaoyang	432	65	●	●	700	●	O	●	●	●
Shangri La's China World	270	World Tde Ctr	687	56	●	●	900	●	O	-	●	●
The Palace Hotel	260-340	Wangfujing	518	59	●	-	450	●	O	●	●	●
Grand Hotel Beijing	260	Centre	161	57	-	-	250	●	O	-	●	-
Beijing Hilton	250	Dipl. Dist	335	24	●	-	180	●	O	●	●	●
Great Wall Sheraton	225	Chaoyang	900	104	●	●	1500	●	O	-	●	●
Shangri La Hotel	200	Zoo/Negs Bdg	538	19	●	●	800	●	O	●	●	●
Holiday Inn Crowne Plaza	200	Centre	380	-	●	-	220	●	O	-	●	●
Traders Hotel	200	World Tde Ctr	288	1	-	-	200	●	O	-	●	●
Jianguo Hotel Beijing	190	Centre	287	61	●	-	200	●	O	-	●	●
Jing Guang New World	190	Centre	469	22	●	-	450	●	O	-	●	-
Guangdong Regency Beijing	180	Centre	400	-	-	-	200	●	●	-	●	-
Chang Fu Gong (New Otani)	180	Centre	480	20	●	-	1500	●	O	●	●	-
Beijing New Century	170	South	630	33	-	-	900	●	●	●	●	-
Beijing Toronto (Jinglun)	170-200	Centre	638	22	●	●	300	●	O	-	●	●
Radisson SAS Hotel	160	Chaoyang	338	10	●	●	300	●	O	-	●	-
Gloria Plaza Hotel	160-190	Centre	377	46	●	-	250	●	O	-	●	●
Sara Hotel Beijing	150-170	Wangfujing	400	26	●	-	150	●	O	-	●	●
The Garden Hotel	150-170	Centre	486	-	●	-	280	●	●	●	-	●
Holiday Inn Lido Beijing	150	Jiangtai Rd	890	21	●	-	600	●	●	●	●	●
Angler's Rest (Diaoyutai)	140	San Li He	302	-	-	-	-	-	-	-	-	-
Grand View Garden	140	Xuan Wu	380	4	●	-	600	●	O	-	●	●
Kunlun Hotel	130	Chaoyang	758	-	●	-	800	●	-	-	-	-
Holiday Inn Downtown	130	Xichengu	347	9	●	-	-	●	O	-	●	-
Novotel Beijing	130	Centre	291	3	●	-	180	●	-	-	●	-
Swissotel KH Macau Center	125-150	HK-Macau Ctr	357	90	●	-	400	●	O	●	●	●
Mövenpick Hotel	115	Airport	391	36	●	-	200	●	-	●	●	-
Beijing Hotel	110	Shopping Ctr	900	-	●	-	-	-	-	-	-	-
Asia Hotel Jinjiang	90	North	263	26	●	●	200	●	-	-	-	-
Capital Hotel	85-110	Centre	243	53	-	-	-	●	O	-	●	●
Jin Lang Hotel Beijing	75-130	Dong Cheng	550	-	●	-	-	-	-	-	-	-
Beijing International	65-85	Centre	1158	72	●	●	500	●	O	●	●	●
Chains City Hotel Beijing	60-75	Chaoyang	45	175	-	-	-	●	-	-	●	-

Guangzhou Hotel Reference Table

Hotel	Single Room Rate (From) US$	Location	Number of Rooms	Number of Suites	Conference Facilities	Exhibition Space	Largest Banquet	Business Centre	Swimming Pool (O=Indoor)	Tennis Court	Health Club	Video Films
White Swan Hotel	140	Shamian Isd	843	33	●	-	300	●	●	●	●	●
China Hotel	140	Centre	717	171	●	●	840	●	●	●	●	●
Holiday Inn City Centre	130	Centre	391	40	●	-	500	●	-	●	-	-
The Garden Hotel	130	Centre	1033	79	●	●	1100	●	O	●	●	-
Guangdong International	115	North	660	142	-	-	-	●	O	●	●	-
Plaza Canton	90	Centre	786	28	●	-	350	●	O	●	●	-
Dong Fang Hotel	90	Trade Fair	1207	78	●	-	500	●	O	●	●	●
Furama Hotel Guangzhou	85	Centre	360	-	●	●	200	●	O	-	●	-
Equatorial Guangzhou	85	Centre	300	4	●	-	600	●	-	-	●	-
The Landmark	75	Centre	677	53	-	-	-	●	-	-	-	-
Central Hotel	70-85	Exhib Ctre	192	39	●	-	600	●	-	-	●	-
Baiyun (White Cloud)	38	Haunshidong	704	14	●	-	500	●	-	-	●	-

CHINA - Hotels

Shanghai Hotel Reference Table

Hotel (listed in price order)	SINGLE ROOM RATE (From) US$	LOCATION	NUMBER OF ROOMS	NUMBER OF SUITES	CONFERENCE FACILITIES	EXHIBITION SPACE	LARGEST BANQUET	BUSINESS CENTRE	SWIMMING POOL (O=Indoor)	TENNIS COURT	HEALTH CLUB	VIDEO FILMS
Shanghai Hilton	280	Shantou Ent Ctr	713	70	●	●	400	●	O	●	●	●
Garden Hotel	210	Centre	500	-	-	-	1200	●	O	-	●	●
Portman Shangri-La	200	Shanghai Ctre	546	49	●	●	350	●	●	●	●	●
Shanghai JC Mandarin	200	Bus. Centre	479	34	●	●	500	●	O	●	●	●
Hotel Sofitel Hyland	200	Centre	322	67	●	●	360	●	-	-	●	●
Westin Tai Ping Yang	200	Hongqiao	539	39	●	●	1200	●	O	●	●	●
Holiday Inn Crowne Plaza	190	Diplomatic qtr	467	29	●	-	500	●	O	●	●	●
Jinjiang Tower	190	Centre	568	48	●	-	600	●	O	-	●	●
Sheraton Hua Ting Hotel	190	Outskirts SW	730	40	●	●	1100	●	O	●	●	●
Equatorial Shanghai	180	Centre	526	46	●	●	350	●	O	●	●	●
Shanghai Worldfield Conv Ctr	160	Chang Ning	342	19	●	●	800	●	●	-	●	●
Yangtze New World	160	West	550	3	●	-	800	●	●	●	●	●
Shangai New Asia Tomson	160	Pudong	416	6	●	-	400	●	●	●	●	●
Jinjiang Hotel	150	Centre	510	-	●	-	1500	●	-	-	●	-
Peace (Heping) Hotel	150	Bund	408	12	-	-	450	●	-	-	●	-
Radisson SAS Langsheng Htl	150	Centre	380	37	●	●	200	●	-	-	●	●
Hotel Nikko Longbai	150	Hongqiao	329	63	●	-	500	●	O	●	●	●
Galaxy Hotel Shanghai	140	W Suburbs	592	65	●	-	1100	●	-	-	●	●
Regal Shanghai	135	Suburbs	378	37	●	-	400	●	-	-	●	●
City Hotel	110	Centre	169	11	-	-	200	●	-	-	●	●
Jianguo Hotel	95	Xuhui	411	64	●	-	800	-	-	-	●	●
Novotel Shanghai Yuan Lin	80	Botanical Gdn	223	-	-	-	300	●	O	●	●	●
Shanghai Hotel	80	W Central	528	23	●	-	500	●	-	-	-	-

Rest of China Hotel Reference Table

Hotel	SINGLE ROOM RATE (From) US$	LOCATION	NUMBER OF ROOMS	NUMBER OF SUITES	CONFERENCE FACILITIES	EXHIBITION SPACE	LARGEST BANQUET	BUSINESS CENTRE	SWIMMING POOL (O=Indoor)	TENNIS COURT	HEALTH CLUB	VIDEO FILMS
Holiday Inn Crown Plaza	170	Chengdu	400	33	●	●	500	●	O	●	●	●
New World Bei Fang	155	Harbin	300	29	●	-	200	●	●	-	-	-
Holiday Inn Dalian	150	Dalian	268	20	●	-	200	●	O	●	●	-
Dragon Hotel	120	Hangzhou	558	-	●	-	650	●	●	●	●	●
Shangri-La Hotel Shenzhen	122	Shenzhen	523	30	●	●	425	●	●	●	●	-
Sunshine Hotel	121	Shenzhen	308	-	●	-	400	●	●	-	●	-
Hyatt Regency Xian	120	Xian	299	10	●	-	450	●	-	-	●	-
Shangri La Golden Flower	120	Xian	464	46	●	-	500	●	●	-	●	-
Citic Ningbo	120	Ningbo	280	8	●	●	280	●	O	-	●	-
New World Shenyang	120	Shenyang	213	33	●	●	250	●	●	-	●	-
Shangri-La Hotel Hangzhou	110	Hangzhou	240	47	●	-	400	●	-	-	●	-
The Landmark	110	Shenzhen	330	16	●	-	300	●	●	-	●	-
Holiday Inn Guilin	110	Guilin	259	-	●	-	400	●	O	-	●	-
Pan Pacific Wuxi Grand	110	Wuxi	330	12	●	-	500	●	●	-	-	-
Bamboo Grove Hotel	110	Suzhou	423	21	●	●	280	-	-	●	●	●
Sheraton Guilin	110	Guilin	414	27	●	-	150	●	O	●	●	-
Holiday Inn Kunming	100	Kunming	252	-	●	-	150	●	O	-	●	-
Shantou International	100	Shantou	330	20	●	●	300	●	-	●	●	●
Huiquan Dynasty Hotel	99	Qingdao	500	-	●	-	1350	●	O	●	●	-
Central Hotel	98	Nanjing	288	6	-	-	-	●	●	●	●	-
Hotel Nikko Longbai	95	Hongqiao	419	-	-	-	-	-	-	-	-	-
Forum Hotel	92	Shenzhen	516	35	●	-	800	●	●	-	●	●
Holiday Inn Urumqi	90	Urumqi	380	3	●	-	300	●	●	-	●	-
Sheraton Xian Hotel	90	Xian	434	16	●	●	260	●	O	●	●	-
Windsor Guishan Hotel	90	Guilin	669	17	●	-	860	●	O	-	-	-
Grand Lijiang Hotel	90	Lijiang	125	2	●	-	-	-	-	-	-	●
King World Hotel	80	Kunming	316	4	●	-	800	●	O	-	●	-
Continental Hotel	80	Shenzhen	220	-	●	-	500	●	-	-	●	-
Xian Lee Gardens	80	Xian	287	10	●	-	100	●	-	-	●	-
Bell Tower Hotel Xian	75	Xian	219	101	●	-	300	●	-	-	●	-
Green Lake Hotel	70	Kunming	302	6	●	-	500	●	●	-	●	●
Holiday Inn Lhasa	63	Lhasa	463	2	●	-	-	●	O	-	-	-

Hotels

Beijing

Angler's Rest (Diaoyutai) B
2 Fucheng Road, Sanlihe
Tel: 6803 1188; Tlx: 22798 DYTGH CN;
Fax: 6801 3362

Asia Hotel D
8 Xinzhong Xi Jie, Gonti North Rd
Tel: 6500 5227; Tlx: 210597; Fax: 6500 8001

Beijing Hilton
1 Dong Fang Road, North Dong Sanhuan Road, Chaoyang District, Beijing 100027
Tel: (10) 6466 2288; Fax: (10) 6465 3073

Strategically located in the Sanlitun Diplomatic District with easy access to the city centre, the hotel is only a short distance from the Agricultural Exhibition Centre. the China International Exhibition Centre, You Yi Shopping Centre and a 9-hole golf course.

Accommodation and rates
220 King single/double, 115 twin rooms US$ 250-330; 24 suites US$360-1900 (Subject to 15% surcharge and government tax of RMB 12 per room per night)

Credit cards accepted:
Amex, JCB, Diners Club, Mastercard, Visa

Meeting & banqueting facilities
8 meeting/conference rooms, capacity up to 260; audio-visual equipment available; largest reception 180 seated or 200

Room services
Airconditioning, colour TV, direct-dial telephone (ext. in bathroom), hairdryer, laundry/valet service, minibar, music/radio/alarm clock, safety deposit box, tea/coffee making facilities, 24-hr room service, video films, non-smoking rooms available

Business & other services
Business centre, executive floor, express checkout, airport pickup, translation service, car parking, car rental, travel centre, taxi service, handicap facilities, guided tours, newsstand/shops

Sports & Recreation
Fitness centre/gym, jacuzzi/whirlpool, massage, sauna, indoor swimming pool, tennis, squash

Restaurants
Atrium Café (145) - à la carte/buffet/international/asian, open 0630-1300; *Genji* (62) - Japanese, open 1130-1400/1800-2200; *Louisiana* (68) - American specialities, open as above, closed Sunday lunch; *Sui Yuan* (145) - Cantonese/Dim Sum, open 1130-1400/1730-2200

Overseas Sales Representatives:
Hilton International Sales Offices; Hilton Reservations Worldwide

Beijing Hotel D
33 East Chang An Ave, 10004
Tel: 6513 7766; Tlx: 22426; Fax: 6513 7307

Beijing International D
9 Jiannai Daije
Tel: 6512 6688; Tlx: 211121; Fax: 6512 9972

Beijing New Century B
6 Southern Road, Capital Gym
Tel: 6849 2001; Fax: 6849 1107

Beijing Toronto (Jinglun) B
3 Jianguimennai, 100020
Tel: 6500 2266; Tlx: 210012; Fax: 6500 2022

Capital Hotel D
3 East Qian Men Street, 100006
Tel: 6512 9988; Tlx: 222650; Fax: 6512 0309

Chains City Hotel Beijing D
No 4, Gongti Donghu, Chaoyang District,
Tel: 6500 7799; Tlx: 210530; Fax: 6500 7668

Chang Fu Gong (New Otani) B
26 Jianguomenwai St, 100022
Tel: 6512 5555;Tlx:210466; Fax: 6513 5346

China World Hotel A
No 1 Jianguomenwai Ave, 10004
Tel: 6505 2266;Tlx: 211206; Fax: 6505 0828

Gloria Plaza Hotel B
No 2 Jianguomenwai Avenue, 100022
Tel: (10) 6515 8855; Fax: (10) 6515 8533

Grand Hotel Beijing
35 East Chang An Avenue, 100006
Tel: 6513 7788; Tlx: 210454 BHPTW CN;
Fax: 6513 0048/49

Its unique location amid the splendour of Imperial Palace provides easy access to Beijings commercial centre. It offers luxurious suites and rooms that blend ancient Chinese with modern western decor, facilities for business and pleasure, elegant bars and restaurants.

Accommodation and rates:
44 double; 117twin US$ 260-300; 57 suites US$ 380-2700 (Subject to 10% service charge and 5% government tax)

Credit cards accepted:
Amex, JCB, Diners Club, Federal Card, Great Wall, Mudan & Jinsui

Groups
8 meeting/function rooms, capacity 10-300; largest reception 250 seated/400 cocktail

Room services
Airconditioning, colour TV, direct-dial telephone (ext. in bathroom), hairdryer, laundry/valet service, minibar, music/radio/alarm clock, safety deposit box, tea/coffee making, trouser press, 24-hr room service

Business & other services
Business centre, express checkout, airport pickup, translation service, car parking, car rental, taxi service, barber shop/beauty salon, newsstand/shops

Sports & Recreation
Fitness centre/gym, jacuzzi/whirlpool, massage, sauna, indoor swimming pool.

Restaurants
Red Wall Cafe (128) - Continental/ buffet, open 0700-midnight; *Rong Yuan* (123) - Sichuan Cuisine, open 1130-1400/1800-2200; *Ming Yuan* - Cantonese (98) - open as above; *Old Peking* (110) - Chinese, open as above.

Overseas Sales Representatives:
Hong Kong. Tel: (+852) 2530 0572; Fax: (+852) 2810 8844

CHINA - Hotels

Grand View Garden Hotel C
88 Nan Cai Yuan St, 100054
Tel: 6353 8899;Tlx: 22688; Fax:6353 9189

Great Wall Sheraton Hotel A
N Donghuan Road, 100026
Tel: 6500 5566;Tlx: 22002; Fax: 6500 1919

Guangdong Regency Hotel B
2 Wangfujing Avenue, 10006
Tel: 6513 6666; Tlx: 210453; Fax: 6513 4248

Holiday Inn Crowne Plaza ◯ A
48 Wangfujing/Sengshixikou Rd
Tel: 6513 3388; Tlx: 210676 HICPBJ CN; Fax: 6513 2513

Holiday Inn Downtown Beijing C
No 98 Beilishi Lu, Xicheng Qu, 100037
Tel: 6832 2288; Tlx: 221045; Fax: 6832 0696

Holiday Inn Lido Beijing ◯ B
Jichang Road, Jiang Tai Road, 100004
Tel: 437 6688; Tlx: 22618; Fax: 437 6237

Jianguo Hotel Beijing ◯
Jianguomenwai Dajie, 100020
Tel: (86-10) 6500 2233; Tlx: 22439 JGHBJ CN; Fax: (86-10) 6500 2871/6501 0539

Located on Jianguomenwai Dajie near the diplomatic quarter in the heart of Beijing's business district, the Jianguo hotel is only 30 minutes from the Beijing Capital Airport and 10 minutes from the famous Tiananmen Square.

Accommodation & rates
243 superior rooms, US$ 190; 44 executive rooms, US$ 240; 61 suites, US$ 290-370.
Subject to 15% service & US$1 tax

Credit cards accepted:
Amex, Diners Club, JCB, Mastercard, Visa

Groups
7 meeting/function rooms, capacity 160 theatre-style; audio-visual equipment available; 293 sq m exhibition space; largest reception 200 seated or 400 cocktail

Room services
Airconditioning, colour TV, direct-dial telephone (ext. in bathroom) laundry/valet service, minibar, safety deposit box, 24-hr room/meal service, non-smoker bedrooms, video films

Business & other services
Business centre, executive floor, express checkout, airport pickup, translation service, car parking, car rental, travel centre, taxi service, guided tours, newsstand/shops, barber shop/beauty salon

Sports & Recreation
Fitness centre/gym, indoor swimming pool, massage

Restaurants & Coffee Shops
The Four Seasons (194) - Chinese, open 1130-1400/1800-2200; *The Café (106)* -Continental, open 0600-0030;*Charlie's Bar*, open 1100-0030; *Justine's* , - Continental, open 0600-0930/noon-1430/1800-2230;*The Lobby*

Overseas Sales Representatives:
Swiss-Belhotel International Hong Kong. Tel: (852) 2838 3855; fax: (852) 2893 9555; Utell International; Pacific Management USA, toll-free (800) 553 3638; Tri Hotel Marketing UK

Jing Guang New World Hotel B
Hu Jia Lou, Chao Yang Qu, 100020
Tel: 6501 8888; Tlx: 210489; Fax: 6501 3333

Jin Lang Hotel Beijing D
75 Chong Nei St, Dong Cheng, 10005
Tel: 6513 2288; Fax: 513 6809/6810

Kempinski Hotel Beijing Lufthansa Center ◯
50 Liangmaqiao Rd, Chaoyang District, 100016
Tel: 6465 3388; Fax: 6465 3366

Located 10 kms northeast of City Centre, 10 minutes' driving time, 25 kms from the international airport. Diplomatic quarters in the vicinity. 10 minutes to the Forbidden City and Tiananmen Square.

Accommodation & rates:
432 single/double/twin, US$ 280-300; 65 suites, US$ 360-400. Subject to 15% surcharge and City devt tax of $1 per pax per night

Credit cards accepted:
Amex, Diners, JCB, Mastercard, Visa

Groups
6 meeting/function rooms, capacity 1500 pax; audio-visual equipment available; largest reception 700 banquet/1000 cocktail

Room services
Airconditioning, colour TV, direct-dial telephone (ext. in bathroom) laundry/valet service, minibar, safety deposit box, trouser press, 24-hr room/meal service, non-smoker bedrooms

Business & other services
Business centre, executive floor, express checkout, airport pickup, translation service, car parking, travel centre, taxi service, guided tours, newsstand/shops

Sports & Recreation
Fitness centre/gym, jacuzzi, jogging track, massage, sauna, indoor swimming pool, tennis, squash

Restaurants & Coffee Shops
Symphony (68) - Continental, open 1200-1400/1800-2200; *Imperial Garden (86)* - Chinese, open 1130-1400/1730-2200; *Seasons (186)* - International, open 0600-midnight; *Paulaner Brauhaus (176)* - German, open 1130-0100

Overseas Sales Representatives
Frankfurt tel: 49610 500258; fax: 49610 251562. Japan tel: 81 3525 8011; fax 81 3525 2308. Hong Kong tel: 852 2848 7397; fax: 852 2877 2002. London tel: 44181 307 7693; fax: 44181 544 9893. New York tel: 1-212 697 8600; fax: 1-212 697 5153

Kunlun Hotel C
2 Xin Juan Nan Lu, Chao Yang Dist
Tel: 6500 3388; Tlx: 210327; Fax: 6500 3228

New Century B
Capital Stadium, South Road No 6, 100044
Tel: 6849 2001; Fax: 6849 1103

Hotel New Otani Chang Fu Gong B
26 Jianguomenwaidajie
Tel: 6512 555; Tlx: 210466; Fax:6513 9810

Novotel Beijing D
88 Dengshikou, Dongcheng Dist, 100006
Tel: 6513 8822; Fax: 6513 9810

The Palace Hotel A
8 Goldfish Lane, Wangfujing, Beijing 100061
Tel: 6512 8899 Tlx: 222696 PALBJ CN; Fax: 6512 9050

SAS Radisson Hotel Beijing ◯ C
6a East Beisanhuan Rd, Chaoyang 100028
Tel: 6466 3388;Tlx: 211241; Fax: 6465 3186

CHINA - Hotels 55

Mövenpick Hotel
Xiao Tianzhu Village, Shunyi County, PO Box 6913 (Airport).
Tel: (10) 6456 5588; Fax hotel: (10) 6456 5678; Fax guests 6456 1234
E-mail: bjmphtlc@iuol.cn.net. Internet: http://www.allhotels.com/a/moven.bj

Located off the main highway and just 5 minutes from the airport, 427 rooms inc. duplex suites, six restaurants and bars, unique resort facilities; travel and ticketing service.

Accommodation & rates
391 rooms, single occ.US$ 115-150; twin/double occ. US$ 150-185; 36 suites US$ 180-235; Subject to 15% service & tax charge

Credit cards accepted:
Amex, Diners, Master, JCB, Eurocard, Visa

Groups
7 meeting/function rooms, capacity 10-200; audio-visual equipment available; 252 sq m exhibition space; largest reception 200 seated or 300 cocktail

Room services
Airconditioning, colour TV, direct-dial telephone (ext. in bathroom) laundry/valet service, minibar, safety deposit box (concierge), 24-hr room/meal service, non-smoker bedrooms, video films

Business & other services
Business centre, airport pickup, translation service, car parking, travel centre, taxi service, barber shop/beauty salon, guided tours, newsstand/shops

Sports & Recreation
Billiards/snooker, fitness centre/gym, golf (nearby), jacuzzi, jogging track, massage, sauna, swimming pool, tennis, riding (nearby)

Restaurants & Coffee Shops
Mövenpick (120) - Continental, open 0600-2300; *Harlekin* (40) - Contemporary Western, open 1800-2300; *Chopsticks* (90) - Chinese, open 0700-0900/1130-1445/1730-2200; *Boulevard Café* (60) - cakes/snacks, open 0630-midnight

Overseas Sales Representatives
Asia-Pacific: HK tel: (852) 2815; fax: 2815 3236; Utell; Delton; USA: 1 800 34 Hotel.

Shangri-La Hotel Beijing ◌ B
29 Zizhuyuan Road, 100081
Tel: 6841 2211; Tlx: 222231 SHABJ CN; Fax: 6841 8002/3/6

Swissôtel HK Macau Center ◌ B
Dong Si Shi Tiao Li Joao Quio, PO Box 9153, Beijing 100027
Tel: 6501 2288; Tlx: 222527; Fax: 6501 2501

Traders Hotel C
1 Jian Guo Men Wai Avenue, Da Bei Yao, 100004
Tel: 6505 2277; Tlx: 222981; Fax: 6505 0818

Chengdu

Yinhe Dynasty Hotel C
99 Xia Xi Shun Cheng Street, 610016
Tel: (28) 661 8888; Fax: (28) 674 8837

Chongqing

Holiday Inn Yangtze Chongqing
15 Nan Ping Bei Lu, 630060 ◌ C
Tel: (811) 280 3380; Fax: (811) 384 3085

Dalian

Furama Hotel Dalian B
74 Stalin Road, 116001
Tel: (411) 263 0888; Fax: (411) 280 4455

Holiday Inn B
18 Sheng Li Square, 116001
Tel: (411) 280 8888; Fax: (411)280 9704

Guangzhou

Baiyun Hotel (White Cloud) E
367 Huanshidong
Tel: 8333 3998; Tlx: 44327; Fax: 8333 6498

Central Hotel D
International Exhibition Center, 33 Ji Chang Lu, Sanyuanli
Tel: 8667 8331;Tlx: 44664; Fax: 8666 2316

Dong Fang Hotel D
120 Liu Hua Rd, 510016
Tel: 8666 9900; Tlx: 44439; Fax: 8666 2775

Hotel Equatorial D
931 Renmin Bei Road
Tel: 8667 2888; Tlx: CN 44168; Fax: 8667 2583

Furama Hotel Guangzhou D
316 Chnagdi Lu, 510210
Tel: 8186 3288; Fax: 8186 3388

China Hotel
Lia Hua Lu, Guangzhou
Tel: 8666-6888; Tlx: 440888 CHLGZ CN; Fax: 8668 6698

A 5-star deluxe business hotel situated in the heart of Guangzhou, adjacent to the Guangzhou Trade Exhibition Centre and close to the railway station and the international airport.

Accommodation & rates
717 single/double rooms, US$ 140-210; 171 suites US$ 210-1500 (except trade fair periods: April 14-30 & Oct 14-30)

Credit cards accepted:
Amex, Diners, Master, JCB, Great Wall, Visa

Meeting & conference facilities
15 meeting/function rooms, capacity 30-1500; audio-visual equipment available; 1272 sq m exhibition space; largest reception 70 tables or 1500 cocktail

Room services
Airconditioning, colour TV, direct-dial telephone (ext. in bathroom), hairdryer, laundry/valet service, minibar, tea/coffee making, safety deposit box, 24-hr room/meal service, non-smoker bedrooms, video films

Business & other services
Business centre, executive floor, airport pickup, translation service, car parking & rental, travel centre, taxi service, barber shop/beauty salon, newsstand/shops

Sports & Recreation
Fitness centre/gym, indoor games, jogging track, massage, sauna, outdoor swimming pool, tennis

Restaurants & Coffee Shops
Four Seasons (304) - Cantonese fine dining, open 0730-1430/1800-2200; *Food Street* (542) - Cantonese, open 0730-1330; *Veranda Coffee Shop* (250) - American & Chinese, open 0630-midnight; *Roof Restaurant* (46) - Fine dining American Grill, open 1800-2230

Overseas Sales Representatives
Utoll international, Renaissance and New World Hotels International

The Garden Hotel   C
368 Huanshi Dong Lu, 510064
Tel: 8333 8989;Tlx:44788 ; Fax: 8335 0367

Guangdong Internatonal   C
339 Hangshi Dong Lu, 510060
Tel: 8331 1888;Tlx: 44556; Fax: 8331 1666

Holiday Inn City Centre Guangzhou   C
Huanshi Dong, Overseas Chinese Village,
28 Guangming Lu
Tel: 8776 6999;Tlx:441265;Fax: 8775 3126

Hotel Landmark Canton   D
8 Qiaoguang Lu, 510115
Tel: 8335 5988; Tlx: 441288; Fax: 8336 6197

Parkview Square Hotel   D
960 Jie Fang Bei Lu, 510030
Tel: 8666 5666; Tlx: 441088; Fax: 8667 1741

Ramada Pearl   C
9 Ming Yue Yi Road, 510600(on river)
Tel: 8737 2988; Fax: 8737 7481

The White Swan   ○ C
1 Nan Jie, Shamian Island, 510133
Tel: 8188 6968; Tlx: 44668; Fax: 8186 1188

Guilin

Guishan Hotel   D
Chuan Shan Lu, 541004
Tel: (773) 581 3388; Tlx: 48443; Fax: (773) 581 4851

Guilin Park Hotel   D
No 1 Luosi Hill, Laoren Shan Qian
Tel: (773) 282 8899; Tlx: 48498; Fax: (773) 282 2296

Holiday Inn Guilin   C
14 South Ronghu Rd, 541002
Tel: (773) 282 3950; Tlx: 48456; Fax: (773) 282 2101

Hong Kong Hotel Guilin   D
8 Xihuan Yi Rd, 541002
Tel: (773) 383 3889; Tlx: 48454; Fax: (773) 383 2752

Sheraton Guilin   C
Bing Jiang Nang Rd, 541001
Tel: (773) 282 5588; Tlx: 48439; Fax: (773) 282 5598

(*Hotel Classification:* **A** after name of hotel =over US$ 200 per person per night; **B** = between US$ 150-200; **C** = between US$ 100-150; **D** = between US$ 50-100; **E** = under US$ 50; ¶ = prices on application..
○ after name = PATA member

Hangzhou

Dragon Hotel   C
Shuguang Rd, 310007
Tel: 799 8833; Tlx: 351048; Fax: 779 8090

Shangri-La Hotel   C
78 Beishan Road, 310007
Tel: 797 7951; Tlx: 35005; Fax: 707 3545

Kunming

Green Lake Hotel   D
6 South Chi Hu Road, Kunming 650031, Yunnan
Tel: (0871) 515 8888; Tlx: 64073 GLHTC CN; Fax: (0871) 515 7867

Holiday Inn Kunming   C
25 Dong Feng E Rd, 650011
Tel: 316 5888; Tlx: 64151; Fax: 313 5189

King World Hotel   D
28 Beijing Road S, 650011
Tel: 313 8888; Tlx: 64143; Fax: 313 1910

Lhasa (Tibet)

Holiday Inn Lhasa   D
1 Minzu Lu Lhasa, 850000
Tel: (891) 63 32221; Tlx: 68010; Fax: (891) 6335796

Lijiang

Grand Lijiang Hotel   ○
Xinyi Street, Dayan Town, Lijiang, Yunnan Province
Tel: (888) 512 8888; Fax: (888) 512 7878

Grand Lijiang Hotel is located near the old town centre of Lijiang in one of the most beautiful areas of Yunnan Province in Southwest China, now easily accessible by air, just 45 minutes flying time from Kunming.
Grand Lijiang Hotel is within walking distance of many places of interest for visitors and offers beautiful views over the old town and the Jade Dragon Snow Mountain Range beyond.

Accommodation and rates
127 guestrooms, US$ 90-120; suites US$ 300. Rates subject to 15% service charge

Credit cards accepted
Visa, Amex, Diners, Mastercard

Groups
Meeting/function rooms with audio-visual facilities, capacity 50; largest reception 50 seated or 100 cocktail

Room services
Airconditioning, colour TV, direct-dial telephone (ext. in bathroom), hairdryer, laundry/valet service, minibar, music/radio/alarm clock, safety deposit box, tea/coffee making facilities, trouser press, 24-hr room/meal service, non-smoker bedrooms available, video films + satellite TV

Business & other services
Express checkout, airport pickup, translation service, car parking, car rental, travel centre, taxi service, guided tours.

Restaurants & Coffee Shops
Jade River Restaurant (140) - International & Thai, open 0600-1400/1700-midnight; *Snowbird Restaurant* (140) - Chinese, open 1130-1400/1800 -2200; *Lobby Lounge* (40) - Snacks, beverages, open as above.

Overseas Sales Representatives
Head Office: M Grand Hotel Company Limited, 11th fl, Boonpong Tower, 1193 Phaholyothin Road, Phayathai, Bangkok 10400, Thailand. Tel: (662) 272 3940-41; Fax: (662) 272 3943

Nanjing

Central Hotel   C
75 Zhongshan Road, 210005
Tel: (25) 440 0888/440 0666; Tlx: 342351 CHNJ CN; Fax: (25) 441 4194

Jinling Hotel   ○ C
Xin Jie Kou Square, 210005
Tel:445 5888; Tlx: 34110; Fax: 771 4695

Nanjing Hotel   E
259 North Zhonghshan Rd, 210003
Tel: 330 2302; Tlx: 34102; Fax: 330 6998

Qingdao

Huiquan Dynasty   C
9 Nanhai Rd, 266003
Tel: 287 3366; Tlx:2871122; Fax: 287 1122

CHINA - Hotels   57

Ningbo

Citic Ningbo International Hotel
1 Jiangdong Bei-Lu, Ningbo, Zhejiang 315040
Tel: (574) 775 7888; Fax: (574) 733 4738

Located in the heart of Ningbo's financial district, in close proximity to major shopping centres. Overlooking Lingqiao Bridge and Fenghua River. 2 kms from Railway Station & 15 kms from airport. The first and only international managed hotel in the city.

Accommodation & rates
288 single/doubles, US$ 120-175; suites US$ 220-1100

Credit cards accepted
Visa, Amex, Diners, JCB, Mastercard

Groups
4 meeting/function rooms with audio-visual facilities, capacity 12-450; 748 sq m exhibition space; largest reception 280 seated or 600 cocktail; KTV and theme rooms available

Room services
Airconditioning, colour TV, direct-dial telephone (ext. in bathroom), hairdryer, laundry/valet service, minibar, music/radio/alarm clock, safety deposit box, tea/coffee making facilities, 24-hr room/meal service, non-smoker bedrooms available, video films

Business & other services
Business centre, executive floor, express checkout, airport pickup, translation service, car parking & rental, travel/tours service, taxi service, barber shop/beauty salon, newsstand/shops.

Sports & Recreation
Billiards/snooker, fitness centre/gym, golf & indoor games, jacuzzi/whirlpool, massage, sauna, indoor swimming pool, bowling

Restaurants & Coffee Shops
Rome (95) - Italian, open 1130-1400/1730-2230; *Imperial Court* (120) - Cantonese & Hot Pot, open as above; *Promenade Cafe* (87) - Continental/Asian open 0600-0200.

Overseas Sales Representatives
Byron International Hotels & World Hotels & Resorts

Shanghai

City Hotel Shanghai C
No 5-7 Shan Xi Rd (South), 200020
Tel: 6255 1133; Tlx: 30031 SCH CN; Fax: 6255 0611

Hotel Equatorial Shanghai B
65 Yanan West Road, 200040
Tel: 6248 1688; Tlx: 33948 EQUAT; Fax: 6248 1773/4033

Galaxy Hotel C
888 Zhong Shan Road West, 200051
Tel: 6275 5888; Tlx: 33176; Fax: 6275 0039

Garden Hotel A
58 Maoming Road South, 200020
Tel: 6415 1111; Tlx: 30157; Fax: 6415 8866

Holiday Inn Crowne Plaza B
388 Pan Yu Road, 200052
Tel: 6280 8888;Tlx: 30310; Fax: 6280 8545

Hua Ting Sheraton Hotel A
1200 Cao Xi, Bei Lu, 200030
Tel: 6439 1000; Tlx: 33589 SHHTH CN; Fax: 6255 0830

Jianguo Hotel D
439 Cao Xi Rd, 200030
Tel: 6439 9299; Fax: 6439 9433

Jinjiang Hotel C
59 Maoming Road South, 20020
Tel: 6258 2582; Fax: 6472 5588

Jinjiang Tower B
161 Changle Road, 20020
Tel: 5415 1188; Tlx:33652; Fax: 6415 0048

Nikko Longbai Hotel B
2451 Hongqiao Rd, 200335
Tel: 255 9111; Tlx: 30138; Fax: 255 9333

Novotel Shanghai Yuan Lin D
201 Bai Se Road, 200231
Tel: 6470 1688; Tlx:32680; Fax: 6470 0008

Ocean Hotel D
1171 Dong Daming Road, 200082
Tel: 6545 8888; Tlx:30333; Fax: 6545 8993

Peace (Heping) Hotel C
20 Nanjing Dong Road, 200002
Tel: 6321 1244; Tlx:33914; Fax: 6329 0300

Portman Shangri-La A
1376 Nanjing Xi Lu, 200040
Tel: 6279 8888;Tlx: 33272; Fax: 6279 8999

Regal Shanghai C
1000 Qu Yang Rd, 200437
Tel: 6542 8000;Tlx: 33952; Fax: 6544 8400

Shanghai Hilton
250 Hua Shan Road, 200040
Tel: 6248 0000; Fax: 6248 3848

Located in the heart of Shanghai city and within walking distance of the commercial and entertainment area. Only 20 minutes' drive from the Shanghai Hong Qiao International Airport.

Accommodation and rates
642 rooms, 71 business studios, 70 suites. Single occ. US$ 280-300; double/twin US$ 300-350; suite US$ 400-2000
Rates include 15% service charge

Credit cards accepted
Visa, Amex, Diners, JCB, Master, Gt Wall

Meeting & conference facilities
6 meeting/function rooms with audio-visual facilities, capacity 1000; 500 sq m exhibition space; largest reception 400 seated or 600 cocktail; theme parties by arrangement

Room services
Airconditioning, colour TV, direct-dial telephone (ext. in bathroom), hairdryer, laundry/valet service, minibar, music/radio/alarm clock, tea/coffee making facilities, 24-hr room/meal service, non-smoker bedrooms available, handicap rooms available

Business & other services
Business centre, executive floor, express checkout, airport pickup, translation service, car parking & rental, travel service, via concierge, taxi service, barber shop/beauty salon, newsstand/shops

Sports & Recreation
Fitness centre/gym, jacuzzi/whirlpool, massage, sauna, indoor swimming pool, squash, tennis

Restaurants & Coffee Shops
Atrium Cafe (154) - Continental, open 0600-2200;*Shanghai Express* (204) - Shanghainese, open 24 hrs; *Sichuan Court* (87) - Sichuan, open 1800-2230; *Suiyuan* - Cantonese, open 1130-1400/1800-2300; *Da Vinci's* (80) - Italian, open 1800-2230 (Sundays also 1130-1400)

Overseas Sales Representatives
Hilton International Sales Offices; Hilton Reservations Worldwide

Shanghai Worldfield Convention Hotel
2106 Hong Qiao Road, Chang Ning District, 200335
Tel: 6270 3388; Fax: 6270 4554

Shanghai's only convention centre and hotel complex is conveniently located in the Hong Qiao commercial area. Ten minutes from the airport and 290 minutes from the Pudong Development Zone by car. Shanghai Worldfield Convention Hotel is the ideal choice for business travellers and the perfect venue for all types of meetings and conventions.

Accommodation and rates
139 singles, US$ 160-220; 193 twin, US$ 170-250; 19 suites US$ 320-1000.
Rates subject to 15% service charge

Credit cards accepted
Visa, Amex, Diners, Mastercard

Groups
18 meeting/function rooms with audio-visual facilities, capacity 3300; 927 sq m exhibition space; largest reception 800 seated or 1000 cocktail.

Room services
Airconditioning, colour TV, direct-dial telephone (ext. in bathroom), hairdryer, laundry/valet service, minibar, music/radio/alarm clock, safety deposit box, tea/coffee making facilities, trouser press, 24-hr room/meal service, video films

Business & other services
Business centre, executive floor, express checkout, airport pickup, translation service, car parking & rental, travel service, taxi service, barber shop/beauty salon, newsstand/shops, guided tours

Sports & Recreation
Fitness centre/gym, jacuzzi/whirlpool, jogging track, massage, sauna, outdoor swimming pool

Restaurants & Coffee Shops
Poolside Coffee Shop (110) - Western & Oreintal, open 24 hours; *Jin Garden* (92) - Cantonese, open 1100-1430/1700-2230; *Ginza* (96) - Japanese, open as above; *Hong Kong Bistro (52)* - Chinese & snacks, open 0700-2230

Overseas Sales Representatives
Worldfield Co Ltd, suite 3006-7 Natwest Tower, Times Square, 1 Mattheson St, Causeway Bay, Hong Kong. Tel: (852) 2506 9028; Fax: (852) 2506 1550

Radisson Lansheng SAS Hotel   C
(formerly Regal Shanghai F T Hotel)
1000 Qu Yang Road, 200437
Tel: 6542 8000; Tlx: 33952 REGBC; Fax: 6544 8400

Shanghai JC Mandarin   A
1225 Nam Jin Xi Lu, 200040
Tel: 6279 1888;Tlx:33939; Fax: 6279 1822

Shanghai Hotel   D
505 Wulumuqi Bei Lu, 200040
Tel: 6248 0088; Tlx:33295; Fax: 6248 1506

Shanghai New Asia Tomson Hotel B
777 Zhang Yang Road, Pu Dong
Tel: 5831 8888; Fax: 5831 7777

Silk Road Hotel   D
777 Qu Yang Road
Tel: 6554 9988; Fax: 6554 8528

Hotel Sofitel Hyland Shanghai   B
505 Nanjing Rd East, 20002
Tel: 6351 5888; Tlx:30386; Fax:6351 4088

Westin Shanghai   B
5 Zun Yi Nan Road, Hongqiao Dev't Zone
Tel: 6275 8888; Tlx:33345; Fax: 6275 5420

Yangtze New World Hotel   B
2009 Yan An Xi Rd, 200335
Tel: 6275 0000; Tlx:33675; Fax: 6275 0750

Shantou

Shantou International Hotel
Jin Sha Lu, Shantou City, Guangdong Prov
Tel: (0754) 8251212; Tlx: 45475; Fax: (0754) 8252250

Shanghai Hilton, Lobby Pavilion

Worldfield Convention Center, Shanghai

Shenyang

New World Hotel Shenyang
No 2 Nanjing Nan Street, heping District, Shenyang 110001
Tel: (24) 386 9888; Fax: (24) 386 0018

Situated at the junction of the Zhonghua Road and Nanjing Street in the city centre of Shenyang. Just a few minutes' walk to the Shenyang South Railway Station and Liaoning provincial museum and 30 minutes from the airport.

Accommodation & rates
3 single/138 double/82 twin US$ 120-155; 33 suites US$ 200-1600

Credit cards acepted:
JCB, Diners, Amex, Mastercard, Visa

Groups
4 meeting/conference rooms, capacity 8-350, with audio-visual equipement; 390 sq m exhibition space; largest reception 250 seated/350 cocktail

Room services
Airconditioning, colour TV, direct-dial telephone, hairdryer, laundry/valet service, minibar, safety deposit box, tea/coffee making, trouser press, 20-hr room/meal service, non-smoker bedrooms, video films

Business and other services
Business centre, executive floor, express checkout, airport pickup, translation service, car parking & rental, travel service, taxi service, barber & beauty shop, guided tours, newsstand/shops

Sports & Recreation
Fitness centre/gym, indoor games, massage, sauna, outdoor swimming pool

Restaurants & Coffee Shops
Coffee Shop (135) - Western/Oriental, open 0630-midnight; *Lumingchum* (120) - Chinese Liao, open 1130-1400/1730-2200; *Dynasty* (130) - Cantonese, open as above

CHINA - Hotels

Overseas Sales Representatives
Europe. UK tel: 44-1293-824124; Germany tel 49-6196-4960; France tel 33-1-47-887172; USA: travel tel: 1-407-898-8333; corporate 1-203-535-1224; Asia-Pacific Japan tel: 81-3-3239-6824; Australia tel: 61-3-9699 2122

Shenzhen

Century Plaza Hotel ○ **C**
KinChit Road, 518001
Tel: (755) 232 0880; Fax: (755) 233 4060

Continental Hotel Shenzhen **D**
Shang Bu North Road, Shenzhen
Tel: (755) 226 3838; Fax: (755) 226 4139

Forum Hotel **D**
68 Heping Road, Shenzhen
Tel: (755) 558 6333; Tlx: 420199; Fax: (755) 556 1700

The Landmark Hotel **C**
2 Nanho Road, Shenzhen, Guangdong
Tel: (755) 225 4615; Fax: 222 7558

Marina Ming Wah **D**
Gui Shan Road, 518067
Tel: (755) 668 9968; Fax: (755) 668 6688

Nanhai Hotel **E**
Szechou Special Industrial Zone, 518069
Tel: 669 2888; Tlx: 420879; Fax: 669 2440

Shangri-La Hotel Shenzhen **B**
East Side, Railway Station, Jianshe Road, Shenzhen 518001
Tel: (755) 233 0888; Fax (755) 233 0870

Sunshine Hotel **D**
1 Jiabin Road, Shenzhen
Tel: (755) 223 3888; Fax: (755) 222 6719

Suzhou

Bamboo Grove Hotel **C**
Zhu Hui Road, Suzhou 215006
Tel: (512) 202 5601; Fax: (512) 203 8778

Tianjin

Hyatt Tianjin **B**
Jie Fang North Road, 300042
Tel: (22) 331 8888; Tlx: 23270; Fax: (22) 331 1234

Sheraton Tianjin **B**
Zi Shan Road, He Xi District, 300074
Tel: 334 3388; Tlx: 23353; Fax: 335 8740

Tianjin Crystal Palace **D**
28 You Yi, Hexi District, 300061
Tel: (22) 835 6666; Tlx: 23387; Fax: (22) 835 8886

Urumqi

Holiday Inn Urumqi **D**
168 N Xinhua Rd, 830002
Tel: (0991) 281 8788; Tlx:79161; Fax: 281 7422

Hotel World Plaza **D**
2 Beijing S Rd, Xinjiang 830011
Tel: (991) 383 6400; Fax: (991) 383 6399

Wuhan

Holiday Inn Tian An Wuhan ○ **B**
888 Jie Fang Da Dao, Wuhan 430022
Tel: (27) 586 7888; Fax: (27) 584 5353

Wuxi

Pan Pacific Wuxi Grand Hotel
1 Liangqing Road, Wuxi, Jiangsu Province
Tel: (86) 510 580 6789; Fax: (86) 510 270 0991; E-mail: wx.pwgh2@publicl.wx.js.cn

Guests at the legendary City of Canals' premier hotel enjoy world-class service and comfort combined with the best of Chinese cuisine and culture.

Accommodation and rates
374 rooms and suites; single/twin $115-129 (+ 10% service & 5% govt tax charge)

Credit cards accepted
Visa, Amex, Diners, JCB, Mastercard

Groups
4 meeting/function rooms; banqueting hall seating up to 500

Room services
Airconditioning, colour TV, direct-dial telephone, minibar, music/radio/alarm clock

Business and other services
Business centre, shopping arcade, barber & beauty shop, clinic and post office.

Sports & Recreation
Pool, sauna, mini-gymnasium, indoor games

Restaurants & Coffee Shops
Four restaurants offering Wuxi, Cantonese, Beijing, Western and Japanese cuisine.Bar and lounge, discotheque and karaoke bar.

Overseas Sales Representatives
Pan Pacific Hotels & Resorts worldwide.
SRS Steigenberger Resrvation Service

Xian

Bell Tower Hotel **D**
SW Corner of Bell Tower, 710001
Tel: 727 9200; Tlx: 70915; Fax: 721 8767

Dynasty Hotel **D**
55 Huan Chang Xi Road North, 710082
Tel: 721 2718; Tlx: 700233 ; Fax: 721 2728

Grand New World **D**
48 Lian Hu Rd, 710002
Tel: 721 6868; Tlx: 700215; Fax: 721 9754

Holiday Inn Xian **D**
Huan Zhen Dong Road, 710048
Tel: 333888; Tlx: 70043; Fax: 335962

Hyatt Regency Xian **C**
158 Dong da Jie, 710001
Tel: 723 1234; Tlx: 70048; Fax: 721 6799

Jianguo Hotel Xian **D**
20 Jin Hua Nan Lu, 710048
Tel: 323 8888; Tlx: 700209; Fax: 323 5145

Shangri-La's Golden Flower Hotel ○ **C**
8 Chang Le Rd West, 710032
Tel: 323 2981; Tlx: 70145; Fax: 323 5477

Sheraton Xian **D**
12 Feng Gao Rd, 710077
Tel: 426 1888; Tlx: 70032; Fax: 426 2983

Xian Lee Gardens Hotel **D**
No 8, Laodong South Road, 710068
Tel: (29) 426 3388; Tlx: 700315; Fax: 426 3200

Xiamen

Holiday Inn Crowne Plaza **D**
12-8 Zhen Hai Rd, 361001
Tel: (592) 202 3333; Fax: (592) 203 6666

The Marco Polo Xiamen **C**
Hubin Bei Road (N), Yuan Dang West Lake, 361012
Tel: (pre-opening) (592) 507 5320; Fax: (592) 507 5236

Zhuhai

Zhuhai Holiday Resort **E**
Zhuhai Special Economic Zone, 519000
Tel: 333 2038; Tlx: 456230; Fax: 333 2036

Zhuhai Hotel **E**
Jingshan Rd, 519000
Tel: 333 3718; Tlx: 456218; Fax: 333 2339

(*Hotel Classification:* **A** *after name of hotel* =over US$ 200 per person per night; **B** = between US$ 150-200; **C** = between US$ 100-150; **D** = between US$ 50-100; **E** = under US$ 50; ¶ = prices on application.. ○ after name = PATA member

Restaurants

Many of the best restaurants are located in the hotels described above. We give below a short selection of main city restaurants, popular with business clientele, where advance booking is recommended.
Note: *Out of hotel restaurants normally close at 9 pm.*

Beijing

Beijing "Sick Duck" Kaoyadian
13 Shifuyuan, off Wangfujing St;
tel: 6525 1642

Beijing "Big Duck" Kaoyadian
Hepingmen, 14 Qianmen St, tel: 6301 8833

Beijing "Old Duck" Kaoyadian
32 Qianmen St, Tel: 6511 2418

Beijing Ren Ren
18 East St, Qianmen. Tel: 6511 2671

Beijing Hot Pot Beef & Seafood Restaurant *(Hongkong Cuisine)*
146 West Zhushikou St, Xuanwu Dist,
Tel: 6633 3220/6301 1069

Chongwenmen Kaoyadian *(Beijing Duck)*
2 Congwenmen St, tel: 6675 0505

Donglaishun Fanzhuang *(Moslem/Chinese)*
6 Donghuamen/Dongfeng Market, off Wangfujing St, tel: 6555 0069

Doosan Restaurant *(Korean)*
206, 2nd fl, Central Building, Hualong Street. Tel: 6512 9130

Feng Ze Zuan *(Shandong/N China)*
83 Zhushikou Street/Qianmen St
Tel: 6333 2828

Fanshan Fandian
Hortensia Island, Beihai Park, tel: 6401 1889

Hongbinlou Fanzhuang *(Moslem Chinese / Duck)* 82 W Changan St, tel: 6665 6404

Imperial Garden *(Chinese)*
Kempinski Hotel Beijing Lufthansa Center. 50 Liangmaqiao Rd, Chaoyang
Tel: 6465 3388

Jinyang Fanzhuang *(Shaanxi)*
241 Zhusikhou West St, tel: 633 1669

Justine's *(Continental)*
Jianguo Hotel, Jianguomenwaidajie.
Tel: 6500 2233

Maxims and Minims *(European)*
2 Quianmen E St, tel: 6754 003/6512 2211

Sichuan Fandian *(Sichuan)*
51 West Rongxian Hutong, tel: 6665 6348

Summer Palace *(Chinese)*
China World Hotel, 1 Jianguimenwai Avenue.
Tel: 6505 2266

Syin "Super Duck" Beijing Kaoya Dian
Xinhua Rd South, tel: 6633 4422

Symphony *(International)*
Kempinski Hotel Beijing Lufthansa Center, 50 Liangmaqiao Rd, Chaoyang. Tel: 6465 3388

Windows on the World *(International)*
CITIC Building, 19 Jianguomennai,
tel: 6500 3335/6500 2255

Guangzhou

Banxi Restaurant
151 Xiangyang Yi Lu, tel: 8188 9318

Beiyuan (North Garden) Restaurant
320 Dongfeng St, tel: 8333 2471

Datong Restaurant
63 Yanjiang Rd, tel: 8188 5365

Dongjiang Restaurant
41 Zhongshan S Rd, tel: 8333 5568

Guangzhou Restaurant
South Wenchang Rd/2 Xiuli Rd, tel: 8188 7136

Nanyuan (South Garden) Restaurant
120 Quianjin Lu, tel: 8555 0532

Yu Yuan
90 Liwan Nan Road, tel: 8188 8552

Shanghai

Bamboo Garden *(Sichuan)*
3rd fl Jinjiang Hotel, 59 South Maoming Rd
Tel: 6258 2582

Chengdu Restaurant *(Sichuan)*
795 Huahai Rd. Tel: 6437 6412

Fangshan Tang (Qing Imperial Style)
Dahua Hotel, 914 Yanan Rd. Tel: 6252 3079

Friendship Restaurant *(Cantonese)*
5th fl, Shanghai Exhibition Centre, 1000 Yanan Zhong Lu. Tel: 6258 1959

Huating Restaurant *(Western/Chinese)*
62 Songshan Rd (off Huahai Rd).
Tel: 6626 3998

Lao Fandian (Old Town) Restaurant *(Shanghai)*
242 Fuyou Rd. Tel: 6628 9850

Luyuegun Restaurant *(Sichuan/Jiangsu)*
763 Nanjing Road. Tel: 6653 7221

Meilongzhen Restaurant *(Sichuan)*
1081 Nanjing Rd West. Tel: 6256 2718

The Red House (Western)
37 Shaanxi Rd South. Tel: 6256 5748

Sky Blue Revolving Restaurant *(Int'l)*
Jin Jiang Tower Hotel, 161 Changle Lu.
Tel: 6433 1984

Tianjin Guan *(Tianjin)*
1029 Huahai Rd. Tel: 6637 3992

Windows on the World *(Cantonese)*
27th fl, Ruijin Bldg, 205 Maoming Nan Lu. Tel: 6433 6309/6433 6310

Xinja *(Cantonese)*
719 Nanjing Rd East. Tel: 6322 4393

Yangzhou Restaurant *(Shanghai)*
308 Nanjing E Rd. Tel: 6322 2777

Xian

East Asia Restaurant *(Suzhou/Wuxi)*
46 Luomashi Street. Tel: 718410

Jufengyuan Restaurant *(Sichuan)*
151 Jiefang Road. Tel: 23185

Tang Dynasty Music Restaurant
39 North Section, Chang'an Rd. Tel: 751633

Airline Offices

Beijing

Aeroflot
3 Jianguomenwai Ave, Beijing
Tel: 6500 2412/6657 8901; Fax: 6664 4623

Air China
Capital Airport, Beijing 100621
Tel: 6456 3230; Fax: 6456 3831

Asiana
Jianguo Hotel Rm 134, Jianguomenwai
Tel: 6506 5227; Fax: 6506 5229

Air France
China World Trade Centre, 1 Jianwai Dajie
Tel: 6505 1818. Fax: 6505 1435

All Nippon Airways
China World Trade Centre, 1 Jianwai Dajie
Tel: 6505 3311; Fax: 6505 1188

British Airways
Rm 210, 2nd fl, Scite Tower, Jianguomenwai
Tel: 6512 4070/5; Fax: 6512 4085

Cathay Pacific
Jianguo Hotel, 5 Jianguomenwai
Tel: 6500 3399/6233 2742

China International Airlines
15 West Chang'an St. Tel: 6601 7755

China United Airlines
A14 Fuxing Rd, Haidian District, 100036
Tel: 6678 4584

Dragonair
L 107, 1/7 China World Trade Centre Tower, 1 Jianguomenwai De Jie.
Tel: 6505 4343; Fax: 6505 4347

Finnair
102 Scite Tower, 22 Jianguomenwai
Tel: 6512 7180; Fax: 6512 7182

Japan Air Lines
Chang Fu Gong Office Bldg,
Jianguomenwai Ave; Tel: 6513 0888

Lufthansa
50 Liangmaqiao, Beijing 100016
Tel: 6465 4488

Malaysia Airlines
Lot 115a/b, West Wing Offices, China World Trade Centre, Jianguomenwai Ave, 100004;
Tel: 6505 2681-3; Fax: 6505 2680

Northwest
Suite 104 China World Trade Centre, 1 Jianguomenwai Dajie
Tel: 6505 3504; Fax: 6505 5147

Qantas
Rm 120B, Yansha Centre No 50 Maqiao Rd, Chaoyang Dist, Beijing
Tel: 6467 3337; Fax: 6466 9494

SAS
G/F Scite Tower, 22 Jianguomenwai Dajie.
Tel: 6512 0575; Fax: 6512 0577

China Airline Departures & Offices

Singapore Airlines
L109 Shopping Arcade, China World Trade Centre. Tel: 6505 3133; Fax: 6505 1178

Swissair
2nd fl, Scite Tower 22, Jianguomenwai
Tel: 6512 3555; Fax: 6512 2288

Thai International Airways
Rm 207-209 Scite Tower, Jianguomenwai
Tel: 6512 3881-3

United Airlines
Suite 204, Scite Tower 22, Jianguomenwai
Tel: 6512 8888; Fax: 6512 3456

Shanghai
Air China
600 Huashan Road, Shanhai. Tel: 6237 7888 Fax: 6327 2762

China Eastern Airlines
Hongqiao Airport, 200335
Tel: 6258 7830; Fax: 6255 8668

Dragonair
202 Level 2, West Tower, Shanghai Centre, 1376 Nanjing Rd (W), 200040
Tel: 6279 8093; Fax: 6279 7189

Northwest Airlines
Rm 207, 2f, East Wing Shanghai Centre, 1376 Nanjing Rd (W), 200040
Tel: 6279 8088; Fax: 6279 8807

Shanghai Airlines
Bei Da Men, Hongqiao Airport, 200035
Tel: 6268 8558; Tlx: 33536 SALCN

Singapore Airlines
Rm 208, 2F, East Wing Shanghai Centre, 1376 Nanjing Rd (W), 200040
Tel: 6279 8008; Fax: 6279 0028

Thai Airways International
201 Shanghai Centre, 1376 Nanjing Rd W 200840.Tel: 6279 7170; Fax: 6279 7179

United Airlines
Suite 204 Shanghai Centre, 1376 Nanjing Rd, 200040.Tel: 6279 8009; Fax: 6279 8853

Guangdong Province
Air China
980 Jiefang N. Rd, Guangzhou. Tel: 668 1399 Fax: 668 1286

China Southern Airlines
Baiyun Airport, Guangzhou
Tel: 8657 8901; Fax: 8665 0797

Shenzhen Airlines
Ling Ziao Garden, Shenzen Airport, Bao An Dist. Tel: 8777 7241; Fax: 8777 7242

Singapore Airlines
The Mezzanine Foyer, Garden Hotel, 368 Huanshi Dong Rd, Guangzhou 510064
Tel: 8335 8886; Fax: 8335 6699

Thai Airways International
M/F M04, The Garden hotel, 368 Huanshi Rd (E), Guangzhou 5100
Tel: 8382 3986; Fax: 8382 4348

China Airline Departures

Below is a list of main departures and frequencies from China's International Airports as of February 1997. **Direct Flights Only.**
Airline Abbreviation Codes: **AY** = Finnair; **AZ** = Alitalia; **BA** = British Airways; **BI** = Royal Brunei Airlines; **CA** = Air China; **CJ** = China Northern Airlines; **CP** = Canadian Airlines;**CZ** = China Southern Airlines; **ET** = Ethiopian Airlines; **GA** = Garuda Indonesia; **GP** = China General Aviation; **G8**= Air Great Wall; **H4** = Hainan Airlines; **HK** = Swan Airlines; **HR** = China United Airlines; **HY** = Uzbekistan Airways; **IR** = Iranair; **JD** = Japan Air System; **JL** = Japan Airlines; **JS** = Air Koryo; **KA** = Dragonair; **K4** = Kazakhstan Airlines; **LO** = Lot Polish Airlines; **LY** = El Al; **MF** = Xiamen Airlines; **NH** = All Nippon Airways; **MU** = China Eastern Airlines; **NX** = Air Macau; **NW** = Northwest Airlines; **OM** = Air Mongol -MIAT; **OZ** = Asiana Airlines; **PK** = Pakistan Int'l Airlines; **QF** = Qantas; **RO** = Tarom; **SC** = Shandong Airlines; **SF** = Shanghai Airlines; **SU** = Aeroflot; **SZ** = China Southwest Airlines;**SK** = Scandinavian Airline Systems; **TG** =Thai International;**TK** = Turkish Airlines; **UA** = United Airlines; **VN** = Vietnam Airlines; **WH** = China Northwest Airlines; **XO** = Xinjiang Airlines; **X2** = China Xinhua Airlines; **X7** = Chita Avia; **Z2** = Zhongyuan Airlines; **3Q** = Yunnan Airlines; **3U** = Sichuan Airlines; **4G** = Shenzhen Airlines.
Figures in brackets after destinations refer to the days of the week. (2,4,6) therefore indicates that departures take place on a Tuesday (the 2nd day of the week, a Thursday & a Saturday)

BEIJING (PEK)
Almaty (ALA)
K4 (3,5)
Amsterdam (AMS)
CZ (2,5) KL (4,7)
Addis Ababa (ADD)
ET (1)
Bandar Seri Begawan
BI (4,1)
Bangkok (BKK)
CZ (3,5,6) TG (1,2,4,5,7) CA (1,4,7)
Berlin (SXF)
CA (5)
Brussels (BRU)
MU (3,6)
Bucharest (BUH)
RO (7)
Chengdu (CTU)
SZ (daily) 3U (daily) CA (daily) CJ (2,7)
Chicago (CHI)
MU (4,7)
Chita (HTA)
SU (3) X7 (3)
Chongqing (CKG)
3U (4,7) CA (1,3,6,7) SZ (daily)
Copenhagen (CPH)
SK (1,2,4,7) CA (2,5)
Dalian (DLC)
CA (daily) CJ (daily)
Delhi (DEL)
ET (1)
Frankfurt (FRA)
CA (2,4,6,7)
LH (1,3,4,5,6,7))
Fukuoka (FUK)
CA (1,3,4,6,7) MU (2,7)
Fuzhou (FOC)
CA (daily) CJ (6) IV (3,6),
MF (1, 2,3,5,6,7)
Guangzhou (CAN)
WH (daily) CA (daily) CZ (daily) XO (3,5,7) SF (4,7)
Guilin (KWL)
CZ (1,2,3,5,6) WH (1,3,4)
Hangzhou (HGH)
CA, MU (daily) SF (1,5)
Hanoi (HAN)
CZ (1,4)
Harbin (HRB)

X2 (4,7) CA (daily) CJ (daily) 3U (1,5) WH (1,5)
SZ (7) XO (2) HK (1,2,3,4,6)
Helsinki (HEL)
AY (1,5)
Hong Kong (HKG)
KA, CZ, CA (daily)
Islamabad (ISB)
PK (1,5)
Jakarta (JKT)
GA (1) CA (2,4)
Karachi (KHI)
CA (4) PK (1,5)
Kiev (IEV)
6U (3)
Kuala Lumpur (KUL)
MH (2,4,5,6,7) CZ (2,4,5,7)
Kunming (KMG)
CA (3,4,6,7) 3Q (daily)
Kuwait (KWI)
SZ (4,7)
CA (4)
London (LHR)
CA (4,7) BA (2,4,7)
Los Angeles (LAX)
CA (4,7) NW (1,3,6)
MU (1,2,3,5,6)
Macau (MFM)
NX (daily)
Madrid (MAD)
MU (3,6)
Manila (MNL)
CZ (2,5)
Melbourne (MEL)
CA (1,5)
Milan (MIL)
CA (3,6) AZ (1,4)
Montreal (YMQ)
CP (4)
Moscow (MOW)
SU (2,4,5,6) CA (1,4)
Munich (MUC)
MU (2,5)
Nagoya (NGO)
JL (2)
Nanjing (NKG)
CA, MU (daily) GP (2,6,7)
SF (2,4,7) H4 (3,5,7) CZ (1,2,5,6)
New York (EWR)
UA (daily)
New York (LGA)
NW (2,5,7)

New York (JFK)
CA (3,5)
Ningbo (NGB)
CA (daily) H4 (daily) SZ (4,7)
Novosibirsk (OVB)
SU (2,4,5,6)
Osaka (OSA)
CA (2,3,4,5,6,7) JL (2,3,5,6)
MU (2,5) NH (4,7)
Paris (CDG)
CA (1,3,5) AF (2,5,6,7)
Pusan (PUS)
CA (1,4) OZ (2,4,7)
Pyongyang (FNJ)
JS (2,6) CJ (3)
Qingdao (TAO)
MU, CA (daily) SC (1,3,4,6)
Rome (FCO)
CA (3,6) AZ (1,4)
San Diego (SAN)
NW (1,3,6)
San Francisco (SFO)
CA (2,5,6)
Sanya (SYX)
CJ (2,4,6,7)
Seattle (SEA)
MU (4,7)
Seoul (SEL)
CA (daily) OSZ (1,2,4,5,7)
KE (1,2,3,5,6,7)
Shanghai (SHA)
CA (daily) MU (daily)
SF (daily) XO (2,4,6) CJ (daily)
Shantou (SWA)
CZ (daily) CA (daily) CJ (3,6)
Sharjah (SHJ)
CZ (3,6)
Shenyang (SHE)
CJ (daily) CA (daily) WH (2,6)
Shenzhen (SZX)
CZ (1,3,4,6,7) CA, 4G (daily)   HK (1,3,6) CJ (2,4,5,7)
Singapore (SIN)
CA (1,2,3,5,6) SQ (daily)
CZ (1,3,4,5,7)
Stockholm (STO)
CA (2,5)
Sydney (SYD)
CA (1,5)

CHINA - Airline Departures

Tashkent (TAS)
HY (3,7)
Tehran (THR)
IR (1,4)
Tel Aviv (TLV)
LY (6)
Tokyo (TYO)
CA, UA, NH (daily) NW (1,3,6) JL (1,3,4,5,6,7) PK(4,7)
Ulan Bator (ULN)
CA (2,5) OM (1,3,6)
Urumqi (URC)
XO (daily) CZ (3,6)
Vancouver (YVR)
CA (1) CP (1,3,4,5)
Vienna (VIE)
OS (1,3)
Warsaw (WAW)
LO (5)
Wenzhou (WNZ)
CA (daily) CJ (7) WH (1)
Wuhan (WUH)
CA, CZ (daily) WH (1,3,6)
Xiamen (XMN)
CZ (5) CA (1,2,3,4,6)
MF (daily)
Xi'an (XIY)
CA (daily) WH (daily) SZ (3,7)
Yangon (RGN)
CA (3)
Zhuhai (ZUH)
CZ (daily) CA (246) WH (136)
Zurich (ZRH)
CA (7) SR (2,4,7)

GUANGZHOU (CAN)

Amsterdam (AMS)
CZ (2,5)
Bangkok (BKK)
CZ (1,3,5) TG (1,2,4)
Beijing (PEK)
CZ (daily) SF (4,7) CA (daily) WH (daily) XO (3,5,7)
Changsha (CSX)
CZ (daily) SZ (2,5,7)
Changzhou (CZX)
XO (3,5) CZ (daily)
Chengdu (CTU)
CZ (daily) 3U (daily) SZ (daily)
Chongqing (CKG)
CZ (daily) 3U (daily) SF (daily) SZ (daily)
Dalian (DLC)
CZ (2,5) CJ (daily)
Dandong (DDG)
CZ (4,7)
Dayong (DDG)
CZ (4,7)
Fuzhou (FOC)
MU (2,4,6) CZ (2,3,6,7) IV (1,5) CJ (1,3,6) MF (daily)
Guilin (KWL)
CZ (daily)
Guiyang (KWE)
SZ (daily) CZ (1,2,4,6,7)
Haikou (HAK)
CZ (daily) H4 (daily) SF (2,6)
Hangzhou (HGH)
CZ,MU (daily) SF(2,4,6) 3Q (4)
Hanoi (HAN)
VN (2,5,7)
Harbin (HRB)
CZ (1,4) HK (1,2,3,5,7) CJ (daily) SZ (2,3,5,6)
Ho Chi Minh (SGN)
VN (2,5,7) CZ (3,6)
Hong Kong (HKG)
CZ (daily)
Jakarta (CGK)
GA (1,3) CZ (3,6)
Jilin (JIL)
CZ (3,7)
Jinan (TNA)
MU (daily) CZ (daily) SC (2,3,4,6)
Jinghong (JHG)
3Q (3,6)
Kuala Lumpur (KUL)
CZ (2,3,5,7) MH (1,2,4,6,7)
Kunming (KMG)
CZ (daily) 3Q (daily) SZ (3,6)
Manila (MNL)
CZ (2)
Melbourne (MEL)
CA/QF (5)
Nanchang (KHN)
CZ (2,4,6,7) MU (daily)
Nanjing (NKG)
MU (daily) SF (1,3,5) CZ (daily) CJ (2,4,5,7)
Ningbo (NGB)
MU (1,3) CZ (2,4,6,7) SZ (1) H4 (daily)
Osaka (OSA)
CZ (1,3,5) JD (1,4,6) H4 (1,3,4,6,7)
Penang (PEN)
CZ (2,4)
Phnom Penh (PNH)
VJ (3,6)
Qingdao (TAO)
CZ (1,2,4,6) MU (daily) SC (1,4,7)
Shanghai (SHA)
CZ, MU, SF (daily)
Shantou (SWA)
CZ (daily) CJ (3,4,7)
Shenyang (SHE)
CZ (2,4,5,7) CJ (daily)
Singapore (SIN)
CZ (1,4,6) SQ (4,7)
Surabaya (SUB)
CZ (3,6)
Sydney (SYD)
CA/QF (3,5)
Tianjin (TYN)
CA (daily) CZ (2,6)
Urumqi (URC)
XO (daily)
Vientiane (VTE)
CZ (4)
Wenzhou (WNZ)
MU (2,5) CZ (1,3,4,6,7) SF (2,4,7) CJ (1,2,3,6) WH (2,4,5) HK (2,5)
Wuhan (WUH)
CA (daily) CZ (daily) WH (3,7)
Xiamen (XMN)
MF (daily) CZ (daily) CJ (1,3,5) SZ (1) MU (2,3,4,6,7)
Xi'an (SIA)
CZ (daily) WH (daily)

SHANGHAI (SHA)

Bangkok (BKK)
MU (1,3,5) TG (2,4,6,7)
Beijing (BJS)
CA, SF, MU, CJ (daily) XO (2,4,6)
Brussels (BRU)
MU (3,6)
Changchun (CGQ)
CJ (1,3,4,5,6,7)
Chengdu (CTU)
3U (daily) SZ (daily) SF (1,2,4,5,6)
Chicago (CHI)
MU (4,7)
Chongqing (CKG)
3U (1,3,5) SZ (daily) SF (3,7)
Dalian (DLC)
CJ (daily) SF (3,7) CA (7) H4 (3,4,6) 4G (2,5)
Frankfurt (FRA)
CA (2,6,7) LH (1,4,6)
Fukuoka (FUK)
MU (2,4,5,7) CA (1,4,7)
Fuzhou (FOC)
MU (daily) SF (2,4,6) MF (daily) IV (daily)
Guangzhou (CAN)
CZ (daily) SF (daily) MU (daily) CA (3)
Guilin (KWL)
MU (daily) SF (1,3,5) WH (1,5)
Haikou (HAK)
MU (1,2,3,4,5,6) CZ (2,3,5,6,7) H4 (daily) SF (1,3,5)
Harbin (HRB)
SF (2,4,5) CJ (daily) 4G (3,6) WH (2,4,7) HK (2,4,6)
Hiroshima (HIJ)
WH (2,5)
Hong Kong (HKG)
MU (daily) KA (daily)
Kathmandu (KTM)
RA (3,7)
Kuala Lumpur (KUL)
CZ (1,4)
Kunming (KMG)
3Q (daily) SF (1,2,3,5,6,7) MU (2,3,5,6) SZ (2,6)
Los Angeles (LAX)
MU (1,2,3,5,6) NW (4) CA (4,7)
Macau (MFM)
NY (daily)
Madrid (MAD)
MU (3,6)
Melbourne (MEL)
CA (1)
Munich (MUC)
MU (2,5)
Nagasaki (NGS)
MU (1,5)
Nagoya (NGO)
WH (daily)
New York (JFK)
CA (3,5)
Ningbo (NGB)
MU (daily) H4 (1,2,3,4,5,6)
Osaka (OSA)
MU (1,3,4,6,7) CA (daily) JL (1,3,4,6,7) NH (1,2,3,4,5,7)
Paris (CDG)
CA (3,5)
Pusan (PUS)
MU/KE (1,3,5,6)
Quingdao (TAO)
SF (6,7) MU (daily) SC (1,3,6,7) SZ (1,3,5,7)
San Francisco (SFO)
UA (daily) CA (2,5,6)
Seattle (SEA)
MU (4,7)
Seoul (SEL)
MU (daily) OZ (daily)
Shantou (SWA)
MU (daily) CZ (daily) SF (3,6) MF (1,4)
Shenyang (SHE)
SF (1,3,5,6) CJ (daily)
Shenzhen (SZX)
MU (daily) SF (1,3,4,5,7) CZ (daily) 4G (2,3,5,6) SC (3,6) CJ (1,5)
Singapore (SIN)
MU (1,2,4,6) SQ (daily)
Sydney (SYD)
CA (1,3) MU (2,5)
Tianjin (TSN)
CA (daily)
Tokyo (TYO)
MU (daily) NW (4) CA (1,2,3,4,5,7) UA (daily) JL (daily)
Urumqi (URC)
XO (1,2,3,4,6,7)
Vancouver (YVR)
CA (1)
Wenzhou (WNZ)
MU (3,7) SF (daily)
Wuhan (WUH)
MU (daily) CZ (daily) 3Q (1,5)
Xiamen (XMN)
MU (daily) MF (daily) SF (1,3,5) SZ (3,7)
Xi'an (SIA)
SF (1,3,6) WH (daily)
Yantai (YNT)
SF (1,2) SZ (1,2,3,4,6,7) SC (5) MU (2)
Zhuhai (ZUH)
SF (2,6) CZ (daily) WH (2,4,7)
Zurich (ZRH)
SR (2,4,7)

What's the link between business and the Asia Pacific?

BRITISH AIRWAYS
The world's favourite airline

http://www.british-airways.com

Major Exhibitions in China 1997/8

Date	Exhibition	Venue	City	Organiser
April 16-19	**PATA Mart**	Beijing	CWH	PATA SF
April 20-24	**PATA Conference**	Beijing	CWH	PATA SF
May 6-9	**Microelectronics Shanghai**	SIEC	Shanghai	Reed
May 27-31	**Shanghaitex '97** - 7th Multinational Exhibition on Textile Industry	SIEC	Shanghai	Adsale
May 27-31	**SITNE '97** - Shanghai Int'l Techtextiles, Nonwovens and Machinery Exhibition	SIEC	Shanghai	Adsale
June 11-16	**Auto Shanghai '97** - 7th Int'l Automobile & Manufacturing Technology Exhibition	SIEC	Shanghai	Adsale
Jul 30 - Aug 2	**PROPAK China 98** - 3rd Int'l packaging, food & Pharmaceutical Processing & Supplies Exhibition **METALPAK China 97** - 2nd Int'l Canmaking & Canning Technology & Supplies Exhibition **BEVTEK And BREWTEK** China 97 - 3rd Int'l Beverage & Brewing Production, Bottling & Packaging Technology & Supplies Exhibition **FIC 97 - Food Ingredients China 97** - 2nd Int'l Food Ingredients & Additives Technology Exhibition & Conference	SIEC	Shanghai	OES/TMN
Aug 26-29	**FHC 97 - Food & Hotel China 97** - incorporating **Bakery & Confectionery China 97** and **Drinks China**	SIEC	Shanghai	OES/TMN
Sept 9-12	**Building Shanghai '97** - Shanghai Int'l Exhibition on Building Materials, Services and Interior Decoration	SIEC	Shanghai	Adsale
Sept 9-12	**Security China '97** - Int'l Exhibition on Public Safety Security and Fire Control	SIEC	Shanghai	Adsale

(Continued overleaf)

Venues: **BIEC/CIEC** = China International Exhibition Centre, Beijing. Fax: (10) 6467 6811; **CFTC/GFTC** = China/Guangzhou Foreign Trade Center & Exhibition Hall, 117 Lunhua Rd, tel: 6667 7000; **SEC/SIEC** = Shanghai (International)Exhibition Centre, 1000 Yanan Zhong Lu, tel: 327 6060; **CWH** = China World Hotel, No 1 Jianguomenwai Ave, 1004 Beijing, tel: 6505 2266; Fax: 6505 0828

Organisers: **Adsale** Exhibition Services Ltd, 4th Fl, Stanhope House, 734 King's Road, North Point, Hong Kong, tel: (852) 2811 8897; tlx: 63109 ADSAP HX; fax: (852) 2516 5024. **MFreeman** = Miller Freeman Asia Ltd, 102-5 Stanhope House, 738 King's Road, Quarry Bay, Hong Kong. Tel: (852) 2827 5121; Fax: (852) 2827 7064. **OES /TMN**= Overseas Exhibition Services/ International Expo Management Pte Ltd, 11 Manchester Square, London W1M 5AB. Tel: (+44) 0171 486 1951; Fax: (+44) 0171 413 8210/2 Handy Road, Fl 14-10 Cathay Building, Singapore 0922. Tel: (+65) 339 2633; Fax: (+65) 338 6542. **The Montgomery Network**, Room 505 Block C, Shanghai Jia Hua Business Centre, 808 Hong Qiao Road, Shanghai 200030. Tel: (+86) 21 6486 3266; Fax: (+86) 21 6486 4681. **PATA SF** = PATA San Francisco, 1 Montgomery Street, Telesis Tower, San Francisco, California, 94101-439, USA. Tel: (415) 986 4646; Fax: (415) 986 3458. **Reed**= Reed Exhibition Companies, 29 offices worldwide of which USA 255 Washington Street, Newton MA 02158, tel: (617) 630 2260; fax: (617) 630 2197. Hong Kong: 19th Fl, 8 Commercial Tower, 8 Sun Yip Street, Chaiwan tel: (852) 2824 0330; fax: (852) 2824 0246. UK: Oriel House, 26 The Quadrant, Richmond-upon-Thames, Surrey TW9 1DL, tel: (181) 910 7910; fax: (181) 940 2171.

CHINA - Major Exhibitions

Date	Exhibition	Venue	City	Organiser
Sept 23-26	**Power China 97** - incorporating Enviro Tech China 97	SIEC	Shanghai	OES/TMN
Sept 23-26	**Elenex China 97** - incorporating Luminex China 97 and Securitex China 97	SIEC	Shanghai	OES/TMN
Oct 14-18	**Chinaplas '97** - 11th Int'l Exhibition on Plastics and Rubber Industries	SIEC	Shanghai	Adsale
Oct 21-25	**Leather China '97** - 6th International Exhibition on Leather Industry and Shoe Making	CIEC	Beijing	Adsale
Nov 3-5	**Shanghai International Non-Wovens Conference & Exhibition 97**	Intex	Shanghai	MFreeman
Nov 11-14	**ETC-Environmental Technology China '97** - 3rd Int'l Exhibition on Environmental Protection, Pollution Control and Green Production Technology	SIEC	Shanghai	Adsale
Nov 11-14	**EP China '97** / Shanghai - Int'l Exhibition on Electric Power and Electrical Engineering	SIEC	Shanghai	Adsale
Nov 11-14	**Woodmac China 97** - 2nd Int'l Forestry and Woodworking Machinery and Supplies Exhibition	SIEC	Shanghai	OES/TMN
Nov 11-14	**Furnitek China 97** - 2nd Int'l Exhibition of Machinery and Accessories for Furniture Production, Upholstery and Furnishings	SIEC	Shanghai	OES/TMN
Nov 11-15	**PT/Wireless Comm Beijing '97** - 2nd Beijing Int'l Wireless Communications Exhibition	CIEC	Beijing	Adsale
Nov 12-15	**CIHEX**: The China International Hardware & Houseware Expo	CIEC	Beijing	Reed
Nov 12-15	**CHINABEX** - Architectural interiors/exteriors, building management systems and services, building materials, engineering products and services	CIEC	Beijing	Reed
Dec 2-5	**Marintec China**	SIEC	Shanghai	MFreeman
March 1998	**Furniture China '98** - 7th International Exhibition on Furniture Manufacturing		Beijing	Adsale
March 1998	**WM Fair China '98** - 7th Int'l Exhibition on Woodworking Machinery		Beijing	Adsale
March 1998	**Building South China '98**		Guangzhou	Adsale
March 1998	**PFP Expo-Printing South China '98**		Guangzhou	Adsale
March 1998	**PFP Expo-Drinkmac & Pack '98**		Guangzhou	Adsale
April 1998	**NEPCON Beijing**	CIEC	Beijing	Reed
April 1998	**China Electronics**	CIEC	Beijing	Reed

Background

Ancient Times. From antiquity to AD 1840

From archeological findings we know that China's history goes back some 500,000 years. The first dynasty in established Chinese history was the *Xia*, established in the 21st century BC, heralding the beginning of a slave society in China. The following *Shang* (16-11th century BC) and the *Western Zhou* dynasties (1100-170 BC) saw further development of this society. Then came the *Spring and Autumn* and *Warring States* period (770-221 BC), a period of evolution from slave to feudal society.

In 221 BC Qin Shi Huang, the First Emperor of the *Qin* Dynasty, ended the rivalry amongst the independent principalities in the *Warring States* period and established the first centralised, unified, multinational state in Chinese history. Subsequently one dynasty replaced the other. They included the *Han*, (206 BC-220 AD), *Wei* (220-265) and *Jin* (265-420), *Southern and Northern Dynasties* (420-589), *Sui* (581-618), *Tang* (618-907), *Five Dynasties* (907-960), *Song* (960-1279), *Yuan* (1271-1368), *Ming* (1368-1644) and *Qing* (1644-1911). Until the Opium War in 1840, China had been a feudal society for close to 2000 years.

Ancient China was fairly well developed in both economy and culture. During the apex of the Chinese feudal society - the *Han* and *Tang* dynasties - agriculture, handicrafts, weaving and shipbuilding were well advanced. Transportation both by land and water was convenient; extensive economic and cultural relations were established with Japan, Korea, India, Persia and Arabia. Meanwhile famous thinkers in ancient China such as Lao Zi and Confucius were influencing the traditional Chinese culture and even world civilisations. Sun Zi's *Art of War* remains an invaluable reference work; Cao Xuequin's *Dream of Red Mansions* is considered the representative work of classical Chinese literature.

Great achievements were also made in the fields of astronomy, geography and mathematics, with the Gan Shi Xing Jing Catalogue of Stars, produced in the *Warring States* period, being the first such record. Also in the *Han* Dynasty, Zhang Heng

invented the armillary sphere and seismograph and Zu Chongzhi in the *Northern & Southern Dynasties* period is credited with being the first mathematician to calculate the value of Pi to seven decimal places.

Modern Period. 1840-1919

The Opium Wars, which started in 1840, were a turning point in Chinese history. They originated because China took exception to Britain's policy of paying for locally produced goods and commodities in opium. After the treaty of Nanking in 1842, China was forced to cede Hong Kong Island to Britain. Kowloon was on a 155-year lease.

The revolution of 1911, a bourgeois democratic one led by Dr Sun Yat Sen (regarded as the father of Modern China) ended the rule of the *Qing* Dynasty. Thus the monarchy which had been in existence for 2000 years came to an end and the provisional government of the Republic of China was founded. However China was split with Yuan Shikai, the head of the northern warlords, fighting emerging communist and agrarian forces in the south.

Contemporary Period. 1919-present

Between 1919-1921 Marx-inspired revolutionaries started challenging northern-dominated imperialism and feudalism. The Communist Party of China, which rules to the present day, was founded by Mao Zedong. Struggles with the nationalists, later led by Chiang Kai Shek, included the Northern Expedition (1924-27), and the Agrarian Revolutionary War (1927-37). In 1935 the communists were forced westwards by the advancing nationalists to the Shaanxi mountains. This retreat, which cost the communists 90,000 lives out of the 100,000 forced into the mountains became known as the *Long March*. It is the survivors of this march, including the recently deceased Deng Xiao Ping, who were to rule China from 1949.

The Nationalists and Communists briefly united during the second world war to fight the common enemy - Japan. But on Japan's defeat in 1945 the two sides resumed hostilities and Chiang Kai Shek, leader of

the Nationalists, was eventually forced in 1949 to flee with his *Kuomintang* party to the offshore island of Taiwan, where his heirs and successors still rule. The People's Republic of China was founded on 1st October 1949 under the leadership of Mao Zedong. Foreigners were expelled and there followed a period of isolation until his death in 1975. Since then, latterly under the leadership of Deng Xiao Ping, China has opened up both to overseas visitors and investors, has joined the United Nations, retains *Most Favoured Nation* trading status with the USA and is a fully fledged member of the global economic community.

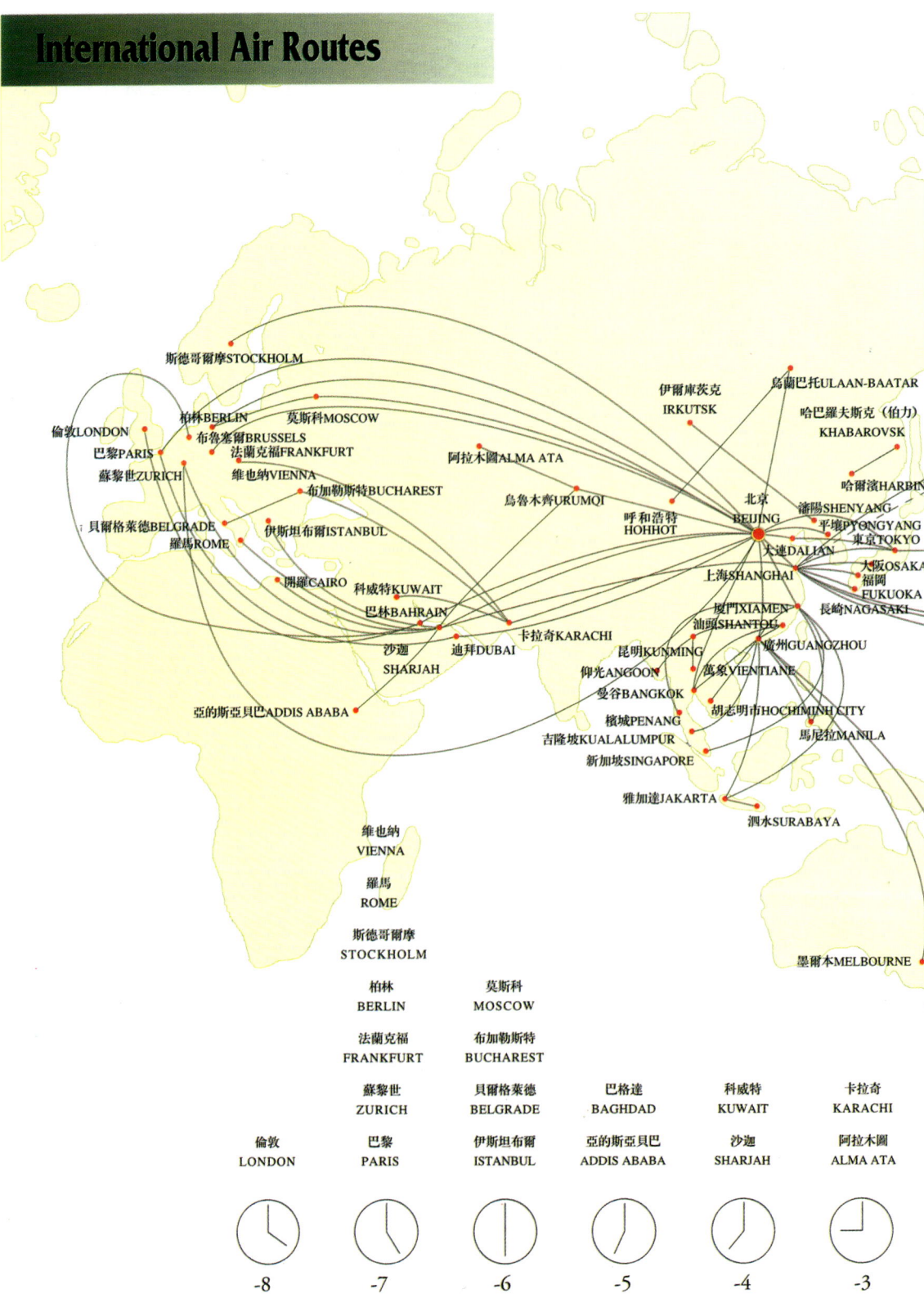

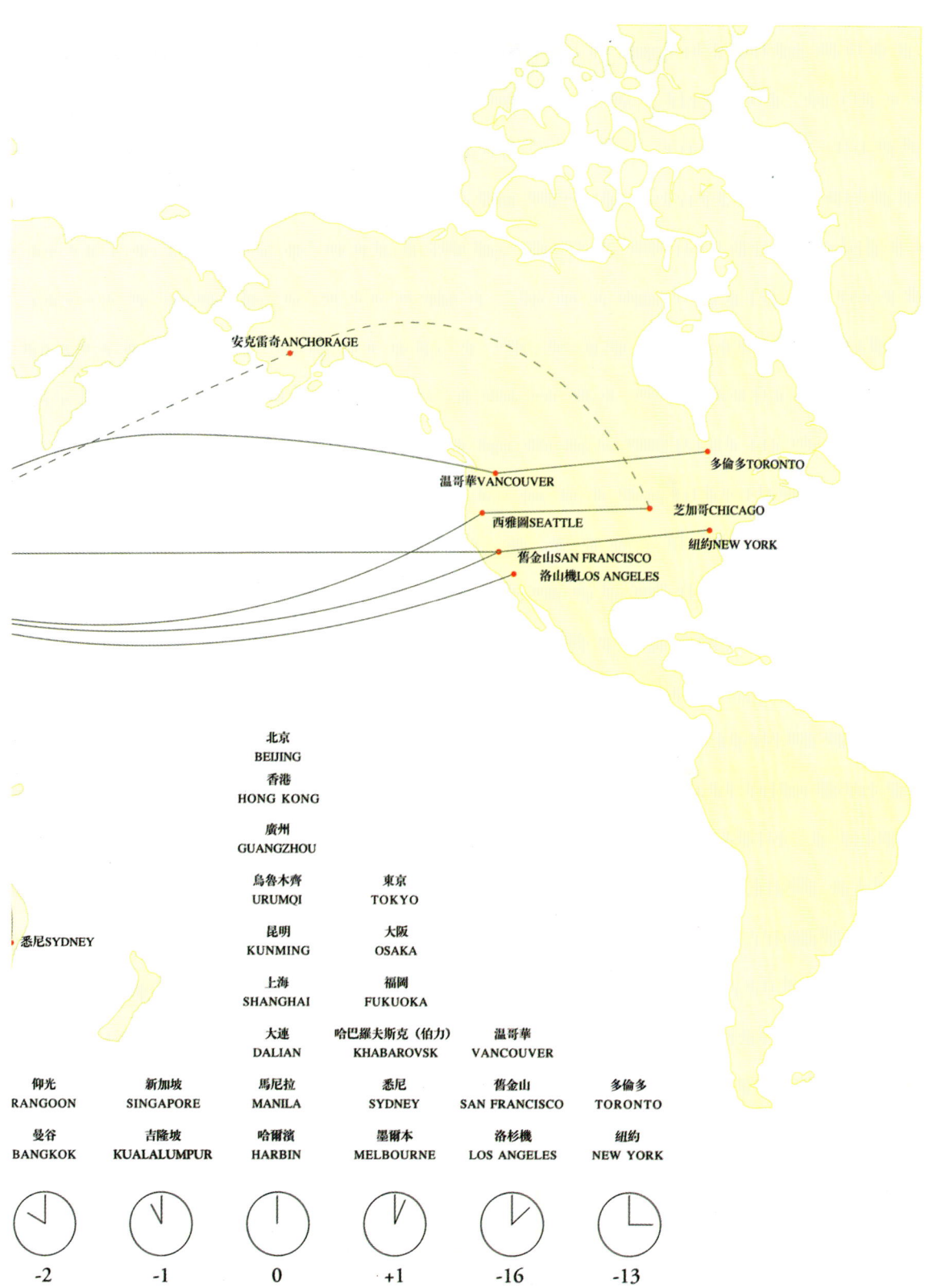

Events for Visit China '97

PATA Chapters World Congress is being held in Shanghai April 15-17. **PATA Travel Mart** takes place in Beijing April 16-19th; **PATA Conference** is being held in Beijing April 20-24th 1997. The three events will bring together some 3000 Travel Industry professionals from around the world and will be a showcase for the China Tourist Industry.

International Tourism Exchange in Hong Kong, May 29th - June 1st sees 50% of the exhibition area devoted to China.

Carnivals. From June 30th to July 6th, Beijing, Shanghai, Shenzhen and Zhuhai, as well as 12 National Holiday Resorts, will organise carnivals and exhibitions showing different cultures.

16 Special Tours and 35 Best Tourist Attractions, including the Great Wall, Huangshan Mountain, Three Gorges Tour and Silk Road Tour are being highlighted.

Photography Contest Hong Kong July 1st 1997. A Grand Prize awaits the best article or photograph associated with this historic moment when Hong Kong returns to Chinese administration.

China Tourist Festival will be held in Guangzhou in September and October.

Celebration of World Tourism Day will take place on September 27th in Pudong, Shanghai.

Shopping Festivals and Souvenir Exhibitions will take place from August to October 10th in ten tourist cities

Regional Short Visits are being organised such as to Suzhou, to Northeast China for ski-ing at Yabuli in Heilongjiang Province and around Songhua and Beida lakes in Jilin province.

Four Season Festival Tours to such popular festivals as the Flower Show around the Spring Fair in Guangzhou, the Beer Festival in Qingdao, Shandong province, the Grape Festival in Turpan (Xinjiang) and the Ice Sculpture Festival in Harbin.

Foreign and Chinese Symphony Concerts.
In September overseas and Chinese symphony orchestras will perform at the Great Wall, the Temple of Heaven and at the Summer Palace. From August to October songs and dances from the various eras of Chinese culture will be performed in the Imperial Ancestral Temple (today's Workers' Cultural Palace) of the Forbidden City.

There are more than 50 regional festivals in 1997 in all parts of China. Details from China National Tourist Offices worldwide.

Fiji

What to See

Old Suva still retains the marks of its colonial past with some fine colonial buildings. Take your time and walk around this intriguing city. Lautoka, too, survives in something of a time warp.

A number of local firms such as Sun Tours, offer island tours of varying duration. A highly recommended full-day tour is trip through the lush Sigatoka Valley and the Kula Bird Park. A visit to the Emperor Goldmine is also worth considering. Another place not to be missed is the Garden of the Sleeping Giant which plays host to Fiji's largest orchid collection and is located just 6.5 km north of Nadi International Airport.

A trip to the North - mainly the island of Vanua Levu - makes an ideal weekend break away from the hustle and bustle of the more heavily marketed Viti Levu.

Shopping

Fiji is a thriving duty free area largely run by the nation's Indo-Fijian community. The usual concessionary items are on offer - cameras, camcorders, watches, hi-fi equipment etc. Expect to haggle over prices in some outlets. Casual clothes - as befits Fiji's hot climate - are a good buy. Suva's Cumming Street is probably the best thoroughfare for duty-free goods. *Proud's* and *Tappoo Duty Free* are among the well known outlets. No fixed tariffs here, so be ready to pay less than the asking price.

For more in the way of local colour try *Suva Municipal Market* - the South Pacific's largest. The market offers a seemingly endless supply of exotic tropical produce. The *Ratu Sukuna House* is arguably the best place to buy local wood carvings, tapa cloth and woven goods at fixed rates. Cheaper prices, 'though, can be found at the *Municipal Curio and Handicraft Centre*, but expect to haggle.

Getting Around

In addition to its international services, Air Pacific offers local flights from Nadi to Suva, and Labasa on Vanua Leva. Domestic and privately-owned carrier Fiji Air Serves most outlying islands from Suva's Nausori Airport. Sunflower Airlines 'though, flies from Nadi to a range of Northern destinations. Flights take about one hour.

Suva, Ovalau, Koro, Savu Savu and Taveuni are connected by a luxury ferry twice per week. Be warned - the ship takes two days to reach Taveuni. It is possible to catch a smaller ferry that departs daily from Suva to Nabouwali.

Visitors are spoilt for choice in terms of car rental (see following page), with all the major firms represented plus a selection of purely local operators. There is a good sealed (paved) highway from Rakiraki to Suva via Korovou. The maximum speed limit on highways is 80 kph - in town 50 kph. Taxis are difficult to find, even in Suva.

Entertainment

Suva has its fair share of noisy discos, such as *Lucky Eddie's* and *Rockefeller's* which are located alongside each other on Victoria Parade. Reasonably smart clothing is required to gain entry to these two establishments.

In essence, Fiji features four basic styles of cuisine - Local, European, Indian and Chinese. Try Fijian lovo-cooked food which is prepared in an earth oven and usually comprises pork, plus various native root crops such as dalo and kumala. Seafood is also plentiful.

Leisure

For golfers, the Pacific Harbour Golf & Country Club - about 50 km west of Suva - boasts a challenging Robert Trent Jones-designed 18-hole course. The club is open to non-members and is generally considered to be the South Pacific's finest. Closer to Suva, the Fiji Golf Club also has an 18-hole course; although not up to the standard of Pacific Harbour.

The Pacific Harbour is the only hotel to feature its own 18-hole course; although others have free membership to nearby clubs - like the Nadi Airport Golf Club.

Or take a trek through Fiji's Central Highlands. For the reasonably energetic, these operate during the dry season (May-October) and last up to 10 days; although tours of a shorter duration are available. Other island treks operate on a year-round basis. All meals are provided and are cooked in traditional Fijian style.

Other tours that involve horse-riding, hiking, boating, white-water rafting on Fijian *bilibili* bamboo rafts are available for the more adventurous.

Firms such as Savusavu's Sea Fiji provide all-inclusive sail/dive charters aboard yachts of up to 15 metres. Each has a local skipper/guide with guests participating in sailing, meal preparation and housekeeping.

Arrival & Departure

Nadi International Airport is nearly 200km from Suva - a hot four-and-a-half hour bus ride in fact, but just 12km from the resort of Nadi on the west coast of Viti Levu. *Sharma's* and *Fiji Express* operate buses to and from Nadi hotels for about F$12.50. Many of the major resort hotels are probably 100km or so from the airport. *Queen's Coach* offers a twice-daily bus service, while firms such as *Fiji Express* serve many of the leading hotels.

Many of the big internationally-known hotels operate courtesy buses to and from Nadi, so there is little need to catch a taxi. In any case a taxi could set you back around US$80 - about ten times the price of the bus.

Nausori Airport is just 18km from Suva and can be used for connections to Nadi or outlying islands. Some short-haul international flights also serve the airport.

There is no tax on domestic departures, but expect to pay F$10 in local currency for any international flight to the ticketing agent at the check-in counter.

Fiji Key Fact File

Passport Requirements:
All visitors must have a valid passport and return air tickets. Permits are granted on arrival for a stay of one month and these may be extended for up to six months. Visas are not required for Commonwealth or EC/EFTA citizens excluding those from Portugal or those staying less than 3 hours

Currency:
Fiji dollar (F$). 100 cents = F$1.

Exchange Rates: *(March 1997)*
US$ 1 = F$ 1.42; £1 = F$ 2.30

Currency Restrictions:
There are no restrictions on the amount of foreign currency visitors may bring into the country. Export of foreign currency is limited to F$ 100.

Electricity Supply:
240 volts 50 cycles AC

Language:
Fijian and Hindi are spoken widely, with English understood by most people.

Time:
GMT + 12; EST + 15 hrs

IDD Code: 679
No area codes applicable

Business Hours:
Commercial offices are open from 0800-1300 to 1400-1630 Monday to Friday. Government offices as above but until 1600 hrs Friday.
Banking hours are 0930-1500 Monday through Thursday; 0930-1600 Fridays.
Shops are generally open 0800-1630 Monday to Friday (some close for lunch 1-2 pm); Saturday 0830-noon; shops in hotels often to 2100 hrs.

Customs & Entry:
A visitor may bring in the following items duty free: 200 cigarettes or 250 grams of cigars or 250 grams of tobacco plus one litre of liquor or two litres of wine or two litres of beer. Up to F$100 per passenger of any duty assessed goods. Dangerous drugs and narcotics, indecent and obscene material, firearms and ammunition, meat and meat products, plants and goods for commercial use are all banned.

Health Requirements:
Fiji is free from tropical diseases. Inoculations will not be required unless a traveller is entering from a designated infected area. Typhoid & polio inoculation recommended. Water heavily chlorinated but drinkable unboiled; milk, meat etc safe.

Climate/best time to visit:
Tropical with dry weather May to October. Rainy season December to April (when rainwear recommended); otherwise lightweight suit for business. Min. year round 24C, max 30C. Humidity averages 70%.

National Holidays 1997
1 January New Year's Day; 28 March Good Friday; 31 March Easter Monday; 15 June HM The Queen's Birthday; 2 August Bank Holiday; 7 October Fiji (Independence) Day; 14 August Prophet Mohammed's Birthday; 11 November Prince Charles' Birthday; 25/26 December Christmas & Boxing Day.

Car Hire

Avis
PO Box 9088, Nadi Airport
Tel: 722688/313833; Tlx: 5187; Fax:790482

Budget Rent A Car
PO Box 12170, Suva
Tel: 315899/722735; Tlx: 2483; Fax: 302450

Central Rent A Car
PO Box 468, Suva.
Tel: 311866/Airport 722711; Tlx: 2415

Hertz
c/o Global Tours Ltd. Nivis Motors. Cnr Ratu Mara/Golf Link Roads, Nabua, Suva
Tel: 383677; Tlx: 2237; Fax: 370212

Khan's Rental Cars
PO Box 299, Nadi Airport.Tel: 701009; Fax: 780159

Letz Rent a Car
PO Box 9353, Nadi Airport.
Tel: 722803; Tlx: 5396; Fax: 790188

National Car Rentals
PO Box 9101, Nadi Airport
Tel: 722740; Tlx: 2511

Roxy Rentals
PO Box 9529, Nadi Airport
Tel: 700710; Tlx: 5248; Fax: 780039

Satellite Rentals
PO Box 9635, Nadi Airport
Tel: 701911; (24 hrs) 722219

Sharma's Rentals
PO Box 1042, Nadi
Tel: 701055; Fax: 780038

Skyline Car Rentals
PO Box 9056, Nadi Airport
Tel: 723980; Fax: 790254

Sheik's Rent A Car
PO Box 9373, Nadi Airport
Tel: 723535/723140; Fax: 790231

Thrifty Car Rentals
PO Box 9268, Nadi Airport
Tel: 722935; Tlx: 5143 ROSIE;Fax:790460

UTC Rent A Car
PO Box 9172, Nadi Airport
Tel: 722811; Tlx: 5171 UTC; Fax: 7223430

Airline Offices

Air Caledonie International
PO Box 159, Suva.Tel: 301928; Tlx: 2465

Air Nauru
PO Box 2317, Suva.Tel: 313731; Tlx: 2340 NASA

Air New Zealand
Box No.340, Suva.Tel: 312444; Fax: 302294

Air Pacific
Private Mail Bag, Suva.Tel: 386444/790777; Tlx: 2131 AIR PAC; Fax: 370120

Canadian Airlines
PO Box 1257, Suva.Tel: 311844/722400; Tlx: 2169 SITA SUVA; Fax: 790145

Qantas
PO Box 1144, Suva.Tel: 313888/722888; Tlx: 2160 QF SUVA; Fax:790388

Sunflower Airlines
PO Box 9452 Suva. Tel: 723408/723555; Tlx: 5183; Fax: 790085

Departures from Nadi International Airport

To the airports printed in bold type. Figures in brackets after airline codes signify (1), departing on Monday, the first day of the week and so on. Departures were correct as at January 1996. Travellers are advised to check with the airline offices listed below. Only direct flights, without change are listed.

Airline Code Abbreviations: CP = Canadian Airlines; **CW** = Air Marshall Airlines; **FJ** = Air Pacific; **IE** = Solomon Airlines; **KE** = Korean Air; **NZ** = Air New Zealand; **ON** = Air Mauru; **PC** = Fiji Air; **PI** = Sunflower Airlines; **PH** = Polynesian Airlines; **QF** = Qantas; **SB** = Air Caledonie International

Apia (APW)
FJ (2,5,6) PH (5)
Auckland (AKL)
CP (7) NZ,FJ (daily) KE (2,4,7)
Brisbane (BNE)
FJ,QF (1,2,4,6,7)
Christchurch (CHC)
FJ,NZ (7)
Honiara (HIR)
FJ,IE (7)
Honolulu (HNL)
NZ (1,3,4,5,6) CP (5)
Kandavu (KDV)
PI (daily), PC (1,5)
Labasa (LBS)
PI,PC (daily)
Los Angeles (LAX)
QF (2,4,6) NZ (1,3,4,6) FJ (2,6)
Majuro (MAJ)
CW (4,6)
Melbourne (MEL)
QF,FJ (3,5,7)
Nagoya (NGO)
NZ (1,4,6)
Nauru Island (INU)
ON (4)
Noumea (NOU)
SB (2)
Osaka (OSA)
FJ (1,4)
Port Vila (VLI)
FJ,NF (4,7)
Rarotonga (RAR)
NZ (3)
Seoul (SEL)
NZ (2,4) KE (2,4,7)
Suva (SUV)
PI,PC (daily) FJ (1,2)
Sydney (SYD)
QF/FJ (2,3,4,5,6,7)
Taveuni (TVU)
PI,PC (daily)
Tokyo (TYO)
FJ (1,4) NZ (1)
Tongatapu (TBU)
FJ (1,3,4,6) WR (1,4,6)
Toronto (YTO)
NZ (5)
Vancouver (YVR)
NZ (5)
Wellington (WLG) FJ,NZ (6)

Restaurants

Most eating in Fifi takes place in the restaurants of the hotels featured on the following pages. Nevertheless, for those seeking a change of scene, we give below a small selection of both hotel and ethnic restuarants in Nadi and Suva.

Nadi

Chopsticks (Cantonese)
Half mile north of Skylodge Hotel.
Tel: 700178

The Garden View (Seafood)
The Regent of Fiji Resort Hotel, PO Box 441. Tel: 780000

Kanatale Restaurant (Continental/Fijian)
Travellers Beach Resort. Tel: 723322

Maharaj Restaurant (Indian)
Nataly's Arcade, Namaka (Nr. Skylodge Hotel) Tel: 722962

The Ocean Terrace (French)
The Regent of Fiji Resort Hotel, PO Box 441. Tel: 780000

Vale ni Kuro Restaurant (French/Fijian/Indian)
Fiji Mocambo Hotel. PO Box 9195. Tel: 722000

Suva

Aberdeen Grill (Steak/seafood)
Noble House, 16 Bau St. Tel: 304322

Curry Place (Indian)
16 Pratt St. Tel: 313000

Kampong Ku (Malaysian)
Suva Courtesy Inn. Tel: 312300

Lantern Palace (Cantonese)
Cnr Pratt & Joske Sts. Tel: 314633

Ming Palace (Cantonese)
Old Town Hall, Victoria Parade. Tel: 315111. Closed Sunday

Red Lion Restaurant (Internatonal)
215 Victoria Parade. Tel: 312968

Scott's Restaurant (European)
Scott's Hotel, 16 Bau St. Tel: 312833

Seoul House Restaurant (Korean)
Southern Cross Hotel. Tel: 314233

Tiko's Floating Restaurant (Seafood)
Alongside Stinson Parade. Tel: 313626

Wan-Q Restaurant (Cantonese)
2nd fl, 25 Cumming St. Tel: 313314

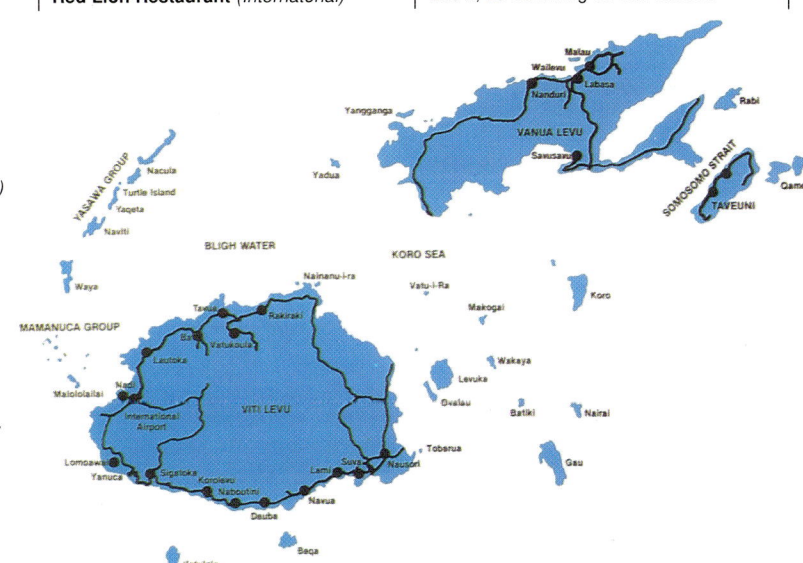

Fiji Hotels

Mamanuca Group

Castaway Island Resort ○ A
PO Box 91, Qaito Island, Castaway Island
Tel: 661233; Tlx: 5224; Fax: 665753

Club Naitasi Resort D
PO Box 10044 Nadi Airport, Malolo Island.
Tel: 720178; Tlx: 5201; Fax: 720197

Mana Island Resort ○ A
PO Box 610, Mana Island
Tel: 661210; Tlx: 5216; Fax: 662713

Plantation Island Resort C
PO Box 9176 Nadi Airport
Tel: 722333; Tlx: 5223; Fax: 721100

Treasure Island Resort ○ C
PO Box 2210, Bligh Waters, Lautoka
Tel: 666999; Tlx: 5189; Fax: 666955

Toberua Island

Toberua Island Resort B
Toberua Island PO Box 567 Suva
Tel: 49177/302356; Tlx: 2350; Fax: 302215

Taveuni

Garden Island Resort E
PO Box 1, Waiyevo, Taveuni
Tel: 880286; Tlx: 8277; Fax: 880288

Dive Taveuni Resort B
PO Box Matei, Taveuni (Garden Island)
Tel: 880441; Tlx: 8291; Fax: 880466

Qamea Island Beach Club B
PO Box Taveuni, Taveuni
Tel: 880220; Tlx: 8277; Fax: 880920

Vanua Levu

Fiji Islands Resort C
c/o PO Private Bag, Savu Savu
Tel: 850188; Fax: 850340

Viti Levu

Beachcomber Island Resort ○ C
1 Wahu St, Lautoka. PO Box 364
Tel: 661500; Fax: 664496

Dominion International Hotel ○ D
Queens Rd, PO Box 9178, Nadi
Tel: 722255; Tlx: 5176; Fax: 720187

Fiji Mocambo Hotel ○ C
PO Box 9195, Nadi Airport
Tel: 722000; Tlx: FJ 5147; Fax: 720324

Metro Inn Fiji E
Queens Road, Martibar, Nadi
Tel: 720088; Fax: 720522

Mokusigas Island Resort D
Nanan-I-Ra.
Tel: 666377/694449; Fax: 694404

Nadi Travelodge D
PO Box 9203, Nadi Airport
Tel: 790277 Tlx: 5186; Fax: 790191

Naitasi Resort ○ B
Malolo Island, PO Box 10044
Tel: 723999; Tlx: FJ 5201; Fax: 720197

The Naviti ○ C
Naviti Bay, PO Box 29, Korolevu
Tel: 530444; Tlx: FJ 3236; Fax: 530343

Pacific Harbour International Hotel
PO Box 144, Pacific Harbour, Deuba D
Tel: 450022; Tlx: 3234; Fax: 450262

Raffles Gateway D
PO Box 9891 (opposite airport)
Tel: 722444; Tlx: 5177; Fax: 790620

Raffles Tradewinds Hotel C
PO Box 3377 Lami, Suva (Queens Road)
Tel: 362450; Tlx:2152; Fax: 361464

The Reef Resort ○ C
PO Box 173, Sigaboka, Coral Coast
Tel: 520044; Tlx: 4242; Fax: 520074

The Regent of Fiji B
PO Box 9081, Nadi
Tel: 750000; Tlx: 5214; Fax: 750259

Sheraton Fiji Resort A
PO Box 9761, Nadi Airport
Tel: 750777; Tlx: FJ 5303; Fax: 750818

Sheraton Vomo Island Resort D
PO Box 5650 Lautoka
Tel: 667955; Fax: 667997

Skylodge Hotel D
PO Box 9222, Nadi Airport
Tel: 722200; Tlx: 5148; Fax: 720212

Sonaisali Island Resort ○ C
Private Mail Bag PO, Nadi
Tel: 706011; Fax: 706092

Sukhdeo Hotel of Fiji ○ E
PO Box 750, Suva
Tel: 314944; Fax: 302944

Suva Courtesy Inn D
PO Box 112, Suva
Tel: 312300; Tlx: 2272; Fax: 301300

Suva Travelodge C
Victoria Parade, PO Box 1357, Suva
Tel: 301600; Tlx: 2159;
Fax: 300251

Hotel Tanoa ○ D
PO Box 9211 Nadi
Tel: 722300; Tlx: 5174; Fax: 660761

Tokatoka Resort Hotel D
PO Box 9305 Nadi Airport
Tel: 790222; Fax: 790400

Vatuele Island Resort B
PO Box 9936, Nadi Airport
Tel: 720300; Fax: 720062

The Warwick Fiji C
Queens Rd, Korolevu, PO Box 100
Tel: 530555; Tlx: 3237; Fax: 530010

Wakaya Island

The Wakaya Club A
Tel: 440128; Fax: 440406

Yanuca Island

Shangri-La's Fijian Resort ○ B
Private Mailbag (NAP 0353), Nadi Airport
Tel: 520155; Tlx: FJ 4241; Fax: 500402

Yasawa Group

Turtle Island Lodge A
Turtle Island, PO Box 9317, Nadi Airport
Tel: 663889; Tlx: 5197; Fax: 790007

Yasawa Island Lodge A
Yasawa Island
Tel: 663364; Fax: 665044

Explanation of codes in hotel entries

A after name of hotel = room rate over US$200 per person per night; **B** = between $150-200; **C** = between 100-150; **D** = between $50-100; **E** = under $50; ¶ = prices on application. ○ = Member of Pacific Asia Travel Association

Prices are only a guide and we recommend travellers to check with individual hotels before booking.

COUNTRY REPORT
HONG KONG '97

Hong Kong

Doing Business

Hong Kong entered 1997 and its highly-publicised date with destiny - the June 30 handover over of rule from Britain to China - in a curiously ambivalent way.

While the Hang Seng Index performed its usual imitation of a yo-yo, taking a daily roller coaster ride on new investments or quick profit taking, the business community shrugged its shoulders as if to say: what's done is done. A change of flag is not immediately going to alter the change of play.

Confidence was growing that China would tread softly, softly during its initial period in control, not wanting to kill the golden goose that generated more than US$360bn in trade, a GDP of nearly US$160bn and a per capita income of nearly US$23,000 the previous year - all under a foreign flag by people who had fled the new controller's previous strictures. Politically also, said observers, a smooth takeover and minimal interference with the established workings of Hong Kong would assist China in its longer-term plans to bring Taiwan back into the fold.

At street level, trust in China's promises largely to leave legislative and other established procedures alone for the next 50 years remained sceptical but, in practical business terms, Hong Kong held its feet firmly on the ground during the early months of the year. Given the general consensus that business and industry would be allowed to get on with it as usual, overall trading remained bouyant, helped by progress with the new airport and ancillary port facilities at Chek Lap Kok.

The giant trading and finance companies which brought so much wealth to the colony, making it the most successful transit port in the world, and responsible for minimally 30% of all China trade, had either shifted base elsewhere or stayed to face the inevitable - and climbed into bed with the mainland.

Two years earlier, in 1995, 20 of the territory's wealthiest business leaders had founded the Better Hong Kong Foundation to encourage inward investment into the 21st century, each chipping in HK$5mn. As another mark of confidence, the Hong Kong Conference and Exhibition Centre was completing a 26,000 sq.m extension in preparation for a World Banking Conference in September 1997.

Observers believe that while China's political ideology may remain as staunch as ever, its newly-opened free market economy will continue to flourish, providing powerful joint venture opportunities for both Hong Kong and overseas investors. The free-for-all incentives - such as a minuscule tax base, extensive tax holidays, (formerly) low labour costs and unfettered trading controls - that initially made Hong Kong such a magnet for investors, are fast being adopted by the mainland, not just in its Special Economic Zones but as the trading fabric of all China.

Shenzhen, a stone's throw from Hong Kong's border at Lo Wu, is today indistinguishable from the colony itself: packed skyscrapers and a sea of bamboo scaffolding testifying to capitalism and potential fortune. Money talks and Shenzhen preceded Shanghai, China's original trading centre, in establishing its own metal futures exchange.

Business barriers and border controls between Shenzhen and Hong Kong, and between Hong Kong and its new Pearl River Delta development partners Macau and Guangdong Province have all but disappeared, although most foreign visitors to Hong Kong still require a separate visa to visit China.

A super highway is nearing completion between Hong Kong and cosmopolitan Guangzhou, the principal city of Southern China, and massive port and leisure construction is planned around the coast. The combined potential trading and manufacturing power of the area is considered enormous, with Hong Kong the established gateway, financial conduit and rendezvous point for China's burgeoning private sector which has absorbed an estimated 30 million people in recent years and is expected to double in size within the next decade.

Hong Kong may still be cautious of the whims and dictats of Beijing but is confident its unique entrepreneurial drive, expertise and acumen will never be stifled, simply honed and adapted to a broader canvass of opportunity. Hong Kong, anyway, has always survived on its wits, the security of tenure of its 6 mn residents and close to 10 mn annual visitors being no more than a daily round of hard work, finding a bargain and striking a deal.

Competition and the inherent work ethic make Hong Kong an aggressive, hard-nosed place to conduct business.But they have also brought the territory a thriving social life and some of the finest hotels and restaurants in the world.

Hong Kong works hard and plays hard, proud to display individual success with a glitzy, glamorous and increasingly expensive lifestyle that apes well-bred society and the chic salons of Europe. The tai-pans of business are to be found not just in their offices atop the glass skyrises of Central or Kowloon but also at exclusive clubs, aboard yachts, in boxes at horseracing meetings or chasing the fairways along golf courses. For them, this is not downtime but part of the workaday business/leisure mix during which deals are still struck faster than anywhere else in Asia.

The business visitor needs to be both slick and quick. Old Chinese habits die hard, face must be saved and often the fungshui spiritual adviser consulted. But the net result of doing business in Hong Kong continues to be a blend of opportunism and gambling. The change of political rule may have shifted the goalposts, but the capitalist game and aims remain the same.

Business awareness, etiquette and practice

Western influence in Hong Kong has produced ways of doing business that are similar to other major business capitals.

However, the local culture should not be ignored: some Western businessmen consult the Chinese geomancers *(Fung Shui)* before setting up office (if only to please their Chinese workforce). Working a five-and-a-half-day week is common although newly arrived expatriates often feel obliged to work Sundays in order to keep pace with Hong Kong's frenetic business environment. Business cards are distributed liberally as a method of developing a network of professional contacts.

Business dress is formal; suits and ties are required whatever the weather (remember, most offices are air conditioned).

Appearances of wealth are considered important in a territory dedicated to making money: business contacts are ostentatiously wined and dined. As in many parts of the world (but perhaps here more than elsewhere), personal friendships and family ties oil the wheels of business.

After July 1st 1997

We have prepared a quick checklist for business travellers and tourism professionals, in consultation with the Hong Kong Tourist Association, to answer the most frequently posed questions about 'after the handover'.

Visas/Entry. No change. See Key Fact File
Currency. No change. The HK$ will still be internationally convertible and linked to the US dollar.
Language. No change. English will continue to be the official language. Signage will continue in English and Chinese.
Business. Hong Kong will remain a free port and the HKSAR will remain an independent member of the World Trade Organisation. The Hong Kong Tourist Association will retain its autonomy for the promotion of Hong Kong.
Security/Judiciary. The same British-trained police force will remain in place. The Judiciary will remain independent with a Final Court of Appeal in Hong Kong.
Politics. The HKSAR will be governed by a legislative council made up of Hong Kong people, democratically elected. Mr Tung Chee-hwa, fromer shipping magnate, who will be the chief executive, has stated that he will not join the communist party. Anson Chan, at present Chief Secretary, is to be his deputy, providing continuity.
Border Controls between China and Hong Kong will be maintained.
Army presence. The PLA will maintain a garrison in Hong Kong, no larger or more obvious than the British Garrison hitherto.
Freedom of Press. Under the Basic Law, existing rights including freedom of speech are safeguarded. In 1996 there was a pronouncement from Beijing that it would curtail subjective reporting of events but would allow factual objective reporting.

Tourism Update

General

The Hong Kong Tourist Association lists a range of superlatives to describe the territory's attractions - such as having the largest number of Rolls-Royces per-capita. This theme can be part-matched for the travel industry. By certain international measures, its airport is the biggest in Asia, its main airline one of the three largest, and its visitor count the highest.

Hong Kong has been the leading destination in Asia for almost 10 years. In 1993, arrivals from China were added into the count, then the overall total topped 10 million in 1995, and in 1996 continued to grow at a rapid pace - about 15%.

In 1996, China grew at 3% to 2.3 million, but its total was passed after spectacular 41% growth from Japan to 2.4 million. Third market Taiwan grew at 3%, taking its total to 1.8 million. Of others in the top five, the US managed a fractional growth, but the UK was up 10%. Looking likely to move into the top five in 1997 was Korea, which grew 12%.

Two main concerns are capacity at the airport and hotels. The airport reached its comfortable capacity in 1993 - of around 24 million passengers annually. The territory's new airport is not due to open until 1998.

Growth of business visitors will depend how the international business community interprets the change of sovereignty in 1997; at present it is largely positive. If this mood remains, then the visitor total in 2000 could be 15 million. But an important aspect of this is the number of visitors from China. Travel is controlled at present, but if controls are lifted, the number of travellers from China could grow by as much as Hong Kong could handle, as there is strong demand in China to visit Hong Kong.

As the territory moves towards 1997, the links with China increase. One example is a tourism promotional body for the Pearl River Delta - an area encompassing Hong Kong, Shenzhen and Guangzhou in China, and Macau. The region could become an important factor in regional tourism. The budget of the NTO is approximately US$25 million, of which US$23 million is for marketing.

Aviation

Hong Kong's aviation profile went through an important evolution in 1996 when shares in the main airline, Cathay Pacific and its associate airline Dragonair, changed hands. As a result, an important China-government company, CITIC, now holds 25% of Cathay's shares, and the long-established owner, Swire Pacific, let its shareholding fall below 50%. Cathay may get a competing airline from its former associate, Dragonair, the Hong Kong-based regional airline but with a strong concentration on China. A majority of Dragonair's shares now rest with interests from China, including 36% from aviation interests. The most significant of these is CNAC, a company that is ultimately owned by the Civil Aviation Administration of China - which is the division of the Chinese government that controls aviation development in China.

Most observers believe that when Dragonair ceases to be managed by Cathay Pacific, it will challenge its former part-owner by applying to operate routes that compete with Cathay. There is no fixed date for the ending of the management contract, but some analysts believe this will happen in 1997.

A slowdown for Cathay Pacific traffic in

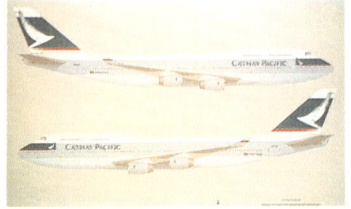

1991 was reversed the following year, and there has been good growth since then - the number of seats sold topped 10 million in 1995. But at Dragonair the number of seats sold increased only 3% in the year, to 1.6 million. The reason for Dragonair's slow growth is believed to have been related to capacity limitations on its flights into China, its main route area. Dragonair has been expected to sell shares to the public, but dates have been put back, and it now looks unlikely before end 1997.

Shortage in airport capacity for local and foreign airlines remains a major concern. Not enough additional passenger capacity can be obtained from the current Kai Tak airport for the believed demand. So this may mean use of nearby airports - such as Shenzhen in China, and Macau. Both are 60 minutes away from the centre of Hong Kong by fast sea ferries. Hong Kong's airport has already passed its design capacity, and so growth was expected to be slight. But in fact, there was 8% growth in 1995, taking the passenger total to 27,313,376, and so keeping its position as the busiest international airport in Asia Pacific. Throughout 1996 growth continued at about the same pace.

The new airport, currently named Chek Lap Kok, is due to open in April 1998, initially with one runway - meaning capacity will be little changed from the current airport. However, the second runway is due to be completed later in 1998.

Hotels

Hong Kong's hotels continue to do well, with year-round occupancy in 4-star hotels at well over 80% and revenue earnings per room are the second-highest of the major centres in Asia after Tokyo.

However, until recently, local property regulations encouraged investors to favour office buildings rather than hotels. That resulted in an almost total stop to building new hotels; with the closing of some existing hotels, there will have been no net increase in the number of hotel rooms for the five years through 1997.

In fact, the number of rooms in Hong Kong nearly doubled over the past decade, but by 1993 a period of under-capacity started. There has been around 33,000 rooms since 1992 and in 1997 there are expected to be 35,000 rooms -- only 1000 more than in 1993.

Relief is due from the year when the airport is due to open, in 1998. At that time, another 3500 rooms are due to open, representing a 10% increase in just one year.

Because of this shortage of rooms, discretionary travel into Hong Kong, including that part organised through the travel industry, will be capacity-constrained almost until the end of this century. Not only are hotel rooms in short supply, but there are only two periods - July/August and a short time around January/February - when there is adequate available capacity.

As with shortage of capacity at the airport, a partial solution for hotels might include using hotels in neighbouring Macau and Shenzhen.

New projects due to open in the next few years in Hong Kong include: International World with 500 rooms; the Mega Tower with 2400 rooms; the Royal Park with 700 rooms; and at the new airport, another Regal with 990 rooms.

There have been few important changes at the existing hotels, but one was ending the franchise agreement with Kempinski for the Furama hotel; the hotel retains its independent management, but it now has a reservations agreement with Inter-Continental Hotels. Also, towards the end of 1996 an agreement was made between Century Hotels and Delta Hotels, which may develop into a link between the Century in Hong Kong, and another that is now an associate, the Ritz-Carlton.

What to See

Among the territory's ever increasing list of attractions is the HK$325 million Hong Kong Science Museum in Tsim Sha Tsui East, which opened in April 1991. Among the Museum's top exhibits is a DC3 called *Betsy* - Cathay Pacific's first-ever aircraft.

The HK$390 million Hong Kong Park also opened its gates to visitors for the first time in 1991. Located on the site of the old Victoria Barracks in Central, the Park covers 10 hectares and includes the region's largest greenhouse and a spectacular aviary, which alone cost HK$21 million.

Annual events to try and coincide visits with are *The Sevens* - Hong Kong's world famous seven-a-side rugby tournament, which takes place in early April. It should be noted that tickets are difficult to come by for this highlight of the territory's sporting calendar. In June visitors can thrill to the colourful sight of the annual dragon boat

HONG KONG - Introduction

races off the Tsim Sha Tsui waterfront.

A trip worth considering is the *Land Between Tour* - a seven-hour journey through rural Hong Kong. There are many others that cater for a wide range of interests.

Shopping

Hong Kong attracts over 10m visitors a year; most are tempted by some of the best shopping facilities in the world. In terms of variety, value and service, Hong Kong is no longer the cheapest city in the region but it is a freeport with no sales tax or import duty and only marginal freight costs. Only tobacco, alcohol, perfume, cosmetics and cars incur any kind of duty - so this leaves a wide range of duty-free goods for shoppers.

A word of caution:- To get the best from what's on offer try to deal with those shops that display the HKTA membership sign in their windows (a red junk) as not everything in Hong Kong is as genuine as it might look.

Located at the bottom of the Kowloon peninsula, Tsim Sha Tsui offers probably the best collection of shops and air-conditioned malls. Most shoppers head for Nathan Road's Golden Mile, a crowded assortment of stores. Others might prefer the air-conditioned comfort of the huge new shopping malls like Times Square in Causeawy Bay, Cityplaza at Taikoo Shing or Pacific Place. At the open air stalls along Peking Road/

Canton Road, 'seconds' of Ralph Lauren shirts and other brand names can be picked up for a song.

For look-alike Gucci, Rolex etc brand names at a fraction of the normal price, try Stanley Market on Hong Kong Island. For Chanel and other lookalike leather goods try Bag Lane near Central MTR station.

Duty Free Shoppers Hong Kong Limited operates several general merchandise outlets at the Airport and six downtown stores in popular tourist areas like Tsimshatsui, Victoria Peak and Jumbo Floating Restaurant. Latest branch is the DFS Galleria in Sun Plaza, Tsimshatsui. As well as a wide assortment of liquor offered at the lowest prices in Hong Kong, the stores carry an extensive selection of quality branded items and holiday mementoes.

Hong Kong Place, the largest shopping centre in Southeast Asia, opened on two floors (200,000 sq ft) in Whampoa Gardens, East Kowloon in August 1991. The ground floor Metro Gallery contains 57 shops selling imported world brand names; the lower ground floor Hong Kong Street houses 70 shops divided into 'streets' depicting Hong Kong's famous specialities: one 'street' for audio-visual equipment, another for jade and jewellery, another for garments and so on.

The renovated Western Market opened in 1992 in Central. It has four levels of shops, selling mostly historical and ethnic Chinese materials, and restaurants. At the end of Nathan Road in Kowloon is the enormous Ocean Terminal shopping centre. It comprises three interconnecting complexes - the Ocean Terminal, Ocean Centre (which even has a Marks & Spencer) and

Harbour City, with perhaps 600 shops in all.

Over in Causeway Bay there is an opportunity to sample some of Hong Kong's many department stores - some local, some Japanese and a few Friendship stores from mainland China. Lane Crawford's (owned by the late Sir Y K Pao's World International Group) is perhaps the best known of the stores. The retailer has three stores in Tsim Sha Tsui and one each at Causeway Bay and Queen's Road Central.

Another shopping centre to look out for is The Landmark on Des Voeux Road Central, which specialises in modern Hong Kong designer wear. The Japanese stores tend to cater for expatriate Japanese shoppers and Japanese tourists. Mitsukoshi at the Hennessy Centre, Hong Kong Daimaru (Causeway Bay) and Hong Kong Matsuzakaya (Central and Causeway Bay) are three of the leading Japanese outlets. Isetan of Japan - close to the Sheraton Hotel - has arguably the cheapest Japanese goods.

Close to the Klasse department store is Jardine's Bazaar - one of Hong Kong's liveliest markets selling a variety of Chinese products. It is particularly good in the evening and a visit to the Bazaar can be combined with a meal in one of the area's many fine restaurants.

A TASTE FOR THE EXTRAORDINARY.

最近いいね

CHANGE

DUTY FREE SHOPPERS HONG KONG LIMITED

DFS GALLERIA AT SUN PLAZA, 8 PEKING ROAD, TSIMSHATSUI, KOWLOON, HONG KONG

The only merchandise offered for sale in our outlets in Hong Kong that is liable to duty in Hong Kong is liquor and tobacco. Duty on this merchandise has been paid except on sales to sea-departing passengers.

Electrical goods: Hong Kong is a good place to buy computers, cameras and a wide range of electronic equipment - hi-fis, VCRs and televisions are all good value. Fierce competition between suppliers keeps prices low for both imported and locally- made electrical goods.

Watches: Almost every make of watch is sold in Hong Kong so don't rush into buying the first one you see. With Hong Kong's duty free prices and volume sales, prices are cheap. On the downside make sure that the watch is not a fake and that it has a worldwide guarantee. It is a good idea to contact the watchmaker's sole agent to check out prices before spending big money.

Jewellery: Hong Kong is a trading centre in gold, precious stones and jewellery. All jewellers must stamp their gold products with the accurate gold content (above 8K) and it is advisable to shop at HKTA (Hong Kong Tourist Association) member shops. Diamond prices are generally lower than those elsewhere. Jade, too, is popular. A good place to buy is the Jade Market on Canton Road in Yaumatei, where both the real thing (jadeite and nephrite) is for sale alongside so-called "new jade" from Taiwan. Cultured pearls, quartz and amethyst are all good value.

Leather goods: Shoes and handbags can be found from European - designer items to cheaper Hong Kong produced made-to-order merchandise. Makers of custom-made shoes will keep your foot measurements on file so that you can order by post in the future.

Furs and ivory: These will not appeal to everyone. Hong Kong is among the world's largest exporters of fur garments and local craftsmenship is said to be high. By buying direct from the supplier, prices are kept to minimum. The importation of ivory was banned finally in the summer of 1989 in response to worldwide pressure.

Suits: Hong Kong was once the home of the 24-hour tailor. But for a more considered job, tailors usually require longer. Hong Kong has gone steadily upmarket in recent years and the colony now rivals London's Savile Row for the crown of the world's top tailors. *Sam's* (opposite the Mosque on Nathan Road), for instance, is popular with royals, film stars and politicians.

Equivalent garments for female executives are becoming increasingly common. Most major shops accept credit cards, but you will either get a discount for paying cash or shopkeepers will add up to 8% for their use.

Getting around

The great thing about Hong Kong is that it's so easy to get around and what's more travel is cheap, safe and reliable.

Local taxis are remarkably inexpensive

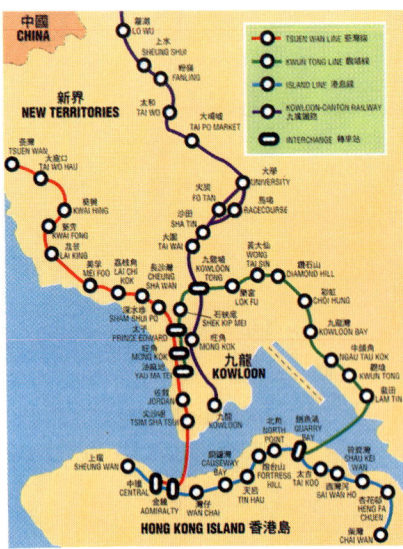

- the flag fall is just HK$13 and you will be hard pressed to pay more than HK$50 for any journey on Hong Kong Island. Public transport is equally superb and unbelievably cheap. Fares on the Star Ferry that links Kowloon with Hong Kong have just gone up to HK$1.70 for an upper-deck seat! A tram costs only HK$1.20 for a journey the entire length of Hong Kong Island - a great way to see the bustling heart of the territory.

The MTR subway system is inexpensive (highest fare HK$11) and spotlessly clean, but crowded during peak periods - so be prepared for a squash. Its four lines total 520 km and link up with KCR station at Kowloon Tong for journeys into China. Special 'stored value' tickets are available to save queuing for every trip.

Hong Kong Yaumatei Ferries (HKY) has a number of inter-island services to Lamma, Lantau, Cheung Chau, Peng Chau and Po Tai plus a range of cross-harbour trips, which can often be quicker than taking the MTR.

The famous Peak Tram (a 'must' on a clear day) costs HK$12 for adults and $4 for children under 12.

Jetfoils and hoverferries depart from Central and Kowloon to Macau. The two main firms offering "flights" are Far East Hydrofoil and Hong Kong Macau Hydrofoil. Trips to Macau across the Pearl River Estuary take about 60 minutes.

Car rental is not recommended as other forms of transport are so good. It is also difficult to park in either Kowloon or Hong Kong Island. In fact, car hire is only probably worthwhile for trips to the New Territories.

Entertainment

Variety is the essential ingredient of Hong Kong's nightlife - if you want it, the territory has it from girlie bars to grand or Chinese opera. Although what's on offer is a somewhat tamer version than that available in the fleshpots of Bangkok or Manila.

Some of the best drinking places are those frequented by resident expatriates - mostly on Hong Kong Island.

Heavy rock aficionados can find some good music at the *Wanch* folk club in lively Wanchai. Lan Kwai Fong, Central contains a cluster of clubs and pubs including the *Quo Quo* jazz club and *Club 1997* for dancing. *JJs* in the Grand Hyatt is a lively disco/entertainment club and *Joe Bananas* in Wanchai offers live music. *The Jazz Club* in D'Aguilar St, Central has visiting celebrities playing. One of the longest-established Kowloon clubs is the *Bottoms Up* bar in Hankrow Road. Another popular Kowloon-side pub is *Mad Dog* at 32 Nathan Road. *Cotton (Jazz) Club* is open nightly on the ground floor of the Kimberley Hotel in Kowloon.

Eating out is an essential ingredient of any visit to Hong Kong and the best Chinese cooking in the world is supposed to be found in the territory. (See *Hong Kong Restaurants* following the *Hong Kong Hotels* section of this publication). Several international hotels feature top-floor restaurants with views over the territory. Floating restaurants are a further option (like the *Jumbo* in Aberdeen Harbour). Many feature set menus for dinner, and pre lunch the *dim sum* should be sampled.

Hong Kong's impressive-looking Cultural Centre in Kowloon hosts many of world's leading orchestras, dance companies and visiting theatre groups plus a sprinkling of performances by Chinese orchestras. There are also concerts at the HK Arts Centre and Academy for Performing Arts in Wanchai.

Leisure

Summer 1994 saw the opening of the HK$850 mn Hong Kong Stadium in Wanchai. It has a capacity of 40,000 for sporting events or concerts and 75% of it is covered by a strking split dome roof.

Perhaps surprisingly, golf features high on the list of weekend pursuits of many busy executives and Hong Kong has some challenging courses. Both the nine-hole Deepwater Bay and Fin Ling with its three 18-hole courses are run by the venerable Royal Hong Kong Golf Club. The Clearwater Bay Golf & Country Club is perhaps the most picturesque and the Discovery Bay course sits atop a mountain on Lantau Island. Visitors can play on some of these courses. Then there is the Johnnie Walker Classic every December to draw some of the world's finest golfers to the territory. A 25,000 sq ft Golf Workshop Centre opened in 1993 at 40 Sun Wong Toi, near Kai Tak Airport.

Horse racing has a fanatical following among the betting-mad locals. Take a trip to the fabulous Sha Tin (in the New Territories) or Happy Valley (on Hong Kong Island) racecourses to soak up the atmosphere - and even win a few dollars. Meetings are held on Wednesdays and Saturdays during the September-June racing season. The Hong Kong Tourist Association offers a HK$468 day ticket including lunch or dinner and entrance to the members' enclosure.

Ocean Park (admission including a visit to the Middle Kingdom adults HK$130, children $65) opened a 3.5 acre *Kids' World* addition in 1993. In 1992, a new thrill ride named **Top Spin** proved a further attraction and **Ocean Park Tower** opened.Ocean Park has a five year HK$600 million investment plan.

On summer weekends, Hong Kong's 235 outlying islands are a haven for sun-worshippers and water sports lovers. But during the week many of these beaches are largely deserted. Deepwater Bay, Repulse Bay and Stanley on the south side of Hong Kong Island are among the most popular. Cheung Sha on Lantau Island is the territory's longest beach, yet it remains one of Hong Kong's best-kept secrets. Cheung Chau is another good island for sandy beaches. Lamma Island, meanwhile, is a great place for peace and quiet. It also has some fine water-side restaurants.

Arrival & Departure

Kai Tak Airport is located in Kowloon and is on a good day about 10-20 minutes from the hotel district around Nathan Road.

Trips over onto Hong Kong Island depend on the traffic situation through the Cross-Harbour Tunnels, but allow up to 45 minutes.

Taxis cost about HK$41 to/from Kowloon side; HK$81to/from Hong Kong side inc.cross harbour tunnel fee.Hotel limousines cost about HK$200; many hotels provide free shuttle buses. Airbuses leave every 15 minutes for hotels in Kowloon (HK$9) and Hong Kong Island (HK$14).There is no MTR connection to the airport.

Immigration control at Kai Tak has speeded up in recent years with computerisation but early afternoons and evenings are the peak time forEuropean arrivals and it can be difficult to find a taxi at this time. Seasoned travellers nip upstairs to grab a taxi from the **Departures** floor.

Departure tax from Kai Tak has been re-increased to HK$ 100 for adults; children under 12 are exempt . To Macau it's HK$22.

Hong Kong Key Fact File

Passport Requirements:
All Visitors must have a valid passport. Nationals from a number of countries in North America, Western Europe and some Asian states are permitted 30-day visa-free visits. Three months visa-free visits are granted to a further 25 or so countries, which include the UK's dependent territories and all Commonwealth countries. UK nationals get a six-month no visa stay.

Currency:
Hong Kong dollar (HK$). 100c = 1HK$.

Exchange Rate: *(March 1997)*
US$1 = HK$7.75(fixed); £1 = HK$12.65

Currency Restrictions:
None

Electricity Supply:
200 volts/50 cycles AC

Language:
Cantonese and English. English is used in government and business.

Time:
GMT + 8 hours; EDT + 13 hours

IDD Code: 852.
'2' was added before all business and leisure fixed line numbers from 1.1.95.

Business Hours:
Commercial offices are open 0900-1700 Monday to Friday; 0900-1200 Saturdays. Government offices are open 0900-1300 and 1400-1700 Monday to Friday; 0900-1300 Saturdays.
Shops are usually open 1000-2100 including Sundays (except in Central, where the hours are 1000-1800 Monday to Friday). Banks are open 0930-1600 Monday to Friday; 0930-1200 Saturdays.

Customs & Entry:
Duty-free allowance comprises 200 cigarettes, one litre of spirits, 60 millilitres of perfume and 250 millilitres of toilet water. Firearms must be declared and handed over to the authorities during any stay.

Health Requirements:
An international certificate of vaccination against cholera is only necessary if you have visited an infected area 14 days prior to arrival in Hong Kong.

Climate: Hong Kong's climate is subtropical: hot and humid in summer (May-September 28°C - 82°F; humidity 83%) with clear autumns (average temp. Sept-Dec 23°C - 73°F; humidity 73%) and mild winters (Dec-Feb 15°C - 59°F; humidity 75%); spring is marked by fog and rain (March-May 21°C - 70°F - humidity 84%). The typhoon season lasts July to September.

Best time to visit:
Busiest tourist months are April-June and September-November when hotels normally charge 'high season' rates. Other months are classified as 'low' season. There is no 'dead' business season but European expatriates tend not to be available over Christmas and in July/August Western school holiday periods.

National Holidays 1997
1 January day following New Year's Day; 6-8 February Chinese New Year; 28/31 March Good Friday/Easter Monday; 5 April Ching Ming Festival; 9 June Tuen Ng Festival; 28/30 June HM The Queen's Birthday; 1/2 July HK Returns to China; 18 August Sino-Japanese War Victory Day; 17 September Day following Chinese Mid-Autumn festival; 1/2 October National Day & day following; 10 October Chung Yeung Festival; 25/26 Dec. Xmas

Hong Kong Hotel Reference Table

Hotel (listed in price order)	Single Room Rate (Hong Kong $)	Location	Number of Rooms	Number of Suites	Conference Facilities	Exhibition Space	Largest Banquet Number	Business Centre	Swimming Pool (0 = indoor)	Tennis Court	Health Club	Video Films
Mandarin Oriental	3000-4800	Central	491	40	●	●	250	●	●	-	●	-
Grand Hyatt HK	2800-3600	Wanchai	550	23	●	●	1200	●	○	●	●	●
The Regal Hongkong Hotel	2800-3800	Causeway Bay	393	32	●	-	500	●	○	-	●	●
The Peninsula	2700-4300	Kowloon	246	54	●	●	140	●	○	-	●	●
Hong Kong Renaissance	2500-3350	Kowloon	473	27	●	●	400	●	●	-	●	●
JW Marriott Hotel Hong Kong	2500-3500	Admiralty	579	29	●	●	520	●	●	-	●	●
Hotel Conrad	2500-3400	Admiralty	467	46	●	●	700	●	●	-	●	●
Island Shangri-La	2400-3250	Admiralty	552	34	●	●	500	●	●	-	●	●
The Regent HK	2400	Kowloon	544	58	●	●	840	●	●	-	●	-
Ritz Carlton Hong Kong	2400-3800	Central	187	29	●	●	230	●	●	-	●	●
Sheraton HK Hotel	2350-2750	Kowloon	703	95	●	●	480	●	●	-	●	●
Royal Garden	2250-3100	Kowloon	375	47	●	●	460	●	●	●	●	●
The Excelsior	2200-3100	Causeway Bay	869	22	●	●	450	●	-	●	●	●
The Hong Kong Hotel	2200-3100	Kowloon	670	84	●	●	300	●	●	-	●	-
Hyatt Regency HK	2200-3100	Kowloon	716	17	●	-	-	●	-	-	●	●
Hotel Nikko	2200-3400	Kowloon	462	18	-	-	-	●	●	-	●	●
Grand Stanford Harbour View	2200-3500	Kowloon	580	12	●	●	210	●	●	-	●	●
The Park Lane	2200-3400	Causeway Bay	785	24	●	●	240	●	-	-	●	●
The Harbour Plaza	2100-3200	Hunghom	385	30	●	●	400	●	●	-	●	●
Regal Kowloon Hotel	2100-2800	Kowloon	558	34	●	●	360	●	-	-	●	●
New World Harbour View	2030-2700	Wanchai	822	40	●	●	460	●	●	●	●	●
Kowloon Shangri-La	2000-3500	Kowloon	689	-	●	●	600	●	●	-	●	●
New World Hotel	2000-2700	Kowloon	585	42	-	-	-	●	●	-	●	●
Holiday Inn Golden Mile	2000-2500	Kowloon	591	9	●	●	540	●	●	-	●	●
Furama Hong Kong Hotel	1950-3300	Central	481	44	●	●	550	●	-	-	●	●
The Prince Hotel	1800-3200	Kowloon	350	51	●	●	-	●	-	-	●	-
The Marco Polo	1800-2100	Kowloon	384	55	●	●	00	●	-	-	●	-
Miramar Hotel	1700-2800	Kowloon	436	23	●	●	1104	●	○	-	-	●
Regal Airport Hotel	1700-2200	Kai Tak	368	21	●	●	200	●	-	-	●	●
Century Hong Kong	1700-2100	Wanchai	492	24	●	●	190	●	●	-	●	●
Grand Plaza Hotel	1650-2400	Quarry Bay	248	40	●	-	-	●	○	-	●	-
The Park Hotel	1600-2100	Kowloon	410	40	●	-	-	●	-	-	-	●
Regal Riverside Hotel	1600-2100	Shatin N.T.	786	44	●	●	800	●	●	-	●	●
Luk Kwok Hotel	1500-1700	Wanchai	198	-	●	-	150	●	-	-	●	-
The Wharney Hotel	1500-1900	Wanchai	280	55	●	-	85	●	●	-	●	●
The Charterhouse	1450-2000	Wanchai	237	4	-	-	-	●	-	-	-	-
Gold Coast Hotel	1400-1950	Castle Peak NT	440	10	●	●	1200	●	●	●	●	●
City Garden Hotel	1400-2000	North Point	609	8	●	-	200	●	●	-	●	●
Kimberley Hotel	1400-1900	Kowloon	420	70	●	●	240	●	-	-	●	-
Royal Park Hotel	1300-1800	Shatin N.T.	430	12	●	●	180	●	●	●	●	●
South Pacific Hotel	1300-1900	Wanchai	286	7	●	●	108	●	-	-	-	-
Kowloon Hotel	1300-2200	Kowloon	679	26	-	-	-	●	-	-	●	-
Eaton Hotel	1300-2280	Kowloon	438	30	●	●	144	●	●	-	●	●
Grand Tower Hotel	1300-1950	Mong Kok	536	13	●	●	130	●	-	-	●	-
Hotel Windsor	1300-1600	Kowloon	165	1	●	-	200	●	-	-	-	-
Newton Hotel Hong Kong	1300-2200	North Point	352	10	●	-	60	●	●	-	-	-
Majestic Hotel	1300-1700	Kowloon	377	9	●	●	40	●	-	-	●	-
Ramada Hotel Kowloon	1300-2200	Kowloon	203	2	●	-	50	●	-	-	●	-
Guangdong Hotel	1200-1500	Kowloon	234	11	●	●	108	●	-	-	-	-
The Wesley Hong Kong	1200-1900	Wanchai	251	-	-	-	-	●	-	-	●	●
Metropole Hotel	1180-1780	Kowloon	479	8	●	●	200	●	-	-	●	●
Hotel Concourse	1180-2080	Mong Kok	425	5	●	-	-	●	-	-	●	-
Prudential Hotel	1150-1850	Kowloon	416	18	●	-	-	●	●	-	●	-
Empire Hotel	1100-1700	Wanchai	306	35	-	-	-	●	-	-	●	●
Royal Pacfific Hotel/Towers	1100	Kowloon	645	28	●	●	200	●	-	-	●	●
Kowloon Panda	1100-1600	Tsuen Wan	1026	-	●	●	390	●	●	-	●	●
BP International Hotel	1050-1450	Kowloon	535	11	●	●	1200	●	-	-	●	●
Stanford Hotel	1050-1500	Kowloon	194	-	●	-	340	●	-	-	-	●
Imperial Hotel	1100-1400	Kowloon	208	7	-	-	-	●	-	-	-	-
Royal Plaza Hotel	950-1150	Mongkok	100	-	-	-	-	●	-	-	●	-
Newton Hotel Kowloon	920-1300	Mong Kok	168	8	-	-	-	●	-	-	●	-
Silvermine Beach Hotel	860-1080	Lantau Isd	130	-	●	-	-	-	●	-	●	-

Hong Kong Hotels

B P International
No 8 Austin Road, Tsimshatsui, Kowloon
Tel: 2376 1111; Tlx: 48375 BPIHK HX;
Fax: 2376 1333;
E-mail: reservations@megahotels.com.hk
Internet: http://www.hwtour.com/bpi

Your hotel on the Park. BP International, the hotel that presents the many facets of fascinating Hong Kong. Enjoy the modern comforts of its 535 rooms and suites. Relax amidst sweeping views of grand Victoria Harbour and the surrounding Kowloon cityscape. Walk out of our doors into the pulse of Tsimshatsui. Dine, shop and do business in this hub of Hong Kong. Take a leisurely stroll through neighbouring Kowloon Park, an oasis of green in the city. In a land of contrasts, these two sides are yours to experience...in one single hotel - BP International, the ultimate in conven-ience and location.

Accommodation & rates
535 single/double/family rooms, HK$ 1050-1450; corporate rooms HK$ 1500-1700; 11 suites, HK$ 2300-2800.Subject to 10% service charge and 5% government tax

Credit cards accepted:
Amex, Diners, JCB, Mastercard, Visa

Groups
Meeting/conference room - capacity 1200, audio-visual facilities; 960 sq m exhibition space; largest reception 2000 cocktail.

Room Services
Airconditioning, colour TV + satellite, direct-dial telephone, hairdryer, self-service laundry, radio/alarm, safety deposit box, trouser press, vending machines, facilities for handicapped.

Business & other services
Executive floor, airport pickup, car parking & rental, taxi service, newsstand/shops,

Sports & Recreation
Fitness centre/gym, outdoor swimming pool nearby

Restaurants & Coffee Shops
Cafe by the Park (120) - Coffee shop, open 0630-2300; *Flamingo Lounge* (60) - Drinks & snacks, open 1630-0100.

Overseas Sales Representatives
Steigenberger Reservations System

Century Hong Kong Hotel
238 Jaffe Rd, Wanchai
Tel :2598 8888; Fax: 2598 8866

Conveniently located in Wanchai, a fast developing and prominent commercial district. Minutes' walk from MTR station and connected by a covered walkway to the Hong Kong Convention & Exhibition Centre. In the heart of Hong Kong's bustling nightlife and shopping district.

Accommodation:
234 single/double, 258 twin, 24 suites

Rates:
Single HK$ 1700-2100; Double/twin HK$ 1900-2300; Suite HK$ 3800-7800
Subject to 10% service charge and 5% tax

Credit cards accepted:
Amex, Diners, JCB, Mastercard, Visa

Groups
7 meeting/conference rooms - capacity 300; boardroom; audio-visual equipment available; 305 sq m exhibition space; largest reception 190 seated/260 cocktail

Room Services
Airconditioning, colour TV + satellite & video films, IDD telephone, hairdryer, laundry/valet service, minibar, music/radio/alarm clock, safety deposit box, tea/coffee making facilities, trouser press, non-smoker bedrooms available, 24-hr room service, voice messaging; dataport & modem connectivity.

Business & other services
Business centre, executive floor, express checkout, airport pickup, translation service, car parking, newsstand, tour desk, bank

Sports & Recreation
Fitness centre/gym, outdoor swimming pool, golf driving lane

Restaurants & Coffee Shops
Century Cafe (166) - Asian/International, open 24 hours; *Jaffe's Italian Food* (70) - Italian, open noon-1500/1830-2300; *AK's Lounge* (40) - Coffee Shop, open 1100-0100; *Lobby Lounge* (38) - Snacks, open 1000-2200

Overseas Sales Representatives
Utell, Delton Reservation Systems, Aviation & Tourism International, Century International Hotels

The Charterhouse   B
209-219 Wan Chai Road, Wanchai
Tel: 2833 5566; Fax: 2833 5888

City Garden Hotel   C
231 Electric Road, North Point
Tel: 2887 2888; Fax: 2887 1111

Hotel Concourse
22 Lai Chi Kok Road, Mongkok, Kowloon
Tel: 2397 6683; Tlx: 46841; Fax: 2381 3768

Located right adjacent to Nathan Road, the heart of Kowloon, Hotel Concourse is surrounded by fabulous shopping centres and entertainment venues.The Mass Transit Railway Station nearby provides easy acess to nearly every part of the territory.

Accommodation & rates
26 double/399 twin, HK$1180-2080 (single occ. from HK$1180); 5 suites from HK$2800. Subject to 10% service charge and 5% government tax

Credit cards accepted:
Amex, Diners, JCB, Mastercard, Visa

Groups
4 meeting/conference rooms - capacity 12-30; audio-visual equipment available; 960 sq m exhibition space; largest reception 340

Room Services
Airconditioning, colour TV, IDD telephone (ext. in bathroom deluxe rms), hairdryer,

laundry/valet service, minibar, music/radio, tea/coffee making facilities, non-smoker bedrooms available, pay movies, fax machines in deluxe riooms

Business & other services
Executive floor, airport pickup, translation service, car parking, taxi service, travel centre, guided tours, newsstand/shops

Restaurants & Coffee Shops
Cafe Concourse (110) - International, open 0630-0100; Daewongak (102) - Korean, open noon-1500/1800-2300; Lychee Garden (336) Chinese, open 0800-1500/1800-2300; Cheers Lounge (68) - Bar & Karaoke, open 1700-0130

Overseas Sales Representatives
China Travel Service

Conrad International Hong Kong A
Pacific Place, 88 Queensway, Central
Tel: 2521 3838; Tlx:69678; Fax: 2521 3888

Eaton Hotel Hong Kong ○
380 Nathan Rd, Kowloon
Tel: 2782 1818; Tlx: 42862 EATHK HX; Fax: 2782 5563

Situated at Downtown Kowloon, directly on the golden mile of Nathan Road, Eaton Hotel is conveniently located near the Jordan subway station, just a few steps away from street markets and nightlife activities. It is a modern 21-storey hotel which offers up-to-date business and recreational facilities.

Accommodation & rates
15 single, 216 double, 207 twin, HK$ 1350-2280; 30 suites HK$ 2700. Subject to 10% service charge and 5% government tax

Credit cards accepted:
Visa, Mastercard, JCB, Diners, Amex

Meeting & banqueting facilities
Meeting/conference room, capacity 130; audio-visual equipment available; 185 sq m exhibition space, largest reception 144 seated/160 cocktail

Room services
Airconditioning, colour TV, direct-dial telephone, hairdryer, laundry/valet service, separate computer & fax lines, separate shower cubicle, electric curtains, minibar, music/radio/alarm clock, safety deposit box, tea/coffee making facilities, non-smoker bedrooms available, video films.

Business & other services
Business centre, express checkout, airport pickup, translation service, car parking/rental, taxi service, barber shop/hairdresser, newsstand/shops.

Sports & recreation
Fitness gymnasium, outdoor swimming pool

Restaurants & Coffee Shops
Coffee Shop (120) - International, open 0630-0100; Yat Tung Heen (370) - Cantonese, open 1100-1500/1800-2300 (0900-1500 Suns/Pub Hols); Astor Café (156) - International, open 0630-1230; Lobby Lounge (30) - Drinks/snacks, open noon-0100; Planter's Bar (55) - Drinks/snacks, open 1500-0100 (-0200 Fri/Sat/PHs)

Overseas Sales Representatives:
Utell International; MMI International

The Excelsior ○
281 Gloucester Road, Causeway Bay
Tel: 2894 8888;Tlx:74550 EXCON HX; Fax 2895 6459; E-mail: cecilia@exhkg.com.hk

Located in Causeway Bay, the heart of Hong Kong's shopping, dining and entertainment centre, the 900-room Excelsior is ideally situated by Victoria Harbour and accessible to all forms of transport. Three executive floors and 6 restaurants, lounges and bars cater to travellers' various needs.

Accommodation & rates:
448 double, 421 twin, 22 suites. Single/double/twin HK$ 2200-3100; suite HK$ 3800-8000.Subject to 10% service charge and 5% government tax

Credit cards accepted:
Amex, Carte Blanche, Diners Club, JCB, En Route, JAL Card, Mastercard, Visa,

Meeting & banqueting facilities
6 meeting/conference rooms, 800-4500 sq ft; audio-visual equipment available; 80/96 sq m exhibition space; largest banquet 30 tables - 450 persons

Room services
Airconditioning, colour TV, direct-dial telephone, hairdryer, laundry/valet service, minibar, music/radio/alarm clock, safety deposit box, tea/coffee making, 24-hr room service, video films, non-smoker bedrooms available

Business & other services
Business centre, executive floor, express checkout, airport pickup, translation service, car parking, car rental, taxi service, barber shop/hairdresser, beauty salon, guided tours, newsstand/shops, flower shop

Sports & Recreation
Fitness centre/gym, jacuzzi/whirlpool, massage, sauna, indoor tennis

Restaurants & Coffee Shops
Café on the 1st (202) - Continental, open 0630-0100; Lounge on the 1st (144) - Continental, open 0700-0200; Dickens Bar (180) - English Pub, open 1100-0200(Sats/prePH -0300);Yee Tung Heen (200) - Chinese, open 1100-1430/1800-2300; TOTTS Asian Grill & Bar (252) - Asian, open noon-0100 (-0200 Sats/PHs); Camino (50) - Italian, open noon-1430/1800-2300

Overseas Sales Representatives
Mandarin Oriental Hotel Group

Empire Hotel Hong Kong ○ C
33 Hennessy Road, Wanchai
Tel: 2866 9111; Fax: 2861 3121

Gold Coast Hotel B
1 Castle Peak Road, Castle Peak Bay
New Territories
Tel: 2452 8888; Fax: 2440 7368

Grand Hyatt Hotel A
1 Harbour Road, Wanchai
Tel: 2588 1234; Tlx: 233 1234 GH HX; Fax: 2802 0677

Grand Plaza Hotel B
2 Kornhill Road, Quarry Bay
Tel: 2886 0011; Tlx: 67645 GPH HX; Fax: 2886 1738

Grand Stanford Harbour View ○ B
70 Mody Road, Tsimshatsui, Kowloon
Tel: 2721 5161; Tlx: 38670 HX; Fax: 2732 2233

Grand Tower Hotel C
627-641 Nathan Rd, Kowloon
Tel: 2789 0011; Tlx: 31602 ; Fax: 2789 0945

Guangdong Hotel ○ C
18 Prat Avenue, Tsimshatsui
Tel: 2739 3311;Tlx: 49067; Fax: 2721 1137

Holiday Inn Golden Mile ○ C
50 Nathan Road, Tsimshatsui, Kowloon
Tel: 2369 3111; Tlx: 56332; Fax: 2369 8016

The Hong Kong Hotel ○ A
Harbour City, Kowloon
Tel: 2113 0088; Fax: 2113 0011

Hyatt Regency Hong Kong A
67 Nathan Road, Kowloon
Tel: 2311 1234; Tlx: 43127 HX; Fax: 2739 8701

HONG KONG - Hotels

Hotel Furama Hong Kong
1 Connaught Rd Central
Tel: 2525 5111; Tlx: 73081; Fax: 2845 9339

Ideally situated in the Central District, the Hotel Furama is within easy walking distance of shopping, entertain-ment and commercial centres. All 517 rooms and suites offer spectacular views of the Peak or Victoria Harbour and feature up to date facilities for both tourist and business traveller.

Accommodation & rates
234 single/double, HK$ 1950-3300; 247 twin HK$ 1950-2700; 44 suites HK$ 3500-9500.Subject to 10% service charge and 5% government tax

Credit cards accepted:
Airplus, Amex, Carte Blanche, Diners Club, En Route, JCB, Mastercard, OTB, Visa

Meeting & conference facilities
13 meeting/conference rooms with full audio-visual facilities, capacity up to 1000; 1120 sq m exhibition space; largest reception 550 seated or 1000 cocktail.

Room services
Airconditioning, colour TV, direct-dial telephone, laundry/valet service, minibar, music/radio/alarm clock, electronic safe, tea/coffee making, trouser press, 24-hr room/meal service, video films, non-smoker bedrooms

Business & other services
Business centre, express checkout, airport pickup, translation service, car parking, travel centre + tours, taxi service, barber shop/beauty salon, newsstand/shops

Sports & Recreation
Fitness centre/gym, jacuzzi/whirlpool, sauna/steamroom, jogging track

Restaurants & Coffee Shops
The Rotisserie (66) - Continental, open 0700-2300; *La Ronda Restaurant & Lounge* (350) - International, open noon-1500/1730-2230;*The Island Restaurant* (125) - Chinese, open as above; *Café Chater* (133) - International, open 0630-0100; *Lau Ling Bar* & *Lobby Lounge*, drinks, snacks - open 1000-0100 Mon-Fri (0200 Sats); closed Sundays

Overseas Sales Representatives:
Utell International. Lufthansa offices

The Harbour Plaza
20 Tak Fung Street, Hunghom, Kowloon
Tel: 2621 3188; Fax: 2621 3311

The Harbour Plaza is located along Whampoa waterfront with 415 guestrooms, 2 Harbour Club Executive Floors and a fitness centre, extensive meeting, function and banquet rooms

Accommodation & rates
159 single, HK$ 2100-3200; 226 double/twin rooms, HK$2250-3350; 30 suites HK$ 4200-28000. Subject to 10% service charge & 5% gov't tax

Credit cards accepted:
Amex, Diners, JCB, Mastercard, Visa

Meeting & banqueting facilities
4 meeting/function rooms, capacity 28-450, with audio-visual equipment; 1020 sq m exhibition space; largest reception 400 banquet or 700 cocktail.

Room services
Airconditioning, colour TV, direct-dial telephone (ext. in bathroom), hairdryer, laundry/valet service, minibar, music/radio/alarm clock, non-smoker bedrooms available, safety deposit box, 24-hr room service, video films, tea/coffee making, trouser press

Business & other services
Business centre, executive floor, express checkout, airport pickup, translation service, car parking, car rental, taxi service, travel centre + tours, barber shop/beauty salon, newsstand/shops, guided tours, gift shop, flower shop, babysitting, free shuttle

Sports & Recreation
Fitness centre/gym, jacuzzi/whirlpool, jogging track, massage, sauna, outdoor swimming pool

Restaurants & Coffee Shops
The Promenade (181) - Coffee Shop, open 0630-midnight; *The Grill* (64) - Steaks & seafood open noon-2200; *Robotayaki* (79) - Japanese barbecue, open noon-2300; *Hoi Yat Heen* (240) - Cantonese, open 1130-2300; *Pit Stop* (234) - Fun pub/ snacks, open noon-0100; *Whampoa Lounge* (86) - Aft.tea/cocktails, open 1430-0100

Hong Kong Renaissance Hotel
8 Peking Road, Tsimshatsui, Kowloon
Tel: 2375 1133; Tlx: 45243 RRHK HX; Fax: 2375 6611; E-mail: renhotel@hk.linkage.net

Located in the business and shopping area of Tsimshatsui on the Kowloon peninsula, the 17-storey hotel offers 5-star accommodation with a business centre, swimming pool, award-winning restaurants and bars.

Accommodation & rates
473 single/double/twin rooms HK$ 2550-3350 (single occ. HK$ 2350-3150); 27 suites HK$ 3600-14800. Subject to 10% service charge and 5% government tax

Credit cards accepted:
Amex, Mastercard, Diners, Visa, JCB

Meeting & banqueting facilities
5 meeting/function rooms - capacity 8-550; full audio-visual facilities; 480 sq m exhibition space; largest reception 400 banquet, 550 cocktail.

Room services
Airconditioning, colour TV, direct-dial telephone (ext. in bathroom), hairdryer, laundry/valet service, minibar, music/radio/alarm clock, safety deposit box, 24-hr room service, non-smoker bedrooms available, pay movie, on-screen message and room bill.

Business & other services
Business centre, executive floor, express checkout, airport pickup, translation service, car parking & rental, taxi service, guided tours, babysitting

Sports & Recreation
Fitness centre/gym, massage, sauna, swimming pool (outdoor), solarium

Restaurants & Coffee Shops
T'ang Court (90) -Cantonese, open Mon-Sat noon-1500/1800-2300 (Sun 1100-1500/1800-2300); *Bostonian* (130) - American Bar & Restaurant, open Mon-Sat noon-midnight (Sun 1130-);*Sun's Cafe* (127) International, open 0630-0100; *Lobby Lounge* (60) - Snacks/drinks, open 1000-midnight; *Poolside Bar*, open daily 0700-2100

Overseas Sales Representatives:
Renaissance worldwide reservation and sales offices. Utell international worldwide and all airline CRS system.

The Island Shangri-La A
Supreme Court Road, Pacific Place
Tel: 2877 3838; Tlx:70373; Fax: 2521 8742

HONG KONG - Hotels 81

JW Marriott Hotel Hong Kong ◌ **A**
Pacific Place, 88 Queensway
Tel: 2810 8366; Tlx: 66899; Fax: 2845 0737

The Kimberley Hotel ◌ **B**
28 Kimberley Road, Tsimshatsui, Kowloon
Tel: 2723 3888; Tlx: 43198; Fax: 2723 1318

The Kowloon Hotel ◌ **B**
19-21 Nathan Road, Kowloon
Tel: 2369 8698; Fax: 2739 9811

Kowloon Panda Hotel ◌
No 3, Tsuen Wah Street, Tsuen Wan, Kowloon
Tel: 2409 1111;Tlx: 47611; Fax: 2761 9070
E-mail: reservations@megahotels.com.hk
Internet: http://www.hwtour.com/panda

Kowloon Panda Hotel, Hong Kong's largest, located in the centre of Hong Kong, has 1026 rooms with 55 suites. Amenities include Asian, European and Chinese cuisine, bars and lounges for relaxation, swimming pool, health club and sauna, in-house movies, private karaoke rooms, business centre, shopping centre, function rooms, exclusive Mega Executive Floors, apartelle suites and many more.... Kowloon Panda Hotel, where comfort, friendliness, service and relaxation meet.

Accommodation & rates:
1026 single/double/twin, HK$ 1100-1450; 52 suites, HK$ 2100-3100.
Subject to 10% service charge and 5% government tax

Credit cards accepted:
Amex, Diners, Visa, Mastercard, JCB

Meeting & banqueting facilities
11 meeting/function rooms - capacity 18-1200; audio-visual equipment available; 733 sq m exhibition space; largest reception 700 banquet or 1200 cocktail.

Room services
Airconditioning, colour TV, direct-dial telephone, hairdryer, laundry/valet service, minibar, music/radio/alarm clock, tea/coffee making facilities, trouser press, 24-hr room service, video films, non-smoker bedrooms, Japanese-style bath tubs on 24-26 floors.

Business & other services
Business centre, executive floor, express checkout, airport pickup, translation service, car parking & rental, travel centre + tours, taxi service, barber shop/beauty salon, newsstand/souvenir shop

Sports & Recreation
Fitness centre/gym, massage, sauna, squash & tennis (nearby), swimming pool (outdoor)

Restaurants & Coffee Shops
Chianti (110) - Italian, open 1200-1500/1800-2300;*Yung Yat Ting* (500) - Elegant Chinese, open 1100-1500; *Yuet Loy Heen* (600) - Casual Chinese, open 0730-1500/1800-2230; *Coffee Shop* (320) - Open 0630-midnight

Overseas Sales Representatives:
Utell International, Golden Tulip Hotels, KLM Offices worldwide

Kowloon Shangri-La ◌ **A**
64 Mody Road, Tsimshatsui East, Kowloon
Tel: 2721 2111;Tlx: 36718; Fax: 2723 8686

Luk Kwok Hotel ◌ **B**
72 Gloucester Road, Wanchai
Tel: 2866 2166; Tlx: 69628 HX; Fax: 2866 2622

Majestic Hotel **C**
348 Nathan Road, Kowloon
Tel: 2781 1333; Tlx: 43255 MJHHX; Fax: 2781 17

Marco Polo Hotel **A**
Harbour City, Kowloon
Tel: 2113 1888; Tlx:40077; Fax: 2113 0022

Hotel Classification: **A** *after name of hotel = over US$ 200 per person per night;* **B** *= between US$ 150 - 200;* **C** *= between US$ 100 - 150;* **D** *= between US$ 50 - 100 ;* **E** *= under US$ 50;* ¶ *= prices on application.* ◌ *= PATA member.*

Mandarin Oriental's swimming pool

Mandarin Oriental Hong Kong ◌
5 Connaught Road, central
Tel: 2522 0111; Tlx: 73653 MANDA HX; Fax: 2810 6190
E-mail: s.cairns@mohkg.com.hk

Mandarin Oriental Hong Kong has magnificent views of Victoria Harbour. The hotel is set in the heart of Central, the commercial and banking district and is within three minutes' walk of some of Hong Kong's finest shopping and entertainment.

Accommodation & rates:
445 double, 46 single rooms, HK$ 3000-4800; 40 suites HK$ 6000-22000.
Subject to 10% service charge and 5% government tax

Credit cards accepted:
Amex, Visa, JCB, Diners, Mastercard, Eurocard

Meeting & banqueting facilities
11 meeting/function rooms - capacity 40-400 with audio-visual facilities; 470 sq m exhibition space; largest reception 250 banquet or 1000 cocktail.

Room services
Airconditioning, colour TV/video films, direct-dial telephone (ext. in bathroom), hair dryer, laundry/valet service, minibar, music/radio, safety deposit box, 24 hr room/meal service, non-smoker bedrooms available

Business services
Business centre, express checkout, airport pickup, translation service, car parking & rental, travel centre, taxi service

Other services
Barber shop, book kiosk, beauty salon, flower and gift shop

Sports & Recreation
Fitness centre/gym, massage, sauna, swimming pool (indoor)

Restaurants & Coffee Shops
Pierrot (60) - French, open 1200-1500/1900-2300; *Man Wah* (60) - Cantonese, open 1200-1500/1830-2300; *Mandarin Grill* (140) - Western, open 0700-2300; *Clipper Lounge* (180) - Western, open 0730-2330; *The Café* (120) - Western/Asian, open 0630-0100

Overseas Sales Representatives
Mandarin Oriental Hotel Group, Leading Hotels of the World, Utell

The Metropole Hotel ◌ **B**
75 Waterloo Road, Kowloon
Tel: 2761 1711; Fax: 2761 9070

Hotel Miramar Hong Kong
130 Nathan Road, Tsimshatsui, Kowloon
Tel: 2368 1111; Tlx:44661; Fax: 2369 1788

Centrally located at the heart of Hong Kong's tourist and shopping centre - Tsimshatsui - Hotel Miramar is just a step away from the Star Ferry and underground Mass Transit Railway Station, giving access to most parts of the territory.

Accommodation & rates
22 single, 72 double, 342 twin, HK$ 1700-2800; 23 suites, HK$ 4200-16000.
Subject to 10% service charge and 5% government tax

Credit cards accepted:
Amex, Diners, JCB, Mastercard, Visa, Federal Card

Meeting & conference facilities
8 meeting rooms, capacity 1200, with audio-visual facilities; 1285 sq m exhibition space; largest reception 1104 seated/1500 cocktail

Room services
Airconditioning, colour TV, direct-dial telephone (ext. in bathroom), hairdryer, laundry/valet service, minibar, music/radio/alarm clock, safety deposit box, 24-hr room service, non-smoker floors available, tea/coffee making, trouser press, video films

Business & other services
Business centre, executive floor, express checkout, airport pickup, kiosk, translation service, car parking & rental, travel centre + tours, taxi service, barber shop

Sports & Recreation
Fitness centre/gym, massage, sauna, squash, swimming pool (indoor)

Restaurants & Coffee Shops
Foyer Cafe (112) - Western/Asian, open 0700-midnight; *Princess Bar* (70) - drinks/snacks with live band, open noon-0200. Other outlets in Miramar Shopping Centre.

Overseas Sales Representatives
Utell International Worldwide, Milford International Marketing Services Inc.

New World Harbour View
1 Harbour Road, Wanchai
Tel: 2802 8888; Tlx: 68967 NWHVH HX; Fax: 2802 8833

Situated above the impressive Hong Kong Convention & Exhibition Centre, this 862-room hotel is central to Hong Kong's business and shopping districts. It also offers 11000 dq m of recreational area, including tennis courts, outdoor pool, golf driving range and three jacuzzis.

Accommodation & rates:
32 Single HK$ 2030-2700; 440 double/350 twin HK$ 2030-3350; 40 suites HK$ 4500-14000.Subject to 10% service charge and 5% government tax

Credit Cards Accepted
Amex, Visa, Mastercard, Diners, JCB.

Meeting & banqueting facilities
7 meeting/function rooms - capacity 16 - 350; 4 boardrooms; full audio-visual facilities; 656 sq m exhibition space; largest reception 456 banquet, 800 cocktail.

Room services
Airconditioning, colour TV, direct-dial telephone (ext. in bathroom), hairdryer, laundry/valet service, minibar, music/radio/alarm clock, safety deposit box, 24-hr room service, non-smoker bedrooms available, video films, fax machines, laser/compact disc players (some rooms), Asis, Meridien Mail

Business & other services
Business centre, executive floor, express checkout, airport pickup, translation service, car parking, car rental, travel centre, taxi service, barber shop/hairdresser, beauty salon, guided tours, newsstand/shops, florist, banking & concierge

Sports & Recreation
Fitness centre/gym, golf driving range, jacuzzi/whirlpool, jogging track, massage, sauna, squash, swimming pool (outdoor), tennis, children's playground

Restaurants & Coffee Shops
Lobby Lounge (138) - Carvery Lunch/Buffet, open 0800-0100; *Coffee Shop* (198) - International/Japanese/SE Asian, open 0630-0030; *Dynasty* (216) - Cantonese, open noon-1500/1830-2300;

Oasis Lounge (105) - Snacks/drinks,slim 'n trim lunch buffet, open noon-1430/1700-0200; *Scala* (48) - Continental, open noon-1500/1900-midnight.

Overseas Sales Representatives
Utell International, Renaissance Worldwide Sales Offices, Renaissance Worldwide Reservations

Newton Hotel Hong Kong C
218 Electric Road, North Point
Tel: 2807 2333; Tlx: 726281; Fax: 2807 1221

Newton Kowloon Hotel C
58-66 Boundary St, Mong Kok, Kowloon
Tel: 2787 2338; Fax: 2789 0688

New World Hotel A
22 Salisbury Road, Kowloon
Tel:2369 411; Tlx: 35860; Fax: 2369 9387

Hotel Nikko Hongkong A
72 Mody Road, Tsimshatsui East, Kowloon
Tel: 2739 1111;Tlx: 31302; Fax: 2311 3122

The Park Hotel B
61-65 Chatham Road, Kowloon
Tel: 2366 1371; Tlx: 45740 Fax: 2739 7259

The Park Lane Hong Kong B
310 Gloucester Road, Causeway Bay
Tel: 2890 3355;Tlx: 75343; Fax: 2576 7853

The Pearl Garden ¶
30-36 Nanking Street, Yaumatei

Pearl Island Hotel ¶
304-314 Des Voeux Rd West, Central
Tel: 2521 6262; Fax: 2537 1800

The Peninsula Hong Kong A
Salisbury Road, Tsimshatsui, Kowloon
Tel: 2366 6251; Tlx: 43821 PEN HX; Fax: 2722 4170

Prince Hotel A
Harbour City, Kowloon
Tel: 2736 1888; Tlx: 50950 ; Fax: 2736 0066

The Prudential Hotel C
222 Nathan Road, Tsimshatsui, Kowloon
Tel: 2311 8222; Tlx:46752; Fax: 2311 1304

Ramada Hotel Kowloon C
73-75 Chatham Road, Tsimshatsui, Kowloon
Tel: 2311 1100; Fax: 2311 1304

HONG KONG - Hotels

Regal Airport Hotel   B
Sa Po Road, Kowloon
Tel: 2718 0333; Tlx: 40950 HOMRA HX;
Fax: 2718 4111

The Regal Hongkong Hotel   A
88 Yee Wo Street, Causeway Bay
Tel: 2890 6633; Tlx: 62932; Fax:2 881 0777

The Regal Kowloon Hotel   A
71 Mody Road, PO Box 98760,
Tsimshatsui East, Kowloon
Tel: 2722 1818; Tlx: 40955 HOMRO HX;
Fax: 2369 6950

Regal Riverside Plaza   A
Tai Chung Kiu Road, Shatin, New Territories
Tel: 2649 7878; Fax: 2637 4748

The Regent Hong Kong   A
Salisbury Road, Kowloon
Tel: 2721 1211; Tlx: 37134 REG HX; Fax: 2739 4546

The Ritz-Carlton Hong Kong ◌ A
3 Connaught Road, Central
Tel: 2877 6666 ; Fax: 2877 6778

The Royal Garden ◌
69 Mody Road, Tsimshatsui East, Kowloon
Tel: 2721 5215; Fax: 2369 9976
E-mail: htlinfo@theroyalgardenhotel.com.hk

10 minutes from airport, at the centre of the city's shopping, dining and entertainment area.100-foot high landscaped Garden Atrium, 422 rooms and suites with Executive Floor, Mediterranean Sky Club on rooftop features year round pool, tennis court,high-tech fitness centre, 5 meeting rooms. A Pan Pacific affiliated hotel.

Accommodation & rates:
136 double, 239 twin, HK$ 2250-3100 (single occ. $2100-2950); 47 suites, HK$ 3700-10000.Subject to 10% service charge and 5% government tax

Credit cards accepted:
Amex, CB/Diners, Mastercard, Visa

Meeting & banqueting facilities
4 meeting/function rooms - capacity 16 - 350; full audio-visual facilities; ; largest reception 456 banquet, 800 cocktail.

Room services
Airconditioning, colour TV, direct-dial telephone (ext. in bathroom), hairdryer, laun- dry/valet service, minibar, music/radio/alarm clock, safety deposit box, 24-hr room service, non-smoker bedrooms available, video films

Business & other services
Business centre, executive floor, express checkout, airport pickup, translation service, car parking, car rental, travel centre, taxi service, barber shop/beauty salon, guided tours, newsstand/shops

Sports & Recreation
Fitness centre/gym, jacuzzi/whirlpool, putting green, massage, sauna, swimming pool (indoor), tennis

Restaurants & Coffee Shops
American, Cantonese and European Restaurants.

Royal Pacific Hotel & Towers   C
China-Hong Kong City, 33 Canton Road, Tsimshatsui, Kowloon
Tel: 2736 1188; Tlx:44111; Fax: 2736 1212

Royal Park Hotel ◌ C
8 Pak Hok Ting Street, Shatin N.T.
Tel: 2601 2111; Tlx: 45776;; Fax: 2601 3666

Sheraton Hongkong Hotel & Towers A
20 Nathan Road, Tsimshatsui, Kowloon ◌
Tel: 2369 1111;Tlx: 45813 ; Fax: 2739 8707

Silvermine Beach Hotel   C
Silvermine Bay, Mui Lo, Lantau island
Tel: 2984 8295; Fax: 2984 1907

Stanford Hotel ◌ C
118 Soy Street, Mongkok, Kowloon
Tel: 2781 1881; Fax: 2388 3733

The Wesley Hotel Hong Kong   C
22 Hennessy Road, Wanchai
Tel: 2866 6688; Tlx: 47666 WESHK HX
Fax: 2866 6633

The Wharney Hotel Hong Kong   B
61-73 Lockhart Road, Wanchai
Tel: 2861 1000; Tlx: 82590 RINN HX; Fax: 2865 1010

Windsor Hotel ◌ B
39-43a Kimberley Road, Tsimshatsui,
Tel: 2739 5665; Tlx: 44419 ; Fax: 2311 5101

South Pacific Hotel

South Pacific Hotel   B
23 Morrison Hill Road, Wanchai
Tel: 2572 3838; Tlx: 78186 SPHHK HX;
Fax: 2893 7773
E-mail: hinfo@southpacifichotel.com.hk

Strategically located in Hong Kong's business district - Wanchai - next to Causeway Bay premier shopping, dining and entertainment complexes, surrounded by street markets, authentic colour and oriental atmosphere with the famed trams and airport bus stopping outside the hotel.

Accommodation & rates:
22 sdingle, HK$ 1300-1900; 50 double, 214 twin, HK$ 1450-1900; 7 suites, HK$ 3500-4800. Subject to 10% service charge and 5% government tax

Credit cards accepted:
Amex, Mastercard, Diners, JCB, Visa

Meeting & banqueting facilities
Three meeting rooms - capacity 120, with audio-visual equipment; 148 sq m exhibition space; largest reception 108 seated or 180 cocktail.

Room services
Airconditioning, colour TV + satellite, direct-dial telephone, hairdryer, laundry/valet service, minibar, music/radio/alarm clock, safety deposit box, tea/coffee making, non-smoker bedrooms available

Business services
Business centre, executive floor, airport pickup, taxi service, translation service, travel centre, car parking

Restaurants & coffee shops
La Pacifica (84) - International, open 0630-midnight; *Swatow Garden Restaurant* (180) - Chiu Chow cuisine, open 1130-1500/1800-2330; *Starlight Lounge* (116) - open 1700-0100; *Piano Lounge* (34) open 1400-2300

Overseas Sales Representatives:
Utell International

---

*Hotel Classification: **A** after name of hotel = over US$ 200 per person per night; **B** = between US$ 150 - 200; **C** = between US$ 100 - 150; **D** = between US$ 50 - 100 ; **E** = under US$ 50; ¶ = prices on application.*
◌ *after name of hotel = PATA member*

Restaurants

Chinese (Cantonese)

Dynasty Restaurant
Hotel Victoria, Shun Tak Centre,
Connaught Road Central.Tel: 2540 7228
Eagle's Nest
Hilton Hotel, 2 Queens Road, Central
Tel: 2523 3111
East Ocean Seafood Restaurant
3/F, Harbour Centre, 25 Harbour Road,
Wanchai.Tel: 2893 8887
East Ocean Seafood Restaurant
B-1, East Ocean Centre, Tsimshatsui East
Tel: 2723 8128
Flower Lounge Restaurant
Harbour City, 11 Canton Road,
Tsimshatsui.Tel: 2722 1800
Fook Lam Moon Restaurant
459 Lockhart Road G/F, Causeway Bay
Tel: 2891 2639
Fook Lam Moon Restaurant
53-59 Kimberley Road, Tsimshatsui
Tel: 2366 0286
Guangzhou Garden Restaurant
4/F, Two Exchange Square, Central
Tel: 2525 1163
Island Restaurant
Hotel Furama Kempinski, 4/F, 1
Connaught Road, Central. Tel: 2525 5111
Jade Garden Restaurant
53 Paterson Street, Causeway Bay
Tel: 2577 8282
Jade Garden Restaurant
25-31 Carnarvon Road, Tsimshatsui
Tel: 2722 6888
Jumbo Floating Restaurant
Wong Chuk Hang, Aberdeen Harbour
Tel: 2553 9111
Lai Kar Heen
Ritz Carlton Hotel, 3 Connaught Rd
Central.Tel: 2877 6666
Lotus Garden Restaurant
6-8 Prat Avenue, Tsimshatsui
Tel: 2723 8818
Man Wah Restaurant
Mandarin Oriental Hotel, 5 Connaught
Road, Central.Tel: 2522 0111
Maxim's Palace Chinese Restaurant
World Trade Centre, 1/F, Causeway Bay
Tel: 2576 0288
Miramar Tsui Hang Village Restaurant
Hotel Miramar, 15/F Keewan Tower, 132-134 Nathan Road, Kowloon
Tel: 2368 1111
Mythical China Restaurant
Level 2, Western Market, Desvoeux Rd
Tel: 2815 4170
Neptune Seafood Restaurant
G/F 6 Tonnochy Road, Wanchai
Tel: 2893 2008
North Park Restaurant
Grd Fl, Lockhart Hse, 440 Jaffe Rd,
Causeway Bay. Tel: 2891 2940
Sea Palace Floating Restaurant
Shum Wan, Wong Chuk Hang, Aberdeen
Harbour.Tel: 2552 7340
Shang Palace
Basement, Shangri-La Hotel, 64 Mody Rd,
Tsimshatsui East, Kowloon.Tel: 2721 8524
South Villa Restaurant
58-60 Cameron Road, Tsimshatsui,
Kowloon.Tel: 2721 5431-4
Tai Pak Floating Restaurant
Shum Wan, Wong Chuk Hang, Aberdeen
Harbour. Tel: 2552 5953
Tai Woo Restaurant
15-19 Wellington Street, Central
Tel: 2524 5618
T'ang Court
Hong Kong Renaissance Hotel, 8 Peking
Rd, Tsimashatsui. Tel: 2375 1133
Tao Yuan Restaurant
3/F Great Eagle Centre, 23 Harbour Road,
Wanchai. Tel: 2573 8080
Yung Kee Restaurant
32-40 Wellington Street, Central
Tel: 2523 2343

Chiu Chau

Chiuchow Garden Restaurant
Basement, Connaught Centre, Central
Tel: 2525 8246
Golden Island Bird's Nest
3-4 F, 25 Carnarvon Road, Tsimshatsui
Tel: 2369 5211
Manning Chiu Chow Restaurant
1/F, Asian House, 1 Hennessy Road,
Wanchai. Tel: 2529 7669
Universal Restaurant
6-8 Hysan Ave, Causeway Bay
Tel: 2576 2727

Peking

Beijing Restaurant
34-36 Granville Road, Tsimshatsui
Tel: 2366 9968
China Garden Restaurant
1/F, 45-47 Carnarvon Road, Tsimshatsui
Tel: 2366 0408
New American Restaurant
179 Wanchai Road, Wanchai
Tel: 2575 0458
Peking Garden Restaurant
3/F, Star House, Tsimshatsui
Tel: 2369 8211
Spring Deer
42 Mody Road, Tsimshatsui, Kowloon
Tel: 2723 3673

Shanghai/Szechuan

Cleveland Szechuen Restaurant
6 Cleveland Street, Causeway Bay
Tel: 2576 3876
Great Shanghai
26 Prat Ave, Tsimshatsui, Kowloon
Tel: 2366 8158
Lotus Pond Restaurant
15 Harbour City, Phase IV, Canton Rd,
Tsimshatsui.Tel: 2724 1088
Shanghai Garden Restaurant
G30/G33, 115-124 & 126 Hutchison
House, Central.Tel: 2523 8322
Shanghai Grand Restaurant
4/F, Island Shopping Centre, 1 Great
George Street, Causeway Bay
Tel: 2890 6828
Sichuan Garden Restaurant
3/F Gloucester Tower, The Landmark,
Central.Tel: 2521 4433
Sze Chuen Lau Restaurant
466 Lockhart Road, G/F, Causeway Bay
Tel: 2891 9027
Ziyang Szechuen Restaurant
G/F, 45D Chatham Road S, Tsimshatsui,
Kowloon.Tel: 2368 7177

Indian

The Ashoka Restaurant
G/F, 57 Wyndham Street, Central
Tel: 2524 9623
New Delhi Restaurant
Mezzanine Floor, 52 Cameron Road,
Tsimshatsui, Kowloon
Viceroy of India
2/F, 30 Harbour Road, Wanchai
Tel: 2572 7227

Indonesian

New Indonesian Restaurant
500 Lockhart Road, Causeway Bay
Tel: 2892 0328

Japanese

Ah-So Japanese Restaurant &Sushi Bar
159 Craigie Court, World Finance Centre,
Harbour City, Tsimshatsui, Kowloon
Benkay Japanese Restaurant
1st basement, Gloucester Tower, The
Landmark, Central.Tel: 2521 3344
Hong Kong Kanetanaka Co Ltd
22/F, East Point Centre, 545-563
Hennessy Road, Causeway Bay
Tel: 2833 5617
Matsubishi Restaurant
F & G, G/F, 440 Jaffe Road, Causeway
Bay.Tel: 2892 7221
Matsuzaka Restaurant
UG 23-28 South Seas Centre, Tsimshatsui
East, KowloonTel: 2724 3057
Nadaman Restaurant
2nd basement, Shangri-La Hotel, 64 Mody
Rd, Tsimshatsui East, Kowloon
Tel: 2372 1211

Thai

Sawasdee Thai Restaurant
Grd Fl, 1 Hillwood Road, Kowloon
Tel: 2372 5577

Western

Au Trou Normand
Grd Fl, 6 Carnarvon Rd,
Tsimshatsui, Kowloon.Tel: 2366 8754
Baron's Table *(German)*
Holiday Inn Golden Mile, Nathan Road,
Kowloon.Tel: 2369 3111

Belvedere *(Seafood)*
Holiday Inn Harbour View. Tel: 2721 5161

Bentley's Seafood Restaurant & Oyster Bar
B4 Basement, Prince's Building, Central
Tel: 2868 0881

Brasserie 97
9 Lan Kwai Fong, Central. Tel: 2526 0303

Camargue
5 Lan Kwai Fong, Central. Tel: 2525 7997

Capriccio *(Italian)*
Hong Kong Renaissance Hotel 2nd Fl, 8 Peking Rd, Shimshatsui, Kowloon
Tel: 2311 3311 ext 2260

Casa Mexicana *(Mexican)*
G/F Victoria Centre, 15 Watson Road, Causeway Bay East
Tel: 2566 5560

Chalet *(Swiss)*
Royal Pacific Hotel, 33 Canton Rd, Tsimsahatsui, Kowloom
Tel: 2736 1188 ext 2717

Chesa
Peninsula Hotel, Tsimshatsui
Tel: 2366 6251

The Chinnery
Mandarin Oriental Hotel, 5 Connaught Rd
Tel: 2522 0111

Cordon Bleu Restaurant
New World Centre, 1st Fl Shopping Arcade, Tsimshatsui. Tel: 2366 8933

Gaddi's
Peninsula Hotel, Tsimshatsui
Tel: 2366 6251

Grissini *(Italian)*
Grand Hyatt Hotel, 1 Harbour Rd, Wanchai
Tel: 2588 1234

Jimmy's Kitchen Ltd
G/F, 1 Wyndham Street, Tel: 2526 5293

Lalique
Royal Garden Hotel, 69 Mody Road, Tsimshatsui East, Kowloon
Tel: 2721 5215

Landau's Restaurant Ltd
G/F, 257 Gloucester Road, Causeway Bay
Tel: 2891 2901

La Ronda *(Eastern/Western)*
30th Fl, Hotel Furama Kempinski, 1 Connaught Rd Central
Tel: 2525 5111 ext. 50213

La Rose Noire *(French)*
8-13 Wo On Lane, 1st Fl, Central
Tel: 2526 5965

La Taverna *(Italian)*
1-2 On Hing Terrace, Wyndham Street, Central. Tel: 2522 8904

La Taverna *(Italian)*
34-38 Ashley Road, Tsimshatsui
Tel: 2369 1945

Mandarin Grill
Mandarin Oriental Hotel, 5 Connaught Road, Central. Tel: 2522 0111

Margaux
Shangri-La Hotel, 64 Mody Road, Tsimshatsui East, Kowloon
Tel: 2723 8686

Maxim's Restaurant
Basement, Connaught Centre, Central
Tel: 2525 7977

Napoleon Restaurant Ltd *(French)*
UG/F, Princess Wing, Hotel Miramar, 134 Nathan Road, Tsimshatsui, Kowloon
Tel: 2368 6861

Ocean City Restaurant & Night Club
New World Centre level 3, Tsimshatsui
Tel: 2369 9688

Pierrot Restaurant
Mandarin Oriental Hotel, 5 Connaught Road, Central
Tel: 2522 0111

Plume Restaurant
Regent Hotel, 18 Salisbury Road, Tsimshatsui, Kowloon
Tel: 2721 1211

Rigoletto *(Italian)*
16 Fenwick Street, Wanchai
Tel: 2527 7144

Sammy's Kitchen Ltd *(French)*
G/F, 204-6 Queen's Road West, Western
Tel: 2548 8400

Stanley's
86 Stanley Main Street, Stanley
Tel: 2813 8873

Toscano's *(Italian)*
Ritz Carlton Hotel, 3 Connnaught Rd
Tel: 2877 6666

Valentino Ristorante Italiano *(Italian)*
G/F, 60 Cameron Road, Tsimshatsui, Kowloon
Tel: 721 6653

The Verandah
Repulse Bay Hotel, Repulse Bay
Tel: 812 2722

Verandah Grill
The Peninsula Hotel, Salisbury Road, Tsimshatsui, Kowloon
Tel: 366 6251

Other

Bodhi Vegetarian Restaurant
388 Lockhart Rd, Causeway Bay
Tel: 573 2155

Golden Bull *(Vietnamese)*
L1, New World Centre, 18 Salisbury Rd, Tsimsahtsui
Tel: 2369 4617

Paterson Singapore Restaurant
62-64 Paterson St, Causeway Bay
Tel: 890 6833

Sun Hung Cheung Hing Restaurant *(Mongolian)*
35 Kimberley Rd, Tsimshatsui
Tel: 369 3435

HONG KONG - Airline Offices/Car Hire

Airline Offices

(first numbers = reservations; 2nd = flight information)

Air China
34 Fl, United Centre, 95 Queensway, Central.Tel: 2861 0288 Fax: 2522 1183

Air France
Alexandra House, Chater Road, Central Tel: 2522 3131

Air India
10th floor, Gloucester Tower, Central Tel: 2521 4321

Air Lanka
c/o Airline Marketing Services (HK), Room 505, 5th floor, Bank of America Tower, 12 Harcourt Street, Central. Tel: 2525 2171/8

Alitalia
2101 Hutchinson House, 10 Harcourt Road, Central. Tel: 2523 7047

All Nippon Airways
Room 902, Fairmont House, 8 Cotton Tree Drive, Central. Tel: 2810 4333

British Airways
c/o Jardine Airways, 30th floor,, Alexandra House, Chater Road, Central Tel: 2868 0303/2868 0768

CAAC
Room 6023, Gloucester Tower, 11 Pedder Street, Central. Tel: 2521 6416

Canadian Airlines
17th floor, Swire House, Central Tel: 2868 3123/2769 8391

Cathay Pacific
Swire House, 9 Connaught Road, Central Tel: 2747 1888/2747 1234

China Airlines
Ground floor, St George's Building, 2 Ice House Street, Central. Tel: 2868 2299

Dragonair
19th floor, Wheelock House, 20 Pedder Street, Central. Tel: 2736 0202/2738 3388

Garuda Indonesia
Fu House, 7c Ice House Street, Central Tel: 2840 0000/2522 9071

Gulf Air
1305 Shui Centre, 8 Harbour Road, Central. Tel: 2868 0832/528 0531

Japan Air Lines (JAL)
Gloucester Tower, The Landmark, 11 Pedder Street, Central. Tel: 2523 0081

KLM
Fu House, 7 Ice House Street, Central Tel: 2525 1255/6/2522 0081

Korean Air
Ground floor, St George's Building, Ice House Street, Central. Tel: 2523 5177

Lufthansa
6th floor, Landmark East, 12 Ice House Street, Central.Tel: 2868 2313/2769 7967

Malaysia Airlines
Room 1306, Prince's Building, Chater Road, Central. Tel: 2521 8181/2769 7967

Northwest Airlines
Room 2908, Alexandra House, 16-20 Chater Road, Central. Tel: 2810 4288

Philippine Airlines
Room 1802, Swire House, Central Tel: 2522 7018/2769 8111

Qantas
Swire House, 11a Chater Road, Central. Tel: 2524 2101/2525 6206

Royal Brunei
Room 1406, Central Building, 3 Pedder Street, Central.Tel: 2747 1888/2522 3799

Royal Nepal
Room 1406, Central Building, Central Tel: 2369 9151/2747 7888

Singapore Airlines
Shop 115, The Landmark, 5-17 Pedder Street, Central.Tel: 2520 2233/2769 6498

South African Airways
Room 702, New World Office Building West Wing, 18 Salisbury Road, Kowloon Tel: 2846 7879/2868 0768

Swissair
8th floor, Admiralty Centre Tower II, 18 Harcourt Street, Central Tel: 2529 3670/2769 8864

Thai Airways International
122-124 World Wide Plaza, 19 Des Voeux Rd Central Central.Tel: 2529 5601/2426 5204

United Airlines
29th floor, Gloucester Tower, 11 Pedder Street Central, Central Tel: 2810 4888

Car Hire

Ace Car Hire Service
Ground floor, 2 Shun Yung Street, Hunghom, Kowloon.Tel: 2363 3155

Avis (Headquarters & HK side Office)
Bonaventure House, 85 Leighton Road, Causeway Bay.Tel: 2890 6988; Tlx: 66456 AVSHK HX; Fax: 2895 3686
+ Offices in Kowloon (tel: 2334 6007)

Hertz *(Chauffeur drive only)*
Morning Star Travel Service Ltd, Room 1535, Star House, 3 Salisbury Rd, Kowloon Tel: 2736 9111; Fax: 2736 9235

Holiday Car Hire Company Ltd
Ground Floor, 237a Prince Edward Road, Mongkok, Kowloon

National Car Rental
Upper Ground Floor, 11 Inter-Continental Plaza, 94 Granville Road, Tsimshatsui, Kowloon.Tel: 2367 1047

Toyota Rent-a-Car
1063 King's Rd, Quarry Bay. Tel: 2562 2226

Trinity Rent-a-Car Ltd
Ground Floor, 653 King's Rd, North Point Tel: 2563 6117

What's the link between business and the Asia Pacific?

BRITISH AIRWAYS
The world's favourite airline

http://www.british-airways.com

Hong Kong Airline Departures 1997

Below is a list of main departures and frequencies from Kai Tak International Airport to the destinations in bold type. Figures in brackets after destinations refer to the days of the week. (2,4,6) therefore indicates that departures to that destination take place on a Tuesday (the second day of the week), a Thursday and a Saturday. Departures were correct as at February 1997 but travellers are recommended to check departures with the airline office concerned, listed on the previous page. Only direct connections are shown.

Airline Abbreviation Codes: AC = Air Canada; **AF** = Air France; **AI** = Air India; **AN** = Ansett; **AZ** = Alitalia; **BA** = British Airways; **BG** = Biman Bangladesh; **BI** = Royal Brunei; **BR** = EVA Airways; **CA** = Air China; **CI** = China Airlines; **CJ** = China Northern; **CO** = Continental Airlines; **CP** = Canadian Airlines Int'l; **CZ** = China Southern Airlines; **CX** = Cathay Pacific; **EG** = Japan Asia Airways; **EK** = Emirates; **F6** = China National Aviation; **GA** = Garuda; **GF** = Gulf Air; **JL** = Japan Airlines; **KA** = Dragonair; **KE** = Korean Air; **KL** = KLM; **LH** = Lufthansa; **LY** = El Al; **MH** = Malaysia Airlines; **MK** = Air Mauritius; **MU** = China Eastern Airlines; **NG** = Lauda Air; **NH** = All Nippon Airways; **NW** = Northwest; **NZ** = Air New Zealand; **OZ** = Asiana Airlines; **PR** = Philippine Airlines; **PX** = Air Niugini; **QF** = Qantas; **RA** = Royal Nepal Airlines; **RG** = Varig; **SA** = South African Airways; **SK** = Scandinavian Airline System; **SR** = Swissair; **SQ** = Singapore Airlines; **SU** = Aeroflot; **SZ** = China Southwest; **TG** = Thai Airways; **UA** = United Airlines; **UB** = Myanmar Airways; **UL** = Air Lanka; **VJ** = Royal Air Cambodge; **VN** = Vietnam Airlines; **VS** = Virgin; **XO** = Xinjiang Airllines; **8L** = Grandair

Abu Dhabi (AUH)
GF (3,6)
Adelaide (ADL)
CX (2,6)
Amsterdam (AMS)
CX (2,4,5,7) KL (1,3,5,6,7)
Auckland (AKL)
NZ (2,4,7) CX (4,5,6)
Bahrain (BAH)
GF (1,4,7) CX (2,4,5)
Bandar Seri B (BWN)
BI (3,7)
Bangkok (BKK)
NG (3,7) CP (1,3,5,7) CX, GF, TG, CI, QF (daily) JL (3,5,7) UL (1,4,6)
Beijing (PEK)
CA (daily) CZ (daily) KA (daily)
Bombay (BOM)
AI (2,3,5,6,7) CX (1,3,4,7) SR (1,3,5)
Boston (BOS)
NW (1,4,6)
Brisbane (BNE)
CX (3,6) QF (1,2,3,4,7)
Cairns (CNS)
QF (3,4,5,7) CX (2,3,5,6)
Cape Town (CPT)
SA (1,3)
Cebu (CEB)
CX (2,4,7) PR (1,3,5,6)
Changsha (CSX)
KA (2,5,6)
Chengdu (CTU)
KA (2,3,7) SZ (1,2,4,5,6)
Chiang Mai (CNX)
TG (2,4,7)
Chicago (CHI)
UA (daily)
Chongqing (CKG)
SZ (1,2,4,6)
Colombo (CMB)
UL (1,4,6) CX (2,6)
Copenhagen (CPH)
SK (2,4,6,7)
Dalian (DLC)
CA (1,3,5) KA (2,6)
Delhi (DEL)
AI (2,3,5,6,7) UA (daily)
Denpasar-Bali (DPS)
GA (3,5,6) CX (3,6)
Denver (DEN)
UA (1,2,3,4,5,7)
Detroit (DTW)
UA (daily)
Dhaka (DAC)
KA (2) BG (1,5)
Dubai (DXB)
CX (1,2,3,4,5,7) EK (1,2,3,4,5,6)
Frankfurt (FRA)
CX (daily) LH (daily)
Fukuoka (FUK)
CX (daily) JL (daily)
Fuzhou (FOC)
MU (daily)
Guam (GUM)
CO (1,5)
Guangzhou (CAN)
CZ (daily)
Guilin (KWL)
KA (daily)
Guiyang (KWE)
SZ (1,5)
Haikou (HAK)
KA (daily)
Hangzhou (HGH)
KA (1,2,3,5,7) MU (daily)
Hanoi (HAN)
CX/VN (daily)
Hiroshima (HIJ)
KA (1,2,3,4,5,7)
Ho Chi Minh (SGN)
VN (daily) CX (daily)
Jakarta (JKT)
CX (daily) GA (daily) CI (daily)
Johannesburg (JNB)
SA (1,3,6) CX (3,5,7) RG (4,7)
Kagoshima (KOJ)
JL (1,4)
Kaohsiung (KHH)
CI,KA (daily)
Kathmandu (KTM)
RA (2,6)
Kota Kinabalu (BKI)
KA/MH (daily)
Kuala Lumpur (KUL)
CI (daily) CX (2,3,4,5,6,7) MH (daily)
Kuching (KCH)
KA/MH (1,3,4,6)
Kunming (KMG)
CZ (daily) KA (4,7)
Lanzhou (LHW)
WH (2,5)
London (LHR)
BA (2,5,7) CX (daily) VS (1,3,5,6,7)
Los Angeles (LAX)
UA,CX (daily)
Manchester (MAN)
CX (daily)
Manila (MNL)
CX,PR (daily) BA (1,3,4,6) AF (1,2,4,5) EK (1,3,5,7) SR (4,7) AZ (3,5) CP (2,4,6) 8L (3,5,7)
Mauritius (MRU)
CX/MK (1,4)
Melbourne (MEL)
QF (5) AN (2,3,5,6,7)
Montreal (YMQ)
CP (daily)
Moscow (MOW)
SU (3,7)
Muscat (MCT)
GF (2,5)
Nagoya (NGO)
CX (daily) JL (daily)
Nanjing (NKG)
KA (daily)
New York (JFK)
NW (daily) UA (daily)
Ningbo (NGB)
MU (daily) KA (4,7)
Okinawa (OKA)
JL (2,6)
Osaka (OSA)
CX, JL (daily) AI (3,7) NH (daily)
Paris (CDG)
AF (1,2,4,5) CX (daily)
Penang (PEN)
CX (2,5,6) MH (2,5)
Perth (PER)
CX, QF (daily)
Phnom-Penh (PNH)
KA (2,6) VJ (1,5)
Phuket (HKT)
KA (1,4,6) TG (2,3,5,7)
Port Moresby (POM)
PX (1,5)
Rio de Janeiro (RIO)
RG (4,7)
Rome (FCO)
AZ (3,5,7) CX (2,4,5,6)
Saipan (SPN)
CO (1)
San Francisco (SFO)
SQ, UA, (daily)
Sao Paulo (SAO)
RG (4,7)
Sapporo (SPK)
CX (4,5,7)
Seattle (SEA)
NW (1,4,6)
Sendai (SDJ)
KA (1,3,4,6,7)
Seoul (SEL)
CX, KE,TG, OZ (daily)
Shanghai (SHA)
KA,MU (daily)
Shantou (SWA)
CZ (daily)
Shijiazhuang (SJW)
CA (4)
Singapore (SIN)
CI,CX,SQ,QF,UA (daily) GA (2,4,7)
Subic Bay (SFS)
8L (5)
Surabaya (SUB)
GA (2,3,4,6,7) CX (2,4)
Sydney (SYD)
CX,QF (1) AN (2,3,5,6,7)
Taipei (TPE)
CI,CX,EG,TG (daily) SQ (3,7) BA (2,5,7) BR (daiily)
Tel Aviv (TLV)
LY (4)
Tianjin (TSN)
CA (daily) KA (1)
Tokyo (NRT)
CX,JL,NH,NW,UA (daily) EG (daily)
Toronto (VYZ)
CP, CX (daily)
Vancouver (YVR)
CP (daily) CX (daily) AC (1,3,5,7)
Vienna (VIE)
NG (3,7)
Wenzhou (WNZ)
MU (1,4,6)
Wuhan (WUH)
WH (2,5)
Xiamen (XMN)
CZ, KA (daily)
Xian (SIA)
KA (1,5) WH (2,4,6,7)
Yangon (RGN)
UB (1,5)
Yantai (YNT)
MU (2,6)
Zhengzhou (CGO)
CZ (3,5,7)
Zurich (ZRH)
CX (1,3,4,5,6) SR (1,3,4,5,6,7)

Major Exhibitions in Hong Kong 1997

Date	Exhibition	Venue	Organiser
April 21-24	**Asia Pacific Leather Fair** - Raw Materials & Manufacturing	HKCEC	MF
April 28-30	**Asia Pacific Leather Fair** - Fashion & Finishes Products	HKCEC	MF
May 6-9	HOFEX 97 - incorporating **Wines & Spirits Asia 97, Hotex, Bakery & Confectionery, Asian Int'l Seafood Show, Hospitality Interiors**	HKCEC	HKES
May 20-22	**MIDEM - Asia**: The International Record Music Publishing and Video Music Market	HKCEC	Reed
May 29-June 1	**International Travel Expo Hong Kong '97**	HKCEC	ITE
June 4-7	**Asia Pacific Merchandise Fair**	HKCEC	MF
June 11-14	**A/E/C Systems Hong Kong** - the 1st Annual Computer Show for the Design & Construction Industry	HKCEC	Reed
June 11-14	**IBEX**: Hong Kong International Building & Construction Exposition	HKCEC	Reed
June 19-22	**Hong Kong Jewellery & Watch Fair**	HKCEC	MF
July 16-19	**Sports & Recreation 97**	HKCEC	MF
Sept 3-7	**Hong Kong Jewellery & Watch Fair**	HKCEC	MF
Sept 29 - Oct 1	**Asia Pacific Leather Fair** - Fashion & Finished Products - Autumn	HKCEC	MF
Oct 6-8	**Cosmoprof Asia 1997**	HKCEC	MF
Oct 22-25	**Asian IT Expo 97** - 8th Asian Information Technology Exhibition	HKCEC	Adsale
Oct 31-Nov 3	**Hong Kong International Furniture Fair**	HKCEC	MF
Oct 31 -Nov 3	**Hong Kong International Lighting Fair**	HKCEC	MF
Nov 4-7	**Asia Communitech 97, Asia Networks, Asia Broadcast** - Telecommunications, Wireless technology, networking, sound, & film	HKCEC	HKES
Nov 20-23	**Intermedia Hong Kong** - computer hardware and software, networks	HKCEC	Reed
Nov 20-22	**Cable & Satellite Asia** - Hardware & software for broadcasting	HKCEC	Reed
Nov 19-21	**Sign & Screen Printing Asia 97**	HKCEC	MF
Dec 9-11	**Incentive Travel & Convention Meetings Asia**	HKCEC	MF

Venue. HKCEC = Hong Kong Convention & Exhibition Centre, 1 Harbour Road, Wanchai. Tel: 2844 3422.

Organisers:
Adsale. Adsale Exhibition Services Ltd, 4/F Stanhope House, 734 King's Road, North Point, Hong Kong. Tel: 2811 8897; Fax: 2516 5024. **BITF** = Business and Industrial Trade Fairs Ltd, 18th fl, First Pacific Bank Centre, 51 Gloucester Road, Wanchai, Hong Kong. Tel: 2865 2633; Tlx: 64882; Fax: 2866 1770/2865 5513. **ITE** = International Travel Expo Hong Kong Ltd, Rm 1712B Fortress Tower, 250 Kings Road, North Point, Hong Kong. Tel: 2508 6655; Fax: 2510 7016. **MF** = Miller Freeman Asia Ltd, 102-5 Stanhope House, 738 King's Road, Quarry Bay, Hong Kong. Tel: 2827 7064; Fax. 2511 7063. **HKES** = Hong Kong Exhibition Services, Unit 902, 9th Fl, Shiu Lam Bldg, 23 Luard Road, Wanchai, Hong Kong. Tel: 2804 1500; Fax: 2528 3103. **Reed** = Reed Exhibition Companies, 19th F, 8 Commercial Tower, 8 Sun Yip Street, Chaiwan, Hong Kong. Tel: 2824 0330; Tlx: 62270 CEG HX; Fax: 2824 0246.

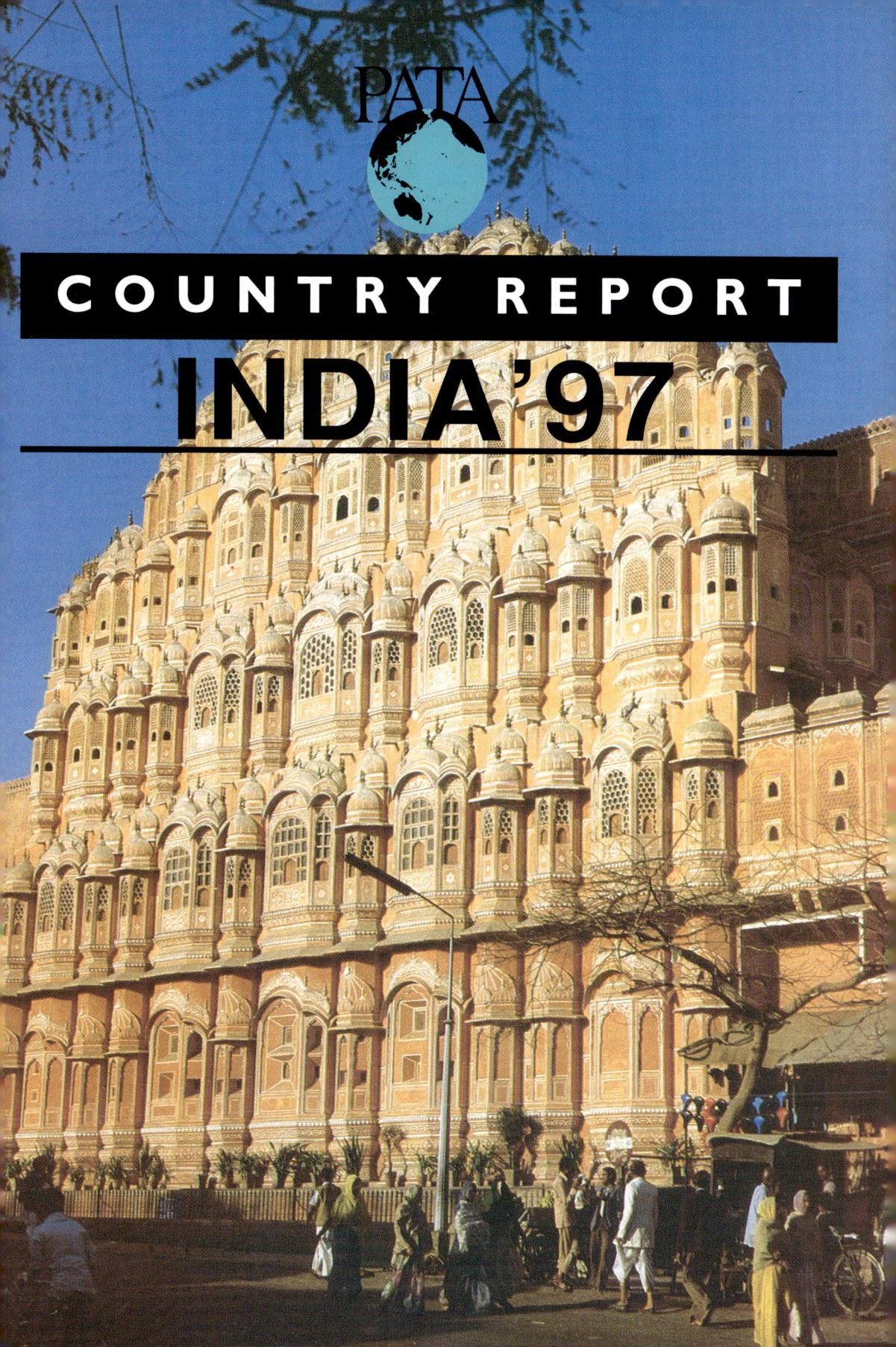

India

Doing Business

Investment Policy

India's open door policy to foreign investment got back on course in 1997 after a period in political limbo. Instigated in 1991 and responsible for several years of burgeoning economic growth, the policy was hit by a rising tide of nationalism, chiefly from the Hindu National Party, which advocates no foreign participation in India, in the run up to the 1996 general election, prompting many other potential investors to rethink their plans about the country. Many investors took a step back and adopted a 'wait and see' policy while the country went to the polls.

In the event, the new coalition government, with some adjustments, advocated the continuation of economic reforms, boosting what had been a lacklustre period for the Mumbai stock exchange and prompting analysts to predict that foreign investment and production would revive in the second half of 1997.

The lack of overseas confidence in India began as early as 1994. While efforts were being made by the outgoing government to lure back investors during late 1995, fears of nationalism had also turned India's stock market jittery. After a promising start to 1995, the market had plunged 25% by mid-year and remained static in the run up to the elections. Real GDP growth, meanwhile, fell below the forecast 5.7% for 1995, compared with 5.5% in 1994 and 3.8% in 1993, further underlining the first fault in the growth spiral brought about by reforms.

India attracted an estimated US$1.3 billion in foreign investment in 1994, a small amount compared with countries like China or Indonesia but significant for a country that until the beginning of the decade was a virtual no-go area for foreign business and on the brink of defaulting on its vast foreign debt.

Since 1991 and the introduction of reforms, India had swiftly paid off an emergency International Monetary Fund loan ahead of schedule and large multinationals like Coca Cola had ploughed millions of dollars into a market of more than 900 million consumers, including a growing middle class of about 200 million, thirsty for overseas goods, management, input or participation.

Understanding local as much as national politics is the key to investment, say analysts, a clear warning that some states are more open to foreign participation than others. They say every foreign business enterprise, however small, must be considered in provincial rather than national terms. For, whatever the federal rules and regulations, most decisions are taken at a provincial level.

This same diversity of opinions and attitudes shaped by local politics, with local control, needs to be taken into account by individual business visitors as they explore a vastly fragmented market whose only common strands require finding a good local agent and an Indian partner in good standing. Red tape may generally have been halved through liberalisation, but India still presents a bureaucratic minefield to the unwary at local, provincial and, ultimately, national level.

Most Indian companies, as well as state agencies, field large squads of minor executives and reaching decision makers can take days, or even weeks, before an idea or a plan can be properly presented or receive attention.

Old British etiquette is deemed a business essential by executives who are otherwise fond of deriding their old colonial masters for saddling them with such complicated officialdom. Appointments should always be made well in advance, in writing, with reconfirmation days before - but don't always expect a reply.

Contradictions are part of everyday Indian business life and the visitor must be prepared for deals which are seemingly signed, sealed and delivered to fall through at the last minute for any one of a thousand apparently inexplicable reasons, usually one of the myriad permits required in triplicate.

An Aladdin's Cave of opportunity India may again be, but traversing the always twisting and turning tunnel towards its business jewels can be time-consuming and exhausting. The same is true of getting around. Airports and flights have improved in recent years, thanks to an influx of private carriers. So have hotels, due to increasing competition and international management.

But prices for the captive business market are high, and not generally matched by services which too often can be non-existent, slow or erratic. Indian executives shrug and accept the shortcomings and beg patience and understanding from visitors. It is easy to comply. Indians generally are generous hosts, excellent conversationalists and avid whisky drinkers.

Business awareness, etiquette and practice

Social/meetings: All visitors should remove footwear when entering Hindu, Sikh, Muslim or Jain places of worship. Photography is prohibited or restricted in the case of protected monuments, wildlife sanctuaries, women, airports, bridges, railway stations or beggars. Greeting should be done by tilting the head and folding hands together rather than by a hand-shake. Never offer the left hand in greeting or in giving anything. Women are generally confined to the background in Indian homes.
Business: English is widely used in commercial circles. Indian businessmen welcome visitors and are very hospitable. Most entertaining is done in hotels or private clubs. Officialdom and bureaucracy is overpowering. It is usual to tip waiters, guides and drivers but not civil servants (since this could be seen as a bribe).
Dress: Suit and tie not essential for business meetings, except for board meetings and important social functions. Female business travellers should avoid wearing trousers, short skirts or tight clothing.

Tourism Update

General Developments

The number of visitors into India increased 12.6% in 1995 to 2,123,683, passing the two million level. The target for 2000 is five million, and the government expects to spend US$11.7 million to reach that total. In an interview, the director-general of tourism targetted a 20% increase in 1996, with the largest growth coming from Asia; but overall growth that year was running at about 7%.

The country's main market in 1995 was still the UK, with a 11.4% increase to 334,827. It was followed by Bangladesh, up 12.8% to 318,474, and the US, up 15.2% to 203,343. The big growth in the top five was from Sri Lanka, up 28.3% to 114,157. The fifth largest market, Germany, increased only 4.3% to 89,040.

There is also a special effort to encourage domestic travel, now at 100m trips annually. Domestic traffic has become an important share of business for the industry, even for the deluxe hotels. For instance, it represents 30% of business at the Delhi Hilton, and Hilton forecasts 40% domestic at its Madras hotel, due to open in 1997. In five years, Hilton believes domestic traffic at its Indian hotels could be 50-60%.

Despite its relatively-small size, India is one of the top five markets with the largest growth in agency locations (others are Indonesia, Malaysia, Taiwan, Thailand).

IATA's BSP plan (a centralised billings system) for travel agencies, was launched in India in 1996, and was expected to have 1200 agency participants by mid-1997. The number of tickets issued is expected to increase 6% yearly.

In the services sector, four bidders were shortlisted to take over duty-free from state-owned India Tourism Development Corporation. ITDC was paying airports US$1400 (Rs50,000) per square metre annually.

And there are plans to expand the country's luxury-train routes.

India plans to install satellite navigation technology for FANS - which means greater flexibility and capacity in airways - the highways of the sky. The first region due to be operational is Calcutta, which will allow more airways to be opened around the Bay of Bengal, which has been a bottleneck. At its peak, 100 flights daily operate through the area controlled by Calcutta. This FANS development could at least double capacity.

Aviation

There has been liberalization on domestic air services, and a number of private airlines are offering services to challenge the long-established domestic airline, Indian Airlines.

The strongest of the newcomers is Jet Airways, established only in 1992. At end-1996 it was operating 12 B737s of various models, and it ordered 10 more B737s -- four -400s, and six -800s (a stretched version of the -400). Deliveries are due to start in 1997 and continue through 2000. But some new challengers have had difficulties.

Modiluft, leasing aircraft as part of an alliance with Lufthansa, lost aircraft in 1996 following a dispute with Lufthansa over aircraft lease payments. East West, the first leading contender, had to return three of its eight aircraft to the lessor, and suspended flights in 1996. And another previously-growing challenger, Damania, was taken over by NEPC.

A proposal by Singapore Airlines and Tata Industries (whose founder created what is now Air India) to form a domestic airline still awaits government approval.

This has meant tough competition for government-owned Indian Airlines, which has now been losing money since 1989. A study in 1996 proposed 50% privatisation.

Air India is also going through change. Currently operating nearly 30 aircraft, the airline hopes to start operating 10 more aircraft - either A340s or B777s - from 1998. The aim is to have a 54-aircraft fleet by 2000.

In 1998, the first of the new aircraft will be based in Delhi. This is the first time aircraft will be based outside Mumbai (bombay) and it will enable the airline to reduce some of its multi-stop intercontinental flights.

Inside Air India's aircraft, the number of business-class seats has been reduced from 25 to 22 to allow a 2x2x2 configuration, and PTVs have been installed in first- and business-class in A310s and B747-400s.

A number of new routes are planned. Chicago and Zurich were added in 1996, and Bandar Seri Begawan, Madrid, Seoul, and Sydney were to be added before the end of 1997.

An important development in 1996 was a no-strike agreement with the unions, which helped the airline to achieve a 90% on-time departure rate. Air India expects 15-16% growth in the year through March 1997, meaning it will have sold more than 3 million seats.

In other news, both All Nippon Airways and Japan Airlines have added routes Tokyo-Delhi, and JAL has also started Osaka-Delhi.

Hotels

About 36,000 more hotel rooms are planned in the categorised sector, compared with 56,000 rooms now (and 200,000 in total). The relative shortage of 4-5 star accommodation in Delhi in 1996 allowed the municipality to impose a further 10% 'luxury tax' on top hotels' rates. And many international groups have moved in.

Hilton signed with Bharat Hotels in 1996, taking over Bharat's Holiday Inn Crowne Plaza in Delhi, and two projects in Mumbai and Goa. The agreement could bring Hilton hotels to Ahmedabad, Bangalore, Calcutta, Chandigarh, Cochin, Hyderabad and Jaipur. The Madras Hilton is now due to open in July 1997. Hilton also plans a 300-room beach club, near the city.

Radisson, which ended its contract with

ITDC at the start of the 1990s, signed with Overseas Indian company Saraf Industries to develop 20 hotels in South Asia countries including India.

Two Country Inns (part of the Radisson group) are being built in Mumbai and Delhi, and the company is looking for hotels in Bangalore, Calcutta, Madras, Pune & Surat. And India's Leela group finally signed at end-1996 for Four Seasons to manage its 248-room Goa hotel, its second hotel being built in Mumbai, and a new one in Bangalore. Leela is also looking for projects in Delhi and Madras, with both likely to be managed by Four Seasons.

Century Hotels has signed with the Mahindra Group to manage Mahindra's Guestline hotels under the brandname *Guestline Century*. It has hotels in Bangalore, Mumbai, and Tirupati, projects in Kolhapur, Lonawala, Udaipur, Vijaywada, and sites in four other centres.

Marriott's plans for a Delhi property have foundered but they are hoping to open a Jaipur hotel in 1998 or 1999. Meanwhile Sydney-based SPHC have not managed to find partners for Travelodges they wanted to open in Goa and Bangalore.

In Agra, the 83-room Howard Park Plaza, part of the Park Plaza group, has opened. And the Mughal Sheraton is adding 65 rooms, convention centre, and other facilities.

Among the local groups, Oberoi plans to open in 1997 the first of planned deluxe resorts in India - the 71-room Rajvilas in Jaipur.

Following a concept introduced by Amanresorts, its Jaipur resort will have 52 rooms, 14 luxury tents and two villas. Also, despite the apparent impasse with Accor (Oberoi has the franchise for Accor brands in India), a Novotel is due in Jaipur in 1997.

But Oberoi is developing its own similar Trident brand at a more rapid pace.

India's Welcomgroup (14 hotels and 2500 rooms, of which seven are Sheraton franchises) plans to add 1500-2000 rooms over the next five years. This will include 100 more rooms at its Maurya Sheraton in Delhi, and two 450-room hotels - near Mumbai airport, and Calcutta - both due end-1998. It also has a site for a 300/350-room Bangalore hotel. All three should be Sheratons. Welcomgroup is also adding small hotels in Visakhapatnam, Jaisalmer, and a palace property in Kota. Also, it wants hotels in Cochin and Goa, and a second in Delhi.

The country's largest private group, Taj Hotels, added four small hotels in 1996.

What to See

In India there is never a shortage of things to see. Starting from the Taj Mahal, then to the Red Fort at Agra, Fatehpur Sikri, Khajuraho, the palaces of Rajasthan and the beautiful lakes of Udaipur, New Delhi, Kashmir and the houseboats on Dal Lake and Goa the list seems to go on and on.

In New Delhi just wonder at the Lutyens dream of the capital city and its broad avenues and splendid buildings. Then compare this with the crowded streets and Moghul architecture of Old Delhi close by. In fact the Moghuls left a string of forts and palaces right across Northern India, including the Taj Mahal (which is, of course, a mausoleum), the pink city of Jaipur in Rajasthan and the yellow city of Jaisalmer in the same state plus the old ghost city of Fatehpur Sikri which are all grouped together in an area known as the Golden Triangle.

While in business-like Bombay there is the Gateway of India close to the Taj Mahal Hotel, its magnificent central railway station and university buildings. It's also possible to pay a visit to Bombay's glamorous film studios. There are also the caves at Elephanta. Calcutta, the old British capital, has perhaps some of India's finest colonial architecture although much of it is now in a poor state of repair.

Up in the foothills of the Himalayas there is Shimla, the British summer capital of India and a place designed for complete relaxation. To the north, in the Kulu Valley you can experience the tranquility of the mountains.

Goa, too, is an ideal place in which to relax. This former Portuguese colony has an atmosphere of its own: street cafes, white-washed churches and overhanging balconies. Many Indians still consider a trip to Goa as a visit to a foreign country.

Over on the other coast in easy-going Madras there are a number of sights to consider - Fort St George, built by the British East India Company, the San Thome Cathedral and any number of Hindu temples.

There is never a dull moment in India's former RAJ capital and largest city and Calcutta leaves no one unaffected by its teeming streets, people and cultures. From Calcutta it's possible to take the train up to Darjeeling, the last leg of which takes place on a miniature railway which winds its way through deep jungles, tea gardens and pine forests - truly one of the world's great journeys.

India's wildlife parks provide shelter to a wide variety of fauna. The tiger can be glimpsed in some jungle locations. Then there are several species of deer, wild boar and some of the world's best bird sanctuaries.

Shopping

Indian craftsmen have been perfecting their skills for centuries. Each region of the subcontinent has its own specialities from hand-crafted silk, through carpets to the finest Moghul jewellery. The goods on offer are often exotic and beautifully made. The bazaars are the best places to find to goods at competitive prices, but expect to haggle. Otherwise, you can try the state-run emporia where there are fixed prices.

Delhi, Bombay and other big cities have areas specialising in certain handmade items, such as jewellery, leather goods, clothes, fabrics, carpets etc. Spices and Indian tea are also worth buying. Indian craftsmen are famous for the quality of their workmanship and you will find remarkably good value for money from many of the shops that sell these locally-made goods.

For quality items, then it's probably just as well to buy from the shopping arcades that grace most large hotels. Similar shops can be found elsewhere and often have cheaper prices as there is no fixed rental to pay to the hotel.

Opposite the exclusive Bombay Gymkhana Club there is an entire street that sells western clothes at only a fraction of what they would cost in Europe or North America. Many are end-runs of garments destined for export and many stalls have the latest fashions. The street is also good for children's wear. In the streets around the Taj Mahal Hotel there are any number of small shops and stalls selling almost everything including pirated videos and books.

In Delhi, the Connaught Place area is considered to be best area to buy as well as the nearby Janpath Lane, which offers garments and jewellery. The Cottage Industries Emporium just off Janpath offers hassle-free shopping at controlled prices. The Mini Market off Janpath is good for things like woollen shawls, skirts and mirror work. The Hauz Khas village, next to a spectacular restored Moghul fort, opened in 1992 and offers designer label shops, most open til 10 pm, in an historic setting as well as a choice of restaurants.

Expect to haggle even in the best stores, so if you have an Indian friend take him or her along to assist you in the bargaining process. And remember, it's forbidden to export antiques and art objects over 100 years old.

Getting Around

Indian Airlines has an extensive network stretching the length and breadth of the subcontinent and extending to neighbouring states such as Sri Lanka and the Maldives.

It can often be difficult to find a seat on some of these services - especially during peak periods. IC's in-flight service also leaves much to be desired; its adherence to schedules can also be a bit erratic.

The only alternative is Indian State Railways, which offers an equally impressive route system which is the world's second largest. Air-conditioned trains ply between the big cities and some journeys take two days or more. Rail travel is a great way of seeing India and outside AC (air-conditioned) class it's cheap, but the trains are slow and are best suited to those with time to spare. In any case, AC class is often more expensive than the air fare for the same journey so it's not highly recommended for business travellers.

A train journey strongly recommended if

time allows is the *Palace on Wheels*, an air-conditioned luxury train that takes a week to tour Rajasthan via Delhi-Jaipur-Chittorgarh-Udaipur-Jasailmer-Jodhpur-Agra-Delhi. Prices are US$ 300 per night per person sharing between September-April only.

A ride in an Indian taxi comes complete with its fair share of the thrills and excitement through the crowded streets, but miraculously you always seem to get to where you want to go. Beggars can be a nuisance at traffic lights. Fares are incredibly cheap, even though some drivers may try to overcharge foreigners. The metered fare often has no relation to the final figure, which must be worked out on a separate cardboard sheet that is secreted under the dashboard. Also remember that most taxis do not have air-conditioning.

Many business visitors prefer to hire a car and driver for the day as this saves the hassle of finding a taxi in the street and is only marginally more expensive than taking individual rides. Most rented cars are *Ambassadors* - a version of the British 1950s Hillman - extremely reliable but seldom air-conditioned. Car rental is not really an option with the congestion of many parts of Bombay, Calcutta and Delhi. Neither are three-wheeled auto-rickshaws. which are in any case not allowed into the centre of cities such as Bombay. They are also extremely dangerous and it's worth noting that Delhi recorded nearly 2000 road deaths in 1992 - or around five a day.

Entertainment

Unless you look hard for it, India's nightlife is generally quiet and laid-back. Both Bombay and Delhi appear to go to bed early as most entertaining is done at home. Indians will often invite foreign business guests to their homes rather than taking them to a restaurant. Many Indians believe that home cooking is far superior to what is available from restaurants outside and the wives of local executives often go to great lengths to prepare meals for visitors.

Delhi, Bombay, Calcutta and Madras all claim to have some of India's best restaurants. In Bombay, there is the *Khyber* close to the Taj Mahal Hotel, which itself boasts both excellent Chinese and Indian restaurants. In fact, India has some surprisingly good Chinese restaurants. But even a city the size of Bombay only has five or six first-class independent restaurants that are not linked to the major hotels. (see the *Restaurant Selection* following India Hotels in this publication).

There are one or two discos and these are usually located in the big hotels. In Delhi, for example, there is *Annabelles* at the Hilton and *CJ's* at the Meridien. Many others appear to have closed only to be replaced by expensive supper clubs with live bands and dance-floors.

Most leading hotels have good bars, with excellent service although not much in the way of foreign drinks. Local beer is good - particularly in Bangalore, while Indian whisky seems to be an acquired taste. Otherwise there do not appear to be many places to go for a casual drink.

Amazingly, both Bombay and Delhi have their own home-grown red light districts. The intensely depressing "cages" in Bombay house sad-looking young prostitutes from the countryside. While in Delhi there is the notorious GB Road strip, which many old hands claim to be superior to Bombay.

Furthermore, the evening papers sometimes run ads for so-called cabarets, which are just euphemisms for cheap strip joints. But this is not the Patpong Road and these dingy places are best left to locals.

Leisure

The good news is that leisure facilities are fast improving throughout India and are becoming more widely available outside the preserves of the old colonial club network. India now has a spectacular variety of sports from which to choose, many of which are geared to foreign visitors.

Cricket is the national sport and is followed passionately, if not to say obsessively, by most locals. Most of the big cities have large cricket stadiums where in winter international matches can be seen. Field hockey is also popular and soccer is now attracting bigger crowds, particularly in states such as Bengal and Kerala.

Horse racing has a devoted following and can be seen on tracks that are largely a hangover from the British Raj. The same goes for polo. Bird-watching, fishing and other pursuits can easily be arranged.

Most large international-class hotels cater for health enthusiasts with gymnasia and saunas. Others have good swimming pools.

Down in Bangaram in Lakshadweep (a group of islands off the coast of Cochin), there is probably some of the world's best diving plus sail-boarding and snorkelling.

All motor-power watersports are banned in the area so there is no water-skiing or paragliding. India's top beach resorts in Goa, at Kovalam in the far south, Madras and Juhu Beach, Bombay are all well prepared for watersports.

In the Himalayas, hill trekking and white-water rafting attract the more adventurous. There are also opportunities for skiing in Kashmir (political conditions permitting) and ice-skating. There is also ballooning, hang-gliding and gliding plus fishing for trout and salmon in the mountain streams. Fishing is also possible in the mountains in the southern states of Tamil Nadu and Kerala. India has many fine golf courses, mainly remaining from British colonial days.

Arrival & Departure

Bombay's International Airport is 37km north of the city. A bus service operates to the Air India office for Rp 50. But better to get a taxi (about Rps 225) into the city. Journey time is about 30 minutes.

Delhi's Indira Gandhi International Airport is 21km south-west of the city. Beware of having to pay by credit card for any overweight at check-in. There seems to be only one dispenser in the airport and this is a 15-minute walk away! Journey time is about 40 minutes and fares about Rp 200. Delhi and Bombay airports have duty free shops both for in- and outgoing passengers.

From Calcutta, a 24-hour bus service operates to the Indian Airlines' city office for Rp 10. Alternatively a taxi costs about Rp125.

Madras' airport is some 14 kms from the city and a one-way taxi costs about Rp 110.

The Indian government levies a Rps 150 tax on all departing passengers to surrounding states - Bhutan, Pakistan, Nepal, Sri Lanka, Nepal, Bangladesh, Burma, Afghanistan and the Maldives. There is a Rps 300 tax on passengers taking flights to countries further afield.

Useful Addresses

Main Chambers of Commerce & Associated Bodies (National)

All India Exporters Chamber
Janmabhoomi Chambers, 29 Walchand Hirachand Marg, Fort, Bombay 40001
Associated Chambers of Commerce & Trade of India
Allahabad Bank Bldg, 17 Parliament St, New Delhi 110001. Tel: 310704; Tlx: 031-61754; Fax: 312193
Bombay Chamber of Commerce
Po Box 473, Mackinnon Mackenzie Bldg, 4 Shoorji Vallabhdas Marg, Ballard Estate, Bombay 400038. Tel: 264681; Tlx: 011-73571
Calcutta Chamber of Commerce
18H Park Street, Calcutta
Bengal Chamber of Commerce & Industry
PO Box 280, Royal Exchange, 6 Netaji Subhas Rd, Calcutta 70001; Tel: 20-8393; Tlx: 021-7369
Bengal National Chamber of Commerce & Industry
23 R N Mukherjee Rd, Calcutta 70001
Delhi Chamber of Commerce
Delbar Bldg, D B Gupta Rd, Pahargani, New Delhi 110055
Federation of Andhra Pradesh Chamber of Commerce & Industry
11-6-841 Red Hills, PO Box 14, Hyderabad 500004
Federation of Chambers of Commerce and Industry of India
Federation House, Tansen Marg, New Delhi 110001. Tel: 331 92521
Indian Motion Pictures' Association
Sandhurst Bldg, Sardar Vallabhai Patel Rd, Bombay 40004
Madras Chamber of Commerce
Dare House Annexe, 44 Moore St, Madras 600001. Tel: 451451/451871; Tlx: 41-7306
Punjab, Haryana & Delhi Chamber of Commerce
PHD House, Thapar Fl, 4/2 Siri Institutional Area. Opp. Asian Games Village, Delhi 110055
Southern India Chamber of Commerce & Industry Indian Chamber Bldgs, PO Box 1208, Esplanade, Madras 600108

Police/Hospitals/Post Offices (Delhi)

EmergencyEmergency Police: dial 100; ambulance dial 102
All India Institute of Medical Sciences
(Also 24-hour chemist). Ansari Nagar, Sri Aurobindo Marg, New Delhi. Tel: 61123
Kalvati Saran Childrens' Hospital
Bangla Sahib Road. Tel: 353408
St Stephen's Hospital
Tess Hazan. Tel: 2511 488
Head Post Office
Parliament Street. Tel: 385605. (Open 0100-1830 Mon-Sat.)
Eastern Court Post Office
Jan Path. Tel 3321878. (Open 1000-1830 Mon-Sat)
Central Telegraph Office
Easter Court, Jan Path. Tel: 332 4010. (Open 24 hrs)
Overseas Communication Service
Bangla Sahib Road. Tel: 186 or 187. (Open 24 hrs)

Air Couriers

DHL: Bombay (22) 261 3996/822 4055
Calcutta (33) 242 6936;
Madras: (44) 234 9771;
New Delhi: (11) 689 8273;
Federal Express: Bombay (22) 422 1588
TNT Worldwide Express: Bombay (22) 839 1597; Delhi (11) 461 0981; Madras: (44) 827 7722. **UPS**: Bombay (22) 611 4404

Car Hire

Budget:
Bombay (22) 493 9726/493 9730
New Delhi: (11) 371 5657; Central Reservations (11) 331 8600; Fax: 371 2990
Europcar Interrent: Tel: Delhi 647 4835
Wheels (Hertz Self- and Chauffeur-Drive): Tel: Bombay (22) 202 3734; Fax: 204 6365

Tourist Offices

Government of India Tourist Office
88 Jan Path, New Delhi. Tel: 332 0088
India Tourist Dev't Corporation, L-block Connaught Place, New Delhi.Tel: 3320005

India Key Fact File

Passport Requirements:
All visitors, except those from Bhutan and Nepal, require a visa. Certain parts of the country - mostly in the North-East are 'restricted areas' and require special permits. For visiting Bhutan itself, visitors require a visa from the Royal Bhutan Government or their missions in Delhi or New York.

Currency:
Rupee (RS). 100 Paise = 1 RS

Exchange rate:
US$1 = RS 36. £1 = RS 58.2 *(March 97)*

Currency restrictions:
No restrictions on the importation of foreign currency or travellers' cheques. However receipts must be kept of all currency transactions made during a stay, so that residual Indian currency may be reconverted on departure.

IDD Code: 91 *followed by....*
Agra 562; Ahmedabad 272; Allahabad 532; Bangalore 812; Baroda 265; Bhopal 755; Bombay 22; Calcutta 33; Cochin 484; Goa 832; Hyderabad 842; Jaipur 141; Madras 44; Mangalore 824; New Delhi 11; Poona 212; Srinagar 194; Trivandrum 471.

Electricity Supply:
220 volts AC 50 HZ

Language: Hindi and English

Time:
GMT + 5.5 hours; EST + 10.5 hours

Business hours:
Commercial offices: 0930-1700 (Mon-Fri); 0930-1300 (Sat).
Banks: 1000-1400 (Mon-Fri); 1000-1230 (Sat).
Shops: 0930-1800 Monday to Saturday

Customs & Entry:
Duty free allowance is 200 cigarettes (or 50 cigars or 250 gms of tobacco); alcoholic liquor up to 0.95 litres. Narcotics, weapons, plants, gold and silver bullion and non-current coins are prohibited.

Health Requirements:
Yellow fever vaccination certificate if arriving from an infected area; inoculations against Cholera and Typhoid recommended; malaria exists - no certificate required but course of pills recommended; do not eat ice cream, undercooked meat, unpeeled fruit or vegetables, drink tap water or have ice in drinks.

Climate/best time to visit:
Hot and tropical with variations according to region. Coolest from mid-November to mid-March (Delhi 7-20°C; Bombay/Madras 20-30°C; Calcutta 15-25°C). Hottest April-June (Delhi 28-40°C; Bombay/Madras 27-35°C; Calcutta 24-34°C). Monsoon rains in most regions June-September. Best months for business visits: October to March.

National Holidays 1997
26 January Republic Day; IIdu'l Fitr Feb 9; Good Friday March 28; Idu'z zuha (Bakrid) April 18; Mahavir Jayanti April 20; Buddha Purnima May 22; 15 Aug Independence Day; 2 Oct Mahatma Gandhi's birthday; Oct 11 Vijaya Dasami ; Oct 30 Deepavali ; Nov 14 Guru Nanak's Birthday ; 25 Dec Christmas Day.
Other local festivals and special events.

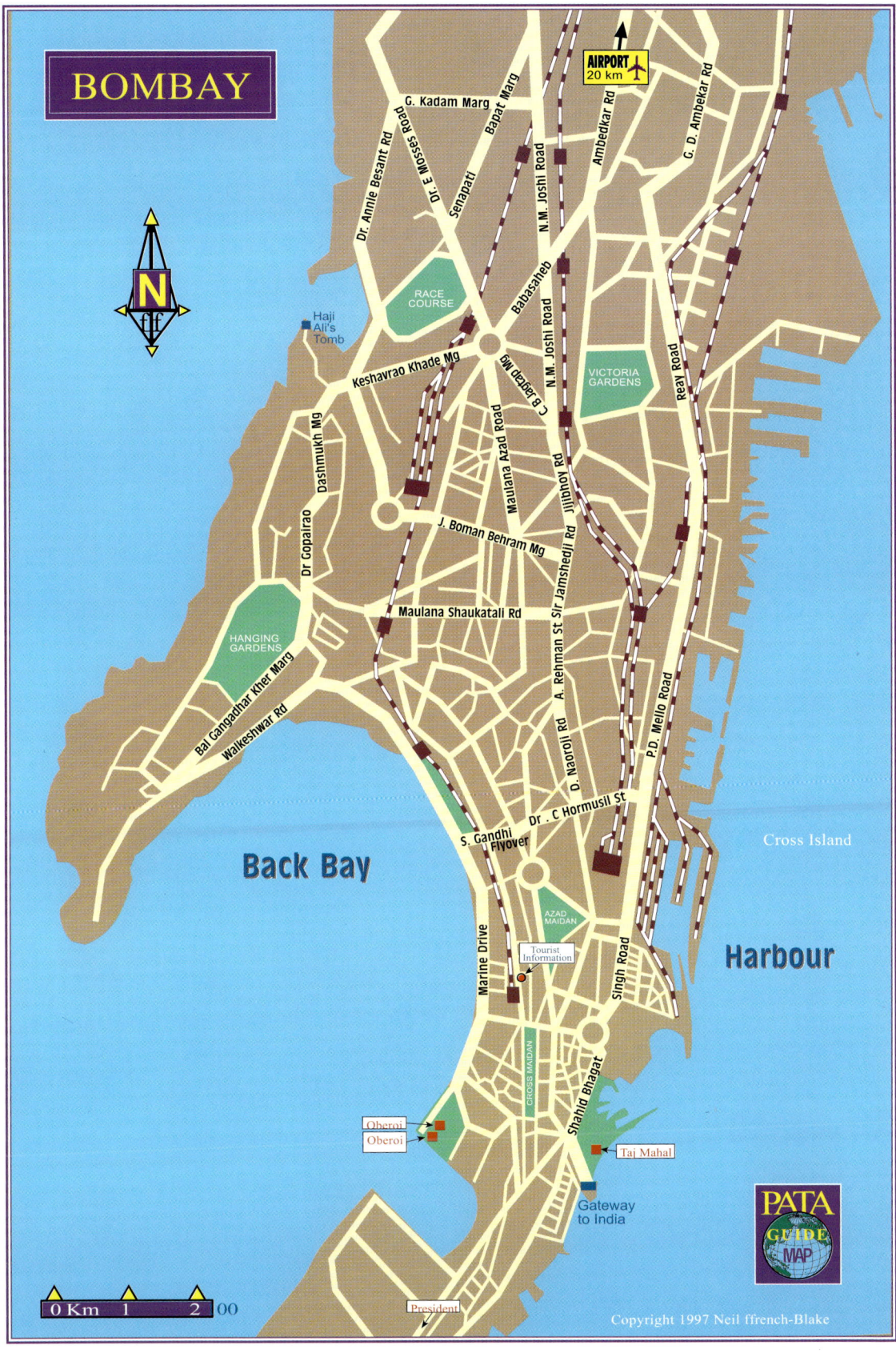

Bombay (Mumbai) Hotel Reference Table

Hotel (listed in price order)	SINGLE ROOM RATE From (US$)	LOCATION	NUMBER OF ROOMS	NUMBER OF SUITES	CONFERENCE FACILITIES	EXHIBITION SPACE	LARGEST BANQUET NUMBER	BUSINESS CENTRE	SWIMMING POOL (0 = indoor)	TENNIS COURT	HEALTH CLUB	VIDEO FILMS
The Oberoi Bombay	305-335	Nariman Pt	315	22	●	●	2000	●	●	-	●	-
Taj Mahal	265	Colaba	554	46	●	-	-	●	●	-	●	-
The Oberoi Towers	260-285	Nariman Pt	630	20	●	-	3000	●	●	●	●	●
Hotel President	225	Colaba	299	20	●	-	700	●	●	-	●	●
Leela Kempinski Hotel	195-235	Airport	282	-	-	-	-	-	-	-	-	-
Taj Inter-Continental	190	Colaba	306	-	●	-	500	●	●	●	●	●
Holiday Inn Juhu Beach	165-275	Juhu Beach	176	15	●	●	180	●	●	●	●	●
Wmgroup Searock Sheraton	150-215	Bandra	401	99	●	●	300	●	●	●	●	●
Ambassador Hotel	120	City	127	-	-	-	-	-	-	-	-	-
Ramada Hotel Palm Grove	120	Juhu Beach	113	-	-	-	-	-	●	●	-	-
Sun-N-Sand Hotel	111	Juhu Beach	124	-	-	-	-	-	-	-	-	-
Fariyas Hotel	107	Colaba	83	-	●	-	-	-	-	-	-	-
Centaur Juhu Beach	88	Juhu Beach	288	-	●	-	200	-	●	●	●	-
Centaur Hotel	80	Airport	288	-	-	-	-	-	●	-	-	-
Hotel Nataraj	54	Marine Dr.	83	-	-	-	-	-	-	-	-	-
Hotel Horizon	35	Juhu Beach	161	-	-	-	-	-	-	-	-	-
West End Hotel	35	Marine Ls	80	-	-	-	-	-	-	-	-	-
Diplomat Hotel	22	Colaba	52	-	-	-	-	-	-	-	-	-
Airport Plaza	20	Airport	81	-	-	-	-	-	-	-	-	-

Delhi Hotel Reference Table

Hotel	SINGLE ROOM RATE From (US$)	LOCATION	NUMBER OF ROOMS	NUMBER OF SUITES	CONFERENCE FACILITIES	EXHIBITION SPACE	LARGEST BANQUET NUMBER	BUSINESS CENTRE	SWIMMING POOL	TENNIS COURT	HEALTH CLUB	VIDEO FILMS
New Delhi Hilton	325-425	New Delhi	445	-	●	-	550	●	●	-	●	●
The Oberoi New Delhi	305	New Delhi	259	31	●	-	-	●	●	●	●	●
Taj Palace New Delhi	275-350	New Delhi	421	34	●	●	450	●	●	●	●	●
Ashok Hotel	225	Chanakyapuri	460	111	●	●	3000	●	●	●	●	●
Hyatt Regency Delhi	275-310	Ramakrishna'm	518	19	●	●	500	●	●	●	●	●
Le Meridien New Delhi	275-300	New Delhi	355	59	●	-	500	●	●	●	●	-
Wmgroup Maurya Sheraton	245-330	New Delhi	534	72	●	●	450	●	●	●	●	●
Taj Mahal Hotel	245-330	New Delhi	271	26	●	-	150	●	●	●	●	●
Best Western Surya	230	Friends Colony	203	27	●	●	500	●	●	O	●	●
The Park Hotel	220	Parliament	230	-	●	-	300	●	●	-	●	●
Claridges Hotel	145	Chanakyapuri	140	-	●	●	900	●	●	-	●	●
Parkroyal	125	Nehru Place	240	6	●	●	400	●	●	-	-	●
Samrat Hotel	120	Chanakyapuri	235	2	●	●	800	-	●	-	●	●
Hotel Siddarth	120-150	Pusa Road	98	-	●	●	350	-	●	-	●	●
Radisson Hotel Delhi	95-110	Nat H'way 8	258	-	-	-	-	-	-	-	-	-
The Oberoi Maidens	85	Civil Lines	53	-	●	-	-	-	●	●	-	-
Hotel Vasant Continental	70	Ramakrishna'm	110	-	●	●	600	●	●	-	●	●

Rest of India Hotel Reference Table

Hotel	SINGLE ROOM RATE From (US$)	LOCATION	NUMBER OF ROOMS	NUMBER OF SUITES	CONFERENCE FACILITIES	EXHIBITION SPACE	LARGEST BANQUET NUMBER	BUSINESS CENTRE	SWIMMING POOL	TENNIS COURT	HEALTH CLUB	VIDEO FILMS
The Oberoi Bangalore	225	Bangalore	130	-	●	-	250	●	●	●	●	●
Madras Hilton	200-275	Madras	237	-	●	●	500	●	●	-	●	●
Oberoi Grand	205-235	Calcutta	210	11	●	●	450	●	●	-	●	●
Taj Bengal Calcutta	205-300	Calcutta	219	11	●	-	800	●	●	●	●	●
Park Hotel	200	Calcutta	150	17	●	●	500	●	●	-	-	-
The Lake Palace	180-200	Udaipur	59	15	●	●	200	-	●	-	●	●
Taj West End Hotel	180-250	Bangalore	129	10	●	●	850	●	●	●	●	●
Wmgroup Mughal Sheraton	175-290	Agra	300	15	●	●	400	●	●	●	●	●
Taj Coromandel	170-270	Madras	201	-	●	●	500	●	●	-	●	●

Rest of India Hotel Reference Table

Hotel (listed in price order)	Single Room Rate From (US$)	Location	Number of Rooms	Number of Suites	Conference Facilities	Exhibition Space	Largest Banquet Number	Business Centre	Swimming Pool (0=indoor)	Tennis Court	Health Club	Video Films
Rambagh Palace	155-275	Jaipur	102	4	●	-	1000	●	●	●	●	-
Welcomgroup Umhaid Bhavan	145-180	Jodhpur	206	12	●	-	500	-	●	●	●	●
Wmgp Windsor Manor Sheraton	145-275	Bangalore	240	12	●	●	500	●	●	●	●	●
Welcomgroup Chola Sheraton	140-230	Madras	98	2	●	●	800	●	●	-	●	●
Welcomgroup Park Sheraton	140-230	Madras	291	9	●	●	850	●	●	●	●	●
Hotel Airport Ashok	140	Calcutta	136	12	●	●	1000	●	●	-	-	●
Jai Mahal Palace	137-175	Jaipur	96	18	●	-	150	●	●	●	-	●
Connemara Hotel	127	Madras	150	-	●	-	500	●	●	●	●	●
Wmgroup Rajputana Palace	125	Jaipur	201	17	●	-	500	●	●	●	●	●
Aquada Hermitage Villas	125	Goa	-	40	●	-	-	-	●	●	●	-
The Taj Mahal Hotel	125-140	Lucknow	1115	4	●	-	1000	●	●	●	●	●
Cidade de Goa	120	Goa	210	-	●	-	-	●	●	●	●	●
The Cecil	115-145	Simla	71	8	●	-	-	-	-	-	-	-
The Oberoi Clarkes	112	Simla	39	-	●	-	100	-	-	-	-	-
Kovalam Ashok Beach Resort	110-150	Kovalam	185	8	●	●	300	●	●	●	●	●
Hotel Ashok	110-120	Bangalore	163	16	●	-	500	●	●	●	●	●
Taj View Hotel	110	Agra	100	4	●	-	350	●	●	●	●	●
Taj Holiday Village	105-200	Goa	142	-	●	-	-	-	●	●	●	●
iv Newas Palace Hotel	105	Udaipur	-	33	-	-	-	-	●	-	-	-
Fort Aquada Beach Resort	105	Goa	106	24	●	-	250	●	●	●	●	●
Fisherman's Cove	103	Madras	100	-	●	-	-	-	●	●	●	-
The Oberoi Palm Beach	100	Gopalpur	20	-	●	-	-	-	●	●	-	-
Holiday Inn Bangalore	100-110	Bangalore	200	-	●	-	-	●	●	-	●	-
Novotel Agra	100	Agra	140	3	●	-	-	-	●	-	-	-
Hotel Clarks Shiraz	95-115	Agra	235	2	●	-	500	-	●	●	-	-
Hotel Clarks Amer	95-115	Jaipur	200	2	●	-	500	-	●	●	-	-
The Trident	95	Madras	158	10	●	-	150	●	●	-	●	●
Hotel Clarks Varanasi	95-115	Varanasi	260	-	●	-	150	-	●	-	●	●
Grand Kakatiya Hotel/Towers	90-160	Hyderabad	200	12	●	●	800	●	●	-	●	●
Malabar Hotel	90	Cochin	100	-	●	-	-	-	-	-	-	-
Welcomgroup Vadodara	85	Baroda	102	-	●	-	500	-	-	-	-	-
Krishna Oberoi	79-100	Hyderabad	256	15	●	-	900	●	●	●	●	●
The Trident	77	Ahmedabad	85	3	●	-	-	●	●	-	●	-
Hyderabad Gateway	75-95	Hyderabad	124	-	-	-	-	-	-	-	-	-
Welcomgroup Royal Castle	75-85	Khimsar	14	-	-	-	-	-	-	-	-	-
Hotel Taj Ganges	75	Varanasi	104	16	●	-	150	-	●	-	●	-
Oberoi Bhubaneswar	75	Bhubaneswar	60	5	●	-	-	-	●	●	●	-
Wmgp Usha Kiran Palace	65-75	Gwalior	27	-	●	-	-	-	-	●	-	-
Welcomgroup Bay Island	61-64	Andamans	48	-	●	-	100	-	●	-	-	-
Taj Residency	60	Bangalore	159	5	●	●	1000	-	●	-	●	●
Goa Renaissance Resort	54	Goa	118	10	●	-	400	●	●	●	●	-
Welcomgroup Rama Int'l	50-95	Aurangabad	102	-	●	-	-	-	●	-	-	-
Lalitha Mahal Palace	50	Mysore	46	8	●	-	60	-	●	●	●	-
Welcomgroup Maurya-Patna	50-80	Patna	80	-	●	-	-	●	●	-	-	-
Best Western Kenilworth	48	Calcutta	110	-	-	-	200	●	-	-	-	-
Best Western Howard Plaza	42	Agra	81	-	-	-	-	-	●	-	-	-
Best Western Mela Plaza	38-46	Ghaziabad	102	-	●	-	-	-	-	-	●	-
Gateway Hotel	38	Bangalore	90	8	●	-	300	●	●	-	●	-
Majorda Beach Resort	37	Goa	108	-	●	-	500	-	●	●	●	●
Samode Palace	35	Jaipur	50	-	-	-	-	-	●	-	-	-
Best Western Vicerory	34	Cochin	25	-	●	-	70	-	-	-	-	-
The Jass Oberoi	33	Khajuraho	94	-	●	-	-	-	●	-	-	-
The Trident	33-66	Agra	143	-	-	-	-	-	-	-	-	-
Best Western Rama Inn	30	Baroda	59	-	-	-	-	-	-	-	●	-
Centaur Lake View Hotel	30	Srinagar	251	3	●	-	-	-	●	-	-	-
The Oberoi Palace	30	Srinagar	101	-	●	-	250	●	-	-	-	-
Blue Diamond Hotel	30	Poona	114	-	-	-	-	-	●	-	●	●
Hotel Savera	30	Madras	125	-	-	-	-	-	●	-	-	-
Cama Hotel	30	Ahmedabad	55	-	●	-	-	●	●	-	-	-
Best Western Kenilworth	29-34	Bhubaneswar	110	-	-	-	-	-	●	-	-	-

India Hotels

Agra

Agra Deluxe Hotel   D
Fathebad Road, 282001
Tel: (562) 360110; Fax: (562) 331330

Hotel Clarks Shiraz   ○   D
54 Taj Rd, 282001
Tel: (562) 361421-29; Tlx: 0565-211;
Fax: (562) 331 2990

The Trident
Tajnagri Scheme, Fatehabad Road, 282001
Tel: (562) 368282; Tlx: 356 NOVIN;
Fax: (562) 360217

The Trident Agra is a garden hotel in the city of the Taj Mahal. As a prelude to both the product and the city, the hotel conceptualises the grandeur of the great Moghul emperors. Built from red sandstone, the Trident has all modern amenities to match the structure.

Accommodation & rates
143 rooms, Rp 1195-2350 + 23.25% tax

Credit cards accepted:
Amex, Diners, Bank America, Mastercharge, Visa

Meeting & conference facilities
Two meeting/conference rooms, capacity 60 persons each

Room services
Airconditioning, colour TV, direct-dial telephone, laundry/valet service, minibar, safety deposit box, 24-hr room/meal service, non-smoker bedrooms available

Business & other services
Car rental, travel centre, barber shop/beauty salon, newsstand/shops, secretarial services

Restaurants & Coffee Shops
La Brasserie (98) - Multi-Cuisine, open 0600-midnight

Taj View Hotel   C
Taj Ganj, Fatehabad Road, 282001
Tel: (0562) 331841; Fax: (0562) 361860

Rates quoted are subject to change without notice and are liable to 23.25% gov't tax (expenditure tax 10%; luxury tax 7%; sales tax on food 6.25%).

Welcomgroup Mughal Sheraton
Taj Ganj, Agra 282001, Uttar Pradesh
Tel: (562) 361701; Tlx: 056 - 5210;
Fax: (562) 361730

Spread across 24 acres, winner of the Aga Khan Award for excellence in architecture, clopse to Fatehpur Sikri in the city of the Taj Mahal. 12 kms from airport

Accommodation & rates*
300 rooms and suites. Single US$ 175-290; double US$ 190-305; suite US$ 700-725. Group tariff single US$ 130-178; double US$ 135-185

Credit cards accepted:
All major

Meeting & conference facilities
Four meeting/conference rooms, capacity 20-400, with audio-visual facilities; 3350 sq m exhibition space; largest reception 400

Room services
Airconditioning, colour TV, direct-dial telephone (ext. in bathroom), hairdryer, laundry/valet service, music/radio/alarm clock, safety deposit box, non-smoker bedrooms available, 24-hr room/meal service, video films, voice messaging

Business & other services
Business centre, executive floor, express checkout, airport pickup, car parking & rental, travel centre, taxi service, barber shop/beauty salon, newsstand/shopping arcade, guided tours

Sports & recreation
Tennis, badminton, mini-golf, croquet, jogging track, archery, darts, chess, health centre, biliards, home theatre, children's room, yoga, outdoor swimming pool, bird watching, royal horse carriage, folk entertainment, weekend disco

Restaurants & Coffee Shops
Mahjong Room (39) - Chinese,open 1230-1500/1930-2200; *Taj Bano* (176) - Multi-cuisine, open 0600-0900; *Nauratna* (76) - Indian, open 1230-1445/1930-2345; *Bagh - E-Bagar* (95) - Continental, open 0600-2245

International Sales Representatives
ITT Sheraton Worldwide

Ahmedabad

The Trident
Airport Cross Roads, Hansol, Ahmedabad
Tel: (79) 786444; Tlx: 121-6501 TAT;
Fax: (79) 7864454

The Trident Ahmedabad is strategically located and is close to the airport with easy access to Gandhinagar, the Naroda Industrial Area and a 20-minute drive from the city centre. The Trident is an elegant, low rise hotel designed around a landscaped central courtyard and with all modern facilities.

Accommodation & rates
61 singles Rp 2750; 24 doubles, Rp 3000; 3 suites Rp 4000-5000. + 25.75% tax

Credit cards accepted:
Amex, Andhra Bank Card, Central Card, Citibank, Diners, Mastercard, Visa

Meeting & conference facilities
Two meeting/conference rooms, capacity 100 persons each

Room services
Airconditioning, colour TV, direct-dial telephone, laundry/valet service, music/radio/alarm clock, 24-hr room/meal service

Business & other services
Business centre, airport pickup, car parking, travel centre, barber shop/beauty salon, newsstand/shops

Sports & recreation
Golf, massage, sauna, tennis

Restaurants & Coffee Shops
Ja Caranda (60) - Continental, Chinese & Indian, open 0600-0200; *Namada* (40) - Indian, open 1930-2300

Overseas Sales Representatives
Oberoi Hotels Worldwide Offices

Cama Hotel   ○   E
Khanpur Rd, 380001
Tel: (79) 550 5281; Fax: (79) 550 5285

Amritsar

Ritz Hotel   E
45 The Mall, 143001
Tel: (183) 66027; Tlx: 384242

Andamans

Welcomgroup Bay Island, Port Blair D
Marine Hill, Port Blair, Andaman & Nicobar

(Continued)

Islands 744101.Tel: (03192) 20881;
Tlx: 069 5207; Fax: (03192) 21389

Aurangabad

Taj Residency D
8N 12 Cidco, 431003
Tel: (240) 33501-5; Tlx: 745356; Fax: (240) 331223

Welcomgroup Rama International D
R-3, Chikalthana, Aurangabad 431210, Maharashtra
Tel: (240) 485441-4; Tlx: 0745-212; Fax: (240) 484768

Bangalore

Hotel Ashok
Kumara Kraupa High Grounds, 560001
Tel: 226 9462/225 0202; Tlx: 0845 2433; Fax: 225 0033. Internet: http://www.indiatourism.com *or* http://www.indianhotels.com

The gentle, graceful ambience of Bangalore, India's garden city, is amply reflected in its first 5-star hotel, the Ashok, one of the finest luxury hotels in southern India. Located on ten spacious acres in the High Grounds area of Bangalore.

Accommodation & rates
163 double, 16 suites. Single US$ 110-120; double/twin US$ 120-140; suite US$ 150-399

Credit cards accepted:
Amex, Visa, Citibank, Diners etc

Groups
5 meeting/function rooms, capacity 20-550; largest reception 5000

Room services
Airconditioning, colour TV, direct-dial telephone (ext. in bathroom), hairdryer, laundry/valet service, minibar, safety deposit box, trouser press, 24-hr room/meal service, in-house video films

Business & other services
Business centre, executive floor, express checkout, airport pickup, car parking & rental, travel & tour centre, taxi service, barber shop/beauty parlour, newsstand/shops

Sports & Recreation
Fitness centre/gym, golf (adjacent), tennis, massage, sauna, outdoor swimming pool

Restaurants & Coffee Shops
Coorg (90) - 24-hour coffee shop; *Lotus* (110) -Continental/Indian/Mughal, open 1230-1500/1930-2300; *Mandarin* (85) -

Chinese, open 1000-midnight; *Hibiscus (60)* cocktail bar, open 1100-1430/1730-2300

Overseas Sales Representatives
Amadeus Marketing SA Madrid, Spain thru' Indian Hotel Resrvation Services (IHRES)

Oberoi Hotel Bangalore
37-39 M G Road, Bangalore 560001
Tel: (80) 558 5858; Tlx: 8696 OBBL IN; Fax: (80) 558 5960

Located in the heart of Bangalore's commercial and shopping district, this prestigious hotel's exclusive business facilities make it an ideal choice for the discerning corporate traveller. The hotel is within walking distance of Ulsor Lake, Cubbon Park and the State Legislature.

Accommodation & rates
130 rooms, single US$ 225; double US$ 255; suite US$ 325-575. All + 25.75% tax

Credit cards accepted:
Amex, Diners, Bank America, Mastercharge, Eurocard, Visa

Meetings & conference facilities
Three meeting/conference rooms, capacity 30-250; audio-visual equipment available; largest reception 250 seated or cocktail

Room services
Airconditioning, colour TV, direct-dial telephone (ext. in bathroom), hairdryer, laundry/valet service, minibar, 24-hr room/meal service, trouser press, video films

Business & other services
Business centre, airport pickup (on request), car parking, travel centre, barber shop/beauty salon, newsstand/shops

Sports & Recreation
Golf (can be arranged), massage, sauna, swimming pool (outdoor), tennis

Restaurants & Coffee Shops
Le Jardin (76) - Multi-Cuisine, open 24 hours; *The Szechwan Court* (86 + 20) - Chinese, open 1230-1500/1930-2330; *The Polo Club* (96) - Bar, open 1100-2300

Taj Residency D
41/3 Mahatma Gandhi Rd, 560001
Tel: 5584444; Tlx: 845 8367; Fax: 5584748

The Taj West End
Race Course Road, 560 001
Tel: (080) 225 5055; Fax: (080) 220 0010

Located close to the city centre, set amidst 20 acres of magnificent gardens, the Taj West End offers round the clock service, tennis courts, walking tracks and the finest dining in the city.

Accommodation & rates
53 single US $180-250; 76 double US$ 200-250; 10 suites US$ 400-600.
All + 25.75% tax

Credit cards accepted:
All major

Meeting & conference facilities
Six meeting/conference rooms, capacity 18-850; audio-visual equipment available; 541.3 sq m exhibition space; fully equipped banquets with modern technology for conferencing

Room services
Airconditioning, colour TV, direct-dial telephone (ext. in bathroom), hairdryer, laundry/valet service, minibar, music/radio/alarm clock, safety deposit box, tea/coffee making, 24-hr room/meal service, trouser press, video films, non-smoker bedrooms

Business & other services
Business centre, executive floor, express checkout, airport pickup (on request), car parking & rental, travel centre, taxi service, barber shop/beauty salon, newsstand/shops

Sports & Recreation
Fitness centre/gym, golf, jacuzzi/whirlpool, jogging track, massage, sauna, swimming pool (outdoor), tennis

Restaurants & Coffee Shops
Paradise Island (120) - Thai/Oriental, open 1230-1500/1930-2345; *Mermaid Barbecue* (120) - Indian, open 0630-2345; *Garden Café* (53) - Bar, open 1000-0100

Gateway Hotel on Residency Road
66 Residency Road   D
Tel: (080) 558 4545 Tlx: 845 2567;
Fax: (080) 5584030

Holiday Inn Bangalore   E
PO Box 174, 28 Sankey Road, 560052
Tel: (812) 226 2233; Tlx: 0845-2354; Fax: (812) 226 7676

Welcomgroup Windsor Manor Sheraton & Towers
25 Sankey Rd, Bangalore 560052, Karinataka
Tel: (80) 226 9898; Tlx: 0845-8209;
Fax: (80) 226 4941

Styled as an imperial residence, 10 kms from the airport and 5 kms from the city centre. Features 240 rooms and suites with a block of Sheraton Towers comprising 100 rooms and 89 luxury suites

Accommodation & rates
240 rooms & suites. Single US$ 145-275; double US$ 160-290; suite US$ 375-800. All + 23.25% tax

Credit cards accepted:
All major

Meetings & conference facilities
Four meeting/conference rooms, capacity 500; largest reception 500

Room services
Airconditioning, colour TV/CCTV, IDD telephone, (ext. in bathroom), hairdryer, laundry/valet service, minibar, music/radio/alarm clock, safety deposit box, 24-hr room service, trouser press, video films (on request), voice messaging

Business & other services
Business centre, executive floor, express checkout, airport pickup, car parking & rental, travel centre, taxi service, barber shop/beauty salon, newsstand/shopping arcade, guided tours

Sports & Recreation
Fitness centre/gym, golf (on request), sauna, outdoor swimming pool, tennis

Restaurants & Coffee Shops
Wellington Room (85) - Continental/Avadh, open noon-1500/2000-midnight; *Nelson Room* (66) - Coffee Shop, open 1930-2300; *Royal Afghan* (50) - North West Frontier, open 1130-1500; *Royal Derby* (50) - Bar, open 1100-1500/1800-2300

International Sales Representatives
ITT Sheraton Worldwide

Bangaram

Bangaram Island Resort   D
Laccadive Islands, 682003
Tel: (484) 668221; Fax: (484) 668001

Baroda

Best Western Rama Inn   E
Sayaji Ganj, Baroda 390005
Tel:(0265) 330132;Tlx:01756668;Fax: 333523

Welcomgroup Vadodara   D
RC Dutt Road, Baroda 390005, Gujarat
Tel: 330033; Tlx: 175-525; Fax: 330050

Bhopal

Hotel Lake View Ashok   E
Shamla Hills, 462013
Tel: (755) 541600;Tlx: 0705-303; Fax: 553399

Bhubaneswar

Best Western Swotsi   D
103 Janpath, 751001
Tel: (0674) 404178; Fax: (0674) 407524

The Oberoi
Post RRL, CB1 Nayapalli, 751013, Bhubesanwar, Orissa
Tel: (0674) 440890-7; Tlx: 6348 HOB IN; Fax: (0674) 440898

Situated amidst fifteen acres of landscaped gardens, the Oberoi has a sense of majesty. The fine sculptureal work in evidence throughout the interiors is inspired by the famous temple architecture of Orissa.

Accommodation & rates
Single US$ 75; double US$ 90; suite US$ 120-155. All + 25.75% tax

Credit cards accepted:
Amex, Diners, Bank America, Mastercharge, Eurocard, Visa

Welcomgroup Windsor Manor Sheraton

Meetings & conference facilities
Two meeting/conference rooms, capacity 35-150; audio-visual equipment available

Room services
Airconditioning, colour TV, IDD telephone, (ext. in bathroom), laundry/valet service, music/radio/alarm clock, 24-hr room service, video films, refrigerator, room fax

Other services
Travel centre, newsstand/shops

Sports & Recreation
Indoor games, jogging track, outdoor swimming pool, tennis

Restaurants & Coffee Shops
Pushpanjali (76) - Multi-cuisine, open 0600-2300; *Chandini* (56) - Indian, open 1930-2300; *Madhusala* (33) - open 1100-2300

Bombay/Mumbai

Hotel Airport Plaza   E
70 C Nehru Rd, Villa Parle E, 400099
Tel: 612 3390; Tlx:11-71365 Fax: 612 7564

Ambassador Hotel   C
Churchgate Ext, 400020
Tel: 204 1131; Tlx: 11-82918; Fax: 204 0004

Centaur Hotel   ○   E
Bombay Airport, 400050
Tel: 611 6660; Tlx: 11-71171

Centaur Juhu Beach Hotel   ○   E
Juhu Tara Rd, 400099
Tel: 611 3040; Tlx: 11-78181; Fax: 6116343

Fariyas Hotel   ○   E
25 off Arthur Bunder Rd, Colaba 400005
Tel: 204 2911; Tlx: 11-83272; Fax: 234992

Hotel Horizon   ○   E
37 Juhu Beach, 400049
Tel: 611 7979; Tlx:11-71218; Fax: 6116715

The Oberoi
Nariman Point, Mumbai 400021
Tel: 202 5757; Tlx: 84153/82335 OBBY IN;
Fax: 204 3282/204 1505

One of the most distinguished hotels in the East. The hotel overlooks the ocean and is located in the heart of the business district. The spacious rooms are tastefully appointed with separate dressing areas. There is a personal butler to attend to your every need; excellent restaurants to pamper your palate.

Accommodation and Rates:
274 single US$305-335; 41 double US$ 330-360; 22 suites US$660-1800.
All + government taxes.

Credit cards accepted:
Amex, Visa, Eurocard, JCB, Mastercharge, Diners Club, Bank America

Meeting & conference facilities
Five meeting/function rooms - capacity 50 - 1000; audio-visual equipment available; largest banquet 2000

Room services
Airconditioning, colour TV, direct-dial telephone (ext. in bathroom), hairdryer, laundry/valet service, minibar, safety deposit box, 24-hr room service, trouser press

Business & other services
Business centre, executive floor, express checkout, airport pickup, translation service, car parking, car rental, taxi service, barber shop/beauty salon, guided tours, newsstand/shopping arcade

Sports & Recreation
Swimming pool, fitness centre/gym, sauna, massage, golf, jacuzzi/whirlpool, tennis, squash, outdoor swiming pool

Restaurants & Coffee Shops
Cafe Royal (90) - French, open 1930-0100; *The Outrigger* (116) - Polynesian, open 1230-1445/1930-2315; *Mewar* (72) - Indian, open 1230-1445/2000-2345; *The Palms* (140) - Coffee shop, open 24 hours; *Casa Mexicana* (72) - Mexican/Tex-Hex, open 1230-1500/1930-2345; *Lancers Bar* (97) - Cocktails, open 1100-2330; *La Brasserie* (106) - European & Oriental, open 0700-midnight; *Kandahar* (82) - North West Frontier, open 1230-1445/2000-2345; *La Rotisserie* (84) - French grill, open 1230-1445/1930-2245; *Bayview Bar* (72) - Cocktails &c, open 1100-1445/1800-2400

The Oberoi Towers
Nariman Point, Mumbai 400021
Tel: 202 4343; Tlx: 82337/82340/84153-54 OBBY IN; Fax: 204 3282/204 1505

The Oberoi Towers - towering above the skyline, is centrally located in the heart of India's bustling business capital, Mumbai i.e. Nariman Point, Marine Drive and the main promenade within the business and shopping district and overlooking the Arabian Sea.

Accommodation and Rates:
650 rooms, single/double US$260-285; suites US$ 525-950. All + government taxes

Credit cards accepted:
Amex, Diners, Bank America, Mastercard, Visa, Mastercharge, Eurocard

Groups
Six function rooms, capacity 8-3000 with audio-visual equipment; largest reception 3000

Room services
Airconditioning, colour TV, direct-dial telephone (ext. in bathroom), hairdryer, laundry/valet service, minibar, music/radio/alarm clock, safety deposit box, trouser press, 24-hr room service, non-smoker bedrooms, video films.

Business & other services
Business centre, airport pickup, car parking & rental, travel centre, taxi service, beauty salon/barber shop, guided tours, newsstand/shops

Sports & Recreation
Fitness centre/gym, massage, sauna, swimming pool (outdoor), tennis, sailing, horse riding

Restaurants & Coffee Shops
See Oberoi Hotel entry (left)

The Oberoi

The Oberoi Towers

Holiday Inn　　　　　　　○　B
Balraj Sahani Marg, 400049
Tel: 620 4444; Tlx: 78411; Fax: 620 4452/670 1710

Hotel President　　　　　○　A
90 Cuffe Parade, Colaba, 400005
Tel: 215 0808; Tlx: 11-84135 PRES IN; Fax: 215 1201

Ramada Hotel Palm Grove　○　C
Juhu Beach, 400049
Tel: 611 2323; Tlx: 11-71419; Fax: 611 3682

Sea Green South Hotel　　○　C
145a Marine Drive, 400020
Tel: 282 1613; Fax: 282 1662

Shalimar Hotel　　　　　　○　D
August Kranti Marg
Tel: 363 1311; Tlx: 11-75087; Fax: 363 0605

Sun-N-Sand Hotel　　　　○　C
39 Juhu Beach, 400049
Tel: 620 1811; Tlx: 11-78406; Fax: 620 2170

The Taj Mahal Hotel　　　　○
Apollo Bunder, Calaba, Mumbai 400001
Tel: 202 3366; Tlx: 11-82442 TAJB IN; Fax: 287 2711

Opened in 1903. It has been described as "The finest caravansari in the East". Overlooking the Gateway of India and the Arabian Sea, it offers a wonderful welcome to Bombay City with an idyllic blend of traditional hospitality and contemporary comforts.

(Leading Hotels Logo)

Accommodation & rates
600 rooms, including 46 suites. New Wing - standard rooms - US$ 240 + 20% tax

INDIA - Hotels   105

single/US$ 265 + 20% tax double. (Traditional Old Wing - standard rooms - US$ 290 + 20% tax single/US$ 315 + 20% tax double. Suites US$ 650-1650 + tax

Credit cards accepted:
Diners, Mastercard, Amex, JCB, Visa

Meeting & conference facilities
11 meeting/function rooms, capacity 20-2500; with full audio-visual facilities and comprehensive conference facilities

Room services
Airconditioning, colour TV, direct-dial telephone (ext. in bathroom), laundry/valet service, minibar, music/radio, safety deposit box, wake-up call, 24-hr room service

Business & other services
Business centre, car parking, car rental, travel desk, barber shop/beauty salon, shopping arcade, art gallery, bookshop

Sports & Recreation
Swimming pool, fitness centre/gym, massage, steambath, hydrotherapy. Squash and tennis can be arranged

Restaurants & Coffee Shops
Zodiac Grill/Lounge Bar - Contemporary European, open 0730-1000/1230-1500/1900-midnight; *Golden Dragon* - Chinese (Szechuan), open 1230-1500/1900-midnight; *Tanjore* (92) - Indian, open 1230-1500/1830-midnight; *Shamiana* - 24 hours coffee shop; *Sea Lounge* - light meals lounge, open 1000-midnight.

Overseas Sales Representatives:
Taj International Sales Offices, Utell International (worldwide), Leading Hotels of the World (worldwide), Supereps International, London

Welcomgroup Searock Sheraton B
Land's End, Bandra 400050
Tel: 642 5454; Tlx: 011-71230; Fax: 640 8046

West End Hotel   **E**
45 Marine Lines, 400020
Tel: 203 9121; Tlx: 11-82892; Fax: 205 7506

 after name of hotel = member of Pacific Asia Travel Association. Photographs generally refer to the properties whose descriptions **follow** them.

Calcutta

Hotel Airport Ashok
Calcutta Airport, 700052
Tel: (33) 511 5111 (20 lines); Fax: 511 9137
Internet: http://www.indiatourism.com or
http://www.indianhotels.com

For business travellers and those in transit through the great commercial metropolis of Calcutta, Hotel Airport Ashok provides an ideal stopover, offering all facilities and comforts of an international hotel and business centre. Just one km from international and domestic airport.

Accommodation
136 rooms; 12 suites

Rates:
Single occupancy US$ 140; twin US$150; suite US$ 260-350

Credit cards accepted:
Amex, Mastercard, Visa

Meeting & conference facilities
2 meeting/function rooms - capacity up to 300; audio-visual facilities available; 718 sq m exhibition space; lush poolside lawns available for reception/banquet up to 1000 pax

Room services
Airconditioning, colour TV, laundry/valet service, music/radio/alarm clock, safety deposit box, 24-hr room service, trouser press

Business & other services
Business centre, express checkout, airport pickup, car parking, car rental, taxi service, newsstand/shops

Sports & Recreation
Outdoor swimming pool, jogging track

Restaurants & Coffee Shops
Durbar (64) - Indian, Mughal, open noon-1500/1950-midnight; *Coffee Shop* (86) - Indian/Continental, open 24 hours; *Pavilion Bar* (33) - open 1100-2230

Overseas Reservation Consolidator:
Amadeus Marketing SA, Madrid, Spain thru' Indian Hotel Reservation System (IHRES)

Best Western Kenilworth **D**
86A-1 Gautamnager, 751014
Tel: (33) 223403; Tlx: 21-2395; Fax: (33) 242 5136

Hindusthan International   **C**
235/1 Acharya Jagadish Bose Blvd, 700020
Tel: 247 2394; Tlx: 21-7164; Fax: 247 2824

The Oberoi Grand
15 Jawaharlal Nehru Road, 700013
Tel: 249 2323/249 0181; Tlx: 21-5919/5971/5937 OBCL IN; Fax: 291 1217

The hotel is a Victorian landmark in the very heart of bustling Calcutta, its marbled corridors, majestic columns and antique crystal chandeliers creating a perfect blend of tradition with contemporary elegance.

Accommodation
122 double, 88 twin, 11 suites

Rates:
Single from US$ 205; double from US$ 235; suites US$ 375-575

Credit cards accepted:
Amex, Eurocard, Visa, Mastercard, Diners, Bank America, Eurocard, Oberoi Hotels Card

Meeting & conference facilities
Three meeting/banqueting rooms, capacity up to 1000

Room services
Airconditioning, colour TV, IDD telephone (ext. in bathroom), hairdryer, laundry/valet service, minibar, safety deposit box, trouser press

Business & other services
Business centre, car rental, travel centre, taxi service, barber shop/beauty salon, newsstand/shops, chemist

Sports & Recreation
Fitness centre/gym, massage, sauna, squash, outdoor swimming pool

Restaurants & Coffee Shops
La Brasserie (96) - Coffee Shop, open 24 hours; *The Ming Court* (98) -Szechuan, open 1230-1430/2030-2330; *La Rotisserie* (64) - Continental, open as above; *Gharana* (74) - Rajasthani, open as above; *Chowdinghee* (42) - Snacks/bar, open 1100-2300
                                    The Oberoi Grand

The Park Hotel   **A**
17 Park Street, 700 016
Tel: 249 3121/249 7336; Fax: 249 7343

Taj Bengal Calcutta
34b Belvedere Rd, Alipore, 700 027
Tel: 248 3939; Tlx: 21-4776 TAJC IN; Fax: 248 1766/8805; E-mail: tajbengal.
calcutta@tajgroup.sprintrpg.emsvsnl.net.in

Located in Alipore, the elite residential area of Calcutta, the hotel opened in October '89. It is an oasis of luxury, offering guests a lush, dramatic and spacious lobby. It offers standard and deluxe rooms, besides an entire Club Floor for the discerning traveller. It also offers a choice of suites, each individually appointed. All rooms are equipped with minibars and safes.

Accommodation & rates
219 single/double twin, US$ 225-230 (single occ. $ 205-300); 11 suites, US$ 375-600. All + government tax.

Credit cards accepted:
Diners, Mastercard, Amex, JCB, Visa

Meeting & conference facilities
8 meeting/function rooms, capacity 20-800; with full audio-visual facilities and comprehensive conference facilities

Room services
Airconditioning, colour TV, direct-dial telephone (ext. in bathroom), laundry/valet service, minibar, music/radio/alarm clock, safety deposit box, 24-hr room service, non-smoker bedrooms, video films

Business & other services
Business centre, executive floor, express checkout, translation service, car parking, car rental, travel desk, taxi service, barber shop/beauty salon, shopping arcade

Sports & Recreation
Fitness centre/gym, jacuzzi/whirlpool, massage sauna, outdoor swimming pool. Squash, tennis, golf, riding and horse racing can be arranged with nearby clubs

Restaurants & Coffee Shops
The Esplanade (120) -24-hour coffee shop; *Chinoiserie* (82) - Sichuan-style Chinese, open 1230-1500/1930-midnight; *Sonargaon* (120) - Indian, open as above; *The French Restaurant* (32), open as above; *Junction* (60) - Bar & snacks, open 1100-midnight; *Incognito* (100) - discothèque, open 2100-0200; *Poolside Barbecue* (50) - Indian/Continental, open 1930-midnight

Overseas Sales Representatives:
Taj International Sales Offices, Utell International (worldwide), Leading Hotels of the World (worldwide), Supereps International, London

Cochin-Ernakulam

Best Western South Asia Resort   E
Silver Sand island, Vittila, Cochin 682019, KerAla
Tel: (0484) 318357/8; Fax: (0484) 354226

Taj Malabar Hotel   D
Willingdon Island, 682009
Tel: 666811; Tlx: 885-6661; Fax; 668297

Darjeeling

Oberoi-Mt Everest Hotel   E
29 Gandhi Rd Tel: (0354) 2616

Delhi/New Delhi

Ashok Hotel
50-B Chanakyapuri, 110021
Tel: 611 0101; Tlx: 031-72075;
Fax: 687 3216/687 6060
Internet: http://www.indiantourist.com or
         http://www.indiahotels.com

Ashok is a five-star deluxe hotel and the flagship of the Ashok Group. Set in a prime location of Delhi's diplomatic enclave and within walking distance of the President Estate, Delhi Racecourse. Also nearby is the large Nehru Garden.

Accommodation & rates
166 singles US$ 225; 294 double/twin US$ 290; 111 suites US$ 320-1000

Credit cards accepted:
Visa, Mastercard, Amex, Diners, Citibank, Standardch, Mercard

Groups
8 conference rooms, capacity 18-2200 with audio-visual equipment; exhibition space available; largest reception 3000 (front lawns)

Taj Bengal Calcutta

Room services
Airconditioning, colour TV, direct-dial telephone (ext. in bathroom), laundry/valet service, music/radio/alarm clock, safety deposit box, trouser press, 24-hr room service, video films

Business services
Business centre, translation service (on request), car parking & rental, travel centre, taxi service

Other services
Barber shop/beauty salon, guided tours, newsstand/shops, shopping arcade

Sports & Recreation
Fitness centre/gym, minigolf, jacuzzi/whirlpool, jogging track, massage, sauna, outdoor swimming pool, tennis

Restaurants & Coffee Shops
Frontier (65) - Indian/Northwest Frontier, open 1300-1430/2000-2315; *Durbar* (70) - Indian, open 1230-1445/2000-2330; *Tokyo* (52) - Japanese, open 1230-1445/1930-2235; *Jewel of East* (103) - Chinese, open 1230-1445/1930-2330; *Coffee Shop*, open 24 hours

Overseas Reservations Consolidator
Amadeus Marketing SA, Madrid, Spain thru Indian Hotel Resrvation Services (IHRES)

Claridges Hotel   ◌   E
12 Aurangzeb Rd, 110001
Tel: 301 0211; Tlx: 65526; Fax: 301 0625

Hyatt Regency Delhi   ◌
Bhikaji Cama Place, Ring Road, 110066
Tel: 618 1234; Tlx: 031-61512 HYT; Fax: 618 6833

Located in the vicinity of Delhi's exclusive residential and commercial complex, Hyatt Regency Delhi is 15 minutes from the city centre and 25 minutes from the International Airport

Accommodation & rates
518 rooms, single/twin/double US$ 275-310; 19 suites US$ 550-1300

Credit cards accepted:
Visa, Mastercard, Amex, Diners, Citibank, JCB

Meeting & conference facilities
6 meeting rooms, capacity 760 with audio-visual equipment; 510 sq m exhibition space available; largest reception 500 seated or 700 cocktail

Room services
Airconditioning, colour TV, direct-dial telephone (ext. in bathroom), hairdryer,

laundry/valet service, minibar, music/radio/alarm clock, safety deposit box, 24-hour room/meal service

Business & other services
Business centre, executive floor, express checkout, airport pickup, translation service, car parking & rental, travel centre, taxi service, barber shop/beauty centre, guided tours, newsstand/shops

Sports & Recreation
Fitness centre/gym, golf (on request), jacuzzi/whirlpool, jogging track, massage, sauna, outdoor swimming pool, tennis

Restaurants & Coffee Shops
La Piazza (80) - Italian, open 1230-1430/1930-2330; *Dehli Ka Aangan* (104) - Indian, open as above; *TK's Oriental Grill* - open 1230-1445/1930-2345; *Coffee Shop* open 24 hours; *Polo Lounge* (75) - Bar, open 1100-midnight

Overseas Reservation Consolidator
All Hyatt hotels worldwide

Le Meridien New Delhi
Windsor Place, Janpath, Delhi 110001
Tel: 371 0101; Tlx: 031-65312 HOME IN; Fax: 371 4545

Located in the heart of the capital city. Spread over 20 floors, displaying glass curtain exterior, the hotel is strategically situated in the major commercial district, within close proximity of main tourist attractions and shopping. Areas include five restuarants, disco, health club and outdoor pool.

Accommodation & rates
355 single/double US$ 275-300; 59 suites from US$ 500.

Credit cards accepted:
All major - Amex, Diners, Mastercard, Visa

Meeting & conference facilities
6 meeting rooms - capacity 40-800, with audio-visual euipment; largest reception 500 banquet or 1000 cocktail.

Room services
Airconditioning, colour TV, direct-dial telephone (ext. in bathroom), hairdryer, laundry/valet service, music/radio/alarm clock, safety deposit box, 24-hour room/meal service

Business services
Business centre, executive floor, express

checkout, airport pickup, car parking & rental, travel centre, taxi service

Other services
Barber shop/hairdresser, beauty salon, guided tours, newsstand/shops

Sports & Recreation
Fitness centre/gym, jacuzzi/whirlpool, jogging track, massage, sauna, outdoor swimming pool, tennis

Restaurants & Coffee Shops
Golden Pheonix (120) - Chinese, open 1230-1500/1930-2345; *Pierre* (54) - French, open as above; *Le Belvedere* (104) - Continental, open as above; *Pakwan* (90) - Indian, open as above

Overseas Reservation Consolidator
Meridien & Forte Hotels, 166 High Holborn, London WC1V 6TT

New Delhi Hilton
Barakhamba Avenue, Connaught Place, 110001
Tel: 332 0101; Tlx: 031-61186 HIND IN; Fax: 332 5335

Located in the heart of New Delhi's main commercial and shopping district - Connaught Place, the hotel is ideal for business as well as leisure travellers, offering deluxe & execututve floor rooms along with luxurious suites and a host of guest facilities.

Accommodation & rates
445 twin/double rooms, US$ 325-425 (single occ. $ 295-395)

Credit cards accepted:
Visa, Amex, Diners, Citibank, JCB, BOB Canara

Meeting & conference facilities
6 meeting rooms, capacity 25-600 with audio-visual equipment; largest reception 550 seated or 600 cocktail

Room services
Airconditioning, colour TV, direct-dial telephone (ext. in bathroom), hairdryer, laundry/valet service, minibar, music/radio, safety deposit box, 24-hour room/meal service, non-smoker bedrooms, video films

Business & other services
Business centre, executive floor, express checkout, airport pickup (charged), car parking & rental, travel centre, taxi service, babrber shop/beauty centre, newsstand/shops

Sports & Recreation
Fitness centre/gym, jacuzzi/whirlpool, massage, sauna, outdoor swimming pool

Restaurants & Coffee Shops
The Grill Room (40) - Continental, open lunch & dinner; *Noble House* (110) - Chinese, open lunch & dinner; *Baluchi* (110) - Indian, open lunch & dinner; *The Rendezvous* (140) - Multi cuisine, open 24 hours; *Annabelles* - Discothèque, open 2130-0230; *The Lounge Bar* (60) - open 1100-midnight

Overseas Sales Representatives:
Hilton International Co

New Delhi Parkroyal A
Nehru Place, 110019
Tel: 622 3344; Fax: 622 1143

The Oberoi
Dr Zakhir Hussain Marg, 110003
Tel: 436 3030; Tlx: 63222/74019 OBDL IN; Fax: 436 0484/436 4758

The capital's most gracious host, the hotel has every comfort and convenience for the international corporate traveller. An air of tranquil ease marks the elegant lobby. The interiors refurbished in vibrant colours present an ambience of warm hosptaility.

Accommodation & rates
290 rooms, single US$ 305; double US$ 335; suite US$ 575-1500

Credit cards accepted:
Visa, Mastercard, Amex, Diners, Citibank, Standardch, Mercard, BOB Card, Andhra Bank Card, Carte Blanche, JCB, Oberoi Hotels Card, Grindlays-Visa-Classic, Eurocard

(continued)

Meeting & conference facilities
8 meeting/conference rooms, capacity up to 400

Room services
Airconditioning, colour TV, direct-dial telephone (ext. in bathroom), hairdryer, laundry/valet service, minibar, trouser press, safety deposit box , 24-hr room service, video films

Business & other services
Business centre, fax and PC rental, car rental, travel centre, barber shop/beauty salon, newsstand/shops, bank, chemist

Sports & Recreation
Fitness centre/gym, jacuzzi/whirlpool, jogging track, tennis, massage, sauna, outdoor swimming pool

Restaurants & Coffee Shops
Taipan (104) - Chinese, open 1230-1500/ 2000-midnight; *Baan Thai* (54) - open as above; *La Rochelle* (64) - French, open as above; *Kandhar* (74) - India, open as above; *The Palms* (64) - Coffee Shop, open 24 hours.

The Oberoi Maidens
7 Sham Nath Marg, 110054
Tel: 291 4841; Tlx: 66303/78163 OMDLIN; Fax: 291 5134

This historic turn of the century hotel, situated amidst spacious gardens in the heart of old Delhi is renowned for its gracious elegance and old world charm.

Accommodation & rates
53 rooms. Single US$ 85; double US$ 105 (plus taxes)

Credit cards accepted:
Amex, Eurocard, Visa, Mastercard, Diners, Bank America

Groups
Meeting room for 150 persons

Room services
Airconditioning, colour TV, IDD telephone, laundry/valet service, 24-hour room/meal service, refrigerator

Sports & Recreation
Indoor swimming pool, tennis

Restaurants & Coffee Shops
The Curzon Room (50) - Multi-cuisine, open 1300-1500/1900-2300; *The Garden Terrace* (32) - Coffee Shop, open 0700-2300

The Park Hotel   ○ D
15 Parliament Street, 110001
Tel: 373 3737; Fax: 373 2025

Radisson Hotel Delhi   C
Delhi-Jaipur National Highway 8, 110 037
Tel: 685 4550; Fax: 686 2954

Hotel Samrat
Chanakayapuri, 110021
Tel: 603030; Tlx: 317 2126; Fax: 688 7047
Internet: http://www.indiatourist.com or
http://www.indianhotels.com

Set in beautifully landscaped gardens which it shares with Delhi's landmark Ashok Hotel, the Samrat is an elegant stone and marble structure built around a central flower-filled atrium and open air corridor. Fountains and water channels run through the lobby and the gardens.

Accommodation & rates
39 double/196 twin, US$ 140 (single occ. $ 120); 2 suites US$ 375-400; 13 apartments to lease only

Credit cards accepted:
Visa, Mastercard, Amex, Diners, Citibank, Standardch, Mercard

Groups
4 meeting/conference rooms, capacity 40-1000; largest reception 800 seated/cocktail; exhibition space; poolside for parties

Room services
Airconditioning, colour TV, direct-dial telephone (ext. in bathroom), hairdryer, laundry/valet service, music/radio/ alarm clock, safety deposit box, 24-hr room service, video films

Business & other services
Car parking & rental, travel centre, taxi service, barber shop/beauty salon, guided tours, newsstand/shops

Sports & Recreation
Fitness centre/gym, jacuzzi/whirlpool, tennis, massage, sauna, outdoor swimming pool

Restaurants & Coffee Shops
Baradari (80) - Indian & Mughal, open 1300-1400/2000-2300; *Gardenia Coffee Shop* (90) - open 24 hours

Overseas Reservation Consolidator
Amadeus Marketing SA, Madrid, Spain thru Indian Hotel Reservation Services (IHRES)

Hotel Siddarth   D
3 Rajendra Place, 110008.Tel: 571 2501; Tlx: 031-77125; Fax: 578 1016

The Surya, a Best Western Hotel ○
New Friends Colony, Delhi 110 055
Tel: 683 5070; Fax: 683 7758

The Surya is a part of the largest hotel chain in the world - Best Western USA - a chain spread across more than 50 countries. It is conveniently located with regard to Delhi's prime commercial attractions, a mere 25 minutes' drive from th airport and 15 minutes from Connaught Place (main shopping mall). The Surya Best Western is the obvious choice with the corporate business traveller.

Accommodation
203 double rooms; 27 suites

Rates:
Single/double US$ 230; suite $350-900

Credit cards accepted:
Amex, Andhra Bank, Visa, BOB, Carte Blanche, Central Card, Diners, Citibank, Eurocard, ANZ Grindlays, Visa Classic, JCB, Mastercard, Standard Chartered

Meeting & conference facilities
Five conference rooms - capacity 10 - 10,000; audio-visual equipment available; 900 sq m exhibition space; largest reception 500 seated or 1000 cocktail

Room services
Airconditioning, colour TV, direct-dial telephone (ext. in bathroom), hairdryer, laundry/valet service, minibar, music/radio, safety deposit box, 24-hr room service, video films + satellite, butler service

Business & other services
Business centre, executive floor,

INDIA - Hotels

secretarial services, express checkout, airport pickup, translation service, car parking, car rental, travel centre, taxi service, barber shop/beauty salon, guided tours, newsstand

Sports & Recreation
Fitness centre/gym, golf, indoor games, jacuzzi/whirlpool, jogging track, massage, aerobics & yoga, sauna, squash & tennis on request, swimming pool (outdoor)

Restaurants & Coffee Shops
Sampan (120) - Szechuanese/Cantonese/Polynesian, open 1230-1500/2030-0100; *Le Cafe* (80) - Coffee Shop, open 24 hrs; *Viceroy* (60) - Continental/Grill, open 1930-0130; *Sikandra* (50) - Mughali/Frontier, open 1200-1500/2000-midnight; *The Atrium* (60) - Pizzas, snacks etc, open 1100-2300; *French Crust* - Confectionery/Bakery, open 0900-2100

Overseas Sales Representatives:
Best Western worldwide including... France. Tel: (1) 4487 4080; fax: (1) 4487 4084. Res'n toll-free 0590 4490; res'n fax (10392) 3340 3851
Germany. Tel (96196) 4720; fax: (6196) 472412. Res'n toll-free 0130 4455; res"n fax (6196) 41377
UK. Tel (0181) 541 0033; fax: (0181) 547 3941. Toll free 0800 393130; fax (3531) 667 0020
Japan. Tel (03) 5442 0611; fax: (03) 5442 0620. Res'n toll-free 0120 42 1234
North America. (freefone) 1-800 528 1234; fax: 602 780 6099; tlx: 187227
South Africa. Tel: (11) 339 4865; fax: (011) 339 2474; tlx: 421741

Hotel Vasant Continental ○ D
Vasant Vihar, New Delhi 110 057
Tel: 678800; Tlx: 031-72386/72263; Fax: 687 3842

Explanation of codes in (short) hotel entries. **A** *after name = single room over US$ 200 per night;* **B** *= between $150-200;* **C** *= between $100-150;* **D** *= between $50-100;* **E** *= under $50;* ¶ *= on application.*

Further copies of this **Country Report** and the complete 1997/98 Asia-Pacific Business Travel Guide are available from the publisher (Priory Public-ations Ltd) at PO Box 24, Brackley, Northants NN13 5FA, UK. Fax: [+44] 1280 850576. The guide can also be viewed on the Internet under http://travel.cm-net.com/pata

The Taj Mahal Hotel
Number One, Mansingh Road, 110 011
Tel: 301 6162; Tlx: 031-4758 TAJD IN; Fax: 301 7299

Exceptionally situated in the heart of Lutyens' Delhi, the hotel is host to the most important business, social and political gatherings. Exclusively designed to satisfy the discerning business traveller's needs, the hotel enjoys a reputation of providing distinguished hospitality

Accommodation & rates
271 single/double/twin, US$ 245-380 (single occ. $ 245-330); 26 suites, US$ 600-900. All plus 20% government tax

Credit cards accepted:
Amex, Diners, Mastercard, Visa

Meeting & conference facilities
Six conference rooms - capacity 8-400; audio-visual equipment available; largest reception 150 seated or 400 cocktail

Room services
Airconditioning, colour TV, direct-dial telephone (ext. in bathroom), hairdryer, laundry/valet service, minibar, music, safety deposit box, trouser press, 24-hr room service, video films

Business & other services
Business centre, executive floor, express checkout, airport pickup, translation service, car parking, car rental, travel centre, taxi service, barber shop/beauty salon, newsstand/shops

Sports & Recreation
Fitness centre/gym, golf, tennis, jacuzzi, massage, sauna, outdoor swimming pool

Restaurants and Coffee Shops
Machan - 24 hour coffee shop; *Captain's Table* - Bar/Cntinental, open 1230-1445/1700-2345; *House of Ming* - Chinese, open 1230-1500/1930-2245; *Haveli* - Indian, open as above; *Casa Medici* - Italian, open as above

Overseas Sales Representatives
Taj International Sales Offices; Leading Hotels of the World; Utell International

Taj Palace Hotel
Sardar Patel Marg, Diplomatic Enclave, 110021
Tel: 301 0404; Tlx: 031-62761 TAJS.IN; Fax: 301 1252

Located in six acres of landsacped gardens, ten minutes from the city centre and the airport. The hotel combines attractive functionality with stylishness in a happy symbiosis. In Taj tradition, you will find the congenial atmosphere of a true business hotel with a special emphasis on cuisine.

Accommodation & rates
8 single rooms, US$ 275-350; 413 double/twin, US$ 300-380; single/double suites, US$ 425-950. All plus 20% government tax

Credit cards accepted:
Amex, Diners, Mastercard, Visa, BOB card

Meeting & conference facilities
12 conference rooms - capacity 8-1400; audio-visual equipment available; 1007 sq m exhibition space; largest reception 450 seated or 1400 cocktail

Room services
Airconditioning, colour TV, direct-dial telephone (ext. in bathroom), hairdryer, laundry/valet service, minibar, music, safety deposit box, 24-hr room/meal service, non-smoker bedrooms, video films

Business & other services
Business centre, executive floor, express checkout, airport pickup, translation service, car parking, car rental, travel centre, taxi service, barber shop/beauty salon, newsstand/shops

Sports & Recreation
Fitness centre/gym, golf, tennis, jacuzzi, massage, outdoor swimming pool

Restaurants & Coffee Shops
Isfahan (160) - 24-hour coffee shop; *Tea House of the August Moon* (175) - Cantonese/Szechuan open 1230-1500/1930-midnight; *Handi* (180) - Indian, open as above; *Orient Express* (36) - French/Continental, open as above

Overseas Sales Representatives
Taj International Sales Offices; Leading Hotels of the World; Utell International

INDIA - Hotels

Welcomgroup Maurya Sheraton ○
Dipomatic Enclave, 110021
Tel: 301 0101; Tlx: 031-61447; Fax: 301 0908

Located in the exclusive Diplomatic Enclave, it depicts the first dynasty of Empire Builders - the 'Mauryan Dynasty'. It has 500 rooms and suites, an exclusive health club, speedy check-in, business lounges, round-the-clock business centre and exclusive Sheraton Towers

Accommodation & rates*
450 kingsize single/double rooms; 84 twin, 46 suites. Single US$ 250-475; double US$ 275-450; suite US$ 450-1100 (single occ. $ 245-330); 26 suites, US$ 600-900.

Credit cards accepted:
All major

Meeting & conference facilities
Four meeting/banquet rooms, capacity 1200+; audio-visual equipment available; largest reception 450 seated/1200 cocktail; 3 commitee rooms, lawns & poolside areas

Room services
Airconditioning, colour TV, direct-dial telephone (ext. in bathroom), hairdryer, laundry/valet service, minibar, music, safety deposit box, trouser press, 24-hr room service, video films (Towers rooms)

Business & other services
Business centre, Cyber Club, executive floor, express checkout, airport pickup (charged), car parking & rental, travel centre & tours, taxi service, barber shop/beauty salon, newsstand/shopping arcade, florist

Sports & Recreation
Fitness centre/gym, golf & tennis by arrangement, jogging track, massage, sauna, outdoor swimming pool, opti-golf

Restaurants and Coffee Shops
Bukhara (150) - Northwest Frontier, open 1230-1445/1930-2345; *Pavilion* (120) - Multi-cuisine/buffet, open 24 hours; *Dum Pukht* (15) - Indian, open as above; *West View* (57) - Continental, open 1930-midnight; *Bali Hai* (150) - Chinese, open 2000-0030; *Night Club* - live band dance floor

Overseas Sales Representatives
ITT Sheraton Worldwide

Ghaziabad

Best Western Mela Plaza Hotel   E
C-3 Rajnagar District Centre, 201001
Tel: (11) 872 2255; Fax: (11) 871 6421

Goa

The Fort Aquada Beach Resort
Sinquerim, Bardez, 403515
Tel: (0832) 276201-09; Fax: (0832) 276044

Built on the ramparts of a 16th century Portuguese fortress, the hotel offers a stunning view of the Arabian Sea and endless miles of the golden Calanquite beach. The ancient ramparts of the fort enclose the main wing of the hotel.

Accommodation & rates
82 double/ 24 twin US$ 230 pp; 24 suites ¶

Credit cards accepted:
Amex, Diners, Mastercard,Visa

Groups
Two meeting/conference rooms, capacity 170; audio-visual equipment available; largest banquet 250 (open air)

Room services
Airconditioning, colour TV, direct-dial telephone (ext. in bathroom), hairdryer, laundry/valet service, minibar, music/radio, safety deposit box, video films

Business & other services
Business centre, express checkout, airport pickup, translation service, car parking & rental, travel centre, barber shop/beauty salon, guided tours, newsstand/shops

Sports & Recreation
Billiards/snooker, fitness centre/gym, golf, indoor games, jacuzzi/whirlpool, massage, sauna, squash, outdoor swimming pool, tennis, watersports

Restaurants & Coffee Shops
Sea Shell (138) - Indian/Cont'l, open 1230-1430/1930-2230; *Raampon* (40) - Goan, open as above; *Trattoria* (52) - Italian, as above; *Anchor Bar* (68) -Coffee Shop, open 0700-0200

Overseas Sales Representatives:
Taj Worldwide Offices

The Aquada Hermitage Villas   B
Sinquerim, Bardez 403515
Tel: (832) 276201-09; Tlx: 019-4291; Fax: (832) 276044

Cidade de Goa   C
Vainguinim Beach, 403004
Tel: (832) 221133; Tlx: 0194-257 DONA IN; Fax: (832) 223303

Holiday Inn Resort Goa   C
Mobor Beach, Cavelossim, Salcete 403731
Tel: (834) 746303-7; Fax: 746333

Leela Beach Goa   ○   C
Mobor, Cavelossim, Salcette M03731
Tel: (834) 246383; Fax: (834) 246352

Majorda Beach Resort   E
Majorda, Salcette, Goa 403713
Tel: 730203-4/220751-2; Tlx: 196234 MBR IN; Fax: 730212

Oberoi Bogmalo Beach Goa   E
Bogmalo, Dabolim Arpt, 403806
Tel: 513281; Tlx: 091 297; Fax: 512510

Renaissance Goa Resort   ○   D
Survey No 132, Fatrade, Salcette 403721
Tel: (832) 745208; Fax: (832) 745225

The Taj Holiday Village   D
Sinquerim, Bardez, Goa 403519
Tel: (0832) 276201-10;Fax: (0832)276045

45 minute drive from the airport. The Taj Holiday Village comprising of 142 centrally a/c rooms, in terracotta roofed cottages, scattered among palm trees in acres of lanscaped gardens.

Accommodation & rates
142 single/double, US$ 105-200; suites US$ 300

Credit cards accepted:
Amex, BOB card, Mercard, Bank of India, Diners, Andhra Bank, Central Bank, Visa, Mastercard, Taj Group card

Meeting & conference facilities
Meeting/conference rooms, capacity 40; audio-visual equipment available

Room services
Airconditioning, colour TV, hairdryer, laundry/valet service, minibar, music/radio, safety deposit box, trouser press

Business & other services
Business centre, express checkout, car parking & rental, travel centre, taxi service, barber shop/beauty salon, guided tours

INDIA - Hotels

Sports & Recreation
Billiards/snooker, fitness centre/gym, 5-hole golf, indoor games, jacuzzi/whirlpool, jogging track, massage, sauna, squash, outdoor swimming pool, tennis, watersports

Restaurants & Coffee Shops
Beach House (130) - Goan/Continental, open 1230-1430/1930-2230; *Banyan Tree* (138) - Thai & Chinese, open as above; *Caravela* (110) -Coffee Shop, open 0730-2330

Overseas Sales Representatives:
Taj Worldwide Offices

Gopalpur-on-Sea

The Oberoi Palm Beach
District of Gianjam, Orissa State 761002
Tel: (6812) 82021/3; Tlx: 673-234 HOPB; Fax: (6812) 82300

The Oberoi Palm Beach is situated on one of the finest unspoiled beaches in India. A haven of seclusion for the holiday maker. The panoramic view of the Bay of Bengal, the distant hills and pine forests forming a picturesque backdrop, make it a perfect resort.

Accommodation & rates
20 rooms, single US$ 100; double US$ 150

Credit cards accepted:
Amex, Diners, Bank America, Eurocard, Mastercard,Visa

Meeting & banqueting facilities
Two meeting/conference rooms, capacity 45 & 55 persons

Room services
24 hour room/meal service, video room, laundry

Other services
Car rental

Sports & Recreation
Tennis, watersports

Restaurants & Coffee Shops
Dining room serving Indian & European cuisine

Gwalior

Welcomgroup Usha Kiran Palace   E
Jayendraganj, Lashkar, Gwalior 474009
Tel: 323213; Tlx: 0786 274; Fax: 321103

Hyderabad

Holiday Inn Krishna   C
Rd No 1, Banjara Hills, 500034
Tel: (40) 393939; Fax: (40) 392684

Hyderabad Gateway   D
Road No 1, Banjara Hills 500 034
Tel: 222222; Tlx: 042 56947; Fax: 222218

The Krishna Oberoi   C
Road No 1, Banjara Hills, 500034
Tel: (40) 392323; Tlx: 0425-6931/6850 OBH IN; Fax: (40) 393079

The Krishna Oberoi is located on Banjara Hills, a green, picturesque and smart residential area, 1½ kms from the main business district. Situated on the highest point in the city amidst 10 acres of lush green gardens with water cascades, lagoons and fountains, the hotel offers a superb panoramic view of the city and its skyline from each of its rooms.

Accommodation & rates
256 rooms, single US$ 70-100; double US$ 70-130; suite US$ 200-450

Credit cards accepted:
Amex, Diners, Bank America, Eurocard, Mastercard,Visa

Groups
Three meeting/conference rooms, capacity up to 1200, with aidio-visual facilities; largest banquet 900

Room services
Airconditioning, colour TV, direct-dial telephone (ext. in bathroom), laundry/valet service, minibar, safety deposit box, trouser press, 24-hour room/meal service, video films

The Oberoi Palm Beach

Business & other services
Business centre, executive floor, car rental, travel centre, barber shop/beauty salon, guided tours, newsstand/shops

Sports & Recreation
Fitness centre/gym, golf, indoor swimming pool, tennis

Restaurants & Coffee Shops
Firdaus (64) - Indian, open 1230-1445/1930-2245; *Szechuan Garden* (76) - Chinese, open as above; *Gardenia* (75) - Indian & Continental, open 0700-0045; *Golconda Bar* (40) -Snacks & cocktails, open 1100-2245

Overseas Sales Representatives:
Oberoi Worldwide Offices

Taj Residency   E
Rd No 1 Banjara Hills, 500034
Tel: 399 9999; Tlx: 4256947; Fax: 392218

Jaipur

Hotel Clarks Amer   E
Jawaharlal Nehru Rd, Jaipur 302 009
Tel: (141) 550616; Tlx: 0365 2276; Fax: (141) 550013

Holiday Inn Jaipur   D
Amer Rd, Jaipur 302002
Tel: (141) 609000; Fax: 609090

The Jai Mahal Palace Hotel
Jacob Rd, Civil Lines, 302006
Tel: (0141) 371616; Tlx: 0365-2254; Fax: (0141) 365237; E-mail: jmpgm.jap/taj group

A magnificent palace, once the home of the Prime Minister of Jaipur. Located downtown, close to main shopping centre and historical monuments

Accommodation & rates
96 single/double/twin rooms; single US$ 37-175; double US$ 72-200; suite US$ 375-475

Credit cards accepted:
All major

(continued)

Meeting & conference facilities
Three meeting/conference rooms, capacity 10-150, with audio-visual facilities; largest reception 150 indoor/1500 outdoor

Room services
Airconditioning, colour TV, direct-dial telephone (ext. in bathroom), hairdryer, laundry/valet service, safety deposit box, trouser press, 24-hour room/meal service, video films

Business & other services
Business centre, express checkout, airport pickup (on request), translation service, car parking & rental, travel centre, barber shop/beauty salon, guided tours, newsstand/shops

Sports & Recreation
Jogging track, massage, outdoor swimming pool

Restaurants & Coffee Shops
Gulab Mahal (90) - Multi-cuisine, open 0630-1030/1230-1430/1930-2330; *Hana Mahal* (35) - open air 24-hour coffee shop; *Rang Mahal* (45) - Bar, open 1130-02330

Overseas Sales Representatives:
Taj Worldwide Offices

The Rambagh Palace
Bhawani Singh Rd, 302005
Tel: (141) 381919; Tlx: 0365-2254/2147 RBAG IN; Fax: (141) 381098

A magnificent palace spread over 47 acres of garden, the former residence of the Maharaja of Jaipur. Centrally located, near the shopping area and historical monuments. 11 kms from the aiport. Has very fine suites and rooms

Accommodation & rates
102 single/double rooms; single US$ 155-275; double US$ 175-275; 4 suites US$ 525-675

Credit cards accepted:
Amex, Visa, Mastercard

Meeting & conference facilities
Two meeting/conference rooms, capacity 20-200, with audio-visual facilities; largest reception 1000 banquet or cocktail

Room services
Airconditioning, colour TV, direct-dial telephone (ext. in bathroom), hairdryer, laundry/valet service, minibar, music/radio/alarm clock, trouser press, 24-hour room/meal service

Business & other services
Business centre, airport pickup, car parking & rental, travel centre, taxi service, barber shop/beauty salon, guided tours, newsstand/shops

Sports & Recreation
Fitness centre/gym, golf, jacuzzi/whirlpool, jogging track, massage, sauna, squash, indoor swimming pool, tennis, *Panghai* cultural theatre from October-April

Restaurants & Coffee Shops
Neel Mahal (50) - Coffee shop, open 24 hours; *Suvarna Mahal* (140) - Indian, Chinese & Continental, open 0630-0900/1230-1430/1930-2230

Overseas Sales Representatives:
Taj Worldwide Offices, Utell International, Superreps International London

Hotel Samode Palace   D
Gangapole, Samode 303806 Dis't, Jaipur
Tel: (141) 602407; Fax: (141) 602370

Welcomgroup Rajputana Palace Sheraton
Palace Road, Jaipur 302006, Rajasthan
Tel: (141) 360011; Tlx: 0365-2489; Fax: (141) 367848

Centrally located and in the Haveu concept of construction. 15 kms from Sanganere Airport. Close to business and shopping locations

Accommodation & rates
218 rooms and suites. Single US$ 135-200; double US$ 150-220; suites US$ 340-700. Group tariff single $ 115-150; double $ 120-165

Credit cards accepted: All major

Meeting & conference/banqueting
Surya Vanshi Mahal, capacity 500 in U shape; 150 in double U shape/800 for a reception; open theme party terrace - 400

Room services
Airconditioning, colour TV/CCTV, direct-dial telephone (ext. in bathroom), hairdryer, laundry/valet service, minibar, music/radio/alarm clock, safety deposit box, 24-hour room/meal service

Business & other services
Business centre, executive floor, express checkout, airport pickup, translation service, car parking & rental, travel & tour centre, taxi service, barber shop/beauty salon, guided tours, newsstand/shopping arcade

Sports & Recreation
Fitness centre/gym, massage, sauna, outdoor swimming pool, tennis

Restaurants & Coffee Shops
The Chandravanshi (108) - Coffee shop, open 24 hours; *Jal Mahal* (154) - Multi-cuisine, open noon-1500/1930-midnight; *Sheesh Mahal* (64) - Bar; *Peshawri* (70) - Northwest Frontier, open as above

Overseas Sales Representatives:
ITT Sheraton Worldwide

Jodhpur

Welcomgroup Umaid Bhawan Palace   B
Jodhpur, Rajasthan 342006
Tel: (0291) 33316; Tlx: 0552-202; Fax: (0291) 35373

Khimsar

Welcomgroup Royal Castle   D
PO Box Khimsar, District Naguar, Khimsar
Tel: 28; Tlx: (New Delhi) 031-65217; Fax: via 91-11 301 2892

Kovalam

Kovalam Ashok Beach Resort
Thiruvananthapuram 695527, Kerala
Tel: (0471) 480101; Tlx: 0435-6216; Fax: (0471) 481522
Internet: http://www.india.tourist.com or
       http://www.indianhotels.com

Set amidst 65 acres of coconut plantation, fanned by balmy breezes, the private beach caressed by the azure blue Arabian waters, the Resort is one of the finest holiday destination. Offers luxurious

accommodation - cottages, sea facing rooms and palatial suites. Recreational facilities include three outdoor pools, health club, water sports, tennis.

Accommodation & rates
10 double/175 twin US$ 125-165 (single occ. $110-150); 8 suites US$ 180-450

Credit cards accepted:
Amex, ITDC, Diners, Central Mastercard, Visa/Cancard, BOB Card, India Card, Citibank, Andhra Bank

Meeting & banqueting facilities
Four meeting/conference rooms, capacity 15-500; audio-visual equipment available; 200 sq m exhibitin space; largest reception 300 seated or 500 cocktail; S I booths; theme parties up to 2000 pax; beach barbecue

Room services
Airconditioning, colour TV, direct-dial telephone (ext. in bathroom), laundry/valet service, minibar, music/radio/alarm clock, safety deposit box, 24-hour room/meal service, non-smoker bedrooms, video films

Business services
Business centre, express checkout, car parking & rental, travel centre, taxi service

Other services
Barber shop/hairdresser, beauty salon, guided tours, newsstand/shops, doctor on call, bank on premises

Sports & Recreation
Fitness centre/gym, indoor games, massage, outdoor swimming pool, tennis, watersports, daily cultural events

Restaurants & Coffee Shops
Shells (120) - Indian/Continental, open 1300-1500/1930-2215; *Coffee Shop* (48) - open for snacks 24 hours; *Grove* (80) - Continental/regional, open 0600-2200; *Beach* (60) - regional, open 0700-1900; *Osheen* (48) - Chinese/steaks/sizzlers,open 2000-2245; *Admiral Bar* - open 1100-2300; *Beer/Ice Cream Parlour,* open 1100-1900

Overseas Reservation Consolidator
Amadeus Marketing SA, Madrid, Spain thru' Indian Hotel Reservation Services (IHRES)

Explanation of codes in (short) hotel entries. *A* after name = single room over US$ 200 per night; *B* = between $150-200; *C* = between $100-150; *D* = between $50-100; *E* = under $50; ¶ = on applcation. Prices are a guide only and in some cases were supplied to us in 1996. Travellers are recommended to check with individual hotels before booking.

Khajuraho

The Jass Oberoi
By Pass Road, Khajuraho, 471606
Tel: (7686) 2085-7; Tlx: 150-1202 OBKH IN; Fax: (7686) 2088

Situated close to the sensuous 10th-century temples, the hotel is set amidst landscaped gardens. The white marble lobby and the rooms with private balconies have an ambience that is distinctly Indian. Besides admiring the temple architecture, one can go boating or fishing in nearby lakes.

Accommodation & rates
94 rooms and suites; single US$ 33; double US$ 65

Credit cards accepted:
Amex, Visa, Mastercard, Eurocard, Bank America, Diners

Meeting & conference facilities
Two meeting/conference rooms, capacity 150

Room services
Airconditioning, colour TV, laundry/valet service, 24-hour room/meal service

Other services
Car rental, travel centre, newsstand/shops

Sports & Recreation
Indoor swimming pool

Restaurants & Coffee Shops
Apsara (72) - Indian & Continental, open 0700-2230; Temple Bar (45) , open 1000-2300

Overseas Sales Representatives:
Oberoi Worldwide Offices

Photographs normally refer to the hotels whose details follow them. Alternatively a photograph may fall **within** an extended entry. Figures in brackets after names of restaurants in long hotel entries signifies number of covers/seats available.
◯ after name = Associated Hotel Member of the Pacific Asia Travel Association.

Lucknow

The Taj Mahal Hotel
Vipin Khand, Gomti Nagar, 226 010
Tel: (0522) 393939; Tlx: 0535-2418 TAJL IN; Fax: (0522) 392282

Built on 33 acres of landscaped gardens, on the banks of the river Gomti, the Taj Mahal Hotel has a low line colonial style of architecture. It offers luxurious accommodation and a wide range of recreational facilities.

Accommodation & rates
1110 rooms including 5 deluxe & 4 suites. Single US$ 125-140; twin/double US$ 145-160; deluxe US$ 250-275; suite US$ 300

Credit cards accepted:
Amex, Visa, Mastercard, Diners

Meeting & conference facilities
Four meeting/conference rooms, capacity 20-1000, with audio-visual facilities; largest reception 1000 banquet or cocktail

Room services
Airconditioning, colour TV, direct-dial telephone (ext. in bathroom), hairdryer, laundry/valet service, minibar, music/radio/alarm clock, safety deposit box, 24-hour room/meal service, video films

Business services
Business centre, airport pickup, car parking & rental, travel centre

Other services
Barber shop/hairdresser, beauty salon, newsstand/shops

Sports & Recreation
Fitness centre/gym, golf, indoor games, jacuzzi/whirlpool, jogging track, massage, outdoor swimming pool, tennis,

Restaurants & Coffee Shops
The Sahib Café (90) - Indian/Continental/Chinese, open 0600-2330; *Oudhyana* (92) - Awadhi Indian, open 1230-1430/1930-2330; *Mehfil* (45) - Bar, open noon-2330; *Poolside Barbecue* (60) - regional, open 0700-1900; *Osheen* (35) - Indian/Continental Grills, open 1930-2330

Madras/Chennai

Connemara Hotel D
Binny Road, 600 002
Tel: 852 0123; Tlx: 41 8197; Fax: 852 3361

The Fisherman's Cove D
Covelong, Chingleput District, 603112
Tel: 4113 44304; Tlx: 4000204; Fax: 4113 44303

Madras Hilton *(opening mid-1997)*
G T S Road, Madras 600018
Pre-opening tel/fax: (44) 234 7621

Scheduled for opening in the second quarter of 1997, this hotel is slated to be one of the finest in Madras. Set amidst beautifully landscaped gardens, it will offer comprehensive facilities & services, including executive floor rooms, luxurious suites & meeting rooms for 2000 upwards

Accommodation & rates
237 rooms and suites, US$ 200-275

Credit cards accepted:
All major

Meeting & conference facilities
Five meeting/conference rooms, capacity up to 750, with audio-visual facilities; 920 sq m exhibition space; largest reception 500 banquet or 750 cocktail

Room services
Airconditioning, colour TV, direct-dial telephone (ext. in bathroom), hairdryer, laundry/valet service, minibar, music, safety deposit box, 24-hour room/meal service, video films

Business & other services
Business centre, executive floor, express checkout, airport pickup, car parking & rental, travel centre, taxi service, barber shop/hairdresser, beauty salon, newsstand/shops

Sports & Recreation
Fitness centre/gym, jacuzzi/whirlpool, massage, sauna, outdoor swimming pool

Restaurants & Coffee Shops
Euro Asian Restaurant (140) - open 24 hours; *Indian Restaurant* (75), open lunch & dinner; *Fun Pub* (100) Bar/dancing/bbq

Overseas Sales Representatives
Hilton International Co

Quality Inn Aruna D
144 Sterling Road, 600 034
Tel: 825 9090; Fax: 825 8282

Taj Coromandel
17 Nungambakkam High Rd, 600 034
Tel: 827 2827; Tlx: 041-7194/6720 TAJM IN; Fax: 825 7104

Centrally located and with easy access to shopping and entertainment centres. Luxurious accommodation and the finest cuisine in town. Also boasts of a modern business centre, health club, beauty salon and swimming pool.

Accommodation & rates
201 rooms & suites. Single US$ 170-270; double US$ 190-300; suite US$ 310-650

Credit cards accepted:
Amex, Visa, Mastercard, Diners

Meeting & conference facilities
Five meeting/conference rooms, capacity 20-50, with audio-visual facilities; largest reception 500 seated or 1000 cocktail

Room services
Airconditioning, colour TV, direct-dial telephone (ext. in bathroom), hairdryer, laundry/valet service, minibar, music/radio/alarm clock, safety deposit box, 24-hour room/meal service, non-smoker bedrooms available, video films

Business services
Business centre, executive floor, express checkout, airport pickup (charged), car parking & rental, travel centre, taxi service

Other services
Barber shop/hairdresser, beauty salon, newsstand/shops, guided tours

Sports & Recreation
Fitness centre/gym, golf (nearby), jacuzzi/whirlpool, massage, sauna, outdoor swimming pool

Restaurants & Coffee Shops
Mysore (77) - Indian/Continental, open 1230-1500/1930-midnight; *Golden Dragon* (82) - Chinese, open as above; midnight; *The Patio* (44) - Continental, open as above; *The Pavilion* (90) - Coffee Shop, open 24 hours

Overseas Sales Representatives
Taj Hotels Worldwide

The Trident
1/24 GST Road, Madras 600027
Tel: 234 4747; Fax: 234 6699

The Trident is professionally managed by the Oberoi group of hotels. It is situated five minutes from the domestic/internatioal airport and 20 minutes from the central business district and shopping areas.

Accommodation & rates
166 rooms & suites. Single US$ 105-130; twin/double US$ 120-150; suite US$ 225-350

Credit cards accepted:
All major

Meeting & conference facilities
Five meeting/conference rooms, capacity up to 150, with audio-visual facilities;

Room services
Airconditioning, colour TV, direct-dial telephone (ext. in bathroom), hairdryer, laundry/valet service, minibar, safety deposit box, trouser press, 24-hour room/meal service, video films

Business & other services
Business centre, newsstand/shops

Sports & Recreation
Fitness centre/gym, golf (nearby), outdoor swimming pool

Restaurants & Coffee Shops
Maratha Coffee Shop (74) - Indian/Continental, open 24 hours; *Shanghai* (68) - Szechuan, open 1230-1500/1930-midnight; *Thanjavur* (68) - Indian Tandoori, open as above; *Arlot Bar* (49) - open noon-midnight

Overseas Sales Representatives
Oberoi Hotels Worldwide

Further copies of this **Country Report** and the complete 1997/98 Asia-Pacific Business Travel Guide are available from the publisher (Priory Public-ations Ltd) at PO Box 24, Brackley, Northants NN13 5FA, UK. Fax: [+44] 1280 850576. The guide can also be viewed on the Internet under **http://travel.cm-net.com/pata**

INDIA - Hotels

Welcomgroup Chola Sheraton
10 Cathedral Rd, Chennai 600034
Tel: 828 0101; Tlx: 041-6660;
Fax: 827 8779

Located in the city centre, 13 kms from Meenambakkam Airport, close to Mahabalipuram Beach Resort with temples and dance festivals. Kanchipuram, City of Silk, is also very close by.

Accommodation & rates
100 rooms and suites. Single US$ 140-230; double US$ 150-240; suite US$ 400. Group tariff - single $ 115, double $ 127. Subject to 6% sales tax; 20% luxury tax on FIT tariff; 20% expenditure tax

Credit cards accepted:
All major

Meeting & banqueting facilities
Large hall for up to 800; three smaller rooms Poolside area; terrace gardens

Room services
Airconditioning, colour TV, direct-dial telephone (ext. in bathroom), hairdryer, laundry/valet service, minibar, music, safety deposit box, 24-hour room/meal service, trouser press

Business & other services
Business centre, executive floor, airport pickup (charged), car parking & rental, travel & tour centre, taxi service, barber shop/hairdresser, beauty salon, newsstand/shopping arcade

Sports & Recreation
Fitness centre/gym, golf/tennis (can be arranged), jogging track, massage, sauna, outdoor swimming pool

Restaurants & Coffee Shops
Peshawri (52) -Northwest Frontier, open 01230-1500/1930-midnight; *Sagari* (75) - Chinese, open as above; *Mercara* (66) - Coffee Shop, open 24 hours

International Sales Representatives
ITT Sheraton Worldwide

---

*Explanation of codes in (short) hotel entries. **A** after name = single room over US$ 200 per night; **B** = between $150-200; **C** = between $100-150; **D** = between $50-100; **E** = under $50; ¶ = on applcation*

Welcomgroup Park Sheraton Hotel & Towers
132 TTK Road, PO Box 1453, Chennai 600034.Tel: (44) 499 4101; Tlx: 041-23188; Fax: (44) 499 7201

Five kms from the city centre, 10 kms from Anna Airport. Close to Mahabalipuram (Beach Shore Temple). Exclusive Sheraton Tower rooms.

Accommodation & rates
300 rooms and suites. Single US$ 140-230; double US$ 150-240; suite US$ 280-750. Group tariff - single $ 115, double $ 127. Subject to 6% sales tax; 20% luxury tax on FIT tariff; 10% expenditure tax

Credit cards accepted:
All major

Meeting & banqueting facilities
Four meeting/banqueting rooms, capacity 800+

Room services
Airconditioning, colour TV, direct-dial telephone (ext. in bathroom), hairdryer, laundry/valet service, minibar, music/radio/alarm clock, safety deposit box, 24-hour room/meal service, trouser press

Business & other services
Business centre, executive floor, airport pickup (charged), car parking & rental, travel & tour centre, taxi service, barber shop/hairdresser, beauty salon, newsstand/shopping arcade

Sports & Recreation
Fitness centre/gym, jogging track, tennis, massage, sauna, outdoor swimming pool, executive 'Towers' health & dining club

Restaurants & Coffee Shops
Gatsby (86) - Multicuisine/coffee shop (converts to discotheque at weekends) open 24 hours;
Residency (122) - buffet, open 1230-1500/1930-midnight;
Dakshin (96) - South Indian, open as above;
Bolan Bar (57) - open noon-midnight

International Sales Representatives
ITT Sheraton Worldwide

Mangalore

Welcomgroup Manjarun   E
Old Port Road, Mangalore 575001
Tel: 420420; Fax: 420585

Mysore

Lalitha Mahal Palace Hotel
Mysore, 570011.
Tel: (0821) 571265-276; Tlx: 0846-217; Fax: (0821) 571770
E-Mail: http://www.indiatourist.com or http://www.indianhotels.com

Set amidst palaces, collonaded markets, statue circles, temples and lakes is the prestigious Lalitha Mahal Palace Hotel, with 54 rooms with original atmosphere and charm and modern luxury of the highest standard with impeccable service.

Accommodation & rates
2 single US$ 50-120; 12 double, 32 twin US$ 60-150; 8 suites US$ 180-620

Credit cards accepted:
Amex, ITDC, Diners, Central Mastercard, Visa/Cancard, BOB Card, India Card, Citibank, Andhra Bank

Meeting & banqueting facilities
2 meeting/conference rooms, capacity 150/35; largest reception 60 seated/300 cocktail

Room services
Airconditioning, colour TV, direct-dial telephone (ext. in bathroom), laundry/valet service, minibar, music, safety deposit box, 24-hour room/meal service, trouser press, video films

Business & other services
Car parking & rental, travel centre, taxi service, barber shop/hairdresser, beauty salon, guided tours, newsstand/shops, doctor on call, helipad, shopping arcade, meditation room, information desk

Sports & Recreation
Billiards/snooker, fitness centre/gym, golf, indoor games, jogging track, massage, sauna, outdoor swimming pool, tennis

Restaurants & Coffee Shops
Restaurant (110) - Indian/Continental, open 0600-2300; *Tea Lounge* (30) - Chinese, open 1100-1330/1500-2000

Overseas Reservation Consolidator
Amadeus Marketing SA, Madrid, Spain thru Indian Hotel Reservation Services (IHRES)

Patna

Welcomgroup Maurya-Patna   D
1 Fraser Road, S Gandhi Maidan, 800001
Tel: (0612) 222061; Tlx: 022-352

Poona/Pune

Blue Diamond Hotel   ○   E
11 Koregaon Road, 411001
Tel: (0212) 625555; Fax: (0212) 627755

Hotel Nandanvan   ○   E
13 Wilson Garden, Motilal Talera Marg, 411001.Tel: (0212) 55251-2; Tlx: 145-454

Shimla

The Cecil
The Mall, Shimla 171001
Tel: (0177) 201725/6242; Tlx: 0391-2170 BCU; Fax: (0177) 211024

The Cecil is the only luxury hotel in the Himalayas. It is situated at the quiet end of the Mall in the capital city of Himachal Pradesh. The hotel has stunning views of the Himalayan forests and peaks on both sides

Accommodation & rates
71 doubles, US$ 115-145; 8 suites US$ 165-200

Credit cards accepted:
All major

Meeting facilities
Two meeting rooms, capacity 30 each

Room services
Airconditioning, colour TV, direct-dial telephone, minibar, 24-hour room/meal service

Other services
Car parking & rental, library

Sports & Recreation
Billiards/snooker, fitness centre/gym, indoor games, outdoor swimming pool

Restaurants & Coffee Shops
The Restaurant (40) - Indian & Continental; *The Lounge* (100) - Atrium Bar; *The Beer Garden*

The Oberoi Clarkes

The Oberoi Clarkes
The Mall, Shimla 171001
Tel: (0177) 212991; Tlx: 206 OBCL IN; Fax: (0177) 211321

The Oberoi Clarkes, with the elegance of an earlier era, is located on Shimla's main shopping promenade, the Mall. the hotel has spacious rooms, tastefully furnished, with attached baths and colour televisions

Accommodation & rates
39 doubles, US$ 112

Credit cards accepted:
Amex, Diners, Visa, Bank America, Mastercharge, Eurocard

Meeting facilities
Meeting rooms, capacity 75-100 persons

Room services
Airconditioning, colour TV, hairdryer, 24-hour room/meal service, video films

Other services: Car rental

Sports & Recreation
Nearby: golf, hiking, trekking, ice skating, roller skating, ski-ing

Restaurants & Coffee Shops
Dining Room (80) - Indian, Continental, Mughal, Chinese, open 0730-2300; *Bar* (12) - Snacks, drinks, open 1100-1500/1900-2300

Srinagar

Hotel Broadway   E
Maulana Azad Rd, 190001
Tel: (194) 75621-3; Tlx: 375-212

Centaur Lake View Hotel   E
Chashmeshabi, on Dal Lake, 190001
Tel: (194) 75631; Tlx: 375-205

The Oberoi Palace   E
Gupkar Rd, 190001
Tel: (194) 71241-2; Tlx: 1375-201

Welcomgroup Ghurka Houseboats   E
PO Box 57, Nagin Lake 19001
Tel: (194) 75229; Tlx: 375-286

Udaipur

Shiv Niwas Palace Hotel   D
City Palace, 313001
Tel: (0294) 28239-41; Tlx: 033-226

The Lake Palace
PO Box No. 5, Pichola Lake, 313001
Tel: (0294) 527961; Tlx: 0335-203 LPAL IN; Fax: (0294) 527974;
E-mail: LPU.UDP/TAJGTOUP

Arising like a mirage out of the turquoise waters of the Pichola Lake, the Lake Palace was erected on a natural foundation of four acres of rock. Here amidst the calm waters of the Pichola, you can get away from the noise and confusion of onshore activity...escape into the lifestyle of Rajasthan's royalty and quite simply live like a king.

Accommodation & rates
1 single US$ 180-200; 15 double, 43 twin US$ 200-220; 15 suites US$ 310-660

Credit cards accepted:
Amex, Bank of America, Diners,Mastercard, Visa/Cancard, BOB Card, India Card, Citibank, Andhra Card, ANZ Grindlays, Vijaya Bank, Hercard, Std Chartered

Meeting & banqueting facilities
Meeting/conference rooms, capacity 40, with audio-visual facilities; 650 sq ft exhibition space; *Gangaur Boat, Lily Pond, Mewar Terrace* - venues for private dinners

Room services
Airconditioning, colour TV, direct-dial telephone (ext. in bathroom), hairdryer, laundry/valet service, minibar, music, safety deposit box, video films

Other services
Express checkout, car parking & rental, travel centre, taxi service

Sports & Recreation
Fitness centre/gym, massage, outdoor swimming pool

Restaurants & Coffee Shops
Neelkamal (110) - Indian/Continental, open 1930-2230; *Jharokha* (80) - Indian/Continental, open 0600-0930/1230-1430; *Amrit Sagar* (52) - Bar, open 1100-2300

Overseas Sales Rpresentatives
Taj Hotels Worldwide

Varanasi

Best Western Ideal   E
The Mall Cantt, 221 001.Tel: (542) 348250
Tlx: 545-204; Fax: (542) 42947

Hotel Clarks Varanasi   E
The Mall, Varanasi 221002
Tel: 0542 46771; Tlx: 0545 2276; Fax: 0542 42947

Hotel Taj Ganges   D
Nadesar Palace Grounds, 221002
Tel: 342481; Tlx: 545219; Fax: 348067

"Think India. Think Taj."

The Taj Mahal Hotel, Bombay: old world elegance with modern style.

"The Taj Group offers you more and varied ways to enjoy the wonders of India than any other hotel group, quite simply, because we are larger than all the rest. TAJ LUXURY HOTELS: eight international grand luxe hotels, in all major cities, led by the legendary Taj Mahal Hotel, Bombay. TAJ RESIDENCY HOTELS: superb business hotels located in the heart of India's key commercial centres. TAJ LEISURE HOTELS: idyllic Beach Resorts, the majesty of genuine Palaces, intimate Garden Retreats in beautiful, natural surroundings and delightful Cultural Centre Hotels in places with historic attractions."

Lake Palace, Udaipur: unimaginably opulent, uniquely tranquil.

TAJ LUXURY HOTELS: The Taj Mahal Hotel, Bombay; The Taj Mahal Hotel, New Delhi; Taj Palace Hotel, New Delhi; Taj Bengal, Calcutta; The Taj West End, Bangalore; Taj Coromandel, Madras; The Taj Mahal Hotel, Lucknow; Taj Samudra, Colombo.

TAJ RESIDENCY HOTELS: Taj Residency, Bangalore; Taj Residency, Hyderabad; Taj Residency, Visakhapatnam; Taj Residency, Aurangabad; Taj Residency, Ernakulam; Taj Residency, Indore.

TAJ PALACE HOTELS: Rambagh Palace, Jaipur; Jai Mahal Palace, Jaipur; Lake Palace, Udaipur.

TAJ RESORT HOTELS: The Aguada Hermitage, Goa; Fort Aguada Beach Resort, Goa; Taj Holiday Village, Goa; Fisherman's Cove, Madras; Em-boo-dhu Fin-olhu Island Resort, Maldives.

TAJ GARDEN RETREATS: Taj Garden Retreat, Madurai; Taj Garden Retreat, Coonoor; Taj Garden Retreat, Kumarakom; Taj Garden Retreat, Varkala.

TAJ CULTURAL CENTRE HOTELS: Taj-View Hotel, Agra; Taj Ganges, Benares; Hotel Chandela, Khajuraho; Hotel de L'Annapurna, Kathmandu; Taj Malabar, Cochin.

THE TAJ GROUP *of* HOTELS

This is not an exhaustive list of properties.

THE TAJ GROUP. INDIA'S *first*. SOUTH ASIA'S *finest*.   FAX CENTRAL RESERVATIONS BOMBAY: (91-22) 283 7272
OR CALL **UTELL** INTERNATIONAL OR YOUR TRAVEL PLANNER.

A colourful directory of the Hotels is available. Please fax your request to (91-22) 283-7272 quoting "PATABTG"

India Airline Departures & Offices

Below is a list of departures from Bombay, Delhi and Madras airports to the destinations in bold type. Figures in brackets after destinations refer to the days of the week. (2,4,6) therefore indicates that departures to that destination take place on a Tuesday (the second day of the week), a Thursday and a Saturday. Departures were correct as at February 1997 but should be checked with the airline offices listed on the facing page. Only direct connections are listed.

Airline abbreviation codes: **AC** = Air Canada; **AF** = Air France; **AI** = Air India; **AZ** = Alitalia; **BA** = British Airways; **BG** = Biman Bangladesh; **B3** = K.D. Air Corps; **CD** = Alliance Air; **CX** = Cathay Pacific; **DY** = Alyemda Democratic Yemen Airways; **D2** = Damania Airways; **D5** = NEPC Airlines; **EK** = Emirates; **FF** = Tower Air; **FS** = Archana Airways; **GK** = Go One Airways; **HM** = Air Seychelles; **IY** = Yemenia Airways; **KB** = Druk Air; **LH** = Lufthansa; **LY** = El Al; **M9** = Modiluft; **RO** = Tarom; **TG** = Thai Airways; **T5** = Avia Comp Turk; **ET** = Ethiopian Airlines; **GF** = Gulf Air; **IC** = Indian Airlines; **KL** = KLM; **KU** = Kuwait Airways; **MS** = Eqyptair; **PF** = Vayudoot; **QF** = Qantas Airways; **Q7** = Qatar Airways; **RA** = Royal Nepal Airlines; **RB** = Syrian Arab Airlines; **RJ** = Royal Jordanian; **SA** = South African Airways; **SR** = Swissair; **SQ** = Singapore Airlines; **SU** = Aeroflot; **SV** = Saudia; **S2** = Sahara India Airlines; **TK** = Turkish Airlines; **UL** = Air Lanka; **WY** = Air South; **Y2** = Alliance Airlines; **4S** = East West Airlines; **6U** = Air Ukraine; **7J** = Tjik Air; **9W** = Jat Airways.

BOMBAY (BOM)

Abu Dhabi (AUH)
AI (2,3,4,5,6,7) GF (daily) RB (3)
Addis Ababa (ADD)
ET (2,4,6)
Aden (ADE)
IY (1,7)
Ahmedabad (AMD)
IC,9W (daily) D2 (2,4,6) AI (4,6)   4S (1,2,3,4,5,6)
Amsterdam (AMS)
KL (2,4,6) FF (4,7)
Athens (ATH)
BG (6)
Aurangabad (IXU)
IC (3,4,6,7) 4S (1,3,5,7) D5 (daily)
Bahrain (BAH)
AI (1,2,4) GF (1,3,4,5,6,7)
Bangalore (BLR)
IC/D2/9W/4S/M9 (daily) AI (4,6) D5 (2,4,6)
Bangkok (BKK)
AI (2,5) CX (1,2,4,5)
Bhavnagar (BHU)
IC (1,2,4,6) D5 (3,5,7)
Bhopal (BHO)
IC (1,2,4,5)
Bhuj (BHJ)
IC (2,3,5,6)
Cairo (CAI)
MS (7) KE (3)
Calcutta (CCU)
AI (5) IC,D2 (daily) 9W (1,3,4,5,6,7) M9 (1,2,3,4,5,6)
Calicut (CCJ)
IC,9W,4S (daily)
Cochin (COK)
IC/9W/4S/M9 (daily)
Coimbatore (CJB)
4S (1,2,3,4,5,7) 9W (daily) IC (2,5,6,7)
Colombo (CMB)
UL (1,4)
Damascus (DAM)
RB (3)
Dar-es-Salaam (DAR)
AI (3,5)
Delhi (DEL)
AI,IC,9W,M9,4S.S2 (daily) D2 (3,5,7)
Dhahran (DHA)
AI (1,3,4,5) SV (2,5,6,7)
Dhaka (DAC)
BG (4,7)
Doha (DOH)
AI (1,2,4) GF (daily) Q7 (6)
Dubai (DXB)
AI/EK (daily) BG (3,6) CX (1,3,4,7) HM (5)
Durban (DUR)
AI (3,7,)
Entebbe (EBB)
AI (1)
Frankfurt (FRA)
AI (1,3,4,6,7) LH (2,4,5,6,7)   DL (daily)
Geneva (GVA)
AI (3,6)
Goa (GOI)
AI (1) D2/IC/9W/M9 (daily) 4S (2,4,6,7)
Gwalior (GWL)
IC (1,2,4,5)
Hong Kong (HKG)
AI (2,5,6) CX (1,2,4,5) SR (1,3,5)
Hyderabad (HYD)
4S,IC,9W (daily) D2 (3,5,7) AI (2,3,4,5,6)
Indore (IDR)
IC (1,2,4,5) D2 (daily)
Jaipur (JAI)
M9, IC (daily) 4S (2,4,5,7)
Jakarta (JKT)
AI (7)
Jamnagar (JGA)
IC (1,2,4,7) D5 (3,5,6)
Jeddah (JED)
AI (2,3,4,5) SV (1,4,6)
Jodhpur (JDH)
IC (1,3,5,6) M9 (daily)
Johannesburg (JNB)
SA (2,6) AI (3,7)
Kandla (IXY)
D5 (1,4)
Karachi (KHI)
IC (3,7) PK (1,2,3,4,7) UL (3)
Kathmandu (KTM)
RA (1,5)
Keshod (IXK)
D5 (2,7)
Kuala Lumpur (KUL)
AI (4,6)
Kuwait (KWI)
KU (daily) AI (1,4,7) AZ (2)
London (LGW)
GK (3)
London (LHR)
AI,BA (daily)
Lucknow (LKO)
IC (2,4,6) S2 (daily)
Madras (MAA)
AI,IC,4S,9W (daily) D5 (2,4,6) AI (1,2,4,5,6,7) D2 (2,3,4,5,6,7)
Madurai (IXM)
IC (2,5,6,7) 4S (daily)
Manchester (MAN)
SQ (1,5) AI (1,4)
Mangalore (IXE)
IC,4S,9W (daily)
Mauritius (MRU)
AI/MK (1,2,3,5)
Muscat (MCT)
AI (2,3,4,5,7) GF (daily) WY (2,4,5,6,7)
Nagpur (NAG)
IC (daily) 4S (1,2,3,4,5,6)
Nairobi (NBO)
AI (1,3,5) KQ (1,3,5,7)
New York (JFK)
AI,DL (daily) FF (4,7)

Osaka (OSA)
AI (2,6)
Paris (CDG)
AF (1,2,6) AI (2,4,5,6,7)
Perth (PER)
AI (1,4)
Poona (PNQ)
D5,D2 (daily)
Porbandar (PBD)
D5 (2,7)
Rajkot (RAJ)
IC (2,3,5,6) D5 (1,2,4,6)
Riyadh (RUH)
AI (1,2,3,4,5,7) SV (1,2,3,5,6,7)
Rome (FCO)
AZ (2,4,7)
Sanaa (SAH)
IY (3,5)
Seoul (SEL)
KE (3)
Sharjah (SHJ)
DY (1) IC (3,6) GF (4) IY (5)
Singapore (SIN)
AI,SQ (daily)
Tehran (TEH)
IR (5)
Tel Aviv (TLV)
LY (3,7) AI (2,6)
Tokyo (NRT)
AI (2,3,5,6)
Toronto (YYZ)
AC (2,5,7)
Trivandrum (TRV)
AI (1,2,3,5,6,7) IC,4S (daily)
Udaipur (UDR)
M9 (daily) IC (1,3,4,5,6,7)
Vadodara (BDQ)
IC,D5 (daily)
Varanasi (VNS)
IC (2,4,6)
Zurich (ZRH)
SR (2,4,6,7)

DELHI (Indira Gandhi International) (DEL)

Abu Dhabi (AUH)
GF (1,3,6,7) AI (2)
Addis Ababa (ADD)
ET (2)
Adler/Sochi (AER)
SU (2)
Agra (AGR)
IC ,M9 (daily)
Ahmedabad (AMD)
9W,IC (daily) AI (3,7) M9 (1,2,3,4,5,6) S2 (1,2,4,5,6,7)
Allahabad (IXD)
UZ (1,2,4,6)
Alamaty (ALA)
KA (2,5)
Amman (AMM)
RJ (1,4,6)
Amritsar (ATQ)
IC (1,3,6) AI (2,4)
Amsterdam (AMS)

KL (1,3,5,7) BG (2,6) AI (2,7)
Aurangabad (IXU)
IC (3,4,6,7)
Bagdogra (IXB)
IC (2,4,6,7) S2 (3,6,7)
Bahrain (BAH)
GF (2)
Bangalore (BLR)
IC, 4S, 9W (daily)
Bangkok (BKK)
TG (1,2,4,6,7) AI (2) SU (3,5) IC (4,7)
Bhopal (BHO)
FS (1,2,3,4,5,6)
Bhubaneswar (BBI)
IC (daily)
Bombay (BOM)
AI,IC,4S,M9,9W,S2 (daily) D2 (3,5,7)
Bucharest (BUH)
RO (1,6)
Calcutta (CCU)
IC,M9 (daily) AI (1) S2 (1,2,3,4,5,7) 4S (1,2,3,4,5,6)
Chandigarh (IXC)
F5 (1,3,5)
Cochin (COK)
IC (daily)
Colombo (CMB)
UL (4,6)
Copenhagen (CPH)
AI, SK (1,3,5)
Damascus (DAM)
RB (1)
Dhahran (DHA)
SV (2)
Dhaka (DAC)
BA (1,2,4,5) BG (1,4)
Doha (DOH)
GF (1,3,5)
Dubai (DXB)
EK (daily) AI (2,4,7)
Dusahanbe (DYU)
W5 (5,7)
Frankfurt (FRA)
AI (1,2,4,5,6,7) LH (daily) DL (1,2,4,6)
Geneva (GVA)
AI (3,6) SR (2)
Goa (GOI)
9W,M9,IC (daily) S2 (1,2,3,4,5)
Guwahati (GAU)
9W,IC (daily) S2 (6,7)
Gwalior (GWL)
IC (1,2,4,5)
Hong Kong (HKG)
UA (daily) AI (2,3,5,6,7)
Hyderabad (HYD)
IC (daily) S2 (1,2,4,5,6)
Indore (IDR)
UZ (daily) IC (1,2,3,4,5,6)
Jaipur (JAI)
M9 (daily) IC (1,3,4,5,6,7) Q2 (3,5,7) S2 (1,2,4,5,6,7)
Jakarta (JKT)
AI(3)

INDIA - Airline Departures

Jammu (IXJ)
  M9, IC (daily)
Jeddah (JED)
  AI (2,3) SV (2,6)
Jodhpur (JDH)
  IC (1,3,5,6)
Karachi (KHI)
  PK (3,5,7) MH (1,4)
Kathmandu (KTM)
  RA (daily) IC (daily)
Khajuraho (HJR)
  M9,IC (daily)
Kiev (IEV)
  6U (1,5)
Kuala Lumpur (KUL)
  MH/AI (1,4) AI (6)
Kuwait (KWI)
  KU (1,2,3,4,6) IC (1,3)
Lahore (LHE)
  PK (1,2,4,6)
  IC (3,5,6,7)
London (LHR)
  BA,UA (daily) TG (3,5,6)
  AC (1,3,5,7) AI (1,3,4,5,7)
Los Angeles (LAX)
  UA (daily)
Lucknow (LKO)
  IC (1,2,3,5) S2,UZ (daily)
Ludhiana (LUH)
  F5 (1,2,3,4,5,6)
Madras (MAA)
  M9,D2,IC,4S (daily) AI (3,6)
Manchester (MAN)
  AI (1,5)
Moscow (MOW)
  SU (2,3,4,5,6) AI (7)
Muscat (MCT)
  GF (2,5,6,7) AI (2) IC (2,4,6)
Nagpur (NAG)
  IC (1,2,4,5,6,7)
New York (JFK)
  UA (daily) BG (2,6) AI (1,3,4,7)
Osaka (OSA)
  AI (3,7)
Paris (CDG)
  AF (3,4,5,7) AI (1,2,5,6,7)
Paro (PBH)
  KB (1,4)
Patna (PAT)
  IC (daily) S2 (1,2,4,5,6,7)
Poona (PNQ)
  IC (daily)
Raipur (RPR)
  IC (1,2,4,5,7) F5 (2,4,6)
Ranchi ((IXR)
  IC (daily)
Riyadh (RUH)
  SV (4,6)
Rome (ROM)
  AI (3,5,6)
Sharjah (SHJ)
  RB (1) IC (1,3)
Simla (SLV)
  F5 (1,3,5)
Singapore (SIN)
  SU (1) AI (1,3,4,6) SQ (3,5,7)
Srinagar (SXR)
  IC,M9 (daily)
Tashkent (TAS)
  HY (2,3,5,6,7)
Tel Aviv (TLV)
  LY (2)
Tokyo (TYO)
  AI (2,3,6)
Toronto (YTO)
  AC (7) AI (2,5,7)
Trivandrum (TRV)
  IC (daily) AI (6,7)
Udaipur (UDR)
  M9 (daily) IC (1,3,4,5,6,7)
Vadodara (BDQ)
  IC (1,2,5,7)
Vancouver (YVR)
  AC (1,3,5,7)
Varanasi (VNS)
  M9, IC (daily) S2 (1,2,3,5,6,7)
Zurich (ZRH)
  SR (2,4,6)

MADRAS (MAA)

Abu Dhabi (AUH)
  GF (2,4)
Ahmedabad (AMD)
  IC (1,3,5,7)
Bahrain (BAH)
  GF (7)
Bangalore (BLR)
  IC (daily) DS (1,2,3,4,5,6)
Bhubaneswar (BBI)
  IC (2,7)
Bombay (BOM)
  IC,9W,4S (daily) AI (1,2,3,5,6,7)
  D2 (1,2,4,5,6,7) D5 (1,3,5)
Calcutta (CCU)
  IC (daily) D2 (1,2,4,5,6,7)
Calicut (CCJ)
  IC (daily)
Cochin (COK)
  D5 (daily) IC (1,4,5)
Coimbatore (CJB)
  D5 (daily) IC (1,3,5,7)
Colombo (CMB)
  UL (daily) IC (daily)
Dar-es-Salaam (DAR)
  AI(3)
Delhi (DEL)
  IC,4S (daily) AI (2,4,5,7)
Dhahran (DHA)
  SV (1,5) AI (4,6)
Doha (DOH)
  Q7 (2)
Dubai (DXB)
  AI (5,7)
Durban (DUR)
  AI (3)
Frankfurt (FRA)
  LH (1,4)
Goa (GOI)
  IC (2,4,6) D5 (2,4,6)
Hyderabad (HYD)
  IC (daily) D5 (1,3,5)
Jakarta (JKT)
  AI (2,3,7)
Jeddah (JED)
  SV (1)
Johannesburg (JNB)
  AI (3)
Kuala Lumpur (KUL)
  MH (1,2,3,4,5) AI (3,4,6) IC (3,7)
Kuwait (KWI)
  AI (2,5)
London (LHR)
  BA (3,5,7) AI (2,5,6)
Madurai (IXM)
  IC (2,4,6) D5 (daily)
Muscat (MCT)
  GF (2,4,7)
New York (JFK)
  AI (2,6)
Paris (CDG)
  AI (2,5)
Poona (PNQ)
  IC (1,3,5) D5 (2,4,6)
Port Blair (IXZ)
  IC (2,4,6)
Riyadh (RUH)
  SV (3,5)
Singapore (SIN)
  SQ (2,4,5,6,7) AI (daily) IC (3,7)
Trivandrum (TRV)
  IC (daily)
Vishakhapatna (VTZ)
  IC (1,3,5)

Airline Offices

(R=reservations; F =flight info'n)

Air Canada
Bombay tel: (R) 202111; (F) 6435653 New Delhi: (R) 604755

Air France
Bombay tel: (R) 2025021; (F) 6328070. Calcutta tel: 296161 New Delhi tel: (R) 604775; (F) 5452294

Air India
Bombay tel: (R) 2024142; (F)6329090.Calcutta tel: (R) 442356; (F) 572611.New Delhi tel: (R) 3311225; (F) 548261 Madras tel: (R) 474477; (F) 474488

Air Lanka
Bombay tel: (R) 223288; (F) 632 7050. Calcutta tel: 431730; New Delhi tel: 332 7909

Alitalia
Bombay tel: (R) 222112; (F) 6329082.Calcutta tel: (R)432140 New Delhi tel: (R)331 1019

British Airways
Bombay tel: (R) 2820888; (F) 832 29061-4. Calcutta tel: 293430; Madras tel: 855 4680.New Delhi tel: (R) 565 2077; (F) 332 7428

Cathay Pacific
Bombay tel: (R) 2029112-3; (F) 6321965-6.Calcutta tel: 293211; New Delhi tel: 3323919

Garuda Indonesian Airways
Bombay tel: (R) 243825; (F) 869832. Madras tel: 867957

Gulf Air
Bombay tel: (R) 2024067; (F) 6327588. Madras tel: 867872; New Delhi tel: 3324293

Indian Airlines
Bombay tel: (R) 2023031; (F) 6144433. Calcutta tel: (R) 200731 (F) 569611.New Delhi tel: (R) 3310071; (F)5483535.Madras tel: (R) 4788339; (F) 433954

Japan Airlines
Bombay tel: 233136; Calcutta tel: 297920.N Delhi.Tel: (R) 3327104; (F) 5452083.Madras tel: 867957

Korean Airlines
New Delhi tel: (R) 3329561; (F) 3323676

Lufthansa
Bombay tel: (R) 2020887; (F) 6321485.Calcutta tel: 299354: Madras tel: 869095.New Delhi tel: (R) 3327268; (F) 5452063

Philippine Airlines
Bombay tel: 224580. New Delhi tel: (R) 3325888; (F) 3325890

Qantas
Bombay tel: (R) 2029297; (F) 6127219.Calcutta tel: (R) 442394; (F) 440718.Madras tel: (R) 478649; (F) 478860.New Delhi tel: (R) 3329732; (F) 3320070

Royal Nepal Airlines
Calcutta tel: 298534. New Delhi tel: (R) 3325222; (F) 5452093. Madras tel: (R) 471195; (F) 477905

Singapore Airlines
Bombay tel: (R) 2023365; (F) 632786 Calcutta tel: (R) 299293; (F) 291525.New Delhi tel: (R) 3320145; (F) 5452011.Madras tel: (R) 862871; (F) 861872

Thai Airways International
Bombay tel: (R) 215207; (F) 214180.Calcutta: 299846; Madras: 450400
New Delhi tel: (R) 332 3608; (F) 548 2672

United Airlines
Bombay tel: 614 6583; New Delhi tel 331 5013. Madras tel: (R) 868377; (F) 862569

What's the link between business and the Asia Pacific?

BRITISH AIRWAYS
The world's favourite airline

http://www.british-airways.com

DO NOTHING AND BE REWARDED

When doing business in India, may we suggest you put aside thoughts of profit margins and balance sheets (at least for a time) and concentrate instead on holidays.

The Tantric form of yoga postulates that *yoga* (discipline) and *bhoga* (enjoyment) are one and the same, but that it takes nothing less than a *vira* (hero) to address and incorporate both. (Some authorities feel the English proverb "all work and no play etc" puts the idea over just as succinctly).

If your life is a little too dominated by the discipline of work and a spot of *bhoga* would not go amiss, then holidaying in India may make a *vira* out of you yet.

If beaches and sun are the key we've got masses of both, but there's also plenty to occupy the most acquisitive (and inquisitive) mind. A civilisation over five thousand years in the making, history at every turn, forts and palaces without number, mausoleums and temples beyond reckoning.

Cometh the hour, calleth the man (or woman). Phone us on 01233 211999 for our free 32 page colour brochure, or see your local travel agent for full details of holidaying in India.

INDIA

ONLY 9 HOURS AWAY

INDIA TOURIST OFFICE, 7 CORK STREET, LONDON WIX 2LN FAX: 0171- 494 1048.

COUNTRY REPORT
INDONESIA '97

Indonesia

Doing Business

Investment climate

An economic growth rate of 8.2% was forecast for 1997/98, maintaining Indonesia's position as one of the fastest growing economies in Southeast Asia - a giant, diverse product market that many would like to enter but few really understand.

Patience is vital to doing business in Indonesia. Patience with family hierarchies, business webs and intrigue; with the unremittingly sultry climate; with often gridlock traffic; with notorious unpunctuality; with seemingly endless red tape; with compulsory one-on-one meetings that often appear to be going nowhere. And with the anticipated full implementation of wide-sweeping trade reforms which potentially make Indonesia Asia/Pacific's biggest ever pot of gold for foreign investors.

In June 1994, the Suharto government announced a dramatic turnaround in its rules allowing foreigners to own and control businesses in Indonesia, followed in 1995 by the introduction of new corporate and capital markets legislation, new tax rate cuts, and reforms aimed at abolishing cheap labour but improving worker productivity and competitiveness.

The reforms, designed to fight tough competition for overseas investment from China and Vietnam as well as decentralise development away from Jakarta, effectively opened up many of Indonesia's formerly restricted sectors to foreign participation. But while they immediately helped foreign project approval levels to soar to a record US$24 billion in 1994, $6 billion more than the predicted level, most analysts believe their full viability and impact will not be felt until the end of the government's current five year plan in late 1998. Other foreign investors and legal experts have argued that

the measures do not go far enough. While, for example, 100% foreign ownership, with only a minimal share divestment after 15 years - instead of a maximum 80% with 51% sold on after 20 years as previously - is permitted in nine formerly restricted sectors, including urgently needed power generation, ports, mass media, transport and water treatment, the turnaround time for foreign investment approvals is still slow; sectors such as retail, advertising, foodstuffs, distribution and wholesale trading remain off limits, and foreign ownership of locally-listed shares still has a ceiling of 49%.

And while the top personal and corporate tax rate has been reduced from 35% to 30% or lower, foreign companies face a capital gains tax on the sale of assets in Indonesia. There is no longer any capital gains tax on the sale of shares on the Indonesia stock exchange but a new witholding tax on the gross of the sale value of the shares has been imposed. Witholding taxes are also being levied on services performed outside Indonesia.

Also of concern to investors amid an otherwise internationally-acclaimed package of reforms, are costs. Inflation topped a record 11.6% during 1996, more than double the five-year plan target of 5%, because of increases in wages, high prices and international pressure on the Rupiah. Depending on location, government-mandated minimum wage rates for workers increased more than threefold in late 1994 and by a further 10% in April, 1995. Private sector wages grew by up to 35% in 1995/96.

Indonesia's US$42bn budget for 1997/98 includes measures to maintain economic growth while curbing inflation, helping production from villages and boosting the mining sector. But growing concerns about the clampdown on East Timor's efforts to gain autonomy and Suharto's continuing preference shown to family business ties have not helped Indonesia's image abroad.

Business etiquette

A local agent is essential, if only to help you through the quagmire of bureaucracy which imposes itself on everyday dealings. Indonesians are generally polite and courteous but steadfastly refuse to be hurried. They recognise urgency but foreigners do themselves no favours by showing irritation, frustration or anger - or expecting results from any single meeting. Dealings by fax or phone are rare. One-on-one meetings, by prior appointment, are essential, but punctuality is unimportant and may require a wait for hours for an initial discussion covering little more than personal trivia. An instant or direct yes or no to proposals are rare. Compromise and an ability to wait for a reply, sometimes for weeks, are essential. Positions of power are frequently occupied by women. A handshake is the accepted greeting for both men and women but the left hand is regarded as unclean and its use, when eating, should be avoided.

In cities, Western business attire is the norm. Although predominantly Muslim, Indonesia is religiously tolerant, although it is wise to avoid pork and alcohol when entertaining for fear of causing offence. Lunchtime business entertaining is popular. Evening functions tend to end early.

Religious tolerance also means that many different holidays are observed, with shops and offices shut tight. Check holiday times before you go but be aware also that government offices are not always open during their advertised times.

Tourism Update

General Developments

Visitor growth in Indonesia has been good - double digits for most of the past five years, near-doubling the total in the past five years. However, only 60% of Indonesia's visitors arrive by air; most of the balance is sea traffic from Singapore into the nearby islands of Bintan and Batam.

Total visitors increased 7.9% to 4,324,229 in 1995. Arrivals from Singapore grew, despite the fact it is already 25% of the total, partly as a result of new airlines and city-pairs between the two countries, and growth of sea travel into Batam for the Bintan resort (see below). The total increased 2.9% to 1,046,533. There was also strong growth from Malaysia, up 37.8% to 511,903. That market was closely followed by Japan, which increased 2.1% to 486,278, then Taiwan, up 11.1% to 352,797. The fifth-largest market was Australia, up 5.0% to 320,494.

Average length of stay is approximately 11 days. Visitor arrivals are projected to reach 6-6.5 million in 1998 - the end of the country's current five-year development plan.

Growth in 1996 was expected to be above 15%. Jakarta, Medan, and Surabaya are primarily business travel destinations, and the other main gateways (which are Bali/Denpasar, and Batam/Bintan) are predominantly tourist.

The worldwide reputation of Bali has encouraged other tourism developments in the country. The NTO would like to repeat the success of Bali by developing other resort areas or regions in the country. The island of Lombok close to Bali, has grown in popularity, with a number of hotel developments - even though this was not one of the designated areas.

The entry point of Batam is a special case. It is 30 minutes by ferry from Singapore, and most of its visitors originate from there. Batam has had a large share of the recent growth in total visitor arrivals in Indonesia.

A huge resort, Bintan Resort, in an area that is one-third the size of Singapore itself, is being built on the island of Bintan, a neighbour island to Batam and included in the same entry point. Part of the resort has been completed and some hotels and golf courses opened, and the complex was opened officially in 1996. Hotels under construction there include a Club Med and Shangri-La. Although there were only just over 100,000 visitors there in 1996, the target is for one million in 2000. The budget of the NTO is approximately US$10 million, of which US$8 million is for marketing.

Airlines

Until recently, Garuda Indonesia Airways was the country's only international airline, and on domestic routes it was also a major operator, along with its subsidiary, Merpati Nusantara. Now there is major change, with three local airlines operating on regional international routes, and Merpati loosening and possibly breaking its connection to Garuda.

Garuda itself has embarked on a major programme to become more market-responsive, concentrating on passenger service. In 1996 it also announced a major aircraft order - for 17 B737-300/500s and six B777-200s.

Sempati, which previously operated only on domestic routes, is adding more international routes, some in competition with Garuda and both Sempati and Merpati, the Garuda subsidiary, have been granted longhaul international routes. Towards the end of 1996, Merpati started flights to Melbourne in Australia. Current route plans show a concentration on Jakarta, as well as a break-out from mainly secondary routes.

INDONESIA - Introduction

Delayed, after being due to start in 1996 were flights Jakarta-Hong Kong. International route plans for 1997 include Jakarta-Singapore, as well as routes from Jakarta to Guangzhou, Jeddah, and Seoul. Merpati also has a sizeable fleet addition plan. Before the end of 1996 it wanted to acquire six B737s, six F28s, five BAe146s, plus one A310 and two A300-600s.

Mandala is the third sizeable domestic airline that has started regular international flights within the region. On domestic routes, airlines have been allowed to operate a wider range of aircraft. Towards the end of 1996, both Merpati Nusantara and Sempati Air were given permission to buy wide-body aircraft. The choice was expected to be between the A340 and B777, with operations to start in 1998. At the end of 1996, Merpati signed to lease up to 10 BAe146s, with five expected to be operating by mid-1997. The airline planned to use them on domestic routes, but possibly on some regional international flights as well.

Travel activity has grown throughout the country, not just in the main centres of Jakarta and Bali. The city of Surabaya has become another major international gateway, and airlines are adding routes to other locations.

Growth of traffic at Jakarta airport has been strong in recent years, particularly so in 1994, when it grew 18%. But international traffic at the newer international gateway of Surabaya is taking some growth from Jakarta, where there was a 2.2% drop in 1995 to 4,584,275 passengers.

After high growth in 1994, Garuda's growth in 1995 eased off. The number of seats sold increased only 1.6% to 3.1 million, and RPKs increased 2.9% to 14.7 million.

Hotels

Growth in the number of attractions in the country will help growth in inbound travel. The development planned for the Riau islands could have an important impact on travel patterns in Southeast Asia when this reaches a reasonable size -- probably around 2000.

Plans have been made to build 16,000 rooms on the tourism island of Bintan and 12,000 on Batam - which has an international industrial centre and airport as well as some tourist resorts. Also, sizeable expansion of the hotel sector is planned, and not just in the Riau islands; much is concentrated in Jakarta and Surabaya, as

well as in Bali. There has been steady growth in hotel room counts, but a surge is expected over the next three years. It is estimated in 1995 there was a 13% increase to 65,000 rooms in star-graded hotels. Occupancy in Jakarta was around 65% in 1995, but is believed to have lost as much as 10 points in 1996. In Bali, occupancy remained steady at around 60%, even through many new hotels are being built there also.

Hotel projects due to open in the country over the period 1996-98 include the following: In **Bali**, the Melia Benoa with 128 rooms, which is its second in the Nusa Dua area; Meridien with 300 rooms; Ritz Carlton with 323 rooms; and Royal Nikko with 398 rooms. There are also a number of developments in Bali in the style set by Amanresorts - small grandluxe resorts. These include the Bali Chedi with 80 rooms (in fact, the Chedi is a brandname for a group with links to Amanresorts); Chedi Ubud with 60 rooms; Four Seasons Resort with 46 rooms; and Melia with 40 rooms in Ubud. Melia also opened some deluxe villas in the grounds of its existing Melia Bali hotel.

In **Bandung**, projects include the Bumi Hyatt with 256 rooms, and the Radisson with 200 rooms.

On **Bintan** island, Allamanda with 200 rooms, Club Med with 300 rooms, and Rasa Indah (part of the Shangri La group) with 400 rooms.

Projects in **Jakarta** and satellite cities: Acacia with 210 rooms; Sheraton Bandara (near the airport) with 225 rooms; Bhagawan with 100 rooms; Conrad with 686 rooms; Dusit Mangga Dua with 400 rooms; JW Marriott with 400 rooms; Marco Polo with 400 rooms; Gran Melia with 428 rooms; Peninsula with 400 rooms; Westin with 500 rooms.

In **Surabaya**, Century with 265 rooms; Conrad with 321 rooms; Holiday Inn Crowne Plaza with 300 rooms; Inter Continental with 350 rooms; Majapahit (a restored heritage hotel, managed by Mandarin Oriental) with 150 rooms; and Sheraton with 316 rooms.

What to see

Most seasoned visitors to Indonesia will confirm that Jakarta is hardly picture postcard stuff and in fact the city has little to recommend it. Although the old Dutch quarter in the south of the city is a surprisingly pleasant place in which to walk among the colonial-style buildings.

Much better then to get out of Jakarta. Highly recommended is a trip to Taman Mini Indonesia Indah where 27 pavilions celebrate the country's many diverse provinces in miniature.

Ragunan Zoo is also a good side trip. It houses the Komodo dragon - the world's largest reptile. Then there's the botanical garden at Bogor, which is also the site of the summer palace of the former Dutch East Indies governor-general. Yogjakarta is the home of the royal palace, while Borobudur is the world's largest Buddhist monument.

An alternative means of seeing the country is to take a cruise with an operator like *Spice Island Cruises* who organise trips to the Ujung Kulon Game reserve and to see the Komodo dragon. Other points off the beaten track include the Way Kambas elephant grounds in South Sumatra.

Shopping

Compared with rival Asian destinations, Indonesia is not yet a shoppers' paradise. With Hong Kong, Singapore, Thailand and Korea close at hand, few items could be said to be a bargain. Part of the problem is that there is a local sales tax on most consumer goods and so these are more expensive than, say, Singapore. It's also difficult to locate some normally familiar items such as those used in personal hygiene, which are also costly if you insist on the imported original. In terms of locally-made goods, most visitors go for *batik* - in either ready-to-wear form or by the metre. Other items to look out for involve traditional craftwork: *rattan*, basketweaving, silver, leather, woodcarving and jewellery.

But where to buy? The Pasar Seni, Taman Impian Ancol Complex is as good a place as anywhere. Most hotel shopping arcades feature at least one store that sells local crafts or *batik*. So-called antiques can be found in the shops on and around Jalan Surabaya, but if you do come across the real thing, it's liable to be pricey. Outside the capital, goods are often cheaper and the authenticity of the product is more reliable.

Getting around

Between them domestic carriers Merpati Nusantra and newcomer Sempati operate an extensive network covering the entire length of the archipelago. Merpati, for instance, flies to over 120 destinations. The national carrier, Garuda, also offers a special 30 or 90-day 8-city touring ticket.

Despite the best efforts of the government to liberalise domestic air travel, internal flights are often full and it is advisable to book well in advance. As a workable alternative, the Indonesian railway system covers the main islands and offers overnight sleeper services between some cities. The Bima Express with air-conditioning, a dining-car and sleeper accommodation leaves Jakarta for Yogyakarta, Solo and Surabaya. But most trains are slow and time keeping remains a problem.

Car rental is not recommended, in fact hire companies are reluctant to let foreigners out on the roads by themselves. So instead most visitors opt for a chauffeur-drive service or taxi. Traffic congestion can be chronic in Jakarta and parking is difficult.

There is no shortage of taxis in Jakarta and the other big cities and drivers are just as likely to pester you while you are waiting or walking on streets in order to get a fare. More and more taxis have air-conditioning, but it's not the general rule. Neither have meters won universal approval from drivers.

Entertainment

Clearly, Jakarta is out-gunned by Hong Kong, Manila and Bangkok in the exotic nightlife stakes. Nevertheless, the city has a style of its own and if you look hard enough it's possible to find something to suit all tastes.

Hotel discos - the *Pitstop* at the Sari Pan Pacific is among the best - are one of the few places to find any western-style entertainment. Away from the big hotels, Jakarta has a lively "Latin Quarter" in Glodok and Chinatown, which has hostess clubs where girls will drink and dance with customers.

Two of Jakarta's best drinking spots are the *Jaya Pub* and the *Green Pub*. Both treat their customers to jazz and other western music in the evenings and are popular with expatriate and local alike. As for

restaurants, Jakarta has a few worth visiting: steakhouses such as the *Gandy* and *Black Angus* in the Menting area; the *Oasis* on Jalan Raden Saleh Raya; the *Java Garden* on Jalan A.M.Sangaji and for Indian food the *Orient Express* on Jalan Majapahit. (See *Restaurants* after the *Hotels* section of Indonesia for more Eating Out suggestions).

Leisure

Public sports facilities are in short supply in Jakarta, so it's best to look to the big hotels for tennis courts and swimming pools. The Borobudur Inter-Continental, the Hilton, the Hyatt Aryaduta, Indonesia, Mandarin Oriental and Pan-Pacific all have fitness clubs and there are jogging tracks at some others.

For golf, there has been an incredible boom in course building in recent years - 20 having opened since 1990 in the Jakarta-Bogor area alone. See below for details of Priory Publications Ltd's *South East Asia Golf Guide* and its extract *Golf in Indonesia* for a complete guide to playable courses. Bali has three golf courses - a nine-hole course at the Hotel Bali Beach in Sanur, the 18-hole championship Bali Handara Country Club in the central mountains and the Robin Nelson-designed 18-hole Bali Golf & Country Club in Nusa Dua.

Anglers and surfers, too, should head for Bali - the leisure seekers' paradise. In Bali it's possible to charter teak schooners for single days or up to a month in order to cruise through the Spice Islands. Bali International Yacht Club at Benoa charters out both crewed and bareboat yachts as well as offering deep-sea fishing and scuba diving. Bali's terrific underwater visibility and dramatic drop-offs makes it an ideal spot for diving. Sulawesi and North Sumatra too have good beaches with plenty of watersports. Indonesia is not short of hill resorts where it is possible to arrange hiking, climbing and pony trekking trips through the mountains.

Arrival & Departure

Jakarta's Soekarno-Hatta International Airport (CGK) is sited 26 km west of the city. It has three terminals - two international and one domestic.

Clearing customs and immigration can often be a problem, so allow at least 30 minutes to get through. The taxi ride into the city takes about one hour, costs about Rp 25,000 and is now reasonably well controlled. Look out for the blue taxis that are operated by recognised companies such as *Steady Safe*, *Kosti Jaya* or *Blue Bird*. Buses cost Rp 3000 pr person. Some hotels operate shuttle buses, but expect to pay Rp5,000 plus. An air-conditioned car might be five times the price, though.

A Rp 21,000 tax is levied on international departures from Jakarta and Rp 20,000 from Bali. Domestic departure tax is Rp 8000 from Jakarta, Rp 7000 from Bali and Rp 5/6000 from other airports.

INDONESIA - Introduction

Useful Addresses

Business Services

Business Advisory Indonesia
Suite 304, Kuningan Plaza, Jalan Rasuna Said Kav C-11 - 14, Jakarta
Tel: 517696; Tlx: 62151

Jakarta Executive Service Centre
Menara Duta Bldg, Jalan H R Rasuna Said
Tel: 516202

Manggala Business Center
Jalan Jend, Gatot Subroto Ged. Tel: 5700279

Pusat Data Business Indonesia (Databanks)
Jalan Kartini 54-i, Jakarta Tel: 6391998

Summa International
2nd Fl, Menara Duta, Jalan Rasuna Said Kav B-9, Jakarta. Tel: 517839; Tlx: 45504

World Trade Centre Club
16th Fl, Wisma Metropolitan II, Jalan Jenderal Sudirman. Tel: 5781302

Government Departments

Central Bureau of Statistics. Tel: 372808

Government Department of Information
Tel: 360113

Indonesian Chamber of Commerce & Industry (KADIN)
Gedung Chandra, 4th Fl, Jalan M H Thamrin 20, Jakarta Tel: 324000 or 324064

Directorate General of Tourism
81 Jalan Kramat Ray. Tel: 310 3117

Investment Coordinating Board (BKPM)
Jalan Gatot Subroto 6, Jakarta
Tel: 512008, Telex: 4561 BKPM IA

Jakarta Chamber of Commerce/ Industry
Kadin Jaya Graha, Jln IH Jaunda 38.
Tel: 365609

Jakarta Convention Centre
Jln Jend. Gatat Subroto, PO Box 4916, Jakarta Pusat (10049)
Tel: 572 6000; Fax: 572 6253

National Development Information Office. Tel: 517193

Trade Ministry (Dept Perdagangan)
5 Jalan M I Ridwan Rais. Tel: 348667

Hospitals, Police

Medikaloka Clinin
Kuningan Plaza, Jalan Rasuna Said, Kuningan
Tel: 520 0387

Metropolitan Clinic/Central Hospital
Cipto Mangunkusumo, 71 Jalan Diponegoro
Tel: 330808/344003

Pertamina Hospital
Jalan Kyai Maja. Tel: 707214
Metropolitan Medical Centre (Dental) Wisata Office Tower, Jalan Thamrin. Tel: 320408

Police Department
Tel: 587771. In emeregency dial 110

Air Couriers

DHL:
Jakarta. Tel: (21) 822 4055

Federal Express:
Jakarta. Tel: (21) 522 4636

TNT Express Worldwide:
Jakarta . Tel: (21) 520 1157

UPS:
Tel: (21) 778 427 381

Indonesia Key Fact File

Passport Requirements:
All visitors to Indonesia must be in possession of a valid passport. Visitors from most West European states, Australia, New Zealand, the US, Canada, nationals from Saudi Arabia, Egypt, Kuwait, UAE & Turkey and from ASEAN states do not need a visa. For others, a 30-day visa is required. Proof of onward travel essential.

Currency: Rupiah (Rp). 100 sen = 1 Rp

Exchange Rates:
US$1 = Rp 2397; £1 = Rp 3911 *(May 97)*

Currency Restrictions:
No restriction on the import of foreign currency and travellers' cheques, but the import or export of local currency over Rp 50,000 is prohibited.

Electricity Supply:
Most hotels use 220 volts/50 cycles. In the provinces 110 volts is more common.

Language: Bahasa Indonesian

Time:
GMT + 7 (Java, Sumatra, Bali); GMT + 8 (Kalimantan, Sulawesi, Timor); GMT + 9 (Moluccas, Irian Jaya); EDT five hours later in each case.

IDD Code = 62
Area codes: Bali 361; Balikpapan 542; Bandung 22; Banyuwangi 333; Jakarta 21; Manado 431; Medan 61; Padang 751; Palembang 711; Pamekasan 324; Semarang 24; Surabaya 31; Tegal 283; Tretes 343

Business Hours:
Commercial offices operate staggered hours, between 0800-0900 to 1600-1700. Some open Saturday mornings.
Government offices open 0800-1500 Monday to Thursday; 0800-1130 Friday and 0800-0200 Saturdays.
Shops are open 0900-1000 to 2100-2200.
Banks open 0800-0830 to either 1200 or 1400.

Customs & Entry:
Indonesia allows a maximum of two litres of alcohol, 200 cigarettes or 50 cigars or 100 gramms of tobacco and a "reasonable amount" of perfume. Cars, photographic equipment and typewriters are admitted provided they are taken out again on departure.

Health Requirements:
International certificates of valid smallpox, cholera/ yellow fever vaccinations required only if arriving from infected areas. Water and milk should be boiled before drinking.

Climate/Best Time to Visit
Hot and tropical all year round (min 23°- max 30°C); humidity at a high of 85% (Jan) and a low of 71% (Sept). Mountain areas cooler. Wet seasons Dec-Jan (up to 300mm rainfall per month). Difficulty travelling/eating out/making appointments with Muslims in daylight hours in Ramadan.

National Holidays 1997:
1 January New Year's Day; 9/10 February* Start of Ramadan; 8-9 March* Juma tul Wida/Eid-el-Fitr; March 28 Good Friday;9 May Ascension of Jesus Christ; 19 May Waisyak Day; 14 April* Eid al-Adha; 28 July; August 17 Independence Day;18 July* Birthday of the Prophet Mohammed; 8 December; December 25 Xmas.

(Muslim holiday dates may vary by one or two days according to the moon)

Indonesia Hotel Reference Table

Hotel (listed in price order)	Single Room Rate (US $)	Location	Number of Rooms	Number of Suites	Exhibition Space	Largest Banquet Number	Business Centre	Swimming Pool (0 = indoor)	Tennis Court	Health Club	Video Films
Banyan Tree Bintan	460-560	Riau Arch.	27	-	●	-	●	●	●	●	●
Amanduri	430-800	Bali	29	-	-	-	-	●	●	-	-
Kupu Kupu Barong	305-635	Ubud	-	19	●	-	-	●	-	●	-
Grand Hyatt Jakarta	265-295	Jakarta	518	24	●	500	●	●	●	●	●
The Regent Jakarta	265	Jakarta	360	18	●	912	●	●	●	●	●
Four Seasons Resort	245	Bali	147	-	-	-	●	●	●	●	●
The Oberoi Bali	240-295	Bali	60	15	●	-	-	O	●	●	●
Sedona Hotel Bintan	240-290	Riau Arch.	401	15	-	240	-	●	●	●	-
Majapahit Mandarin Oriental	225	Surabaya	47	103	●	350	●	●	-	●	-
Sheraton Sengigi Beach Resort	220-300	Lombok	149	-	●	-	●	●	-	●	-
Shangri-La Hotel Jakarta	220-270	Jakarta	669	30	●	2300	●	●	●	●	●
Gran Melia	210-270	Jakarta	100	-	●	-	●	●	-	-	-
Oberoi Lombok	204-320	Lombok	30	20	●	-	-	●	●	●	-
Le Meridien Jakarta	190	Jakarta	228	24	●	450	●	●	●	●	●
Borobodur Inter-Continental	190	Jakarta	649	235	●	1000	●	●	●	●	●
RitzCarlton	190-310	Bali	323	-	●	-	●	●	●	●	●
Melia Panorama	188	Riau Arch.	191	-	●	-	●	●	-	●	-
Bali Inter-Continental	185-295	Bali	250	-	●	200	●	●	●	●	●
Mandarin Oriental	180-235	Jakarta	415	10	●	450	●	●	-	●	●
Puri Ratih Bali	180-195	Bali	-	25	-	-	-	●	●	-	-
Aryaduta Hyatt Jakarta	180-210	Jakarta	331	28	●	800	●	●	●	●	●
Jakarta Hilton International	180-220	Jakarta	1080	82	●	680	●	●	●	●	●
Nusa Dua Beach Hotel	180-210	Bali	380	38	●	216	●	●	●	●	-
Melia Bali Sol	176	Bali	90	38	●	250	●	●	●	●	●
Bali Cliff Resort	170	Bali	200	-	-	50	●	●	●	●	-
Sahid Jaya Hotel/Tower	170-200	Jakarta	750	66	●	1000	●	●	●	●	-
Grand Hyatt Bali	170-255	Bali	656	41	●	-	●	●	●	●	●
Sheraton Lagoon Nusa Bch	165	Bali	276	19	●	130	●	●	●	●	-
Sheraton Nusa Indah Resort	165-250	Bali	340	29	●	1500	●	●	●	●	-
Bali Hilton	160-230	Bali	537	-	●	400	●	●	●	●	●
Dai Ichi Hotel Jakarta	160-220	Jakarta	350	18	●	500	●	●	-	●	-
Four Seasons	160-265	Jakarta	170	-	●	400	●	●	●	●	-
Sari Pan Pacific	160-230	Jakarta	375	25	●	350	●	●	-	●	●
Bali Imperial	160-276	Bali	110	28	●	150	●	●	-	●	-
Hyatt Regency Surabaya	159-250	Surabaya	500	24	●	540	●	●	●	●	●
Bali Hyatt Hotel	155-175	Bali	387	-	●	450	●	●	●	●	●
Matahari Beach Resort	154	Bali	30	2	-	-	-	●	-	●	-
Sanur Beach Hotel	150	Bali	405	20	●	70	●	●	●	●	-
Bintang Bali	140	Bali	384	17	●	250	●	●	●	●	●
President Hotel	140-150	Jakarta	315	-	●	-	●	●	-	●	-
Sheraton Surabaya Hotel/Towers	140-325	Surabaya	369	-	500	●	●	●	●	●	●
Shangri La	140-200	Surabaya	380	9	●	3000	●	●	●	●	●
Holiday Inn Crowne Plaza	139	Jakarta	352	-	●	300	●	●	-	●	●
Holiday Inn Bali Hai	135	Bali	200	-	-	-	●	●	●	●	-
Hotel Horison	135-155	Jakarta	350	-	●	-	●	●	●	●	●
Bali Padma	130-185	Bali	400	-	●	420	●	●	●	●	●
Le Meridien Bali	130-190	Bali	-	21	●	450	●	●	●	●	●
Bali Tropic Palace	130-150	Bali	103	-	-	-	-	●	-	●	-
Indonesia Hotel	130-150	Jakarta	537	17	●	550	●	●	●	●	●
Imperial Century Hotel/Resort	130-180	Tangerang	146	39	●	-	●	●	●	●	-
Dusit Balikpapan	130	Kalimantan	189	-	●	400	●	●	●	●	-
Hotel Santika Beach	121-131	Bali	150	11	●	90	●	●	-	●	-
Hotel Kartika Chandra	120-135	Jakarta	200	-	●	-	●	●	●	●	-
Omni Batavia	120-150	Jakarta	213	8	●	700	●	●	-	●	●
Ciputra Hotel	120-135	Jakarta	325	5	●	120	●	●	-	●	●
The Acott Jakarta	120-170	Jakarta	-	198	●	-	●	●	●	●	●
Bali Dynasty Hotel	120-150	Bali	255	12	●	80	●	●	-	●	-
Pertamina Cottages	120-140	Bali	255	-	-	500	-	●	●	●	-
Balisani Suites Hotel	120-140	Bali	100	3	-	-	-	●	-	-	-
Amburrukmo Palace Hotel	115-135	Yogyakarta	245	14	●	600	●	●	-	●	-
Hotel Aquila Prambanan	115-135	Yogyakarta	179	12	●	270	●	●	●	●	-
Hotel Ciputra Semarang	115	Semerang	179	28	●	100	●	●	-	●	-
Dusit Mangga Dua	115-185	Jakarta	321	23	●	450	●	●	-	●	-
Melia Purosani	115	Yogyakarta	280	16	●	600	●	●	●	●	-
Wisata International	115-120	Jakarta	215	2	-	-	-	●	-	●	-
The Grand Bali Beach	110-150	Bali	562	-	-	-	●	●	●	●	-
Grand Hotel Preanger	110-170	Bandung	187	6	●	250	●	●	-	●	-
Natour Garuda Hotel	110	Yogyakarta	120	-	●	100	-	●	-	-	-
Natour Hotel Simpang	110-154	Surabaya	124	5	●	-	-	●	-	-	-
Putri Bali Hotel	110-125	Bali	425	-	●	-	●	●	●	●	-
Hotel Atlet Century Park	105-140	Jakarta	479	17	●	420	●	●	●	●	●
Tiara Medan Hotel & Conv Ctre	100	Medan	148	11	●	600	●	●	-	●	-
Patra Surabaya Hilton Int'l	73	Surabaya	80	40	●	400	●	●	●	●	●
Jayakarta Hotel	70-110	Jakarta	420	5	●	250	●	●	-	●	-

Indonesia Hotels

Bali

Amanduri A
Ubud, Bali
Tel: (361) 975335; Fax: (361) 975333

Bali Clarion Suites C
Jln Dalem Tarukan, 7 Taman Mumbul
Tel: (361) 773808; Fax: (361) 773737

Bali Hilton
PO Box 46, Nusa Dua Beach, 80631
Tel: (361) 771102; Tlx: 35862; Fax: 771616

Situated on 11.5 hectares of landscaped gardens along Nusa Dua Beach, with Balinese theme courtyards and a giant lagoon, the hotel has a 300-metre beachfront and is adjacent to a new 18-hole golf course.

Accommodation & ates:
537 rooms. Single US$ 160-230; double/twin US$ 175-260; suite US$ 425-950. Subject to 21% service & government tax

Credit cards accepted:
Visa, Amex, JCB, Diners, Mastercard

Meeting & conference facilities
5 meeting/conference rooms, capacity 1065; largest reception (ballroom) 400 banquet, 700 cocktail.

Room services
Airconditioning, colour TV, direct-dial telephone (ext. in bathroom), hairdryer, laundry/valet service, minibar, music/radio/ alarm clock, safety deposit box, trouser press, 24-hr room/meal service, video films, non smoker bedrooms available

Business & other services
Business centre, Ayodha club, express checkout, airport pickup, car parking & rental, travel centre + tours, taxi service, newsstand/shops, barber shop/beauty salon

Sports & Recreation
Billiards/snooker, indoor games, massage, outdoor swimming pool, fitness centre/

gym, golf (adjacent), sauna, jacuzzi/ whirlpool, spa, jogging track, water sports, tennis, squash

Restaurants & Coffee Shops
Lagoona (250) - Seafood/traditional, open 0700-2300; *Surfers Corner* (60) - Snacks, open 1000-1800; *Genji* (118) - Japanese, open 1800-2200; *Waterfall* (247) - Coffee Shop, open 24 hours

Overseas Sales Representatives:
Hilton International /Hilton Reservations

Bali Cliff Resort B
Pura Batu Pageh, Nusa Dua
Tel: 771992; Fax: 771993

Bali Dynasty Resort D
Jalan Kartika Plaza, PO Box 2047, Kuta 80361
Tel: 752403/4; Tlx: 35366 BDHTL IA; Fax: 752402

Bali Imperial Hotel
Jalan Dhyana Pura, Legian Beach,
(PO Box 384), Denpasar 80001
Tel: (361) 730730; Tlx: 35652 BIHDPS IA; Fax: (361) 730545

Luxurious accommodation from rooms and suites through to self-contained private bungalows set in lush, tropical gardens. Complete convention and banquet facilities. International restaurants offering European, Teppanyaki and Indonesian cuisine, swimming pools, tennis courts and relaxation room (including sauna, jacuzzi & steambath).

Accommodation & rates
110 single/double/ twin, US$ 160-176; 28 suites US$ 300-330; villa US$ 400-2000

Credit cards accepted:
Visa, Amex, Diners, Mastercharge, JCB, BCA

Meeting & conference facilities
Three meeting/conference rooms, capacity 15-360, with audio-visual facilities; largest reception 150 banquet, 360 cocktail

Room services
Airconditioning, colour TV + hbo, direct-dial telephone (ext. in bathroom), hairdryer, laundry/valet service, minibar, music, safety deposit box, tea/coffee service, 24-hr room/meal service, non-smoker bedrooms available

Business & other services
Express checkout, airport pickup, car parking, car rental, taxi service, barber shop/beauty salon, guided tours, newsstand/shops

Sports & Recreation
Relaxation room, jacuzzi/whirlpool, massage, sauna, tennis, 2 outdoor swimming pools, shuttle service to Kuta, putting green

Restaurants & Coffee Shops
Cafe Imperial (120) - Coffee shop, open 0600-0100; *Pisces Seafood and Teppanyaki Restaurant* (96), - open 0600-2300

Overseas Sales Representatives:
Leading Hotels of the World; Imperial Hotel Tokyo, tel 03 3504 1111; fax 071 3581 9146; Imperial Sales Offices: London - tel 0171 355 1775, fax 0171 355 1776; New York - tel 212 692 9001, fax 212 867 0244; Los Angel-es - tel 213 627 6214, fax 213 239 2404

Bali Hyatt Hotel C
PO Box 392, Sanur 80001
Tel: 281234; Tlx: 35127; Fax: 287826

Bali Inter-Continental Resort B
Jalan Uluwatu 45, Jimbaran 80361
Tel: 701888; Fax: 701777

Balisani Hotel D
Jalan Padma Utara, Legian, PO Box 2011 Kuta, Denpasar
Tel: 752314; Fax: 752313

Balisani Suites Hotel D
Batubelig Beach, Krobokan Bali. PO Box 193/DPS Denpasar
Tel: 730550; Fax: 730655

Bali Tropic Palace C
34a Jalan Prataman, 80361
Tel: 772130; Tlx: 35861; Fax: 772131

Bintang Bali Hotel C
Jl Kartika Plaza, PO Box 1068
Tel: 753292; Tlx: 35833 BIBA; Fax: 753288

INDONESIA - Hotels

Bali Padma Hotel ⊙
Jln Padma No 1, Legian PO Box 1107, Bali
Tel: (361) 752111; Tlx: 35624; Fax: 752140

On Legian Beach, away from the hustle and bustle of Kuta but conveniently within walking distance to restaurants and shopping area.

Accommodation & rates
400 rooms, single US$130-185; double/twin US$ 140-195; suite US$ 195-1785

Credit cards accepted:
Amex, Diners, Mastercard, Visa, JCB

Meeting & conference facilities
3 meeting/conference rooms - capacity 12-300 pax; audio-visual facilities available; largest reception 420 seated,720 cocktail

Room services
Airconditioning, colour TV, direct-dial telephone, hairdryer, laundry/valet service, minibar, music/radio, safety deposit box, 24-hr room/meal service

Business & other services
Business centre, airport pickup, car parking & rental, travel centre, taxi service, barber shop/beauty salon

Sports & Recreation
Fitness centre/gym, massage, sauna, squash, swimming pool (outdoor), tennis

Restaurants & Coffee Shops
Taman Ayun (130) - International coffee shop, open 24 hours; *Kurumaya* (54) - Japanese, open 1800-2300; *Batavia* (90) - Asian, open as above; *Pizzaria* (50) Italian, open 1000-2200

Overseas Sales Representatives:
Mac Marketing Services, Dai 2 Matsuoaka Bldg 3F, 2-14-6 Ginza, Chuo-ku, Tokyo. Tel: (03) 3544 0340; Fax: (03) 3544 0323

Four Seasons Resort Bali A
Jimbaran, Denpasar 80361
Tel: 701010; Fax: 701020

Grand Bali Beach ⊙ C
Jln Hangtuah, Sanur 80001
Tel: 288511; Tlx: 35138; Fax: 287917

Grand Hyatt Bali A
P.O. Box 53 Nusa Dua
Tel: 771234; Tlx: 35863; Fax:772038

Holiday Inn Bali Hai ⊙ C
Jln Wana Segara 33, PO Box 2054, Kuta Beach 80361
Tel: 753035; Fax: 754548/9

Intan Bali Village ⊙ C
PO Box 1089, Tuban 80361
Tel: 730777; Fax: 730778

Kartika Plaza Beach Hotel ⊙ C
Jln Kartika Plaza, PO Box 3084, 80030
Tel: 751067; Tlx: 35142; Fax: 752475

Kul Kul Resort D
Jln Pantai Kuta, PO Box 3097, Denpasar 80030
Tel: 752520; Tlx: 35505;Fax: 752519

Kupu Kupu Barong ⊙ A
Kedewatan (overlooking Sayan Valley), Ubud
Tel: 975478; Tlx: 23813; Fax: 975079

Kuta Palace Hotel ⊙ C
Jln Pura Bagus Teruna, Legian, Denpasar
Tel: 751433-6 Tlx: 35234; Fax: 752074

Matahari Beach Resort B
Permuteran Singaraja, Bali

Melia Bali Hotel ⊙ B
PO Box 1048, Tuban, Nusa Dua
Tel: 771510; Tlx: 35237; Fax: 771360

Melia Benoa C
Jalan Pratama, Tanjung Benoa, Bali
Tel: 361 771714; Fax: 361 771713

Hotel Nikko Bali B
Jln Raya Nusa Dua Selatan, Nusa Dua
Tel: 773377; Fax: 773388

Nusa Dua Beach Hotel ⊙ B
PO Box 1028, Denpasar
Tel: 771210; Tlx: 32506 IA; Fax: 771229

Hotel Patra Jasa Bali ⊙ C
Tuban Beach, 80001
Tel: 751161; Fax: 752030

Pertamina Cottages ⊙ C
Tuban Beach, PO Box 121, 80001
Tel: 751161; Tlx: 35131; Fax: 752030

Putri Bali Hotel ⊙ C
PO Box 301, Nusa Dua, 80363
Tel: 771020; Tlx: 35247; Fax: 771139

Radisson Bali C
Jln Hang Tuah 46, Sanur, Bali
Tel: (361) 281781; Fax: (361) 281782

Le Meridien Nirwana Golf & Spa Resort
Jalan Raya Tanah Lot, Desa Boraban, Kediri, Tabanan, Bali
Tel: 243691; Fax: 812398

Fully integrated luxury resort located on the south west coast of Bali. featurung 18-hole Greg Norman designed golf course and thalassotherapy spa. Overlooking the famous Tanah Lot temple.

Accommodation & rates
Single US$ 130-190; double/twin US$ 140-190; 21 suites US$ 220-350

Credit cards accepted: All major

Meeting & banqueting facilities
Four meeting/conference rooms - capacity 600; audio-visual facilities available; 575 sq m exhibition space; largest reception 450 seated/600 cocktail; Balinese amphitheatre

Room services
Airconditioning, colour TV, direct-dial telephone (ext. in bathroom), hairdryer, laundry/valet service, minibar, music/radio/alarm clock, safety deposit box, tea/coffee making, 24-hr room/meal service, non-smoker bedrooms available

Business & other services
Business centre, airport pickup, car parking & rental, translation service, travel centre + tours, taxi service, barber shop/beauty salon, newsstand/souvenir shop

Sports & Recreation
Fitness centre/gym, indoor games, jacuzzi/whirlpool, jogging track, massage, sauna, squash, swimming pool (outdoor), tennis, spa, 18-hole Greg Norman golf course

Restaurants & Coffee Shops
Sedana (150) - Continental, open 0600-2300; *Nirwana* (70) - South-East Asian, open 1800-2330; *Pool Grill* (80) - Seafood & pizza, open 1100-1600; Masks Fun Pub (80) - Light snacks, open 1800-0200; *Balinese Amphitheatre* (150) - Indonesian, open 1800-2300

Overseas Sales Representatives:
Worldwide Forte/Le Meridien Sales Offices

The Oberoi
Legian Beach, Jalan Kayu Aya, PO Box 3351, Denpasar 80001, Bali
Tel: (361) 730361; Tlx: 35352/35125 OBHOTL IA; Fax: (361) 730791

The Oberoi Bali is set in 30 acres of verdant tropical gardens on Legian Beach, one of the best surfing beaches on the island. The thatched roof lanai cottages and private villas recreate the atmosphere of a typical Balinese village.

Accommodation & rates
60 lanai cottages, US$ 240-295; 15 villas US$ 485-800

Credit cards accepted:
Amex, Diners, Mastercard, Visa, Eurocard

Meeting & conference facilities
Meeting/conference room - capacity 1000, with audio-visual facilities available

Room services
Airconditioning, colour TV, direct-dial telephone (ext. in bathroom), hairdryer, laundry/valet service, minibar, safety deposit box, trouser press, non-smoker bedrooms available, 24-hr room/meal service

Business & other services
Business centre, airport pickup, car rental, travel centre, barber shop/hairdresser, shops

Sports & Recreation
Fitness centre/gym, golf, indoor games, , sauna, swimming pool (indoor), tennis

Restaurants & Coffee Shops
Kura Kura (100) - Continental/Asian, open 1900-2230; *Frangipani Cafe* (60) - Seafood specialities, open 0700-1100/1200-1900; *Kayu Bar (40)* - Tropical cocktails, open noon-midnight; *Amphitheatre* (70) - Buffet dinners, open 1915-2300; *Pool Deck* - snacks & drinks, open 0900-1800

Overseas Sales Representatives:
Oberoi Sales Offices Worldwide

Rama Palace D
Jln Pantai Kuta, PO Box 293, Denpasar 80001. Tel: 752208; Fax: 753078

Ritz Carlton Bali A
Jln Karang Mas Sajahtera, Jimbaran 80364
Tel: 361 702122; Fax: 361 702123

Santrian Beach Cottages D
Jln Tamblingan, No. Banjar Semawang
Tel: 288181; Tlx; 35169; Fax: 288185

Hotel Santika Beach
Jln Kartika, PO Box 1008, Tuban, Bali
Tel: 751267; Tlx: 35277; Fax: 751260

Right on the sands of Tuban Resort, near Kuta, the hotel overlooks the dazzling blue ocean and is surrounded by acres of unspoiled tropical gardens. A peaceful retreat into paradise is yours at this heavenly hotel.

Accommodation & rates
56 double, 94 twin US$ 121-131 (single occ. $100-110); 11 suites US$ 181-373

Credit cards accepted:
Amex, Diners, Mastercard, Visa

Meeting & banqueting facilities
2 meeting/conference rooms - capacity 25; audio-visual facilities available; largest reception 90 seated, 200 cocktail.

Room services
Airconditioning, colour TV, direct-dial telephone, hairdryer, laundry/valet service, minibar, music/radio/alarm clock, safety deposit box, tea/coffee making, 24-hr room service, video films

Other services
Express checkout, airport pickup, car parking & rental, travel centre + tours, taxi service, newsstand/souvenir shop

Sports & Recreation
Massage, swimming pool (outdoor), chess, childrens pool, tennis, table tennis

Restaurants & Coffee Shops
Tampaksiring (78) - Oriental, open 24 hrs; *Uluwatu* (60) Seafood, open 0900-2300; *Kaiser* (51) - Indonesian, open 1600-2300

Overseas Sales Representatives:
Steigenberger Reservation Service (SRS)

Sanur Beach Hotel C
Box 3279, Denpasar 800032
Tel: 288011; Tlx: 35135; Fax: 287566

Sheraton Laguna Nusa Dua Beach
77 Nusa Dua, Kuta 80363 B
Tel: 771327-8; Tlx: 35851; Fax: 771326

Sheraton Nusa Indah Resort B
PO Box 36, Nusa Dua, Bali
Tel: 771906/7; Tlx: 35369; Fax: 771908

Surya Beach Hotel D
Jalan Mertasari, PO Box 3476
Tel: 288833; Tlx: 35810; Fax: 287303/772

Java - Bandung

Aerowisata Preanger C
Jalan Asia Afrika 81, PO Box 1220
Tel: (22) 431631; Tlx: 28570 GHPBDO; Fax: (22) 430034

Hotel Panghegar D
Jalan Merdeka 2, Bandung, West Java 40111
Tel: (022) 432286; Tlx: 28276; Fax: (022) 431583

Savoy Homann Panghegar Heritage Hotel D
Jalan Asia Afrika 112, Bandung 40261
Tel: (022) 432244; Tlx: 28425; Fax: (022) 436187

Sheraton Bandung C
Jln Ir Haji Juanda 390
Tel: 250 0303; Tlx: 28882; Fax: 250 0301

Java - Jakarta

Hotel Atlet Century Park
Jln Pintu Satu, Senayan, Jakarta 10270
Tel: 571 2041; E-mail:hacp@rad.net.id; Fax: 571 2139/ (reservations 571 2094)

Located in the heart of Jakarta's business district, the hotel is surrounded by parks and the open green spaces of Jakarta. A short stroll from the hotel are Jakarta Convention Center, Sudirman Business District and Plaza Senayan, the biggest shopping center in town; also Senayan Sports Complex, sport hall, golf course, and golf driving range.

Accommodation
222 single/double, 257 twin, 17 suites

Rates:
Single US$ 105-140; Double/twin US$ 115-150; Suite US$ 250-500

(continued)

INDONESIA - Hotels

Credit cards accepted:
Amex, Diners, Mastercard, Visa, JCB

Meeting & conference facilities
6 meeting/conference rooms - capacity 12-700 pax; audio-visual facilities available; 1264 sq m exhibition space; largest reception 420 seated, 720 cocktai.

Room services
Airconditioning, colour TV+ video, direct-dial telephone, hairdryer, laundry/valet service, minibar, music/radio/alarm clock, safety deposit box, trouser press, non-smoker bedrooms, 24-hr room service

Business & other services
Business centre, executive floor, express checkout, airport pickup, translation service, car parking & rental, taxi service, newsstand/shops, drugstore

Sports & Recreation
Fitness centre/gym, golf nearby, jogging track, massage, sauna, swimming pool (outdoor), tennis

Restaurants & Coffee Shops
Senayan Cafe (130) - Indonesian/Asian/International, open 0600-1000/1200-1430/1800-2130; *Nogiku* - Japanese, open 1100-1400/1800-2200

Overseas Sales Representatives:
Utell International Worldwide Services, Delton Reservation System, Century & Delta International Hotels

The Acacia Jakarta D
Jl ramat Raya 73-81, Jakarta 10450
Tel: 390 3030; Fax: 390 3388

Ancol Travelodge ○ C
Jalan Lodan Timur 7 (Taman Impian), 14430
Tel: 640 5461; Fax: 640 5645

The Ascott Jakarta C
Golden Triangle, Jln Kebong Kacang Raya, 10240.Tel: 391 6868; Fax: 391 3368

Aryaduta Jakarta Hotel B
44-46 Jalan Prapatan, Jakarta 10110
Tel: 386 1234; Tlx: 46220; Fax: 380 9900

Hotel Borobodur Inter-Continental A
PO Box 1329, Jalan Lapangan Banteng, Selatan, 10710.Tel: 380 5555; Tlx: 44156 BDO IA; Fax: 580 9195

Hotel Ciputra Jakarta ○ C
Jalan S Parman, PO Box 6282, 11062
Tel: 566 0640; Fax: 568 1616

Dusit Mangga Dua
Jln Mangga Dua Raya, PO Box 4349, 11043
Tel: 612 8811; Tlx: 41422 DUSIT; Fax: 612 8822; E-Mail: dusit mg2@rad.net.id

Located on the site of Old Chinatown, a shopper's paradise paradise, surrounded by over 4000 shops, retail and wholesale. The area still retains the charm of traditional bazaars, Dusit Hotel offers world class services and facilities

Accommodation & rates
321 single/double, US$ 115-185; 23 suites, US$ 230-1000 .
Subject to 21% govt tax & service charge

Credit cards accepted:
Amex, Visa, Mastercard, Diners

Meeting & conference facilities
Six meeting/function rooms - capacity 30-600, with aidio-visual facilities; 1380 sq m exhibition space; largest reception 450 banquet, 1500 cocktail.

Room services
Airconditioning, colour TV, direct-dial telephone, hairdryer, laundry/valet service, minibar, music/radio/alarm clock, safety deposit box, 24-hr room/meal service, non-smoker bedrooms available, video films

Business & other services
Business centre, executive floor, express checkout, airport pickup, car parking, taxi service, barber shop/beauty salon, newsstand/shops

Sports & Recreation
Fitness centre/gym, jacuzzi/whirlpool, sauna, massage, outdoor swimming pool

Restaurants & Coffee Shops
Kafe Mangga Dua (140) - Vietnamese/Thai/International, open 0600-1000/1100-2100; *Dusit Patisserie* (25), open 0800-2100; *Pagoda* (260) - Cantonese/Szechuan, open 1100-1500/1800-2300; *Taman Tirta* (30) - bbq restaurant, open 1130-1500/1800 onwards; *Lobby Bar* (43), open 1100-2000; *Equinox* (100) - Nightclub, open 2100-0200 (-0300 Fr-Sat)

Overseas Sales Representatives: Utell

Dai Ichi Hotel Jakarta B
135 Jln Senen Raya, 10410
Tel: 344 2828; Fax: 344 2929

Hotel Equatorial Jakarta B
Jl H Fachrudin 3, Jakarta 10250
Tel: 230 3636; Fax: 230 0880

Four Seasons Resort B
Jln Jend Sudirman, 12190
Tel: 520 6880; Fax: 521 4884

Gran Melia Jakarta A
Jln H R Rasuna Said Kav, X-O, 12950
Tel: 526 8080; Fax: 526 8181

Grand Hyatt Jakarta A
Jalan M H Thamrin, Jakarta 10230
Tel: 390 1234; Tlx: 61534; Fax: 334321

Holiday Inn Crowne Plaza
Jalan Gatot Subroto Kav 2-3, Jakarta 12930
Tel: 526 8833; Fax: 526 8832;
E-Mail: holiday@indosat.net.id

The first international 5-star hotel from the airport, located in the financial district, surrounded by a myriad of offices, entertainment and commercial complexes.

Accommodation & rates
352 rooms, from US$ 139.
Subject to 21% service charge and tax

Meeting & banqueting facilities
Eight meeting/function rooms, capacity 10 to 1200, with audio-visual equipment; 490.5 sq m exhibition space; largest banquet 300 seated or 1100 cocktail.

Room services
Airconditioning, colour TV, direct-dial telephone (ext. in bathroom), hairdryer, laundry/valet service, minibar, music/radio/alarm clock, 24-hour room/meal service, non-smoker bedrooms, video films.

Business & other services
Business centre, executive floor, express

checkout, car parking & rental, taxi service, travel centre, barber shop/hairdresser, newsstand/shops

Sports & Recreation
Fitness centre/gym, massage, sauna, outdoor swimming pool.

Restaurants & Coffee Shops
Beranda Kafe (230) - Continental, open 24 hours; *Plaza de Espana* (150) - Spanish, open lunch & dinner; *Loone Jin* (150) - Cantonese, open lunch & dinner; *Sen Nari* (60) - Japanese, open as above

Overseas Sales Representatives:
Holiday Inn Worldwide Sales Offices

Imperial Century Hotel & Resort
401 Bulevar Jend. Sudirman, LIPPO Karawaci 1300, Tangerang 15811
Tel: (021) 546 0101; Fax: (021) 546 0201
E-Mail: IMENTRY@RAD.NET.ID

Conveniently located in Lippo Karawaci, a new destination for business and leisure, with easy access to the central business district of Jakarta.

Accommodation & rates
102 double/44 twin rooms US$ 130-180; 39 suites (inc. Medieteranean-style cabanas) US$ 260-600.
Subject to 21% service charge & gov't tax

Credit cards accepted:
Amex, Diners, Mastercard, Visa

Meeting & conference facilities
Meeting/conference rooms - capacity 12-400; audio-visual equipment available

Room services
Airconditioning, colour TV + CCN & Int'l channels, direct-dial telephone, hairdryer, laundry/valet service, minibar, alarm clock, safety deposit box, 24-hr room service, non-smoker bedrooms available

Business & other services
Business centre, airport pickup, car parking, taxi service

Sports & Recreation
Fitness centre/gym, jacuzzi/whirlpool, spa, massage, sauna, 2 swimming pools, tennis, squash, rock climbing

Restaurants & Coffee Shops
Choice of five restaurants including *RJ's Sports Bar & Grill,* Japanese & Chinese and Intercontinental restaurants.

Overseas Sales Representatives:
Sterling Hotels & Resorts (WR), Delton Reservaton System; Century International Hotels

Jakarta Hilton International
PO Box 3315, Jalan Jend Gatot Sudirman, Jakarta 10002
Tel: 570 3600; Fax: 573091/573089

Situated in a lush garden setting of 32 acres, the hotel is located at a main crossroads, near major business districts and just minutes from downtown Jakarta.

Accommodation & rates:
1104 rooms. Main hotel single US$ 180, double US$ 195; Garden Tower single US$ 200-215; Lagoon Garden suite US$ 310-2000.
Subject to 21% gov't tax & service charge

Credit cards accepted:
Mastercard, Visa, Diners, Amex

Meeting & conference facilities
17 meeting/function rooms, capacity up to 1050, with audio-visual equipment; 6000 sq m Exhibition Hall; largest banquet 680 seated or 1050 cocktail. (Jakarta Convention Centre with seating for 4000 available)

Room services
Airconditioning, colour TV, direct-dial telephone (ext. in bathroom), hairdryer, laundry/valet service, minibar, in-room fax, alarm clock, safety deposit box, 24-hr room service, trouser press, non-smoker & disabled bedrooms available

Business & other services
Business centre, executive club floor, express checkout, airport pickup, translation service, car parking, car rental, tour & travel centre, taxi service, barber shop/hairdresser, newsstand/shops, guided tours, drugstore, florist, Indonesian Bazaar, Post Office

Sports & Recreation
Massage, sauna, outdoor swimming pool, fitness centre/gym, squash, tennis, jogging track, jacuzzi/whirlpool

Restaurants & Coffee Shops
Taman Sari (104) - Continental, open lunch & dinner; *NipponKan* (120) - Japanese, open as above; *Lotus* (120) - Halal Chinese, open as above; *Peacock Cafe* (124) - open 24 hours; *Sriwedari* (80) - International, open 0700-2300

Overseas Sales Representatives
Hilton International Sales Offices; Hilton Reservations Worldwide

Hotel Jayakarta
PO Box 5024, 126 Jalan Hayam Wuruk, Jakarta 11150. E-Mail: jhr@indo.net.id
Tel: 649 6760; Fax: 629 5000

Located in the centre of this capital city, close to the business district, major shopping centres, entertainment district and historic Batavia.

Accommodation & rates
50 double/ 370 twin US$ 80-120 (single occ. $70-110); 5 suites US$ 150-500
Subject to 10% service charge & 11% tax

Credit cards accepted:
Amex, JCB, Mastercard, Visa

Meeting & banqueting facilities
Five meeting rooms, capacity 200 with audio-visual facilities; 1000 sq m exhibition space largest reception 250 seated/1000 cocktail

Room services
Airconditioning, colour TV, direct-dial telephone, hairdryer, laundry/valet service, minibar, music, safety deposit box, tea/coffee making, 24-hr room/meal service

Business & other services
Business centre, executive floor, airport pickup, translation service, car parking & rental, travel & tour centre, taxi service, barber shop/beauty salon, newsstand/shops

Sports & Recreation
Fitness centre/gym, massage, sauna, outdoor swimming pool

Restaurants & Coffee Shops
Coffee Shop (90) - International, open 24 hours; *Jayakarta* (450) - Chinese, open 1100-1430/1700-2300

Overseas Sales Representatives:
Golden Tulip Worldwide; Utell

INDONESIA - Hotels

Hotel Horison ◯ C
Jaya-Ancol, PO Box 3340, Jakarta 10022
Tel: 640 7000; Tlx: 42824 HORIZ JKT;
Fax: 640 6123

Hotel Indonesia ◯ C
PO Box 54, Jalan M Thamrin
Tel: 320008; Tlx: HTLIND IA; Fax: 321508

Hotel Kartika Chandra ◯ D
PO Box 85, Jalan Gotot Subroto
Tel: 525 1008; Tlx: 62474; Fax: 520 4238

Hotel Kartika Plaza D
10 Jln M L Thamrin, PO Box 2081, 10310
Tel: 314 1008; Tlx: 61893; Fax: 322547

Mandarin Oriental, Jakarta ◯
Jalan M H Thamrin, PO Box 3392, 10310
Tel: 314 1307; Tlx: 61266 MANDA IA; Fax: 314 8680; E-mail: silviav@mojkt.co.id

Located in the heart of the financial and commercial district and easily accessible from all directions. Guestrooms have in-house movies, minibar, IDD telephones, large safes, electronic door locks and individually controlled airconditioning. Five restaurants, a bar & lounge are also available in the hotel as well as a 24-hour business centre, fitness centre and swimming pool.

Accommodation & rates
415 rooms; US$ 180-235; 10 suites US$ 480-1500

Credit cards accepted:
Amex, BCA, Diners, Mastercard, Visa

Meeting & banqueting facilities
9 meeting/conference rooms - capacity up to 500 (theatre syle); audio-visual equipment available; ballroom; largest reception 450 seated or 1000 cocktail

Room services
Airconditioning, colour TV (+ CNN/HBO/ABN/Star TV), direct-dial telephone with voicemail (ext. in bathroom), hairdryer, laundry/valet service, minibar, music/radio/alarm clock, safety deposit box, tea/coffee making facilities, 24-hr room service, non-smoker bedrooms available, video films

Business & other services
Business centre, exclusive floor, airport pickup, translation service, car parking & rental, travel centre & tours, taxi service, barber shop/beauty salon, newsstand/book kiosk, flower shop and cigar divan

Sports & Recreation
Fitness centre/gym, massage, sauna, outdoor swimming pool

Restaurants & Coffee Shops
Xin Hwa (85) - Sichuan, open noon-1430/1830-2230; *KafeKafe* (165) - Coffee Shop, Asian and Western, open 24 hours; *The Lounge* (70) - Light refreshments/snacks, open 1000-2300; *Pool Bar* (60) - Western & Asian, open 0700-1800; *Zigolini* (108) - Italian, open 1130-0230/1830-2030; *Chequers* (97) - Fun pub/bar, open 0700-0100; *Tokio Joe* - Japanese sushi bar

Overseas Sales Representatives:
Mandarin Oriental Hotel Group

Le Meridien Jakarta
Jl Jenderal Sudirman Kav. 18-20, 10220
Tel: 251 3131; Fax: 571 1633

Ideally located in the centre of Jakarta's "Golden Triangle" of business and shopping. Directly opposite the World Trade Centre and with a full range of business and leisure facilities, Le Meridien is the perfect location for visitors to Jakarta.

Accommodation & rates
133 double, 95 twin, US$ 190; 24 suites US$ 280-750

Credit cards accepted:
Amex, Diners, Mastercard, Visa, JCB

Meeting & banqueting facilities
12 meeting/conference rooms - capacity 10-600; audio-visual equipment available; 920 sq m exhibition space; largest reception 450 seated or 1000 cocktail

Room services
Airconditioning, colour TV + cable, direct-dial telephone (ext. in bathroom), hairdryer, laundry/valet service, minibar, music/radio/alarm clock, safety deposit box, tea/coffee making facilities, 24-hr room/meal service, non-smoker bedrooms available, voicemail

Business & other services
Business centre, express checkout, airport pickup, translation service, car parking &

rental, concierge, taxi service, newsstand/shops, patisserie

Sports & Recreation
Fitness centre/gym, massage, sauna, outdoor swimming pool

Restaurants & Coffee Shops
La Brasserie (157) - European, open 24 hours; *Lemon Grass* (63) - S-E Asian, open Sun-Fri noon-1430/daily 1830-2230; *Aoi* (130) - Japanese, open 1100-1430/1800-2230

Overseas Sales Representatives:
Le Meridien Reservations International

Omni Batavia Hotel
Jl Kali Besar Barat No 46, PO Box 4922, Jakarta 11049
Tel: 690 7926; Fax: 6904092

Located in the busy "Kota" area of great historical significance and easily reached by all modes of transport. Approx. 20 minutes' drive from Jakarta's international airport and from the Golden Triangle business district.

Accommodation & rates
26 single rooms, US$ 120-150; 10 double, US$ 160-190; 207 twin, US$ 120-190; 8 suites, US$ 250-500

Credit cards accepted:
Amex, Diners, Mastercard, Visa, JCB

Meeting & banqueting facilities
6 meeting/conference rooms - capacity 60-1500; largest reception 700 seated or 1500 cocktail

Room services
Airconditioning, colour TV + video, direct-dial telephone (ext. in bathroom), hairdryer, laundry/valet service, minibar, music/radio/alarm clock, safety deposit box, tea/coffee making facilities, trouser press, 24-hr room/meal service, non-smoker bedrooms

Business & other services
Business centre, executive floor, express checkout, airport pickup, translation

service, car parking & rental, travel & tour centre, taxi service, newsstand/shops

Sports & Recreation
Fitness centre/gym, jogging track, massage, sauna, outdoor swimming pool

Restaurants & Coffee Shops
Spice Market (135) - European, open 0600-0100; *Brown Bar* (108) - Bar, open 1600-0100; *Lotus Court* (300) - Chinese, open 1100-1400/1800-2230; *Sun Deck Terrace* (50) - open 1800-2230

Overseas Sales Representatives:
Hong Kong - regional sales office; Singapore - regional sales office; Taiwan - general sales agent; Japan - general sales agent; Thailand - general sales agent; Shanghai - general sales agent; Beijing - general sales agent; Los Angeles - regional sales office; UK - regional sales office; Germany - regional sales office

Hotel Marcopolo   C
19 Jalan Cik Di Tiro,
Tel: 325409; Tlx: 46607 ; Fax: 310 7138

Millenium Sirih Jakarta   B
Jln Fachrudin 3, Jakarta 10250
Tel: 230 3636; Fax: 230 0880

The President Hotel ○   C
59 Jalan M H Thamrin, Jakarta 10350
Tel: 230 1122; Tlx: 61401 PREHOJKT;
Fax: 314 3631

The Regent Jakarta   A
Jalan H R Rasuna Said, 12920
Tel: 252 3456; Fax: 252 4480

Sabang Metropolitan Hotel ○ D
11 Jln H Agus Salim, Jakarta 10110
Tel: 384 0050; Fax: 384 3546

Sahid Jaya Hotel & Tower ○ B
86 Jalan Jenderal Sudirman, Jakarta 10220
PO Box 1041/Jkt 10001.Tel: 570 4444; Tlx: 65635 SAHID IA; Fax: 573 3168

Shangri-La Jakarta   A
Jalan Jend Sudirman Cav 1, Jakarta 10220
Tel: 570 7440; Fax: 570 3530

Wisata International Hotel ○   C
PO Box 2457, Jalan M Thamrin, 10230
Tel: 230 0406; Tlx: 61787; Fax: 230 0578

○ = Member of Pacific Asia Travel Association

Sari Pan Pacific Hotel ○
Jalan M H Thamrin 6, Jakarta 10340
Tel: 323 707; Fax: 323 650;
E-mail: dewisuli@panpac.co.id

Noted for its cuisine and warm welcome, the Sari Pan Pacific is located in the city centre, right in the heart of the business and entertainment district.

Accommodation
400 rooms and suites, inc. 3 special Pacific floors and 3 Penthouse floors

Rates:
Single US$ 165-195; double US$ 185-215;
Subject to 21% service charge and tax

Meeting & banqueting facilities
Seven meeting/function rooms, capacity 10 to 800, with audio-visual equipment; 400 sq m exhibition space; largest banquet 350 seated or 800 cocktail.

Room services
Airconditioning, colour TV, direct-dial telephone, in-room fax machine & wet-bar in Penthouse Floor rooms, laundry/valet service, minibar, music/radio, 24-hour room service, video films.

Business & other services
Business centre, executive floor, airport shuttle, car parking, car rental, taxi service. Barber shop/hairdresser, newsstand, drugstore, gift shop

Sports & Recreation
Executive health centre, massage, sauna, outdoor swimming pool.

Restaurants & Coffee Shops
Fiesta Coffee Shop (200) - open 24 hours; *Keyaki* (180) - Japanese Restaurant, open 1130-1500/1900-2300; *Melati Mediterranean Bar & Grill* (70) - open noon-1500/1900-2030, dining (-0100 for bar)

Overseas Sales Representatives:
Pan Pacific Hotels & Resorts Worldwide;
SRS Steigenberger Reservation Service

Hotel Classification: A *after name of hotel =* over US$ 200 per person per night;
B = between US$ 150 - 200; **C** = between US$ 100 - 150; **D** = between US$ 50 - 100 ; **E** = under US$ 50; ¶ = prices on application. ○ = PATA member.

Java - Semarang

Hotel Ciputra Semarang
Simpang Lima, PO Box 1288, Semarang 50134
Tel: (24) 449888; Fax: (24) 447888

The only international hotel in Semarang, ideally located in the heart of the city. 10 minutes away from the airport and the city's thriving business district, shopping area and industrial zone.The hotel's location in front of Ciputra Mall,Semarang's largest and most comprehensive shopping mall, provides direct access to exclusive shops, restaurants, banks and cinemas.

Accommodation & rates
97 double/82 twin US$115; 28 suites US$150-500
Subject to 10% service charge & 11% tax

Credit cards accepted:
Amex, BCA, Diners, Mastercard, Visa

Meeting & banqueting facilities
3 meeting rooms, capacity 150, with audio-visual facilities; 160 sq m exhibition space; largest reception 100 seated/150 cocktail

Room services
Airconditioning, colour TV, direct-dial telephone (ext. in bathroom), hairdryer, laundry/valet service, minibar, music/radio/alarm clock, 24-hr room/meal service, non-smoker bedrooms available, video films

Business service
Business centre, executive floor, express checkout, airport pickup, translation service, car parking & rental, travel centre, taxi service, executive lounge

Other services
Barber shop/beauty salon, guided tours, newsstand

Sports & Recreation
Fitness centre/gym, massage, outdoor swimming pool

Restaurants & Coffee Shops
The Gallery (92) - Western/Asian, open 0600-2330; *Marble Court/Chips Bar* (47) - Snacks, open 0800-midnight; *Pool Bar* (32) - Snacks, open 1000-2000

Overseas Sales Representatives:
Swiss Belhotel International Hong Kong,
tel (852) 2836 5555; fax: (852) 2893 9555

Patrajasa Hotel-Motel ○   D
Jln Sisingamangaraja, Semarang 50232
Tel: (024) 314441; Tlx: 22286 PATRAS IA;
Fax: (024) 314448

INDONESIA - Hotels

Java - Solo

Kusuma Sahid Prince Hotel   D
20 Jalan Sugiyopranato, Solo 57101
Tel: (0271) 46356; Tlx: 25274 KSPH IA;
Fax: (0271) 44788

Java - Surabaya

Altea Hotel Mirama   D
Jln Raya Darmo No 68076, Surabay
60012/PO Box 1232
Tel: (31) 582501-4; Fax: 571943

Garden Palace Hotel   D
Jalan Yos Sudarso II
Tel: (031) 352 1001; Tlx: 34184 GPHSB IA; Fax: (031) 513 6111

Hyatt Regency Surabaya   B
Jalan Jend. Basuki Rakhmat 124/128
Tel: 511234; Tlx: 34316; Fax: /512038

Natour Hotel Simpang   D
1-3 Jalan Permuda, PO Box 36
Tel: 42151; Tlx: 31607 IA; Fax: 510356

Hotel Majapahit Mandarin Oriental
65 Jalan Tunjungan, Surabaya 60275
Tel: (31) 545 4333; Fax: (31) 545 4111

Originally built in 1910 by the Sarkies Brothers, the Majapahit is a government protected historic landmark. Today, the hotel, with its prime central location, offers guests Surabaya's largest and most spacious rooms in a garden courtyard setting. Coupled with Mandarin Orietal"s legendary service, the Majapahit is a true oasis of hospitality in the midst of Indonesia's second largest city.

Accommodation & rates
22 single, 25 twin US$ 98-108; 103 suites US$ 128-1500. Subject to 10% service charge and 11% gov't tax

Meeting & banqueting facilities
9 meeting/function rooms, capacity to 500, with audio-visual equipment; 420 sq m exhibition space; largest banquet 350 seated or 500 cocktail.

Room services
Airconditioning, colour TV, direct-dial telephone (ext. in bathroom), hairdryer, laundry/valet service, minibar, alarm clock,

safety deposit box, tea/coffee making, trouser press, 24-hour room/meal service, non-smoker bedrooms

Business services
Business centre, express checkout, airport shuttle, translation service, car parking & rental, taxi service

Other services
Barber shop/hairdresser, beauty salon, newsstands/shop, guided tours

Sports & Recreation
Fitness centre/gym, jacuzzi/whirlpool, massage, sauna, steam, outdoor swimming pool, tennis. Access to golf course

Restaurants & Coffee Shops
Indigo Restaurant (140) - open 0600-0100 (Sat -0300); *Sarkies Seafood Restaurant* (140) - open noon-1430/1830-2230 (Sun from 0830); *Shima Japanese Restaurant* (104) - open noon-1430/1830-2230

Overseas Sales Representatives:
Mandarin Oriental Int'l Sales Offices, Utell, Leading Hotels of the World

Patra Surabaya Hilton International
Jalan Gunungsari, Surabaya 60224
Tel: (031) 568 2703; Fax: (031) 568 2081
E-Mail: SUBHIL@rad.net.id

Only 20 minutes from the airport, 15 minutes from the city centre, set amidst 15 acres of lush green, landscaped gardens, with a large pool and beside Yani golf course.

Accommodation & rates
40 single/twin de luxe US$ 73; 40 double/de luxe US$ 83; 40 suites US$ 120
Subject to 10% service charge & 11% tax

Credit cards accepted:
Amex, JCB, Diners, Mastercard, Visa

Meeting & banqueting facilities
Argopuro room, capacity 600 theatre-style; largest reception 400 seated/450 cocktail; Bromo room, capacity 120 theatre-style; largest reception 80 seated/100 cocktail

Room services
Airconditioning, colour & satelliteTV, direct-dial telephone (ext. in bathroom), hairdryer, laundry/valet service, minibar, music/radio/alarm clock, 24-hr room service, radio, hairdryer, safety deposit box, tea/coffee making, non-smoker bedrooms, video films

Business & other services
Business centre, express checkout, airport pickup, car parking & rental, taxi service, newsstand/shops

Sports & Recreation
Golf (adjacent), massage, outdoor swimming pool, tennis

Restaurants & Coffee Shops
Kedai Jepara (100) - Japanese, open 0600-midnight; *The Beer Garden* (60) - Local/international, open 0900-midnight (from 0700 Sat/Sun)

Overseas Sales Representatives:
Hilton International Sales Offices. Hilton Reservations Worldwide

Radisson Plaza Suite Hotel   C
Jalan Permuda 31-37, 60271
Tel: 516833; Fax: 516393

Sahid Surabaya   D
Jln Sumatra 1-15
Tel: (31) 522711; Tlx: 34391; Fax: 516292

Shangri-La   B
Jalan May Jmd Sungkoto 120, 60256
Tel: (31) 566 1550; Fax: (31) 566 1570

Sheraton Surabaya Hotel/Towers   B
Jalan Embong Malan 25-31, 60261
Tel: 546 8000; Fax: 546 7000

Java - Tretes

Natour Bath Hotel Tretes   D
2 Jalan Pesanggrahan, Tretes, Pasuruan,
Tel: (0343) 81777; Tlx: 31689; Fax: 510156

Java - Yogyakarta

The Acacia Yogyakarta   C
Jln Laksda Adisucipto (Jl Solo) 38, 55001
Tel: (274) 566 222; Fax: (274) 566 220

Benakutai Hotel   C
Jalan A Yani, PO Box 299
Tel: (542) 31896; Tlx: 37102; Fax: 31823

After an exhilarating day at the magnificient Borobudur...

Discover Yogyakarta's most comfortable deluxe hotel. The hotel with the extra large lobby, extra large room, extra large bed. For the luxury of space...

HOTEL AQUILA PRAMBANAN YOGYAKARTA

Jl. Adisucipto (Jl. Solo) No. 48
Po. Box. 82, Babarsari 55281
Yogyakarta, INDONESIA.

ACCOMODATION
- 191 Deluxe rooms including Aquila Club Floor.
- 4 Executive Suites, 5 Studio Suites, 2 Junior Suites.
- 1 Presidential Suite with Jacuzzi.
- Check-out time : 13.00 hrs.

FACILITIES AND SERVICES
Business Centre
Safe deposit boxes
Daily laundry & dry cleaning
Drugstore and souvenir shops
Tour and travel counter
Airport transfer & meeting services
Multi-lingual hotel staff
In-room entertainment : CNN, France Int'l, Australia Int'l, HBO & Local Channels
Major credit cards accepted.

RECREATION FACILITIES
- Joanne Drew Health Club
- Outdoor Swimming pool
- Children's playground
- Table tennis
- Tennis courts & 18-holes golf course located 5 minutes away

RESTAURANT AND BAR
- Chin Chin Lounge   • Taman Sari Cafe
- Serayu Seafood Restaurant (Cantonese and Szechuan Cuisine)
- The Pub   • Japanese Corner

BANQUET & CONFERENCE
	Min	Max
Kalasan Ballroom	60	650
Sambisari	24	100
Sewu	12	25

HOTEL RESERVATION
Yogyakarta :
Tel : (62)-(274) 565100 Direct
Tel : (62)-(274) 565005
Fax : (62)-(274) 565009
Jakarta :
Tel : (62)-(21) 7982360
Fax : (62)-(21) 7970006
Europe :
Swiss Sales
Alte Obefelderstrasse 57
CH-8910 Affoltern a.A.
Tel : (41-1) 7617434
Fax : (41-1) 7617262

Ambarrukmo Palace Hotel C
Jln Laksda Adiscupito, PO Box 1010
Tel: (274) 566488; Fax: 563283

Melia Purosani C
Cnr Jl Suryotomo/Jl Suryatmajan, POB 1246
Tel: (274) 58952/3; Fax: (274) 588071/73

Hotel Natour Garuda C
60 Jalan Malioboro, 59271
Tel: (0274) 66353; Tlx: 25174; Fax (0274) 63074

Yogya International Hotel D
Jalan Laksda, Adisucipto No 38, PO Box 215, Yogyakarta 55001
Tel: (0274) 64727; Tlx: 25162 YPP YKIA; Fax: (0274) 64171

Kalimantan (Borneo)

Altea Hotel Benakutai C
Jalan P Antasari, PO Box 200, Balikpapan, East Kalimantan
Tel: 23522; Tlx: 37102 ; Fax: 23893

Dusit Balikpapan C
Jalan Jend Sudirman, 76114
Tel: (542) 20155; Fax: (542) 20150

Lombok

Holiday Inn Resort C
Jln Sengigi Lombok, 83125
Tel: (364) 93444; Fax: (364) 93185

The Oberoi
Medana Beach, Tanjung, PO Box 1096, Mataram 83001, West Lombok
Tel: (370) 38444; Fax: (370) 32496

The Oberoi Lombok is a village style resort on Medana Beach, 45 minutes' drive north west of Mantaram Airport. The hotel is easily accessible via two main roads leading from Mantaram through mountainous rain forests or along scenic rugged coastline.

Accommodation & rates
30 luxury terrace pavilions US$204-320; 20 luxury villas US$ 320-850,
Subject to 21% service & gov't tax.

Credit cards accepted:
Amex, Diners, Mastercard, Visa, JCB

Meeting & banqueting facilities
Meeting/conference rooms - capacity 30

Room services
Laundry/valet service, minibar, music/radio/alarm clock, 24-hr room/ meal service, safety deposit box, video films,

Other services
Beauty salon

Sports & Recreation
Snooker, fitness centre/gym, indoor games, jacuzzi/whirlpool, massage, sauna, swimming pool, tennis, watersports

Restaurants & Coffee Shops
Sunbird Open Air Restaurant (60) - open 0700-1100/noon-1900; *Beach Barbecue* (60) - Seafood, open 1900-2200; *Lambung* (100) - Asian & Continental, open 1900-2230; *Amphitheatre* (70) - themed buffet, open 1915-2300; *Tokek Cocktail Bar* (40) - open noon-midnight

Overseas Sales Representatives:
Oberoi Hotels Worldwide

Sengigi Beach Hotel D
PO Box 2, Lombok 83001
Tel: (0364) 93210-9; Tlx: 35340; Fax: 93200

Sheraton Sengigi Beach Resort A
PO Box 1154, Mataram 83015, Nusa Tenggara Barat
Tel: 93333; Tlx: 35761; Fax: (364) 93140

Riau Archipelago
Near Singapore

Banyan Tree Bintan A
Tanjong Said, Riau Archipelago
Tel: (771) 81348; Fax: (771) 81348

Melia Panorama B
Sei Jodoh, Batam Island
Tel: (778) 452888; Fax: 452555

Hotel Mutiara Panghegar D
Jalan Jos. Sudarso 12, Pakanbaru, Riau
Tel: 23637; Fax: 23380

Sedona Hotel Bintan Lagoon A
Tel: (65) 338 8944; Fax: (65) 338 6696

Sulawesi (Celebes)

Century Hotel Manado ¶
Jalan Sam Ratulangi No 458, Manado
Tel: (c/o) (21) 572 0462; Fax: (21) 571 2139

Manado Beach Hotel D
Tasik Ria, PO Box 1030, Manado
Tel: (0431) 67001; Tlx: 74321; Fax: 67007

Novotel Resort Toraja D
PO Box 80, Rantepao, South Sulawesi
Tel: (423) 21192; Fax: (423) 21666

INDONESIA - Hotels/Restaurants/Car Hire/Airline Offices

Hotel Victoria Panghegar   D
Jalan Jendral Sudirman 24, Ujung Pandang
Tel: (0411) 311863; Cable: Victoria UPJ; Fax: (0411) 312468

Sumatra

Biliton Beach Hotel   D
c/o Aerowisata Marketing Centre, Jalan Prapatan 32, Jakarta 10410
Tel: (21) 231 0002; Fax: (21) 231 0003

Danau Toba International   D
17 Jalan Iman Bonjol, PO Box 490, Medan
Tel: 327000; Tlx: 51167 HDTI MDN IA

Hotel Bumi Minang   ¶
c/o Aerowisata Marketing Centre, Jalan Prapatan 32, Jakarta 10410
Tel: (21) 231 0002; Fax: (21) 231 0003

Hotel Tiara Medan   ○ E
PO Box 328, Jalan Cut Mutlagh, Medan
Tel: 574 6000; Tlx: 51721 GRIYA MDN; Fax: (061) 510176

Polonia Hotel   ○ D
14 Jalan Jenderai Sudirman, Medan
Tel: 535111; Tlx: 20152; Fax: 538870

Hotel Pusako   D
Jln Soeharno Hatta No 7, PO Box 69, Bukittingigi, West Sumatra
Tel: (752) 22111; Tlx: 55569; Fax: 21017

Hotel Sandeja International   ○ E
Jalan Kapten A Rival 6193, PO Box 16, Palembang
Tel: 27778/20634; Tlx: 27429

Restaurants

Outside Jakarta, the most reliable restaurants tend to be in the big hotels described in the foregoing pages. Below we list some of the most popular Jakarta dining places, where advance booking is advisable and where credit cards are accepted.

Ambiente *(Italian)*
Hyatt Aryaduta Hotel, 2nd fl, 444-48 Jln Prapatan. Tel: 376008
Le Bistro *(French)*
75 Jalan K H Wahid Hasyim. Tel: 364272

Casablanca
Kununigan Plaza, Jn Ras. Said. Tel: 514800
Club Noordwjik *(Western & Indonesian)*
5 Jalan Ir H Juanda. Tel: 353909
Club Room *(Western)*
Mandarin Oriental Hotel. Tel: 321307
Jayakarta Grill *(European)*
Sari Pan Pacific Hotel. Tel: 323707
Memories *(Western)*
Ground Fl, Wisma Indocement, Jalan Jendel Sudirman. Tel: 5781008
Oasis *(Western & Indonesian)*
47 Jalan Raden Saleh. Tel: 326397
Le Parisien *(French)*
Aryaduta Hotel, Jn Prapatan. Tel: 376008
Plaza de Espana *(Spanish)*
Holiday Inn Crowne Plaza, Jln Gatot Subroto, kav 2-3. Tel: 526 8833
Rugantino *(Italian)*
28 Jalan Melawai Raya. Tel: 714727
Taman Sari *(Indonesian)*
Jakarta Hilton hotel, Jalan Jenderal Gatot Subroto. Tel: 587981
Town Club *(Seafood)*
16th Fl, Wisma Metropolitan II, 31 Jalan Jenderal Sudirman. Tel: 5781659

Car Hire

Avis
Jln Diponegro 25 (Head Office), Jakarta
Tel: 334495/332900; Tlx: WISTA IA; Fax: 331845. + 10 branches at leading hotels &c
Budget
Jakarta JKTAA, Jln Gelong Baru 35
Tel: 591720/593897/596230
Hertz *(chauffeur drive only)*
P T Varista International, Hertz Int'l Licensee, Kanindo Plaza 4th fl, Jln Jend, Gatot Subroto Kav.23, Jakarta 12930
Tel: 518090; Fax: 518093
National Car Rental
Kartika Plaza Hotel, 10 Jln M H Thamrin, Jakarta. Tel: 333423/333425/322849 + branches at Denpasar and Medan.

Airline Offices

*(*Domestic carriers)*
Air China
Wisma Tamara, suite 802, Jln J Sudirman kav 24, Jakarta 12920. Tel: 520 6467-70
Bouraq Indonesia Airlines*
Jalan Angkasa, Jakarta
Tel: 659 5326/600 1557/600 1558

British Airways
c/o P T Kandida Persada, 10th fl, World Trade Centre Bldg, Jalan Jenderal Sudirman Kav 29/31. Tel: 521 1500
Cathay Pacific
Hotel Borobudur Inter-Continental, 3rd floor. Tel: 380 6660/663 8868
China Airlines
Wisma Dharmala Sakti M.I. Floor, Jln Jend Sudirman 32a. Tel: 588005/588285/588304
Garuda Indonesia
(Head Office) Danareska Bldg, 13 Jalan Angkasa Kemayoran. Tel: 3801901/3806276
(Sales Office) Wisma Dharmala sakti, Jln Jend Sudirman 32. Tel: 588707/588797
Japan Air Lines (JAL)
Mid Plaza Bldg, Jl Jend Sudirman Kav 10-11, Jakarta. Tel: 5703883/5703189/5781708
KLM
Hotel Indonesia, Jln M H Thamrin, Jakarta
Tel: 320708/322008
Lufthansa
Panin Centre Building 2nd fl, Jln Jenderal Sudirman 1. Tel: 710241/710251
Malaysian Airlines
Hotel Indonesia Grd Fl, Jln M H Thamrin
Tel: 320909
Mandala Airlines*
Jalan Veteran 1/34, Jakarta. Tel: 368107
Merpati Nusantara Airlines*
Jalan Angkasa 2, Jakarta 10720
Tel: 417404/416608
Philippine Airlines
Hotel Borobudur Inter-Continental Jalan Banteng Selatan. Tel: 370108
Qantas
Bank Dageng Negara Building, Jalan MH Thamrin 5. Tel: 327707/326707/327538
Royal Brunei
Room 8, Bali Arcade Ground floor, Hotel Indonesia, Jln MH Thamrin.Tel: 327214
Sempati Air
Grd floor, Terminal Bldg, Halim Perdana Kusuma Airport, Jakarta 13610
Tel: 809 4407; Fax: 809 4420
Saudia
Ground floor, Wisma Bumi Putra, Jln Jenderal Sudirman 75.Tel: 5782336/5780873
Singapore Airlines
Grd Fl, Chase Plaza, Jln Jen Sudirman Kav 21. Tel: 584021/584011
Thai International Airlines
BDN Bldg, Jln M H Thamrin. Tel: 320607
UTA
Gedung Java, Jln M H Thamrin (PO Box 2658). Tel: 323507/5202262-3

What's the link between business and the Asia Pacific?

BRITISH AIRWAYS
The world's favourite airline

http://www.british-airways.com

Aircraft Departures

Below is a list of frequencies and departures from Denpasar (Bali) and Jakarta to the destinations in bold type. Figures in brackets after destinations refer to the days of the week. (2,4,6) therefore indicates that departures to that destination take place on a Tuesday (the second day of the week), a Thursday and a Saturday.

Departures were correct as at February 1997 but travellers are advised to check with the offices listed above. Only direct flights, without plane changes are listed.

Airline Abbreviation Codes: AF = Air France; **AI** = Air India; **AN** = Ansett Australia; **BA** = British Airways; **BI** = Royal Brunei Airlines; **BO** = Bouraq Indonesia Airlines; **BR** = EVA Airways; **CA** = Air China; **CI** = China Airlines; **CO** = Continental Airlines; **CX** = Cathay Pacific; **CZ** = China Southern Airlines; **EG** = Japan Asia Airways; **EK** = Emirates; **GA** = Garuda Indonesia; **GF** = Gulf Air; **HY** = Uzbekistan Airways; **JL** = Japan Airlines; **KE** = Korean Air; **KL** = KLM; **KU** = Kuwait Airways; **LH** = Lufthansa; **LT** = LTU International Airways; **MH** = Malaysian Airlines; **MI** = Silk Air; **MZ** = Merpati Nusan-tara Airlines; **NC** = National Jet; **NZ** = Air New Zealand; **PK** = Pakistan International Airways; **PR** = Philippine Airlines; **QF** = Qantas; **RI** = Mandala Airlines; **RJ** = Royal Jordanian; **SG** = Sempati Air; **SQ** = Singapore Airlines; **SU** = Aeroflot; **SV** = Saudia; **TG** = Thai Airways International.

DENPASAR BALI (Ngurah Rai) (DPS)

Abu Dhabi (AUH)
GA (3,5,7) LT (6)
Adelaide (ADL)
GA (4,7) AN (6)
Ambon (AMQ)
MZ (daily)
Amsterdam (AMS)
GA (1,3,6,7) KL (3,7)
Auckland (AKL)
GA (1,4) NZ (3,6)
Balikpapan (BPN)
SG (daily)
Bandar Seri B (BWN)
BI (1,2,3,7)
Bandung (BDO)
MZ (daily)
Bangkok (BKK)
GA (4,6,7) TG(3,5,6,7) LH (6,7)
Biak (BIK)
MZ (daily)
Brisbane (BNE)
AN (7) GA (4,5,7)
Broome (BNE)
NC (1)
Cairns (CNS)
GA (2,6)
Darwin (DRW)
GA (2,6) AN (4,6,7) QF (1,2,4,6)
Dili (DIL)
MZ (daily)
Frankfurt (FRA)
GA (1,5,6) LH (6,7)
Fukuoka (FUK)
GA (1,4,7)
Guam (GUM)
CO (1,2,3,5,6)
Hobart (HBA)
AN (4)
Hong Kong (HKG)
GA (3,5,6)
Jakarta (JKT)
GA,SG, RI, MZ,JL (daily)
EG (1,2,3,5,6,7)
Jayapura (DJJ)
MZ (daily)
Johor Bahru (JHB)
MH (1,3)
Kaohsiung (KHH)
BR,GA (2,5)
Kuala Lumpur (KUL)
GA/MH (daily)
Kupang (KOE)
MZ, BO (daily)
London (LGW)
GA (5,7)
Mataram (AMI)
MZ,BO,SG (daily)
Maumere (MOF)
BO (daily)
Medan (MES)
GA (3)
Melbourne (MEL)
GA (2,4,6,7) QF (1,2,5)
AN (4,6)
Munich (MUC)
LT (6)
Nagoya (NGO)
GA (1,2,3,5,6)
Osaka (OSA)
GA (2,4,6) EG (5)
Paris (CDG)
GA (2,6)
Perth (PER)
AN (6,7) GA (1,2,5,7)
QF (2,6,7) SG (4,7)
Port Headland (PHE)
MZ (5)
Rome (FCO)
GA (4,6)
Semarang (SRG)
MZ (daily)
Seoul (SEL)
GA (1,2,3,6,7)
Singapore (SIN)
GA,SQ,BO (daily) NZ (3,6) KL (3,7)
Sorong (SOQ)
MZ (1,4,6)
Surabaya (SUB)
MZ,BO,SG,GA (daily)
Sydney (SYD)
AN (4,6,7) QF (1)
Taipei (TPE)
GA/CI (daily)
Tembagapura (TIM)
MZ (2,3,5,7)
Tokyo (TYO)
GA, JL (daily) NH (3,6)
Ujung Pandang (UPG)
MZ,GA (daily)
Waingapu (WGP)
BO (daily)
Yogyakarta (JOG)
GA, RI, (daily)
Zurich (ZRH)
GA (2,7)

JAKARTA (Soekarno-Hatta) (JKT)

Abu Dhabi (AUH)
GA (5) GF (1,4)
Adelaide (ADL)
GA (4,7)
Ambon (AMQ)
RI (daily) SG (daily)
Amman (AMM)
RJ (1,4)
Amsterdam (AMS)
GA (1,4,5,7) KL (6,7)
Auckland (AKL)
GA (1,4)
Bahrain (BAH)
GF (5)
Balikpapan (BPN)
BO, SG,GA (daily)
Banda Aceh (BTJ)
GA (daily)
Bandar Lampung (TKG)
MZ (daily)
Bandar Seri B (BWN)
BI (3,4,5,7)
Bandung (BDO)
MZ, SG (daily)
Bangkok (BKK)
GA (2,3,6,7) TG (daily)
Banjarmasin (BDJ)
SG,BO,MZ,GA (daily)
Batu Besar (BTH)
SG, GA, BO (daily)
Beijing (BJS)
CA (3,6) GA (7)
Bengkulu (BKS)
MZ, RI (daily)
Biak (BIK)
MZ (1,2,4,5,6) GA (3,5,7)
Bombay (BOM)
AI (3,7)
Brisbane (BNE)
GA (4,5,7) QF (3,6)
Broome (BME)
NC (1)
Cairns (CNS)
GA (2,6)
Darwin (DRW)
GA (2,6) NC (6)
Denpasar-Bali (DPS)
GA,SG,MZ,RI,JL (daily)
Dhahran (DHA)
GA (4) SV (7)
Dili (DIL)
MZ (1,3,5,6) SG (2,5,7)
Dubai (DXB)
EK (1,2,4,7) SU (4)
Frankfurt (FRA)
GA (1,3,4,5)
Fukuoka (FUK)
GA (3,6,7)
Guangzhou (CAN)
CZ (4,7) GA (3,7)
Ho Chi Minh (SGN)
GA (2,5)
Hong Kong (HKG)
CX,GA, CI (daily)
Honolulu (HNL)
GA (1,3,5,6,7)
Jambi (DJB)
MZ, RI (daily)
Jayapura (DJJ)
SG,MZ (daily) GA (3,5,7)
Jeddah (JED)
GA (1,3,5) SV (1,2,4,5)
Johor Bahru (JHB)
MH (3,6)
Kaohsiung (KHH)
CI (2,3,5,7)
Karachi (KHI)
PK (2,6)
Kuala Lumpur (KUL)
GA, MH (daily) BA (2,3,4,6,7)
GF (1,4,5)
Kupang (KOE)
SG (2,5,7) MZ (2,4,7)
Kuwait (KWT)
KU (1,3,6)
London (LGW)
GA (5,6)
Los Angeles (LAX)
GA (1,3,5,6,7)
Madras (MAA)
AI (3,7)
Malang (MLG)
MZ (daily)
Manado (MDC)
GA, SG, BO, RI, MZ (daily)
Manila (MNL)
GA (2,4) PR (daily)
Mataram (AMI)
SG (daily) GA (1,4,6)
Mauritius (MRU)
MK/SQ (6)
Medan (MES)
GA,BO,SG,RI,MZ (daily)
Melbourne (MEL)
GA (1,2,3,5,6,7) AN (6)
Minneapolis (MSP)
NW (1,3,5)
Moscow (MOW)
SU (4)
Muscat (MCT)
GF (5)
Nagoya (NGO)
GA (1,2,4)
Osaka (OSA)
GA (3,5,7) EG (1,2,3,5,6,7)
Padang (PDG)
MZ,SG,RI,GA (daily)
Palangkaraya (PKY)
MZ (daily)
Palembang (PLM)
MZ,RI,BO,GA (daily)
Palu (PLW)
MZ, BO (daily)
Pangkalpinang (PGK)
MZ, RI (daily)
Paris (CDG)
GA (2,4)
Pekanbaru (PKU)
SG,MZ, GA (daily)
Perth (PER)
SG (2,3,6) GA (daily) QF (2,4,7)
Pontianak (PNK)
MZ, RI, GA (daily)
Riyadh (RUH)
SV (2,3,6,7) GA (2,4,7)
Semarang (SRG)
MZ,SG,RI,GA (daily)
Seattle (SEA)
NW (1,3,5)
Seoul (SEL)
GA (2,3,4,6,7) KE/GA (2,3,4,7) KE (2,4,6,7)
Singapore (SIN)
GA, LH, SQ, TG, SG, MI, KL, QF (daily) EK (2,4,7) RJ (5) AI (3,7)PK (2,6) AF (1,2,4,6) UB (2,5)
Solo City (SOC)
GA,SG (daily)
Surabaya (SUB)
GA,RI,MZ,SG,BO (daily)
Sydney (SYD)
GA (daily) AN (3)
Taipei (TAI)
CI (daily) BR (daily) GA (1,2,4,5) SG (1,5)
Tokyo (NRT)
GA,JL (daily) NH (3,7)
Ujung Pandang (UPG)
GA, RI, SG, MZ, BO (daily)
Xiamen (XMN)
CA (3,5)
Yangon (RGN)
UB (2,5)
Yogyakarta (JOG)
GA, SG, BO, MZ, RI (daily)

Major Exhibitions in Jakarta 1997

Date	Exhibition	Venue	Organiser
April 23-26	**Communications Technology Indonesia 97** - 7th Int'l Telecommunications Exhibition	JIEC	OES/TMNI
April 23-26	**Business Communications Indonesia 97** - 9th Int'l business communications, networking, internet & office equipment show	JIEC	OES/TMN
April 23-26	**Mobile Communications Indonesia 97**	JIEC	OES/TMN
April 23-26	**Broadcast Technology Indonesia 97** -3rd Int'l broadcast, sound, film, video & lighting exhibition	JIEC	OES/TMN
April 23-26	**Cable & Satellite Indonesia 97**	JIEC	OES/TMN
April 23-26	**Marine Indonesia 97** - 9th Int'l marine, shipping equpment	JIEC	OES/TMN
April 23-26	**Transport Technology Indonesia 97** - 4th Int'l urban transport, rail & freight cargo handling exhibition	JIEC	OES/TMN
April 23-26	**Truck Indonesia 97** - 4th Int'l Commercial Vehicle exhibition	JIEC	OES/TMN
July 23-26	**NETWORKS** - Computer Exhibition	Jakarta	MFreeman
July 23-26	**IMTEC** - Int'l machine tool technology exhibition	Jakarta	PTPeraga
Sept 2-6	**Packaging & Food Processing Indonesia 97** - 12th Int'l; packaging & food processing exhibition	JIEC	OES/TMN
Sept 2-6	**Cantech Indonesia 97** - Int'l Canmaking & Canning Show.	JIEC	OES/TMN
Sept 2-6	**Printing Indonesia 97** - 5th Int'l printing machinery, equipment & suppliers exhibition	JIEC	OES/TMN
Sept 2-6	**Plastics & Rubber Indonesia 97** - 12th Int'l plastics & rubber machinery processing & handling exhibition	JIEC	OES/TMN
Sept 18-22	**Manufacturing Indonesia 97** - 10th Int'l manufacturing machinery exhibition incorporating **Machine Tool Indonesia 97** & **Welding Indonesia 97**	JIEC	OES/TMN
Sept 25-28	**INDOBEX** - Int'l building & construction expo	Jakarta	IIR
Nov 5-8	**Int'l Electrical Exhibition**	Jakarta	PTPam

Venues: BICC = KEC = New Jakarta International Exhibition Centre, Kemayoran, Jakarta. **JCC** = Jakarta Convention Center, Jl Jend. Gatot Subroto, PO Box 4916, Jakarta Pusat 10049, tel: 572 6000; Fax: 572 6523; **JFK** = Jakarta Fairground Kemayoram

Organisers: IIR = IIR Exhibitions Pte Ltd, 101 Cecil Street 09-03, Tong Eng Bldg, Singapore 069533. Tel (65) 2270688 Fax (65) 2270913. **JCB** = Jakarta Convention Bureau, Mashill Tower 20th level, Jalan Jenderal Sudirman KAV 25, Jakarta 12920, tel: 526 7685; fax: 526 7689. **MFreeman** = Miller Freeman/PT Napindo Mediapratama, Trade Mart Bldg, 3rd Fl 330A, Jakarta Fairgrounds, Jakarta. Tel (62) 21 4218531; Fax (62) 21 4218534 . **OES** = Overseas Exhibition Services, 11 Manchester Square, London W1m 5AB, tel: (+44) 171 486 1951; fax: (+44) 171 413 8222. **PTPam** = PT Pamerindo Buana Abadi, Bank Bumi Daya Plaza, Unit 2102, 21st fl, Jln Imam Bonjol 61, Jakarta 10310, tel: 325560; fax: 331223. **PTPeraga** = PT Peraga Nusantara Jaya Sakti, Jl P Jayakarta 141 Blok B/9, Jakarta, 10730 Tel (62) 21 6493727 Fax (62) 21 6390062.. **Reed** = World Trade Centre Complex, Wisma Metropolitan 1, 10th fl, Jln Jendral Sudirman Kav 29, Jakarta 12920. Tel: 571 2487; fax: 571 2488.

Something in you is drawn to a world where drinking & driving has entered ancient tradition.

Indonesia, a world of extraordinary spectacle.

Indonesia has more than 300 cultures, each with its own rites and festivals, across 17,000 islands. On Madura, the special diet for racing bulls is eggs, chilli and honey - washed down with strong beer. The bulls, not obviously affected, can reach 50 kph in the traditional festival race called *karapan sapi*. On the island of Sumba, worms rising from the sea are the signal for ranks of horsemen to engage in furious mock battle, in a rite called *pasola*. These unique festivals, and more, are played out against some of Nature's most incredible creations: volcanic landscapes, lush plains, turquoise seas.

For holiday information, mail the coupon to: Indonesia Tourist Promotion Office, PO Box 486, Weybridge, Surrey, United Kingdom KT1 5 2YF. Or visit the Indonesia website at http://www.visit-indonesia.com

Mail to receive our free brochure, "Discover Our Islands."

Name

Street Address, Apt. #, City

State/Province, Country, ZIP/Postal Code

INDONESIA
— A WORLD ALL ITS OWN —
Indonesia Tourism Promotion Board

Japan

Doing Business

General Climate

Work hard and prosper together was always a maxim instilled in Japanese workers. So also was the belief that once they had secured a job, they would have it for life. Both credos, along with the homogeneous conviction that Japan must unswervingly be self-sufficient, have been taking a severe drubbing recently.

As domestic economic blight dragged into its sixth year in 1997, with no immediate end in sight, public confidence in the 'Japanese way' reached a new low; banks and industry were forced to let more 'lifetime' workers go and the country -perhaps for the first time with any real enthusiasm or commitment - began seriously to open its doors to foreign influence and investment.

By January 1997 - with the economic outlook still shaky, the stock exchange hitting a 10-year low, real estate prices falling, the insurance industry on the verge of collapse and the top five banks showing no sign of being able to fund an estimated US$73bn in oustanding development loans -government issued a stern warning to trade and industry: economic revival, it said, depends on old, entrenched attitudes and attachments being changed forever; on a radical re-allocation of capital and labour and on a new brand of flexibility and financial spread.

Yet the government itself was accused by some analysts of being fickle. While some success had been achieved in bringing down the high value of the Yen, which had led to a massive flight of capital, it remained protected from falling to more feasible trading levels. And while a spartan budget for fiscal 1997/98 was introduced, it carried the sting of an increase from 3% to 5% in consumption tax. The resulting general mood remained gloomy, with analysts predicting growth of 1.5%-2% at best for the year. And while many business visitors believe in Japan's apparent new readiness to deal on a level international playing field, they are nonetheless still faced with entrenched and implacable ways of doing business.

Although westernised in many ways, Japan remains the most 'foreign' of Asia's business markets. Outwardly, there are few barriers, save the need for patience, politeness, a good interpreter and an appreciation of customs that sometimes are curious to modern Japanese themselves.

Yet, above all, it can be hard, if not impossible, to rapidly secure a business answer, whether a direct yes or no, from often endless and seemingly pointless meetings. Critics claim the Japanese love of meetings - rich in ceremony, long silences and the in-depth study of *meishi* (name cards) - plus meetings about arranging further meetings owe allegiance not to the notorious inscrutability of the nation but to an inherent reluctance or fear of dealing with foreigners or to making the first move.

In many Japanese companies, the ultimate power and decision-making, even on apparently minor issues, rests with just one man, or woman, and gaining the appropriate nod takes time. Protocol demands the average visitor spends long hours with middle-management 'salary men', both in the office and after hours, before access is granted to the inner sanctum, there to repeat the process. Meetings can stretch from office to restaurant, where drinks flow and a greater measure of informality can be shown as part of lengthy business courtships.

However, the years of recession have been kind in one respect to the visiting business traveller. The slowdown in domestic business travel has prompted many top hotels to bring down rates and broaden their markets with special packages for overseas visitors. In addition, many more *ryokan* (local inns) and *minshuku* (guest homes) catering for, and being marketed to, international business travellers.

Domestic air and rail discounts are also more widespread, and travel on the subway (always faster than taxis in major cities) is regarded as both suitable and practical for all ranks.

An added bonus is that many Japanese executives no longer expect to be entertained in very expensive supperclubs. In general, entertaining at mid-market *yakatori* (kebab) houses, or similar, followed by an evening at a karaoke bar is deemed appropriate by a people who, on their homeground at least, are learning, perhapsfor the first time, how to live on a budget.

Business awareness, etiquette and practice

Japanese manners and customs are very different from those in the West. Meetings tend to be long and formal; also to carry on into the evening at bars or restaurants where the atmosphere is more relaxed. It is customary when entering a Japanese house or restaurant to remove shoes.

When a Japanese person says 'yes', this means 'I hear you, I understand' rather than 'I agree with you'. Remember: in Japanese culture, the more vague one is, the more polite one is. Chivalry towards women is not developed and Japanese men will defer, within their own companies, to senior and older personnel.

English is not widely spoken outside business circles. Be punctual for appointments and allow plenty of time to get around Tokyo if taking taxis.

Large supply of business cards printed in both Japanese and English is important. Do not be in a rush to do your business in Japan, allow more than a stopover. Tips should not be given in the form of loose change but rather as a small financial gift, and then given with some ceremony. Smoking is more widely tolerated than in the West.

Tourism Update

General

Despite the high costs in Japan, the destination has been resilient - particularly for travellers from other parts of Asia. This is partly because of consumer demand - many people want to see the country they have heard so much about, and partly because the industry has packaged travel to Japan efficiently so that tour prices are reasonably priced.

But although travel to Japan dropped 3.5% in 1995 to 3,345,274, partly because of the strong yen, early figures indicated a recovery in 1996, with the provisional total at 3.8 million growth, up almost 15%. Average length of stay is approximately 14 days. Japan counts visitors by their passports, not by where they live. Market sources most affected by this system is American passport holders (which is overstated when compared with a by-residence count). The British total is separated, as many of those visiting Japan are living in Hong Kong, a British colony until July 1997. 57% of tourists in 1996 came from Asia. Taiwan increased by 25%, Singapore by 45%, with South Korea again sluggish at only 1.1% up. The Japanese National Tourist Organisation has initiated a ten-year programme *Welcome Plan 21*, aimed to attract 7 million visitors by the year 2005. The increase of 14.7% in 1996 is put down to both the weakening of the Yen against other currencies and the realism of hoteliers and tour operators in lowering their prices.

The inbound travel business is likely to continue to face high costs in Korea, which affect primarily the discretionary segment of the travel market (the largest). A positive factor of that airport capacity shortage in Tokyo might encourage more to visit other parts of Japan, where prices are not as high as in the big cities. Much of the leisure travel into Japan is by travellers from Asia, and this is the market that might be more comfortable with an itinerary that covers other parts of Japan. The budget of the NTO is approximately US$33 million.

Aviation

Japan's main international airline is Japan Airlines, whose subsidiaries include Japan Asia Airways, and the main domestic airline is All Nippon Airways - which is now also expanding rapidly on international routes. The third airline is Japan Air System, which concentrates on domestic routes.

New airlines are planned. Skymark wants to launch domestic low-fare services in 1998, and another airline start-up is Hokkaido International Airlines.

In response to the potential challenge from Skymark, both JAL and JAS announced plans in early 1997 to form domestic low-fare subsidiaries. JAL sold 9.0% more seats in 1995, taking the total to 10.2 million, and RPKs increased 11.0% to 54.8 billion. Growth at ANA was faster -- seats sold up 24.7% to 2.1 million, and RPKs up 22.1% to 12.8 billion. Growth continued at a rapid pace in 1996 -- around 17% for JAL and again around 24% for ANA.

ANA is adding a number of international routes, and it is also likely that there will be more dual designation. For instance, there are more than 25 different routes between Japan and Korea. The opening of Osaka Kansai airport relieved pressure on Tokyo Narita airport, but Narita is still limited by its single runway, and curfew. Studies for a third Tokyo airport are already being undertaken.

Passenger traffic at Kansai, opened in 1994, is currently about 25% of the country's total, compared with about 55% at Narita. In 1995 there was a 2.9% increase in passengers at Narita, taking its total to 23.4 million, and Kansai increased 235.5% to 8.15 million. Even though Narita's growth is capacity constrained, passenger growth ran around 6% in 1996, and at Kansai the rate was above 25%.

Hotels

There has been steady growth in hotels in Japan over the past five years - about 4,000 more rooms each year, and growing about 4.0% in 1995 to 145,877. The number of rooms in *ryokan*, traditional Japanese inns, which reached 100,000 in 1994, increased slightly (0.6%) to 102,220 in 1995.

For most hotels, international visitors represent a small percentage of business. As many as 70% of a hotel's customers are likely to be travellers from Japan itself. In addition, many hotels get as much as 70% of their revenue from food and beverage (particularly from banquet and wedding receptions), compared with generally below 50% in other countries in Asia. And the source of such business is primarily local.

Foreign hotel groups have expanded into Japan, and a number of international groups have announced new plans. Two international hotel companies are owned by Japanese companies - Inter-Continental, and Pan Pacific (operating in Japan under the Tokyu name).

And both Japan's major airlines have hotel subsidiaries. JAL has Nikko Hotels, and ANA has a company of the same name, ANA Hotels. JAL has also begun to develop a network of budget hotels, geared primarily at the business traveller, and called JAL City Hotels. The first were in Japan, but one is also in Indonesia.

New openings in 1997 included the 485-room Pan Pacific in Yokohama, the 292-room Ritz Carlton Osaka, 61-room Holiday Inn Sapporo, 361-room Ana gate Tower in Osaka and the Accor Sofitel Tokyo with 71 rooms in a daring post-cubism architectural style. Projects planned to open between 1997 and before 2000 include Grand Hyatt in **Fukuoka** with 420 rooms; in **Osaka**, the Imperial with 400 rooms, and the Ritz Carlton with 300 rooms; in **Tokyo**, the planned Meridien Grand Pacific with 884 rooms has been delayed.

What to see

Most visitors to Japan are struck by the dramatic contrast between the country's modern, high-tech, image and the rural backwaters where life hardly seems to have changed in decades. This contrast between old and new is even evident in the big cities. As Japan's commercial and political centre, Tokyo, perhaps, best illustrates this situation as it is home to both the traditional values associated with the Imperial Palace and vast areas of modern high-rise and endless shopping malls and expensive stores. In fact, the Palace is very close to the busy Marunouchi Business District and usually at the top of list when it comes to sightseeing in Tokyo. But the Palace is only open to visitors twice a year and even the most charitable would not describe it as a particularly stunning building.

Away from the Palace, Tokyo has its fair share of interesting old temples and some good museums. The Asakusa Temple is the oldest in the city and is worth a visit. Probably the best museum is the Goto Art Museum (named after late railway baron Keita Goto), which is home to an excellent collection of ancient scrolls and a fine selection of Japanese and Chinese paintings. In Marunouchi, there is the Idemitsu Gallery with its fascinating collection of ceramics, paintings and bronzes. It also overlooks the Imperial Palace and was set up by one Sazo Idemitsu, founder and chairman of the Idemitsu Oil Company. The Tokyo National Museum has what is generally accepted as the world's best collection of Asian art and is in fact Japan's largest.

As you might expect, Japanese botanical gardens are probably the finest anywhere. With its large carp, running streams and small ornamental bridges, the six-hectare Koishikawa Korakuen should not be missed by gardeners or anyone else for that matter. However, Korakuen is better known by locals for its giant baseball stadium and amusement park.

Tokyo Disneyland, which celebrated its 11th birthday in 1994, launched a new attraction - the *Disney Party Gras Parade* during 1991. The Parade can be seen daily at 1500. Studio Tours - an adjacent theme park - is now underway.

To see the real Japan it is important to get out of Tokyo and probably the most popular side trip is to the ancient capital of Kyoto, which can be reached easily by *shinkansen* bullet train in under three hours. Kyoto was the nation's capital as recently as 1868 and still retains its own Imperial Palace. In addition the city has no less than 1,600 Buddhist temples plus some 400 Shinto shrines, three palaces, 60 temple gardens and any number of museums. The local office of the JNTO can arrange special visits to any of the palaces or temples.

Among the other big cities opportunities for sightseeing are somewhat limited as some were partly destroyed by Allied bombing during World War II and large scale development has torn the heart out of others. But Osaka has some good museums, including the Fujita Art Museum, and the Shitennoji Temple (founded 593) is thought to be Japan's oldest.

Shopping

Tokyo has a well-deserved reputation for high prices, but it should also be remembered that many items are of excellent quality as is the almost legendary standards of service in many stores from immaculately uniformed girls in white lace gloves.

Japanese department stores are at the forefront of the drive to provide customers with the highest quality. Seibu and Mitsukoshi are two the best-known names and are lavishly equipped with goods to satisfy even the most discerning shopper and the pair even have their own theatres.

The Japanese are among the world's most fashion-conscious consumers and vie for the latest French and Italian designer-label offerings. Increasingly, though, young Japanese designers have sprung to the world's attention and their fashion houses can be found in the upmarket Aoyama district. Many smaller shops sell good clothes and it's not always necessary to pay the inflated prices of Aoyama.

Ginza is a much better place to for more mainstream shopping with a broad range of outlets from top department stores to those shops selling local goods such as kimono silk and porcelain to Italian-imported leather items. Other areas to consider are Kanda Jimbocho, which is known for its books, the old Shitamachi area (for antiques), Shinjuku and Akihabara are best known for cameras and the latest Japanese electricals.

It's worth noting that foreigners (accompanied by their passports) are eligible for a tax rebate of up to 40 percent on the wholesale price by shopping in an authorised tax-free store, often found in hotel arcades as well as some shopping areas. Tax-free electrical stores are plentiful in Akihabara.

Getting Around

Following the mid-eighties liberalisation of the internal air system, Japan's domestic airline network is probably the region's most comprehensive Three airlines dominate the market ANA, JAS and flag carrier JAL, which has become increas-

ingly active locally. It's worth noting the fact that the majority of domestic flights use Tokyo's Haneda Airport and not Narita.

The national rail system provides stiff competition for the airlines' domestic flights, especially over distances of less than 600 km where Japan's famous *shinkansen* bullet trains offer an alternative. These now run Tokyo-Yamagata, as well as Tokyo-Morioka, Tokyo-Niigata and Tokyo-Fukuoka. There are five other grades of express and not so express trains.

In Tokyo the subway is usually thought of as the cleanest, safest and most efficient in the world - if overcrowded. However station names are written up in English and lines/trains are colour-coded. Buses, by contrast, are painfully slow as they make their way through Tokyo's heavy traffic.

As for taxis, very few drivers speak any English so it's important to get your destination written down in Japanese before departing. Car rental is best reserved for out-of-town trips as traffic congestion, non-English signs, the excessive number of traffic lights and a distinct lack of parking spaces make driving difficult.

Entertainment

As a rule, Tokyo's nightlife tends to start early (as office workers rush from their desks to various drinking haunts) and finish early (as the same workers hurry to catch trains back to the suburbs).

But some well-defined areas do offer a refuge for late-night revellers such as Roppongi with its discos and all-night clubs. Discos tend to be pricey, but this disguises the fact that drinks and sometimes food are included in the entry fee. The *Lexington Queen* and *Samba Club* in Roppongi always rate highly.

Yoshiwara is a run-down area of cheap bars and massage parlours, but Shinjuku's Kabukicho is more up-market. Generally, though, a night out is likely to be expensive especially if you end up in an expense-account type hostess bar.

Tokyo is over-endowed with bars, beer halls and brasseries. The traditional Japanese pub, or *nomiya*, is found in most neighbourhoods and is recognisable by its red lantern hanging outside. *Nomiya* serve food with beer and *sake*. On a larger scale, beer halls offer a less intimate place to socialise.

Expats have a habit of congregating is a few select bars in the city - some of which are modelled on British pubs. If you feel the need for western company then *Maggie's Revenge*, *Charleston* and *Berni Inn* in Roppongi are all worth checking out. Among hotel pubs, many old-timers swear by the *Orchid Bar* at the Okura.

Karaoke, which has recently caught on in the West, is still very much part of the Japanese social scene but the thought of having to sing to backing music in front of a large audience may not be to everyone's taste. Most neighbourhoods have at least one *Karaoke bar*. The *Lorelei* in Ginza, the *Roaring 20'* and *Saint Julian* all come with a recommendation.

For those that like their entertainment a little more restrained, Tokyo has no less than five symphony orchestras and there are classical concerts almost every night.

Leisure

After a hard week at the office or factory, the Japanese take their leisure time very seriously. Golf has become one the nation's top pursuits, but due to a scarcity of land, courses are few and far between. As a result many players are confined to multi-storey driving ranges with real golf only played on overseas trips.

Golf club membership and green fees are both exorbitant and as a visitor it will be difficult to get near a course. It's not unusual for Japanese players to pay US$200 for a round, so if a local contact or associate invites you, this is indeed a compliment and should not be refused as he will be paying.

Otherwise, Japan Grey Line offers a full-day golf tour every weekday except Monday. This, too, is expensive but does allow visitors to play at the exclusive Fuji Ace Golf Club.

Baseball is as popular in Japan as it is in the US and has been played locally since 1873. The season lasts April-October. Tokyo has two major horse-racing tracks which hold year-round meetings. Betting is government controlled. Ski-ing is popular on the island of Hokkaido.

Cycling is surprisingly popular, especially with the gambling fraternity which organises betting on races at places such as Tokyo's main stadium Kawasaki Keirinjo. A growing number of firms rent out bikes to visitors and this is a great way of seeing Tokyo or any of the other big cities.

A visit to one of the six big annual *basho*, or sumo tournaments is recommended. These last 15 days and are held in Tokyo (January, May and September) and three other cities - Nagoya (July), Osaka (March) and Fukuoka (November). Non "ring-side" tickets are usually available on the day of the match.

Many (but by no means all- see *Hotel Reference Table* following this digest) of Tokyo's leading hotels have excellent swimming pools and well-equipped fitness centres. Two good jogging tracks are the 5km Imperial Palace Course and the shorter Yoyogi Park Course.

Theme parks have become increasingly popular in Japan. There is a Disneyland in Chiba and Tokyo itself has seven: Namco Wonder Eggs (involving computer graphics), the Dr Jeekan's (computer games), the indoor Sanrio Puroland, the Geopolis, the Tokyo Sesame Place. the Daytona Park and the futuristic Amazing Square.

Arrival & Departure

Tokyo's Narita Airport is located about 60km north-east of the city. The new Narita Express Train offers a non-stop link between the airport and Tokyo station. Journey time is just 53 minutes. Trains run every hour from early morning to mid-evening. Single fare is ¥2890.

Otherwise, there is the express bus which connects Narita with the Tokyo City Air Terminal (TCAT) and costs ¥2600. From here it is possible to get a taxi to your ultimate destination. There are also Airport Limousine Buses directly to downtown hotels, leaving hourly and costing ¥2600-3500. Either way, travellers should allow three hours between leaving their hotel and take-off time and 2½ hours from touchdown time to any appointment they might have in central Tokyo, as customs and immigration procedures can take time. Haneda Airport for domestic and Taiwan departures is only 10 km SW of the city centre. "Passenger service facility charge" is ¥2000 on all departing passengers from Narita Children between 2-11 pay half this figure. International flights from other airports are toll free.

JAPAN - Introduction

Useful Addresses

Banks, government agencies

Bank of Japan Exchange Control and Foreign Investment Division
2-1-1 Nihonbashi-Honggokucho, Chuo-ku, Tokyo. Tel: 3279 1111

Center for Inducement of Industry to Rural Areas, Senkoku Choson Kaikau, 1-11-35 Nagado-chu, Chiyoda-ku, Tokyo. Tel: 3580 1668

Hokkaido-Tohoku Development Finance Public Corporation
Koko Bldg, 1-9-3 Otemachi, Chiyoda-ku, Tokyo. Tel: 3270 1651

Japan Chamber of Commerce & Industry
2-2 Marunouchi, 3-chome, Chiyoda-ku, Tokyo. Tel: 3283 7500

Japan Development Bank
Planning Dept Bureau for Regional Development, 1-9-1 Otemachi, Chiyoda-ku, Tokyo. Tel: 3270 3211

Japan External Trade Organisation (JETRO)
2-5 Toranomon, 2-chome, Mianto-ku, Tokyo 107. Tel: 3582 5511; Tlx: J 24378; Fax: 3582 0656

Japan Federation of Importers' Organisations
Nihonbashi Daiwa Bldg, 6-1 Nihonbashi Honcho, 1-chome, Chuo-ku, Tokyo. Tel: 3270 2020

Japan Foreign Trade Council
World Trade Centre Building, 4-1 Hamamatsu-cho, 2-chome, Minato-ku, Tokyo 105. Tel: 3435 5952

Japan Industrial Location Centre
1-4-2 Toranomon, Minato-ku, Tokyo. Tel: 3502 2361/2366

Japan Junior Chamber of Commerce
1-14-3 Irakawa-cho, Chiyoda-ku.Tel: 3324 5601

Japan Regional Development Corporation
Sales Promotion Division, Toranomon Mitsui Bldg, 3-8-1 Kasumigaseki, Chiyoda-ku, Tokyo. Tel: 3501 5211

Ministry of International Trade & Industry (MITI)
Industrial Location Guidance Division, 1-3-1 Kasumigaseki, Chiyoda-ku, Tokyo. Tel: 3501 0645

Osaka Chamber of Commerce & Industry
Uchihommachi, 58-7 Hashizumechi, Higashi-ku 540, Osaka. Tel: 3944 6412

Osaka Municipal Centre for Business & Trade
Osaka Municipal Office, 3-20 Nakanoshima 1-chome, Kita-ku, Osaka. Tel: 32623261/3208 8181

Tokyo Chamber of Commerce & Industry
Tosho Bldg, 2-2 Marunouchi 3-chome. Tel: 3283 7601

US Chamber of Commerce
7th Fl, No 2 Fukide Bldg, 4-1-21 Toranomon, Minato-ku, Tokyo. Tel: 3433 5381

Post Offices, Hospitals

Central Post Office. Tokyo Station Plaza, Chiyoda-ku, Tokyo. Tel: 3284 9527

Tokyo International Post Office
2-3-3 Otemachi, Tokyo. Tel: 3241 4891

Japan Red Cross Hospital (Nisseki Iryo Centre)
4-1-22 Hiro, Shibuya-ku, Tokyo. Tel: 3400 1311

St Luke's International Hospital (Seiroka Byoin)
1-10 Akashi-cho, Chuo-ku, Tokyo. Tel: 3541 5151

Tourist Information

Japan National Tourist Organisation (JNTO)
Tokyo Kotsu Kaikan Bldg, 2-10-1 Yurakucho, Chiyoda-ku, Tokyo. Tel: 3216 1901

Japan Travel Bureau (JTB)
Foreign Tourist Dept, 3rd Fl, Nitteshu-Nihonbashi Bldg, 1-13-1 Nihonbashi, Chuo-ku, Tokyo. Tel: 3276 7771

Osaka Tourist Information Office
1-1 Umeda, 3-chome, Osaka 2189. Tel: 3345 2189

Tokyo Tourist Information Centre (TIC)
B1F, Tokyo Int'l Forum, 3-5-1 Marunouchi, Chiyoda-ku, Tokyo 100. Tel: 3201 3331

Air Couriers

DHL: Fukuoka (092) 473 4541;Hiroshima (082) 295 6140;Kobe (078) 251 8661; Kyoto (075) 661 7255; Nagasaki (0958) 478145; Nagoya (052) 582 2580; Osaka (06) 262 9290;Tokyo (03) 5479 2580

Federal Express: Tokyo (03) 3521 4300

TNT Express Worldwide: Japan Head Office (03) 5445 1300/01;Hiroshima (82) 234 9221;Nagoya (052) 937 4831;Narita Airport (476) 32 6593;Osaka (06) 448 4730 Tokyo (03) 5821 3291;Yokohama (045) 313 9177. **UPS:** Okinawa (81) 4732 71040.

Japan Key Fact File

Passport Requirements:
A valid passport is required by all visitors. Business visas are required for those travelling for commercial reasons. Nationals of Austria, Germany, Ireland, Liechtenstein, Mexico, Switzerland and the UK (except territories) are exempted from obtaining a visa for up to six months as long as they refrain from "any remunerative activity." Nationals from a large number of other countries including USA may stay for up to three months.

Currency: Yen (Y)

Exchange Rate:
US$ 1 = Y 121; £1 = Y 197 *(May 1997)*

Currency Restrictions:
No restrictions on the import of foreign and Japanese currencies. The export of foreign currencies is also unlimited, but Yen exports are restricted to Y 5 million.

Electricity Supply:
100 volts AC/60 cycles in West Japan and 100 volts AC50/cycles in East Japan.

Language:
Japanese; some English spoken in commercial circles.

Time:
GMT + 9 hours; EDT + 14 hours

IDD Code: 81
Area codes: Fukuoka 92; Hiroshima 82; Kawasaki 44; Kobe 78; Kyoto 7; Nagasaki 958; Nagoya 2; Naha 988; Osaka 6; Sapporo 11; Tokyo 3; Yokohama 468.

Business Hours:
Commercial and government offices: 0900-1700 Monday to Friday; 0900-1200 Saturdays. (Govt. offices close 2nd & 4th Sats) Shops: Most department stores open 1000-1800 weekdays and 1000-1830 Saturday and Sunday. Each store closes once a week, but on different days in any one area.
Banks: Banking hours are from 0900-1500 Monday to Friday. Post Offices 0900-1700.

Customs & Entry:
Duty-free allowance comprises three bottles of 760cc each of alcohol, 400 cigarettes or 500 grams of tobacco or 100 cigars for persons aged over 19 years and only half the amounts for residents; two ounces of perfume and gifts and souvenirs up to the value of Y 200,000 or its equivalent.

Health Requirements:
No inoculations are required to enter Japan from any country.

Climate:
Japan boasts four distinct seasons: winter, spring, summer and autumn. The country's four main islands stretch through 25 degrees of longtitude and as a result the cimate varies from subtropical in the south to subarctic in northern Hokkaido. Tokyo is hot in summer, (min. 20° - max 30°C) with cool winters (min. 14° - max 9°C). Rain falls mainly in the summer and typhoons can be experienced during September.

National Holidays 1997:
January 1 - New Year's Day; Jan 15 - Coming of Age Day; Feb 11 - National Foundation Day; March 21 - Vernal Equinox Day; April 29 - Greenery Day; May 3 - Consitution Memorial Day; May 5 - Children's Day; July 20 - Marine Day; Sept 15 - Respect for the Aged Day; Sept 23 - Autumnal Equinox Day; Oct 10 - Health-Sports Day; Nov 3 - Culture Day; Nov 23 - Labour Thanksgiving Day; Dec 23 - Emperor's Birthday.

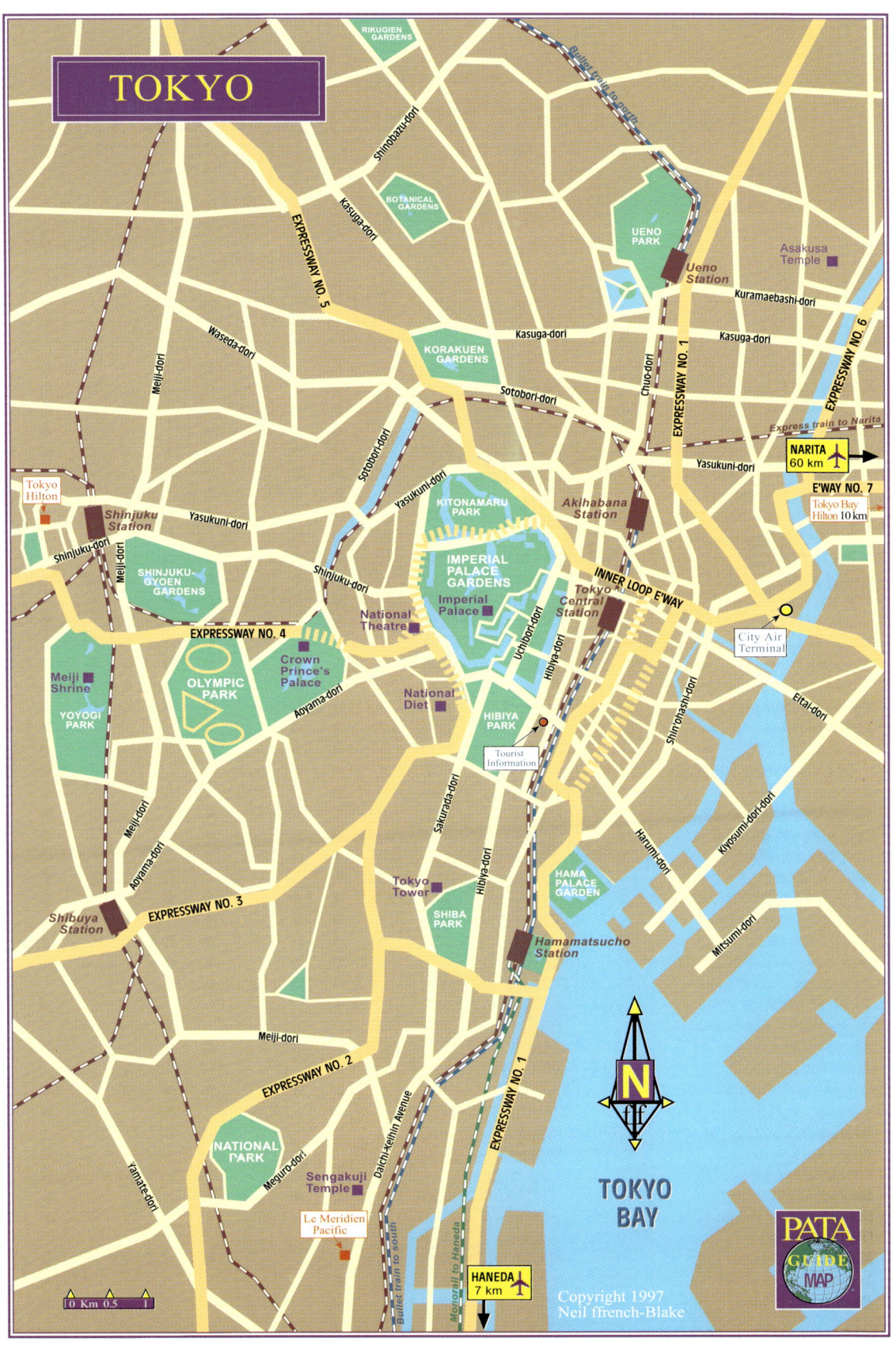

Tokyo Hotel Reference Table

Hotel (listed in price order)	SINGLE ROOM RATE (x 1000 YEN)	LOCATION	NUMBER OF ROOMS	NUMBER OF SUITES	CONFERENCE FACILITIES	EXHIBITION SPACE	LARGEST BANQUET NUMBER	BUSINESS CENTRE	SWIMMING POOL (0 = indoor)	TENNIS COURT	HEALTH CLUB	VIDEO FILMS
Hotel Seijo	48-72	Chuo-ku	80	-	-	-	150	●	-	-	-	●
Park Hyatt Tokyo	40-51	Shinjuku-ku	175	3	●	●	500	●	●	-	●	●
Imperial Hotel	35-61	Chiyoda-ku	1064	76	●	●	3500	●	●	-	●	●
Four Seasons Hotel	34-60	Chinzan-So	286	-	●	-	-	●	-	-	-	●
Sheraton G'de Tokyo Bay	32-52	Tokyo Bay	782	-	●	●	1300	●	●	●	●	●
Tokyo Rennaissance Hotel	31-50	Chuo-ku	197	9	●	●	400	●	-	-	-	●
Ginza Nikko Hotel	31-55	Chuo-ku	112	-	●	●	70	●	-	-	-	●
Century Hyatt Tokyo	31-39	Shinjuku-ku	776	24	●	●	1400	●	●	-	●	●
Capitol Tokyu Hotel	30.5	Chiyoda-ku	479	-	●	●	1000	○	●	-	-	●
Hotel Okura	28-40	Minato-ku	831	79	●	●	3000	●	●	-	●	●
The Westin Tokyo	28-40	Megoru-ku	430	15	●	●	500	●	-	-	-	●
The Manhattan	28-58	Chiba	117	14	●	●	250	●	●	-	●	●
Dai-Ichi Hotel	27-34	Minato-ku	275	-	●	-	300	●	-	-	-	●
Ginza Tokyu	26.3	Chuo-ku	440	-	●	-	500	●	-	-	-	●
The New Otani	26-30	Chiyoda-ku	2047	9	●	●	10000	●	●	●	●	●
Tokyo Bay Hotel Tokyu	25-40	Tokyo Bay	750	53	●	●	745	●	●	●	●	●
Tokyo Bay Hilton Int'l	26-49	Tokyo Bay	684	56	●	●	770	●	●	●	●	●
Akasaka Prince	24-35	Chiyoda-ku	636	124	●	●	-	●	-	-	-	●
The Palace Hotel	24-29	Chiyoda-ku	404	5	●	●	-	●	-	-	-	●
Inter-Continental Tokyo Bay	24	Tokyo Bay	331	8	●	●	250	-	-	-	-	●
Ana Hotel Tokyo	23-26	Minato-ku	900	2	●	●	870	●	○	-	-	●
Tokyo Prince Hotel	23-25	Minato-ku	466	1	●	●	1500	●	○	-	-	●
Tokyo Hilton Internat'l	22-37	Shinjuku-ku	750	53	●	●	745	●	○	●	●	●
Rhiga Royal Waseda	22-38	Waseda	123	4	●	●	300	●	-	-	-	●
Miyako Hotel	22-25	Minato-ku	483	17	●	-	-	-	○	-	-	●
Le Meridien Pacific	22-30	Minato-ku	913	41	●	●	1500	●	●	-	-	●
Akasaka Tokyu Hotel	21	Chiyoda-ku	566	-	●	●	-	●	-	-	-	●
Royal Park Hotel	21-41	City Air T'l	450	-	●	●	500	●	○	-	●	●
New Takanawa Prince	21	Minato-ku	1000	-	●	●	-	●	●	-	●	●
Keio-Plaza Inter-Cont'l	20-30	Shinjuku-ku	1462	23	●	●	1000	●	●	-	-	●
Takanawa Prince	20	Minato-ku	444	34	-	-	-	-	●	-	-	●
Roponggi Prince Hotel	19.5	Minato-ku	216	12	-	-	-	-	●	-	-	●
Haneda Tokyu Hotel	21	Ota-ku	303	4	●	●	-	●	-	-	-	●
Hotel Takanawa	18-21	Minato-ku	132	-	●	●	-	●	-	-	-	●
Hotel Grand Palace	17-28	Chiyoda-ku	462	4	●	●	-	●	-	-	-	●
Holiday Inn C PMetropolitan	17-21	Toshima-ku	818	-	●	-	1000	●	●	-	●	●
Holiday Inn Tokyo Yaesu	17-20	Chuo-ku	119	-	●	-	-	●	-	-	-	●
Shiba Park Hotel	16-19	Minato-ku	400	-	●	-	-	●	-	-	-	●
Shinjuku Prince	15-16	Shinjuku-ku	571	-	●	●	200	●	-	-	-	●
Ginza Dai-Ichi Hotel	15-21	Chuo-ku	800	-	●	●	-	●	-	-	-	●
Sunshine City Prince	14-21	Toshima-ku	1166	-	●	●	1000	-	-	-	●	●
Diamond Hotel	12-19	Chiyoda-ku	471	-	●	-	-	●	-	-	-	●
Miyako Inn Tokyo	10.8	Minato-ku	405	-	-	-	-	-	-	-	-	●
Tokyo Hotel Urashima	10	Chuo-ku	982	-	●	-	-	●	-	-	-	●
Shinagawa Prince	9	Minato-ku	1273	-	●	-	300	-	-	-	-	●

Rest of Japan Hotel Reference Table

Hotel (listed in price order)	SINGLE ROOM RATE from (x 1000 YEN)	LOCATION	NUMBER OF ROOMS	NUMBER OF SUITES	CONFERENCE FACILITIES	EXHIBITION SPACE	LARGEST BANQUET NUMBER	BUSINESS CENTRE	SWIMMING POOL (0 = indoor)	TENNIS COURT	HEALTH CLUB	VIDEO FILMS
Kyoto Takaragaike Prince	31-37	Kyoto	322	-	-	-	-	●	-	-	-	●
Imperial Osaka	27-37	Osaka	373	17	●	-	2000	●	●	●	●	●
Ritz Carlton Osaka	27-34	Osaka	266	26	●	-	500	●	O	-	●	●
Hankyu International	27-30	Osaka	146	22	●	-	500	-	O	-	●	●
Sapporo Renaissance	27-36	Sapporo	200	10	●	●	500	●	●	-	●	●
Kyoto Prince	27-33	Kyoto	100	-	-	-	-	-	-	-	-	-
Hankyu International	27-33	Osaka	146	22	●	●	1000	●	-	-	●	-
Hotel New Otani	27	Osaka	506	53	●	-	500	●	●	-	●	●
Hakone Prince	26-45	Hakone	373	-	-	-	-	-	-	-	●	-
Karuizawa Prince	26	Karuizawa	632	-	-	-	-	-	-	●	-	-
Yokohama Grand Interc'l	26-40	Yokohama	559	41	●	●	430	●	●	-	●	●
Hyatt Regency Osaka	26-30	Osaka	500	-	●	●	500	●	●	-	●	●
The Westin Osaka	25-33	Osaka	256	48	●	●	500	●	●	-	●	●
Hilton Osaka	26-36	Osaka	469	57	●	●	800	●	O	●	●	●
Kawana Hotel	25-47	Ito	140	-	●	●	1000	-	●	●	-	●
Shimoda Prince	24-47	Shimoda	135	-	-	-	-	-	●	●	-	●
Nikko Prince Hotel	22	Nikko	60	18	-	-	-	-	●	●	-	●
Shimoda Tokyu Hotel	22	Shimoda	127	6	●	●	-	●	O	●	-	●
Kyoto Brighton	21-34	Kyoto	183	-	●	●	-	●	-	-	-	●
Nagoya Hilton	21-27	Nagoya	423	28	●	-	800	●	O	●	●	●
Holiday Inn Yokohama	21-23	Yokohama	187	-	●	-	1500	-	●	-	●	-
Yokohama Prince	20	Yokohama	404	37	●	●	500	●	●	-	●	●
New Otani Makuhari	20-43	Chiba	382	36	●	●	1000	●	-	●	●	●
New Furano Prince	20-27	Furano	114	-	-	-	-	●	●	●	-	●
Yokohama Tokyu	19.5	Yokohama	219	3	●	●	-	●	-	-	-	●
Hotel New Grand	19-31	Yokohama	191	-	-	-	-	-	-	-	-	-
Hakuba Tokyu Hotel	19	Hakuba	73	-	-	-	-	-	-	-	-	-
Holiday Inn Nankai-Osaka	18-21	Osaka	225	4	●	-	300	-	●	-	●	●
The Hotel Yokohama	18	Yokohama	168	-	-	-	-	-	-	-	-	-
Hotel Nikko Kansai Airport	18-27	Osaka	576	-	●	-	-	-	-	-	-	-
Yumoto Fujiya Hotel	18-25	Hakone	87	1	●	●	150	-	●	-	●	-
Manza Prince Hotel	17-33	Gunma	194	-	-	-	-	-	-	-	-	-
Rhiga Royal Narita	17-26	Narita	495	5	●	●	500	●	-	-	-	-
Hotel Okura Kobe	17-21	Kobe	489	-	●	-	-	●	-	-	-	-
Okinawa Harbourview	17-25	Okinawa	360	8	●	●	450	-	●	-	-	-
Fukuoka Hotel (Ana)	17-21	Fukuoka	99	-	●	-	-	-	-	●	●	-
Nankai South Tower	17-26	Osaka	548	-	●	●	550	●	-	-	-	-
Hotel Nikko Osaka	17-21	Osaka	654	-	●	●	-	●	-	-	-	-
New Otani Hakata	16-32	Fukuoka	436	8	●	●	-	●	-	●	●	-
Naha Tokyu Hotel	16	Okinawa	208	2	●	●	-	●	●	-	-	-
Palace on the Hill Okinawa	16-21	Naha	145	-	●	-	400	●	●	-	●	-
Narita Winds Hotel	16	Narita	313	8	●	●	300	●	●	●	-	-
Ana Hotel Osaka	16-20	Osaka	500	-	●	●	550	●	O	-	-	●
The Plaza Hotel	16-23	Osaka	401	17	●	●	1800	●	●	●	-	-
Holiday Inn Crowne Plaza	16-24	Toyohashi	505	-	●	-	-	●	●	-	-	-
Holiday Inn Tobu Narita	15-27	Narita	250	4	●	-	400	-	●	-	●	-

Rest of Japan Hotel Reference Table

Hotel (listed in price order)	SINGLE ROOM RATE from (x 1000 YEN)	LOCATION	NUMBER OF ROOMS	NUMBER OF SUITES	CONFERENCE FACILITIES	EXHIBITION SPACE	LARGEST BANQUET NUMBER	BUSINESS CENTRE	SWIMMING POOL (0 = indoor)	TENNIS COURT	HEALTH CLUB	VIDEO FILMS
Sapporo Tokyu	15	Sapporo	263	-	●	●	-	●	-	-	-	●
Osaka Tokyu Hotel	15	Osaka	340	-	●	●	-	-	●	-	-	-
Nagoya Tokyu Hotel	15	Nagoya	553	15	●	●	2000	●	O	-	●	●
Ana Hotel Sapporo	15-19	Sapporo	412	2	●	●	350	-	-	-	-	-
Miyako Hotel Osaka	14.3-16	Osaka	557	29	●	●	700	●	●	-	●	●
Kyoto Tokyu Hotel	14	Kyoto	429	4	●	●	-	●	●	-	-	-
Hakata Tokyu Hotel	14	Fukuoka	266	3	●	●	-	●	-	-	-	●
Royal Hotel	14-25	Osaka	1350	-	●	●	-	-	●	-	●	●
Hotel Narita Tokyu	14.8	Narita	710	2	●	●	280	-	●	●	●	●
Okinawa Grand Castle	14-27	Okinawa	314	4	-	-	-	-	O	-	-	-
Hotel Kajima No Mori	14-45	Karuizawa	46	4	●	-	80	-	-	●	-	-
Ana Hotel Narita	14-16	Narita	438	4	●	●	280	●	O	●	●	●
Narita View Hotel	14-18	Narita	504	4	●	●	-	●	●	●	●	-
The Plaza Hotel	13-29	Osaka	401	17	●	●	1800	●	●	●	-	-
Kobe Portopia Hotel	13-17	Kobe	533	17	●	●	-	●	●	●	●	●
Sapporo Grand Hotel	13-16	Sapporo	617	-	●	●	-	-	-	-	-	-
Hotel Fujita	13.5	Kyoto	189	-	-	-	-	-	-	-	-	●
Hotel Nagoya Castle	13	Nagoya	253	-	●	●	-	-	●	-	-	-
Nishetsu Grand	13-18	Fukuoka	301	-	-	-	-	-	●	●	-	-
Toyo Hotel	12.5-17	Osaka	576	-	●	●	350	●	-	-	-	●
Sendai Tokyu Hotel	12.5	Sendai	302	-	●	●	-	●	-	-	-	-
Kyoto Grand Hotel	12-17	Kyoto	574	3	●	●	-	-	O	-	-	-
Ana Hotel Hakata	12-18	Fukuoka	351	5	●	●	450	-	O	-	●	-
Nagasaki Tokyu	12	Nagasaki	224	2	●	●	-	●	-	-	-	●
Sapporo Prince	11-16	Sapporo	195	27	-	-	-	●	-	-	-	●
Okayama Tokyu Hotel	11.5	Okayama	237	3	●	●	1000	●	●	-	-	●
Nasu Royal Hotel	15	Nasu	110	-	●	●	-	-	●	●	-	-
Osaka Grand	11.5-18	Osaka	350	-	-	-	-	-	-	-	-	-
Rhiga Royal Hiroshima	11-13	Hiroshima	486	5	●	●	350	●	●	-	●	●
Ana Hotel Kyoto	11-16	Kyoto	296	7	●	●	700	-	●	-	-	●
International Hotel	11-14.5	Kyoto	300	-	●	-	500	-	-	-	-	-
Miyako Hotel	10-15	Kyoto	366	140	●	●	-	●	-	●	-	●
Hakata Miyako Hotel	10-14	Fukuoka	269	-	-	-	-	-	-	-	-	●
Kobe Harborland New Otani	10-16	Kobe	235	-	-	-	-	-	-	-	-	-
Holiday Inn Kyoto	10-13	Kyoto	268	2	●	●	500	●	●	●	●	-
Ana Hotel Hiroshima	10-13	Hiroshima	423	8	●	●	600	●	O	-	●	-
Moriguchi Prince	10	Osaka	177	-	-	-	-	-	-	-	-	●
Dai-Ichi Osaka	10-13	Osaka	475	-	-	-	-	-	-	-	-	-
Station Plaza	10-12.5	Fukuoka	248	-	-	-	-	-	-	-	-	-
Kagoshima Tokyu	10	Kagoshima	206	2	●	●	-	●	●	-	-	●
Holiday Inn Kanazawa	10-16	Kanazawa	170	3	●	-	250	-	●	-	-	●
International Hotel	9	Nagoya	260	3	●	●	-	-	-	-	-	●
Holiday Inn Nagasaki	9-30	Nagasaki	84	-	●	-	100	●	-	-	-	●
Okura Hotel Niigata	8.5-10	Niigata	303	-	-	-	-	●	-	-	-	-
Kurashiki Kokusai	8-17 s	Kurashiki	70	1	●	●	120	●	-	-	-	-
Ana Hotel Matsuyama	7.5-10	Matsuyama	333	2	●	-	-	-	-	-	-	●

Japan Hotels

Fukuoka

Ana Hotel Hakata C
3-3-3 Hakataekimae, Hakata-ku, Fukuoka 812
Tel: 471 7111; Tlx: 722288 ANAFUK J; Fax: (092)472 7707

Fukuoka Hotel Umino Nakamichi (Ana Hotel) B
18-25 Nishitozaki Oaza Higashi-ku, 811-03
Tel: (092) 603 2525; Fax: (092) 603 2828

Hakata Miyako Hotel C
2-1-1 Hakataeki, Higashi 812
Tel: (092) 441 3111; Tlx: 724585; Fax: (092) 481 1306

Hakata Tokyu C
1-16-1 Tenjin, Chuo-ku, Fukuoka 810
Tel: (092) 781 7111; Tlx: 723295 THCFUK J; Fax: 092 781 7198

Hakata Tokyu Annex D
10-13 Tenjin, 1-chome, Chuo-ku, Fukuoka 810
(092) 723 7111; Tlx: 723489 THCAFU J

The New Otani Hakata B
1-1-2 Watanabe-dori, Chuo-ku, Fukuoka City 810
Tel:(092) 714 1111; Tlx: 726567 OTANIH J; Fax: 715 5658

Nishitetsu Grand Hotel C
6-60 Daimyo, 2-chome, Chuo-ku, Fukuoka City, Kyushu
Tel: (092) 771 7171; Tlx: 723351 NGH J; Fax: 092 751 8224

Station Plaza Hptel D
1-1 Hakata Ekimae 2-chome,Hakat-ku 812
Tel: 431 1211; Fax: 431 8015

Hakone

Fujiya Hotel B
359 Miyanoshita, Hakone 250-04
Tel: (0460) 22211; Tlx: 389 2718; Fax: 22210

Palace Hotel Hakone B
1245 Sengokubara, Hakone 250-06
Tel: (0460) 48501; Tlx: 389 2765; Fax: (0460) 48500

Hakone Prince C
144 Motohakone, Hakone-Machi 25005
Tel: (460) 31111; Tlx: 3892609; Fax: (460) 37616

Hiroshima

Ana Hotel Hirsohima C
7-20 Naka-machi, Naka-ku, 730
Tel: (082) 241 1111; Tlx: 652751; Fax: (082) 241 9123

Hiroshima Prince B
23-1 Motoujina-machi, Miniami-ku, 734
Tel: 256 1111; Fax: 256 1134

Rhiga Royal Hotel Hiroshima C
6-78 Moto-machi, Naha-ku 730
Tel: 502 1121; Fax: 228 5415

Karuizawa

Hotel Kajima No Mori B
Hanareyama, Karuizawa 389-01, **Nagano** Province
Tel: (0267) 42 3535; Tlx: 332 8676; Fax: (0267) 42 5335

Karuizawa Prince Hotel B
Karuizawa-machi, Kitsaki-gun, **Nagano** 389-01
Tel: 0267 441111; Tlx: 332 8660: Fax:427139

Kobe

Kobe Harborland New Otani C
1-3-5 Higashi-Kawasaki, 1-chome, 650
Tel: (078) 360 1111; Fax: 360 7799

Kobe Portopia Hotel C
6-10-1 Minatojima-Nakamachi, Chuo-ku 650
Tel: (078) 302 1111; Tlx: 5622 112; Fax: (078) 302 6877

Hotel Okura Kobe B
2-1 Hatobacho, Chuo-ku, 650
Tel: (078) 333 0111; Tlx: 5622 123; Fax: (078) 333 6673

Kyoto

Ana Hotel Kyoto C
Horikawa-dori, Nijoj-mae, Nagaka-ku, Kyoto 60
Tel: 231 1155; Tlx: 542 3181 J; Fax: 231 5333

Hotel Fujita Kyoto C
Kamo Riverside Nijo, Nakagyo-ku
Tel: (075) 222 1511; Tlx: 5422 571; Fax: (075) 256 4561

Hotel Gimmond ◯ D
Takakura Oike St, Nagakyo-ku, Kyoto 604
Tel: 221 4111; Tlx: 5423 219; Fax: 221 8250

Holiday Inn Kyoto D
36 Nishihiraki-cho, Takano, Sakyo-ku, Kyoto 606.Tel: (075) 721 3131; Tlx: 5422 251; Fax: (075) 781 6178

International Hotel Kyoto ◯ C
Nijyo, Horikawa-dori, Nakagyo-ku
Tel: (075) 222 1111; Tlx: 5422 158; Fax: (075) 231 9381

Kyoto Brighton Hotel ◯ A
Shinmachi-Nakadachiuri, Kanigyo-ku
Tel: (075) 441 4411; Tlx: 5422 690; Fax: (075) 431 2360

Kyoto Century D
680 Higashishikoji-cho, Shikoji-sagaru, Shimogyu-ku, Kyoto 600.Tel: (075) 351 0111; Tlx: 5422 380; Fax: 343 3721

Kyoto Hotel D
Oike-Kawaramachi, Nagagyo-ku, Kyoto City, Honshu
Tel: (075) 211 5111; Tlx: 5422 126 YOTEL J; Fax: (075) 254 2529

Kyoto Grand Hotel ◯ C
Higashi-Horikawa-Shikoji, Shimogyo-ku, Kyoto 600, Honshu
Tel: (075) 341 2311; Tlx: 5422 551; Fax: (075) 341 3073

Kyoto Park Hotel ◯ D
Mawari-cho, 644-2, Saniyu-Sandgendo, Higashiyama, Kyoto 605
Tel: (075) 525 3111; Tlx: 5422 777; Fax: (075) 551 4350

Kyoto Prince Hotel D
43 Matsubara-cho, Shimogamo, Sakyo-ku, Kyoto 606.Tel: 781 4141; Tlx: 5422 611 J; Fax: 781 4150

Kyoto Royal Hotel ◯ C
Kawaramachi, Sanjo-agaru, Nakagyo-ku, Kyoto 604. Tel: (075) 223 1234; Tlx: 5422 888; Fax: (075) 223 1702

Kyoto Takaragaike Prince Hotel A
Takaragaike, Sakyo-ku, Kyoto-shi, Kyoto 606
Tel: 712 1111; Tlx: 5423 261 KYTPRH J; Fax: 712 7677

Kyoto Tokyu Hotel ◯ C
Horikawa-Gojo, Shimogyo-ku, Kyoto 600, Honshu
Tel: (075) 341 2411; Tlx: 5422 459 THCKYO J; Fax: (075) 341 2488

New Miyako Hotel ◯ C
Hachijo-guchi, Kyoto Station 601
Tel: 661 7111; Tlx: 5423 211;Fax: 661 7135

The Westin Miyako Hotel ◯ B
Sanjo-dori Keage, Higashiyama-ku, Kyoto 605, Honshu
Tel: (075) 771 7111; Tlx: 5422 132 MIYAKO J; Fax: 751 2490

Nagasaki

Holiday Inn Nagasaki D
6-24 Doza Machi, **Nagasaki**
Tel: (958) 281234; Tlx: 7525 25; Fax: (958) 280178

Nagasaki Tokyu C
1-18 Minamiyamate-cho, **Nagasaki 850**
Tel: 251501; Tlx: 752762; Fax: 235167

Nagoya

Hotel Nagoya Castle C
3-19 Hinokuchicho, Nishi-ku, 451
Tel: (52) 521 2121; Tlx: 59787 CASTLE J; Fax: 331 3313

Nagoya Dai-Ichi Hotel D
3-27-5 Meieki, Nakamura-ku, 450
Tel: 581 4411; Fax: 581 4427

Nagoya Hilton
3-3, Sakae 1-chome, Naka-ku, Nagoya City, Aichi 460
Tel: (052) 212 1111; Tlx: 422 2121 HILNGO J; Fax: (052) 212 1225

A 28-storey, 451-room luxury hotel, one of the tallest buildings in Nagoya. The centre of business, shopping and entertainment area of Nagoya city.

Accommodation
23 rooms, 28 suites

Rates:
Single ¥ 21000-27000; Double/twin ¥ 29,000-36,000; Suite ¥ 55,000-250,000
Subject to service charge and government tax

Credit cards accepted:
Amex, Diners, Mastercard, Visa, JCB

Meeting & banqueting facilities
10 meeting/function rooms - capacity up to 1200 with full audio-visual facilities; 971 sq m exhibition space; largest reception 800 seated or 1000 cocktail.

Room services
Airconditioning, colour TV, direct-dial telep-hone (ext. in bathroom), hairdryer, laundry/valet service, minibar, music/

radio/alarm clock, tea/coffee making facilities, 24-hr room/meal service, non-smoker bedrooms, video films, data jack for PCs

Business services
Business centre, executive floor, express checkout, translation service, car parking, car rental, travel centre, taxi service.

Other services
Barber shop/hairdresser, beauty salon, guided tours, newsstand/shops, camera shop, shopping arcade

Sports & Recreation
Fitness centre/gym, indoor games, jacuzzi, jogging track, massage, sauna, indoor swimming pool, tennis court

Restaurants & Coffee Shops
The Seasons (84) - French, open 1130-1400/1700-2130; *Genji* (104) - Japanese, open as above; *Dynasty* (136) - Chinese, open as above; *The Terrace* (160) - Coffee Shop, open 0630-2300; *The Gallery* (235) - Lobby Lounge, open 1000-2300

International Hotel Nagoya D
3-23-3, Nishiki, Naka-ku, Nagoya 460
Tel: 961 3111; Tlx: 444 3720; Fax: 962 5937

Nagoya Kanko Hotel C
19-30 Nishiki 1 chome, Naka-ku, Nagoya 460
Tel: (052) 251 2411; Tlx: 59946; Fax: (052) 231 7719

Nagoya Tokyu Hotel C
4-6 Sakae, Nagoya 460
Tel: 251 2411; Tlx: 442 2046; Fax: 251 2422

Narita

Ana Hotel Narita B
68 Horinouchi, Narita 28601. Tel: (0476) 331311; Tlx: 3762167; Fax: 330244

Holiday Inn Tobu Narita B
320-1 Tokko, Narita-shi, Chiba 286-01
Tel: (0476) 321234; Tlx: 3762 133; Fax: (0476) 320617

Marroad International Hotel C
Narita. Tel: (0476) 302222; Fax: (0476) 329112

Narita Winds Hotel B
560 Tokko, Narita-shi 286-01
Tel: (0476) 33 1111; Fax: (0476) 331108

Hotel Narita Tokyu
31 Oyama, Narita City, Chiba 286-01
Tel: (0476) 330109; Fax: (0476) 330148

A refreshing retreat for travellers both entering and leaving Japan, the Hotel Narita Tokyu is just minutes from Narita Airport.

Accommodation
393 single, 8 double, 309 twin, 2 suites

Rates:
Single ¥ 14800; double/twin ¥ 24000-29000; suite ¥ 80000
Service charge included; subject to 3% consumption tax

Credit cards accepted:
Amex, Diners, Mastercard, Visa, JCB

Meeting & banqueting facilities
7 meeting/function rooms; 433 sq m exhibition space; largest reception 280 seated or 380 cocktail.

Room services
Airconditioning, colour TV, direct-dial telephone, hairdryer, laundry/valet service, minibar, music/radio/alarm clock, safety deposit box, video films

Other services
Airport pickup, car parking, beauty salon, newsstand/shops.

Sports & Recreation
Gym, jacuzzi, massage, sauna, indoor & outdoor swimming pools, tennis court

Restaurants & Coffee Shops
Japanese, Chinese, French Restaurant,Bar

Overseas Sales Representatives
Pan Pacific Hotels & Resorts; SRS Steigenberger Resrvation Service

Narita View Hotel C
700 Kosuga, **Narita City 286-01**
Tel: 0476 21 3111; Tlx: 3762 123 NVHNRT J; Fax: 0476 32 1078

Rhiga Royal Hotel Narita B
456 Kosuga, 286-01
Tel: (476) 331121; Fax: (476) 330700

Niigata

Okura Hotel Niigata D
6-53 Kawabata-cho, Niigata 951
Tel: (025) 224 6111; Tlx: 3122 815; Fax: 224 7060

○ = member of Pacific Asia Travel Association

JAPAN - Hotels

Okinawa

Naha Tokyu   B
1002 Ameku, **Naha 900,** Okinawa Pref.
Tel: 8682151; Tlx: 795216 TOTEL J; Fax: 8687895

Okinawa Grand Castle Hotel   C
1-132-1, Yamanawa, Shuri, **Naha City,** Okinawa
Tel: (0988) 86 5454; Tlx: 795375 OKAOGC J; Fax: 0988 87 0070

Okinawa Harborview Hotel   C
2-46 Izumizaki, **Naha** 900
Tel: (098) 8532111; Tlx: 795236 HVHHJ; Fax: (098) 8346043

Okinawa Miyako Hotel   C
40 Matsukawa, Naha, **Okinawa 902**
Tel: (098) 887 1111; Fax: (098) 886 5591

Okinawa Renaissance Resort   A
3425-2, Nakohbaru, Yamada, Onna-Son Kunigami-gun, 904-04
Tel: (098) 965 0707; Fax: (098) 965 5011

Osaka

Ana Hotel Osaka ○   B
1-3-1 Dojimahama, Kita-ku, Osaka 530
Tel: 347 1112; Tlx: 5236 884 ANAOES J; Fax: 348 9208

Ana Gate Tower Hotel Osaka   B
1 Rinkuorai-Kita, Izumisano City, 598
Tel: 460 1111; Fax: 460 1177

Hotel Hankyu International   A
19-19 Chayamachi Kita-ku, 530
Tel: 377 2100; Fax: 377 3628

Hilton Osaka   B
8-8 Umeda 1-chome, Kita-ku, Osaka 530
Tel: (06) 347 7111; Tlx: 524 2201 HIOSAK J; Fax: (06) 347 7001

In the centre of the business, shopping and entertainment area of Osaka's busy Umeda district. Easy access to major public and private railways and subways through hotel's basement. 58 km from new Kansai Airport with direct limousine bus to the hotel.

Accommodation & rates
469 standard rooms, 57 suites.
Single ¥26000-¥36000; double/twin ¥ 32000-45000; suite ¥ 70-300,000. Subject to 10% service charge and government tax

Credit cards accepted:
Amex, Diners, Visa, JCB

Meeting & banqueting facilities
15 meeting/function rooms -capacity 4-800 with audio-visual facilities; 823 sq m exhibition space; largest reception 800

Room services
Airconditioning, colour TV, direct-dial telephone (ext. in bathroom), hairdryer, safety deposit box, laundry/valet service, minibar, music/radio/alarm clock, tea/coffee making facilities, trouser press, 24-hr room/meal service, non-smoker bedrooms, video films

Business & other services
Business centre, executive floors, translation service, car parking, car rental, travel centre, taxi service.

Other services
Barber shop/hairdresser, beauty salon, guided tours, newsstand/shops, florist

Sports & Recreation
Fitness centre/gym, jacuzzi/whirlpool, massage, sauna, indoor swimming pool, tennis court

Restaurants & Coffee Shops
Checkers (180) - Cafe restaurant, open 0630-midnight; *Genji* (124) - Japanese, open 0700-2230; *Dynasty* (118) - Chinese, open as above; *The Seasons* (84) - Continental, open as above

Overseas Sales Representatives
Hilton International Worldwide

Holiday Inn Nankai-Osaka   B
No 15-5, 2-chome, Shinsaibashisuji, Chuo-ku, Osaka 542. Tel: (06) 213 8281; Tlx: 5222 939; Fax: (06) 213 8640

Hyatt Regency Osaka   A
1-13 Nanko Kita, 530
Tel: 612 1234; Fax: 944 7598

International Hotel Osaka ○   D
Uchihonmachi, Higashi-ku, 540
Tel: (06) 941 2661; Tlx: 5222 939; Fax: (06) 941 5362

Miyako Hotel Osaka   ○
6-1-55 Uehommachi, Tennoji-ku, Osaka 543
Tel: 773 1111; Tlx: 527 7555 MYKOSA J; Fax: 773 3322; E-Mail: wimal@mbox.kyoto-inet.or.jp

Luxury hotel in downtown Osaka, located next to subway and Kintetsu Railway Stations with easy access to any part of the city and beyond. 50 minutes from the new Kansai International airport by direct limousine. Spacious rooms with all modern amenities at affordable prices.

Accommodation & rates
208 singles, ¥14,300-16,500; 66 doubles, ¥26,000-29000; 283 twin, ¥22,000-31,900; 29 suites. ¥40,000-60,000. Service charge included. Subj. to 5% consumption tax.

Credit cards accepted:
Amex, Diners, Mastercard, Visa, JCB,

Meeting & banqueting facilities
27 meeting/function rooms - capacity 5-1400; audio-visual facilities available; 3706 sq m exhibition space; largest reception 700 seated or 1200 cocktail.

Room services
Airconditioning, colour TV, direct-dial telephone (ext. inbathroom), hairdryer, laundry/valet service, minibar, music/radio/alarm clock, tea/coffee making facilities, trouser press, 24-hr room/meal service, non-smoker bedrooms, video films, newspaper, Yukata

Business & other services
Business centre, executive floors, car parking, travel centre, taxi service, barber shop/ beauty salon, guided tours, newsstand/shops, florist

Sports & Recreation
Fitness centre/gym, massage, sauna, indoor swimming pool, squash

Restaurants & Coffee Shops
Ciel Bleu (48) - French, open 1130-1400/ 1700-2200; *Miyako* (119) - Japanese, open 0700-1000/1130-1430/1700-2200; *Shisen* (128) - Chinese, open 1130-1430/1700-2200; *Matsusaka* (22) - Teppanyaki, open 1130-1500/1700-2200; *Montmartre* (136) - Coffee Shop, open 0630-midnight; *La Mer* (48) - French/Seafood, open 1130-1430/ 1700-2200; *Top of Miyako* (111) - Lounge Bar, open 1130-1600/1700-2200; *Le Havre* (120) - Bar, open 1700-0100.

(continued)

Overseas Sales Representatives
SRS Steigenberger Reservation Service.
Supranatonal

Imperial Hotel Osaka   A
8-50 Tenmabushi, 1-chome, Kita-ku, 530
Tel: 881 1111; Fax: 881 1200

Moriguchi Prince Hotel   D
1 Kawahara-cho, Moriguchi-shi, Osaka 670
Tel: (06) 994 1111; Tlx: 529 4070; Fax: 994 1100

Nankai South Tower Hotel   B
5-1-60 Naniwa, Chuo-ku, Osaka 540
Tel: 646 1111; Tlx: 526 7717;Fax: 648 0331

Hotel New Hankyu Osaka   D
1-35 Shibata 1-chome, Kita-ku, osaka 530
Tel: (06) 372 5101; Tlx: 5233 830 OHTLNH; Fax: (06) 374 6885

Hotel New Otani Osaka   A
1-4-1, Shiromi, Chuo-ku, Osaka 540
Tel: (06) 941 1111; Tlx: 5293 330 OTNOSK J; Fax: (06) 941 9769

Hotel Nikko Osaka   B
7 Nishinocho, Daihojicho, Minami-ku, Osaka 542.Tel: (06) 244 1111; Tlx: 5227 575; Fax: 245 2432

Osaka Grand Hotel   C
3-18 Nakanoshima 2-chome, Kita-ku 530
Tel: 202 1212; Fax: 227 5054

Osaka Terminal Hotel   C
3-1-1 Umeda Kita-ku, Osaka 530
Tel: (06) 344 1235; Tlx: 5233 738; Fax: (06) 344 1130

Osaka Tokyu   C
7-20, Chaya-machi, Kita-ku, Osaka 530
Tel: 373 2411; Tlx: 523 6751; Fax: 376 0343

The Plaza Hotel   C
2-2-49 Oyodo-Minami, Oyodo-ku, Osaka 531.Tel: (06) 453 1111; Tlx: 524 5557 PLAOSA; Fax: 454 0269

Rhiga Royal Hotel Yotsubashi   D
10-12 Shinmachi 1 chome, Nishiku
Tel: 534 1211; Fax: 534 6360

The Ritz-Carlton Osaka   A
2525 Umeda, Kita-ku, 530
Tel: 0120 853201

Royal Hotel   D
5-3-68, Nakanoshima, Kita-ku, Osaka 530
Tel: (06) 448 1121; Tlx: 63350 HOTEL J; Fax: 448 4414

Toyo Hotel   D
3-16-19 Toyosaki, Oyodo-ku
Tel: (06) 372 8181; Tlx: 5233 886; Fax: (06) 372 8101

The Westin Osaka   A
11-20 Oyod-Naka, Kita-ku, Osaka 531
Tel: (06) 440 1111; Fax: (06) 440 1100

Sapporo

Hotel Alpha Sapporo   B
S 1, W 5, Chuo-ku, 060. Tel: (011) 221 2333; Tlx: 935345; Fax: (011) 221 0819

Ana Hotel Sapporo   C
2-9, Kita 3, Nishi-1, Chuo-ku, Sapporo 060
Tel: 221 4411; Tlx: 934712 SZENHL J; Fax: 222 7624

Sapporo Renaissance Hotel   C
1-1 Toyohira, 4-jo 1-Chome, Toyohira-ku, Sapporo 062.
Tel: 821 1111; Fax: 842 6191

Sapporo Grand Hotel   C
4 Nishi, Kita-1, Chuo-ku, Sapporo
Tel: 261 2311; Tlx: 932613; Fax: 232 5164

Sapporo Prince Hotel   C
11 Minaminijonishi, Chuo-ku, Sapporo 060
Tel: 241 1111; Tlx: 933949 SAPPRI J; Fax: 231 5994

Sapporo Tokyu   B
Nishi 4-chome, Chuo-ku, Sapporo 060
Tel: 231 5611; Tlx: 934510 THCSAP J; Fax: (011) 251 3515

Shizuoka/Shimoda

Kawana Hotel   B
1459, Kawana, Ito, Shizuoka Pref. 438
Tel: (557) 45 1111; Tlx: 392 7565; Fax: (557) 45 3834

Shimoda Prince Hotel   A
1547-1 Shirahama, Shimoda-shi, 415
Tel: (558) 222111; Tlx: 393 9754; Fax: (558) 227584

Shizuoka Terminal Hotel   D
56 Kurogan-chu, 420
Tel: (0542) 544141; Tlx: 3962 111; Fax: (0542) 553721

Shimoda Tokyu   A
5-12-1 Shimoda-shi, Shimoda 415
Tel: (558) 222411; Tlx: 392 9732; Fax: (558) 224970

Tokyo

Akakura Kanko Hotel   A
7-1-3-chome, Ginza, Chuo-ku
Tel: 2558 72501; Fax: 2558 72678

Akasaka Prince Hotel   A
1 Kioicho, Chiyoda-ku, Tokyo 102
Tel: 234 1111; Tlx: 3232 4028 AKAPRH J; Fax: 3262 5163

Akasaka Tokyu Hotel   A
2-14-3, Nagatacho, Chiyoda-ku, Tokyo 100
Tel: 3580 2311; Tlx: 3222 4310 THCAKA J; Fax: 3580 6066

Ana Hotel Tokyo   A
12-33 Akasaka, 1-chome, Mianto-ku,Tokyo 107
Tel: 3505 1111; Tlx: 242 4625 ANAETH J; Fax: 3505 1155

Capitol Tokyu Hotel   A
2-10-3 Nagata-cho, Chiyoda-ku, Tokyo 100
Tel: 3580 4511; Tlx: 24290 THCCAP J; Fax: 3581 5822

Century Hyatt Tokyo   A
2-7-2 Nishi-Shinjuku, Shinjuku-ku, Tokyo 160
Tel: 3349 0111; Tlx: 29229 CENHYATT J; Fax: 3344 5575

Dai Ichi Hotel Tokyo   A
2-6, 1-chome, Shimbashi, Minato-ku 105
Tel: 3501 4411; Tlx: 222 2233; Fax: 3595 2634

Dai-ichi Hotel Tokyo Bay   A
1-8 Maihama, Urayasu-shi, Chiba 279
Tel: (0473) 55 3333; Tlx: 299 332; Fax: (0473) 55 3366

Diamond Hotel   C
25 Ichiban-cho, Chiyoda-ku
Tel: 3263 2211; Tlx: 2322 764; Fax: 3263 2222

Four Seasons Hotel Chinzan-so   A
10-8 Sekiguchi, 2-chome,112
Tel: 3943 2222; Fax: 3943 2300

Ginza Dai-ichi Hotel   A
8-13-1, Ginza, Chuo-ku, Tokyo 104
Tel: 3542 5311; Tlx: 252 3714; Fax: 3542 3030

Ginza Nikko Hotel   A
8-4-21, Ginza, Chuo-ku, Tokyo 104
Tel: 3571 4911;Tlx: 252 2812; Fax: 3571 8379

Ginza Tokyu   A
5-15-9 Ginza, Chuo-ku, Tokyo 104
Tel: 3541 2411; Tlx: 252 2601; Fax: 35416622

Hotel Grand Palace   B
1-1 Idibashi 1-chome, Chiyoda-ku
Tel: 3264 1111; Tlx: 2322 981; Fax: 3230 4985

JAPAN - Hotels

Haneda Tokyu Hotel A
2-8-6, Haneda-kuko, Ota-ku, Tokyo 144
Tel: 3747 0311; Tlx: 246 6560;
Fax: 3747 0366

**Holiday Inn Crowne Plaza
Metroplitan Tokyo** B
6-1 Nishi-Ikebukuro 1-chome, Toshima-ku, 171. Tel: 3980 1111; Tlx: 2722 787;
Fax: 3980 5600

Holiday Inn Tokyo Comm. Centre B
1-13-7 Hatchobori, Chuo-ku, Tokyo 104
Tel: 3553 6161; Tlx: 252 3748 HJOLITK J;
Fax: 3553 6040

Hotel Seiyo Ginza A
1 Ginza, Chuo-ku, Tokyo 104
Tel: 3535 1111; Tlx: 252 3118; Fax: 3535 1110

Imperial Hotel A
1-1-1 Uchisaiwaicho, Chiyoda-ku, Tokyo 105
Tel: 3504 1111; Tlx: 26816 IMPHO J; Fax: 3581 9146

Hotel Inter-Continental Tokyo Bay
1-14 Kaigan, Minato-ku, 105 A
Tel: 5404 2222; Fax: 5404 2111

Le Meridien Pacific
3-13-3 Takanawa, Minato-ku
Tel: 3445 6711; Tlx: 22861 HOTELPAC J;
Fax: 3445 5733

Conveniently located in scenic Shinagawa, Le Meridien Pacific Hotel rises high above a beautiful area of Tokyo srill rich and lush with greenery. The hotel is 15 minutes from either Tokyo Central Station or Haneda Domestic Airport.

Accommodation
255 single, 256 double, 402 twin, 41 suites

Rates:
Single ¥22,000-30500; double/win ¥ 25,000-33,000; suite ¥ 50-300,000. Subject to 10% service charge and 8.8% government tax

Credit cards accepted:
Amex, Carte Blanche, Diners, Eurocard, Mastercard, Visa, JCB etc

Meeting & banqueting facilities
19 meeting/function rooms - capacity up to 2500; full audio-visual facilities and exhibition space available; largest reception 1000-1500 seated/2500 cocktail

Room services
Airconditioning, colour TV, direct-dial telephone (ext. in bathroom), hairdryer, laundry/valet service, minibar, music/radio/alarm clock, trouser press, non-smoker bedrooms available, video films

Business services
Business centre, translation service, car parking, car rental, travel centre, taxi service

Other services
Barber shop/hairdresser, beauty salon, guided tours, newsstand/shops

Sports & Recreation
Massage, sauna, outdoor swimming pool

Restaurants & Coffee Shops
Piccolo Mondo (172) - Coffee House, open 0600-0100; *Ukidono* (168) - Continental, open breakfast/lunch/dinner; *Boeuf d'Or* (116) - French, open lunch & dinner; *Ro-Lan (138)* - Chinese, open lunch/dinner

Overseas Sales Representatives:
Meridien Hotels & Resorts. Utell, Tokyo (toll-free) 0120 475 777

Keio Plaza Inter-Continental A
2-2-1, Nishi-Shinjuku 2-chome, Shinjuku-Ku, 160. Tel: 3344 0247; Tlx: 26874 J;
Fax: 3345 8269

The Manhattan A
2-10-1 Hibino, 261. Makuhari Convention Centre, China Prefecture
Tel: (0432) 751111; Fax: (0432) 750011

Miyako Hotel Tokyo A
1-1-50, Shiroganedai, Minato-ku, Tokyo 108 Tel: 3447 3111; Tlx: 242 3111 MYKTKY J; Fax: 3447 3133

Miyako Inn Tokyo C
3-7-8 Mita, Minato-ku, 108
Tel: 3454 3111; Fax: 3454 3397

The New Otani Tokyo A
4-1, Kioicho, Chiyoda-ku, Tokyo 102
Tel: 3265 1111; Tlx: 24719 HTLOTANI J;
Fax: 3221 2619

New Takanawa Prince Hotel A
3-13-1, Takanawa, Minato-ku, Tokyo 108
Tel: 3442 1111; Tlx: 242 7418 TAKPRH J;
Fax: 3444 1234

Hotel Okura A
2-10-4 Toranomon, Minato-ku, 105
Tel: 3582 0111; Fax: 3582 3707

The Palace Hotel A
1-1-1, Marunouchi, Chiyoda-ku, Tokyo 100
Tel: 3211 5211; Tlx: 222 2580 PALACE J;
Fax: 3211 6987

Park Hyatt Tokyo A
3-7 Nishi-Shinjuku, Shinjuku-ku160
Tel: 5322 1234; Fax: 5322 1288

Rhiga Royal Hotel Waseda A
1-104-19 Totsuka-machi, 169
Tel: 5285 1121; Fax: 5285 4321

Roppongi Prince Hotel A
3-2-7 Roppongi, Minato-ku, Tokyo 106
Tel: 3587 1115; Tlx: 2427231; Fax: 3667 1111

Royal Park Hotel A
2-1-1 Nihonbashi-Kakigara, 103
Tel: 3667 1111; Tlx: 2523788; Fax: 3665 7212

Sheraton Grande Tokyo Bay Hotel
1-9 Maihama, Urayasu, Chiba 279 A
Tel: 047355 5555; Tlx: 2993 155 SGTBH J; Fax 047355 5566

Shiba Park Hotel B
1-5-10, Shibakoen, Minato-ku, Tokyo 105
Tel: 3433 4141;Tlx: 242 2917; Fax: 5470 7519

Shinagawa Prince Hotel C
4-10-30 Takanawa, Minato-ku, Tokyo 108
Tel: 3440 1111;Tlx: 242 5178; Fax: 3441 7092

Shinjuku Prince Hotel B
1-30-1 Kabuki-cho, Shinjuku-ku, Tokyo 160
Tel: 3205 1111; Tlx: 2324733; Fax: 3205 1952

Hotel Sofitel Tokyo C
2-1-48 Ikenohata, Taito-ku, 110
Tel: 5685 7111; Fax: 5685 6171

Hotel Sunroute Tokyo C
2-3-1 Yoyogi, Shibuya-Ku, Tokyo 151
Tel: 3375 3211; Tlx:2322 288; Fax: 3379 3040

Sunshine City Prince Hotel C
3-1-5 Higashi Ikebukuro, Toshima-ku, Tokyo 170.Tel: 3988 1111; Tlx: 272 3749;
Fax: 3988 7878

Hotel Takanawa B
2-1-17 Minato-ku, Takanawa 108
Tel: 5488 1000; Tlx: 2422553; Fax: 5488 1005

Takanawa Prince Hotel A
3-13-1 Takanawa, Minato-ku, Tokyo 108
Tel: 3447 1111; Tlx: 242 3232; Fax: 3446 0849

Tokyo Bay Hilton
1-8 Maihama, Urayasu-chi, Chiba 279
Tel: (473) 55 5000; Tlx: 299 3108 TKBAY J; Fax: (473) 55 5019

Tokyo Bay Hilton is an official hotel of Tokyo Disneyland, and enjoys the best of both worlds. Nestling in peaceful Tokyo Bay, with stunning views of the ocean, it is just minutes from the heart of Japan's bustling capital, Tokyo.

Accommodation & rates
684 rooms, 56 suites. Single ¥26,000-49000; double/twin ¥ 33,000-56,000; suite ¥88,000-330,000. Subject to 10% service charge and 8.8% government tax

(continued)

Credit cards accepted:
Amex, Diners, Mastercard, Visa, JCB, Bank Card

Meeting & banqueting facilities
16 meeting/function rooms - capacity 1580; with full audio-visual facilities; 1278 sq m exhibition space; largest reception 770 seated or 1200 cocktail.

Room services
Airconditioning, colour TV, direct-dial telephone (ext. in bathroom), hairdryer, laundry service, minibar, music/radio/alarm clock, tea making facilities, 24-hr room/meal service, non-smoker bedrooms available

Business services
Business centre, executive floor, translation service, car parking, car rental, taxi service, courier service

Other services
Barber shop/hairdresser, beauty salon, newsstand/shops, hotel shuttle to/from Disneyland

Sports & Recreation
Fitness centre/gym, jogging track, massage, sauna, outdoor & indoor swimming pools, squash, tennis, aerobics studio

Restaurants & Coffee Shops
Carousel (202) - Coffee Shop, open 0630-midnight; *Matsukaze* (186) - Japanese, open 0700-1030/1130-1430/1730-2230; *Dynasty* (149) - Chinese, open 1130-1430/1730-2230; *Piazza Roma* (96) - Italian, open as above; *Chandu's* (90) - Indian, open as above; *Ma Maison* (74) - Continental, open as above; *Sazanami* (109) - Barbecue, open as above

Overseas Sales Representatives:
Hilton International Worldwide

Tokyo Bay Hotel Tokyu   A
1-7 Maihama, Urayasu-shi, 279
Tel: (473) 552411; Tlx: 299 3111; Fax: (473) 500109

Tokyo Hilton International
6-2 Nishi-Shinjuku, 6-chome, Shimjuku-ku, Tokyo 160
Tel: 3344 5111; Tlx: 232 4515 HILTON J; Fax: 3342 6094

Located on the west side of Tokyo's Shinjuku district - the city's prominent modern business, shopping and entertainment sector. Only a block away from Tokyo Metropolitan Government offices.

Accommodation and rates:
754 rooms, 53 suites. Single ¥27,000-35,000; double/twin ¥ 30,000-38,000. 53 suites ¥45,000-200,000. Subject to 10% service charge and 8.8% government tax

Credit cards accepted:
Amex, Diners, Mastercard, Visa, JCB

Meeting & banqueting facilities
18 meeting/function rooms - capacity 20-1365 with full audio-visual facilities; 932 sq m exhibition space; largest reception 745 seated or 1365 cocktail.

Room services
Airconditioning, colour TV, direct-dial telephone (ext. in bathroom), hairdryer, laundry/valet service, minibar, music/radio/alarm clock, safety deposit box, tea/coffee making facilities, 24-hr room/meal service, non-smoker bedrooms available, video films

Business services
Business centre, executive floor, express checkout, translation service, car parking, car rental, travel centre, taxi service, library

Other services
Barber shop/hairdresser, beauty salon, guided tours, newsstand/shops, drugstore

Sports & Recreation
Fitness centre/gym, massage, sauna, indoor swimming pool, tennis

Restaurants & Coffee Shops
Checker's (208) - buffet, pasta, open 0600-midnight; *Musashino* (118) - Japanese, open 1130-1500/1730-2200; *Dynasty* (164) - Chinese, open as above; *The Imari* (102) - Continental, open as above

Overseas Sales Representatives:
Hilton International Worldwide

Tokyo Hotel Urashima   D
5-23-2 Harumi, 104
Tel: 3533 3111; Tlx: 252 4297; Fax: 3533 5336

Tokyo Prince Hotel   A
3-3-1 Shiba Park, Minato-ku, Tokyo 105
Tel: 3432 1111; Tlx: 242 2488; Fax: 3434 5551

Tokyo Renaissance Hotel Ginza Tobu   A
14-10, Ginza 6-chome, Chuo-ku, Tokyo 104 Tel: 3546 0111; Tlx: 252 3388; Fax: 3546 8990

Yokohama

Holiday Inn Yokohama   B
77 Yamashita-cho, Naka-ku, Yokohama
Tel: (45) 681 3311; Tlx: 382 2758 J; Fax: (45) 681 5082

Hotel New Grand   C
10 Yamashitacho Naka-ku, 231
Tel: (045) 681 1841; Tlx: 3823 411; Fax: (045) 681 1895

The Hotel Yokohama   B
6-1 Yamashita-cho, Naka-ku
Tel: 662 1321; Tlx: 3822 061; Fax: 662 3536

The Pan Pacific Hotel Yokohama
(Opening August 1997. Pre-opening address:) 6f, Sakuragicho AN Building, 6-113 Aioi-cho, Naku-ku, Yokohama 231
Tel: (45) 641 0020; Fax: (45) 641 0023
E-Mail: nejat@mxs.meshnet.or.jp

Part of an ambitius new urban development project on prime waterfront land in Yokohama, the hotel offers panoramic views of the surrounding greenery and sea. located on Queen's Square at Minato Mirai 21.

Accommodation and rates:
485 rooms. Rates to be announced

Credit cards accepted: All major

Meeting & banqueting facilities
17 meeting/function rooms; largest reception 700 seated or 1200 cocktail.

Room services
Airconditioning, colour TV, direct-dial telephone (ext. in bathroom), hairdryer, laundry/valet service, minibar, music/radio/alarm clock, tea/coffee making facilities, 24-hr room/meal service, non-smoker bedrooms available

JAPAN - Hotels/Restaurants

Business & other services
Business centre, executive floor, translation service, car parking, barber shop/beauty salon, newsstand/shops, chapel, wedding shrine, flower shop, photo studio

Sports & Recreation
Fitness centre/gym, jacuzzi/whirlpool, massage, indoor swimming pool

Restaurants & Coffee Shops
All-day dining (180), Japanese (120), Chiese (210), Theme (90) Restaurants and Tea Lounge (100) to be opned.

Overseas Sales Representatives:
Pan Pacific Hotels & Resorts Worldwide; SRS Steigenberger Reservation Service.

Yokohama Grand Inter-Continental ◌ **A**
1-1 Minatomirai, Nishi-ku, **220 Yokohama**
Tel: 223 2222; Tlx :239 76012; Fax: 223 2292

Yokohama Prince **A**
13-1, Isogo 3-chome, Isogo-ku, **235**
Tel: (045) 751 1111; Tlx: 382 3727; Fax: (045) 753 8811

Yokohama Tokyu **A**
1-1-12, Minami-Saiwai, 1-chome, Nishi-ku
Tel: 311 1682; Tlx: 382 2264; Fax: 311 1084

Other areas

New Furano Prince **D**
18-6 Kitanomine-cyo, **Furano-shi 076**
Tel: (167) 234111; Tlx: 929280 FURANO J; Fax: (167) 223430

Hakone Prince Hotel **C**
144 Motohakone, Ashigarashimo-gun, **Hakone-machi 250-05**, Kanagawa Pref.
Tel: 460 37111; Tlx: 389 2609; Fax: 37616

Hotel de Yama **A**
80 Motohakone Kanagawa, **Hakone-machi** Tel: 0460 36321; Tlx: 389 2734 HYAMA J; Fax: 0460 37419

Hotel Classification: **A** *after name of hotel = over US$ 200 per person per night;*
B *= between US$ 150 - 200;* **C** *= between US$ 100 - 150;* **D** *= between US$ 50 - 100 ;*
E *= under US$ 50;* ¶ *= prices on application.* ◌ *after name of hotel = PATA member.*

Hakuba Tokyu **A**
Happo, Hakuba-mura, Kita-Azumi-gun, **Hakuba 399 093,** Nagano Pref.
Tel: 261 72 3001; Tlx: 334 5410; Fax: 261 72 5349

Hokone Prince Hotel **C**
1435-91, Ajiroguchi, Matsubara-chi, **Hokone-shi 522**, Shiga
Tel: 261111; Tlx: 548 6664; Fax: 32419

Kagoshima Tokyu **C**
22-1 Komoikeshinmachi, **Kagoshima 890**
Tel: 572211; Tlx: 782284; Fax: 576083

Holiday Inn Kanazawa **D**
1-10 Horikawa-cho, **Kanazawa-shi**
Tel: (0762) 23 1111; Tlx: 5122 288; Fax: 0762 23 1110

New Sky Hotel **D**
2 Higashi-amidaji-cho, **Kumamoto 860**
Tel: (096) 354 2111; Tlx: 762254 NEWSKY J; Fax: (096) 354 8973

Kurashiki Kokusai Hotel **D**
1-44, 1-chome, **Kurashiki City 710**
Tel: 0864 22 5141; Tlx: 5933 158 KKHTL J; Fax: 0864 22 5192

Ana Hotel Matsuyama **D**
3-2-1 Ichiban-cho, **Matsuyama 790**
Tel: 335511; Tlx: 584 2013 MANAHO J; Fax: 216053

Nasu Royal Hotel **C**
3375-7, Takaku-Otsu, Nasu-machi, **Nasu-gun**, Tochigi Pref. 325-04.Tel: (02877) 82001; Tlx: 352 4112; Fax: 81360

Nikko Prince Hotel **A**
2485 Shobugahama, Chugushi, **Nikko 321-16**, Tochigi Pref.
Tel: (288) 550661; Fax: 0288 550669

Okayama Tokyu **C**
2-18, Daiku 3-chome, **Okayama City 700**,
Tel: 0862 332411; Tlx: 592 2332; Fax: 238763

Sendai Tokyu **C**
2-9-25 Ichiban-cho, **Sendai 980**, Myagi Pref.
Tel: 262 2411; Tlx: 852393; Fax: 262 4109

Holiday Inn Crowne Plaza Toyohashi **D**
141 Fujisawa-cho, **Toyohashi-shi**, Aichi
Tel: (0532) 48 3131; Tlx: 432 2126, Fax: 0532 46 6672

Hotel Mt Fuji **D**
1360-83 Yamanaka, Yamanakako Village, Minamitsuru-gun, **Yamanashi Pref.401 05**
Tel: (555) 62 2111; Tlx: 3385 481; Fax: 555 62 3177

Restaurants

Tokyo boasts over 45,000 restaurants, ranging from eel and blowfish centres to the most sophisticated French, Swiss, Italian and Chinese tables. Below we have given a sample of those most popular with western business people, where credit cards are accepted and where advance booking is essential. Osaka boasts Japan's most expensive restaurant **(Kicho)** *while Kyoto has a reputation for serving the best* **kaiseki** *cuisine in the country.*

Tokyo - non-Japanese

Al Porto *(Italian - kaiseki style)*
24-9 Nishi-Azubu 3-chome, Minato-ku. Tel: 3403 2916

Ashoka *(Indian)*
2nd fl, Pearl Bldg, 7-9-18 Ginza, Chuo-ku Tel: 3572 2377

Attore *(Italian)*
Hotel Seijo Ginza, 1-11-2 Ginza, Chuo-ku Tel: 3535 1111

Aux Six Herbes *(French)*
7-13-10 Roppongi, Minato-ku. Tel: 3479 2888

Bistro Lotus *(French)*
B1 JBP Bldg, 8-17 Roppongi 6-chome, Minato-ku. Tel: 3403 7666

Borsalino *(Italian)*
8-21 Roppongi 6-chome, Minato-ku. Tel: 3401 7751

Brasserie Bernard *(French)*
7th Fl, Kajimaya Bldg, 7-14-3 Roppongi, Minato-ku. Tel: 3405 7877

Chez Inno *(French - nouvelle cuisine)*
3-2-11 Kyobashi, Chuo-ku. Tel: 3274 2020

Crescent Restaurant *(French)*
Crescent House, 1-8-20 Shiba Park, Minato-ku. Tel: 3436 3211-4

Heichinrou *(Cantonese)*
Fukoku Seimei Bldg, 28th fl, 2-2-2 Uchisaiwai-cho, Chiyoda-ku Tel:3508 0555

Ile de France *(French)*
Com Roppongi Bldg, 3-11-5 Roppongi, Minato-ku. Tel: 3404 0384

Imari *(French)*
2nd Fl, Tokyo Hilton International Hotel, 6-2 Nishi-Shinjuku 6-chome, Shinjuku-ku. Tel: 3344 5111

I Piselli *(Italian-Japanese)*
1st Fl Nikko Palace Hotel, 5-2-40 Minami-Azabu, Minato-ku. Tel: 3442 9771

Isolde *(French)*
2nd Fl, Hokushin Bldg, 3-2-1 Nishi-Azabu. Tel: 3478 1055

Joel *(French)*
2nd Fl, Kyodo Bldg, 5-6-24 Mianami-Aoyama, Minato-ku. Tel: 3400 7149

Ketel's (German)
5-5-15 Ginza, Chuo-ku
Tel: 3571 5056

Keyaki Grill
Capitol Tokyu Hotel, 10-3 Nagato-cho 2-chome, Chiyoda-ku. Tel: 3581 4511

La Belle Epoque (French)
12th Fl, Hotel Okura, 2-10-4 Toranomon, Minato-ku. Tel: 3505 6073

La Columba (Italian)
2-1-33 Kudan Minami, Chiyoda-ku. Tel: 3230 1938

L'Orangerie (French)
Hanae Mori Bldg, 5th fl, Minato-ku, 3-6-1 KitaAoyama. Tel: 3407 7461

La Tour d'Argent (French)
2nd Fl, Hotel New Otani, 4-1 Kioi-cho, Chiyoda-ku. Tel: 3239 3111

L'Ecrin (French)
B1, Mikimoto Bldg, 4-5-5 Ginza, Chuo-ku. Tel: 3561 9706

Le Trianon (French)
Akasaka Prince Hotel, 1-2 Kioi-cho, Chiyoda-ku. Tel: 3234 1111

Lohmeyer's (German)
5-3-14 Ginza, Chuo-ku. Tel: 3571 1142

Maxim's de Paris (French)
B3 Sony Bldg, 5-3-1 Ginza, Chuo-ku. Tel: 3572 3621

Metropole (Chinese)
TV Asahi-dori, 6-4-5- Roppongi, Minato-ku. Tel: 3405 4400

Mireille (French - Provencal)
3-1-6 Azabudai, Minato-ku. Tel: 3586 9050

Moti (Indian)
2nd Fl, Akasaka Floral Plaza, 3-8-8 Akasaka, Minatoku. Tel: 3584 3760

Pachon (French)
29-18 Sarugaku-cho, Shibuya-ku. Tel: 3476 5025

Patata (Italian)
2-9-11 Jingumae, Shibuya-ku
Tel: 3403 9664

Petit Point (French)
TGK Bldg, 4-2-48 Minami-Azabu, Minato-ku. Tel: 3440 3667

Prunier (French)
Top Fl, Kasumigaseki Bldg, Chiyoda-ku. Tel: 3581 9161

Sabatini di Firenze (Italian)
5-3-1 Ginza, Chuo-ku
Tel: 3573 0013

Spago (Californian)
5-7-8 Roppongi, Minato-ku. Tel: 3423 4025

Star Hill (Chinese)
B1 Capitol Tokyu Hotel, 10-3 Nagato-cho 2-chome, Chiyoda-ku. Tel: 3581 4511

Stockholm (Swedish)
Sweden Centre Bldg B1, 6-11-9 Roppongi, Minato-ku.Tel: 3403 9046

Tokhalin (Chinese)
6th Fl, Hotel Okura, 2-10-4 Toranomon, Minato-ku. Tel: 3505 6068

Tokyo Joe's (American)
Akasaka 8-1 Bldg B1, Nagato-cho 2-13-5, Chiyoda-ku. Tel: 3508 0325

Tokyo - Japanese

Goemon
1-1-26 Komagome, Bunkyo-ku.
Tel: 3811 2015

Hassan
B1 Denki Bldg, 6-1-20 Roppongi, Minato-ku. Tel: 3403 8333

Inagiku
2-9-8 Nihonbashi Kayabacho, Chuo-ku. Tel: 3669 5501

Inakaya
3-12-7 Akasaka, Minato-ku. Tel: 3586 3054

Isehiro
1-5-4 Kyobashi, Chuo-ku. Tel: 3281 5864

Mon Cher Ton Ton (Teppanyaki)
3-12-2 Roppongi, Minato-ku. tel: 3402 1055

Nadaman (Ryotei)
Hotel New Otani, 4 Kioi-cho, Chiyoda-ku. Tel: 3265 7591

Seryna
3-12-2 Roppongi, Minato-ku. Tel: 3403 6211

Takamura
3-4-27 Roppongi, Minato-ku. Tel: 3585 6600

Tempura Tenichi
Namiki-dori, 6-6-5 Ginza, Chuo-ku. Tel: 3571 1949

Tochigaya (Game)
1-3-15 Nishi Shinjuku. Tel: 3342 5871

Yama-no-Chaya
2-10-6 Nagato-cho, Chiyoda-ku. Tel: 3581 0585

Zakuro
1-7 Kyobashi, Chuo-ku. .
Tel: 3563 5031

Osaka - non-Japanese

Alaska
13th Fl, Asahi Shimbun Bldg, Nakanoshima 3-chome, Kita-ku. Tel: 231 1351

Bistro Vingt Cinq
25 Taihoji-machi, 25 Nishino-cho, Minami-ku. Tel: 245 6223

Colosseo (Italian)
3-2-6 Minami semba, Minami-ku.
Tel: 252 2024

Haiwhan (Chinese)
11Fl, Midosuji Bldg, 8 Nishi Shimuzu-machi, Minami-ku. Tel: 281 0080

Osaka Joe's (American)
2nd Fl, IM Excellence Bldg, 1-11-20 Sonezaki-shinchi, Kita-ku. Tel: 344 0124

Rose Room (French)
ANA Sheraton Hotel, 1-3-1 Dojimahama, Kita-ku. Tel: 347 1112

Osaka - Japanese

Hanayagi
22 Higashi Shimizu-machi.Tel: 271 8028

Kicho
3-23 Koraibashi, Higashi-ku. Tel: 231 1937

Kitamura
46 Higashi Shimuzu-machi, Minami-ku. Tel: 245 4129

Yamate ya Rinsa
19th Fl Acty Bldg, 3-11-1 Umeda, Kita-ku. Tel: 345 3535

Kyoto

Ashiya (American)
4-172-13 Kiyomizu, Matsubara, Higashiyama-ku. Tel: 541 7961

Gion Suehiro (Japanese)
570-46 Gion-machi-minamigawa, Higashiyama-ku. Tel: 781 2248

Manyoken (Western)
Fuyacho, Shijo, Shimogyo-ku. Tel: 221 1022

Minokichi (Japanese - kaiseki)
Dobutsuenmae-dori, Sanjo-agaru, Sakyo-ku. Tel: 771 4185

Car Hire

Avis *(Sales Office)*
2nd fl, Landic No. 3 (Head Office),
Akasaka Bldg, 2-3-2 Akasaka, 2-chome,
Minato-ku, Tokyo 107
Tel: (03) 3583 0911; Fax: (03) 3583 6850

Budget Rent A Car
5th floor, Nikko Gotanda Building,
2-29-5 Nisshi-gotanda, Shinagawa-ku,
Tokyo
Tel: (03) 3779 0543; Tlx: 2466991
(+ branches throughout Japan)

Hertz Japan Limited
7-8 Motoakasaka 1-chome, Minato-ku,
Tokyo 107
Tel: (3) 3796-8002/8201; Fax: 3796-8290/8291

Japa-ren
2-12-7 Shinjuku, Shinjuku-ku,
Tokyo
Tel: (03) 3354 5531

New Japan Rent-a-Car
6-20 Jingumae, Shibuya-ku,
Tokyo
Tel: (03) 3400 2296

Nippon Rent-A-Car (National Car Rental)
5-5 Kamiyama-cho, Shibuya-ku, Tokyo
Tel: (03) 3468 7126
(English speaking desk)
(+ branches throughout Japan)

Zenkoku Rent-a-Car Association
7th floor, Nakanishi Building,
2-5-6 Nishi-Kanda, Chiyoda-ku,
Tokyo Tel: (03) 3262 3076

Airline Offices

Aeroflot
Tatsunuma Building 3-19, 1-chome, Yaesu
Chuo-ku, Tokyo
Tel:(03) 3271-5311/ 3434 9671

Air France
15th floor, New Aoyama Building,1-1
Minami -Aoyama,1-chome, Minato-ku,
Tokyo
Tel:(03) 3475-1511

Air India
6th floor, Hibiya Park Building, 1-8-1
Yurako-cho,Chiyoda-ku, Tokyo 100
Tel:(03) 3214-1981

Air Lanka
Dowa Building, 7-2-22 Ginza, Chuo-ku, 104
Tel:(03) 3573-4261

Air New Zealand
Room 110, Shin Kokusai Building,3-4-1
Marunochi, Chiyoda-ku, Tokyo 100
Tel:(03) 3287-1641

Alitalia
Tokyo Club Building, 2-6 Kasumigaseki
3-chome, Chiyoda-ku, Tokyo 100
Tel:(03) 3580-2181

All Nippon Airways
Yanmar Tokyo Building, 2-1-1 Yaesu
Chuo-ku, Tokyo
Tel:(03) 3272-1212

British Airways
Sanshin Building, 4-1Yurakucho, 1-chome,
Chiyoda-ku, Tokyo
Tel:(03) 3214-4161/3593-8811

CAAC (Air China)
Motoazabu 3-4-38, Minato-ku, Tokyo
Tel:(03) 3505-2021

Canadian Airlines
8-1 Yurakucho, 1-chome,Chiyoda-ku,
Tokyo
Tel:(03) 3281-7426

Cathay Pacific
Toho Twintower Building,N05-2 Yuraku-
cho, 1-chome, Chiyoda-ku, Tokyo
Tel:(03) 3504-1531

China Airlines
1st floor, Matsuoka Building
Shimbashi 5-22-10 Minato-ku, Tokyo
Tel:(03) 3436-1661

Continental
Suite 242, Kokusai Building,1-1
Marunouchi, 3-chome, Chiyoda-ku, Tokyo
Tel:(03) 3592-1631

Delta
Room 243, Kokusai Building ,Tokyo
Tel:(03) 5275-7000

Egyptair
Palace Building, 1-1-1 Marunochi
Chiyoda-ku, Tokyo
Tel:(03) 3211-4521

Finnair
NK Building, 2-14-2 Kojimachi
Chiyoda-ku, Tokyo
Tel:(03)3222-6801

Garuda
Room 1518, 15th floor, Kasumigaseki Bldg,
2-5 Kasumigaseki,3-chome, Chiyoda-ku,
Tel:(03) 3593-1181/5

Iberia
Room 924/5, HibiyaPark Building
1-8-1 Yuraku-cho,Chiyoda-ku, Tokyo 100
Tel:(03)3213-4306

Iran Air
Habitation House, 1-3-5 Akasaka
Minato-ku, Tokyo
Tel:(03) 3586-2101

Japan Air Lines
Daini Tekko Building,1-8-2 Marunouchi
Chiyoda-ku, Tokyo
Tel:(03) 3457-1121/5259-3777 (Int)
    (03) 3456-2111(Dom)

Japan Air System (formerly Toa Domestic)
18 Mori Building 3-13
Toranomon, 2-chome
Minato-ku, Tokyo 105
Tel:(03) 3438-1155/3747-8111

'98 WINTER OLYMPIC GAMES EVENT SCHEDULE (schedule subject to alteration)

Event	distance from Nagano (kms)	07	08	09	10	11	12	13	14	15	16	17	18	19	20	21	22
Opening Ceremony	0	■															
Alpine Skiing (Men)																	
Downhill	44		■														
Combined Downhill	44			■													
Combined Slalom	59																
Super G	44							■									
Giant Slalom	55											■					
Slalom	59														■		
Alpine Skiing (Women)																	
Downhill	44						■										
Combined Downhill	44								■								
Combined Slalom	59																
Super G	44										■						
Giant Slalom	55													■			
Slalom	59																■
Cross Country Skiing (Men)	37			■		■				■			■			■	
Cross Country Skiing (Women)	37		■			■		■			■			■			
Ski Jumping	43					■					■		■				
Nordic Combined	44							■	■								
Freestyle - Moguls	23		■			■											
Freestyle - Aerials	23												■				
Snowboarding																	
Giant Slalom (Men)	59		■														
Half Pipe (Men/Women)	41				■												
Giant Slalom (Women)	59			■													
Speed Skating (Men)	12		■	■			■			■			■			■	
Speed Skating (Women)	12			■	■			■		■			■			■	
Figure Skating	6			■		■		■	■		■			■		■	
Ice Hockey (Men)	12		■	■	■	■	■	■	■	■	■	■	■	■	■	■	
Ice Hockey (Women)	12		■	■		■		■		■		■					
Bobsleigh	21								■	■					■	■	
Luge (Men)	21			■	■												
Luge (Women)	21					■	■										
Biathlon (Men)	56			■						■				■			
Biathlon (Women)	56		■			■					■						
Curling	66		■	■	■	■	■	■	■	■	■	■	■				
Closing Ceremony	0																■

KLM
Yurakucho Denki Building 7-1,1 -chome, Yurakucho,Chiyoda-ku, Tokyo
Tel:(03) 3216-0771

Korean Air
Room 113-5, Shinkokusai Building
4-1 Marunochi, 3-chome, Tokyo
Tel:(03) 3211-3311

Lufthansa
Tokyo Club Building,2-6 Kasumigaseki
3-chome, Chiyoda-ku, Tokyo
Tel:(03) 3580-2111

Malaysia Airlines
Hankyu Express Building
3-3-9 Shinbashi,Minato-ku, Tokyo 105
Tel:(03) 3503-5961

Northwest Airlines
Imperial Hotel
1-1 Uchisaiwai-cho
1-chome, Chiyoda-ku, Tokyo 100
Tel:(03) 3432-6000

PIA
Room 102, Hibiya Park Building
1-8-1 Yurakucho, Chiyoda-ku, Tokyo
Tel:(03) 3216-6511

Philippine Airlines
8th floor, Sanno Grand Building
14-2-2 Nagatacho,Chiyoda-ku, Tokyo
Tel:(03) 3593-2421

Qantas
Tokyo Chamber of Commerce Building,2-3-3
Marunouchi, Chiyoda-ku, Tokyo.Tel:(03) 3593-7000

Sabena
Akasaka 2-2-19, Minato-ku,Tokyo
Tel:(03) 3585-6151

SAS
Toho Twin Tower Building 5-2
1-chome, Yuraku-cho
Chiyoda-ku, Tokyo
Tel:(03) 3503-8101/5

Singapore Airlines
Yarukucho Building,10-1 yuraku-Cho
1-chome, Chiyoda-ku, Tokyo
Tel:(03) 3213-3431

Swissair
Hibiya Park Building,8-1 Yurakucho, 1-chome,Chiyodu-ku, Tokyo
Tel:(03) 3212-1016

Thai International
Asahi Seimei Hibiya Building
1-5-1 Yuraku-cho
Chiyoda-ku, Tokyo 100
Tel:(03) 3503-3311

United Airlines
Kokusai Building,
3-1-1 Marunouchi
Chiyoda-ku, Tokyo 100
Tel:(03) 3817-4411

Virgin Atlantic
Tel: (03) 3435-8330

Japan Airline Departures

Below is a list of departures and frequencies from Japan's main international airports to the destinations in bold type. Only direct flights are listed. Figures in brackets after destinations refer to the days of the week. (2,4,6) therefore indicates that departures to that destination take place on a Tuesday (the second day of the week), a Thursday and a Saturday. Departures were correct as at February '97.

Airline Abbreviation Codes: **AA** = American Airlines; **AC** = Air Canada; **AF** = Air France; **AI** = Air India; **AY** = Finnair; **AZ** = Alitalia; **BA** = British Airways; **BG** = Biman Bangldesh; **BI** = Royal Brunei Airlines; **CA** = Air China (CAAC); **CI** = China Airlines; **CO** = Continantal Airlines; **CP** = Canadian Airlines; **CX** = Cathay Pacific; **DL** = Delta; **EG** = Japan Asia Airways; **EL** = Air Nippon; **FJ** = Air Pacific; **GA** = Garuda Indonesia; **IB** = Iberia; **IR** = Iran Air; **JD** = Japan Air Sysem; **JL** = Japan Airlines; **KE** = Korean Air; **MH** = Malaysian Airlines; **MS** = Egyptair; **MU** = China Eastern Airlines; **NH** = All Nippon Airways; **NU** = Japan Transocean Air; **NW** = Northwest Airlines; **NZ** = Air New Zealand; **OM** = MIAT - Mongolian Airlines; **OS** = Austrian Airlines; **OZ** = Asiana Airlines; **PK** = Pakistan International Airlines; **PR** = Philippine Airlines; **RA** = Royal Nepal Airlines; **RG** = Varig; **SN** = Sabena; **SQ** = Singapore Airlines; **SR** = Swissair; **TG** = Thai Airways; **TK** = Turkish Airlines; **UA** = United Airlines; **UL** = Air Lanka; **VP** = VASP; **VS** = Virgin; **3X** = Japan Air Commuter.

FUKUOKA (Fukuoka) (FUK)

Aomori (AOJ)
JD (1,3,5,6)
Auckland (AKL)
JL, NZ (1,6)
Bangkok (BKK)
JL/TG (2,4,7)
Beijing (PEK)
CA (1,3,4,6,7) MU (4,5)
Brisbane (BNE)
QF (1)
Cairns (CNS)
QF (1,3,5,7)
Cheju (CJU)
OZ (2,4,5,6,7)
Christchurch (CHC)
JL, NZ (1)
Colombo (CMB)
UL (4)
Dalian (DLC)
CA (3,6) NH (1,6)
Denpasar-Bali (DPS)
GA (1,4,7)
Fukue (FUJ)
EL (daily)
Fukushima (FKS)
EL (daily)
Guam (GUM)
CO (daily)
Hakodate (HKD)
JL (daily)
Hiroshima (HIJ)
JD (2,4,7)
Hong Kong (HKG)
CX (daily) JL (daily)
Honolulu (HNL)
NW,JL (daily)
Iki (IKI)
EL (daily)
Izumo (IZO)

3X (daily)
Jakarta (JKT)
GA (1,4,7)
Kagoshima (KOJ)
EL (daily) JD (daily) 3X (daily)
Kochi (KCZ)
JD (daily)
Komatsu (KMQ)
EL (daily)
Kuala Lumpur (KUL)
MH (3,5,7)
Manila (MNL)
PR (2,4,7)
Matsumoto (MMJ)
JD (daily)
Matsuyama (MYJ)
JD (daily)
Melbourne (MEL)
QF (3,5)
Memambetsu (MMB)
JD (2,4,7)
Miyazaki (KMI)
JD (daily)
Morioka (HNA)
JD (1,3,6)
Nagoya (NGO)
NH (daily) JL (daily) JD (daily)
Nanki Shirhma (SHM)
3X (1,4,6)
Niigata (KIJ)
NH (daily)
Okinawa (OKA)
NH (daily) JL (daily)
Osaka (OSA)
NH, JL, JD (daily)
Penang (PEN)
MH (3,5)
Pusan (PUS)
JL (3,6) KE (daily) OZ (5,7)
Saipan (SPN)
CO (1,4,5,7)
Sapporo (SPK)

What's the link between business and the Asia Pacific?

BRITISH AIRWAYS
The world's favourite airline

http://www.british-airways.com

JL (daily) NH (daily) JD (daily)
Sendai (SDJ)
JD (daily)
Seoul (SEL)
JL (daily) KE (daily) OZ (daily)
Shanghai (SHA)
MU (2,4,5,7) CA (1,4,7)
Singapore (SIN)
SQ (daily)
Taipei (TPE)
CI, CX, EL, BR (daily)
Takamatsu (TAK)
3X (daily)
Tokushima (TKS)
3X (daily)
Tokyo (HNA)
NH (daily) JL (daily) JD (daily)
Toyama (TO)
EL (daily)
Tsushima (TSJ)
EL (daily)
Yamagata (GAJ)
JD (2,4,7)
Yonago (YGJ)
3X (2,3,5,7)

OSAKA (Itami) (OSA)

Akita (AXT)
JD (daily)
Amami O Shima (ASJ)
JD (daily)
Amsterdam (AMS)
KL (daily)
Aomori (AOJ)
JD (daily)
Asahikawa (AKJ)
JD (daily)
Auckland (AKL)
NZ (1,2,4,5,6,7)
Bandar Seri Bagawan (BWN)
BI (3,6)
Bangkok (BKK)
TG, JL (daily) NH (1,3,4,5,6,7)
Beijing (BJS)
JL (2,3,5,6) MU (2,5) CA (daily) NH (4,7)
Bombay (BOM)
AI (3,7) NH (4,7)
Brisbane (BNE)
QF (1,2,4,5,7) JL (1,3,5,6) AN (1,3,4,6,7) NZ (2,7) NH (1,5)
Cairns (CNS)
JL (2,4,7) QF (6)
Cairo (CAI)
MS (1,5)
Cebu (CEB)
PR (4,7)
Cheju (CJU)
KE (1,3,4,5)
Chicago (CHI)
UA (daily)
Christchurch (CHC)
JL/NZ (1,6) NZ (7)
Copenhagen (CPH)
SK (2,5,7)
Dalian (DLC)
NH (1,4,6,7) CA (3,6)
Delhi (DEL)
AI (3,7) JL (7)
Denpasar-Bali (DPS)
GA (3,5,7) EG (daily)
Denver (DEN)
UA (daily)

Detroit (DTW)
NW (daily)
Frankfurt (FRA)
LH (2,3,5,7) JL (1,3,5) NH (3,7)
Fukuoka (FUK)
NH (daily) JL (daily) JD (daily)
Fukue (FUJ)
EL (2,3,5,7)
Fukushima (FKS)
JL (daily)
Guam (GUM)
UA, CO, NH, JL (daily)
Guangzhou (CAN)
JD (1,4,6) CZ (1,3,5)
Hakodate (HKD)
NH (daily) JL (1,3,5,7)
Helsinki (HEL)
AY (4,6)
Ho Chi Minh (SGN)
VN (2,3,4,6,7) JL (2,3,4,5,6,7)
Hong Kong (HKG)
CX, JL (daily) NH (daily) AI (3,7)
Honolulu (HNL)
NW (daily) JL (daily) UA (daily)
Ishigaki (ISG)
NU (daily)
Istanbul (IST)
TK (3,6)
Izumo (IZO)
JD (daily) 3X (daily)
Jakarta (JKT)
GA (3,5,7) EG (1,2,3,5,6,7) NW (2,4,7)
Kagoshima (KOJ)
NH (daily) JD (daily) JL (daily)
Kaohsiung (KHH)
EG (2,5,7)
Kathmandu (KAT)
RA (3,7)
Kochi
JD, EL (daily)
Kuala Lumpur (KUL)
MH (1,3,4,6) NH (1,4,6) JL (daily)
Kumamoto (KMJ)
NH (daily) JL (daily)
Kushiro (KUH)
JD (daily)
Kwangju (KWJ)
OZ (5,7)
Langkawi (LGK)
MH (3)
London (LHR)
BA (1,3,5,6,7) JL (1,2,4,6,7) NH (2,6)
Los Angeles (LAX)
JL, UA, NW (daily) VP (3,7)
Manila (MNL)
NW, TG (daily) PR (3,6)
Matsumoto (MMJ)
JD (daily)
Matsuyama (MYJ)
NH (daily) JL (daily)
Melbourne (MEL)
AN (1,3,4,6,7) QF (6)
Memambetsu (MMB)
NH (daily)
Milan (MIL)
NH (1,5) JL (2,7) AZ (2,4,7)
Minneapolis (MSP)
NW (1,3,5,6)
Misawa (MSJ)
JD (daily)
Miyako Jima (MMY)
EL (daily)
Miyazaki (KMI)
NH (daily) JD (daily) JL (daily)

Morioka (MRW)
JD (daily)
Moscow (MOW)
SU (1,6)
Munich (MUC)
LH (1,4,6)
Nadi (NAN)
FJ (1,4)
Nagasaki (NGS)
NH (daily) JD (daily) JL (daily)
New York (JFK)
UA (daily)
New York (LGA)
NW (daily)
Niigata (KIJ)
JD (daily) NH (daily)
Obihiro (OBO)
JD (daily)
Oita (OIT)
NH, JL (daily)
Oki (OKI)
3X (daily)
Okinawa (OKA)
NH (daily) JL (daily) JD (daily)
Paris (CDG)
AF (daily) JL (daily)
Penang (PEN)
MH (4,6)
Pusan (PUS)
JL (daily) KE (daily) OZ (5,7)
Qingdao (TAO)
NH (3,6) MU (2,5)
Rome (ROM)
NH (1,3,4,7) JL (2,7) AZ (2,4,7)
Saipan (SPN)
CO (daily)
Sao Paulo (SAO)
VP (3,7)
San Francisco (SFO)
UA (daily)
Sapporo (SPK)
NH (daily) JL (daily) JD (daily)
Seattle (SEA)
NW (1,3,5,6)
Sendai (SDJ)
NH (daily) JL (daily)
Seoul (SEL)
JL, KE, NH, OZ (daily)
Shanghai (SHA)
CA (2,5,6,7) JL (1,3,4,6,7) MU (1,3,4,6,7) NH (1,2,5,7)
Shonai (SYO)
NH (daily)
Singapore (SIN)
NH,JL,SQ (daily)
Sydney (SYD)
JL(daily) NH (1,5) QF(1,2,4,5,7) AN (1,3,4,6,7)
Taipei (TPE)
CX,EG (daily) SQ (3,5,6,7)
Takamatsu (TAK)
EL (daily)
Tanega Shima (TNE)
3X (daily)
Teagu (TAE)
KE (2,5)
Tokushima (TKS)
JD (daily) 3X (daily)
Tokyo (HND)
NH (daily) JL (daily) JD (daily)
Tokyo (NRT)
NH (daily) JL (daily)
Toronto (YYZ)
AC (daily)
Toyama (TOY)

JAPAN - Airline Departures

NH (Daily)
Toyooka (TJH)
3X (daily)
Tsushima (TSJ)
EL (1,4,6)
Ulaan baatar (ULN)
OM (6)
Vancouver (YVR)
AC (daily) NH (daily)
Vienna (VIE)
NH (1,5) OS (1,5)
Yamagata (GAJ)
JD (daily)
Yangon (RGN)
NH (2,5,7)
Yonago (YGJ)
3X (daily)
Zurich (ZRH)
SR (1,4,6)

TOKYO (Narita) (NRT)
(Departures from Haneda followed by *)
Akita* (AXT)
NH (daily) JL (daily)
Amami O-shima* (ASJ)
JD (daily)
Amsterdam (AMS)
JL (daily) KL (1,2, 4,5,6)
Aomori* (AOJ)
JD (daily) NH (daily)
Asahikawa *(AKJ)
JD (daily) NH (daily)
Atlanta (ATL)
DL (daily) JL (1,3,6)
Auckland (AKL)
NZ (1,3,6,7) JL (1,5) NZ/JL (2)
Bangkok (BKK)
AI (3,6) MS (3,6) JL, NW, TG, UA (daily) BG (5) PK (2,6) NH (1,3,5,6,7)
Barcelona (BCN)
IB (1,3,5)
Beijing (PEK)
CA, MU, UA, NH (daily) PK (1,5) NW (2,5,7) JL (1,2,4,5,6,7)
Bombay (BOM)
AI (3,4,6,7)
Boston (BOS)
AA (1,2,4,5,6,7) NW,UA (daily)
Brisbane (BNE)
JL, QF (1,2,3,4,5,7) NH (2,4,6)
Brussels (BRU)
SN (1,3,6)
Cairns (CNS)
JL (daily), QF (1,2,3,5,6,7)
Cairo (CAI)
MS (3,6)
Calcutta (CCU)
AI (6)
Calgary (YYC)
CP (4,5)
Cebu (CEB)
PR (3,4,7)
Cheju (CJU)
KE (1,2,4,5,6,7)
Chicago (ORD)
JL, NW (daily)
Christchurch (CHC)
NZ (1,2,6) NZ/JL (2)
Chiang Mai (CNX)
TG (1,4,6)
Colombo (CMB)
UL (1,4)

Copenhagen (CPH)
SK (1,3,4,6,7)
Dalian (DLC)
NH (2) CA (1,4,7)
Dallas/Ft Worth (DFW)
AA (daily) DL (1,2,4,5,6,7)
Darwin (DRW)
QF (1)
Delhi (DEL)
AI (3,4,7) JL(4) NH (1,5)
Denpasar-Bali (DPS)
GA (daily) JL (daily) NH (3,6)
Detroit (DTT)
NW (daily)
Dhaka (DAC)
BG (5)
Frankfurt (FRA)
JL (daily) LH (daily) NH (2,4,6)
Fukuoka *(FUK)
JL (daily) NH (daily) JD (daily)
Guam (GUM)
JL, CO , NW (daily)
Hachijo Jima (HAC)
EL (daily)
Hokadate* (HKD)
NH (daily) JL (daily)
Helsinki (HEL)
AY (3,7)
Hiroshima* (HIJ)
NH (daily) JD (daily) JL (daily)
Hong Kong (HKG)
CX (daily) EG (daily) JL (daily) NW (daily) UA (daily) NH (daily)
Honolulu (HNL)
JL,NW,UA,CO (daily) CI (1,2,3,5,6)
Houston (HOU)
NW (daily)
Ishigaki (ISG)
NU (daily)
Islamabad (ISB)
PK (1,5)
Istanbul (IST)
TK (2,4)
Iwami (IWJ)
EL (daily)
Izumo* (IZO)
JD (daily)
Jakarta (JKT)
GA (daily) JL (daily) NH (3,6)
Kagoshima* (KOJ)
JD (daily) JL (daily) NH (daily)
Kaohsiung (KHH)
EG (1,3,5)
Karachi (KHI)
PK (1,2,5,6)
Kitakyushu* (KKJ)
JD (daily)
Kochi* (KCZ)
NH (daily)
Komatsu* (KMO)
NH (daily) JD (daily) JL (daily)
Kona (KOA)
JL (1,4,7)
Kota Kinabalu (BKI)
MH (4)
Kuala Lumpur (KUL)
JL (daily) MH (daily)
Kuching (KCH)
MH (1)
Kumamoto* (KMJ)
NH (daily) JL (daily) JD (daily)
Kushiro* (KUH)

NH (daily) JD (daily)
Lima (LIM)
RG (1)
London (LHR)
NH,BA,JL (daily) VS (1,2,3,5,6, 7) SU (1,6)
Los Angeles (LAX)
JL, KE, NH,NW,SQ,UA (daily) MH (1,4,6)DL (1,2,4,5,6,7) RG (1,3,5)
Madrid (MAD)
IB (1,3,5,6)
Manila (MNL)
MS (3) JL,NW, PR (daily) PK (2,6)
Matsuyama* (MYJ)
JL (daily) NH (daily)
Memeambetsu* (MMB)
JD (daily) NW (daily)
Mexico City (MEX)
JL (1,4)
Miami (MIA)
AA (daily) UA (daily)
Milan (MIL)
AZ (1,3,5,6,7) JL (1,5)
Minneapolis (MSP)
NW (daily)
Misawa* (MSJ)
JD (daily)
Miyako Jima * (MYE)
EL (daily) NU (daily to MMY)
Miyazaki* (KMI)
JD (daily) NH , JL (daily)
Moscow (SVO)
SU (daily) NH (2) JL(3) IB (1,3,5,6)
Nadi (NAN)
FJ (1,4) NZ (3)
Nagasaki* (NGS)
JD (daily) NH (daily) JL (daily)
Nagoya (NGO)
NH (daily) JL (daily)
Nakashibetsu* (SHB)
EL (daily)
Nanki Shirhma* (SHM)
JD (daily)
New York (JFK)
NH, JL, NW, UA (daily) DL (4,5,6)
New York (EWR)
UA (daily)
New York (LGA)
AA (daily)
Noumea (NOU)
AF (2,3,5,7) JL (2,3,5,7)
Obihiro* (OBO)
JD (daily)
Oita* (OIT)
JD (daily) NH (daily) JL (daily)
Okayama* (OKJ)
NH (daily)
Okinawa* (OKA)
NH (daily) JL (daily) JD (daily)
Orlando (ORL)
DL (1,2,4,5,6,7) AA (daily)
Osaka* (OSA)
JL (daily) NH (daily) JD (daily)
Oshima (OIM)
EL (daily)
Papeete (PPT)
AF (1)
Paris (CDG)
SU (2,3,5,7) AF, JL (daily) NH (daily)

Penang (PEN)
MH (1,5)
Perth (PER)
QF (1,3,6)
Portland (PDX)
DL (daily)
Pusan (PUS)
JL (2,3,4,5,7) KE (1,2,4,5,6,7)
Rio de Janeiro (GIG)
RG (1,3,5,6)
Rome (FCO)
SU (4,6) AZ (1,3,5,6,7) JL (1,3,4,5,6)
Saipan (SPN)
CO (daily) JL (daily) NW (daily)
Salt Lake City (SLC)
DL (1,2,4,5,6,7)
San Diego (SAN)
NW (daily)
San Francisco (SFO)
JL,NW,UA (daily)
San Jose (SJC)
AA (1,2,4,5,6,7)
Sao Paulo (GRU)
JL/RG (6) RG (1,3,5,6) JL (1,4,6)
Sapporo* (SPK)
JL (daily) JD (daily) NH (daily)
Seattle (SEA)
NW (daily) AA (daily)
Seoul (SEL)
JL,JD, KE, NW, UA(daily) OZ (2,3,5,6,7)
Shanghai (SHA)
CA,JL, MU, UA (daily)
Shonai (SYO)
NH (daily)
Singapore (SIN)
UA, SQ, JL, NW (daily) BG (5) NH (1,3,4,6,7)
Stockholm (STO)
SK (2,5)
Sydney (SYD)
NH (daily) JL, QF (daily)
Taipei (TPE)
CI, CX, EG, NW (daily) SQ (1,2,4)
Takamatsu* (TAK)
NH (daily) JD (daily)
Tehran (THR)
IR (1,4)
Tokushima (TKS)
JD, NH (daily)
Toronto (YYZ)
CP (daily)
Tottori (TTJ)
NH (daily)
Toyama* (TOY)
NH (daily)
Ube* (UBJ)
NH (daily)
Vancouver (YYZ)
CP (daily) JL (daily)
Vienna (VIE)
NH/OS (1,3,6)
Washington (IAD)
NH (1,3,5,7)
Washington (DCA)
NW (daily)
Yamagata (GAJ)
NH (daily)
Yonago (YGJ)
EL (daily)
Zurich (ZRH)
JL (daily) SR (3,4,5,6,7)

Major Exhibitions in Japan 1997

Date	Exhibition	Venue	City	Organiser
May 1-5	**West Japan Import Fair 97**	WJGEC	Fukuoka	WJITEA
May 9-13	**Tour Expo 97** - in conjunction with TABI FAIR 97 Trade fair centered on world travel	Intex	Osaka	OITFC
May 14-16	**Osaka Int'l Jewellery Fair**	APTC	Osaka	MFreeman
May 21-24	**COMMUNET 97** - personal communications exhib.	Intex	Osaka	OITFC
May 21-24	**TECHNO-PIA '97** - Automatic machines and technology exhibition	Intex	Osaka	NKS
May 21-23	**Expo Nonwovens Asia 97**	Intex	Osaka	MFreeman
June 5-8	**37th West Japan Machine & Tool & Industrial System Fair**	WJGEC	Fukuoka	WJITEA
June 5-8	**West Japan Multi Media Fair 97**	WJGEC	Fukuoka	WJITEA
June 18-20	**Expo Paper Asia 97**	TIEC	Arlake	MFreeman
June 18-20	**CIM Japan** - computing technology, planning & control systems & the Industrial Virtual Reality show	TIEC	Tokyo	Reed
June 18-20	**Design Engineering Japan** - CAD/CAM/CAE systems	TIEC	Tokyo	Reed
July 2-4	**Fine Process Technology Japan** - Devices and production technology for production line eqpt.	TIEC	Tokyo	Reed
July 9-11	**CASE Japan** - CASE tools, GUI development tools, visual programming tools, other consulting companies	TIEC	Tokyo	Reed
Sept 19-23	**19th West Japan Chinaware Festa**	WJGEC	Fukuoka	WJITEA
Oct 7-13	**OTEMAS** - 6th Int'l textile machinery show	Intex	Osaka	OITFC
Oct 15-17	**Eco-Technology Expo 97**	WJGEC	Fukuoka	WJITEA
1988 April 24-29	**Messe-bition 98** - 23rd Osaka Int'l Trade Fair	Intex	Osaka	OITFC
April 15-18	**CMM JAPAN & JSP 98** - 5th Converting & special printing machinery/materials conf. & exposition	NCC	Chiba	ICS

Venues: APTC = Asia and Pacific Trade Centre, Osaka. **Intex** = Osaka Internatonal Exhibition Centre; **TIEC** = Tokyo Internatinal Exhibition Center, 3-12 Ariake, Koto-ku, Tokyo 135. Tel: 3531 3371; Fax: 3531 1344; **NCC** = Nippon Convention Centre (Makuhari Messe) 2-1 Nakase, Mihama Mihama-ku, Chiba 261. Tel: 043 296 0001; Fax: 043 296 0529. **WJGEC** = West Japan General Exhibition Center, 3-7-1 Asano, 3-chome Kokurakita-ku, Kitakyusyu, 802, Japan Tel: 093-511-6848; Fax: 093-521-8845.

Exhibition Organisers: ICS = Int'l Communications Specialists Inc, Kasho Bldg, 2-14-9, Nihonbashi, Chuo-ku, Tokyo 103. Tel: 03 3273; Fax: 03 3273 2445. **JES** = Japan Exhibition Services, Seshimo Bldg 301 8-8, Kohraku 2-chome, Bunkyo-ku, Tokyo 112, tel: 3814 8655; fax: 3814 8687. **MFreeman** = Miller Freeman, 907 Gt Eagle Centre, 25 Harbour Rd, Hong Kong, tel: (852) 2827 5121; fax: 2511 7063. **NKS** = The Nikkan Kogyo Shimbun, Osaka, 2-16 Kitahama Higahi, Chuo-ku, Osala 540. Tel: 06 946 3384; Fax: 06 946 3389. **OITFC** = Osaka International Trade Fair Commission, 1-5 102, Nanko-kita, Suminoe-ku, Osaka 559, tel (06) 612 3773, fax (06) 612 8585; **Reed** = Reed Exhibition Companies, 18th Fl, Shinjuku Nomura Bldg, 1-26-2 Nishsishinjuku, Shinjuku-ku, Tokyo 163, tel: 3349 8501; fax 3345 7929; tlx 27280 RECJPN. **TITFC** = Tokyo Int'l Trade Fair Commission, 4-7-24 Harumi, Chuo-ku, Tokyo 104, tel: 3531 3371; fax: 3531 1344. **WJITEA** = West Japan Industry & Trade Exhibition Association. 7-1 Asano 3-chome, Kokurahita-ku, Kitakyushu, 802, Japan. Tel: (093) 511-6848; Fax: (093) 521-8845.

North Korea

Doing Business

The business/political scene

Overseas businesses waiting for trade liberalisation in North Korea following the death of Kim Il-Sung were kept guessing for much of 1995. By year's end it was still not clear whether 'The Great Leader's' successor Kim Jong-Il had officially taken control of the country, so infrequent were his public appearances or statements, or whether even he would actually instigate a transformation from a centralised to a market economy as was initially expected.

The expectant business climate was not helped by a continued on-off international settlement over the position of North Korea's nuclear plants, resolution of which was considered vital before trade discussions could either begin or be taken a stage further by existing investors.

In October 1995 North Korea signed a US$ 4.5 billion deal for nuclear power stations with the US, part of a package of incentives designed to get North Korea to scrap its nuclear weapons programme.

However the North continues to mass troops on the border with the South, possibly in a bid to divert domestic attention away from the famine which is said to have left the 1995 harvest 3.5mn tons short.

The continued political standoff was said by observers to be particularly frustrating for large international conglomerates hoping to use both Beijing and the South Korean capital, Seoul, as stepping stones into a country whose basic infrastructural and commercial needs are said to rank alongside those of China 20 years ago.

In 1992/3 North Korea passed a series of foreign investment laws, including the *Foreign Enterprise Act* which finally made it possible for wholly-owned foreign companies to set up in free trade zones. The first zone was set up along the Tumen river, bordering Russia and China but this has been put on hold pending clarification of the nuclear issue. Since 1994 North Korea has been boosting foreign exchange earnings (otherwise dependent on weapons' sales) by exporting workers to logging camps in Siberia. Unfortunately for the regime, many of these have sought political asylum in Moscow en route to South Korea.

1996 saw the defection of a senior North Korean government official to the south and a further shortfall of about 2.5m tonnes (or 50%) in the autumn grain harvest. The US and even South Korea have donated grain to help ease the shortage, which observers are concerned could lead to a further outflow of hungry refugees. The UN World Food Programme has appealed for a further 100,000 tonnes of food aid and the US hopes this will be enough to get Pyongyang back to security talks with the South, in an attempt to finally sign a peace treaty.

Business etiquette & practice

Discretion and a low political profile are advised. Business is not allowed to be conducted in a North Korean office, so will be discussed in the evening. Business suit required with tie. No tipping. Do not touch a North Korean woman. Even shaking hands can be construed as an 'immoral act'. Do not compromise your hosts by giving them foreign coins or photographs of yourself as this could have political repercussions.

Tourism Update

Gaining a business or tourist visa for North Korea requires at least 10 days advance notice to overseas representatives and probably the easiest method of visiting the country on an exploratory business trip is to take one of the official four to eight-day tours offered through travel agents in various Asian capitals, notably Hong Kong and Tokyo — costing about US$200-a-day inclusive of hotel accommodation, most meals and compulsory guide/interpreter. In 1995 North Korea joined PATA (the Pacific Asia Travel Association) and in April 1997 exhibited for the first time at an international travel show - the PATA Travel Mart in Beijing.

Special permits are required for travel outside Pyongyang, a spacious and green, if somewhat uninspiring, city built from scratch following the Korean War. Beyond the official state trade offices in the capital, foreign business revolves around the lobby of the 500-room Koryo Hotel in the heart of the city, a deluxe property including secretarial, translation and postal services.

Other hotels of international standard include the Ptonggang, Sosan, Ryanggang and Chongnyon. A grade below are the Taedonggang, Pyongyang, Changgwangsan and Haebangsan. In aviation terms the North does still not allow the South to overfly its territory, although the North Korean Civil Aviation Authority has now submitted plans to the ICAO for the opening up of its skies to other carriers.

What to See

Travel outside Pyongyang is very difficult to arrange. In the capital, which was built from scratch after the Korean War of 1953, main monuments to the proletarian struggle are the Tower of the Juche Idea, the Arch of Triumph, the Grand Monument and the Chollima Statue. There is, however, a good museum of artefacts and drawings from Korea's past: The Korean Central History Museum. Tours are strictly guided and circumscribed but may take you to institutions such as the Maternity Hospital, the Embroidery Institute or Mangyondae where Kim Il Sung was born. The Movie Studio is not on the official circuit but can be visited on request and will provide a fascinating insight into the mentaility of the regime.

Outside the capital your tour may take in Myohyangsan - three hours' distant by train, where the International Friendship Exhibition is housed. This is a line up of gifts from other dictators to Kim Il Sung and Kim Jong-Il. Just outside the IFE is the Buddhist temple Pohyonsa, consisting of several small pagodas and a large hall housing Buddha images.

Kaesong is interesting for its burial mounds of Korean kings and queens and for its Sonjuk (12th century) bridge and Pyochung Stele shrine.

Panmunjon is the northern side of the

truce village which you may have visited from South Korea. You will also be taken to the Wall - a 248 km concrete bunker 'built by the Americans' across the peninsula. South of Wonsam on the East Coast is what many consider some of Korea's most famous scenery - the Kumgungsam (Diamond Mountain) area of outstanding natural beauty. Also near Wonsan City on the East Coast is Lake Sijung, famous for its mud clinics.

The Kuryong Falls and Samil Lake are spectacular by any standards and Paekdusan (Mount Paekdu) astride the Chinese/Korean border at 2744 metres is the highest mountain in the whole of Korea and is revered both North and South, purporting to be the fountainhead of all Korean life, and, predictably, claimed by the North to have been where Kim Jong-Il was born.

Shopping

There are precious few consumer goods for sale; souvenirs like stamps and ginseng are available, although the latter is more reasonably priced in South Korea. Strangely, department stores look well stocked form the outside, but the doors are locked from the inside and there are no shoppers in them. Popular buys also include snake liquor, embroidery, ceramics and North Korean paintings. Koryo celadons, *insam* and its products are also good buys. Some imported brandies and cigarettes are cheaper than in their countries of origin, due to low duties. Most of the major hotels have souvenir shops. Otherwise, shopping is limited to the foreign exchange outlets of Diplomatic, Ragwon, Taesong, Taedon or the Pyongyang Department Store No.1.

Getting Around

All public transport in Pyongyang costs 10 Won; the subway is something of a showcase on the Soviet model with bronze sculptures, murals, mosaics chandeliers and marble steps and platforms, and should be experienced. Buses and trams are extremely crowded. Taxis can be booked from tourist hotels and the fare is approx. 2 Won per km. There are no regular scheduled domestic flights. Occasionally a charter to Paekdusan is laid on for W2000. Traffic is very sparse in the countryside as North Koreans need permission to move freely around their own country. Trips to centres outside the capital will most probably be arranged for you in ornate 1950s-era sleeping cars - a special train service for foreigners. Unlike China, there is no mass ownership of bicycles amongst the population. All tours will be accompanied by an official guide, necessary, apart from political reasons, because there are no maps or street signs.

Entertainment & Leisure

Pyongyang features little in the way of restaurants or entertainment. Recommended restaurants include the Korean/Chinese eaterie at the Taedonggang Hotel; the *Diplomatic Club* on the east bank of the Teadong River; the *Ansan Club* opposite the Potonggang Hotel and Koryo Hotel outlets. The Koryo, Diplomatic Club and Changgwangsan Hotel, which has a Saturday night disco, and Karaoke Bar, opposite the Koryo, are favoured evening rendezvous for foreigners. The National Restaurant is a supperclub with nightly Korean folk performances. The Pyongyang Grand Theatre and East Pyongyang Grand Theatre provide regular concerts and cultural performances. The Koryo Hotel also has a dance hall (cover charge W25) and a billiards room which is a popular meeting place for diplomats and journalists. A night at the revolutionary Korea opera or at one of the circuses will be remembered.

North Korea Key Fact File

Passport Requirements:
Visas are issued by the North Korean embassies in Moscow or Beijing or, more reliably, by the DPR Korea-Macau International Tourist Office in Macau (see later *addresses*). The fee is US$15

Currency:
Won (W). 100 jon = W1

Exchange Rates: *(May 1997)*
US$ 1 = W2.15; £1 = W3.50

Currency Restrictions:
Currency forms are made out at the time you get your visa or at your point of entry and have to be produced on departure. Only German, French, US, UK and Japanese currency can be exchanged in the country; cash gets a better exchange rate than travellers' cheques. Money must be exchanged at hotels.

Electricity Supply:
220 volts 60 Hz

Language:
Korean. Very few people speak English or another foreign language.

Time: GMT + 9; EST + 12 hrs

IDD Code: 850
No area codes applicable

Customs & Entry:
A reasonable amount of tobacco or alcoholic beverages may be imported on entry. The importation of binoculars, wireless sets, arms, ammunition, explosives, drugs, plants and seeds is prohibited.

Business Hours
Officially 9 am to 6 pm Monday to Saturday

Health Requirements:
Yellow fever and malaria inoculation not necessary; cholera, typhoid and polio advised. Most Koreans drink their water unboiled. Western medicines are in short supply

Climate/best time to visit:
Similar to South Korea, only with colder winters. July/August max temp 28° (also the rainy season). December/January temp average 2° C; Spring & Autumn mild and dry, av. temp 10-20)°C.

National Holidays 1997
1 January New Year's Day; February 16 Kim Jong - Il's birthday; March 8 International Women's Day; 15 April Kim Il Sung's birthday; May 1 May Day; August 15 Anniversary of Liberation; September 9 Independence Day; October 10 Anniversary of the foundation of the Korean Workers Party; December 27 Anniversary of the Constitution

Arrival & Departure

Pyongyang is connected by air with Beijing via Air China once weekly or Koryo Air, the North Korean carrier, twice weekly. Fares are about US$120 if bought in North Korea but $274 if bought in China. Khabarovsk-Pyongyang has Aeroflot or Koryo Air and between Moscow and Pyongyang. Passengers are advised to book flights well in advance and to reconfirm departure when arriving in the country. Sunan International Airport is 30 kms, about 20 minutes, west of Pyongyang by taxi. Airport departure tax is W13 payable when you reconfirm with your tour operator, rather than at the airport.

There are four trains per week to and from Beijing via Tianjin and other North Chinese cities, which take 23 hours to make the journey and cost some US$ 115 in 'soft sleeper' (first) class.

Useful Addresses

Visa issue

Embassy of the Democratic People's Republic of Korea
Ritan Beilu, Jianguomenwai, Chaoyang District, Beijing. Tel: 6532 1186

DPR Korea-Macau International Tourism Company
23rd floor, Nam Yan Commercial Centre, 57-9 Rua da Praia Grande, Macau
Tel: (853) 333355/333939

Embassy of the Democratic People's Republic of Korea
PO box Ulitsa Mosfilmovskaya 72, Moscow
Tel: 578 7580; Tlx: 413272

Tourism Information

Ryohaengsa (Korean International Travel Company)
Central District, Pyongyang
Tel: (2) 381 7201; Tlx: 5998 RHS KP; Fax: (2) 381 7607

Kumgangsan International Tourist Company
Central District, Pyongyang. Tel: 31562

Hotels

Pyongyang

Pyongyang Koryo Hotel A
Changwang Street.
Tel: (2) 381 4406; Tlx: 38027/8 KORYO KP; Fax: (2) 381 4422
500 rooms, IDD telephone; restaurants, bar

Potonggang Hotel B
4 kms from city centre. Tel: 48301
161 rooms

Ryanggang Hotel B
4 kms from city centre. *330 rooms*
Tlx: 38039 RYANGGANG KP;
Fax: (2) 381 3594

Changwangsan Hotel C
Chollima Street. Tel: 48366
326 rooms

Pothongang Hotel C
Otan Kangan Street. *170 rooms*
Tel: 381 4461; Tlx: 38030/1; Fax: 381 4428

Taedonggang Hotel C
Okryu Street. Tel: 381 3346
60 rooms

Tongmyong Hotel D
52 rooms. Fax: (2) 332 0703

Yanggakdo International Hotel C
1001 rooms.

Myohyangsan

Hyangsan Hotel A
228 rooms. Tlx: 24029 HYANGSAN KP

Kumgangsan

Songdowon Hotel C
164 rooms. Tlx: 24012 SONH KP

Kumgangsan Hotel C
240 rooms. Tlx: 24012 SONH KP;
Fax: (2) 381 3582

Paekdusan area

Hyesan Hotel B
Samjiyon Hotel B
Onsupyong Hotel C

> **Explanation of codes in hotel entries. A** after name of hotel = room rate over US$200 per person per night; **B** = between $150-200; **C** = between 100-150; **D** = between $50-100; **E** = under $50; ¶ = prices on application. Prices include local tours and transport.

Koryo Hotel

Mt Paekdu

South Korea

Doing Business

General Climate

Despite easing relations and winning the protracted propaganda war with North Korea, South Korea's government entered an election year under a black cloud in 1997. Allegations of scandal and corruption prompted President Kim Young Sam into a widespread reshuffling of his cabinet in a bid to regain public confidence.

At the same time a national strike was called in a bid to repeal a new labour law making it easier for employers to dismiss workers.

During the first two weeks of the year, violent demonstrations accompanied mass worker walkouts, including 'necktie' office workers, from the country's primary auto, shipbuilding and other industries, costing an estimated US$2bn in lost production and dramatically slowing the economic progress of one of Asia's most formidable industrial powers. The government insisted the new law was essential to curb trade union wage demands and keep economic growth on track. It argued that across the board wage rises of 12% in the previous two years had escalated labour costs to an untenable level, making Korean exports uncompetitive.

Although the stock exchange remained steady and analysts were predicting the economy would rebound in the second half of 1997 prior to the December election, the strikes heralded another hiccup in the transformation of the country from one of Asia's poorest to one of its wealthiest. Back in the early 1960s, much of South Korea still lay in the ashes of war. With few natural resources but full of grit, determination and the optimum use of international loans, the country set a development course which few observers believed could be achieved - but nonetheless has been achieved beyond the expectations of even Koreans themselves.

Success may have been bought at the expense of true democracy but, by any standards, the transformation has been remarkable. Per capita income spiralled from US$85 in the early 1960s to more than US$13,000 in 1996 and South Korea emerged from nowhere to join the world's top 20 trading nations. Korea became a member of OECD in 1996.

By 1995, South Korea's GNP was said to be the size of Russia's. Double digit economic growth throughout the 1980s dipped into single figures in the early and mid-1990s, levelling off at an estimated 7.7% for 1997. But the economy, along with a threatened outflow of too much capital, accompanying the lifting of restrictions on Koreans travelling abroad, were held in check and nurtured by liberalised foreign investment controls plus domestic austerity measures, improving GDP but with consumer spending growing at only moderate pace. The OECD sees growth rates levelling off at 5-6% per annum rate for the rest of the 90s, in comparison to the 8-10% rate of recent years.

But the path to progress has rarely been smooth for South Korea, whose politics are as fiery as the national determination. Nascent democracy, epitomised by violent demonstrations over the years, has been paid only lip service by successive rulers.

Public honesty and efficiency are frequently brought into question. And highly-publicised government efforts to root out endemic corruption in banking and industrial contracting have met with little success.

Four or five big *chaebol*, or conglomerates, control much of South Korean business life and rare is the business visitor who does not find him of herself dealing either directly or indirectly with one of these giants, so widespread are their tentacles in every facet of manufacturing or commerce. Business is treated seriously, and formally, requiring the visitor to be well-prepared and pre-acquainted, via a local agent, with company lines of communication, seniority and rank during what inevitably will involve protracted meetings involving much ceremony and, initially, much small talk as you are personally 'sized-up'.

Social invitations should be treated as precisely that, rather than as an excuse, unless asked, to continue business discussions in more convivial surroundings. After hours, South Koreans are not generally as outgoing with foreigners as their counterparts in Japan - but a banquet at a *kinsaeng* (geisha) house at the invitation of a senior ranking official should not be refused, even if you are picking up what will be a gargantuan bill.

The Itaewon district of Seoul, with a big variety of bars, restaurants and nightlife, is the most cosmopolitan area for entertaining. Itaewon forms part of the old section of the city, separated from a new commercial area by the Han River.

Seoul traffic is frequently congested. Using the subway, which has English signage, is often quicker and easier than taking taxis which have a reputation for serious overcharging, despite official efforts to bring them under control.

Seoul has an excellent but expensive range of deluxe hotels and ancillary services. Dining out can be a delicious eastern challenge in South Korea but general entertainment is thoroughly westernised. Baseball is the number one sport. Christianity has a powerful following, evident through various sects and actions. In 1995, for example, no fewer than 35,000 couples from one sect were married at the same time in a stadium. But then South Korea makes a big noise in everything it does.

Business etiquette

Like Japan, business is treated formally in Korea and business travellers are expected to arrive punctually, wearing a suit and tie.

English is widely, if hesitatingly, spoken in commercial circles. Socialising is carried out much more in the home than in Japan. However, shoes should be removed before entering and do not raise business matters until your host does. Men sit cross-legged on the floor and women sit with their legs tucked beneath them. Despite

SOUTH KOREA - Introduction

this posture, it is considered impolite to stretch your legs. Give and receive gifts only with the right hand. Also like the Japanese, Koreans defer to age and position -in cars, the right-hand rear seat is the position of greatest seniority. Service charges are usually included in bills.

Tourism Update

General developments

Although Korea has a shorter travel season - cold winters keep most leisure travellers except skiers away for four months of the year - its overall total has reached almost four million.

The industry has made strong efforts to expand inbound travel, but exterior factors have also had an impact. The slowdown in travel between Korea and Taiwan, in both directions, followed Korea's diplomatic recognition of Beijing in 1992. This ended not only diplomatic ties and flights by airlines of the two countries, but also other travel facilitation such as visa issuance.

A *Visit Korea Year* promotion ran in 1994 but despite incentives (such as visa liberalisation, discount offers, etc) the 4 million visitors target was not achieved mainly because flights from Taiwan by the national airlines were not restarted.

Visitor arrivals increased 4.8% in 1995 to 3.8 million, but in 1996 there was a 2% fall to 3.7 million. Average length of stay is approximately five days.

The largest market, with nearly 45% of the total, was those with Japanese passports, but that was the main reason for the overall drop in 1996. Japanese fell 8% to 1.5 million, but Americans increased 11% to 399,000.

The next largest is Overseas Koreans - those travelling on Korean passports, but not living in Korea. These figures were not immediately available for 1996.

The Chinese total showed a good increase, for the third year running; it was up 12% to 200,000 in 1996. The Taiwanese market dropped still further, and compares with its peak of 296,000 in 1992. It was targeted to recover to reach 300,000 in 1994, but is still well short, dropping 12% to 115,000. The NTO targets 7 million visitors by 2000.

Efforts by the NTO to encourage travel over recent years include expositions, its *Visit Korea* promotion, and promoting the country's special-interest attractions, from mountaineering to shopping. The NTO's budget is approximately US$214 million.

Airlines

In 1989 the country's second airline, Asiana, started on international routes, one year after having been formed. This was significant for aviation in Korea and it still has an important effect. Asiana is now about one-third the size of Korean Air in fleet size, but near matches it in some route areas - such as to the US. Fierce competition between the two has helped spur outbound travel, and it is likely that there would be fewer visitors if Korea did not have both airlines.

Traffic at Korean Air has shown a steady increase every year for the past five years. This is impressive as the airline has faced strong competition from Asiana. In 1995, Korean Air recorded a 7.8% increase to 6.9 million seats sold, and a 14.0% increase in RPKs to 29,179 million. Korean Air took delivery of its first A330-300 Airbus in March 1997, the first of 13 to be delivered by the year 2000. It has another 35 Boeings on order by the end of the millenium. In march KE added a fifth London-Seoul Boeing 747-400 weekly frequency. In 1996, Asiana ordered 18 A321s for delivery starting 1998 and up to 2005.

Traffic at the airport matches the overall travel figures - most international flights leave from Seoul, although there are also routes from Cheju and Pusan in Korea to Japan. This was a sizeable increase on the international passenger total at Seoul's Kimpo airport. Growth there was 12.7% in 1995, taking the international count to 13,369,486. Growth was slightly slower in 1996, probably just over 10%.

Important for the future are plans to build a new airport for Seoul. This is expected to encourage airlines, particularly from North America, to use the airport s a hub for flights to other parts of Asia. It will be 52km from Seoul, with two runways. It is due to open in 2000, and is expected to handle 27 million passengers that year (domestic and international).

Hotels

A sizeable growth in hotels took place in time for the Summer Olympic Games in 1988. Construction slowed after this, and the travel industry is now concerned about a shortage of rooms in Seoul.

In the country overall, there was a 1.0% increase in the number of rooms in 1995 to 44,479. Most, about 17,000, were in Seoul, with another 4500 in Cheju. Of new hotels, the 402-room Ritz-Carlton opened in 1995 in Seoul; it was a partial rebuild of what was the Nam Seoul hotel, with a new wing.

Others announced to open in 1997 are: the 228-room Novotel Ambassador Kuro in **Seoul**; a 325-room Haeundae Grand and 900-room Lotte in **Pusan**; and a 208-room Holiday Inn in **Mokpo**. On **Cheju** island, a 312-room Renaissance is due in 1997, and a 500-room Lotte in 1998. In 1997 the Nam Seoul (under the same ownership as the Ritz-Carlton in Seoul) reopened as the 370-room Holiday Inn Crowne Plaza after being refurbished. More projects are expected as the island has been earmarked for more tourism development.

Two major corporate groups, Hyundai and Daewoo, are reported to be looking for opportunities to build new hotels, most probably in **Seoul**. There is also development at some of the country's ski resorts. **Muju Resort**, for instance, due to host an international ski event in 1997, has increased the number of slopes from 23 to 42. And **Phoenix Park Resort** is adding a hotel and aims to become a year-round resort.

According to figures from *Travel Business Analyst*, four-star hotels in Seoul recorded an 83% occupancy in 1995 at an average room rate of US$159. In 1996 these figures were running at 79% at US$173.

What to See

The first impression of Seoul is one of dull modern buildings and road congestion, but the city has its fair share of unexpected gems. Seoul has some fine old palaces, the most popular of which is Ch'ang-dokkung. It was rebuilt in 1611 and was in fact the royal residence until as recently as 1910. The palace has many royal relics and a collection of rare portraits.

Nearby, Ch'anggyonggung Palace has only just been fully restored to its former glory. A past official residence of King Kojong, Toksugung Palace, is equally attractive but is now best known for its splendid peony and chrysanthemum gardens. There are several other palaces that are well worth taking time out to visit.

No trip to Seoul is complete without a visit to Namdaemun - Seoul's Great South Gate. The Gate is considered to the nation's number one national treasure. Also recommended is the National Museum of Modern Art, the Seoul Sejong Cultural Center with its theatrical acts, musical performances and exhibitions by top Korean and sometimes foreign performers.

Outside Seoul, Chungnam Tourist Resort Complex on Chejudo is certainly worth a visit and its 11-hectare Yeomiji Botanical Gardens, which opened in October 1989, are certainly a must.

Lotte World also opened in 1989 and is the world's largest indoor theme park. It is located in Chamsil in the southeastern part of Seoul, close to the subway station with the same name on Line No.2. The complex is linked to its outdoor sister attraction - Magic World, built over Sokch'onhosum Lake. Entrance fee: adults W4,500, children W2,500. A second US$600 million Lotte World is due for completion in Pusan in 1993.

A visit to the almost surreal United United Command Advance Camp at P'anmunjom right on the DMZ that splits the two Koreas in half should be given a high priority. View such exotic sights as the *"Third Tunnel of Aggression,"* and wonder how the war has not restarted on a visit to the *"Conference Room"* that straddles the border.

It is here that frosty meetings between two sides still take place, but be careful not to make any sudden movement in this highly sensitive area where one soldier from each side stands off against his opposite number over an empty room. But given the recent thaw in east-west relations, P'anmunjom's days may well be numbered.

Shopping

Every visit to Seoul should include a trip to Itaewon - the city's excellent shopping district. In fact the entire area which grew up catering for foreigners now sells everything from sportswear and jogging shoes to leather and eel skin products.

Itaewon's best bargains are those items which are mass produced locally for export, such as Reebok trainers and ski-wear, golf-shoes and tennis racquets. As its name suggests, *Electroland*, is a massive multistorey department store that specialises in electronics - videos, computers and televisions.

Alternatively, Tongdaemun Market is Seoul's most colourful market-place and spreads across a 10-block section of the city. The market is especially good for shoes, fabrics such as silk, clothes, furniture, bedding, electronics and sports equipment. Namdaemun Market is close to Seoul's South Gate and smaller than Tongdaemun, but is much closer to the downtown hotel district. It is acclaimed for it's fine food and fish.

Seoul and other cities have a number of duty free shops, some of which specialise in the sale of fur. Major department stores open 1030-1930, but smaller shops tend to open from early morning till late evening every day of the week. Prices are fixed, so there is no haggling in the big stores.

For Korean antiques head down to the Hwang-hak-dong market on the eastern side of downtown Seoul - take the Subway Line No.1 or 4 to Tong-daemun station. Ignore the rather run-down buildings and street stalls that appear to have missed out on the city's rebuilding blitz and seek out some keenly-priced Korean curios, pottery, furniture et al. Similarly, *Insadong* or *Mary's Alley* is another area famed for its antiques and fine Korean art and handicrafts.

It's worth remembering that Value Added Tax (at 10 per cent) is levied on most goods Credit cards are accepted at major hotels, department stores and restaurants.

Getting Around

Both Korean Air and Asiana provide a fairly comprehensive domestic network linking 12 major cities. KE still operates the widest system and the most frequencies; although newcomer OZ is catching up fast. The longest journey time is about 60 minutes.

Four clean and efficient subway lines now serve Seoul. Line 1 runs through the heart of the city, connecting Seoul's two most important rail termini. Line 2 is a circular line that operates both above and under ground. Lines 3 and 4 criss-cross the city and connect both sides of the Han-gang River, passing through the downtown area. One way tickets inside the city cost just W 200.

The Korea National Railroad operates fast, reliable and moderately-priced services which run to a strict timetable. The rail network is not affected by road congestion and is often a more secure means of travelling around the country. The super-express *Saemaul-ho* trains ply between the main cities.

Taxis are plentiful and reasonably cheap and come in two sizes - the smaller taxis and medium-sized 88 cabs, which are bigger and more comfortable and naturally more expensive. There are taxi stands in most areas of Seoul. You can also hail a taxi in the street or you can obtain an 88 taxi by phone. An increasing number of drivers understand basic directions in English, but many visitors continue to complain about drivers refusing to pick up passengers unless they are going in the right direction. Also it is important to agree a fare in advance as there have been many complaints of overcharging in recent years.

Buses are the most common means of transport in Seoul. They are frequent and reliable and charge a fare of W 140 regardless of distance. These buses are often crowded and are clearly numbered. In addition there are city express buses, which stop less frequently.

Car rental is becoming more commonplace among visiting executives, especially those with business outside Seoul. Roads in Seoul are clogged with traffic and self-drive is not highly recommended. Much better to hire a car and driver at a cost of around W 20,000 a day.

Since September 1990, a new twice-weekly car ferry has connected Inchon with Weihai in China. The journey time is 17 hours and one-way ticket prices range upwards from US$ 90. A second car ferry route opened in March between Inchon and Tientsin (twice-weekly) by Cosmo Tiger Corporation. The crossing time is 27 hours. A sixth ferry route to Japan opened in December 1990 with a new link between Pusan and Hakada.

Entertainment

Seoul, in particular, has a lively and mixed nightlife embracing both local and western-style entertainment from discos to opera and ballet.

The shopping areas of Itaewon and Myong-dong are the principal areas in which discos, bars and club are concentrated.

The two areas are especially popular with US service personnel from the nearby Yongsan garrison; although efforts are being made to take them both up market.

Otherwise many of the hotels have their own bars and night clubs, with *Ninth Gate Lounge* at the recently refurbished Westin Chosun and the *Bobby London* at the Hotel Lotte popular. Most local bars operate a "happy hour" which for some reason last two hours between 6-8pm and during which drinks are not necessarily cheaper. Hostess bars are to be found around Seoul, often geared to (Japanese) business travellers.

Korea's long history of theatrical productions results in classical local dramas as well as the latest Broadway shows. It is also possible to seek out classical music concerts. Opera and ballet are usually performed at the smart Sejong Cultural Center or at the National Theater in Namsan Park.

Aside from many local restaurants serving Korean cooking, the city has a wide variety of US, Continental, Chinese and Japanese cuisine. The more select restaurants accept credit cards.

Korea has several licensed casinos. These tend to be located in the major hotels in Seoul, Inchon, Taejon, Pusan and Cheju.

Leisure

Major spectator sports include baseball and soccer. Golf is becoming increasingly popular among Korean executives and the country now has more than 40 courses.

Most tourist hotels in resort areas have either their own courses or easy access to them.

As one of the few states in the PATA area to experience chilly winters, Korea is emerging as a top ski centre as it starts to market its cold and snowy climate. The season lasts from early December to early-March and special events to accompany the snowfall are worth looking out for, such as the Snow Festival and the Snowman Contest. Korea has seven superbly equipped resorts - many of them close to Seoul - and there is no shortage of nightlife.

A particular favourite side trip for many visitors is a weekend break in Chejudo - Korea's honeymoon island. The island combines rugged mountain scenery with some of Korea's beaches with a Mediterranean-type climate. Visitors will find rural tranquillity after the hectic pace of weekday Seoul. Chejudo also boasts a vast array of leisure activities - swimming, tennis and golf plus restaurants, bars and casinos. Koreans are keen sea fishermen and Chejudo is considered one of the best spots. Daily flights from Seoul take about an hour and cost W40,300 one-way.

Arrival & Departure

Korea has three international airports - Seoul's Kimpo, Kimhae in Pusan and on the holiday island of Chejudo in the south. Pusan and Cheju are only gateways for short-haul flights, mainly from Japan.

Allow 40 minutes to get from Kimpo to Seoul's downtown area by taxi (ca.W12000), longer by airport bus which costs W 600. There are two airport express buses - Nos. 600 and 601, which connect Kimpo with the major hotels in Seoul. Passengers departing on Northwest, Asiana, Cathay and Aeroflot can now check inat the Korea City Air Terminal. Anyone can report to the KCAT; buses leave for Kimpo every 10 minutes between 0605-2215 hrs. Departure tax on international flights is W8000.

Korea Key Fact File

Passport Requirements:
All visitors to Korea must have a valid passport. Travellers with confirmed outbound ticket can stay for 15 days without a visa. EEC Nationals may stay up to 60 days without a visa; most other countries 90 days; nationals from japan and South Africa require a visa for all visits.

Currency:
South Korean Won(W); 100 chon = 1W

Exchange Rates:
US$ = 864W; £1 = 1410 W (*May 1997*)

Currency Restrictions:
Up to US$5,000, or its equivalent, can be brought in provided it is declared on arrival. Unused local currency can be reconverted upon presentation of certificate of Foreign Exchange purchases up to the amount changed.

Electricity Supply:
110 and 220 volts, AC 60 Hz (110 volt supply gradually being phased out)

Language:
Korean, some Chinese, Japanese and English also spoken.

Time:
GMT + 9; EDT + 14 hours

IDD Code: 82
Area codes: Cheju 641; Ch'onan 417; Ch'ongju 431; Chonju 652; Ch'ungju 441; Inchon 32; Pusan 51; Seoul 2; Taegu 53; Taejon 42

Business Hours:
Commercial offices are open 0900-1200, 1300-1800 Monday to Friday; 0900-1300 Saturdays.
Government offices are open 0900-1200, 1300-1700 Monday to Friday; 0900-1300 Saturdays.
Banks are open 0930-1630 Monday to Friday; 0930-1300 Saturdays.

Customs & Entry:
Duty-free allowance comprises two bottles of alcohol not exceeding 1,520cc; 400 cigarettes, 50 cigars, 200 grammes of pipe tobbaco and 100 grammes of other tobacco.

Health Requirements:
No vaccinations are needed to enter South Korea from any country. Vaccinations against cholera and yellow fever are recommended for visitors arriving from infected areas.

Climate/Best time to visit:
South Korea experiences four very distinct seasons marked by cold dry winters (min. -10°, max 2°C) and hot, wet summers (min. 18°, max 30°C - humidity 80%). February to June best months for business visits; Autumn best for tourism.

National Holidays 1997:
1-2 January New Year's Holiday; 6-8 February Lunar New Year; 1 March Independence Movement Day; 5 April Arbor Day; 5 May Children's Day; 14 May Buddha's Birthday; 6 June Memorial Day; 17 July Constitution Day; 15 August Liberation Day; 15-17 September Ch'usok (Korean Thanksgiving) Day; 3 October National Foundation Day; December 25 Christmas Day.

Useful Addresses

Public Offices & Organisations

American Chamber of Commerce
Sogong-dong, Chung-gu, Seoul.Tel:753 6471

Association of Foreign Trading Agents of Korea
Dong Jln B/D, 218 Hankang-ro, 2-ka, Yongsan-ku, Seoul
Tel: (2) 792 1581; Fax: (2) 785 4373

Central Bank (Bank of Korea)
110, 3 ka, Namdaemun-ro, Chuing-ku. Tel: 759 4114

Federation of Korean Industries
28-1 Youido-dong, Yongdungpo-gu, Seoul. Tel: 783 0821; Tlx: 25544; Fax: 784 1340

Korea Chamber of Commerce & Industry
45, 4-ga Namdaemun-ro, Chung-gu, Seoul. Tel: 757 0757; Tlx: 25728 CHAMBER K

Korea World Trade Center,Korea Exhibition Center,Yongdongdaero, Samsong, Seoul. Tel: 553 7907

Korea Export Industry Corporation
Kongdanno, Kurogongdan, Seoul.
Tel: 856 5781

Korea Federation of Small Businesses
Youido Plaza, Seoul. Tel: 785 0010; Tlx: 734 2731; Fax: 737 3713

Korea National Tourism Corporation
10, Ta-dong, Chung-gu, Seoul. Tel: 757 6030; Tlx: KOTOUR K 28555; Fax: 757 5997

Korea Overseas Development Corporation
Taehakno, Wonnam-dong, Seoul. Tel: 764 0161

Korea Tourist Association
9F Kyongwun Bldg, 70 Kyungwun-dong, Chongno-gu. Tel: 757 2345

Korea Trade Promotion Corporation
159 Samsundong, Kangnam-ku Seoul
Tel: 551 4181

Korea Traders' Association
10-1, 2-ga Hoehyon-dong, Chung-gu, Seoul. Tel: 77141; Tlx: K 24265; Fax: 754 1337

Post Office, Police, Hospitals

Seoul Central Post Office
Ch'ungmuro, Chung-gu, Seoul. Tel: 776 0014

Seoul Metropolitan Police Dept
Namdaemunno 3-ga, Seoul. Tel: 755 4400/ 774 8800. *Emergencies:* Tel: 112

Koryo General Hospital
P'yong-dong, Chongno-gu, Seoul. Tel: 739 3211

Seoul National University Hospital
Yongondong, Chongno-gu, Seoul. Tel: 760 2114

St Mary's Hospital
Youido-dong, Yongdungp'o-gu, Seoul. Tel: 789 1114

Air Couriers

DHL: Seoul (02) 716 0001; Pusan (51)444921; Inchon (032) 428 5611; Pohang (051) Taegu (053) 235735; Ulsan (0522) 722884
Federal Express: Seoul (02) 333 8000
UPS: Seoul (02) 366 53651
TNT Express Worldwide: (02) 660 161/ 669 0422; Pusan (51) 554 6661

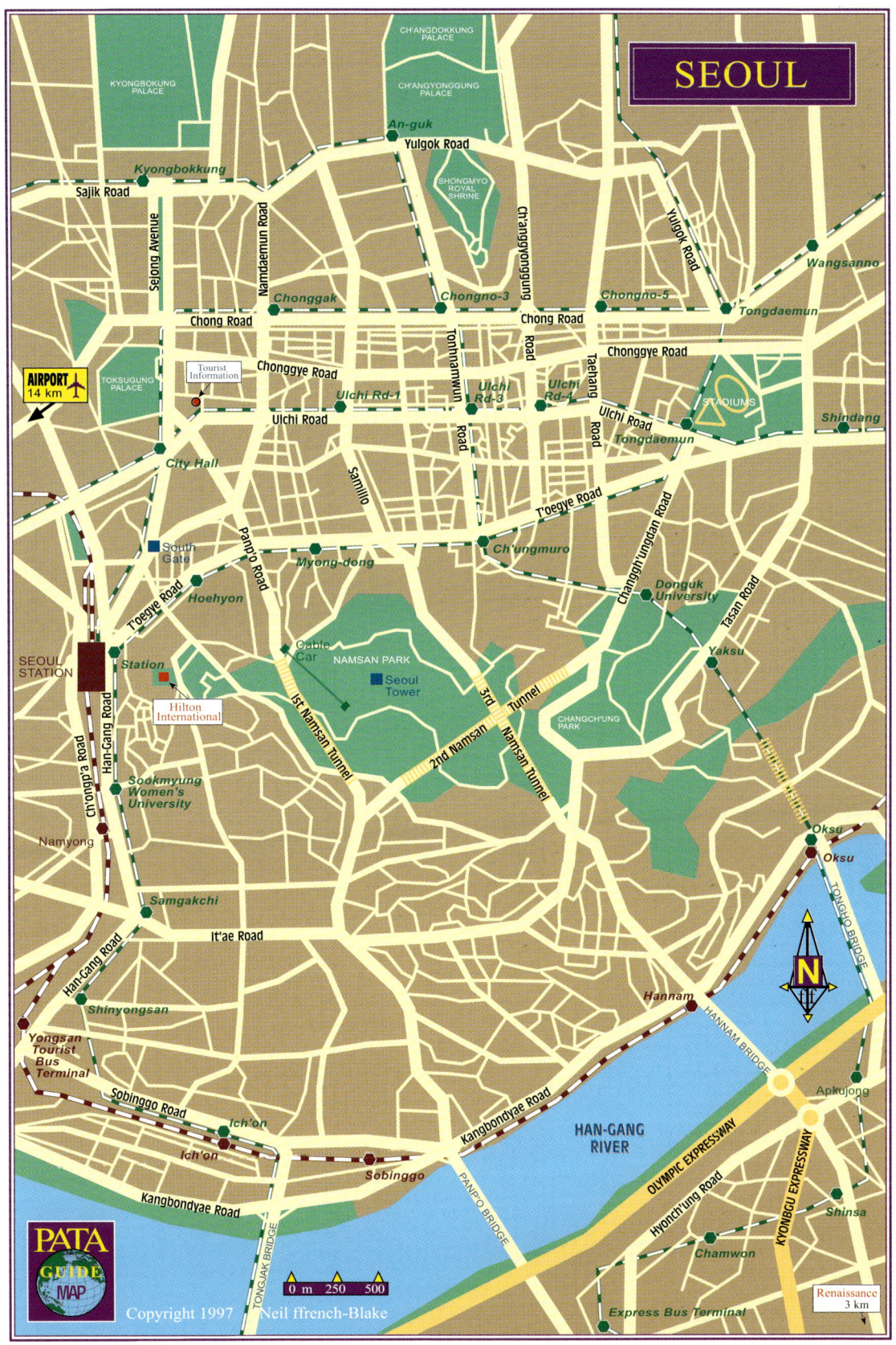

South Korea Hotel Reference Table

Hotel (listed in price order)	SINGLE ROOM RATE (US $)	LOCATION	NUMBER OF ROOMS	NUMBER OF SUITES	CONFERENCE FACILITIES	EXHIBITION SPACE	LARGEST BANQUET NUMBER	BUSINESS CENTRE	SWIMMING POOL (0 = indoor)	TENNIS COURT	HEALTH CLUB	VIDEO FILMS
Seoul Inter-Continental	250	Seoul	379	221	●	●	1400	●	O	-	●	●
Seoul Renaissance Hotel	238	Seoul	471	19	●	●	730	●	O	-	●	●
Seoul Hilton International	237-300	Seoul	653	43	●	●	2000	●	O	-	●	●
Hotel Shilla	230	Seoul	640	53	●	●	2000	●	●	-	●	●
Sheraton Walker Hill	230	Seoul	600	30	●	●	1000	●	●	●	●	●
Westin Chosun Hotel	220	Seoul	463	17	●	●	450	●	O	-	●	●
Hotel Lotte	220	Seoul	1369	115	●	●	1500	●	O	-	●	●
Ritz Carlton Seoul	212	Seoul	352	50	●	●	400	●	O	-	●	●
Hotel Lotte World	211	Seoul	489	45	●	●	1500	●	O	-	●	●
Seoul Plaza Hotel	207	Seoul	530	11	●	●	350	●	-	-	-	●
Novotel Ambassador	195	Seoul	329	9	●	●	250	●	O	-	●	●
Amiga Hotel	195	Seoul	190	10	●	-	350	●	O	-	●	●
Cheju Shilla	185	Cheju-do	330	-	-	-	400	-	O	●	●	●
Sofitel Ambassador	183	Seoul	400	50	●	●	600	●	-	-	●	●
Koreana Hotel	183	Seoul	280	2	●	-	290	●	-	-	●	●
Swiss Grand Hotel	170	Seoul	361	39	●	●	1200	●	O	-	●	●
Sejong Hotel	170	Seoul	235	-	●	●	300	●	-	-	●	●
Grand Hyatt Seoul	165	Seoul	604	32	●	●	2000	●	●	●	●	●
Nam Seoul Washington	155	Seoul	189	17	●	-	-	●	-	-	●	●
Ramada Olympia Hotel	150	Seoul	271	29	●	-	1000	●	O	-	●	●
Kyongju Hilton	150	Kyong-ju	274	50	●	●	600	●	●	●	●	●
Hotel President	150	Seoul	303	20	●	-	400	●	-	-	●	●
Hyatt Regency Pusan	146	Pusan	326	38	●	-	300	●	O	-	●	●
Kolon Hotel	146	Kyongju	309	7	●	-	1000	-	●	●	●	●
Seoul Garden Hotel	146	Seoul	348	5	●	●	600	●	-	-	●	●
Seoul Royal Hotel	146	Seoul	274	26	●	●	200	●	-	-	●	●
Hotel New World	145	Seoul	197	19	●	-	-	●	O	-	●	●
Hotel Capital	145	Seoul	269	18	●	-	-	●	O	-	●	●
Westin Chosun Beach	140	Pusan	280	10	●	●	500	●	●	●	●	●
Hotel Riviera Seoul	125	Seoul	227	23	-	-	-	●	-	-	●	●
Hotel Riverside	125	Seoul	226	4	●	-	300	-	-	-	●	●
Pacific Hotel	122	Seoul	115	5	●	-	-	-	-	-	●	●
Seoul Palace Hotel	120	Seoul	278	6	●	-	-300	●	-	-	●	●
Taedok Hotel Lotte	116	Taejon	60	9	●	-	400	-	-	-	●	●
Paradise Beach Hotel	115	Pusan	250	38	●	●	200	●	●	-	●	●
New Seoul Hotel	89	Seoul	208	9	-	-	-	-	-	-	●	●
Kyongju Tokyu (Concorde)	107	Kyongju	272	31	●	-	1200	-	-	-	-	●
Hotel Riviera Yusung	107	Chung'-do	36	91	-	-	-	-	-	-	-	-
Dragon Valley	106	Kangnam-ku	26	165	-	-	-	-	O	●	●	-
Hamilton Hotel	103	Seoul	127	12	●	-	-	●	●	-	-	●
Kyongju Chosun Hotel	100	Kyongju	239	61	●	●	-	●	-	●	●	●
Hotel Core	100	Chollabuk-do	56	54	-	-	-	-	-	-	-	-
Hyatt Regency Cheju	97	Cheju-do	185	15	●	●	300	●	O	-	●	●
Seoulin Hotel	96	Seoul	203	4	●	-	-	●	-	-	●	●
Cheju Grand Hotel	95	Cheju-do	524	35	●	●	700	-	●	-	●	●
Commodore Dynasty Hotel	94	Pusan	298	18	●	-	490	-	●	-	●	●
New Seoul Hotel	89	Seoul	208	9	-	-	-	-	-	-	●	-
Hotel Kumho	88	Taegu	65	29	-	-	-	-	-	-	-	-
Cheju Prince Hotel	83	Cheju-do	170	50	-	-	-	●	●	-	●	●
Cheju Namseoul	85	Cheju-do	159	23	●	●	150	●	O	-	●	●
Tower Hotel	79	Seoul	205	-	●	-	300	●	-	●	●	●
Ulsan Koreana Hotel	75	Ulsan City	143	1	●	●	200	●	-	●	●	●
Bugok Royal Hotel	70	Kyong'sam-do	44	114	-	-	-	-	-	-	-	-
Phoenix Hotel	64	Pusan	96	110	-	-	200	-	-	-	-	-
Hotel Sorabol	49	Pusan	152	10	-	-	200	-	-	-	-	-

South Korea Hotels

Pusan

Commodore Hotel D
743-80 Youngju-dong, Chung-ku
Tel: (51) 466 9101; Tlx: 53717 COMOTEL K; Fax: 462 9101

Hotel Lotte Pusan §
503-15 Pujeon-Dong, Pusanninku
Tel: (51) 810 1000; Fax: 810 5609

Hyatt Regency Pusan C
1405-16, Chung-dong, Haeundae-gu
Tel: (51) 743 1234; Tlx: 52668; Fax: 743 1250

Paradise Beach Hotel ☼ C
1408-5 Chong-dong, Haeundae-ku
Tel: 742 2121; Tlx: PARABH K 52145; Fax: 742 2100

The Phoenix Hotel D
8-1, 5-ga, Nampo-dong, Chung-gu
Tel: 245 8061; Tlx: K 53704; Fax: 241 1523

Hotel Sorabol C
37-1, 1 ga, Taechong-dong, Chung-gu
Tel: 463 3511-19; Tlx: 3827; Fax: 463 3510

Westin Chosun Beach Hotel ☼ C
737, Woo 1-dong, Haeundae-ku
Tel: (51) 742 7411; Tlx: 53718 CHOSUNB K; Fax: 742 1313

Seoul

Hotel Amiga A
248-7 Nonhyon-Dong, Kangnam-gu, 135010
Tel: 3440 8010; Fax: 3440 8025

Hotel Capital D
22-76 It'aewon-dong, Songp'a-gu
Tel: 792 1122; Tlx: HCAPITL K 23502; Fax: 796 0918

Grand Hyatt Seoul B
747-7 Hannam-dong, Yongsan-ku
Tel: 797 1234; Tlx: 24136 HYATT K; Fax: 798 6953

Hamilton Hotel C
119-25 Itaewon-dong, Yongsan-ku, Seoul 140
Tel: 794 0171; Tlx: 24491; Fax: 795 0457

Hotel Inter-Continental Seoul ☼ A
Young Dong PO Box 975, Seoul 135-609
Tel: 555 5656; Tlx: K34254; Fax: 559 7991

Koreana Hotel ☼ C
61, 1-ga, Taep'yongno, Chung-gu
Tel: 720 9911/20; Tlx: 26241 KOTEL K; Fax: 734 0665

Hotel Lotte ☼ A
1 Sogong-dong, Chung-ku, CPO Box 3500, Seoul 100-070
Tel: 771 1000; Tlx: K 23533/4 LOTTEHO; Fax: 752 3758

Hotel Lotte World A
40-1, Chamshil-dong, Songpa-ku, Songpa PO Box 66, Seoul
Tel: 419 7000; Tlx: K 33728 LOTTEHW; Fax: 417 3655/6

Metro Hotel E
199-33, 2-ka, Eulchiro, Chung-ku, Seoul 100 192
Tel: 752 1112; Tlx: 26486; Fax: 757 4411

Nam Seoul Washington Hotel B
602-4 Yeok San-dong, Kangnam-gu
Tel: 552 7111; Tlx: 25019 K; Fax: 556 8855

New Seoul Hotel ☼ D
29-1, 1-ka, Taipyung-ro, Chung-ku
Tel: 735 9071-9; Tlx: 27220; Fax: 735 6212

Hotel New World B
112-5 Samsong-dong, Kangnam-gu
Tel: 557 0111; Tlx: K 33226; Fax: 557 0141

Novotel Ambassador Seoul ☼ C
603 Yoksam-Dong, Kangnam-ku, 135-080
Tel: 567 1101; Fax: 564 4573

Olympia Hotel Seoul B
108-2 Pyonchang-Dong, 110012
Tel: 287 6000; Fax: 396 6633

Pacific Hotel D
31-1 Nam San Dong, Chung-ku
Tel: 777 7811; Tlx: 26249; Fax: 755 5582

Hotel President ☼ D
188-3. 1-ka, Ulchiro, Chung-gu
Tel: 753 3131/9; Tlx: K 27521; Fax: 752 7417

Ramada Olympia Hotel Seoul ☼ B
108-2, P'yonch'ang-dong, Chongro-ku
Tel: 287 6000; Tlx: RAMADA K 23171; Fax: 396 6633

The Ritz-Carlton Seoul A
602 Yeok Sam-Done, Kangnam-Ku
Tel: 3451 8000; Fax: 556 8855

Hotel Riviera Seoul ☼ D
53-7, Ch'ongdam-dong, Kangnam-gu
Tel: 541 3111; Tlx: K 32465; Fax: 546 6111

Hotel Riverside C
6-1, Chamwon-dong, Socho-gu, 13400
Tel: 543 1001; Tlx: 22063 RIVTEL K; Fax: 514 7998

Savoy Hotel E
23-1, 1-ka, Chungmu-ro, Chung-ku
Tel: 776 2641; Tlx: 23222; Fax: 755 7669

Sejong Hotel ☼ C
61-3, 2-ga, Ch'ungmuro, Chung-gu
Tel: 773 6000; Tlx: 27265 SEJONTE K; Fax: 771 4179

Seoulin Hotel C
149 Sorin-dong, Chongno-gu
Tel: 732 0181; Tlx: 28510 SEOULIN K; Fax: 732 2774

Seoul Garden Hotel C
169-1, Tohwa-dong, Map'o-gu
Tel: 717 9441; Tlx: SGARDEN K 24742; Fax: 715 9441

Seoul Hilton ☼
395, 5-ga, Namdaemun-ro, Chung-ku
Tel: 753 7788; Tlx: 26695 KHILTON; Fax: 754 2510

Nestling in the foothills of Mt Namsan and with commanding views of the city, the Seoul Hilton is locatd at the heart of the business district and is a short stroll from the bustling Namdaemun Market. The majestic Kyungbok Palace is close by, and a 20-minute shuttle bus takes you to the shopping district of Itaewon.

Accommodation
696 rooms, inc. suites & executive floor

Rates:
Single US$ 237-300; double US$ 262-325; suite US$ 527-937.
Subject to 11% tax and 10% service charge

Credit cards accepted:
Amex, Diners, Master, Visa, JCB

Meeting & conference facilities
9 meeting/conference rooms, capacity up to 5000 pax with full audio-visual facilities; 2368 sq m exhibition space; largest reception 2000 seated or 3500 cocktail.

Room services
Airconditioning, colour TV, direct-dial telephone (ext. in bathroom), hairdryer, laundry/valet service, minibar, music/radio/alarm clock, safety deposit box, 24-hr room service, shoeshine service, trouser press, non-smoker bedrooms available, pay video channels

178 SOUTH KOREA - Hotels

Business services
Business centre, executive floor, express checkout, translation service, car parking, car rental, travel centre, taxi service, courier services

Other services
Barber shop/hairdresser, beauty salon, guided tours, newsstand/shops, free shuttle to Itaewon, duty free shop

Sports & Recreation
Billiards/snooker, fitness centre/gym, golf driving range, jacuzzi, massage, sauna, jogging track (summer only) indoor swimming pool, aerobic studio

Restaurants & Coffee Shops
Garden View (123) - popular priced coffee shop, open 0600-midnight; *Genji* (60) - Japanese, open noon-2200; *The Phoenix* (108) - Chinese, open as above; *Sura* (40) - Korean, open as above; *Il Ponte* (83) - Italian, open as above; *The Seasons* (75) - French, open noon-2230; *Orangerie* (250) - international buffet, open 0700-2200

Overseas Sales Representatives:
Hilton International Worldwide

Seoul Palace Hotel   C
63-1 Panp'o-dong, Soch'o-gu
Tel: 532 0101; Tlx: 22657 PALACHL K; Fax: 532 0399

Seoul Plaza   A
23, 2-ga, T'aep'yongno, Chung-gu
Tel: 771 2200; Tlx: 24424 PLAZAHL K; Fax: 755 8897

Sheraton Walker Hill   A
San 21, Kwangjang-dong, Songdong-gu
Tel: 453 0121/0131; Tlx: 28517 WALKHTL K; Fax: 452 6867

Hotel Shilla   ○ B
202, 2-ga, Changch'ung-dong, Chung-gu
Tel: 233 3131/230 3114; Tlx: 24160 SHILLA K; Fax: 233 5073

Hotel Sofitel Ambassador   ○ B
342-1, Shinsa-dong, Kangnam-gu
Tel: 270 3111; Tlx: 22063; Fax: 272 0773

○ = Allied Hotel Member of the Pacific Asia Travel Association (PATA)

Seoul Renaissance Hotel   ○
676, Yoksam-dong, Kangnam-ku, 135-080
Tel: 555 0501; Tlx: RAMDAS K 34392; Fax: 553 8118

The 23-storey hotel is located south of Han river in the heart of the Kangnam commercial district, close to the Korea Exhibition Center, Korea World Trade Center and Olympic Park.

Accommodation
212 single; 259 twin; 19 suites; 7 Korean-style ondol

Rates:
Single/double/twin W195,000-340,000; suite W420,000-2,500,000

Credit cards accepted:
Amex, Diners, JCB, Mastercard, Visa

Meeting & conference facilities
8 meeting/function rooms, capacity up to 1740; with full audio-visual facilities; 1562 sq m exhibition space; largest reception 730 seated or 1200 cocktail; 6 private dining rooms

Room services
Airconditioning, colour TV, direct-dial telephone (ext. in bathroom), hairdryer, laundry/valet service, minibar, music/radio/alarm clock, safety deposit box, 24-hr room service, non-smoker bedrooms available, computer modem

Business services
Business centre, executive floor, express checkout, translation service, car parking/rental, travel centre, taxi service, free shuttle bus service to Itaewon shopping district

Other services
Barber shop/hairdresser, beauty salon, guided tours, newsstand/shops

Sports & Recreation
Indoor games, golf (driving range), fitness centre/gym, jogging track, massage, sauna, squash, tennis, indoor swimming pool

Restaurants & Coffee Shops
Noblesse (140) - Speciality Restaurant/bar, open 1200-1500/1800-2230; *Toscana* (75) - Italian, open as above; *Kabin* (110) - Chinese, open as above til 2200; *Sabiru* (78) Korean, open as above; *Ilroduri* (152) - Japanese, open 0700-1000 & as above.

Overseas Sales Representatives:
Renaissance and Stouffer worldwide sales offices - Australia fax: (61) -2-251-8491; Europe fax: (44) 1293 823 923; Hong Kong fax: (852) 877 6600; Japan fax: (81) 3-3239 6986; North America fax: (1) 312 372 4560; USA/Canada fax: (1) 216 349 2687

Seoul Royal Hotel   D
6, 1-ga, Myong-dong, Chung-gu
Tel: 756 1112; Tlx: 27239 ROYAL K; Fax: 756 1119

The Swiss Grand Hotel   ○ B
201-1 Hongeun-dong, Suhdaimoon-ku
Tel: 356 5656; Tlx: 34322 SGHSEL K; Fax: 356 7799

Tower Hotel   C
5-5 San, 2-Ka, Chang Chung-dong, Chunggu
Tel: 236 2121; Tlx: 28246; Fax: 235 0276

The Westin Chosun Hotel   ○ A
CPO Box 3706, 87 Sogong-dong, Chung-ku
Tel: 771 0500; Tlx: CHOSUN K24256; Fax: 756 8848/752 1443

Other areas

Bugok Royal Hotel   D
215-1, Komun-ri, Pugok-myon, Ch'angnyong-gun, **Kyongsangnam-do**
Tel: (0559) 36 5181; Fax: (0559) 36 6427

Cheju Grand Hotel   ○ C
263-15, Yon-dong, **Cheju**
Tel: (064) 47 5000; Tlx: 66712 GRANHTL K; Fax: 42 3150

Cheju Namseoul Hotel   D
291-30 Yondong, Cheju City, **Chejudo**
Tel: (064) 42 4111; Fax: (064) 46 4111

Cheju Prince Hotel   ○ D
731-3 Seohong-Dong, Cheju-si, **Cheju-do**
Tel: (064) 32 9911; Fax: (064) 32 9900

Cheju Shilla Hotel   B
3060 Saekdal-dong, Cheju-do
Tel: 33 4466; Fax: 33 2823

Do Go Spa Hotel   E
180-1, Kigok-ri, Togo-myon, Asan-gun, **Ch'ungch'ongnam-do**
Tel: (0418)43 5511; Fax: 43 5520

Hotel Core D
627-3, So-nosong-dong, Chonju, **Chollabuk-do**
Tel: (0652) 85 1100/(02) 713 3814; Tlx: HANSHIN K 66613; Fax: 0652 85 5707

Dragon Valley Hotel ○ B
1 Nonhyun-Dong, Kangnam-ku
Tel: 511 1562-5; Tlx: 24270; Fax: 548 2458

Hotel Kumho D
28 Haso-dong, Chung-gu, **Taegu**
Tel: (053) 252 6001; Tlx: K 54545; Fax: 253 4121

Hotel Riviera Yusung C
478, Pongmyong-dong, So-gu, Taejon-shi, **Ch'ungch'ongnam-do**
Tel: (042) 823 2111; Fax: 822 5250

Hyatt Regency Cheju B
3039-1 Saekai-dong, Seogwipo-si, **Cheju-do**, (Choongmoon Beach)
Tel: (064) 33 1234; Tlx: 66749 NAMJU K; Fax: 064 32 2039

Kyongju Hilton B
370 Shinpyong-Dong, Kyongju City, Kyungsangbuk-do
Tel: (561) 745 7788; Fax: (561) 745 7799

In the south-eastern area of the Korean peninsula, the Kyongju Hilton is located in the Pomun Lake Resort, four miles notheast of Kyongju City. In the leisurely, tranquil and historic atmosphere, the 2750 acre resort consists of golf course, shopping arcades, Shilla village, Kyongju World Amusement Park. For families, as well as the rich historic relics of the ancient capital city of the Shilla..

Accommodation
274 rooms, 50 suites

Rates:
Single/double/twin W165,000; suite W200,000-210,000.
Subject to 10% tax & 10% service charge

Credit cards accepted:
Amex, Diners, Mastercard, Visa

Groups
7 meeting/function rooms, capacity up to 1050, with full audio-visual facilities; 758 sq m exhibition space; largest reception 600 seated or 900 cocktail.

Room services
Airconditioning, colour TV, direct-dial

telephone, hairdryer, laundry/valet service, minibar, music/radio/alarm clock, safety deposit box, tea/coffee making facilities, 24-hr room service, non-smoker bedrooms available, video films, satellite TV

Business services
Business centre, executive floor, express checkout, airport pickup, translation service, car parking/ rental, travel centre, taxi service

Other services
Barber shop/hairdresser, beauty salon, guided tours, newsstand/shops, duty free shop

Sports & Recreation
Fitness centre/gym, massage, sauna, outdoor/ indoor swimming pools, tennis, squash, golf course nearby

Restaurants & Coffee Shops
Lakeside (132), buffet/continental, open 0700-2300; *Genji* (95); Japanese, open noon-2230; *Silkroad* (84), Chinese; *Okpiri* (46) - Korean, open as above.

Kolon Hotel ○ D
111-1, Ma-dong, Kyongju, **Kyongsangbuk-do**
Tel: (0561) 2 9001/11; Tlx: 54469 K; Fax: 43 6331

Kyongju Chosun Hotel ○ C
410, Shinp'yong-dong, Kyongju, **Kyongsangbuk-do**
(0561) 745 7701; Tlx: 54328/54467 CHOSUNK K; Fax: 408349

Kyongju Tokyu Hotel ○ C
410, Shinp'yong-dong, Kyongju, **Kyongsangbuk-do**
Tel: (0561) 429901; Tlx: 54328; Fax: 429916

Taedok Hotel Lotte D
382 Doryong-dong, Yusong-ku, Taejon
Tel: (042) 865 7000; Fax: (042) 862 0059

Ulsan Koreana Hotel D
255-3, Songnam-dong, Chung-gu, Ulsan City 690-00, **Kyongsangnam-do**
Tel: (0522) 44 9911/20; Tlx: 52550 KOTEL K; Fax: 0522 44 1665

Hotel Classification: **A** *after name of hotel = over US$ 200 per person per night;* **B** *= between US$ 150 - 200;* **C** *= between US$ 100 - 150;* **D** *= between US$ 50 - 100;* **E** *= under US$ 50;* **§**= *prices on application.*

Restaurants

Many of Korea's best ethnic, Japanese, Chinese and Western-style restaurants are situated in the international and business class hotels listed above. Below we list a selection both of these and of other town centre restaurants popular with business people, where credit cards are accepted, and where prior booking is recommended.

Seoul - Korean

Asadal
Plaza Hotel, 23 Taepyong-no 2-ka, Chung-ku. Tel: 771 2200

Bright Moon Hall
Sheraton Walker Hill Hotel, San 21, Kwanggjang-dong, Songdong-gu. Tel: 453 0121

Gardenia
2nd Fl, Hotel Lotte, 1 Sogong-dong, Chung-gu. Tel: 771 1000

Lee Hak
52-13, Myong-dong 2 ga, Chung-gu. Tel: 776 1561

Ka Ya Rang
239-4, It'aewon-dong, Yongsan-gu. Tel: 797 4000

Korea House *(Theatre-Restaurant)*
80-2, P'il-dong 2-ga, Chung-gu.
Tel: 266 9101

Mu Gung Hwa
Lower level, Hotel Lotte, 1 Sogong-dong, Chung-gu. Tel: 771 1000

Nak San Garden
1-36, Tongsung-dong, Chongno-gu.
Tel: 742 7470

Po Suk Yung *(Theatre-Restaurant)*
Hotel Lotte, 1, Sogong-dong, Chung-gu.
Tel: 771 1000

Sanchon
2-2, Kwanhun-dong, Chongno-gu.
Tel: 735 1900

Samwon Garden
Apkujongdong. Tel: 544 5351

Sorabol
2nd Fl, Hotel Shilla, 202 Changch'ung-dong 2-ga, Chung-gu. Tel: 233 3131

Taewongak
323, Songbuk-dong, Songbuk-gu. Tel: 762 0034

Seoul - non-Korean

Ariake *(Japanese Kaiseki)*
2nd Fl, Hotel Shilla, 202 Changch'ung-dong 2-ga, Chung-gu. Tel: 233 3131

Ashoka *(Indian)*
Hamilton Hotel, 119-25 Itaewon-dong, Yongssan-ku. Tel: 794 0171

Baron's Restaurant (French)
Hotel Inter-Continental, 159-1 Samsong-dong, Kangnam-gu.
Tel: 553 8181 ext 7631.

Benkay (Japanese)
Lower level, Hotel Lotte, 1 Sogong-dong, Chung-gu. Tel: 771 1000

Bohemian (American & French)
27-2, Youido-dong, Yongdungp'o-gu.
Tel: 783 8867

Chalet Swiss (Swiss)
104-4, It'aewon-dong, Yongsan-gu.
Tel: 797 9664

Dah Han Gerth (Chinese)
130-17 Chamwon-dong, Soch'o-gu.
Tel: 590 0266

Daesanghae (Chinese)
Koreana Hotel, 61, 1-ga, Taep'yongno, Chung-gu. Tel: 720 9911

Dongbosong (Chinese)
50-8 Namsan-dong 2-ga, Chung-gu.
Tel: 755 2727

Four Seasons (French)
Seoul Hilton International, 395 5-ga, Namdaemunro, Chung-gu. Tel: 753 7788

Hugo's (French)
Hyatt Regency Seoul Hotel, 747-7 Hannam-dong, Yongsan-ku. Tel: 798 0061

Il Ponte (Italian)
Seoul Hilton International, 395 5-ga, Namdaemunro, Chung-gu. Tel: 753 7788

L'Abri (French)
1-Bun-ji, 1ka Chongro, Chongru-gu.
Tel: 739 8830

La Cantina (Italian)
Lower level, Samsung Bldg, 50 Ulchiro 1-ga, Chung-gu. Tel: 777 2579

Man Dang (Japanese)
662-7, Yoksam-dong, Kangnam-gu.
Tel: 566 1858

Moghul Restaurant (Pakistani & Indian)
116-2, It'aewon-dong, Yongsan-gu.
Tel: 796 5501

Momoyama (Japanese)
Hotel Lotte World, 40-1, Chamshil-dong, Songpa-ku. Tel: 419 7000

9th Gate (French)
Westin Chosun Hotel, 87 Sogong-dong, Chung-gu. Tel: 771 0500

Paengni Hyang (Chinese)
DLI Bldg, 57th Fl, Yoido-dong, Yongdungpo-gu. Tel: 789 5741

Sunwon Restaurant (Japanese)
Seoulin Hotel, 149 Sorin-dong.
Tel: 732 0181

Shanghai (Chinese)
Lower level, Hotel Lotte, 1 Sogong-dong, Chung-gu. Tel 771 1000

World Trade Centre Club (Western & Chinese)
10-1, Hoehyon-dong 2-ga, Chung-gu.
Tel:755 4863

Yesterday (European)
Westin Chosun Hotel, 87 SoKong-dong, Chung-gu. Tel: 771 0500

Pusan

Chung Tap Grill (International)
36 Namp'o-dong 2-ga, Chung-gu. Tel: (051) 23 0071

Dong Baek (Japanese)
2nd Fl, Hotel Sorabol, 37-1, Taech'ong-dong 1-ga, Chung-gu. Tel: 463 3511

Ever Spring Park (Korean)
178-7, Onch'on-dong, Tongnae-gu. Tel: 53 1800

Keum Mun (Chinese - Szechuan)
2nd Fl, Hotel Sorabol, 37-1, Taech'ong-dong 1-ga, Chung-gu. Tel: 463 3511

Kyongju

Geo Goo Yang (Korean)
220 Shinp'yong-dong. Tel: (0561) 42-8624

Hobanjang (Korean)
Kyongju Tokyu Hotel, 410 Shinp'yong-dong. Tel 42-9901

King's Arms (Western)
1st Fl, Kyongju Tokyu Hotel, 410 Shinp'yong-dong. Tel: 42-9901

Lotus (Japanese)
2nd Fl, Kyongju Kolon Hotel, 111-1 Ma-dong. Tel: 42-9001

Cheju

Fontainebleau (Western)
Cheju Grand Hotel, 263-15 Yon-dong.
Tel: (064) 42-3321

Haewon (Korean)
Hyatt Regency Cheju, 3039-1 Saektal-dong, Sogwip'o. Tel: 32-2001

Umibe (Japanese)
Hyatt Regebcy Cheju, 3039-1 Saektal-dong. Tel: 32-2001

Airline Offices

Air France
Room 236, Chosun Hotel
87 Sogong-dong, Chung-gu, Seoul
Tel:(02) 753-2574/773 3151

All Nippon Airways (ANA)
c/o Room 102, Kum Jeong Building
192-11, I-ka Eulji-Ro, Chung-ku, Seoul 100
Tel: (02) 752-5500

Asiana Airlines
Tel: (02) 774 4000

British Airways
Han Young Air Agencies, Rm 238 Westin Chosun Hotel, 87 Sokong-dong, Chungku, Seoul. Tel (02) 774 5511-5/664 4123-4

Cathay Pacific
Room 701, Kolon Building.
45 Mugyo-dong, Chung-gu, Seoul
Tel: (02) 779-0321/6

China Airlines
Room 211, Chosun Hotel
87 Sogong-dong, Chung-gu, Seoul
Tel:(02) 755-1523/5

Garuda Indonesia
Seoul. Tel (02) 773 2092/3

Japan Air Lines(JAL)
Room 202, Paiknam Building
188-3 1ga Ulchiro, Chung-gu, Seoul
Tel: (02) 757-1711/4

KLM
Room 110, Chosun Hotel
87 Sogong-dong, Chung-gu, Seoul
Tel:(02) 753-1093/5

Korean Air
KAL Building.41-3 Sosomun-dong, Chung-gu, Seoul
Tel: (02) 755-2221/756 2000

Lufthansa
Room 601, Center Building
91 Sogong-dong, Chung-gu, Seoul
Tel: (02) 777-9655

Malaysia Airlines
14th floor, Dongbang Life Insurance Mn Bldg
150 2-ga T'aep'yongno, Chung-gu, Seoul
Tel:(02)777-7761

Northwest
7-9th floor, In-Joo Building
111-1 Sorin-dong, Chongno-gu, Seoul
Tel:(02)734-7800

Singapore Airlines
Room 202, Chosun Hotel
87 Sogong-dong, Chung-gu, Seoul
Tel:(02)755-1226

Swissair
Oriental Chemical Building
50 Sogong-dong, Chung-gu, Seoul
Tel:(02)757-8901

Thai Airways
Room 223, Chosun Hotel
87 Sogong-dong, Chung-gu, Seoul
Tel:(02)779-2621/5

United Airlines
Room 1503, Anguk Ins.Bldg, 87 1-ga
Ulchiro, Chung-ga, Seoul.Tel:(02)757-1691

Car Hire

Arirang
Kangso-gu, Seoul. Tel: (02) 695 0340

Avis
Head Office: 21-1, 1st Ga, Euija-Ro,
Choong-Gu, Seoul
Tel: (02) 737 7878; Tlx: K 32125; Fax: (02) 739 9009 (+ seven other branches)

Changwon
Seoul.Tel: (02) 556 2008

'88 Rent-a-Car
Kangso-gu, Seoul.Tel: (02) 699 3885/7

Hertz Self and Chauffeur Drive
Kumho & Co Inc
20th fl, Asiana Bldg, # 10-1,2-Ka,
Hoehyun-dong, Chung-ku, Seoul 100 052.
Tel: 758 1567; Fax: 773 3084
Represented in all major cities. For reservations, refer to Seoul.

The Korea Express
Map'o-gu, Seoul. Tel: (02) 719 7295/7

Korean Rent A Car
Seoul. Tel: (02) 585 0801/5

New Korea
Yongdungpo-gu, Seoul. Tel: (02) 676 0031

Sambo Rent A Car (National)
Yongsan-gu, Seoul. Tel:(02) 797 5711

Seoul Rent a Car
Kangdong-gu, Seoul. Tel: (02) 474 0011/3

Sungsan
Yongsan-gu, Seoul. Tel: (02) 552 1566/7

VIP Rent-a-Car
Tel: (02) 557 8081

Major Exhibitions in Seoul 1997

Date	Exhibition	Venue	Organiser
April 12-15	**KIECO 97** - 16th Korea Int'l Exhibition for Computers, Software etc.	KOEX	KED
April 24 -May 1	**SMS '97** - Seoul Motor Show	KOEx	KAMA
May 7-10	**SEOUL FOOD '97** - Seoul Int'l food technology exhibition	KOEX	KTIPA
May 15-18	**EXPO COMM/WIRELESS KOREA '97**	KOEX	KOEX
May 15-19	**SEOUL BOOK FAIR '97** - Seoul Int'l Book Fair	KOEX	Korean PA
June 8-11	**ENVEX '97** - Int'l exhibition on environmental technologies	KOEX	MoE
July 10-13	**JEWELEX '97** - Seoul Int'l Jewellery & watch show	KOEX	KOEX
July 18-21	**GLASS KOREA '97** - 4th Int'l glass industry technology exhibition	KOEX	KTFL
Aug 2-6	**FOODEX KOREA '97** - Korea Int'l Kitchen and food expo	KOEX	KOEX
Sept 30-Oct 3	**COSMETICS FAIR '97** - The Korea Int'l cosmetics fair	KOEX	Korean IECA
Oct 16-19	**KOBA '97** - 7th Korea Int'l broadcast & audio visual equipment show	KOEX	Hankook
Nov 9-11	**NEPCON KOREA** - 13th exhibition for manufacturers of PCB/LCD semiconductors and related equipment and materials	KOEX	Reed
Dec 12-15	**SEOUL STOFF '97** - Seoul Int'l Textile Fair	KOEX	KFTE

Hankook = The Hankook Ilbo, 14 Chunghak-dong, Chongno-gu, Seoul 100-180,tel: 02-739 5272; fax: 02-738 1048. **KIETPC** = Korea Int'l Exhibition & Trade Promotion Co-operative, 371-22 Shinsu-Dong, Map'o-gu, Seoul 121-110, tel: 02-718-7771; fax: 02-3272 7771. **KAMA** = Korea Autombile Manufacturers Assocation. tel:782 1360; **KED** = Korea Economic Daily tel:360 4506. **KFTE** = Korean Federation of Textile Industries, 16th Fl, Textile Center, 944-31, Taechi 3-dong, Kangnam-gu, Seoul 135-283; **KOEX** = Korea Exhibition Center, World Trade Center,159 Samsung-dong, Kangnam-gu, Seoul 135-731 tel: 551 1171-6. **KTIPA** = Korea Trade-Investment Promotion Agency. tel: 551 4414; **Korean IECA** = International Exhibitions & Conferences Association.tel: 761 2512. **Korean PA** = Publishers Association. tel: 551 1126. **KTFL** = Korea Trade Fairs Ltd. tel: 783 8261. **Kortst** = Korea Tourist Association, 11th Fl, Saman Bldg, 945 Taech'i-dong, Kangnam-gu, Seoul 135-280, tel: 02-556 2356; fax: 02-556 3818. **Kotra** = Korea Trade Promotion Corporation, 159 Samsong-dong, Kangnam-gu, Seoul 135-731, tel: 02-551-4416; fax: 02-557 5784. **MoE** = Ministry of Environment, Kwacheon 427-760. tel: 504 9236. **Min Const/Tra** = Ministry of Construction & Transportation. **Reed** = Reed Exhibition Companies - Korea, Rm 501, Kumsan Bldg 17-1 Yoido-Dong,Youngdeungpo-ku, Seoul, tel 785 4771, fax 785 6118. **TSICEC** = Taegu Sungsea Industrial Complex Exhibition Center.

Korea Airline Departures

Below is a list of international departures and frequencies from Pusan and Seoul to the destinations in bold type. Figures in brackets refer to the days of the week. (2,4,6) therefore indicates that departures to that destination take place on a Tuesday (the second day of the week), a Thursday and a Saturday. Only direct flights, without changing planes, are listed. Correct at February 1997.

Airline Abbreviation Codes: AF = Air France; **AN** = Ansett Australia; **BA** = British Airways; **CO** = Continental ; **CX** = Cathay Pacific; **DL** = Delta Air; **GA** = Garuda; **HY** = Uzbekistan Airways; **JL** = Japan Airlines; **KE** =Korean Air; **KL** = KLM; **LY** = El Al; **MH** = Malaysian Airlines; **NZ** = Air New Zealand; **NW** = Northwest Airlines; **OS** = Austrian Airlines; **OZ** = Asiana Airlines; **QF** = Qantas; **SU** = Aeroflot; **SR** = Swissair; **TG** = Thai Airways; **UA** = United; **VN** = Vietnam Airlines; **VP** = VASP.

PUSAN (Kimhae International) (PUS)

Beijing (BJS)
OZ (2,4,7) CA (1,4)
Cheju (CJU)
OZ (daily) KE (daily)
Fukuoka (FUK)
JL (3,6) KE (daily) OZ (5,7)
Guam (GUM)
KE (3,5,7)
Kuala Lumpur (KUL)
MH (3,5)
Kwangju (KWJ)
OZ (daily)
Manila (MNL)
PR (4,7)
Nagoya (NGO)
KE (1,3,5,7) JL (2,4,6)
Osaka (OSA)
KE, JL (daily) OZ (5,7)
Saipan (SPN)
OZ (3,5,7)
Sendai (SDJ)
OZ (3,5)
Seoul (SEL)
OZ (daily) KE (daily)
Shanghai (SHA)
KE/MU (1,3,5,6)
Tokyo (NRT)
JL (2,3,4,5,7) KE (1,2,4,5,6,7)

SEOUL (Kimpo International) (SEL)

Amsterdam (AMS)
KL (3,5,6,7) KE (1,4,6)
Anchorage (ANC)
KE (2,4,7)
Atlanta (ATL)
KE (1,3,5) DL (daily)
Auckland (AKL)
KE (daily) NZ (3,4,5,6,7)
Bahrain (BAH)
KE (1)
Bangkok (BKK)
OZ, KE,TG (daily)
Beijing (BJS)
KE (1,2,3,5,6,7) CA (daily) OZ (1,2,4,5,7)
Bombay (BOM)
KE (2,5)
Boston (BOS)
KE (1,3,5)

Brisbane (BNE)
QF (2,4) KE (1,3,5,6) NZ (1,6) AN (2,3,5) AN/KE (2) KE/NZ (2,3,5)
Brussels (BRU)
OZ (3,6) OS (3)
Cairns (CNS)
OZ (3,6,7) QF (3,6,7)
Cairo (CAI)
KE (1)
Cheju (CJU)
OZ (daily) KE (daily)
Chicago (CHI)
KE (1,3,4,5,7) UA (daily)
DL (1,3,5)
Chinju (HIN)
KE (daily) OZ (daily)
Christchurch (CHC)
KE (2,4,5,7)
Cincinnati (CVG)
DL (daily)
Dalian (DLC)
CJ (1,3,5,7)
Dallas (DFW)
DL (daily) KE (1,4,6)
Denpasar-Bali (DPS)
GA (2,3,4,5,7) KE (7)
Detroit (DTT)
NW (1,3,4,6) OZ (1,3,4,6)
Frankfurt (FRA)
KE (2,3,5,6,7) LH (1,3,5,6,7)
Fukuoka (FUK)
JL (daily) KE (daily) OZ (daily)
Guam (GUM)
CO (2,3,4,6,7) KE, OZ (daily)
Hanoi (HAN)
VN (2,4,7)
Hiroshima (HIJ)
OZ (1,3,5,6) JL (2,4,6)
Ho Chi Minh (SGN)
OZ (2,4,6,7) KE (3,7)VN (1,2,3,5)
Hong Kong (HKG)
OZ, CX,KE, TG (daily)
Honolulu (HNL)
KE,UA, DL, NW, OZ (daily)
Jakarta (JKT)
GA (daily) KE (1,3,5,6,7) KE/GA (2,3,4,7)
Jeddah (JED)
KE (1)
Kagoshima (KOJ)
KE (1,3,6)
Kangnung (KAG)

KE (daily) OZ (daily)
Khabarovsk (KHV)
OZ (3) SU (7)
Komatsu (KMQ)
JL (1,5)
Kota Kinabalu (BKI)
MH (1)
Kuala Lumpur (KUL)
KE (2,5,7) MH (1,3,5,6,7)
Kuching (KCH)
MH (6)
Kumamoto (KMJ)
KE (1,6)
Kunsan (KUV)
KE , OZ (daily)
Kwangju (KWJ)
OZ, KE (daily)
London (LHR)
KE (1,3,5,6) BA (2,4,6)
Los Angeles (LAX)
KE, OZ, NW, UA (daily) TG (1,3,5,6) VP (2,4) PR (1,3,5,6,7)
Macau (MFM)
KE (3,5,7) OZ (2,5,7)
Madrid (MAD)
IB,KE (1,4)
Manila (MNL)
KE (daily) PR, UA (daily)
OZ (1,2,3,4,6,7)
Minneapolis (MSP)
NW (2,3,5,7)
Moscow (MOW)
SU (3,5) KE (3,7)
Nadi (NAN)
KE (1,3,6) NZ (7)
Nagoya (NGO)
KE, JL, OZ (daily)
New York (JFK)
NW, KE, OZ (daily) DL (1,3,5,7)
Niigata (KIJ)
KE (1,4,5,7)
Okayama (OKJ)
KE (1,3,5,7)
Okinawa (OKA)
OZ (4,7)
Osaka (ITM/KIX)
KE, JL, OZ, NH, UA (daily)
Paris (CDG)
AF (1,4,6) KE (1,3,5,7)
Phuket (HKT)
KE (1,4,7)
Pohang (KPO)
OZ, KE (daily)
Portland (PDX)

DL (daily)
Pusan (PUS)
OZ (daily) KE (daily)
Qingdao (TAO)
KE (1,2,4,6,7) CA (daily)
Rome (FCO)
KE,AZ (2,4,6)
Saipan (SPN)
CO (2,3,4,6,7) OZ, KE (daily) NW (1,2,3,4,5)
San Francisco (SFO)
KE (2,3,4,5,6,7), UA,OZ (daily)SQ (2,3,4,5,7) NW (1,2,3,5,6)
Sao Paulo (SAO)
VP (2,4) KE (3,5,7)
Sapporo (SPK)
KE (1,3,4,5,7)
Seattle (SEA)
OZ (1,3,4,6,7)
Sendai (SDJ)
OZ (1,2,4,6,7)
Shanghai (SHA)
OZ, MU (daily)
Shenyang (SHE)
KE (2,3,5,7) CJ (1,2,4,6)
Singapore (SIN)
OZ, KE,SQ (daily)
Sydney (SYD)
KE (daily) QF (4,6,7) OZ (2,4,5,6,7) AN (2,7)
Taegu (TAE)
KE (daily) OZ (daily)
Taipei (TPE)
CX,CO,TG,UA (daily) SQ (1,3,4,5)
Tashkent (TAS)
HY (1,5)
Tel Aviv (TLV)
KE (3)
Tianjin (TSN)
KE (1,3,4,6)
Tokyo (NRT)
KE,NW,UA,JL,JD (daily) OZ (2,3,5,6,7)
Toronto (YYZ)
KE (2,4,7) AC (2,4,6,7)
Ulsan (USN)
KE (daily) OZ (daily)
Vancouver (YVR)
KE (2,4,5,7) AC (2,4,5,6,7) SQ (1,6)
Vienna (VIE)
OS,OZ (3,6)
Washington DC (WAS)
KE (1,3,5,7) DL (1,3,5,7)
Zurich (ZRH)
KE (2,7) SR (2,5)

What's the link between business and the Asia Pacific?

BRITISH AIRWAYS
The world's favourite airline

http://www.british-airways.com

Laos

Doing Business

General Climate

In the six years since the hammer and sickle was discreetly removed from the national flag and an economic policy of '*chin thanakan mai*', or 'new thinking', was introduced, little seems to have changed much in Laos. Outwardly, at least.

There are more cars and more new paving on the once broad and pristine boulevards of the capital, Vientiane, but ultimately it remains a sleepy, one-horse town — perhaps the last such example of Old Asia. Assigned tourist guides, a requirement for most visitors, still mix fierce political dogma with their thorough knowledge of local history and culture. And you will probably be paying as much, or more, for your sub-standard hotel room as you would for five star quality virtually anywhere else in Asia.

Fifteen years of bankrupt communist rule from 1975-1990 is taking longer to overcome than many westerners thought, primarily because the 1991 transition by Laos from a centralised to a liberalised economy has not been matched by an equivalent shift in political thinking. Laos knows its new 'popular democracy' must play at *glasnost* and succour foreign revenue, but not at any cost. Outsiders, and all the inherent diseases of democracy, are still treated with the utmost suspicion by an embattled, hard-line one party government which wants aid and trade but not the accompanying dictats.

Beneath the surface, however, slow progress appears to be being made. Although official statistics are hard to come by, the privatisation of farms and state-owned businesses is estimated to have helped cut inflation from 80% in the late Eighties to less than 7% today. Timber concessions have been awarded to Chinese, Malaysian and Taiwanese firms. Foreign investment, chiefly in garments and tourism facilities, is said to be growing, and economic potential is foreseen in gold, precious stones, coal and iron.

Although one of the 10 poorest countries in the world, with an annual per capita income of about US$180 plus extensive overseas aid for its 4.1 million population, Laos can feed itself. But more rapid development is said by analysts to be hamstrung by a still top-heavy bureaucracy and a shortage of skilled workers.

All foreign trade is handled by the Dept of Foreign Trade in the Ministry of Commerce. The country has large untapped reserves of tin, zinc, lead, iron ire and timber but at present the economy is largely agricultural. Russia, Vietnam and Thailand are Laos' main trading partners.

The country's chief foreign revenue earners to date have been hydro-electric power from the Nam Ngum and Xeset dams producing electricty to neighbouring countries and fees from the estimated 80 international airlines which overfly Laotian air space, chiefly en route between Bangkok, Hong Kong and Tokyo.

Aid from the former Soviet Union has been replaced by economic ties with Japan, the US, France, Germany, Australia and Thailand. The influence of the latter two countries is most overt to most first time visitors. As well as supplying education, temple restoration and other assistance, Australia ploughed US$30 million into construction of the 'Friendship Bridge' which opened in 1994 across the Mekong River between Tha Dua, just south of Vientiane, and Nong Khai in Thailand's I-San province. And it is still predominantly Thais, an estimated 400-a-day during the first year of operation, who have been using the bridge to develop new businesses in Laos, principally in the textile and tourism sectors.

Although sharing the '*wai*' form of greeting, Buddhist principles, numerous festivals and erratic public offices, in pace, mood, attitudes and lifestyles, landlocked Laos is far removed from its most capitalist neighbour and former enemy, Thailand. But when it comes to new business, the two have become intrinsically entwined.

Etiquette & practice

The Laos are a gentle, unhurried people. Accepted form of greeting is the *nop* (like the Thai *wai*), also used as an expression of thanks, regret or saying goodbye, but it is acceptable for Westerners to shake hands. One should not touch a person's head, nor point one's toe at a person or object. French, rather than English is the language of commerce. Lightweight suit, shirt and tie for business meetings.

Tourism

General Developments

Laos is happy to count its tourists in the thousands rather than the millions. Arrivals have risen from 37,000 in 1991 to more than 346,000 in 1995, and the target is 500,000 by 2000. At present 90% are from Thailand, with 15% from Vietnam and 1% each from China, Australia and Japan. The Tourism Authority is targeting other ASEAN countries (Laos is set to join later in 1997), Japan, Australia, Europe and the US.

Athough Vientiane and Bangkok are closely linked in terms of business and leisure, Laos is no admirer of the way Thailand has developed its tourism. The national tourism administration officially discourages backpackers and actively pursues a policy of issuing visas only to high-spending visitors on cultural group tours; the overall aim being to discourage crime, prostitution, uncontrollable development, environ-mental damage and all the other pitfalls of mass tourism.

Laos has official representation in France, Sweden, the US, Japan, China, Vietnam, Cambodia and Myanmar — but Thailand is the acknowledged gateway, both for visa issue and for officially-appointed tour agencies. Getting a business visa requires an official invitation and lengthy processing. But exploratory business can usually be undertaken with a tourist visa, requiring up to one week's prior notice, a good supply of passport photographs plus an official fee, exclusive of agency commission, of about US$12 in advance or US$30 on arrival. If you intend getting a visa on arrival, fax confirmation is required at your international point of departure. Organized tours range upwards in price from about US$250 for one night to $580 for four nights, inclusive of hotel, internal transport and some meals for one person.

Tourists visas usually are valid for 15 days, allowing extra time in the country following a tour, provided arrangements are made in advance. Laos is stunningly picturesque, a sparsely-populated land of mountains, lakes and rivers made all the more enticing by its long closure to the outside world. Tribes and culture are the main visitor attractions, supported by delicious Laotian food (mostly fresh riverfish or vegetarian and milder than Thai), and shopping for finely-woven textiles and handicrafts.

Vientiane is a slow-paced city with traces of flamboyant French and drab Russian architecture; some fascinating monuments and temples; a good variety of restaurants; an uninspiring selection of mid-market hotels and a lively but tame nightlife, consisting mainly of a growing string of riverside bars and bistros. The capital is usually combined on tours with the northern cultural capital of Luang Prabang, a cool mountain town liberally sprinkled with magnificent temples and launch point for boat rides up and down a rushing tributary of the Mekong.

Other organised tours go to the historic Plain of Jars, a high plateau scattered with 2,000-year-old funeral urns, and Xieng Khouang, an ancient town whose 1,500 buildings were razed by American bombing during the Southeast Asian war. Less explored — and exploited — but also available on organised tours is the southern area of Laos, including the culturally scenic Thakhek, the mountainous Ho Chi Minh Trail, the old French town of Saravan and the fertile Bolovens Plateau.

What to See

Vientiane. Buddhist temples abound in Vientiane, of which Pha That Luang , 3 km northeast of the city, is the best known. It was built on a religious site dating back to the 3rd century and the central great *stupa* was built in 1566. Other stupas and Wats are the black That Dam, Wat Mixai, Wat Si Saket, Wat Si Muang and Wat Ong Teu Mahawithan with its ornate doors. Haw Pha Kaew (Wat Phra Kéo) was originally the home of the Emerald Buddha and now houses supposedly the oldest stone Buddha in the country amongst its spectacular galleries and sculptures. One of Vientiane's most prominent landmarks is the *Patuxai* or Victory Gate, rather a drab structure built in 1975 to commemorate those who died during the communist takeover. The Revolutionary Museum celebrates the triumphs of the Pathet Lao Revolutionary forces and the Viet Minh over the French. Excursions around the capital: Buddha Park is 24 km east; Tad Leuk Waterfall is a two-hour four-wheel drive journey but is worthwhile for its setting and rare birds and plants in the surrounding jungle. Houei Nhang Forest Reserve contains rare bird species also, plus red-bellied squirrels, porcupines, rare civet and barking deer. North of Vientiane are the Dau Song caves and Lao Pako Ecotourism Lodge.
Luang Prabang. The capital until 1975, the City of the Golden Buddha is not at present connected by road to Vientiane but is delightfully welcoming. Wat Xieng Thong is the most spectacular of the many wats; the Royal Palace Museum, music room, private chapel, reception room of the king, throne room and royal library should not be missed. Two hours up the Mekong river from Luang Prabang are the spectacular limestone *Pak Ou* Caves (Tham Ting). In between Vientiane and Luang Prabang near Phonsavan is the *Plain of Jars*, where over 300 stone rice receptacles, over 2000 years old, still repose in the midst of idyllic countryside.

Shopping

Handicrafts are a good buy in Vientiane with Somsri, the Textile Centre, the Handicraft Centre, Kanchana Boutique, Lao Pathana or Phonethip Handicrafts and Ceramics the best outlets. For gems, MM Bari stocks precious stones from the North; Vanxay Art Handicrafts, Nguyen Ti Selto and Nan Xuan sell antiques.

Getting Around

There are international flights into and out of Vientiane from Bangkok, Ho Chi Minh, Phnom Penh and Khunming (PRC). Lao Aviation flies domestically between provincial capitals.

The Mekong river is navigable on 1330 of its 2030 kilometres in the country. River taxis, often quicker than jeeps, can be hired for US$4 per hour. Only 1620 km of the 3390 km national road network is paved with the major artery being Road No. 13 linking Pak Mong in the North via Luang Prabang, Vientiane, Savannakhet to Khong in the South. Cars or jeeps can be hired through your hotel. Laotian drivers are optimistic about the intentions of oncoming traffic and should not be imitated! Buses are very cheap but very unreliable. By 1997 the road to Luang Prabang should all be paved and buses from Bangkok will ply it.

Jumbo taxis (*jamboh*) can be hired for urban travel for about US$1 for a 4-km journey; car taxis do not cruise but can be found outside most tourist hotels. Three-wheelers (*samlors*) are slightly cheaper than taxis. Motorbikes under 100 cc can be rented for US$10-12 per day in some provincial capitals. There are no trains as yet.

Entertainment & Leisure

Undeveloped, as in Cambodia, but several beer gardens have sprung up in recent years. Discos in Vientiane include Vienlatry Mai, the Dao Viang, Feeling Well and Seng Aloune, Olympic, the Saysana Club and the Anou Cabaret. Discos have recently opened in the Chaleune Hotel and in the Saysana Hotel. There are live bands nightly in the Santiphab Hotel and at the Nokkeo Latrymai. There is a night club at the Dok Buoathang Restaurant. Bars popular with men on their own include *Les Rendezvous des Amis*, the *Purple Porpoise* and the *James Bond* Bar.

Traditional French restaurants include *Le Santal* (opp. Wat Ong Teu), *La Vendome* on Thanon Lupeng and the pricey *Arawan* on the Fountain Circle. Laotian food is available at the *Soukevarm* Restaurant off Thanon That Dam, *Dao Vieng* on Thanon Heng Boun, *1st May Restaurant* on the Phag Kham Quay, *Somchan's* on Thanon Luang Prabang and the *Mekong* on Tha Deua Road; there are plenty of food stalls in the streets and cheap Laotian cafés. Indian food is available at the *Taj* Indian Restaurant on Thanon Pang Kham and Thai food at the *Thai Food Garden* Restaurant on Luang Prabang Road. Pricey Chinese restaurants include *Lani's* at 281 Settathirat and *Hong Kong* Restaurant at 80/4 Samsenthai Road. There is a *Sakura* Japanese Restaurant in Luang Prabang Road and an Italian at *Giarrosto L'Opera* in Namphu Square.

Lao traditional dance can be seen at the *Natasin Lao School* on Thanon Phoun Hang. Tennis equipment can be hired at the Vientiane Tennis Club and overseas visitors can swim for 900 kip at the Lanexang Hotel. Table tennis, squash, swimming, snooker and a sauna are available at the Australian Club (belonging to the Australian Embassy) for members and their guests. Herbal saunas can be had in some of the *wats* (temples) - Wat Sri Amphorn and Wat Sokpaluang, for example. The new Van Sana Hotel on Phonthan Road has a Lao sauna.

Arrival & Departure

Wattay Airport is 3 km west of Vientiane and takes 15 minutes to reach by taxi. Fares are about $6 (5500 kip). Buses run from Thanon Luang Prabang, about 150m south of the air terminal, for 250 kip. Departure tax is US$5.

In April 1994 the *Friendship Bridge* was opened, financed by Australian money, between Thailand and Laos, replacing the former ferry entry point. Bus fares from the Laotian side of the bridge to the capital cost 10 baht (US$0.40); taxis cost $4 and buses $1.50. Other road border checkpoints which are open are Boten (between Laos and China), Savannekhet (Laos-Thailand) and Dand Savanh (Laos-Vietnam).

Laos Key Fact File

Passport Requirements:
All visitors must have a valid passport and return air tickets. Visas are obligatory and can be obtained from Laotian consulates and embassies abroad. A business visa can usually be obtained by a sponsoring company in Laos. A tourist visa can be obtained through your travel agency. In an emergency, a tourist visa can be issued through a travel agency at an approved border crossing.

Currency: New Kip

Exchange Rates: *(May 1997)*
US$ 1 = kip 920; £1 = kip 1497

Currency Restrictions:
There are no restrictions on the amount of foreign currency visitors may bring into the country but once dollars have been changed into local currency, they cannot be bought back on departure. The Thai baht is as freely traded as the local kip. Banks charge 2% commission on money changed; hotels give a worse exchange rate than banks such as the Banque pour Commerce Exterieure. Visa and Amex credit cards are accepted at the top hotels and restaurants only.

Electricity Supply:
220 volts, 50 cycles AC (110 in rural areas)

Language:
Lao (similar to Thai). English, French and some Russian spoken in business

Time:
GMT + 7; EST + 10 hrs

IDD Code: 856
Area codes: Vientiane 21; Luang Prabang 71

Business Hours:
Commercial offices are open from 0800-1200 and 1400-1700 Monday to Friday; 0800-1200 on Saturdays.
Banking hours are 0830-1630 Monday through Friday; 0830-1100 Saturdays.
Shops are generally open 0800-1200 Mon-Friday; 0800-1200 Saturday.

Customs & Entry:
A visitor may bring in the following items duty free: 500 cigarettes or 500 grams of cigars or 250 grams of tobacco plus one litre of liquor or two litres of wine or two litres of beer.

Health Requirements:
Yellow fever vertificate required if entering from a designated infected area. Typhoid, malaria and cholera inoculation recommended. All water and milk should be boiled before consumption; meat and fish should be well cooked. Rabies present.

Climate/best time to visit:
Hot and tropical with the rainy season between May and October. Dry season between November and April with temperatures 15-25° C. is the best time to visit. Tropical and washable cotton clothing suitable all year. Lightweight suit, shirt and tie for business. Humidity is 70% in March; 87% in July.

National Holidays 1997
1 January New Year's Day; April 14-16 Lao New Year; May 1 International Labour Day; December 2 National Day. Many local festivals throughout the year.

Luang Prabang

Mittaphap Hotel E
PO Box 50 (Thanon Phuvao).Tel: (71) 217233
AC.Restaurant & swimming pool to re-open

Mouang Luang Hotel D
BounKhong Road. Tel/Fax: (71) 212790
Pool, conference room. 35 AC rooms

Phu Vao Hotel D
PO Box 50, Luang Prabang
Tel: (71) 212194; Fax: (71) 212534
59 AC rooms with telephone, minibar. Pool, vehicle rental, meeting room, bar, Restaurant.

Hotel Sisouvannaphoum E
Thanon Phothisalat. Tel: (71) 212200
20 rooms, 5 suites. Lao restaurant, bar

Villa de la Princesse D
Thanon Sakkalin. Tel: (71) 7041
11 rooms with AC. Restaurant. Bicycle hire

Vientiane

Asian Pavilion Hotel E
379 Samsenthai Road. Tel: 213430; Fax: 213432.*45 rooms, meeting room, restaurants*

Belvedere Hotel D
Unit 9, Bane KM2, Khonta Toong, Samsenthai Road, Sikhotabong District, PO Box 585, Soi Nongno
Tel: (21) 213570/4; tlx: 4363; fax: 213572/9
223 AC rooms, satellite TV, IDD. Pool, gym, tennis, conference facilities, restaurants

Ekalath Metropole Hotel E
Samsenthai Rd, Chanthabuly District, PO Box 3179
Tel: (21) 3420/1; Fax: (21) 3421
33 rooms with AC, colour TV, telephone. Melody Club, Lao & Inte'l Restaurant.

Lanexang Hotel D
Thanon Fa Ngum
Tel: (21) 4102/4/6/7; Fax: (21) 4108
30 rooms with AC. Swimming pool, badminton, souvenir shop, restaurants.

New Apollo Hotel E
Luang Prabang Rd, Chanthabuly District. PO Box 102.Tel/Fax: (21) 3343/4462/3244
75 AC rooms, with minibar, telephone, colour TV, . Gift shop, nightclub, restaurants.

Novotel Hotel C
Unit 9, Samsenthai Road, PO Box 585.
Tel: 213570; Fax: 213572
242 AC rooms, business centre, swimming pool, tennis, sauna & massage

River View Hotel E
Khaemkhong Road, Sikhotabong District, PO Box 636
Tel: (21) 216224/9123; Fax: 216232/9127
32 double rooms with AC, minibar, telephone, colour TV, laundry service. Restaurants.

Royal Dokmaideng D
Lanexang Avenue, Chanthaboul District, PO Box 3925
Tel: (21) 214455/4477; Fax: (21) 214454
83 rooms with AC, minibar, satellite TV. Night club, karaoke, swimming pool, gift shop, conference facilities, Lao and Chinese restaurants.

Tai-Pan Hotel D
2-12 Francois Hginn St, Chanthabouly District.
Tel: (21) 216906; Fax: (21) 216223
36 rooms with AC, minibar, colour TV, telephone, laundry service. Night Club, Lao & International Restaurant.

Vansana Hotel D
Phonthan Road, PO Box 881
Tel: (21) 414189/413171
39 rooms with AC, minibar, telephone, satellite TV. Restaurants, Lao sauna, pool.

Explanation of codes in hotel entries
C after name of hotel = room rate overUS$100 per person per night; D = between $50-100; E = under $50; ¶ = prices on application. Prices are only a guide and we recommend travellers to check with individual hotels before booking.

Useful Addresses

Air Couriers
DHL Worldwide Delivery service: Nongno St, Sikhotabong District, PO Box 2924; tel: (21) 216830; fax: (21) 215414
Lao Freight Forwarder, KM3, Tha Deua Road, PO Box 3145; tel: (21) 313321/ 313351; fax: (21) 314831
TNT Express Worldwide, Lanexang Ave; tel/fax: (21) 214361.**UPS**: Tel: (21) 414792

Airline Offices
Aeroflot
409 Samesenthai (near Lanexang Hotel); tel: (21) 213501
Air France
c/o Lao Aviation Booking Office
China Southern Airlines
c/o Lao Aviation Booking Office
Lao Aviation
Thanon Pang Kham. Tel: (21) 212093/4; fax: (21) 219719.
Lao Aviation Booking Office.
43/1 Thanon Settathirat. Tel: (21) 218710; fax: (21) 212056

Thai Airways International
Thanon Pang Kham. Tel: (21) 219231
Vietnam Airlines
c/o Lao Aviation Booking Office

Business Centre
Burapha, 14 Thanon Fa Ngum. Tel: (21) 212604; fax: (21) 212604

Car Hire
Lanexang Hotel, Thanon Fa Ngum. Tel: (21) 213672
International Consultants, Thanon Samsenthai. Tel: (21) 213106
Burapha, 14 Thanon Fa Ngum. Tel: (21) 212604

Emergencies
Dial: 3352
Police: 41 2536

English Language Newspaper
Vientiane Times
Pangkham Street, Vientiane
Tel: (21) 216364; fax: (21) 216365

Hospitals
International Medical Clinic, bank of Mekong river, Fa Ngum Road;
tel: 21 4018/21 4022/21 4025
Australian Embassy Clinic, Nehru St Phonexay; tel 41 3603/3610/31 2343
Swedish Clinic, Swedish Embassy, Sok Paluang. Tel: 31 5015

Investment Corporation
Lao Investment Promotion Corporation (LIPCO). Building 1, Thanon Luang Prabang, PO Box 795. Tel: (16) 9645; fax: (16) 9646/4163

Legal Services
DFD (Dirksen Flipse Doran). PO Box 2920, Bldg 1, Luang Prabang Rd. Tel: (21) 216927-9; fax: (21) 216919

Post Office/Telephone Office
Post: Thanon Khou Viang
International telephone: Thanon Settathirat; open 0800-2200

PATA Travel Agent
Sodetour
PO Box 70, Vientiane. Tel: (21) 6134/5689; fax: (21) 216313; tlx: 4316 LS

Tourism Authorities etc
National Tourism Authority of Laos
Lane Xang Avenue, PO Box 3556
Tel: (21) 212248/212251/212769;
Fax: (21) 212769
Lao National Tourism
Intersection Thanon Pangkam/Settathirat, PO Box 2912. Tel: (21) 3254/2998; tlx: 4348 MICOM LS/4492 TE VTE LS
Vientiane Tourist Office
Sithan Neua Bldg 11, Thanon Luang Prabang. Tel: (21) 4041; fax: (21) 5911

Macau

Doing Business

Despite growing competition from other destinations in the region, Macau will probably always be best known as the gambling capital of Asia/Pacific. But one thing its city fathers have been taking no chances on is the territory's future as a gateway and key trading hub for the emergent Pearl River Delta region.

Old Asia hands with a penchant for cobblestone streets, pastel mansions and subsidised wines may rue the outwardly changing face of the old Portuguese-administered enclave, currently in the process of doubling its tiny 21.45 sq.kms through reclaimed land and the construction of vast skyrise industrial and housing estates.

But, in Macanese eyes, the die was cast long ago for its reversion to Chinese rule in 1999. Unlike neighbouring Hong Kong, which noisily went to the wire with China on a raft of democratic principles, Macau has quietly and successfully negotiated its future role as a Special Administrative Region with its own government, laws and economic system of free trade and low taxation. For business visitors, this spells a potentially easy and profitable new conduit to China.

The opening in late 1995 of its international airport, with a direct bridge link to China, plus the launch of its own regional airline have ostensibly given Macau operational independence from its former British neighbour and the opportunity to strengthen an already dynamic economy with rapidly improving standards of living and one of the highest GDPs in Asia/Pacific.

Macau's traditional economic base, led by gambling/tourism plus textile and garment exports, is expanding in response to burgeoning business in the Pearl River Delta and southern Guandong regions of China. On the one hand, Macau provides financial and communications services-- with more than 20 banks and high standards of telecommunications. On the other, it is determined to maintain its industrial base by upgrading facilities to produce higher value added goods alongside government-sponsored technical training courses for local workers in the manufacture of garments and accessories, toys and electronics, furniture and ceramics, rubber and leather goods.

As well as being a member of GATT and ESCAP, Macau is particularly well placed for business between Europe and China. Thanks to its Portuguese ties, the territory enjoys trade privileges with the EU and is a base for Asia's Euro-Infocentre which provides information on European trade laws and regulations.

As a growing site for trade fairs with good exhibition facilities and an increasingly varied choice of meetings venues and international standard hotels, Macau is an ideal shop window and conduit for two-way trade with China, its top investor. Currently, there are more than 200 Chinese companies in Macau. In addition, the neighbouring Zuhai Special Economic Zone of Guandong Province maintains several offices in Macau to help potential overseas investors.

Zuhai and the big new Gaolan port, twice the size of Hong Kong harbour, under development to the west of the Pearl River Delta, are linked directly with Macau's new airport by a system of railway lines, highways and bridges to speed the throughput of people and goods to and from China.

Macau is also planning to develop as China's premier playground with a new array of leisure facilities. Gaming helps maintain the territory with a powerful financial base. Money supply rocketed by almost 700% between 1984 and 1993, when cash in circulation and overnight bank deposits reached a record US$2.6 billion, and grew to $6.7 billion with additional savings and term deposits.

Business etiquette & awareness

Lightweight suits are recommended for business meetings and outings to restaurants and nightclubs (where most entertaining is done). Spirits are welcomed as gifts in return for hospitality. Appointments should be made ahead of time and punctuality observed. 10% is normally added automatically to bills but small extra tips for good service are appreciated.

Tourism Update

General Developments

Macau's visitor pattern is finally changing, thanks to the opening of its first airport, and growth of outbound travel from China.

Arrivals in Macau in 1996 registered an overall growth of 5.14%, despite the fact that Hong Kong fell by 7.3%. International traffic was up by 40%, making a total of 8.15 mn visitors. In the previous year arrivals had dropped 1% to 7.8 million, mainly due to an 8% drop in the Hong Kong market.

In modern times, Macau has had one dominant source of visitors - neigbouring Hong Kong residents, which is explained by the ease of access, proximity, and a strong attraction for gambling.

Nevertheless, with the opening of the Macau's International Airport, this pattern is likely to change. The Hong Kong share had been falling through the 1980s, down to 78% in 1994, 73% in 1995, and 64% in 1996. A market that is becoming prominent is the Taiwanese (9.3% share, registering a growth of 171%) the second largest in 1996, followed by P R China and Japan. In 1995 Chinese visitors overtook Japanese, moving from 3% share to 7.4%.

At the start of 1997 the national tourism organisation began appointing new representatives around the world, having terminated contracts with its existing representatives at the end of 1996. The Macau Tourist Information Bureaus overseas were closed in 1996, to be replaced by MGTO-appointed representatives.

Aviation

Macau, which opened its first airport only in November 1995, is becoming an important gateway to China with flights to twelve cities there - Beijing, Changsha, Chongqing, Fuzhou, Guilin, Qingdao, Shanghai, Wuhan, Xian, Xiamen and Zhengzhou.

In 1996, Air Macau started flying to Bangkok, Kaohsiung, Xiamen and increased frequencies to Shanghai and Taipei. Up to June 1997 it had started flights to Qingdao and Wuhan and in July it will start flights to Manila. It currently operates two A320s and four A321s. The airline's traffic is dominated by Taiwan-originating passengers, mostly in transit for China. One estimate is that 30% of Taiwan-China traffic (totalling over 1.5 million one-way trips, and travelling mainly via Hong Kong), will go via Macau. Flight frequency from Taiwan built up rapidly. By April 1997 there were already 80 flights weekly to Taipei - with Air Macau operating 42 Eva Airways 24, and Trans Asia 14. To Kaohsiung there are 28 flights weekly.

Macau's marketing reprsentative in Taiwan expected visitor arrivals from Taiwan to increase 50% in 1996; in fact, growth was almost three times faster than that. Other flights have been started. Air Portugal (TAP) flies to Macau with a stop in Bangkok; the airline does'nt fly into Hong Kong, neither is Lisbon served directly from Hong Kong. Also, Korean Air started flying from Seoul and Singapore Airlines and Malaysia Airlines from Singapore and Kuala Lumpur respectively. North Korea's airline, Air Koryo, also operates into Macau as a stop on its Bangkok route and All Nippon Airways operates charters. Xiamen Airlines started charters too in 1997.

Macau's airport authority planned to launch Express Link in mid-1997, allowing passengers to bypass Macau immigration and customs and to travel, with their baggage, direct from the airport by 'sealed bus' to the jetfoil terminal for transfer to Hong Kong. The authority also has space at the HK jetfoil terminal for airline check-in counters for air travel from Macau airport.

Hotels

Macau is becoming an important gateway to southern China, having already a comprehensive China air route network. Hoteliers report that most inbound traffic, even that from Southeast Asia, is in transit to China.

In 1996 there was a 8.76% increase in the number of hotel overnights, which probably suggests a gradual change in market patterns. Also, business from China to Macau is beginning to be noticed. Even the Mandarin Oriental Hotel, which has the second-highest room rate in Macau, is getting China custom. Its share is only about 6%, but yield is probably the highest; currently, most customers are paying at rack rate.

According to figures from Travel Business Analyst, four-star hotels in Macau recorded a 64% occupancy in 1995 at an average room rate of US$85. In 1996 these figures were running at 71% at US$82 - which indicates that the airport was bringing in some lower-yield traffic.

Despite the opening of the airport, announcements of plans for new hotels have been few, with only the Grandview opening in 1997. There was a burst of activity earlier when the Holiday Inn, New World and New Century (not part of the Century group) opened. Part of the reason is believed to be the seasonality of current business - where rooms are full at weekends, but half empty during the week. There are reports, however, that a 500 room Sheraton resort will open July 1999 in Praia Grande Bay.

What to see

The ruins of St Paul's church (the facade of which has now been fully restored) is the territory's best-known sight. The church dates back to the early 16th century, but was totally destroyed by fire in 1835 - only the façade remaining.

The *Senado* Square, located in the heart of the city, is a pedestrian zone covered with wave patterned cobble stone with historic buildings like the *Leal Senado* (Municipal Council) and the tourism office, among others, and is well worth a visit. Aside from its western Christian links, Macau has some fine Chinese temples: the Temple of the Goddess A-Ma, at the foot of Barra Hill, is considered by most experts to be one of the territory's finest examples. It too has been restored to its former glory. Other temples to see are Lin Fong and Kun Iam. The museums (Maritime, Grand Prix, Wine and Sacred Art) are certainly worth a visit.

Shopping

Macau is a duty free area and as such most items on sale are competitively priced. So look out for bargains such as cameras, watches and electrical goods. But don't pay the asking price as you will be expected to haggle over the cost of most goods.

The main shopping streets are located along Avenida do Infante D. Henrique and Avenida Almeida Ribeiro. These two thoroughfares are good for more upmarket items. Try Macau's flea market around the Rua das Estalagens for something cheaper.

Entertainment

Macau's many casinos provide plenty of entertainment for the Hong Kong Chinese and other visitors, but are often packed to the rafters at weekends. In any case, there is more to do in Macau than just gamble.

For example, the French-style Crazy Paris Show at the Mona Lisa Hall can be caught every night for 120 patacas and is always a favourite among first-time visitors.

The Skylight Disco at the Hotel Presidente provides a good cabaret. Hotel Lisboa's Mikado Nightclub has been popular, but fashions change and either of these two may no longer be in vogue.

The traditions of Macau's culinary crossroads, nurtured over four centuries, continue to flourish in hundreds of restaurants. They range from elegant dining rooms and palatial banqueting halls to European Inns and Chinese Cafés. All offer ample helpings with fresh ingredients at reasonable prices, with friendly service and a relaxed, unhurried atmosphere.

For Macanese food (a distinctive style combining many contrasting cuisines) try *A Lorcha, Balichao, Henri's Galley, Alfonso III* and *Fat Sui Lau*. All sorts of Chinese cooking can be found in Macau; try *Long Kei* or *Fook Lam Mun*. Portuguese, Italian, Korean, Thai, Japanese, African and Vietnamese cuisine can also be sought out in the territory.

Leisure

For Hong Kong residents, Macau is little more than an Asian Las Vegas - a giant casino across the Pearl River. But for foreign tourists, Macau represents more than just the freedom to gamble.

The Macau Jockey Club holds meetings at its sparkling new track and grandstand on the Taipa course. The Club runs flat races from September to June on both grass and all-weather tracks. The course is open to all racegoers and includes restaurants, a sauna swimming pool, spa and a gym.

The popular Macau Canidrome now holds the world's richest greyhound race. Meetings are held every Tuesday, Thursday, Saturday and Sunday. Entry fee is just two patacas or 80 patacas for a six-person box.

The annual Macau Grand Prix Formula 3, motor cycle and saloon car racing is held late-November around the city's streets. Other annual events include the Macau International Music Festval (Oct/Nov) and the (mostly local) Macau Arts Festival, held in February/March.

Otherwise, the Hyatt Regency has a squash court as do the Oriental Macau and the Royal Health Club. All charge entry fees to non-guests. Macau also has two public swimming pools. The Hac Sa Sports & Recreation complex on Coloane Island has an Olympic-size pool, roller hockey pitch, roller skating rink and an 18-hole mini golf course.

The 18-hole Macau Golf & Country Club, opened in January 1993 at the Westin Resort in Coloane, is ideal for enthusiasts. Besides the Zhongshan golf course - across the border in China - is another option preferred mainly by local businessmen and visiting Japanese tourists.

Getting around

Locally, Macau's nearly 600 taxis (which carry a cream-coloured roof - yellow for radio call cabs) are probably the best means of transport. But watch for surcharges for luggage and journeys to (although not back from) Taipa and Coloane Islands. Happy Mokes and Avis Rent a Car supply mini moke-type cars for hire. Avis also has saloon cars suitable for business trips. There is no shortage of buses linking various parts of the territory.

Arrival & departure

Macau International Airport opened in November 1995 and has direct flights to twelve Chinese cities, Lisbon, Seoul, Korea, Taipei and Bangkok among others. *(See Macau Aviation section).*

Visitors travelling to Macau from Hong Kong can choose from helicopters, the world's largest fleet of jetfoils, jumbo-cats, jet-cats, high-speed ferries and hover-ferries. The routes from Kowloon and Hong Kong Island can be very busy at weekends. Many visitors also arrive overland from Guangzhou. There are also ferry services. Hong Kong charges a departure tax on passengers coming to Macau of HK$ 26. The departure tax Macau-Hong Kong is HK$ 25.

At present access from Hong Kong is either by Jetfoil, taking 55 minutes and costing from HK$142 (first class), Jumbo Cats, costing from $128 (60 mins), and TurboCats and TriCats also costing from HK$128. East Asia Airlines inaugurated helicopter connections in November 1990. Flights depart 16 times daily and the round trip costs HK$1206 on weekdays or HK$1310 on weekends. Like the Jetfoil, departures are from Shun Tak Centre, Hong Kong (tel: 859 3359).

A seventh 306-seat jumbo-catamaran was delivered during 1994 to Hong Kong Macau Hydrofoil Company. A catamaran links Macau with Shenzhen - one of China's Special Economic Zones- once-a-day taking 90 minutes. The Macmosa ferry operates a weekly service between Macau and Kaohsiung, Taiwan.

Macau Key Fact File

Passport Requirements:
All visitors must have a valid passport. 14-day visas can be obtained on arrival or in Hong Kong for HK$100 (individual); HK$50 child or member of group of 15 or more or HK$ 200 for families. EU nationals and citizens of Brazil, Canada, USA, Japan, ASEAN countries, Australia, New Zealand, S Korea, Norway, Switzerland, Uruguay, S Africa, India, Poland & Mexico do not require a visa.

Currency:
Pataca. 100 avos = 1 Pataca

Exchange Rates: *(May 1997)*
US$1 = 7.9 Patacas; £1 = 12.8 Patacas

Currency Restrictions: None

Electricity Supply:
110 volts, 50 cycles to the "old" section of Macau and 220 volts, 50 cycles to the "new" sections and islands.

Language:
Officially Portuguese and Chinese, with Cantonese the most widely spoken. English is Macau's third language and is generally used in trade, tourism and commerce.

Time: GMT + 8 hours; EDT + 13 hours

IDD Code: 853 (No further codes applicable)

Business Hours:
Commercial offices are open 0900-1300, 1430-1730 Monday to Friday; 0900-1300 Saturdays.
Shops are open Monday to Sunday 1000-1900.
Banks are open 0930-1630 Monday to Friday; 0930-1200 Saturdays.

Customs & Entry:
Only rudimentary customs controls exist. There is a 5 percent *ad valorem* duty on imported electrical goods. There are no duties on outgoing goods or any restrictions on the amount carried, but in reality Hong Kong customs regulate the amount of duty-free items brought into the Crown Colony.

Health Requirements:
International inoculation certificates are not normally required unless cholera has been detected either in Macau or Hong Kong or in an area recently visited by a person arriving in Macau.

Climate/best time to visit:
Hot and humid - especially May-September, with an annual average temperature of 22.5°C (July hottest at 28.6°C; January coolest at 14.6°C av.) and relative humidity ranging between 67-83% per cent for most of the year. Wettest month: June.

Business/social etiquette
Lightweight suits recommended for business meetings and outings to restaurants and nightclubs (where most entertaining is done); appointments should be made ahead and punctuality observed; 10% service is added to most hotel and restaurant bills, but further tipping appreciated if warranted.

National Holidays 1997
January 1 New Year's Day; February 6-8 Chinese New Year; April 5 Ching Ming Festival; 28/30 March Good Friday/Easter Day; April 25 Anniversary of the Portuguese Revolution; May 1 Labourers'Day; June 9 Dragon Boat/Tun Ng Festival; June 10 Camoes Day/Portuguese Communities Day; 17 June Feast of St John the Baptist; September 28 Day following Mid-Autumn Festival; October 1 National Day of the People's Republic of China; October 5 Republic Day; October 10 Festival of Ancestors (*Chung Yeung*) November 2 All Souls Day; December 1 Restoration of Independence Day; December 8 Feast of Immaculate Conception; December 22 Winter Solstice; December 24-5 Christmas

MACAU - Hotels 191

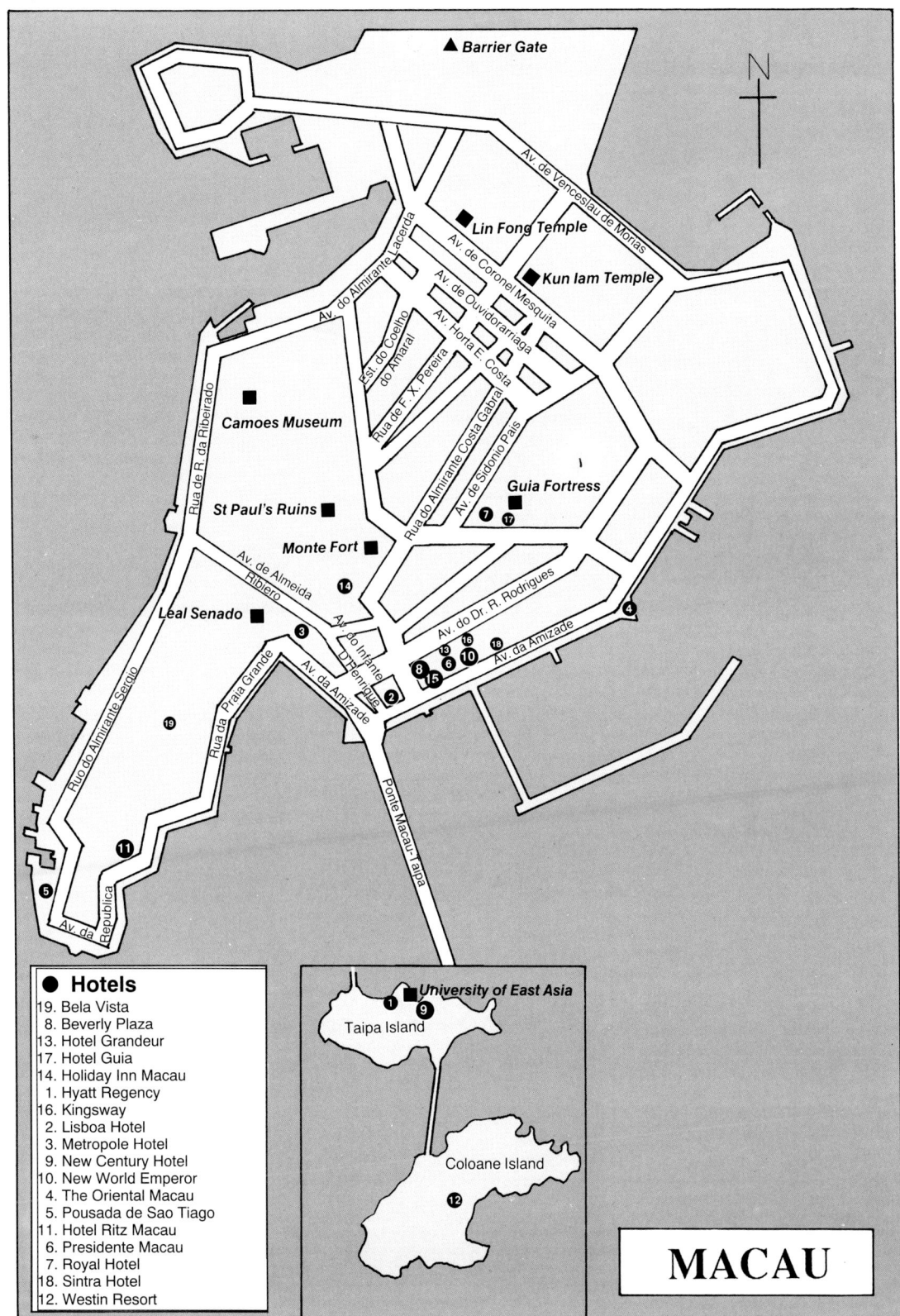

Macau Hotels

Hotel Bela Vista
8 Rua do Comendador Kou Ho Neng
Tel: (853) 965333; Fax: (853) 965588
E-mail: belavist@macau.ctm.net

Situated amidst elegant landscaped gardens on the slope of Colina da Penha, the century old Hotel Bela Vista commands impressive views of Praia Grande Bay. This enchanting boutique hotel has been part of the history of th Portuguese enclave since the late 1800s and, following its complete restoration, offers Macau's finest accommodation and dining experience.

Accommodation & rates:
4 guest rooms, HK$ 2000-3450;
4 suites, HK$ 2200-5250;

Credit cards accepted:
Amex, Bank Americard, Diners Club, Eurocard, OTB, Visa, Mastercard

Meeting & banqeting facilities
Private dining room with capacity for 16; largest reception open terrace 100 seated/ 350 cocktail

Room services
Airconditioning, colour TV, direct-dial telephone, hairdryer, laundry/valet service, minibar, radio, in-room safe, 24-hr room service

Business & other services
Free arrival and departure shuttle, postal services, travel & tour desk, baby sitting, car parking & hire, taxi service, bank

Sports & recreation
Guests can use the sport & recreation facilities of the Mandarin Oriental Macau

Restaurants & Coffee Shops
Bela Vista (60) - International, Portuguese/ Macanese, open 0700-2200

Overseas Sales Representatives:
Mandarin Oriental Hotel Group, Leading Hotels of the World, Utell International, Small Luxury Hotels

Hotel Beverly Plaza Macau C
Avenido do Dr Rodrigo Rodrigues
Tel: (853)782288; Tlx: 88345; Fax: 780704

Hotel Fortuna C
Rua da Cantao
Tel: (853)786333; Fax: (853) 786363

Hotel Grandeur Macau ○ C
Rue de Peguim, Outer Harbour
Tel: (853)781233; Fax: (853) 785896

Hotel Grandview D
(Pre-opening numbers)
Tel: (853) 82005; Fax: (853) 837777

Hotel Guia D
Estrada do Eng. Trigo 1-5
Tel: (853) 513888; Fax: (853) 559822

Holiday Inn Macau ○ C
Rua de Pequim, S-N
Tel: (853) 783333; Fax: (853) 782321

Hyatt Regency Macau ○ C
2 Estrada Almirante Marques Esparteiro, PO Box 3008, Taipa Island
Tel: (853) 831234; Tlx: 88512; Fax: 830195

Kingsway Hotel D
Rua de Luis Gonzaga Gomes
Tel: (853) 702888; Fax: (853) 702828

Lisboa Hotel ○ D
Ave. da Amizade, PO Box 85
Tel: (853) 377666; Tlx: 88203 HOTEL OM; Fax: (853) 567193

Mandarin Oriental Macau ○
956-1110 avenida da Amizade
Tel: (853) 567888; Fax: (853) 594589

Conveniently situated at the city's prime location on the seawall of the outer harbour, Mandarin Oriental Macau is close to Macau's International Airport and the China border, within walking distance from the ferry terminal, entertainment and shopping districts. Guest rooms face either the magnificent views of the South China Sea or the wooded hillside of the Guia fortress.

Accommodation & rates:
105 doubles, 302 twin, HK$ 1300-1900;
28 suites, HK$ 3800-20000

Credit cards accepted:
Amex, Diners Club, Eurocard, Mastercard, Visa, Barclaycard, Bank Americard, OTB

Meeting & banqueting facilities
15 meeting/function rooms, capacity 8 to 300, with audio-visual facilities; largest reception 236 seated/300 cocktail

Room services
Airconditioning, colour TV + video & satellite, direct-dial telephone with personal voicemail, fax & modem ports, hairdryer, laundry/valet service, minibar, safety deposit box, tea/coffee making facilities, 24-hr room service, non-smoker bedrooms available

Business & other services
Business centre, executive floor, express checkout, shuttle bus service, car parking & rental, baby sitting, travel centre, taxi service, barber shop/beauty salon, guided tours, newsstand/shops, foreign exchange, postal service, medical service

Sports & recreation
Fitness centre/gym, aerobics studio, tennis, massage, squash, outdoor swimming pool

Restaurants & Coffee Shops
The Mezzaluna - Italian, open 1230-1500/ 1830-2300 (closed Monday); *Cafe Girassol* - Coffee Shop, open 24 hours (Thursday til midnight only); *The Dynasty* -Cantonese, open 0800-1500/1800-2300

Overseas Sales Representatives:
Mandarin Oriental Hotel Group, Leading Hotels of the World, Utell International

Macau Masters Hotel D
Rua das Lorchas, 162
Tel: (853) 937572; Fax: (853) 937565

Metropole Hotel ○ D
62-63a Rua da Praia Grande
Tel: (853) 388166; Tlx: 88356 CTSOM; Fax: (853) 330890

Nam Yue Hotel C
International Centre, Av Dr Rodrigo Rodrigues.
Tel: (853) 726288; Fax: (853) 726726

New Century Macau ○ C
Av. Padre Tomas Pereira No 889, Taipa
Tel: (853) 831111; Fax: (853) 832222

New World Emperor Hotel ○ C
Rua de Xangai, Macau
Tel: (853)781888; Tlx: 88832; Fax: 782287

Pousade de Coloane D
Praia de Cheoc Van, Coloane
Tel: (853)882143; Tlx: 88251; Fax: 882251

Pousada da Sao Tiago ◐ C
Fortaleza de S Tiago de Barra, Avda da Republica.
Tel: 378111; Tlx: 88376 Fax: 552170

Hotel Presidente Macau ◐ D
355 Ave da Amizade
Tel: 553888; Tlx: 88440; Fax: 552735

Hotel Ritz Macau ◐ C
Kou Ho Neng, Macau
Tel: 339955; Tlx: 88316 ; Fax: 317826

Hotel Royal ◐ C
Estrada da Vitoria 2-4
Tel: 552222; Tlx: 88514 ; Fax: 563008

Hotel Sintra ◐ D
Avenida Dom Joao IV
Tel: 710111; Fax: 510527

The Westin Resort Macau B
Estrada de Hac Sa, Ilha de Coloane
Tel: 871111; Fax: 871122

Restaurants

456 Shanghai *(Chinese)*
Lisboa Hotel, Ave. da Amizade. Tel: 377666
Adam's Apple *(Continental)*
38 Avenida Sidonio Pais. Tel: 581366
Afonso III *(Portuguese)*
11a Rua Central. Tel: 586272
A Lorcha *(Portuguese)*
289 Rua Almiralte Sergio. Tel: 313195
Ban Thai *(Thai)*
1 Rua Henrique Macedo. Tel: 372050
Beira Mar *(Continental with dancing)*
Jai Alai Stadium. Tel: 383866/381770
Caçarola *(Portuguese)*
8 Rua das Gaivotas, Coloane.Tel: 882226
Dynasty *(Chinese)*
Mandarin Oriental Hotel, Ave. da Amizade. Tel: 567888
Fat Siu Lau *(Macanese)*
64 rua da Felicidade. Tel: 573585
Fernando *(Portuguese)*
9 Praia de Hác Sá, Coloane. Tel: 882264
Fok Lam Mum *(Chinese)*
63a Ave da Amizade. Tel: 386388
Jade Garden *(Chinese)*
Rua dr. Pedro J Lobo. Tel: 82005
Kwun Hoi Heen *(Cantonese)*
Westin Resort Macau, Estrada de Hac Sa, Ilha de Colane.Tel: 871 1111
La Forteleza *(International)*
Pousada de Sao Tiago Hotel, Ave. da Republica. Tel: 78111

Long Kei *(Cantonese)*
7b Largo do Senado. Tel: 573970
Leung Un *(Italian)*
46 Rua da Cunha, Taipa Island. Tel: 27061
Maxim's (Henri's Galley) *(International)*
4 Ave da Republica. Tel: 562231
O Pescador *(Seafood)*
Hyatt Regency Hotel, PO Box 3008, Taipa Island. Tel: 321234
Pinocchio's *(Local)*
4 Rua do Sol, Taipa Island. Tel: 327128
Pun Kai *(Cantonese & Dim Sun)*
44 Rua da Praia Grande. Tel: 75934/88737
Portugues *(Portuguese)*
16 Rua do Campo. Tel: 375445
Shangri-La *(Continental)*
13a Grd Fl, Av Horta e Costa. Tel: 564706
Silver Court *(Chinese)*
New Century Hotel, Taipa. Tel: 831111
Solmar *(Portuguese)*
11 Rua da Praia Grande. Tel: 574391
Toscana *(Italian)*
GP Building, Av de Amizade. Tel: 726637

Airline Offices

Air Macau
693 Avenida da Praia Grande, Tai Wah Bldg 9-12th fl.Tel: 396 6888; fax: 396 6466
Asiana Airlines
Mezzanine Level, suite 22-24, Macau Int'l Airport. Tel: 861400; fax: 861404
China Northern Airlines, China Northwest Airlines
Corporation Group Macau Co Ltd, 7-9 Avenida de D Joao IV, Centro Commercial Iat Teng Hou, 5th fl. Tel: 711888; fax: 711824
Eva Airways
Rm 6, Mezzanine Floor, Macau Airport
Tel: 861330; fax: 861324
Korean Air
Mezzanine Fl, rooms 15-18, Macau Intern'l Airport. Tel: 861480; fax: 861485
Malaysia Airlines
Bank of China Bldg, 18th fl - B/C, Macau. Tel: 787898; Fax: 787883
Singapore Airlines
Luso Int'l Bank Bldg, 10th fl, Room 1001. Tel: 711728; fax: 711732
Tap Air Portugal
Lojas S & T, Dynasty Plaza Lote 8 (A 2/C), NAPE, Macau. Tel: 750408; fax: 750409
TransAsia Airways
11th fl B-C, Macau Finance Centre 244-246, Rua de Pequin.
Tel: 701777; Fax: 701565

Useful addresses

Air Couriers
DHL: Tel: 372828; **UPS**: Tel: 273 53535;
TNT: Tel: 2331 2663; Fax: 2331 2266

Associacao dos Exportadores e Importadores de Macau (Export/Import Assoc.)
Av Inf D Henrique 60-62, 3rd fl, Macau
Tel: 375859; Telex: 88216; Fax: 512174

Air Macau
PO Box 1910, Ava Dr Rodrigo Rodrigues 10th fl, Edif. Nam Kwong.
Tel: 713724/5/6; Fax: 713728

AMCM - Autoridade Monetaria e Cambial de Macau
R Pedro Nolasco da Silva 45, Macau
Tel: 325416; Telex: 88479; Fax: 325433

Associacao Industrial de Macau (Macau Industrial Association)
17th floor, AIM Building, Rua Dr Pedo Jose Lobo 34-36. Tel: 574125; Telex: 88542 AIMAC OM; Fax: 578305

CAM - Macau Airport Company
Av de Mario Soares,Edif. Banco da China 29th fl. Tel: 785448; Fax: 785465

Car Hire
Avis Rent a Car
Shopping Arcade Car Park, Mandarin Oriental Hotel.Tel: 555686; 567888 ext. 3004; Tlx: 76228 HX; Fax: 314112
Happy Rent A Car
64 Istmo Ferreira do Amaral G/F, Macau
Tel: 439393; Fax: 439696 or
New Century Hotel Car Park - tel 831212

**Departamento de Promocao de Exportacoes
(Macau Export Promotion Department)**
8th floor, Luso Internacional Building, Rua Dr Pedro Jose Lobo 1-3. Tel: 378221; Telex: 88413 DPE OM; Fax:590309
Direccao dos Servicos de Economia
(Macau Economic Services)
25th floor, Luso Internacional Building, Rua Dr Pedo Jose Lobo 1-3. Tel: 562622; Telex: 88413 dpe om; Fax: 590309

Governor's Office
Palacio do Governo, Rua da Praia Grande. Tel: 565555; Telex: 88201 govma om

IPIM - Macau Investment Promotion Office
R Dr Jose Pedro Lobo, 1-3, Edif Banco Luso Int'l 7th fl. Tel: 712660/340090; Fax: 712659
Macau Business Centre
Grd Fl, Edificio Ribiero, Loja D, PO Box 138. Tel: 373379/511631/323598; Tlx: 88251 MBC OM; Fax: 511631
Macau Government Tourist Office
9 Largo do Senado, PO Box 3006, Macau
Tel: 315566; Tlx: 88338 ; Fax: 510104.
also at Macau Maritime Terminal. Tel: 726416/7
World Trade Center Macau
R de Pequiem 183, 5th Fl, A-B, Edif Marina Plaza. Tel: 562151/565225; Telex: 88831 WTC OM; Fax: 563398

DON'T YOU WISH YOU WERE HERE?

Dining and wining can also be an event in Macau

The Bela Vista Hotel - a touch of nostalgia

Yesterdays traditions are alive, for today and tomorrow

Dragon dance at the ruins of St. Paul's

Fun and Action all year round

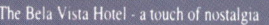
Gateway to China

City of Culture

MACAU

MACAU GOVERNMENT TOURIST OFFICE
9 Largo do Senado, PO Box 3006, Macau. Tel: (853) 315566; Fax: (853) 510104;
Internet: http://macau.tourism.gov.mo
1 Battersea Church Road, London SW11 3LY. Tel: (44) [0] 171 771 7006; Fax: (44) [0] 171 771 7059

COUNTRY REPORT
MALAYSIA '97

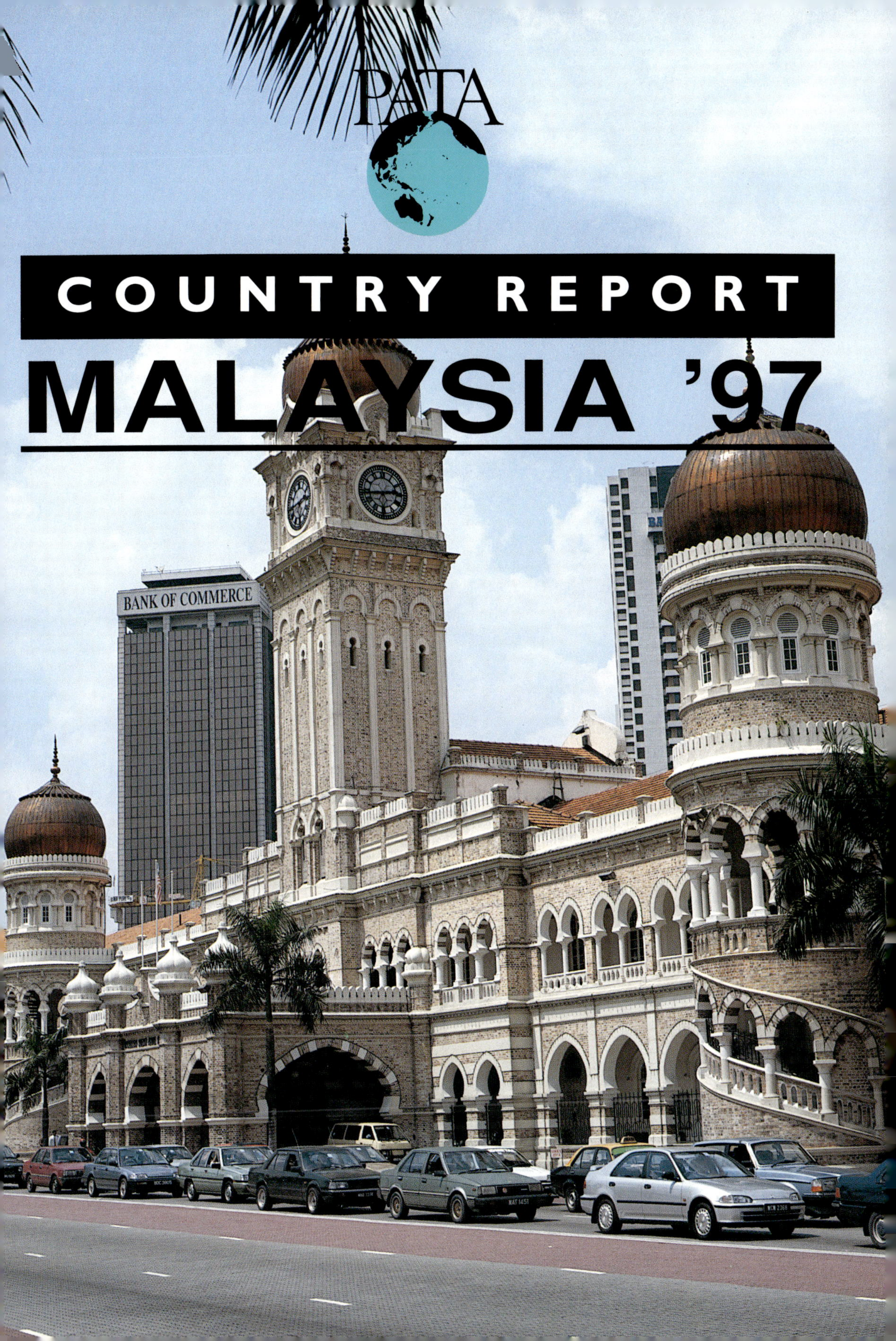

Malaysia

Background

General climate

If any underlying resentments remain between Malaysia's Malay and Chinese peoples over shares of the country's rich natural spoils, then they are hard to detect but always worth bearing in mind when exploring potential business partnerships.

The racial tensions of the early 1970s that led to the march of the Bumiputras and shift of economic as well as political power and decision making to the majority Malays may seem, on the surface at least, all but forgotten as Malaysia heads inexorably towards another economic boom.

Yet they are worth remembering if only for the business visitor to understand and be patient with the sometimes unexpected intervention of extra bureaucracy and lengthy decision making in a business climate that is otherwise wide open to foreign participation.

Once deemed as moody, introspective and slow to cooperate with the outside world, Malaysia in the past 10 years has become a powerful base for new high-tech industries, building on its rich natural mainstays of oil/gas, tin, rubber, palm oil and, latterly, tourism.

Kuala Lumpur, the capital and financial conduit for all main industries, is today unrecognisable from the slow, provincial garden city of the early 80s. It exudes wealth and affluence, with a burgeoning and ever-expanding middle class proud to display all the trappings of economic success - gold watches, mobile phones, glittering shopping malls and shiny, late model cars.

Success has also brought a completely different look and feel to a city once easy to get around. Despite massive new highway projects, traffic jams are part of daily life, exacerbated by countless new multi-purpose complex developments such as the twin Petronas Towers, soaring to 1,475 feet - 21 feet higher than the Sears Tower in Chicago - to become the tallest building in the world.

New city ring roads plus a light rail transit linking downtown commercial centres are expected eventually to ease traffic problems - at least in the wake of the 1998 Commonwealth Games, deadline date for much of the new construction. But a shortage of taxis, particularly at peak hours or when it is raining, plus a general lack of parking space, makes scheduling more than two or three business calls per day difficult.

Business etiquette

Being punctual for business meetings is important to Malaysians, as is showing respect for their staunchly Islamic principles. The ways of doing business are predominantly Western, with largely formal attire for both men and women and English widely spoken. But the means are Eastern, requiring more than a passing prior knowledge of family connections and hierarchy.

Even if your business is generated through a Chinese Malaysian, or an Indian, it more than likely will require the higher approval of a Malay. Knowing who's who through a good local agent and having command of titles that are often long and complex can prove a definite advantage in smoothing the passage of any given project.

Malaysia could never claim to be as squeaky clean as Singapore, its former federation partner and competitor, although corruption officially is frowned upon. Gifts and entertaining are acceptable.

Malaysian restaurants are admirably varied and generally first class, whether you are in the gourmet dining room of a hotel or at a street market. Nightlife, while far from being racy, also is varied, ranging from supperclubs with cultural shows through discos and jazz clubs to, a particular business favourite, karaoke.

Apart from KL's traffic jams, the general infrastructure for doing business is excellent, with a surplus of good top of the range hotels at sometimes bargain rates; efficient telecommunications plus an advanced network of highways speedily linking main centres across Peninsular Malaysia.

Again outside KL (where some hotels provide chauffeur-drive cars by the hour, day or week at low rates), Malaysia is an easy country to visit using car hire as an alternative to the also comprehensive, expanding and generally efficient domestic air network.

Tourism Update

General Developments

Malaysia has a number of tourism centres, of which the main ones are the capital Kuala Lumpur, Penang, Kota Kinabalu, and Kuching.

In general, the East Malaysia state capitals of Kota Kinabalu and Kuching are centres for adventure travel (and Sarawak has recently begun to promote eco-tourism), Penang is for beaches, and Kuala Lumpur for more urban and developed attractions. There are numerous other secondary attractions including the country's national parks, the east coast beaches, Melaka, Langkawi etc.

As the country's economy and infrastructure grow - such as the new 900km North-South tollway - the more opportunities there will be for the tourism industry.

New attractions in Kuala Lumpur include a communications tower, the Menara, which opened in 1996, and a light train project.

There was a large increase in visitor arrivals in 1990 when a *Visit Malaysia Year* promotion was held. But this was followed by a fall the following year. A similar VMY promotion took place in 1994, and this also helped push visitor arrivals growth into double digits. There was no drop in 1995, but the increase was only 3.8%, taking the total to 7,468,749. Figures for 1996 were not available at the time of going to press.

Malaysia's visitor arrival counts are high relative to most other regional destinations because the Malaysia Tourism Promotion Board counts categories of visitors across the land border with Singapore, although the equivalent is not counted in, for instance, the visitor arrival total for Singapore. For this reason, Malaysia's total should not be compared with Singapore's, but the basis is similar for Thailand's visitor count.

Of the major market sources for Malaysia in 1995, Singapore increased 1.5% to 4,537,347, Thailand fell 1.5% to 530,160, Japan at 15.5% grew fast, to 330,725, Taiwan also grew fast, at 17.3%, to 293,896, and Indonesia grew 3.6% to 233,996. The number of inbound travellers was expected to reach 12.5 million in 2000 on the 7.5 million base in 1995.

The inbound visitor profile is expected to show positive results as a result of Malaysia Airlines' route expansion and Malaysia's increasing range of attractions. Average length of stay is approximately five days. The budget of the MTPB is approximately US$40 million.

Airlines

There were important changes in aviation starting 1996, which have been interpreted as the start of liberalisation of air transport in the country.

The first, actually created towards the end of 1995, was the creation of Saeaga Airlines as a joint-venture between the Sabah and Sarawak governments and another company. Saeaga began by flying within the states of East Malaysia, but it was expected to start shorthaul international flights, probably by early 1997, and it was also considering flights to Australia. The airline was also expected to order 10 B737-700 aircraft before the end of 1996.

The other development is potentially more significant. Air Asia was formed almost five years ago to be a new international airline operating regional flights. However, changes in its governmental sup-

port caused plans to be changed, making it a ground operator, handling airlines at airports, and not an airline itself. But in 1996, the original aim was reinstated and the company was given permission to start flights, but using the name Pacific Eagle. The plan was for regular charter flights, starting before the end of the year, over Kuala Lumpur-Kota Kinabalu-Taipei. Other routes planned were to two holiday resorts - Pattaya in Thailand, and Subic Bay in the Philippines.

Pacific Eagle also has plans to start longhaul flights, to the US and Europe, but not until 2000. Its second B737 was due in January 1997; both are leased for a three-year period.

In yet another change in the aviation scene, Malaysia Airlines was expected to take a greater equity share in Pelangi Air, a third-level airline which almost 10 years earlier devised plans to operate regional routes in competition with Malaysia Airlines. Despite all this other airline activity, Malaysia Airlines has also grown much in terms of capacity, with longhaul expansion to Africa and Latin America. Malaysia Airlines has become the first airline to buy the new long-range 777-200X aircraft. The airline wants to operate non-stop from Kuala Lumpur to Chicago, Los Angeles and New York.

Traffic growth in 1994 and 1995 was also rapid. In 1995, seats sold increased 11.5% to 5.7 million, and RPKs increased 16.9% to 19.3 billion. Malaysia Airlines operates domestic as well as international flights, and its fleet - from light planes to B747-400s - illustrates this.

At Kuala Lumpur airport, the international passenger total increased 6.8% to 6,985,622. A key factor in development of aviation are plans to build a new airport for Kuala Lumpur at Sepang, 50km from Kuala Lumpur. This is due to open in 1998 and will have an initial annual capacity for 25-30 million passengers.

Hotels

Hotels are spread around the country in the many tourism and business centres, although there is now significant development planned for Kuala Lumpur. But at the same time, international hotel groups have begun to open hotels around the country, and this is likely to expand tourism around the country also.

There has been strong growth in the number of hotels throughout Malaysia over the past five years -- an average of over 10% per year. In 1995, the increase was 15.9%, taking the total to 76,373. This was above demand as occupancy in Kuala Lumpur in 1996 was about five percentage points below the 1995 figure of 77%.

There have been moves over the past few years to establish a new resort destination at Langkawi, north of Penang, and this is expected to continue as more hotel rooms open there, although progress is limited by the lack of international flights.

Another new resort is being built at Karambunai, 35 km from Kota Kinabalu in East Malaysia. the first of as many as 10 new hotels is the luxury 500-room Nexus, planned to open late 1997; another could be the 3-star, 300-room Muara Hotel. There are also plans for a golf course, apartments, condominiums etc.

As noted above, there is major addition of hotels in the capital Kuala Lumpur, and analysts forecast that the city will have more rooms than it needs for the number of travellers expected for as long as five years. This would mean that there would be discounting of hotel tariffs for much of this period.

Hotel projects due over the period 1997-98 include the following: In **Cameron Highlands**, the Equatorial Hill Resort with a total 410 rooms. In **Kuala Lumpur**, the Byron with 238 rooms; Conrad with 600 rooms; a Formula 1 (an economy brand name of the Accor hotel group) with 80 rooms; Grand Hyatt Duta with 572 rooms; Mandarin Oriental with 645 rooms; Renaissance with 400 rooms; Ritz Carlton with 248 rooms; Rockman's Regency with 323 rooms and Sheraton Towers with 400 rooms. At Sepang International Airport a Pan Pacific International is due to open December 1997. In **Kuching**, the Byron with 300 rooms. In **Melaka**, the Century Mahkota with 617 rooms; Equatorial with 496 rooms; Hyatt Regency Duta with 220 rooms and 1 260-room Pan Pacific. And in **Penang**, the Century with 950 rooms; Regalis Park with 320 rooms; Swiss Inn with 200 rooms and Pan Pacific Leader with 373 rooms. In **Kota Kinabalu** a 500-room Pan Pacific.

What to See

For lovers of beautiful buildings, then Kuala Lumpur has more than its fair share and is probably one of the best cities in Asia to view such architecture. Monuments to the genius of little-known architect A.C.Norman include: the Railway Station, which is a real gem, the mock tudor delights of the Royal Selangor Club (known locally as *The Spotted Dog*), the Sultan Abdul Samad Building, the Keretapi Tanah Melayu Railway Office and the Survey Office.

The city also boasts some fine mosques. The two best examples are the Masjid Negara and the Masjid Jame. Just north of KL are the famous Batu Caves with a Hindu shrine at the top of 200 steps.

For a weekend break away from KL, there's really only two choices - either the beach resorts of Penang and Langkawi or the cool mountain air of the Malaysia's upland areas. The Cameron Highlands has some of the best known hill country and some excellent hotels and good golf courses.

Penang is less than an hour's flight from KL and a great short-break destination. Not to be missed are the funicular railway up 770-metre Penang Hill in George Town and the city's snake temples. Down in the south, a trip to Malacca can be combined with a visit to Singapore. Malacca - a former Dutch and Portuguese trading post - has a particularly interesting colonial quarter.

Shopping

In terms of shopping, Malaysia offers great value for money. For quality stick to the fancy shopping malls and pricey hotel arcades, but if you are looking for a bargain or inexpensive gifts then the street stalls are your best bet. Haggling is an every day part of the buying process on the street, so don't be shy in asking for a price perhaps 50 per cent below the seller's starting figure.

Malaysia is not awash with locally-made goods, although pewter appears a particularly good buy. Batik, *kain songet* (hand-woven silk with a gold and silver weave) and handicrafts are also worth looking out for, but better buys are probably available elsewhere in the region.

One of the best areas to shop for batik is along Jalan Ipoh, to the north of the central business district. There are many other stores to chose from and, if you want handicrafts, then the government-run Karyaneka Handicraft Centre is as good as anywhere.

Like Singapore, Kuala Lumpur has any number of smart new air-conditioned shopping complexes that sell quality goods such as designer-label clothes and export-quality electrical goods. Examples are Star Hill Centre in the town centre, The Mall, opposite the Putra World Trade Centre and, further out of town, One Utama.

Locally-made goods are certainly worth seeking out as they are much cheaper than comparable items in North America or Europe. Major stores include: *Metro Jaya* (Bukit Bintang Plaza), *Mun Loong* (Kuala Lumpur Plaza and Kota Raya), *Yaohan* (The Mall and Bandar Park-OUG) and *Pakson Grand* (Sungai Wang Plaza).

At the other end of the spectrum, local street markets offer outstandingly good value. The Jalan Cheng Lock or the Central Market is particularly recommended, as is the *Pasar Malam* (night market).

Getting Around

Malaysia Airlines and Pelangi Air both offer domestic airline services to a wide range of local destinations. There are at least 11 flights a day between KL and Penang, for example. MHS Aviation offers a 9-seater executive jet (max. operating range 3700 kms) and helicopter services for the business traveller.

Car hire is highly recommended and best used for trips outside KL and Penang. Most car rental companies have their offices in hotels. KL is one of the few cities in the region where car rental can prove an attractive alternative to taxis and public transport services. Outside KL, the Malaysian road system is excellent and traffic congestion is minimal.

The country's rail network is as good as any in South East Asia, with trains running between major towns in Peninsular Malaysia and to Thailand and Singapore. Day and night trains operate on the main line between Butterworth and Singapore via Ipoh. There is also a line that goes up the east coast from Singapore, and Gemas in Johore, to Kota Bharu. This route links up again with the main Bangkok to Butterworth line at Haadyai, southern Thailand. It's well worth making a seat reservation before travelling.

A good way to see the country is by taking the Eastern and Oriental Express train which runs from Singapore to Bangkok, taking two nights and one day for the 1943-km journey. The train departs three timres per fortnight in either direction. Side trips can be taken en route to Penang or Kuala Lumpur. There are 14 accommodation cars, 3 restaurants, bars etc and 3 grades of cabin, all with private facilities. One-way fare starts at $1170. The timings allow the train to pass through the most scenic parts of Malaysia during daylight hours. September 1995 saw the addition of a steamer leg *The Road to Mandalay*, a spectacular journey up the Irrawaddy from Yangon to Mandalay in Myanmar.

Taxis are black in colour and sport yellow roofs with H or HW licence plates. The majority have air-conditioning. The fare is M$1.50 for the first 2km and an additional 20c for each 200 metres further. It's important to remember that there is a 50 per cent surcharge after midnight and before 0600. By and large, most drivers have a good working knowledge of the city and speak quite passable English.

The first phase of a new Light Rail Transit system opened in the capital in 1996.

Inter-city taxis are shared and you pay just for a seat with fixed rates. Buses are in abundant supply and are generally uncrowded and clean. Long-distance buses are also available.

Ferries operate between Butterworth and Penang (although the Penang Bridge has tended to supersede this service) and between Kuala Perlis and the resort island of Pulau Langkawi. There is also a service from Penang and between Mersing and Pulau Tioman.

Entertainment

In contrast with other capital cities in the area, Kuala Lumpur has little in the way of outrageous nightlife. In fact, KL is quiet and easy going, with the country's Islamic religion influencing social behaviour. But Malaysia is not Saudi Arabia or Iran and there are plenty of bars and discos for those out to enjoy themselves. The only difference is that all this happens in a more restrained manner than in some neighbouring states.

Malaysian cuisine comprises three main types - Malay, Indian and Chinese. Seafood, chicken, local fruits and rice and the key local staples. Most large hotels have Continental, Malay and Chinese restaurants or at least these styles on the menu. The best satay can be found at Kajang, about 15 km from KL, which attracts hordes of locals. *Nonya* cooking from the Straits-born Chinese is another local speciality.

Leisure

Almost all the leading hotels have well equipped fitness centres and swimming pools, with top marks going to the Hilton, Pan Pacific and Shangri-La. Joggers should head for the Lake Gardens, west of the city. As befits a former British colony, there is no shortage of golf clubs. More than 50 are described in Priory Publications' *South East Asia Golf Guide* and its section *Golf in Malaysia*, which is available free of charge from the Malaysian Tourism Promotion Board. Otherwise, a trip up into the Genting or Cameron Highlands gives a welcome breather from the humidity of KL in the summer.

For participants and spectators there is cricket, rugby and hockey that is played on the Padang at weekends, according to season. Soccer and badminton as the country's two most popular sports. Horse race meetings are held at the Selangor Turf Club Race Course at weekends.

Arrival & Departure

Kuala Lumpur's Subang International Airport is 22.5 km from the city centre and a taxi ride costs a M$20-25. A taxi coupon system ensures that no one is going to be overcharged. Journey time is about 50 minutes. The bus from Subang to KL is just M$1.50 and departs from Kelang Bus Station. Hotel shuttle buses also operate.

Departure tax is M$20 tax on all international flights, M$5 to Singapore and on domestic flights.

Discover the delights of South-East Asia on the most leisurely and stylish form of transport - The Eastern & Oriental Express.

Contact telephone numbers:
Singapore (65) 323 4390; USA (toll-free) (800) 524 2420; UK (171) 928 6000

Malaysia Key Fact File

Passport Requirements:
All visitors must be in possession of a valid passport. Commonwealth citizens (except Indian nationals) plus nationals of a few small European states do not not require a visa. Citizens from most of the rest of Western Europe and the US may stay up to three months without a visa. Most other nationals (but not those from the former Eastern bloc) can get a 14-day visa.

Currency:
Malaysian ringgit or dollar (M$). 100 cents = 1M$

Exchange Rate: US$ 1 = M$ 2.48; £1 = M$ 4.05 *(March 1996)*

Currency Restrictions: None

Electricity Supply:
220-240 volts AC

Language:
Bahasa Malaysia (Malay). English is very widely understood and used in business. Chinese dialects and Tamil also spoken by ethnic minorities.

Time:
GMT + 8; EDT + 13

IDD code: 60
Georgetown 4; Ipoh 5; Johor Bahru 7; Kota Kinabalu 88; Kuala Lumpur 3; Kuantan 60; Kuching 82; Malacca 6; Pahang 5; Penang 4, Perak 5; Sandakan 89; Taiping 5

Business hours:
Commercial offices: 0800/0830-1615/1630 Monday to Friday; 0800/0830-1230/1245 Saturdays.

Government offices: 0900-1600 Monday to Friday; 0900-1300 Saturdays. Many offices take a long break for lunch on Fridays.

Shops: 0830-1830 in peninsular Malaysia (many open later 'though).
Banks: 1000-1500 Monday to Friday; 0930-1130 Saturdays - with regional variations.

Customs & Entry:
The duty-free allowance is 1 quart bottle of liquor, 225 gramms of tobacco or 200 cigarettes plus goods to the value of M$200.

Health Requirements:
Visitors arriving from infected countries require yellow fever vaccination certificate.

Climate/best time to visit:
No distinct seasons, with year-round tropical warm, humid weather (min. 24°C, max. 32°C). Rainfall is generally heavy - 200 - 400 mm per month (wettest August-Nov).

National Holidays 1997
1 January New Years Day; 7-9 February Chinese New Year; 9 January* start of Ramadan; 9 February Hari Raja Puasa; 18 April Hari Raya Haji; 1 May Labour Day; 8 May Muharram; 26 May Spring Bank Holiday; 31 May Vesak Day; 7 June HM The King's Birthday; 17 July Prophet Mohamed's Birthday; 25 August Summer Bank Holiday; 31 August National Day; 30 October Deepavali; 25/26 December Christmas. *(*Moslem Holidays-may vary acc to moon)*

Useful Addresses

Government Agencies/Depts

Federation of Malaysian Manufacturers
17th floor, Wisma Sime Darby, Jalan Raja Laut, PO Box 12194, 50350 Kuala Lumpur
Tel: (03)293-1244; Telex:3237 fmm

Kuala Lumpur Visitors' Centre
3 Jalan Sultan Hishanuddin. Tel: 230 1369

Malay Chambers of Commerce & Industry
17th floor, Plaza Pekeliling, 2 Jalan Tun Razak, 50400 Kuala Lumpur
Tel: (03) 441-8522; Telex:30954 dewana

Malaysian Industrial Development Authority (MIDA)
6th floor, Wisma Damansara, Jalan Semantan, PO Box 10618, Kuala Lumpur 50720. Tel: (03) 255 3633; Telex: 30752 ; Fax: (03) 255-7970

Malaysian Industrial Development Finance Behad (MIDF)
195a Jalan Tun Razak, Peti Surat 12110, 50939 Kuala Lumpur. Tel: (03) 261-1166, 261-0066; Telex: 30534 midf

Malaysian International Chamber of Commerce & Industry
10th floor, Wisma Damansara, Jalan Semantan, PO Box 10192, 50706 Kuala Lumpur. Tel: (03) 254-1690, 254-2117; Telex: MA 32120 COMER

Ministry of Finance
Jalan Sultan Hishanuddin. Tel: 254 6066

Ministry of Information
Jalan Raja Laut. Tel: 274 5333

Ministry of Trade & Industry
Jalan Sultan Hishanuddin. Tel: 254 8044

Malaysia Tourism Promotion Board
26th Fl, Menara Dato' Onn, Putra World Trade Centre, Jalan Tun Ismail, 50480 Kuala Lumpur. Tel: 293 5188; Tlx: MTDC KL MA 30093; Fax: 293 5884

Secretarial Services

Ansacom
Lot 138, 1st Fl, Wisma HLA, Jln Raja Chulan. Tel: 242 8780

Hospitals, Post Office, Police

Subang Jaya Medical Centre
1 Jalan Subs. 12, 1a Subang Jaya, Selangor
Tel: 734 1212

University Hospital
Petaling Jaya, Selangor. Tel: 756 4422

General Post Office
Dayabumi Complex, Jalan Sultan Hishamuddin. Tel: 274 1122

Police
Jalan Pudu Police Station, off Jalan Bandar
Tel: 985 0222 (or 999 in emergency)

Air Couriers

DHL: Ipoh (05) 538043; Johore Bahru (07) 243211; Kota Kinabalu (088) 214769; Kuala Lumpur (03) 757 1166; Penang (04) 619413
Federal Express: Tel: Kuala Lumpur (03) 800 6363
TNT Express Worldwide: Ipoh (05) 253 2606; Johore Bahru (07) 3344988; Kota Kinabalu (88) 219950; Kuala Lumpur (03) 755 7744; Kuantan (09) 528893; Melaka (06) 283 2410; Penang (04) 642 0939
UPS: Kuala Lumpur (03) 794 2311

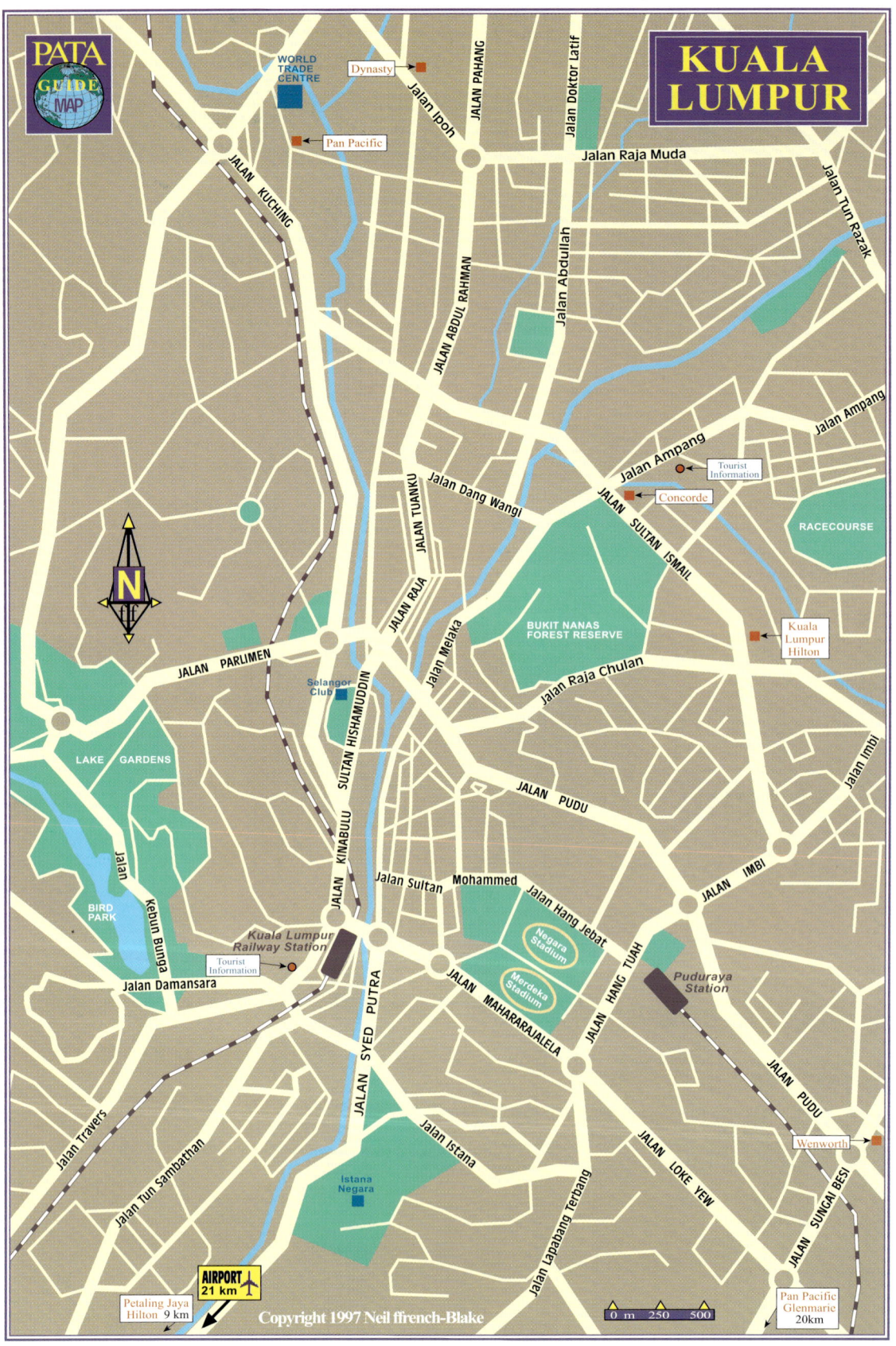

Kuala Lumpur Hotel Reference Table

Hotel (listed in price order)	SINGLE ROOM RATE (M$)	LOCATION	NUMBER OF ROOMS	NUMBER OF SUITES	CONFERENCE FACILITIES	EXHIBITION SPACE	LARGEST BANQUET NUMBER	BUSINESS CENTRE	SWIMMING POOL (0 = indoor)	TENNIS COURT	HEALTH CLUB	VIDEO FILMS
Marriott Kuala Lumpur	490	Jln Bintang	515	-	●	-	500	●	●	-	●	●
Renaissance Kuala Lumpur	460-520	Jln Ismail	399	-	●	-	500	●	●	-	●	●
Regent of Kuala Lumpur	455-520	Jl Ismail	452	17	●	●	400	●	●	●	●	●
Shangri-La Kuala Lumpur	400-550	Jl Ismail	686	35	●	●	1300	●	●	●	●	●
Hotel Istana	390-440	Jl Chulan	439	77	●	●	1600	●	●	●	●	●
Hotel Nikko Kuala Lumpur	390-430	Jln Ampang	470	-	●	-	500	●	●	-	●	●
Crown Princess	380-500	Jl Tun Razak	480	50	●	●	1600	●	●	●	●	●
Pan Pacific Hotel	380	Putra WTC	526	15	●	●	420	●	●	●	●	●
Hyatt Regency Saujana	340	Airport	370	16	●	-	200	●	●	●	●	●
Kuala Lumpur Parkroyal	340-370	Jl Ismail	296	41	●	●	550	●	●	●	●	●
Micasa Hotel Apartments	340-420	Jl T Razak	-	240	●	-	80	●	●	●	●	●
New World Hotel	330	Jln Ampang	500	21	●	●	1200	●	●	●	●	●
Pan Pacific Int'l Airport Htl	TBA	Airport	439	-	●	●	1000	●	●	-	●	-
Pan Pacific Glenmarie Rst	330-450	Jln Putra	272	19	●	●	350	●	●	●	●	●
Hilton Kuala Lumpur	320-380	Jl Ismail	501	87	●	●	1800	●	●	●	●	●
Pearl International	320-360	Jln Klang	550	13	●	-	750	●	●	-	●	●
Melia Kuala Lumpur	310-345	Jl Imbi	300	2	●	-	240	●	●	-	●	●
Holiday Inn City Centre	300-340	Jl Ismail	250	-	●	-	200	●	●	-	●	●
Holiday Inn on the Park	300-340	Jl Pinang	200	-	●	-	150	●	●	-	●	●
Ming Court Vista Hotel	300	Jl Ampang	390	57	●	●	550	●	●	●	●	-
Petaling Jaya Hilton	300-320	Pet'g Jaya	554	10	●	●	700	●	●	-	●	●
The Legend Hotel & Aptmts	300-400	Jln Putra	609	-	●	-	1000	●	●	●	●	●
Hotel Equatorial	280-300	Jl Ismail	275	15	●	-	350	●	●	-	-	●
Sucasa Hotel Apartments	280-410	Jl Ampang	-	142	●	-	90	●	●	●	●	●
Dynasty Hotel KL	275-390	Jl Ipoh	591	18	●	-	500	●	●	-	●	●
Concorde Hotel KL	260-460	Jl Ismail	586	24	●	-	765	●	●	-	●	●
Melia Kuala Lumpur	250-300	Jln Imbi	302	-	●	-	250	●	●	-	●	●
Subang Airport Hotel	250	Airport	157	-	-	-	-	-	-	-	-	-
Swiss Garden Hotel	250	Jl Pudu	302	12	●	-	110	●	●	-	●	●
Federal Hotel	230-310	Jl Ismail	450	-	●	-	700	●	●	●	●	●
Grand Continental	215	Jl Belia	243	85	●	●	300	●	O	-	●	●
The Merlin Subang	195	Airport	162	-	-	-	-	-	-	-	-	-
Kuala Lumpur Mandarin	190	Jl Ismail	150	2	●	●	200	●	-	-	-	-
Radisson Plaza	184-260	Jl Ampang	280	-	-	-	-	-	-	-	-	-
The Plaza Hotel	175-200	Jl R Laut	160	7	●	-	140	●	●	-	●	-
Wenworth Hotel	160-220	Jl Yew	246	4	●	-	200	-	●	-	-	-
The Plaza Hotel	150	Jln R Laut	160	-	-	-	-	-	-	-	-	-
Swiss Inn Kuala Lumpur	135-170	Jl Ismail	110	-	-	-	-	-	-	-	-	-

Rest of Malaysia Hotel Reference Table

Hotel	Single Room Rate (M$)	Location	Number of Rooms	Number of Suites	Conference Facilities	Exhibition Space	Largest Banquet Number	Business Centre	Swimming Pool	Tennis Court	Health Club	Video Films
The Datai	610-690	Langkawi	94	14	●	-	500	●	●	●	●	●
Radisson Tanjung Rhu Resort	600-1200	Langkawi	-	138	-	-	-	-	●	-	●	●
Berjaya Tioman Beach Resort	390-490	Tioman Isd	370	10	●	●	400	-	●	●	●	●
Penang Mutiara Beach	368-443	Penang	440	85	●	-	-	●	●	●	●	●
Hyatt Regency	350-550	Johor Bahru	406	-	-	-	600	●	●	-	●	●
Riviera Bay Resort	350	Malacca	450	-	-	-	-	-	●	●	●	●
Shangri-La's Tanjung Aru Rt	340-420	K Kinabalu	500	37	●	●	600	●	●	●	●	●
Holiday Inn Crowne Plaza	320	Johor Bahru	186	154	●	-	500	●	●	●	●	●
Pan Pacific Pangkor	320-800	Pangkor Isd	240	-	-	-	-	-	●	●	●	●
Puteri Pan Pacific, ('Kotaraya')	320-420	Johor Bahru	475	25	●	-	500	●	●	-	●	●
Berjaya Redang Beach Resort	320-350	Redang Isd	252	-	-	-	-	-	-	-	-	-

Rest of Malaysia Hotel Reference Table

Hotel (listed in price order)
TBA = rates to be announced

Hotel	Single Room Rate (M$)	Location	Number of Rooms	Number of Suites	Conference Facilities	Exhibition Space	Largest Banquet Number	Business Centre	Swimming Pool (0 = indoor)	Tennis Court	Health Club	Video Films
Sheraton Penang (ex-Merlin)	315	Penang	255	38	-	-	500	●	●	●	●	●
Shangri-La's Rasa Sayang Rst	310-390	Penang	500	14	●	●	700	●	●	●	●	●
Pan Pacific Sutera	TBA	K Kinabalu	499	-	●	-	800	●	●	●	●	●
Hyatt Kinabalu	310-400	K Kinabalu	315	20	●	●	500	●	●	●	●	●
Pan Pacific Malacca	TBA	Malacca	260	-	●	-	500	●	●	●	●	●
Pan Pacific Leader Hotel	TBA	Penang	373	-	-	-	-	●	●	●	●	●
Holiday Inn Kuching	305	Kuching	133	37	●	●	450	●	●	●	●	●
Kuching Hilton	305	Kuching	132	37	●	-	450	-	●	●	●	●
Sandakan Renaissance Htl	305-490	Sandakan	104	16	●	-	370	-	●	●	●	●
Awani Kyal Beach/Golf Resort	300	K Terengganu	278	9	●	-	320	●	●	●	●	●
Hotel Sofitel Palm Resort	300	Johor Bahru	330	-	●	-	-	●	●	●	●	●
Malacca Renaissance	300-425	Malacca	295	16	●	●	-	●	●	●	●	●
Penang Parkroyal	295-380	Penang	333	-	-	-	-	●	●	●	●	●
Holiday Inn Damai Beach	290	Kuching	302	-	●	-	180	●	●	●	●	●
Riverside Majestic	290-310	Kuching	250	-	●	●	1200	●	●	-	●	●
Pelangi Beach Resort	286-396	Langkawi	300	2	●	-	-	●	●	●	●	●
Shangri-La Hotel Penang	285-310	Penang	431	16	●	●	900	●	●	●	●	●
Holiday Inn Shah Alam	280-310	Selangor	145	9	●	●	700	●	●	●	-	●
Hotel Equatorial	280-305	Penang	415	-	●	-	1000	●	●	●	●	●
Berjaya Langkawi Beach Resort	280-350	Langkawi	394	-	-	-	600	-	●	●	●	-
Damai Lagoon Resort	276	Kuching	226	30	-	-	-	-	●	●	●	-
Rhiga Royal Hotel Miri	265-390	Miri	225	-	-	-	-	-	●	●	●	●
Holiday Inn Miri	260-280	Miri	168	-	-	-	-	-	●	●	●	●
Sheraon Langkawi Beach Rst	260-480	Langkawi	264	-	-	-	-	-	●	●	●	-
Tapa Nyal Island Resort	260	Malacca	145	-	-	-	-	-	●	●	-	-
Shangri-La's Golden Sands	255-345	Penang	395	-	●	●	240	●	●	●	●	●
Holiday Inn Penang	250-300	Penang	151	9	●	●	100	●	●	-	●	●
Malacca Village Paradise Resort	250	Malacca	134	11	●	-	-	●	●	●	●	-
Hyatt Regency Kuantan	245-290	Kuantan	185	-	●	-	250	●	●	●	●	●
The Legend Resort	240-320	Kuantan	248	-	-	-	-	-	●	●	●	●
Casuarina Beach Hotel	240	Penang	175	3	-	-	-	-	●	-	-	-
Bayview Beach Resort	235-275	Penang	364	82	●	●	350	●	●	●	●	-
Genting Hotel	230-300	Genting Hds	669	31	-	-	-	●	●	●	●	●
Royal Casuarina Hotel	220	Ipoh	182	16	●	●	1000	●	●	-	●	●
Crown Prince Penang	210-240	Penang	250	30	●	●	230	●	●	-	●	●
Equatorial Hill Resort	210-300	Cam. Highlands	510	-	●	●	600	●	O	●	●	●
Ferringhi Beach Hotel	200-225	Penang	312	37	●	●	350	●	●	-	●	-
Novotel Penang	200-280	Penang	286	32	●	●	500	●	●	●	●	●
Klana Resort	200-260	Seremban	198	15	●	●	900	●	●	●	●	●
City Bayview Hotel	190-220	Penang	146	14	●	●	200	●	●	-	●	-
Hotel Perdana	190-220	Kota Bahru	110	26	●	●	500	●	●	●	●	●
Burau Bay Resort	190-220	Langkawi	150	-	●	●	80	-	●	●	●	-
Strawberry Park Resort	185	Cam. Highlands	103	39	●	-	-	-	●	●	●	-
Langkawi Island Resort	180-200	Langkawi	213	-	-	-	-	-	●	●	●	●
Merlin Inn Resort	180-220	Kuantan	106	-	●	-	300	-	●	●	●	●
Desaru View Hotel	180	Johor Bahru	134	-	-	-	-	-	●	●	●	-
Primula Besut Resort	180	K Trengganu	264	27	●	●	1000	●	●	●	●	-
Eastern & Oriental	165-230	Penang	100	-	●	-	650	●	-	-	-	-
Ming Court Beach	160	Pt Dickson	159	12	●	-	400	●	●	-	●	-
Hilton Batang Ai Longhouse	160-180	Kuching	88	12	●	-	200	-	●	-	-	-
Merlin Inn Resort	160-170	Cameron Hds	62	-	-	-	-	-	-	-	-	●
Hotel Shangri-La	160-180	K Kinabalu	122	-	-	-	-	-	●	-	●	●
Palm Beach Resort	155-205	Penang	138	-	●	-	200	-	●	-	-	-
Coral Beach Resort	150-220	Kuantan	158	4	●	-	400	-	●	-	●	-
Capital Hotel	150-165	K Kinabalu	102	-	-	-	-	-	-	-	-	-
Premier Hotel	150	Sibu	145	7	●	●	300	●	-	-	-	●
Ye Olde Smokehouse Inn	150	Cam Highlands	13	-	-	-	-	-	-	-	-	-
Hotel Jesselton	140-160	K Kinabalu	27	-	-	-	-	-	-	-	-	-
Desaru Golf Hotel	130	Kota Tinggi	90	6	●	-	400	-	●	●	●	-
Aurora Hotel	120-140	Kuching	69	10	●	-	-	-	●	-	-	-
Golf Course Inn	110-140	Cameron H'ds	28	7	●	-	200	-	●	●	●	●
The Murni Hotel	92-104	Kota Bahru	40	-	-	-	-	-	-	-	-	-
The Borneo Hotel	90-120	Kuching	40	-	●	-	-	-	●	-	-	-
Grand Continental Melaka	80-128	Malacca	63	84	●	-	300	●	●	-	●	-

Malaysia Hotels

Cameron Highlands/Ipoh/ Pahang area (West Malaysia)

Equatorial Hill Resort Cameron Highlands
P.O. Box 78, 39100 Kea Farm, Brinchang, Cameron Highlands, Pahang Darul
Tel: (05) 499 1777; Toll-free: 800 3106; Fax: (05) 496 1333

Situated in Kea Farm, about 15 minutes' drive up from Tanah Rata. Spread over 13 acres of beautiful landscaped gardens, the Resort is sited on a knoll, 1628m above sea level. Its cool climate (15ºC to 25ºC) makes the resort a refreshing holiday retreat.

Accommodation & rates:
510 superior rooms & suites; rooms M$ 210-300; suites M$ 350-500
Subject to 10% service charge and 5% government tax

Credit cards accepted:
Mastercard, Visa, Amex, Diners

Meeting & banqueting facilities
7 meeting/function rooms, capacity 20 to 80; audio-visual equipment available; 8000 sq m exhibition space; largest reception 400-600 seated/500 cocktail; Grand Cameron Ballroom capacity 500-600

Room services
Colour TV, direct-dial telephone, hairdryer, laundry/valet service, minibar, safety deposit box, tea/coffee making facilities, trouser press, video films

Business & other services
Business centre, car parking, travel desk, taxi service

Sports & recreation
Billiards/snooker, indoor swimming pool, fitness centre/gym, indoor games, sauna, tennis, squash

Restaurants & coffee shops
Cricket Bar Lounge (100) - Bar/live band, open 1100-midnight (w/ends/pub.hols 0100); *Coffee Shop* (133) - Continental/local, open 0700-2330; *Golden Phoenix* (200) - Chinese, open 1830-midnight (Sat/Sun +0800-1400); *Singalot Karaoke Pub Lounge* (210-250), open 1700-midnight; *Food Bazaar*, Hawker cuisine, open 1000-2200 (w/ends/pub. hols)

Overseas Sales Representatives
Kuala Lumpur tel: (3) 264 7866/261 7777; fax: (3) 264 7663/263 2300. Japan Osaka tel: (6) 209 8437; fax: (6) 209 8439. Japan Tokyo tel: (3) 3542 2826; fax: 3546 8234. Beijing tel: (10) 6776 7436; fax: 6776 7441. Taipei tel: (2) 571 5491/3; fax: (2) 571 5499. Hong Kong tel: 2368 1922; fax: 2366 7621; E-mail: heihkso@netvigator.com. Corporate Sales & Mktg Office KL tel: (3) 732 0431; fax: (3) 235 8089; E-mail: corpoff@equatorial-int.com.sg

Hotel Excelsior ○ ¶
43 Jalan Clarke, 30300 Ipoh, Perak
Tel: 536666; Fax: 536912

The Garden Inn E
Tanah Rata, Pahang, Cameron Highlands
Tel: (05) 941911/941680

Genting Hotel D
Genting Highlands Resort, Ipoh 69000
Tel: (03) 211 1118; Tlx: 30482 GENTOL MA; Fax: (03) 211 1888

The Golf Course Inn E
PO Box 46, Tanah Rata, Pahang, Cameron Highlands, 39007
Tel: (05) 901411; Tlx: 32821; Fax: 901462

Merlin Inn Resort D
Cameron Highlands, Tana Rata 39007
Tel: (05) 491 1211; Tlx: 44253; Fax: (05) 491 1178

The Royal Casuarina Hotel D
18 Jalang Gopeng, Ipoh 30250, Perak.Tel: (05) 255 5555; Tlx: 44573; Fax: 255 8177

Strawberry Park Resort D
Lot 195/196 Tanah Rata 39000, Pahang Darul Makmur, Cameron Highlands
Tel: (05) 491 1166; Tlx: 44507 SPMCH MA; Fax: (05) 491 1949

Johor Bahru (West Malaysia)

Desaru Golf Hotel D
PO Box 50, 81907 Kota Tinggi,
Tel: (07) 821107; Tlx: 60500; Fax: 821480

Desaru View Hotel D
PO Box 71, Kota Tinggi 81907,
Tel: (07) 822 1221; Fax: (07) 822 1237

Holiday Inn Crowne Plaza ○ C
Jalan Dato Sulaiman, Century Garden, 80990 Johor Bahru Tel: (07) 332 3800; Tlx: MA 60790 HOLJB; Fax: (07) 331 8884

Hyatt Regency C
2 Jalan Sungai Chat, 80720
Tel: (07) 222 1234; Fax: (07) 223 2718

Puteri Pan Pacific,"The Kotaraya"
P.O. Box 293, 80730 Johor Bahru ○
Tel: (07) 223 3333; Fax: (07) 223 6622;
E-mail: panpjjb@po.jaring.my

Located in the heart of the city's commercial and government centre. Overlooking the straits of Johor and five minutes' drive from the causeway to Singapore.

Accommodation & rates:
500 rooms & suites; single M$ 320-420; double/twin M$ 350-450; suite M$ 450-1600.Subject to 10% service charge and 5% government tax

Credit cards accepted:
Mastercard, Visa, Amex, Diners

Meeting & banqueting facilities
9 meeting/function rooms; audio-visual equipment available; largest reception 500 seated/800 cocktail

Room services
Airconditioning, colour TV, direct-dial telephone (ext. in bathroom), hairdryer, laundry/valet service, minibar, music/radio/alarm clock, safety deposit box, tea/coffee making facilities, 24-hr room service,non-smoker & non-alcoholic floors available, video films.

Business & other services
Business centre, complimentary shuttle, limousine/car rental, travel desk, florist

Sports & recreation
Swimming pool, fitness and sports centre, sauna, massage, tennis, squash

Restaurants & coffee shops
4 restaurants offering Malay, Chinese, Continental, Italian and Western cuisine; poolside bar/dining area; pub/lounge for cocktails/entertainment

Overseas Sales Representatives
Pan Pacific Hotels & Resorts

Hotel Sofitel Palm Resort C
Senai Johor, 81250
Tel: (7) 599 6000; Fax: 599 7028

Kota Kinabalu (Sabah)

Best Western Berjaya Palace D
1 Jalan Tangki, Karamunsing, 88997
Tel: (088) 211911; Fax: (088) 211600

Hotel Capital D
23 Jln Haji Saman, PO Box 1223, 88813
Tel: (88) 231999; Tlx: 80699; Fax: 237222

The Pan Pacific Sutera Hotel Kota Kinabalu *(Opening December 1997)*
Pre-opening office: Pan Pacific Hotels & Resorts, 7 Raffles Boulevard, #01-050 Marina Square, Singapore 039595
Tel: (65) 339 4688; Fax: (65) 339 5787
E-Mail: etan@panpac.com.sg

Set within the Sutera Harbour project, which consists of golf courses, hotels, condominiums, residential properties and a boating marina.

Accommodation and Rates
499 rooms. Prices to be announced
Subject to 10% service charge and 5% government tax

Credit cards accepted:
All major

Meeting & banqueting facilities
Four meeting/function rooms, capacity 200; audio-visual equipment available; largest reception 800

Room services
Airconditioning, colour TV, direct-dial telephone (ext. in bathroom), hairdryer, laundry/valet service, minibar, safety deposit box, tea/coffee making facilities, 24-hr room service

Business & other services
Business centre, executive floor, express checkout, translation service, car parking, taxi service, newsstand/shops

Sports & Recreation
Fitness centre/gym, massage, swimming pool (outdoor), tennis, boating marina

Restaurants & Coffee Shops
All Day dining (190), *Chinese* (180), *Japanese* (170), *Lobby Lounge* (70) restaurants to be opened

Overseas Sales Representatives
Pan Pacific Hotels & Resorts Worldwide; SRS Steigenberger Reservation Service

Hyatt Kinabalu International C
Jalan Datuk Salieh Sulong, 88994
Tel: (088) 221234; Tlx: 80036 HYATKK MA; Fax: (088) 225972

Shangri-La's Rasa Ria Resort C
Pantai Dalit Beach, PO Box 600, 89208 Tuaran, Sabah
Tel: (88) 258885; Fax: (88) 258886

Shangri-La's Tanjung Aru Resort C
Locked Bag 174, 88744 Kota Kinabalu
Tel: (088) 58711/225800; Tlx: 80751 TABHOT MA; Fax: (088) 217155

Hotel Shangri La D
75 Bandaran Berjaya, PO Box 11178, 88819
Tel: (088) 212800; Tlx: 80001 HOSHAN MA; Fax: (088) 212078

Kuala Lumpur

Concorde Hotel Kuala Lumpur
2 Jalan Sultan Ismail, 50250
Tel: 244 2200; Tlx: 20226 CONKUL; Fax: 244 1628

A 610-room business hotel within Kuala Lumpur's "Golden Triangle", the city's main business and shopping district. Concored Hotel, Kuala Lumpur offers first class accommodation with restaurant, meeting and shopping facilities to international business travellers.

Accommodation and Rates
316 double/270 twin rooms M$ 260-460; 24 suites M$400-2000
Subject to 10% service charge and 5% government tax

Credit cards accepted:
Amex, JCB, Mastercard, Visa

Meeting & banqueting facilities
19 meeting/function rooms, capacity 35-765; audio-visual equipment available; 800 sq m exhibition space; largest reception 765

Room services
Airconditioning, colour TV, direct-dial telephone, laundry/valet service, minibar, music/ radio/alarm clock, 24-hr room service, safety deposit box (Concorde rms upwards), video films.

Business & other services
Business centre, executive floor, car parking, car rental, travel centre, taxi service, secretarial services, offices to rent, barber shop/beauty salon, newstsand, shopping arcade

Sports & Recreation
Fitness centre/gym, massage, swimming pool (outdoor)

Restaurants & Coffee Shops
Xin Cuisine (360) - Cantonese/Dim Sun, open Mon-Fri 1130-1430/1830-2200, Sat/Sun/Pub Hols 0900-1430/1830-2200; *Melting Pot Cafe* (200) - Asian/Continental, open 24 hours; *Spices* (130) - Asian "nouvelle cuisine", open 1130-1430/1800-2230; *Crossroads Lounge* (110) - Refreshments etc, open 1130-0100; *Espresso Bar* (30) - Deli, open 1000-2000; *Pool Terrace* (80) - Snacks, open 1000-1900.

Overseas Sales Representatives:
Delton Global Resevations

The Crown Princess C
City Square Complex, Jalan Tun Razak, 50400. Tel: 262 5522; Tlx: MA 28190 TCPHL; Fax: 262 4492

Dynasty Hotel Kuala Lumpur
218 Jalan Impoh, 51200
Tel: 443 7777; Fax: 443 6868

Located strategically along one of Kuala Lumpur's most well known landmarks - Ipoh Road or Jalan Ipoh, the Dynasty is within convenient reach of government offices, the central business district, Putra World Trade Centre and shopping malls.

Accommodation and Rates
315 double, 276 twin MS$ 275-390; 18 suites from M$ 490-690.
Subj. to 10% service charge & 5% govt tax

Credit cards accepted:
Amex, Mastercharge, Visa, Diners, JCB

Meeting & banqueting facilities
6 meeting/function rooms, capacity up to 1200; audio-visual facilities available; 540 sq m exhibition space; largest reception 500 seated or 1000 cocktail. Projection booth, stage, dance floor, decorative parties

Room services
Airconditioning, colour TV, direct-dial telephone (ext. in bathroom), hairdryer, laundry/valet service, minibar, music/radio/alarm clock, non-smoker bedrooms available, safety deposit box, tea/coffee making facilities, 24-hr room service, video films, fax outlet in deluxe rooms

MALAYSIA - Hotels 207

Business services
Business centre, express checkout, airport pickup, car parking, office studios

Other services
Guided tours, newsstand/shops

Sports & Recreation
Fitness centre/gym, massage, sauna, swimming pool (rooftop)

Restaurants & Coffee Shops
Aseana (150) - South East Asian, open 24 hours; *Primavera* (80) - Mediterranean, open noon-2230; *Tang Palace* (650) - Chinese, open 1130-2230

Hotel Equatorial ○ C
Jalan Sultan Ismail, 50250
Tel: 261 7777; Tlx: 30263; Fax: 261 9020

Federal Hotel ○ D
35 Jalan Bt Bintang, 55100
Tel: 248 9166; Tlx: MA 30429 FEDTEL; Fax: 248 2817

Hotel Grand Continental D
Jalan Belia/Jalan Raja Laut, 50350
Tel: 293 9333; Tlx: 28200; Fax: 293 9732

Hilton Kuala Lumpur
Jalan Sultan Ismail, PO Box 10577, 50718
Tel: 248 2322; Tlx: 30495; Fax: 244 2157

Strategically located in the golden triangle and within walking distance of the capital's commercial, banking and shopping district, the 36-storey Kuala Lumpur Hilton stands majestically on a 5-hectare hillock. The hotel is within 30 minutes from Subang Int'l Airport.

Accommodation and Rates
581 rooms; 195 singles M$ 320-400; 306 doubles M$ 350-430; 87 suites M$580-3800 Subject to 10% service charge and 5% tax.

Credit cards accepted:
Amex, JCB, Diners, Mastercard, Visa

Meeting & banqueting facilities
17 meeting/function rooms, capacity 50-1800; audio-visual facilities available; largest reception 1800 seated or cocktail

Room services
Airconditioning, colour TV, direct-dial telephone (ext. in bathroom), hairdryer, laundry/valet service, minibar, music/radio/alarm clock, non-smoker bedrooms available, safety deposit box, tea/coffee making facilities, trouser press, 24-hr room service, video films, handicapped rooms

Business services
Business centre, executive floor, express checkout, airport pickup, car parking, car rental, travel centre, taxi service

Other services
Barber shop/hairdresser, beauty salon, guided tours, newsstand/shops, boutiques

Sports & Recreation
Fitness centre/gym, golf (nearby), massage, sauna, swimming pool (outdoor), tennis, squash

Restaurants & Coffee Shops
Planters Inn (180) - 24 hours, local & continental; *Melaka Grill (80)* - Continental Fine Dining, open lunch & dinner; *Tsui Yuen* (180) - Chinese, open as above; *Gourmet House & Cafe* - deli,pastries etc, open 0730 (0930 at weekends) -1930.

Overseas Sales Representatives
Hilton Reservations Worldwide; Hilton International Sales Offices

Holiday Inn City Centre ○ C
PO Box 11585, Jalan Raja Laut, 50750
Tel: 293 9233; Tlx: 28130; Fax: 293 9634

Holiday Inn on the Park D
PO Box 10983, Jalan Pinang, 50732
Tel: 248 1066; Tlx: 30239; Fax: 248 1930

Hyatt Saujana Hotel & Country ○
Club D
Subang Int'l Airport Highway, 46710, PO Box 111 Petaling Jaya
Tel: 746 1188; Tlx: 37903; Fax: 746 2789

Hotel Istana ○ B
37 Jalan Raja Chulan, 50200
PO Box 12919, 50792 Kuala Lumpur
Tel: 241 9988; Tlx: 31621 ISTANA; Fax: 244 1245

Kuala Lumpur Mandarin Hotel D
2-8 Jalan Sultan Ismail, 50000
Tel: 230 3000; Tlx: 32143; Fax: 230 4363

The Legend Hotel & Apartments ○
Putra Place, 100 Jalan Putra, 50350 C
Tel: 442 9888; Tlx: MA 3208; Fax: 443 0700

Marriott Kuala Lumpur ○ A
Jalan Bukit Bintang
Tel: 245 9000; Fax: 245 3000

Melia Kuala Lumpur ○ C
16 Jalan Imbi, 55100 Kuala Lumpur
Tel: 242 8333; Tlx: 21117; Fax: 242 6623

Micasa Hotel Apartments
368 B Jalan Tun Razak, 50400
Tel: 261 8833; Tlx: 21362; Fax: 261 1186

Ming Court Vista Kuala Lumpur ○
Jalan Ampang, PO Box 11295, 50450 C
Tel: 261 8888; Tlx: 32621 MINGKL MA; Fax: 262 3428

New World Hotel B
128 Jalan Impang, 50450
Tel: 263 6888; Fax: 264 8868

Hotel Nikko Kuala Lumpur B
165 Jalan Impang, 50450
Tel: 261 1111; Fax: 261 1122

Pan Pacific KL International Airport Hotel *(Opening December 1997)*
(Pre-opening) Pan Pacific Hoels & Resorts
7 Raffles Boulevard, #01-050 Marina Square, Singapore 039595
Tel: (65) 339 4688; Fax: (65) 339 5787
E-Mail: etan@panpac.com.sg

The first hotel to open at the new Kuala Lumpur International Airport in Sepang. Developed around the concept of an "urban oasis"; abundant foliage, lush tropical plants and water features will ne the highlight.

Accommodation and Rates
439. Rates to be announced

Credit Cards accepted: All major

Meeting & banqueting facilities
10 meeting/function rooms, capacity 360; audio-visual equipment available; largest reception 1000 banquet; video conferencing facilities

Room services
Airconditioning, colour TV, direct-dial

(continued)

telephone (ext. in bathroom), hairdryer, laundry/valet service, minibar, safety deposit box, tea/coffee making facilities, 24-hour room/meal service

Business and other services
Business centre, executive floor, express checkout, car parking, taxi service, newstand/shops

Sports & Recreation
Fitness centre/gym, jacuzzi, massage, spa, sauna, outdoor swimming pool

Restaurants & Coffee Shops
All Day Dining (280); *Theme Dining* (160) - *Restaurant/Pub* (180); *Lobby Lounge* (60); all to be opened.

Overseas Sales Representatives
Pan Pacific Hotels & Resorts Worldwide; SRS Steigenberger Reservation Service

The Pan Pacific Glenmarie Resort Kuala Lumpur
Jalan Glenmarie, off Jalan Lapangan Terbang Antara Subang, PO Box 8354, Kelana Jaya, 46788, Peteraling Jaya, Selangor
Tel: (3) 703 1000; Fax: (3) 704 1000

Set amidst lush, tropical greenery, 7 minutes' drive from the International Airport and 26 minutes' drive from the city. The resort features 291 guest rooms and suites, overlooking golf and garden views.

Accommodation and Rates
272 single/double rooms, M$ 330-450; 19 suites, M$ 600-1500.Subject to 10% service charge & 5% govt tax

Credit cards accepted:
Amex, Visa, Diners, Mastercard, JCB

Meeting & banqueting facilities
13 meeting/function rooms, capacity 10-500; 50 sq m exhibition space; largest reception 350 seated or 500 cocktail

Room services
Airconditioning, colour TV (with CNN channel), direct-dial telephone, hairdryer, laundry/valet service, minibar, music/radio/alarm clock, safety deposit box, tea/coffee making, 24-hr room service, video films

Business & other services
Business centre, airport pickup, translation service, car parking & rental, taxi service Barber shop/hairdresser, beauty salon, guided tours, newsstand/shops

Sports & Recreation
Billiards/snooker, fitness centre/gym, golf, indoor games, jogging track, massage, sauna, squash, swimming pool (outdoor), tennis, night golf, 33-bay driving range

Restaurants & Coffee Shops
Rendezvous - Karaoke Lounge, open 1500 -2300; *Kites Restaurant* - International, open 24 hours; *The Glen (Lounge)* - Drinks/Deli lunches, open 1100-midnight;*Pool Bar* - Local/Western, open 1000-1900; *Cender-awasih* - Chinese, open noon-1430/1900-2230; *Garden Terrace* - Snacks, open 0700 -2300; *Pine Terrace* - Drinks, snacks, open noon-2000

Overseas Sales Representatives
Pan Pacific Hotels and Resorts

Parkroyal Kuala Lumpur   C
Jl Sultan Ismail, 50250
Tel: 242 5588; Tlx: 30486; Fax: 241 5524

Pan Pacific Hotel Kuala Lumpur
Jalan Putra, PO Box 11468, 50746
Tel: 442 5555; Tlx: 33706; Fax: 441 7236

Located in the heart of the city of Kuala Lumpur and conveniently placed near the best shopping complex and the Putra World Trade Centre, the hotel has 571 luxuriously appointed rooms and suites, furnished with all the comforts of a 5-star hotel.

Accommodation
179 deluxe king, 287 deluxe twin, 31 Pacific Floor king, 29 Pacific Floor twin, 15 suites

Rates:
Single/double M$ 380; twin/double M$ 410; Suite M$ 750-1300.
Subject to 10% service charge and 5% government tax

Credit cards accepted:
Amex, Diners, Mastercard, Visa, JCB

Meeting & banqueting facilities
7 meeting/conference rooms, capacity 20-500, with audio-visual equipment; 600 sq m exhibition space; largest reception 420 banquet or 550 cocktail.

Room services
Airconditioning, colour TV, direct-dial telephone, hairdryer, laundry/valet service, minibar, in-room safe, tea/coffee making facilities, trouser press, 24-hr room service, non-smoker bedrooms, video films.

Business & other ervices
Business centre, executive floor, car parking, taxi service, travel centre, barber shop/beauty salon, newsstand/shops

Sports & Recreation
Fitness centre/gym, jacuzzi/whirlpool, massage, sauna, squash, swimming pool (outdoor), tennis.

Restaurants & Coffee Shops
Selera Coffeehouse (250) - open 24 hrs; *Keyaki* (144) - Japanese, open 1200-1430/1830-2230; *Hai Tien Lo* (200) - Chinese, open as above

Overseas Sales Representatives
Pan Pacific Hotels & Resorts

Pearl International Hotel   C
Pearl Point Shopping Mall, Babu 5, Jalan Klang Lama, 58000
Tel: 783 1111; Fax: 783 2211

Petaling Jaya Hilton International
2 Jln Barat, 46200 Petaling Jaya, Selangor
Tel: 755 9122/755 3533; Tlx: MA 36008; Fax: 755 3909

Strategically located on the Federal Highway near the industrial centres, factories and residential areas in Petaling Jaya, the first satellite town of Malaysia. The hotel is situated midway between the Subang International Airport and Kuala Lumpur.

Accommodation & rates:
554 rooms.Single M$ 300-320; Double/twin M$ 320-340. 10 suites M$480-510; (Royal M$1200). Subject to 10% service charge and 5% government tax

Credit cards accepted:
Amex, Diners, Mastercard, Visa, JCB

Meeting & banqueting facilities
16 meeting/conference rooms, capacity 10-1000, with complete audio-visual equipment; 751 sq m exhibition space; largest reception 700 banquet or 1000 cocktail.

Room services
Airconditioning, colour TV, direct-dial telephone (ext. in bathroom), hairdryer, laundry/valet service, minibar, music/radio/alarm clock, safety deposit box, tea/coffee making facilities, 24-hr room service, non-smoker bedrooms, video films.

Business services
Business centre, executive floor + clubroom lounge facility, Japanese floor, express checkout, airport pickup, translation service, car parking, car rental, taxi service, executive board room

MALAYSIA - Hotels

Other services
Barber shop, beauty salon, newsstand/shops, gift shop, florist, men's tailor shop

Sports & Recreation
Fitness centre/gym, jacuzzi/whirlpool, massage, sauna, swimming pool (outdoor)

Restaurants & Coffee Shops
Paya Serai (270) - Local & Western, open 0600-0300 Mon-Thurs/24 hours Fri-Sun; *Genji* (85) - Japanese, open noon-1430/1900-2230; *Toh Yuen* (135) - Chinese, open as above; *Uncle Chilli's* (160) - Fun Pub, open 1130-0200; *Pool Terrace*.

Overseas Sales Representatives:
Hilton International Sales Offices; Hilton Reservations Worldwide

Plaza Hotel Kuala Lumpur ○ D
Jalan Raja Laut, 50350
Tel: 298 2255; Tlx: 30987 Fax: 292 0959

Radisson Plaza Hotel B
Jalan Ampang
Tel: 466 8866; Fax: 466 9966

The Regent of Kuala Lumpur B
160 Bukit Bintang, 55100
Tel: 241 8000; Tlx: 33912; Fax: 242 1441

Renaissance Kuala Lumpur ○ B
Cnr Jln Sultan Ismail/Jln Ampang, 0450
Tel: 264 8877; Fax: 264 8868

Shangri-La Kuala Lumpur ○ B
11 Jalan Sultan Ismail, 50250
Tel: 232 2388; Tlx: SHNGKL MA 30021; Fax: 230 1514

Subang Airport Hotel ○ D
Kompleks Airtel Fima, 47200 Subang, KL
Tel: 746 2122; Tlx: 37964;Fax: 746 1097

Sucasa Hotel Apartments C
222 Jalan Ampang, 50450 Kuala Lumpur
Tel: 451 3833; Tlx: MA 32209; Fax: 452 1031

Swiss-Garden Hotel C
No 117 Jalan Pudu, 55100 Kuala Lumpur
Tel: 241 3333; Tlx: MA 30819; Fax: 241 5555; Toll-free (Malaysia/Sing) 800 3093

Swiss Inn Kuala Lumpur D
No 62 Jalan Sultan, 5000 Kuala Lumpur
Tel: 232 3333; Fax: 201 6699

Hotel Classification: **A** *after name of hotel = over US$ 200 per person per night;* **B** *= between US$ 150 - 200;* **C** *= between US$ 100 - 150;* **D** *= between US$ 50 - 100;* **E** *= under US$ 50.* ¶ *= Prices on application* ○ *after name of hotel = PATA member*

Hotel Wenworth Kuala Lumpur ○
Jalan Yew, 55100 Kuala Lumpur
Tel: 983 3888; Fax: 982 8088

Located just minutes away from KL's Golden Triangle, 30 minutes away from Subang International Airport and just off the North-South Highway interchange.

Accommodation & rates
45 singles M$ 160-220; 201 doubles M$ 180-280; 4 suites M$ 280-480

Credit cards accepted
Visa, Mastercard, Amex, Diners, JCB

Meeting & banqueting facilities
Three meeting/function rooms, capacity 250 persons; audio-visual equipment available; largest reception 200 seated or 250 cocktail

Room services
Airconditioning, colour TV, direct-dial telephone, hairdryer, laundry/valet service, minibar, music/radio/alarm clock, safety deposit box, tea/coffee making, non-smoker bedrooms available, electronic door lock system, room/meal service 0700-0200

Business & other services
Airport pickup, car parking & rental, taxi service, newsstand/shops, florist

Sports & Recreation
Massage, sauna, jacuzzi, swimming pool (outdoor), spa

Restaurants & Coffee Shops
Palm's Cafe (150) - International/Local, open 0700-0200; *Wenworth Court* (250) - Cantonese, open 1130-1430/1830-2230; *Peebles Lounge* (100) - Karaoke & music machine, open 1130-0100

Kuala Terengganu (West M'a)

Awana Kijal Beach & Golf Resort A
Sales Office: 23rd fl, Wisma Genting, Jalan Sultan Ismail, 50250 Kuala Lumour
Tel: (03) 262 3555; Fax: (03) 261 6611

Berjaya Redang Beach & Golf Resort C
PO Box 126, Main Post Office, 20928 Kuala Terengganu, Redang 20300
Tel: (09) 697 3988; Fax: (09) 697 3899

Hotel Grand Continental ¶
Jln Sultan Zaind Aliadia, Diarah 8, Kuala Terengganu. (Pre-opening office)
c/o (03) 298 8999; Fax: (03) 293 2968

Kuantan (Western Malaysia)

Coral Beach Resort D
152 Sungai Karang, Besarah 26100
Tel: (09) 587544; Tlx: 50307; Fax: (09) 587543

Hyatt Regency Kuantan ○ C
Telok Chempedak, Kuantan 25050, Pahang
Tel: (09) 5661234; Tlx: 50252; Fax: 567 7577

The Legend Resort C
Lot 1290, Mukim Sungai, Karang, Cherating 26080, Kuantan
Tel: (09) 439439; Fax: (09) 439400

Merlin Inn Resort Kuantan D
Telok Chempedak, Kuantan 25700, Pahang
Tel: (09) 5141388; Tlx: 50285; Fax: 513 3001

Hotel Perdana Sdn Bhd ○ D
PO Box 222, Jln Mahmud, 15720 Kota Bharu, Kelantan
Tel: (09) 748 5000; Fax: (09) 744 7621

Kuching (Sarawak)

The Borneo Hotel E
Tabuhan Rd, Kuching
Tel: 244122; Tlx: 70389; fax: 254848

Hilton Batang Ai Longhouse Resort
c/o The Kuching Hilton, Jalan Tunku Abdul Rahman, PO Box 2396, 93748 Kuching
Tel: (082) 248200; Tlx: MA 70184 ; Fax: (082) 238546

Built according to the tribal Iban architectural designs, the resort is situated by the shores of freshwater Batang Ai Lake, some 275 km from Kuching Airport. Day trips to Iban longhouses along the Engkari and Ulu Ai rivers and the Batang Ai National Park are possible from the resort.

Accommodation & rates
26 doubles, 62 twin M$160-180; 12 suites M$220-240.Subject to 10% service charge & 5% government tax

(continued)

MALAYSIA - Hotels

Credit cards accepted:
Amex, Visa, Mastercard, Diners, JCB, Eurocard

Groups
3 meeting/function rooms, capacity 200; largest reception 200 seated/220 cocktail

Room & other services
Airconditioning, TV, minibar, tea/coffee making facilities, non-smoker bedrooms, tour desk

Sports & recreation
Fishing, board games, cycling, trails etc

Restaurants & coffee shops
Nanga Mepi (200) - Western/Chinese; *Wong Irup Bar* (60) - Malay/Local, open 0700-1100

Overseas Sales Representatives
Hilton International/Resrvations Worldwide

Damai Lagoon Resort Hotel C
Teluk Penyuk, Santubong, PO Box 3159, Kuching 93762
Tel: (82) 846900; Fax: (82) 846901

Holiday Inn Damai Beach D
PO Box 2870, 93756 Kuching, Sarawak
Tel: (082) 411777; Tlx: MA 70081; Fax: (082) 428911

Holiday Inn Kuching ◌
PO Box 2362, Jalan Tunku Abdul Rahman, 93100. Tel: (082) 423111; Tlx: MA 70086; Fax: 426169

Kuching Hilton

Kuching Hilton
PO Box 2396, Jalan Tunku Abdul Rahman, 93748 Kuching
Tel: (082) 248200; Tlx: 70184; Fax: (082) 428984

Located along Kuching's spectacular river front promenade with panoramic views of the Sarawak river and Fort Margherita, within walking distance to commercial and shopping area, 15 km to the airport.

Accommodation and rates
26 single M$ 305; 26 double M$ 325; 81 twin M$115-325; 37 suites M$700
Subject to 10% service charge & 5% government tax

Credit cards accepted:
Amex, Diners, Mastercard, Visa, JCB, Eurocard

Groups
9 meeting/function rooms, capacity 10-500 with audio-visual facilities, capacity 40-360; Grand Ballroom, capacity 450 seated or 500 cocktail

Room services
Airconditioning, colour TV, direct-dial telephone (ext. in bathroom), hairdryer, laundry/valet service, minibar, music/radio/alarm clock, safety deposit box (exec floor), tea/coffee making facilities, 24-hr room room service, video films, non-smoker bedrooms

Business & other services
Executive floor, express checkout, car parking, travel centre, taxi service, medical clinic, barber shop/beauty salon, newsstand/shops

Sports & recreation
Billiards/snooker, health club/gym, jacuzzi, jogging track, massage, sauna, outdoor swimming pool, tennis

Restaurants & Coffee Shops
Waterfront Cafe - International, open 0600-0100; *Steakhouse* - Western, open 1830-2300; *Toh Yuen* - Chinese, open 1130-1430/1830-2230; *Margherita Lounge* - cocktails, open 1500-0100 (Sun-Mon)/1500-0200 w'end/pub.hols; *Peppers* - Karaoke/discotheque, open 1700-0100

Overseas Sales Representatives:
Hilton International/Reservations Worldwide

Hotel Classification: **A** *after name of hotel = over US$ 200 per person per night;* **B** *= between US$ 150 - 200;* **C** *=between US$ 100 - 150;* **D** *= between US$ 50 - 100;* **E** *= under US$ 50; ¶= prices on application.* ◌ *= PATA member.*

Riverside Majestic Hotel Kuching ◌
Jln Tunku Abdul Rahman,PO Box 2928, Kuching, Sarawak
Tel: (082) 247777; Tlx:70088; Fax: 425858

Langkawi Island

Berjaya Langkawi Beach Resort C
Teluk Burau, 07000 Langkawi
Tel: (04) 959 1888; Fax: (04) 959 1886

Burau Bay Resort ◌ C
Teluk Burau, 07000 Langkawi, Kedah
Tel: (04) 959 1061; Fax: (04) 959 1172

The Datai B
Jalan Teluk Datai, 07000 Langkawi, Kedah
Tel: (04) 959 2500; Fax: (04) 959 2600

Langkawi Island Resort E
Jln Pantai Dato Sayed Omar, 07000 Pulau Langkawi, Kedah
Tel: (04) 788209; Tlx: 42044; Fax: 788414

Pelangi Beach Resort ◌ C
Lot 1226 Pantai Cenang, Mukim Kedawang, 07000 Langkawi, Kedah
Tel: (04) 955 1001; Tlx: 42189; Fax: (04) 955 1122

Radisson Tanjung Rhu All Suite Resort C
Lot 1476, Tanjung Rhu, 17000 Langkawi
Tel: (04) 959 1033; Fax: (04) 959 1899

Sheraton Langkawi Beach Resort C
Teluk Nibong, 07000 Langkawi, Kedah
Tel: (04) 955 1901; Fax: (04) 955 1968

Malacca (Western Malaysia)

Allson Klana Resort Seremban D
PT 4388 Jalan Penhulu Cantik, Taman Tasik Seremban, 70100 Seremban
Tel: (06) 729600; Fax: (06) 739218

The Malacca Village Resort C
Ayer Keroh, Malacca 75450
Tel: 232 3600; Tlx: 62854; Fax: 232 5955

Hotel Grand Continental Melaka E
20 Jalan Tun Sri Lanang, 75100 Malacca
Tel: (06) 240088; Fax: (06) 248125

Malacca Renaissance Hotel C
Jalan Bendahara, PO Box 105, 75720 Malacca
Tel: (06) 284 8888; Tlx: 62966 RAMADA MA; Fax: (06) 2849269

Riviera Bay Resort B
Jalan Tanjung Kling, 76400
Tel: (06) 315 1111; Fax: (06) 315 3333

Tapa-Nyai Island Resort C
PO Box 356, Malacca
Tel: (06) 242088; Fax: (06) 243588

Pan Pacific Hotel Malacca
(Opening December 1997). Pre-opening address: c/o Pan Pacific Hotels & Resorts, 7 Raffles Boulevard, # 01-050 Marina Square, Singapore 039595
Tel: (065) 339 4688; Fax: (065) 339 5787;
E-Mail: etan@panpac.com.sg

Presenting the old world charm of olden Malacca, integrating the local heritage with the Portuguese and Dutch influence into a design concept that will make this hotel the preferred business hotel in Malacca Town.

Accommodation and Rates
260 rooms. Rates to be announced

Credit cards accepted:
All major

Meeting & banqueting facilities
5 meeting/banqueting rooms; audio-visual equipment available; largest reception 500

Room services
Airconditioning, colour TV, Idd telephone (ext. in bathroom), hairdryer, laundry/valet service, minibar, safety deposit box, tea/coffee making facilities, 24-hr room service

Business & other services
Business centre, executive floor, express checkout, translation service, car parking, taxi service, newsstand/shops

Sports & Recreation
Fitness centre/gym, massage, sauna, outdoor swimming pool, spa

Restaurants & Coffee Shops
All-day dining (120); *Theme dining* (160), *Lobby Lounge* (80, *Pub* (80) Restaurants to be opened

Overseas Sales Representatives:
Pan Pacific Hotels & Resorts; SRS Steigenberger Resrvation Service

Miri (Sarawak)

Holiday Inn Miri D
Brighton Centre. PO Box 2295, 98008 Miri
Tel: (85) 420788; Fax: 419999

Rihga Royal Hotel Miri C
Jalan Temenggong Datuk Oyong Lawai
Tel: (85) 421121; Fax: (85) 421099

Pangkor Island

Pangkor Laut Resort A
Pangkor Laut Island, 32200 Lumut, Perak
Tel: (5) 699 1100; fax: (5) 699 1200

The Pan Pacific Resort Pangkor
Teluk Belanga (Golden Sands), 32300
Tel: (05) 685 1399; Fax: (05) 685 2390
E-mail: res@pprp.po.my

This secluded island resort just off the west coast of Malaysia is superbly situated between a lush tropical forest and a golden sandy beach.

Accommodation and Rates
240 rooms (de luxe, Pacific Wing, chalets, suites & bungalows). Single/twin rate M$ 320-800 + 10% service charge and 5% gov't tax

Credit cards accepted:
Amex, Diners, Eurocard, Mastercard, Visa

Groups
6 meeting/banqueting rooms; audio-visual equipment available

Room services
Airconditioning, colour TV. tea/coffee making facilities, minibar, hairdryer

Other services
Ferry and shuttle service

Sports & Recreation
Two swimming pools, private beach, 3 - hole golf course, tennis, beach volleyball, bicycles, watersports, hiking trails

Restaurants & Coffee Shops
Newly renovated restaurants, lounge, poolside Bar

Overseas Sales Representatives:
Pan Pacific Hotels & Resorts; SRS Steigenberger Reservation Service

Penang (Western Malaysia)

The Bayview Beach Resort ○
Batu Ferringhi Beach, 11000 Penang
Tel: (04) 881 2123; Tlx: MA 41325 BAYBRP; Fax: (04) 881 2140

Casuarina Beach Hotel ○ D
25a Lebuh Farquar, Georgetown 10200, Northern Penang
Tel: (04) 363161; Tlx: 40322; Fax: 374124

City Bayview Hotel D
25a Farquar Street, 10200 Penang
Tel: (04) 263 3161; Tlx: 40322; Fax: 263 4124

Crown Prince Hotel Penang ○ D
Jalan Tanjung Bungah, Penang 11200
Tel: (04) 890 4111; Fax: (04) 890 4777

Eastern & Oriental (E & O) Hotel D
10 Farquar Street, PO Box 399 10750 ○
Penang Tel: (04) 263 0630; Tlx: 40270 ENDO MA; Fax: 263 4833

Hotel Equatorial Penang ○ D
1 Jalan Bukit Jambul, 11900 Penang
Tel: (04) 643 8111; Tlx: 40665;
Fax: (04) 644 8000

Ferringgi Beach Hotel D
12.5 km Batu Ferringhi Rd, 11100 Batu Ferringhi, Penang
Tel: (04) 890 5999; Tlx: 40634 FERIEL MA; Fax: (04) 890 5100

Shangri-La's Golden Sands Resort
87 Batu Feringgi Beach, PO Box 222, ○
11100 Penang C
Tel: (04) 881 1911; Tlx: 40627 GOSAND MA; Fax: (04) 881 1880

Holiday Inn Penang D
Batu Ferringgi Beach, 11000 Penang
Tel: (04) 8811611; Tlx: 40952; Fax: 881 1389

Novotel Penang ○ D
Tanjung Bunga, 11200 Penang
Tel: (04) 890 3333; Tlx: 40310 ORCHEL MA; Fax: (04) 890 3303

Palm Beach Resort D
Batu Feringgi Beach, 11100 Penang
Tcl: (04) 881 1621; Fax: (04) 881 1051

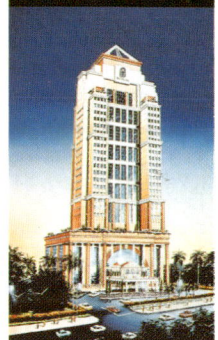

The Pan Pacific Leader Hotel Penang
(Opening December 1997). Pre-opening address: c/o Pan Pacific Hotels & Resorts, 7 Raffles Boulevard, # 01-050 Marina Square, Singapore 039595
Tel: (065) 339 4688; Fax: (065) 339 5787;
E-Mail: etan@panpac.com.sg

A landmark on the Penang Island skyline, the hotel will retain the original concept of the city's British heritage in interior and exterior design, recalling the charm of classical hotels of the colonial era.

Accommodation and Rates
373 rooms. Rates to be announced

Credit cards accepted:
All major

(contineud)

MALAYSIA - Hotels

Groups
6 meeting/banqueting rooms; audio-visual equipment available

Room services
Airconditioning, colour TV, IDD telephone (ext. in bathroom), laundry/valet service, minibar, safety deposit box, tea/coffee making facilities, hairdryer, 24-hr room/meal service

Business & other services
Business centre, executive floor, translation service, car parking, taxi service, newsstand/shops

Sports & Recreation
Fitiness centre/gym, massage, sauna, outdoor swimming pool

Restaurants & Coffee Shops
All-day dining (120); *Chinese* (160), *Japanese* (160); *Pub* (80) Restaurants to be opened

Overseas Sales Representatives:
Pan Pacific Hotels & Resorts;
SRS Steigenberger Resrvation Service

Penang Continental Hotel   D
5 Penang Rd, Po Box 525, Georgetown,
Tel: 863 6388; Tlx: 40098; Fax: 863 8718

Penang Mutiara Beach Resort ☼ C
1 Jln Teluk Bahang, 11050 Penang
Tel: 885 2828; Tlx: 40829; Fax: 885 2829

Penang Parkroyal Hotel   C
Batu Ferringhi Beach
Tel: (04) 881 1133; Fax: (04) 881 2233

Shangri-La's Rasa Sayang Resort☼
PO Box 735, Batu Feringgi Beach,11100 C
Tel: (04) 881 1811; Tlx: 40065; Fax: (04) 881 1984

Sheraton Penang   B
3 Jalan Laut, Georgetown 10050
Tel: (04) 226 7888; Fax: (04) 226 6615

Sandakan (Sabah)

Sandakan Renaissance Hotel C
Km 1, Jalan Utara, PO Box 275, 90007 Sandakan
Tel: (89) 213299; Fax: (89) 271271

Sibu (Sarawak)

Premier Hotel   E
PO Box 1064, Sibu 96000
Tel: (084) 323222; Tlx: 72073 MA; Fax: (084) 323399

Hotel Classification: A *after name of hotel = over US$ 200 per person per night;* **B** *= between US$ 150 - 200;* **C** *=between US$ 100 - 150;* **D** *= between US$ 50 - 100;* **E** *= under US$ 50;* ¶*= prices on application.* ☼ *= PATA member.*

Western Malaysia other areas

Berjaya Tioman Beach Resort ☼ C
Pulau Tioman, 86807.Tel: (09) 414 5445;
Tlx: 50279; Fax: (09) 414 5718

Hotel Equatorial Bangi   ¶
Off Persiran Bandar, 43650 Bandar Baru Bangi, Selangor
Tel: (3) 677 2222; Fax: (3) 677 2888

Holiday Inn Resort Pedu Lake   D
Po Box 1, 06300 Kuala Nerang, Kedah
Tel: (04) 730 4888; Fax: (04) 730 4488

Holiday Inn Shah Alam   C
Plaza Perangsang, Persiaran Perbanda, Selangor 40000
Tel: (03) 550 3696; Tlx: 39859; Fax: (03) 550 3913

Ming Court Beach Hotel   D
Teluk Kamang, Port Dickson 71050
Tel: (06) 662 5244; Tlx: 63952; Fax: (06) 662 5899

The Murni Hotel   E
Jalan Dato Pati, Kotah Bahru, Kelantan
Tel: (09) 748 2399; Fax: (09) 744 7255

Primula Beach Resort   D
PO Box 43, Jalan Persinggahan, Kuala Terengganu 20904
Tel: (09) 622 2100; Fax: (09) 623360

Ye Olde Smokehouse   D
PO Box 77, 39007 Cameron Highlands
Tel: (05) 491 1215; Fax: (09) 491 1214

Restaurants

Malaysian cuisine appeals to most palates, being something of a cross between Thai and Chinese. Kuala Lumpur hotels offer reliable international menus; sidewalk stalls offer satay and other local specialities. This is a KL selection popular with business people which accept most credit cards and where advance booking is advisable.

Bangles (*Indian*)
60 Jalan Tunku Abdul Rahnman.
Tel: 298 3780

La Bussola (*Italian*)
Wilayah Shopping Centre, Jalan Dang Wangi. Tel: 291 5832

The Castell (*European - bistro*)
81 Jalan Bukit Bintang. Tel: 242 8328

Le Coq d'Or (***European/Malay***)

121 Jalan Ampong. Tel: 242 9732
Copper Grill (*European*)
Menara Promet Bldg, Jalan Sultan Ismail.
Tel: 243 8057
Country Kitchen (*Chinese*)
21 Jalan Barat, Petaling Jaya.
Tel: 256 6312
Eden Village (*Malaysian/Seafood*)
260 Jln Raja Chulan. Tel: 241 4027
Edo Kirin (*Japanese*)
Regent of Kuala Lumpur, 160 Jln Bukit Bintang. Tel: 241 8000
Hai Tien Lo (*Chinese*)
Pan Pacific Hotel, Jalan Chow Kit Barow.
Tel: 442 5555
Happy Valley Seafood (*Chinese/Seafood*)
Menara Promer Bldg, Jalan Sultan Ismail.
Tel: 241 1264
Inn of Happiness (*Chinese*)
Hilton Hotel, Jalan Sultan Ismail.
Tel: 242 2122
Jothy's (*Indian*)
21b/c, Jalan Barat, Petaling Jaya.
Tel: 757 5819
Koryo-Won (*Korean*)
Kempleks Antarabangsa, Jalan Sultan Ismail. Tel: 242 7655
Kwali Indonesian Restaurant
Plaza Yow Chuan, Jalan Pekeliling
Tel: 242 0580
Lafite (*European*)
Shangri-La Hotel, 11 Jalan Sultan Ismail.
Tel: 232 2388
Mahsuri Dining Hall (*French*)
Carcosa Seri Negara, Taman Tasek Perdana. Tel: 230 6766
Melaka Grill (*European/Malay*)
Hilton Hotel, Jalan Sultan Ismail.
Tel: 242 2122
Nadaman (*Japanese*)
Shangri-La Hotel, 11 Jalan Sultan Ismail.
Tel: 232 2388
Ranch Grill (*American*)
Regent Hotel, Jalan Sultan Ismail.
Tel: 242 5588
Restoran Embassy (*Cantonese/Seafood*)
243 Jln Ampang. Tel: 457 3803
Rive Gauche (*European*)
34 Jalan Ampang. Tel: 201609
Suasa (*International*)
Regent Hotel, Jalan Sultan Ismail.
Tel: 242 5588
Tai Thong (*Cantonese*)
51 Jln Barat (off Jalan Imbi). Tel: 248 8621
La Terrasse (*French*)
388 Jln Tun Razak. Tel: 248 4243

Car Hire

Avis
Head Office: 40 Jalan Sultan Ismail, Kuala Lumpur. Tel: (03) 242 3500; Tlx: MA 30002; Fax: (03) 243 3809
Offices in Ipoh, Johore Bahru, Kota Baru, Subang Int'l Airport KL, Kuantan, Malacca, Penang.

Budget Rent-a-Car
Central Resrvations Headquarters
20 Jalan Telawi Bangsar Baru, Kuala Lumpur 59100. Tel: (03) 242 5159;
Tlx: 36283; Fax: 242 9362

City Car Rentals
Hotel Regent, Jalan Sultan Ismail Kuala Lumpur 50250. Tel: (03) 242 0240

Express Rent-a-Car
2nd floor, Bangunan Sateras, 152 Jalan Ampang, Kuala Lumpur 50450 Tel: (03) 242 4113

Hertz Self and Chauffeur Drive
Pernas Sime Darby Rent a Car Sdn Bhd 214a 2nd Fl, Kompleks Antarabangsa, Jalan Sultan Ismail, 50250 Kuala Lumpur. Tel: 248 6433; Tlx: 8430956; Fax: 242 8481

Kasina Rent-A-Car
No 195, Block G, Mukim 12, Sungai Tiram, 11900 Penang. Tel: (04) 841842; Fax: (04) 842654. Also at Federal Hotel Kuala Lumpur, tel (03) 244 9968; fax (03) 244 9972.

National Car Rental (Europcar)
Lot 8, Mid-Level floor, Jalan Sultan Ismail Kuala Lumpur
Tel: (03) 261 9397; Tlx: 30596 easb ma

Sintat Rent-a-Car
Lobby floor, Holiday Inn, Jalan Pinang Kuala Lumpur 50450 Tel: (03) 248 2388

SMAS Rent-a-Car
3rd floor, Menara Tun Razak, Jalan Raja Laut Kuala Lumpur 50350 Tel: (03) 293 6233

Thrifty Car Rental
Holiday Inn on the Park, Jalan Pinang Kuala Lumpur 50450. Tel: (03) 248 2388; Tlx: MA 30544; Fax: (03) 274 5171

Toyota Rent-a-Car
145-3c Jalan Sungei Besi
Kuala Lumpur 57100 Tel: (03) 243 8142

Airline Offices

Air India
Bangunan Ankasa Raya, 123 Jalan Ampang, Kuala Lumpur 50450
Tel: (03) 242-0166

Air Lanka
UG4 Bangunan Perangsang Segemai, Jalan Kampong Attap, Kuala Lumpur 50460
Tel: (03) 274-0211

Biman
Ground floor, Bangunan Angkasa Raya, Jalan Ampang, Kuala Lumpur 50450
Tel: (03) 242 7671

British Airways
Letterbox M3, Mezzanine Floor, Plaza See Hoy Chan, Jalan Raja Chulan, Kuala Lumpur. Tel: (03) 232 5797

Cathay Pacific
Ground floor, Mui Plaza, Jalan P. Ramlee Kuala Lumpur 50250. Tel: (03) 238-3377

China Air Lines
64 Jalan Bukit Bintang, Kuala Lumpur
Tel: (03) 242 7344

Garuda
1st floor, Angasa Raya Building, 123 Jalan Ampang, Kuala Lumpur 50450 Tel: 241 0811

Japan Air Lines (JAL)
1st floor, Pernas International, Lot 1157, Jalan Sultan Ismail, Kuala Lumpur
Tel: (03) 261-1722

KLM
Shop 7, Ground floor President House, Jalan Sultan Ismail, Kuala Lumpur 50250
Tel: (03) 242-7011

Korean Air
Ground floor, Wisma MPI, Jalan Raja Chulan, Kuala Lumpur. Tel: (03) 242-8311

Lufthansa
3rd floor, Pernas International Building Jalan Sultan Ismail, Kuala Lumpur 50250
Tel: (03) 261-4666

Malaysia Airlines
33rd floor, Bangunan MAS, Jalan Sultan Ismail, Kuala Lumpur 50250
Tel: (03)261 0555

Philippine Airlines
104-107 Wisma Stephens, Jalan Raja Chulan, Kuala Lumpur. Tel: (03) 242 9040

PIA
Ground floor, Angkasa Raya Building 123 Jalan Ampang Kuala Lumpur 50450
Tel: (03) 242 5444

Qantas
6th floor, UBN Tower, Jalan P. Ramlee Kuala Lumpur 50250. Tel: (03) 238-9133

Royal Brunei
1st floor, Wisma Merlin, Jalan Sultan Ismail Kuala Lumpur 50250. Tel: (03) 242-6511

Royal Jordanian
8th floor, Mui Plaza, Jalan P. Ramlee Kuala Lumpur 50250. Tel: (03) 248-7500

Singapore Airlines
Wisma Singapore Airlines, 2/4 Jalan Dang Wangi, Kuala Lumpur 50100
Tel: (03)292 3122

Thai
Ground floor, Bangunan Kuwasa, 5 Jalan Raja Laut, Kuala Lumpur 50350
Tel: (03)293-7133/292 7100

United Airlines
Kuala Lumpur
Tel: (03) 261 1433

(On-line carriers only)

What's the link between business and the Asia Pacific?

BRITISH AIRWAYS
The world's favourite airline

http://www.british-airways.com

Malaysia Airline Departures

Below is a list of departures and frequencies from Kuala Lumpur and Penang International Airports to the destinations in bold type. Figures in brackets after destinations refer to the days of the week. (2,4,6) therefore indicates that departures to that destination take place on a Tuesday (the second day of the week), a Thursday and a Saturday. Only direct flights are shown and were correct as at February 1997.

Airline abbreviation codes: AI = Air India; **AK** = Island Air; **AN** = Ansett Australia; **BA** = British Airways; **BG** = Biman Bangladesh; **BI** = Royal Brunei Airlines; **BR** = EVA Airways; **CI** = China Airlines; **CX** = Cathay Pacific; **CZ** = China Southern Airlines; **GA** = Garuda Indonesia; **HY** = Uzbekistan Airways; **IC** = Indian Airlines; **IR** = Iran Air; **J8** = Berjaya Air; **JL** = Japan Airlines; **KE** = Korean Air; **KL** = KLM; **LH** = Lufthansa; **LZ** = Balkan; **ME** = MEA; **MH** = Malaysian Airlines; **MK** = Air Mauritius; **NZ** = Air New Zealand; **PK** = PakistanInternational Airlines; **PR** = Philippine Airlines; **QF** = Qantas; **RJ** = Royal Jordanian; **SG** = Sempati Air; **SQ** = Singapore Airlines; **SU** = Aeroflot; **SV** = Saudia; **TG** = Thai International; **UL** = Air Lanka; **UT** = UTA; **VN** = Vietnam Airlines; **9P** = Air Pelangi; **L6** = Air Maldives; **VS** = Virgin Atlantic.

KUALA LUMPUR (Subang International) (KUL)

Abu Dhabi (AUH)
GF (1,4)
Adelaide (ADL)
MH (1,3,6) VS (3,6)
Alor Setar (AOR)
MH (daily)
Amman (AMM)
MH/RJ (1,4)
Amsterdam (AMS)
KL (1,3,7) MH (4,5,7)
Auckland (AKL)
MH (2,4,6)
Bahrain (BAH)
GF (6)
Banda Aceh (BTJ)
9P (2,5)
Bandar Seri B (BWN)
MH (3,4,6) BI (daily)
Bangkok (BKK)
MH/TG (daily) LH (1,4) NH (1,4,6)
Beijing (BJS)
CZ (1,3,5,6) MH (2,4,5,6,7)
Beirut (BEY)
MH/ME (3,7)
Bombay (BOM)
AI (5)
Brisbane (BNE)
MH (1,3,5,6) QF (3,7)
Buenos Aires (BUE)
MH (3,7) AR (3,7)
Cairns (CNS)
MH (4)
Cape Town (CPT)
MH (3,5,6,7)
Cebu (CEB)
MH (4,7)
Chiang Mai (CNX)
MH/TG (3,7)
Colombo (CMB)
MH/UL (1,5)
Darwin (DRW)
MH (1,4)
Delhi (DEL)
MH/AI (3,7)
Denpasar-Bali (DPS)
GA/MH (daily)
Dhaka (DAC)
BG (1,5,6) MH (3,5,7) EK (2,4,7)
Dubai (DXB)
MH (2,3,5,6,7)
Frankfurt (FRA)
LH (1,4) MH (4,5,7) CI (1,4)
Fukuoka (FUK)
MH (3,5,7)
Guangzhou (CAN)
MH (1,2,4,6,7) CZ (2,3,5,6)
Hanoi (HAN)
MH (1,6) VN (1,5)
Hat Yai (HDY)
TG/MH (2,4,5,6,7)
Ho Chi Minh (SGN)
MH/VN (daily)
Hong Kong (HKG)
CI (daily) CX (daily) MH (daily)
Ipoh (IPH)
MH (daily) 9P (2,4,6,7)
Islamabad (IPH)
PK (4)
Istanbul (IST)
MH (2,5)
Jakarta (JKT)
GA, MH (daily) BA (2,3,4,6,7)
GF (1,4,5) AN (1,2,3,5,6,7)
Jeddah (JED)
MH (5,7) SV (3,6)
Johannesburg (JNB)
MH (3,5,6,7)
Johor Bahru (JHB)
MH (daily) 9P (1,3,5,6,7)
Kaohsiung (KHH)
MH (daily) CI (1,2,4,6) BR (2,4,6)
Karachi (KHI)
MH (3,7) PK (1)
Kerteh (KTE)
9P (daily)
Kota Bharu (KBR)
MH (daily) 9P (daily)
Kota Kinabalu (BKI)
MH (daily) AK (1,3,4,5,6,7)
Kuala Terengg (TGG)
MH (daily)
Kuantan (KUA)
MH (daily)
Kuching (KCH)
MH (daily)
Labuan (LBU)
MH (daily)
Lahore (LHE)
PK (4)
Langkawi (LGK)
MH (daily)
London (LHR)
MH,VS (daily)
Los Angeles (LAX)
MH (1,3,4,5,6,7)
Macau (MFM)
MH (1,3,5)
Madras (MAA)
AI (2,5) MH (1,2,3,4,5,7) IC (3,7)
Madrid (MAD)
MH (2,5)
Male (MLE)
L6 (3) MH (1,6)
Manila (MNL)
MH (daily) PR (2,4,6,7) KL (6)
Mauritius (MRU)
MK/MH (3)
Medan (MES)
GA, MH (daily) SG (2,3,6)
Melbourne (MEL)
MH,AN (1,2,3,4,6,7)
VS (1,3,4,6,7) QF (3)
Miri (MYY)
MH (daily)
Moscow (MOW)
SU (3,5)
Munich (MUC)
MH (1,4)
Muscat (MCT)
GF (6)
Nagoya (NGO)
MH (3,6,7)
Osaka (KIX)
MH (2,3,5,7) NH (3,5,7) JL (daily)
Padang (PDG)
9P (daily)
Palembang (PLM)
9P (1,3,6)
Paris (CDG)
MH (1,4,6)
Pekanbaru (PKU)
9P (daily)
Penang (PEN)
MH (daily) 9P (2,5)
Perth (PER)
MH (daily)
Phnom-Penh (PNH)
VJ (2,4,6) MH (1,3,5,7)
Phuket (HKT)
MH/TG (daily)
Pusan (PUS)
MH (1,6)
Rome (ROM)
MH (2,7)
Seoul (SEL)
KE (2,5,7) MH (1,2,4,6,7)
Shanghai (SHA)
CZ (1,4)
Sibu (SBW)
MH (daily)
Singapore (SIN)
MH/SQ (daily) QF (3,5,7) JL (daily) GA (1,3,4,7)
Surabaya (SUB)
MH (daily) SG (1,3,4,6) GA (1,3,4,7)
Sydney (SYD)
MH (1,2,4,5,6,7) QF (3,5,7)
VS (1,4,5,7) AN (daily)
Taipei (TAI)
CI/MH/BR (daily) AK (1,4,6)
Tashkent (TAS)
HY (7)
Tawau (TWU)
MH (daily)
Tehran (THR)
MH/IR (2,6)
Tioman (TOD)
9P,J8 (daily)
Tokyo (NRT)
JL, MH (daily)
Ujung Pandang (UPG)
MH (2,5)
Vancouver (YVR)
CP,MH (3,5)
Vienna (VIE)
MH (2,4)
Vientiane (VTE)
MH (1,3)
Xiamen (XMN)
CZ (4,7)
Yangon (RGN)
UB (3,6) MH (2,5)
Zurich (ZRH)
MH (4,7) CI (1,4)

PENANG (Internat'l) (PEN)

Banda Aceh (BTJ)
9P (2,5)
Bangkok (BKK)
MH/TG (daily)
Guangzhou (CAN)
CZ (3,5)
Hong Kong (HKG)
CX (2,3,5,6,7) MH (2,5)
Johor Bahru (JHB)
MH (daily)
Kota Bahru (KBR)
9P (daily)
Kuala Lumpur (KUL)
MH (daily) 9P(2,5)
Kuching (KCH)
MH (daily)
Langkawi (LGK)
MH (daily)
Madras (MAA)
MH (3)
Medan (MES)
MH (daily) SG (1,4,5,7)
Miri (MYY)
MH (daily)
Phuket (HKT)
TG/MH (3,5,7)
Singapore (SIN)
MH (daily) SQ (daily) BR (daily)
Taipei (TPE)
BR (daily)
Xiamen (XMN)
CZ (3)

Major Exhibitions in Malaysia 1997

Date	Exhibition	City	Venue	Organiser
May 6-9	**Elenex Malaysia 97** - 2nd Malaysian int'l exhibition of electrical power general transmission	K.Lumpur	PWTC	MES
June 4-8	**ITM 97 Industry Tradefair Malaysia** - Int'l fair of industrial development & technology: series of exhibitions including: **Materials Handling 97, Pneumatics & Hydraulics 97, Printing/Packaging 97**	K.Lumpur	PWTC	MES
June 4-8	**IMX 97 Machinetool Malaysia 97** - incorporating: **Metal Cutting 97, Sheet Metal 97, Mould & Die 97, Metrology 97, CAD/CAM 97, Weldtech 97**	K. Lumpur	PWTC	MES
June 17-20	**NEPCON Malaysia** - All aspects of microelectronics	K. Lumpur	PWTC	Reed
June 17-20	**ENEX Malaysia** - Electrical manufacturing & installation equipment and systems	K. Lumpur	PWTC	Reed
July 14-17	**OGM 97** - 7th Malaysian oil, gas and petrochemical engineering exhibition - incorporating: **Instrument Malaysia 97**.	K.Lumpur	PWTC	MES
July 14-17	**Environmex**/Watermex Malaysia 97 - Int'l environment technology exhibition	K. Lumpur	PWTC	MES
July 29-31	**Software Development Asia 97**	K.Lumpur	Shangri-la	MFreeman
Aug	**Multimedia Asia** - for investors in & developers of Multimedia Super Corridor in Malaysia	K. Lumpur	PWTC	Reed
Sept 9-12	**AEC Systems Malaysia** - Computer show for the design & Construction Industry	K. Lumpur	PWTC	Reed
Sept 24-27	**FHM 97** - 4th Int'l exhibition of food, agricultural products, drinks, hotel, & catering	K, Lumpur	PWTC	MES
Nov 26-29	**Telecom Malaysia 97** - incorporating: MobileComm Malaysia 97, Network Malaysia 97, Multimedia Malaysia 97.	K. Lumpur	PWTC	MES
Nov 26-29	**Mobilecomm Malaysia 97** - Int'l cellular, radio & satellite communications exhibition	K. Lumpur	PWTC	MES
1998 21-24 April	**Defence Services Asia 98 (DSA 98)**	K. Lumpur	PWTC	MES

Venues:
PWTC = Putra World trade Centre, Jalan Tun Ismail, Kuala Lumpur, tel (03) 442 2999; tlx PUTRA MA 28100; fax (03) 442 2959.
Shangri-La Hotel, 11 Jalan Sultan Ismail, 50250 Kuala Lumpur; Tel: 232 2388; Fax: 230 1514

Organisers:
MES = Malaysian Exhibition Services Sdn Bhd, 468-1B, Batu 3, Jalan Ipoh, 51200 Kuala Lumpur, tel (03) 441 0311; fax (03) 443 7241.
MFreeman = Miller Freeman Asia Ltd, 102-5 Stanhope House, 738 King's Road, Quarry Bay, Hong Kong. Tel (852) 2827 5121; Fax (852) 2827 7064
Reed = Reed Exhibitions, 19th Floor, Menara Utama UMBC, Jalan Sultan Sulaan, 50000 Kuala Lumpur. Tel (603) 201 8100; Fax (603) 201 6100.

Myanmar

Doing Business

Beneath a continuing international outcry, principally from the US and UK, over alleged human rights abuses and the enforcement of slave labour, the Union of Myanmar made solid progress on the business front in 1996/97. Economic reforms together with a series of liberalised laws, rules and regulations enacted by the State Law and Order Restoration Council were attracting growing investment, particularly from Singapore and other neighbouring ASEAN countries which, despite vocal disapproval from the West, were preparing to welcome the former Burma into their economic partnership. By late 1995, approved foreign investment in Myanmar had topped US$3bn. In order, oil and gas; hotels and tourism; fisheries; real estate development; mining; manufacturing; transport and agriculture were the main sectors attracting foreign investment.

Despite the often vociferous actions of anti-Myanmar protesters, the UK was the top investor, pumping US$666mn into 18 of total 162 foreign investment projects underway in the country. Singapore came a close second, with more than US$568 mn in 34 different projects. France, Thailand, the US, Malaysia, Japan, The Netherlands, Austria and Hong Kong comprised the remaining countries in the Top 10 foreign investor list.

Although the highly-publicised standoff between SLORC and the followers of pro-democracy activist and Nobel peace Prize winner Daw Ang Suu Kyi continued into 1997, the ruling junta had largely succeeded in uniting most of the many disparate tribal provinces which make up the Union of Myanmar. Only a large part of Shan State, whose people ally themselves to Thailand, remained off-limits to foreign inspection and investment.

Myanmar's Investment Commission permits enterprises that have between 35% and 100% of foreign capital amounting to US$500,000 to establish production companies or US$300,000 for service companies. Joint ventures can apply for three year tax exemptions and other tax breaks. By agreed international law, they are guaranteed full repatriation of funds and that there will be no nationalisation by the state on expiry of their terms of contract.

Myanmar has privatised some of its formerly struggling State Economic Enterprises and reformed the management or marketised its remaining SEE's. Restrictions on agricultural activities have been reduced and private traders and enterprises, co-operative societies and joint venture enterprises have been allowed to engage in the domestic procurement, transportation, milling, storing and marketing of agricultural products, including rice.

Mechanisation of agriculture is deemed a priority. Machinery, construction and building materials are encouraged imports. Food and beverages and other personal and household items are also permitted imports. Rice and textiles are controlled exports, along with 28 other products prohibited to export through border trade. Telecommunications, electricity and energy supply are other priority projects in which foreign input and expertise is being encouraged as Myanmar attempts to modernise and industrialise with an open market economy after 20 years of zero growth.

Despite demonstrations by its workers in Los Angeles in early 1997, US company Unocal said it would continue with a major pipeline project through Myanmar to Thailand. Unocal president John Imle said the well-being of Myanmar's economy through foreign joint ventures would encourage the well-being of its people.

Unocal was building schools and hospitals for workers and had an ethical and moral responsibility to influence the behaviour of the government, he said.

Tourism, another priority sector and target for overseas anti-Myanmar activists, also continued to progress during 1996/97, albeit without any real help from a hastily-assembled and underfunded 'Visit Myanmar Year' which ran for only six months during the peak winter season. Visitors, mostly Japanese and continental Europeans in search of Myanmar's unmatched Buddhist culture and sights, increased from 140,000 in 1995 to 150,000 in 1996 and is aiming for 200,000 in 1997, progressing gradually towards a target of 500,000 by 2000 under a United Nations plan. More notable during the period was a huge influx of new joint venture international hotels. As recently as the early 1990s, Myanmar had only 900 rooms around the country. By early 1997, there were 4,500 beds in Yangon alone, with an additional 35 hotel projects approved nationwide.

Business awareness

Most business activity centres around the capital, Yangon and, to a lesser extent, the commercial capital of Mandalay. Thanks to furious building, the skylines of both cities are changing literally every few months. Despite overseas perceptions, politics are not a taboo subject. All Myanmese, whatever their political affiliations or standing, are proud and often outspoken people keen to share their views with outsiders. Given the services of a well-connected local agent, deals can often be struck far quicker than in neighbouring countries. Formal business attire and punctuality are recommended in Yangon. Hotel and restaurant service is willing but basic, although rapidly improving, as is the choice of domestic ground and air travel. A visa is essential for most visitors. Hotel and air fares are pegged to the official dollar/*kyat* (local currency) exchange rate of about $1=5*kyat*. Tourists should dress respectfully to conform with local customs. Footwear in the precincts of pagodas and temples is strictly forbidden. Light tropical clothing is suitable year round, unless visiting the hill stations.

Tourism Update

General

The government, having only had a Tourism Ministry since 1992, said it hoped the "*Visit Myanmar Year 1996*" promotional event would help attract 230,000 foreign visitors to Myanmar — although its original target was 500,000. The 1996 total was put at 150,000, earning US$70 million. Monitoring was complicated by the fact that VMY was not a calendar year; it actually started in November 1996. Early indications were for an increase of over 50%, which would actually take the annual total to around 230,000. But much of the growth was coming not from tourists — the main target of a Visit promotion — but from increased business travel.

In 1996 Diethelm Travel, Thailand's big inbound travel agency, opened branch offices in Bagan and Mandalay; it already had one in the capital Yangon. Another Thailand-based company, Fantasea Divers, may start a water-tour programme in the south of Myanmar. And Exotissimo, a French agency, became the third joint-

venture agency to win a licence for tourism services. And the 'Road to Mandalay' cruiser started plying the Ayerawaddy River. Operated by the same company that runs the Orient Express train, 'Mandalay' has 60 berths. Myanmar's entry into Asean (Association of South East Asian Nations) in 1996 will have a positive impact on travel, such as by allowing freer flow of Asean nationals into the country, and participation in Asean travel exhibitions, trade shows and other promotions. Also, entry requirements have been eased. Visas are issued for 18 days rather than seven up to the start of the 1990s. And the previous requirement that forced each visitor to change at least US$200 at the official exchange of US$1 to K6, has been changed to US$300 but at the market rate, which is over K100. By end-1996, 550 licences had been issued for tourism services, 392 for hotels, 1465 travel and tour operators, and 2091 tourist guides.

Aviation

There have been many recent developments in aviation. Flight frequencies have increased, particularly to Bangkok and Singapore, and charter flights were allowed over Yangon/Mandalay-

Burma (Myanmar) ~ unparalleled beauty, unspoiled charm, unforgettable cultural treasures. Quite unlike any land you know!

From the simplest FIT, to the most elaborate incentive package and inclusive tours, EPG can meet all of your travel requirements in Myanmar. EPG boasts hands-on Western management and a highly-trained local staff, which guarantee Myanmar's most reliable services at competitive prices.

EPG TRAVEL COMPANY LTD.

YANGON
Tel: + 951 296 205
Fax: + 951 298 685

BANGKOK
Tel: + 662 895 3170
Fax: + 662 895 3171

LONDON
Tel: + 44 1923 249 910
Fax: + 44 1923 218 649

E-mail: IEPG@ mozart.inet.co.th.   OR   E-mail: BURMA@ larry-of-london.demon.co.uk

Chiangmai and Yangon-Phuket. Royal Brunei Airlines started a Bandar Seri Begawan-Yangon-Abu Dhabi-London route, operating twice weekly with Boeing B767s. German airline Condor ran some ad hoc charters in winter 1996, but was unable to get permission for a regular series. Its flights may not restart in winter 1997.

The state-owned Myanmar Airways joined with foreign investors in 1993 to operate on its international routes as Myanmar Airways International. April 1997 saw a Memorandum of Understanding signed between Myanmar Airways and Indonesian aircraft manufacturer IPTN to launch a joint venture airline for "border area development" in Myanmar. ITPN builds 30/40 seater aircraft. Meanwhile Air Mandalay, partly owned by Singapore interests, began operating in 1994 on domestic routes and to Chiangmai in Thailand. Also, there are plans to launch another domestic airline, Yangon Airways. Air Mandalay targetted 180,000 seat sales in 1996, with four 69-seat ATR72s. Business has been good. Loads in the peak winter (May-August is low season) were up to 50%, but the airline's breakeven is only at 38%. Druk Air has started flights Yangon-Bangkok-Paro, as well as Malaysia Airlines on Yangon-Kuala Lumpur, and Lao Aviation on Yangon-Vientiane. And All Nippon Airways plans to add a route to Yangon from Tokyo. The government is studying whether to build a new airport for Yangon. Also, the government signed a contract with Thai company, Italthai, to expand and improve Mandalay International Airport; work is due to be finished in 1999.

Hotels

Hotel growth in Myanmar is rapid. Before 1988, the last major change in government, the country had 20 hotels with 914 rooms. Now there are 409/9276; foreign investors plan 40/7649 and locals a further 472/10,856—averaging 23 rooms per hotel, so many are like village resthouses. The resulting total is about 950/27,600. Foreign investment in hotels totals over US$7 billion, and there are many foreign management groups with hotels open or opening. They include Accor, Amanresorts, New World, Shangri-La, Sedona, Concorde, Equatorial. Those opening in 1996 in Yangon include the Ramada Yangon International Airport with 121 rooms, the Sedona with 430 rooms, and the Traders (part of the Shangri-La group) with 400 rooms. A new hotel, the Baiyoke Kandawgyi in Yangon, changed its name shortly after opening in 1996 to Kandawgyi Palace.

In the capital Yangon hotel projects included Amara with 250 rooms, now delayed three years until 1999; Equatorial with 359 rooms, due in mid 1997; the Nikko Royal Lake, with 200 rooms in May 1997; the Shangri-La with 450 rooms in 1998; the Sofitel with 270 rooms in 1997; the Yangon with 340 rooms in 1997; and Yuzana with a 200-room extension in 1998. Also, Malaysian company Idris Hydraulic is building two hotels. Names are not finalised but one is currently named Idris Shwegondine, with 250 rooms, and the other Idris Laharpyin, with 350 rooms. Opening dates have not been set. In Bagan, both Hilton and Novotel are reported to be building hotels with about 200 rooms, and Mandarin Oriental's resort, with 120 rooms, was due to open by the Ayerawaddy river in 1997. In Kawthaung, the US$44 million Salon Island Resort is due to open 700 rooms around 1999. In Mandalay, Sedona planned a 300-room hotel to open mid 1997.

By country the following number of hotel investment projects were in place at end 1996: Singapore 10, Thailand 8, Japan 3, Hong Kong 3, Malaysia 4, Others 32.

A major new resort complex is planned for Salon Island; the first phase to consist of a 250-room US$30m hotel; the second, costing $200m, comprising a round-island railway and airstrip.

What to See

Yangon. First stop in the capital (formerly Rangoon) should be the 2500 year-old Shwedagon pagoda. This richly gilded Buddhist stupa lies 6.5 km north of the city centre and rises 100 metres from the top of Singuttara Hill. The treasure vault is said to contain the sacred relics of the Buddha. Another notable pagoda is the Sule pagoda, near the Strand hotel. It is reputed to be 2250 years old and stands 48 metres high. The sacred hair of the Buddha is said to be enshrined in its vault. Also worthy of a visit is the Kaba Aye pagoda, 11 km north of the city centre, which was built only in 1954, and its neighbouring Great Sacred Cave. The Mae La Mu pagoda, 13 km northeast of the city centre has beautiful images depicting scenes from Buddha's previous lives surrounding it. As well as Buddhist pagodas, Yangon has places of worship for Hindus, Jews, Chinese, Muslims and Christians, testifying to the country's religious tolerance. Apart from the famous pagodas, Rangoon Zoo makes a good family trip, housing rare species of birds, reptiles, apes, wild beasts and crodilies. The National Museum in Pansodan displays the Mandalay regalia, belonging to the last Burmese kings and returned to Myanmar in 1964 by the British. Orchid lovers will enjoy the horticultural gardens at Mingaladon, 16 km north of the city centre, which houses more than 115,000 different species. It is part of the 120-acre National Park.

100 miles east of the capital is **Kyaiktiyo** with the legenday perching pagoda on the

Discover the delights of South-East Asia on the most leisurely and stylish form of transport - The Eastern & Oriental Express.

Contact telephone numbers:
Singapore (65) 323 4390; USA (toll-free) (800) 524 2420; UK (171) 928 6000

Golden Rock, reached after a 7-mile hike. The rock is said to be held in place by a strand of Buddha's hair enshrined in the pagoda atop it.

Mandalay is the cultural capital of Myanmar and its second biggest city with 600,000 inhabitants. Its centre used to be Mandalay Palace, the last residence of Burmese kings, but this was largely destroyed by allied bombing in the second world war. The moat, some walls and wooden pavilions survive and the precincts house the Cultural Museum, a model of the original palace. Near the palace wall is Mandalay (or Sagaing) Hill, covered with pagodas and monasteries and topped with a colossal standing image of Buddha. An enduring example of Mandalay skills can be seen in the Schwenandaw monastery, with its fine wood-carving. Nearby is the Kuthodaw Pagoda, which houses the entire Buddhist scriptures carved onto 729 marble slabs, constituting the world's biggest book. Other notable pagodas are the Shwe Kyi Myint, the Mahamumi or Arakan, the Eindawya and the Sandamuni, with impressive gold leaf.

Excursions around Mandalay should take in **Mingun** with its huge unfinished pagoda and 90-tonne bell, said to be the largest ringing bell in the world. Also the former capitals of **Amarapura** and **Bagan** (or Pagan). The latter was the 11th century capital and cradle of Burmese civilisation. Ruins of the ancient city cover 16 square miles along the banks of the Irrawaddy. In its heyday there were said to be millions of pagodas - now more than 2000 remain, the most spectacular being the 11th-century Ananda Temple with 80 bas reliefs depicting the final life cycle of Buddha and the 215-ft high Thatbyinnyu Temple, affording an excellent panorama of the Bagan plains. Between Bagan and Mandalay is the celebrated hilltop monastery of **Mount Popa**, said to be the dwelling place of the 37 nats (spirit gods).

200 miles east of Bagan in Shan State is **Inle Lake**, famous for its floating villages, colourful markets and native Inhas who row their small boats with their legs.

Nearby are the celebrated **Pindaya Caves**. Amongst the stalacmites and stalctites are nearly 9000 Buddhist statues, placed there by devotees over hundreds of years. The neighbouring **Meditation Caves**, access-ible only through foot-high entrances provide a peaceful retreat for worshippers.

Shopping

Handicrafts are the best buys in Myanmar. Bogyoke market in Yangon (formerly known as Scott Market) is one of the best centres, where Mandalay silk longyis, Shan woven bags, Burmese slippers, wood and ivory carvings, lacquerware and silverware make the best presents. Gems, rubies, sapphire, jade, pearls and other precius metals are best bought at the government-run Diplomatic Shop on Sule Pagoda Road. Quality is officially guaranteed and their export is permitted. All payments have to be in US dollars. Other gem emporia are to be found at the FMI centre in Bogyoke Street and at the Gems Museum. There are two foreign owned depart-ment stores: SKS and Daewoo. The best place for curios and antiques is Curio da City at 35 Bahan Road and for art the Burma Art Centre at 187 Bogyoke Market and Lokanath Art Shop in Phayre Street. In Mandalay the Zegyo bazaar offers bags, jewellery and lacquerware and the Mandalay Night Bazaar near the railway station is a mecca for bargain hunters.

In general bargaining is the norm, so feel free to ask for a discount where prices are not marked. Be careful, though, when dealing with pavement vendors.

Getting Around

Yangon Airways flies regularly from the capital to Mandalay, Bagan, Kawrhaung in the extreme South, Tachilek in the east and Putao in the far north. Internal air tickets must be purchased in US dollars. Car hire is available from the major hotels or Myanmar Travel & Tours can rent you a limousine and driver for about US$50 per day in town. Buses are crowded and not air conditioned; trishaws are plentiful and cheap and a popular tourist experience. There is a good railway network with two classes of fare - upper and ordinary, with upper being three times the standard fare. On the Yangon-Mandalay line, the best time to take the neat and clean Japanese-bult express is 6 am. The journey takes some 11 hours; there is an alternative sleeper service departing Yangon 1815.

Entertainment & Leisure

Yangon has very little night life. Some of the new hotels have discos and there is the Palace Club for singing and dancing at City Central Plaza in Latha Township. But Myanmar is a land of festivals and between November and April (the dry season) these glittering events are held in the open air. Called *pwes*, they are concerts of dance and music with classical and dramatic performances of themes drawn from Buddhist culture . There are cinemas in Yangon and Mandalay which show Burmese, Western, Indian and Japanese movies.

Soccer is Myan-mar's most popular sport and the Aung San stadium, near the Thamada Hotel is the venue for major events played between June and February. The national sport is *chin-lone* or cane-ball, where a shutlecok-type ball has to be kept in the air using only feet, head or shoulders.

A number of western and Japanese-style **recreation clubs** have sprung up in Yangon in the past two years including the *BMB Club* at 126 Dhamazedi Road (karaoke and music), the *Cave Music Club* at the Kandawgwi Hotel, *Club Hollywood* at

Summit Parkview Hotel, *Dynamite Karaoke Lounge* at Royal Lake, *Palace Club* as noted above and *Raffles Recreation Centre* at 5th fl, F Bloc, Theingizay, Shwedagon Pagoda Road. **Swimming** is available at *Kokkine* (34 Saya San Rd) and the *National Swimming Pool* (U Wisara Rd, Dgn). **Golf** is available at *City Golf Resort* (Thri Mingalar St), *Okkala Golf Resort* (cnr Waizeyantar St/Gandama St, South Okkala) and at Yangon Golf Club (Lower Mingladon Road). **Tennis** can be played at Theinbyu Court in Banyadala Road, and yachting at Yangon Sailing Club (132 Inya Road). *Harbour Point Recreation Club* opened in 1996 with a membership joining fee of US$500 and annual subscription of $100. It is situated at Myanandar Park, Pansodan, Seikkan Township and offers fine dining, a fitness centre, billiard room and a jewel mart. Members may bring three guests each. Best English language bookshop is the Mandalay Book Agency at 80 (m) Kanbawza Lane 1, Bhn.

Photographs in this section by courtesy of Lawrence of London

Arrival & Departure

Visitors arrive in Myanmar by air or sea. Mingaladon Airport is 20 km north of Yangon. Only Thai nationals are allowed to use the land crossing in the southeast of the country at present, and most of those cross and re-cross daily for work purposes. Individual business travellers should get from Yangon Airport to their hotel by taxi or governemnt car and these cost between 150-200 Kyats, to be negotiated. International Departure Tax is US$6.

Myanmar Key Fact File

Passport Requirements:
All visitors must have a valid passport. Visas are obligatory. Nationals from Taiwan and North Korea are refused admission. Tourist visas, valid for up to 28 days, are usually organised by inbound travel agencies. Children over seven, even if on parents' passports, require separate visas. Business visas should be applied for at Myanmar embassies in home countries and can usually be extended in the country. and embassies abroad.

Currency: Kyat. 100 pyas = 1 kyat

Exchange Rates: *(February 1997)*
US$ 1 = 6 kyat (Official); £1 = 4.5 kyat

Currency Restrictions:
There are no restrictions on the amount of foreign currency visitors may bring into the country but they must be declared on arrival and once dollars have been changed into local currency, they cannot be bought back on departure. The importation of local currency (Kyats/FECs) is prohibited.

Electricity Supply:
20/230 volts, 50 cycles AC (110 in rural areas)

Language:
Myanmar. English widely understood in business and tourism circles. Cantonese, Mandarin and Fukienese also used in business.

Time:
GMT + 6.5 hrs; EST + 9.5 hrs

IDD Code: 95
Area codes: Yangon 1, Mandalay 2, Bagan 62

Business Hours:
Government offices (inc. the Post Office) are open from 0930-1630 without a break Monday to Friday.
Banking hours are 1000-1400 Monday through Friday. Military working hours are generally 0800-1500.
Government shops follow office hours; small private ones open longer. Commercial businesses normally work 0900-1700 Mon-Friday; 0900-noon Saturdays.

Customs & Entry:
A visitor may bring in the following items duty free: 400 cigarettes or 0.5 lbs of tobacco plus two quarts of liquor and one pint bottle of perfume or Eau de Cologne.

Health Requirements:
Yellow fever vertificate required if entering from a designated infected area. Typhoid, malaria and cholera inoculation recommended. All water and milk should be boiled or bottled before consumption; meat and fish should be well cooked.

Climate/best time to visit:
Best time to visit is from October to February. The dry seasonruns from mid-February to mid-May. The rainy season is from mid-May to mid-October. Hottest month is April when temperatures reach 45° celcius. Tropical lightweight clothing year round except when travelling to hilly areas.

National Holidays 1997/98
4 January Independence Day; February 12 Union Day; March 2 Peasants' Day; March 27 Armed Forces Day; April Maha Thingham-Water Festival. April 17 Myanmar New Year; May 1 Workers Day; Lao New Year; May 1 International Labour Day; May 21 tbc Eid al Adha; July 19 Martyrs' Day; November Tazaungdaing Festival; December 1 National Day; December 25 Christmas. Many local Buddhist festivals, governed by the moon's cycle throughout the year.

Myanmar Hotels

Bagan

Free Bird Hotel E
Cnr Kha-Ye/Myatlay Sts, New Bagan East
Tel: (62) 294941; Fax: (01) 275638/284823

Kaytumadi Dynasty Hotel E
Myatlay Road
Tel: (62) 70123; (01) 225714/226962

Kumudara Hotel E
Cnr Dawna St/5th St, Pyu Saw Hti Qtr,
Kyansittha Area, New Bagan
Tel: (62) 70080/70081

Mandalay

Emerald Land Inn E
No 9, 14th Street
Tel: (2) 26990

Mandalay Swan C
Cnr 26/68th Streets
Tel: (2) 22498/9; Fax: (95) 35677

Mya Mandala E
Cnr 27th/96th Streets
Tel: (2) 21283

Novotel Mandalay Hotel C
9 Kwin (416b), 10th St (foot of Mandalay Hill), Aung Myay Tha Zan T/S
Tel: (2) 35638; Fax: (2) 35639

Sedona Hotel Mandalay C
Pre-opening office: 230 Victoria St, Fl 06-06, Singapore.
Tel: (65) 338 8944; Fax: (65) 338 6696

Yangon (Rangoon)

Alfa Hotel D
41 Nawaday St. Tel: 240127; Fax: 240134

Asia Hotel E
44 Golden Valley. Tel: 526495; Fax: 550755

Bagan Inn E
29 Pho Sein St. Tel: 550489; Fax: 549660

Barani Hotel E
71 Minyekyawswa. Tel: 220854; Fax: 223104

Central Floating Hotel C
No 1,2 Wah-Dan Jetty
Tel: 227288/227422; Fax: 227577

Central Hotel D
335-357 Bogyoke Aung San Street
Tel: 29007/78472; Fax: 88003/72324

Hotel December E
89 Pyi Daung Su Yeiktha St
Tel: 221943; Fax: 289960

Jade Pavilion Inn D
126 A Dhammazedi St
Tel: 286021; Fax: 553062

Kandawgyi Palace Hotel B
Kan Yai Tha Road (on the Royal Lake)
Tel: 249225-9; Fax: 280412/242776

Mya Neik Nyo Royal C
20 Pa Le Road. Tel: 548310; Fax: 665052

Mya Neik Royal Supreme D
23-25 Kabaaye Pagoda Road
Tel: 553818; Fax: 665052

Nawarat Concorde C
257 Insein Road, 11052 (between city/airport). Tel: 667888; Fax: 667777

New World Inya Lake C
37 Kaba Aye Pagoda Road
Tel: 662866; Tlx: 21502; Fax: 665537

Ramada Hotel C
Airport Estate, Mingaladon Township
Tel: 666699; Fax: 663575

Savoy Hotel B
129 Dhammazedi Road
Tel: 526289; Fax: 524891/2

Sedona Hotel Yangon A
No 1 Kaba Aye Pagoda Road, Yankin Township. Tel: 666900; Fax: 666911;
E-Mail: sedona@singnet.com.sg

Strand Hotel A
92 Strand Road. Tel: 243377/281532;
Tlx: 21220; Fax: 289880

Summit Parkview B
250 Ahlone St. Tel: 227966; Fax: 227993

Traders Hotel Yangon C
Cnr Sule Pagoad Rd/Bogyoke Aung San Rds. Tel: 227757/60; Fax: 228226/227989

Hotel Windsor D
31 Shin Saw Pu Road, Sanchaung PO
Tel: 511216/7; Fax: 511218

Yangon City D
No 1a Kaba Aye Pagoda Rd
Tel: 667751; Fax: 667763

> **Explanation of codes in hotel entries**
> **A** after name of hotel = rack single room rate over US$200 per person per night; **B** = between $150-200; **C** = between US$100-150; **D** = between $50-100; **E** = under $50

Useful Addresses

Air Couriers
DHL Worldwide
Tel: (1) 71385
TNT Express Worldwide,
Tel: (1) 75424/30940
UPS. C/o Wahwah Co Ltd. Tel: (2) 45813

Airline Offices
Air France
69 Sule Pagoda Rd, PO Box 1050 Yangon
Tel : (1) 74199/70376
Myanmar Airways International
104 Kannar Road, Yangon
Tel: (1) 89772-4
Silk Air
537 Merchant Street, Yangon
Tel: (1) 84600
Thai International
Dawie House, 441-5 Mahabandoola St,
Yangon. Tel: (1) 75936

Business Centre
Indochina Business Centre
326a Pyay Road, Sanchaung, Yangon
Tel: (1) 527660; Fax: (1) 527665

Car Hire (with driver only)
Flora Myanmar
269 1st fl, Anawrahtar Road, Lanmadaw T/S, Yangon. Tel: (1) 227740; Fax: 287806
Asia Lion Travel & Tours
79, 2nd fl,Kyaikkasan St, Tamwe Township, Yangon
Tel: 549681; Fax: 297500
EPG Travel Company Ltd
28 Bogalayzay Street, Botahtaung Towns'p
Tel: 296205; Fax: 298685

Ambulance/Hospitals
Saydamar World Care Ltd
55 Saya San Road, Bahan. Tel: 550998
Aea International Clinic
Nawarat Hotel, 257 Insein Rd. Tel: 667888
Aung Zay Health Care Centre
Cnr Thein Phyu Rd/Anawratha Rd, Yangon
Tel: 294638/294572

National Tourist Office
Directorate of Hotels & Tourism
77/91 Sule Pagoda Road, Yangon
Tel: 284949; Fax: 289064

Business Contacts
Myanmar Investment Commission
653/691 Mercaht Road, Yangon
Tel: 272219/272009
Union of Myanmar Chamber of Commerce & Industry
78-86 Bo Sun Pat St, Pabedan Townsh'p
Tel: 277103

Nepal

Tourism/What to see

Nepal welcomed 360,000 tourists in 1996, half of which came from India. With *Visit Nepal Year 1998*, the country hopes to exceed 500,000 arrivals.

Kathmandu is a wonderful place in which to walk or cycle through the streets and past the old wooden buildings and temples. Of particular interest is the Royal Palace and the Jaganath Temple in Durbar Square.

For those with little time to spare, Royal Nepal Airlines offers an extremely popular "Mountain Flight" - an hour-long Himalayan circuit giving unparalleled views of the peaks including Mount Everest.

The only other way to get a close look at the mountain is to fly into Lukla and take a hill trek - seven days is the shortest duration. Lukla is also the gateway to the Namche Bazar area - 200 km or so out of Kathmandu - the home of Nepal's legendary Sherpas. The government is opening new trekking areas and it is now possible to reach the still unspoilt area around Mount Kanchenjunga - the world's third-highest peak.

For non-trekkers venturing out of

Kathmandu, Pokhara is probably the most popular destination. Sited next to a lake with Annapurna in the distance, Pokhara's location says it all.

The Royal Chitwan National Park is another must. Bordering the Rapti River, the Park was once the private hunting ground of government ministers. In 1962 it became a wildlife sanctuary and now has over 100 tigers and more than 400 rhinos plus the odd leopard, sloth, elephant, monkey and other creatures of the jungle. It also boasts over 350 species of bird. Many experts believe Chitwan is the best wildlife sanctuary in Asia. It is possible to explore the park in either a 4x4 vehicle or on the back of an elephant. There are other wildlife parks, such as the Royal Bardia Wildlife Reserve in the western Terai, the Lake Rara National Park and the Sagarmatha National Park (in which Everest is located) in the extreme northeast, which are also worth a visit. But go to Chitwan first.

Shopping

Kathmandu has a host of tourist shops in the centre of town and in the arcades of the big hotels. Items to look out for include jewellery, carpets, clothes and local handicrafts.

As is the norm elsewhere, carpet shops are happy to handle overseas shipments. Antiques can be taken out of the country only with special permission. For old curios and artwork the shops on Durbar Marg are probably your best bet as prices are cheap and some stores take credit cards (usually just Amex).

For quality local clothing there's *Durga Design* and *Roof of the World*, which sells classy sweaters and stylish dresses. The Tibetan Refugee Center is also worth a visit if you want traditional handicrafts from across the border.

Getting around

Royal Nepal Airlines and now Nepal Airways, Everest Air and Nicon Air fly to 40 locations throughout the country. RA operates from a domestic terminal near Tribhuvan International Airport.

Domestic fares are not expensive, but it is advisable to book early during peak periods. It is also important to reconfirm tickets at least 72 hours before departure and arrive at the domestic terminal at least 90 minutes before departure. The airport is inclined to become a melée of departing passengers.

There are no trains in Nepal. Taxis (those with black-and-white licence plates) and auto-rickshaws (three wheelers) with meters are available in Kathmandu. The night

taxi stand is located at Bhugol Park. A surcharge of 50 per cent is levied on all night taxi rides. Taxis cost about Rs 1,050 a day.

Local buses for different parts of the Kathmandu Valley can be found at Shahid Gate and Ratna Park.

Only chauffeur-drive car or jeep hire is available and you will be expected to pay for this service in foreign currency. A car with driver can work out expensive for trips out of Kathmandu, so it is often cheaper to fly.

Entertainment

Nepal is no Thailand and Kathmandu no Bangkok, so don't expect to find any sort of wild nightlife in the city. In fact, Kathmandu is fairly quiet in the evenings.

There are few goods bars - the best is probably *Rumdoodle* at the Hotel Shanker and the bar at the Yak & Yeti. Expect bars to close by 2300 and then it's off to bed. Otherwise, the *Casino Nepal* in the Oberoi Hotel is open 24 hours a day. The Hotels Annapurna, Everest and Yak and Yeti now also have casinos. Foreign visitors can get Indian Rs 100 worth of chips free upon presentation of their passport and airline ticket stub within seven days of arrival. After three days they may come back and apply for a further Rs 100.

Kathmandu's cinemas screen Nepali, Indian and Western movies. The National Theatre Hall *(Rathtriya Nach Ghar)* stages dramas and folklore programmes. The Nepal Association of Fine Arts frequently organises art exhibitions. Look out for performances of traditional Nepalese dances by the New Himalchuli Cultural Group in the Hotel Shanker compound. While the Everest Cultural Society performs classical folk dances every day at the Hotel de L'Annapurna.

Kathmandu not only offers local cooking (slightly less spicy than Indian), but also restaurants selling Tibetan, Indian, Japanese, Chinese and Continental food. Expect to eat early, though, as many restaurants shut up shop at 2200.

Leisure

Nepal may be unsophisticated, but it does have a golf course - the nine-hole Royal Golf Club near the airport, which is open to member-sponsored guests. The Gokarna Safari Golf Club is 10km northeast of Kathmandu.

Cycling is popular and is a good way to see Kathmandu, but organised trips are possible to points further afield. Keen anglers are free to fish for snow trout in the Terai river and many of the nation's valley lakes. You can also fish along the Sunkosi river between October-March - no licence is required. Yoga and horse-riding are also on offer. Most major hotels offer tennis and swimming.

For adventure holidays the famous Tigre Tops or Temple Tiger Camps, offering inclusive big game holidays are hard to beat. Otherwise hill-trekking is a favourite among visitors. As is pony trekking. Trekking is usually undertaken from October to May but note that a permit is needed for trekking outside designated areas.

White-water rafting down the glacier-fed rivers of Nepal is increasing in popularity. The Sunkosi is a good place to start, the Trisuli river is often crowded. The country has three river systems that cut through the narrow gorges of the Mahabharat Range. Trips are from one to five days duration.

Daily one-hour sightseeing flights from Kathmandu along the Himalayas to Mount Everest operate during October-May.

Arrival & Departure

Kathmandu's International Airport is situated 8km from the city. Delays in clearing customs are often caused by the registration of temporarily imported electrical goods, such as computers.

Taxis from the airport into Kathmandu cost upwards of Rs50 - negotiable with the driver. A bus service operates from Tribhuvan International Airport to New Road Gate and vice versa. It costs Rs20. The bus calls at many of the big hotels and runs between 0800-2200. Some hotels also operate shuttle buses. International airport departure tax is Rs700 per passenger.

Restaurants

Many cuisines are on offer in Kathmandu, although 'beef' will more usually mean buffalo. The selection below, both inside and outside the main hotels, mostly accept American Express cards and advance booking is recommended.

Arniko Room *(Chinese/Tibetan)*
Hotel de l'Annapurna, Durbar Marg. Tel: 221711

Chimney Restaurant *(Russian/Continental)*
Yak & Yeti Hotel. Durbar Marg. Tel: 413999

Coppers *(Western)*
Kaisermahal, Thamel

Far Pavilion *(Indian)*
Everest Hotel, Baneswor. Tel: 220567

Fuji Restaurant *(Japanese)*
Kanti Path (opp. American Embassy). Tel: 225272

Ghar-E-Kabab *(Indian/Nepalese)*
Hotel de l'Annapurna, Durbar Marg. Tel: 221711

Golden Gate Restaurant *(Chinese)*
Durbar Marg (opp. Indonesian Bank). Tel: 223705

Kokonor *(Western)*
Hotel Shangri La, Lazimpat. Tel: 412999

Greenlands Vegetarian Restaurant
Woodlands Hotel, Durbar Marg.
Tel: 220123

Moti Mahal *(Indian)*
Durbar Marg. Tel: 225647

Naachghar *(Nepalese)*
Yak & Yeti Hotel, Durbar Marg. Tel: 413999

Ras Rang *(Chinese)*
Opp. Hotel Ambassador. Tel: 414432

Rumdoodle *(Western - bar & food)*
Thamel, Nr Kathmandu Guest House. Tel: 226138

Sunkosi *(Nepalese/Tibetan)*
Durbar Marg. Tel: 215299/220299

Nepal Key Fact File

Passport & Visa Requirements:
All visitors, except Indian nationals, must hold a passport and a valid visa. A 15-day visa is also granted upon entry, upon presentation of two photographs and the fee.

Currency: Nepali Rupee.

Exchange Rate:
US$1 = Nr 57; £1 = Nr 92.7 *(Mar 1997)*

Currency Restrictions:
Any amount imported over US$2,000 must be declared on entry. Non-Indian visitors are not allowed to import or export Indian currency. Foreign currencies must be exchanged ony through the banks or authorized exchange dealers. Export of local currency is prohibited. Only 10% of any local currency left over on departure can be re-exchanged.

Electricity Supply: 220 volts/50 cycles

Language:
Nepali. Some Engish spoken in business and the tourist industry.

Time:
GMT + 5.45 hrs; EDT + 10.45

IDD Code: 977 *followed by...*
Kathmandu/Patan 1; Pokhara 61; Nepalguni 81

Business Hours:
Government offices are open 1000-1700 Sunday to Thursday February to mid-November; 1000-1600 Sunday to Thursday mid-November to February.
Banks are open from 1000-1430 Sunday to Thursday; 1000-1200 Fridays.
Office hours are 1000-1700 Mon- Friday.

Customs & Entry:
Duty-free allowance comprises 200 cigarettes and 50 cigars, plus 1.15 litres of alcohol. Carrying narcotics, arms and ammunition is strictly forbidden.

Health Requirements:
Yellow Fever inoculation certificate required if arriving from an infected area; cholera, typhoid, malaria inoculations advised. Boil all water and milk and avoid unpeeled fruit and ice cubes. Eat meat when it is hot. Leeches present after monsoon time. Rabies present.

Climate/best time to visit:
Spring and autumn most pleasant seasons. Monsoon June to October. Oct-May best business months to visit. Lightweight clothes with umbrella June-Aug; Oct-March lightweight clothes for Kathmandu, coat and warm clothing for mountains. Winter min. 0°, max 17°C; July-Aug min. 18°, max. 26°C.

National Holidays 1997
11 January Prithivi Jayanti or National Unificatin day; 29 Jan Martyr's day; 12 Feb Sri Panchami or Sarswoti puja; 18 Feb Democracy day; 7 March Siva Ratri; 7 April Ghode Jatra; 13 April New Year's day; 15,16 April Chaite Dasain; 22 May Buddha Jayanti; 18 Aug Raksha Bandhan; 25 Aug Krishnastami; 15 Sept Indra Jatra; 2 Oct Ghatasthapana; 8-15 Oct Bada Dasain; 30 Oct Laxmipuja (cow festival); 1 Nov Govardan Paja; 2 Nov Bhai Tika; 7 Nov HM Queen's Birthday; 8 Nov Consitution day; 29 Dec HM King's Birthday.

Useful addresses

Airline Offices

Aeroflot Russian Airlines
PO Box 5640, Kamaladi. Tel: 226161/227399
Biman Bangladesh
Durbar Marg, Kathmandu. Tel: 222544
British Airways
Annapurna Intl Pte Ltd, Durbar Marg, Kathmandu. Tel: 222266/226611
Cathay Pacific
Kamaladi, Kathmandu. Tel: 411725
China Southwest Airlines
PO Box 4907, Kamaladi.
Tel: 411302; Fax: 419778
Indian Airlines
Durbar Marg, Kathmandu. Tel: 419649
Nepal Airways
Hattisar, Kamalpokhari, Kathmandu
Tel: 412388; Fax: 410134
PIA Durbar Marg, Kathmandu. Tel: 223102
Royal Nepal
RNAC Bldg, Kantipath, Kathmandu.
Tel: 220757/214640; Tlx: 2212
Singapore Airlines
Durbar Marg, PO Box 482. Tel: 220759
Thai International
Durbar Marg, Kathmandu. Tel: 223566/224917

Car Hire

Avis
(Chauffeur driven service only)
Yeti Travels Pvt Ltd, PO Box 76, Durbar Marg, Kathmandu. Tel: 221234/221754; Tlx: 2204 YETI NP; Fax: 1-226153
Branches at De l'Annapurna, Mayalu, Soaltee and Yak & Yeti Hotels.

Air Couriers

DHL. Tel: (1) 222358
TNT Express. Tel (1) 470351 / 212637
UPS. Tel: (1) 225 854 / 216 215

Government/Commercial

Federation of Nepalese Chambes of Commerce
Tripureswar, PO Box 269, Kathmandu
Tel: 212096/215920; Tlx: 2476 NP

Nepal Chamber of Commerce
2 Nepal Bank Building, Dharmapath, PO Box 198, Kathmandu. Tel: 212005/213318
Tlx: 2349; Fax: 228324

National Planning Commission
Singh Durbar, PO Box 1284, Kathmandu

Tourism, banks, post office emergency, secretarial

Department of Tourism
Tripureswor, Kathmandu Tel: 211293.
Tourist Information Centre
New Road, Basantpur. Tel: 220818
International Convention Centre
New Baneswore, Kathmandu.
Tel: (1) 228799; fax: (1) 474912

Bir Hospital
Thundikel Parade Ground. Tel: 226963

American Express/Thomas Cook
Yeti Travels, Hotel Mayalu, Jamal Tole, Durbar Marg, Kathmandu. Tel: 221234

General Post Office
Sundhara, Lower Kanti Path, Kathmandu

Security Exchange Centre
Dilli Bazar, GPO Box 1550, Kathmandu
Tel: 411031
Police: Tel: 226998/226999
Ambulance: Tel: 211959
Worldwide Communications **Secretarial Services** Pvt Ltd
New Road Gate, New Road, PO Box 3513, Kathmandu Tel: 225565/227710; Tlx: 2716

Nepal Hotels

Kathmandu

Hotel de l'Annapurna ○ C
Durbar Marg, PO Box 140
Tel: 221711; Tlx: 2205; Fax: 225236

Bluestar Hotel ○ D
Tripureswar, PO Box 983
Tel: 228833; Tlx: 2322; Fax: 226820

Dwarika's Kathmandu Village Hotel D
Battisputali, PO Box 459
Tel: 414770; Tlx: 2239

The Everest Hotel C
PO Box 659, Baneswor, Kathmandu
Tel: 220567; Tlx: 2260; Fax: 226088

Hotel Blue Diamond D
Jyatha, Thamel PO Box 2134
Tel: 226320; Fax: 226392

Hotel Himalaya D
Sahid Sukra Marg, PO Box 2141
Tel: 523900; Tlx: 2566; Fax: 523909

Hotel Malia ○ D
Lekthnath Marg, PO Box 787, Kathmandu
Tel: 418385/410320; Tlx: 2238; Fax: 418382

Hotel Narayani ○ D
PO Box 1357, Kathmandu
Tel: 525015; Tlx: 2262; Fax: 521291

Novotel Kathmandu ¶
Laximpat Box 324, Kathmandu
Tel: 419358/223045; Fax: 224001

Hotel Shangri-La ○ D
Lazimpat, PO Box 655
Tel: 412999; Tlx: 2276; Fax: 414184

Hotel Shanker D
Lazimpat, PO Box 350
Tel: 410151/412973; Tlx: 2230; Fax: 412691

Hotel Sherpa ○ D
PO Box 901, Durbar Marg
Tel: 222585/6; Tlx: 2636; Fax: 222346

Soaltee Holiday Inn Crowne Plaza
Tahachai, Kalimati, PO Box 97 ○
Tel: 272555; Tlx: 2203; Fax: 272201/27 2205

*Hotel Classification: **A** after name of hotel = over US$ 200 per person per night; **B** = between US$ 150 - 200; **C** = between US$ 100 - 150; **D** = between US$ 50 - 100 ; **E** = under US$ 50; **§**= prices on application; ○ = PATA member.*

Summit Hotel ○
Kopundole Height, Lalitpur. PO Box 1406
Tel: 521894; Tlx: 2342; Fax: 523737

The Summit lies 10 minutes south of what is now an overcrowded Kathmandu. Standing on a ridgeline looking north across the city to the Himalayas, it offers a unique old world charm with the friendliest staff, most beautiful gardens and the best food in Kathmandu.

Accommodation and rates
72 twin US$ 20-85; 4 suites from US$ 100

Credit cards accepted
Amex, Visa, Mastercard

Groups
Two conference/function rooms, capacity 25-30; audio-visual equipment available; largest reception 100 seated or 200 cocktail

Room services
Direct-dial telephone, laundry/valet service, 24-hr room service, non-smoker bedrooms

Business & other services
Business centre, airport pickup, translation service, car parking, travel centre, taxi service, beauty salon, newsstand/shops

Sports & Recreation
Golf nearby, sauna, outdoor swimming pool, tennis nearby

Restaurants & Coffee Shops
Himalayan (75) - Continental, open 0700-2230; *Naachgar* (60) - Chinese/Nepalese, open 1800-2230; *Garden, Terrace, Poolside Bar*

Overseas Sales Representatives
Nepal Reizen, Holland. Tel: (20) 624 7580

Hotel Woodlands Dynasty Plaza ○
Durbar Marg, PO Box 760, Kathmandu D
Tel: 220623; Tlx: 2282; Fax 225650

Hotel Yak & Yeti ○ C
Durbar Marg, PO Box 1016
Tel: 222635/413999; Tlx: 2237; Fax: 227782

Hotel Yellow Pagoda ○ D
Kantipath, Po Box 373
Tel: 220337; Tlx: 2268; Fax: 228914

Meghauli

Tiger Tops Tharu Safari Resort A
Royal Chitwan National Park
Tel: (1) 415659; Tlx: 2216; Fax: (1) 414075

Pokhara

New Crystal Hotel ○ E
Naghdunga, Pokhara Valley (Postal address: PO Box 1253 Kathmandu).Tel: (61) 20035/6; Tlx: 6004; Fax: (1) 228028

Hotel Mount Annapurna E
PO Box 12 Pokhara Airport
Tel (61) 20027/20037; Fax: (61) 20027

Airline Departures

*Below is a list of principal departures from Kathmandu (Tribhuvan) International Airport to the destinations in bold type. Figures in brackets after destinations refer to the days of the week. (2,4,6) therefore indicates that departures take place on a Tuesday a Thursday and a Saturday. Departures were correct as at February 1997 but travellers are advised to check times as timetables are liable to change .
Airline abbreviation codes: **BG** = Biman Bangladesh; **IC** = Indian Airlines; **KB** = Druk Air; **LH** = Lufthansa; **PK** = Pakistan International Airlines; **Q7** = Qatar Airways; **RA** = Royal Nepal Airlines; **SQ** = Singapore Airlines; **SU** = Aeroflot; **SZ** = China Southwest. **TG** = Thai International; **E2** = Everest Air; **3Z** = Necon Air; **7E** = Nepal Airways.*

Bangkok (BKK)
RA (2,3,5,7) TG (1,3,5,6,7)
Calcutta (CCU)
IC (1,2,4,5,6)
Delhi (DEL)
RA (daily) IC (daily) KB (3,7)
Dhaka (DAC)
BG (1,3,5,7) SQ (4,7)
Dhangarhi (DHI)
RA (2,6)
Doha (DOH)
Q7 (6)
Dubai (DXB)
RA (3,5,7)
Frankfurt (FRA)
RA (3,5,7) LH (1,3,7)
Hong Kong (HKG)
RA (2,6)
Jankapur (JKR)
3Z (daily)
Karachi (KHI)
LH (1,3,7) PK (1,2,4,5)
London (LGW)
RA (5,7)
Moscow (MOW)
SU (6)
Osaka (OSA) RA (3,7)
Paris (ORY) RA (3)
Shanghai (SHA)
RA (3,7)
Singapore (SIN)
RA (3,7) SQ (4,7)

New Zealand

What to See

In a land dominated by wide open spaces and where the cities have still to mature, it is to the country's many natural wonders and to a countryside filled with fat woolly sheep and munching dairy cows that visitors look first. New Zealand has some truly excellent national parks, some of the world's best geysers and springs and unique flora and fauna.

Most New Zealanders consider Rotorua the country's greatest attraction. Rotorua is 240km south of Auckland and is famed for its thermal activity - weird geysers and bubbling mud-pools, and its scenic beauty. It's possible to bath in the hot thermal pools and what better way to relax after a hard day's sightseeing? Many hotels and motels have their own thermal pools.

Tongariro National Park is the most popular national park in the North Island and is about 100km south of Taupo. The park is home to three just-about-active volcanoes and was originally a gift from the Maori people to the British crown.

Also on North Island, the Waimangu thermal valley should not be missed. This is a massive boiling lake with geysers. Half-day mini-bus trips to the area can be organised.

Other national parks to look out for are: the Mount Cook National Park, which is dominated by the nation's highest peak and huge glaciers; Mount Aspiring National Park is south of Mount Cook and is a wild and rugged area; Fiordland National Park is a huge expanse of virgin territory and is probably New Zealand's best.

As for Auckland - New Zealand's biggest city, there is the Auckland War Memorial Museum, which houses memorabilia from two World Wars. There are also Maori items such as the only surviving war canoe which forms part of display of native art and culture. In 1998 the NZ$300 mn Museum of New Zealand is due to open on the new waterfront.

Shopping

It's generally accepted that greenstone jewellery and sheepskin products are the best buys. New Zealand sheepskins make excellent floor coverings, jackets, toys and car seat covers. Maori weapons, ornaments and jewellery are also popular.

Don't expect to find smart designer clothes in any great numbers; although Auckland, Wellington and Christchurch do have some fine shops. Given the freight costs involved, imported items tend to be expensive; especially if goods have arrived from, say, Europe.

In Auckland, many of the best shops are located either in or close to Queen Street. Queens Arcade, a recently refurbished thoroughfare, houses 45 shops. Close by, the Downtown Shopping Centre has around 70 stores under one roof, including a duty-free outlet. The Plaza Shopping Centre is the best place to find speciality stores. Many items are sold duty-free to visitors throughout the country. Credit cards are widely accepted.

Getting Around

New Zealand has a reliable and efficient internal air network with the domestic arm of flag carrier Air New Zealand (NZ) and Ansett New Zealand (ZQ) competing for business. NZ operates mainly B737s and F27s on its local flights, while ZQ is increasingly relying on BAe146s to maintain its services. Mount Cook Airlines operates on a number of South Island routes as well as operating daily to the North Island. Its subsidiary Mount Cook Landline operates the largest coach network in South Island.

As an alternative to air and coach travel there is New Zealand Railways. Both Wellington and Auckland have commuter networks. Buses also operate the length and breadth of the country. A regular ferry service connects North and South Island between Wellington and Picton. It takes around 3.5 hours.

New Zealand's roads are happily uncrowded and driving the long distances between cities can be a real pleasure; although it's not an especially quick way of getting around. As such, car rental is highly recommended and all of the well-known international firms operate in the country.

City taxis do not cruise for hire and must be hired from a recognised rank or by phone. All are metered and tipping is not particularly necessary.

Entertainment

New Zealand lays claim to a handful of professional theatre groups. These are resident in the larger cities - Auckland, Wellington, Christchurch, Dunedin and Palmerston North. The country has 10 major public art galleries. The Royal New Zealand Ballet performs throughout the country. Maori concerts are often staged in the larger hotels, at the Maori Cultural Theatre and elsewhere. Some hotels also offer Maori feasts where food is cooked in underground ovens. Eating out is relaxed and informal in keeping with life in New Zealand.

Gambling is illegal, so there are no casinos or poker machines. Horserace betting is allowed and bets can either be placed at the course or in any one of the so-called TAB high street offices.

Leisure

The entire range of sports in on offer, from white-water river rafting through surfing and golf. Hunting and fishing are also in abundance.

With plenty of space for everyone to indulge his or her passion, even quite small towns have good golf courses at which visitors are usually welcome. Green fees vary, but be prepared to pay up to NZ$20 for a round.

Both North and South Islands have excellent ski-ing facilities with the season lasting from July through to early October. There are opportunities for both Nordic and Alpine ski-ing.

With a long coastline, surfers have a wide choice of beaches. The very best waves can be found in Northland on the west coast of the North Island, the Bay of Plenty, Gisborne and on the east coast of South Island.

As you would expect, deep sea fishing is one of New Zealand's best assets. The coastal waters seem to teem with fish - swordfish, various varieties of marlin, shark and kingfish, but the prime spot is considered to be off the east coast of North Island. Boats can be chartered at a number of points. Good trout fishing can be found in the country's many under-fished rivers and lakes. A special trout fishing licence is available for NZ$50 from any NZTP. Lake Taupo in the middle of the North Island is known worldwide for its abundant trout. It is said that over 700 tonnes of trout are taken from the lake each year. While Lake Tarawera has a reputation for producing more big trout than any other lake in the world.

Arrival & Departure

Auckland International Airport is 22km outside the city and is the nation's chief gateway; Christchurch airport is 10km from the city.

Taxis operate into Auckland from the airport and cost upwards of NZ$35. Journey time is ca. 35 minutes. *Airporter* buses leave every 30 minutes from the International Terminal, calling at all principal city hotels and the city air terminal - cost NZ$9. Shuttle buses also operate 24 hours at a cost of NZ$8.

Taxis from Christchurch can be picked up from outside the terminal and a ride into the city centre should cost from around NZ$20. *Canride* buses leave for the city centre on the hour at a cost of NZ$3. Journey time is 15 minutes. Wellington Airport is 8 km from the city and a taxi costs NZ$15; bus to the Rail Station is NZ$4.50. International departure tax is NZ$20.

New Zealand Key Fact File

Passport Requirements:
Passports are required by all visitors to New Zealand. These must be valid for at least three months. All visitors (except Australians) need temporary permits, which are applied for on arrival. UK, EEC, Japanese and USA visitors do not need a visa for visits of up to 3 months.

Currency:
New Zealand dollar (NZ$). 100 cents = NZ$1

Exchange Rates:
US$ 1 = NZ$ 1.46; £1 = NZ$ 2.23 *(March 1996)*

Currency Restrictions:
None on foreign or local currency.

Electricity Supply:
230 volts AC.

Language:
English. Maori is also spoken.

Time:
GMT + 12; EDT + 17. In summer this is advanced one hour.

IDD dialling code: 64
Area codes: Auckland 9; Christchurch 3; Dunedin 24; Hamilton 71; Invercargill 21; Palmerston North 63; Rotorua 73; Wellington 4.

Business hours:
Commercial offices 0830-1700.
Government offices: hours are more flexible than commercial offices.
Banks are open from 0930-1630 Monday to Friday.
Shops are open from 0900-1750 Monday to Thursday and from 0900-2100 on Fridays. In some areas, particularly city suburbs, late-night shopping occurs on Thursday. Many shops are also open on Saturdays in cities and resort areas.

Customs & Entry:
Duty-free allowance comprises 200 cigarettes or equivalent in cigars/tobacco; one litre of spirits and 4.5 litres of wine (equivalent to six 750ml bottles) and one bottle containing not more than 1,125ml of spirits or liqueur. Goods up to the value of NZ$500 are free of duty. Many agricultural products are banned.

Health Requirements:
Visitors do not need any vaccination certificates.

Climate/best time to visit
New Zealand enjoys an oceanic, temperate climate, uninfluenced by any land mass. Warm sunny summers are followed by mild and wetter winters. Sub-tropical in the north to temperate in the south. Some snow in the extreme south in winter. Average temperature Nov-Feb 10-18C; June-Aug 3-10C. Humidity 70%. Best months for business visits Feb-April and Oct-November; tourist visits Feb-Mar, Oct-Nov busiest times. January tends to be the holiday month for New Zealanders (equivalent of August in Europe).

National Holidays 1997
1-2 January New Year's Day; 6 February Waitangi Day; 28/30/31 March Good Friday/April Easter Monday; 25 April ANZAC Day; 2 June Queen's Birthday; 27 October Labour Day; 25/26 December Christmas Day/Boxing Day. Each province also celebrates its European settlement foundation day as a local holiday.

Useful Addresses

Business

Auckland Chamber of Commerce
PO Box 47, 2 Courthouse Lane, Auckland 1
Tel: 303 1969; Tlx: 2326

British-New Zealand Trade Council
PO Box 3029, Level 3, Eagle House, 150-154 Willis St, Wellington

Department of Trade & Industry
Bowen State Building, Bowen St, Wellington 1

New Zealand Bureau of Importers & Exporters
PO Box 9248, 12 Courthouse Lane, Auckland1. Tel: (09) 377 1273

Trade Ministry
Ministry of Trade & Industry
99 Queen St, Auckland. Tel: (9) 303- 3189

Convention/Exhibition Centre
Aotea Center, Aotea Square, Queen St, Auckland. Tel: (9) 307 5091

Auckland Waterfront

Air Couriers

DHL. Auckland tel: (09) 636 5000
Christchurch tel: (03) 365 5543
Wellington tel: (04) 801 5135
Federal Express
Auckland (09) 256 8300
TNT Worldwide Express
Auckland (09) 275 0549; Wellington tel(04) 471 2746; Christchurch tel: (3) 366 7344
UPS
Auckland (09) 275 4009/275 4006

Secretarial Services

Private Secretary.
10 Durham St E, Auckland. tel: (9) 799142

Tourism

Auckland Visitors' Bureau
299 Queen St, Auckland. tel: (9) 303 1899

New Zealand Tourist Office
99 Queen Street, Auckland 1
Tel: (09) 798180

New Zealand Tourist Office
65 Cathedral Square, Christchurch
Tel: (03) 379 4900

New Zealand Tourist Office
25-27 Mercer Street, Wellington
Tel: (04) 739269

Emergencies etc

Auckland City Medical Center
Lister Bldg, Victoria St. Tel (9) 379 9635

Auckland Hospital
Park Rd, Grafton. Tel: (9) 379 7440
Police/Ambulance. Dial 111

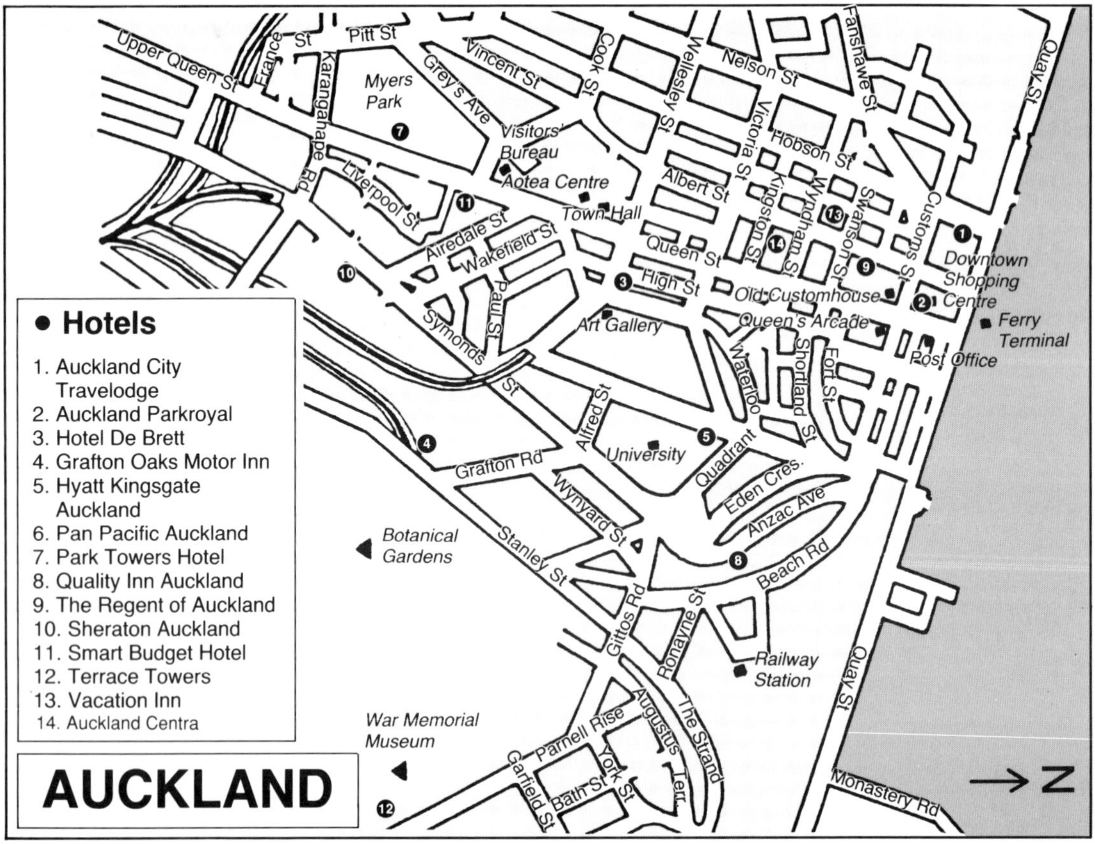

AUCKLAND

● Hotels

1. Auckland City Travelodge
2. Auckland Parkroyal
3. Hotel De Brett
4. Grafton Oaks Motor Inn
5. Hyatt Kingsgate Auckland
6. Pan Pacific Auckland
7. Park Towers Hotel
8. Quality Inn Auckland
9. The Regent of Auckland
10. Sheraton Auckland
11. Smart Budget Hotel
12. Terrace Towers
13. Vacation Inn
14. Auckland Centra

NEW ZEALAND - Hotels

New Zealand Hotel Reference Table

Hotel (listed in price order) * = all meals included. Previous names in brackets.	SINGLE ROOM RATE (NZ$)	LOCATION	NUMBER OF ROOMS	NUMBER OF SUITES	CONFERENCE FACILITIES	EXHIBITION SPACE	LARGEST BANQUET NUMBER	BUSINESS CENTRE	SWIMMING POOL (0 = indoor)	TENNIS COURT	HEALTH CLUB	VIDEO FILMS
Huka Lodge	560*	Taupo	-	17	-	-	-	-	•	•	•	•
Solitaire Lodge	400-500*	Rotorua	-	10	-	-	-	-	-	-	•	•
Wellington Parkroyal	320	Wellington	230	2	-	-	-	•	-	-	•	•
Stamford Plaza (Regent)	305	Auckland	313	19	•	•	500	•	•	-	-	•
Lake Rotorua Lodge	300	Rotorua	-	9	-	-	-	-	-	-	-	•
Hotel du Vin	295-345	Auckland	46	-	-	-	-	-	-	-	-	•
Parkroyal Christchurch	290-360	Christchurch	300	-	•	•	500	•	-	-	•	•
Noah's Christchurch Hotel	285	Christchurch	203	5	•	-	220	•	-	-	-	•
Queenstown Parkroyal	275	Queenstown	140	-	•	•	260	•	-	-	-	•
Hyatt Auckland	270	Auckland	275	-	•	•	300	•	-	-	•	•
Novotel Auckland (Parkroyal)	265	Auckland	189	-	•	-	300	•	•	-	-	•
Sheraton Auckland	265-375	Auckland	422	9	•	•	500	•	•	-	•	•
Auckland City Travelodge	250	Auckland	196	-	•	-	200	•	•	-	-	•
Millbrook Resort	250-270	Queenstown	20	-	-	-	-	-	•	•	•	•
Auckland Centra	245-265	Auckland	252	-	•	-	-	•	-	-	•	•
Sheraton Rotorua Hotel	245-340	Rotorua	130	-	•	-	200	•	•	-	•	•
Carlton Hotel Auckland	240-360	Auckland	275	11	•	•	800	•	-	•	-	•
Plaza International	240-275	Wellington	200	-	•	-	-	-	-	-	-	•
Tongariro Lodge	235	Taupo	-	10	-	-	-	-	-	•	-	•
Centra James Cook Hotel	235	Wellington	244	16	•	-	250	•	-	-	-	•
The George Hotel	230-350	Christchurch	-	54	•	-	-	-	-	-	-	•
Quality Resort Lake Rotorua	202-225	Rotorua	227	-	•	-	-	-	•	•	•	•
Quality Hotel Anzac Ave	196-220	Auckland	110	-	•	-	120	-	-	•	-	•
Quality Inn Plimmer Tws	190-320	Wellington	94	-	•	•	200	•	-	-	-	•
Chateau on the Park	190	Christchurch	199	-	•	-	280	•	•	•	•	•
Lakeland	185	Queenstown	182	-	•	-	-	-	•	-	-	•
Te Anau Travelodge	185-200	Te Anau	109	3	•	-	100	-	•	-	-	•
Quality Hotel Rose Park	175-394	Auckland	117	-	•	-	350	-	-	-	-	•
Quality Hotel Oriental Bay	170-200	Wellington	117	-	•	-	100	-	O	-	-	•
Michael Fowler Hotel	165-245	Wellington	39	-	•	-	-	-	-	-	-	•
Quality Hotel Durham St	165-185	Christchurch	160	-	•	-	160	-	-	-	-	•
Quality Hotel Rose Park	162-189	Auckland	117	-	•	•	200	•	-	-	-	•
Holiday Inn Queenstown	160-275	Queenstown	150	-	•	-	-	-	•	•	•	•
Kingsgate Logan Park	160	Auckland	222	-	•	-	-	-	•	-	-	•
Quality Hotel Queenstown	155-195	Queenstown	100	-	•	-	80	-	•	-	-	•
Grand Chancellor (Quality Airport)	154-320	Auckland	158	2	•	-	200	•	•	-	•	•
Cotswold Inn	150	Christchurch	71	-	•	-	-	-	•	-	-	•
Quality Hotel Willis St	142-155	Wellington	84	-	•	-	500	-	O	-	-	•
Grafton Oaks Motor Inn	135	Auckland	44	-	•	-	-	-	-	-	-	•
Pacific Park	135	Christchurch	66	-	•	-	-	-	-	-	-	•
Quality Hotel Palm'n North	129-175	Palmerston N	154	-	•	-	150	•	-	-	-	•
Park Towers Hotel	129	Auckland	108	-	•	-	-	-	-	-	-	•
Quality Hotel Dunedin	128-150	Dunedin	54	-	•	-	120	-	-	-	-	-
Hotel De Brett	125	Auckland	25	-	•	-	-	-	-	-	-	-
THC Rotorua Internat'l	125-160	Rotorua	124	-	•	-	-	-	•	-	-	-
Bay Plaza Hotel	120-150	Wellington	114	1	•	•	100	-	-	-	-	-
Central City Motor Inn	120	Wellington	49	-	-	-	-	-	-	-	-	•
City Travelodge (Avon Hotel)	120	Christchurch	113	-	•	-	-	-	•	-	-	•
Airport Travelodge	118-140	Christchurch	155	-	•	-	-	-	•	-	-	•
Burma Motor Lodge	113	Wellington	63	-	-	-	-	-	-	-	-	-
Port Nicholson Hotel	110	Wellington	30	-	-	-	-	-	-	-	-	-
St George Hotel	105	Wellington	90	-	•	-	-	-	-	-	-	•
Lake Plaza Rotorua	100-130	Rotorua	200	-	•	-	-	-	•	-	•	•
Terrace Towers	95-120	Auckland	24	-	-	-	-	-	-	-	-	•
Hotel Russley	88-99	Christchurch	69	-	•	-	-	-	•	-	-	•

New Zealand Hotels

Auckland

Auckland City Travelodge   B
96-100 Quay St
Tel: 377 0349; Fax: 307 8159

Auckland Parkroyal   D
8 Customs St, PO Box 1707
Tel: 377 8920; Tlx: 2231; Fax: 307 3739

Auckland Vacation Inn   D
87 Campbell Rd, Greenlane
Tel: 641269; Tlx: 2781; Fax: 668115

Hotel De Brett   D
Cnr Shortland & High Sts, PO Box 237
Tel: 303 2389; Tlx: 60267; Fax: 303 2300

Carlton Hotel Auckland   B
Mayoral Drive & Vincent St
Tel: 366 3000; Fax: 366 0121

Grafton Oaks Motor Inn   D
121 Grafton Rd
Tel: 309 0167; Fax: 377 5962

Hotel du Vin   B
Lyons Rd, Mangatawhiri Valley
Tel: 233 6314; Fax: 233 6215

Hyatt Auckland   B
Princes St, PO Box 3938
Tel: 366 1234; Fax: 303 2792

Novotel Auckland   B
8 Customs Street
Tel: (9) 377 8920; Fax: (9) 307 3739

Park Towers Hotel   D
3 Scotia Place, 1
Tel: 309 2800; Tlx: 63645; Fax: 302 1964

Quality Hotel Anzac Avenue ○ C
150 Anzac Ave, PO Box 3272
Tel: 379 8509; Fax: 379 8582

Quality Hotel Rose Park   D
100 Gladstone Rd, Parnell, PO Box 37441
Tel: 377 3619; Fax: 303 3716

Quality Hotel Airport Auckland   D
Cnr Kirkbridge/Ascot Rds, PO Box 53339
Tel: 275 7029; Fax: 275 3322

The Regent of Auckland   B
Albert St, Private Bag
Tel: 309 8888; Tlx: 60079; Fax: 379 6445

Sheraton Auckland Hotel/Towers   B
83 Symonds St, PO Box 2771
Tel: 379 5132; Tlx: 60231; Fax: 377 9367

Terrace Towers Apartments   D
258 Parnell Rd, 68199
Tel: 793130; Tlx: 63645: Fax: 792092

Christchurch

Chateau on the Park   C
189 Deans Avenue, PO Box 8161,
Tel: (3) 348 8999; Tlx: 4806; Fax: (3) 348 8990

Christchurch Airport Plaza   C
Cnr Memorial Ave/Orchard Rd
Tel: (3) 358 3139; Tlx: 4258; Fax: 358 3029

Christchurch City Travelodge   C
356 Oxford Terrace, PO Box 13063
Tel:(3) 379 1180; Tlx: 4382; Fax: 366 7590

Cotswold Inn   C
88-90 Papanui Rd
Tel: (3) 355 3535; Tlx: 4160; Fax: 355 6695

The George Hotel   B
50 Park Terrace, PO Box 13063
Tel: (3) 379 4560; Tlx: 4654; Fax: 366 6747

Hawthornden Lodge   C
2 Hawthornden Rd
Tel: (3) 358 5610

Noahs Hotel Christchurch   A
Cnr Worcester St/Oxford Terrace
Tel: (3) 379 4700; Tlx: 4875; Fax: 3795357

Pacific Park Christchurch   D
263 Bealey Ave
Tel: (3) 379 8660; Tlx: 4965; Fax: 366 9973

Parkroyal Christchurch   B
Cnr Durham & Kilmore Sts, 1544
Tel: (3) 365 7799; Tlx: 40079; Fax: 365 0082

Quality Hotel Durham St   D
Cnr Durham & Kilmore Sts
Tel: (3) 338 0511; Tlx: 40194; Fax: 366 6302

Hotel Russley   D
73 Roydvale Ave
Tel: 358 8289; Tlx: 4464; Fax: 358 3953

Dunedin

Quality Hotel Dunedin   D
Upper Moray Place, PO Box 5119
Tel: (03) 477 6784; Fax: (03) 474 0115

Te Anau Travelodge   C
PO Box 185, Te Anau
Tel: (3) 249 7411; Fax: (3) 249 7947

Hamilton

Ambassador Motor Inn   E
86 Ulster St, PO Box 9501
Tel: (07) 839 5111; Tlx: 21299; Fax: 839 5104

Nelson

Quality Hotel Nelson   D
Trafalgar Square, PO Box 248
Tel: (03) 548 2299; Fax: (03) 546 3003

New Plymouth

Quality Hotel New Plymouth   D
State Highway 3, Bell Block, PO Box 7165
Tel: (06) 755 0379; Fax: (06) 755 1616

Palmerston North

Coachman Hotel   D
134 Fitzherbert Ave
Tel: (6) 357 3059; Tlx: 31382; Fax: 356 6692

Quality Hotel   D
110 Fitzherbert Avenue, PO Box 502
Tel: (6) 356 8059; Fax: (06) 356 8604

Queenstown

Holiday Inn Queenstown ○ C
Salisbury Rd, Fernhill
Tel: (3) 442 6600; Tlx: 5513; Fax: 442 7354

Lakeland   C
14-18 Esplanade
Tel: (3) 442 7600; Tlx: 5604; Fax: (3) 442 9653

Millbrook Resort ○ C
Mallaghans Road, PO Box 160
Tel: 441 7000; Fax: 442 1145

Quality Hotel Queenstown   C
Frankton Road/Adelaide St
Tel: (3) 442 8123; Tlx: 5704; Fax: 442 7472

Queenstown Parkroyal   B
Beach Street
Tel: 442 7800; Tlx: 5346; Fax: 442 8895

Hotel Classification: **A** *after name of hotel = over US$ 200 per person per night;* **B** *= between US$ 150 - 200;* **C** *= between US$ 100 - 150;* **D** *= between US$ 50 - 100* **E** *= under US$ 50;* ¶ *= prices on application These prices are only a guide and we recommend visitors to check rates with individual hotels before booking.* ○ *= PATA member.*

Quality Resort Terraces   C
48 Fankton Rd, Queenstown
Tel: (3) 442 7950; Fax: 442 8066

Rotorua

Lake Plaza Rotorua   D
6 Eruera St, PO Box 884
Tel: 348 1174; Tlx: 2247; Fax: 346 0238

Lake Rotoroa Lodge   B
Lake Rotoroa Rd 3, Murchinson, Lake
Rotoroa.Tel & Fax: 6454 39028

Quality Hotel Rotorua   D
Fenton Street, PO Box 1045
Tel: (07) 348 0199; Fax: (07) 346 1973

Quality Resort Lake Rotorua   D
Cnr Enuera & Hinemaru Sts
Tel: (7) 347 1234; Fax: (7) 348 1234

Royal Lakeside Hotel Rotorua   C
9-11 Tutanekai St, Rotorua
Tel: (7) 346 3888; Fax: (7) 347 1888

Sheraton Rotorua Hotel   C
Fenton St, PO Box 983
Tel: 348 7139; Tlx: 2656; Fax: 348 8378

Solitaire Lodge Rotorua   A
Ronald Road, Lake Tarawera Rd 5, .Tel:
(07) 362 8208; Fax: (07) 362 8445

THC Rotorua International Hotel   D
Froude St, PO Box 1048
Tel: 348 1189; Tlx: 2427; Fax: 347 1620

Taupo

Huka Lodge   A
Huka Falls Rd.Tel: (647) 378 5791; Tlx:
63229; Fax: (647) 378 0427

Tongariro Lodge   C
Turangi PO Box 278, Lake Taupo
Tel: (6474) 67946; Fax: 68860

Wellington

Bay Plaza Hotel   E
40-44 Oriental Parade, Oriental Bay
Tel: 385 7799; Fax: 385 2936

Burma Motor Lodge   D
Burma Road, PO Box 13155
Tel: 478 4909; Tlx: 31202; Fax: 478 4901

Central City Motor Inn   D
130 Victoria St, PO Box 11-814
Tel: 385 4166; Tlx: 30655; Fax: 385 4167

Michael Fowler Hotel   C
51-61 Cable St
Tel: 385 2809; Tlx: 30634; Fax: 385 2483

Oriental Park Hotel   D
360 Oriental Parade, Oriental Bay
Tel: 385 9949; Fax: 384 5443

Plaza International Hotel   C
148-176 Wakefield St, PO Box 1843
Tel; 473 3900; Tlx: 30343; Fax; 473 3929

Port Nicholson Hotel   D
Cnr Cambridge Terr/Wakefield St
Tel & Fax: 384 5903; Tlx: 31481

Quality Hotel Oriental Bay   C
73 Roxburgh St, PO Box 9555
Tel: 385 0279; Fax; 384 5324

Quality Hotel Plimmer Towers   D
Cnr Boulcott/Gilmer Sts, PO Box 10-148
Tel: 473 3750; Fax: 473 6329

Quality Hotel Willis Street   D
355 Willis St, PO Box 27241
Tel: 385 9819; Fax: 348 1234

St George Hotel   E
Cnr Willis & Boulcott Sts, PO Box 11327
Tel/fax: 473 9139; Tlx: 3674

James Cook Centra Hotel   C
147 The Terrace, PO Box 2429
Tel: 499 9500; Fax: 499 9800

Wellington Parkroyal   B
Grey St/Featherston St
Tel: 472 2722; Tlx: 30650; Fax: 472 4724

Restaurants

*New Zealand restaurants have increased in variety and sophistication in recent years. Home produced steak, lamb and seafood are world-famous and New Zealand wine, like its Australian counterpart, particularly white, is well worth trying. Liquor is not sold at supermarkets or stores in New Zealand but wine can be bought at wine shops and beer or spirits at the "bottle stores" of hotels or, in larger quantities, from liquor wholesalers. Only hotel guests can be served liquor on Sundays. The code **BYO** following the name of the restauarnt in the selection below signifies that the restaurant in question is not licensed, but that diners may bring in their own bottles.*

Auckland

Antoine's *(French)*
333 Parnell Road. Tel: 798756

Ariake *(Japanese)*
Quay Towers, Cnr Albert/Customs Sts
Tel: 792377

Chinatown *(Chinese)*
8 Lorne St. Tel: 366 1642

Da Gino *(Italian)*
66-68 Pitt St. Tel: 770973

Gamekeeper's *(Game/Local)*
29 Ponsonby Road. Tel: 789052

Hoffman's *(European)*
70 Jervois Road, Herne Bay. Tel: 762049.
Closed weekends.

Longchamps *(French)*
Regent of Auckland Hotel, Albert St
Tel: 309 8882

Mai Thai *(Thai)*
57b Victoria St. Tel: 303 2550

Matisse *(French)*
223 Parnell Rd, Parnell. Tel: 799300

New Orient *(Cantonese/Yum Cha)* **BYO**
Strand Arcade, Elliott St. Tel: 797794

Number Five *(French - nouvelle cuisine)*
5 City Road. Tel: 7630410

Rick's Cafe Americain *(European)* **BYO**
Victoria Park Market. Tel: 399074

Top of the Town *(Continental)*
Hyatt Kingsgate Hotel, Princes St
Tel: 366 1234

Union Fish Company *(Seafood)*
16 Quay Street. Tel: 796745

Vinnie's (Italian)
166 Jervois Rd, Herne Bay. Tel: 765597

Yamato *(Japanese)*
183 Karangahape Rd. Tel: 771424

Christchurch

Aggie's *(International)*
263 Bealey Ave. Tel: 379 8660

Kurashiki *(Japanese)*
Cnr Colombo/Gloucester Sts. Tel: 67092

Leinster *(Game)*
158 Leinster Rd. Tel: 358 8866

Sorbonne *(French Provincial/NZ)* **BYO**
Arts Centre, Rolleston Ave. Tel: 350 566

Waitangi Room
Noah's Hotel, Oxford Terrace. Tel: 379 4700

Rotorua

Colonel's Retreat *(International)*
Little Village, Tyon St, Whakarewarewa.
Tel: 81519

Hoo Wah *(Cantonese)* **BYO**
82 Ervera St. Tel: 85025

Rumours *(French - nouvelle cuisine)*
81 Pukuatua St. Tel: 477277

Wellington

Akiyoshi *(Japanese)* **BYO**
103 Willis St. Tel: 731189

Coachman *(Game/Seafood)*
97 The Terrace. tel: 738170

Nicholson's *(European)*
Rotunda Pavilion. 245 Oriental Parade.
Tel: 843835

Le Normandie *(French/NZ)*
116 Cuba St. Tel: 845000

(continued)

232 NEW ZEALAND - Restaurants/Airline Offices/Car Hire

Pierre's Restaurant *(French)* **BYO**
342 Tinakori Rd. Tel: 726238

Plimmer House *(Beef/Seafood)*
99 Boulcott St. Tel: 721872

Yangtze Restaurant *(Cantonese)* **BYO**
Cnr Jervois Quay/Williston St. Tel: 728002

Airline Offices

On-line only. Auckland unless otherwise indicated.

Aerolineas Argentinas
5th Fl, Air New Zealand Hse, 1 Queen St, Auckland.Tel: 379 3675

Air New Zealand
Air New Zealand House, Quay St, Private Bag, Auckland
Tel: 366 2400/367 2323

Air Pacific
National Mutual Ctre Bldg, PO Box 3628, 43 Shortland St, Auckland
Tel: 792404/798476

Ansett New Zealand
PO Box 3735, Auckland
Tel: 376950/796409

British Airways
154 Queens St, Qantas House, Auckland
Tel: (9) 356 8690

Canadian Airlines
1st Fl, Southpac Tower,
45 Queen Street, Auckland
Tel: 390735/393620

Cathay Pacific
3rd floor, General Buildings,
29-31 Shortland Street, PO Box 1313, Auckland. Tel: 790044/790833

Continental/Air Micronesia
7-9 Albert Street, Auckland
Tel: 795680/394144

Cook Islands International
Auckland. Tel: 733078

Hawaiian Airlines
87 Queen St, PO Box 279, Auckland
Tel: 793798

Japan Airlines
15th Fl, Quay Tower, 29 Customs Street West, Auckland.Tel: 799906

Lufthansa
9th floor, Royal Insurance Building
109 Queen Street, PO Box 1427, Auckland. Tel: 31527/9

Mount Cook Line New Zealand
47 Riccarton Road, Christchurch
Tel: (3) 348 2099; Fax: (3) 343 8159

Polynesian Airlines
Auckland.Tel: 794824

Qantas
154 Queen Street, Auckland
Tel: 790306/32506

Singapore Airlines
Lower Ground Floor, West Plaza Building, Cnr Customs & Albert Street,Auckland
Tel: 793209/303 2129

Thai International
2nd floor, West Plaza Building, Cnr Customs & Albert Street, Auckland 1
Tel: 796455

United Airlines
NZI Building, 3 Shortland Street, PO Box 3319, Auckland C1 NZ.. Tel: 793800

Car Hire

Avis
Bldg 4, 666 Gt South Rd (Head Office) Central Park, Private Bag 9, Penrose, Auckland
Tel: (09) 525 1982; (Airport 792545); Tlx: 2543; Fax: (09) 370269
Offices in 29 towns and cities

Budget Rent-a-Car
Central reservations:
Pte Bag 1, Auckland
Tel: (09) 309 6739; Fax: (9) 309 4180
+ 61 locations throughout New Zealand

Guthreys Pacific
PO Box 22-255, Christchurch

Henderson Rental Cars
9 Dora St, PO Box 21-012, Henderson,
Auckland. Tel: (09) 836 8089; Tlx: 21580

Hertz New Zealand Limited
46-48 Lichfield St, Christchurch
Tel: (03) 379 9888,(Airport 303 4924); tollfree 0800 655955; Tlx: 744437; Fax: (03) 379 9416.*Also*: 154 Victoria St West, City, Auckland. Tel: (9) 307 3546/7

Letz Rent-A-Car
51-53 Shortland Street, PO Box 2752, Auckland.Tel:(09) 939 0145; Tlx: 604424; Fax:(09) 397518

National Car Rental
Newmans Car Rentals, PO Box 22-413, Oatahuhu, Auckland
Tel: (09) 275 3409; Tlx: 2622

Percy Rent-a-Car
219 Hobson St, PO Box 5364, Auckland
Tel: (09) 31122; Tlx: 60097

What's the link between business and the Asia Pacific?

BRITISH AIRWAYS
The world's favourite airline

http://www.british-airways.com

Pacific Islands

Background

American Samoa

The Territory of American Samoa is under the direct jurisdiction of the United States of America and is administered by the US Department of the Interior, Office of Territorial and International Affairs. American Samoa does some ninety per cent of its foreign trade with the United States with tuna fishing, canning and processing the principal export generator.

American Samoa does have a tourist industry though this has developed relatively slowly compared with that of the other Pacific Islands. The island had 15,970 visitors in 1992. The population is 51,000 of which ninety percent are Samoan with the remainder from Europe and Tonga. American Samoa's agriculture is tropical and bananas, coconuts, yams, papayas, copra and pineapples are grown. Apart from the tuna industry, meat canning and handicrafts are the other principal industries.US$.

Cook Islands

The Cook Islands cover a total land area of 240 square kilometres and have a population of approximately 18,000 (1993). The majority of the population are ethnic Polynesian though a few Europeans live there also.

The Cook Islands are self governing in free association with New Zealand. The islands economy is predominantly agriculturally based and fruit, clothing and copra are exported to New Zealand and Japan. To date, economic development has been held back because the islands are so isolated with poor transportation links. As a result, a trade deficit has meant that the Cook Islanders are increasingly dependent on

foreign aid and money sent by relatives living abroad. In 1992 the islands were reliant on one cargo ship and there were no major transport aircraft. The islands received 50,000 visitors in 1992. Capital is Avarua (on Rarotonga); lanuguage is Maori (with English largely used) and currency is the NZ$. (US$=1.46).

Guam

Situated 1250 miles east of the Philippines, Guam is an unincorporated territory of the USA and is under the jurisdiction of the US government acting through a Governor who is head of government.

The island's economy is largely dependent on US military spending and tourism earnings. Tourism has developed rapidly with a hotel construction boom during the 1980s and again in the mid-90s. There were over 1mn visitors in 1996. GNP per capita in 1996 was $17,000 and exports consist of transhipments of petroleum products, drinks, food and manufactured goods.

Industry is relatively developed compared to other Pacific Islands - Guam boasts a moderately sophisticated indigenous construction industry, printing and publishing, textiles and food processing industries. Most citizens speak English but Japanese and Chamorro are also widely spoken. Capital is Agana and currency is US$.

Micronesia

Situated 1000 miols north-east of Papua New Guinea, the Federated States of Micronesia cover a total area of some 700 square kilometres and include four main island groupings - Yap, Pohnpei, Truk and Kosrae - totalling 607 islands altogether. Micronesia's topography varies from high mountainous islands to coral atolls. In 1992 Micronesia had a population of some 115,000 and Micronesia is a constitutional government in free association with the United States of America. There are no formal political parties and the economy is based mainly on subsistence farming, fishing and limited exploitation of minerals. A tourism industry is developing though it has to date been hindered by the islands' remote location.

Other main industries are fish processing and the manufacture of small arts and craft items from pearls and shells. Coconuts, copra, cassava, black pepper and sweepotatoes are grown and chickens and pigs are farmed. Micronesia is very heavily dependent on financial assistance from the USA. Currency is US$. Languages are English, Japanese and local dialects.

New Caledonia

New Caledonia is an overseas territory of France with a population of 175,000 in 1992. It is therefore under the jurisdiction of the French Government although a referendum on independence is due in 1998.

Much of the island's food is imported as most of New Caledonia is unsuited to farming. However the territory does boast significant mineral deposits - particularly nickel. It is estimated that New Caledonia has some 25% of the world's known nickel resources, though in recent months this has not helped the territory's economy due to a downturn in world demand. Per capita GNP stood at about $6000 in 1992 and principal exports are nickel metal and ore mainly to France, the USA and Australia. New Caledonia had 81,000 tourist arrivals in 1992, the vast majority from metropolitan France. Capital is Noumea; currency is the French Pacific Franc (US$1 = 102 CFP); languages are French, English and local dialects.

Solomon Islands

The Solomon Islands is a constitutional monarchy led by a UK style of government with a cabinet chosen by parliament and headed by a prime minister. The head of state is the Queen of England, Elizabeth II, but she is represented on the islands by the governor general, Sir George Lepping. The legal system is also styled on the British legislature and main political parties include the Peoples' Alliance Party, the Labour Party, the Liberal Party, the National Front for Progress and the United Party. The Prime Minister of the Solomon Islands is currently Solomon Mamaloni and Sir Baddeley Devesi is Deputy Prime Minister.

The Solomon Islands are predominantly agriculturally based and farming, fishing and forestry are the main economic activities on the islands. Agriculture accounts for about sixty per cent of GDP. The Islands also enjoy an abundance of natural mineral resources particularly lead, gold, nickel and zinc. Principal exports are fish, timber and copra and Japan is the Solomon Islands' biggest trading partner followed by the UK, Thailand and Australia. There were some 10,000 tourist arrivals in 1992. Capital is Homiara, currency Solomon Islands Dollar (US$1 = 3.63 SI$) and official language is English.

Tonga

The island of Tonga is a constitutional monarchy and the King still has real influence on the country's political system. The island's cabinet is appointed by the King (King Taufa'ahau Tupou IV) who has ruled since December 1965. Over seven feet tall, citizens of Tonga are not supposed to look this mighty monarch in the eye, 'though weighing in at some twenty stone, it might be difficult to miss him. There are thirty three other nobles in the kingdom, most of whom are the king's cousins.

The island's main trading partners are Australia, New Zealand, Japan, Fiji and the USA and Tonga imports much of its food, particularly from New Zealand. Tonga's main exports are bananas, coconuts, cassava, yams and vanilla beans. Tonga enjoys a tropical climate and is an archipelago of 170 islands. Tropical cyclones frequently batter Tonga, particularly between October and April.

Tourism is the island's principal source of hard currency (there were 19,000 arrivals in 1992) though Tonga remains dependent on external aid largely because of the country's trade deficit. In 1991 the country's total external debt stood at US $50.9 million and the current account deficit stood at US$4.13 million. Inflation in the same year stood at 10.6 per cent having risen from 4.1 per cent in 1989.

The main ports are Nukualofa, Neiafu, and Pangai and Tonga's merchant navy has four ships. Nukualofa has a number of small hotels and B & B's. The only large hotel in the kingdom is the International Dateline which was built in 1966 to house guests for the coronation and is a stone's throw from the royal palace. Tongans are religious, so everything is shut on Sundays. Capital is Nuku'alofa, languages Tongan and English and the currency is the Pa'anga (US$1 = 1.29 T$).

Vanuatu

The name Vanuatu means *'The Land that has always existed.'* Vanuatu (previously called New Hebrides and a French/English condominium) is a republic and is situated about 500 miles West of Fiji. Consisting of 13 large islands and about sixty smaller ones, it is a member of the Commonwealth of Nations and in 1981 became the 155th country to join the United Nations. English is the main business language and the economy is primarily based on tropical agriculture, tourism and finance. The main crops are copra, and cocoa though fish and forestry are becoming increasingly important to the islands' economy.

Vanuatu is generally regarded as politically stable and its legal and political systems are based on that of the United Kingdom (UK). The Council of Ministers consists of members selected by the prime minister who is in turn elected by Parliament. The main political parties are the Union of Moderate Parties, the Tan Union, the National United Party, the Melanesian Progressive Party and the Vanua'aku Pati. The regional legislature is controlled by the National Council of Chiefs.

Tourism has increasingly become a mainstay of the the Vanuatu economy - in 1996 65,000 tourists visited the islands compared with some 40,000 in 1991.Capital is Vila; currency the Vatu (US$1 = 113 VT) and languages French, English and Pidgin.

Western Samoa

Otherwise known as 'the Cradle of Polynesia', the Independent State of Western Samoa is a constitutional monarchy ruled by a native chief. The current Chief of State is Chief Susuga Malie-toa Tanumafili II and the country's main political parties are the Samoan National Development Party and the Human Rights Protection Party.There are two main islands on Western Samoa - Savai'i and Upolu and total land area is 2,850 square kilometres.Western Samoa is predominantly Christian and its legal system is based on a mixture of English common law and the island's own customs. The economy is mainly agriculturally based but tourism is becoming an increasingly important industry, with 38,600 arrivals in 1992. Main exports are copra, fish and coconut oil. Cigarettes have recently become an important source of revenue though Western Samoa is dependent on overseas aid to a large extent - in 1992 China agreed to lend US $7 million for an international conference centre at Apia. The country's merchant navy consists of one roll-on-roll-off ship and there are three main transport aircraft and three airports. Western Samoa is a member of the United Nations and the World Health Organisation.It was devastated by Cyclone Ofa in 1990 and Cyclone Val in 1991 and this caused a 1 per cent decline in GDP

Capital is Apia, languages Samoan and English ;currency Western Samoan Dollar (US$= 2.48 S$).

PACIFIC ISLANDS - Introduction

What to See

Each island has its own, often unique, natural beauty and visitors are likely to be attracted to this rather than anything man made. Most of the towns and cities across the Pacific are a disappointment - sprawling with little character. As you would expect, there are one or two exceptions - Noumea in **New Caledoni**a is one that combines the best of the Pacific with the elegance of French colonial influences.

To get to see some of the natural beauty, it's often wise to get into a boat or even a submarine. From **Guam**, for instance, it's possible to take a ride in a submarine, which dives to around 50 metres on the coral reefs.

The Aquarium de Noumea in **New Caledonia** is reputed to hold the world's most interesting collection of tropical marine life. The city also boasts a botanical gardens and a zoo.

The **Tonga** National Centre is arguably one of the South Pacific's best exhibitions with its insight into the island's native culture. The Cultural Centre in Port Vila gives a good account of **Vanuatu**'s history.

The **Solomon Islands** is easily the best place to see some of the key battle sites of World War II. Guadalcanal, the location of one the fiercest encounters of the war in the Pacific, is certainly worth a visit. Unfortunately many battle sites are not marked and finding you way to places such as Red Beach and Bloody Ridge is far from easy. The Solomon Islands Peace Memorial sits atop Mt Austen. It is Japanese built.

Shopping

Almost all the islands of the Pacific are proud of their handicrafts and many have government-run shops or cooperatives selling locally-made products. The quality tends to vary, though.

Again, the Tonga National Centre is an excellent place from which to buy direct from the craftsmen themselves. Quality is truly first class with Tonga tapa cloth, mats, carvings, shell jewellery and other exquisite items all in demand. Honiara (in the Solomons) is equally good for handicrafts, such as baskets and woodcarvings. These are of excellent quality and represent real value for money.

Hong Kong-based Duty Free Shoppers (DFS) opened a store in Tumon Bay, Guam in 1996.

In New Caledonia it's possible to buy the latest French designer fashions; although prices are on the high side. Duty-free shops with their red, white and blue signs offer discounts of up to 30 percent on French goods and electrical items. Many other islands, such as the Cook Islands, have duty-free shops.

Getting Around

Inter-island air service are generally good and getting better every year as island airlines increase flights around the region. It may not be possible to fly directly between each island group, but with a stop-over, there are few places that can't be reached within 24 hours.

The region's ferries tend to be small and offer only services between islands in the same group. Many of these ferries call at several islands en route so journeys often take several days. Fine if you have the time, otherwise it's much better to fly.

Taxis are available in all the capitals and on some outlying islands. Prices vary from expensive to remarkably cheap.

Car rental is possible with all the big companies represented. Even quite small islands offer car hire, but rates throughout the Pacific are high; reflecting the high freight costs of shipping cars to the area and of high import taxes in many states. Obtaining fuel outside the main towns can be a problem.

Some islands have a good public transport system (buses), a few smaller ones only rely on taxis. Where buses do exist they tend to cater for rural dwellers on shopping trips to town so comfort and speed are not always priorities.

Entertainment

Don't expect exotic nightlife anywhere in the Pacific. Many towns shut up shop at 1700 and appear to go straight to bed. Many urban residents tend to go home for dinner with the family and, maybe, a video.

Many tourist hotels host traditional floor shows, which is often the limit of the nightlife on many islands. Other nights are taken up with feasts or barbecue dinners.

Noumea has a number of fashionable discos as befits a French colony. Some are private and are not open to visitors unless accompanied by a member. Noumea also boasts the Pacific's only gambling establishment - the Casino Royal. Port Vila has a disco at the Inter-Continental named Ravenga.

Obviously, Noumea is also the place to find the very best in French cooking. But the islands also boast some good Vietnamese, Tahitian and Indian restaurants, not to mention Chinese cuisine. Vietnamese restaurants have also sprung up on other towns, such as Vanuatu's Port Vila. The town has equally good Chinese food.

In Tonga, Nuku'alofa is just beginning to sprout a selection of ethnic eating places (for example, there are now three Chinese restaurants) to add to the local fare and the hotel feast nights.

Leisure

Being surrounded by warm clear and inviting water on all sides, it's only natural that visitors quickly gravitate towards the many water sports on offer. Diving and snorkelling are particularly popular, with many islands providing opportunities to dive on Second World War wrecks.

Truk in the Caroline Islands, Yap in the Federated States of Micronesia are highly recommended. So are various sites around the Solomon Islands and unspoilt Tonga. In fact, the Solomons sells themselves as the top scuba diving destination with an excellent assortment of tropical fish, coral and some of the best-kept wrecks in the Pacific. Divers from around the world are attracted to Honiara to view the Japanese battleships and the many fighter aircraft at rest in the shallow waters around the islands.

Then there is sailboarding, sailing, water-skiing and beach volleyball. Big-game fishing is also readily available. Look a little harder and you may find horse-riding, bowls and squash.

In terms of spectator sports, Rugby Union is popular on islands such as the Samoas, which has an especially fearsome team. While water-sports, tennis and yachting, canoeing and big game fishing are the chief attractions of islands such as the Samoas, Tonga and the Cook Islands.

There are a number of golf courses in the northern islands, where the US influence is strongest. Tonga also has a course at Manamo'ui. The Sheraton Cook Islands opened an 18-hole golf course soon after it opens in December 1991. There is already the Rarotonga Golf Club, which welcomes visitors.

Honiara has tennis, squash and a rather flat nine-hole golf course. Noumea: tennis, a nine-hole golf course at Dumbea, squash and sailing.

Vanuatu claims snorkelling and diving as its two top attractions, but there is also sailing, tennis,squash and golf at the 18-hole course at the Inter-Continental Island Inn, the Whitesands Resort & Country Club (18 holes) and the less impressive Port Vila Golf & Country Club with just nine holes.

Arrival & Departure

American Samoa: Pago Pago International Airport is 11 km from the city centre. Taxi fare is around US$ 6, though hotels normally arrange buses at a nominal fee. There is no departure tax.

Cook Islands. Raratonga Airport is 4½ km from Avarua. Most hotels run courtesy coaches. Departure tax is NZ$ 20 for adults; NZ$ 10 for children 2-11 years; infants free.

Guam: Guam International Airport (Tamuning) is 3.2km from Agana. Most hotels provide free transfers. No departure tax.

Micronesia: Palau departure tax US$3 ($2 transit passengers); Yap US$ 10.

New Caledonia: Tontouta Airport is 47km northwest of Noumea. The taxi fare is a hefty CFP5,000. An express bus will cost CFP1,500. As an overseas territory of France, there is no departure tax.

Solomon Islands: Honiara International Airport (Henderson Field) is 11km from Honiara. Taxi fare from airport to downtown is SI$6; the RED Bus will cost SI$4. An airport departure tax of SI$20 (in local currency) is levied on all departing passengers (except infants and transit who travel free).

Tonga: All passengers leaving on international flights pay a T$15 tax at Fua'amotu Airport, which is 24km from Nuku'alofa. Hotel buses meet many visitors, but a taxi into the capital will cost T$12.

Vanuatu: Bauer Field Airport is sited 6km north of Port Vila. Tour Vanuatu bus to and from hotels available at VT 3000; taxis also available. A departure tax of VT1,500 is levied on all international flights and VT200 on domestic departures.

Western Samoa: Faleolo Airport is 34 km from Apia. The taxi fare into town is WS$20. The bus ride is only WS$5. Departure tax is set at WS$26.

Car Hire

Avis
American Samoa. Tel: (684) 633 1276; Fax: (684) 633 1277.
Cook Islands. Tel: (682) 22833; Fax: (682) 21040; Tlx: 772 62021.
Guam. Tel: (671) 646 1803; Fax: (671) 649 2847.
Kiribati. Tel: (686) 21090; Fax: 21451.
New Caledonia. Tel: (687) 275484; Tlx: ADANG 3123.
Saipan, **Micronesia**. Tel: (670) 234 1701/ 234 1701; Fax: (670) 234 1570.
Solomon Islands. Tel: (677) 30211; Fax: (677) 30084.
Tonga. Tel: (676) 23344; Fax: (676) 23833
Vanuatu. Tel: (678) 24816/22570; Fax: (678) 24464
Western Samoa. Tel: (685) 20957; Fax: (685) 22468.

Budget Rent A Car
Cook Islands. Tel: (682) 20895; fax (682) 20888.
Guam. Tel: (671) 646 5494; Fax: 6471014
New Caledonia. Tel: (687) 262009
Solomon Islands. Tel: 23205/66326
Tonga. Tel: (676) 23510
Vanuatu. Tel: (678) 3170/2522; Fax: 3543.
Western Samoa. Tel: (685) 20561; Fax: (685) 22284

Pavitts U-Drive
American Samoa. Tel: (684) 699 1456

Hertz Self Drive (Guam & Saipan)
New Era Inc, Airport Road, Tamuning.
Guam. Tel: 646 5875; Fax: 649 9024
New Caledonia. Tel: (687) 261822; fax: (687) 261219; tlx: 7063045
Vanuatu. Tel: (678) 22244/22016; Fax: (678) 3685l Tlx: 7711019.

Rental Cars (Cls) Ltd
Cook Islands. Tel: (682) 24442/24441; Fax: (682) 24446

Thrifty Car Rental
Guam. Tel: (671) 646 1871; Fax: (671) 649 7226; **Saipan.** Tel: (670) 234 3051; Fax: (670) 234 3052; **Pohnpei** (691) 320 2551; Fax: (691) 320 2389.

Pacific Islands Hotels

American Samoa

Rainmaker Hotel D
PO Box 996, Pago Pago 96799
Tel: (684) 633 4241; Tlx: 782511; Fax: (684) 633 5959

Cook Islands

Aitutaki Resort Hotel ◌ D
PO Box 342, Aitutaki
Tel: (682) 31203; Tlx: RS 62003; Fax: 31202

Rarotongan Resort Hotel ◌ C
PO Box 103, Rarotonga
Tel: (682) 25800; Tlx: 62003: Fax: (682) 25799

Sheraton Cook Islands Resort A
Private Bag, Rorotonga.
Tel: (682) 28850; Tlx: 6020;Fax: (682) 25401

Guam

Cocos Island Resort ¶
PO Box 7174, Tamuning
Tel: (671) 828 8691; Fax: 828 8697

Guam Hilton
Tumon Bay, PO Box 11199 Tamuning, Guam 96931.
Tel: (671) 646 1835/7912; Fax: (671) 646 6038; E-mail: guamhilt@ite.net

The Guam Hilton is a beachfront resort situated on 32 acres of tropical landscaped gardens on the western end of Tumon Bay. The hotel features a total of 691 guestrooms and suites, including the 13-storey "Magalahi Tower" and is Guam's largest.

Accommodation
376 twin, 281 king, 34 suites

Rates:
Single US$ 210-290; double/twin US$ 240-

320; suites US$ 325-1000
All rates liable to 13% occupancy tax.

Credit cards accepted:
Amex, Diners, Mastercard, Visa

Meeting & banqueting facilities
5 meeting/function rooms, capacity up to 400; audio-visual facilities available; largest reception 500 seated/700 cocktail

Room services
Airconditioning, colour TV, direct-dial telephone (ext. in bathroom), hairdryer, laundry/valet service, minibar, music/radio/alarm clock, safety deposit box, tea/coffee making facilities, non-smoker bedrooms available, video films, voice messaging, modem, E-mail hook-up access

Business & other services
Business centre, executive floor, express checkout, airport pickup, translation service, car parking, taxi service, newsstand, shopping arcade

Sports & Recreation
Fitness centre/gym, sauna, outdoor swimming pool, tennis

Restaurants & Coffee Shops
Islander Terrace (220) - Buffet, open 0600-midnight; *Roy's Restaurant* (110) - Euro-Asian cuisine, open 1800-2200; *Genji* (110) - Japanese, open 0700-1000/1130-1400/1800-2200, closed Sunday lunch; *Dynasty* - Chinese, open June 1130-1400/1800-2200

Overseas Sales Representatives:
Hilton International Sales Offices, Hilton Reservations Worldwide

Guam Dai-Ichi C
801 Pale San Vitores Road, 96910
Tel: 646 5881; Tlx: 7006118; Fax: 646 6729

Guam Plaza Hotel C
1328 San Vitores Rd, 96931
Tel: 646 7803; Tlx: 6274; Fax: 646 7809

Guam Reef Hotel B
1317 Pale San Vitores Rd, Tanuming
Tel: 646 6881; Tlx: 6329; Fax: 646 5200

Guam Hotel Okura ◌ C
185 Gun Beach Rd, Tumon 96911
Tel: 646 6811; Tlx: 6242; Fax: 646 1403

Hyatt Regency Guam A
1155 Pale San Vitores Rd, Tamuning 96911
Tel: 647 1234; Fax: 647 1235

Hotel Nikko A
245 Gun Beach Road, Tumon 96931
Tel: 649 815; Fax: 649 8817

Onward Agana Beach Hotel B
PO Box 12697, 96931
Tel: 647 7777; Fax: 649 2226

Pacific Islands Club C
PO Box 8946, Tanuming 96911
Tel: 646 9171; Tlx: 6135; Fax: 646 5762

Pacific Star Hotel A
6273 San Vitores Rd 96931,PO Box 6097
Tel: 649 7827; Tlx: 6696; Fax: 649 9335

Palace Hotel Guam A
470 Fahrenholt Ave, 96911
Tel: 646 2222; Fax: 649 5211

Pia Marine A
193 Tumon Lane, 96911
Tel: (671) 646 7422; Fax: (671) 646 3931

Micronesia, Federated States

Village Hotel D
PO Box 339, Kolonia 96941, Pohnpei
Tel: (691) 320 2797; Fax: (691) 320 3797

Truk Continental Hotel ◌ C
PO Box 340, Weno 96942, Chuuk
Tel: 330 2727; Tlx: 6831; Fax: 330 2439

Nauru

Meneng Hotel E
PO Box 298, Menteng District
Tel: (674) 3210; Tlx: 33092; Fax: 3595

New Caledonia

Club Mediterranee C
Anse Vata, BP 115 Noumea
Tel: (687) 261200

Hotel Ibis C
8 Baie des Citrons, BP 819, Noumea
Tel: (687) 262055; Tlx: 3152; Fax: 262044

Le Lagon Hotel D
143 rte de l'Anse Vata, PO Box 440 Noumea
Tel: 261255; Tlx: 706 3017 : Fax: 261244

Le Meridien Noumea
Pointe Magnin, BP 1915, Noumea Cedex 98846, New Caledonia

Located directly on the beach and overlooking one of the world's most beautiful lagoons, each of Le Meridien Noumea's 253 guest rooms offers a private balcony with a view of the ocean.

Accommodation & rates
253 single/double,150 twin US$ 250; 13 suites US$415-1200
Subject to 3% government tax

238 PACIFIC ISLANDS - Hotels

Credit cards accepted:
Amex, Visa, Diners, Mastercard, JCB

Meeting & conference facilities
3 meeting/function rooms, capacity 600; audio-visual equipment available, largest reception 300 seated or 450 cocktail;

Room services
Airconditioning, colour TV, direct-dial telephone (ext. in bathroom), hairdryer, laundry/valet service, minibar, music/radio/alarm clock, safety deposit box, tea/coffee making facilities, 24-hr room/meal service, non-smoker bedrooms, video films

Business & other services
Business centre, express checkout, translation service, shops, car parking & rental, travel centre + tours, taxi service, newsstand/shops

Sports & Recreation
Billiards/snooker, fitness centre/gym, indoor games, massage, sauna, outdoor swimming pool, tennis

Restaurants & Coffee Shops
Sextant (210) - International, open 0630-1000/1800-2200; *Fare* (100) - Light meals, open 1130-1400; *Hippocampe* (61) - Gourmet, open 1130-1400/1900-2200; *Shogun* (64) -Japanese, open 1130-1400/1800-2300

Overseas Sales Representatives
Forte/Meridien regional sales offices: Europe, asia, Australia/New Zealand, USA

Hotel Mocambo D
Baie des Citrons, PO Box 678 Noumea
Tel: (687) 262701; Tlx: 148; Fax: 263877

Noumea Village Hotel D
1 rue de Sebastopol, Noumea
Tel: (687) 283006; Tlx: 3808; Fax: 273220

Nouvata Parkroyal B
123 Promenade R Laroque, BP 137 Noumea
Tel: (687) 262200; Tlx: 3145; Fax: 261677

Noumea Novotel C
BP 4230 Rocher a la Voile, Noumea
Tel: (687) 286688; Tlx: 3118; Fax: (687) 285223

Novotel Malabou Beach Resort C
Baie de la Nehoue, BP 4, Poum
Tel: (687) 356060; Fax: (687) 356070

Paradise Park Motel D
34 rue du R P Roman, PO Box 9 Noumea
Tel: (687) 272541; Tlx: 131; Fax: 276131

Norfolk Island

Cascade Gardens Apartments D
New Cascade Rd, PO Box 15, NI 2899
Tel: (6723) 22625; Tlx: 30003; Fax: 22785

Hillcrest Gardens Hotel D
Queen Elizabeth Ave, NI 2899
Tel: (6723) 22255; Tlx: 32026; Fax: 22909

South Pacific Resort Hotel C
Taylors Rd, Burnt Pine, 12899
Tel: (672-3) 3154; Tlx: 32006; Fax: 2907

Northern Marianas

Hafadai Beach Hotel C
PO Box 338 Chalan Kanoa, Saipan 96950
Tel: (670-234) 6495; Tlx: 616

Hyatt Regency Saipan A
PO Box 87 CHRB Micro Beach Rd, Saipan MB 96950
Tel: (670) 234 1234; Tlx: 783659 HYATT SPN; Fax: (670) 234 7745

Nikko Hotel Saipan A
PO Box 152, CHRB 9650
Tel: 322 3311; Tlx: 760702; Fax: 322 3144

Pacific Islands Club B
PO Box 2370, Garapan, Saipan 96950
Tel: 234 7976; Tlx: 783715; Fax: 234 6592

Rota Resort & Country Club B
Songsong Village, Po Box 871 Rota CM 96951
Tel: (670-532) 3561; Fax: 532 3562

Saipan Beach Hotel D
PO Box 1029, Garapan, Saipan
Tel: (670-234) 6412; Tlx: SBH SPN 694

Saipan Diamond Hotel B
PO Box 66, Susupe 96950
Tel: (670-234) 5900; TlX: 762; Fax: (670) 234 5909

Palau

Palau Pacific Resort
PO Box 308, Koror, Palau 96940
Tel: (680) 488 2600; Fax: (680) 488 1601/ 488 1606

This vacation mecca for snorkelling and scuba divers is situated on a white sandy beach and is noted for its tranquil ambience and pristine beauty.

Accommodation and rates
160 rooms and suites; single/twin from US$ 195-600

Credit cards accepted:
Amex, Carte Blanche, Diners, Mastercard, Visa, JCB

Meeting & banqueting facilities
Function/meeting rooms, capacity to 120; audio-visual equipment available; largest reception 300 pax

Room services
Airconditioning, pay for view TV, direct-dial telephone, hairdryer, in-room safe, minibar, laundry/valet service, mini-bar music/radio/alarm clock, room service

Business & other services
Business centre, boutiques, beauty/barber shop

Sports & Recreation
Beach, outdoor swimming pool, tennis, watersports, massage, PADI 5-star dive center, dive boats, fitness centre/spa pools, underwater photo center

Restaurants & Coffee Shops
2 restuarants offering International/Pacific Rim cuisine; beach bar, lounge/entertainment

Nikko Hotel Palau C
PO Box 310, 96940
Tel: 488 2486; Tlx: 8938; Fax: 488 2878

Solomon Islands

Solomon Kitano Mendana Hotel D
Mendana Ave, PO Box 384, Honiara
Tel: (677) 20071; Tlx: HQ 66315; Fax: (677) 23942

Uepi Island Resort E
Morovo Lagoon via Seghepa, PO Box 169 Western Province
Tel: (via) (61) 77 725022; Tlx: (Aus) 47205; Fax: (61) 77 213315

Tonga

Friendly Islander Motel D
PO Box 142 Nuku'Alofa
Tel: (676) 23810; Tlx: 66208; Fax: (676) 24199

International Dateline Hotel ◯ D
PO Box 39, Vuna Rd, Nuku'Alofa
Tel: (676) 23411; Tlx: 66223; Fax: 23410

Best Western Pacific Royale D
PO Box 74 Nuku'Alofa
Tel: (676) 23344; Tlx: 66205; Fax: 23833

PACIFIC ISLANDS - Hotels

Vanuatu (New Hebrides)

Irriki Island Resort C
PO Box 230 Port Vila
Tel: (678) 23388; Tlx 1080; Fax: 23880

Le Meridien Port Vila Resort & Casino
Tassiriki Park, PO Box 215, Port Vila
Tel: (678) 22040; Fax: (678) 23340

Situated on 50 acres of lagoon front property amongst tropical gardens, with our own private island. The resort now offers deluxe accommodation in two wings and a wide range of complimentary watersport activities, tennis and a 9-hole golf course. Vanuatu's only international casino is located at the resort.

Accommodation & rates
150 single/double/twin US$ 115-130; suite US$180-250
All rates subject to 10% government tax

Credit cards accepted:
Amex, Diners, Mastercard

Meeting & conference facilities
Two meeting/function rooms, capacity 320; audio-visual equipment available, largest reception 220 seated or 320 cocktail; own private island for theme parties

Room services
Airconditioning, colour TV, direct-dial telephone, laundry/valet service, music/radio/alarm clock, safety deposit box, tea/coffee making facilities, 24-hr room/meal service, non-smoker bedrooms, video films

Business & other services
Executive rooms, express checkout, shops, airport pickup, car parking & rental, travel centre + tours, taxi service, newsstand

Sports & Recreation
Golf, indoor games, jogging track, outdoor swimming pool, tennis, casino, watersports

Restaurants & Coffee Shops
Shell's Restaurant - International, open 24 hours; *La Verandah* - Theme nights/ à la carte/buffet, open 0700-1000/1800-2100; *Poolside* Restaurant, open 1130-1400

Overseas Sales Representatives:
Forte and Meridien Hotels & Resorts. Utell

Windsor International Hotel D
Rue de Picardi, Efate. PO Box 810 Port Vila
Tel: (678) 2150; Tlx: 1065; Fax: 2678

---

*Hotel Classification: **A** after name of hotel = over US$ 200 per person per night; **B** = between US$ 150-200; **C** = between US$ 100-150; **D** = between US$ 50-100; **E** = under US$ 50; ¶ = prices on application. ⚪ = PATA Member.*

Western Samoa

Aggie Grey's Hotel ⚪ D
PO Box 67 Apia
Tel: (685) 22880; Tlx: 257; Fax: (685) 23626

Hotel Kitano Tusitala D
Beach Rd, PO Box 101, Apia, Upolu
Tel: (685) 21122; Tlx: 226; Fax: (685) 23562

Sinalai Reef Resort B
PO Box 1510, Apia
Tel: (685) 25191; Fax: (685) 20285/25490

International Airline Departures

Below is a list of departures from the Pacific Islands to the international destinations in bold type. Figures in brackets after destinations refer to the days of the week. (2,4,6) therefore indicates that departures take place on a Tuesday (the second day of the week), a Thursday and a Saturday. Departures were correct as at February 1997 but travellers are advised to check times as timetables are liable to change. Only direct flights, without change, are listed.

Airline abbreviations codes :
AF = Air France; **CO** = Continental Air; **IE** = Solomon Airlines; **IW** = AOM French Airlines; **JL** = Japan Air; **KE** = Korean Air; **NH** = All Nippon Air; **NW** = Northwest Airlines; **NZ** = Air New Zealand; **ON** = Air Nauru; **OZ** = Asiana Air; **PH** = Polynesian; **PX** = Air Niugini; **SB** = Air Caledonie Int'l; **UA** = United Air; **WR** = Royal Tongan Airlines; **ZU** = Freedom Air

From RAROTONGA (RAR): (Cook Islands)
Auckland (AKL)
 NZ (4,5,6)
Honolulu (HNL)
 NZ (1)
Los Angeles (LAX)
 NZ (1,7)

From GUAM (GUM) :
Denpasar Bali (DPS)
 CO (1,2,3,5,6)
Fukuoka (FUK)
 CO (daily)
Hong Kong (HKG)
 CO (1,5)
Honolulu (HNL)
 CO (daily)

Kaohsiung (KHH)
 CO (6)
Manila (MNL)
 CO (daily) ON (2,3)
Nagoya (NGO)
 CO, NW (daily)
Nauru Island (INU)
 ON (2,4)
Osaka (OSA)
 NH,CO,UA,JL (daily)
Pohnpei (PNI)
 ON (2,4) CO (1,3,5,7)
Pusan (PUS)
 KE (1,4,6)
Saipan (SPN)
 CO,NW,ZU,JL (daily)
Sapporo (SPK)
 CO (daily)
Sendai (SDJ)
 CO (daily)
Seoul (SEL)
 KE,OZ (daily) CO (2,3,4,6,7)
Taipei (TPE)
 CO (daily)
Tokyo (TYO)
 CO,NW,JL (daily)

From NOUMEA (NOU) - New Caledonia
Auckland (AKL)
 NZ (6) SB (4,7)
Brisbane (BNE)
 SB(6,7) QF (6,7)
Colombo (CMB)
 IW (5)
Paris (ORY)
 IW (5)
Sydney (SYD)
 SB, QF (1,2,5,6,7) IW (5)
Tokyo (TOU)
 AF (1,3,4,6) JL (1,3,4,6)

From HONIARA (HIR) - Solomon Islands
Auckland (AKL)
 IE (2)
Brisbane (BNE)
 IE,QF (2,5,7)
Port Moresby (POM)
 IE, PX (3,7)

From TONGATAPU (TBU) - Tonga
Auckland (AKL)
 WR (1,3,5) PH (2) NZ (3,5)
Honolulu (HNL)
 NZ,WR (2)
Los Angeles (LAX)
 NZ (2)
Sydney (SYD)
 WR (5) PH(2)

From APIA (APW) - Samoa
Auckland (AKL)
 NZ (1,5,6,7) PH (1,4,5,6,7)
Honolulu (HNL)
 NZ,PH (6)
L Angeles US (LAX)
 NZ (6)
Melbourne (MEL)
 PH (2)
Sydney (SYD)
 PH (1,4)
Wellington (WLG)
 PH,NZ (2)

PACIFIC ISLANDS - Hotels

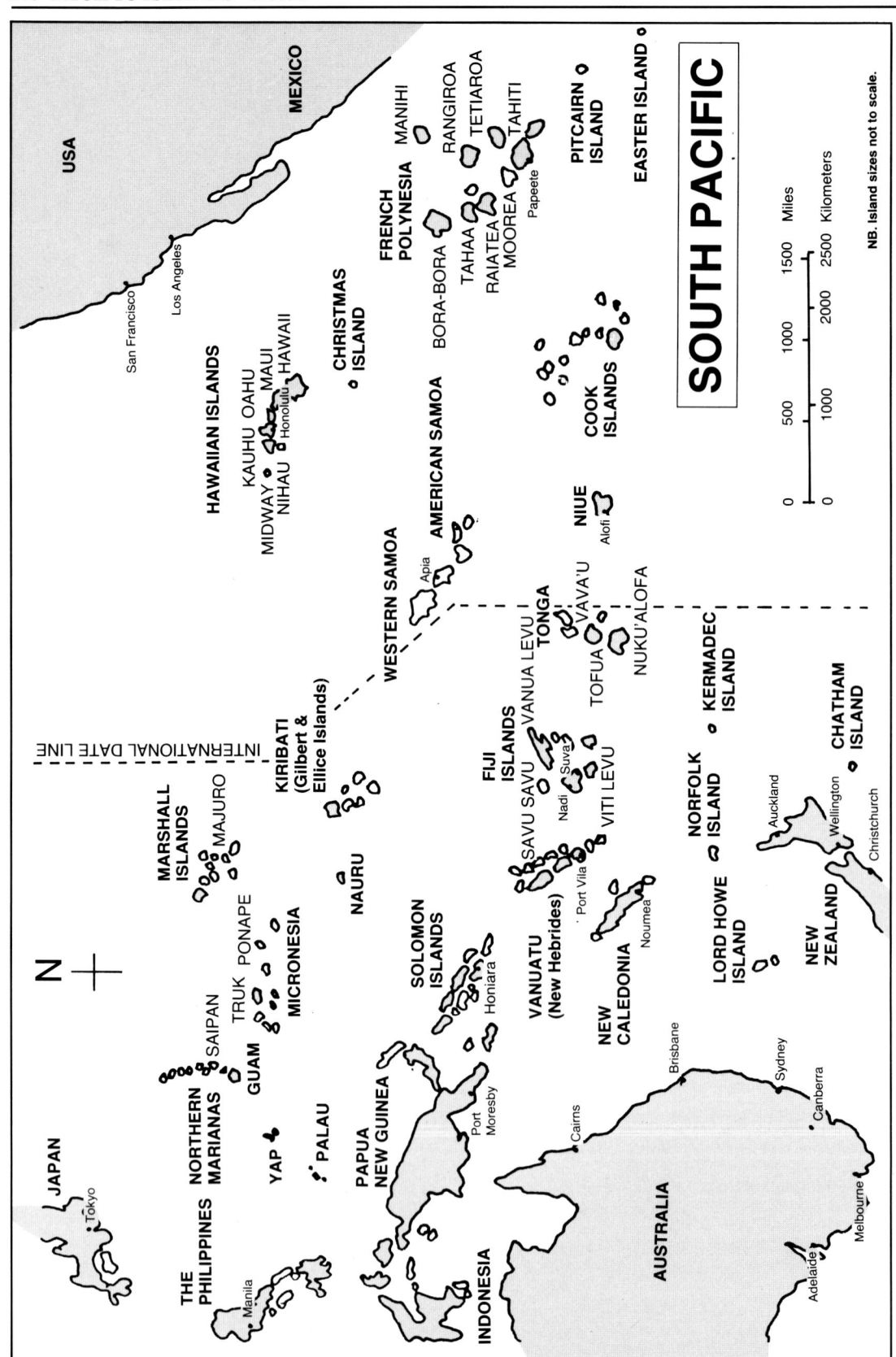

Pakistan

What to See

It's often easy to overlook Karachi as a city which has little to recommend it except for the teeming hordes that make up its 7m population. But there are one or two nuggets, though, for the visitor such as the National Museum in the centre of Burns Garden and the grim Parsee Tower of Death. Karachi also has some reasonable beaches like French Beach at Hawkes Bay about 40km from the city and a good zoo.

Moenjodaro, some 430 km north of Karachi, was once the site of a flourishing Indus Valley civilisation, which appears to have ended in 1700 BC. The site has been restored and is made of baked red bricks.

In the still wild North West Frontier province there is the fascinating Swat Valley and Chitral.

Much of Pakistan's natural beauty is in the north. The area is being increasingly opened up to foreign investors. The 1,000km Karakoram highway to China must rank as one of the world's great road journeys as it climbs up past the peaks such as K2 - the world's second highest mountain and its huge glaciers - and makes for a great long weekend away. Access to the Upper Northern Territory is only possible during the summer months as some parts of the area are closed for up to nine months a year.

Shopping

Handicrafts are among the best buys, particularly Persian-type carpets which are rated highly by experts. Embroidery and leatherwork can be found in most towns. Leather bags, jackets and shoes are all inexpensive. Furthermore, there are sellers of brass and copperware, jewellery and items made from Onyx. Pottery, too, is popular with foreign visitors but can often be too bulky to transport home.

In terms of sports goods, Pakistan produces excellent squash racquets and cricket bats at competitive prices.

Lahore and Peshawar both have first-rate bazaars where it is possible to find an extensive range of locally-produced goods including precious and semi-precious stones. Karachi, too, is a good place to find interesting items with the Jodia Bazaar behind Boulton Market, the new Linquat Market and the central Bohri Bazaar all highly rated. There is also the government-run Sind Handicraft Centre, which has fixed prices, but visitors should expect to haggle in the bazaars for a good deal.

Duty-free shops can be found in Karachi and Lahore. In Karachi there is concessionary shopping at a store on Airport Road as well as an outlet at the airport itself. In Lahore, the only duty-free store is in the city centre.

Getting around

PIA offers an extensive domestic network, with better-than-daily frequencies between the major cities - Karachi, Peshawar, Multan, Islamabad and Lahore.

Flights to the remoter regions of the north, which are often cut off by snow in winter, are subsidised by the government in order to maintain transport links. Poor weather conditions often delay flights to the north so it's important to check with PIA before departing. Seat availability is limited so you should book well in advance if you wish to travel north.

The big cities are linked by rail, but trains tend to be overcrowded so you must reserve first class air-conditioned accommodation a few days before departure. Sleepers, too, must be reserved. AC class is more than double the price of first class. The train takes 19 hours between Karachi and Lahore, 26 hours to Rawalpindi and 32 hours to Peshawar. Express trains will do the journey more quickly, though.

Buses are also crowded but can be an alternative to the train for short trips.

Taxis are fitted with meters, but you are unlikely to find one that works. So you must agree a price before setting off and as a rule of thumb allow R2.50 per km.

Car rental is becoming more commonplace, but driving conditions still leave much to be desired for "rookie" western drivers. It is therefore advisable to hire a car with a driver. This takes the hassle out of negotiating the traffic-choked streets within cities such as Karachi where road signs are difficult to find. The sheer weight of people, carts, animals and other vehicles combine to ensure that driving in town is not for the faint hearted.

Entertainment

Pakistan is a strict Islamic country and as such alcohol is difficult to come by. As a general rule, foreign visitors can only get a drink supplied to their hotel room. Most hotel bars appear to have long since closed down.

As a result, nightlife is somewhat stunted, not to say boring, compared with neighbouring India. The big cities have cinemas which show films in English.

Karachi has a mix of eating places across a broad price range. (See *Restaurants* following *Hotels* in this chapter). Many of the best restaurants are located in the major hotels. But for a change of scene *Agha's Tavern, Hill Park* and *Farooq's* are highly recommended by westerners for their local cooking. The city has some surprisingly top-class Chinese restaurants, while the *Horse Shoe* and *Khekashan 11* are known for their international cuisine.

Unfortunately, restaurants in hotels or elsewhere do not serve alcohol and this tends to make them rather dull. In the countryside it is often possible to by-pass the strict no-alcohol ban.

Leisure

Don't expect to find Pakistan particularly relaxing. First-class leisure facilities are limited unless you can gain access to the good local clubs - many of which are a hangover from British rule. Nevertheless, most large hotels have their own swimming pools, some have fitness centres. Karachi's Holiday Inn even has a sauna, tennis and squash.

Women should take care when swimming and exercising so as not to offend local sensibilities or to bring unwelcome attention to themselves. The Princess of Wales has recently been criticised for having an above-the-knee hemline whilst visiting a mosque.

Squash is popular and Pakistan has a fine record as the top nation in the sport. Cricket and field hockey are followed keenly by locals and matches take place during the winter. Beyond spectator sports, there is little else to do.

Get out of Karachi and Lahore and it's a different story. In the north, Pakistan offers mountaineering, trekking, rafting and angling. All these activities require a special permit from the Ministry of Home Affairs in Islamabad.

Trout is plentiful in the Northern Territory. Fishing licences must be obtained from the Bureau of Fisheries in a number of towns. For foreigners the licence fee is Rs32 and small fish must be put back. Equipment can be hired.

Arrival & Departure

Karachi Airport is the chief international gateway into Pakistan and is 18km north-east of the city. Some flights from the Gulf and India arrive direct to Lahore and Islamabad.

PIA is supposed to operate a bus between the airport and downtown Karachi, but this service has an unreliable reputation. Expect to pay up to Rs150 for a taxi. Most taxis have meters, but many either don't work or are not used by drivers. So it is important to agree on a fare before setting off. Mini-buses cover the same route for just Rs10.

Passengers pay a Rs 480 tax on departure for international flights and a fee of Rs 20 on domestic services.

Pakistan Key Fact File

Passport Requirements:
All visitors must have a valid passport. Visas and return tickets are required by all visitors.

Currency: Pakistan Rupee. 100 paisa = R1.

Exchange Rates:
US$1 = 40 Pr; £1 = 65.4 Rp (*May 1997*)

Currency Restrictions:
Visitors may only import up to 100 Pakistani rupees, but may bring in any amount of foreign currency or travellers cheques. Only 100 rupees may be exported; although visitors may take out any amount of foreign exchange brought in less that encashed by an authorized dealer/money changer in Pakistan.

Electricity Supply: 220 volts AC

Language:
Urdu is the national language; but English is used officially, in commercial circles and in the big cities. Regional languages include Sindhi, Punjabi, Baluchi, Pushto, Saraiki and Hindko.

Time: GMT + 5; EDT + 10

IDD Code: 92, *followed by....*
Area codes: Faisalabad 411; Gujranwala 431; Hyderabad 221; Islamabad 51; Karachi 21; Lahore 42; Multan 61; Peshawar 521; Quetta 81; Rawalpindi 51; Sialkot 432; Sukkur 71.

Business Hours:
Commercial offices are open from 0900-1300; 1400-1700 Saturday to Wednesday.
Government offices are open from 0830-1300; 1330-1500 Saturday to Thursday in Winter; til 1430 only in Summer.
Banks are open 0900-1300 Monday to Thursday and 0900-1100 Saturday and Sunday.
Shops are open from 0900-1830 Saturday to Thursday.

Customs & Entry:
Duty-free allowance comprises 200 cigarettes or 50 cigars or 0.5lbs of manufactured tobacco. Perfumed spirits and toilet water up to 0.5 pint. Gifts up to the value of rupees 500. The import of liquor in any quantity is strictly forbidden.

Health Requirements:
Vaccination against typhoid, para typhoid and poliomyelitis is recommended. Cholera and yellow fever vaccinations are required for visitors arriving from infected and endemic areas. A malaria risk exists all year in areas below 2000 metres and anti-malaria tablets must be taken. Advisable to boil all water and milk and not to eat unpeeled fruit.

Climate/best time to visit:
Diverse, with extreme regional variations. Summer starts in mid-April, with May, June and July the hottest months as temperatures hit 45°C on the plains (Karachi min. 27° - max 34°C). The monsoon is from mid-July to mid-September, with most of the rain falling in the hills. Mountain areas are naturally much cooler. Karachi temperatures in winter range from 12 min to 25°C. max. November to March most pleasant season.

Airport Departure:
Departing businessmen may not leave Pakistan without producing an income tax certificate stating that they have no liabilities under the *Income Tax Act* or *Business Profits Act*. Details from regional Chambers of Commerce - see *Useful Addresses* section, below.

National Holidays 1997
6 February* Juma tul Wida; 8-10 March* Eid ul Fitr; 23 March Pakistan Day; 14 April* Eid-al-Azha; 20/21 May* 9 & 10th Muharram*; 14 August Independence Day; 18 July Eid-i-Milad-un-Nabi*; 6 September Defence of Pakistan Day; 11 September Death Anniversary of Quaid-i-Azam; 9 November Iqbal Day; 25 December Birthday of Quaid-i-Azam and Christmas;
(**Moslem Holidays* - *dates may vary by one or two days according to the moon*)

Pakistan Hotels

Bhurban

Pearl Continental   C
GPO Box 16, Murree Hills
Tel: (via) 51 427082-8; Fax: (via) 51 427081/427092

Faisalabad

Faisalabad Serena Hotel   C
Club Rd, PO Box 443, 38000
Tel: 411 600428; Tlx: 43453; Fax: 411 629235

Gilgit

Gilgit Serena Lodge   D
Jutial
Tel: (572) 2331; Tlx: 23924; Fax: 572 2525

Hyderabad

Fataz Hotel   E
Thandi Sarak, 71000
Tel: (221) 23425-9; Fax: (221) 22342

Islamabad

Best Western Regency Hotel   E
Islamabad Club Road
Tel: (51) 815 7915; Fax: 212013

Holiday Inn Islamabad   D
Municipal Rd, Ramra, 44000
Tel: 827311; Tlx: 5643; Fax: 273273

Islamabad Marriott   B
Aga Khan Rd, Shalimar 5, PO Box 1351
Tel: 568 0111; Tlx: 5740; Fax: 820648

Karachi

Airport Hotel   E
Stargate Rd, 25200
Tel: (21) 457 0141; Fax: (21) 457 3800

Avari Towers   C
Fatima Jannah Rd, Karachi 4
Tel: 525261; Tlx: 21400; Fax: 568 0310

Beach Luxury Hotel ◌   E
Tamizuddin Khan Rd, PO Box 0227,74000
Tel: 561 1031; Tlx: 23899; Fax: 561 0673

Holiday Inn Crowne Plaza   B
Sharjah-el-Faisal, 0408
Tel: 520211; Tlx: 24267; Fax: 568 3146

Karachi Marriott   C
9 Abdullah Haroon Road, GPO Box 10444
Tel: 568 2011; Fax: 568 1610

Hotel Mehran   E
Shar-reh-E-Faisal, 75530
Tel: 515061; Tlx: 20616; Fax: 515311

Hotel Metropole   E
Club Rd, 75520
Tel: 512051; Fax: 568 4301

Midway House   E
Stargate Rd, Airport
Tel: 457 0371; Tlx: 25860; Fax: 457 1815

Pearl Continental Hotel   B
Club Rd, PO Box 8513
Tel: 568 5021; Tlx: 21713; Fax: 568 1835/568 2655

Plaza International Hotel   E
Dr Dawood Pota Rd
Tel: 520351; Tlx: 25706; Fax: 568 3055

Sheraton Karachi Hotel & Towers ◌   B
Club Rd, PO Box 3918, 75530
Tel: 568 1021; Tlx: 25255; Fax: 568 2875

Lahore

Ambassador Hotel   E
7 Davis Rd
Tel: 301861; Tlx: 44424

Avari Hotel   B
87 Shahrah-e-Quaid Azam, 54000
Tel: 636 5366; Tlx: 44678; Fax: 636 5367

Holiday Inn Lahore   C
25-26 Egerton Road, 54000
Tel: 636 7879; Tlx: 44469; Fax: 631 4515

Pearl Continental Hotel ◌   B
Shahrah-e-Quaid-e-Azam, 54000
Tel: (042) 636 0210; Tlx: 44877/44167 PEARL PK; Fax: (042) 636 2760/636 8694

Uganda Hotel   E
45 McLeod Road
Tel: 368097

Peshawar

Dean's Hotel   E
Islamia Rd
Tel: 76481/79781-2/76483-4; Tlx: 52442

Hotel Classification. **B** = single room between US$150-200 per night; **C** = Single room between US$ 100-150; **D** = between $ 50-100; **E** = under $50.
◌ *After name of hotel = PATA Member*

Pearl Continental Hotel   B
Khyber Rd
Tel: (0521) 276361; Tlx: 52389; Fax: 276465

Quetta

Quetta Serena Hotel   D
Shahrah-e-Zarghoon, PO Box 109
Tel: (081) 820071; Tlx: 78221; Fax: 820070

Rawalpindi

Pearl Continental Hotel ◌   B
The Mall
Tel: 566011; Tlx: 5736/54063 PEARL PK; Fax: 563927/566008

Shalimar Hotel   D
PO Box 93, Shaddar Rd
Tel: 562901-20; Tlx: 5764; Fax: 566061

Restaurants

Restaurants in fundamentalist Pakistan are not licensed. Non-Moslem visitors are allowed to drink alcohol, but only in their hotel rooms. To get a liquor licence, apply for a Tourist Certificate at the Tourist Office in Club Road, Karachi and you may then be sent to the excise and Tax Office on Shahrah-i-Iraq Rd. Alternatively, if staying in a hotel, a liquor permit can be signed and Rp 60 will be added to your bill.
Many of the best known restaurants are in the big hotels listed above; below we give a selection of mainly out-of-hotel restaurants in Karachi for a change of scene.

ABC Restaurant *(Chinese)*
Zaibun-Nisa Street. Tel: 511442
Agha's Tavern *(Local)*
North Western Hotel, 26 Beaumont Rd.
Tel: 510843
Albustan *(Seafood)*
Sheraton Hotel, Club Rd. tel: 521021
The Casbah *(Seafood/Lebanese)*
Beach Luxury Hotel, Tamizuddin Khan Rd.
Tel: 551031
Farooq Restaurant *(Local)*
Off Zaibun-Nisa Street. Tel: 511031
Four Seasons Restaurant *(Chinese)*
Hotel Metropole, Club Rd. Tel: 512051
Fujiyama *(Japanese)*
Avari Renaissance Towers Hotel
Fatima Jannah Rd, Tel: 525261
Hong Kong Restaurant *(Chinese)*
Abdullah Haroon Road. Tel: 511971
Horse Shoe Restaurant *(International)*
Shahrah-e-Faisal (Drigh Road/Airport Rd).
Tel: 432939
Kowloon Restaurant *(Chinese)*
Allama Iqbal Road, PECHS. Tel: 435010
Le Marquis *(French)*
Sheraton Hotel, Club Rd. Tel: 521021
Maxim's Restaurant *(International)*
Main Clifton Rd. Tel: 532588
Pirate Isles *(Barbecue)*
Taj Mahal Hotel, Shahrah-e-Faisal. Tel: 520211
Shezan Restaurant *(International)*
Abdullah Haroon Rd. Tel: 526715

Car Hire

Islamabad
Access
44-E, Blue Area, Office Tower Plaza
Tel: 815535/815521
Avis Rent-a-Car
Walji's Bldg, 10 Khayabam Srwdy, PO Box 1088.Tel: (51) 214345/210745; Tlx: PK 5769/5836; Fax: (51) 210762 + branches
International Transport Organisation
No 4, Blk E, School Rd, F-6/3, Po Box 1287Tel: 825541; Tlx: PK 5652

Karachi
Akbar Tours
Kutchery Road. Tel: 51468
Avis
Airport -Tel: 526295; Town - 14 Services Club Bldg, Mereweather Road.Tel: 526985

Peshawar
Khyber Turizm
1 Saddar Rd, Hotel International Bldg
Tel: 75109; Tlx: PK 52314 KTLPE

Rawalpindi
Avis Rent-a-Car
7 Rahim Plaza, Murree Rd. Tel: 68879
Khyber Turizm
Hotel Shalimar, Aziz Bahti Rd. Tel: 562901
Sitara Travel Consultants
25-6 Shalimar Plaza, Off The Mall, PO Box 63. Tel: 64750; Tlx: PK 5751 STARA

Useful Addresses

Business
Chamber of Commerce & Industry
Aiwan-i-Tajarat, PO Box 4158, Karachi 2
Tel: 226091-5; Tlx: 23613 KCCI PK
Export Promotion Centre
48 I & T Centre, Aab Para, Islamabad
Tel: 26723/27348; Tlx: 5614 EXPOM PK
Export Promotion Centre
Chamber of Commerce Bldg, 11 Sharee Aiwan-e-Tijarat, Lahore-3. Tel: 65107; Tlx: 44548 EXPOM PK
Export Promotion Bureau
Hirani Centre, 1,1 Chundrigar Rd, Karachi
Tel: 214022; Tlx: 23877 EXPOM PK
Export Promotion Bureau
Sarhad Chamber of Commerce Bldg, GT Road, Peshawar.Tel: 64153
Faisalabad Chamber of Commerce & Industry
MCB Building 5th Fl, Circular Rd, Faisalabad. Tel: 23039/32583
Federation of Pakistan Chambers of Commerce
Shahrah Firdousi, Main Clifton, Karachi 6
Tel: 532179/532198; Tlx: 25370 FPCCI PK
Lahore Chamber of Commerce & Industry
11 Shahra-i-Aiwani Tijarat, Lahore
Tel: 305538-40; Tlx: 44833 LCCI
Ministry of Commerce
Block A, Pakistan Secretariat, Islamabad
Tel: 825078; Tlx: 5859
Overseas Investors Chamber of Commerce & Industry
Chamber of Commerce Bldg, PO Box 4833, Talpur Rd, Karachi.Tel: 222557-8
Pakistan Industrial Development Corporation.PIDC House, Karachi
Tel: 511080/524571-79
Rawalpindi Chamber of Commerce/ Ind'try
108 Adamjee Rd, Rawalpindi
Tel: 67598/62155-B; Tlx: 5547 RCCI PK

Tourism Information Centres

PTDC Information Centre
International Arrival Lounge, Terminal 2, Karachi Airport,Club Road, Karachi City
PTDC
H-2, St 61, F-7/4, PO Box 1465,Islamabad 44000.Tel: 811001-4; Tlx: 54356 PTDCPK
Tourist Information Centre
Club Road, Karachi.Tel: 510234
Tourism Div.Min. of Culture & Tourism
13-Tu Commercial Area, F 7/2
Tel: 824597/826108

Air Couriers
DHL. Tel: Karachi 4543470
TNT Express Worldwide. Tel: Karachi 431005-7; Lahore (042) 631 0346 /636 0222
UPS. Tel: Karachi 111 3232 / 454 0710

Police (foreigners) & Post Office:
1, 1 Chundrigar Road, Karachi. Tel: 233737/210771

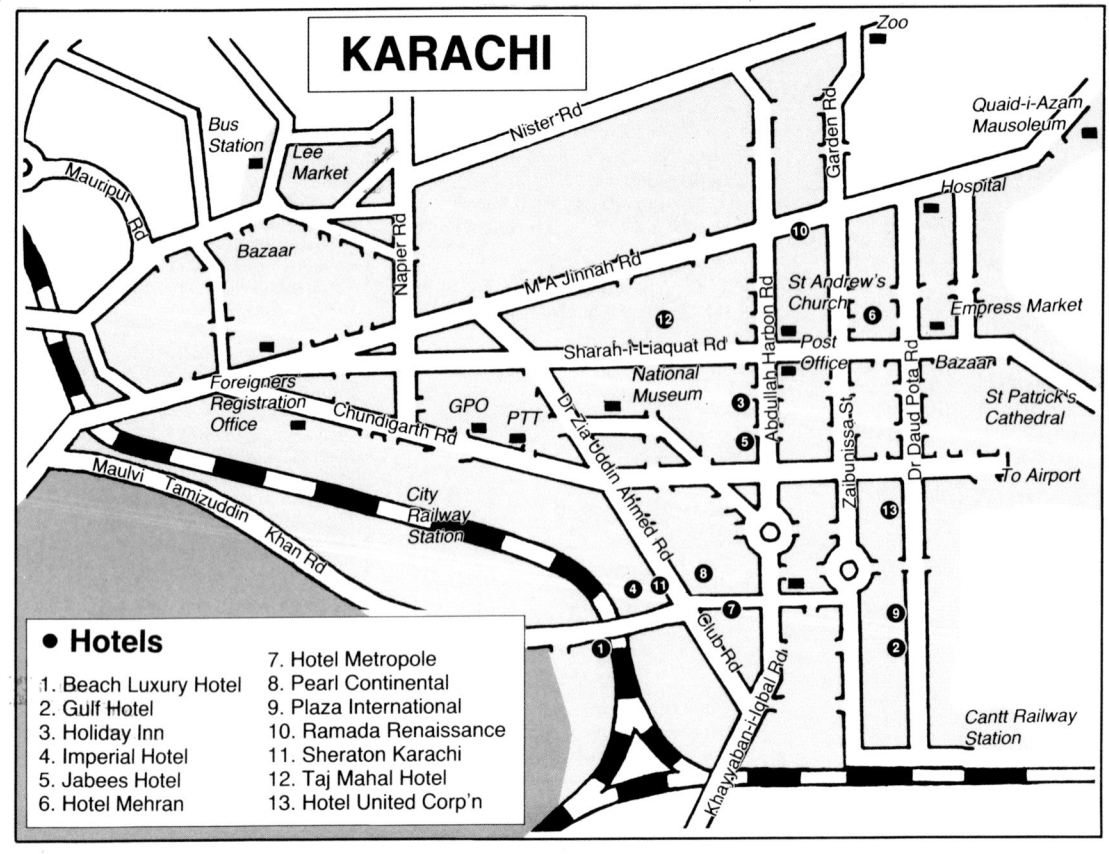

KARACHI

• Hotels
1. Beach Luxury Hotel
2. Gulf Hotel
3. Holiday Inn
4. Imperial Hotel
5. Jabees Hotel
6. Hotel Mehran
7. Hotel Metropole
8. Pearl Continental
9. Plaza International
10. Ramada Renaissance
11. Sheraton Karachi
12. Taj Mahal Hotel
13. Hotel United Corp'n

Papua New Guinea

Doing Business

General climate

Visitors planning a sortie into Papua New Guinea should bone up on what it was like to do business in Australia in the old days. With few modern adjustments and rather more manners, PNG offers the same environment today. In other words forthright, hard bargaining and no bull.

Fashioned on a number of international influences but owing its ultimate business and political *modus operandi* to Australia, PNG represents perhaps the Pacific's final frontier, rich in untapped minerals and opportunities yet acutely aware of not selling its potential down the proverbial river.

Many are the multinationals who have honed in on what they imagined was an easy pot of gold, only to be sent packing by a country surprisingly well-educated in the ways of the business world and confident of its future role as the Pacific's next major growth area. Gold, copper and huge supplies of high quality hardwood timber all lie at the end of a business rainbow governed by fierce national preservation orders and confused by disparate local controls. Vast distances and a lack of basic infrastructure beyond some good domestic air services and adequate hotels are factors which can drain the enthusiasm of any but the most determined business interloper. Another discouraging factor is that PNG gives priority, and consequently appropriate incentives, to oil and gas generation, both of which reached capacity in the past two years against depleted world price markets; as well as to new technology - it has a high-tech university - rather than to the immediate further exploitation of minerals and timber.

Often fragile politics also aid some eventual disinterest or disinvestment in an economy which is based on private enterprise but seen by analysts not to have capitalised fully on its potential, resulting in depleted foreign exchange reserves and slower than expected growth.

Marginally rising unemployment has done little to aid civil rest in a country with a poor record for crime and an even worse reputation overseas. The visitor to the capital, Port Moresby, needs to be aware that it can be unsafe to walk alone at night, argue the odds with a 'taxi' driver or even travel in a car without the doors locked. Yet in this same city, as in others in PNG, it is not uncommon to be turfed out of an hotel dining room for not being properly attired or to attend private house parties with white-gloved butlers and waiters. At the same time, it is considered quite proper to attend a business meeting without a jacket yet totally improper to be unpunctual, ill-prepared or casual in approach or attitude.

In many respects, Port Moresby is redolent of its near Australian neighbour, Darwin — that is to say a city proud of its pioneering status on the edge of a new frontier but eager also to be counted as a modern and sophisticated commercial centre with all the attendant niceties and leisure pursuits. As with many other aspects of PNG, such dreams have yet to become reality.

March 1997 saw the resignation of Prime Minister Sir Julius Chan plus the Finance and Defence ministers in the wake of protests against his hiring of mercenaries to put down the long running rebellion in secessionist Bougainville.

Tourism Update

General Devlopments

In mid-1995, Papua New Guinea signalled its intention of becoming a serious player on the international tourism circuit. The PNG Tourism Promotion Authority launched a campaign to capture a larger slice of tourist arrivals from around the world enjoyed by neighbouring Indonesia and Australia. The TPA launched its campaign through the Pacific Asia Travel Association, hoping that PATA would find ways of expanding visitor traffic to all three member nations of the designated *Arafura Tourism Zone*, which PNG shares with Indonesia and Australia. The TPA presented to PATA a survey carried out by its representatives in Europe, Japan and North America in which it claimed to identify a 'large number' of people who would visit PNG if access was improved. " *If tourists coming down from Japan or Europe to either Australia or Indonesia could return via PNG, then our country - as one of the last great untouched tourist destinations in the world - would reap a tourism bonanza,"* said a spokeswoman for the TPA. She added that this would not happen unless all three members of the *Arafura* Zone could improve accessibility, reduce the costs of travel to and within PNG and work more closely together as an industry.

The TPA said the key to attracting more tourists would be establishing regular flights into PNG via Jayapura, across the Indonesian border in Iran Jaya. This would allow PNG to tap into the Australia-Bali tourist route, say with flights from Cairns via Bali to Jayapura and stopovers in Milne Bay, Madang, New Britain, New Ireland, Goroka, Sepik, Mt. Hagen and Vanimo - effectively all the areas of PNG geared to larger visitor numbers.

With Indonesia in 1995 looking at the viability of direct flights from Cairns or Darwin to Irian Jaya, the TPA said it wanted Air Niugini to be allowed to put reciprocal arrangements in place to enable PNG to gain maximum benefit. The PNG tourism authority stressed that the country was now in position to service a growing tourism industry, with both its Wingti and Chan governments deciding that tourism development should be given a high level of priority.

PNG's TPA was established in June 1993 with the objectives of marketing the country as an international holiday destination and developing tourism product and infrastructure to international standards. Since its inception, the TPA has developed a clear strategy in marketing and development, attending overseas trade shows — latterly as part of the high profile *Visit South Pacific Year '95* campaign — and assisting the tour trade to develop new itineraries. Recognising that Australia will continue to be PNG's biggest market for short-term visitor arrivals, mostly for business purposes, it began focusing tourism marketing attention in 1995 on Europe, Japan and North America as representing the largest potential source of new leisure business.

Europeans, particularly Germans, are viewed as being interested in the last frontier aspects of PNG while Japanese are thought to favour seeing orchids, birds of paradise and World War Two monuments.

Arrivals for the first 10 months of 1994 showed significant gains for PNG. Overall visitor count rose 19.3% to 33,007 compared with 27,672 during the same period of 1993. Arrivals from Japan rose 54.7% to 1,959 and from Europe by 40.0% to 5,233. North American traffic increased 4.3% to 3,644 during the period and from the rest of Asia (excluding Japan) by 3.6% to 4,211. Arrivals from the major market, Australia, increased 6.1% to 13,905 compared with 13,103 during the corresponding period of 1993. Short-term arrivals statistics for the nine-month period January-September period of 1994 showed more visitors in all three main sectors — business, holiday and visiting friends and relatives. Business traffic increased from 11,631 to 14,769; holiday traffic from 7,391 to 8,024 and VFR from 3,850 to 5,435. There was a large drop in ' other' reasons for visiting from 1,822 to 353. -

Airlines

Papua New Guinea's flag carrier Air Nuigini(PX) has been through a quiet period consolidating its international network. It flies at present to Singapore, Hong Kong/Manila, Cairns, Brisbane/Sydney and Honiara in the Solomons. Developments for 1997 include the commencement of a weekly scheduled service between Port Moresby and Kansai (Osaka) in Japan. This replaces the present charter service.

Domestically the carrier replaced its two Dash 7 aircraft with two new Dash 8 200B aircraft and purchased a further Fokker F28-4000 for domestic and island-hopping routes.

Talair, once considered the world's largest third level carrier, bowed out in May 1993 citing declining sales and disputes with the government for ending services.

In the wake of Talair's decision to ground its aircraft, the government offered the carrier's routes to a range of local operators: Airlink, Islands Nationair, Islands Aviation, Trans Islands Airways, MAF and Milne Bay Air.

The break up of Talair had a beneficial impact on Air Nuigini's inter-provincial services.

What to see

The majority of PNG's sights are natural rather than man made. In fact there are few noteworthy colonidal-style buildings as the capital, Port Moresby, only dates from 1886. The town does house, however, the National Museum and Art Gallery, which features examples of PNG's varied tribal life styles. It is also the site of the National Parliament Building - a mix of modern architecture and traditional design - which opened in 1984.

There are two major national parks at Variarata on the Sogeri Plateau near Port Moresby and the McAdam National Park close to Bulolo.

Relics of World War II and of the Japanese partial occupation of the country provide a certain fascination for many visitors. Rabaul on the northern tip of New Britain has perhaps the best collection of war memorabilia as this was the headquarters of the invading Japanese forces until 1945.

The Sepik River, which runs no less than 1,126km, also comes with a high recommendation for a thrilling trip through the country's still undiscovered heart. The timeless simplicity of the Sepik with their many different languages and clans provide both a mystery and fascination for visitors.

If you get up to Goroka in the Eastern Highlands then it is worth visiting the J.K.McCarthy Museum, which many consider better than the National in Port Moresby.

Held each August or September, the Highlands Show at either Goroka or Mount Hagen is the nation's biggest festival - these so-called *singsings* feature song, dance and local rituals. The Chicago Tribune has referred to it as *"One of the 12 Travel Wonders of the World"*.

Trans Niugini Tours (*see below*) runs a Special Interest Tour to the Mount Hagen Cultural Show; also special interest tours including Diving, Reef & Rainforest and Adventure.

Shopping

Department stores and Western-style malls are out in Papua New Guinea but local handicrafts are a good buy and PNG's art-forms are as diverse as they are distinctive. Visitors can buy for a few dollars locally produced artefacts that sell for hundreds of dollars in the West! Many of the larger hotels (see *listings* following this chapter) sell a fine selection of quality local merchandise.

Pottery, *bilums* (natural fibre strings bags), weaponry, masks, bowls and musical instruments are popular with visitors. Although most of these items are made in small villages, they are obtainable from shops in the bigger cities.

PNG Art on Spring Garden Road is a well-known and respected outlet and is prepared to ship items worldwide on behalf of customers.

Visitors are not allowed to take out of the country any bird of paradise plumes, stone objects (except axes) or artefacts manufactured before 1960 without an export permit.

Getting Around

The most convenient, and often the only way, to move around PNG is by air. As a result, PNG has an excellent internal air network stretching from Kieta in the east to Tabulil in the Hindenburg Range on the border with Indonesia's Irian Jaya in the west.

Domestic airlines, such as Air Nuigini (PX) and Douglas Airways, network most major cities with a highly efficient and regular service. With the demise of Talair, Trans Niugini Tours have bought two aircraft to service their lodges at Tari, Karawari and Timbunke from Mount Hagen. These are known as TNT Air Transfers and aircraft used are a 9-seater Brittan Norman Islander and a 5-seater Beechcraft Baron.

PX introduced its "Visit Papua New Guinea" air-pass in September 1991. It is now called the "Adventure Airpass". It costs US$299 and includes four flight coupons, offers cheap internal travel as long as the visitor arrives in PNG on board a PX flight and stays less than 30 days. Additional flight coupons may be purchased for US$50 each.

On Bougainville, in normal times Bougair provides the largest number of flights.

Although air and sea connections are important in a nation with a rugged terrain and many outlying islands, a good highway network does connect the Highland provinces to Morobe and Madang.

Driving in the Highlands is not without its problems, so exercise caution before hiring a vehicle. The large car rental firms - Hertz, Budget and Avis - have offices in Port Moresby and some of the other big towns. Outside Port Moresby, smaller companies also compete with the "big three." Some of the main towns even have taxis, most with meters.

Entertainment

The National Theatre Company and Raun Raun Theatre Company perform a number of plays and participate in arts festivals at home and overseas. The National Tourism Entertainment Centre at the National Arts School Campus is the base for the Tambaran Group. In Madang the Haus Tambaran Group performs cultural dances and plays at hotel venues.

Some of the larger hotels and clubs up and down the country hold weekly discos. Visitors to Port Moresby would be well advised to stick to their hotel as venturing out at night is not always recommended.

Leisure

Sport of every kind is on offer. Of particular significance is PNG's spectacular scuba diving on vividly coloured coral reefs.

The Walindi Plantation Resort, for example, is rated one of the world's top diving spots. World War II shipwrecks and downed aircraft submerged in crystal-clear water, sunken live volcanoes, grazing dugong and slow-swimming giant turtles make this one of the very best diving locations. Trans Niugini Tours runs special 7-day dive packages at Malolo Plantation Lodge near Madang and at Wailindi in New Britain. They have also introduced a 7-day 'Reef and Rainforest' cultural and ecological itinerary.

Trekking and climbing in highland areas is also popular with clearly defined trails up into the mountains. White Water Rafting is conducted on the Watut River, close to Bulolo and also on some other rivers. It is best to do these things through officially recognised tour operators. To do otherwise

---

A SHORT HOP FROM AUSTRALIA!

PAPUA NEW GUINEA

A unique experience, a world away in a land of cultural and natural wonders. Encounter the spectacular, highly photogenic dances of the colourful Huli Wigmen at **Ambua Lodge**, recipient of the PATA's Pacific Heritage Award.
Explore primeval rainforests at **Karawari Lodge** or dive to the wrecks and colourful reefs from **Malolo Plantation Lodge**, Madang.
Cruise aboard the luxury 18-passenger **MV Sepik Spirit** visiting traditional villages along the Sepik and Blackwater rivers. For the more adventurous, choose from trekking and sea kayaking.
For information, contact:
TRANS NIUGINI TOURS - PO Box 371, Mt Hagen, Papua New Guinea
Tel: (675) 542 1438; Fax: (675) 542 2470; E-mail: 100250.3337@compuserve.com
or contact your nearest Air Niugini office

could prove both expensive and potentially dangerous. On the coast, big game fishing is on hand for skipjack tuna and marlin. Then there is barramundi and a variety of tropical fish closer to the shore.

The better hotels have tennis courts. In Madang there is even a golf course. Bowls, horse riding and racing, swimming, yachting and motor sports are all available.

Arrival and Departure

Port Moresby's Jacksons International Airport and Mount Hagen Airport are the nation's two international gateways; although flights to the Solomon Islands go (in normal times) via Kieta in Bougainville. Jacksons is just 11 km from downtown Port Moresby and the journey from downtown takes 15-20 minutes.

Taxis can be hailed from the front of the terminal. The fare into Port Moresby is about K20. Budget, Hertz and Avis all have desks in the domestic arrivals area. Expect to change a small amount of foreign exchange into Kinas to pay for your visa (K15). K15 is payable as departure tax.

Useful Addresses

Business

Papua New Guinea Chamber of Commerce and Industry
PO Box 1621, Port Moresby Tel: 3213057

National Investment & Dev't Authority
PO Box 5033, Boroko, Na.l Capital District

Lae Chamber of Commerce
PO Box 265 Lae.Tel: 4722340; Fax: 4726038

Papua New Guinea Dept of Trade &Industry
Central Government Offices, PO Wards Strip, Waigini, National Capital District

Port Moresby Chamber of Commerce
PO Box 1764, Pt Moresby. Tel: 3213077

Tourism

National Tourist Office
Embassy Drive, Waigini. (PO Box 7144 Boroko) .Tel: 325 1269; Tlx: 23472 PNGTB; Fax: 325 9447

PNG Tourism Promotion Authority
Po Box 1291, Port Moresby.Tel:320 0211

Tourist Association of New Guinea
c/o Islander Hotel, PO Box 1981, Boroko
Tel: 315 5955

Trans Niugini Tours Pty Ltd
PO Box 371, Mt Hagen
Tel: 352 1438; Tlx: 52012; Fax: 352 2470

Air Couriers

DHL.Port Moresby Tel: 325 9866
TNT Express Worldwide Tel:325 2411
UPS.Tel: 321 2185/321 2350

Airline Offices

Air Niugini
PO Box 7186, Boroko
Tel:3273200; Tlx: NE 22225; Fax: 3273482

Cathay Pacific Airways
PO Box 1711 Port Moresby
Tel: 3214486; Tlx 22269; Fax: 3211017

Continental/Air Micronesia
PO Box 928, Hohola
Tel: 321 4766; Fax: 321 4750

Douglas Airways Pty Ltd
PO Box 1179 Boroko
Tel: 325 3499; Fax: 325 3751

Islands Nationair
Jacksons Airport, Port Moresby PO Box 488
Tel: 325 4055/325 2501; Fax: 325 5059

Qantas
PO Box 330, Port Moresby
Tel: 321 1200; Tlx: 22298; Fax: 323 1073

Singapore Airlines
PO Box 1162, Port Moresby
Tel: 3213975; Fax: 3213998

Papua New Guinea Key Fact File

Passport Requirements:
All visitors need a valid passport. Those intending to stay for no more than 30 days are issued a visa on arrival. For longer visits, visas need to be obtained from a PNG consular office before arrival. Visas are only issued to visitors from a select group of countries - mainly regional, UK & Commonwealth, Western Europe, Japan, Thailand and North America. Visa fees are K15.

Currency:
Kina. 100 toea = 1 kina

Exchange rate:
US$1 =1.39 kina; £1= 2.26 kina (May 1997)

IDD Code: 675
No area codes required

Currency restrictions:
Free import of local currency although it must be re-exchanged on departure.

Language:
There are over 820 languages. The main ones are Tok Pisin and Hiri Motu. English is the official and commercial language.

Time:
GMT + 10 hours: EDT + 15 hours.

Business hours:
Commercial offices: usually 0800-1630 Monday to Friday. Government offices: 0745-1600
Shops: Monday to Fridays 0800-1700; Saturdays 0800-1200.
Banks: Monday to Thursday 0900-1400; Friday 0900-1700.

Customs & Entry:
Duty free allowance is 200 cigarettes or equivalent; one litre of spirits plus 250 ounces of perfume. A limit of K200 per passenger (over 18) on other dutiable items. Narcotics, etc are prohibited as are various types of weapons. Domestic pets are prohibited as are agricultural items and animals.

Health Requirements:
Certificates of vaccination against yellow fever or cholera are required by travellers over one year of age coming **from or** through infected areas. Malaria is the only serious health risk. Advisable to boil water in rural areas.

Climate/best time to visit:
Generally warm all year round, (Port Moresby min. 24º, max. 32ºC) but varies acc. to geographical terrain. Port Moresby is comparatively dry with an average rainfall of 1,200mm a year split between wet (Dec to March) and dry seasons. Humidity 77% in Summer. By comparison Lae has 4,617mm a year. Throughout the year the Highlands enjoy a climate similar to late spring in temperate zones.

Public Holidays 1997:
1 January New Years Day; 28 March Good Friday; 31 March Easter Monday; 10 June HM The Queen's Birthday; 23 July Remembrance Day; 16 September Independence Day; 25 December Christmas Day; 26 December Boxing Day.

PNG Hotels

Bulolo

Pine Lodge   D
c/o PO Box 707 Madang
Tel:474 5220; Tlx: 82707; Fax: 4745284

Goroka

Bird of Paradise Hotel   D
PO Box 12
Tel: 732 1144; Tlx: 52022; Fax: 732 1007

Kainantu

Kainantu Lodge   E
PO Box 31 Tel: 737 1020-1; Tlx: NE 77632; Fax: 737 1229

Kavieng

Kavieng Hotel   E
Coronation Drive, PO Box 4
Tel: 942199; Tlx: 94924

Kieta

Davara Motel   D
PO Box 241, Toniva Beach, N. Solomons
Tel: 956175; Tlx: 95852; Fax: 956218

Kimbe

Walindi Plantation   C
PO Box 4, West New Britain Province
Tel: 935441

Lae

Coral Sea Huon Gulf Motel   C
Markham Road, PO Box 612
Tel: 472 4844; Tlx: 44187; Fax: 472 3706

Lae International Hotel   C
4th St, PO Box 2774
Tel: 472 2000; Tlx: 42473; Fax: 472 2534

Coral Sea Melanesian Hotel   C
PO Box 756, Lae
Tel: 472 3744; Tlx: 44187; Fax: 472 3706

Madang

Coral Sea Coastwatchers Motel   D
Coralita St, PO Box 324
Tel: 852 2684; Fax: 852 2716

Jais Aben Resort Nagara Harbour   D
Nagada, PO Box 105 Madang
Tel: 852 3311; Fax: 852 3560

Madang International Resort Hotel   E
Coastwatchers Ave, PO Box 111 Madang
Tel: 852 2655; Tlx: 42471; Fax: 852 3325

Malolo Plantation Lodge   C
c/o PO Box 371 Port Moresby
Tel: 542 1438; Tlx: 52012; Fax: 542 2470

Coral Sea Smugglers Resort   D
Modilon Rd, PO Box 303
Tel: 852 2744; Tlx: 82722; Fax: 852 2267

Mount Hagen

Ambua Lodge   B
Tari, c/o PO Box 371
Tel: 542 1490; Tlx: 52012; Fax: 542 2470

Coral Sea Highlander Hotel   D
PO Box 34, Mount Hagen
Tel: 542 1355; Tlx: 55108; Fax: 542 1216

Karawari Lodge ◌   B
Karawari. c/o PO Box 371
Tel: 542 1438; Tlx: 52012; Fax: 542 2470

Plumes and Arrows Inn   D
Kagamuga, PO Box 86
Tel: 545 1555; Tlx: 52088; Fax: 545 1546

Popondetta

Coral Sea Lamington Lodge   C
PO Box 27, Popondetta, N. Province
Tel: 329 7152; Fax: 329 7470

Port Moresby

Boroko Lodge   D
PO Box 1033, Boroko
Tel: 325 6677; Fax: 325 4585

The Ela Beach Hotel   B
Ela Beach Rd, PO Box 799
Tel: 321 2100; Tlx: 23236; Fax: 321 2434

Coral Sea Gateway Hotel   C
Morea Tobo Rd, PO Box 1215 Boroko
Tel: 325 3855; Tlx: 23082; Fax: 325 4585

Islander Travelodge   C
Waigani Drive, PO Box 1981
Tel: 325 5955; Fax: 321 3835

Loloata Island Resort   D
Boroko (Loloata Island) PO Box 5290
Tel: 325 1369; Fax: 325 8933

Port Moresby Travelodge ◌   B
Hunter St, PO Box 1661
Tel: 321 2266; Tlx: 22248; Fax: 321 7534

Rabaul

Motel Kaivuna   D
Mango Ave, PO Box 395
Tel: 982 1766; Tlx: 92982; Fax: 982 1832

Rabaul Travelodge   D
Mango Ave, PO Box 449, 92975
Tel: 982 2111; Tlx: 92975; Fax: 982 2104

Wabag

Wabag Lodge   D
PO Box 2
Tel: 571069

Weam

Bensbach Wildlife Lodge   C
c/o PO Box 371 Mount Hagen
Tel: 352 1438; Tlx: 52012; Fax: 352 2470

Sepik Motel   D
Hill St, PO Box 51
Tel: 856 2388; Tlx: 86143

Wewak

Sepik International Beach Resort   E
Boram Rd, PO Box 152
Tel: 862388; Fax: 862701

◌ after name of hotel = Allied Hotel Member of the Pacific Asia Travel Association.
A = price over US$200 per night; **B** = between $150-200; **C** = between $100-150; **D** = between $50-100; **E** = under US$50 per head per night. ¶ = Prices on application.

Restaurants

It is not recommended to venture too far outside hotels at night in Papua New Guinea. Nevertheless, for the intrepid, two Port Moresby restaurants commend themselves:

The Galley Restaurant *(Seafood)*
Aviat Club, Aviat Street. Tel: 321 2167

Oyster Bar *(Seafood)*
Hugo Bldg, Angau Drive, Boroko.
Tel: 325 6711

Car Hire

Avis Rent-A-Car
PO Box 1533, Port Moresby
Tel: 325 8299; Tlx: 22279; Fax: 325 3767
(+ 10 branches throughout PNG)

Budget Rent-A-Car
PO Box 503, Port Moresby
Tel: 325 4111; Tlx: 23019; Fax: 325 7853
(+ 8 regional branches in hotels etc)

Hertz Self Drive
Alva Motoring Pty Ltd, PO Box 4126, Jacksons Int'l Airport. Tel: 325 4499; Fax: 325 6985
Mimimum age 25; home driving licence acceptable; driving is on the left.

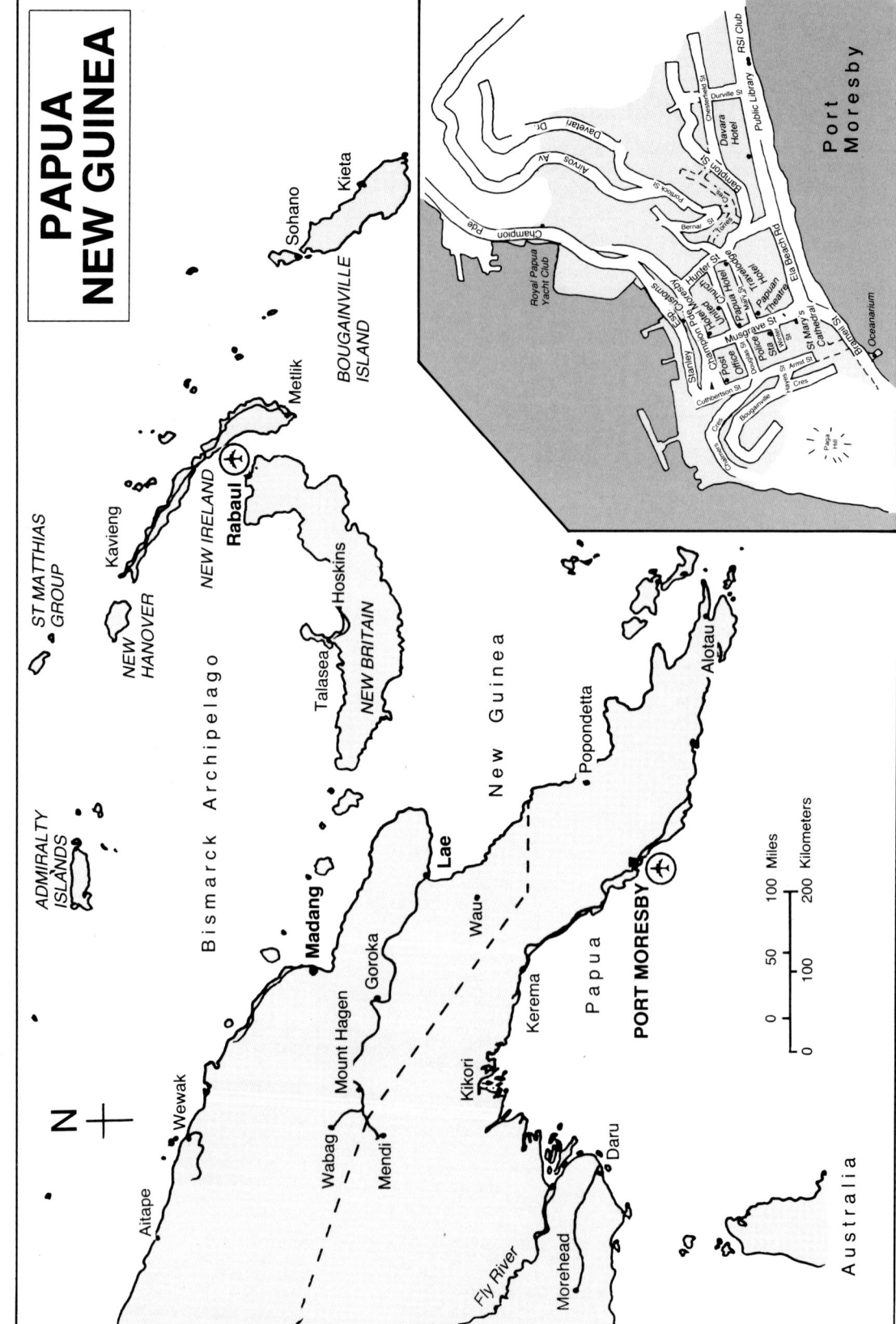

COUNTRY REPORT
PHILIPPINES '97

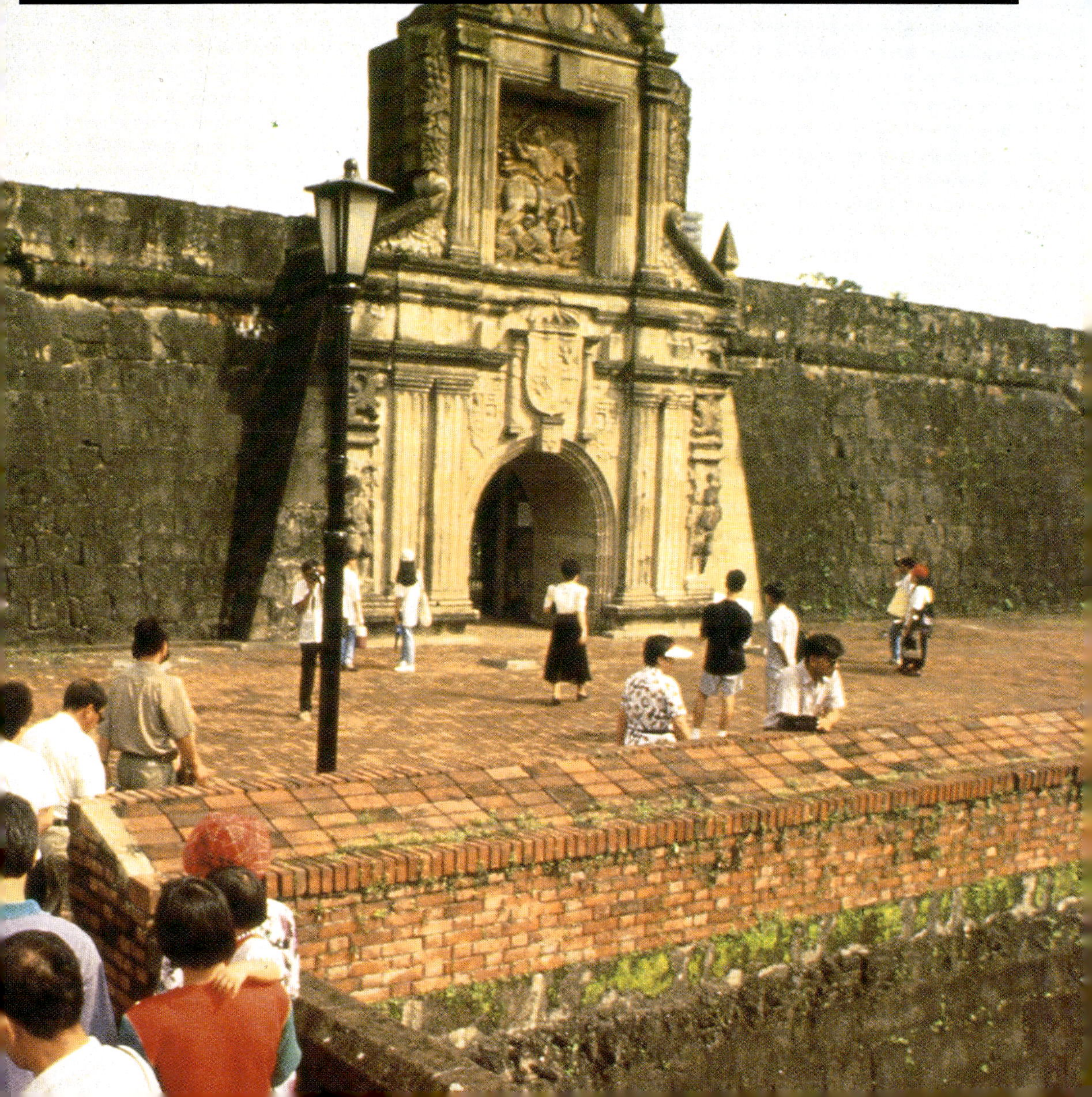

Philippines

Doing Business

General Climate

Continued political and economic stability under the Ramos government during 1996/7 strengthened interest in the Philippines as an investment opportunity. Economically, the country was one of Asia's strongest performers during the year, with 7% growth forecast for 1997, helping to stoke interest in Manila as one of the region's primary financial and trading centres. The export-led growth was bought at the cost of a burgeoning trade deficit and inflation of 8.8% in 1996. Real GDP growth increased to 5.05%, from 4.7% and President Ramos has forecast 8% GNP for 1997 but the Asian Development Bank predicts 5.5% GDP growth in 1996 and 5.7% in 1997.

Reserves in 1996 hit the US$10.25 billio mark despite a widening trade deficit (US$5.04 billion) and the balance of payments for first half 1996 showed a US$2.5 billion surlpus, 1000% better than the same period in 1995. The Central Bank is now an independent monetary authority on the European model and oversees the banking sector. International Monetary Fund proposals to impose a package of tax reforms on the Philippines helped the international business community to keep faith in a country still viewed as being 'on probation'.

Traditionally, the Philippines has been judged as volatile in international business circles, a factor not helped by the Filipino *penchant* for weaving bureaucratic red tape plus a long-standing shortage of power resulting in still too frequent 'brownouts' — despite a World Bank-inspired programme to generate enough power for industrialisation and commercialisation of the country's inestimable natural resources and virtually limitless workforce.

Other fears still to be overcome include revived communist or southern area Muslim fundamentalist insurgency coupled with unforeseen future natural calamities (to which the Philippines is sadly prone).

Vigorous campaigns to attract offshore equity, including widely-publicised mid-1990s globetrotting trips by President Ramos, have attracted new investment, mostly from Japan, Korea and Taiwan. Yet much of the foreign equity succoured by the Philippines remains offshore as a cautious international business community continues to adopt its 'wait and see' approach to long-term opportunities.

Subject to a myriad of international aid programmes, the Philippines government makes few excuses about looking after its own first. The state and private sectors live in uneasy harmony. Locals take precedence in all investment transactions, often making it difficult for foreigners to count on any short-term gain, despite a tranche of potential tax breaks and corporate incentives offered by the Board of Investment.

Small entrepreneurs are actively being encouraged to create more national wealth and employment through manufacturing and high-tech assembly, and rural families are being assisted in broadening their agricultural productivity to include high-yield exports crops such as orchids and asparagus to supplement staples such as shrimp.

Filipinos themselves are often viewed as being as volatile as their surroundings. On the one hand they are seen as being gregarious, warm-hearted and entertaining hosts, on the other as often unreliable business partners forced into under counter dealings by a system and social order bred on cant and corruption.

As is common in Asia, Philippines has a business hierarchy born of real power being retained by a network of families, requiring the services of good local agent and an approach demanding who you know rather than what you know or have to offer. The interloper needs to be careful which business partner to back in a climate fraught with internecine politics yet currently making overt play of cleaning up crime along with business and exposing tax evasion and corruption in high places. American colonial habits and attitudes make a strange and intriguing mix with the Spanish and Chinese heritage of Filipinos. The style is a fusion of gambling to get rich quick with an acceptance that the bet will probably lose, so have a nice *mañana* anyway.

Lately, rival Cebu claims to offer an easier, less restrictive and more freewheeling investment climate than Manila. Tourism projects account for much of the new foreign investment in both cities and visitors today are assured of at least sophisticated accommodation, improved transport and some world class recreational facilities, if less in the way of industrial or agricultural opportunities.

Business etiquette & practice

Business customs follow the Western manner, with formal attire and a preference for entertaining, with both formal and informal discussions taking place over lunch or dinner, either 'at home' or in a hotel or one of the many smart restaurants around Manila's 'Green Belt'. Small presents are frequently given and appreciated in return, such as gift-wrapped chocolates, cakes or donuts to which many Filipinos appear addicted. Despite the outwardly hectic pace of life, business is rarely rushed in Philippines. Public holidays and religious festivals are frequent, with offices closed for sometimes days at a time to cater to parades and, another Filipino love, musical events.

PHILIPPINES - Introduction

Tourism Update

General developments

Growth in visitor arrivals in the Philippines continued in double-digits in 1995. The increase was 11.8%, to 1,760,163, following on from three similarly good years. And growth in 1996 was running over 10%. Average length of stay is approximately 11 days. Predictions for 1996 are for over 2 million visitors, with 2.3 mn being the target for 1997. Earnings from tourism are expected to grow by 10-14% in 1997 to reach US$3 billion.

Market sources are defined by the residence of the visitor, except for one category - Overseas Filipinos - which is those visitors travelling on Filipino passports but living outside the Philippines. Most OFs (over 50%) are believed to be resident in the US.

The two leading market sources - US and Japan - are much larger than the others, and both grew well in 1994 and 1995 although the fastest-growing market was Korea. The US grew at 10.3% to 342,189, followed by Japan, which grew at 16.3% to 323,199. These were followed by Taiwan, up 21.0% to 190,423, Overseas Filipinos, down 5.8% to 149,903, and Korea, up 24.2% to 121,559. The official target to attract 10.5 million visitors for 2001 has been reduced to 3.94 million in 2000. The budget of the NTO is approximately US$17 million.

The Philippines is now working to a tourism master plan, which follows the standard World Tourism Organization pattern of *cluster* development of visitor attractions. The *clusters* are based on Luzon, including Palawan; the Visayas, including the central island areas; and Mindanao. Each cluster should have one or more international gateway. In Luzon these are Manila, Laoag, San Fernando, and Subic Bay airport. In the Visayas, the airport at Cebu. And for Mindanao, the airports of Davao and Zamboanga. Few of these are international airports at present.

There is some expansion in the tourism plant, with a large number of vehicles due to be added. However, some vehicles are for general transport, not just for the travel business.

Aviation

Following domestic air deregulation in 1994, a number of new companies have started air services, joining the flag carrier, Philippine Airlines. The biggest among them is Grand Air; others include Air Philippines, Asian Spirit, Cebu Pacific, and Star Asia. All operate domestic routes but some want to expand into international routes.

Grand Air has become the country's second international airline. It started international flights to Hong Kong and Taipei in 1996; plans to add Seoul (which has no direct service) and Singapore before end-1996 have been delayed. The airline, headed by a former PAL president, also wants to fly to Los Angeles via the longer trans-

Pacific route - round the curve of the globe through Honolulu. Grand, part of the Panlilio group which also owns hotels in the country, operates B737 and A300 aircraft and is due to take delivery of seven aircraft (believed to be A320s) starting from 1998; this order has not yet been announced by Airbus.

Air Philippines is due to take delivery of B737s, and start international flights to Hong Kong, Kuala Lumpur, Singapore, and Taipei starting from end 1996 and into 1997. Cebu Pacific, part of the John Gokongwei group, has bought four DC9s, and applied for rights to operate on some Asian routes and to the US. Asian Spirit operates 50-seat aircraft to smaller centres in the country. And Star Asia, which is currently concentrating on flying to local tourist resorts, is headed by a former under-secretary of the tourism department. Of the smaller airline companies, Region Air, based in Cagayan de Oro, bought two Embraer aircraft for delivery at end-1996.

But Philippine Airlines is not standing still. It is now planning a major aircraft renewal programme, and in 1996 announced it expected to spend US$2 billion on 20 aircraft, including four B747-400s. Original orders have had to be cut back due to payment and benefit demands from its workers. Traffic growth for Philippine Airlines has been running at about 5% since 1993. In 1995, seats sold increased 5.2% to 2.5 million, and RPKs increased 2.5% to just under 12 billion. Seat sales growth ran faster in 1996 - above 10% and possibly close to 14% - but RPK growth was still at around 5%. For both 1996 and (predicted) 1997 PR's losses are expected to be 1.7 billion pesos (US$65.3 mn). Some of the predicetd route expansions to China, India, South Africa and Eastern Europe have had to be postponed. But the airline started non-stop services to London and Rome in October 1996.

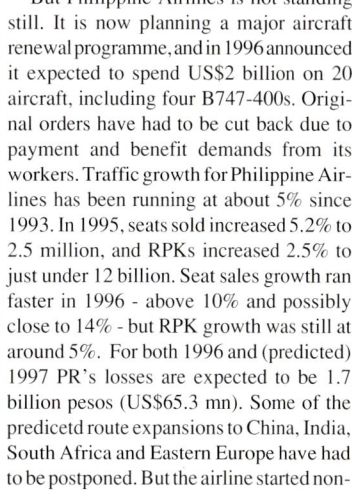

After firmer growth in 1992 and 1993, Manila's airport topped 6 million passengers in 1994, and increased about 5.0% in 1995 to 6.4 million. In 1996 growth was running in double-digits - around 14%. There are still access road problems to the airport and the third runway, due to be seconded from a nearby air base, has yet to materialise.

Hotels

After a long gap, there has been steady growth in hotels. These include resort areas, such as the star-rated Plantation Bay in 1996 in Cebu, and the Delta Dream Resort. The Plantation Bay resort, with 200 rooms and the lowest rack rate at US$210, targets 75% occupancy in 1997 at an average room rate of US$160-170.

In Batangas City the first Days Hotel

opened with 112 rooms. Four more Days Hotels are planned in secondary cities 1997 - 1999. And in the former Clark Air Base nearer to Manila, the Holiday Inn Resort Clark Field opened in 1996. And in the capital and suburbs, Century Imperial Palace Suites opened in Quezon City. These new hotels and others opening helped increase inventory figures starting 1993. Official figures show a 50% increase in rooms in 1994 and a 13% increase in 1995 to 21,815 rooms. Over 50% of the country's rooms are in Metro Manila.

A number of interesting new projects are planned, which sees more foreign groups becoming involved in locations outside Manila. These include a Sheraton in Boracay with 448 rooms, due in 1997; a Marco Polo in Davao with 250 rooms in 1998; a Century in Subic with 150 rooms in 1997 and a Delta-Century in Makati 1997, plus a proposed giant 17200-room development in the 250-hectare Samal Resort to be built over eight years, with rooms in hotels, resort units, etc.

The Accor group, which signed to take over four hotels in the Philippines in 1996, has others planned for Baguio (two), Cebu, and Davao. And presently it is considering proposals for 20 other projects, most of them resorts.

Marriott has announced plans to build two hotels in Cebu. The 304-room Marriott, part of the Cebu Business Park, is due to open in 1998; it is owned by Ayala Land. The other is the 325-room Mactan Island Marriott Resort, due to open in 1999; this is part of the 14 ha Porto Bello Cove Resort.

And the new Singapore-based hotel group, Regalis (part of Liang Court Hospitality) has earmarked the Philippines as one of its three prime target areas for development, along with China and Vietnam. It hopes to have 15 by 2000.

Also, the Department Of Tourism has endorsed the addition of 24 villas at the Amanpulo grandluxe resort in Palawan. Owned by the Soriano family by Seven Seas Resorts & Leisure, the project cost is P260m; the first villa is due in 1999.

Official statistics show occupancy levels of classified hotels in Metro Manila increased 5% in 1995, from 59% to 62%. Occupancy of deluxe hotels throughout the Philippines was 67%, up from 62% in 1994. However, guests average stay was 2.5 nights at these hotels, compared with 2.6 nights in 1994. According to figures from *Travel Business Analyst*, four-star hotels in Manila recorded a 63% occupancy in 1995 at an average room rate of US$107. In 1996 these figures were running at 72%/US$111.

What to See

Manila is a sprawling city of great contrasts between the flashy and affluent business centre in Makati, which is sometimes called "The Wall Street of the Philippines" to the slums in the streets nearby.

Among the many historical sights still to be found in the city is the Malacanang Palace. This graceful mansion dates back around 200 years and has housed many governor generals, both Spanish and American and more latterly eight Philippine presidents. The mansion is home to the world famous Imelda Marcos shoe collection and has been kept exactly as it was left when the Marcos family fled the Philippines for Hawaii back in 1986.

Intramuros, the old Spanish settlement built behind thick walls, dates back to the 16th century and was a closed community that ruled the archipelago for four centuries. Similarly, Fort Santiago is an old Spanish garrison containing the memorabilia of national hero Dr Jose Rizal.

The Ayala Museum & Aviary on Makati Avenue is an insight into Philippine culture. Its most famous attraction is its set of dioramas depicting the culture of the Philippines in miniature.

Outside Manila some spots to consider include the site of particularly ferocious battle between Filipino-US troops and the Japanese during World War II at Corregidor in Manila Bay. Further afield, the Tagaytay and Taal volcano is a popular destination for locals during the summertime.

Shopping

The Philippines represents good value for foreign visitors, with particular emphasis on locally-made clothes and shoes and handicrafts as bargains.

The upmarket Makati district has the highest concentration of the country's finest department stores, fashion boutiques, jewellery and outlets selling antiques. Harrison Plaza is a trendy shopping complex and F.B.Harrison in Malate is home for the major department stores plus a sprinkling of specialist shopes.

The Pistang Pilipino Complex is a market along A. Mabini Street selling all kinds of handicrafts - wood carvings, coral products, shellcraft and popular rattan furniture pieces. The Makati Commercial Center sells

a similar array of locally-made items. As does the Nayong Pilipino Museum, which sells quality antiques that, unlike many others in the city, are actually genuine.

Crowded Mabini Street in the heart of the so-called "tourist belt" is full of interesting shops selling handicrafts, antiques, shells, paintings, pottery and souvenirs.

The modern shopping complex in Greenhills along Ortigas Avenue is home to any number of boutiques selling clothes, sports equipment and home furnishings. The Marikina Shoe Expo is a small shopping village selling expensive shoes made in nearby Marikina municipality - Imelda Marcos, eat your heart out !

Getting Around

The domestic arm of national carrier Philippine Airlines flies to more than 40 destinations outside Manila. Following deregulation in 1994, new airlines Southeast Air, Star Asia, Grand Air, Pacific Air and All Asia Air are also plying domestic routes.

Filipinos rely on the faithful and exotic looking *jeepney* as a cheap and reliable means of travelling around Manila and beyond. But *jeepneys* are often crowded, stop frequently and are uncomfortable over long journeys. But businessmen are well advised to stick to taxis.

Even so, most taxis are in a poor state of repair, but on the credit side most drivers have a reasonable knowledge of English and fares are cheap. Some of the better hotels provide guests with their own taxis, which are generally smarter than those available direct from the street.

Car rental companies operate throughout the country. Self-drive is not highly recommended in Manila where traffic congestion makes driving difficult, but is a worthwhile option for destinations outside

the city. A driver can be hired for something like 30 per cent over the basic car hire rate. Ferries to outlying island are cheap and frequent, but it's advisable to buy a first-class air-conditioned cabin for overnight trips.

Entertainment

Manila's nightlife is often of the hot and frenzied variety. Nightclubs in Makati include *Giraffe* at Ayala Bank Building, *Hard Rock Cafe* and *TGI Friday*. English-style pubs include the *Prince of Wales* and *San Mig*. But don't be surprised to find burly guards at the doors of some and notices to *'leave your weapons outside'*! Ermita's red light district has been closed down by mayoral decree and has re-surfaced to an extent in Pasay City. Better clubs are to be found around P Burgos Street in Makati.

But Manila has more to offer than just sleazy night-clubs. The Cultural Center of the Philippines is the best place to view opera, ballet, concerts and recitals by foreign and local artists. The Maynila Restaurant at the Manila Hotel stages colourful Filipino music and dance every night except Sunday. The Pistahan sa Plaza has a Barrio Fiesta three times a week at the poolside.

Several theatres feature English and Tagalog plays, dances, musicals and concerts during the season. The Rizal Theater on Ayala Avenue is probably the best known.

Outside the large hotels, Manila has some good restaurants. For native dishes (short on spice, but strong on seafood) try the Kamayan on Pasay Road or the Ang Hang on the ground floor of Sunvar Plaza; the *Patio Esperanza* specialises in Filipino-Spanish cuisine and located on the corner of P.Burgos and Kalayaan Avenue. Look harder and you will find Indian, Italian, Middle Eastern, Chinese and Japanese cooking.

Leisure

Manila can offer visitors a wide range of sports. Golf courses and tennis courts are especially good and health clubs provide saunas, jacuzzis and massage. Sailing enthusiasts who are members of yacht clubs elsewhere need only to show their membership cards to be able to use local facilities. Jogging is popular with the Roxas Boulevard and Rizal Park the top spots.

Look to Manila's country clubs to provide the very best in leisure facilities. The Alabang Country Club and the Canlubang & Country Club are two to consider.

There are over 50 superb, playable golf courses in the Philippines. Details are in Priory Publications Ltd' recently published *South East Asia Golf Guide*. An extract from this guide *Golf in the Philippines* is available free of charge from the Philippines Department of Tourism in either Manila or London.

Arrival & Departure

Manila has two airports - Ninoy Aquino International handles overseas flights while Manila Domestic is adjacent to NAIA.

NAIA is situated 13km from the city centre. The taxi fare will cost P100 plus(use official metered cabs); Metro Manila Transit Love Bus costs P12. Departure tax is P500.

Useful Addresses

Government Departments & Agencies

American Chamber of Commerce
Corinthian Plaza, Makati. Tel: 818 7911

Department of Tourism
Dept. of Tourism Bldg, T. M. Kalaw Street, Rizal Park, Manila Tel: 599031; Tlx: 40183

Foreign Investments Assistance Center
385 Senator Gil. J. Puyat Avenue, Makati.
Tel: 818 1831

Ministry of Tourism
Agrifina Circle, Rizal Park, Manila.
Tel: 501703/599031

Ministry of Trade and Industry
361 Senator Gil. J. Puyat Ave, Makati.
Tel: 818 5701

Philippine Chamber of Commerce
Chamber of Commerce Bldg, Manila.
Tel: 403082

Trade Ministry (Board of Investments)
Dept Trade & Industry, Industry & Investment Bldg, Makati. Tel: 868403

United National Information Office
PO Box 2149. Tel: 850611

Conventions/Exhibitions

Cultural Centre of the Philippines
Roxas Blvd. Tel: 832 1125

Fairs & Exhibitions Company (Fairexpo)
CCP Complex, Roxas Boulevard, Metro Manila. Tel: 833 4482

Philippine Convention/Visitors Corporation
4th Fl, Legaspi Towers 300, suite 10-17
Roxas Boulevard, Metro Manila.Tel: 575031

Philippine Center for International Trade

Exhibitions
Cultural Center, Metro Manila. Tel: 832 0304

Professional Events Organiser
CCP Complex, Roxas Boulevard, Metro Manila. Tel: 883 2019

Post Offices, Hospitals, Police

Manila Central Post Office
Liwasang Bonifacio, Intramuros.
Makati Central Post Office
Buendia Ave (Gil. J. Puyat Ave)

Makati Medical Centre
2 Amorsolo St, Makati. Tel: 815 9911

Police. Emergencies. Tel: 599011
Public Information Desk. Tel: 702593

Air Couriers

DHL. Tel: (63-2) 834 0418
Federal Express: (2) 833 7586/9
TNT Express Worldwide: (2) 897 3457
UPS. (2) 832 1565/832 1569

Philippines Key Fact File

Passport Requirements:
All visitors require a valid passport. Nationals of countries that have diplomatic relations with the Philippines and staying less than 21 days do not require a visa provided they have a return ticket.

Currency:
Philippine Peso (P). 100 centavos = 1P

Exchange Rates:
US$1 = 26.3 P; £1 = 43 P (*May 1997*)

Currency Restrictions:
No restrictions on the amount of foreign currency visitors can bring into the Philippines. Travellers with more than US$3,000 (or its equivalent) must declare it to the Central Bank. The import of local currency is forbidden and departing passengers are restricted to exporting just P500.

Electricity Supply:
Generally 220 volts AC/60 cycles (except in Baguio where it is 110 volts)

Language:
Pilipino (Tagalog) - English widely used in business, government, in schools and in everday communications. Nationwide there are 111 languages and dialects. Spanish is still spoken fluently by a great number of Filipinos.

Time:
GMT + 8 hours; EDT + 13 hours

IDD Code: 63
Area codes: Bacolod 34; Baguio 442; Cagayan de Oro 8822; Ceby 32; Dagupan 48; Davao 35; Iloilo 33; Manila 2; San Pablo 43

Business Hours:
Commercial offices are open 0900-1200/1400-1800 Monday to Friday; 0800-1200 Saturdays.
Government offices are open 0730-1130, 1230-1630 or 0900-1200, 1300-1800 Monday to Friday.
Shops are open 0900-1200, 1400-1930 Monday to Saturday.
Banks are open 0900-1500 Monday to Friday.

Customs & Entry:
Duty-free allowance comprises 400 cigarettes or two tins of smoking tobacco; two one-litre bottles of alcohol plus a reasonable amount of personal effects.

Health Requirements:
A yellow fever vaccination is required upon arrival for passengers from infected areas, except for children under one year.

Climate/best time to visit:
Tropical in lowland areas, with high humidity and heavy rainfall. Year-round temperatures remain in a band 21-28C. Hilly areas can be much cooler. October to March, when Manila is at its coolest, is considered the best time to visit. Seasons: Cool and dry - November to Feb; Hot and mainly dry March to June; Wet - July to October.

National Holidays 1997
January 1 New Year's Day; 25 February Edsa Revolution Anniversary; 27/28 March Maundy Thursday/Good Friday; 9 April Day of Valour; May 1 Labour Day; June 12 Independence Day; 28 August National Heroes Day; 1 November All Saints' Day; 30 November Bonifacio Day; December 25 Christmas Day; December 30/31 Rizal Public Holiday/Special Public Holiday.

Car Hire

Self-drive car rental costs between P1000-2500 per day, including insurance and maintenance. depending on type of car. Chauffeur-driven car rental costs from P2000-6000 for a 16-hour day.

Avis Rent-A-Car (G&S Transport Corp)
311 P Casal, San Miguel, Metro Manila
Tel: 741 6126/741 0438; Tlx: 29755 AVIS PH; Fax: 741 3053
Branches in Angeles, Baguio, Cebu Airport & Magellan Hotel, Ninoy Aquino Airport, Manila Hotel, Peninsula Hotel, Olongapo City.

Bonsai Transportation Services
1035 J Bocobo St, Ermita, Manila
Tel: 587838/582406

Budget
Central Resrvations Headquarters, Manila.
Tel: 833 4155/831 8276; Fax: 832 0931
(+ branches at Peninsula Hotel, Inter-Continental Hotel, Ninoy Aquino Airport and Nayong Pilipino Compound)

Cattleya Limousine Service
Riasjac Building, Juana Osmena Street, Cebu City. Tel: 57201

Hertz Self and Chauffeur Drive
Executive Cars Inc
Cnr Roxas Blvd/Airport Rd, Baclaran, Paranaque, Metro Manila
Tel: 832 0520; Fax: 832 0525....

...Represented in all major cities. For reservations, refer to Metro Manila (above)
Pacific Rent-A-Car
Ground floor, Garden Hotel, Makati,
Tel: 818-7742; Tlx: 63902 ETPMGH PN

Venture Tours & Transport Services
Sundowner Hotel, 1430 A Mabini St, Ermita, Manila. Tel: 521 2041/521 8794

Philippines Hotel Reference Table

Hotel (listed in price order) * (M) after location = part of Metro Manila	SINGLE ROOM RATE (US$)	LOCATION	NUMBER OF ROOMS	NUMBER OF SUITES	CONFERENCE FACILITIES	EXHIBITION SPACE	LARGEST BANQUET NUMBER	BUSINESS CENTRE	SWIMMING POOL (0 = indoor)	TENNIS COURT	HEALTH CLUB	VIDEO FILMS
The Manila Peninsula	250-285	Makati (M)	500	22	●	●	500	●	●	●	●	-
Shangri-La Hotel	220-285	Makati (M)*	699	-	●	●	1750	●	●	●	●	●
Mandarin Oriental	240-270	Makati (M)	444	20	●	●	600	●	●	-	●	●
New World Hotel	220-230	Makati (M)	600	11	●	-	500	●	●	-	●	●
Shangri-La's Edsa Plaza	190-270	Mandaluyong (M)	435	4	●	●	830	●	●	●	●	●
The Manila Hotel	180-225	Rizal Park (M)	506	64	●	-	1300	●	●	●	●	●
Century Park Sheraton	180-230	Makati (M)	440	60	●	●	500	●	●	-	●	-
Manila Diamond Hotel	180-320	Ermita (M)	510	-	●	●	400	●	●	●	●	●
Inter-Continental	170-190	Manila	400	30	●	●	600	●	●	●	-	●
Nikko Manila Garden	170-220	Makati (M)	523	44	●	●	660	●	●	-	●	●
Heritage Hotel	170-190	Manila	460	7	●	●	574	●	●	-	●	●
Westin Philippine Plaza	165-245	Manila	625	53	●	●	1500	●	●	●	●	●
Manila Galeria Suites	160-170	Pasig	-	40	-	-	-	-	-	-	-	-
Holiday Inn Manila Pavilion	150-200	Ermita (M)	537	52	●	●	850	●	●	-	●	●
Mercure Philippine Village	150-190	Airport (M)	269	13	●	-	900	●	●	-	●	-
Shangri-La Mactan Isd Rst	145-280	Cebu	359	-	●	●	500	●	●	●	●	●
Hyatt Regency Hotel	130	Pasay (M)	232	33	●	●	400	●	●	-	-	●
Badian Island Beach	130-140	Cebu City	26	24	●	●	100	-	●	●	-	-
Sofitel Grand Boulevard	130-210	Manila	478	32	●	-	50	●	●	-	●	●
Traders Hotel	130-150	Pasay (M)	275	28	●	●	550	●	●	-	●	●
Admiral Hotel Manila	120-130	Manila	95	13	●	-	250	●	-	-	●	-
Manila Midtown Hotel	120-165	Manila	438	162	●	●	3000	●	●	●	●	●
Bayview Park Hotel	110	Manila	265	10	●	-	250	●	●	-	●	●
Century Imperial Palace Stes	100	Quezon (M)	-	204	●	-	1000	-	●	-	●	-
Cebu Plaza Hotel	95-110	Cebu City	398	22	●	-	800	●	●	●	●	●
Insular Century Hotel Davao	115-155	Davao City	152	5	●	-	1000	●	●	●	-	●
Puerto Azul Beach Htl	85-140	Ternate	593	75	●	●	300	●	●	●	●	●
Punte Baluarte Hotel	77-110	Batangas	177	3	●	●	260	●	●	●	-	●
Alegre Beach Resort	75	Cebu	40	-	●	-	-	-	●	●	●	●
Marbella Marine Beach	65-90	Ternate	84	6	●	-	240	-	●	●	●	-
Century Citadel Inn	60	Makati(M)	72	45	●	-	100	●	●	-	-	-
Magellan International	55-70	Cebu City	180	20	●	●	500	●	●	-	-	●
Midland Plaza Hotel	42-44	Manila	85	14	●	-	-	●	-	-	●	-

Hotels

Manila

Admiral Hotel Manila
2138 Roxas Blvd, Malate, Manila 1004
Tel: 521 0905; Fax: 522 2018;
E-mail: admiral@philonline.com.ph

City Center hotel facing Manila Bay, it has a Spanish style of architecture which withstood World War II. The hotel is rich in history and considered one of Manila's historical landmarks. World famous American and European personalities stayed in the hotel.

Accommodation & rates
110 single/double/twin US$ 120-140 (single occ. US$ 110-130); 13 suites US$ 200-500

Credit cards accepted:
Visa, Mastercard, Amex, JCB, Diners

Meeting & banqueting facilities
6 meeting/function rooms, capacity 10-350, with audio-visual equipment; largest reception 350 seated or 450 cocktail

Room services
Airconditioning, colour TV, direct-dial telephone (ext. in bathroom), hairdryer, laundry/valet service, minibar, safety deposit box, non-smoker bedrooms available

Business & other services
Business centre, express checkout, airport pickup, car parking & rental, travel centre, taxi service, barber shop/beauty salon, newsstand/shops

Sports & Recreation
Fitness centre/gym, outdoor swimming pool

Restaurants & Coffee Shops
The Mariner (100) - Filipino/International, open 0600-2330; *Kaigun* (30) - Japanese, open 0700-2300; *Lobby Café* (40) - Continental/snacks, open 24 hours

This ***Philippines Country Report*** is an extract from the 1997/8 Asia-Pacific Business Travel Guide, published by Priory Publications Ltd of PO Box 24 Brackley, Northants NN13 5FA, UK. Fax: (+44) 1280 850576

Bayview Park Hotel Manila ◯ C
1118 Roxas Boulevard, cnr United Nations Avenue, Manila
Tel: 526 1555; Fax: 521 2674

Century Citadel Inn Makati D
5007 P Burgos Street, Makati, Metro Manila
Tel: 897 2370; Fax: 897 2666

Century Park Sheraton A
PO Box 117, Vito Cruz, Cnr M Adriatico St, Malate
Tel: 522 1011; Tlx: 41085; Fax: 521 3413

Delta Sunrise Hotel ¶
Makati. Pre-opening office
Tel: 890 4433; Fax: 897 2225

Holiday Inn Manila Pavilion C
United Nations Avenue/Cnr Maria Orosa St, Ermita, Manila 1000
Tel: 526 1212; Fax: 522 3531

Hyatt Regency Hotel C
2702 Roxas Boulevard, Pasay
Tel: 833 1234; Tlx: 45327; Fax: 833 5913

Hotel Inter-Continental Manila ◯ B
1 Ayala Avenue, PO Box 731, D 3117
Tel: 815 9711; Tlx: 45005; Fax: 817 1330

Nikko Manila Garden Hotel B
4th Quadrant, Makati Commercial Centre
Tel: 801 4101; Tlx: 45883; Fax: 817 1862

The Heritage Hotel

Hotel Classification.
A *after name of hotel* = single room rate over US$200 per night; **B** = between US$ 150-200; **C** = between US$ 100-150;
D = between US$ 50-100; **E** = under US$50;
¶ = prices on application.
Number in brackets after restaurant name = no of seats. ◯ = PATA member.

Admiral Hotel

The Heritage Hotel, Manila
Roxas Blvd/cnr Edsa, Pasay City, Manila
Tel: 891 8888; Fax: 891 8833

Conveniently located on the Bay and in close proximity to major commercial districts, the hotel is only minutes' away from the Ninoy Aquino International Airport. The brand new 5-star Heritage Hotel Manila offers a total freedom from the bustling city life and is an ideal alternative from the daily traffic surrounding the Makati area. Amidst the beautiful sea front and bay fresh atmosphere, the hotel's exceptional facilities make it a perfect home for both business and holiday travellers.

Accommodation & rates
440 rooms. Single/double superior US$ 200-220; deluxe US$ 220-240; exec. room US$ 280; exec. suite US$ 400

Credit cards accepted:
Visa, Mastercard, Amex, Diners

Meeting & banqueting facilities
5 meeting/function rooms, capacity 20-500; audio-visual equipment available; largest reception 574 seated/600 cocktail

Room services
Airconditioning, colour TV, direct-dial telephone (ext. in bathroom), hairdryer, laundry/valet service, minibar, music/radio/alarm clock, safety deposit box, 24-hr room service, video films/cable TV, tea/coffee making in deluxe rooms/suites, non-smoker rooms, handicapped rooms

Business services
Business centre, executive floor, express checkout, airport pickup, translation service, car parking & rental, taxi service, travel centre, helicopter landing pad

Other services
Barber shop/hairdresser, beauty salon, newsstand/shops, doctor's clinic

Sports & Recreation
Fitness centre/gym, jacuzzi, massage, sauna, outdoor swimming pool, casino

Restaurants & Coffee Shops
Hua Ting (220) - Cantonese, open 1130-1500/1830-midnight; *Restaurant Riviera* (280) - Western/Oriental, open 24 hours; *L'Opera Lounge* (80) - PM tea/cocktails, evening ballroom dancing open 1000-0200

Overseas Sales Representatives
Anasazi Travel Resources (ATR), CDL International Hotels Ltd

Mandarin Oriental Manila
Makati Avenue, Makati 1226, Metro Manila
Tel: 893 3601; Tlx: 63756 MANDA PN;
Fax: 817 2472;
E-mail: bcentre@globe.com.ph

Located in the heart of Makati, a bustling city in the Metro Manila metropolis, and the country's primary financial and business district. Bounded by Makati and Senator Cil Puyat Avenues, Mandarin Oriental Manila is only 10 minutes' away from Ninoy Aquino International Airport and only a 5-minute bus ride to the shopping centres and entertainment area.

Accommodation & rates
464 rooms; single US$ 240-270, double/twin US$ 260-290; suite US$ 340-1900

Credit cards accepted: Visa, Mastercard, Amex, JCB, Bankamerikard, Diners

Meeting & banqueting facilities
10 meeting/function rooms, capacity 10-700, with audio-visual equipment; 635.5 sq m exhibition space; largest reception 600 seated or 1000 cocktail; theme parties, Chinese banquets and outside catering available

Room services
Airconditioning, colour TV (+pay per view), direct-dial tel-ephone (ext. in bathroom), facility for fax modem, fax in all suites, hairdryer, laundry/valet service, minibar, music/radio, safety deposit box, 24-hr room/meal service, non-smoker rooms, bidet, free newspapers, voicemail

Business & other services
24-hour business centre, executive floor, Cathay Pacific Citycheck express checkout, airport pickup, car (valet) parking, travel centre, taxi service, barber shop/hairdresser, beauty salon, guided tours, newsstand/shops, photo shop, flower shop, valet shop, disabled facilities

Sports & Recreation
Fitness centre, massage, sauna, swimming pool (outdoor)

Restaurants & Coffee Shops
The Brasserie (126) - Filipino/Asian/Western, open 0700-midnight; *Captain's Bar* (120) - Continental, open 0700-0200 (1000-0200 Sun); *Tin Hau* (170) - Chinese, open noon-1430 (1100-1500 Sun)/1830-2130; *Tivoli Grill* (90) - Californian/Asian, open 0700-1900 Mon-Fri/noon-1430 daily/1930-2230 daily; *Clipper Lounge* (60) - Asian, open 1100-2100 Mon-Fri; *Cake Shop & Delicatessen* (32), open 0700-1900; *Poolside* (100), Snacks, open 0600-2000.

Overseas Sales Representatives
Mandarin Oriental Sales Offices

The Manila Hotel
One Rizal Park, PO Box 307, 1099Manila
Tel: (63-2) 527 0011; Fax: (63-2) 527 0022-24; Internet: http://www.travelweb.com/summit.html

Built in 1912 and beautifully nestled among such sights as the historic Intramuros, Rizal Park and Manila Bay, the Manila Hotel houses the restored edifice completely restructured and refurbished in the same distinctive classic architecture as the original structure. With 510 luxurious rooms and suites, the hotel offers one executive floor at the Macarthur Club, eight speciality restaurants and two bars, a sports/health club complex, two tennis courts, one squash court, men's and ladies' gym, sauna, outdoor swimming pool, golf simulator and games room.

Accommodation & rates
510 rooms and suites. Single US$ 200-230; twin/double US$ 225-255; suite US$ 300-2000

Credit cards accepted:
Amex, Visa, Diners, Mastercard, JCB

Meeting & banqueting facilities
8 meeting/function rooms, capacity up to 1800 with audio-visual facilities; 135 sq m exhibition space; largest reception 1300 seated or 2000 cocktail

Room services
Airconditioning, remote controlled colour TV + satellite & pay TV, radio, direct-dial telephone (ext. in bathroom), hairdryer, laundry/valet service, minibar, in-room safe, trouser press, 24-hour room/meal service, Ving card electronic lock system

Business & other services
Business centre, express checkout, airport pickup, translation service, car rental, taxi service, barber shop/beauty salon, flower shop, newsstand/shops,

Sports & Recreation
Fitness centre/gym, indoor golf simulator, indoor games, jacuzzi, massage, sauna, swimming pool (outdoor), squash, tennis

Mandarin Oriental

Restaurants & Coffee Shops
Champagne Room - French speciality restaurant, open noon-1500/1900-2300; *Roma Ristorante Italiano* - Italian, open as above; *Ginza Japanese Restaurant* - open as above; *Maynila* - Ballroom dancing with buffet dinner, open Mon/Wed/Fri 1900-0100; *Cafe Ilang Ilang* - open 0600-0100; *Lobby Lounge* - Businessman's lunch/cocktails/snacks/live music; *Pool Bar* - refreshing drinks

Overseas Sales Representatives:
Summit International Hotels, Utell, Seahong Air Travel, World Travel Consultants

Manila Diamond Hotel B
Roxas Blvd/Cnr Dr J Quintos St, 1000
Tel: 526 2211; Tlx: 62791; fax: 526 2255

Manila Galeria Suites B
Ortigas Ave, Pasay City
Tel: 633 7111; Fax: 633 2824

Manila Midtown Hotel C
Pedro Gil Street, PO Box 4252, Manila
Tel: 521 7001; Tlx: 27797 MNLMID PH;
Fax: 522 2629

Mercure Hotel Millenium Plaza C
Makati Ave/Cnr Eduque St, Makati 1200
Tel: 899 4718; Fax: 899 4755

Midland Plaza Hotel E
M Adriatico Street, Ermita
Tel: 525 9003; Tlx: 64018; Fax: 521 8122

New World Hotel A
Esperanza St/Cnr Makati Ave, Makati
Tel: 811 6888; Fax: 811 6777

The Peninsula Manila A
Cnr Ayala/Makati Avenues, Makati
Tel: 812 3456; Tlx: 22507; Fax: 815 4825/

Shangri-La's Edsa Plaza Hotel A
Garden Way, Ortigas Center, Mandaluyong
Tel: 633 8888; Tlx: 62616; Fax: 631 1067

Shangri-La Hotel, Manila A
Cnr Ayala/Makati Avenues, Makati
Tel: 813 8888; Fax: 813 5499

Sofitel Grand Boulevard Hotel C
(formerly Silahis International)
1990 Roxas Boulevard, Manila
Tel: 526 8588; Fax: 524 2526/526 0111

*Photographs normally refer to the properties whose details **follow** them. Alternatively a photograph may appear **within** a full entry.*

PHILIPPINES - Hotels

Mercure Hotel Philippine Village Airport Manila
Nayong Pilipino Complex, Pasay City
Tel: 833 8080; Fax: 833 8248

The Mercure Hotel Philippine Village Airport Manila is Manila's only airport hotel. It is conveniently located just two kms from the Ninoy Aquino International Airport (NAIA) and less than 3 kms from the Domestic Airport.

Accommodation & rates
269 single/double/twin US$ 150-190 9single occ. US$ 130-170); 13 suites US$ 240-282

Credit cards accepted:
Visa, Mastercard, Amex

Meeting & banqueting facilities
8 meeting/function rooms, capacity 30-700, with audio-visual equipment; largest reception 900 seated or 1100 cocktail

Room services
Airconditioning, colour TV, direct-dial telephone, laundry/valet service, minibar, music/radio/alarm clock, trouser press, 24-hr room/meal service, non-smoker rooms

Business services
Business centre, airport pickup, car parking & rental, travel centre, taxi service

Other services
Barber shop/hairdresser, beauty salon, newsstand/ shops

Sports & Recreation
Fitness centre, massage, sauna, swimming pool (outdoor)

Restaurants & Coffee Shops
Saranggola (120) - International Coffee Shop, open 24 hours; *Kagetsu* (150) - Japanese + Sushi Bar, open 1100-1430/ 1800-2230; *Par Avion* (30) - Bar, open 1700-0100

Overseas Sales Representatives
Accor Hong Kong Regional Office

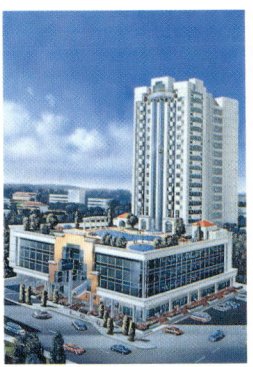

The Pan Pacific Manila
(Opening December 1997)
Pre-opening office: Adriatico Consortium Inc. Cnr M Adriatico & Gen Malvar Sts, Malate, Manila
Tel: 526 6515; Fax: 526 6503
E-mail: amcburnie@compass.com.ph

A business hotel set in the Spanish-style international sector of Manila Bay. A new concept of hotel.

Accommodation & rates
250 rooms. Rates to be announced

Credit cards accepted:
All major

Meeting & banqueting facilities
4 meeting/function rooms, capacity 300, with audio-visual equipment

Room services
Airconditioning, colour TV, direct-dial telephone (ext. in bathroom), hairdryer, laundry/valet service, minibar, safety deposit box, 24-hr room/meal service

Business & other services
Business centre, executive floor, express checkout, car parking, taxi service, newsstand/shops

Sports & Recreation
Fitness centre, massage, sauna, swimming pool (outdoor), spa

Restaurants & Coffee Shops
Approx. 30 different food and beverage outlets available at the Podium Block

Overseas Sales Representatives
Pan Pacific Hotels & Resorts Worldwide; SRS Steigenberger Reservation Service

Traders Hotel   C
3001 Roxas Boulevard, Pasay City 1305
Tel: 521 7961; Fax: 522 3985

Westin Philippine Plaza   B
CCP Complex, Roxas Boulevard, Manila
Tel: 832 0701; Fax: 832 3485

Hotel Classification. **A** *after name of hotel = single room rate over US$200 per night;* **B** *= between US$ 150-200;* **C** *= between US$ 100-150;* **D** *= between US$ 50-100;* **E** *= under US$50;* ¶ *= prices on application.*

Other areas

Badian Island Beach Hotel   C
Badian Island, Badian **Cebu**
Tel: (32) 254 6309/253 6452; Fax: (32) 253 3385/254 7429

Cebu Plaza Hotel   D
Nivel Hills, Lahug, **Cebu City**
Tel: 231 1231; Tlx: 24861; Fax: 312071

Century Imperial Palace Suites   C
Timog Corner, Tomas Morato Street, **Quezon City**
Tel: (2) 897 2370; Fax: (2) 897 2403

Insular Century Hotel Davao
PO Box 144, Lanang, 8000 **Davao City**
Tel: (82) 234 3050; Fax: (82) 62959
E-mail: ichdavao@weblinq.com

Insular Century Hotel Davao is a business resort hotel with a garden setting nestled along the Gulf of Davao and offering excellent service, first class amenities and tropical ambience.

Accommodation & rates
152 single/double/twin, US$ 135-175 (single occ $ 115-155); 5 suites, US$ 270-655, Inclusive of 10% value added tax

Credit cards accepted:
Amex, Visa, Diners, Mastercard, All major...

Meeting & banqueting facilities
7 meeting/function rooms, capacity 40-600, with audio-visual facilities; largest reception 1000 at garden banquet.

Room services
Airconditioning, cable TV, direct-dial telephone, hairdryer, laundry/valet service, minibar, safety deposit box, trouser press, babysitter, 24-hr room/meal service,

Business & other services
Business centre, airport pickup, car rental & parking, travel centre + tours, taxi service, newsstand, curio shops

Sports & Recreation
Golf (pitch & putt), jogging track, swimming pool (outdoor), tennis, jetty, basketball

Restaurants & Coffee Shops
Orchid Cafe (80) - International, open 0600-0100; *La Parilla* (80) - Seafood/grills, open 1900-2300; *Vinta Music Bar* (50) - open 1700-0100; *Badjao Pool Bar* (20) - Tropical drinks/snacks, open 0800-1900.

Overseas Sales Representatives:
Aviation Tourism International, Delton Reservations System, Utell, Century International Hotels

PHILIPPINES - Hotels/Restaurants/Map

Eurasia Holiday Resort D
Badian Island, Badian, **Cebu**
Tel: 61396/74611; Tlx: 6288 BADIAN PU

Club Panoly Resort D
Punta Bunga, Yapac, **Boracay Island**
Tel: 536 0682; Tlx: 66064; Fax: 586928

Magellan International Hotel ◯ E
Gogordo Avenue, Lahug, **Cebu** City
Tel: 74613; Tlx: 24729; Fax: 812 6958

Marbella Marina Beach Resort D
Beach Front, Ternate, **Cavite**
Tel: 815 8385; Tlx: 63457

Novotel Puerto Azul Resort ◯ D
PO Box 7773 NAIA Airmail Exchange
Center, **Pasay City**, Ternate, Cavite
Tel: (63-2) 525 9248; Fax: (63-2) 536 1584

Punta Baluarte Hotel D
Calatagan, **Batangas**
Tel: 818 3185; Tlx: 14545; Fax: 819 5867

Shangri-La's Mactan Island Resort B
PO Box 86, Punta Engano, Lapu-Lapu City,
Mactan Island, **Cebu** Tel: (63-32) 310288;
Tlx: 62644; Fax: 311688

Restaurants

Eating out is very important to the Filipino buisnessman and restaurants are cheap by Western standards. Below we give a small selection of restaurants in Manila which are suitable for business entertaining, accept credit cards, and where prior booking is advisable.

Abelardos (French/Continental)
Westin Philippine Plaza Hotel, Roxas Blvd.
Tel: 832 0701

Au Bon Vivant (French)
1133 L. Guerrero, Ermita St. Tel: 503405

Baron's Table (European)
Holiday Inn, 3001 Roxas Boulevard.
Tel: 597961

Benkay (Japanese)
Manila Garden Hotel, Makati Commercial Centre. Tel: 857911

Champagne Room (French)
Manila Hotel, Rizal Park. Tel: 470011

Chesa (Swiss)
Peninsula Hotel, Makati Avenue.
Tel: 8193456

Hua Ting (Cantonese)
Heritage Hotel, Roxas Blvd/Cnr Edsa,
Pasay City. Tel: 891 8888

La Taverna (Itaian)
1602 Adriatico. Tel: 585372

L'Hirondelle (International)
Mandarin Hotel, Makati. Tel: 816 3601

Maynila (Filipino)
Manila Hotel, Rizal Park. Tel: 527 0011

Nielson Tower (European/Filipino)
7929 Makati Avenue,i. Tel: 817 1180

Old Manila (European/Filipino)
Peninsula Hotel, Makati Avenue, Makati.
Tel: 819 3456

Pavilion Court (Chinese)
Manila Pavilion, United Nations Avenue,
Ermita. Tel: 522 2911

Prince Albert (European)
Inter-Continental Hotel, Tel: 815 9711

Szechuan House (Chinese)
Aloha Hotel, 2150 Roxas Bvd. Tel: 599061

Sud (European)
Century Park Sheraton Hotel, Vito Cruz/
Cnr. M. Adriatico St, Malate. Tel: 522 1011

La Tasca (Spanish)
Legaspi Street, Makati. Tel: 868586

Tempura-Misono (Japanese)
Hyatt Regency Hotel, 2702 Roxas Blvd.
Tel: 831 2611

Tin Hau (Chinese)
Mandarin Oriental Hotel, Makati Avenue
Tel: 816 3601

Map by David Burles. Reproduced by kind permission of Columbus Press Limited

Philippines Airline Departures & Offices

Below is a list of departures and frequencies from Ninoy Aquino International Airport to the destinations in bold type. Figures in brackets refer to the days of the week. (2,4,6) therefore means that departures to that destination take place on a Tuesday (the second day of the week), a Thursday and a Saturday. Departures correct as at February 1997. Only direct flights, without change, are shown.
Airline abbreviation Codes. **AF** = Air France; **AZ** = Alitalia; **BA** = British Airways; **BI** = Royal Brunei Airlines; **BR** = EVA Airways; **CI** = China Airlines; **CO** = Continental Airlines; **CX** = Cathay Pacific; **CZ** = China Southern Airlines; **EK** = Emirates; **GA** = Garuda Indonesia; **GF** = Gulf Air; **JL** = Japan Airlines; **KE** = Korean Air; **KL** = KLM; **KU** = Kuwait Airways; **LH** = Lufthansa; **MH** = Malaysian Airlines; **MS** = Malaysian Airlines; **NW** = Northwest Airlines; **OZ** = Asiana Airlines; **ON** = Air Nauru; **PK** = Pakistan Int'l Airlines; **PR** = Philippine Airlines; **PX** = Air Niugini; **QF** = Qantas; **Q7** = Qatar Airways; **SQ** = Singapore Airlines; **SR** = Swissair; **SV** = Saudia; **TG** = Thai International; **UA** = United Airlines; **VN** = Vietnam Airlines; **5J** = Cebu Pacific Air; **8L** = Grand Int'l Airways.

Departures

Abu Dhabi (AUH)
PR (1,2,4) GF (6)
Amsterdam (AMS)
KL (1,3)
Bacolod (BCD)
PR (daily) 5J (daily)
Baguio (BCD)
PR (daily)
Bahrain (BAH)
GF (4)
Bandar Seri B (BWN)
PR (2,4,6,7) BI (1,2,3,5,6)
Bangkok (BKK)
MS (3) PR (1,2,3,4,5,6) KL (3) PK (2,6) TG,LH (daily) AZ (2,5)
Beijing (PEK)
CZ (3,6)
Boston (BOS)
NW (daily)
Brisbane (BNE)
PR (5) QF (4)
Bu Suanga (USU)
GX (daily)
Butuan (BU)
PR (1,3,5,7)
Cagayan d'Oro (CGY)
PR, 5J (daily) 8L (1,3,5,6,7)
Cairo (CAI)
MS (3) PR (3)
Catician (MPH)
GX (daily)
Cebu (CEB)
5J,PR,8L (daily)
Chicago (CHI)
UA,NW (daily)
Cotabato (CBO)
PR (daily)
Culion (CUJ)
GX (6)
Cuyo (CYO)
GX (1,3,5)
Davao (DVO)
5J,8L,PR (daily)
Dhahran (DHA)
PR (1,3) SV (2,5,7)
Dipolog (DPL)
PR (1,2,4,5,6)
Doha (DOH)
GF (3) Q7 (6,7)
Dubai (DXB)
PR (1,3,4,7) EK (1,2,4,6,7)
Dumaguete (DGT)
PR (daily)
Frankfurt (FRA)
PR (1,2,3,4,5,6)
Fukuoka (FUK)
PR (2,4,7)
Gem Santos (GES)
PR (1,2,4,5,6)
Guam (GUM)
CO (daily) ON (2,3)
Guangzhou (CAN)
CZ (3)
Ho Chi Minh (SGN)
VN,PR (2,4,6) VN (1,5)
Hong Kong (HKG)
CX, PR (daily) AF (1,2,4,5) BA (1,3,4,6) SR (4,7) CP,8L (3,5,7)
Honolulu (HNL)
PR (1,2,3,5,7)
Iloilo (ILO)
PR (daily) 5J (daily)
Jakarta (JRT)
PR (daily) GA (3,5)
Jeddah (JED)
SV (1,4,7) PR (1,4)
Kalibo (KLO)
PR (daily)
Kaohsiung (KHH)
CI (daily) PR (1,3,4,5,6,7)
Karachi (KHI)
PK (2,6)
Koror (ROR)
CO (2,4,6)
Kota Kinabalu (BKI)
MH (1,3,5) PR (2,4,6,7)
Kuala Lumpur (KUL)
MH (daily) PR (2,4,6,7) KL (6)
Kuching (KCH)
MH (1,4)
Kuwait (KWI)
PR/KU (1,3,4,6)
Laoag (LAO)
PR (2,4,5,6)
Legaspi (LGP)
PR (daily)
London (LHR)
PR (1,3,5,7)
Los Angeles (LAX)
NW (daily) PR (daily)
Lubang
GX (3,7)
Melbourne (MEL)
PR (2,3,4,6,7)
Muscat (MCT)
GF (1,5)
Naga (WNP)
PR (daily)
Nagoya (NGA)
JL (1,5)
Nauru Island (INU)
ON (2,3)
New York (EWR)
Pr (2,4,5,6)
Osaka (OSA)
TG,NW (daily) PR (3,6)
Paris (CDG)
AF (1,2,4,5) PR (2,4,6)
Port Moresby (POM)
PX/PR (1,5)
Pohnpei (PNI)
ON (2,3)
Pto Princesa (PPS)
PR (daily)
Pusan (PUS)
PR (4,7)
Riyadh (RUH)
PR (2,4,7) SV (daily)
Roxas (RXS)
PR (daily)
Saipan (SPN)
CO (1,2,4,6)
San Francisco (SFO)
PR,UA (daily)
San Jose Phil (SJI)
PR (daily)
Seoul (SEL)
KE,UA,OZ (daily) PR (1,3,4,5,6,7)
Singapore (SIN)
PR (daily) SQ (daily)
Sydney (SYD)
PR (daily) QF (3,6)
Tacloban (TAC)
PR,5J (daily) 8L (1,3,5,6,7)
Tagbilaran (TAG)
PR (daily)
Taipei (TPE)
CI,PR,BR (daily) MH (3,4,6,7) 8L (2,4,6,7)
Tokyo (NRT)
MS (3) JL,NW,PR (daily) PK (2,6)
Toronto (YTO)
CO (3,5,7,8)
Tuguegarao (TUG)
PR (daily)
Vancouver (YVR)
CP (daily) PR (2,4,5,6)
Virac (VRC)
PR (daily)
Xiamen
CZ (2,6,7) PR (1,2,4,5)
Zamboanga (ZAM)
PR (daily)
Zurich (ZRH)
SR (4,7)

Airline Offices

on line carriers only

Air France
7th floor, Century Tower, 100 Tordesilla Street, Sacedo Village, Makati, Manila. Tel: 815 6790
British Airways
Ground floor, Filipino Merchants Building, 135 Dela Rosa Street, Legaspi Village, Makati, Manila. Tel: 817 4571/817 0361-4
China Air Lines (CAL)
2nd floor, Manila Pavilion Hotel, UN Avenue, Ermita. Tel: 590086-89
Cathay Pacific
Gammon Centre, 126 Alfaro Street, Salcedo Village, Makati. Tel: 815-9401/815 9417
Garuda
Ground floor, Manila Peninsula Hotel, Makati Avenue, Manila. Tel: 862458/862265
Japan Air Lines (JAL)
Hotel Nikko Manila Garden, EDSA Cor, Pasay Rd, Makati Tel: 810 9776
KLM
8th floor, Athenaeum Building, 160 Alfaro Street, Salcedo Village, Manila. Tel: 815 4790
Korean Air
Ground floor, LPL Plaza, 124 Alfaro Street, Salcedo Village, Makati, Manila. Tel: 815-9261
Lufthansa
Legaspi Park View Condominium, 134 Legaspi Street, Legaspi Village, Makati. Tel: 810 4596/810 5089
Malaysian Airlines
Ground floor, Legaspi Towers 300, Roxas Boulevard, Manila Tel: 571596
Pakistan International Airlines
3110 Domestic Airport Rd, Pasay City. Tel: 832 2731/832 2732
Philippine Airlines
Grd Fl, Colonnade Bldg, Carlos Palanca St, Legaspi Vill., Makati Tel: 818 0502
Qantas
Ground floor, China Bank Building, 8745 Paseo de Roxas, Makati, Metro Manila Tel: 815-9491
Swissair
2nd Fl, Country Space 1 Bldg, Sen. Gil Puyat Ave, Makati Tel: 818 8351
Thai International
2nd Fl, Country Space 1 Bldg, Sen. Gil Puyat Ave, Makati Tel: 815 8421
United Airlines
Pacific Star Bldg, Makati Ave, Makati. Tel: 818 5421

Major Exhibitions & Conventions in the Philippines 1997/8

Date*	Exhibition	Venue	Organiser
May 15-18	**Horticulture and Agricultural Exhibition**		HQLink
June 18-21	**BIO-Search 97** - Natural and organic products.	PTTC	CITEM
July 9-12	**Mining Philippines 97** - Int'l Mining & Minerals Recovery	WTC	PIEC
July 9-12	**Elenex Philippines 97** - Int'l Electrical Equipment & Power generation exhibition	WTC	PIEC
July 9-12	**Building Services Philippines 97** - Int'l Building Services, equipment and products exhibition	WTC	PIEC
Sept 17-20	**Powertrends 2000** - Power Systems & Energy	WTC	INTERFAMA
Oct 9-12	**FAME** Gifts & Houseware Market Week - gifts & decorative accessories, houseware, domestics and textiles etc.	WTC	CITEM
Nov 5-8	**FOODTEC** - Food Processing & Agricultural Technology		BITF
Nov 5-8	**INTERPLAS** - Plastics Packing & Printing Exhibition		BITF
1998 Feb 18-21	**Food & Hotel Philippines 98** - Int'l Hotel, Catering Equipment, Food and Drink Exhibition	WTC	PIEC
March 11-15	**ProPak Philippines 98** - Int'l Packaging & Food Processing Machinery, Equipment & Materials, & Printing for Packaging	WTC	PIEC
April 29-2	**Building Materials Philippines 98** - Int'l exhibition for building materials, equipment and products	WTC	PIEC

Venues
PTTC = Philippines Trade Training Center, CCP Complex, Manila.
World Trade Centre, Manila.

Organisers
BITF = Business & Industrial Trade Fairs Ltd, 4/F Amtel Building, 144-148 Des Voex Road Central, Hong Kong. Tel: (286) 52633; Fax: (286) 61770
CITEM = Center for International Trade Expositions and Missions, International Trade Centre, Roxas Boulevard, Sen. Gil Puyat Avenue, 1300 Pasay City, Metro Manila, Tel: 833 1284/833 1277; Fax: 832 3965
HQ Link = HQ Link Philippines Inc, Unit B8/F Cacho Gonzalez Bldg, 101 Aguirre St, Legaspi Village, Makati, Metro Manila, tel: 810 3694; fax: 815 3152.
INTERFAMA = 1 Maritime Square, 09-36, World Trade Centre, Singapore 0409 Tel: (276) 6933; Fax: (27) 6811
PCOC = Philippine Congress Organizing Center, 2/F Physicians Tower, 533 United Nations Avenue, Ermita, Metro Manila, tel: 521 4892; fax: 522 1090.
PIEC = PIEC Inc (The Montgomery Network) Units 908 & 909, 9th Floor, PS Bank Tower, Sen Gil Puyat Avenue, Makati CIty 1200, Metro Manila. Tel: (2) 759 3229/30/50; Fax: (2) 759 3228

What's the link between business and the Asia Pacific?

BRITISH AIRWAYS
The world's favourite airline

http://www.british-airways.com

Bradt Publications
in Asia Pacific

* thoroughly researched * regularly updated
* getting there * getting around * maps
* hotels, restaurants, nightlife
* red tape * media & communications * language
* background information
* sports, culture, places to visit

COUNTRY GUIDES

Guide to Burma   *Nicholas Greenwood*
ISBN 1 897323 21 6   £12.95   304 pages, 40 colour photos
"A rare travel book. ... I highly recommend it."   *John Pilger*

Guide to Laos & Cambodia   *John R Jones*
ISBN 1 898323 22 4   £10.95   352 pages, colour photos
"Everything about it works superbly"   Reader's letter

Guide to Philippines   *Stephen Mansfield*   (May 1997)
ISBN 1 898323 58 5   £11.95   304 pages, colour photos
A complete guide to all the main islands and island groups

Guide to Vietnam   *John R Jones*
ISBN 1 898323 11 9   £11.95   422 pages, colour photos
Everything from history and hotels to festivals and pagodas

RAIL GUIDES

Australia & New Zealand by Rail   *Colin Taylor*
ISBN 1 898323 46 1   £10.95   224 pages, colour photos

India by Rail   *Royston Ellis*   (3rd edition: March 1997)
ISBN 1 898323 49 6   £11.95   256 pages, colour photos

Sri Lanka by Rail   *Royston Ellis*
ISBN 0 946983 77 1   £10.95   240 pages

For a fast and efficient mail order service, contact Bradt Publications
Dept AP, 41 Nortoft Road, Chalfont St Peter, Bucks SL9 0LA, England
Tel/fax: + 44 1494 873478

PHILIPPINES

DAVAO
The Best of the Islands

DEPARTMENT OF TOURISM T.M. Kalaw Street, Rizal Park, Manila, Philippines, P.O. Box 3451 Mal., Phil., Tel: 523-8411 • Fax: 521-7374 • Cable: DEPTOUR • Telex: 40183 DEPTOUR PM 66412 MOT PN 40435BT PROM PM

PHILIPPINE CONVENTION & VISITORS CORPORATION 4th Floor, Suite 10-17, Legaspi Towers 300, Roxas Blvd., Manila, Phillipines P.O. Box EA-459 Tel.: 525-9318 to 32 • Fax: (632) 5216165

LONDON Embassy of the Philippines, Department of Tourism, 17 Albemarle St., London W1X 4LX United Kingdom • Tel: (0171) 499-5443 / 499-5652 • Fax: (0171) 499-5772

COUNTRY REPORT
SINGAPORE '97

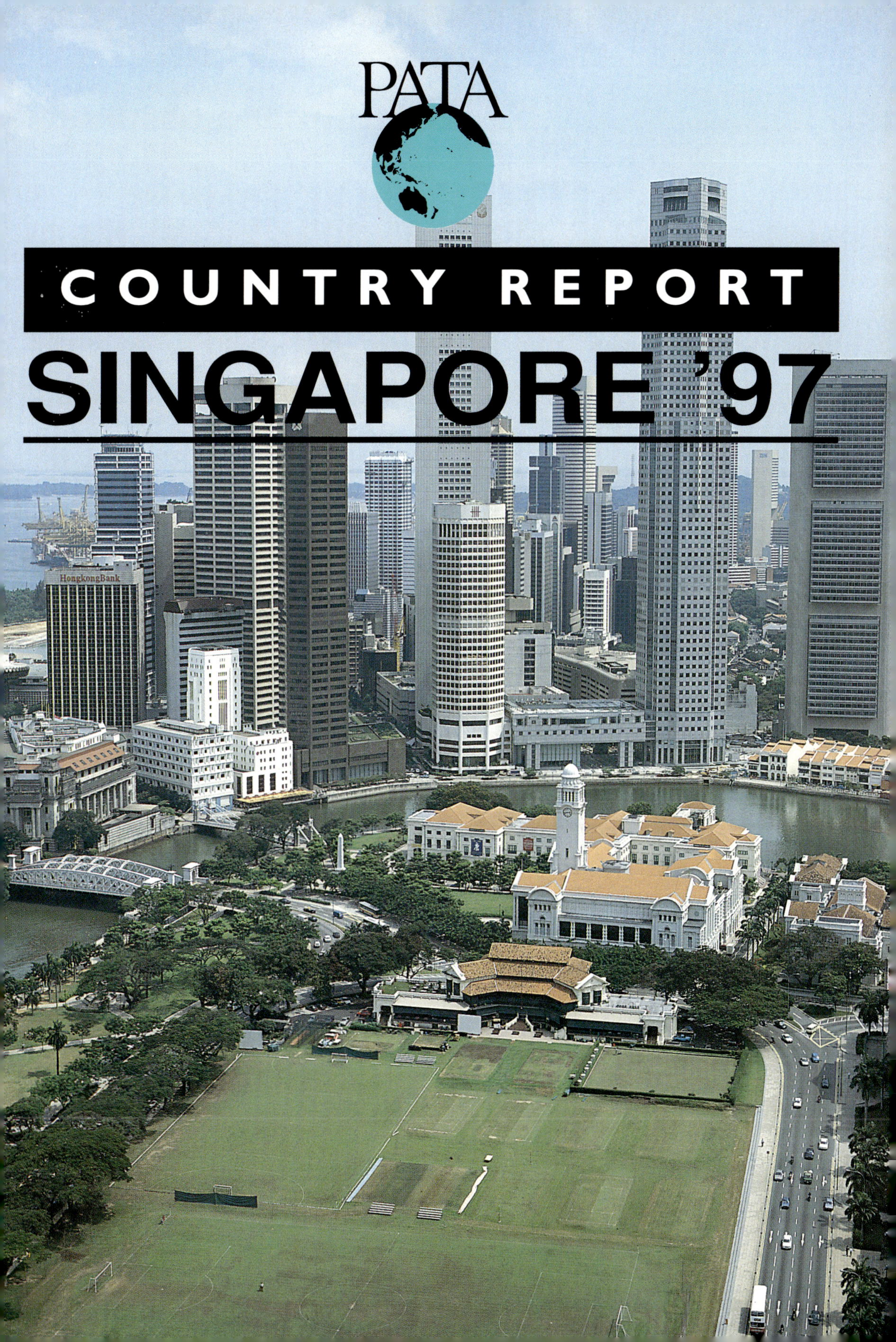

Singapore

Business Scene

General Climate

Singapore was made for doing business. Devoid of any natural resources of its own, the phenomenal economic success of the republic has been built on free trade and largely unfettered foreign investment.

Despite being reprimanded by the US in early 1997 for allegedly making politically incorrect pre-election comments, the government's strict guidance of citizens in its drive for nationhood and clean living in no way infringes on a business climate that is open, competitive and free of corruption.

Telecommunications and utilities are among very few sectors not yet fully open to investment and the Economic Development Board offers a variety of tax incentives and assistance programmes for the development of pioneer industries.

The EDB has met with particular success in recent years with an incentive programme to attract increased production of the arts, including films, in Singapore in line with some easing of formerly stringent censorship laws and a policy of creating new and diversified industries - both within Singapore itself and in neighbouring countries.

As a port city with six free trade zones for storage and the re-export of dutiable and controlled goods, plus advanced air and sea containerisation facilities, Singapore is widely mooted as a major regional trade successor to Hong Kong after 1997.

Singapore's advanced general infrastructure has earned it an unmatched reputation among the international business community as the place in Asia that 'works'. The city state is compact, safe and easy to get around, with good transport, comfortable hotels, widespread leisure facilities, offices that open on time and trained, efficient staff.

Less attractive to these same travellers, although increasingly less so, are Singapore's still strict censorship laws and codes governing personal behaviour, including the banning of chewing gum and imposition of heavy fines for jaywalking, littering, smoking anywhere but in the open air and failing to flush the lavatory. Singaporeans appreciate the common sense behind authoritative government dictats which have earned them not only one of the highest standards of living in Asia with corresponding lifestyles, but also a clean, responsible and disciplined society.

Voicing genuine admiration for the Singaporean 'way' is appreciated, but visitors should keep criticisms to themselves. With 6-10% annual economic growth that barely faltered through world recession, Singaporeans are proud of their achievements and can appear arrogant and dismissive of other, less successful but more liberal attitudes.

Business etiquette

The code for doing business is western and formal in everything but dress. In respect of the hot, humid climate, standard business attire is shirt and tie or blouse and skirt.

Unlike elsewhere in Asia, small talk is an unnecessary precursor to getting down to business. Shake hands, shoot from the hip and expect straightforward, no-nonsense answers. Bribery is taboo, with severe penalties imposed for corruption. But business entertaining is popular, mostly in hotels and restaurants and sometimes in private homes, when a small, inexpensive gift is appreciated.

Currently, Singaporeans are addicted to fun pubs, discos and karaoke lounges. Going along with business partners could help smooth negotiations but is not imperative.

Eating is a Singaporean preoccupation and entertaining at a good restaurant is an acceptable alternative. The choice of restaurants and cuisines, and general quality of food, is among the finest in Asia. Seafood is a particular speciality. Another acceptable alternative for business talks outside the office is golf. Singapore has 18 courses and most decision makers belong to one or more clubs. For those not interested in sightseeing (old colonial buildings, botanic gardens and theme parks) time off can be spent in or around the inexpensive resorts of Johor Bahru, across the causeway in Malaysia, or in Batam or Bintan islands, each a short hydrofoil ride south of Singapore in Indonesia's Riau Islands.

Tourism Update

General Developments

Singapore's inbound travel business is strong and, despite the country's small size, the number of visitor arrivals makes it one of the three largest destinations in the region - by most systems of measuring - after Hong Kong and Thailand.

The destination has recorded steady growth in visitor arrivals over most of the past five years, and the total increased 3.5% in 1995 to 7,137,255. Previously, the Singapore Tourist Promotion Board presented all arrivals from Asean as a grand total, but it now breaks out the separate market sources. This shows that arrivals from Indonesia topped 1 million in 1995. Before this, analysts had estimated that Malaysia was the largest Asean market.

Other fast-growing sources that year were Taiwan and Korea. Japan, still the largest market source, increased 6.3% to 1,179,007 in 1995, with Indonesia close behind, increasing 4.5% to 1,050,181. Malaysia was up 4.3% to 681,164 (this excludes land-based travel, which would take the total into tens of millions), Taiwan 10.3% to 563,333, and Korea 21.2% to 350,999. The average length of stay for all visitors is approximately 2.9 days.

1996 saw a 2.2% increase in arrivals to 7.3 million. Japan, the main source, was down 0.6% to 1.172 mn; UK (8th source) was down by 8.3% to 288,500; Taiwan

(4th) down by 6.2% to 528,500 visitors but there were healthy increases from Malaysia + 3% to 700,750, South Korea (5th) +9.5% to 384,500, USA (6th source) +8.2% to 374,000, Hong Kong (9th) +3.1% to 288,500; China (11th) + 12.2% to 226,700 and India (12th) + 8.3% to 204,200.

Singapore has worked hard to enhance its tourism product, and this was expected to maintain growth. At the start of 1996, the STPB targetted a total of 10 million visitor arrivals in 2000. The STPB's budget is approximately US$82 million.

One example of the product change is Suntec City, a major complex comprising conference and exhibition centre, hotels, offices and other commercial outlets. It is now attracting good international exhibition and conference business. Some of the attractions added recently include a 37-metre Merlion Viewing tower, Wonder Golf theme park, Volcano Land, Fantasy Island water park, all on Sentosa island, plus Chijmes (sic), a convent square converted into a shopping and entertainment complex but with cultural enhancements.

A further massive new 60,000 sq metre exhibition centre is planned for Changi, near the airport - first phase due to open in 1999 - and will be the biggest such venue in South-East Asia. Phase 2 with a further 40,000 sq m will open at a later stage.

There are also plans to develop the Singapore river into a world-class destination. 13 new hotel sites have been designated for opening by the year 2000 and two major new shopping centres opened early 1997 - Riverside Point and Central Mall.

Airlines

Despite the small size of the country and its population, Singapore's aviation sector is among the biggest in Asia Pacific and the world by some measures. The country's airline, Singapore Airlines, is the largest in Asia Pacific in terms of revenue passenger kilometres (the number of kilometres travelled by passengers) on international routes, although the next two airlines, Cathay Pacific and Japan Airlines, are very close in terms of size and the country's Changi airport is in the top three in terms of international passengers, just behind Hong Kong and Tokyo Narita. This position is complemented by the country's increasingly-liberal aviation policies, which improve the chances that Singapore will capture growth from and into the Southeast Asia region.

By early 1997 SIA had ordered 77 Boeing 777s - 34 on firm order and the remainder as options at a cost of US$1.7 billion.

Singapore Airlines also has a subsidiary, Silk Air, which operates regional flights into a number of regional destinations - tourist and business. Silk's growth, in terms of new routes, is related to pla
airline, although currently it has been operating only shorthaul routes.

Singapore also has another airline - Region Air. Although the company was originally planned to operate as a regional airline in competition with Singapore Airlines and/or Silk Air, it was licensed only for some charter flights. It also leases aircraft out to other airlines in the region.

Even with this other airline activity, Singapore Airlines continues to increase its traffic steadily -- its preferred rate of growth is 7-8% annually. In 1995 it sold more than 10 million seats, growing 8.5% to reach 10.8 million. And RPKs increased 7.7% to 48.4 billion. In the same period Silk Air sold 642,000 seats, and 801 million RPKs.

The number of travellers passing through Singapore's Changi airport topped 20 million in 1994. And by 1995, the international passenger total at the airport had increased 7.2% to 23,196,240. The airport is important for regional growth, and has been expanded to ensure there is always sufficient capacity for the expansion of airline flights. It is one of the few airports in the region that is not capacity-constrained. At the end of 1996, the decision was taken to add a third terminal at the airport, with opening planned for 2005. This will have a capacity for 20 million passengers annually, as the two existing terminals, making 60 million total.

Hotels

Singapore's hotels have a good reputation for high standards and reasonable rates. There has not been a rapid increase in hotel rooms in Singapore over the past five years, but now more are being added.

In what is almost the regular business cycle for hotel development in Asia, Singapore's last growth period was in the second half of the 1980s, and there is due to be another with double-digit growth in hotel rooms starting in 1996 and running for at least the following two or three years. In 1995, the total number of rooms increased 5.3% to 28,544.

Occupancy in 1996 increased from 75.6% in 1995 to 80.7% in 1996, according to *Travel Business Analyst* at US$130 average room rate in four-star hotels, and 70% at US$148 in five-star hotels. This compares with about 70% at US$140 in 1995 for four-star hotels, and just under 70% at US$165 for five-star hotels. Most of the difference in terms of rate is a result of the strength of the Singapore dollar, which meant that in US dollar terms, there was a drop in 1996.

Several important hotels have opened in the past two years - they include the Inter-Continental, Ritz-Carlton, Negara, and Traders (part of the Shangri-La group). In addition, the Marriott was opened following refurbishing of the hotel previously known as Dynasty.

Other new openings in 1997 include the Conrad International with 500 rooms; the Merchant Court (managed by Raffles International) with 476 rooms and the Grand Plaza. Due 1997/98 are the Kings Centre with 560 rooms; New World with 520 rooms; Rockman's Inn with 110 rooms; and a 541-room extension to the Cockpit.

Already becoming considered as part of Singapore as a destination, is the Bintan Resort project - on the nearby Indonesian island of Bintan, only 30 minutes by fast ferry from Singapore. There is a substantial Singaporean ownership of the resort, and the first two hotels opened there are Singapore-based. In 1996 a local company, part of Liang Court, added a hotel division. Named Regalis, there will be two divisions, Regalis Court is three-star, Regalis Park is four-star. The emphasis will be on three-star hotels, and the target is to have 15 hotels open by 2000.

What to see

After years of criticism from purists for ripping out the heart of old Singapore, the authorities have finally acted to halt the destruction of the city and encourage conservation and restoration.

1991 marked a turning point and a spruced up Raffles Hotel threw open its doors to both guests and tourists in September. It is set to regain its position as one of the island's top attractions. Its faded elegance is no more and visitors will find many of the hotel's favourite bars and restaurants meticulously refurbished.

Anyone who visited Singapore before demolition of the much-loved, though slightly seedy, Bugis Street will welcome the government's attempts to revive the outdoor bars and small eating places in the area. But it is doubtful whether it will be able to recapture the area's charming decadence of old.

In any case, new sights are on offer. One of the latest is the S$80 million Haw Par Villa - a kind of Chinese mythological theme-park. Entry fee is S$16 (S$10 children).

Underwater World and the Tang Dynasty Village - Asia's largest historical theme park - opened in November 1991 with further attractions - the Asian Village and Sentosa Riverboat- added in 1992. The S$100 million Village covers a 12-hectare site is a recreation of the ancient city of Chang-An - capital of the Chinese Tang Dynasty of 1,300 years ago. The Village is located in Jurong (near the famous Bird Park), about 20 minutes from the central business district. The entrance fee is US$8-10 per person

The Malay Village re-opened after refurbishment in January 1994. The revived Clarke Quay Festival Village, with 176 retail outlets and 17 eating places opened November 1993.

Shopping

Almost half the annual S$6 billion spent annually by visitors to Singapore goes on shopping, according to an STPB-commissioned survey. The island is 'tops' for electronics at cheap prices. Almost everything on sale is duty free, so imported French and Italian designer clothes and Japanese consumer goods represent remarkably good value from the smart stores along Orchard and Scotts Road.

Most shops open seven days a week and stay open until 2130 at night. Certain streets and areas have gained a reputation for particular types of merchandise. For example, Coleman Street and High Street are renowned for their electronics stores; Scotts

and Plaza Singapora have carved out a reputation in the same sector. For batik and silk, then it's the Singapore Handicraft Centre or Arab Street. Like Hong Kong, most of the speciality Chinese stores sell readymade silk garments.

The Peninsula Shopping Centre is considered the best for sports equipment; although Coleman Street also specialises in leisure gear. Chinese Emporia tend to sell cheaper non-branded Taiwan and Korean sports items.

Shoppers should look for the red square Merlion DECAL logo in the windows of stores as this means that they are associate members of the STPB where customers can shop with confidence. These shops have been endorsed for their service, fair prices and the quality of products on offer.

But away from Orchard Road and the other fancy stores, haggling over prices is still a way of life and Lucky Plaza is particular well-known for its discounts. The goldsmiths in Chinatown's South Bridge Road do not offer fixed prices either.

Getting around

As a small, compact and well-run island which discriminates against private cars and has an excellent public transport system, it could not be easier to get around. .

Singapore has more than 10,000 taxis (including some 'London' cabs). All are metered, air-conditioned and offer an inexpensive and efficient means of transportation. Initial flagdown fare is S$2.40 with a surcharge for trips into the Central Business District (CBD). There are further levies on luggage and for groups of more than two people; for calling a taxi by telephone and for travel between midnight and 0600.

Many visitors find it more practical to use the Mass Rapid Transit (MRT) system to move around the city. The MRT comprises 42 stations along a 67km route and consists of two lines running north-south and east-west. Trains operate every six minutes during peak periods.

SINGAPORE - Introduction

Car rental is more practical than in most Southeast Asian cities. Driving is on the left side and the wearing of seat belts in compulsory.

There two types of buses - either red and white or orange and yellow. Fares are charged on a zonal basis and it's important to retain your ticket as inspectors check for fare dodgers on a regular basis. Small ferries and water taxis connect Singapore with its outlying islands. Ferries for Sentosa leave every 15 minutes from the World Trade Centre.

September 1993 saw the inauguration of the Eastern and Oriental Express train which runs between Singapore and Bangkok, taking two nights and one day fro the 1943-km journey. There are 14 accommodation cars, 3 restaurants & bars and 3 grades of cabin, all with private facilities. One way fare starts at US$ 1170. There is now an extension of the Rail Journey by steamer called the *Road to Mandalay* up the Irrawaddy river in Myanmar.

Entertainment

While most old-timers recognise that Singapore is not what it was, the island still has much to offer if in a more subdued form than in the past.

Singapore has a thriving English-language theatrical tradition, with plays often staged at the Victoria Theatre. From time to time, some of the island's top hotels stage their own theatre/dinner evenings featuring overseas touring companies.

Orchard Road cinemas show the latest Hollywood releases, while local Chinese, Malay and Tamil language movies are also on offer. The Singapore Symphony Orchestra has regular performances in the delightful Victoria Concert Hall. Culture vultures will also find smaller ensembles performing around Singapore, often during the lunch period - the Botanical Gardens is a well known haunt.

Leisure

Given that Singapore is home to some of the world's very best hotels, there is no shortage of sports and leisure facilities. All hotels feature swimming pools and many also saunas, steambaths and well-equipped gyms. At weekends a great way to relax is to take a walk into the heart of Singapore and watch the rugby and cricket being played on the Padang. Spectators are welcome.

Singapore has some great golf courses. The Singapore Island Country Club has two 18-hole courses. There are 13 other courses including two out on Sentosa Island, where visitors can find two 18-hole courses and some fine sandy beaches. Alternatively visitors can pop over the causeway to Johor Bahru in Malaysia or take the hydrofoil to Bintan Resort in the Riau Archipelago for further golf. All the courses mentioned in this book are described in Priory Publications' *South East Asia Golf Guide*. For racegoers, there are Saturday meetings at the Bukit Timah Road Racetrack.

Arrival & Departure

Changi International Airport changed its name to Airtropolis in 1990. The airport is generally acclaimed as the world's best and travellers should experience few problems. The airport's spacious second terminal (T2) opened in November 1990 at a cost of S$650 million and aims to allow passengers to clear the airport within 20 minutes of arrival.

There is now a S$15 airport tax for departing passengers to all other countries. It is possible to prepay your airport tax at either your hotel, the downtown airline office or with a travel agent. Taxis into the City Centre cost S$18-23 (+50% surcharge midnight-6 am) and take about 30 minutes. Bus No 390 costs $1.50.

Discover the delights of South-East Asia on the most leisurely and stylish form of transport - The Eastern & Oriental Express.
Contact telephone numbers:
Singapore (65) 323 4390; USA (toll-free) (800) 524 2420; UK (171) 928 6000

Car Hire

Ace Tours & Car Rentals Pte Ltd
Hotel Asia, 37 Scotts Road, Singapore 0922
Tel: 235-3755, 235-6618

Avis Rent-a-Car
PO Box 40, Orchard Point (Head Office), Singapore. Tel: 737 9477; Tlx: RS 50000; Fax: 235 4958
Branches at Changi Airport tel: 542 8855 and Boulevard Hotel tel: 737 1668

Blue Star Car Rentals & Tours Pte Ltd
262 Balestier Road, 02-19 Balestrier Complex, Singapore 1232
Tel: 253 4661; Fax: 252 8760

Budget Rent-a-Car
Central Reservations, Pan Pacific Hotel, 7 Raffles Boulevard, 0103
Tel: 339 4388; Fax: 339 4190

City Car Rentals & Tours(Pte) Ltd
02-20 Hotel Miramar, 401 Havelock Road, Singapore 0316
Tel: 733-2145, 733-0655; Fax: 733 3403

Elpin Tours & Limousine Services Pte Ltd
Level 3, Pico Creative Centre, 20 Kallang Avenue, 1233 Tel: 292 2388; Fax: 291 1511

Friendly Tour Corporation Pte Ltd
Fringe Car Park M, Holland Road/ Dempsey Road, Singapore 1024
Tel: 474-2292, 475-9035

Hertz Self and Chauffeur Drive 280 Sime Darby Services Pte Ltd.280 Kampong Arang Road, Tanjong Rhu 1543, Singapore Tel: 447 3388; Fax: 345 7247

Ken Air
227 Orchard Road, Fl 04-41 Specialist Shopping Centre, 0923
Tel: 737 8282; Fax: 733 5513

Letz Rent a Car
110 Killiney Road, Unit 01-02, Singapore0923
Tel: 733-8688, 733-6222; Fax: 732-8342

Ng Transport & Tourist Service Pte Ltd
01-02 Hotel Royal, 36 Newton Road, Singapore 1130 Tel: 253-7698; Tlx: 27158

Orchard Rent-a-Car
Orchard Towers, 0923. Tel: 235-8775

San's Tours & Car Rentals
100 Kim Seng Road Fl 02-05/07, Kim Seng Shopping Centre, Singapore 0923
Tel: 734-9922; Fax: 734 1039

Sintat Rent-a-Car Pte Ltd
60 Bendemeer Road, 1233
Tel: 295 2211; 295 1678

Sunrise Car Rentals Pte Ltd
109 Bukit Timah Road, Singapore 0922
Tel: 336-0626

Singapore Key Fact File

Passport Requirements:
For most visitors, visas are not required for stays under 14 days. EC and Commonwealth citizens do not need a visa at all, providing sufficient funds for duration of stay and onward ticket can be shown.

Currency:
Singapore dollar(S$). 100 cents = 1S$.

Exchange Rates:
US$1 = S$1.40; £1 = S$2.14 (*March 1996*)

Currency Restrictions:
There are no restrictions on the movement of either local or foreign currency. The movement of gold, however, must be declared to the Trade Development Board.

Electricity Supply:
200-240 volts AC/50 cycles; 400 volts AC 50 cycles for industry. Most hotels have a transformer to reduce the voltage to 110-120 volts, 60 cycles when necessary.

Language:
English is the official language and is used in business and government. Three other official languages: Mandarin, Malay and Tamil.

Time:
GMT + 8 hours; EDT + 13 hours

Business Hours: Commercial offices open 0900-1300, 1400-1700 Monday to Friday; 0900-1200 Saturdays.
Government offices open 0800-1300, 1400-1700 Monday to Friday; 0800-1300 on Saturdays.
Shops open 0900-1800 or even 2000, especially in major shopping complexes. Banks open 1000-1500 Monday to Friday, 0930-1130 Saturdays.

Customs & Entry:
Visitors (except those arriving from Malaysia) can bring in one litre of spirits, a litre of wine, a litre of beer, 200 cigarettes or 50 cigars or 250 grams of tobacco. Changi Airport has a duty-free shop for *arriving* passengers. Controlled drugs, video cassettes, obscene publications and endangered species of wildlife are prohibited.

Health Requirements:
Vaccination certificates are required for yellow fever or cholera if travelling from infected area.

Climate/best time to visit:
Tropical; with warm, humid and wet weather throughout the year. Temperatures remain between 27C and 29C all year round.

National Holidays 1997
1 January New Year's Day; 7/8 February Chinese New Year; 9 February Hari Raya Puasa; 28 March Good Friday; 18 April Hari Raya Haji; 1 May Labour Day; 21 May Vesak Day; 9 August National Day; 31 October Deepavali; 25 December Christmas Day.

Useful Addresses

Government Departments & Agencies

Ecomonic Development Board (EDB)
24th floor, Raffles City Tower 24-00, 250 North Bridge Rd, 0617. Tel: 336 2288

Ministry of Trade & Industry
8 Shenton Way Fl 48-01 Treasury Building, 0106. Tel: 225 9911; Fax: 323 9260

National Productivity Board
2 Bukit Merah Central, NPB Building 0315 Tel: 278 6666; Fax: 278 6665

Primary Production Department
5 Maxwell Rd, Fl 02-/03-00 Tower Block MND Complex, 0106.
Tel: 222 1211; Fax: 220 6068

Registry of Companies & Businesses
10 Anson Rd Fl 01-01/15 International Plaza, 0207. Tel: 227 8551; Fax: 225 167

Singapore Federation of Chambers of Commerce & Industry
47 Hill Street 03-01, 0617. Tel: 338 9761

Singapore International Chamber of Commerce
Denmark House 05-00, 6 Raffles Quay, 0104. Tel: 224 1255

Singapore Manufacturers' Association
SMA House, 20 Orchard Road
Tel: 338 8787

Singapore Professional Association
Fl 09-11, World Trade Centre, 1 Maritime Square, Tel: 272 9100

Trade Development Board
1 Maritime Square Fl 10-40 Lobby D, World Trade Centre, Telok Blangah Road, 0409. Tel: 271 9388; Fax: 274 0770

Tourism & Travel

Singapore Association of Convention & Exhibition Organisers & Suppliers
Robinson Road, PO Box 594.
Tel: 732 6613

Singapore Hotel Association
11 Dhoby Ghaut, Fl 15-04 Cathay Bdg
Tel: 336 2955

Singapore Tourist Promotion Board
Raffles City Tower, 250 North Bridge Road Fl.36-04, 0617. Tel: 339 6622;
Tlx: STBSIN RS 33375; Fax: 339 9423

STPB Tourist Information Centre
Fl 02-34, Raffles Hotel Arcade, 238 North Bridge Road, 0617. Tel: 334 1335

Business/Translation Bureaux

Interlingua Tranlsations
71 Robinson Road, Fl 05-01, 0106
Tel: 222 3755; Fax: 224 9188

Worldwide Business Services
111 North Bridge Road 11-04. Tel: 336 6577

Conventions & Exhibitions

Singapore Conference Hall
Shenton Way, City. Tel: 222 9711

Singapore Convention Bureau.
235 6611
World Trade Centre
Maritime Square, 0409. Tel: 274 7111

Post Office, Hospitals, Police

Singapore General Post Office
Tel: 532 3753
The Orchard Point Post Office. B 1-16/17, 160 Orchard Road. Tel: 737 4424
American Hospital Tel: 345 1516
National University Hospital 772 5000
Central Police Station
Tel: 535 2725 (or in emergency 999)

Air Couriers

DHL.Tel: 285 8888
Federal Express-Tel: 743 2626
TNT -Tel: 742 9000/ 542 3321
UPS - Tel: 326 2222

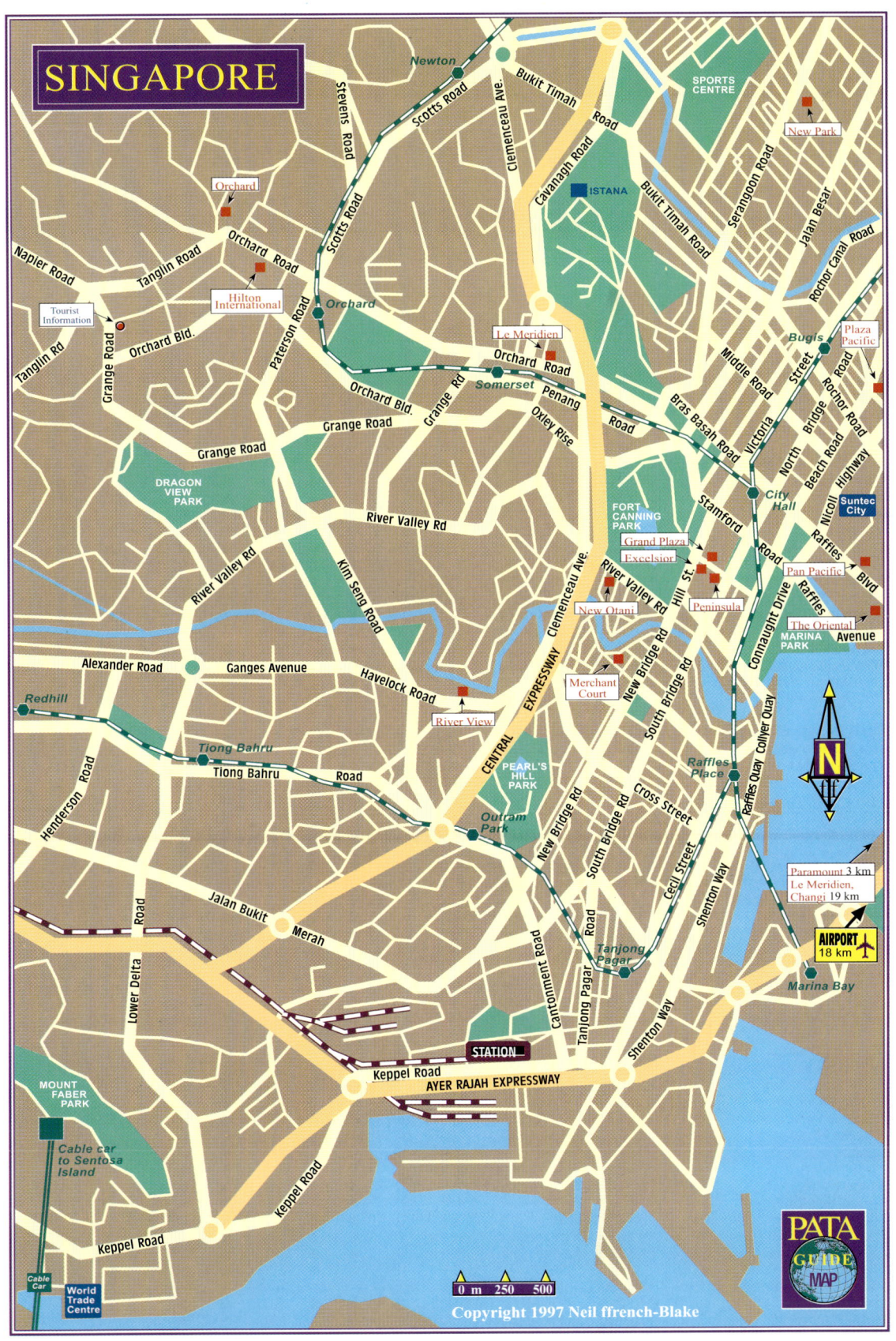

Singapore Hotel Reference Table

Hotel (listed in price order)	Single Room Rate (S$)	Location	Number of Rooms	Number of Suites	Conference Facilities	Exhibition Space	Largest Banquet Number	Business Centre	Swimming Pool (0 = indoor)	Tennis Court	Health Club	Video Films
Raffles Hotel	65	Raffles City N	-	104	●	●	300	●	●	-	●	●
Ritz Carlton Millenia	430	Marina Ctre	587	23	●	●	1000	●	●	●	●	●
Four Seasons Hotel	420	Orchard Rd	211	43	●	●	300	●	●	●	●	●
Goodwood Park	385	Orchard Rd	123	112	●	●	300	●	●	-	●	-
The Beaufort Singapore	380	Sentosa Isd	175	39	●	-	250	●	●	●	●	●
Sheraton Towers	370-475	Orchard Rd	358	52	●	●	500	●	●	-	●	●
Hyatt Regency	370-430	Orchard Rd	698	-	●	●	700	●	●	●	●	●
Conrad International	360-400	Marina Centre	47	26	●	●	380	●	●	-	●	●
The Oriental	360-400	Marina Sq	418	100	●	●	600	●	●	●	●	●
Regent of Singapore	340-365	Tanglin	441	-	●	-	550	●	●	-	●	●
Shangri-La Hotel	340-460	Tanglin	758	60	●	●	1000	●	●	●	●	●
Singapore Marriott	330-365	Orchard Rd	351	22	●	●	550	●	●	-	●	●
Inter-Continental Singapore	325-425	Bugis Jctn	323	83	●	●	450	●	●	-	●	●
Marina Mandarin	315-380	Marina Sq	575	-	●	●	800	●	●	●	●	●
Le Meridien Singapore	300-330	Orchard Rd	349	58	●	●	480	●	●	-	●	●
Pan Pacific Hotel	300-400	Marina Sq	800	-	●	●	800	●	●	●	●	●
Mandarin Singapore	300-320	Orchard Rd	1075	75	●	●	1060	●	●	●	●	●
Marco Polo Hotel	300-400	Tanglin	570	30	●	●	170	●	●	-	●	●
Hilton International	300-320	Orchard Rd	423	16	●	●	600	●	●	-	●	●
Royal Holiday Inn Cr Plaza	300-430	Orchard Rd	493	-	●	-	300	●	●	-	●	-
Carlton Hotel	300-320	Raffles City	469	8	●	●	350	●	●	-	●	●
Westin Stamford/Plaza	300-315	Raffles City	2049	80	●	●	3000	●	●	●	●	●
Holiday Inn Park View	290-310	Orchard Rd	300	12	●	-	200	●	●	-	●	●
Orchard Hotel	290-400	Orchard Rd	674	6	●	●	1000	●	●	-	●	●
Grand Plaza Hotel	280-330	Raffles City	338	3	●	●	500	●	●	-	●	-
Hotel Negara Singapore	280-320	Orchard Rd	196	4	-	-	-	-	●	-	-	-
The Duxton Hotel	280-330	Chinatown	38	11	-	-	-	●	-	-	-	●
The Elizabeth	280-340	Orchard Rd	241	4	●	-	-	●	●	-	●	●
Ana Hotel Singapore	270-360	Tanglin	437	19	●	●	220	●	●	-	●	●
Crown Prince Hotel	260-299	Orchard Rd	288	15	●	●	100	●	●	-	●	●
Merchant Court Hotel	260-290	City	476	-	●	-	-	●	●	-	●	●
Hotel New Otani	260-300	N Chinatown	386	22	●	●	500	●	●	-	●	●
Imperial Hotel	250-270	N Chinatown	529	32	●	●	400	●	●	-	●	●
Boulevard Hotel	250-400	Orchard Rd	510	10	●	●	170	●	●	-	●	●
Melia at Scotts	245-285	Orchard Rd	213	32	●	●	100	●	●	-	●	●
Orchard Parade Hotel	240	Tanglin	322	-	●	●	400	●	●	-	-	●
The York Hotel	230-390	Orchard Rd	400	-	●	●	-	●	●	-	-	-
Apollo Hotel	230-240	N Chinatown	323	22	●	●	180	●	●	-	●	●
Plaza Hotel	230-310	Raffles City	347	3	●	●	1000	●	●	-	●	●
The Amara Hotel	230-310	City	324	14	●	●	500	●	●	-	●	●
The Ascott Singapore	220-340	Orchard Rd	-	177	-	-	-	-	●	●	●	●
Hotel Phoenix	220-250	Orchard Rd	289	16	●	-	80	●	-	-	●	●
Novotel Orchid Inn	220-240	Dunearn Rd (N)	450	3	●	●	220	●	●	-	●	●
Cairnhill Hotel	210-280	Orchard Rd	195	-	-	-	-	●	●	-	●	●
Meridien Changi	210-270	Airport	275	4	●	-	400	●	●	●	●	●
Peninsula Hotel	210-230	Raffles City	299	8	●	●	300	●	●	-	●	●
Paramount Hotel	210-230	East Coast	250	-	●	●	140	●	●	-	●	●
New Park Hotel	200-220	Little India	531	20	●	●	500	●	●	-	●	●
Harbour View Dai Ichi	200-340	City	408	8	●	●	350	●	-	-	●	●
Furama Hotel	200-220	Chinatown/City	356	-	●	●	-	●	●	-	●	●
Excelsior Hotel	200-260	Raffles City	259	12	●	-	160	●	●	-	●	●
Hotel Miramar	190-210	N Chinatown	333	9	●	●	120	●	●	-	●	●
Kings Hotel	190-230	Orchard Rd	312	4	●	●	120	●	●	-	-	●
Allson Hotel Singapore	190-215	Raffles City	423	28	●	●	400	●	-	-	●	●
Shangri-La's Rasa Sentosa Rst	180-230	Sentosa Isd	450	9	●	●	500	●	●	-	●	-
River View Hotel	180-210	N Chinatown	464	8	●	●	350	●	●	-	●	●
Golden Landmark	170-240	Raffles City	393	6	●	●	240	●	●	-	●	●
The Concorde Hotel	170	N Chinatown	497	18	●	●	450	●	●	-	●	●
Albert Court Hotel	170-190	Tanglin	135	1	-	-	-	●	-	-	-	●
Ladyhill Hotel	170-210	Tanglin	180	2	●	●	80	●	●	-	-	-
Hotel Equatorial	160-180	Bukit Timah	220	8	●	-	300	●	●	-	●	●
The Garden	140-190	Orchard Rd	216	-	-	-	-	-	●	-	●	●
Hotel Royal	140	Newton Road	307	23	●	●	150	-	●	-	●	●

SingaporeHotels

Albert Court Hotel ◌ C
180 Albert Street, 189971
Tel: 339 3939; Tlx: 24109Fax: 339 3252

Allson Hotel Singapore ◌ C
101 Victoria Street, 188018 (Raffles City Area). Tel: 336 0811; Fax: 339 7019

Amara Hotel Singapore ◌ B
165 Tanjong Pagar Road, 085539
Tel: 224 4488; Fax: 224 3910

ANA Hotel Singapore ◌ B
16 Nassim Hill, 258390 (Tanglin area)
Tel: 732 1222; Fax: 737 6684

Apollo Hotel Singapore C
405 Havelock Road, 169633 (Chinatown)
Tel: 733 2081; Tlx: 21077 ; Fax: 733 1588

The Ascott Singapore B
6 Scotts Road, 228209
Tel: 735 6868; Fax: 733 7561

Banyan Tree Bintan Resort ◌ A
(Pre-opening office) Wah Chang House, 211 Upper Bukit Rd, Neil Road, 2158
Tel: 462 2022; Fax: 469 9082

The Beaufort Singapore A
2 Bukit Manis Rd, Sentosa Island 099891
Tel: 275 0331; Fax: 275 0228

Boulevard Hotel ◌ B
200 Orchard Boulevard, 248647
Tel: 737 2911; Tlx: 21771; Fax: 737 8449

Cairnhill Hotel ◌ C
19 Cairnhill Circle, 229767
Tel: 734 6622; Fax: 235 5598

Carlton Hotel ◌ A
76 Bras Basah Rd, Cnr Victoria St, 189558 (Opposite Raffles City Convention Centre)
Tel: 338 8333; Fax: 339 6866

The Concorde Hotel ◌ C
317 Outram Road, 169075 (North Chinatown) Tel: 733 0188; Tlx: RS 50141 CHSIN; Fax: 733 0989

Conrad International Centennial A
2 Temasek Boulevard, 038982
Tel: 334 8888; Fax: 338 8264

Crown Prince Hotel ◌ B
270 Orchard Road, 238857
Tel: 732 1111; Tlx: 22819; Fax: 732 7018

Hotel classification in (short) entries:
A after name of hotel = single room rate over US$ 200 per night; **B** = between $ 150-200; **C** = between $100-150; **D** = between $50-100; ¶ = prices on application. ◌ = PATA Allied Hotel Member.

The Duxton Hotel ◌ A
83 Duxton Road, 0208
Tel: 227 7678; Fax: 227 1232

The Elizabeth Hotel ◌ A
24 Mount Elizabeth Road, 228518
Tel: 738 1188; Tlx: 22538 ELITEL; Fax: 732 3866

Hotel Equatorial ◌ C
429 Bukit Timah Road, 259737
Tel: 732 0431; Fax: 737 9426

Excelsior Hotel ◌
5 Coleman Street, 179805
Tel: 338 7733; Tlx: 20678; Fax: 339 3847

Centrally located, the Excelsior Hotel overlooks Fort Canning Park, Singapore River and the Harbour. It is within close proximity to the business and entertainment district, major convention centres and many exciting places of interest.

Accommodation & rates
259 single/double/twin rooms, S$ 220-260; 12 suites, S$ 400-680. Subject to 10% service charge and 4% government tax

Credit cards accepted:
Amex, Visa, Mastercard, Diners, JCB

Meeting & banqueting facilities
3 function/banquet rooms, capacity 200, with audio-visual facilities; largest banquet 160 seated/200 cocktail

Room services
Airconditioning, colour TV, direct-dial telephone, hairdryer, laundry/valet service, minibar, music/radio/alarm clock, safety deposit box, tea/coffee making facilities, 24-hr room/meal service, video films, in-room guest system

Business & other services
Business centre, airport pickup, car parking, taxi service, barber shop/beauty salon, guided tours, newstand/shops

Sports & Recreation
Outdoor swimming pool, fitness centre/gym, massage, sauna, karaoke lounge in next door Peninsula Hotel, 6th level

Restaurants & Coffee Shops
Cafe Excelsior (100) - Local & Western, open 0600-0100; *Hana* (80) - Japanese, open 1100-1430/1800-2230; *Shanghai*

alace (320) - Chinese, open noon-1430/1830-2230; *Annalakshmi* (120) - Indian, open 1130-1500/1800-2130.

Overseas Sales Representatives
LRI/Anaasazi (UK). Tel: (44-171) 495 0700; Fax: (44-171) 491 3135

Four Seasons Hotel Singapore A
190 Orchard Rd, 248646
Tel: 734 1110; Fax: 235 5131

Furama Singapore Hotel ◌ B
10 Eu Tong Street, 059804 (Chinatown/City)
Tel: 533 3888; Tlx: RS 28592; Fax: 534 1489

The Garden, Singapore ◌ C
14 Balmoral Road, 259800
Tel: 235 3344; Tlx: 50999 Fax: 235 9730

Golden Landmark Hotel ◌ C
390 Victoria Street, 0718
Tel: 297 2928; Tlx: RS 38291; Fax: 298 2038

Goodwood Park Hotel ◌ A
22 Scotts Road, 228221 (Orchard Road)
Tel: 737 7411; Fax: 732 8558

Grand Central Hotel D
22 Orchard/Cavenagh Rd, 229617
Tel: 737 9944; Fax: 733 3175

Harbour View Dai-Ichi Hotel ◌ C
81 Anson Road, 079908 (City)
Tel: 224 1133; Tlx: 40163; Fax: 222 0749

Holiday Inn Park View Singapore B
11 Cavenagh Road, 229616 (Orchard ◌ Road).Tel: 733 8333; Tlx: Rs 55420; Fax: 734 4593

Hyatt Regency Singapore ◌ A
10-12 Scotts Road, 228211 (Orchard Road). Tel: 738 1234; Fax: 732 1696

Imperial Hotel Singapore ◌ C
1 Jalan Rumbia, 239616 (North Chinatown).Tel: 737 1666; Tlx: RS 21654 IMPHTI; Fax: 737 4761

Hotel Inter-Continental Singapore A
80 Middle Road, Bugis Junction, 188966
Tel: 338 7600; Fax: 338 7366

Kings Clarion Hotel C
403 Havelock Road, 169362 (Chinatown)
Tel: 733 0011; Tlx: 21931 KINGTEL RS; Fax: 732 5764

(*Grand Plaza* and *Hilton* Hotels - see next page)

Grand Plaza Hotel Singapore
10 Coleman Street, Singapore 179809
Tel: 336 3456; Fax: 339 9311

Grand Plaza Hotel sits resplendently on the corner of Coleman Street and Hill Street, close to landmarks such as St Andrews Cathedral, Fort Canning Park, National Library, Arts Centre, Raffles City, Marina Square and Suntec City. Dining and entertainment outlets at Boat Quay and Clarke Quay are a five-minute walk away whilst the Orchard Road shopping haven and Central Business District can be easily accessed by a five-minute drive and the City MRT Station is a mere 5-minute walk away.

Accommodation & rates
338 rooms, single S$ 280-330, double US$ 300-360. 3 luxurious suites US$ 600-1200.

Credit cards accepted:
Amex, Mastercard, Visa, JCB, Diners

Meeting & banqueting facilities
Three meeting/conference rooms, capacity 20-500 pax, with full audio-visual facilities; 700 sq m exhibition space; largest reception 500

Room services
Airconditioning, colour TV + movie channel + CNN + Teletext, direct-dial telephone (ext. in bathroom), hairdryer, laundry/valet service, minibar, music/radio/alarm clock, safety deposit box, tea/coffee making, 24-hr room service, workdesk

Business & other services
Business centre inc Internet access, car parking, guided tours, taxi service, newsstand/shops, pharmacy/drugstore, comp. shuttle to Orchard Road & shops

Sports & Recreation
Fitness centre/gym, massage, sauna, swimming pool (outdoor), St Gregory Marine Spa

Restaurants & Coffee Shops
St Gregory's Brasserie - Buffet, Mediterranean, continental, local; Hau Yuen - Cantonese; Jugglers Lounge - bar with live entertainment; Pool Terrace - cocktails/light snacks

Overseas Sales Representatives
Utell International Reservations .
Japan tel (03) 3461 8585; fax (03) 3461 8550;

Hilton International Singapore
581 Orchard Road, Singapore 238883
Tel: 737 2233; Tlx: RS 21491; Fax: 732 2917

Right in the heart of the business, entertainment and shopping district of Singapore; on fashiobale Orchard Road, 25 minutes from Changi International Airport.

Accommodation & rates
423 rooms, single S$300-320; twin S$ 330-350; 16 suites S$ 480-580; Hilton Exec Club single S$380, twin S$ 420, club suite S$ 680; presidential suite S$ 1800 Subject to 10% service charge and 4% government tax

Credit cards accepted:
Amex, Diners Club, JCB, Mastercard, Visa

Meeting & banqueting facilities
10 meeting/conference rooms - capacity 10-600, with full audio-visual facilities; 625 sq m

---

Fine Vacations For The Mind, Body And Spirit

Escape from your daily routine and be pampered in the luxurious surroundings of our hotels. In their own unique way, each creates an unbeatable experience that makes your holiday an unforgettable one. With extraordinary, gentle service that brings to realisation your ideal of a dream vacation. One that assures you thorough enjoyment for your mind, body and spirit.

Grand Plaza Hotel. Elegance blending with the heart of culture and the arts, close to financial and convention centres.

GRAND PLAZA HOTEL
- 338 rooms & suites
- Executive floor with exclusive lounge
- Leisure amenities: Marine spa with full spa facilities, fitness centre & swimming pool
- Business facilities: Full business centre, function/seminar & banquet rooms
- F&B outlets: Brasserie, Chinese restaurant, lounge & wine bar

Plaza Hotel. A stone's throw from among the world's best convention facilities, yet an oasis of leisure and entertainment.

PLAZA HOTEL
- 350 rooms & suites
- Penthouse floors with exclusive lounge
- Leisure amenities: Fitness & resort club with fully equipped gyms, beauty spa, outdoor jacuzzi and swimming pool
- Business facilities: Full business centre, function/seminar & banquet rooms
- F&B outlets: Coffee house, Chinese restaurant, nostalgia lounge, karaoke theme lounge

New Park Hotel. A tourist's delight set amidst historical attractions of the Lion City. Yet conveniently close to business.

NEW PARK HOTEL
- 531 rooms & suites
- Penthouse floors
- Leisure amenities: Gym, swimming pool & wading pool
- Business facilities: Function/seminar & banquet rooms
- F&B outlets: Coffee house, Chinese restaurant, leisure lounge, Asian pub, poolside restaurant

PLAZA PACIFIC
HOTELS & RESORTS

Corporate & Marketing Office: The Plaza #04-301 Beach Road Singapore 199591 Tel: (65) 298 0011 Fax: (65) 297 3591
E-Mail Address: pphrcorp@singnet.com.sg

SINGAPORE - Hotels

exhibition space; largest banquet 600 seated or 700 cocktail.

Room services
Airconditioning, colour TV, direct-dial telephone (ext. in bathoom), hairdryer, laundry/valet service, minibar, music/radio/alarm clock, non-smoker floors/Japanese floors available, safety deposit box, tea/coffee making facilities, 24-hr room service, video films/CNN, trouser press

Business & other services
Business centre, executive floor, express checkout, car parking & rental,barber shop/beauty salon, shopping arcade, car parking, car rental, taxi service, courier service, wheelchairs, post office, doctor (nearby)

Sports & Recreation
Fitness centre/gym, outdoor swimming pool, sauna, massage

Restaurants & Coffee Shops
Checkers Brasserie (160) - Asian, open 0630-0100; *Harbour Grill & Oyster Bar* (75) - Continental, open 1230-1430 Mon-Fri/1900-2230 Mon-Sat; *Inn of 6th Happiness* (150) Cantonese, open noon-1430/1900-2230; *Tradewinds* (140) - Rooftop & Muslim bbq, open 1000-2330

Overseas Sales Representatives:
Hilton Reservations Worldwide; Hilton International Sales Offices

Holiday Inn Park View Singapore B
11 Cavenagh Road, 0922 (Orchard Road)
Tel: 733 8333; Fax: 734 4593

Ladyhill Hotel C
1 Ladyhill Road (Tanglin), 258670
Tel: 737 2111; Fax: 739 4606

Mandarin Singapore A
333 Orchard Road, PO Box 135, 238867
Tel: 737 4411; Fax: 732 2361

Marina Mandarin Singapore A
6 Raffles Boulevard, Marina Square, 039594
Tel: 338 3388; Fax: 339 4977

Le Meridien Singapore
100 Orchard Road, 0923
Tel: 733 8855; Tlx: 50163 HOMERI; Fax: 732 7886

Le Meridien Singapore, strategically located along the legendary Orchard Road, in the heart of the business, shopping and entertainment district. Le Meridien is large enough to offer all amenities guests expect from a hotel today.

Accommodation & rates
407 guestrooms and suites, single S$ 300; double/twin S$ 330; suite S$ 1400-1800. Subject to 10% service charge & 4% government tax

Credit cards accepted:
Amex, Diners Club, JCB, Mastercard, Visa

Meeting & banqueting facilities
10 meeting/conference rooms - capacity 20-200, with audio-visual facilities; largest banquet 480 seated or 800 cocktail.

Room services
Airconditioning, colour TV, direct-dial telephone (ext. in bathroom), hairdryer, laundry/valet service, minibar, music/radio/alarm clock, safety deposit box, tea/coffee making facilities, 24-hr room service, non-smoker bedrooms, video films

Business & other services
Business centre, executive floor, express checkout, car parking, newsstand/shops, car parking, taxi service, travel centre

Sports & Recreation
Fitness centre/gym, sauna, outdoor swimming pool

Restaurants & Coffee Shops
Cafe La Terrasse - International/Local, open 0400-0100; *Chez Georges* (150) - Provincial French, open noon-1430/1900-2230

Overseas Sales Representatives
Forte & Meridien Hotels & Resorts

Le Meridien Changi Singapore
1 Netheravon Road, 508502 (Airport)
Tel: 542 7700; Tlx: RS 36042 HOMRA; Fax 542 5295;E-mail:meridien@singnet.com.sg

The only four-star hotel close to Changi International Airport and Ferry terminal to Indonesian Islands. Complimentary airport meet & greet service and shuttle service to airport/ferry terminal/downtown provided. Beach and sporting facilities within walking distance

Accommodation & rates
275 rooms; single S$ 210-270; double/twin S$ 240-290; suite S$ 380-750. Subject to 10% service charge and 4% government tax

Credit cards accepted:
Amex, Visa, Mastercard, JCB, Diners

Meeting &bnaqueting facilities
11 meeting/function rooms, capacity 400, with full audio-visual facilities; 396 sq m exhibition space; largest reception 400

Room services
Airconditioning, colour TV, direct-dial telephone, hairdryer, laundry/valet service, minibar, music/radio/alarm clock, safety deposit box (some rooms), non-smoker bedrooms available, 24-hr room service, video films, tea/coffee making facilities, voicemail & Internet services

Business & other services
Business centre, express checkout, airport pickup, car parking, taxi service, newsstand/shops

Sports & Recreation
Golf, squash, tennis (nearby), indoor games, outdoor swimming pool

Restaurants & Coffee Shops
The Verandah (60) - Steakhouse, open 1200-1430/1900-2200 (closed Suns/Pub Hols);*The Changi Cafe* (180) - Local/International, open 24 hours; *Lotus* (110) - Karaoke lounge, open 1700-0100 (-0200 Fri/Sat)

Overseas Sales Representatives
Forte and Meridien Hotels & Resorts

Merchant Court Hotel Singapore
20 Merchant Road, Singapore 058281
Tel: 337 2288; Tlx: RS 20396; Fax: 334 0606; E-Mail: mchotel@singnet.com.sg

The first urban resort in Singapore, Merchant Court is locted in the city centre, along the bank of the Singapore river and next to the financial and business district. Resort-style facilities include a free-form swimming pool and a fully-equipped health spa and fitness centre set amidst lush landscaping.

Accommodation & rates
476 rooms. Superior rooms S$ 260 single/S$ 290 double; deluxe rooms S$ 290 single/S$ 320 double; Merchant Club rooms S$ 320 single/S$ 350; Studio rooms S$ 350 single/S$ 380 double; Suites S$ 810-1500. Subj to 14% service/tax charges

Credit cards accepted:
Amex, Diners, JCB, Mastercard, Visa

Room services
Airconditioning, colour TV, direct-dial telephone (ext. in bathroom), voicemail, hairdryer, laundry/valet service, minibar, alarm clock, in-room safe, tea/coffee making facilities, pay movies, non-smoking & handicapped rooms available

Business & other services
Business centre, exececutive floor, express checkout, translation service, Internet access, car parking & rental, taxi service, barber shop/beauty salon, newsstand/shops, travel agency

Sports & recreation
Fitness centre/gym, jacuzzi, massage, sauna, outdoor swimming pool

Restaurants & Coffee Shops
Ellenborough Market Cafe (160) - Local/international, open 0700-midnight; (high tea available 1530-1730 Sat/Sun/Pub Hols); *Crossroads Bar* (32) - Open 1100-midnight; *Poolside Bar* (80), open 0700-2300

Overseas Sales Representatives:
Sterling Hotels & Resorts

Melia at Scotts   B
45 Scotts Road, 228232
Tel: 732 5885; Tlx: 36811; Fax: 732 1332

Hotel Miramar   C
401 Havelock Road, 169631 (Chinatown)
Tel: 733 0222; Fax: 733 4027

Hotel Negara Singapore   A
10 Claymore Road, 229540
Tel: 737 0811; Fax: 737 9075

Hotel New Otani Singaore
177a River Valley Road, 179031 (North Chinatown).
Tel: 338 3333; Tlx: RS 20299 SINOTA; Fax 339 2854; E-Mail: newotani@singnet.sg

Located next to Singapore River and Clarke Quay. Minutes from Orchard Road, near the business district and Chinatown. Well-furnished rooms with panoramic view of city and harbour. Next to major shopping complex. 25 minutes from the airport.

Accommodation & rates
386 rooms, 22 suites.Single S$ 260-300; Double S$ 280-320; Suite S$ 450-800

Credit cards accepted:
Amex, Diners, JCB, Mastercard, Visa

Meeting & banqueting facilities
Four meeting/conference rooms, capacity 20-630 pax, with full audio-visual facilities; 500 sq m exhibition space; largest banquet 500 seated or 630 cocktail.

Room services
Airconditioning, colour TV, direct-dial telephone (ext. in bathroom), hairdryer, laundry/valet service, minibar, music/radio/alarm clock, non-smoker bedrooms available, safety deposit box, tea/coffee making facilities, 24-hr room service, video films.

Business & other services
Business centre, express checkout, car parking, car rental, taxi service, gift shop

Sports & Recreation
Fitness centre/gym, massage, sauna, swimming pool (outdoor), complimentary river cruises & guided temple tours

Restaurants & Coffee Shops
Trader Vic's (190) - International, open 1130-1430/1830-2230; *Taikan-En* (200) - Chinese, open as above; *Senbazaru* (120) - Japanese, open as above; *River Terrace* (180) - Snacks/Local/Western, open 0630-0200.

Overseas Sales Representatives:
Sabre, Apollo/Galileo, System One/Amadeus, Worldspan

New Park Hotel Singapore
181 Kitchener Road, Singapore 208533
Tel: 291 5533; Fax: 297 2827

New Park Hotel is an international class hotel strategically and conveniently located just 10 minutes away from the Businss District and Orchard Road and 25 minutes from Changi International Airport. It is a 10-minute drive to Marina Square, Millenia Walk, convention and exhibition centres at Raffles City and Suntec City. Situated along Kitchener Road, New Park Hotel's proximity to some of the island's most beautiful mosques, temples and ethnic shops offers a unique cultural experience for guests.

Accommodation & rates
531 rooms; single S$200-220, double/twin S$ 220-300, Penthouse rooms & suites S$330-700

Credit cards accepted:
Amex, Diners, Mastercard, Visa, JCB

Meeting & banqueting facilities
3 meeting/function rooms, capacity 30-500 with full audi0-visual facilities; 1500 sq m exhibition space; largest reception 500

Room services
Airconditioning, colour TV, direct-dial telephone, hairdryer, minibar, tea/coffee making facilities, 24-hr room/meal service

Business & other services
Business centre, car parking, taxi service, newsstand/shops, guided tours, comp. shuttle to Orchard Rd/major shopping areas

Sports & Recreation
Fitness centre/gym,18-metre swimming pool, sun deck, steam bath

Restaurants & Coffee Shops
New Park Cafe -Buffets/Western/Local/Oriental; *Hax Xiang* -Cantonese; *Pool Terrace* - Light snacks/steamboat buffet; *Chances* - Lounge/bar with Internet facilities; *181* - Asian Pub - karaoke etc.

Overseas Sales Representatives
Utell International Reservations . Japan tel (03) 3461 8585; fax (03) 3461 8550

SINGAPORE - Hotels

Novotel Orchid ○ C
214 Dunearn Road, 299526
Tel: 250 3322; Tlx: NOVSIN RS 21756;
Fax: 250 9292

Orchard Hotel Singapore ○
442 Orchard Road, Singapore 238879
Tel: 734 7766; Tlx: 35228; Fax: 733 5482
E-mail: HoEsther@cdl.hl.infonet.com.
Orcharde@Singnet.com.sg

The 680-room hotel is located in the shopping and entertainment belt, with close proximity to banks, embassies and a five-minute walk to the Mass Rapid Transit.

Accommodation & rates
694 rooms, 6 suites. Single S$ 290-400; twin/double S$ 320-430; suites, S$ 600-650. Subject to 10% service charge, 3% gov't & services tax and 1% cess.

Credit cards accepted:
Amex, Diners Club, Carte Blanche, Visa, JCB

Groups
11 meeting/conference rooms, capacity 10-1200; full audio-visual facilities; 1234 sq m exhibition space; largest reception 1000 seated or 1200 cocktail.

Room services
Airconditioning, colour TV, direct-dial telephone (ext. in bathroom), haidryer, laundry/valet service, minibar, music/radio/alarm clock, safety deposit box, tea/coffee making, trouser press, 24-hr room/meal service, non-smoker bedrooms, video films

Business & other services
Business centre, executive floor, express checkout (Club floor), airport pickup (charged), car parking, taxi service, travel centre, bnarber shop/beauty salon, newsstand/shops

Sports & Recreation
Fitness centre/gym, outdoor swimming pool

Restaurants & Coffee Shops
Ficus Cafe (157) - Taiwanese, open 0700-0100; *Hua Ting* (200) - Chinese, open 1100-1500/1800-2300; *Orchard Sidewalk Cafe* (110) - open 0700-0100; *Lobby Lounge/Tea Lounge* (71) - open 1100-2300

Overseas Sales Representatives
Anasazi Travel Resources Inc, Sterling Hotels & Resorts

Marco Polo Hotel ○ A
247 Tanglinn Road, 247935
Tel: 474 7141; Tlx: RS 21478 CMPS; Fax: 471 0521

Orchard Parade Hotel B
442Tanglin Road, 247905
Tel: 737 1133; Fax: 733 0242

The Oriental Singapore ○
5 Raffles Avenue, Marina Square, 039797
Tel: 338 0066; Fax: 339 9537
E-mail: reserve@orsin.com.sg

The Oriental Singapore is the only Mandarin Oriental Hotel group property in Singapore. Overlooking the Singapore harbour, the hotel is connected to Marina Square Mall and Marine Leisureplex, Suntec City Mall and Millenia Walk. The Oreintal is 15 minutes by car from Changi International Airport and 5 minutes from the financial and commercial districts.

Accommodation & rates
143 single/double, 275 twin, S$ 360-400; 100 suites, S$ 420-3600
Subject to 10% service charge, 3% gov't & services tax and 1% cess.

Credit cards accepted:
Amex, Diners Club, Mastercard, Visa, Airplus, JCB

Meeting & banqueting facilities
13 meeting/conference rooms, total capacity 880; audio-visual facilities; 2196.5 sq m exhibition space; largest reception 450 seated or 1000 cocktail.

Room services
Airconditioning, colour TV, direct-dial telephone (ext. in bathroom) with voicemail, haidryer, laundry/valet service, minibar, music/radio/alarm clock, safety deposit box, tea/coffee making facilities (club floors), 24-hr room service, video films, non smoker bedrooms

Business & other services
Business centre, executive floor, express checkout, airport pickup, translation service, car parking & rental, taxi service, travel centre, newsstand/shops

Sports & Recreation
Fitness centre/gym, golf (can be arranged), jacuzzi/whirlpool, jogging track, massage, sauna, aerobics, outdoor swimming pool, tennis

Restaurants & Coffee Shops
Liana's (80) - Californian, open noon-1430/1830-2230; *Cherry Garden* (120) - Hunan/Szechuan, open noon-1430/1830-2300; *Cafe*

Palm (144) - International/local, open 0630-midnight; *Pronto* (80) - Italian, open 0700-2200

Overseas Sales Representatives
UK: Ms Julia Camp, Area Director of Sales, Europe

Pan Pacific Singapore
7 Raffles Boulevard, Marina Square, 039595.
Tel: 336 8111; Fax: 339 1861
E-mail: panpac@pacific.net.sg

There is never a dull moment here with choices as wide and diverse as the Pacific itself for fine dining, shopping and discovering the many delights of this exciting ASEAN gateway city.

Accommodation & rates
800 guest rooms & suites; special Pacific floor. Single/double S$ 300-400; suite S$ 420-1600. Subject to 10% service charge and 4% government tax

Credit cards accepted:
Amex, Diners Club, Mastercard, Visa, JCB,

Meeting & banqueting facilities
19 meeting/function rooms - capacity up to 800 with full audio-visual facilities; largest banquet 800 seated or 1000 cocktail.

Room services
Airconditioning, colour TV, direct-dial telephone (ext. in bathroom), hairdryer, laundry/valet service, minibar, music/radio/alarm clock, safety deposit box, tea/coffee making facilities, non-smoker and disabled bedrooms available, 24-hr room service, video films, voltage 220v

Business & other services
Business centre, executive floor, express checkout/checkin for *Passages* and *PCI* card members, shuttle to Central Business District, car parking & rental, taxi service, newsstand/shops, currency exchange

(continued)

Sports & Recreation
Fitness centre/gym, golf putting green & range, jacuzzi/whirlpool, solarium, jogging track, massage, sauna, squash, swimming pool (outdoor), tennis, children's playground

Restaurants & Coffee Shops
8 food & beverage outlets serving Cantonese, local, Halia, Deli, Japanese, all-day Singaporean & international dining; Poolside Bar; Cocktail lounge

Overseas Sales Representatives:
Pan Pacific Hotels & Resorts Worldwide. SRS Steigenberger Reservation Service

The Paramount Hotel
25 Marine Parade, Singapore 449536
Tel: 344 5577; Fax: 447 4131

Paramount Hotel is conveniently located in the East Coast, within easy rach of multi-storey shopping plazas, seafodd restaurants and clear long beaches, just minutes away, perfect for aquatic pursuits - all within walking distance from the hotel.

Accommodation & rates:
166 single/double/twin S$ 210-230; 13 suites S$ 350-450; 71 Exec. Club rooms S$ 245-275. Subject to 10% service charge and 4% government tax

Credit cards accepted:
Amex, Diners, Mastercard, Visa, JCB

Meeting & banqueting facilities
Two meeting/function rooms, capacity up to 160 with audio-visual equipment; largest reception 140 seated or 160 cocktail

Room services
Airconditioning, colour TV, direct-dial telephone, hairdryer, laundry/valet service, minibar, music/radio/alarm clock, safety deposit box, tea/coffee making facilities, video films, 24-hr room/meal service, in-room Guestserve system

Business & other services
Business centre, executive floor, airport pickup, shops, taxi service, car parking, barber shop/beauty salon, guided tours

Sports & Recreation
Fitness centre/gym, outdoor swimming pool, massage, sauna

Restaurants & Coffee Shops
Cafe Vanda (130) - Local/Western, open 0600-0100; Paramount Restaurant (470) - Chinese, open 1130-1500/1830-2300

Overseas Sales Representatives
LRI/Anasazi (UK) Tel: (44-171) 495 0700; Fax: (44-171) 491 3135

Peninsula Hotel
3 Coleman Street, 179804 (Raffles City area). Tel: 337 2200; Tlx: RS 21169 PENHOTE; Fax: 339 3580

The Peninsula Hotel stands in a prized spot on Coleman Street. Centrally located, it is only 10 mins away from the business and leisure district and convention centres. With an MRT station just around the corner, we are easily accessible from Singapore's many exciting spots.

Accommodation & rates
299 single/double/twin rooms S$ 210-230; 8 suites S$ 330-420. Subject to 10% service charge and 4% government tax

Credit cards accepted:
Amex, Diners, Mastercard, Visa, JCB

Meeting and banqueting facilities
Meeting/function room, with audio-visiual equipment, capacity up to 300 for cocktails

Room services
Airconditioning, colour TV, direct-dial telephone, hairdryer, laundry/valet service, minibar, music/radio/alarm clock, safety deposit box, tea/coffee making, video films, 24-hr room service, in-room Guestserve system

Business & other services
Business centre, airport pickup, shops, car parking, taxi service, barber shop/beauty salon, guided tours, newsstand/shops

Sports & Recreation
Fitness centre/gym, massage, sauna, outdoor swimming pool, Karaoke Lounge

Restaurants & Coffee Shops
Coleman's Cafe (122) - Local & Western, open 24 hours

Overseas Sales Representatives
LRI/Anasazi (UK) Tel: (44-171) 495 0700; Fax: (44-171) 491 3135

Hotel Phoenix Singapore   C
Orchard Road/Somerset Road, 238858
Tel: 737 8666; Fax: 732 2024

Plaza Hotel Singapore
7500A Beach Road, 0719
Tel: 298 0011; Fax: 296 3600

Guests at Plaza Hotel will enjoy its strategic location and modern facilities. Convention and exhibition centres at Raffles City and Suntec City are a mere 10-minute walk from the hotel, while the Central Business District and Orchard Road shopping haven are a mere five-minute drive. For the health and beauty conscious, our fully equipped Plaza Fitness Club is available for an invigorating workout or a therapeutic beauty session.

Accommodation & rates:
350 rooms, single S$ 230-310; Double/twin S$ 250-340; Suite S$ 370-550.
Subject to 10% service charge and 4% government tax

Credit cards accepted:
Amex, Diners, Mastercard, Visa, JCB

Meeting and banqueting facilities
Five meeting/function rooms, capacity 20-1000 with audio-visual facilities, exhibition space available, largest reception 1000

Room services
Airconditioning, colour TV + CNN & Video,

direct-dial telephone, minibar, music/radio/ alarm clock, tea/cofee making, 24-hr room service

Business & other services
Business centre, shops, car parking, taxi service, guided tours, newsstand/shops, comp. shuttle Orchard Road/Shops

Sports & Recreation
Plaza fitness club, outdoor swimming pool, aerobics, squash, beauty spa, health bar

Restaurants & Coffee Shops
Cafe Plaza - Western/Asian/Oriental buffet; *Dou Hua* - Sichuan; *Club 5* - Music & dance lounge

Overseas Sales Representatives
Utell International Reservations. Japan tel: (03) 3461 8585; fax (03) 3461 8550

Raffles Hotel ○ A
1 Beach Road, 189673
Tel: 337 1886; Tlx: RS 39028 RINTL; Fax: 339 7650

Regent of Singapore ○ A
Cuscaden Road, 249715 (Tanglin area)
Tel: 733 8888; Tlx: 37248; Fax: 732 8838

Ritz Carlton Millenia A
7 Raffles Avenue, Singapore 039799
Tel: 337 8888; Fax: 338 0003

River View Hotel ○
382 Havelock Road, 169629 (Chinatown)
Tel: 732 9922; Tlx: RS 55454 RVHTEL; Fax: 732 1034

At the gateway between the Nation's tropical riverline origins and its computerised high-tech urban metropolis, lies the River View Hotel. With her beautiful landscaped garden cafe terrace along the historic Singapore river, she is set in the heart of the nation's cultural history.

Accommodation & rates
111 single/double, S$ 180-210; 353 twin, S$ 200-230; 8 suites, S$ 350-500
Subject to 10% service charge and 4% government tax

Credit cards accepted:
Amex, Visa, Mastercard, Diners Club, JCB

Meeting & banqueting facilities
5 meeting/function rooms, capacity 20 to 380, with audio-visual equipment; 384 sq m exhibition space; largest reception 350

Room Services
Air condirtioning, colour TV, direct-dial telephone (ext. in bathroom), hairdryer, laundry/valet service, minibar, music/radio/ alarm clock, tea/coffee making facilities, trouser press, non-smoker bedrooms available, 24-hr room service, video films, non-smoker bedrooms available

Business & other services
Business centre, car parking, taxi service, guided tours, newsstand/shops, drugstore, complimentary shuttle to Orchard Road

Sports & Recreation
Fitness centre/gym, mini-golf, massage, sauna, swimming pool (outdoor)

Restaurants & Coffee Shops
River Garden Terrace (260) - International, open 24 hours; *River Palace* (250) - Szechuan, open noon-1430/1830-2230; *Ginga* (90) - Japanese, open as above

Overseas Sales Representatives:
Malaysia - tel: (60-3) 248 6104; fax: (60-3) 9951. Macau - tel: (853) 378688; fax: (853) 569045. Hong Kong - tel: (852) 2543 3345; fax: (852) 2542 0824; tlx: 63851 LATINHX

Hotel Royal ○
36 Newton Road, 307964 (Orchard Road - N)
Tel: 253 4411; Fax: 253 8668;

Royal Holiday Inn Crowne Plaza ○ B
25 Scotts Road, 228220 (Orchard Road)
Tel: 737 7966; Fax: 737 6646

Shangri-La Hotel, Singapore ○ A
Orange Grove Road, 258350 (Tanglin area)
Tel: 737 3644; Fax: 733 1029/733 7220

Shangri-La's Rasa Sentosa Resort C
101 Siloso Road, Sentosa, 098970
Tel: 275 0100; Fax: 275 0355; Tlx: 20817

Sheraton Towers Singapore B
39 Scotts Road, 228230 (Orchard Road).Tel: 737 6888; Tlx: RS 36882 SSCSIN; Fax: 737 1072

Singapore Marriott Hotel ○ A
25 Scotts Road, 238865 (Orchard Road)
Tel: 735 5800; Fax: 735 9800

Stamford Inn D
Tel: 332 2222; Fax: 334 9633

The Westin Plaza/Stamford ○ C
2 Stamford Road, 178882 (Raffles City)
Tel: 338 8585; Tlx: RS 22206; Fax: 338 2862

The York Hotel ○ B
21 Mount Elizabeth Rd, 228516 (Orchard Rd). Tel: 737 0511; Fax: 732 1217

Restaurants

Aziza's Restaurant *(Malay)*
36 Emerald Hill Rd.
Tel: 235 1130

The Beefeater *(European)*
417 River Valley Rd.
Tel: 737 8425

Casablanca *(Continental)*
7 Emerald Hill.
Tel: 235 9328

Domus *(International)*
Sheraton Towers Hotel, 39 Scotts Rd, 0922.
Tel: 737 6888

Fook Yuen Seafood Restaurant
290 Orchard Road, Fl 03-05 Tha Paragon. Tel: 235 2211

Fourchettes *(International)*
Oriental Hotel, 6 Raffles Boulevard, Marina Square, 0103.
Tel: 338 0066

Gordon Grill *(International)*
Goodwood Park Hotel, 22 Scotts Road, 0922.
Tel: 737 7411

Harbour Grill *(French)*
Hilton Hotel, 581 Orchard Road, 0923.
Tel: 737 2233

House of Sundanese *(Indonesian)*
55 Boat Quay, 0104.
Tel: 534 3775

Hugo's *(French)*
Hyatt Regency Hotel, 10-12 Scotts Road, 0922. Tel: 733 1188

Inn of Happiness *(Cantonese)*
Hilton Hotel, 581 Orchard Road, 0923.
Tel: 737 2233

Golden Phoenix Sichuan *(Sichuan)*
Hotel Equatorial, 2nd floor, 429 Bukit Timah Rd, 1025. Tel: 732 0431

Jawa Timur Permai *(Malay)*
Chiaixt Hong Bldg, 7th fl 110 Middle Rd.
Tel: 337 5532

Kelong Thomson Restaurant *(Cantonese)*
Thomson Plaza, Upper Thomson Road.

Kinara North Indian Shore Cuisine
57 Boat Quay, 0104
Tel: 533 0412;

Latour *(French)*
Shangri-La Hotel, 22 Orange Grove Road, 1025. Tel: 737 3644

Li Bai *(Chinese)*
Sheraton Towers Hotel, 39 Scotts Road, 0922.
Tel: 737 6888

Lido Palace *(Theatre Restaurant)*
Concorde Hotel Shopping Centre, 317 Outram Road, 0316.
Tel: 732 8855

Marco Polo *(French/Sea)*
Marco Polo Hotel, 247 Tanglin Road, 1024.
Tel: 474 7141

Mayflower *(Chinese)*
DBS Bldg, Shenton Way.
Tel: 220 3133

Maxim's de Paris *(Fr.)*
Regent of Singapore Hotel, 1 Cuscaden Road
Tel 733 8888

Meisan Restaurant *(Chinese - Szechuan)*
Royal Holiday Inn Hotel, 25 Scotts Road, 0922.
Tel: 737 7966

Moti Mahal *(Indian)*
18 Murray St.
Tel: 221 4338

Nadaman Restaurant *(Japanese)*
Shangri-La Hotel, 22 Orange Grove Road, 0915. Tel: 737 3644

The Neptune *(Theatre Restaurant)*,Collyer Quay. Tel: 224 3922

Omar Khayyam *(Indian)*
55 Hill Street

Palm Grill *(International)*
Westin Plaza Hotel, 2 Stamford Road, 0718.
Tel: 338 8585

Pasta Fresca *(Italian)*
30 Boat Quay, 0104
Tel: 532 6283

Pete's Place *(Italian)*
Hyatt Regency Hotel, 10-12 Scotts Rd, 0922.
Tel: 733 1188

Pine Court *(Peking)*
Mandarin Hotel, 333 Orchard Road, 0923.
Tel: 737 4411

Le Restaurant de France *(French)*
Hotel Meridien, 100 Orchard Road, 0923.
Tel: 733 8555

Restaurant 1819 *(Cont'l)*
B1, Tuan Sing Towers, 30 Robinson Road, 1130.
Tel: 223 4033

Salero Bagindo *(Indonesian)*
Fl.03-239, 6 Raffles Boulevard, Marina Square, 0103.
Tel: 338 1389

The Seafood Place
Pan Pacific Hotel, 7 Raffles Blvd.Tel: 336 8111

Suntory *(Japanese)*
Fl.06-01, Delfi Orchard, 402 Orchard Road, 0923.
Tel: 732 5111

Swatow Teochew Restaurant *(Chinese)*
5th Fl, Centrepoint Shopping Plaza, 176 Orchard Road, 0922.
Tel: 235 4717

Tropicana *(Theatre [Chinese] Restaurant)*
Scotts Road.
Tel: 737 6433

Wen's Place *(Malay)*
101-A Block 4, Queen's Rd. Tel: 474 8250

Departures from Changi International Airport

To the **airports** printed in bold type below. Flights correct as at February 1997. Figures in brackets after airline codes (see below) signify (1) departing on a Monday (first day of the week) and so on to (7) = Sunday. Only direct flights, without change, are listed.

Main Airline Abbreviation Codes: AF = Air France; **AI** = Air India; **AY** = Finnair; **AZ** = Alitalia; **BA** = British Airways; **BG** = Biman Bangladesh; **BI** = Royal Brunei; **BO** = Bouraq Indonesia Air; **BR** = EVA Air; **CA** = Air China; **CI** = China Air; **CK** = Gambia Air; **CX** = Cathay Pacific; **CZ** = China Southern; **DL** = Delta Air; **EK** = Emirates; **GA** = Garuda; **GF** = Gulf Air; **HM** = Air Seychelles; **IC** = Indian Air; **JL** = Japan Air; **JU** = Yugoslav Air; **KE** = Korean Air; **KL** = KLM; **KU** = Kuwait Air; **LH** = Lufthansa; **ME** = Xiamen Air; **MH** = Malaysian Air; **MI** = Silk Air; **MK** = Air Mauritius; **MS** = Egyptian; **MU** = China Eastern; **MZ** = Merpati Nusantara Air; **NG** = Lauda Air; **NH** = All Nippon Air; **NW** = Northwest Airlines; **NZ** = Air New Zealand; **OK** = Czechoslovak Air; **OS**=Austrian; **OZ** = Asiana Air; **PK** = Pakisatn Int Air; **PR** = Philippine Air; **PX** = Air Niugini; **QF** = Qantas; **RA** = Royal Nepal; **RJ** = Royal Jordanian; **SA** = South African Airways; **SG** = Sempati Air; **SK** = Scandinavian Airline System; **SQ** = Singapore Airlines; **SR** = Swissair; **SU**= Aeroflot; **SV** = Saudia; **SZ** = China Southwest; **TG** = Thai Int; **TK** = Turkish Airlines;**UA** = United Airlines; **UL** = Air Lanka; **VJ**=Royal Air Cambodge;**VN** = Vietnam Air; **3Q** = Yunnan Air; **9P** = Air Pelangi;

Abu Dhabi (AUH)
GA (6)
Adelaide (ADL)
SQ (1,3,5,7)
Amman (AMM)
RJ (3,6)
Amsterdam (AMS)
GA (1,6) KL (1,2,4,5,6,7) SQ (daily)
Athens (ATH)
SQ (2,5)
Auckland (AKL)
NZ (2,3,5,6,7) SQ (daily)
Bahrain (BAH)
GF (1,3,5,7) OK (3)
Bandar Seri B (BWN)
BI (daily) SQ (daily)
Bandung (BDO)
MZ (daily)
Bangalore (BLR)
AI (1,4)
Bangkok (BKK)
SQ,CX,TG,SK (daily) GA (2,4,6) RA (1,4) NZ (2,5) BG (1,3,5,7) SR (1,3,4,5,7) AZ (3) AY (1,5) OZ (1,3,4,5) KE (1,3,4,6) TK (1,3,5) OK (1,3) QF (2,4,6,7) AF (5)
Beijing (PEK)
SQ (daily) CA (2,3,4,6,7) CZ (2,4,5,7)
Berlin (SXF)
SQ (3,7)
Bombay (BOM)
AI,SQ (daily) QF (3,5,7)
Boston (BOS)
UA (daily)
Brisbane (BNE)
QF (daily) SQ (1,2,4,6)
Brussels (BRU)
SQ (5,7)
Cairns (CNS)
QF (1,2,3,5,6,7) SQ (1,2,6)
Cairo (CAI)
SQ (1,3,6) MS (4,7)
Calcutta (CCU)
SQ (2,5) BI (6)
Cape Town (CPT)
SQ (2,4,5)
Cebu (CEB)
MI (2,3,5,6,7)
Chengdu (CTU)
SZ (2,6)
Chiang Mai (CNX)
MI (2,5,7)
Chicago (CHI)
UA (daily)
Christchurch (CHC)
NZ (2,3,5,6,7) SQ (2,4,6,7)
Christmas Is (XCH)
NC (1,5)
Colombo (CMB)
UL (1,3,5,6) SQ (2,3,5,7) EK (1,3,5,6)

Copenhagen (CPH)
SQ (3,6,7)
Darwin (DRW)
QF (1,2,3,5,6,7) SQ (2)
Delhi (DEL)
SU (1) AI (2,4,6) SQ (3,5,7)
Denpasar-Bali (DPS)
SQ,GA, BO (daily) KL (3,7) NZ (3,6) QF (1,4,7)
Detroit (DTT)
UA (daily)
Dhahran (DHA)
SQ (3,6)
Dhaka (DAC)
BG (1,3,4,5,7) SQ (2,3,4,5,7)
Dubai (DXB)
EK (1,2,3,4,5,6) BI (3,5,6) SQ (1,3,5,6) SU (3,5)
Durban (DUR)
SQ (3,6)
Frankfurt (FRA)
GA (1,5,6) LH (2,4) SQ (daily)
Fukuoka (FUK)
SQ (daily)
Geneva (GVA)
SR (3,4,7)
Guangzhou (CAN)
SQ (4,7) CZ (2,5,7)
Hangzhou (HGH)
SQ (3)
Hanoi (HAN)
SQ/VN (1,3,6) VN (daily)
Hat Yai (HDY)
MI,TG (daily)
Helsinki (HEL)
AY (1,5)
Hiroshima (HIJ)
SQ (1,3,5,6)
Ho Chi Minh (SGN)
SQ/VN (1,3,4,5,7) GA (2,5)VN (daily)
Hong Kong (HKG)
CI, CX, SQ, UA, QF (daily) GA (1,3,6)
Islamabad (ISB)
PK (4)
Istanbul (IST)
TK (1,3,5) SQ (3,6)
Jakarta (JKT)
GA,KL,SG,SQ,TG,MI,LH (daily) PK (2,6) EK (1,2,4) AI (3,7) RJ (1), AF (1,2,4,6) QF (4,6) UB (2,5)
Jeddah (JED)
SV (2,4)
Johannesburg (JNB)
SQ (2,3,4,5,6,7)
Kaohsiung (KHH)
CI (daily) BR (1,3,5,7) SQ (1,3,5,6,7)
Karachi (KHI)
PK (1,3,5) SQ (1,3,5)
Kathmandu (KTM)
RA (1,4) SQ (4,7)

Khabarovsk (KHV)
SU (3)
Kota Kinabalu (BKI)
MH (daily) SQ (2,6)
Kuala Lumpur (KUL)
MH,SQ,JL (daily) QF (3,5,7)
AI (2,5) IC (4) GA (1,3,4,7)
Kuantan (KUA)
MH/MI (3,5,7)
Kuching (KCH)
MH (daily) SQ (3,6)
Kunming (KMG)
MI (4,7) 3Q (3,4,6,7)
Kuwait (KWI)
KU (2,4,7)
Lahore (LHE)
PK (4)
Langkawi (LGK)
MH/MI (daily)
London (LHR)
BA, SQ (daily) BI (3,5)
Los Angeles (LAX)
SQ (daily) UA (daily)
Macau (MFM)
SQ (2,5)
Madras (MAA)
AI (1,2,3,5,6,7) SQ (1,3,4,5,6,7) IC (1,4,6) BA (4,7)
Madrid (MAD)
SQ (1,6)
Mahe Island (SEZ)
HM (2,5)
Male (MLE)
EK (2,4,6) SQ (daily)
Manado (MDC)
MI (1,4)
Manchester (MAN)
SQ (1,4,7)
Manila (MNL)
PR (daily) SQ (daily)
Mataram (AMI)
MI/SG (daily)
Mauritius (MRU)
MK/SQ (3,6,7)
Medan (MES)
GA (daily) MI (daily)
Melbourne (MEL)
GF (2,4,6,7) SQ (daily) NG (1,4,6) QF (1,4,6,7) EK (2,4,6)
Moscow (SVO)
SU (1,3,5)
Nagoya (NGO)
JL (1,4,7) SQ (daily)
New York (JFK)
SQ, DL (daily)
Osaka (OSA)
JL,NH,SQ (daily)
Padang (PDG)
MZ (1,4,6) MI (2,5,7)
Paris (CDG)
GA (3) SQ (daily) AF (5,6)
Pekanbaru (PKU)
MZ (1,4,6) MI (1,3,5,6)
Penang (PEN)

MH,SQ,BR (daily)
Perth (PER)
BA,QF,SQ (daily) AI (3,5)
Phnom-Penh (PNH)
MI (daily) VJ (1,2,3,5,7)
Phuket (HKT)
TG (daily) MI (daily)
Pontianak (PNK)
MZ (2,5)
Port Moresby (POM)
PX/SQ (4,6)
Prague (PRG)
OK (1,3)
Riyadh (RUH)
SV (2)
Rome (FCO)
AZ (3) SQ (2,4,7)
San Francisco (SFO)
SQ,UA (daily)
Seattle (SEA)
NW (daily)
Sendai (SDJ)
SQ (1,2,5,6)
Seoul (SEL)
KE (1,2,3,4,5,7) SQ (daily) OZ (1,3,4,5)
Shanghai (SHA)
SQ (daily) MU (2,3,5,7)
Shenzhen (SZX)
CZ (7)
Solo City (SOC)
MI/MZ (1,3,6)
Stockholm (STO)
SK (7)
Surabaya (SUB)
GA (1,3,4,7) SQ, BO (daily) KL (3,7)
Sydney (SYD)
QF,SQ, (daily) KL (1,4,6) NG (1,4,6) MS (2,5) NG (1,4,6) GF (2,4,6,7)
Taipei (TPE)
CI, SQ, BR (daily) BI(3,7)
Tioman (TOD)
MI, 9P (daily)
Tokyo (NRT)
JL, SQ, UA, NW (daily) BG (5) NH (1,3,4,6,7)
Trivandrum (TRV)
AI (3,7)
Ujung Pandang (UPG)
MI/BO (1,4,6)
Vancouver (YVR)
SQ (1,6)
Vienna (VIE)
SQ (2,5) NG (2,5,7) OS (2,5)
Vientiane (VTE)
MI (1,3,5)
Wellington (WLG)
NZ (2,3,5,6,7)
Xiamen (XMN)
CA (2,4,7) MI (2,4,6) CZ (1,3,6)
Yangon (RGN)
UB, MI (daily)
Zurich (ZRH)
GA (1,3) SQ (daily) SR (1,3,4,5,7)

Major Exhibitions in Singapore 1997/98

Date	Exhibition	Venue	Organiser
May 14-17	**AIHEX**: Asian International Hardare & Houseware Exposition - architectural hardware, DIY supplies, garden products etc.	WTC	Reed
May 16-18	**Asian Diver Exhibition & Conference**	WTC	MFreeman
May 14-17	**SIBEX**: South East Asian Int'l Bldg & Construction Expo	WTC	Reed
June 3-5	**Pharmaceutical Ingredients Asia**	SICEC	MFreeman
June 26-29	**PC SHOW '97 - SINGAPORE** & **The SOFTWARE SHOW '97**	WTC	LEMS
Jul 22-25	**APP: AsiaPrint** & **APP: AsiaPack**- 10th printing machinery, pre-press, laminating and computer graphics equipment & packaging machinery	WTC	Reed
Sept 16-19	**WoodmacAsia 97** & **Furnitek/Asia 97** - 8th & 3rd respectively int'l exhibitions of woodworking & forestry supplies, & furniture production	WTC	SES
Sept 24-27	**NEPCON/SMT & ASIA ELECTRONICS** - surface mount technology, equiment, materials and services	SICEC	Reed
Oct 21-24	**Industrial Automation/Logismat 97**	WTC	MFreeman
Nov 4-7	**ChemAsia 97** - 10th Asian Int'l instrumentation and equipment show	WTC	SES
Nov 12-15	**Corrugated Asia/Converting Machinery Asia 97**	WTC	MFreeman
1988			
April	**Asian International Gift Fair 98**	WTC	SES
April	**Asian International Stationery Fair 98**	WTC	SES
April 14-17	**Food & Hotel Asia 98** - 11th Asian Int'l exhibition of food, drink and related equipment	WTC	SES

Venues:
SICEC/Suntec = Singapore International Convention & Exhibition Centre, 1 Raffles Boulevard, Suntec City, Singapore 039593. Tel: (65) 337 2888; faxt (65) 431 2222. **WTC** = World Trade Centre, Maritime Square. Tel: 274 7111.

Organisers:
ITF = Internatonal Trade Fairs (S) Pte Ltd, 1 Maritime Square, Fl 09-20 World Trade Centre, Singapore 0409, tel: 278 9166; fax: 274 8670; tlx: RS 55171. **LEMS** = Lines Exposition & Management Services Pte. Ltd, 318-B King George's Avenue, Singapore; tel: (65) 2998611; fax: (65) 2998633. **MFreeman** = Miller Freeman Asia Ltd, 102-5 Stanhope House, 738 King's Road, Quarry Bary, Hong Kong. tel: (852) 2827 5121; fax: (852) 2827 7064. **Reed** = Reed Exhibition Companies (South Asia Headquarters), 1 Lemasek Avenue 17-01, Millenia Tower, Singapore 039192, tel: 338 2002; fax: 338 2112.
SES = Singapore Exhibition Services Pte Ltd, 2 Handy Road, Fl 15-09 Cathay Bldg, Singapore 229233; tel: 338 4747; E-mail: sesinfo @ singnet.com.sg; fax: 339 5651.

What's the link between business and the Asia Pacific?

BRITISH AIRWAYS
The world's favourite airline

http://www.british-airways.com

Sri Lanka

Tourism/What to See

Sri Lanka's arrivals in 1996 were expected to match 1995's 400,000. The Tourism Authority has launched a number of initiatives to reassure travellers of the safety of most parts of the country, in the face of continued reports of fighting in the North-East. In a bid to lure more Asian travellers, the Colombo government is to allow casinos in certain hotels and is developing three golf courses.

At present Sri Lanka's chief attractions are its temples and former capitals. Colombo, like the rest of the Indian subcontinent, has an almost endless list of beautifully-crafted colonial-style official buildings.

But there's plenty for culture vultures, too: Anuradhapura - Sri Lanka's first capital which dates from the 5th century BC and is just over 200km from Colombo; Jetavanaramaya is the tallest of the country's *dagabas;* the Brazen Palace. In addition, there is the Thuparama Dagaba the most ancient of the island's *dagabas*, – built by King Devanampiya and reconstructed in the 1840s; the Samadhi Buddha is a 4th century statue and is acknowledged as a masterpiece.

Mihintale - just 11km east of Anuradhapura - is generally regarded as the cradle of Buddhism in Sri Lanka. The rock is dotted with shrines and rock dwellings. A grand stairway of 1,840 steps made of granite slabs leads to the summit.

Polonnaruwa was the island's medieval capital and is 216 km from Colombo and features a wealth of parks and gardens dotted with shrines. A unique irrigational complex known as the *Sea of Parakrama* watered the city as well as the surrounding plains. Polonnaruwa also boasts many fine old buildings. Some of the restoration work is being funded by Unesco. Other places worth visiting include Dambulla, Yapahuwa and Aluvihara.

Hill-top Kandy is without doubt Sri Lanka's most beautiful town. Situated nearly 500 metres above sea level it also boasts a more pleasant climate. The town's focal point is the golden-roofed Dalada Maligawa where the Sacred Tooth Relic of the Buddha is enshrined. Again major restoration work is being funded by Unesco.

A visit to the National Parks: Yala, Wilpattu (known for leopards and sloth) and Gal Oya (famous for its elephants) make a pleasant day out from Colombo. The Elephant Orphanage on the Kegalle-Rambukkana road is a great chance to see young elephants and the National Zoological Gardens offers a wider variety of wildlife. Sri Lanka also has some fine bird sanctuaries.

Other places of interest to consider include: the Dutch Period Museum, the Bandaranaike Museum and the Colombo Museum. Weligama - about 27km from Galle - is the home of the island's famous stilt fishermen. Galle, itself, has an impressive Dutch fort.

Shopping

Sri Lanka sees itself as a shopper's paradise with a wide range of handicrafts at reasonable prices. The island is also famous for its gems and silverware. Contemporary paintings, dolls, ebony work, brassware, rush and reedware are all popular with visitors.

Most large hotels have their own shopping arcades. The state-run Sri Lanka Handlooms Emporium on Galle Road offers handloom fabrics and furnishing materials together with hand-crafted brass and silverware, jewellery, pottery and coconut fibre products plus leather goods and a variety of traditional arts and crafts. Other government-owned outlets are Viskram Niwasa and Laksala on York Street.

Sri Lanka is the world's leading producer of high quality tea and many shops in Colombo sell locally-grown varieties. Every visitor is allowed three kilos for export duty free. The Sri Lankan Tea Board has sales counters on Galle Road and at Katunayake International Airport, where there is also a duty-free complex.

Getting Around

Only a few taxis or trishaws have meters (fewer still working ones), so arrange the fare beforehand. Expect to pay around Rps15-20 a kilometre - a little more after 2200. Taxis from the main hotels have fixed rates. Unlike India, self-drive cars are available through travel agents and firms such as Quickshaws (Hertz), Mercs Rent-a-Car Tours, Mackinnons (Avis) and Abans (Europcar).

Train and bus transport is inexpensive. Air-conditioned trains operate from Colombo to Kandy and Talawakelle. The Inter-city Express Service is available between Colombo-Kandy and Colombo-Banarawela. The Sri Lankan Transport Board maintains an island-wide bus network with rates are among the world's cheapest.

Scheduled internal air travel is not available; although Inland Air Services will provide fixed-wing and helicopter charter to domestic destinations.

Entertainment

Many large hotels have night clubs which provide dinner/dancing and occasional floor shows. Some of the more popular clubs are: the *Blue Leopard* at the Hotel Taprobane; the *Little Hut* at Mount Lavinia Hotel; the *Supper Club* at Hotel Lanka Oberoi; the Ramada's *Library* and the *Blue Elephant* at the Colombo Hilton.

Colombo has several excellent air-conditioned cinemas showing both western and local films. Sinhala and western plays and Sinhala translations of western plays are staged frequently. Popular theatres include the Lionel Wendt, the YMBA, the John de Silva Memorial and the Lumbini.

The State Dance Ensemble present traditional dance performances from time to time. "Devil" dancing and the well-known Kandyan dances are regularly performed at a variety of venues.

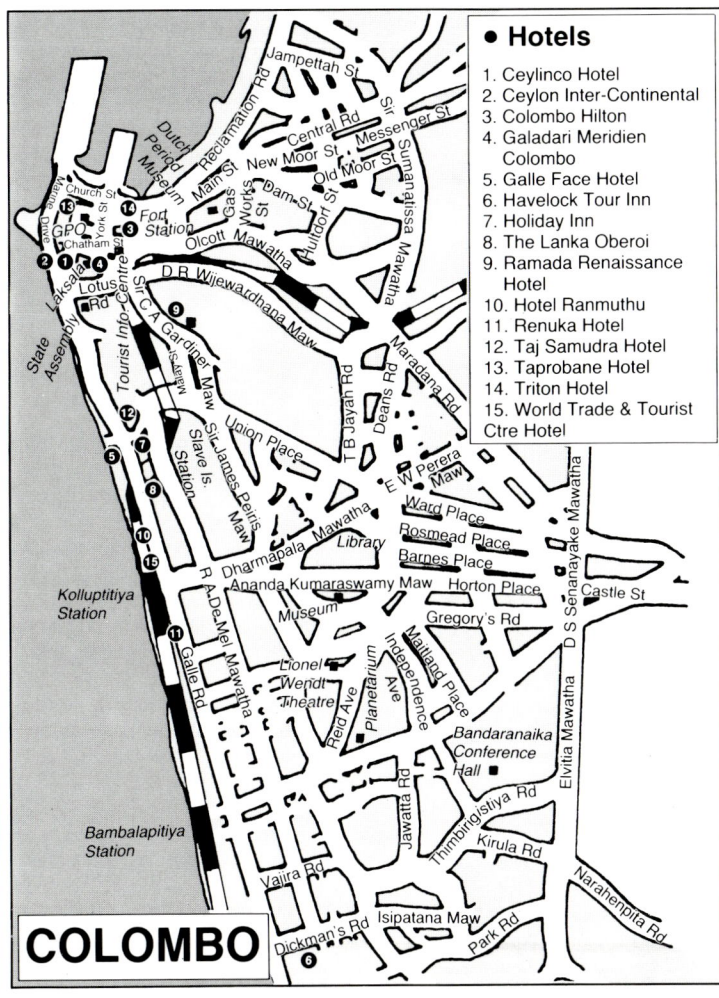

Hotels

1. Ceylinco Hotel
2. Ceylon Inter-Continental
3. Colombo Hilton
4. Galadari Meridien Colombo
5. Galle Face Hotel
6. Havelock Tour Inn
7. Holiday Inn
8. The Lanka Oberoi
9. Ramada Renaissance Hotel
10. Hotel Ranmuthu
11. Renuka Hotel
12. Taj Samudra Hotel
13. Taprobane Hotel
14. Triton Hotel
15. World Trade & Tourist Ctre Hotel

Restaurants

A selection offering specialist cuisine.

Alt Heidelberg German Restaurant
11 Galle Face Court, (opp. Galle Face Hotel). Tel: 421577

Chinese Golden Gate
25 Galle Rd, Col 6. Tel: 582510

Ginza Araliya *(Sri Lankan)*
286 Galle Rd (near Kolluptiya Junction).

Ginza Hohsen *(Japanese)*
Colombo Hilton Hotel. Echelon Square Complex. Tel: 544644 ext 2123

Harbour Room
Taprobane Hotel, 2 York St. Tel: 20391

Hong Kong Restaurant *(Chinese)*
19/1 Daisy Villa, Duplication Rd. Tel: 501606

London Grill *(International)*
The Lanka Oberoi Hotel, 77 Steuart Place. Tel: 437437

Mandarin Palace *(Chinese/Thai)*
28 Longden Place. Tel: 587740

Car Hire

Avis
4 Leyden Bastian Rd (Head Office), Col. 1
Tel: 29881; Tlx: 21124 ; Fax: 547748

Inter Rent
Mercantile Tours (Ceylon), 586 Galle Road, PO Box 1778, Colombo 3. Tel: 500 578/9, 500687/8; Tlx: 22771; Fax: 500688

Mutual Holiday Travel
M4 Hotel Galadari Meridien, 64 Lotus Road, Colombo 1 Tel: 544544, 437122; Tlx: 22334 GALMER CE; Fax: 437122

Tangerine Tours. Tel: 422518/9
Toyota Rent-A-Car. Tel: 713356

Leisure

The island's sport and leisure activities tend to be of the easy-going, unsophisticated variety. The best facilities are to be found at either private clubs or at the large international-class hotels, many of which offer tennis and swimming - some even have health and fitness clubs.

Fishing is available through temporary membership of local clubs. Golf is easy to arrange and there are several good courses. Scuba diving and water-sports are both popular with visitors - especially at the resorts in the south-west of the island.

The Royal Colombo Golf Club offers excellent and challenging golf to non-members. A new golf resort, the Victoria, which will be the island's third is being planned near Kandy. The Ceylon Sea Anglers Club in Trincomalee and the Ceylon Angler's Club can be contacted to arrange a fishing party. The Royal Colombo Yacht Club can also set up fishing trips.

Sri Lanka has over 1,600km of palm-fringed beaches. Best time to visit is November or April on the south-west coast and April to September on the east coast. Bentola and Beruwela are two of the island's best beach resorts.

Arrival & Departure

Colombo International Airport is located 34 km north of the city. Expect a 40-60 minute drive from the airport to the city centre. A special airport bus runs to the city for Rps100. A train runs four times a day. Better, though, to catch an airport taxi, which will charge about Rps600 to downtown Colombo.

A Rps 400 tax, payable in local currency, is charged on departure. The Bank of Ceylon bureau de change counter is open 24 hours.

Sri Lanka Key Fact File

Passport Requirements:
All visitors must be in possession of a valid passport. Nationals of 66 countries (EC countries, Rest of W & E Europe, USA, Canada, Japan, former USSR and most Southeast Asian countries) are exempt from visa requirements if their stay is less than 30 days and the purpose of their visit is touristic. ALL business visitors require a visa.

Currency: Sri Lanka rupee. 100 cents = SLR 1

Exchange Rates:
US$ 1 = 57.5 SLR; £1 = 94 SLR *(May 1997)*

Currency Restrictions:
The import and export of local currency is limited to RS 250. All visitors arriving in Sri Lanka have to declare the amount of foreign currency brought in. All unspent money converted into local currency can be reconverted upon departure. The import of notes from India and Pakistan is forbidden.

Electricity supply:
230-240 volts/50 cycles AC

Language: Sinhala, Tamil (in Northeast) and English all official
Time: GMT + 5.5 hours; EDT + 10.5 hrs

IDD Dialling Code: 94
Area Codes: Colombo 1; Galle 9; Jaffna 21; Kandy 8; Matara 41; Negombo 31; Trincomalee 26.

Business Hours:
Banks are open 0900-1300 Mondays; 0900-1330 Tuesdays-Fridays.
Government offices: 0830-1630 Mon-Fri. Office hours are generally 0830-1630 Monday to Friday.
Shops open 0800 (or 0900) to 1700 Monday to Friday with most also open Saturday mornings.

Customs & Entry:
Visitors are required to re-export articles brought in as personal effects. No antiques, protected flora and fauna and rare books may be exported.

Health Requirements:
Yellow fever and cholera certificates only required if arriving from an infected area. Typhoid/polio inoculation and anti-malaria course advised. Tap water not drinkable. Only eat well-cooked, hot, meat. Avoid ice cubes and unpeeled fruit. Beware of poisonous snakes.

Climate/best time to visit:
Hot and humid year-round. The wet South-West zone experiences some 5,000mm of rainfall; although Colombo has around 2,240mm. The average temperature is between 25C-30C - cooler in upland areas.

National Holidays 1997
23 January* and each full moon Poya day throughout the year *(21 Feb; 23 Mar; 22 April; 21 May; 21 May; 20 June; 19 July; 18 Aug; 16 Sept; 15 Oct; 14 Nov; 13 Dec)*; 14 January Tamil Thai-Pongal Day; 4 February National Day; 9 February* Eid-ul-Fitr; 28 March Good Friday; 13/14 April Sinhala & Tamil New Year; 1 May May Day; 22 May Day following Vesak; 18 July* Holy Prophet's Birthday (Milad-Un-Nabi); 30 October Deepavali Festival; December 25 Christmas Day;

(*Moslem and lunar holidays may vary by one or two days according to the moon's cycle.)

Useful Addresses

Air Couriers

DHL: Tel: 440686
TNT: Tel: 447644/326308
UPS: Tel: 328793

Business

All Ceylon Trade Chamber
212/45, 1-3, Bedhiraja Mawatha, Colombo 1
Tel: 545742/32428

The Ceylon Chamber of Commerce
50 Navam Mawatha, PO Box 274, Colombo 2
Tel: 421745-47; Tlx: 21494 GLOBAL CE 5193; Fax: 449352

Department of Commerce
Rakshana Mandiraya, 4th Fl Vauxhall Street, Colombo 2
Tel: 22311-13; Tlx: 21908 COMECE CE

Federation of Chambers of Commerce & Industry of Sri Lanka
People's Bank Building, 220 Deans Road, Colombo 10. Tel: 599530; Tlx: 22186

Greater Colombo Economic Commission Investment Promotion Department
14 Sir Baron Jayatillake Mawatha, PO Box 1768, Colombo 1

Tel: 434403/448880/447531; Tlx: 21332 ECONCOM CE; Fax: 447995

The Mercantile Chamber of Commerce
19 Arthur's Place, Colombo 4.
Tel: 425451

The National Chamber of Commerce of Sri Lanka
2nd Fl, YMBA Bldg, PO Box 1375, Main Street, Colombo 1. Tel: 545409/25271

The Sri Lanka Chamber of Small Industry
17a Dickman's Road, Colombo 5
Tel: 209788

Sri Lanka Export Development Board
Ramada Renaissance Bldg, 115 Sir Chittampalam A Gardiner Mawatha, Colombo 2
Tel: 438513-15; Tlx: 21457 EXDEV CE

Women's Chamber of Industry & Commerce
10, 1/1, Sir Marcus Fernando Mawatha, Colombo 7. Tel: 495913

Sri Lanka National Council Interrnational Chamber of Commerce,
17a Alfred Place, Colombo 3

Tourism, exhibition centres

Buddhist Information Centre
50 Ananda Cumaraswamy Mawatha, Colombo 7. Tel: 423079

Ceylon Tourist Board
78 Steuart Place, Colombo 3
Tel: 437059-60; Tlx: 21867 TOURBD CE

Post Office, Medical etc

Central Telegraph Office
Duke St, Colombo 1. Tel: 431407

Accident Service
Ward Place, Colombo 7
Tel: 693184/693185 (Ambul'ce tel: 422222)

Hospital Durdans
3 Alfred Place, Colombo 3. Tel: 575205-7
Emergency: Tel: 433333

Sri Lanka Hotels

Ahungalla

Agungalla Triton Hotel E
Tel: (09) 54041; Fax: 54046

Anuradhapura

Miridya Hotel E
Rowing Club Rd
Tel: (025) 2112/2519

Bentota

Bentota Beach House E
PO Box 171
Tel: (034) 75176; Tlx: 21104

Ceysands Hotel E
Aluthgama
Tel: (034) 75073-4; Tlx: 21228 Fax: 447087

Lihiniya Surf Hotel E
Beachfront
Tel: (034) 75126; Fax: 75486

Beruwela

Neptune Hotel Beruwela ○ E
Moragalla
Tel: (034) 76031/2; Tlx: 21788; Fax: 76033

Pearl Beach Hotel E
Tel: (034) 75117-8; Tlx: 21788

Colombo

Hotel Ceylon Inter-Continental ○ D
48 Janadhipathi Mawatha, Colombo 1
Tel: 421221; Tlx: 21188; Fax: 447326

Colombo Hilton ○
Echelon Square Complex, Lotus Road, 1
Tel: 544644/437177/344644; Tlx: 22803-5; Fax: 544657/8

The Colombo Hilton is situated on a seven-acre site facing the Old Parliament Building, overlooking the Beira Lake and the Indian Ocean. The hotel is within walking distance of the business and shopping district and adjacent to the World Trade Centre Twin Towers. It is 32 km from Colombo Airport and just 5 minutes from the bus station, local railway station and Colombo harbour.

Accommodation and rates
194 single/double from US$ 115; 150 twin from US$ 125; 43 suites from US$190
Subj to 10% service charge & 6.4% govt tax

Credit cards accepted:
Amex, Diners, Mastercard, Visa, JCB

Meeting & banqueting facilities
16 meeting/conference rooms, capacity 25-700, with audio-visual equipment; 630 sq m exhibition space; largest reception 650 banquet or 850 cocktail.

Room services
Airconditioning, colour TV, direct-dial telephone (ext. in bathroom), hairdryer, laundry/valet service, minibar, music/radio, 24-hr room service, non-smoking floor, safety deposit box, Japanese floors, video films, satellite TV news, butler service, four executive floors

Business services
24-hour business centre, executive floor, express checkout, airport pickup, translation service, car parking, car rental, courier service, travel centre, taxi service

Other services
Clinic, art gallery, hairdresser, newsagent/drugstore, florist

Sports & Recreation
Fitness centre/gym, indoor games, jacuzzi/whirlpool, joggong track, massage, sauna, squash, outdoor swimming pool, tennis,

Restaurants & Coffee Shops
Lotus (137) - international, open 24 hours; Gables (60) - European, open noon-1430/1900-2300; Ginza Hohsen (120) - Japanese, open 1100-2300; Wok (74) - Chinese, open 1100-1430/1900-2300; Il Ponte (70) - Italian, open 1800-2300; Curry Leaf (60) - Open air Sri Lankan cuisine; Discothèque, Karaoke Bar, Echelon Pub, Thorana Lounge Bar, Poolside Bar, Lounge Bar.

Overseas Sales Representatives:
Hilton International Sales Offices, Hilton Reservations Worldwide

Colombo Renaissance Hotel D
Sir Chittampalam A Gardiner Mawatha, 2
Tel: 544200; Tlx: 22386 RENAIS CE; Fax: 449184

Le Galadari Colombo D
64 Lotus Rd, Colombo 1
Tel: 544544; Fax: 449875

Galle Face Hotel ○ E
2 Kollupitiya Rd, Colombo 3
Tel: 541010-16; Tlx: 21281; Fax: 541072

The Lanka Oberoi ○
77 Steuart Place, Colombo 03
Tel: 421171/320001; Tlx: 21201/21523 OBEROI CE; Fax: 4492801/447933

This deluxe hotel is centrally located overlooking the Beira lake. It has close proximity to the business centre of Colombo and all major diplomatic missions. Its awe-inspriring atrium is decorated with spectacular batik banners.

Accommodation and rates
600 rooms & suites. Single US$ 125-160; double US$ 140-175; suite US$190-700
Subj to 10% service charge & 6.4% govt tax

Credit cards accepted:
Amex, Diners, Eurocard, Bankamerica, Visa, Mastercharge

Meeting & banqueting facilities
8 meeting/conference rooms, capacity to 900

Room services
Airconditioning, colour TV, direct-dial telephone (ext. in bathroom), hairdryer, laundry/valet service, minibar, 24-hr room service, safety deposit box, video films, baby sitter

Business & other services
Business centre, car rental, travel centre, babrber shop/beauty salon, newsstand/shops, wheelchair access

Sports & Recreation
Fitness centre/gym, indoor games, sauna, massage, squash, indoor swimming pool, tennis

Restaurants & Coffee Shops
Ran Malu (200) - Western/Oriental/Chinese, open 24 hours; London Grill (200) - European, open 1930-2230; The Club (65) - Continental, open 0700-2230; The Chapter One (60) - Bar, open 2100-0100; Supper Club Bar/Restaurant (30/85), open 1100-0100

Overseas Sales Representatives:
Oberoi Hotels & Resorts Worldwide

Holiday Inn — D
30 Sir Mohammed Macan Markar
Mawatha, PO Box 1202, Colombo 3
Tel: 422001-9; Tlx: 21200; Fax: 447977

Hotel Ranmuthu — E
112 Galle Road.
Tel: 43986; Tlx: 21839

Renuka Hotel — E
328 Galle Rd
Tel: 573598; Tlx: 22082; Fax: 574137

Taj Samudra Hotel — D
25 Galle Face Centre
Tel: 446622; Tlx: 21729; Fax: 446348

Taprobane Hotel — E
2 York St, PO Box 152
Tel: 20391; Tlx: 21557

Triton Hotel — D
Sir Baron Jayatilaka Mawatha
Tel: 927228; Tlx: 21142

Kalutara

Tangerine Beach Hotel — E
25 St Andrews Rd, Waskaduwa
Tel: (034) 22640; Tlx: 21889; Fax: 22794

Kandy

Chalet Hotel — E
32 Gregory Road.
Tel/Fax: (08) 24353

Hotel Hill Top — E
21 Bahirawakanda
Tel: (08) 24162; Tlx: 21788; Fax: 232459

Hotel Suisse — E
30 Sangaraja Mawatha
Tel: (08) 233024; Fax: (08) 232083

Negombo

Blue Lagoon Tourist Hotel — E
Talahena
Tel: (031) 3004; Tlx: 21494; Fax: 8363

Catamaran Beach Hotel — D
89 Lewis Place
Tel: (031) 2342; Tlx: 21241

Ranweli Holiday Village — E
Waikkai, Kochchikade
Tel: (031) 2136; Tlx: 21716; Fax: 9504

Trincomalee

Hotel Club Oceanic — E
Alles Gardens, Beach
Tel: (026) 2307; Tlx: 21230

Airline Departures

From Colombo to the airports printed in bold type. Flights correct as at February 1997. Figures in brackets after airline codes signify (1) departing on a Monday, (2) Tuesday and so on to (7) Sunday. Airline Codes: BA = British Airways; CX = Cathay Pacific; DE = Condor Flugdienst; IW = AOM French Airlines; GF = Gulf Air; EK =Emir-tes; IC = Indian Air-ines; KL = KLM; KU = Kuwait Airways; LT = LTU; MH = Malaysian Airlines; NG = Lauda Air; PK = Pakistan Int Airlines; Q7 = Qatar Airways; SQ = Singapore Airlines; X6 = Khors Aircompany; RJ = Royal Jord-anian; SU = Aeroflot; SV = Saudia; TG = Thail nternational; UL = Air Lanka; UT = UTA

Abu Dhabi (AUH)
UL (7) GF (6)
Amman (AMM)
RJ/UL (4,6)
Amsterdam (AMS)
KL (3,6) UL (2,4,7)
Bahrain (BAH)
GF/UL (1,5,7)
Bangkok (BKK)
UL (1,4,6) TG (1,4,6) CX (3,7)
Bombay (BOM)
UL (3,7) IC (2,6)
Delhi (DEL)
UL (3,5)
Dhahran (DHA)
SV (7) UL (5)
Doha (DOH)
Q7/UL (4,5)
Dubai (DXB)
UL (1,3,4,7) EK (1,3,4,5,6) BA (3,7)
Durban (DUR)
UL (4)
Düsseldorf (DUS)
LT (1)
Frankfurt (FRA)
UL (3,5,7) DE (1) LT (3)
Fukuoka (FUK)
UL (3)
Hanover (HAJ)
DE (3)
Hong Kong (HKG)
UL (1,4,6) CX (3,7)
Jeddah (JED)
UL (2) SV (7)
Johannesburg (JNB)
UL (4)
Karachi (KHI)
SU (1) PK (3,4) UL (3,7)
Kiev (IEV)
X6 (3)
Kuala Lumpur (KUL)
UL/MH (1,5)
Kuwait (KWI)
KU (1,3,5) UL (2,4,7)
London (LGW)
UL (2,4,6,7)
Madras (MAA)
UL (daily) IC (daily)

Male (MLE)
EK (1,4) UL (1,3,4,5,6,7) NG (2)
Moscow (MOW)
SU (1)
Mumbai/Bombay (BOM)
UL (4,7)
Munich (MUC)
LT (4,6)
Muscat (MCT)
GF/UL (1,4) WY (3)
Paris (PAR)
UL (3,5,7) IW (4)
Riyadh (RUH)
SV (3,5) UL (3)
Rome (ROM)
UL (2,5)
Singapore (SIN)
UL (1,3,5,6) SQ (2,3,5,6,7) EK (2,4,7)
Sydney (SYD)
IW (2,4)
Tokyo (TYO)
UL (3,7)
Trivandrum (TRV)
UL (1,2,4,5,6) IC (1,3,5,7)
Vienna (VIE)
NG (2)
Zurich (ZRH)
UL (2,5,7)

Airline Offices

*On line carriers only

Aeroflot
Hemas Building, 79-81 York St, Colombo 1.
Tel: 325580, 433062

Air Lanka
12 Sir Baron Jayatilake Mawatha/55 Janadhipathy Mawatha, Colombo 1
Tel: 0735555

British Airways
c/o Air Global Ltd, Trans Asia Hotel, 115 Chittampalam Gardiner Mawatha, Colombo 1. Tel: 320231/325975

Cathay Pacific
186 Vauxhall St, Colombo 2
Tel: 334145

Condor Airlines
57a Dharmapala Mawatha, Colombo 07. Tel: 448167

Emirates
64 Lotus Road, Colombo 1.
Tel: 440709

Gulf Air
c/o Mack Air Ltd, 11 York Street, Colombo 1
Tel: 434662, 326633

Indian Airlines
Gaffor Building, 95 Sir B Jayat-ilaka Mawatha. Tel: 323136/329838

KLM
67 Dharmapala Mawatha, Colombo 1.
Tel: 439747/439756

Kuwait Airways
c/o South Asian Travels Ltd, Ceylinco House, Janadh-ipathi Mawatha, Colombo 1
Tel: 445531/438832

LTU International Airways
11a York St, Colombo 1
Tel: 327244/422590

Malaysia Airlines
GSA Mercantile Tours, 51 Janadhipathi Mawatha.
Tel: 445410

PIA
342 Galle Road, Colombo 3
Tel: 573475, 574445

Saudi Arabian Airlines
51-53 Janadhipathi Mawatha, Colombo 1.
Tel: 577242/5

Singapore Airlines
Colombo Hilton, Lotus Road, Colombo 1
Tel: 422711

Thai International
Hotel Ceylon Inter-Continental 48 Janadhipathi M. Tel: 31166

Explanation of codes in hotel entries: D *after name of hotel = room rate between US$ 50-100 per night;* E *= under US$50.* ○ *= PATA member.*

What's the link between business and the Asia Pacific?

BRITISH AIRWAYS
The world's favourite airline

http://www.british-airways.com

COUNTRY REPORT
TAIWAN '97

290 TAIWAN - Introduction

Taiwan

Doing Business

General Climate

Aided by the highly-publicised handover of Hong Kong rule to China, Taiwan managed to maintain a relatively low international political profile in 1996/97, both saving 'face' and openly compromising in its own traditionally volatile relations with the mainland.

Taiwan's first all-party elections in March, 1996 were successfully won by President Lee Teng-hui of the ruling Kuomintang party with what many critics viewed as a 'backtracking, wait and see' version of his earlier calls for 'one China' and independence from the mainland. The proposed opening of direct air and sea links between Taiwan and the mainland during 1997 further helped to smooth relations and forestall the independence issue until 2007, a date earmarked by Beijing's rulers for the issue finally to be resolved.

In the meantime, Taiwan remains a highly favourable venue for foreign investment and trade - made more favourable in recent years as the island republic has attempted to break out of its political isolation with improved incentives for foreigners, including less rigid banking laws, tax holidays for high-tech investors and visa-free stays.

As the 14th largest trading nation in the world, with a GNP rivalling those of Japan and South Korea, the tiny island's 21 million population enjoys high living standards backed up by keen competitiveness and a powerful work ethic.

In recent years capital outflows for Taiwanese investments overseas - chiefly in mainland China - coupled with rising labour costs, have slowed general domestic growth from an average annual 8.5% to 6.2% for the period 1995-1997. But it has also helped to earn diplomatic relations with more than 30 countries, opening up wider avenues of business. There are both advantages and disadvantages to doing business in Taiwan. Advantages include a sophisticated commercial network with excellent transport and communciations - to, from and within all cities - plus an improved choice of hotel accommodation which has fallen in price to a five star average of between US$100-200 per night in direct relation to spiralling rates in rival trade post Hong Kong.

Disadvantages include getting around the polluted, ugly and cluttered capital, Taipei, and dealing with a people who can be dismissive or pre-occupied over relations with the mainland - sometimes to the point of being infuriatingly pedantic and oversensitive. That said, in 1996/97 there were more international flights than ever from destinations all around the world into Taipei's Chiang-kai Shek Airport, tied to a more open official greeting to those wanting to join the economic bandwagon.

Executive visitors won't lack for opportunities, but they need constantly to be on their toes among a predominantly Chinese but also ethnic tribal people who have known the rigours of Portuguese, Dutch, Spanish, French and Japanese colonialism, as well as 40 years of separatism.

Taiwanese business acumen is highly tuned, no less for the general shift from low-cost, mass production to higher quality goods in recent years. Capitalism is a god and you'll need to do your homework and keep your wits to score profits among abacus-acute minds which know their dollars and cents. Unlike in the mainland, English is often spoken and politics are not so much a taboo discussion subject as an open wound requiring much sympathetic soothing and tact on the part of the visitor.

When travelling overseas, Taiwanese are sometimes reputed to behave very casually. Business at home, however, is conducted very formally, from western-style handshaking, the double-handed presentation of name cards and initial, sometimes lengthy, preparation of documents to the ubiquitous final banquet of strange, steaming delicacies, accompanied by repeated mutual toasts to new partnerships, health and prosperity.

Business etiquette

Business is taken very seriously and dress should be impeccable. The difference to the suit and tie requirement is that in Taiwan, rather than in what is frequently referred to as *Communist China*, the air-conditioning is usually turned up full blast to counteract the humid climate. Show deference by greeting the older person at a meeting first and when exchanging cards, be sure to include as much information on them as possible, since status is important. Appointments should be made ahead and punctuality is appreciated (allow plenty of time to get through Taipei traffic!). English is widely used in business circles. Most entertaining is done in restaurants, or in private dining rooms.

10% service charge is included in hotel and restaurant bills; no further tipping is expected, particularly not for taxis.

Tourism Update

General

Taiwan's visitor arrivals staged a long-awaited growth in 1994 - after strong efforts in the industry - which continued into 1995, and, just, in 1996. Average length of stay is approximately eight days.

In 1995 there was a 10% increase to 2.3 million. Japan grew at a double digit rate, taking it to a total of just under one million. Also showing good growth was Thailand. And for Korea, growth continued after a turnaround starting in 1994. Japan was up 11% to 914,000, US up 1% to 290,000, Hong Kong up 2% to 247,000, Thailand up 28% to 147,000, and Korea up 12% to 146,000.

However, growth stalled in 1996. This may have been caused by a political disturbance in early 1996 when China carried out missile tests near Taiwan. Arrivals during this period did not fall (growth was over 4%), but the short-lived negative publicity may have influenced later travel plans.

In 1996 there was a 1.13% increase to 2.4 million. Japan was static, so still just short of 1 million, and the US was also unmoved at 290,000, Hong Kong up 6% to 263,000, but Korea fell 13% to 127,000, and Thailand was also down, 18% to 121,000. This is despite the fact that a number of initiatives to increase the flow of inbound travel - such as visa-free entry for nationals of 12 countries starting from 1994 - had begun to pay off with European arrivals rising 5.37%. In January 1997 the following extra countries were added to the 14-day visa-free entry list: Switzerland, Italy, Poland, Czech Republic and Hungary. Singapore and Hong Kong are thought to be going to be added to the list in 1997.

One new attraction was the official residence of a former president of republican China, Chiang Kai-shek, in a suburb of

Taipei. (Other former residences of Chiang are open to the public in mainland China.)

The budget of the NTO is approximately US$60 million. A 20% cut in its budget in 1996 caused a rethinking on promotional activity. This is part of the reason for promoting Taipei as a convention and business destination. A study in 1996 recommended approval for at least one casino resort.

Meanwhile the tourism authotity is concentrating on promoting local areas outside the capital, such as Puli, the East Coast and the Penghu Islands scenic areas. A Chinese-style Disneyland is being built near Taichung on 198 ha. and will open in 2006.

Airlines

The most significant development for aviation in Taiwan over the past five years was the creation of Eva Airways, a second major international airline, in 1991. In some measures it is already two-thirds the size of the long-established airline, China Airlines.

China Airlines, partially privatised in 1993, also established a subsidiary in 1991, Mandarin Air, and took an ownership share in the long-established domestic airline, Far East Air Transport. And in 1995 CAL introduced a new market image in preparation for the political changes expected in the greater China area over the next few years.

And Eva has also been on the acquisition trail, buying shares in domestic airlines - 30% of Taiwan Airlines, 20% of Great China, and 30% of Makung. At end1996, Eva ordered two B747 400s for delivery in 1997. Also, Trans Asia Airlines (formerly the Foshing domestic airline), was given permission to operate international flights in late 1994. In late 1995 services were started from Taiwan to Macau by Trans Asia and Eva Airways, and then in 1996, Eva Airways and Dragonair from Hong Kong started flying Taiwan-Hong Kong routes. China Airlines hopes to start direct flights Taiwan-China by the end of 1997.

Seats sold at China Airlines increased 13.4% to 5.9 million in 1995, and RPKs increased 11.6% to 16.9 billion. Growth slowed in 1996, but was still about 10%; growth at Eva Airways may have been faster, closer to 15%. CAL expects delivery of four B747-400s and one Airbus A300-600R in 1997.

There has been steady growth in the number of international passengers through Taipei's airport. In 1995, there was a 9.4% increase in the number of international passengers to 12,982,314, and in 1996 this was running about 6%. In late 1996, the government approved a policy to allow passenger helicopter services.

Taiwanese carriers sold 9.7 mn seats, up 11%, in 1996, nearly 60% to Taiwanese nationals. Seats sold on domestic flights increased 24% to 17.6 mn - more than half on two routes Taipei-Kaohsiung and Taipei-Tainan.

Hotels

The hotel business has been doing well, although it has had to deal with a shortage of labour and related wage inflation. Hoteliers have been trying to contain room rates as the strength of the local currency has made them more expensive for foreign visitors.

Inbound travel has also been affected by these price changes, although two categories of visitors - business travellers and those visiting friends or relatives - are less affected.

For tourists, the NTO has been working

on widening the range of attractions. Although there was little change over the past five years in hotel room counts, some new hotels are now opening. Over 20 are planned. In 1995 there was a 2.3% increase in hotel rooms to 20,044. In Taipei, these include the Byron with 269 rooms, and the Lin Yuan (sometimes called the Linden) with 265 rooms. In Kaohsiung, three hotels opened in 1996 - counting the Linden, which opened in the last month of 1995. Others were the Howard Plaza and Grand Hi Lai.

As the international business has slowed, some hotels have moved more to attract the local domestic travellers. **Taichung**, sometimes named Taiwan's cultural capital, is adding hotels - two of various sizes in 1996 (Landis, Howard), with another three due in 1997 (Grand Formosa, Ching Tang, National). Taiwan's Howard hotel group plan to open four more projects between 1996 and 1998 - in **Kaohsiung, Sun Moon Lake, Taipei** (the Howard Prince), and **Kenting**.

According to figures from *Travel Business Analyst*, four-star hotels in Taipei recorded a 78% occupancy in 1995 at an average room rate of US$125. In 1996 these figures were running at 79% at US$135.

What to See

The island is sometimes accused by the travel industry of not having enough attractions for visitors. But this is all changing as investment is poured into a range of new tourist facilities.

Starting with Taipei, which is one of Asia's fastest growing cities, and at the top of the list should be the National Palace Museum. The Museum houses arguably the world's largest and most priceless collection of Chinese art treasures brought over by the Nationalists from the mainland. Other museums worth considering are the National Museum of History and the Taiwan Fine Arts Museum.

The locals are extremely proud of the Chiang Kai-shek Memorial Hall - a 76 metres high marble edifice, which is close to the Presidential Office Building. The 25-tonne bronze statute of the former president looks out on 250,000 square metres of landscaped gardens. The Sun Yat-Sen Memorial Hall is also built in classical Chinese style and is dedicated to the Father of the Republic.

Taipei plays host to any number of exquisite temples. The best of which is arguably the Lungshan (Dragon Mountain). It is open from 0430 to 1030. Why anyone should want to visit the temple at 0430 in the morning has yet to be fully explained.

The island has some excellent national parks. The one closest to Taipei is the Yangmingshan National Park, which covers 11,000 hectares. A new national park is earmarked for the high mountains of northern Taiwan.

For most people's money the *Window on China* - a 1:25 miniature replica of Taipei and mainland China - is the best attraction on the island and is certainly one of the most popular. Further attractions are on their way as a Chinese-style theme park is being planned on the lines of the Sung Dynasty Village in Hong Kong.

If you are planning to take time out from Taipei, then a visit to the 64-island Pescadores *(Penghu)* group is certainly worth considering. These unspoiled islands are set to become the equivalent of Korea's Cheju, with pleasant coastal scenery, unusual cultural attractions, fine sandy beaches and regular air services. The Pescadores has been designated by the Tourism Bureau as the country's *Third Special Scenic Area*. Another is the *East Coast Scenic Area*, and the Taroko Gorge beautification project.

Shopping

Taipei likes to market itself as a shopper's paradise, but this is a slight exaggeration. Nevertheless, the island is well known for its locally-manufactured electrical consumer products such as calculators, watches and audio-visual equipment. To be sure of getting a good buy, it's best to shop at one of the government-approved stores where items are of export quality.

Clothing, too, can be a bargain. Inexpensive casual wear is a particularly good buy. Tailors are usually willing to make up suits within 24 hours. The best are located in the areas around Chungshan North and Linsen North Roads. Many shops specialising in women's clothes are situated on Poai and Hengyang Roads in the Hsimenting district. High-quality, low-priced off-the-rack clothing for men and women can be found in the Tinghao district, which has a number of large stores.

Like Korea, the island produces and exports some of the world's top sports gear and prices here are very competitive with those found around Asia.

Gold, marble, porcelain items are also exceptionally good value. The Chinese Handicraft Mart is as good a place as anywhere from which to buy these goods.

Getting Around

There are no less than five domestic airlines that operate regular flights around the island. Many carriers now use aircraft up to B737 size.

Car rental fees start from around NT$1,500 a day. Chauffeur-drive can also be rented. Leading firms in Taipei include:**Avis**, 333 Ming Sheng E Rd, tel: 500 6633;**Central Auto Service**, 1098 Cheng Teh Rd, tel: 881 9545; **China Rental Co**, 506 MinTzu E Rd, tel: 500 6088; **Mercedes Limousine Service**, 21Alley 5, Hsin Sheng BN Rd, tel: 536 5093; **Taipei Budget Rent-a-Car**, 10 Wen Chang Rd, tel: 831 2906; **VIP Car Rental Co**, 606 Min Chuan E Rd, tel: 713 1111.

All the major cities have a plentiful supply of taxis. Most drivers do not speak English, so it's a good idea to have your destination written down in Chinese before you start out.

The building of Taipei's Mass Rapid Transit subway system, several months behind schedule at end-1994, has further exacerbated the traffic situation in Taipei (where a daily *Quality of Air* bulletin is published in the newspapers).The high-speed rail linking Taipei and Kaohsiung and the tunnel highway connecting Taipei with the east coast, both behind schedule, are all set to improve domestic travel.

Buses from Taipei to, say, Kaohsiung

TAIWAN - Introduction

take only four hours and fares are very reasonable. The railway, though comfortable, seems to take much longer. The Taiwan Railway Administration introduced a business class service on the busy Taipei-Kaohsiung route aboard the daily *Tzuchiang Express*. The train's three business class coaches are fitted with telephones and the fare costs NT$1,004 one way.

Entertainment

There are several good theatre-restaurants where you can enjoy a two-hour floor show. You can book either an early evening or late table. Otherwise restaurants without floor shows tend to close early. So grab an early evening meal at any one of Taipei's first rate restaurants (many consider the city to be the gastronomic capital of Chinese cuisine) and hit the town. Taipei has an excellent selection of bars and discos.

One of the best areas for bars is Shuangcheng Street and from there it's possible to stagger out into the Ching Kuang Night Market for *après* drink snacks. Taipei is quite safe so it is possible to walk even at night. Most foreign movies shown in Taipei are in English with Chinese subtitles; similarly most Chinese films have English subtitles.

Leisure

As the country has become more affluent, so the variety of sports and leisure facilities has grown accordingly. Tennis and golf and both extremely popular locally. Hordes of Japanese players descend on Taiwan to take advantage of its first-class courses and easy access. There are 26 courses open to visitors in Taiwan. The first was opened in 1914. The Taiwan Golf & Country Club at Tamsui is probably the republic's best known course and there are three clubs close to Taipei which accept non-members on special "golf days." There are 300,000 regular players on the island as well as the Japanese visitors, so don't expect to find uncrowded fairways.

To escape the summer heat, there are some fine beaches within easy reach of the big cities, from Chinshan, Green Bay and Fulung in the north to Kenting and Oluanpi in the south. Popular water-sports include sail-boarding, jet-ski riding and water-skiing. Scuba divers are attracted to the bright coral and exotic tropical fish at Oluanpi and Yehliu.

Added to which there is year-round white-water rafting on the Hsiukuluan River. Around 25 companies organise trips on the river and it costs NT$600 for the four-hour trip.

Skiing is possible during January and February at the ski resort on Hohuanshan *(Mountain of Harmonious Joy)* in the Central Mountain Range, just off the Cross-Island Highway.

The island is thought to have some of the world's best sea fishing - a fact supported by the thousands of Japanese anglers that flock to the island. In 1988, the government lifted restriction on sea-fishing and anglers can now fish anywhere within the nation's territorial waters. A day's excursion costs about NT$1,000 a day. However you will need a licence and this is often time-consuming to arrange.

Arrival & Departure

Taipei's Chiang Kai-shek International Airport is located some 40km outside the city. A modern highway links the airport with the city centre and also Kaohsiung and other major cities. A trip from the airport to Taipei generally takes around 50 minutes and the public bus costs NT$ 80. Major hotels provide their own limousines for guests at a cost of around NT$ 1500. Taxis are available for the trip into Taipei, but city-bound you will be charged NT$1500 (around $40) and airport-bound $1000. An airport tax of NT$300 is payable on departure at a desk by the entrance.

Key Fact File

Passport & Visa Requirements:
Visas are no longer required for visitors from USA, Japan, Canada, UK, France, Germany, Austria, Netherlands, Belgium, Luxembourg, Australia & New Zealand, Switzerland, Italy, Poland, Czech Republic and Hungary for visits of up to 14 days. Otherwise multiple entry and exit visas are available for business visitors, valid 6 mths.

Currency:
New Taiwanese dollar (NT$). 100 cents = 1NT$

Exchange Rates:
US$1 = 27.5NT$; £1 = 45NT$ (*May 1997*)

Currency Restrictions:
NT$ 8000 limit on import and export of local currency; free import of foreign currency allowed; export limited to US$ 5000.

Electricity Supply: 110 volts AC/60 cycles

Language:
Mandarin Chinese is the official language. Some English spoken but NOT by most taxi drivers.

Time: GMT + 8 hours; EDT + 13

IDD code: 886
Area codes: Chiai 5; Hengchun 8; Hsinchu 35; Hualien 38; Kaohsiung 7; Keelung 32; Taichung 4; Tainan 6; Taipei 2; Taoyuan 3

Business Hours:
Commercial offices: 0900-1700 Monday to Friday; 0900-1200 Saturdays.
Government offices: 0830-1230, 1330-1730 Monday to Friday; 0830-1230 Saturdays.
Banks: 0900-1530 Monday to Friday; 0900-1200 Saturdays.
Shops: 0900-2100 Monday to Saturday.

Customs & Entry:
Duty free limits are one bottle of alcohol, 200 cigarettes or 25 cigars or one pound of tobacco products

Health Requirements:
Travellers arriving from cholera-infected areas must have a valid vaccination certificate. A smallpox vaccination is no longer required. Typhoid/polio inoculation recommended. No malaria risk.

Climate/best time to visit:
Subtropical with an average annual temperature of around 22C in the north and 24C in the south. June/July maximum in Taipei = 34C. Summer weight clothing is advised from April to November; sweaters are needed from December to March. Humidity is generally high (83% average).

National Holidays 1997
1 January Founding of the Republic of China/New Year's Day; 6-9 February* Chinese Lunar New Year; 29 March Youth Day; 4 April Children's Day; 5 April Tomb-Sweeping Day/Death of President Chiang Kai-shek; 9 June Dragon Boat Festival; 16 Sept* Mid-Autumn (Moon) Festival; 28 September Teacher's Day (Confucius' Birthday); 10 Oct Double Tenth National Day; 25 Oct Taiwan Retrocession Day; 31 Oct Birthday of President Chiang Kai-shek; 12 Nov Dr Sun Yat-sen's Birthday; 25 December Constitution Day.
(**lunar; may vary by a day or two*)

Taiwan Hotel Reference Table

Hotel (listed in price order)	SINGLE ROOM RATE (x 100 NT$)	LOCATION	NUMBER OF ROOMS	NUMBER OF SUITES	CONFERENCE FACILITIES	EXHIBITION SPACE	LARGEST BANQUET NUMBER	BUSINESS CENTRE	SWIMMING POOL (0 = indoor)	TENNIS COURT	HEALTH CLUB	VIDEO FILMS
The Sherwood Taipei	70-88	Taipei	350	45	●	●	144	●	O	-	●	●
Snangri-La's Far Eastern Plaza	69	Taipei	388	44	●	●	312	●	●	-	●	●
Grand Hyatt Hotel	69-85	Taipei	872	58	●	●	1300	●	●	-	●	●
The Grand Formosa Regent	67	Taipei	490	60	●	●	600	●	●	-	●	●
Lai Lai Sheraton	60-80	Taipei	614	72	●	●	1500	●	●	-	●	●
Taipei Hilton	58	Taipei	193	22	●	●	276	●	●	-	●	●
Ritz Hotel Taipei	58	Taipei	200	4	●	●	250	●	-	-	●	●
Holiday Inn Crowne Plaza	56-60	Taipei	300	-	●	-	300	●	-	-	●	●
Asiaworld Plaza	54-70	Taipei	1057	-	●	●	-	●	-	-	-	●
Howard Plaza Hotel	54	Taipei	604	2	●	●	2000	●	●	-	●	●
Westin Caesar Park Hotel	52-59	Kenting	235	-	●	●	-	●	●	●	●	●
Ambassador Hotel	52-64	Taipei	450	21	●	●	900	●	-	-	●	●
Hotel Royal Taipei	50-60	Taipei	182	20	●	●	330	●	-	-	●	●
Magmnolia Hotel	48	Taipei	343	-	●	●	300	●	-	-	●	●
Riviera Hotel	45-53	Taipei	59	53	●	●	120	●	-	-	-	●
Evergreen Laurel Hotel	45-51	Taichung	330	24	●	●	720	●	●	-	●	●
Holiday Garden	38-45	Kaohsiung	290	-	●	●	-	●	-	-	-	●
Ambassador Hotel Kaohsiung	37-46	Kaohsiung	440	17	●	●	960	●	●	-	●	●
The Grand Hotel	37	Taipei	438	82	●	●	1200	●	●	●	●	●
Taipei Miramar	36	Taipei	584	16	-	-	-	-	-	-	-	-
Fortune Dragon Hotel	36	Taipei	312	-	●	-	-	-	-	-	-	●
President Hotel	35-45	Taipei	381	40	●	●	280	●	-	-	●	●
Gloria Hotel	35-45	Taipei	220	-	●	●	-	●	-	-	-	●
Hotel Riverview	35	Taipei	201	-	●	-	-	-	-	-	-	●
Brother Hotel	35-38	Taipei	268	-	●	●	-	●	-	-	-	●
Imperial Hotel	35-48	Taipei	283	44	●	-	300	●	-	●	●	●
Taipei Fortuna Hotel	34-38	Taipei	285	18	●	●	280	●	-	-	●	●
Golden China Hotel	32	Taipei	220	-	●	●	-	●	-	-	-	●
Sun Moon Lake Hotel	30-31	SM Lake	116	-	●	-	-	●	-	-	-	-
Hotel Kingdom	29-32	Kaohsiung	312	-	●	●	-	●	-	-	-	●
CKS Int'l Airport Hotel	26	CKS Airport	496	15	●	-	200	●	O	-	●	●

Useful addresses

Air Couriers

DHL: Taipei (02) 503 6858; Kaohsiung (07) 231 8186;
TNT Express Worldwide: (02) 713 2345/ 712 2234
UPS: (02) 883 3868/ 880 9300

Government Departments/Agencies/Chambers Commerce

Board of Foreign Trade
Tel: (02) 351 0271/391 2311

Central Bank of China
Roosevelt Rd, Sec 1. Taipei. Tel: (02) 393 6161

China External Trade Development Council (CETRA)
7th Fl, 333 Kee Lung Rd, sec 1, Taipei
Tel: 757 6297; Fax: 757 6653

China Productivity Center
340 Tunhua Rd North, Taipei. Tel: 713 7731

Chinese Nat'l Assocn Industry & Commerce
13 F, 390 Fu Hsing S Rd,sec 1, Taipei
Tel: 707 0111; Fax: 701 7601

Confederation of Asia-Pacific Chambers of Commerce & Industry
10th Fl, 122 Tun Hua N Rd, Taipei
Tel: 716 3016; Fax: 718 3683

Government Information Office
Chunghsiao E Rd, Sec 1, Taipei.
Tel: (02) 341 9211

Industrial Development Bureau (MOEA)
109 Hankow Street, Sec 1. Taipei.
Tel: 331 7531

Industrial Development & Incentive Centre
10th Fl, Yumin Bldg, 7 Roosevelt Rd, Sec 1. Taipei. Tel: 394 7213

Inspectorate General of Customs
85 Hsincheng Rd, Sec 1. Taipei.
Tel: (02) 741 3181

International Trade Assocn of the ROC
8 Fl, 148 Chung Hsiao Rd, sec 4, Taipei
Tel: 772 6252; Fax: 752 2411

Ministry of Economic Affairs
15 Foochow St, Taipei. Tel: 351 7271

Ministry of Foreign Affairs
Tel: (02) 311 9292

Taipei Chamber of Commerce
6 Fl, 72 Nan King E Rd, sec 2, Taipei
Tel: 531 8217; Fax: 542 9461

Taiwan Chamber of Commerce
4 Fl, 158 Sung Chiang Rd, Taipei
Tel: 536 5455; Fax: 521 1980

Taipei-US Chamber of Commerce
Rm 1012, Chia hsin Bldg Annexe, 96 Chung Shan North Rd, Sec 2, Taipei.
Tel: 551 2515; Fax: 542 3376

Taipei World Trade Centre
5 Hsinyi Rd, Sec 5, Taipei. Tel: (02) 723 2177; Tlx: 28094/10571; Fax:(02)725 1314

Taiwan International Convention Centre
1Hsin Yi Rd, Sec 5, Taipei. Tel: 723 1535

Taiwan Tourism Bureau
9th Fl, 280 Chungsiao E Rd, Sec 4, PO Box 1490, Taipei. Tel: (02) 721 8541; Tlx: 26408 ROCTB; Fax: 773 5487/781 5399
Tourist Inf'n Hot Line: Tel (02) 717 3737

Taiwan Visitors' Association
111 Minchuan East Rd. Tel: (02) 594 3261

Business Services/Consultants

Central Business Centre (CBC)
8th Fl, Shin Kong World Commercial Bldg 287, Sec 3, Nanking Rd West, Taipei. Tel: (02) 129368, Tlx. 16533 ; Fax: 713 0812

China Management Consultants Inc
37 Fushing N Rd, Sec 2, Taipei. Tel: 331 2862

The New Mall Business Service Centre
Tel: (02) 725 1492; Fax: 723 2196

Taipei International Business Centre (TIBC)
4th Fl, 25 Tunhua South Rd, Taipei. Tel: 775 4352; Tlx: 29242; Fax: 775 4157

Taiwan Invest't & Business Consultants
624 Mingchuan East Rd, Taipei. Tel: 713 3222; Tlx: 27591

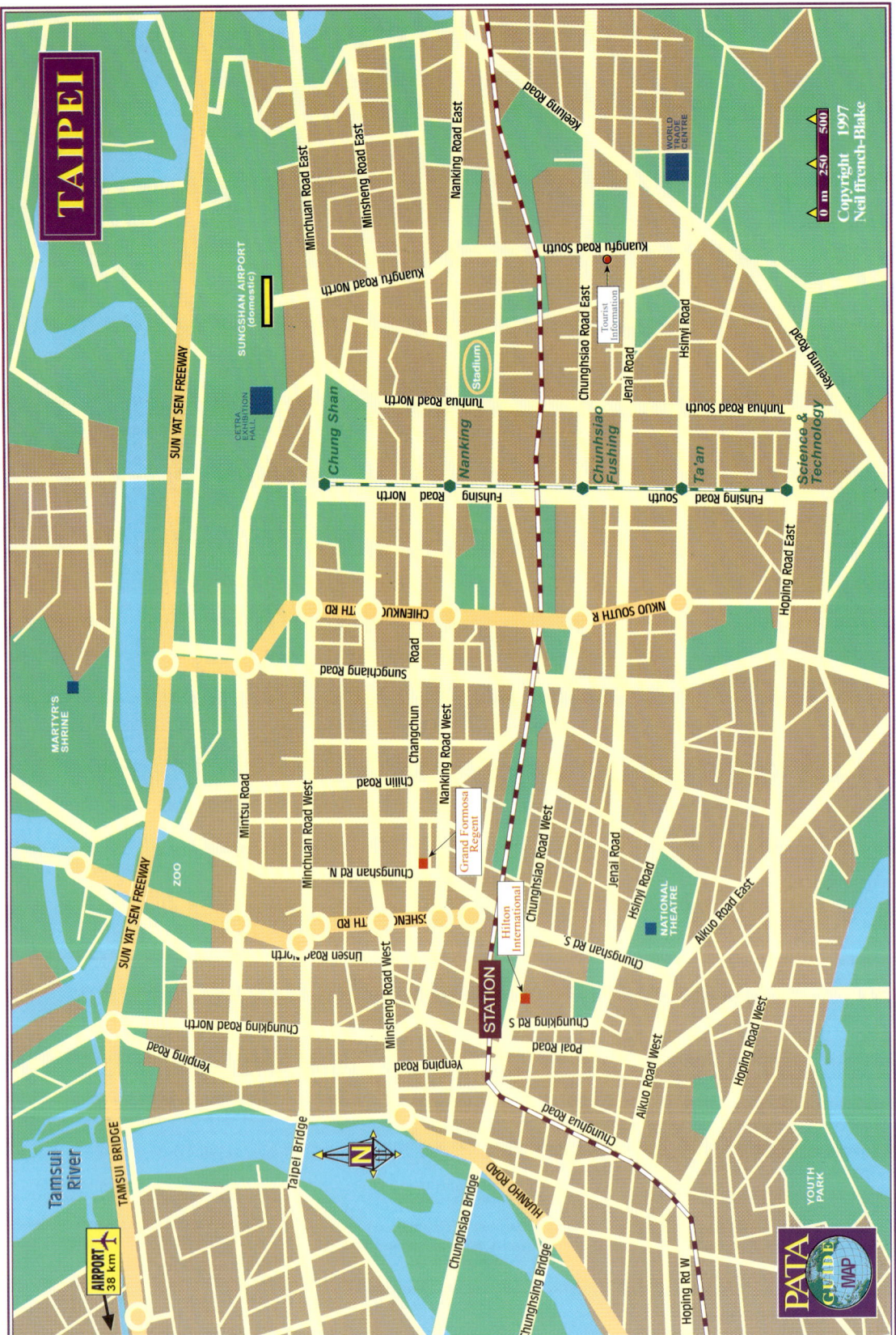

Hotels

Taipei

Ambassador Hotel ◯ B
63 Chungshan North Road, sec 2
Tel: 551 1111; Tlx: 11255; Fax: 536 4814.

Asiaworld Plaza Hotel ◯ A
100 Tun Hwa N Rd
Tel: 715 0077; Tlx: 26299; Fax: 713 4148

Brother Hotel ◯ C
255 Nanking E Rd, Sec 3
Tel: 712 3456; Tlx: 25977/28930 BROHOTEL; Fax: 717 3334

Hotel China C
14 Kuan Chien Rd
Tel: 331 9521-9; Tlx: 21757 CHINATEL; Fax: 381 2349

Hotel China Yangmingshan C
237 Kochih Rd, Yangmingshan (suburbs)
Tel: 861 6661-5; Fax: 861 3885

CKS International Airport Hotel ◯ C
PO Box 66, Taoyuan
Tel: (03) 383 3666; Tlx: 34634; Fax: (03) 383 3546

Fortune Dragon Hotel C
172 Chunghsiao Road, Sec 4
Tel: 772 2121; Tlx: 19794/19795 FODAHTL; Fax: 721 0302

Gloria Hotel C
369 Linshen Rd
Tel: 581 8111; Tlx: TP 11192 GLORITAL; Fax: 581 5811

Golden China Hotel C
306 Sung Chiang
Tel: 521 5151; Tlx: 19550 GOLDNATL; Fax: 531 2914

The Grand Hotel Taipei ◯
1 Chung Shan North Rd, Sec 4
Tel: 596 5565; Tlx: 11646 GRANDHTL; Fax: 594 8243

Grand Hyatt Taipei ◯ A
2 Sung Shou Rd, World Trade Centre
Tel: 720 1234; Tlx: 12738; Fax: 720 1105

Holiday Inn Rebar Crown Plaza ◯ A
32 Nanking East Rd, Sec 5
Tel: 763 5656; Tlx: 14207 HTLREBAR; Fax: 767 9347

Howard Plaza Hotel ◯ B
160 Jenai Rd, Sec 3
Tel: 700 2323; Tlx: 10702/24095 HOPLATEL; Fax: 700 0729

Imperial Hotel ◯ C
600 Lin Shen North Rd, Taipei 104455
Tel: 596 5111; Tlx: 11730; Fax: 592 7506

The Grand Formosa Regent Taipei ◯
41 Chung Shan North Rd, Sec 2.
Tel: 523 8000; Fax: 523 2828

In the heart of Taipei's business, financial and entertainment districts, Grand Formosa Regent offers the city's largest rooms complete with fully marbled bathrooms, soaking tub and separate shower. Service and facilities are so complete that guests need never leave the premises. 10 restaurants, 24-hour multilingual business centre, fully equipped health spa and the city"s best shopping are all on the premises.
Voted 1994,1995 and 1996 "Top Hotel in Taipei" by the readers of Business Traveller Magazine.

Accommodation & rates
490 single/double rooms. King NT$ 6700-8000; twin NT$ 7500-8500; 60 suites NT$ 9600-60,000

Credit cards accepted
Amex, Diners, Mastercard, JCB, Visa & all major credit cards

Meeting & banqueting facilities
9 meeting/function rooms, capacity 8-1000, with audio-visual equipment; 896 sq m exhibition space; largest reception 600 banquet/1000 cocktail

Room services
Airconditioning, colour TV, direct-dial telephone (ext. in bathroom) two lines, hairdryer, laundry/valet service, minibar, music/radio/ alarm clock, safety deposit box, 24 hr room/meal/butler service, tea/coffee making, trouser press (on request), Non-smoker bedrooms, video films

Business & other services
Multilingual business centre, express checkout, airport pickup, translation service, car parking, travel centre, barber shop/beauty salon, taxi service, haute couture shopping arcade, duty free shop

Sports & Recreation
Rooftop swimming pool, fully equipeed health club with massage, sauna & jacuzzi

Restaurants & Coffee Shops
The Court - Coffee Shop, Cajun & Californian, Chinese; *Tsai Yi Lo* - Dim Sun; *The Gallery* - Lobby Lounge; *The Brasserie* - East & West Buffet; *Cafe Studio* - Italian pizza & pasta; *Tsai Fung Shen* - Elegant Cantonese Seafood; *Ming Jiang* - Taiwanese specialities

Overseas Sales Representatives
A Four Seasons Regent Hotel. Formosa International Hotels Group

Lai Lai Sheraton Hotel Taipei ◯ A
12 Chung Hsiao East Rd, Sec 1
Tel: 321 5511; Tlx: 23939 SHANGTEL; Fax: 394 4240

The Leofoo C
168 Changchun Rd
Tel: 507 3211; Tlx: 11182; Fax: 508 2070

Magnolia Hotel ◯ B
166 Tun Wha North Road, 10590
Tel: 712 1201; Fax: 712 2122

President Hotel ◯ C
9 Teh Hwei Street, 10469
Tel: 595 1251; Tlx: 11269 PRESIDENT; Fax: 591 3677

The Ritz Taipei ◯ A
155 Min Chuan E Rd
Tel: 597 1234; Tlx: 27345; Fax: 596 9223

The Riviera Hotel B
646 Lin Sen North Road
Tel: 585 3258; Fax: 596 5160

Hotel Riverview ◯ C
77 Huan Ho Rd, Sec 1
Tel: 311 3131; Tlx: 11609; Fax: 361 3737

Hotel Royal Taipei ◯ B
37-1 Chungshan North Rd, Sec 2
Tel: 542 3266; Tlx: 23915 ROYALHTL TPE; Fax: 543 4897

Santos Hotel C
439 Cheng Teh Rd
Tel: 596 3111; Tlx: 27155 SANTEL; Fax: 596 3120

Shangri-La's Far Eastern Plaza Hotel A
201 Tun Hwa South Rd, sec 2, Taipei 106
Tel: 378 8888; Fax: 377 7777

The Sherwood Taipei ◯ A
111 Min Sheng E Road, sec 3
Tel: 718 1188; Tlx: 13630 SHERWOOD; Fax: 713 0707

Taipei Fortuna Hotel ◯ C
122 Chung Shan N Road, sec 2, Taipei
Tel: 563 1111; Tlx: 21578; Fax: 561 9777

Hotel Classification: A *after name of hotel = over US$ 200 per person per night;* **B** = *between US$ 150 - 200;* **C** = *between US$ 100 - 150;* **D** = *between US$ 50 -100;* **E** = *under US$ 50;* ¶ = *prices on application.* ◯ = *PATA Member Hotel.*

Taipei Hilton
38 Chung Hsiao West Rd, sec 1
Tel: 311 5151; Tlx: 11699; Fax: 331 9944
E-mail: hilton@taipeihilton.transend.com.tw

Located just minutes away from the shopping and entertainment area, the Taipei Hilton offers facilities for meetings and functions for up to 600 persons, four restaurants with one bar, roof garden and jacuzzi pools.

Accommodation and rates
159 single, 34 double NT$5800; executive floor NT$ 6500; 22 suites, from NT$7000. Plus 10% service charge

Credit cards accepted
Visa, Amex, JCB, Diners, Mastercard

Meeting & banqueting facilities
Five meeting/function rooms, capacity 250; 340 sq m exhibition space; largest reception 276 seated/450cocktail

Room services
Airconditioning, colour TV + video, direct-dial telephone (ext. in bathroom), hairdryer, laundry/valet service, minibar, music/radio/alarm clock, safety deposit box, tea/coffee making; non-smoker bedrooms available

Business & other services
Business centre, executive floor, express checkout, airport pickup, translation service, car parking, car rental, taxi service, travel centre, newsstand/shops

Sports & Recreation
Fitness centre/gym, jacuzzi/whirlpool, massage, sauna

Restaurants & Coffee Shops
Checkers (125) - Coffee Shop, open 0600-midnight; *Dynasty Restaurant* (160), Cantonese, open 1200-1430/1800-2130; *Tiffany's* (60) - Taiwanese buffet, open noon-1430 (exc Suns/Pub Hols); *Traders Grill* (180) - Fine dining, open noon-1430/1830-2200; *Galleon* - pub, cocktail lounge, open 1500-0130; buffet lounge noon-1430

Overseas Sales Representatives
Hilton Reservations Worldwide; Hilton International Sales Offices

Taipei Miramar ◯ C
420 Min Chuan Rd East, 10829
Tel: 505 3456; Tlx: 19788; Fax: 502 9173

Other areas

Ambassador Hotel Kaohsiung C
202 Min Sheng 2nd Rd, Kaohsiung
Tel: (07) 211 5211; Tlx: 72105; Fax: (07) 281 1115

Caesar Park Hotel - Kenting ◯ B
6 Kenting Road, **Hengchun**, Ping Tung Hsien
Tel: (08) 886 1888; Tlx: 71882 CAESARKT; Fax: (08) 886 1818

Evergreen Laurel Hotel ◯ B
6 Chung Kang Rd, sec 2, **Taichung**
Tel: (4) 328 9988; Fax: (4) 328 8642

Holiday Garden Kaohsiung C
279 Liu-Ho 2nd Rd, **Kaohsiung**
(07) 241 0121; Tlx: 81948 GARDEN; Fax: (07) 251 2000

Hotel Kingdom C
42 Wu-Fu 4th Rd, **Kaohsiung**
Tel: (07) 551 8211; Tlx: 81938 KINGDOM; Fax: (07) 521 0403

Hotel National C
257 Taichung Kang Rd, 1056, Sec 1, **Taichung**
Tel: (04) 321 3111; Tlx: 51393 NATALHTL; Fax: (04) 321 3124

Plaza International Hotel C
431 Ta Ya Rd, **Taichung**
Tel: (04) 295 6789; Tlx: 57206; Fax: (04) 293 0099

Sun Moon Lake Hotel ◯ C
23 Chung Cheng Rd, 554 **Sun Moon Lake**
Tel: (49) 855911; Tlx: 11144; Fax: 855268

Hotel Tainan D
Cheng Kung Rd, 70001 **Tainan**
Tel: (06) 228 9101; Tlx: 71365; Fax: (06) 226 8502

Hotel Classification: **A** after name of hotel = over US$ 200 per person per night; **B** = between US$ 150 - 200; **C** = between US$ 100 - 150; **D** = between US$ 50 -100; **E** = under US$ 50; ¶ = prices on application. ◯ = PATA Member Hotel. Prices are a guideline and exact rates should be checked with hotels before booking.

Restaurants

Taipei restaurants are good value by Western standards, although drink can add considerably to the bill. Taiwanese cuisine per se is Cantonese/Szechuan with Japanese influences. Below we list a selection of Taipei restaurants popular for business entertaining, where English is spoken, credit cards are accepted and where prior booking is advised.

Beautiful Garden *(Chinese)*
230 Tunhua North Rd. Tel: 715 3921

Canton Garden
Grand Hyatt Taipei. 2 Sung Shou Rd
Tel: 720 1234

Cannes French Restaurant
26-3 Jenai Rd, Sec 3. Tel: 700 6489

Canton Palace & Formosa Seafood Rest't
(Chinese). The Evergreen Laurel Hotel, 6 Taichung Kang Road. Tel: 328 9988

Casa Mia *(Italian)*
628 Linsen N Rd. Tel: 596 4636/591 7478

Les Célébrités *(French)*
Royal Hotel, 37-1 Chungshan N Rd, Sec 2. Tel: 542 3266

The Celestial *(Beijing/Peiping)*
3rd Fl, 1 Nanking West Rd. Tel: 563 2380

Chalet Swiss Restaurant
47 Nanking E Rd, Sec 4. Tel: 715 2702

Chih Yuan Restaurant *(Szechuan)*
96 Chungshan N Rd, Sec 2. Tel: 522 3217

The Chinese Restaurant *(Hunanese)*
Ritz Taipei Hotel, 155 Minchaun East Rd. Tel: 597 1234

Gaylord Restaurant *(Indian)*
328 Sungchiang Rd. Tel: 543 4003-4

Genghis Khan *(Mongolian)*
176 Nanking E Rd, sec 3. Tel: 711 4412

Golden Dragon *(Chinese)*
Grand Hotel, 1 Chung Shan N Rd, sec 4
Tel: 596 5565

Hai Pa Wang *(Taiwanese)*
62 Hsining N Rd. Tel: 521 3252

Jen Hao Cantonese Seafood Restaurant
7th Fl, 197 Chunghsiao E Rd, Sec 4.
Tel: 752 9227-9

Mongol Restaurant *(Japanese)*
998 Minsheng E Rd. Tel: 760 4680

Paris 1930 *(European)*
Ritz Hotel, 155 Minchaun E Rd.
Tel: 597 1234

Peiping Sung-Chu Restaurant *(Taiwanese)*
96 Chunghiao E Rd, Sec 1.Tel: 721 0091-3

Pulau Kelaps Indonesian Restaurant
718 Tingchou Rd. Tel: 391 4717

Rong Hsing *(Szechuan)*
45 Chilin Rd. Tel: 521 5431

The Ruby Restaurant *(Cantonese)*
135 Chungshan N Rd, Sec 2.Tel: 562 0378

Ruffino European Kitchen
2nd Fl, 23-3 Shuangcheng St. Tel: 591 8562

La Seine *(French)*
14 Minchuan E Rd, Lane 550.Tel: 716 9669

Shanghai Court
Grand Hyatt Hotel, Sung Shou. Tel: 720 1234

Shang Palace *(Cantonese)*
Far Eastern Plaza Hotel, 201 Tun Hwas Rd. Tel: 378 3886

Shin Yeh Restaurant *(Taiwanese)*
125 Hsinsheng S Rd, Sec 1. Tel: 741 4162

Suntory Restaurant *(Japanese)*
Far Eastern Plaza Hotel, 201 Tun Hwas Rd. Tel: 376 3247

Tainan Tan Tsu Mien *(Taiwanese)*
31 Huahsi St. Tel: 308 1123-5

Taj Palace Indian Restaurant
2nd Fl, 30 Chungshan Rd, Sec 3. Tel: 598 2984

Tao Jan Ting *(Beijing/Peiping)* 16 Alley 4, Chunghsiao Rd, Sec 4. Tel: 711 4015

Trader's Grill *(European)*
Taipei Hilton Hotel, 38 Chunghsiao W Rd. Tel: 311 5151

Trader Vics *(Polynesian/Continental)*
135 Ming Sheng E Rd. Tel: 545 9999

Ya Yuen Seafood Restaurant *(Cantonese)*
2nd Fl, 26 Changchun Rd. Tel: 543 5513

Zum Fass *(German & Swiss)*
55 Linsen N Rd, Lane 119. Tel: 531 3815

Airline Offices

Asiana Airlines
5th Fl, 65 Chienkuo N Rd, sec 2, Taipei
Tel: 508 1114; Fax: 508 0960

British (Asia) Airways
Taiwan Travel Inc, 5th fl, 98 Nanking E Rd, sec 2. Taipei. Tel: 541 8080

Canadian Airlines International
4 Fl, 90 Chienkuo N Rd, sec 2, Taipei
Tel: 503 4111; Fax: 505 3151

Cathay Pacific
65 Nanking E Rd, sec 3, Taipei
Tel: 712 8228; Fax: 717 6844

China Airlines (CAL)
131 Nanking E Road, Section 3, Taipei
Tel: 715 1212; Fax: 713 5010

Delta Airlines
3 Fl, 50 Nanking E Rd, sec 2, Taipei
Tel: 551 3656; Fax: 531 6984

EVA Airways
1 & 2 Fl, 166 Minsheng E Rd, sec 2, Taipei
Tel: 501 1999; Fax: 501 5999

Garuda
6th fl, 82 Sungchiang Rd, Taipei
Tel: 561 2311; Fax: 531 3436

Japan Asia Airways
2 Tunhua S Road, Taipei
Tel: (02) 776 5151; Fax: 777 2993

KLM Royal Dutch Airlines
2 Fl, 1 Nanking Road E, Section 4, Taipei
Tel: (02) 717 1000; Fax: 717 3767

Korean Air
53 Nanking Road E, Section 2, Taipei
Tel:(02) 521 4242; Fax: 561 1204

Malaysia Airlines
1/2 floor, San Ho Plastic Building, 102 Tun Hwa N Road, Taipei
Tel: (02) 716 8348; Fax: 712 9312

Northwest Airlines
181n Fushing N Rd, Taipei
Tel: 716 1555; Fax: 719 0237

Philippine Airlines
2nd Fl, Chienkuo N Rd, sec 2, Taipei
Tel: 505 3030; Fax: 509 5827

Royal Brunei Airlines
11th Fl, 9 Nanking E Rd, sec 3, Taipei
Tel: 531 2884; Fax: 531 1649

Singapore Airlines
148 Sung Chiang Road, Taipei 104
Tel: (02) 551 6655; Fax: 523 5955

South African Airways (SAA)
12th Fl, 205 Tunhua N Rd, Taipei
Tel: 713 6363; Fax: 713 9478

Thai Airways International
2nd Fl, 150 Fusing N Road, sec 4, Taipei
Tel: (02) 717 5299; Fax: 713 9478

United Airlines
12th Fl, 2 Jenai Rd, sec 4, Taipei
Tel: 325 8868; Fax: 325 5583
**International on line only*

Photographs supplied by courtesy of the Taiwan Tourism Bureau.
Top row (left) Taiwanese Cuisine; (right) Taipei; Bottom row (left) Sun Moon Lake; (right) Taiwan Folk Village

Taipei Airline Departures

Below is a list of departures and frequencies from Chiang-Kai Shek International Airport to the destinations in bold type. Figures in brackets after destinations refer to the days of the week. (2,4,6) therefore indicates that departures to that destination take place on a Tuesday (the second day of the week), a Thursday and a Saturday. Departures were correct as at February 1997 but travellers are advised to check with the Airline Offices on an earlier page as timetables can change without notice. Only direct flights without change are listed.

Airline Abbreviation Codes: AE = Mandarin Airlines; **AN** = Ansett Australia; **BA** = British (Asia) Airways; **B I** = Royal Brunei Airlines; **BL** = Pacific Airlines; **BR** = EVA Airways; **B7** = Makung Airlines; **CI** = China Airlines; **CO** = Continental Airlines; **CP** = Canadian Airlines; **CX** = Cathay Pacific; **EF** = Far Eastern Air Transport; **EG** = Japan Asia Airways; **EL** = Air Nippon; **GA** = Garuda Indonesia; **GE** = Trans Asia Airways; **IF** = Great China Airlines; **KL** = KLM; **LH** = Lufthansa; **LZ** = Balkan; **MH** = Malaysian Airline Systems; **NW** = Northwest Airlines; **NX** = Air Macau; **NZ** = Air New Zealand; **PR** = Philippine Airlines; **QF** = Qantas; **SA** = South African Airways; **SG** = Sempati Air; **SQ** = Singapore Airlines; **SR** = Swissair; **TG** = Thai International; **UA** = United Airlines; **VN** = Vietnam Airlines.

Abu Dhabi (AUH)
AE (1,5) CI/AE (1,5)
Amsterdam (AMS)
CI (1,2,4,5,6) KL (6,7)
Auckland (AKL)
AE (4,7) NZ (6,7) BR (1,3,5,6)
Bandar Seri B (BWN)
BI (3,7)
Bangkok (BKK)
CI,TG,BR (daily) KL (1,2,4,5,6,7) SA (2,7)
Brisbane (BNE)
QF (2,3,7) BR (1,3,5) NZ (2,6)
Cairns (CNS)
QF (2)
Cebu (CEB)
PR (5,7)
Chiang Mai (CNX)
TG (2,4,7)
Christchurch (CHC)
NZ (2)
Denpasar-Bali (DPS)
CI/GA (1,2,3,5,6,7)
Detroit (DTT)
NW (daily)
Frankfurt (FRA)
CI (3,7)
Fukuoka (FUK)
CI,CX,BR,EL (daily)
Guam (GUM)
CO (daily)
Hanoi (HAN)
CI (1,3,4,6,7) VN (1,3,4,6,7)
Ho Chi Minh (SGN)
CI,VN,BR (daily) BL (4,6)
Hong Kong (HKG)
CI, CX,TG,EG,BR (daily) SQ (1,4) GA (3,6)
Honolulu (HNL)
CI (daily) BR (1,3,5)
Hualien (HUN)
GE,EF,B7 (daily)
Jakarta (JKT)
CI (daily) GA (1,2,4,5) BR (daily) SG (2,6)
Johannesburg (JNB)
SA (2,7)
Kaohsiung (KHH)
CI,EF,GE,B7,BR, UI (daily)
Kinmen (KNH)
EF,B7,GE, UI (daily)
Koror (ROR)
CO (4,7)
Kota Kinabalu (BKI)
MH (3,5,7) AK (1,4,6)
Kuala Lumpur (KUL)
CI,MH,BR (daily) AK (1,4,6)
Kuching (KCH)
MH (1,4)
Langkawi (LGK)
MH (2,4,6)
London UK (LHR)
BR (2,4,6) BA (2,5,7)
Los Angeles (LAX)
CI,BR,SQ (daily) MH (3,5,7)
Macau (MFM)
BR,NX, GE (daily)
Makung (MZG)
B7,EF,GE,IF, UI (daily)
Manila (MNL)
CI,PR,BR (daily) MH (1,4,5,7) 8L (2,4,6,7)
Melbourne (MEL)
AN (3,6) BR (4,7)
Nagoya (NGO)
CX (daily) EG (1,3,4,5,7) CI (1,2,4,5,6)
New York (JFK)
CI (1,3,4,6) BR (3,5,7)
New York (EWR)
BR (1,4,6)
Okinawa (OKA)
EG (1,2,4,5,6,7) CI (daily)
Osaka (OSA)
CX,EG (daily) SQ (2,4,5,6)
Panama City (PTY)
BR (3,7)
Paris (CDG)
BR (3,5,7)
Penang (PEN)
BR (daily)
Phuket (HKT)
CI (daily)
Pingtung (PIF)
IF,GE (daily)
Rome (ROM)
AE (1,5), CI/AE (1,5)
Saipan (SPN)
CO (3,6)
San Francisco (SFO)
CI,BR,UA (daily)
Seattle (SEA)
BR (2,4,6,7)
Seoul (SEL)
CX,TG (daily) SQ (2,4,5) CO (2,3,4,6,7)
Singapore (SIN)
CI, SQ, BR (daily) BI (3,7)
Surabaya (SUB)
GA (3,6) BR (3,5,7) GE (1,4,6)
Sydney (SYD)
QF (3,5,6,7) AE (3,5,7) AN (4,7) BR (3,4,6,7)
Taichung (TXG)
IF (daily)
Tainan (TNN)
EF,GE, BR (daily)
Taitung (TTT)
EF,GE,B7 (daily)
Tokyo (NRT)
CI,CX,NW,EG (daily) SQ (1,3,7)
Vancouver (YVR)
CP (3,4,5,6,7) AE (2,4,6,7)
Washington DC (WAS)
NW (daily)
Zurich (ZRH)
CI (3,7)

What's the link between business and the Asia Pacific?

BRITISH AIRWAYS

The world's favourite airline

http://www.british-airways.com

Major Exhibitions & Conferences in Taiwan 1997

Date	Exhibition	Venue	Organiser
1997 April 16-19	**Taipei International Cycle Show** - Bicycles, parts & Accessories	TWTC	CETDC
April 24-27	**TaiSPO 97** - Taipei Int'l SPorting Goods S how	TWTC	CETDC
May 2-5	**TAIPEIBUILD 97** - Int'l Building Material, Hardware & Construction Show	TWTC	CETDC
May 24-28	**TIDEX 97** - Taipei Int'l Design Exhibition - Products, packaging & graphic designs from Taiwan & Abroad, corporate identity systems, design co's	TWTC	CETDC
June 12-16	**Taipei Int'l Food Industry Show**	TWTC	CETDC
Aug 14-17	**TATE**: Taipei Aerospace Technology Exhibition	TWTC	Reed
Aug 22-25	**Int'l Automation Industry Exhibition** also **Int'l Fluid Power Exhibition**, **Int'l Logistics Exhibition**, **Mould & Die Exhibition**, **Paper Products & Equipment**	TWTC	CCI
Oct 6-10	**TAIPEI PLAS 97** - Int'l Plastics & Rubber Industry Show	TWTC	CETDC
Oct 16-21	**Taipei Int'l Electroncs Show** - Consumer electronics, meters & instruments, computers and peripherals, satellite TV products	TWTC	CETDC
Nov 8-11	**Taipei Int'l Medical Equipment & Pharmaceuticals Show**	TWTC	CETDC/OES
Nov 17-21	**TAIPEI PACK 97** - Taipei Int'l Packaging Industry Show	TWTC	CETDC

Venues:
TICC = Taipei International Convention Center, 1 Hsin-Yu Rd, sec 5, Taipei, Taiwan. Tel: 723 2535; fax: 723 2590.
TWTC = Taipei World Trade Center, 5 Hsin-Yi Rd, sec 5, Taipei, Taiwan. Tel: 725 1111; Fax: 725 1314.

Organisers:
CETDC/CETRA = China External Trade Development Council, c/o Taiwan World Trade Centre, 5 Hsin Yi Rd, sec 5, Taipei, Taiwan. Tel: (02) 725 1111; Fax: (02) 725 1314.
Reed = Tai-Den Co Ltd, No 52, 3rd Floor, PO Box 28-309, Fu Kou Road, Shin Lin, Taipei. Tel: (2) 763 4300 Fax: 2) 763 4345
CCI = Chan Chao International, 11 Nan-King E Road, Section 2, Taipei, Tel: (2) 5216727 Fax: (2) 5622 700
CAS-ME = Chinese Assoc'n of Small-Medium Enterprises. Tel: (002) 366 0812.
CNAIC = Chinese National Assoc of Industry & Commerce. Tel: (02) 707 0111.
ITRI = Industrial Technology Research Institute, Union Chemical, tel: (035) 727437; fax: (035) 721321.
NTHU = National Tsing-Hua University. Tel: (035) 715971; Fax: (035)715131.
OES = Overseas Exhibition Services Ltd, 11 Manchester Square, London W1M 5AB. Tel: (+44) 171 486 1951; Fax: (+44) 171 486 8773; Tlx: 24591 Montex G.

All photographs & maps used in this section provided by courtesy of the Taiwan Tourism Bureau

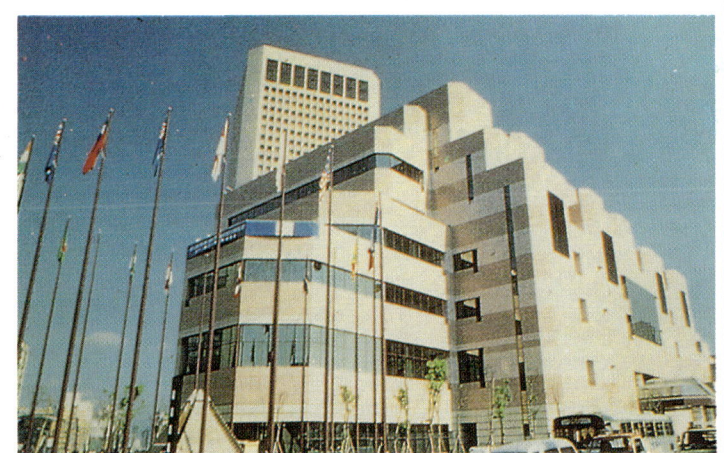

TAIWAN

TAIWAN
AN ISLAND OF FASCINATION

R.O.C. Tourism Bureau
P.O.Box 1490, Taipei, Taiwan, R.O.C.
Tel: (886) 2-349-1635   Fax: (886) 2-773-5487

Overseas Offices:
Singapore   Tel: 65-223-6546/7   Fax: 65-225-4616
Japan   Tel: 81-3-3501-3591   Fax: 81-3-3501-3586
Korea   Tel: 82-2-732-2357/8   Fax: 82-2-732-2359
Hong Kong   Tel: 852-25810933   Fax: 852-25810262
Australia   Tel: 61-2-9231-6942, 9231-6973   Fax: 61-2-9233-7752

(PATA Guid

Tell me more about Taiwan:
Name   Company   Address   City   Country

COUNTRY REPORT
THAILAND '97

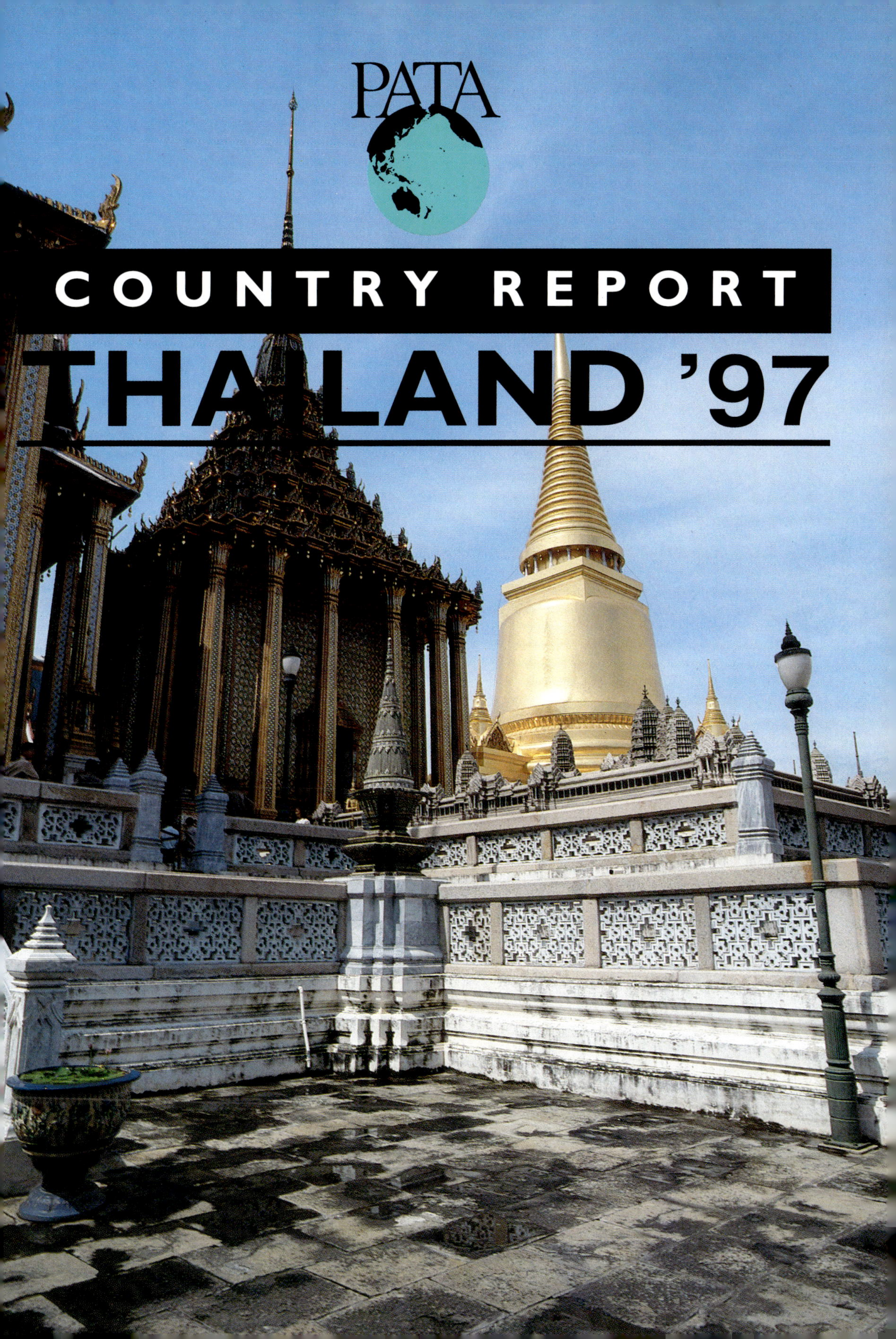

Thailand

Doing Business

The climate in 1997

Rocked by political scandals and rudderless government, Thailand drifted from its familiar bullish economic path during 1996, temporarily losing investor confidence. But with a new government and budget in place, promising to curb public spending and tackle a mounting trade deficit, the country began 1997 with renewed confidence - prompting analysts to predict that Thailand would again becoming one of Asia's top economic performers by late 1997/early 1998.

Back on course as one of the region's 'tigers', Thailand is again shouting business opportunities at every turn. Yet accessing its pots of potential profitability demands caution, stealth and a thorough understanding of a labyrinthine bureaucracy and internecine web of national complexities. Above all it requires patience, not just of a people who cannot be hurried but also of ingrained customs and procedures which doggedly refuse to budge for the onset of the 21st Century.

On the surface, Thailand is all go - racing towards full industrialisation with a rarely dented 8.5% economic growth rate, a burgeoning collection of new export industries and a voracious appetite for imports.

With trade and manufacturing zones such as the hugely sussessful East Coast Industrial Park near Rayong, now being extended - the country is a veritable shop window for investment in industry, infrastructure and partnerships with the emerging markets of Indochina. But it also can be an infuriating business parcel to unravel for all but the most determined of opportunistic shoppers. Thailand is edging only slowly towards full democracy, is stuck with a military still powerful in civilian affairs and suffers frequently fractious politics. It is also saddled with a business hierarchy reluctant to share its spoils.

Foreign investment is welcomed in most major industries, including petrochemicals and construction, but strictly on terms that favour Thai partners in often unfeasible measure.

Establishing the right contacts is vital to any arriving visitor. Incentives and tax breaks are available to overseas investors in areas including agriculture, mining, chemicals, textiles, electronics and tourism, but there are also still many no-go areas. Financing can also prove problematic. Hiring a good local agent is a first step to moving up the long pecking order ladder towards an inner business family sanctum where all but the smallest decisions are taken. Past allegations of widespread corruption in Thai business life may no longer be founded. But it is undoubtedly true the right massaging in the right circles helps speed up projects.

Old Asia 'hands' say the only way to progress is to go with a flow which often can resemble a stop-go switchback rollercoaster ride towards achieving a given goal. Many are the major projects in recent years that have been stalled indefinitely for want of a tickle and nod from the right quarter.

Business etiquette

Behaviour is another telling factor in business. The way overseas visitors conduct themselves is of paramount importance, primarily with respect to a staunchly Buddhist religion, with customs and cultures revolving around family and deference to elders, and always with reverence to the Royal Family who are beyond the tiniest criticism, particularly from a *farang* (foreigner).

Never having been colonised, Thais have adapted to rather than adopted the business mores of the West. Shaking hands is a perfectly acceptable form of greeting instead of the 'wai'(hands clasped as if in prayer with head dipped), but any other form of touching should be avoided, even with friends. Touching the top of a Thai's head is extremely disrespectful, as is sitting cross-legged and pointing the soles of your feet towards a Thai, a Buddhist image or a portrait of the Royal Family.

Thais are extremely hospitable and find it almost impossible to show disrespect to guests. They are very forgiving of gaffes but beneath their ever-present smiles it is equally impossible to know precisely where you stand in a relationship. Sometimes they will say 'yes' because they don't want to cause offence by saying 'no', and only much later will you discover the true answer.

Business negotiations can be laborious and getting a response can take many weeks or months of frustrating inaction, even before the long process of getting the correct permits begins. But losing your temper or showing irritation will get you nowhere. Displays of anger are treated with contempt, despite the serenity on the surface. Politeness and formality are the keynotes, even on social occasions with partners you know.

Business dress is dark jacket and tie, or dress, with polished shoes. Strict punctuality is not vital, which is a relief in congested Bangkok, but never expect your Thai partners to be punctual either. Try to phone ahead if you're running behind time.

Most business entertaining is conducted in hotel restaurants and rarely at Thai family homes. Lunchtime buffets are a popular form of business entertainment, leaving evenings free for other pursuits. Smoking is not taboo, but allow your senior host to light up first or extend permission. Whatever the nationality or style of cuisine chosen, the business tipple of Thailand invariably is old Scotch, drunk in copious quantity with plenty of water or soda.

Tourism Update

General developments

The travel business in Thailand has faced a number of challenges over recent years. It was hit hard when travel fell after the Gulf War, and then the market had to adjust to a rise, fall and rise again, of outbound travel from China.

By 1995 fast growth was re-established when its visitor arrivals total increased 12.7% to 6,951,566. And by one measure - air arrivals - Thailand overtook Singapore that year to become the second-largest in the region after Hong Kong. In 1995, the top two markets, Malaysian and Japanese, grew strongly, and the Chinese market gained some places. Visitors with Malaysian passports increased 19.8% to 1,077,005, those with Japanese passports up 17.8% to 814,706, Taiwanese were up 9.8% to 492,189, Koreans up 23.9% to 456,228, and Singaporean up 11.4% to 430,824. The Chinese market, which has been strong in the past, increased 45.9% to 375,564.

One positive outcome of the addition of hotels in Bangkok (see elsewhere) is that resulting lower rates have encouraged tour companies in other countries to promote travel to Thailand again. However, growth in 1996 slowed, to a rate of just over 4%. The main reason for the change was a slight fall in the largest, closest, but also volatile market - neighbouring Malaysia. Much of this traffic is short-term border crossing to Haadyai in the south of Thailand.

The average visitor to Thailand stays approximately seven days, longer than in many competing destinations because the country has a number of separate destinations - not only Bangkok, but also Pattaya, Phuket, Chiangmai and now also Koh Samui, although this is still small in comparison with Phuket. When the measure is 'visitor nights' (visitors multiplied by the number of nights they stay), Thailand is well ahead of its regional rivals, Hong Kong and Singapore. The budget of the NTO is almost US$100 million. Nearly 9 million visitors are expected in 2000. A boost is expected if Thailand launches a second international airline, as planned, in the next two years.

Thailand is also positioning itself as a gateway to Indochina, and to the Mekong River area and formed a Mekong division in 1997. Although this is now attracting more attention, growth, particularly into the main destination, Vietnam, has not been as rapid as was expected.

Airlines

The merger of international and domestic airlines into Thai Airways in the late 1980s resulted in seamless air services throughout the country, as well as more international flights from centres other than Bangkok.

But in the late 1980s, allegations of political interference and inept management resulted in what is now generally considered to be a decline in standards at Thai. The main charge has been that new aircraft were different types, bringing additional costs in management, training, spares, and operations. A consultants report in 1996 proposed a series of administrative changes, mostly small in themselves, but which overall are expected to revitalise the airline. Dates for implementation are not clear, but 2000 is presumed to be one target.

Although some analysts believe the structure of management and decision-making is still too bureaucratic, many adjustments have been made. In the early 1990s, the government decided to license a privately-owned airline, and operating parameters have now been provided for companies to bid. The new airline would fly domestic and international, even inter-continental. There were some formal bids in 1996, but reportedly not satisfactory to the government, and thus a review seems likely. It could still be in operating in 1998.

Meanwhile, two small domestic airlines, Bangkok Airways and Orient Express, continue to expand their routes. Bangkok Airways has a fleet of seven ATR72s and added the shorthaul international destinations of Yangon and Singapore, flying from secondary airports in Thailand. In 1995 Thai Airways international seats sold increased 10.2% to 7.8 million, and RPKs increased 6.5% to 24.2 billion. In 1996 its traffic was growing at about 10%.

In terms of fleet acquisition, Thai Airways announced plans to buy 21 new aircraft, but dispose of 31 partly in a move to reduce the 14 different aircraft types it has. The aircraft were five A300-600s, four A330s, four B737-400/500s, six B777s, and two B747-400s. Later in the year, however, the government disallowed the order, and said the airline should lease these aircraft rather than buy. Thai

signed marketing agreements with Lufthansa to Europe and with United Airlines across the Pacific, leading to code-share flights to both regions.

Traffic at Bangkok airport dropped in 1991, but has recovered since then. In 1995, the total increased 4.2% to 17,318,289, and was growing at about 6% in 1996.

A new airport is planned for Bangkok (with an opening passenger capacity of 25 million); however, some procedural delays indicate this will not be ready when originally due - for 2000.

Hotels

There are now 50,000 hotel rooms in Bangkok (over 60,000 rooms by a measure that includes small-size operations that might not be considered suitable to the international visitor). That compares with 29,000 in Singapore and 33,000 in Hong Kong, both of which count more arrivals than Bangkok.

The increase in the number of hotel rooms has been sizeable - over 30% over the past five years. Most of the expansion has been in the capital. The country-wide total increased 3.8% in 1995 to 255,573 rooms. Most of the other hotel rooms are in Pattaya, which has 24,000, followed by Phuket 19,000, and Chiangmai 13,000. Koh Samui continues to be developed as a new resort area. Although still small in comparison with Phuket, it now has almost 9000 rooms. There has been some attempt to market the island at the top of the market.

But although there has already been great expansion of hotels, mainly in Bangkok, there are still more to open.

In **Bangkok**, projects due to open between 1997 and 1999 include the All Seasons Place with 400 rooms, Conrad with 400 rooms, the Country Marina Hilton with 375 rooms, Meridien President with 400 more rooms, Marriott with 433 rooms, New World with 430 rooms, Peninsula with 400 rooms, Renaissance Le Concorde with 400 rooms, Sheraton Grande Sukhumvit with 407 rooms, and Sofitel Riverside with 550 rooms.

A Holiday Inn with 200 beds is planned to open mid-1997 in **Chiang Rai.**

In **Phuket** there has been a change in management companies with Mandarin Oriental pulling out of the Phuket Yacht Club and its resort on Koh Samui, and Meridien taking over. Recent expansion work on villas at Amanpuri in Phuket has

now been completed. There are now 30 privately-owned 3-4 bedroom villas available for rental. Each has its own private pool, dining and living area pavilions, and comes with kitchen and maid staff.

According to figures from *Travel Business Analyst*, four-star hotels in Bangkok recorded a 67.2% occupancy in 1995 at an average room rate of US$79. In 1996 these figures improved to 69.7% at US$68. In Phuket, 1995 occupancy was 73% at an average room rate of US$66. In 1996 these figures were running at 71% at US$95. At the top, 5-star level in Bangkok, the hotels ended 1995 at 64% occupancy and US$140 average room rate, and were running fractionally down - 63% at US$139 - in 1996.

The Imperial Queen's Park Hotel. Bangkok

The Imperial Tara Hotel. Bangkok

The Imperial Samui Hotel. Ko Samui

The Imperial Boat House Hotel. Ko Samui

The Imperial Phukaew Hill Resort. Petchaboon

The Imperial Mae Ping Hotel. Chiang Mai

The Imperial Golden Triangle Hotel. Chiang Rai

The Imperial Tara Mae Hong Son Hotel. Mae Hong Son

THE IMPERIAL HOTELS GROUP

The Essence of Thai Hospitality

The Imperial Hotels Group invites you to experience true Thai hospitality in the heart of Bangkok and Chiang Mai, on the shores of the Mekong River at Chiang Rai, in the misty tropical mountains of Petchaboon and Mae Hong Son or on the idyllic island Ko Samui. Our unique mix of modern amenities and traditional Thai charms will easily captivate you.

**Enjoy true Thai hospitality at every Imperial Hotel.
It's a feeling you won't forget.**

THE IMPERIAL HOTELS GROUP
THAILAND

199 Sukhumvit Soi 22, Bangkok 10110 Thailand
Tel. (662)261-9000. Fax. (662)261-9530-4
E-mail address: imperial@ksc.net.th . Internet address: http://www.imperialhotels.com

What to See

Although business visitors to Bangkok see little more than an endless succession of traffic snarl ups, the city is certainly not without its charm and splendour. Its Buddhist temples must rate as among the best in the world.

The Royal Barge Museum on Klong Bangkok Noi is certainly worth taking time out to visit. A great way to see Bangkok is to take a day-long ride on luxury cruiser "Ayutthaya Princess" along the Chrao Phraya river. Daily cruises from Bangkok and Ayutthaya take you to Bang Pa-in' Royal Summer Palace and the ancient ruins of Ayutthaya.

A short ride (about one hour) out of Bangkok is the Damnoensaduak floating market. You will have to get up early because the market is at its busiest between 0600-0900. Not far away is the orange-tiled Phra Pathom pagoda - the world's tallest Buddhist monument.

Increasingly popular with visitors is a trip west of Bangkok to the "Bridge over the River Kwai" - the notorious death railway built by Allied POWs during World War II. But it should be remembered that the film of the same name was in fact shot elsewhere.

Other side trips to consider are to Chiang Mai is the extreme north with its compelling hill tribes. Alternatively, a weekend in Phuket might be enough to recharge the batteries.

Shopping

The best places to shop are on Silom Road and the surrounding streets between Surawongse Road and Sukhumvit Road. Goods are mostly sold from stalls, so expect to haggle over the price and expect to get a discount of between 30-40 per cent.

Fake designer shirts and T-shirts are among the most popular buys and cost, perhaps, B15. There is also a selection of other counterfeit goods such as "Rolex" watches from B300, but expect to pay up to B850 for better quality examples.

The city is particularly well known for its silk and *Jim Thompson's Thai Silk Company* store on Surawongse Road is the most famous and probably the most expensive of the lot. Jim Thompson is revered in many guide books and is generally accredited with kick starting the local silk industry after World War II and being influential in developing new styles. But *Anna Silk, Design Thai* and *Star of Siam* sell equally good silk at lower prices and you will find literally hundreds of shops selling the product.

Jewellery is also worth seeking out, but it is advisable to stick to recognised shops rather than the street stalls. A recent move to label and mark all jewellery products sold in Thailand is a welcome sign for visitors. Labelling details have to include trademarks, weight, trade and mineralogical name and place of production but will be in Thai only; although foreign-language labelling is an option.

For leather goods, go along to the Indra Hotel shopping arcade on Rajprarob Road which specialises in bags and suitcases.

Chiang Mai and the northern hill areas are well known for their handicrafts and silverware where prices are significantly cheaper than those displayed in Bangkok. Stoneware pots, brass ornaments, carved wooden boxes and reproduction antiques are among the items on offer.

Special permission is needed to export antiques and old images of Buddha. TAT manages a new duty-free shop in the Mahathun Plaza building on Ploenchit Rd.

Entertainment

Both Bangkok and Pattaya offer some of the hottest nightlife in Asia. Bangkok's Patpong - the Surawongse Road and Silom Road area - is the obvious *mecca* for those seeking a good time.

The sex shows and girlie bars on and around Silom Road retain an easy-going atmosphere and the area is a lot less seedy than, say, Amsterdam's *Zeedijk* or Hamburg's *Reeperbahn* areas. In fact, a visit to Patpong has become just another stop on the tourist circuit, with some local firms offering all-inclusive Night Tours to the area, with a massage parlour, go-go bar and erotic show all thrown in.

There is, however, the risk of infection and a trip to one of Bangkok's famed massage parlours should be treated with caution. It's a safer bet to follow local advice as to which establishment to choose.

Bangkok's discos are as good as anywhere in the Far East. Try the *Rome Club* on Silom Road, which really gets underway at around 11.30; *Bubbles* at the Dusit Thani is one of the better upmarket nightspots and ranks with the *Talk of the Town* at the Shangri-La. Both demand a cover charge.

Brown Sugar (Soi Sarasin) is a jazz club where food is served; *Blues Bar* (also in Soi Sarasin) is Western and Thai techno-pop (NOT blues), whilst *Round Midnight* in Soi Lang Suan offers live jazz nightly.

Many cinemas show English-language films. To sample some local colour, there is the Thailand Cultural Centre on Ratchadapisek Road for Thai plays, concerts and dance in a rather pleasant atmosphere. Some hotels offer similar cultural evenings.

For a city best known for its raunchy nightlife, it may come as a shock to learn that Bangkok has two highly regarded orchestras - the Philharmonic and the Bangkok Symphony. Furthermore, some top hotels feature feature soothing string quartets and the Siam Inter-Continental often hosts dinner-theatre evenings. The National Theatre is a good place to catch up with Thai music and dance.

As a big cosmopolitan city, Bangkok has restaurants offering most sorts of foreign food at reasonable prices, especially Indian, Chinese and Japanese. Among the top eateries serving international cuisine is Hamilton's *Steak House* and *Ma Maison* at the Hilton International, which has a particularly fine French restaurant and *Genji* - the hotel's Japanese restaurants. Top class Thai restaurants to consider are *Lemon Grass* and *Green Tamarind*.

Leisure

Bangkok offers visitors some challenging golf with several good courses to choose from within easy reach of the capital.

Ekachai Golf & Country Club, which is about 30 minutes (traffic permitting) from the city centre, is as good as any. Both the Royal Thai Army and Thai Royal Navy clubs are open to the public.

Green fees are cheap by Asian standards and this in turn has attracted golf-mad Japanese players in their thousands. Several travel agencies arrange golf tours, such as Diethelm Travel, Thailand Tourist Service and Siam Sept (who arrange three to five day golf packages in association with Accor hotels). See Priory Publications Ltd's *South East Asia Golf Guide* or the extract *Golf in Thailand*, available from TAT offices, for further details of playable golf courses.

Horse-racing takes place on alternate Saturdays at the Royal Turf Club track on Phitsanulok and on the second Sunday of each month at the Royal Bangkok Sports Club.

Most hotels have excellent health clubs, while for water sports it is best to head for Pattaya - now only 30 minutes' away by *Yellowbird* flying boat service.

Getting around

Thai Airways - the domestic arm of big sister Thai International - operates an impressive route network throughout Thailand. In recent years one or two privately-owned airlines have sprung up in competition, such as Bangkok Airways.

The Thai rail system is surprisingly good and offers overnight services to many cities from Bangkok. The Eastern and Oriental Express started the 1943-km, 41-hour journeys between Singapore and Bangkok and Sukhothai in November 1993. There are 14 accommodation cars, 3 restaurants and 3 grades of cabin. One-way fare starts at US$1170.

E & O started five or six night luxury air-conditioned cruises up the Irrawaddy from Yangon (Rangoon) to Mandalay in neighbouring Myanmar from November 1995. These depart weekly and prices start at $1700. This option, added onto the train journey from Singapore to Bangkok, and called the *Road to Mandalay*, provides a fascinating introduction to the unspoiled riverside temples, pagodas and villages of Myanmar. The same company also organises beach hol-iday extensions at Phuket or Krabi, Thailand.

Another option in Thailand is to use air-conditioned Express buses, which depart from one of Bangkok's three main terminals to points throughout the country.

Car hire is not recommended in Bangkok, but outside the capital it can be an attractive option as petrol is subsidised. Many hotels offer their own car and uniformed drivers for guests and will cost around B2,500 for the entire day. The drivers are smart, careful and know their way around the city. Even though catching a taxi is infinitely better than hiring a car, allow plenty of time between appointments as traffic congestion is terrible. If your hotel is on the river side, river taxis are a speedier alternative. The *Airport River Express*, jointly owned by the Oriental, Shangri-La and Royal Orchid hotels offers a one-way part-riverbound trip to the airport for Baht 700 in a bid to beat the traffic jams. The new Dom Muang expressway has also eased congestion.

Many taxi drivers only have a sketchy knowledge of the city and their English can be patchy, so get someone at the hotel to write down your destination in English. It is also important to agree a price before starting your journey. You won't have to pay more than B200 for a trip in town. A tip is not expected.

The three-wheeled *tuk-tuk* is a much cheaper means of getting around the city, but travel can be hot and noisy and is best used in the evenings for the sheer fun of it.

Arrival & Departure

Bangkok's Don Muang International Airport is situated 25 km from the city centre. The journey in and out has improved much in recent years. There is now an arrivals desk selling vouchers for Thai International's own taxis, costing Bt 400. Thai also runs a shuttle bus to the Asia Hotel, leaving every half hour til 9 pm. Airport limos cost from baht 500;the high speed (35 minute) rail link, costs 100 Bt. Departing passengers pay a Bt 350 departure tax on international flights and Bt 30 on domestic.

Discover the delights of South-East Asia on the most leisurely and stylish form of transport - The Eastern & Oriental Express.

Contact telephone numbers:
Singapore (65) 323 4390; USA (toll-free) (800) 524 2420; UK (171) 928 6000

Useful Addresses

American Chamber of Commerce
3rd Fl, Kian Gwan Bldg
140 Wireless Road, Bangkok
Tel: 251 1605

Association of Thai Industries
394/14 Samsen Road
Bangkok 1030. Tel: (02) 282-2482/3

Board of Trade of Thailand
150 Rajbopit Road
Bangkok 10200.Tel: (02) 221-0555

British Chamber of Commerce
Bangkok Insurance Bldg, Rm 206, 302
Silom Road, Bangkok
Tel: 255 8866; Fax: 255 8869

Department of Business Economics
Rajdamnoen Klang Avenue
Bangkok 10200 Tel: (02) 282-6171/9

Department of Export Promotion
22/77 Rachadapisek Road
Bangkok 10900.Tel: (02) 511-5066/77

Department of Foreign Trade (Ministry of Commerce)
Sanamchai Road, Bangkok 10200
Tel: (02) 223-1481/5

Department of Industrial Promotion
Rama VI Road, Bangkok 10400
Tel: (02) 246-0033

Export Service Centre
22-77 Rachadapisek Road,Nng Khen,
Bangkok. Tel: 511 5066

National Econ & Social Devel't Board
962 Krung Kasem Road, Bangkok 10100
Tel: (02) 282-3861

Office of the Board of Investment
16th floor, Thai Farmers Bank Building
400 Praholyothin Road , Bangkok 10400
Tel: (02) 270-1400; Tlx: 82542

Securities Exchange of Thailand
(Stock Exchange). Sinthorn Bldg, Wireless
Rd, Bangkok
Tel: 250 0001-8; Fax: 254 9470

Thai Chamber of Commerce
150 Rajbolit Road, Bangkok 10200
Tel: (02) 225 0086; Fax: 225 3372

Tourism Authority of Thailand
Ratchadamneon Nok Avenue, Bangkok 10100. Tel: 282 1143-7; Tlx: 72059 TAT BKK TH; Fax: 280 1744
Tourist Assistance Centre Tel: 281 3072

Thai Incentive & Convention Association
Rm 1509/2, 15th Fl, Bangkok Bank Bldg,
333 Silom Rd, Bangkok.
Tel: 235 0731; Tlx: 22228; Fax: 235 0730

Air Couriers

DHL. (02) 2070600
TNT Express Worldwide. (02) 249 5702 / (02) 249 0242
UPS. (02) 712 3300

Hospitals/Emergencies

Bangkok Christian Hospital
124 Silom Rd, Bangkok. Tel: 233 6981/9
Bangkok Adventist Hospital
430 Pitsanuloke Rd, Bangkok.Tel: 281 1422
Dental Clinic
7 South Sathorn Rd, Bangkok. Tel: 287 1036
Tourist Police
509 Vorachak Rd, Bangkok. Tel: 195 or 226 6206 (Some English spoken)
Ambulance. Dial 246 0199

Thailand Key Fact File

Passport Requirements:
All visitors must hold a valid passport. Visitors from countries in Europe, S-E Asia and the Middle East do not now require a visa for stays of up to 30 days, provided that they have a fully-paid onward ticket. Visitors from New Zealand, S Korea, Sweden, Denmark and Norway may stay for 90 days without a visa. Tourist visas are usually valid for 90 days. Business travellers staying more than 30 days should enter on a non-immigrant visa rather than a non-renewable tourist visa.

Currency: Baht (B). 100 satong = 1B

Exchange Rates:
US$ 1 = 25.9B; £1 = 42.2 B (*May 1997*)

Currency Restrictions:
No limit on the amount of foreign currency imported; exports of foreign currency in excess of US$ 10,000 are limted to the amount declared on arrival. Visitors may bring in B2,000 (B4,000 per family passport). Exports are limited to B500 per person (B1,000 per family passport).

Electricity Supply: 220 volts AC/50 cyc

Language:
Thai, but English and some other European languages spoken. English is increasingly used in business.

Time: GMT + 7 hours; EDT + 12 hours

IDD dialling code: 66
Area codes: Bangkok 2; Chiang Mai 53; Hua Hin 32; Pattaya 38; Phuket 76

Business Hours:
Commercial offices:0800-1200, 1300-1700 Monday to Friday.
Government offices:0830-1200, 1300-1630 Monday to Friday.
Banks: 0830-1530 Monday to Friday.
Shops: varies, but generally 0800-2100 seven days a week; department stores - 1000-1900.

Customs & Entry:
Duty-free allowance includes one litre of wine or spirits plus cigarettes (only 200), cigars and/or tobacco up to 250 grams in weight. Narcotic drugs, pornographic material and firearms are strictly forbidden. Entry may be refused to persons of unconventional attire or appearance.

Health Requirements:
Unless arriving from an infected area, no vaccinations are required. Cholera, typhoid & malaria precautions advised. Avoid tap water, ice cubes, undercooked meat and vegetables and unpeeled fruit.

Climate/best time to visit:
Two distinct climates: most of the country is tropical savanna, with a tropical monsoon climate in the south. Three clearly defined seasons: hot (March-May), rainy (June-October) and cool (November-February). However, in reality Bangkok is warm with average year-round of 28C. Humidity is high (80% June-Nov). Average rainfall is around 1,500mm. Most popular tourist months: Dec-Feb; best for business Oct-Feb.

National Holidays 1997*
1 January New Year's Day; 25 February Makha Bucha; 6 April Chakri Day; 12-14 April Songkran Festival; 5 May Coronation Day; 11 May Ploughing Ceremony; 24 May Wisakha Bucha; 29 July Asalha Puja; 30 July Khao Phansa; 12 August HM The Queen's Birthday; 23 October Chulalongkorn Day; 5 December HM The King's Birthday; 10 December Constitution Day; 31 December New Year's Eve.
(**Some commercial firms and international organisations may choose to close for the Chinese New Year [7-9 February]and/or for Christmas.*)

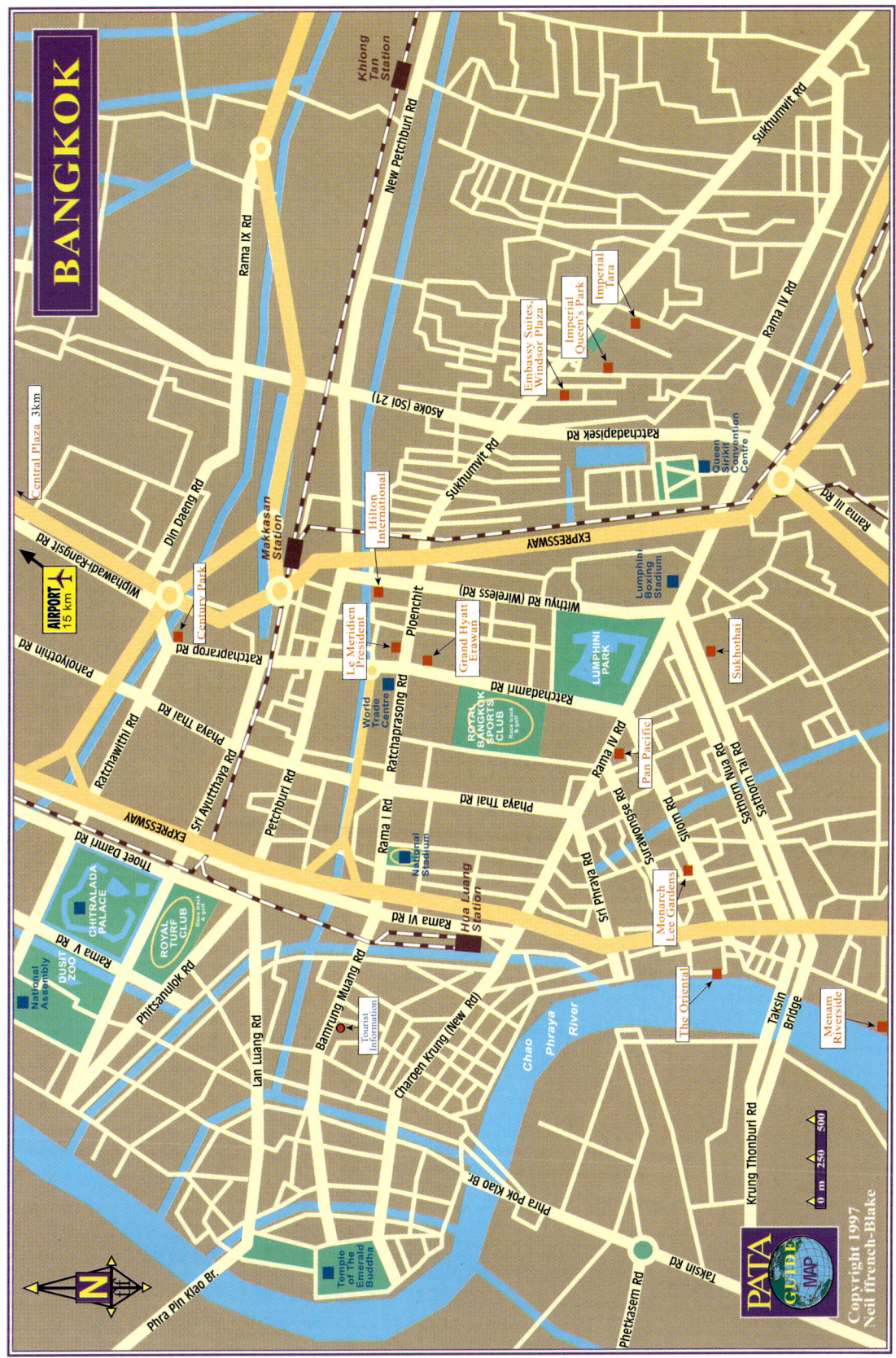

Bangkok Hotel Reference Table

Hotel (listed in price order)	SINGLE ROOM RATE (x 100 Baht)	LOCATION	NUMBER OF ROOMS	NUMBER OF SUITES	CONFERENCE FACILITIES	EXHIBITION SPACE	LARGEST BANQUET NUMBER	BUSINESS CENTRE	SWIMMING POOL (0 = indoor)	TENNIS COURT	HEALTH CLUB	VIDEO FILMS
The Oriental Bangkok	64-79	Oriental Ave	318	78	•	•	450	•	•	•	•	•
Grand Hyatt Erawan	56-67	Rajamri Rd	346	45	•	•	750	•	•	•	•	•
Hilton International	55-65	Nai Lert Park	305	37	•	•	450	•	•	•	•	•
The Dusit Thani	52-67	Rama IV Rd	495	37	•	•	1000	•	•	•	•	•
Sheraton Grande Sukhumvit	50-55	Sukhumvit Rd	445	-	•	-	500	•	•	-	•	•
Embassy Suites Windsor Plaza	50	Sukhumvit Rd	-	463	•	•	1200	•	•	-	•	•
Imperial Hotel	49-54	Wireless Rd	370	15	•	•	800	•	•	•	•	•
Central Plaza Hotel	48-52	Bangkhen	501	106	•	•	3800	•	•	•	•	•
Shangri-La Hotel	48-65	Bangrak	808	47	•	•	1000	•	•	•	•	•
Royal Orchid Sheraton	48	Siphya Rd	770	74	•	•	1500	•	•	•	•	•
The Montien Bangkok	47-66	Suriwongse Rd	393	69	•	•	800	•	•	-	•	•
Evergreen Laurel Hotel	46	Sathorn Rd	115	45	•	•	100	•	•	-	•	•
Pan Pacific Bangkok	46-62	Bangrak	155	17	•	•	200	•	•	-	•	•
Bangkok Renaissance	45	Rama IX Br	400	76	•	•	1000	•	•	•	•	•
The Mansion Kempinski	45-65	Sukhumvit Rd	120	7	•	-	-	•	•	-	•	•
The Sukhothai	45-56	S Sathorn Rd	146	80	•	•	225	•	•	-	•	•
The Regent Bangkok	45-56	Rajadamri Rd	400	39	•	•	600	•	•	•	•	•
Swissôtel B'kk-Felix Arnoma	44-54	World T C	370	33	•	•	500	•	•	-	•	•
Amari Watergate	43	Petchaburi Rd	575	25	•	-	700	•	•	•	•	•
Delta Grand Pacific	43-66	Sukhumvit Rd	400	10	•	•	400	•	•	-	-	•
Marriott Royal Gd'n Riverside	42-57	Thonburi	420	7	•	•	600	•	•	•	•	•
Landmark Hotel & Plaza	41-45	Sukhumvit Rd	360	55	•	-	500	•	•	-	•	•
Novotel Bangkok	41	Siam Square	429	-	•	•	300	•	•	-	•	•
Novotel Lotus	41-48	Sukhumvit Rd	215	9	•	-	250	•	•	-	•	•
The Imperial Queens Park	40	Sukhumvit Rd	1280	120	•	•	1200	•	•	•	•	-
Monarch Lee Gardens	40-50	Silom Rd	422	32	•	-	100	•	•	-	•	•
Rama Gardens Hotel	38-42	V. Rangsit Rd	363	17	•	•	1500	•	•	•	•	•
Amari Airport Hotel	37	Don Muang Apt	383	50	•	•	560	•	•	-	•	•
Tawana Ramada	37-45	Suriwongse Rd	265	22	•	•	1250	•	•	-	•	•
Tara Hotel	37-44	Sukhumvit Rd	196	14	•	•	700	•	•	-	•	•
Hotel Nikko Mahanakorn	36-42	Rachadapisek	582	18	•	•	750	•	•	-	•	•
Siam City Hotel	36-39	Phyathai Rd	460	69	•	•	600	•	•	-	•	•
Century Park Hotel Bangkok	36-45	Ratchaprarop	375	8	•	-	710	•	•	-	•	•
Emerald Hotel	34-40	Huay Kwang	625	-	•	-	1300	•	•	-	•	•
Indra Regent Hotel	34	Rajaparob Rd	469	24	•	•	900	•	•	-	•	•
Siam Inter-Continental	34-49	Rama I Rd	327	35	•	•	2500	•	•	•	•	-
The Menam Riverside Hotel	33-36	Yannawa	351	27	•	•	700	•	•	-	•	•
Royal Princess	33-36	Pomprab	170	-	-	-	200	-	•	-	•	•
Le Meridien President	32-58	Gaysorn Rd	729	20	•	•	950	•	•	-	•	•
Holiday Inn Crowne Plaza	32-44	Silom Rd	697	29	•	•	650	•	•	-	•	•
Amari Atrium	31	Petchaburi Rd	577	-	•	•	220	•	•	-	•	•
Amari Boulevard Hotel	31	Sukhumvit Rd	315	2	•	-	-	•	•	-	-	•
Imperial Tara Hotel	30	Sukhumvit Rd	195	-	•	•	500	•	•	-	•	•
Radisson Hotel Bangkok	30-35	Huay Kwang	440	8	•	-	200	•	•	-	•	•
Asia Hotel	29-33	Payathai Rd	617	33	•	-	1500	•	•	-	•	•
Royal City	29-32	B'mRatchonni	400	-	•	-	1500	-	•	-	•	•
Bel Aire Princess	28-34	Sukhumvit Rd	100	-	•	-	80	•	•	-	•	•
Sol Twin Towers	27-30	Patumwan	632	28	•	-	650	•	•	-	•	•
Mandarin Hotel	27-31	Rama IV Rd	394	6	•	•	1000	•	•	-	•	•
Narai Hotel	27	Silom Rd	464	36	•	-	600	•	•	-	•	•
Royal River Hotel	26-35	Bangplad	458	-	•	•	1200	-	•	-	•	•
The Somerset Hotel	24	Sukhumvit Rd	80	-	-	-	-	•	o	-	•	•
Tai Pan Hotel	24-28	Sukhumvit Rd	150	11	•	-	-	•	•	-	•	•
Silom Plaza	24	Silom Rd	209	10	•	-	-	•	•	-	-	•
Quality Hotel Pinnacle	23	Yannawa	164	5	•	-	80	•	•	-	•	•
Bangkok Palace	23-27	N. Petchburi Rd	500	200	•	-	600	•	•	-	•	•
Palm Court Bangkok	23-27	Sathorn	-	110	•	-	-	•	•	-	-	-
Ambassador Hotel/Conv Ctre	23-32	Sukhumvit Rd	945	41	•	•	2000	•	•	•	•	-
Manohra Hotel	22-24	Suriwongse Rd	466	8	•	-	-	-	•	-	•	•
Bangkok Centre Hotel	20	Rama IV Rd	250	-	•	-	600	-	•	-	-	•
Park Hotel	20-23	Sukhumvit Rd	135	4	-	-	-	•	•	-	•	•

Rest of Thailand Hotel Reference Table

Hotel (listed in price order)	SINGLE ROOM RATE (x 100 Baht)	LOCATION	NUMBER OF ROOMS	NUMBER OF SUITES	CONFERENCE FACILITIES	EXHIBITION SPACE	LARGEST BANQUET NUMBER	BUSINESS CENTRE	SWIMMING POOL (0 = indoor)	TENNIS COURT	HEALTH CLUB	VIDEO FILMS
Chiva Som Int'l Health Rst	104	Hua Hin	57	-	-	-	50	-	●	●	●	●
Santiburi Dusit Resort	65-70	Koh Samui	-	75	-	-	-	-	●	-	●	-
Banyan Tree	65-83	Phuket	-	86	●	-	100	-	-	●	●	-
Phuket Yacht Club	54-66	Phuket	100	10	●	●	50	-	●	●	-	●
Sheraton Gde Laguna Beach	50-80	Phuket	247	87	●	●	250	●	●	●	●	●
Dusit Laguna Resort	45-49	Phuket	235	7	●	●	320	-	●	●	-	●
Baan Taling Ngam	40	Koh Samui	42	9	●	-	50	-	●	●	●	●
Best Western Phuket Island	37-59	Phuket	300	13	●	-	320	-	●	●	●	-
Melia Hua Hin	37	Hua Hin	225	70	●	●	380	●	●	●	●	●
Holiday Inn Phuket	35-42	Phuket	256	21	●	●	250	-	●	●	●	●
Hotel Sofitel Central	35-42	Hua Hin	218	-	●	●	200	-	●	●	-	-
Boathouse Inn/Rest't	34-39	Phuket	33	3	-	-	-	-	●	-	-	●
Allson Rst Samui Euphoria	34-38	Koh Samui	124	8	●	-	280	-	●	●	●	-
Le Meridien Phuket	34	Phuket	470	20	●	●	450	●	●	●	●	●
The Chedi Phuket	33-45	Phuket	110	-	●	-	-	-	●	●	●	-
Chaweng Blue Lagoon	33-38	Koh Samui	61	2	-	-	-	-	●	-	-	-
Phuket Arcadia Hotel	33-36	Phuket	247	8	●	-	-	-	●	●	●	●
Dusit Resort & Polo Club	32-64	Cha-am	290	10	●	-	900	-	●	●	●	-
Swissôtel River Kwai	32-34	River Kwai	228	27	●	-	1000	-	●	●	●	●
Sofitel Raja Orchid K Kaen	31	Khon Kaen	300	5	●	●	2500	●	●	-	●	●
Thavorn Palm Beach	30-43	Phuket	203	7	●	●	400	●	●	●	●	-
Royal Cliff Beach Resort	30-35	Pattaya	420	298	●	●	1500	●	●	●	●	●
Club Aldiana Siam	30-31	Hua Hin	185	-	●	-	200	-	●	●	●	-
Golden Sands Hotel, Cha-am	30-34	Petchaburi	170	56	●	●	600	-	●	●	●	●
Amari Palm Reef Resort	30-46	Samui Isld	104	-	-	-	-	-	●	●	-	●
Dusit Resort Hotel	29-35	Pattaya	271	-	●	-	-	-	●	●	●	●
Karon Villa	29-48	Phuket	323	13	●	●	1000	-	●	●	●	●
Kata Beach Resort	28-34	Phuket	262	19	●	●	350	-	●	-	●	●
Beachcomber	28-33	Koh Samui	60	3	-	-	-	-	●	-	-	●
Clarion Resort Cumsaed	28	River Kwai	42	-	-	-	-	-	●	-	-	-
Karon Beach Resort	28-34	Phuket	81	-	●	-	-	-	●	●	-	●
Rayong Resort Hotel	28-30	Rayong	170	20	●	-	600	●	●	●	●	●
Metropole Hotel	28	Phuket	400	-	●	-	400	●	●	●	●	●
Royal Garden Village	28-31	Hua Hin	160	2	●	-	100	-	●	●	-	●
Cape Panwa Hotel	28-41	Phuket	160	14	●	-	160	●	●	●	●	●
Royal Park Travelodge	27-38	Phuket	115	-	-	-	-	-	●	-	-	-
Phuket Island Resort	26-60	Phuket	277	13	●	-	325	-	●	●	●	●
Swissôtel Felix Karon	26-30	Phuket	118	8	●	-	50	-	-	-	●	●
Royal Paradise Hotel	26-29	Phuket	246	22	●	●	500	●	●	-	●	●
The Maiton Resort	26-41	Phuket	-	75	-	-	-	-	●	●	●	●
The Imperial Phukaew Hill	25	Petchaboon	124	8	●	-	120	-	●	●	●	-
Royal Garden Resort	25-28	Hua Hin	300	-	●	-	120	-	●	●	●	●
Chiang Mai Orchid	24-31	Chiang Mai	257	8	●	●	400	●	●	-	●	●
Montien Pattaya	24-38	Pattaya	300	14	●	-	500	-	●	●	●	-
Amari Coral Beach Resort	24-29	Phuket	194	6	●	-	-	-	●	-	●	●
Westin Chiang Mai	24-32	Chiang Mai	481	45	●	●	600	-	●	●	●	-
Club Andaman Beach Resort	24-41	Phuket	250	-	●	-	160	●	●	-	●	●
Royal Garden Resort	23-30	Pattaya	300	-	●	●	120	-	●	●	●	-
Amari Kata Thani Resort	22-40	Phuket	337	3	●	-	-	-	●	●	●	●
Royal Princess	22-28	Chiangmai	198	-	●	-	200	●	●	-	●	●

Rest of Thailand Hotel Reference Table

Hotel (listed in price order)	SINGLE ROOM RATE (x 100 Baht)	LOCATION	NUMBER OF ROOMS	NUMBER OF SUITES	CONFERENCE FACILITIES	EXHIBITION SPACE	LARGEST BANQUET NUMBER	BUSINESS CENTRE	SWIMMING POOL (0 = indoor)	TENNIS COURT	HEALTH CLUB	VIDEO FILMS
Dusit Island Resort	22-29	Chiang Rai	271	45	●	-	600	-	●	●	●	●
Imperial Boathouse Hotel	22	Koh Samui	182	34	●	●	120	-	●	-	-	●
Quality Resort Jomtien	22	Pattaya	400	-	●	●	800	●	●	●	●	●
Regent Cha-am Beach	22	Petchaburi	508	126	●	-	450	-	●	●	●	●
Phuket Cabana	22-37	Phuket	75	5	●	-	200	●	●	-	●	●
Le Meridien Baan Boran	21-24	Chiang Rai	110	4	●	-	60	-	●	●	●	●
Chaweng Regent Beach	21	Koh Samui	-	288	●	-	287	-	●	-	●	●
Imperial Mae Ping Hotel	20	Chiang Mai	371	-	●	●	220	●	●	-	●	-
Amari Rincome Hotel	19-24	Chiang Mai	154	4	●	-	-	-	●	-	-	-
Siam Bayview Hotel	19-24	Pattaya	254	14	●	●	140	-	●	-	●	-
Siam Bayshore Hotel	19-26	Pattaya	262	9	●	●	200	-	●	●	-	-
Amari Nipa Lodge Hotel	19	Pattaya	150	10	●	-	100	-	●	●	-	●
Suriwongse Zenith	19-21	Chiangmai	166	2	●	●	-	●	●	-	-	-
Asia Pattaya Beach	18-22	Pattaya	270	50	●	-	800	-	●	●	-	-
Vises Patong Hotel	18-22	Phuket	133	3	●	-	160	-	●	-	-	●
Quality Chiang Mai Hills	18-20	Chiang Mai	271	10	●	●	500	●	●	-	●	●
The Merlin Pattaya	18-20	Pattaya	344	16	●	●	400	-	●	●	●	●
Pattaya Park Beach Resort	18	Pattaya	270	-	-	-	-	-	-	-	-	-
Delta Golden Triangle Rst	17	Chiang Rai	71	2	●	●	250	●	●	-	●	●
Sol Jomtien	17-19	Chonburi	137	3	●	-	70	-	●	●	-	-
Amari Orchid Resort Hotel	17-23	Pattaya	228	8	●	-	-	-	●	●	-	-
Comfort Rst Thaton View	17	Chiang Mai	33	-	●	-	150	-	-	-	-	-
Empress Hotel	16-22	Chiang Mai	375	-	-	-	-	-	●	-	●	-
Imperial Tara Mae Hong Sorn	16	Chiang Rai	93	11	●	●	240	-	●	-	●	-
Woodlands Resort	16-18	Pattaya	185	1	●	-	120	-	●	-	-	-
Regent Chiang Mai (Rimkok)	14-19	Chiang Mai	250	6	●	-	-	-	●	●	●	●
Novotel Tropicana	14	Pattaya	172	14	●	-	-	-	●	●	-	●
Pearl Hotel	14-16	Phuket	241	9	●	-	350	-	●	-	-	●
Baiyoke Pattaya Hotel	13-15	Pattaya	112	23	●	-	-	●	-	-	-	●
Wiang Inn	12	Chiang Rai	258	3	●	●	-	-	●	-	-	●
Ambassador City Jomtien	10	Jomtien	500	-	●	-	-	●	●	●	●	●

Thailand Hotels

Bangkok

Alexander Hotel D
3303 (Sukhumvit 71) Ramkhamhaeng Rd,
Huamark, Bangkapi 10240
Tel: 375 0300-40; Fax: 375 2332

Amari Airport Hotel ○ C
333 Chert Wudthakas Rd, Don Muang,
10210. Tel: 566 1020-1; Tlx: 87424-5
AIRHOTEL TH; Fax: 566 1941

Amari Atrium Hotel C
1880 New Petchburi Road, Bangkapi,
Hway Kwang, Bangkok 10310
Tel: 718 2000; Fax: 718 2002

Amari Boulevard Hotel ○ C
17 Sukhumvit Soi 7, 10110
Tel: 255 2930; Tlx: 84033 BLVDHTL; Fax: 255 2950

Amari Watergate B
847 Petchburi Road, 10400
Tel: 653 9000; Tlx: 20108; Fax: 653 9045

Ambassador Hotel & Convention Center ○ C
171 Sukhumvit Rd Sol 11-13, 10110
Tel: 254 0444/255 0444; Fax: 253 4123

Asia Hotel ○ C
296 Phayathai Rd, 10400
Tel: 215 0808; Tlx: 82722/81177 ASIATEL; Fax: 215 4360

Bangkok Centre Hotel D
328 Rama IV Road, 10500
Tel: 238 4980-99; Tlx: 72067; Fax: 236 4848

Bangkok Palace Hotel ○ C
1091/336 New Petchburi Rd, 10400
Tel: 253 0510; Tlx: 74278-79 BANGHIL TH; Fax: 253 0556

Bangkok Renaissance Hotel B
Rama IX Bridge, 3999 Rama III Rd, 10120
Tel: 292 3160; Fax: 292 3164

Bel-Aire Princess C
16 Sukhumvit Rd, sol 5,10110
Tel: 253 4300; Tlx: 20672; Fax: 255 8850

Best Western Baiyoke Suites D
130 Ratprarop Rd, Rattharree, 10400
Tel: 255 0330; Fax: 254 5553

Best Western Jade Pavilion D
30 Sukhumvit, soi 22
Tel: 259 4675; Fax: 258 2328

Central Plaza Hotel ○
1695 Phaholyothin Rd, Chatuchak,10900
Tel: 541 1234; E-mail: centel@ksc5,th.com
Fax: 541 1087; SITATEX: BKKAZCR

The Central Plaza Hotel is only 15 minutes from Bangkok International via Dom Muang tollway. The hotel also provides a shuttle bus service. It features 607 deluxe guestrooms and suites with recreational facilities including an open-air swimming pool, tennis courts, jogging track and the adjacent 18-hole Railway Golf Course. In addition, the shopping centre is located within the Central Plaza Complex.

Accommodation and rates:
501 rooms, 106 suites. Single baht 4800-5200; double/twin baht 5100-5600; suite baht 5600-115,000.
Subject to 10% service charge & 7%VAT

Credit cards accepted
Visa, Diners Club, JCB, Mastercard, Amex

Meeting & banqueting facilities
26 meeting/conference rooms, capacity 10-3800 persons, with full audio-visual equipment; largest reception 3800 seated or 5000 cocktail.

Room services
Airconditioning, colour TV, IDD telephone (ext in bathroom), hairdryer, laundry/valet service, minibar, music/radio/alarm clock, safety deposit box, non-smoker bedrooms available, 24-hr room service, video films/ IBC cable TV, baby cot, wheelchairs

Business services
Business centre, executive floor, express checkout, airport pickup, translation service, car parking, travel centre, taxi service

Other services
Barber shop/hairdresser, beauty salon, guided tours, newsstand/shops, photo shop, flower shop, shopping centre, free shuttle bus service

Sports & Recreation
Fitness/health centre, golf (adjacent), jacuzzi, jogging track, massage, sauna, outdoor swimming pool, tennis (3 courts)

Restaurants & Coffee Shops
Dynasty Chinese Restaurant (200) - open 1130-1400/1800-2230; *Don Giovanni*(120) - Italian, open as above; *Le Danang* (120) - Vietnamese, open 1130-1400/1800-2300; *Suan Bua Restaurant* (150) - Thai, open as above;*Hagi* (120) - Japanese, open 1100-1400/1800-2300; *Chatuchak Cafe* (170) -International, open 24 hrs; *Lobby Lounge* (120), open 1130-midnight.

Overseas Sales Representatives:
Utell International. Aviation & Tourism International (ATI). GTA Global Hotel Services Program

Century Park Hotel Bangkok ○
9 Ratchaprarop Road, Bangkok 10400
Tel: 246 7800-9; Fax: 246 7197

The Century Park Hotel Bangkok is situated in the midst of the commercial and shopping district of bustling Ractchaprarop. An express transit system at the hotel's doorstep brings the airport and major tourist attractions to within an easy ride of the hotel.

Accommodation and rates
383 single/double/twin, baht 3600-4500; suite baht 4800-118000.
Subject to 10% service charge and 7% VAT

Credit cards accepted
Amex, Diners, Mastercard, Visa, JCB

Meeting & banqueting facilities
7 meeting/function rooms, capacity 30-710, with audio-visual facilities; largest reception 710 seated/900 cocktail.

Room services
Airconditioning, colour TV + satellite, bath with sep shower, direct-dial telephone, laundry/valet service, minibar, multi channel radio/music/alarm clock, personal safe, tea/coffee making

Business & other services
Business centre, Century Club exclusive floor, airport pickup, translation service, car parking, travel centre, taxi service, barber/hairdresser, non-smoking floors

Sports & recreation
Clark Hatch fitness centre/gym, outdoor swimming pool

Restaurants & coffee shops
Cafe at the Park - International/local 24-hour coffee shop; *Fountain* (lobby) *Lounge*, drinks, music; *Garden* (poolside) *Terrace* -Thai/light food; *La Patisserie* - Bakery Shop

Overseas Sales Representatives
Utell International, Delton Reservations System, Century International Hotels

City Lodge Bangkok E
Soi 9, Sukhumvit Road, Bangkok 10110
Tel: 253 7705; Fax: 255 4667

The Classic Place Hotel ○ D
1574-1598 New Petchburi Rd, 10310
Tel: 255 4444-9; Tlx: 22007; Fax: 255 4450

Embassy Suites Windsor Palace ○
8-10 Sukhumvit 20, Sukhumvit Rd, 10110
Tel: 262 1234; Tlx 82081; Fax: 258 1522

Each oif our 463 suites has been exquisitely furnished with meticulous attention to detail. Spacious and luxurious, our hotel is the only true all-suite hotel to grace the Bangkok skyline, offering two-room suites for the same price as a regular room in the city's other leading hotels.

Accommodation and rates
463 suites, 5000-65,000 baht
Subject to 10% service charge and 7% VAT

Credit cards accepted
All major

Meeting & banqueting facilities
10 meeting/function rooms, capacity 50-1500; audio-visual facilities available; 130-750 sq m exhibition space; largest reception 1200 seated or 1500 cocktail

Room services
Airconditioning, colour TV, direct-dial telephone (ext. in bathroom), hairdryer, laundry/valet service, minibar, music/radio/ alarm clock, safety deposit box, 24-hr room service, tea/coffee making, trouser press, non-smoker bedrooms, video films

Business & other services
Business centre, executive floor, airport pickup, car parking, travel centre, taxi service, newsstand/shops, tailor shop, heli pad

Sports & Recreation
Fitness centre/gym, whirlpool, jogging track, massage, sauna, outdoor swimming pool, steam room

Restaurants & Coffee Shops
The Golden Palace (200) - Chinese, open lunch & dinner; *The Atrium Cafe* (300) - International, open 24 hours; *The Marco Polo* (250) - Grill room, open lunch/dinner; *The Atrium Lounge* (200) - Beverages, open 1400-midnight

Delta Grand Pacific Hotel ○   B
1 Sukhumvit Soi 19, Bangkok 10110 Tel: 255 2440; Tlx: 20686; Fax: 255 2441

Grand Hyatt Erawan Bangkok
494 Rajdamri Road, Bangkok 10730
Tel: 254 1234; Tlx: 20975 HYATBKKTH; Fax: 254 6308

A leading business hotel located in the heart of Bangkok's business, diplomatic and residential districts. Surrounded by modern shopping centres, opposite World Trade Centre. On the legendary Erawan Shrine site.

Accommodation and rates
250 single/double, 96 twin rooms, baht 5600-6700; suite baht 8500-39500
Subject to 10% service charge and 7% VAT

Credit cards accepted
Amex, Diners, Mastercard, Visa, JCB

Meeting & banqueting facilities
9 meeting/function rooms, capacity 10-1100; 920 sq m exhibition space; largest reception 750 seated/1100 cocktail.

Room services
Airconditioning, colour TV, direct-dial telephone (ext. in bathroom), hairdryer, laundry/valet service, minibar, music/radio/ alarm clock, safety deposit box, trouser press, 24-hr room service, non-smoker bedrooms, HBO

Business & other services
Business centre, executive floor, express checkout, airport pickup, translation service, car parking & rental, travel centre, taxi service, beauty salon, newsstand/ shops, tour operator, per pay view movies, helicopter service

Sports & Recreation
Fitness centre/gym, jacuzzi/whirlpool, massage, sauna, outdoor swimming pool, squash, tennis

Restaurants & Coffee Shops
The Dining Room (210) - Continental/Thai, open 0600-0100; *The Chinese Restaurant* (155) - Cantonese, open 1130-1430/1830-2230; *Spasso* (96) - Italian/Entertainment, open noon-0100 (0230 Fri/Sat); *Ruen Thai Terrace* (72) - Thai, open 1130-1430/1830-2230; *You and Mee* (70) - Noodles, open 1100-2300; *Snax* (73) - All day snacks, open 1000-2000

Overseas Sales Representatives:
Hyatt Hotels & Resorts Sales Offices

Hilton International at Nai Lert Park
2 Wireless Road, Bangkok 10330   ○
Tel: 253 0123; Fax: 253 6509;
E-mail: Hiltopia@hiltonint.com

Centrally located in 8.5 acres of landscaped garden within business, diplomatic and shopping district. The hotel, low rise building with 3 atrium lobbies offers 342 rooms including suites, executive floor with clubroom, fitness center and sport recreation as well as extensive 6 restaurants.

Accommodation and rates
158 double/147 twin, 5500-6500 baht (single occ. baht 5000-6000); 37 suites, 8000-30000 baht.
Subject to 10% service charge and 7% VAT

Credit cards accepted
Amex, Visa, Mastercard, JCB, Diners

Meeting & banqueting facilities
6 meeting rooms, capacity 50-700 (theatre style); audio-visual equipment available; largest reception 450 seated/ 850 cocktail.

Room services
Airconditioning, colour TV, direct-dial telephone (ext. in bathroom), hairdryer, laund -ry/valet service, minibar, music/radio, non-smoker bedrooms available, safety deposit box, trouser press

Business and other services
Business centre, executive floor, translation service, car parking, travel centre, limousine service

Sports & Recreation
Fitness centre/gym, jogging track, sauna, outdoor swimming pool, tennis, squash

Restaurants & Coffee Shops
Suan Suranrom (160)- Thai/Western, open 0600-2300; *Ma Maison* (70)- French, open 1130-1400/1830-2200; *Genji* (130) - Japanese, open as above; *Noble House* (170) - Cantonese, open as above

Overseas Sales Representatives
Hilton International Worldwide

The Dusit Thani
Rama IV Rd, 10500
Tel: 236 0450-9; Fax: 236 6400/236 7238

THAILAND - Hotels

The Emerald Hotel ○ C
99/1 Rachadapisek Rd, Huay Kwang, 10310
Tel: 276 4567; Tlx: 20518; Fax: 276 4555

Evergreen Laurel Hotel Bangkok ○
88 North Sathorn Road, Bangrak 10500 B
Tel: 266 9988/266 7266; Fax: 266 7322

Holiday Inn Crowne Plaza Bangkok
981 Silom Road, Bangkok 10500 ○ C
Tel: 238 4300; Tlx: 82998; Fax: 238 5289

Impala Hotel D
9 Sukhumvit Road, soi 24, 10110
Tel: 259 0053; Tlx: 84056; Fax: 258 8747

Indra Regent Hotel ○ B
120/126 Rajprarop Rd, 10400
Tel: 208 0022; Tlx: 82723; Fax: 208 0388/9

The Imperial Queen's Park Hotel ○
199 Sukhumvit, soi 22
Tel: 261 9000; Tlx: 20326 IMPQPTH; Fax: 261 9546/7; E-mail: Imperial@usc.net.th

37-storey luxury-class hotel located in the city's fastst growing economic, commercial and entertainment area. Overlooking the Benjasiai Park and only minutes from the Queen Sirikit National Convention Center. Three access points to the Airport Expressway.

Accommodation & rates
1400 rooms inc. 120 suites. Single baht 4000; double/twin baht 4400; suite baht 7000. Subject to 10% service charge and 7% government tax

Credit cards accepted
Amex, Diners, Mastercard, Visa

Meeting & banqueting facilities
11 meeting/function rooms, capacity 3000; audio-visual facilities available; 1420 sq m exhibition space; largest reception 1200 seated or 2000 cocktail

Room services
Airconditioning, colour TV, direct-dial telephone (ext. in bathroom), hairdryer, laundry/valet service, minibar, music/radio/alarm clock, safety deposit box, 24-hr room service, non-smoker bedrooms available, trouser press

Business & other services
Business centre, executive floor, airport pickup, barber shop/beauty salon, newsstand/shops, guided tours

Sports & Recreation
Billiards/snooker, fitness centre/gym, squash, jacuzzi/whirlpool, massage, sauna outdoor swimming pool

Restaurants & Coffee Shops
Parkview Restaurant (350) - International/Asian,open 24 hours; *Terrace Shabu-Shabu* (120) - Japanese-style fondu, open 1800-2200; *Cibo Brasserie* (100) - Continental, open noon -1400/1800-2200; *Uncle Ho Vietnamese Restaurant* (80), open as above; *Imperila China Restaurant* (400) - Cantonese, open as above; *Kacho* (400) - Japanese, open as above; *The Sundowners* (90) - Bar/music lounge, open 1900-0200; *Lobby Lounge* (60) - open 1000-2200

Overseas Sales Representatives:
Worldwide: Ana Enterprises Ltd; Europe: Supereps International, London; Japan: MAC Marketing Service

The Imperial Tara Hotel
18/1 Sukhumvit, soi 16
Tel: 259 2900; Tlx: 22613 TARA TH; Fax: 259 2896; E-mail: Imperial@ksc.net.th

City hotel for executive travellers. Situated in the hub of one of Bangkok's fast growing business and entertainment areas; only five minutes from the Benjasiai Park and 15 minutes from the Queen Sirikit National Convention Center. Two access points to the Airport Expressway.

Accommodation & rates
195 deluxe rooms and suites. Single baht 3000; double/twin baht 3300; suite baht 4500. Subject to 10% service charge and 7% government tax

Credit cards accepted
Amex, Diners, Mastercard, Visa

Meeting & banqueting facilities
Four meeting/function rooms, capacity 30-600; audio-visual facilities available; 512 sq m exhibition space; largest reception 500 seated or 600 cocktail

Room services
Airconditioning, colour TV, direct-dial telephone (ext. in bathroom), hairdryer, laundry/valet service, minibar, music/radio/alarm clock, safety deposit box, 24-hr room service, non-smoker bedrooms available

Business & other services
Business centre, airport pickup, barber shop/beauty salon, newsstand/shops, guided tours

Sports & Recreation
Billiards/snooker, fitness centre/gym, jogging track, massage, sauna, outdoor swimming pool, aerobics dance room

Restaurants & Coffee Shops
Tara Coffee Shop (160) - Thai/Chinese/International, open 24 hours; Eurofayre (50) - Continental, open 1130 -1400/1830-2230

Overseas Sales Representatives:
Worldwide: Ana Enterprises Ltd; Europe: Supereps International, London; Japan: MAC Marketing Service

The Landmark of Bangkok ○
138 Sukhumvit Road, Bangkok 10110
Tel: 254 0404; Tlx: 87474; Fax: 253 4259

Mandarin Hotel ○ C
662 Rama IV Road, Bangkok 10500
Tel: 238 0230-58; Tlx: 87689; Fax: 237 1620

Manhattan Hotel E
13 sol 5/15 Sukhumvit Road, 10110
Tel: 255 0166; Tlx: 87272; Fax: 255 3481

Manohra Hotel ○ D
412 Suriwongse Road, Bangkok 10500
Tel: 234 5070; Tlx: 82114; Fax: 237 7662

The Mansion Kempinski B
75/23 Sukhumvit Soi 11, Prakanong 10110
Tel: 255 7200/253 2655; Fax: 253 2329

Marriott Royal Garden Riverside Hotel Bangkok ○ B
257/1-3 Charoen Nakorn Rd, Thonburi 10600
Tel: 476 0021/22; Fax: 460 1805/476 1120

The Montien Bangkok ○ B
54 Surawongse Road, PO Box 1098, 10500
Tel: 233 7060-9/234 8060; Tlx: 81160/82938 TH; Fax: 236 5219/237 7333

Montien Riverside Hotel B
372 Rama 3 Road, Bangklo, 10120
Tel: 292 2999; Fax: 292 2962-4

Narai Hotel ○ C
222 Silom Road, 10500
Tel: 237 0100; Tlx: 81175; Fax: 236 7161

The Menam Riverside Hotel
2074 Charoenkrung Road, Yannawa, 10120
Tel: 688 1000; Fax: 291 9400
E-mail: menamhtl@mozard.inet.co.th
Internet: http://www.siam.net/menam

In Bangkok's main business district and tourist area. 1/2 mile from expressway access. Dom Muang international airport 22 miles. A deluxe riverside hotel set amidst large tropical gardens with giant swimming pool. Overlooks the great Chao Phya river and caters for all leisure & business needs.

Accommodation and rates
256 single, baht 3300-3600; 363 double/twin, baht 3600-3900; 32 triple, baht 4200-4500; 27 connecting rooms, baht 7200-7800; suites, baht 6000-20000.
Subject to 10% service charge and 7% VAT

Credit cards accepted
Amex, Visa, Diners, Mastercard, JCB

Meeting & banqueting facilities
Nine meeting rooms, capacity 50-1200; audio-visual equipment available; 80-875 sq m exhibition space; largest reception 700 seated or 1200 cocktail

Room services
Airconditioning, colour TV (+ Star/CNN), Pay TV, direct-dial telephone (ext. in bathroom), hairdryer, laundry/valet service, minibar, music/radio/alarm clock, safety deposit box, 24-hr room service, non-smoker bedrooms, video films

Business and other services
Business centre, executive floor, express checkout, airport pickup, car parking & rental, travel centre & tours, limousine service, barber shop/beauty salon, newsstand/shops, helicopter service, free shuttle Oriental Pier/River City/World Tr Centre

Sports & Recreation
Fitness centre/gym, jacuzzi/whirlpool, jogging track, massage, outdoor swimming pool, figure centre

Restaurants & Coffee Shops
Chainam Coffee Shop (300) - European/Local, open 24 hours; *La Brasserie* (300) - French/European, open 1100-1430/1800-2300; *Menamtien* (300) - Cantonese/Szechuan, open as above; *Seafood Barbecue* (450) - open 1800-2300; *Japanese Corner* (300), open as above

Le Meridien President Hotel & Tower
971 Ploenjit Rd, Bangkok 10330
Tel: 253 0044; Tlx: 81194; Fax: 253 7565

The most centrally located hotel in Bangkok, in the heart of the shopping district near the Erawan Shrine and World Trade Center with easy access to the Airport Expressway. With 749 de luxe rooms and suites and superb restaurants it has a cosy ambience depicting a truly European flair.

Accommodation and rates
749 rooms. Single 3200-5800 baht; double/twin 3600-5800 baht; suite 6000-17500 baht.
Subject to 10% service charge and 7% VAT

Credit cards accepted
Amex, Visa, Mastercard, Diners

Groups
18 meeting rooms, capacity up to 200; 1500 sq m exhibition space available; largest reception 950 banquet/1100 cocktail; President Garden Terrace, Tower Rooftop Terrace

Room services
Airconditioning, colour TV, direct-dial telephone (ext. in bathroom), hairdryer, laundry/valet service, minibar, music/radio/alarm clock, non-smoker bedrooms, tea/coffee making, safety deposit box, 24-hr room service, video films, trouser press

Business and other services
Business centre, executive floor, express checkout, airport pickup, translation service, car parking & rental, taxi service, travel centre, barber shop/beauty salon, guided tours, newsstand/shops

Sports & Recreation
Fitness centre/gym, jogging track, sauna, massage, outdoor swimming pool, spa

Restaurants & Coffee Shops
Fireplace Grill (86) - Gourmet Grill, open noon-1430/1830-2230; *Cappuccino* (120) Western/Thai, open 0600-midnight; *President's Lounge* (120) - Buffet bkfst/lunch/dinner, open 0630-0100; *Espresso* (188) - Thai/International, open 24 hours; *Summer Palace* (Chinese), *Tsukiji* (Japanese), *Oasis* (Snacks), opened in Tower Wing '97

Overseas Sales Representatives:
Le Meridien Worldwide Sales Offices

The Monarch Lee Gardens Bangkok
88 Silom Road, Bangrak, 10500
Tel: 238 1991; Tlx: 20436; Fax: 238 1999

A 38-storey international superior class hotel. Located within walking distance of the business area on Silom Road in the midst of Bangkok. 40-minutes' ride to the International Airport. Superb cuisine, full banquet facilities, business center & health club

Accommodation and rates
221 single, 201 twin/double rooms, 4000-5000 baht; 32 suites, 7000-16000 baht.
Subject to 10% service charge and 7% VAT

Credit cards accepted
Amex, Visa, Mastercard, Diners, JCB

Meeting & banqueting facilities
Three meeting rooms, capacity up to 180; audio-visual equipment available; 161.5 sq m exhibition space available; largest reception 100 seated or 180 cocktail

Room services
Airconditioning, colour TV, direct-dial telephone (ext. in bathroom), hairdryer, laundry/valet service, minibar, music/radio/alarm clock, non-smoker bedrooms, safety deposit box, 24-hr room service, video films

Business & other services
Business centre, executive floor, express checkout, airport pickup, translation service, car parking & rental, taxi service, guided tours, newsstand/shops

Sports & Recreation
Fitness centre/gym, jacuzzi/whirlpool, massage, massage, sauna, outdoor pool

Restaurants & Coffee Shops
Cafe Royal (86) - Asian/International, open 24 hours; *Teio* (104) - Japanese, open 1130 -1430/1800-2230; above; *Palais de Monarch* (54) - Continental, open as above; *Ti-Jing* (180) - Chinese, open as above.

Le Meridien President Bangkok

Overseas Sales Representatives:
Regional sales offices in Hong Kong and Singapore. Travel Resources Management Group (Sterling) Worldwide

Hotel Nikko Mahanakorn Bangkok A
273 Ratchada-Pisek Road, Huay-Kwang, 10310
Tel: 274 1515; Tlx: 72602; Fax: 274 1500

The Oriental Bangkok ○
48 Oriental Avenue, 10500
Tel: 236 0400-20; Tlx: 82997 ORIENTAL TH; Fax: 236 1937-9

On the banks of Bangkok's Chao Phya - the fabled "River of Kings"- stands the Oriental, which can genuinely lay claim to being one of the world's truly great hotels. The Oriental is renowned for its unique ambience of timeless colonial-style elegance in an exotic Eastern setting. Over its 121 years of existence, it has acted as host and inspiration for such great writers as Joseph Conrad and Somerset Maugham. Every great city has one great hotel. In Bangkok, it's the Oriental.

Accommodation & rates
396 rooms. Single baht 6400-7900; double /twin baht 6700-8400; suite bt 10500-55000
Subj. to 10% service charge and 7% VAT

Credit cards accepted
Amex, Diners, Visa, Mastercard, JCB

Meeting & banqueting facilities
8 meeting/function rooms, capacity 10-500, with full audio-visual facilities; largest reception 450 seated/1000 cocktail; also Thai Cooking School, Oriental Queen, Spa

Room services
Airconditioning, colour TV, direct-dial telephone, hairdryer, laundry/valet service, minibar, safety deposit box, trouser press, 24-hr room service, non-smoker bedrooms available, butler service

Business & other services
Business centre, airport pickup, translation service, car parking & rental, travel centre, taxi service, barber shop/hairdresser, beauty salon, newsstand/shops

Sports & Recreation
Fitness centre/gym, jacuzzi/whirlpool, jogging track, massage, sauna, squash, swimming-pool (indoor & outdoor), tennis

Restaurants & Coffee Shops
Le Normandie (80) - French, open noon-1430/1900-2200; *Lord Jim's* (150) - International/Seafood, open noon-1430/1900-2300; *Sala Rim Naam* (200) - Thai, open as above til 2200; *The Verandah* (140+80) - A la carte, open 0600-midnight (Fri-Sat-0100); *The China House* (135) - Cantonese, open 1130-1430/1830-2230; *BBQ Terrace* (400) - open 1900-2300; *Ciao* (48) - Italian, open 1700-2300; *Terrace Rim Naam* (150) - Thai, open 1630-2300

Overseas Sales Representatives
Mandarin Oriental Group, Leading Hotels

Novotel Bangkok on Siam Square
Siam Square, sol 6, 10330 ○ B
Tel: 255 6888; Tlx: TH 22780; Fax: 255 1824

Novotel Lotus B
1 Soi Daeng Udom, Sukhumvit 33 Rd, 10110
Tel: 261 0111; Fax: 262 1700

Palm Court Bangkok ¶
27 Soi Saladaeng 1, Salthorn 10500
Tel: 267 4050; Fax: 267 4080

The Park Hotel D
6 Sukhumvit, soi 7, Sukhumvit Rd, 10110
Tel: 255 4300; Tlx: 22173; Fax: 255 4309

Peninsula Bangkok A
333 Charoennathorn Road, Klongsan, 10600.Tel: 861 1111; Fax: 861 1112

Quality Hotel Pinnacle D
17 Soi Ngam Duphli, Rama S Rd, Yannawa, Bangkok 10210
Tel: 287 0111; Tlx: 20183; Fax: 287 3420

Radisson Bangkok C
Rama 9 Road, 10310
Tel: 255 0404; Fax: 255 4450

Rama Gardens Hotel ○ C
9/9 Vinhavadi Rangsit Road, Bangkhen, Bangkok 10210.Tel: 561 0022; Tlx: 84250 GARDENS TH; Fax: 561 1025

The Regent of Bangkok ○ B
155 Rajadamri Rd, 10330
Tel: 251 6127; Fax: 253 9195

The Pan Pacific Hotel Bangkok
952 Rama 4 Road, Bangrak, 10500
Tel: 632 9000; Fax: 632 9001
E-mail: panpacificbkk@loxinfo.co.th

Located in the heart of the commercial, financial and entertainment district, on Silom 4 intersection and soaring to 32 storeys, its superb 235 rooms command a panoramic view. Facilities include business centre, health club and pool, an authentic Japanese restaurant, Chinese restaurant and all-day dining.

Accommodation and rates
155 double/twin rooms, baht 5000-6900 (single occ. baht 4600-6200); 17 suites, baht 7500-50000
Subject to 10% service charge and 7% VAT

Credit cards accepted:
Visa, Amex, JCB, Diners

Meeting & banqueting facilities
5 meeting/conference rooms, capacity 40-200; audio-visual equipment available; 67 sq m exhibition space; largest reception 200 seated or 280 cocktail

Room services
Airconditioning, colour TV, direct-dial telephone (ext. in bathroom), hairdryer, laundry/valet service, minibar, music/radio/alarm clock, safety deposit box, tea/coffee making, trouser press, 24-hour room/meal service, non-smoker bedrooms, video films voicemail, TV message viewing, fax in rooms

Business & other services
Business centre, executive floor, airport pickup, translation service, car parking & rental, taxi service, travel centre, newsstand/shops, 24-hour reservations, express delivery service, mobile phone pager

Sports & Recreation
Fitness centre/gym, jacuzzi/whirlpool, massage, sauna, squash, outdoor swimming pool

Restaurants & Coffee Shops
The Keyaki (165) - Japanese, open noon-1430/1800-2230; *Hai Tien Lo* (125) Chinese, open 1130-1430/1800-2230; *Heights Cafe* (150) - International, open 24 hours; Lobby Lounge (56) - Snacks, open 1100-2300

Overseas Sales Representatives:
Pan Pacific Hotels & Resorts Worldwide; SRS Steigenberger Reservation Service

○ = *Member of Pacific Asia Travel Association*

THAILAND - Hotels

Rembrandt Hotel and Plaza ⏾ D
Soi 18, Sukhumvit Road, Bangkok 10110
Tel: 261 7100; Fax: 261 7017

Royal City Hotel C
28 Borom Ratchanri Rd, Bangkok 10700
Tel: 435 8888; Fax: 434 3636; Tlx: 20615

Royal Orchid Sheraton Hotel & Towers ⏾ B
2 Captain Bush Lane, Siphraya, Bangrak, Bangkok 10500. Tel: 266 0123; Tlx: 84491-2 ROYALORCH; Fax: 236 8320

Royal Princess Hotel ⏾ C
269 Lam Luang Road, Pombrab, 10100
Tel: 281 3088; Tlx: 86788; Fax: 280 1314

Royal River Hotel ⏾ C
670/805 Charansanitwong Road, 10700
Tel: 433 0300; Tlx: 22048; Fax: 433 5880

Shangri-La Hotel, Bangkok ⏾ B
89 Soi Wat Suan Plu, New Road, Bangrak, 10500
Tel: 236 7777; Tlx: 84265; Fax: 236 8579

Sheraton Grande Sukhumvit A
250 Sukhumvit Rd, 10110
Tel: 653 0334; Fax: 653 0400

Siam City Hotel ⏾ B
477 Sri Ayuthaya Rd, 10400
Tel: 247 0123; Tlx: 20190 ; Fax: 247 0165

Hotel Siam Inter-Continental ⏾ C
PO Box 2052, 967 Rama I Road, 10330
Tel: 253 0355-7; Tlx: 81155 SIAMINT TH; Fax: 253 2275

The Silom Plaza D
320 Silom Road, 10500
Tel: 236 8441-85/236 0333; Tlx: 21625 SLOMPZA TH; Fax: 236 7566

Sol Twin Towers Hotel C
88 New Rama 6 Road, Rongmuang, 10330
Tel: 216 9555; Tlx: 20399; Fax: 216 9544

Swissôtel Bangkok-Felix Arnoma
99 Rajadamri Road, 10330   B ⏾
Tel: 255 3410; Tlx: 21212; Fax: 255 3456-8

Tai-Pan Hotel ⏾ C
25 Sukhumvit soi 23, Sukhumvit Rd, 10110
Tel: 260 9888; Tlx: 20540 Fax: 259 7908

The Tara B
18/1 Sukhumvit Soi 26, 10110
Tel: 259 2900; Fax: 259 2896

Tawana Ramada ⏾ B
PO Box 1742, 80 Surawongse Rd, 10500
Tel: 236 0361; Tlx: 81167; Fax: 236 3738

Explanation of codes following hotel names.
A = over US$ 200 per person per night; **B** = between US$ 150 - 200; **C** = between US$ 100 - 150; **D** = between US$ 50 -100; **E** = under US$ 50; ¶ = prices on application.

The Sukhothai Bangkok ⏾
13/3 South Sathorn Road, Bangkok 10120
Tel: 287 0222; Fax: 287 4980

Set amidst an oasis of calm on South Sathorn Road, 45 minutes from the airport and minutes' away from major embassies, business centres, shopping districts and tourist attractions. Styled in the manner of grand hotels, 226 rooms including 80 suites overlook lotus ponds and beautifully landscaped gardens which compliment the elegant Thai decor.

Accommodation and rates
99 single/double, 47 twin rooms, US$ 252-317; 80 suites, US$ 384-2162
Subject to 10% service charge & 7% VAT

Credit cards accepted:
Visa, Mastercard, Amex, JCB, Diners

Meeting & banqueting facilities
Six conference rooms, capacity 5-235, with full audio-visual facilities; 515 sq m exhibition space; largest reception 225 seated or 300 cocktail

Room services
Airconditioning, colour TV, direct-dial telephone (ext. in bathroom), hairdryer, laundry/valet service, minibar, safety deposit box, trouser press, 24-hr room service, non-smoker bedrooms available, video films

Business & other services
Business centre, airport pickup (on request), translation service, car parking & rental, taxi service, travel centre, barber shop/beauty salon, newsstand, antique & jewellry shops

Sports & Recreation
Fitness centre/gym, jacuzzi/whirlpool, massage, sauna, outdoor swimming pool, squash, tennis, aerobics

Restaurants & Coffee Shops
La Noppamas (122) - French, open 1130-1430/1830-2330; The Celadon (100) - Thai, open 1100-1500/1800-2230; Terrazzo (40) - Italian, open as above; The Colonnade (90) - Internat'l, open 0600-midnight

Overseas Sales Representatives
Sterling Hotels & Resorts - UK tel 0800 252840; Ameri International - Germany tel (49) 69 771231; fax: (49) 69 771237

---

*This Thailand Country Report is an extract from the **Asia-Pacific Business Travel Guide**, available from Priory Publications Ltd, PO Box 24, Brackley, Northants, UK*

Chiangmai

Amari Rincome Hotel ⏾ D
Huey Kaew Road, 50200
Tel: (53) 221 1044; Tlx: 49314; Fax: 221915

Chiang Mai Orchid C
100-102 Huay Kaew Rd, 50200
Tel: (53) 222099; Tlx: 49337; Fax: 221625

Chiangmai Hills Hotel D
18 Huay Kaew Rd, 5000
Tel: (053) 210030-4; Tlx: 49316 SEAPAL TH; Fax: (053) 210035

Comfort Resort, Thaton River View E
Baan Thaton, Mae Ai, Chiang-Mai 50280
Tel: (053) 510 1781; Fax: (053) 451008

The Empress Hotel D
199 Chang Klan Rd, 50000
Tel: (53) 270240; Tlx: 43516; Fax: 272467

Holiday Garden Hotel D
16/16 Huay Kaew Road, 50000
Tel: 211333; Tlx: 49320 HOLIDAY TH; Fax: 210905

Holiday Inn Green Hills Chiang Mai
24 Chiang Mai-Lampang 50000   ⏾ D
Tel: 220100; Tlx: 49353; Fax: 221602

Mae Ping Hotel D
153 Sridonchai Rd, Chang Klan A Muang
Tel: 270160; Tlx: 49343; Fax: 270181

Melia Suriwongse ⏾ D
110 Changklan Rd, 50000
Tel: 270051-7; Tlx: 49311; Fax: 270063

Pornping Tower D
46-48 Charoenprathet Rd, 50000
Tel: 270099; Tlx: 43557; Fax: 270119

Quality Chiangmai Hills Hotel D
18 Huay Kaew Rd, Chiangmai 50000
Tel: (53) 210030-4; Tlx: 49316 SEAPAL TH; Fax: (53) 210035

Regent Chiang Mai A
Mae Rim Samoeng Rd, 50180
Tel: 298181; Fax: 298190

Royal Princess (Dusit Inn) ⏾ D
112 Changklan Road, Chaingmai 50000
Tel: 281033-43; Tlx: 49325; Fax: 281044

The Westin Chiang Mai C
318/1 Chiang Mai Lampun Road, 50000
Tel: 275300; Fax: 275299

The Sukhothai, Bangkok

THAILAND - Hotels

The Imperial Mae Ping Hotel
153 Sridonchat Road, Chang Klan A
Muang, Chiang Mai 50100
Tel: (53) 270 16080; Tlx: 49343 MAETEL
TH; Fax: (53) 270181;
E-Mail: maeping@chmai.louinfo.co.th

Strategically located in the heart of Chiang Mai, the Mae Ping combines luxury and elegance with the highest standard of personalised hospitality. The atmosphere is one of traditional elegance,complimented by the numerous works of Thai art throughout the hotel.

Accommodation and Rates
371 rooms, single baht 2000; double/twin baht 2400; suite baht 5000
Subject to 10% service charge + 7% VAT

Credit cards accepted: All major

Meeting & banqueting facilities
Three meeting/function rooms, capacity up to 200; audio-visual equipment available; 300 sq m exhibition space; largest reception 220 seated or 300 cocktail

Room services
Airconditioning, colour TV, direct-dial telephone, hairdryer, laundry/valet service, minibar, music/radio, 24-hr room service

Business & other services
Business centre, executive floor, airport pickup, translation service,car rental, travel centre, taxi service

Sports & Recreation
Billiards/snooker, fitness centre/gym, jogging track, massage, outdoor swimming pool

Restaurants & coffee shops
Kampaengdim (240) -International/Asian Coffee Shop, open 24 hours; *Ming Ming* (100) - Cantonese, open 1130-1400/1800-2230; *Venezia* (90) -European, open as above; *Mae Ping Beer Garden & Kantoke* (400/350) - BBQ/Local shows, open 1700-midnight; *Lobby Bar* (60) - ôpen 0600-0100; *Terrace Shabu Shabu* (80) - Japanese fondus, open 1800-2200

Overseas Sales Representatives
Europo: Superreps Int'l; Japan: Mac Marketing Service

Chiang Rai

Dusit Island Resort   D
1129 Kraisorasit Rd, 57000
Tel: (053) 715777; Tlx: 41322; Fax: (053) 715801

Delta Golden Triangle Resort/Hotel
222 Golden Triangle, Chiangsan 57150   D
Tel: (53) 784001; Tlx: 41308; Fax: 784006

Imperial Tara Mae Hong Sorn   D
149 Moo 8, 58000
Tel: 611473; Fax: 611252

Le Meridien Baan Boran Hotel D
The Golden Triangle/Chiang Saen, Chiang Rai 57150. Tel: (53) 784084; Tlx: 49131; Fax: (53) 784090

Wiang Inn Hotel   D
893 Phaholyothin Road, 57000
Tel: (053) 711533; Tlx: 41308 WIANGIN TH; Fax: (053) 711877

Hua Hin

Chiva-Som International Health Resort
73/4 Petchkasem Road, Nongkae, Hua Hin, Prachuabkririkhan 77110
Tel: (32) 536536; Fax: (32) 511154
E-mail: chivasom@ksc9.th.com

This dedicated international health resort, Asia's first, is located on 7 acres of beachside land in Hua Hin. It offers luxury accommodation in Thai-style pavilions or a low rise building, delicious spa cuisine and professional health and beauty treatments for the rejuvenation of mind, body and spirit.

Accommodation and Rates
57 rooms, single US$ 400-480; double/twin US$600-760; single suite US$640-800; double US$1080-1400.
(Rates include all meals + heat-treatment, massage and all leisure activities)
Subject to 10% service charge + 7% VAT

Credit cards accepted
All except JCB, Siam Commercial Bank

Meeting & banqueting facilities
Meeting/function room, capacity 25;largest reception 50 seated or 100 cocktail

Room services
Airconditioning, colour TV, direct-dial telephone (ext. in bathroom), hairdryer, laundry/valet service, minibar, music/radio, safety deposit box, tea/coffee making, non-smoker bedrooms, video films.

Other Services
Express checkout, airport pickup, car parking & rental, travel centre, taxi service, barber shop/hairdresser, beauty salon, newsstand/shops, clinic

Sports & recreation
Fitness centre/gym, indoor games, jacuzzi/whirlpool, jogging track, massage, sauna, outdoor & indoor swimming pools, tennis, ultra modern spa with 15 treatment rooms, 3 Thai massage rooms, 6 hydrotherapy suites, flotation room, jet shower blitz room

Restaurants & Coffee Shops
Dining Room (100) - Spa cuisine, open mealtimes; *Seafront Restaurant* (70) - Healthy snacks, open all day

Overseas Sales Representatives
Insignia Resorts

Club Aldiana Siam   D
9 Parknampran Beach, Hua Hin 97220
Tel: (2) 233 2151; Fax: (2) 237 5680

Dusit Resort & Polo Club   B
1349 Petchkasem Rd, Petchburi 76120
Tel: (32) 520009; Tlx: 78302; Fax: 520296

Golden Sands Hotel Cha-am Beach
Petchkasem Rd, Petchburi 76120   C
Tel: 471985; Tlx: 78303; Fax: 471984

Hotel Sofitel Central Hua Hin   C
1 Damnerkasem Road, 77100
Tel: (32) 512021; Fax: (32) 511014

Melia Hua Hin Hotel
c/o 118/1 Rama 6, Samsennai, Payathai Bangkok 10400.
Tel: (2) 270 0734/278 5415; Tlx: 81059/21185 Tipco TH; Fax: (2) 270 0596
E-mail: MELIA_HUAHIN@mozart.inet.co.th

A perfect property for meeting/seminar and leisure located on the unspoilt beachfront and within walking distance to lcoal night market and easy access to 6 golf courses

Accommodation & rates
52 double/173 twin rooms, baht 3700; 70 suites baht 4400.
Subject to 10% service charge + 7% VAT

Credit cards accepted
Amex, Visa, Mastercard, Diners, SCB

Meeting & banqueting facilities
5 meeting/function rooms, capacity 350; withn audio-visual facilities; 513 sq m exhibition space; largest reception 380 seated or 700 cocktail

Room services
Airconditioning, colour TV, direct-dial telephone, hairdryer, laundry/valet service, minibar, music/radio/alarm clock, safety deposit box, non-smoker bedrooms, video films, separate shower

Business & other services
Business centre, express checkout, airport pickup, car parking, barber shop/beauty salon, newsstand/shops

Sports & Recreation
Billiards/snooker, fitness centre/gym, golf (nearby), indoor games, jacuzzi/whirlpool, massage, sauna, squash, outdoor swimming pool, tennis, water slide

Restaurants & coffee Shops
Goya (80) - Mediterranean, open 0630-2230; *El Patio* (250) - Coffee Shop, open 0600-2300; *White Lotus* (164) - Chinese, open 1730-2230; *Doodles* (207) - Disco/Fun Pub, open 1730-0200

Overseas Sales Representatives
Galileo/Apollo 07481; System One ML HH Q124; Amadeus SMHHQMHH; Utell International; Sabre ME 32264

The Regent Cha-am　　　○　D
849/21 Cha-am Beach, Phetchaburi
Tel: (032) 471890; Tlx: TH 78306; Fax: (032) 471491

Royal Garden Resort Hua Hin ○ C
107/1 Phetkasem Beach Road, 77110
Tel: (032) 511881-4; Tlx: 78309 ROGAHUA TH; Fax: (032) 512422

Royal Garden Village Hua Hin ○ C
43/1Phetkasem Beach Road, Hua Hin 77110
Tel: (032) 520250-6; Tlx: 78314 ROGAVIL TH; Fax: (032) 520259

Koh Samui

Amari Palm Reef Hotel　　　C
14/3 Moo 2 Tampon Boput, Chaweng Beach 84140. Tel: 077) 422015-9; Tlx: 69714; Fax: 422394

Baan Taling Ngam
295 Moo 3, Taling Ngam, Koh Samui, Saruthani 84140
Tel: (77) 423019; Fax: (77) 423220

Beachcomber　　　C
3/1 Moo 2, Chaweng Beach, 84320
Tel: (077) 422041-3; Fax: (077) 422388

Blue Lagoon　　　C
99 Moo 2, Chaweng Beach, 84320
Tel: (077) 422037-40; Fax: (77) 422401

The Imperial Boat House Hotel
83 Moo 5, Choeng Mon Beach, Tumbol Bor-Phut, Koh Samui, Surat Thani 84320
Tel: (77) 425041-52; Fax: (77) 425460-1; E-mail: Imperial@usc.net.th
Located at Choeng Mon Beach, 4 kms from the airport, this unique resort comprises 34 authentic teakwood rice barges converted to "boat suites" and eight low rise southern guestroom buildings.

Accommodation and Rates
182 deluxe rooms, single baht 2200; double/twin baht 2400;boat suite baht 4000
Subject to 10% service charge + 7% VAT

Credit cards accepted:
Amex, Visa, Master, Diners, JCB

Meeting & banqueting facilities
Three meeting/function rooms, capacity up 20- 200; audio-visual equipment available; 210 sq m exhibition space; largest reception 120 seated or 200 cocktail

Room services
Airconditioning, colour TV, direct-dial telephone, hairdryer, laundry service, minibar, tea/coffee making (suites), non-smoker bedrooms, video films, private balconies

Business & other services
Airport pickup, car rental, travel centre, beauty salon, guided tours, newsstand/shops

Sports & Recreation
Billiards/snooker, jacuzzi/whirlpool, outdoor swimming pool, water sports

Restaurants & coffee shops
Captain's Choice (100) -International/Thai/Seafood, open noon-2200; *Garden Terrace* (150) - A la carte & theme nights, open 9730-1030/1930-2200; *Pool Bar* (40) - open 1000-2300; *Lobby Bar* (50) - Cocktail lounge, open 1800-midnight

Overseas Sales Representatives
Europe: Superreps Int'l; Japan: Mac Marketing Service; Canada: Apex Holidays

Chaweng Regent Beach Resort　D
155/4 Chaweng Beach, **Koh Samui**, Suratthani 84140. Tel: (77) 422389-90; Fax: (77) 422222; Bangkok office: Tel: (2) 280 4425-7; Fax: (2) 280 44284062

Santiburi Dusit Resort　　○　A
12/12 Moo 1, Tambon Maenam, 84330
Tel: (77) 425031-8; Fax: (02) 237 4738

Pattaya

Amari Nipa Lodge Resort　　D
Pattaya Beach Resort, Pattaya 20260
Tel: (038) 428161; Tlx: 85958; Fax: 428165

The Asia Pattaya Beach Hotel　D
Cliff Road, Pattaya Beach, 20260
Tel: (038) 250602-6; Fax: (038) 250496

Baiyoke Pattaya Hotel　　　D
557 Phartumnak Road, Moo 10, Tumbul Nongprue Amphur Banglamung, Cholburi 20260. Tel: (038) 423300-2; Tlx: 85929; Fax: (038) 426124

Dusit Resort Hotel　　　C
240 Pattaya Beach Road, Chonburi 20150.Tel: (038) 425611-4; Tlx: TH 20150; Fax: (038) 428239

The Merlin Pattaya　　　D
429 Moo 9, Pattaya Beach Rd, Pattaya City, Chonburi 20260
Tel: (38) 428755-9/421670-2; Tlx: TH 85905; Fax: (38) 421673

Montien Pattaya Hotel　　　C
Pattaya Beach Resort, Chonburi 20260
Tel: 428155; Tlx: 85906 TH; Fax: 423155

Pattaya Palace　　　D
opp. Shinawatra Thai Silk, 20260 Pattaya
Tel: (038) 428409; Tlx: 75904; Fax: 428026

Pattaya Park Beach Resort　　D
345 Jomtien Beach, Cholburi 20260
Tel: (038) 251209; Fax: 251201

Royal Century Pattaya Hotel　E
129/16 M9 Central Pattaya Road, Pattaya City.Tel: (038) 427800-9; Fax: 427 808

Royal Cliff Beach Resort　　○　C
Royal Cliff Bay, Nr. Pattaya City, 20260
Tel: (038) 421421-40; Tlx: CLIFFEX 85907 TH; Fax: (038) 250511/250513

Royal Garden Resort Pattaya ○ D
218 Beach Road, Pattaya 20260
Tel: (038) 423235-9; Tlx: 85909 ROGADEN TH; Fax: (038) 429926

Royal Jomtien Resort　　　C
408 Jomtien Beach Road,Chonburi 20260
Tel: (02) 265 1865; Tlx: 20071 ROYATEL TH; Fax: (02) 254 1869

Siam Bayview Hotel　　○　D
Pattaya Beach, Cholburi 20260
Tel: (038) 423871-7; Tlx: 85921 BAYVIEW; Fax: (038) 423879

Siam Bayshore Resort ◯ D
Pattaya Beach, Cholburi 20260
Tel: (038) 428678-81; Fax: (038) 428730

Town in Town Hotel D
06 Moo 9 Central Pattaya Rd, Pattaya City,
Cholburi 20260
Tel: (038) 426350-4; Fax: (038) 426351
(Bangkok tel: 5398358; Fax: 5395052)

Tropicana Resort D
45 Pattaya Beach Road, 20260
Tel: 428645; Fax: 423031

Woodlands Resort ◯ D
1641 Pattaya-Naklua Rd, Pattaya City,
Chonburi 20150
Tel: 421707; Tlx: 85944; Fax: 425663

Phuket

The Allamanda Phuket ◯ ¶
29 Moo 4, Srisoonthorn Road, 83100
Tel: (76) 324359; Fax: (76) 324360

Amanapuri A
Pansea Beach, Phuket Island
Tel: 324333; Fax: 324100

Amari Coral Beach Hotel D
100 Moo 4, Patong Beach, 83150
Tel: (076) 340106-14; Tlx: 69527
CORALSL TH; Fax: (076) 340115

Bantai Beach Resort E
89/71 Taveewong Road, Patong Beach,
83150
Tel: 321328-9; Tlx: 65509 BANTHAI TH;
Fax: 321330

Banyan Tree Phuket B
PO Box 5, Cherngtalay Amphur Talang,
83110. Tel: (76) 324374; Fax: (76) 324375

Blue Canyon Country Club ◯ ¶
165 Moo 1, Thapkassatri Rd, Maikaw,
Thalang Phuket
Tel: (76) 327440; Fax: (76) 327450

The Boathouse Inn & Restaurant C
Kata Beach, 83100
Tel: (76) 330015; Fax: (76) 330561

The Chedi Phuket C
Pansea Bay, 198 Moo 3 Choeng Talay,
Phuket 83110
Tel: (76) 324017-20; Fax: 324252

Diamond Cliff Resort Hotel C
Kalin Beach, Phuket
Tel: (076) 340501-6; Tlx: 69561 DICLIFF
TH; Fax: (76) 340507

Dusit Laguna Phuket B
390 Srisoontorn Rd, Cherngtalay District,
Amphur Talang, 83100
Tel: (076) 311320-9; Fax: (076) 311174

Karon Beach Resort C
27 Rasda Rd, 83130
Tel: (76) 330006; Fax: (76) 330529

Cape Panwa Hotel, Phuket
27 Mu 8 Sakdidej Road, Cape Panwa,
Phuket 83000.Tel: (076) 391123-5; Tlx:
69569 CAPANWA TH; Fax: (076) 391177

Located on a hilltop with panoramic view of Andaman Sea and with its own private beach, sheltered from extreme harsh weather conditions. The low rise architectural design for those seeking a natural environment.

Accommodation and rates
160 single/double/twin rooms, rate from baht 3000; 14 suites, baht 5300-12500
Subject to 10% service charge and 7% VAT

Credit cards accepted
Amex, Diners Club, Mastercard,
Eurocharge, Visa, JCB

Conference/banqueting facilities
6 meeting/conference rooms, capacity 12 - 200; full audio-visual facilities; largest banquet 160 seated or 200 cocktail

Room services
Airconditioning, colour TV, direct-dial telephone, hairdryer, laundry/valet service, minibar, music/radio/alarm clock, safety deposit box, 24-hour room/meal service, non-smoker bedrooms available, video films

Business & other services
Business centre, expresss checkout, airport pickup, car parking, car rental, travel centre, taxi service, barber shop/beauty salon, newsstand/shops, Panwa Bat Shopping Center

Sports & Recreation
Fitness centre/gym, indoor games, jacuzzi/whirlpool, jogging track, massage, sauna, outdoor swimming pool, water sports, tennis

Restaurants & Coffee Shops
Cafe Andaman (160) - Continental/local, open 0600-midnight; *Top of the Reef* (50) - International/Seafood, open 1900-2300; *Panwa House* (100) - Thai, open 1800-2200; *Uncle Nan's Restaurant* (80) - Italian, open 1100-2300; *The Light House* (74) - Pub, open 1700-0100

Overseas Sales Representatives
Hotel Marketing Company UK,
MM International Hotels - Tokyo

Club Andaman Beach Resort
2 Hadpatong Road, Patong Beach
Phuket 83150. Tel: (76) 340530; Tlx:
69538 ANDAMAN TH; Fax: (76) 340527;
E-mail: cabrhkt@sun.phuket.ksc.co.th

Club Andaman Beach Resort is situated in 15 acres of tropical gardens in the northern and quiet end of Patong Beach,50 metres from Patong Beach and only a few minutes' stroll to the entertainment and shopping district of Patong.

Accommodation and rates
250 single or twin rooms; single baht 2400-4100; twin baht 2700-4400.
Subject to 10% service charge and 7% VAT

Credit cards accepted
Amex, Diners Club, Mastercard, Visa, JTB

Conference/banqueting facilities
1/2 meeting/conference rooms, capacity 100/200; audio-visual equipment available; 252/126 sq m exhibition space; largest reception 160 seated or 210 cocktail

Room services
Airconditioning, colour TV + satellite, direct-dial telephone, hairdryer, laundry/valet service, minibar, music/radio/alarm clock, safety deposit box, 24-hour room/meal service, video films

Business & other services
Airport pickup, car parking, taxi service, barber shop/beauty salon, newsstand/shops, guided tours, gift shop, tailor

Sports & Recreation
Billiards/snooker/pool, fitness centre/gym, golf (nearby), massage, sauna, two outdoor swimming pools, water sports, tennis, games room, aerobics classes

Restaurants & Coffee Shops
The Andaman Restaurant (300) - Continental/Thai/Chinese, open 0630-2300; *Palm Tree Bar* (50) -Snacks, open 1000-midnight; *Lobby Bar* (50), open 1000-0200; *Fun Pub* (70), open 2100-0300; *Club Andaman's Burger* (25), open 1000-2100

Local Sales Office
252/91 16th fl Muang Thai-Phatra Tower II, Ratchadaphisek Rd, Huaykwang, Bangkok 10310. Tel: (2) 693 3245-7; Fax: 693 3249

THAILAND - Hotels

Holiday Inn Resort Phuket ◯
86/11 Thaweewong Road, Patong Beach,
PO Box 158, Phuket 83120
Tel: (076) 321020; Tlx: 69545 HI PHUKT;
Fax: (076) 321435

Set in a palm tree garden beside beautiful Patong Beach and within easy reach of shops, restaurants and nightspots, Holiday Inn Resort Phuket combines Thai flair and hospitality with the international standard comfort for which the group is known. An extensive range of sports and recreational facilities exist within the well tended grounds

Accommodation and rates
32 double, 224 twin rooms, baht 3500-4200 (single occ. baht 3200-3900); 21 suites, baht 4800-11000
Subject to 10% service charge and 7% VAT

Credit cards accepted
Amex, Diners Club, Mastercard, Visa, JCB

Conference/banqueting facilities
6 meeting/conference rooms, capacity 30 - 300 with audio-visual facilities; largest banquet 250 seated or 350 cocktail

Room services
Airconditioning, colour TV, direct-dial telephone, laundry (self-operated)/valet service, minibar, music/radio/alarm clock, safety deposit box, 24-hour room/meal service, non-smoker bedrooms available, video films

Other services
Expresss checkout, airport pickup, car parking, car rental, travel centre, taxi service, barber shop/beauty salon, newsstand/shops

Sports & Recreation
Billiards/snooker, fitness centre/gym, mini-adventure golf, massage, sauna, outdoor swimming pool, tennis

Restaurants & Coffee Shops
Seabreeze Cafe & Terrace (45+90) - International, open 0600-midnight; *Suan Nok* (55) - Thai, open 1800-2200; *Sam's Steakhouse* (50) - Beef & salad bar, open as above; *Pizzeria* (65) - Italian, open 1800-2300

Overseas Sales Representatives
Holiday Inn Worldwide

Karon Villa Phuket/Karon Royal Wing
36/4 Karon Beach, Phuket 83100 ◯ C
Tel: (076) 396139; Fax: (076) 396122

Kata Beach Resort ◯ C
27 Rasda Road, 83130
Tel: (76) 330531; Fax: (76) 330128

Kata Thani Hotel Resort ◯ D
3/24 Patak Rd, Kata N0i Beach, 83100
Tel: 330124-6; Fax: (076) 330426

Kharon Inn Phuket E
Karon Beach, 83000
Tel: (76) 396519; Fax: (76) 396526

The Maiton Resort A
Maiton Island, 100 Moog Tambon, 83000
Tel: (76) 214954; Fax: (76) 214959

Le Meridien Phuket B
PO Box 277, Phuket 83000
Tel: (76) 340460-5; Tlx: 69542 MERIHKT TH; Fax: (76) 340479

Metropole Hotel Phuket ◯ D
1 Soi Surin Montri Road, 83000
Tel: 215050; Fax: 215990

Pearl Hotel ◯ D
42 Montree Road, Phuket 83000
Tel: (076) 211044; Fax: (076) 212911

Patong Merlin D
99/2 Moo 4, Patong Beach, Kathu District 83150. Tel: 340037; Fax: 340394

Phuket Cabana Resort C
94 Taweewongse Rd, Patong Beach, Phuket 83150
Tel: (076) 340138/342100 Tlx: 69544 CABANA TH; Fax: (076) 340178

Phuket Island Resort Hotel ◯ C
73/1 Rasda Rd, Phuket 83000
Tel: 381010-7; Fax: 381018

Phuket Merlin Hotel ◯ E
158/1 Yawaraj Road, Phuket 83000
Tel: 212866-70; Tlx: 65522; Fax: 216429

Phuket Yacht Club ◯ A
Nai Harn Beach, Phuket 83130
Tel: (76) 381156; Tlx: 69532 YACHT TH; Fax: (76) 381164

Swissôtel Phuket-Felix Karon ◯ C
4/8 Patak Road, Karon Beach, Phuket 83100
Tel: (76) 396666-75; Fax: (76) 396853

The Residence C
Kalim Beach, Phuket 83150
Tel: 340456/344; Tlx: 69587; Fax: 340607

Royal Paradise Hotel C
700 Moo 3, Ratutit Road, Patong Beach, Phuket 83150
Tel: (076) 340660; Fax: (076) 340666

Royal Park Travelodge Resort C
Bangtao Beach, Cheung Thalang, 83110
Tel: (76) 324021; Fax: (76) 324243

Sheraton Grande Laguna Beach B
10 Moo 4 Srisoontorn Road, Cherngtalay, Talang 83110.Tel: (76) 324101-7; Tlx: 69519; Fax: (76) 324108

Thavorn Palm Beach Hotel C
128/10 Moo 3, Karon Beach
Tel: 396090; Tlx:69505; Fax: 396555

Vises Patong Hotel C
Soi Sai Nam Yen, Patong Beach 83150
Tel/Fax: 340556-8; Tlx: 69576 XSH TH

Other Areas

The Ambassador City Jomtien ◯ E
21/10 Sukhumvit Road, km 155 Na Jomtien, Sattahip, Cholburi 20250. Tel: (038) 255 501540/601640; Fax: 255731-3

Clarion Resort Cumsaed C
1819 Moo 5, Ladya, **River Kwai** 71190
Tel: (1) 212 4858; Fax: (1) 312 0176

The Imperial Phukaew Hill Resort
99 Moo 5 Pitsanulok-Lomsak Road (Highway 12), Tombol Campson, Amphua Khao Kho, **Petchaboon** 67280
Tel: (2) 551 9304; Fax: (2) 551 9305
E-mail: Imperial@usc.net.th

The Imperial Phukaew Hill Resort is a Swiss-style retreat, hidden among the misty mountains of Petchaboon province, Central Thailand. The resort is occupying a 200-acre site, high up on beautiful Khao Kho mountains and surrounded by many famous scenic attractions.

Accommodation and rates
124 rooms, single/double, from baht 2500. 8 suites from baht 5500.
Subject to 10% service charge and 7% VAT

Credit cards accepted
Visa, Mastercard

Conference & banqueting facilities
Two meeting/conference rooms, capacity up to 200, with audio-visual equipment; largest banquet 120 seated or 200 cocktail

Room services
Airconditioning, colour TV, direct-dial telephone, hairdryer, laundry/valet service, safety deposit box, fireplace and heater

Other Services
Airport pickup, guided tours

Sports & Recreation
Billiards/snooker, jogging track, sauna, outdoor swimming pool, tennis, mountain bikes, picnic area, bbq terrace, karaoke

Restaurants & Coffee Shops
Phukaew Terrace (125) - International/Thai, open 0600-0200; *Kieng Dao Lobby Bar* (30) - open 1145-2200; *Yoo Doi* (80) - Karaoke, open 2000-0200

Overseas Sales Representatives
Europe: Supereps International; Japan: MAC Marketing Services

Imperial Tara Mae Hong Son Hotel
149 Moo 8, Tambon Pang Moo, Muang District, Mae Hong Son, 58000
Tel: (53) 611021; Tlx: 41202 TARA MGN TH; Fax: (53) 611252
E-mail: Imperial@ksc.net.th

First class hotel in the picturesque town of Mae Hong Son, Northern Thailand, located in a teak forest on the edge of town.

Accommodation and rates
93 deluxe rooms. Single baht 1600; double /twin baht 1900; 11 suites, baht 2100
Subject to 10% service charge and 7% VAT

Credit cards accepted
Visa, Mastercard, Amex, Diners, JCB

Conference & banqueting facilities
3 meeting/conference rooms, capacity up to 250, with audio-visual equipment; 252 sq m exhibition space; largest banquet 240 seated or 300 cocktail

Room services
Airconditioning, colour TV, direct-dial telephone, hairdryer, laundry/valet service, minibar, tea/coffee making (suites)

Other Services
Airport pickup, car rental, guided tours, newsstand/shops

Sports & Recreation
Fitness centre/gym, sauna, outdoor pool

Restaurants & Coffee Shops
Golden Teak Restaurant (60/80/90) - Thai/Chinese/European, open 0630-midnight

Overseas Sales Reorenatatives
Europe: Supereps International; Japan: MAC Marketing Services; Worldwide: ANA Enterprises Ltd

Rayong Resort Hotel   D
Laemtarn, Banphe District, Umpur Muang, **Rayong**. Tel: (38) 651000; Fax: (38) 651007

The Regent Cha-Am   ◌   D
849/21 Cha-Am Beach, **Phetchaburi**
Tel: (032) 471480-91; Fax: (032) 471492

Sofitel Raja Orchid Koen Khan ◌ C
9/9 Prachasumran Rd, Amphur Muang **Khoen Khan** 40000
Tel: (043) 322155; Fax: (043) 322218

Swissôtel River Kwai-Felix Kanchanaburi   ◌   C
9/1 Moo 3 Thamakham, Amphur Muang, **Kanchanaburi** 71000.
Tel: (34) 515061; Fax: (34) 515086/515095

Restaurants

In Bangkok top Thai businessmen and ministers often prefer the ordered quiet of a private room at The Oriental or another of the top hotels. Below we give a selection of both hotel and city restaurants of various cuisines which are popular with the business community, where English is spoken and prior booking is advisable

Benkay *(Japanese)*
Royal Orchid Sheraton Hotel, 2 Capt Bush La, Siphya Rd. Tel: 234 5599

La Brasserie *(European - bistro)*
Regent Hotel, 155 Rajadamri Road, 10500. Tel: 251 6127

Bussarucum *(Thai)*
35 Soi Pipat 2. Tel: 235 8915

Captain Bush Grill *(European)*
Royal Orchid Sheraton Hotel, 2 Captain Bush Lane, Siphya Rd.. Tel: 234 5599

Charly's *(European)*
66 North Sathorn Road. Tel: 234 9035

China House *(Cantonese)*
Oriental Hotel, 48 Oriental Avenue, 10500. Tel: 326 0400

Le Cristal *(French)*
Regent Hotel, 155 Rajadamri Road, 10500. Tel: 251 6127

Daikoku *(Japanese)*
960 Rama IV Road. Tel: 233 1495

D'Jit Pochana *(Thai)*
1. 1082 Phahon Yothin Rd. Tel: 279 5000
2. 62 Sukhumvit 20. Tel: 258 1597-8
3. 26/368-80 Don Muang.Tel: 531 1644/2716

Galaxy Nightclub & Restaurant
19 Thanon Phra Ram IV, 10500.
Tel: 235 5000-9

Hamilton's
Dusit Thani Hotel, Rama IV Road, 10500. Tel: 233 1130

Himali Cha-Cha *(Indian)*
1229/11 New Road. Tel: 245 1561

Hoi Tien Lau *(Cantonese)*
308 Suapa Road. Tel: 221 1685

Laikhram *(Thai)*
Soi 49/4, 11/1 Sukhumvit Rd. Tel: 392 5867

Le Banyan *(French/Thai)*
59 Soi 8 Sukhumvit Rd. Tel: 253 5556

Ma Maison
Hilton Hotel, 2 Wireless Road, 10500.
Tel: 253 0123

Mayflower *(Chinese)*
Dusit Thani Hotel, Rama IV Rd, 10500.
Tel: 236 0450

Le Metropolitan *(French)*
135-6 Soi Gaysorn (Nr. President Hotel).
Tel: 252 8364

Neil's Tavern *(European)*
Soi Ruamrudee. Tel: 251 5644

Nick's Number 1 *(European)*
1 Sathorn Road/Cnr. Wireless Road, 10500. Tel: 286 2258

Normandie *(European)*
Oriental Hotel, 48 Oreintal Avenue, 10500. Tel: 236 0400

Shangri-La *(Chinese)*
154 Silom Road. Tel: 234 2045

Sui Siam *(Cantonese)*
Landmark Hotel, 138 Sukhumvit Rd
Tel: 254 0404

La Tache *(International)*
Shangri-La Hotel, 89 Soi Wat Suan Plu, New Road, 10500. Tel: 236 7777

Teikoku Japanese Restaurant
Imperial Hotel, 6-10 Wirel;ess Rd, Ploenchit Rd,. Tel: 254 0023

Thalay Thong *(Thai)*
Siam Inter-Continental Hotel, 967 Srapatum Palace Property, Rama ! Rd, 10330. Tel: 253 0355

Tumpnakthai *(Thai - pavilions)*
131 Ratchadapisek Road, 10310. Tel: 277 8833/277 8855

La Vendôme *(French)*
75/5 Soi, 11/1 Sukhumvit Rd. Tel: 250 1220

Car Hire

Avis
Head Office: 2/12 Wireless Road, Bangkok 10330.Tel: 255 5300-4; Tlx: 72118 avis th; Fax: 253 3734

Grand Car Rent Co Ltd
144/3-4 Silom Road, Bangkok 10500
Tel: 234 9956

Hertz Self and Chauffeur Drive
Premier Inter Leasing Co Ltd. 420 Sukhumvit 71 Road, Prakanong, Bangkok 10110. Tel: 391 0461; Fax: 381 4582
Represented in all major cities. For reservations refer to Bangkok.

Highway Car Rent
6/2 Rama III Road, Bangkok 10500
Tel: 311 7867/235 5132

Krung Thai Car Rent
233-5 Asok-Dindaeng Road, Bangkok 10500.Tel: 245 1525-7/246 0089 5320

Airline Offices

*on line carriers only

Air China
CP Tower, 2 Fl, 313 Silom Rd, Bangrak
Tel: 631 0728-34; Fax: 238 2205

Air France
Ground floor, Charn Issara Tower, 924/51 Rama IV Road, Bkk 10500. Tel: 233 9477

Air India
16th floor, Amarin Plaza, 500 Ploenchit Road, Bangkok 10500. Tel: 256 9614/9

Air Lanka
Ground floor, Charn Issara Tower, 942/34-35 Rama IV Road,Bangkok 10500
Tel: 236 9292/3

Alitalia
8th floor, Boonmitr Building, 138 Silom Road, Bangkok. Tel: 233 4000/4

British Airways
2nd floor, 942/81 Charn Issara Tower, Rama IV Road, Bangkok 10500
Tel: (2) 236 0038 or (38) 607592; Fax: (2) 236 6735

Canadian Airlines
6th floor, Maneeya Center, 518/5 Ploenchit Road, Bangkok 10500
Tel: 251 4521; Fax: 253 5159

Cathay Pacific
5th floor, Charn Issara Tower, 942/136 Rama IV Road, Bangkok 10500
Tel: 233 6105/9/233 9825

China Airlines (CAL)
4th foor, Peninsula Plaza, 153 Rajadamri Road, Bangkok 10500
Tel: 253 4241/4/253 4438; Fax: 253 4791

Delta
Bangkok. Tel: 237 6838

Dragonair
Big Bell Arcade, 866 Ploenchit Road, Bangkok 10500.Tel: 254 7468/9; Fax: 253 7978

Finnair
518/2 Ploenchit Road, Bangkok 10500
Tel: 251 5012/251 5075; Fax: 254 1271

Garuda
944/19 Rama IV Road, Bangkok 10500
Tel: 233 0981/233 3873

Gulf Air
15th floor, 518/5 Maneeya Center, Ploenchit Road, Bangkok 10500
Tel: 254 7931/4

Japan Air Lines (JAL)
Wall Street Tower, Suwarong Road, Bangkok 10500
Tel: 234 2440; Fax: 236 7264

KLM
2 Patpong Road, Bangkok 10500
Tel: 235 5155/9; Fax: 236 6542

Korean Air
Room 306, 3rd floor, Dusit Thani Building, 946 Rama IV Road, Bangkok 10500
Tel: 234 9283/7; Fax: 235 6800

Lauda Air
14th Wall Street Tower, 33/37 14th Fl Wall St Tower Bldg, Suriwongse Road, Bangkok 10500.Tel: 233 2544; Fax: 237 2307

Lufthansa
5th floor, Tilot Pen Building, 331/1-3 Silom Road, Bangkok 10500.
Tel: 234 1350/9

Malaysian Airlines
98-102 Surawongse Roadm, Bangkok 10500. Tel: 236 4705/9

Northwest
4th floor, The Peninsula Plaza, 153 Rajadamri Road, Bangkok 10500
Tel: 253 4822

Philippine Airlines
4th floor, Chonskolnee Building, 56 Suriwongse Road, Bangkok 10500
Tel: 233 2350-2/234 2483/235 2584

Qantas
Charn Issara Building, 942/51 Rama IV Road, Bangkok 10500
Tel: 236 0102/236 9193/5; Fax: 236 9196

Royal Brunei
2nd fl, Charn Issara Tower, 942/51 Rama IV Rd, Bangkok 10500.Tel: 234 0007/0009

Royal Nepal
Sivadon Building, 1/4 Convent Road, Bangkok 10500.Tel: 233 3921/3

Sabena
11th floor, CCT Building, 109 Surawongse Road, Bangkok 10500.
Tel: 233 2020/3

SAS
412 Rama I Road, Bangkok 10500
Tel: 253 8333; Fax: 263 3779

Saudia
Ground floor, CCT Building, 109 Suriwongse Road, Bangkok 10500
Tel: 236 9395/8; Fax: 236 9401

Singapore Airlines
12th floor, Silom Centre Building, 2 Silom Road, Bangkok 10500
Tel: 236 0440; Fax: 236 5304

Swissair
1 Silom Road, Bangkok 10500
Tel: 233 2930/4; Fax: 236 7417

Thai International
89 Vibhavadi Rangsit Road, Bangkok 10900.
Tel: 513 0121/233 8810;
Fax: 235 3746

United
9th floor, 183 Regent House, Rajdamri Road, Bangkok 10500
Tel: 253 0558; Fax: 253 3545

Vietnam Airlines
578-580 Ploenchit Rd, Bangkok
Tel: (2) 251 4242/5439; Fax: (2) 255 3978

Airline Abbreviation codes used in departure tables at right: **AF** = Air France, **AI** = Air India, **AY** = Finnair, **AZ** = Alitalia, **BA** = British Airways, **BG** = Biman Bangladesh, **BI** = Royal Brunei, **BR** = EVA Airways, **CA** = Air China; **CI** = China Airlines, **CP** = Canadian Airlines, **CX** = Cathay Pacific, **CZ** = China Southern Airlines, **DE** = Condor, **EK** = Emirates, **ET** = Ethiopian Airlines, **GA** = Garuda Indonesia, **GF** = Gulf Air; **IC** = Indian Airlines; **JL** = Japan Airlines, **JS** = Air Koryo, **KA** = Dragonair; **KB** = Druk-Air, **KE** = Korean Air, **KL** = Royal Dutch Airlines, **KU** = Kuwait Airways, **LH** = Lufthansa, **LO** = LOT Polish Airlines, **LT** = LTU Int'l; **LY** = El Al, **LZ** = Balkan; **MH** = Malaysian Airlines; **MS** = Egyptair, **MU** = China Eastern, **NG** = Lauda Air, **NH** = All Nippon Airways, **NW** = Northwest Airlines, **NZ** = Air New Zealand, **OA** = Olympic Airways, **OK** = CSA Czechoslovak Airlines, **OX** = Orient Express Air; **OZ** = Asiana, **PG** = Air Nelson, **PK** = Pakistan International Airlines, **PR** = Philippine Airlines, **QF** = Qantas, **QV** = Lao Aviation; **RA** = Royal Nepal , **RG** = Varig, **RJ** = Royal Jordanian, **RO** = Tarom; **SA** = South African Airways, **SK** = Skandinavian Airline System, **SQ** = Singapore Airlines, **SR** = Swissair, **SU** = Aeroflot, **SV** = Saudia, **SZ** = China Southern, **TG** = Thai Airways, **TK** = Turkish Airlines, **UB** = Myanmar Airways; **VJ** = Royal Air Cambodge; **VN** = Vietnam Airlines; **9P** = Pelangi Air.

What's the link between business and the Asia Pacific?

BRITISH AIRWAYS
The world's favourite airline

http://www.british-airways.com

Thailand Airline Departures 1997

To the airports printed in bold type. Flights correct as at February 1997. Travellers are advised to check with the offices on the previous page. Figures in brackets after airline codes (see previous page for code explanation) signify (1) departing on a Monday, (2) Tuesday and so on to (7) Sunday. Only direct flights are shown.

BANGKOK (Don Muang Interntaional) BKK

Abu Dhabi (AUH)
LT (1,3,6) GF (3,6) BI (3)
Addis Ababa (ADD)
ET (2,6)
Amman (AMM)
RJ (1,4,7)
Amsterdam (AMS)
CI (2,3,5,6,7) GA (5,7) KL (2,3,6,7) TG (daily)
Athens (ATH)
OA (3) TG (1,4)
Auckland (AKL)
TG (2,4,6) NZ (2,3,5) LH (2,4,6)
Bahrain (BAH)
GF (1,4,7) OK (2,3) UX (3) RO (2,4)
Bandar Seri Begawan (BWN)
BI (1,3,5,6) TG (2,4,7)
Beijing (PEK)
CZ (3,4,6,7) TG (2,4,5,7) CA (2,4,7)
Berlin (BER)
DE (6) LT (3)
Bombay (BOM)
AI (3,6) CX (1,3,4,7) KE (2,5)
Brisbane (BNE)
BA (2,4,7) TG (1,5) NZ (6) QF (1,3,5)
Brussels (BRU)
TG (1,3,6)
Budapest (BUD)
MA (2,6)
Bucharest (BUH)
RO (2,4)
Buri Ram (BFU)
TG (1,3,5)
Cairns (CNS)
QF (1,3)
Cairo (CAI)
MS (4,7)
Calcutta (CCU)
AI (6) IC (2,4,5,7)TG (1,3,6) KB (5,7)
Chengdu (CTU)
SZ (1,4)
Chiang Mai (CNX)
TG (daily) OX (2,4,6,7)
Chiang Rai (CEI)
TG (daily)
Chittagong (CGP)
BG (5)
Christchurch (CHC)
NZ (6)
Colombo (CMB)
TG (3,5,7) UL (1,4,6) CX (2,6)
Copenhagen (CPH)
SK/TG (daily)
Delhi (DEL)
AI,SU (3) TG (1,3,5,6,7) IC (4,7) NH (1,5)
Denpasar-Bali (DPS)
GA (1,2,5,6) TG (3,5,6,7) LH (6,7)
Dhaka (DAC)
TG (daily) KB (3) RG (1,3,5,7)
Doha (DOH)
QF (7)
Dubai (DXB)
TG (1,3,4,6) EK (1,3,5,7)CX (1,3,4,7) BI (1,6)
Dusseldorf (DUS)
DE (6)
Frankfurt (FRA)
BI (1,3,6) GA (4,7) TG,LH (daily) PR (2,4,6) QF (1,3,5,7) DE (6)
Fukuoka (FUK)
JL/TG (2,4,7)
Geneva (GVA)
SR (3,4,7)
Guangzhou (CAN)
CZ (1,3,6) TG (1,2,4)
Hanoi (HAN)
VN (daily) TG (1,2,3,5,6) AF (1,3,6)
Hat Yai (HDY)
TG (daily)
Helsinki (HEL)
AY (1,5)
Ho Chi Minh (SGN)
AF (2,4,7) VN,TG (daily)
Hong Kong (HKG)
CX,GF,TG,(daily) CP (1,2,4,6) JL (1,4,6) UL (1,4,6) NG (3,7)
Hua Hin (HHQ)
PG (daily)
Islamabad (ISB)
PK (4,7)
Istanbul (IST)
TK (2,4,6) TG (1,4)
Jakarta (JKT)
GA (1,2,4,5,6) TG (daily)
Jeddah (JED)
SV (3,4)
Johannesburg (JNB)
SA (2,7) RG (4,7)
Kaohsiung (KHH)
CI (1,3,4,5,6,7) TG (daily)
Karachi (KHI)
PK (1,2,5,6) TG (2,4,6,7)
Kathmandu (KTM)
RA (1,2,4,5) TG (1,3,5,6,7)
Khon Kaen (KKC)
TG (daily)
Koh Samui (USM)
PG (daily)
Kuala Lumpur (KUL)
TG/MH (daily) NH (3,5,7)
Kunming (KMG)
CZ (2)TG,3Q (daily)
Kuwait (KWI)
KU (2,4,5,7)
Kwangju (KWJ)
KE (2,7)
Lahore (LHE)
PK (4,7) TG (2,4,7)
Lampang (LPT)
TG (daily)
London (LHR)
QF,TG (daily) BR (2,4,6)
London (LGW)
GA (7)
Los Angeles (LAX)
TG (1,3,5,6)
Macau (MFM)
JS (2) NX (3,5,7)
Madrid (MAD)
TG (3,5,7) UX (3)
Manila (MNL)
MS (3) PR (1,3,4,5,6,7) LH,TG (daily) PK (2,6) KL (1,3) AZ (2,5)
Melbourne (MEL)
AZ (4,6,) QF (2,3,5,6,7) TG (3,7) OA (2,5)
Memphis (MEM)
NW (daily)
Moscow (SVO)
SU (1,2,3,5,6,7)
Munich (MUC)
DE (6) LH (1,2,4,5,7) TG (1,2,4,5,7)
Muscat (MCT)
GF (2,5) TG (2,3,4,7)
Nagoya (NGO)
JL/TG (1,6,7) JL (3,5)
Nakhon Phanom (KOP)
TG (daily)
Nakhon Ratcha (NAK)
TG (daily)
Nakon Si Tha (NST)
TG (daily)
Nan (NNT)
TG (daily)
Narathiwat (NAW)
TG (daily)
Osaka (OSA)
JL/TG,JL,TG (daily) NH (1,3,4,5,6,7)
Paris (CDG)
AF (1,2,4,5,7) TG (daily) PR (3,5,7) GA (7)
Paro (PBH)
KB (3,5,7)
Penang (PEN)
MH/TG (daily)
Perth (PER)
QF (5,7) TG (3,5,7)
Phitsanulok (PHS)
TG (daily)
Phnom-Penh (PNH)
VJ,TG (daily)
Phrae (PRH)
TG (daily)
Phuket (HKT)
TG (daily) OX (2,4,6,7)
Prague (PRG)
OK (3)
Pyongyang (FNJ)
JS (2)
Ranong (UNN)
PG (daily)
Rio de Janiero (RIO)
RG (4,7)
Riyadh (RUH)
SV (7)
Rome (FCO)
AZ (1,4,5,7) GA (5,7) TG (1,3,4,5,6,7) QF (2,4,6)
Sakon Nakhon
TG (daily)
San Francisco (SFO)
NW (daily)
Sao Paulo (SAO)
RG (4,7)
Seoul (SEL)
KE (daily) TG (daily) OZ (1,2,3,4,5,7)
Shanghai (SHA)
TG (2,4,6,7) MU (1,3,5)
Shantou (SWA)
CZ (1,2,3,4,5,6)
Shenzhen (SZX)
CZ (7)
Singapore (SIN)
BG (3,7) CX,SQ,TG,SK (daily) GF (1,2,4,6)AY (1,5) OK (1,3) TK (1,3,5) RA (3,7) AZ (3) OZ (1,3,4,5) NZ (2,5) KE (1,3)GA (2,4,6) AF (5) SR (1,3,4,5,7) BG (1,4)
Sofia (SOF)
LZ (2,4)
Stockholm (ARN)
SK,TG (1,2,4,7)
Sukhothai (THS)
PG (daily)
Surat Thani (URT)
TG (daily)
Sydney (SYD)
AZ (4,6) BA (6,7)QF,TG (daily) OA (2,5) NZ (3)
Taipei (TPE)
KL (1,2,4,5,6,7) TG,CI,BR (daily)SR (2,6)
Tashkent (TAS)
HY (2,3)
Tel Aviv (TLV)
LY (2,3,7)
Tokyo (NRT)
AI,MS (3,6) NH (2,3,4,6,7) PK (2,6) BG (4) TG,NW,JL,UA (daily)
Toronto (YYZ)
CP (1,2,4,6)
Trang (TST)
TG (daily)
Ubon Ratcath (UBP)
TG (daily)
Udon Thani (UTH)
TG (daily)
Utapao (UTP)
OX (2,4,6,7)
Vancouver (YVR)
CP (1,2,4,6)
Vienna (VIE)
NG (3,6,7)
Vientiane (VTE)
QV (1,2,3,4,5,7) TG (1,2,4,5,6,7)
Warsaw (WAW)
LO (3,7)
Yangon (RGN)
UB,TG (daily) BG (5) PK (4)
Zurich (ZRH)
SR (1,3,4,5,7) TG (daily)

PHUKET (International) HKT

Abu Dhabi (AUH)
LT (1,3)
Bangkok (BKK)
TG (daily) OX (2,4,6,7)
Frankfurt (FRA)
LT (1) DE (3) TG (1,3,6)
Hanover (HAJ)
DE (3)
Hat Yai (HDY)
TG (daily)
Hong Kong (HKG)
KA (1,4,6)
Ipoh (IPH)
9P (4,7)
Koh Samui (USM)
PG (daily)
Kuala Lumpur (KUL)
MH/TG (daily)
Munich (MUC)
LT (3)
Narathiwat (NAW)
TG (daily)
Penang (PEN)
TG/MH (3,5,7)
Seoul (SEL)
KE (2,5)
Singapore (SIN)
TG, MI (daily)
Taipei (TPE)
CI (daily)
Utapao (UTP)
OX (2,4,6,7)
Vienna (VIE)
NG (6)
Yangon (RGN)
6T (4,7)

Major Exhibitions in Thailand 1997/98

Date	Exhibition	Venue	Organiser
May 22-25	**Propak Asia 97** - 8th International food processing & packaging technology exhibition Incorporating: **CanTech 97**; **PharmaPak 97** and **SeafoodTech 97**	QSNCC	OES/BES
June 5-8	**International Food & Hospitality Show 97** - 6th International Hotel, Catering, Bakery, Food, Beverage & Franchising exbn.	QSNCC	OES/BES
June 24-27	**AARME**: Asian Auto Repair & Maintenance Exbn. plus **AAAE**: Asian Auto Accessories Exbn	BITEC	Reed
July 17-20	**IT TRADE** - Thailand and Indochina's Information Technology Trade Exhibition	QSNCC	Reed
Mid July	**Bangkok International Jewellery Fair**		MF
July 24-27	**INTERPLAS** Thailand - Raw materials, related equipment & manufacturing technology re plastics and rubber. Incorporating **Manufacturing Technology, Welding, Logismat** & **Intermould**.	BITEC	Reed
July 24-27	**TPP: ThaiPackPrint** - Thailand's Int'l General Packaging, Food Packaging and Printing Machinery Event	BITEC	Reed
Oct 23-26	**THAIBEX** - 7th building materials, construction equipment tools, decoration and interior decoration show	QSNCC	Reed
Nov 20-23	**BUILDTECH CONSTECH** - Building & Construction Show		TTF
1988 Feb	**ASIACOMM** - 7th exbn of accessories & materials for data processing, fibre-optics, ISDN, modems, broadcast technology etc	QSNCC	Reed
Feb 11-14	**Oil & Gas Thailand 98** - 6th International Oil & Gas Exploration & Production Exhibition. Incorporating **RLP Thailand, Instrument Thailand** & **Analab Thailand**	QSNCC	OES/BES
Feb 11-14	**Environmex/Watermex Thailand 98** - 2nd Thai Int'l environment management technology, equipment & control systems Exhibition & Conference	QSNCC	OES/BES

Venues:
QSNCC = Queen Sirikit National Convention Centre. New Rajadapisek Road, Klongtoey, Bangkok 10110. Tel: 229 4111; Fax: 229 4253; Shangri-La Hotel, 89 Soi Wat Suan Plu, New Rd Bangrak 10500; tel: 236 7777; fax: 236 8579
BITEC = Bangkok International Trade & Exhibition Centre, Bangkok
Organisers:
OES/BES = Bangkok Exhibition Services Ltd. 62 soi Areesamphen 11, Rama VI Road, Phyathai, Bangkpk 10400. Tel: 271 4722; Fax: 271 3223.
MF = Miller Freeman Asia Ltd, 102-5 Stanhope House, 738 King's Road, Quarry Bay, Hong Kong, tel: (852) 2827 5121; fax: 2827 7064
Reed/Tradex = Reed Exhibition Companies/Tradex. Reed Tradex House, 323 Bond Street, Office Villa, Muang Thong Thani, Chaengwattana, Nonthaburi 11120. Tel: (02) 503 4076 / 503 2199; Fax: (02) 503 4100/1.
TTF = TTF International Co Ltd, 200/12-14 Soi Rankhamhaeng 4, Ramkhamhaeng Road, Suanluang, Bangkok 10250. Tel: (02) 7172477 Fax: (02) 717246668

Pump up your Purchasing power.

Where better to show off your new DKNY than on a romantic boat cruise down the Chao Phraya River at sunset? In an eccentric Moschino then perhaps, a slap-up meal of sizzlin' spicy seafood for starters and dancing till dawn for seconds. Of course, with a classic Ralph Lauren, you might be in the mood for a round on one of our tropical sun-dazzled golf courses. You see, Thailand's perfect for designer shopping; where else could you have such fun afterwards? Besides, you can also get that tan you'll need to wear your revealing new Versace.

Discover your one-stop shopping world at the new Thailand Duty Free shop, located in the heart of Bangkok on the 7th floor of the World Trade Center, Bangkok. Tel. (662) 267-8555. Fax. (662) 267-8551. You will find a fantastic selection of top international brands and Thai products.

THAILAND
DUTY FREE SHOPS

COME TO Thailand EXOTIC EXPERIENCE The SPLENDOURS of A KiNGDOM

For a Free brochure on Thailand, fill in and mail this coupon to : Tourism Authority of Thailand, 372 Bamrung Muang Rd., Bangkok 10100, Thailand. Tel. (66 2) 226-0060, 226-0072 Fax. (66 2) 224-6221 E-mail Address:tat@cs.ait.ac.th

Name: Address: AS/APT/96CPS

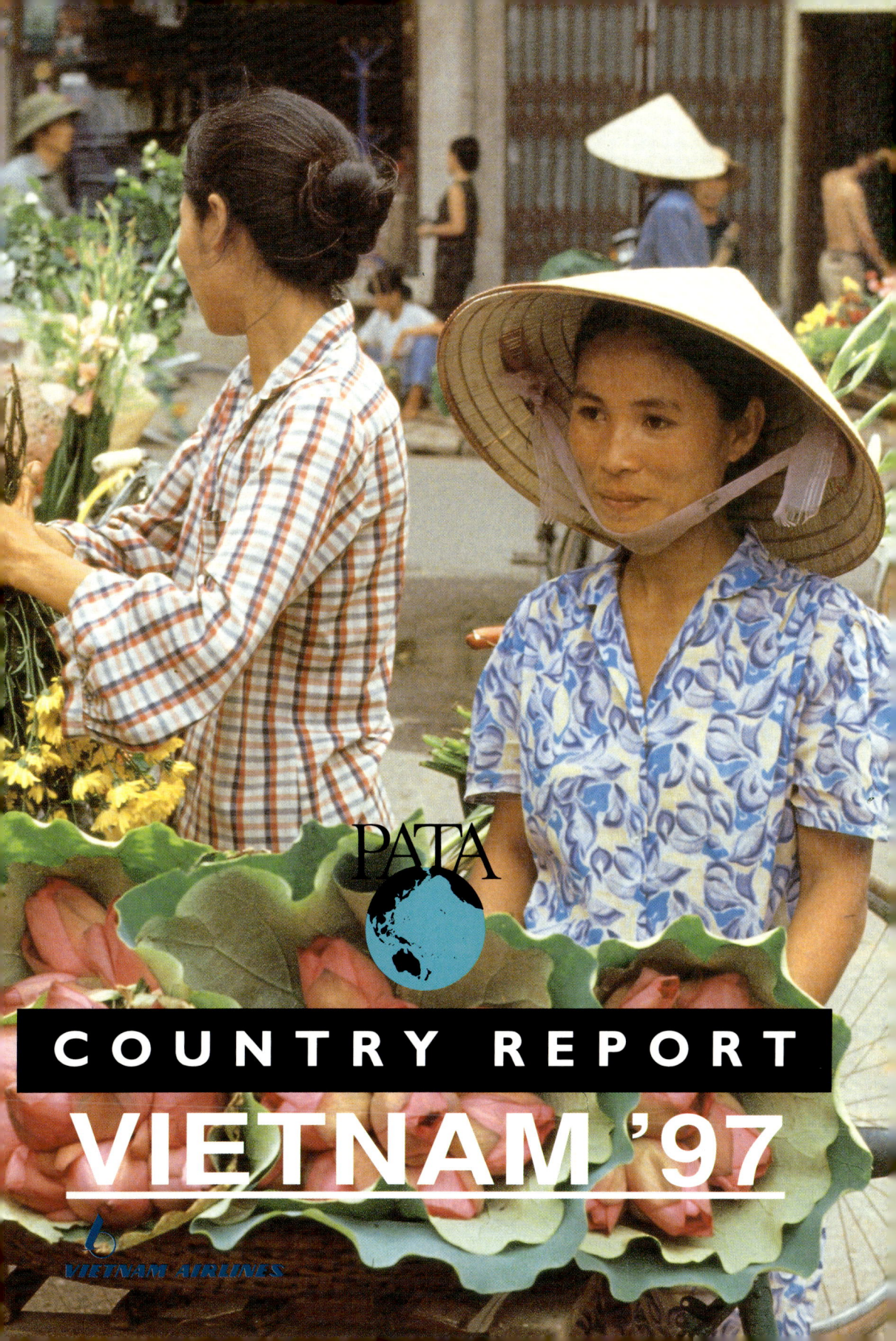

Vietnam

Doing Business

General Climate

More haste, less speed. The final hurdle to Vietnam becoming a fully functioning international business venue was surmounted in 1995 when the US resumed both diplomatic and trade relations with its former enemy.

But by early 1997, the country was still struggling to put its economic and marketing houses in order. While the former standoff with the US had failed to eradicate a good deal of tentative business through the back door into Vietnam during previous years, primarily with Japan, Hong Kong, Taiwan, Singapore, France, the UK and Australia, Vietnam's official regaining of credentials with the world's trading and capital markets was expected to put a proverbial economic firecracker under a country whose *doi moi* (change to the new) policies had achieved only mixed success since its doors were opened to the West in the late 1980s.

An added business incentive was Vietnam's admittance in July 1995 to the Association of South East Asian Nations (ASEAN), an economic union paradoxically formed by neighbouring countries to fend off communist interference from countries like Vietnam. It was the vibrant free market economies of ASEAN countries like Thailand and Malaysia which initially prompted Vietnam's *doi moi* policies: in essence to switch from a stagnating centralised economy and move to a multi-sectoral economy, doubling GDP in the process.

Legalised private ownership, a free private sector and the opening up of markets had all helped Vietnam's economy to grow year on year from stagnation in the late 80s to 8.8% in 1994, with inflation falling from over 200% in 1991 to 15% in 1992 and 5.2% in 1993. In 1992, Vietnam showed a trade surplus for the first time in its history and between 1988 and 1995 the government issued licences for foreign investment projects worth US$9.8 billion, with oil/gas, tourism/hotels and manufacturing being the most favoured sectors.

But aside from sidestepping the obstacles created by the former US embargo, analysts believe growth could have been, and still could be, much more impressive. Vietnamese are generally perceived to be among Asia's most astute and enthusiastic business people. But, say analysts, their zeal continues to be stifled by a procrastinating centralised bureaucracy which tries hard but has failed to keep pace with the free trade principles of *doi moi*, leading to widespread corruption and smuggling.

As a result, many foreign joint venture projects meet an impasse and fall by the wayside while Vietnam's general infrastructure strains to handle new investment interest. Essentially, business travellers face a country of endless opportunity hampered by red tape with changing rules and regulations plus frequent tax revisions - the latest package being introduced in 1997 to encourage more rural investment.

Although sustained growth and big new investment is envisaged and although the privatisation of large state industries is underway, there has been little corresponding relaxation in state bureaucracy. An added problem for investors is high operating costs. Office rentals in Ho Chi Minh City and Hanoi are high due to a continuing shortage of suitably-equipped space and long waiting lists. Many visiting business people have been forced to operate from hotels where, until an easing in 1995/96, demand also far exceeded supply.

Although investment laws are ostensibly among the most liberal in Southeast Asia, many business people claim joint venture rules are stacked in favour of local partners and suitable agreements can be hard to reach, and even harder to police. Little English is spoken.

The business habits of the Vietnamese are much the same as the neighbouring Thais, with non-committal answers and ever-present smiles masking a range of emotions. That said, Vietnam and the Vietnamese exude a thirst for business which foreigners find hard to resist. South Korea's Daewoo corporation, for example, invested more than US$1 billion in the country in 1996/97.

With the doors of opportunity fully open, many hope the infrastructure will now fast improve nationwide to sustain and support the interest shown. With French-style cafes, hotel bars and raucous nightclubs forming the backdrop to most business dealings, amid much toasting, the general mood is still one of frontierland. But it could be some years yet before Vietnam fully harnesses and realises its undoubted potential.

Business etiquette

By Western standards, business practice can appear unsophisticated and basic. However, a high degree of regulation and government control means that bureaucracy and red tape delays can stretch on for days, even weeks.

Although improving, telecommunications are still rudimentary by Western standards, and expensive to the end user. Supplementary charges are normally levied on both incoming and outgoing calls. Business travellers are advised to book incoming calls prior to arrival time to ensure a reasonable line and price.

Most major hotels and restaurants in Ho Chi Minh City and Hanoi, but not yet all, accept main credit cards and travellers' cheques. Elsewhere, the use or acceptance of credit cards or travellers' cheques is limited.

Business cards are a must; local printers can produce an emergency supply if you run out. Handshaking is the normal form of greeting. Business dress is fairly informal - a shirt and tie being perfectly adequate.

Always make appointments well in advance and reconfirm prior to meeting, but don't always expect the Vietnamese to be punctual. A good local agent/translator is essential. Few Vietnamese speak English and only older officials speak French. Tipping is officially prohibited but widely practised, particularly in (former) South Vietnam.

Tourism Update

General Developments

Growth in visitor arrivals in Vietnam slowed somewhat in 1995 after some great leaps in earlier years. But nevertheless, the number is now at the level of an established tourism destination such as New Zealand.

The total increased 19% to 1.2 million in 1995, and 25% in 1996 to 1.6 million. First three monmths of 1997 showed 432,000 arrivals - 1.3% up on the same period a year earlier. The NTO targets 1.9 million for the whole of 1997 and 3 mn by the year 2000. Breakdowns of visitor arrivals are by passport, which overstates certain markets, such as American and British. For instance, it is likely that Hong Kong is the second-largest source in terms of residence. But according to the breakdown by passport in 1995 (no breakdowns for 1996), those with Taiwanese passports were the single largest market, increasing 21.6% to 224,004. This was followed by the French, up 23.3% to 119,202, then Japanese, up 81.0% to 117,763, American, up 28.1% to 54,368, and British, up 40.6% to 51,817.

Overall visitor arrivals show a business share of almost 70%, but that includes visiting friends or relatives - probably half of the business share. Also, part of the 30% is business travellers who prefer to be designated tourists for entry visa purposes.

There is certainly tourism potential in Vietnam, but growth has been held back by high hotel prices, and visas - difficulty in obtaining them, and their high cost (14 days, US$40+; 'express' visas up to US$100). The authorities hope to reduce this cost and also to start visas on arrival in 1997/98.

Avis Rent A Car had hoped to open in Vietnam in 1996, but city demands postponed its plans for that year. It planned to start with between 50 and 100 vehicles in both Hanoi and Ho Chi Minh City.

The Opera House, Hanoi. Photo: Patricia Clanzy

Airlines

The country's national carrier, Vietnam Airlines, continues to grow steadily by adding new routes, and acquiring new equipment. In 1996 it ordered 10 new Airbus A320s and two new Fokker 70s to make up a 27-strong fleet consisting of almost entirely new Western-built aircraft. That same year Vietnam Airlines counted 2.5 million seats sold, including 900,000 on domestic routes, and it also carried 43,000 tons of cargo. That 20% increase was expected to be repeated in 1997. The airline now flies to 22 international destinations and 16 internal destinations (*see page 341*).

Such is the thaw in international relations that flights to USA are envisaged within two years. Also Vietnam Airlines has talked of introducing a Frequent Flyer Plan by the end of 1997.

Pacific Air (Vietnam's semi-private airline) started flights into Macau in 1996 from Ho Chi Minh City, with the return routed through Danang. At end-1995, Trans European Airways of Switzerland signed an agreement to operate B737s for Pacific Air over Ho Chi Minh City-Danang and to add a second B737 in 1996.

Also in 1996, Lauda Air started flying into Ho Chi Minh City, but Emirates stopped. Dubai-based Emirates built its route feasibility for a Dubai-Ho Chi Minh City-Singapore route on winning HCMC-Singapore traffic rights. But although Singapore said yes to rights, Vietnam said no, even though Vietnam Airlines has unrestricted rights on its flights through Dubai to Europe.

There is a possibility that Swissair will add a route into Vietnam in 1997. And among All Nippon Airways hoped-for new routes is Ho Chi Minh City-Osaka Kansai, and/or a code-share with Vietnam Airlines over Hanoi-Osaka Kansai-Tokyo Haneda.

Vietnam Air Services Co (Vasco), a national helicopter company, planned to form a regional scheduled airline in 1996, but there was no progress.

There have been various plans for the improvement of airports in the country, including the main ones of Hanoi and Ho Chi Minh City. Although some were major projects, most development has been at a slower pace. Plans at Ho Chi Minh City are to increase capacity to 5-6 million passengers from the current 2.5 million for the year 2000. At Hanoi, the target was to increase capacity to 2.5 million passengers by 1997.

Hue

Hotels

Vietnam's NTO targets 70,000 international-standard hotel rooms by 2010; currently there are about 42,000.

Opened in Hanoi in 1996 was the Daewoo hotel and a 135-room extension to the Sofitel Metropole; also, the Sofitel was designated the country's first 5-star hotel that year. Other hotels due to open 1997-99 in Hanoi are the long-awaited Grand West Lake with 325 rooms, 150-room New World and Sheraton with 279 rooms.

Major hotels opening recently in Ho Chi Minh City were the Saigon Prince and the Equatorial. Opened in 1997/8 is the delayed Amara Saigon with 309 rooms; the 157-room Garden Plaza; also the 56-room Century Indochine, the Sofitel Plaza and the 335-room Delta Caravelle. In Hanoi the Sheraton is due to open in October. Due 1998/99 in Ho Chi Minh is the Conrad with 300 rooms, Hilton 400 rooms, Park Hyatt Saigon 258 rooms, Plaza 300 rooms, Renaissance 388 rooms, 356-room Ramada Saigon and a 397-room extension to the Continental.

In 1996, the Floating Hotel, the first internationally-managed hotel (at that time, by Southern Pacific) was forced to close, and sailed away! Also, the Mandarin Oriental group pulled out of its 250-room project in the city.

The first post-war international beach hotel, the 200-room Furama Resort on China Beach near Danang, opened in 1997. It is managed by Majestic International Hotels, which also runs the Furama in Hong Kong. Also planned for Danang is a giant China Beach Resort, and a Novotel Tourane with 202 rooms.

The Accor hotel group formed an investment company to develop hotels in Vietnam. They signed to manage the 312-room Sofitel Plaza, due to open late 1997 on Le Duan Boulevard in the centre of Ho Chi Minh City. Indotel will take equity in the Sofitel Metropole in Hanoi, and in three hotels due to open in 1998 - Novotel Danang, Ibis Haiphong, and Novotel Haiphong. Hotel rates in Ho Chi Minh City have fallen 50% over the past three years, from around US$200 for a 4-star hotel to around US$100. A decline in hotel rates is likely to encourage greater growth in tourist traffic. Rates in Hanoi have also fallen from US$200, but not so far.

What to see

The first stop for many visitors to Ho Chi Minh City is Thien Hau Pagoda and the former presidential palace. The National Museum, with its collection of Vietnamese, Khmer and Cham culture, together with its Japanese and Chinese relics, should not be missed, together with the War Crimes Exhibition. A floating restaurant cruise is a great way to see the city and eat at the same time. These depart from opposite the *Cuu Long* (Majestic) Hotel and take about two hours. Also of interest is Cu Chi - the network of underground tunnels in which the Vietcong lived during the Vietnam War.

Those with some time on their hands might consider a trip on the Mekong river or a visit to cool and breezy Dalat - the former French Colonial hill station some 350km from Ho Chi Minh City. It's certainly worth enduring the day's journey across dubious roads, or you can fly via the twice-weekly service.

In Hanoi, a favourite spot is the Ho Chi Minh Mausoleum, the One-Pillared Pagoda and the so-called Temple of Literature. Also worth visiting are the Reunifcation Park, the Zoo and the State Circus. 164 km from Hanoi is the spectacular Ha Long Bay, now being opened to tourism and 300 km west of Hanoi on the Laotian border is the historic Dien Bien Phu, site of the final French-Vietnamese battle in 1954. An attraction now being promoted is the Phong Nha grotto near Dong Hoi in central Vietnam. On the coast of Central Vietnam, Da Nang is famous for its Museum of Cham Art and nearby Marble Mountain, a cave behind a Buddhist monastery with walls of natural marble. 70 km southwest of Da Nang, My Son Valley is the home of the Museum of Cham Culture, recording their history since the 4th century.

112 km from Da Nang is Hue, the ancient Imperial capital. Much of the city was destroyed in the Tet fighting of 1968 but the Dai Noi Citadel, started in 1804, remains. 5 km west of Hue is the Phuoc Duyen Tower and further upstream are the Imperial Tombs of the Nguyen emperors (1802-1925).

Shopping

Ho Chi Minh City and Hanoi lack the shopping malls of other south-east Asian capitals but Duty Free Shopping of Hong Kong opened its first store in Vietnam at 23 Le Loi Street in May 1997. There is also an arrivals Duty Free Shop at Ho Chi Minh airport.

Otherwise bargains are to be found in the array of small shops and street side-stalls which sell all kinds of items - including Vietnam War memorabilia. Best known for second hand flak jackets and Zippo lighters is Dan Sin Market at 104 Nguyen Cong Tru Street. Largest general market is Ben Thanh (Central Market). These shops and stalls also offer trinkets, pens, combs, maps, postcards and pirated tapes. Most tours take in the handicraft workshops in Ho Chi Minh City. The Government is very sensitive about the export of artefacts and it is advisable to obtain from shops certificates stating that any *objet d'art* purchased is not an antique.

It is inadvisable to walk around the streets with too much cash or valuables on you, particularly in Ho Chi Minh City. US$ or Thai Baht are the most readily convertible currency.

Cho Ben Thanh Market

Getting Around

Vietnam Airlines offers a regular service between Ho Chi Minh City, Hanoi, Da Nang, Hue and other cities. Old Tupolev aircraft are gradually being replaced with Boeings and A320s.

Taxis, yellow or white, do cruise the streets. A car with driver can be hired for about US$35 per day, but for those with more time on their hands the old colonial 'cyclo' is as good a way of seeing Ho Chi Minh City as any other means of transport. These charge about US$1 for a single ride and perhaps US$10 for the entire day. Another alternative is the *Honda Om* - basically a hitched lift on the back of one of the thousands of Honda scooters driven by the inhabitants - but make sure your travel insurance is up to date! Buses are not developed or comfortable but trains link Hanoi and Saigon, taking 48 hours to complete the journey, via the coastal towns. Seat prices range from US$48 for a hard seat to US$114 for a Super Class Sleeper.

Entertainment

Ho Chi Minh City's nightlife is fairly wild. *Q Bar* or *The Apocalypse Now* bar in Thi Sach Street are some of the hottest dancing spots in town, although *Hien and Bob's* at 43 Ba Trung Street is quieter and *VIP Club* (with branches in Hanoi and Da Nang) quieter still. *Saigon Headlines* (7 Lam Son Square) offers jazz. *Madame B* and *Miss Saigon* provide interesting entertainemnt which would have been popular with GIs on R & R leave in the old days!

Even Hanoi boasts discotheques now and *Queen Bee* at 42 Lang Ha Street is one of the most popular. Heavy Metal music is available at *Metal Club* (57 Cua Nam - old Kinh Do cinema). A quieter ambience of jazz, blues and Country & Western prevails at *Polite Pub* at 5 Bao Khanh Street.

A growing number of Vietnamese, Chinese and French restaurants are springing up all around Ho Chi Minh City (see *Restaurant* section of this guide - after *Hotels*). Many are now geared to Western tastes and the tourist dollar. Note that restaurants and dance halls close at 10.30 or 11pm, however. Whereas the city's older hotels tend to offer rather sombre surroundings in which to eat; the newer ones are comparable with any in South-East Asia.

Horse racing is still held on Sundays and sometimes Thursdays at track that goes back to French colonial times. Betting is permitted.

Leisure

Leisure facilities are developing fast as new resorts are opened up. Most new joint venture hotels have swimming pools and tennis courts and there are several recently opened golf courses: at Thu Duc, 20 km from Ho Chi Minh is the Lee Trevino 2 x Championship course complex; above Lake Xuan Huong is the 18-hole Dalat Palace Golf Club (and nearby Sofitel); at Phan Thiet, near Ho Chi Minh City, is the Ocean Dunes Golf Club. There are also very unspoiled beaches to explore, such as at Ha Long in the North, with a nearby 9-hole course. The Mekong delta is famous for its rare birds and wildlife.

Ocean Dunes Golf Club

Arrival & Departure

Arrival at Ho Chi Minh City's Tan Son Nhut airport can be chaotic to say the least as the country's bureaucracy greets you head on. So be prepared to wait for your luggage and for long lines at customs and immigration. Take a yellow cab into town and expect to pay around US$10 for the 7km taxi ride from the airport to downtown, but for some reason you have to double this in Hanoi. Agree the fare with the driver in advance and make sure you have your destination written down. An airport tax of US$8 is charged in cash for each international outbound journey and $1.5 for internal flights.

Pagoda of the Heavenly Lady, Hue.
Photo: Patricia Clanzy

Useful Addresses

Government Offices/Ministries

The Economic Institute
175 Hai Ba Trung St, Ho Chi Minh City
Tel: 828 6590

Entry/Exit Permit Dept
40a Hang Bui St, Hanoi. Tel: 825 5798

Foreign Investment Service Company
35-37 Ben Chuong Duong, Quan 1, Ho Chi Minh City.Tel: 895 8061

Ministry of Culture & Information
51 Ngo Quyen St, Hanoi
Tel: 825 3231/825 3234

Ministry of Finance
8 Phan Huy Chu St, Hanoi
Tel: 826 4872

Trade Relations (Foreign Economic Relations Office)
86 Le Thanh Ton, Quan 1, Ho Chi Minh City.Tel: 829 0048

Vietcochamber (Chamber of Commerce)
33 Ba Trieu St, Hanoi.Tel: 825 2961; Tlx: 4264

Tourism Agencies/Ministries

Hanoi Tourist Agency
18 Ly Thuong Kiet, Hanoi. Tel: 8254209

Ho Chin Minh Tourist Agency
1 Dong Khoi, Ho Chi Minh City
Tel: 8295515/8295517

Ministry of Trade & Tourism
31 Tran Tien St, Hanoi. Tel: 825 4950

National Tourist Organisation of Vietnam (Tong cuc Du lich Vietnam)
30a Ly Thuong Kiet, Hanoi
Tel: 256916; Tlx: 411272

Saigontourist Travel Service Center
(Du lich Thanh Pho Ho Chi Minh) 49 Le Thanh Ton, Ho Chi Minh City.Tel:8298914/ 8298129; Tlx: 812745; Fax: 8224987

Vietnamtourist
54 Nguyen Du St, **Hanoi**
Tel: 8257080/8252986; Tlx: 411272 TCDL-VT; Fax: (84.4) 8257583.
69-71 Nguyen Hue, **Ho Chi Minh City**
Tel: (84.8) 829 1276/829 0776; Tlx: 811295 DULIVIN -VT; Fax: (84.8) 8290775
91/1 Nguyen Chi Tanh St, **Da Nang**
Tel: (84.51) 22990/22999; Tlx: 515735 VITOUR VT; Fax: (84.51) 22854

Import/Export Organisation

Cosevina Import-Export and Service Company of Ho Chi Minh City,102 Nguyen Hue.Tel: 8291506/8292391; Fax: 889 1024

Post Office, Hospital, Emergencies

The International Hospital
Kim Lien, Hanoi. Tel: 852 2004

Emergency Center
125 Le Soi St, Dist 1, Ho Chi Minh City
Tel: 829 2071/829 2711

International Post Office
75 Dinh Tien Hoang, Hanoi. Tel: 825 7004
City Post Office, 125 Hai Ba Trung St, Ho Chi Minh City. Tel: 829 3310

Police: Dial 13; **Fire Brigade** - 14; **Ambulance** - 15; **Directory Enquiries** - 16

Air Couriers

DHL: Ho Chi Minh. Tel: 844 6203

TNT: Hanoi. Tel: 826 5750; Ho Chi Minh. Tel: 844 6478.

UPS. Hanoi. Tel: 824 6483

Vietnam Key Fact File

Passport Requirements
Passport and visa required by all visitors. Business visitors have to be invited in by 'sponsors' in Vietnam. Tourists will have a group visa arranged by their travel agent. Three completed application forms needed + three front-on bareheaded 4 x 6 cm photos + fee. Allow 4-6 weeks.
Visas will state which cities the guest may travel to.
Within 48 hours of arrival, all visitors are required to register with local immigration police; most hotels will do this for guests for a fee of US$10.

Currency:
Dong (Dg)

Exchange Rates: *(May 1997)*
US$1 = 11205 Dg; £1 = 18231 Dg

Currency Restrictions:
Import and export of local currency prohibited. No limit on importation of foreign currency but exportation limited to the amount declared brought in on arrival.

Electricity Supply:
220 volts, AC50
(liable to fluctuation).

Language:
Vietnamese (*Quoc Ngu*). French in business/government cadres.

Time: GMT + 7 hours; EST + 12 hours

IDD Code: 84 *followed by....*
Hanoi 4; Da Nang 51; Ho Chi Minh City 8; Hue 54

Business Hours:
Commercial offices and shops open 0730 until 1630 Monday to Saturday. Lunch is normally noon-1300 hrs).
Banks are open 0800-1500 Monday to Friday (til 1300 Saturdays).
Shops are open until late in the evening.

Customs & Entry:
600 cigarettes or 100 cigars or equivalent may be imported; unlimited quantity of alcohol; reasonable quantities of perfume; precious stones or gold (subject to declaration); pornographic magazines may not be imported.

Health Requirements:
Vaccination recommended against tetanus, polio, typhoid and yellow fever. Carry proof of immunization. Malaria risk in rural areas and deltas only. All water potentially contaminated. Avoid local dairy products, under-cooked meat and uncooked vegetables.

Climate/Best Time to Visit:
Tropical monsoon climate with one wet and one dry season. The average temperatures in the South (Ho Chi Minh City) range from 25°C in January to 35° in May with humidity peaking at 80% in July. Temperatures in the North (Hanoi) are more extreme, ranging from 13°C in January to 33°C in June, with humidity peaking at 80% in March. Mid-September to end-December are the most agreeable months for business visits to the North; The South, like Hong Kong, is most pleasant in Spring and Autumn.

National Holidays 1997:
1 January New Year's Day; 7/8 February Tet (Lunar) New Year; 30 April/1 May Liberation of South Vietnam Day/ International Labour Day; 2/3 September Founding of the Socialist Republic of Vietnam /Independence Day.

There are other regional feast days and holidays.

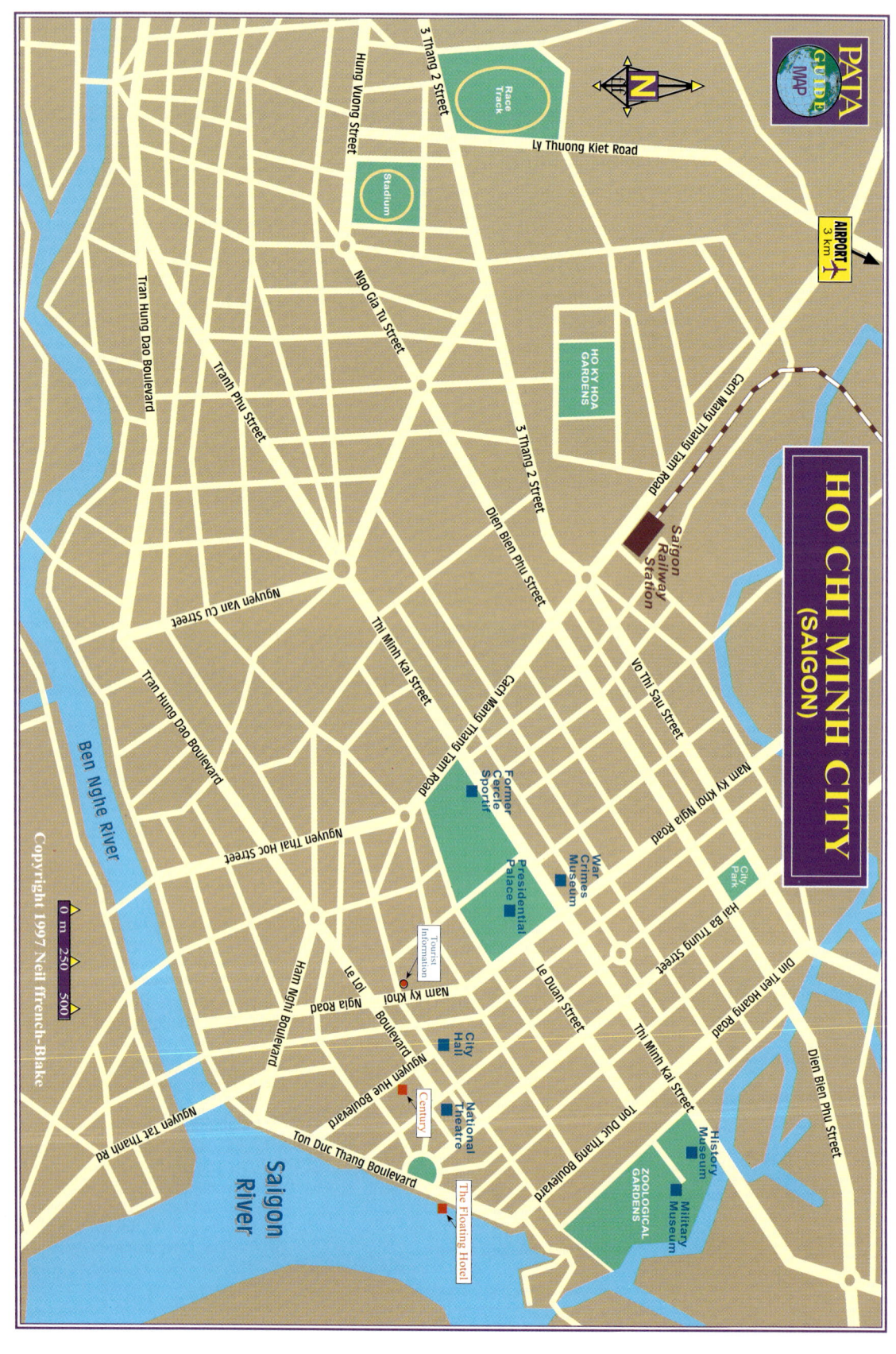

Hotels

Da Lat

Hotel Sofitel Dalat Palace C
12 Tran Phu St, Dalat
Tel: (84-63) 825444; Fax: (84-63) 825666

Da Nang

The Furama Resort ¶
68 Ho Xuan Huang St, Bac My An, Da Nang City
Tel: (51) 847888/847333; Fax: (51) 847666

Phuong Dong (Eastern) E
43 Phan Chau Trinh St
Tel: (51) 821266; Fax: (51) 821666

Thai Binh Duong (Pacific) E
80 Phan Chu Trinh
Tel: 822137/822921

Haiphong

Duyen Hai Hotel ¶
5 Nguyen Tri Phuong St
Tel: 847657/842157; Tlx: 4269

Do Son Resort ¶
Do Son Beach (13 km SE of Haiphong)
Tel: 847486 ext 10; Tlx: 4269

Ha Long

Heritage Halong Hotel ◌ C
88 Halong Road, Bai Chay Beach, Halong City, Quang Ninh Province
Tel: (84-33) 846888; Fax: (84-33) 846718

Hanoi

Bang Sen Hotel E
117-123 Dong Khoi St, Dist 1
Tel: 829 1516; Fax: 829 8076

Capital Garden B
48a Lang Ha Street
Tel: 835 0373; Fax: 835 0363

Daewoo Hotel Hanoi ◌ A
360 Kim Ma St, Ba Dinh Dist
Tel: 831 5000; Fax: 831 5010

Hanoi Horison A
40 Cat Link St.Tel: 733 0808; Fax: 733 0688

Hanoi Hotel (Dan Chu) B
D8 Giang Vo St, Ba Dinh District.
Tel: 845 2270; Fax: 845 9209

Hotel Majestic C
1 Dong Khoi
Tel: 829 5517; Fax: 829 5510

Hotel Sofitel Metropole ◌ A
15 Ngo Quyen, Hoan Kiem
Tel: 826 6919; Fax: 826 6920

Saigon Hotel E
80 Ly Thuong Kiet St
Tel: 826 8505; Tlx: 411259; Fax: 826 6631

Hoa Binh (Splendid) E
27 Ly Thuong Kiet Street
Tel: 253315; Tlx: 411288; Fax: 269818

Thang Loi (Victory) E
Yen Phu Street, West Lake, Ba Dinj
Tel: 268211; Tlx: 411276; Fax: 252800

Ho Chi Minh City

Amara Hotel Saigon B
323 Le Van Sy Street, district 3
Tel: 843 9999; Fax: 843 8888

Century Saigon Hotel
68a Nguyen Hue Blvd, district 1
Tel: (84-8) 829 2959; Fax: (84-8) 822 2958

French colonial boutique hotel situated in the heart of Ho Chi Minh City's business and tourist district. Within walking distance of the city's restaurants, banks, airline offices and tourist attractions.

Accommodation & rates
108 rooms and suites; standard US$ 95; superior US$ 140; deluxe US$ 195; suites US$ 300-450

Credit cards accepted
All major cards

Meeting & banqueting facilities
Three conference/function rooms, capacity 12-50 with audio-visual equipment; largest reception 60 seated/120 cocktail

Room services
Airconditioning, colour TV, direct-dial telephone (ext. in bathroom), hairdryer, laundry/valet service, minibar, music, safety deposit box, 24-hr room service

Business & other services
Business centre, airport pickup, translation service, car rental, travel centre, taxi service, barber shop/hairdresser, newsstand/shops, disco and nightclub

Sports & Recreation
Billiards/snooker, fitness centre/gym, golf (nearby), massage, sauna

Restaurants & Coffee Shops
Colour's Cafe (100) - International, open 24 hours; Lobby Cafe Lounge, Cleo's Karaoke, Starlight Night Club

Overseas Sales Representatives:
Utell International Worldwide, Delton Reservation System, Century International Hotels Hong Kong

Chains First Hotel (De Nhat) D
201/3 Hoang Viet Tan Binh
Tel: (84-8) 844 1199; Fax: (84-8) 844 4282

Ben Thanh (Rex) Hotel ◌ D
141 Nguyen Hue Blvd/1st dist
Tel: 829 2185; Fax: 829 6536

Continental ◌ B
132-134 Dong Khoi/1 Dist
Tel: (8) 829 9201; Tlx: 811344 HOCONT VT; Fax: (8) 824 1772

Cuo Long (Majestic) Hotel E
1 Dong Khoi Rd, 1st District
Tel: 829 5515; Tlx: 812615; Fax: 829 5510

Doc Lap (Caravelle) Hotel E
19-23 Lam Som Square, 1st dist
Tel: 829 3704; Tlx: 811259; Fax: 829 6767

Hotel Equatorial B
242 Tran Binh Trong St, district 5
Tel: 839 0000; Fax: 839 0011

Garden Plaza Hotel ¶
309-311 Nguyen Van Troi, Tan Binh Dist
Tel: 842 1111; Fax: 842 4370

Huu Nghi (Palace) Hotel E
56-64 Nguyen Hue Blvd/1st dist
Tel: 829 2860; Tlx: 811208; Fax: 829 9872

Kimdo International Hotel C
133 Nguyen Hue Ave, district 1
Tel: 822 5914; Tlx: 813168; Fax: 822 5913

Metropole Hotel ¶
148 Tran Hung Dao Ave, 1st district
Tel: 832 2021; Fax: 832 21019

Mondial Hotel E
109 Dong Khai Street/1st dist
Tel: 829 6291; Tlx: 811450; Fax: 829 6324

New World Hotel ◌ A
76 le Lai St, district 1
Tel: 822 8888; Tlx: 811403; Fax: 823 0710

Norfolk Hotel D
117 Le Thanh Ton St, district 1
Tel: 829 5368; Fax: 829 3415/823 0948

Omni Saigon A
251 Nguyen Van Troi St
Tel: 449222; Tlx: 813163; Fax: 449200

Saigon Prince Hotel ◯
63 Nguyen Hue Blvd, district 1
Tel: (84-8) 822 2999; Tlx: 813210 Prince VT; Fax: (84-8) 824 1888

An elegant international boutique hotel catering t the traveller who seeks personalised service and courtesy. Strategically located in the heart of the city, with access to business, government and shopping areas. Offering views overlooking the Saigon river and a short 20-minute drive from the airport.

Accommodation and rates
203 single/105 double/98 twin US$ 180-350; 4 suites from US$ 350

Credit cards accepted
Amex, Visa, Mastercard, Diners

Meeting & banqueting faciliies
Three conference/function rooms, capacity 400; audio-visual equipment available; 264 + 204 sq m exhibition space; largest reception 210 seated or 250 cocktail

Room services
Airconditioning, colour TV, direct-dial telephone (ext. in bathroom), hairdryer, laundry/valet service, minibar, music/radio/alarm clock, safety deposit box, 24-hr room/meal service, no-smoker bedrooms, video films & satellite

Business & other services
Business centre, express checkout, airport pickup, translation service, car parking & rental, travel centre, limousine service, guided tours, newsstand/shops, babysitting

Sports & Recreation
Fitness centre/gym, indoor games, jacuzzi/whirlpool, massage, sauna, waterfall shower

Restaurants & Coffee Shops
Chatterbox (150) - International, open 24 hours; *Lobby Lounge* (60) - Cocktails etc, open 1100-0100; *Club Lido* (120) - Japanese lounge/nightclub, open 1700-0100; *Sushi Ya* (60) - Sushi, open 0700-1000/noon-1400/1830-2300

Overseas Sales Representatives:
Utell Worldwide Resrvations

Sol Chancery Saigon C
196 Nguyen Thi Mink Khai, district 3
Tel: 829 9152; Fax: 825 1464

Hue

Century Riverside Inn Hue
49 Le Loi Street, Hue
Tel: (84-54) 23390; Tlx: 54154 HUEHOTXT; Fax: (84-54) 23309

Located on the bank of the Huong (Perfume) River and close to the city centre with easy access to the major tourist sites of Hue.

Accommodation and rates
19 singles US$ 65; 51 double, 82 twin US$ 85-95; 3 suites US$ 160

Credit cards accepted
Amex, Visa, Mastercard, Diners

Meeting & banqueting facilities
Four conference/function rooms, capacity 150; audio-visual equipment available; largest reception 80 seated or 150 cocktail

Room services
Airconditioning, colour TV, direct-dial telephone (ext. in bathroom), hairdryer, laundry/valet service, minibar, music, safety deposit box, 24-hr room service

Business & other services
Business centre, airport pickup, translation service, car parking & rental, taxi service, barber shop/hairdresser, guided tours, newsstand/shops, visa extension service

Sports & Recreation
Fitness centre/gym, indoor games, massage, outdoor swimming pool, tennis

Restaurants & Coffee Shops
Riverside Cafe (120) - International/Asian/Vietnamese, open 0600-2300; *Bar & lounge* (150) - Cocktails & entertainment, open 1500-2300

Overseas Sales Representatives:
Utell International Worldwide, Delton Resrvation System, Aviation & Tourism Int'l, Century International Hotels

Huang Giang Hotel D
51 Le Loi Street, Hue
Tel: (54) 822122; Tlx: 080554; Fax: (54) 823424

Explanation of codes in (short) hotel entries):
A = single room rack rate over US$200 per night; **B** = $150-200; **C** = $100-150; **D** = $50-100; **E** = under $50; ¶ = Prices on application. ◯ = PATA member.
Number in brackets after restaurant names in full entries = seating capacity.

Restaurants

Below we give a small selection of restauarants in Hanoi and Ho Chi Minh City, both in and outside of hotels. Please note that credit cards are usually not accepted at out-of-hotel restaurants and many of these close at 10.30 pm.

Hanoi

A Little Italian *(closed Mondays)*
81 Tho Nhuom St. Tel: 825 8167

Le Beaulieu *(French)*
Hotel Sofitel Metropole, 15 Ngu Quyen St. Tel: 826 6919 ext. 8028

Club Opera. 59 Ly Thai To St. Tel: 826 8802

The Emerald 53 Hang Luoc St.Tel: 825 9285

Galleon Steakhouse
50 Tran Quoc Toan St. Tel: 822 8611

Gustave Restaurant *(French)*
17 Trang Tien St. Tel: 825 0625

Indochine *(Vietnamese)*
16 NamNgu St. Tel: 824 6097

Kharana *(Indian)*
27 Quoc Tu Giam Street. Tel: 843 3468

La Paix *(Continental)*
Hanoi Daewoo Hotel. 360 Kim Ma St. Tel: 831 5000 ext 3245

La Terrazza *(Italian)*
142 Trieu Viet Vuong St. Tel: 822 7345

No Noodles 51 Luong Van Can St. Tel: 825 7721

The Pear Tree *(Pub + pool tables)*
78 Tho Nhuom St. Tel: 825 7812

Tam Tu *(Thai)*
84 Ly Thuong Kiet St. Tel: 825 1682

Ho Chi Minh City

Cafe Singapore *(Singaporean/Vietnamese).* Amara Saigon Hotel, 323 Le Van Sy Street. Tel: 843 9999

Dynasty Restaurant *(Chinese)*
Saigon New World Hotel, 76 Le Lai St. Tel: 822 8888

La Fourchette *(French)*
5 Ngo Duc Ke St. Tel: 823 1101

Garden Court Restaurant *(open 24 hrs)*
Oscar Hotel, 68 Nguyen Hue St. Tel: 823 1818

Jim Bean. 20 Bis Thi Sach St. Tel: 8251311

Kampachi *(Japanese)*
Hotel Equatorial, 242 Tran Binh Trong St. Tel: 839 0000

Madame Dai's Bibliotheque
84a Nguyen Du St, dist 1. Tel: 823 1438

Maxim's Dinner Theatre
115 Dong Khoi St, dist 1. Tel: 829 6676

Le Petit Bistro *(French)*
58 Le Thanh Ton St, dist 1. Tel: 823 0219

Saigon Banana Leaf
174 Tran Hung Dao, Dist 1. Tel: 833 2484

Seoul Restaurant *(Korean)*
35 Ngo Duc Ke St, dist 1. Tel: 829 4297

Vietnam Airline Departures & Offices

To the destinations in bold type. Departures were accurate as at February 1997 but are liable to change without prior notice. Figures in brackets after destinations signify the days of the week i.e (1) = departing on a Monday; (3) - departing on a Wednesday etc. Only direct connections, without change, are listed.
Airline Abbreviation Codes used in tables beneath: **AF** = Air France; **BL** = Pacific Airlines; **BR** = EVA Airways; **CI** = China Airlines; **CZ** = China Southern Airlines; **GA** = Garuda Indonesia; **JL** = Japan Airlines; **KL** = KLM Royal Dutch Airlines; **LH** = Lufthansa; **MH** = Malaysia Airlines; **NG** = Lauda Air; **OZ** = Asiana Airlines; **PR** = Philippine Airlines; **QF** = Qantas; **QV** = Lao Aviation; **SU** = Aeroflot; **TG** = Thai International; **VJ** = Royal Air Cambodge; **VN** = Vietnam Airlines.

Departures

From Hanoi International Airport (HAN)

Bangkok (BKK)
 VN (daily) TG (1,2,3,5,6) AF (1,3,6)
Beijing (BJS)
 CZ (2,5)
Da Nang (DAD)
 VN (daily)
Dien Bien Phu (DIN)
 VN (2,4,5,7)
Dubai (DXB)
 VN (2,4,5)
Guangzhou (CAN)
 VN (2,5,7)
Ho Chi Minh City (SGN)
 VN (daily) BL (2,3,4,6,7)
Hong Kong (HKG)
 VN (daily)
Hue (HUI)
 VN (daily)
Kuala Lumpur (KUL)
 VN (1,5) MH (1,6)
Melbourne (MEL)
 VN (3,6)
Moscow (MOW)
 SU (3,5) VN (4)
Nanning (NNG)
 CZ (2,5)
Paris (CDG)
 VN (2,5) AF (1,3,6)
Singapore (SIN)
 VN (daily) SQ (1,3,6)
Sydney (SYD)
 VN (3,6)
Taipei (TPE)
 VN (1,3,4,6,7) CI (1,3,4,6,7)
Vientiane (VTE)
 VN (3,4,6,7) QV (2)

From Ho Chi Minh City (SGN)

Amsterdam (AMS)
 KL (1,3)
Bangkok (BKK)
 VN (daily) TG (daily) AF (2,4,7)
Da Nang (DAD)
 VN (daily)
Dubai (DXB)
 VN (1,4,5,6)
Frankfurt (FRA)
 LH (1,3)
Guangzhou (CAN)
 VN (2,5,7) CZ (3,6)
Haiphong (HPH)
 VN (daily) BL (2,4,6)
Hanoi (HAN)
 VN (daily) BL (daily)
Hong Kong (HKG)
 VN (2,3)
Hue (HUI)
 VN (daily)
Jakarta (JKT)
 GA (2,5)
Kuala Lumpur (KUL)
 MH/VN (daily)
Macau (MFM)
 BL (1,5)
Manila (MNL)
 VN (1,2,4,5,6) PR (2,4,6)
Melbourne (MEL)
 QF (6) VN (3,6)
Moscow (MOW)
 VN (5) SU (1)
Novosibirsk (OVB)
 SU (1)
Osaka (OSA)
 VN (1,3,5,6,7) JL (1,3,5,6,7)
Paris (CDG)
 VN (1,4,6) AF (2,4,7)
Phnom Penh (PNH)
 VN (daily) VJ (daily)
Seoul (SEL)
 VN (1,2,3,5) OZ (1,3,5,7)
Singapore (SIN)
 VN (daily) SQ (daily) GA (2,5)
Sydney (SYD)
 QF (3,6) VN (3,6)
Taipei (TPE)
 BL (4) CI (daily) BR (daily) VN (daily)
Vienna (VIE)
 NG (6)
Vientiane (VTE)
 QV (5)

Offices

British Airways
GSA: Hanoi - Jardine Pacific, 16 Han Thuyen St, Hai Ba Trung Dist. Tel: (4) 826 6306. Ho Chi Minh City - Jardine Pacific, 7th fl, 58 Dong Khoi St, dist 1. Tel: (8) 826 6306

Pacific Airlines
77 Le Thanh Ton Street, Ho Chi Minh City
Tel: 823 1285

Vietnam Airlines
Booking Office Hanoi - 1 Quang Trung; tel: 825 0888/825 3842/825 4440
Booking Office Ho Chi Minh - 116 Nguyen Hue; tel: 829 218 or 15b Dinh Tien Hoang tel: 829 9910

Tam Coc (Ninh Binh)

ON VIETNAM AIRLINES NO ONE HAS TO LEARN HOW TO SMILE.

While most airlines have to train their cabin crews on how to relax and be more hospitable, Vietnam Airlines doesn't need to. Politeness, graciousness, and genuine caring, are a way of life in Vietnam. And it shows on the face of every *ao-dai* clad flight attendant. It's one of the reasons why our passenger volume is climbing steadily every year. Another, is our modern aircraft. We have one of the youngest fleets of 767s and A320s in the air. In addition, our flight schedule can now take you to 35 destinations worldwide. In short, the kind of service designed to make you smile. **VIETNAM AIRLINES**

FOR FURTHER INFORMATION CALL: AUSTRALIA 2-252 3303 • BERLIN 49-30 282 4895 • CAMBODIA 2-336 4460 • DUBAI 971-4 680 944 • FRANKFURT 49-69 629 891 • GUANGZHOU 20-8382 7187 • HONG KONG 2810 6680 • JAPAN 6-533 2689 • KOREA 2-319 6648 • LAOS 21-21 7562 • MALAYSIA 3-241 2416/3288 • MONTREAL 1 514-395 4646/50 • MOSCOW 7095251 1949/3964 • PARIS 33-1-445 43900/1 • PHILIPPINES 2-843 4878 • SINGAPORE 65-339 3552 • TAIWAN 2-517 7177 7-227 0209 • THAILAND 2-6569056 • VIENTIANE 856-217 562

Major Hotel Chains in Asia - Pacific

Below we list the head offices of chains, followed by their main reservation or representative offices in the countries where the *Asia-Pacific Business Travel Guide* will be circulating; also city locations of hotels within chains. Exact addresses, telephone numbers etc will be found under individual country sections of this guide, where we have considered that the hotel has both profile and location to suit the business and independent traveller. Telephone numbers are usually those for the individual traveller.
Country code abbreviations in text below:
AUS = Australia; **IN** = Indonesia; **IND** = India; **JN** = Japan; **KO** = South Korea; **MA** = Malaysia; **NZ** = New Zealand; **PK** = Pakistan; **PN** = Philippines; **PRC** = People's Republic of China; **SL** = Sri Lanka; **TD** = Thailand; **TN** = Taiwan.

ACCOR ASIA-PACIFIC

Head Office Asia: Wall Street Tower 23rd fl, 33/117 Surawongse Rd, Bangkok 10500, Thailand. Tel: 267 0810; Fax: 237

Toll-free reservations:
Australia: 1 800 64 2244
France/Belgium: 0 800 10127
Canada/USA: 1 800 221 4542
Switzerland: 155 8022
Hong Kong: tel 800 2509; fax 800 4633
Japan: tel 003 161 6353; fax 003 161 6354
Singapore: tel 800 6161 367; fax 800 6161 202
Other reservations offices:
UK: tel (171) 724 1000; fax (181) 7489116

Hotels in *Sydney (2), Melbourne (3), Brisbane (2), Cairns (2), Adelaide (2), Perth (2) & 23 others in Australia, Beijing, Shanghai, Jakarta, Balikpapan, Seoul (2), Penang, Singapore, Hua Hin, Bangkok, (2), Rayong, Chiang Mai, Agra, Hanoi*

ANA HOTELS INTERNATIONAL

Head Office: Enokizaka Hills 12-20, Akasaka 1-chome, Minato-ku, Tokyo 107, Japan
Tel: (03) 3505 1115; Fax: (03) 3505 1152

Hong Kong. Tel: 2845 4280; Tlx: 69114 ANAHH; Fax: 2845 5106
Singapore. Tel: 734 0835; Tlx: 21819 ANAHS; Fax: 733 2401
UK (for Europe). Tel: (0171) 493 4856;

Tlx: 51 884510; Fax: (0171) 493 5577
USA/Canada. Tel: 800 262 4683 (toll-free)
USA Offices. New York - Tel: (212) 332 1500; Tlx: 141441 ALLNIPPON NYK; Fax: (212) 582 0300. Los Angeles - Tel: (213) 955 7677; Tlx: 244074 ANALRV; Fax: (213) 955 7678. Chicago - Tel (312) 553 9191; Fax: (312) 553 9192

Hotels in *Fukuoka, Hakata, Hakodate, Hirado, Hiroshima, Kanazawa, Kumamoto, Kyoto, Makuhari, Matsuyama, Narita, Niigata, Okinawa (7), Sapporo,Takamatsu, Ube, Yamagata, Yoron, Japan. Gold Coast, (Aus.), Sydney, Bangkok, Beijing, Xian, Guam, Manila, Singapore,Hawaii,Bangkok, Beijing, Sydney, Tokyo, Xian.*

BEST WESTERN

Head Office: 6201 N 24th Parkway, PO Box 10203, Phoenix AZ 850166 USA
Tel: (602) 957 4200; Fax: (602) 957 5643

Hotels *in India (6), Indonesia, Philippines, Taiwan,Thailand (5)*

Australia: Tel: (2) 373 1313 (toll-free); Fax: (02) 264 2062
France: Tel : (1) 4487 4080; Fax: (1) 4487 4084
Germany: Tel: 0130 4455 (toll-free); Fax: (49) 6196 472412
Italy: Tel: 1-6782-0080 (toll-free); Fax: (39-2) 334 3934
Japan: Tel: 0120 421234 (toll-free); Fax: (81-3) 3289 4239
North America: Tel: 1-800-528 1234 (toll-free); Fax: 187527

CENTURY INTER-NATIONAL HOTELS / DELTA HOTELS

Head Office: 20/F Allied Kajima Bldg, 138 Gloucester Road, Wanchai, Hong Kong.
Tel: (852) 2598 8811; Fax: 2598 0022

Reservations:
Hong Kong. Tel: (852) 2507 6635; Fax: (852) 2507-6504
Indonesia. Tel: (62-21) 572 0462; Fax: (62-21) 571 2139
Malaysia. Tel: (603) 262-2999; Fax: (603) 262 6352
E-mail intsales@century.com.hk

Hotels in *Jinan, Wuhan, Xian, Shenzhen, Shanghai, Hong Kong, Pattaya , Bangkok (2), Chiangmai, Ho Chi Minh (2), Jakarta*

(2), *Manado, Surabaya, Melaka, Port Dickson, Makati (2), Quezon City, Cebu, Manila, Davao*

CHOICE HOTELS INTERNATIONAL

Head Office: 10750 Columbia Pike, Silver Spring, Maryland 20901, USA
Tel: (301) 236 5109; Fax: (301) 681 7478
Asia-Pacific Regional Office: Suite 1, Level 3, Kimberly Clark Bldg, 52 Alfred St, Milsons Point, Sydney, NSW 2061, Australia
Tel: (612) 9929 6444; Fax: (612) 9929 8282

Hotels in *Australia (21), India (10), Indonesia (3), Japan (8), New Zealand (16), Singapore (2) and Thailand (10)*

Australia. Tel: 1 800 090 600
USA: Tel: 800 654 6200
France: 05 908536
Germany: 0130 85 5522
Italy: 1 678 72045
Japan: 0031 6163 37
Switzerland: 155 9138
UK: 0 800 444444.

DUSIT THANI GROUP/ KEMPINSKI HOTELS

Head Office: (Dusit Hotels & Resorts) The Dusit Thani, Rama IV Road, Bangkok 10500, Thailand.
Tel: (66 2) 236-0450-9; Fax: (66 2) 236-6400, 236-7238
Corporate Office: (Kempinski) Am Forsthaus Gravenbruch 9-11, 63263 Neu-Isenburg, Germany.
Tel: (49) 61 02 50 02 52; Fax: (49) 61 02 5 29 17

Toll-free reservations:
Australia. 1 800 623 578
France. 0 800 852 852
Germany. 0130 33 39
Hong Kong. 800 8381
Japan. 0120 326 733
UK. 0800 86 8588
USA. 800 426 3135
Singapore. 1 800 735 46 22
Switzerland. 155 0626

Hotels in *Bangkok, Hua Hin, Chiang Rai, Jomtien, Koh Samui, Krabi, Pattaya, Phuket, Balikpapan, Jakarta, Nepal*
(Dusit Hotels & Resorts).
Bangkok (4), Cha-am, Chachoengsao, Chiang Mai, Khon Kaen, Korat, Petchaboon, Rayong, Songkhla
(Royal Princess Hotels & Resorts).
Chang Mai, Kanchanaburi, Nongkhai, Phrae, Songkhla, Prachinburi, Roi-Et,

(continued)

Phitsanulok, Surat Thani **(Thani).**
Bangkok, Beijing, Bombay, Jakarta, Tokyo
(Kempinski)

FOUR SEASONS REGENT HOTELS & RESORTS

Asia-Pacific Head Office. 15th Fl, New World Centre, Salisbury Rd, Kowloon, Hong Kong. Tel: 2366 3361; Fax: 2721 4400

Toll-free reservations:
Australia: 008 022 800
Japan: 0120 001500
Germany: 0130 2332
UK: 0800 282 245
USA & Canada: 800 545 4000
Other reservation centres:
Hong Kong: Tel: 2366 3361; Fax: 2721 4400
Singapore: Tel: 737 3555; Fax: 737 3510

Hotels in *Auckland, Bali, Bangkok, Chiang Mai, Fiji, Hong Kong, Jakarta, Kuala Lumpur, Melbourne, Singapore (2), Sydney, Taipei, Tokyo*

HILTON INTERNATIONAL

Head Office: International Court, 2-3 Rhodes Way, Watford, Herts WD2 4WY, UK. Tel: (01923) 231333; Fax (01923) 2333358
Asia-Pacific Office: Fl 07-02, Palais Renaissance, 390 Orchard Rd, Singapore 238871. Tel: 734 5661; Fax: 733 3305

Toll-free reservations:
Australia. 1-800 22 22 55
Italy. 1678 78346
France. 0590 7546
Germany. 0130 818146
Japan. 0120 489852
UK. 0800 289303
USA .1-800 445 8667

Hotels in *Adelaide, Bali, Bangkok, Beijing, Brisbane, Cairns, Colombo, Guam,Jakarta, Kuala Lumpur (2), Kuching (2)(MA), Kyongju (KO), Melbourne, Nagoya (JN), New Delhi, Madras, Osaka, Perth, Perth, Seoul, Shanghai, Singapore, Surabaya (IN), Sydney (2),Taipei, Tokyo (2)*

HOLIDAY INNS INTERNATIONAL

Regional Head Office Asia-Pacific: 20th fl, Tower 3, China Hong Kong City, 33 Canton Road, Hong Kong. Tel: 2736 6955; Fax: 2375 0957

Australia. Tel 1 800 221 066 (toll-free)
France. Tel 0800 905 999 (toll-free)
Germany. Tel: 0130 815131 (toll-free)
Hong Kong. Tel: 2736 6855; Fax: 2735 2808
Italy. Tel: 1678 77399
UK. Tel: 0800 897121 (toll-free)
US. 1-800 465 4329 (toll-free)

Hotels in *Adelaide, Ahmedabad (IND), Bali, Bangalore (IND), Bangkok, Beijing (2), Bombay, Cairns (AUS), Cheju, Chengdu, Chiang Mai (TD), Chongquing (PRC), Clark Field (PN), Colombo (SL), Dalian (PRC), Damai Beach (MA), Guangzhou, Guilin (PRC), Hamilton Island (AUS), Harbin (PRC), Hong Kong, Hyderabad, I-Lam (TN), Islamabad (PK), Jaipur, Jakarta, Johor Bahru (MA), Kanazawa (JN), Kansai (JN), Karachi, Kathmandu, Karuizawa (JN), Kochi (JN), Kuala Lumpur (2), Kuching (MA), Kunming (PRC), Kyoto, Lahore, Lhasa, Lombok (IN), Macau, Maie Hong Son (TD), Manali (IND), Manila, Melbourne, Miri (MA), Multan (PK), Nagasaki, Naha (JN), Nainital (IND), Narita, Nongkhai (TD), Ooty (IND), Osaka (2), Pedu Lake (MA), Penang (MA), Phuket, Queenstown (NZ), Sapporo (2), Sasebo (JN), Shah Alam (MA), Shanghai, Singapore (2), Surat (IND), Sydney (3), Taipei, Terrigal (AUS), Tokyo (3), Toyohashi (JN), Urumqi (PRC), Wuhan (PRC), Wuxi, Xiamen, Xian (2), Yokohama, Zengzhou (PRC)*

HYATT HOTELS WORLDWIDE

Head Office: The Madison Plaza, 200 W Madison St, Chicago IL 60606, USA
Tel: 312 750 1234; Fax: 312 750 8579

Toll-free reservations:
Australia. 008 222 188
France. 0590 8529
Germany. 0130 2929
Italy. 1678 72021
UK. 01345 581666 (London 0171 5808197)
USA/Canada. 800 233 1234

Hotels in *Adelaide, Gold Coast, Perth (AUS), Auckland, Bali (2), Bangkok, Canberra, Cheju (KO), Coolum (AUS), Fukuoka, Guam, Hawaii (4), Hong Kong (2), Jakarta (2), Johor Bahru, Kota Kinabalu, Kuala Lumpur, Kuantan (MA), Macau, Manila, Melbourne, Nagoya, New Delhi, Osaka, Pusan (KO), Saipan, Seoul, Singapore, Surabaya (IN), Sydney (2), Taipai, Tahiti, Tianjin (PRC), Tokyo (2), Xian.*

INTER-CONTINENTAL HOTELS

Head Office: Devonshire House, Mayfair Place, London W1X 5FH. UK
Tel: 0171 495 2500; Fax: 0171 495 2769

Toll-free reservations
Australia. 008 221 335
France. 05 90 8555
Germany. 0130 853955
Italy. 1678 72070
UK. (outside London) 01345 581444; (London) 0181 847 2277
USA/Canada. 1 800 327 0200

Hotels in *Bali, Bangkok, Bombay, Colombo, Hawaii, Jakarta, Manila, New Delhi, Seoul, Shenzhan (PRC), Sydney, Tokyo, Yokohama, Phnom Penh.*

ITT SHERATON

Head Office: 60 State St, Boston, Massachusetts 02109, USA
Tel: 617 367 3600; Fax: 617 367 5676
http://www.sheraton.com

Toll-free reservations:
Australia: 008 073535
France: 0800 906 535
Germany: 0130 853535
Italy: 1678 35035
Japan: 0120 003535
UK: 0800 353535
USA & Canada - travellers: 800 325 3535 - travel agents 800 334 8484
Hong Kong: 800 8397
Singapore: 1 800 324 1600

Hotels in *Brisbane, Gold Coast, Hobart, Melbourne, Noosa, Perth, Port Douglas, Sydney (2), Townsville (AUS); Beijing, Guilin, Shanghai, Tianjin, Xian (PRC); Dhaka, Cook Islands, Fiji (2), Hawaii (8), Hong Kong; Agra, Andamans, Bangalore, Bombay, Jaipur, Jodhpur, Khimsar, Madras (2), New Delhi (IND), Bandar Lampung, Bali (3), Bandung, Lombok, Yogyakarta (IN);Tokyo, Kobe, Osaka (JN); Karachi (PN), Auckland, Rotorua (NZ); Manila; Seoul; Singapore (2);Taipei; Bangkok, Phuket (TD); Labuan, Langkawi (MA)*

MANDARIN ORIENTAL

Head Office: 281 Gloucester Rd, PO Box 30632, Causeway Bay, Hong Kong
Tel: 2895 9288; Tlx: 86767 MOHG HX; Fax: 2837 3510; E-mail: mandarin-oriental.com

Australia: Tel: (02) 957 5529

HOTEL CHAINS

Germany: Tel: 0130 858508 (toll-free)
Japan: Tel: (03) 3433 3388
Hong Kong: Tel: 881 1288
Singapore: Tel: 339 0033 (collect)
UK: Tel: 0171 537 2988
USA/Canada: Tel: 1 800 526 6566 (toll-free)

Hotels in *Bangkok, Hong Kong (2), Jakarta, Macau (2), Manila, Phuket, Singapore, Surabaya*

MARCO POLO

Head Office: 5/F The Hong Kong Hotel, Harbour City, Kowloon, Hong Kong. Tel: 2118 7232; Fax: 2118 7388

Asia-Pacific: Tel: Hong Kong 2965 1999; Fax: 2 965 1900
France: Tel (1) 4897 9697; fax: (1) 4897 9190
Germany: Tel: (211) 491 0055; Fax: (211) 491 0679
Japan: Tel: (03) 5561 9353; Fax: (03) 5561 9354
UK: Tel: 990 300 200; Fax: (181) 661 1234
US: Toll-free Tel: 800 THE OMNI; Fax: (402) 334 8013
Hotels in *Hong Kong (3), Jakarta, Singapore, Vietnam, Xiamen,*

MARRIOTT

Head Office: 1 Marriott Drive, Washington DC 20058, USA
Tel: 301 380 9000; Fax: 301 380 5728

Worldwide Reservations Offices:
Australia (exc Sydney): 1 800 251259 (toll free) Sydney: (2) 299 1614
France: 0590 8333 (T-F)
Germany: 0130 854422 (T-F)
Hong Kong: 2 841 3000
Japan: (3) 5275 3711
Singapore: 295 6204
UK: 0800 221222 (T-F)
USA/Canada: (800) 228 9290(toll-free)

Hotels in *Hong Kong, Tokyo, Fukuoka, Gold Coast (AUS), Sydney, Bangkok, Singapore*

MERIDIEN HOTELS

(Parent Company Granada Hotels, London)
Head Office: 171 Boulevard Haussmann, 75008 Paris, France
Tel: 4420 5200; Fax: 4289 8243

Reservation Offices (* = toll-free)
UK. (0345) 40 40 40*
France. (05) 40 22 15*
Germany. (0130) 818200*
Italy. (1678) 20088*
Spain. (900) 210934
US & Canada. Tel: 1800 225 5843*
Australia. 0800 331 330*
New Zealand. (0800) 445 577*
Hong Kong. (852) 2366 9996
Japan. (0120) 475 777*
Japan - Tokyo. (81-3) 3475 2364

Hotels in *Bangkok,The Golden Triangle, Koh Samui, Phuket (2), New Delhi, Singapore (2), Jakarta, Port Vila, Noumea, Bali*

MIYAKO HOTELS

Head Office: Sanjo Keage, Higashiyama-ku, Kyoto 605, Japan
Tel: (75) 771 7111; Tlx: 242 3111 MYKTKY J; Fax: (75) 751 2490

Australia: Utell, Sydney: (02) 235 1111
Hong Kong: Utell : 3 722 6432
Singapore: Utell: 338 3488
USA: Tel: 800 336 1136 (toll-free)

NIKKO HOTELS

Head Office: Nichirei Higashiginza Bldg, 10th fl, 69-20 Tsukiji, Chuo-ku, Tokyo 104
Tel: (03) 3248 3007; Tlx: 2424106 JDCNH J; Fax: (03) 3248 3008

Toll-free Reservations
France. Tel 0502 3009; fax: 0145 75 42 35
Germany. Tel 0130 3137; fax: 0211 161216
Mexico. Tel 95-800-NIKKO-US (645 - 5687)
UK. Tel 0800 282502; fax: 0171 724 9180
USA & Canada. Tel 1 800 NIKKO US (645-5687); fax: 1-800-544-4455
Other Reservation Centres
Japan: Tokyo tel (03) 3248 4321; fax: (03) 3248 3020. Osaka tel: (06) 645 7711; fax: (06) 645 7712.

Hotels in *Chitose*, Fukuoka, Ishigaki, Kagawa, Kanazawa, Kansai, Kyoto, Narita*, Niseko*, Okinawa/Naha, Okuma, Onna & Yomitan, Osaka, Tokyo (Japan) and Bali, Bangkok, Beijing*, Guam*, Hong Kong*, Jakarta*, Kuala Lumpur, Manila*, Palau*, Saipan*, Seoul, Shanghai*, Sydney, Taipei*, Xian.* (* = managed)

OBEROI HOTELS

Head Office: 7 Sham Nath Marg, New Delhi 110054, India Tel: (11) 252 5464; Tlx: 66303/78163; Fax: 292 9800

Australia: Tel: (02) 247 6061; 008 802509 (toll-free); Tlx: AA 74339; Fax: (2) 247 8850
France. Tel: 0590 8607 (toll-free).
Germany: Tel: 0130 824222 (toll-free)
Hong Kong: Tel: 800 2595 (Toll-free)
Italy: 1678 25107 (Toll-free)
Japan: Tel: 0120 025725 (T-F); Tokyo 5210 5135; **Singapore:** 737 0005 (T-F).
UK: Tel: (T-F) 0800 515517
USA: Tel: Toll-free (800) 5-OBEROI; NY City Tel: 752 6565; Fax: (212) 758 7367

Hotels in *Melbourne, Bangalore, Bombay (2), Bhubaneswar, Calcutta, Delhi (2),Goa, Gopalpur, Hyderabad, Khajuraho, Lombok, Shimla, Srinagar, Madras (IND) Bali, Colombo.*

PAN PACIFIC HOTELS & RESORTS

Asia-Pacific Office: 7 Raffles Boulevard, Fl 01-050, Marina Square, Singapore 0103
Tel: (65) 339 4688; Fax: (65) 339 5787

Australia: Toll-free (008) 252900 or (02) 264 1122; Tlx: 71979 PPHSYD AA; Fax: (02) 264 3574
Hong Kong: (852) 877 3321; Tlx: 77785; Fax: (852) 877 0052
Japan: Tel: (03) 3214 3001; Tlx: 25467 PHGTOKYO; Fax: (03) 3211 8002
Singapore: Tel: 339 4688; Tlx: 37586 PPHSIN RS; Fax: 339 5787
UK: Tel: (0171) 491 3812; Tlx: 295860 TKKLON G; Fax: (0171) 323 1791
USA/Canada: Toll-free Tel: 800 327 8585/ 800 538 4040; Fax: (714) 966 2040

Hotels in *Bangkok, Dhaka, Hong Kong, Wuxi (PRC), Jakarta, Narita (JN), Johor Bahru, Kuala Lumpur (3), Pangkor; Singapore, Malacca.* New Openings - *Manila, Palau, Yokohama, Penang*

PENINSULA GROUP

Head Office: 8FL, St George's Building, 2 Ice House St, Hong Kong
Tel: 2840 7788; Tlx: 74509 ; Fax: 2845 5508

Australia/New Zealand: Tel: (02) 261 4322; Fax: 264 6826
Europe (exc. UK/Scandinavia): Frankfurt- Tel: (69) 612168; Fax: (69) 623529
Hong Kong & Asia - see Head Office (above)
Japan & Korea: Tokyo - Tel: (03) 5473 7001; Fax: (03) 5473 7002
UK & Scandinavia: London - tel: (0171) 730 0993; fax: (0171) 730 2154
USA New York- tel: (212) 489 9586; Fax: (212) 397 0380
USA (West): Beverly Hills - Tel: (310) 278 8777; Fax: (310) 278 2777

PRINCE HOTELS

Head Office: 8F Seibu Shinjuku Bldg, 30-1 Kabuki-cho, 1-chome, Shinjuku-ku, Tokyo 160, Japan.
Tel: (3) 3205 2600; Fax: (3) 3205 6750

France: Tel: (01) 4579 9230
Germany: (069) 284427
Singapore: Tel: 734 9024
UK: Tel: (0181) 569 7122
USA: Tel: 800 542 8686 (toll-free)
Hotels in *Furano, Hakone, Hikone, Kanazawa, Karuizawa, Kyoto (2), Manza Spa, Matsuzaki-cho, Minakami-Machi, Moriguchi, Narita, Nojiriko, Sapporo, Shiga*

(continued)

Heights, Shimoda, Tazawako, Tokyo (8), Tomakomai, Towada, Yuzawa-Machi, Japan

RENAISSANCE/ RAMADA INT'L/NEW WORLD HOTELS INT'L

Head Office: Gables International Plaza, 2655 Lejeune Rd, suite 800, Carol Gables, Florida 33134, USA
Tel: 305 460 1900; Fax: 305 442 4396
Regional Head Office: 17th fl, New World Tower, 16-18 Queens Rd Central, Hong Kong. Tel: 2526 2233; Fax: 2877 5699

Australia: 008 222 431 (T-F) ;Fax: (2) 251 8586
France: 0590 6540(toll-free)
Germany: 0130 812340 (toll-free)
Italy: 1678 72090 (toll-free)
Hong Kong: Tel:(852) 2525 9966; Fax: 2724 3892
Japan: Tel: 0120 222332 (T-F); Fax: 3 3239 1868
UK; 0800 181737
USA/Canada: 800 468 3571/800 854 7854 (toll-free); Fax: (1) 602 443 6543/216 3493159

Hotels **(Renaissance)**. in *Colombo, Hong Kong, Karachi, Lahore, Malacca (MA), Okinawa, Sapporo (JN), Sendakan (MA),Seoul, Sydney,Tokyo.*
(Hotels) *Adelaide, Bangkok, Bombay, Cairns, Goa, Guangdong, Hong Kong, Korea, Kuantan (MA), Seoul, Surfers' Paradise (AUS), Sydney (3).*
(New World) *Beijing, Guangzhou, Harbin, Ho Chi Minh City, Hong Kong (2), Kuala Lumpur, Macau, Manila, Shanghai, Shenyang (PRC), Tianjin, Xian, Yangon.*

RITZ-CARLTON HOTELS

Corporate Head Office: 3414 Peachtree Road, N.E. Suite 300, Atlanta, Georgia 30326. Tel: (404) 237-5500; Fax: (404) 365-9643

Toll-free reservations:
Australia. 800 252 888
France. 05 90 72 03
Germany. 0130 81 23 34
Hong Kong. 800 2064
Italy. 1678 72076
New Zealand. 0800 44 3030
Singapore. 800 616 1049
Japan (Tokyo). 0120 853 201
UK. 0800 234000
USA/Canada. 800 241 3333

Hotels in *Double Bay, Hong Kong, Seoul, Singapore, Bali, Kuala Lumpur, Osaka*

SHANGRI-LA HOTELS & RESORTS

Head Office: 15F, Nat West Tower, Times Sq, 1 Matheson St, Causeway Bay, Hong Kong
Tel: 2599 3000; Fax: 2599 3131

Toll-free reservations:
Australia: (800) 222448
France: 0800 90 8687
Germany: 0130 856649
Switzerland: 0800 556333
USA/Canada: 800 942 5050
Other reservation centres:
Australia: Tel: (612) 9262 2488; Fax: (612) 9290 2986.
Hong Kong: Tel: (852) 2590 3888; Fax: (852) 2599 3222.
Japan: Tel: (03) 3667 7741; Tlx: 0252 23402 SLITYO J; Fax: (03) 3667 7743.
UK: Tel: (44) 181 747 8484; Tlx: 938839 SHAINT G; Fax: (44) 181 747 8591

Hotels in *Bali, Bangkok, Beijing (3), Beihai (PRC), Chengchun (PRC), Dalian (PRC), Fiji (2), Hangzhou (PRC), Hong Kong (2), Jakarta, Kuala Lumpur, Kota Kinabalu (2), Mactan (PN), Manila (3), Pantai Dalit, Penang (3), Qingdao (PRC),Shanghai, Shenyang, Shenzhen (PRC), Surabaya, Xian, Singapore (3), Taipei, Yangon*

SINGAPORE MANDARIN

Head Office: 33rd Fl, 333 Orchard Road, Singapore 238867
Tel: 235 7788; Tlx: 21528; Fax: 235 6688

Australia/New Zealand: Tel: 2 9231 6744
Europe: Tel London (0171) 583 5212
Hong Kong: Tel: 2735 3222; Fax: 2735 2889
Japan/Korea: Tel: Tokyo (3) 3663 1023
Malaysia: (03) 245 8823; Fax: 243 0823
Singapore: Tel: 235 8588; Fax: 235 4588

Hotels in *Beijing, Singapore (3), Penang, Langkawi (2), Shanghai, Kuala Lumpur, Pahang, Malacca*

SOUTHERN PACIFIC HOTELS CORPORATION

Head Office: 3rd Fl, 7 York St, Sydney 2000, New South Wales. Tel: (02) 290 3033; Tlx: AA 121565; Fax: (02) 290 9855

Australia: Tel: 1 300 363 300 (toll-free)
Japan: Tel; (03) 5275 2611
New Zealand: 0800 801111 (toll-free)
UK: 01345 404040
USA/Canada: 800 835 7742 (toll-free)

Hotels in *Australia (31), Fiji (2),French Polynesia (2), Malaysia (2), New Zealand (20), Papua New Guinea (3),Thailand, Vietnam*

SWISSÔTEL

Head Office: PO Box, CH-8058, Zurich-Airport, Switzerland. Tel: (+41) 1-812 5451; Fax: (+41) 1-810 9490
Hong Kong. Tel: 254 23399; Fax: 2850 4797. **Japan**. Tel: 0120 118058 (toll-free); Fax: (+81) 3 3211 8029. **UK**. 0800 614 145 (toll-free); Fax: (+44) 171 493 6187.
Germany. Tel: 0130 845858 (toll-free)
France. Tel: 05 11 8380 (toll-free)
USA/Canada. Tel: 800 637 9477 (toll-free)
Australia. Tel: 1-800 062155 (toll-free)

Hotels *in Beijing, Seoul, Bangkok, River Kwai & Phuket*

TAJ GROUP OF HOTELS

Head Office: Taj Mahal Hotel, Apollo Bunder, Bombay 400 001, India
Tel: (22) 2023366; Tlx: 11 82442 TAJB IN; Fax: (22) 287 2719

Australia: 008 221176 (toll-free)
France: (1905) 908338 (toll-free)
Germany: 0130 852428 (toll-free). **Japan**: Tokyo (03) 55619353; Fax: (03) 55610354
UK: 0800 282699 (toll-free); Fax: (0171) 4138883
USA: 800 458 8825 (toll-free)

Hotels in *Agra, Aurangabad, Bangalore (2), Bombay (2), Calcutta, Calicut, Chiplun, Cochin, Ernakulam, New Delhi (2), Goa (3), Hyderabad, Jaipur (4), Khajuraho, Lucknow, Madras (3), Mangalore, Nasik, Ootacamund (Ooty- 2), Sawai,Udaipur, Varanasi (Benares), Varkala, Vishkapatnam, India; Colombo, Kathmandu, Maldives*

WESTIN HOTELS & RESORTS

Head Office: Westin Building, 2001 6th Avenue, Seattle WA 98121, USA
Tel: 206 443 5000

Japan: 0120 39 1671 (toll-free, exc. Tokyo)
Australia: Toll-free (008) 803849; (NZ) (0800) 441787
France: 059 908 567 (toll-free)
Germany: 0130 852662 (toll-free) Fax: (69) 5963691; Tlx: (17) 6997435
UK: 0800 282 565 (toll-free); Tlx: 22144; Fax: (171) 408 0268
USA: 1 800 228 3000 (toll-free); Fax: (1) 212 683 6295
Hong Kong: (852) 2803 2333; Fax: 2547 2525

Hotels in *Hawaii, Shanghai, Kyoto, Osaka, Tokyo (2), Seoul, Pusan (KOR), Macau, Manila, Singapore (2), Taipei*

Bradt Publications
in Asia Pacific

* thoroughly researched * regularly updated
* getting there * getting around * maps
* hotels, restaurants, nightlife
* red tape * media & communications * language
* background information
* sports, culture, places to visit

COUNTRY GUIDES

Guide to Burma   *Nicholas Greenwood*
ISBN 1 897323 21 6   £12.95   304 pages, 40 colour photos
"A rare travel book. ... I highly recommend it."   *John Pilger*

Guide to Laos & Cambodia   *John R Jones*
ISBN 1 898323 22 4   £10.95   352 pages, colour photos
"Everything about it works superbly"   Reader's letter

Guide to Philippines   *Stephen Mansfield*   (May 1997)
ISBN 1 898323 58 5   £11.95   304 pages, colour photos
A complete guide to all the main islands and island groups

Guide to Vietnam   *John R Jones*
ISBN 1 898323 11 9   £11.95   422 pages, colour photos
Everything from history and hotels to festivals and pagodas

RAIL GUIDES

Australia & New Zealand by Rail   *Colin Taylor*
ISBN 1 898323 46 1   £10.95   224 pages, colour photos

India by Rail   *Royston Ellis*   (3rd edition: March 1997)
ISBN 1 898323 49 6   £11.95   256 pages, colour photos

Sri Lanka by Rail   *Royston Ellis*
ISBN 0 946983 77 1   £10.95   240 pages

For a fast and efficient mail order service, contact Bradt Publications
Dept AP, 41 Nortoft Road, Chalfont St Peter, Bucks SL9 0LA, England
Tel/fax: + 44 1494 873478

ADVERTISERS INDEX

Admiral Hotel Manila, 259
Adelaide Hilton, 17
Air China, 41
Airport Ashok Hotel, 105
Aquila Prambanan, 138
Ashok Hotel Bangalore, 102
Ashok Hotel New Delhi, 106
Atlet Century Park, Jakarta, 132

Bali Hilton, 130
Bali Imperial, 130
Bali Padma Hotel, 131
Beijing Hilton, 53
Bela Vista Macau, 191
BP International HK, 78
Bradt Publications, 265, 347
Brisbane Hilton, 18
British Airways, 26,29,62,86,119,139,162, 182,213,232,283,288,300,326

Cairns Hilton, 18
Cape Panwa Hotel, 323
Cecil, the, Shimla, 116
Central Plaza Bangkok, 315
Century Park Bangkok, 315
Century Hong Kong Hotel, 78
Century Saigon Hotel, 339
China Hotel, Guangzhou, 55
Chiva Som Int'l Health Resort, 321
Ciputra Semarang Hotel, 136
Citic Ningbo Int'l Zhejiang, 57
Club Andaman Beach Resort, 323
Colombo Hilton, 287
Concorde Hotel, Kuala Lumpur, 206
Concourse Hotel, HK, 78

Dusit Mangga Dua Jakarta, 133
Duty Free Shoppers, HK, 73
Dynasty Kuala Lumpur, 206

Eastern & Oriental Express, 200,218,271,309
Eaton Hotel, HK, 79
Embassy Suites Windsor Palace B'kk, 316
EPG Travel, 217
Equatorial Hill Resort Malaysia, 205
Excelsior Hotel HK, 79
Excelsior Hotel, Singapore, 275

Fort Aquada Beach Resort, Goa, 110
Furama Hotel HK, 80

Government of India Tourist Office,120
Grand Formosa Regent, 297
Grand Hotel Beijing, 53
Grand Hyatt Erawan Bkk, 316
Grand Lijiang Hotel, 56
Grand Plaza Hotel, Singapore, 276
Guam Hilton, 237

Harbour Plaza Hong Kong, 80
Heritage Hotel Manila, 259
Hilton Batang Ai Longhouse Resort, 209
Hilton International Hotels, *Inside back cover*
Hilton Int'l at Nai Lert Park, 316
Hilton International Singapore, 276/7
Hilton Kuala Lumpur, 207
Hilton Osaka, 155
Holiday Inn Crowne Plaza Jakarta, 133
Holiday Inn Resort Phuket, 324
Hong Kong Renaissance Hotel, 80
Hyatt Regency New Delhi, 106

Imperial Boat House Hotel, 322
Imperial Century Tangerang, 134
Imperial Queens Park, Bkk, 317
Imperial Hotel Group, Thailand, 307

Imperial Mae Ping, Chiang Mai, 321
Imperial Phukaew Hill Resort, 324
Imperial Tara Hotel, Bkk, 317
Imperial Tara Mae Hong Son Hotel, 325
Indonesian Tourism Promotion Board, 142
Insular Century Hotel Davao, 261

Jai Mahal Palace, Jaipur, 111
Jakarta Hilton International, 134
Jass Oberoi, Khajuraho, 113
Jayakarta Hotel, Jakarta, 134
Jianguo Hotel Beijing, 54

Kempinski Hotel Lufthansa, Beijing, 54
Kovalam Ashok Beach Resort, 112
Kowloon Panda, 81
Krishna Oberoi, Hyderabad, 111
Kuching Hilton, 210
Kyongju Hilton, 179

Lake Palace Udaipur, 116
Lalitha Mahal Palace Hotel, 115
Lanka Oberoi, the, 287
Le Meridien Changi Singapore, 277
Le Meridien Hotels & Resorts, 5
Le Meridien Jakarta, 135
Le Meridien New Delhi, 107
Le Meridien Nirwana Bali, 131
Le Meridien President, Bangkok, 318
Le Meridien Singapore, 277

Macau Government Tourist Office, 194
Madras Hilton,114
Majapahit Mandarin Oriental, 137
Mandarin Oriental HK, 81
Mandarin Oriental Hotel Group, *Inside Front Cover*
Mandarin Oriental Jakarta, 135
Mandarin Oriental Macau, 191
Mandarin Oriental Manila, 260
Manila Hotel, the, 260
Melbourne Hilton on the Park, 21
Melia Hua Hin Hotel, 321
Menam Riverside Bangkok, 318
Merchant Court Singapore, 278
Mercure Philippine Village Hotel, 261
Miramar Hotel Hong Kong, 82
Miyako Hotel, Osaka, 155
Monarch Lee Gardens, 318
Mövenpick Hotel Beijing, 55

Nagoya Hilton International, 154
Narita Tokyu Hotel, 154
New Delhi Hilton, 107
New Otani Hotel Singapore, 278
New Park Hotel, Singapore, 278
New World Harbour View HK, 82
New World Hotel Shenyang, 58

Oberoi, Bali, 132
Oberoi Bangalore, 102
Oberoi Bhubaneswar, 103
Oberoi Mumbai, 104
Oberoi Clarkes, Shimla, 116
Oberoi Grand Calcutta, 105
Oberoi, Lombok, 138
Oberoi Maidens, New Delhi, 108
Oberoi New Delhi, 107
Oberoi Palm Beach, Gopalpur-on-Sea, 111
Oberoi Towers Mumbai, 104
Omni Batavia Hotel, 135
Orchard Hotel Singapore, 279
Oriental Bangkok, 319
Oriental Singapore, 279

Pacific Asia Travel Ass'n, *outside back cover*

Palau Pacific Resort, 238
Pan Pacific Glenmarie Resort, KL, 208
Pan Pacific Bangkok, 319
Pan Pacific Gold Coast, 19
Pan Pacific Hotels & Resorts, 2
Pan Pacific KL Int'l Airport Hotel, 207
Pan Pacific Kuala Lumpur, 208
Pan Pacific Leader, Penang, 211
Pan Pacific Malacca, 211
Pan Pacific Manila, 261
Pan Pacific Sonargaon, Dacca, 30
Pan Pacific, Singapore, 279
Pan Pacific Resort Pangkor Isl'd, 211
Pan Pacific Sutera, Kota Kinabalu, 206
Pan Pacific Wuxi Grand, 59
Pan Pacific Yokohama, 158
Paramount Hotel Singapore, 280
Patra Surabaya Hilton, 137
Peninsula Hotel Singapore, 280
Perth Parmelia Hilton, 22
Petaling Jaya Hilton Int'l, 208
Philippine Convention/Visitors Bureau, 266
Plaza Hotel Singapore, 280
Plaza Pacific Hotel Group, 276
Puteri Pan Pacific, the Kotaraya, 205

Rambagh Palace, Jaipur, 112
River View Hotel Singapore, 281
Royal Garden Hong Kong, 83

Saigon Prince Hotel, 340
Samrat Hotel New Delhi, 108
Santika Beach Hotel, 132
Sari Pan Pacfic Jakarta, 136
Seoul Hilton, 177
Seoul Renaissance Hotel, 178
Shanghai Hilton, 57
Shanghai Worldfield Conv Centre, 58
South Pacific Hotel, HK, 83
Sukhothai, the, Bangkok, 320
Surya, the, New Delhi, 108
Sydney Airport Hilton, 24
Sydney Hilton, 24

Taipei Hilton Hotel, 298
Taiwan Tourism Bureau, 302
Taj Bengal, Calcutta, 106
Taj Coromandel, Madras, 114
Taj Holiday Village, Goa, 110
Taj Hotel Group, 117
Taj Mahal Lucknow, 113
Taj Mahal Mumbai, 104
Taj Mahal New Delhi, 109
Taj Palace New Delhi, 109
Taj West End, Bangalore, 102
Thai International, 330
Tokyo Bay Hilton, 157
Tokyo Hilton International, 158
Tourism Authority of Thailand, 329
Trans Niugini Tours, 247
Trident, the, Agra, 101
Trident, the, Ahmedabad, 101
Trident, the, Madras, 114

Vietnam Airlines, 342

Welcomgroup Chola Sheraton, 115
Welcomgroup Maurya Sheraton, 110
Welcomgroup Mughal Sheraton, 101
Welcomgroup Park Sheraton Hotel/ Towers, 115
Welcomgroup Rajputana Palace Sheraton, 112
Welcomgroup Windsor Manor Sheraton/ Towers, 103
Wenworth Hotel Kuala Lumpur, 209
Windsor Oberoi, Melbourne, 22